COMICS SHOP

MAGGIE THOMPSON   **BRENT FRANKENHOFF**   **PETER BICKFORD**

Published by

Krause Publications, a division of F+W Media, Inc.
700 East State Street • Iola, WI 54990-0001
715-445-2214 • 888-457-2873
www.krausebooks.com

Our toll-free number to place an order is (800) 258-0929
or visit our online bookstore at http://shop.collect.com.

Library of Congress Control Number: 2010923674
ISBN-13: 978-1-4402-1283-3
ISBN-10: 1-4402-1283-X

Edited by:
Brent Frankenhoff
Maggie Thompson

Designed by:
Sandi Carpenter
Shawn Williams
Heidi Bittner-Zastrow

Printed in China

Thanks!

Thanks, first to you, for buying this book — an evolution of our **Comic Book Checklist and Price Guide, Standard Catalog of Comic Books, and Comics Values Annual** — and also to the many people who helped us put this book together. As ever, there are so many of them to thank that we're bound to miss a few. To anyone who should be thanked but isn't (you know who you are): We're sorry, and you know we couldn't have done this without you.

First and foremost, without the copious contributions of ComicBase developer Peter Bickford, this book simply wouldn't exist. While his research has often paralleled our own, he has also obtained information to which we didn't have access, just as our information has added many titles to his computerized comics database program. This book contains a number of fresh updates obtained through various sources, including many of ComicBase's users.

That brings us to the publishers and individual creators who provided copies of their titles, so that we could maintain a database based on actually published material. We thank them all and encourage others to do the same.

Thanks also to the readers of our other price guides who have been providing additional data on their favorite titles.

Thanks go, as well, to our own behind-the-scenes people, including: Tammy Kuhnle and Steve Duberstein, computer services; Sandi Carpenter in our book production department; graphic designers Heidi Bittner-Zastrow and Shawn Williams; and the entire antiques and collectibles division at Krause Publications.

Most of all, we acknowledge the work of Don Thompson, who nursed this project through the last 11 years of his life. We miss you, Don.

And, again, we thank you all.

Maggie Thompson
Brent Frankenhoff
Iola, Wisconsin
June 8, 2010

Contents

How to Use This Book

Titles are organized alphabetically with number titles alphabetized as if the number were spelled out. (With the exception of *Walt Disney's Comics & Stories*, titles with a writer or artist's name at the beginning are alphabetized by the ***title's name*** with the creator's name moved to the end of the title.)

Running head indicates the last title on the page.

Thumb tab displays the issues' place in the alphabet

Series reviews provides an overview of the title, with additional information and a cover scan.

The publisher and initial year of publication (when known) are displayed.

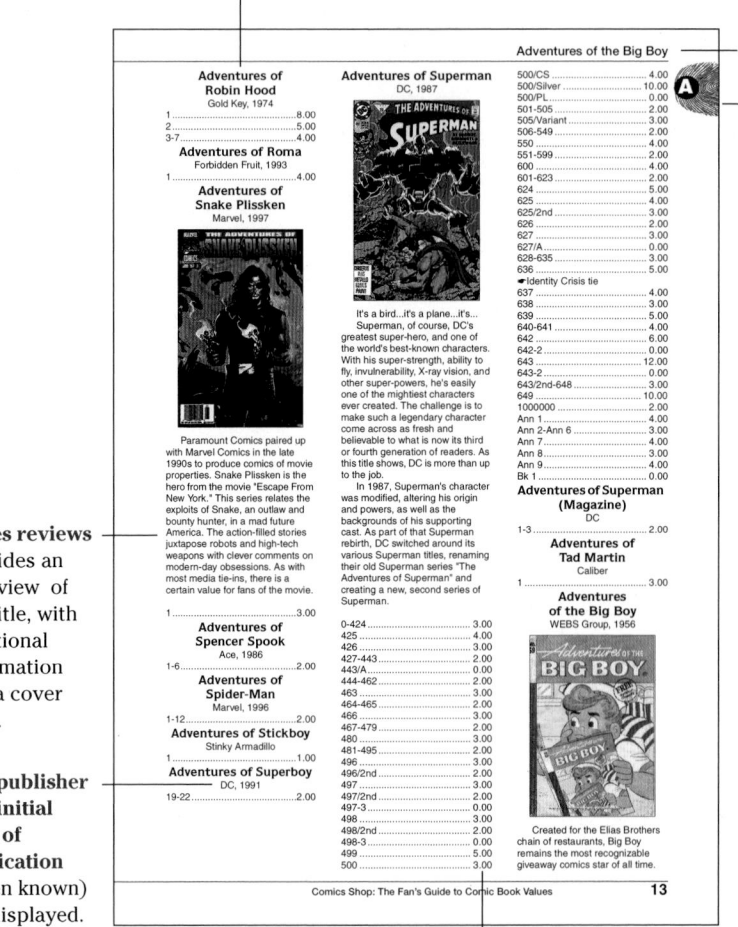

Adventures of the Big Boy

Adventures of Robin Hood
Gold Key, 1974

1	8.00
2	5.00
3-7	4.00

Adventures of Roma
Forbidden Fruit, 1993

1	4.00

Adventures of Snake Plissken
Marvel, 1997

Paramount Comics paired up with Marvel Comics in the late 1990s to produce comics of movie properties. Snake Plissken is the hero from the movie "Escape From New York." This series relates the exploits of Snake, an outlaw and bounty hunter, in a mad future America. The action-filled stories juxtapose robots and high-tech weapons with clever comments on modern-day obsessions. As with most media tie-ins, there is a certain value for fans of the movie.

1	3.00

Adventures of Spencer Spook
Ace, 1986

1-6	2.00

Adventures of Spider-Man
Marvel, 1996

1-12	2.00

Adventures of Stickboy
Stinky Armadillo

1	1.00

Adventures of Superboy
DC, 1991

19-22	2.00

Adventures of Superman
DC, 1987

It's a bird...it's a plane...it's... Superman, of course, DC's greatest super-hero, and one of the world's best-known characters. With his super-strength, ability to fly, invulnerability, X-ray vision, and other super-powers, he's easily one of the mightiest characters ever created. The challenge is to make such a legendary character come across as fresh and believable to what is now its third or fourth generation of readers. As this title shows, DC is more than up to the job.

In 1987, Superman's character was modified, altering his origin and powers, as well as the backgrounds of his supporting cast. As part of that Superman rebirth, DC switched around its various Superman titles, renaming their old Superman series "The Adventures of Superman" and creating a new, second series of Superman.

0-424	3.00
425	4.00
426	3.00
427-443	2.00
443/A	0.00
444-462	2.00
463	3.00
464-465	2.00
466	3.00
467-479	2.00
480	3.00
481-495	2.00
496	3.00
496/2nd	2.00
497	3.00
497/2nd	2.00
497-3	0.00
498	3.00
498/2nd	2.00
498-3	0.00
499	5.00
500	3.00

500/CS	4.00
500/Silver	10.00
500/PL	0.00
501-505	2.00
505/Variant	3.00
506-549	2.00
550	4.00
551-599	2.00
600	4.00
601-623	2.00
624	5.00
625	4.00
625/2nd	3.00
626	2.00
627	3.00
627/A	0.00
628-635	3.00
636	5.00
✒Identity Crisis tie	
637	4.00
638	3.00
639	5.00
640-641	4.00
642	6.00
642-2	0.00
643	12.00
643-2	0.00
643/2nd-648	3.00
649	10.00
1000000	2.00
Ann 1	4.00
Ann 2-Ann 6	3.00
Ann 7	4.00
Ann 8	3.00
Ann 9	4.00
Bk 1	0.00

Adventures of Superman (Magazine)
DC

1-3	2.00

Adventures of Tad Martin
Caliber

1	3.00

Adventures of the Big Boy
WEBS Group, 1956

Created for the Elias Brothers chain of restaurants, Big Boy remains the most recognizable giveaway comics star of all time.

Price guide has prices derived from monitoring online sales, shop sales, and auction sales and are for comics in Near Mint condition. A run of issues with the same Near Mint value are grouped together and includes all issues in that range, including variants.

Greetings!

Hello and welcome to the first edition of *Comics Shop*, our full-color guide with more than 800 pages of comic-book details and pricing. In our pages, you'll find listings for thousands of individual comics and hundreds of background essays — along with examples of some of the covers that pulled so many of us into the hobby of comic-book collecting.

We began compiling comic-book price guides nearly 30 years ago in the pages of *Comics Collector*, a newsstand-distributed sister magazine to the long-established *Comics Buyer's Guide*. That initial price guide evolved, as we added more data and more listings, moved the price guide to the pages of *CBG*, and then circulated it as its own publication. Finally, the information became too cumbersome to cram into a magazine format, so we launched it in book form.

Our book price-guide projects began with the Marvel-licensed *Marvel Comics Checklist and Price Guide, 1961 to Present*, when "Present" was 1993. (Stan Lee provided the foreword. Thanks again, Stan!) Then, we released the *1995 Comic Book Checklist & Price Guide* ("1961-Present"), and it became an annual event, with issue-by-issue listings of comics from the Silver Age to the time of compilation.

We also formed a strategic alliance with Pete Bickford to join with him in data for his *ComicBase*, a computer program for comics-collection maintenance. That enabled us to produce our first *Standard Catalog of Comic Books* in 2002 — expanding our scope to include comics that predated the Silver Age and beginning to introduce essays on many indexed titles. Three more print volumes followed, with content (a separate entry for each issue) eventually swelling to a point that pretty much hit our printer's limits.

The next step was a DVD-ROM format, which we released in 2008. Again, the goal was to provide an issue-by-issue checklist: too bulky even to fit handily in a totebag. So we searched for a way to shrink the information we'd compiled into a portable format that didn't require hardware to use.

Comics Shop is the culmination of all those price guides, offering both longtime collectors and novices a full-color guide to comics they already collect — and those they might want to look for in the future.

Whether you're already collecting or just curious about the whys and wherefores of comic books, we've made this volume for you. After all, while illustrated stories have been produced for centuries, the comic books that we've seen on newsstands and in comics shops are a 20th century art form.

The 1930s and 1940s. While some will put comic-book predecessors as far back as the 19th century (or earlier), the first

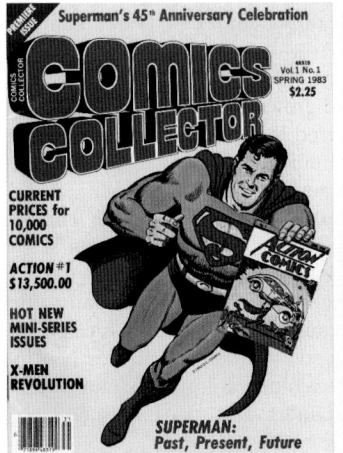

dime comics circulated to newsstands on a monthly schedule were released in the mid-1930s, beginning with *Famous Funnies*.

In 1938, Superman (which had been rejected for newspaper publication multiple times) was published as the star of one of a number of features in *Action Comics* #1, and comics would never be the same. In the next few years, dozens of colorfully clad crimefighters would appear from almost an equal number of publishers.

Of course, super-hero stories were hardly the only genre of picture-stories. There were funny-animal, Western, crime, newspaper-reprint, and many others.

The 1950s. The first super-hero boom ended shortly after World War II, although a few caped crusaders hung on. By the early 1950s, the focus was on horror comics, crime comics, and romance comics, trends which would only last a short while — until Congressional investigations led comics publishers to form the Comics Magazine Association of America and institute its Comics Code seal. That sent comics back to the nursery and instituted pre-publication censorship of their contents.

In 1956, DC began to bring back its abandoned heroes, updating costumes and origins and beginning what would later be called The Silver Age. Those revivals began slowly but quickly picked up steam and reader interest when Marvel followed DC's lead to begin its own line of super-heroes with *Fantastic Four* #1 in late 1961, following that with such titles as *Amazing Spider-Man, Incredible Hulk, Daredevil*, and *The Avengers* in 1962 and 1963.

The 1960s. Marvel's super-hero expansion continued throughout the decade, as readers identified with that company's characters (who had real-life problems) and the salesmanship of editor and scripter Stan Lee. In addition to Marvel and DC, other publishers, including Archie Comics, brought out costumed characters of their own during this decade, but most were relatively short-lived.

The 1960s also saw the creation and expansion of an ongoing comics-collecting community, with amateur magazines and a network of back-issue dealers quickly growing in number.

The 1970s. As America emerged from the late 1960s and began to pay more attention to such social issues as discrimination, pollution, and urban crime, comics followed suit, with Marvel publishing three issues of *Amazing Spider-Man* with an anti-drug story and DC sending two of its heroes — Green Lantern and Green Arrow — on a cross-country trip of self-discovery. This was also the era in which fans who had grown up with comics came of age and entered the field as professionals in increasing numbers, with new ideas and new stories for a new generation.

While readers had been trading comics since the magazines first appeared on store racks, this was the first decade in which standard prices for back issues began to be agreed upon and "official" price guides began to be produced. Amateur magazines continued and were joined by professionally produced newspapers and magazines devoted to the hobby.

The 1980s. The number of comics shops, whose owners could buy comics for a substantial discount, increased. Retailers ordered stock in advance, predicting customers' buying demands. Because their orders were made non-returnably, publishers could eliminate the problems of the newsstand market, in which unsold copies were returned for credit. This meant publishers could print to order.

Thanks to those economics, smaller publishers could come up with viable sales plans. More publishers joined the field, including Dark Horse, Eclipse, Pacific, and First. Later in the decade, the success of *Teenage Mutant Ninja Turtles* encouraged even more small publishers to enter the market — and a bubble was created that quickly burst. The subsequent collapse of that part of the market closed a number of publishers and hurt some shops.

The 1990s. The early 1990s were marked by another boom of independent publishers, led by Image, headed by popular creators who set up their own publishing house. Image was the home for such series as *Spawn, Savage Dragon, Youngblood, Shadowhawk,* and *WildC.A.T.S.* Another major imprint of the early 1990s was Valiant, which reintroduced several adventure heroes previously introduced by Gold Key in the 1960s.

Established super-hero "events" at DC (including 1992's "Death of Superman" and 1993's breaking of Batman's back — they both got better) and Marvel (with a new Spider-Man title in 1990 and a "Clone Saga" in 1994) were part of another boom early in the decade. Part of the action consisted of customers' and retailers' buying entire *cases* of comics hoping to cash in at some future date. Such speculation drove publishers to release variant printings of the highest-selling comics, diluting the market even further and making those cases of comics good for little more than insulation.

The investment bubble inevitably burst,

with huge supplies meeting falling demand.

Another byproduct of the era, comics covers with special features (including glued-on gimmicks, left), are slowly losing their value as those features begin to disintegrate two decades later.

The 2000s. Comics-based movies have, to an extent, resurrected a hobby that was severerly hurt by the speculator boom and bust of the 1990s. The popularity of such films as the Spider-Man trilogy, the Iron Man films, recent Batman films, and other properties — along with the advent of the annual Free Comic Book Day each May and the growing recognition of the excitement of Comic-Con International: San Diego — have made comics cool once again.

In 2010, the sale of three "key" comic books for more than $1 million each (see Page 16) validated the investment potential of specific issues, while calling attention to the hobby as a whole. Third-party comic-book grading has also leveled the playing field for buyers and sellers.

The past few years have also been marked by an increase in families of collectors, in which comics buff Dad is joined by Mom and the kids. Part of that increase in readership is directly attributable to the increase in the number of hardcover and softcover books collecting comic-book storylines in stand-alone packages.

So, whether you're new to collecting (in which case, welcome again to our world) or a longtime fan (in which case, thanks for joining us), there's always something new to discover.

After more than 40 years of collecting and nearly 20 of working in the industry, I still find something new to enjoy every day.

And you can join in those discoveries at *www.cbgxtra.com* and in the pages of *Comics Buyer's Guide*.

— Brent Frankenhoff

Any questions?

Readers have been kind enough to ask many questions about our price guide. To help you make the best use of this volume, we're answering many of them here (and we're answering questions you didn't ask, too, in an attempt to provide more information than you can possibly use).

Is this your first price guide?

Far from it. We've spent nearly 30 years developing a guide so that buyers and sellers of back issues will have help knowing what a consumer with various buying choices can expect to pay, if he's looking — for example — for that issue that will complete his run of the two DC series of *Shade the Changing Man*. The collector will find that even the highest-priced issue in the best condition probably won't cost more than about $4 — and that's the sort of information that can motivate a casual reader to become a collector. (You'll find more on the history of our series of price guides on Page 7.)

Moreover, we try to provide helpful information to people who purchase it in order to have a (yes) guide to buying comics.

This price guide began as a quarterly update of activity in comics published since 1961, as reflected in prices comics shops were likely to charge. Moreover, the focus was pretty much limited to Silver Age super-hero titles — in fact, Silver Age super-hero titles *that were being published when the price guide began*. This meant that such titles as *OMAC*, a title that starred a super-hero but was not still being published by 1983, didn't get listed in that earliest edition. It also meant that so-called "funny animal" titles, "war" titles, and the like were not included.

However, once the listings were begun (not by *Comics Buyer's Guide* staff,

incidentally; the material was started for another publication), Don Thompson took over the compilation. From that point, every effort was made to include every issue of every comic book received in the office. However, since the entries were not on a database and had to be compressed to fit the space available, annotation, dates, and original prices were not usually part of the listing. On the other hand (and because of Don's care, once he took over the project), material which was often overlooked by other reference publishers has been listed from the beginning in the *CBG* listings. *Concrete* and *Teenage Mutant Ninja Turtles*,

Paul Chadwick's creation, Concrete, has appeared in numerous mini-series.

for example, were first listed in **CBG**'s price listings.

In the years since, we've expanded our focus even further, adding in the hundreds of titles published in the 1930s, '40s, and '50s, as well as many lesser-known titles of the Silver Age and beyond. Our cooperative agreement with *ComicBase* has led to the inclusion of hundreds of new titles and issues, as well as a wealth of variant editions.

Pricing information is just *part* of what we offer. In fact, we are increasingly intrigued by the more detailed information you'll find in this book, including character appearances and publishing anomalies. And we continue to fill in remaining information whenever we get it.

Why can't I find a title in your list?

We're working constantly to expand the listings themselves and increase the information on those we already provide. Check out what we have included, and — if you have something we're not listing — please let us

The main Marvel title featuring the wall-crawler is *Amazing Spider-Man.*

know the details!

We need to know the information as given in the indicia of the issue (that's the tiny print, usually on the first few pages, that gives the publishing information): the full title, the number, and the issue month and year — and the U.S. price given on the cover. If there's a significant event (an origin, a birth, a death, *etc.*), please include that, too.

We're also always on the lookout for creator information as it appears in the issue, along with story titles and any other bits of data that we can add to our database. That database doesn't just produce this book, but other price guides as well and is shared with ComicBase, a software package for comics inventory management.

Check, too, on whether you're looking up the title as it appears in the indicia. For example, we list *Vampire Lestat*, not *Anne Rice's The Vampire Lestat*; we list *Mack Bolan: The Executioner*, not *Don Pendleton's Mack Bolan: The Executioner*. Many Marvel titles have adjectives, including *Incredible Hulk* and *Amazing Spider-Man.*

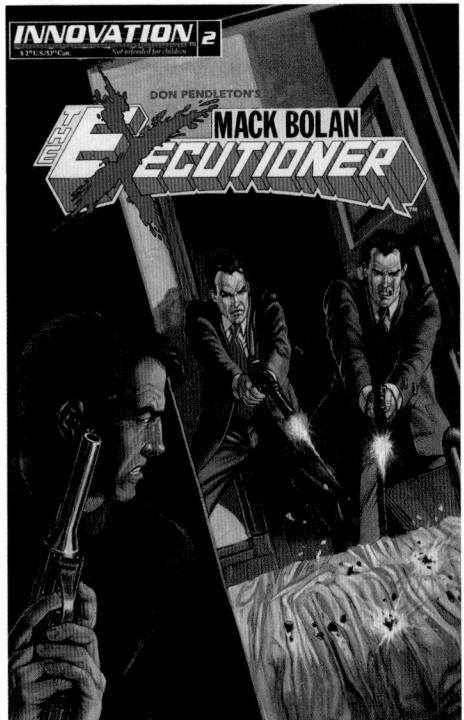

You'll find this title under *Mack Bolan: The Executioner (Don Pendleton's ...)*, not *Don Pendleton's Mack Bolan: The Executioner.*

What's in this book?

Take a look at our "How to Use This Book" piece on Page 6. In addition, we provide quick notes for many individual comics to indicate why they're worth more than issues on either side of them in a given listing.

What are the "Golden Age" and the "Silver Age?"

Comic-book collectors divide the history of comics into the "Golden Age" and the "Silver Age." "Golden Age" indicates the first era of comic-book production — the '30s and '40s. It was a time of incredible creation in the field, when such characters as Superman and Batman first appeared.

"Silver Age" is used to indicate a period of comic-book production of slightly less (nostalgic?) luster than that of the Golden Age. It is usually considered to have begun with the publication of the first revival of a '40s super-hero: the appearance of The Flash in *Showcase* #4 (Oct 1956).

There are additional comics ages, but discussion of those is beyond the scope of this piece.

The Flash's revival in 1956 kicked off what's now known as The Silver Age.

This guide lists #8 and #10. Where's #9?

We haven't seen a copy and can't verify its existence. There was a time when comics collectors could safely assume that issue numbers would run in normal sequence, when no numbers were skipped and when there were no special numbers to confuse completists. That's not the case any more. What we need from those who want to help add to our information is confirmation that an item has *actually been published*.

In the case of multiple variants of a given issue, if they have the same value, they're lumped together in one listing here. For example, the multiple variants of a given Image issue, designated as 1/A, 1/B, 1/C, and so on, could appear as 1/A-1/E in our listings.

So do you own all these comics?

No. Many publishers and collectors have helped us over the years by sending photocopies of indicia, records of publication, annotations, and the like — all of which permitted us to provide collectors with more information every year. What *ComicBase* and we cannot do — and *do* not do — is pull information from other price guides or from announcements of what is *scheduled* for publication. The former would not be proper; the latter leads to errors — the sort of errors that have been known to become imbedded in some price guides' information files.

Every effort has been made to make the notations consistent, but this list has more than 150,000 individual issues coordinated between *ComicBase* and *CBG*, so this can be an arduous task.

Why do some of your listings say (first series), (second series), etc., while others have (Vol. 1), (Vol. 2), and so on? Is there a difference?

Although publishers may begin a series again at #1, they often don't update the volume number in the indicia, which leads to the (first series) and (second series) notations. If the volume number changes (and it's a clear change, as in the case of Marvel's "Heroes Reborn" and "Heroes Return" title restarts), that is what differentiates the series.

After a pair of restarts, Marvel restored *Fantastic Four*'s numbering to its original sequence with #500 in 2003.

On the other hand, when the volume number changes each year (as was the case with some Golden Age and early Silver Age material) but the series number is ongoing in sequence (Vol. 2, #21), then we don't note that change.

Marvel's return to original numbering for *Fantastic Four* and *Amazing Spider-Man* in mid-2003 caused both titles' later listings, beginning with #500 for each, to revert to the respective title's first volume. To help show where the issues from later volumes of those series fall in sequences, we've added parenthetical notations to the original numbers like this: 1 (442).

What are "cover variants"?

These occur when publishers try to increase "collectibility" of and interest in a title by releasing an issue with an assortment of covers. This is in hopes that completists will want to buy multiple copies, instead of just one. (The practice even spread to publications like *TV Guide*.)

So how are these performing as "rare" back issues? So far: poorly. Prices may rise at the time of release, but they usually fall again relatively quickly.

I've heard some of my squarebound comics referred to variously as "bookshelf format," "prestige format," and "Dark Knight format." What's the difference?

Various formats — usually reserved for special projects (mini-series and one-shots) — have different names, depending on the publisher. We use the term "prestige format" generically to indicate a fancier package than the average comic book. Marvel refers to some titles in upscale formats as "bookshelf format," whereas DC initially solicited some of its titles in the format of *Batman: The Dark Knight* as "Dark Knight format." Details of fancy formats can be widely varied.

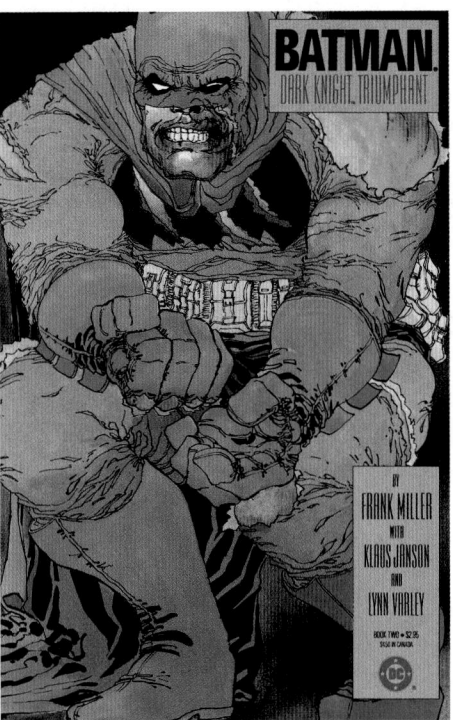

"Dark Knight" format originated in 1986 with DC's four-issue *Batman: The Dark Knight*. The mini-series was printed on glossy stock and squarebound.

I tried to sell my comics to a retailer, but he wouldn't even offer me 10% of the prices you list. Is he trying to cheat me? Are your prices wrong?

Remember, our prices are based on what an informed collector with some choices is willing to pay for a comic book, not necessarily what a shop is charging or paying for that comic book. A shop has huge overhead and needs to tailor its stock to match the interest shown by its customers.

If no one locally is buying comics starring Muggy-Doo, Boy Cat, it doesn't matter that *Muggy-Doo, Boy Cat* is bringing high prices elsewhere in the country.

Comics listed at their original prices may be showing no movement in most comics shops. In such cases, a retailer won't usually be interested in devoting store space to such titles, no matter **how** nice they are or **how** much you're discounting them. We've seen dealers being more selective than ever in what they will buy in recent years.

I'm a publisher, and I'd be willing to buy a hundred copies of my first issue at the price you list. I get calls from all over America from would-be buyers who would pay 10 times the price you give here for out-of-print issues of my comics. What's going on?

A publisher like you hears from faithful fans across the nation. A comics shop deals with a market of one community or smaller. You're dealing with a narrow, focused market of aficionados of your product who are looking for the specific issues they're missing. And with more and more online offerings, those fans find it easier to seek you out. As a result, a publisher who has back issues for sale may get higher prices than readers will find in this checklist. It doesn't mean you're ripping off fans; it means fans looking to buy that material are competing within a nationwide pool; the Internet may eventually put everyone in the same pool.

Can I just order the back-issue comics I want from Comics Buyer's Guide?

This price guide is just that: a guide to the average back-issue prices comics shops

While you can't order back-issue comics directly from us, you can find many of them from the retailers and dealers who advertise in *Comics Buyer's Guide.*

are likely to charge their customers.

We maintain no back-issue stock for sale; we leave that to retailers who specialize in back issues. (Start with your local shops. You'll be able to check out the variety of material available and take a look in advance at what you're buying.)

Comics Buyer's Guide itself is the magazine of the comic-book field. As such, it carries ads from retailers across the country. You can check those ads for specific back issues that you're looking for. You can even take out a "wanted" ad to locate particular items, if that appeals to you. Subscription and advertising information can be found at **www.cbgxtra.com**.

What's the first thing to do when I find a bunch of old comics?

If you've found a box of old comics in the attic and wonder what to do next, the first thing to do is find out what you've got. The same goes when you're looking for what you want to buy.

Here are some basics: Look at the copyright dates; if there are multiple dates, look

at the *last* date. (If they're before 1950, chances are the comics are considered "Golden Age." Comics from the mid-1950s and later are Silver Age or more recent.)

Almost all comics are collected and identified by title and issue number. Look at the indicia, the fine print on the inside front page or inside front cover. That's what you'll use to find a specific issue in this or any other price guide. You'll want to check the issue title as given there — and the issue number.

What's the second thing to look at when I find a bunch of old comics?

Evaluate the condition of the copies. What does the comic book look like? Check the grading guide pages of this price guide, starting on Page 43, to get a feel for the shape your comics are in. If they're beaten up, enjoy them for reading but don't expect to get a lot of money for them.

For this reason, many beginning collectors focus on exactly such poor issues, getting the pleasure of reading without making a heavy investment.

How can I learn more?

Our website, *www.cbgxtra.com*, is a fun and friendly forum for new and longtime collectors to discuss all aspects of comics. But, it's not the only comics-related website out there.

Additional Internet browsing will yield other websites that can answer the myriad questions collectors ask and increase your sources for buying and selling comics. (And *ComicBase* can help in your inventory.)

Surf the Web to find more!

Yes, we're collectors as well, who enjoy going through a box of old comics!

Market Trends

How three $1 million+ comics sales affected the market

Early 2010 was marked by a trio of high-end sales of historically significant comics. Those results have changed everything the world has imagined about comic-book values.

"Now, comic books have entered the realm inhabited by fine art, rare wines, one-of-a-kind jewels, and the like," said Vincent Zurzolo, co-founder of ComicConnect, which on Feb. 22 sold a copy of *Action Comics* #1 (Jun 38, the first appearance of Superman) for $1 million via its website.

Three days after Zurzolo's eye-popping Superman auction, Heritage Comic Auctions sold *Detective Comics* #27 (May 39, the first appearance of Batman) for $1,075,500.

While those two key comics were each graded 8.0 (Very Fine) by Certified Guaranty Company, another copy of Action Comics #1, this time graded 8.5 (Very Fine+), the highest grade received for that issue to date, was sold March 29 for $1.5 million by ComicConnect.

Comic books have been thrust into the conversation of what a well-balanced investment portfolio contains.

Heritage Director of Operations — Comics Division Barry Sandoval told *CBG*, "I think this is a tipping point for comics sales, since we're talking about comics from the 1930s. Supply is limited and, in those higher grades, almost non-existent. Now, if a Silver Age comic book [that is, one distributed after 1955] would sell for $500,000, that would be close to folly in my book, since you never know how many more copies are out there."

Zurzolo said, "I believe people will look back on these sales in the next few years or less and think, 'Boy, that was cheap!' This has happened time and again in the collectibles world. A record price is reached, people gasp, and then, a few years later, they look back and wish they'd bought the book."

The tide raises many boats

How will these events affect pricing overall? ComicBase and Atomic Avenue creator (and *Comics Shop* co-author) Pete

$1,000,000   **$1,075,500**   **$1,500,000**

Action #1 and Detective #27 — Buyer beware!

Action Comics #1 is historically significant because it contains the first appearance of Superman, written by Jerry Siegel and drawn by Joe Shuster.

With Superman jump-starting the super-hero genre and what is known as The Golden Age of comics, the issue has been reprinted several times in the past 72 years, so collectors should be wary of copies presented as the original printing. This is *especially* true of an oversized reprint from the early 1970s that was one of DC's *Famous First Editions* titles. That reprint was roughly the size of a *Life* magazine, and there have been several cases of buyers' being told, "Comics back then were that much bigger than comics of today," and informed that the reprint was the original. (Such sellers would remove the cardboard identifying outer cover, leaving what appeared to be a complete copy of *Action* #1, including the glossy cover and all the original ads.)

Action Comics was an anthology series, containing several stories featuring other characters, and The Man of Steel's first outing was actually a late addition to the package. Long considered one of the "holy grails" of the collecting hobby, copies of the issue in collectible condition have

been selling at gradually higher and higher prices over the years. These 2010 sale surpassed all previous sales by a wide margin. It is estimated that, of its 200,000 copy initial print run, around 100 copies still exist — and approximately half of those have been graded by CGC.

Just shy of a year after Superman's introduction, Batman (written by Bill Finger and drawn by Bob Kane) first appeared in *Detective Comics* #27, another anthology title — and the series whose initials gave DC its identity.

Initially an anthology of mystery stories, *Detective* quickly embraced super-heroes with The Caped Crusader's adventures. The issue hasn't been reprinted as often as *Action* #1, but there is an oversized early 1970s *Famous First Edition* out there, as well as a 1984 reprint. It's estimated that 175,000 copies of this key issue were printed in 1939, with approximately 100 copies surviving and 50 being CGC-graded.

Bickford said his evaluations had already priced *Action Comics* #1 at $1 million in Near Mint (equivalent to CGC 9.4) and had since raised the Near Mint price to more than $1,250,000. (No copies in that condition have ever been reported.)

Detective Comics #27, which his service had previously priced at $225,000 in Near Mint, was at more than $940,000 but was expected to clear the $1 million mark soon. (Sales of other copies of the issue in lesser grades had kept his price-guide estimate from immediately vaulting over the barrier.)

An *eventual* $1 million price for such comics as *Action* #1 and *Detective* #27 has been discussed for years among high-end dealers, including rumors of such a bounty for a Near Mint copy of *Action* #1, but few had expected *two* comics to break the barrier in the same week — with a third adding to the mix within a month and a half.

But what about lower-grade comics? Do these sales affect their price?

Sandoval said he didn't think they would. "Elite collectors tend to want the very best and be bored by second-best," he said. "I personally would love to have the 10th-best

What is CGC?

CGC is the abbreviation for Certified Guaranty Company, an independent grading firm that evaluates comics, gives them a condition grade based on strict criteria and a 10-point scale, and then encapsulates the comic book in a hard plastic holder with the grade prominently displayed. This independent grading levels the playing field for buyers and sellers by establishing a grade that both can agree on and trust. More information is available at ***www.cgccomics.com.***

existing copy of *Detective Comics* #27, but that's just me!"

Zurzolo disagreed. "For books that are rare or lower-grade copies of key issues, you will see an increase in value."

The sales have spurred interest in other comics.

Heritage's *Detective* #27 sale came near the start of a multi-day Signature Sale, and Sandoval said, "We couldn't really focus on that sale too much, since we had the rest of the auction to get through."

"Key" comics

So-called "key comics" are historically significant comics. That is to say, they contain such events as: the first appearance of a character; a major change in that character's life; or a new concept, such as putting several heroes together as a team.

Scarcity and demand can also play into determining a key issue. While the horror, crime, and science-fiction comics produced by E.C. Comics in the early 1950s are highly sought after by many collectors, the real keys (in terms of scarcity) among

all that publisher's releases are the file copies stored away by owner William Gaines at the time and made available to the public in the 1980s.

Gaines' file copies are also an example of

another factor that can determine a key issue: a pedigree. Pedigrees are typically granted to collections that can be identified as belonging to a single collector, who amassed his collection by purchasing his comics from the

The sale did help the firm set a record for a Signature Sale's total results, with a final total of $5.6 million.

Zurzolo said that his pair of *Action Comics* #1 sales has attracted a significant increase in customer interest in other prominent comics. "Customers are calling, looking for certain books," he said, "and not just Superman and Batman.

"These high-end sales produce a certain amount of confidence in our firm, especially for people hesitant to cash in securities and invest in a vintage comic book."

With the security added by CGC's third-party grading service leveling the playing field so that experienced and first-time sellers can identify the items and their quality on an equal basis, it is simpler these days to market such collectibles.

Moreover, unlike many other pop-culture items, most comics are relatively easy for even newcomers to identify to potential buyers.

What's next?

As to the next comic book that might join the $1 million club, Zurzolo said, "The only comics that are worth more are higher-grade copies of *Action Comics* #1."

Sandoval said that he had given the matter some thought in the week or so after his sale and concluded, "Only other copies of *Action* #1 or *Detective Comics* #27 or a really, really nice copy of *Superman* #1 would be a possibility to break into that club.

"I think *Superman* #1 will pass *Marvel Comics* #1 in the price guides soon."

When asked what the *Action Comics* #1 *would* have brought, had it been CGC-graded at 9.4 (Near Mint) or better, Zurzolo said, "I couldn't even *venture* to guess — probably in the multi-millions."

With the *Detective* #27 being only one of two copies graded 8.0 by CGC — and no copies graded higher — Sandoval said he was hesitant to speculate on what a CGC-graded 9.4 (Near Mint) or higher copy might bring.

"This copy was initially graded a Very Fine before CGC put it at 8.0.

"There are comic books that get a nice grade but have a 'blah' appearance that counts against eye appeal — but that *wasn't* the case with this copy and its sharp, bright yellow background."

newsstand, preserving those comics carefully, and retaining many key or rare comics in that original collection.

The most famous of such pedigrees is the Mile High Collection, amassed by Colorado commercial artist Edgar Church in the 1930s and 1940s and discovered by Chuck Rozanski in the 1970s when Church's heirs were clearing the artist's home. Other well-known pedigree collections include (but are not limited to) the Allentown Collection, the Larson Collection, and the Bethlehem Collection.

Since many super-heroes were introduced in the late 1930s and early 1940s, there are many key comics from that time. In addition to Action #1 and Detective #27, other keys of that era include Marvel Comics #1 (Nov 39, first Human Torch, first Sub-Mariner), Detective Comics #38 (Apr 40, first Robin), Superman #1 (Sum 39), Batman #1 (Apr 40), All-Star Comics #3 (Win 40, first teaming of heroes, in The Justice Society of America), All-Star Comics #8 (Jan 42, first Wonder Woman), and Captain America Comics #1 (Mar 41).

What difference does that first impression make?

Getting It Covered

by MAGGIE THOMPSON

What *is* a comic-book cover and what does it *do*? At a recent comics convention panel, artist Michael Golden talked about his job in terms of commercial art: He provides what the publisher wants, which is (in the case of a cover) persuading a shopper to pick up the issue.

Note: That's the *purpose* of a cover.

Donald A. Wollheim (organizer of the first science-fiction convention) produced science-fiction and fantasy paperbacks starting in the 1950s. Among his *many* claims to fame was his discovery that a tiny cover detail could make a difference in sales.

Specifically: If the cover of a Gothic romance novel showed a woman running from a darkened mansion, sales were *higher* if there was a *light* in one of the mansion's windows.

That's the sort of realization that can lead to trends in cover design — and it's the sort of knowledge for which editors and publishers seek all the time.

Once comic-book publishers expanded their contents beyond simple strip reprints, identified by the image of characters buyers already knew, many publishers had to explain what their publication contained.

Nevertheless, publishers whose comics featured beloved characters sometimes didn't provide more than that identification.

As the comics industry and comics-collecting hobbies have evolved, so, too, have comic-book covers. Some typical cover designs fall into such clearly defined categories as:

- The "What Is This?" Cover
- The "It's the Story" Cover
- The "You Know Me!" Cover
- The "What's Going On?" Cover

Of course, those aren't the only types to be found on comics of yesterday and today. Take a look.

The "What *Is* This?" Cover

Jumbo Comics #1 (Sep 38) © 1938 Real Adventure Publishing Co. image courtesy Heritage Comic Auctions

The first monthly comic (*Famous Funnies* #1) had come out four years earlier. (*Jumbo* followed *Action Comics* #1 by three months.) The publisher even had to explain what a comic book was.

The "You Know Me!" Cover

For a while in the 1950s, Dell's *Tarzan* covers consisted of photos of Lex Barker, who starred in five Tarzan films. Kids knew there'd be Tarzan stories inside.

Yikes! The hero is in "not a hoax" peril! How will he escape? Better buy it!

The "What's Going On?" Cover

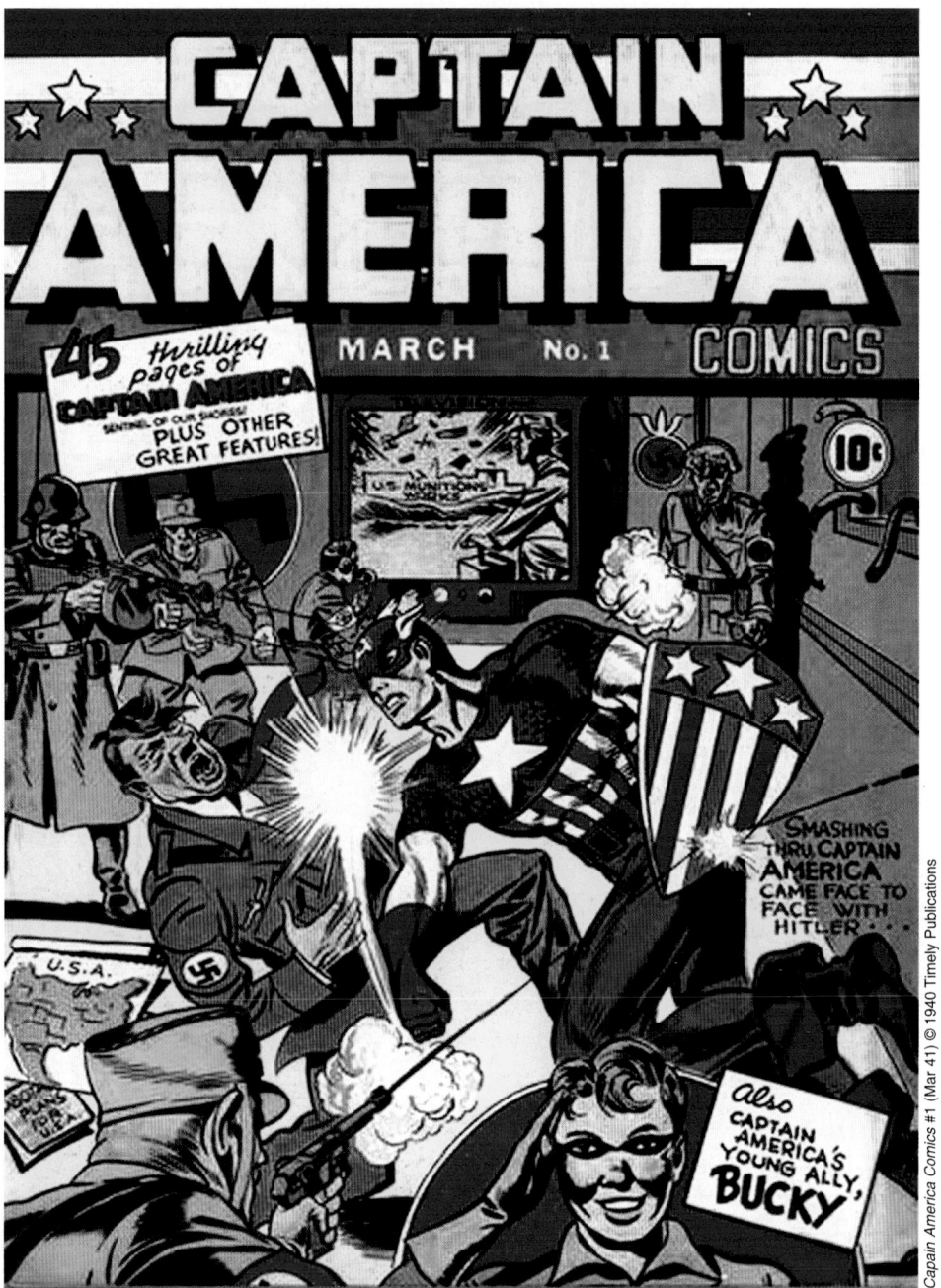

Or maybe it should be called the "Everything but the Kitchen Sink Cover."
Sabotage plans, a TV view of an explosion, guns, Hitler, and more
pack every square inch of the cover. Oh, *and* there's Bucky!
And the United States hadn't even entered the war yet.

The "Read This" Cover

The heck with one big image! Editors get cover credit with Stooges, and readers know what they're buying, thanks to contents page, story summary, *and* bonus gag.

The "Gimmick" Cover

Walt Disney's Vacation Parade #1 (Jul 50) © 1950 Walt Disney Productions

Hey! This cover *moves!*
Sometimes, a cover is there to announce simply:
"Buy this, folks! It's going to be *fun!*"

The "Breaking the Fourth Wall" Cover

We know it's a comic book. *She* knows it's a comic book. So buy it, already.

The "She's *Hot!*" Cover

Hey, the lingerie pages of the Sears catalog are all very well,
but the kid who buys this issue gets "Good Girl Art" *and* a story packed
with jungle action-adventure. Did we mention she's hot?

The "*Yuck!*" Cover

Crime SuspenStories #22 (Apr-May 54) © 1954 L.L. Publishing Co., Inc.

Readers looking for jolts knew what they'd find in this issue.
(Congress called on the publisher to defend this classic cover. He said it *would* have been in bad taste, *if* it had shown the severed portion of the neck.)

The "It's a Variant!" Cover

Is it worth more? Some completists feel compelled to own *all* versions.

What readers these days usually expect is a link between an eye-catching cover and an entertaining story in the issue. When Uncle Scrooge McDuck is shown digging for gold but being startled by an aggressive bear and an armed, angry, elderly lady duck — Well, that's what the readers expected to find in the story "Back to the Klondike." And those readers were not disappointed.

These days, if a wide variety of Lanterns (Red, Blue, Yellow — and, yes, Green) populate a DC cover, readers expect to find it covering a wild story involving, yes, lots of Lanterns. And, if the Red Hulk is on the cover, readers look for crimson coloring on a big guy.

Of course, that's only the beginning of an exploration of what has appeared on comics covers since *Famous Funnies* #1 (July 1934) introduced the monthly 10¢ comic book.

For starters, there are many other categories of cover. Writer Kurt Busiek once suggested, for example, that there were enough covers featuring "Two Guys Hitting Each Other While Falling off a Building" to earn their own genre.

And, of course, there are the "Gimmick" covers. In fact, for a while, there were so many being produced that it was the *Non*-Gimmick covers that were unusual. The category of "Gimmick" covers surely includes:
- infinity covers (in which there's a cover in a cover in a cover, *etc.*)
- gorilla covers (yes, it turned out that having a gorilla on the cover sometimes boosted sales)
- lenticular printing (in which the image shifts depending on the viewing angle)
- atomic-bomb covers

- covers featuring a hologram image
- covers to which the printer has added a fifth ink (in addition to cyan, magenta, yellow, and black)
- diecut covers (with different dimensions than the usual rectangular binding)
- sketch covers (with white space left so that an artist can add an original drawing)
- and ...

Well, what *hasn't* been a gimmick cover?

And, hey, what type of cover — gimmick or not — makes *you* buy a comic book? It is, after all, another aspect of collecting.

The "It's the Story" Cover

What you see on the cover is what you got. There's gold, a grizzly, and a gun-toting gal in this classic Duck story.

The "Don't Get Your Hopes Up" Cover

You knew there had to be a counterpoint to at least one of the cover types, didn't you? Yes, it's the opposite of the "It's the Story" Cover.

In 1952's *Mystery in Space* #9, "The Seven Wonders of Space!" by "Robert Starr" (a penname of Gardner Fox) was the cover story. Clearly, Editor Whitney Ellsworth handed the cover to Fox with instructions to work the cover image into the lead adventure.

The panel shown here is the result: a single panel in which the trapped pair appear in a story that otherwise deals with what amounts to an interplanetary scavenger hunt.

No one ever comments on what's going on in The Great Jewel of Jalar. No one mentions The Diamond Death. The central character is told to retrieve the jewel, and he simply does.

It could be considered

Mystery in Space #9 (Aug–Sep 52) © 1952 National Comics Publications, Inc.

the counterpoint to the "It's the Story" cover in that it *pretends* to be enough of a reason to get the buyer to pick up the issue — but fails to reward the reader for having done so. (Moreover, in this case, the story is pretty mediocre. Comics wouldn't have survived for so long if they did this on a regular basis.)

Nevertheless, it might be fun to collect some comic books in a special file labeled "Horrible Examples." And this issue of *Mystery in Space* could represent a "Horrible Example" of misleading covers.

You *may* have bought it for the *cover* — but what's *inside*?

Now it's time to READ the issue!

by MAGGIE THOMPSON

Do comic-book covers obsess you?

People who don't read comic books could be excused for thinking comics collecting is all about the covers. In *Comics Buyer's Guide*, we even carry a monthly feature in which we focus on 10 covers selected as the subject's favorites.

But are the covers the *reason* we seek out comics? Time after time, collectors tell us that we shouldn't leave comics encapsulated, but should *read* them. Nevertheless, we tend to identify an issue by the cover — and pay higher prices for original cover art than for the original art for the story that cover art was designed to entice the casual customer to buy.

When the cover initially attracts you to an issue, *do* you buy it for that cover — or do you (as do I) — open the cover to see the first interior page (called a "splash page" when it's one big image)? When you're looking at that first page, it's worth noting the tricks that the artist and writer used to entice you to plunk down your money in order to read (and maybe *re*read) the rest.

Let's take a quick glance at a few comics of the past as we think about the matter. Would *you* have bought these issues (which I've picked at whim, albeit not quite at random)? Some of these opening pages were designed to hook the potential purchaser with an introduction to a concept or character; some played on affection for existing characters; some were simply, in effect, the opening paragraphs for an entertaining tale.

Look at them. Read the text. (It should be possible, if you squint.)

Which are most effective?

You might note that the usually anonymous writer Bill Finger actually received prominent contributor credit for his work on *Green Lantern* #2. (And that Mart Nodell's name was misspelled.)

You might note how seldom (at least in these samples) writers received Page One credits. (More recently, they've appeared *somewhere* in the issue — but many Golden and early Silver Age writer's credits never appeared on their creations.)

You might see that Sergio Aragonés even used his *Groo* #1 introductory page to discuss the industry's business models.

But such considerations come in passing. My question remains: Which of these initial pages would have left you unable to put the issue back on the rack? Which, in short, would have made you *buy* the comic book?

Our Gang #24 (Jul 46) © 1946 Loew's Incorporated art by Walt Kelly

It's the first interior page, and writer-artist Walt Kelly tosses off a slew of casual jokes to set up the adventure.

"Here's a Cool Character!"

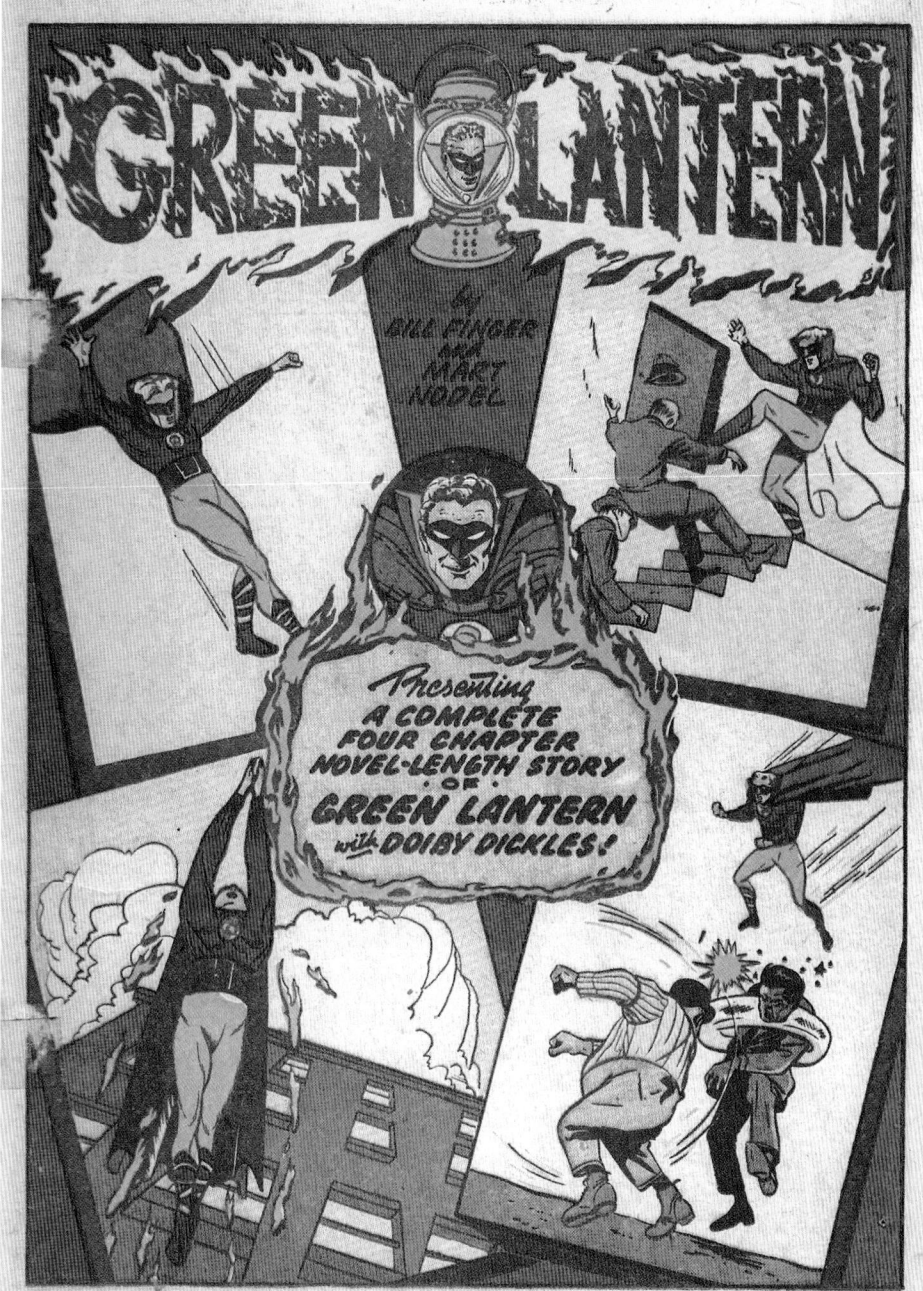

Green Lantern #2 (Winter 42) © 1941 Jolaine Publications, Inc. art by Mart Nodell

Green Lantern had been introduced in *All-American Comics* #16 (Jul 40) a year and a half before this "novel-length" story was published. That meant many readers would want to see more — but new readers needed some idea of what lay ahead.

"Who's in the Story — and Why!"

THE MARVEL FAMILY

The Marvel Family #1 (Dec 45) © 1945 Fawcett Publications, Inc. "The Mighty Marvels Join Forces!" art uncredited

Billy Batson became Captain Marvel in the first issue of *Whiz Comics* (Feb 40), Freddy Freeman became Junior in *Whiz* #25 (Dec 41), and Mary Batson earned her cape in *Captain Marvel Adventures* #18 (Dec 42). Now, they were a family!

"It All Began …"

Dick Ayers turned Magazine Enterprises' The Calico Kid into The Ghost Rider in
***Tim Holt* #11 (Nov 49), then introduced him to new readers in a solo title.**

"Here's the Set-Up!"

Readers knew the characters, so writer-artist Carl Barks simply prepared for action.
This was the one Barks story to be based on a released (October 1952) cartoon.

"Huh? You've Been — *What?*"

It was a chill blustering night at the end of March when Victor Gattling dragged the body into the police station... the body of Joe Endersby, his best friend. Joe Endersby was dead. The two policemen in the station house didn't have to be told that. They could see how his skull was bashed in and how his hair was matted down with thick dried blood. The desk sergeant and the station clerk stared at the shocking grisly sight. But they were more shocked at the words that Victor Gattling croaked hoarsely from his throbbing throat...

MY NAME IS... GASP... *GATTLING...VICTOR GATTLING.* I'VE BEEN *MURDERED*...AND I'VE BROUGHT IN MY *KILLER!*

YOU... YOU'VE BEEN *WHAT?!* MURDERED!?

The desk sergeant cursed and knelt over the still-warm body lying on the station-house floor. The station clerk looked at the man standing before him incredulously...

YOU SAY YOU'VE BEEN *MURDERED?!* BUT YOU'RE *ALIVE!* AND HOW COULD *THIS* GUY *KILL* YOU WHEN HE'S *DEAD!*

@#?*//!! *HE* MUST BE *CRA...*

I'M *NOT CRAZY!* I'M TELLING YOU THE *TRUTH!*

In the early 1950s, E.C. comic books were aimed at older readers and provided sophisticated stories embellished by artists who competed to outdo each other.
Each issue was an anthology of stand-alone short stories,
each designed to grab the reader from the start (and often culminate with a shock).

"Diving into Action"

DOCTOR SOLAR
SOLAR'S
SECRET

A SLED, DESIGNED TO TEST A REVOLUTIONARY NEW ROCKET, SUDDENLY JUMPS ITS TRACKS DURING A TEST RUN IN ATOM VALLEY!

RACING ACROSS THE SAND AT SUPERSONIC SPEED, THE ROCKET BEARS DOWN ON GAIL SANDERS, A NEWCOMER TO THE VALLEY!

DR. SOLAR #1   -627

Doctor Solar, Man of the Atom #1 (Oct 62) © 1962 K.K. Publications, Inc. "Solar's Secret" art by Bob Fujitani

Why wait? Let's just turn back the cover and see him save the woman!
The cover painting had been by science-fiction artist Richard Powers,
but the interiors offered more standard fare.
Note, however, that publisher Gold Key at this point had abandoned panel borders.
And, hey, Doctor Solar didn't get a costume until #5 (Sep 63)!

"Welcome! Let's Talk!"

HOLA! I AM SERGIO ARAGONÉS AND I AM PLEASED TO WELCOME YOU TO THE FIRST ISSUE OF *GROO THE WANDERER!*

FOR MANY YEARS, I HAVE WANTED TO SHARE THE STORIES OF *GROO* WITH THE WORLD... BUT THE COMIC BOOK PUBLISHERS ALL SAID "IF YOU TELL THE TALES IN OUR MAGAZINES, WE OWN THEM, IN TOTAL, FOREVER!"

FOR YEARS, THEY WOULDN'T EVEN *DISCUSS* ANY OTHER ARRANGEMENT. A CREATOR WOULD ASK FOR A TEENSY PERCENTAGE OF HIS CREATION AND BE TOLD NO...

"*SERGIO, IT'S IMPOSSIBLE,*" THEY TOLD ME. THEY HAD *HUNDREDS* OF REASONS WHY AN ARTIST *COULDN'T* SHARE IN THE PROFITS HIS IDEA MADE...

...AND IT *WAS* IMPOSSIBLE UNTIL ALONG CAME NEW PUBLISHERS LIKE *PACIFIC COMICS* OFFERING CREATORS THE SAME RIGHTS THEY GET IN ANY OTHER FIELD.

...AND YOU KNOW WHAT HAPPENED-?

...SUDDENLY, ALL THE PUBLISHERS FOUND A WAY TO DO IT.

AMAZING, NO?

...SO I AM PLEASED NOW TO SHARE THE TALES I'VE WAITED SO LONG TO TELL...

LADIES AND GENTS... MEET GROO...

If *Doctor Solar* was standard fare, *Groo* was clearly not. Cartoonist Sergio Aragonés took readers behind the scenes.

"Imaginative Art, Captivating Text!"

The Swamp Thing character was introduced in *House of Secrets* #92 (Jul 71),
created by writer Len Wein and artist Bernie Wrightson. Writer Alan Moore joined
artists Stephen Bissette and John Totleben to reconstruct the very concept.

"Here's a Stylish, Spooky Set-Up!"

Journal of 1st Sgt.
George Whitman, USA
12/23/44
East Bromwich, England.

We've been here for two days now and it isn't getting any better. All of the men are jittery in this place. Maybe if it had a name. Maybe if the people in the village would even talk about it. But they won't.

Not even telling them there could be a crack team of Nazi commandos lurking about somewheres gets anything out of them. They just look at you like Nazis are maybe the last thing in the world they need to worry about.

If that were true, we wouldn't be here.

Okay--this is what we think we know: Hitler has sent some kind of team to England. I called them commandos, but there's a trio of people from the British Paranormal Society who say they're more than that. They say the Germans are some kind of spook squad. That the krauts are here to perform some kind of spell or something. Summon monsters. Raise the dead.

Yeah, right.

Writer-artist Mike Mignola hooks the reader with a combination of evocative art and tantalizing text.

"It's Not Simple, but You Know You'll Catch On!"

STATURE
(A.K.A. Cassie Lang)

Posted 1 minute ago

MWRAH! HURRH! RRAH! GWRAR!

Posted 30 minutes ago

Ugh. So, we finally made it to Tibet. USAgent and Quicksilver, along with China's super heroes, have been battling a hideously creepy and insanely powerful exiled Inhuman king (like, whew) called The Unspoken. (What kind of name is THE Unspoken anyway? So glad Jonas dropped that "THE" Vision shtick.) It took us long enough to get here. since the Scarlet Witch (who, according to Ronin's lips ((don't ask)), isn't actually the Scarlet Witch) intercepted their distress call!

The crazy Inhuman has released this Xerogen gas that's really starting to cause problems for the Avengers. Unlike Terrigen gas, which upgrades the Inhumans, this gas turns humans into Alpha Primitives. (That's a fancy name for Neanderthals!) It's pretty scary to see my friends acting like primates.

Posted 2 hours ago

While we're running around Infinite Avengers Mansion rounding up bodies to battle the crazy Inhuman guy, Uncle Hank has traveled outside time and space (don't ask me how) to a place he calls… the Overspace. Then, the living embodiment of pretty much everything named him Earth's Scientist Supreme! (I know. So weird, right? You'd totally think it'd be Reed Richards!!) So now it's up to Uncle Hank to save the universe.

Gotta run…time to go kick some Primitives back to the Stone Age!

Previous posts:
- Uncle Hank…gone to the Macroverse. That is SO like him…
- Jocasta and Hank Pym seem to be sharing more than just a friendly connection. Something subatomic?
- Vision has changed his ring on my cell to "My Name is Jonas." Amusing or obnoxious?

THE MIGHTY AVENGERS

THE WASP (HANK PYM)

JOCASTA

THE VISION

HERCULES & AMADEUS CHO

QUICKSILVER (PIETRO MAXIMOFF)

USAGENT (JOHN WALKER)

THREAT

THE UNSPOKEN

The Mighty Avengers #31 (Jan 10) © 2009 Marvel Characters, Inc. art by various

Let's face it: Many of today's stories involve decades of background.
But, hey, in one quick page, you're up to date and can join long-time fans in the fun!

Comic Book Grading Guide

Coming to a consensus on what grade a given comic book is in has been a topic of heated discussion among collectors for many years. When you compare your comics with the images provided here, it's easy to see there are many comics which fall between categories in something of an infinite gradation.

For example, a "Fair" condition comic book (which falls between "Good" and "Poor") may have a soiled, slightly damaged cover, a badly rolled spine, cover flaking, corners gone, tears, and the like. It is an issue with multiple problems but it is intact — and some collectors enjoy collecting in this grade for the fun of it. Tape may be present and is always considered a defect. In addition to the grades shown, *any* defects must be taken into account.

The condition of a comic book is a vital factor in determining its price.

MINT

(Abbreviated **M, Mt**)

This is a perfect comic book. Its cover has full luster, with edges sharp and pages like new. There are no signs of wear or aging. It is not imperfectly printed or off-center. "Mint" means just what it says.

Mint prices are 150% of the Near Mint prices listed in this guide.
[The term for this grade is the same one used for CGC's 10.0 grade.]

NEAR MINT

(Abbreviated **NM**)

This is a nearly perfect comic book.
Its cover shows barely perceptible signs of wear. Its spine is tight, and its cover has only minor loss of luster and only minor printing defects. Some discoloration is acceptable in older comics — as are signs of aging.

Near Mint prices are what are listed in this guide.
[The term for this grade is the same one used for CGC's 9.4 grade.]

VERY FINE

(Abbreviated **VF**)

This is a nice comic book with beginning signs of wear. There can be slight creases and wrinkles at the staples, but it is a flat, clean issue with definite signs of being read a few times. There is some loss of the original gloss, but it is in general an attractive comic book.

Very Fine prices are 66.6% of the Near Mint prices listed in this guide.
[The term for this grade is the same one used for CGC's 8.0 grade.]

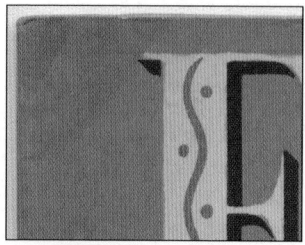  

FINE

(Abbreviated **F, Fn**)

This comic book's cover is worn but flat and clean with no defacement. There is usually no cover writing or tape repair. Stress lines around the staples and more rounded corners are permitted. It is a good-looking issue at first glance.

Fine prices are 33.3% of the Near Mint prices listed in this guide.
[The term for this grade is the same one used for CGC's 6.0 grade.]

VERY GOOD

(Abbreviated **VG, VGd**)

Most of the original gloss is gone from this well-read issue.

There are minor markings, discoloration, and/or heavier stress lines around the staples and spine. The cover may have minor tears and/or corner creases, and spine-rolling is permissible.

Very Good prices are 20% of the Near Mint prices listed in this guide.
[The term for this grade is the same one used for CGC's 4.0 grade.]

GOOD

(Abbreviated **G, Gd**)

This is a very worn comic book with nothing missing.

Creases, minor tears, rolled spine, and cover flaking are permissible. Older Golden Age comic books often come in this condition.

Good prices are 12.5% of the Near Mint prices listed in this guide.
[The term for this grade is the same one used for CGC's 2.0 grade.]

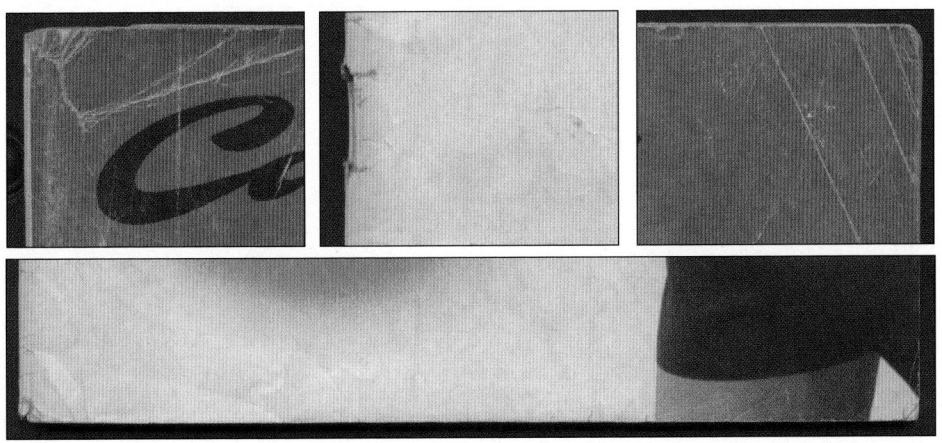

FAIR

(Abbreviated **FA, Fr**)

This comic book has multiple problems but is structurally intact.
Copies may have a soiled, slightly damaged cover, a badly rolled spine, cover flaking, corners gone, and tears. Tape may be present and is always considered a defect.

Fair prices are 8% of the Near Mint prices listed in this guide.
[The term for this grade is the same one used for CGC's 1.0 grade.]

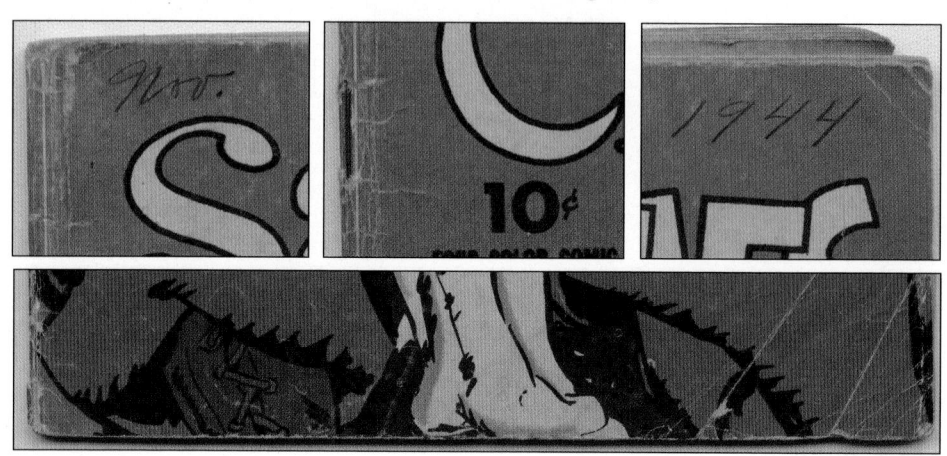

POOR

(Abbreviated **P, Pr**)

This issue is damaged and generally considered unsuitable for collecting.
While the copy may still contain some readable stories, major defects get in the way. Copies may be in the process of disintegrating and may do so with even light handling.

Poor prices are 2% of the Near Mint prices listed in this guide.
[The term for this grade is the same one used for CGC's 0.5 grade.]

Guide to Defects

Theoretically, given a set of grading rules, determining the condition of a comic book should be simple. But flaws vary from item to item, and it can be difficult to pin one label on a particular issue — as with a sharp issue with a coupon removed. Another problem lies in grading historically significant vs. run-of-the-mill issues.

The examples shown here represent specific defects listed. These defects need to be taken into account when grading, but should *not* be the sole determinant of a comic's grade.

(For example, the comics with stamped arrival date, off-center staple are *not* in Mint condition aside from those defects.)

Stamped arrival date and off-center cover and off-center stapling.

Minor defects. Some will not call it "Mint"; some will.

Writing defacing cover.

Marking can include filling in light areas or childish scribbling. Usually no better than "Good."

Clipped coupon.

A square or rectangular piece deliberately removed from the front or back cover or one of the interior pages.
No better than "Fair."

Subscription crease.
Comic books sent by mail were often folded down the middle, leaving a permanent crease. Definitely no better than "Very Good"; probably no better than "Good."

Water damage.
Varies from simple page-warping to staining shown here behind and on the logo. Less damage than this could be "Good"; this is no better than "Fair."

Missing pages and other material.
Ask before taking a comic book out of its bag, but most sellers should allow you to carefully flip through a comic book, looking for such items as clipped coupons from interior pages, scribbling on interior pages, a missing center section, or such lost extra material as trading cards or 3-D glasses.

Rusty staple.
Caused by dampness during storage, rust stains around staples may be minor — or more apparent. No better than "Very Good."

Chunk missing.
Sizable piece missing from the cover (front or back). No better than "Fair."

Multiple folds and wrinkles.
No better than "Fair" condition.

Stains.
Can vary widely, depending on cause. These look like dirt — but food, grease, and the like also stain. No better than "Good."

Tape.
This extreme example of tape damage is used to show *why* tape shouldn't be used on a comic book — or *any* book — for repairs. *All* tape (even so-called "magic" tape) ages badly — as does rubber cement. Use of tape usually means "Fair," at best.

Rolled Spine.
Caused by folding back each page while reading — rather than opening the issue flat. Repeated folding permanently bent the spine. *May* be corrected, but the issue is no better than "Very Good."

*Considered the Holy Grail of comic book collecting, Action Comics # 1 (1938)
features the first appearance of the Jerry Siegel and Joe Shuster creation Superman*

A-1 Comics
Life's Romances, 1944

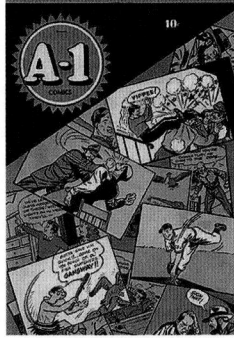

A1 Comics started its run in 1944, publishing a collection of Western, adventure, humor, and crime strips that varied from month to month. Among these were Mr. Ex, Rocky the Stone-Age Kid, and Dotty Dripple.

The title is particularly irksome to indexers in that the first two issues carried no numbering at all. Worse, the later strips such as Tim Holt Western would carry issue numbers marking them as the start of their own titles, instead of a continuation of the larger A-1 Comics title. After issue #17, the A-1 logo was dropped altogether. In a way, this was the reverse of what Four Color Comics (that other nemesis of comic indexers) did when they continued the numbering of the overall series, despite the fact that "Four Color Comics" appeared nowhere at all in the indicia. Only the impossibly high issue numbers indicated that the featured strips were really part of a larger title.

0	200.00
1	100.00
2-4	50.00
5-9	40.00
10-12	34.00
13	135.00
nn	40.00
15	34.00

A1 True Life Bikini Confidential
Atomeka

1	7.00

A1 (Vol. 1)
Atomeka, 1989

1	6.00
2	10.00
3-4	6.00
5	8.00
6	9.00
6/A	10.00
7	8.00

A1 (Vol. 2)
Marvel, 1992

1-4	6.00

A', A
Viz

1	16.00

Aam-Ka-Jutsu
E.C. McGilvray III

1	3.00

Äardwolf
Aardwolf, 1994

1-2	3.00

Aaron Strips
Image, 1997

1-6	3.00

Abadazad
CrossGen, 2004

1	5.00
1/2nd	4.00
2	3.00
3	4.00
3/2nd	3.00

Abbie an' Slats
United Feature, 1948

1	70.00
2	45.00
3-4	40.00

Abbott and Costello
St. John, 1948

1	385.00
2	200.00
3-9	125.00
10	140.00
11-20	80.00
21-30	55.00
31-40	42.00
3D 1	275.00

Abbott & Costello
Charlton, 1968

1	30.00
2-3	20.00
4-10	14.00
11-22	12.00

ABC: A To Z - Greyshirt and Cobweb
DC, 2006

1	4.00

ABC: A To Z - Terra Obscura and Splash Brannigan
DC, 2006

1	4.00

ABC: A To Z - Tom Strong and Jack B. Quick
DC, 2005

1	4.00

ABC: A To Z - Top 10 and Teams
DC, 2006

1	4.00

A.B.C. Warriors
Fleetway-Quality, 1990

A.B.C. stands for Atomic, Bacterial, Chemical. These warriors are robots and can handle it all. Programmed as war machines, these mechanical beings fight for humanity against any number of foes, including the robotic Volgans. Whereas humans would shudder at the horrors of the war they fight, the A.B.C. Warriors are actually programmed to enjoy it.

There are several nice twists here on the familiar theme of "robots as man's programmed death dealers." For one, the A.B.C. Warriors sometimes choose not to kill the robotic foes they fight. They are instead reprogrammed, thus transforming a defeated enemy into a team member. Another unusual turn happens when one of the A.B.C. Warriors decides that hes seen too much killing in his "life" and decides to become a pacifist.

This title originally appeared in the British 2000 A.D.

1-8 .... 2.00

ABC Warriors: Khronicles of Khaos
Fleetway-Quality
1-4 .... 3.00

Abe Sapien Drums of the Dead
Dark Horse, 1998
1 .... 3.00

Abiding Perdition
APComics, 2005
1 .... 3.00
1/A-1/D 4.00
2 .... 3.00
2/A-2/B 4.00

A. Bizarro
DC, 1999
1-4 .... 3.00

A-Bomb
Antarctic, 1993
1-16 .... 3.00

Abominations
Marvel, 1996
1-3 .... 2.00

Above & Below: Two Tales of the American Frontier
Drawn & Quarterly, 2004
1 .... 10.00

Abraham Lincoln Life Story
Dell, 1958
1 .... 16.00

Abraham Stone (Epic)
Marvel, 1995
1-2 .... 7.00

Absolute Vertigo
DC, 1995
1 .... 4.00

Absolute Zero
Antarctic, 1995
1 .... 4.00
2-6 .... 3.00

Absurd Art of J.J. Grandville
Tome
1 .... 3.00

Abyss
Dark Horse, 1989
1-2 .... 3.00

AC Annual
AC

Bill Black, the publisher and head writer of AC Comics, has been very successful at revitalizing a number of second-tier Golden Age characters and combining them with characters of his own. Known primarily for Femforce, an all-woman group, Black brings the fun and exuberance back to comics with straightforward, unpretentious, super-hero deeds and not a small amount of good-girl art.

AC Ann features new stories about characters from decades ago, like American Crusader, Rocketman, and Jet Girl. The back-story, related in a capsule history on each character's pinup page, reveals that they voluntarily underwent suspended animation in Jonathan Weir's Vault of Heroes until such time as the world needed them. Naturally, a crisis precipitated by the Black Shroud necessitated the heroes' reawakening. Now they're back to resume crime fighting in the modern era, though their 1940s attitudes make them something of an anachronism.
-- George Haberberger

1 .... 4.00
2 .... 5.00
3-4 .... 4.00

Accelerate
DC, 2000
1-4 .... 3.00

Accidental Death, An
Fantagraphics, 1993
nn 4.00

Accident Man
Dark Horse, 1993
1-3 .... 3.00

Acclaim Adventure Zone
Acclaim, 1997
1-3 .... 5.00

Ace
Harrier
1 .... 2.00

Ace Comics
McKay, 1937

The cost of amassing a run of Ace Comics keeps many collectors from even starting the project today. Nevertheless, it was one of the best ways for comics buffs of an earlier time to have copies of their favorite King Features Syndicate comic strips. It followed McKay's King Comics by a year, establishing that King's formula of reprinting comic strips in comic-book formats had been an economic success.

The first issue featured the first appearance of Jungle Jim in comic books, and its pages continually featured monthly snippets of top strips of the day. Lee Falk's The Phantom began in #11, and The Ghost Who Walks was an ongoing success, starring on the cover even by the time the series wound to an end in the late 1940s. Although another hit was Hal Foster's Prince Valiant, which began in #26, the primary focus of the series was often on such comedy features as H.H. Knerr's Katzenjammer Kids and Chic Young's Blondie.
-- Maggie

1	2,100.00
2	700.00
3	465.00
4	400.00
5-10	365.00
11	425.00
12-14	245.00
15-20	200.00
21-25	175.00
26	725.00
27-30	180.00
31-36	150.00
37-40	135.00
41-59	105.00
60-79	95.00
80-90	80.00
91-99	68.00
100	85.00
101-119	60.00
120-143	54.00
144-145	80.00
146-148	70.00
149-151	60.00

Ace Comics Presents
Ace, 1987

1-4	2.00

Ace McCoy
Avalon

1-3	3.00

Ace of Spades
ZuZupetal

1	3.00

Aces
Eclipse, 1988

1-5	3.00

Aces High
E.C., 1955

1	120.00
2	90.00
3-5	75.00

Aces High (RCP)
RCP, 1999

1-5	3.00
Ann 1	14.00

ACG Christmas Special
Avalon

1	3.00

ACG's Civil War
Avalon, 1995

1	3.00

ACG's Halloween Special
Avalon

1	3.00

Achilles Storm: Dark Secret
Brainstorm, 1997

1-2	3.00

Achilles Storm/ Razmataz
Aja Blu, 1990

1-4	2.00

Acid Bath Case
Kitchen Sink

1	5.00

Ack the Barbarian
Innovation, 1987

1	2.00

Acme
Fandom House, 1987

1-7	3.00
8	2.00
9	3.00

Acme Novelty Library
Fantagraphics, 1993

1	10.00
1/2nd	4.00
2	7.00
2/2nd-4/2nd	5.00
5-6	4.00
7	7.00
8-13	5.00
14	11.00
16	16.00

Acolyte
Mad Monkey, 1993

1	4.00

Action Comics
DC, 1938

It all started back in 1938 with Action Comics #1. Though it began as an anthology title featuring a number of characters, it cover-featured the first appearance of a certain muscular guy from the planet Krypton - better known to the world as Superman. More than 65 years later, Superman is still going strong, appearing, not only here, but in several other comic titles, including Superman.

Action Comics is where the world first met Clark Kent, Lois Lane, and countless other of the most memorable characters in the world of comics. Over time, the comic book has updated itself somewhat, but the stories remain true to their classic form. Today, Superman still flies the skies over Metropolis, battling evildoers everywhere, fighting for truth, justice, and the American Way.

0	3.00
1	1,000.00
☛1st Superman	
1/2nd	18.00
1/3rd	14.00
1/4th	6.00
1/5th	5.00
1/Ashcan	20,000.00
2	29,250.00
3	19,000.00
4-5	10,600.00
6	15,400.00
7	15,500.00
8-9	6,650.00
10	8,200.00
11-12	4,150.00
13	6,175.00
14	3,825.00
15	6,175.00
16	3,125.00
17	4,350.00
18	3,825.00
19	4,050.00
20	3,825.00
21-22	2,600.00
23	7,300.00
☛1st Luthor	
24-25	2,475.00
26	2,060.00
27-30	1,700.00
31-32	2,600.00
33	7,300.00
☛1st Mr. America	
34-35	2,475.00
36	2,060.00
37-40	1,700.00
41	1,050.00
42	2,600.00
☛1st Vigilante	
43-46	980.00
47	1,300.00
☛1st Luthor cover	
48-52	980.00
53	850.00
54-60	710.00
61-63	630.00
64	750.00
65-70	630.00
71-99	580.00
100	600.00
101	1,200.00
☛A-Bomb cover	
102-126	525.00
127	600.00
128-150	525.00
151-157	480.00
158	750.00
☛Superman origin	
159-161	450.00
162	500.00
163-180	385.00
181-201	340.00
202-220	290.00
221-240	240.00
241	250.00
242	1,200.00

   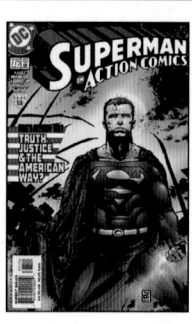

☞1st Brainiac
243-251 ....185.00
252 ....1,200.00
☞1st Supergirl
253 ....425.00
254 ....325.00
255 ....225.00
256-261 ....100.00
262 ....90.00
263 ....100.00
264-266 ....80.00
267 ....650.00
☞1st Colossal Boy
268-270 ....80.00
271-275 ....65.00
276 ....125.00
☞Legion app.
277-284 ....60.00
285 ....100.00
☞Legion app.
286-294 ....60.00
295 ....90.00
296 ....65.00
297 ....90.00
298-299 ....60.00
300-316 ....50.00
317-324 ....40.00
325 ....50.00
326-333 ....40.00
334 ....60.00
335-338 ....40.00
339 ....70.00
340-346 ....40.00
347 ....50.00
348-362 ....40.00
363-373 ....30.00
374-387 ....20.00
388 ....25.00
389-399 ....20.00
400 ....40.00
401-406 ....17.00
407 ....15.00
408 ....20.00
409 ....15.00
410-411 ....13.00
412-415 ....12.00
416-418 ....11.00
419 ....14.00
420-422 ....11.00
423-424 ....10.00
425 ....19.00
426 ....10.00
427-436 ....8.00
437 ....29.00
☞Giant-size issue

438-439 ....8.00
440 ....25.00
☞1st Grell Green Arrow
441 ....12.00
442 ....8.00
443 ....26.00
☞Giant-size issue
444-454 ....7.00
455-465 ....6.00
466 ....7.00
467-481 ....5.00
481/Whitman 10.00
482 ....5.00
482/Whitman 10.00
483 ....5.00
483/Whitman 10.00
484 ....5.00
484/Whitman 10.00
485 ....8.00
485/Whitman 10.00
486 ....5.00
486/Whitman 10.00
487 ....5.00
487/Whitman 10.00
488 ....5.00
488/Whitman 10.00
489 ....5.00
489/Whitman 10.00
490 ....5.00
490/Whitman 10.00
491 ....5.00
491/Whitman 10.00
492 ....5.00
492/Whitman 10.00
493 ....5.00
493/Whitman 10.00
494 ....5.00
494/Whitman 10.00
495 ....5.00
495/Whitman 10.00
496 ....5.00
496/Whitman 10.00
497 ....5.00
497/Whitman 10.00
498 ....5.00
498/Whitman 10.00
499 ....5.00
499/Whitman 10.00
500 ....5.00
500/Whitman 10.00
501 ....5.00
501/Whitman 10.00
502 ....5.00
502/Whitman 10.00
503 ....5.00

503/Whitman 10.00
504 ....4.00
504/Whitman 8.00
505 ....4.00
505/Whitman 8.00
506 ....4.00
506/Whitman 8.00
507 ....4.00
507/Whitman 8.00
508 ....4.00
508/Whitman 8.00
509-544 ....4.00
545-566 ....3.00
567-597 ....2.00
598 ....15.00
☞1st Checkmate
599 ....2.00
600 ....5.00
601-659 ....2.00
660 ....3.00
661 ....2.00
662 ....4.00
662/2nd-682 ....2.00
683 ....3.00
683/2nd 2.00
684 ....3.00
684/2nd-685 ....2.00
685/2nd-685/3rd 1.00
686-687 ....2.00
687/CS 3.00
688-695 ....2.00
695/Variant 3.00
696-699 ....2.00
700 ....3.00
700/Platinum 5.00
701-769 ....2.00
770 ....4.00
771-774 ....2.00
775 ....5.00
775/2nd 4.00
776-799 ....2.00
800 ....4.00
801-810 ....2.00
811 ....5.00
812 ....8.00
812/2nd 2.00
813 ....4.00
814-817 ....3.00
818 ....4.00
819-825 ....3.00
826 ....5.00
☞Inf. Crisis tie
827-828 ....3.00
829 ....6.00
829/Variant 3.00

830	4.00
831-843	3.00
844	6.00
845	5.00
846-849	3.00
850	4.00
851-857	3.00
858	4.00
859-862	3.00
863-875	4.00
1000000	1.00
Ann 1	4.00
Ann 2	3.00
Ann 7	4.00
Ann 8	3.00
Ann 9-12	4.00

A.C.T.I.O.N. Force (Lightning)
Lightning, 1987

1	2.00

Action Girl Comics
Slave Labor, 1994

Sarah Dyer created Action Girl Comics as a sort of springboard for new women cartoonists to use to attract attention. Each issue features the work of numerous cartoonists, each of whom brings an individual style and sensibility to bear. Artistic styles can range from the anime-like characters of Elizabeth Watasin to the more darkly "alternative" work of Carolyn Ridsdale. For her part, Sarah Dyer both coordinates Action Girl and gives new installments of the adventures of the cheerful title character. Readers who are interested in the work of any of these artists can find further biographical and ordering information in the back of each issue.

Overall, Action Girl Comics is a pleasantly hip sampler of the world of women cartoonists. It's a perfect showcase, not only for their work, but for the very idea of artistic independence and self-publishing.

1	4.00

1/2nd-14	3.00
15-19	4.00

Action Planet Comics
Action Planet, 1997

1-3	4.00
Ashcan 1	2.00
GS 1	6.00

Actions Speak (Sergio Aragonés)
Dark Horse, 2001

1-6	3.00

Actual Confessions
Atlas, 1952

13-14	80.00

Actual Romances
Atlas, 1949

1-2	125.00

Ada Lee
NBM

1	10.00

A.D.A.M.
The Toy Man

1	3.00
Ashcan 1	1.00

Adam-12
Gold Key, 1973

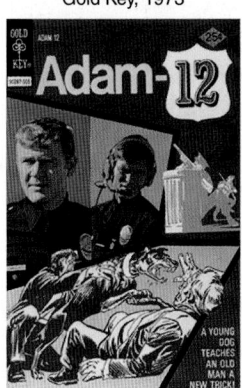

"One Adam-12, One Adam-12!" Those memorable words from the police dispatcher in 1968 ushered in a TV cop show going behind the scenes to view the world of two uniformed policemen assigned to a patrol car. Jack Webb, whose Dragnet series about police detectives had been a major success on both radio and TV, saw to it that his new series (like Dragnet) featured a variety of cases. Some of the stories were played for laughs; some had tension-filled suspense moments. Gold Key delivered a solid comic-book version of the television show

(with a little more mystery and action added for spice) and cool photo covers of the heroes, Pete Malloy and Jim Reed.

-- Rob Salkowitz

1	20.00
2	15.00
3-5	12.00
6-10	10.00

Adam and Eve A.D.
Bam, 1985

1-10	2.00

Adam Bomb Comics
Blue Monkey, 1999

1	2.00

Adam Strange
DC, 1990

1-3	4.00

Adam Strange (2nd series)
DC, 2004

1	10.00
2-3	6.00
4-6	5.00
7	7.00
8	8.00

Addam Omega
Antarctic, 1997

1-4	3.00

Addams Family
Gold Key, 1974

1	60.00
2-3	35.00

Addams Family Episode Guide
Comic Chronicles

1	6.00

Adele & The Beast
NBM, 1990

1	10.00

Adolescent Radioactive Black Belt Hamsters
Eclipse, 1986

1	2.00
1/Gold	3.00
1/2nd-9	2.00

Adolescent Radioactive Black Belt Hamsters Classics
Parody, 1992

1-5	3.00

Adolescent Radioactive Black Belt Hamsters in 3-D
Eclipse, 1986

1-4	3.00

Adolescent Radioactive Black Belt Hamsters: Lost and Alone in New York
Parody

1 ....3.00

Adolescent Radioactive Black Belt Hamsters Massacre the Japanese Invasion
Eclipse, 1989

1 ....3.00

Adolescent Radioactive Black Belt Hamsters: The Lost Treasures
Parody

1 ....3.00

AD Police
Viz, 1994

AD Police is a spinoff from the popular Bubblegum Crisis series. In 2025, Tokyo was utterly destroyed in the Kanto earthquake. Fortunately - or not - the Genom Corporation was all too ready to help rebuild. Within a few years, Genom had risen to become a great economic power in its own right, controlling nearly all of Tokyo.

Among the most popular of Genom's products were the "boomers" - increasingly sophisticated robots with brains modeled after those of humans. The boomers were designed for industry, for extraterrestrial use, and for battle. As a result, they were many times stronger than humans and nearly indestructible. And those electronic brains of theirs, held in check by several levels of blocks to prevent them from going renegade...

This graphic novel is about what happens when those blocks fail...

1 ....15.00
1/2nd 13.00

Adrenalynn
Image, 1999

1-4 .... 3.00

Adult Action Fantasy Featuring: Tawny's Tales
Louisiana Leisure

1-2 .... 3.00

Adults Only! Comic Magazine
Inkwell, 1979

1-3 .... 3.00

Advanced Dungeons & Dragons
DC, 1988

1-36 .... 2.00
Ann 1 .... 3.00

Adventure Comics
DC, 1938

This classic series featured most of DC's favorite heroes and villains in its 45-year run. The Legion of Super-Heroes; Starman; Saturn Girl; the Sandman's sidekick, Sandy; Golden Boy; Hourman; Cosmic Boy; and others made their first appearances in this series. Superboy and Supergirl each starred in its pages for a time, and it was here that Superboy and Lois Lane first met (although Superboy would later encounter and date his mermaid girlfriend Lori Lemaris in this same series).

In December 1972, DC started featuring pure adventure without super-heroes, and in 1974 artist Mike Grell did his first comic-book work for this series. The change in format was short-lived, and, in 1975, DC switched back to the super-hero format, featuring Aquaman, Flash, Wonder Woman, Green Lantern, and many of the first adventures of the later Spectre.

32 .... 2,800.00
33-35 .... 1,450.00

36-39 .... 1,275.00
40 .... 36,000.00
☛1st Sandman
41 .... 4,700.00
42 .... 5,500.00
43 .... 3,200.00
44 .... 5,500.00
45 .... 2,800.00
46-47 .... 4,200.00
48 .... 22,000.00
☛1st Hourman
49-50 .... 1,950.00
51 .... 2,630.00
☛Sandman cover
52 .... 1,600.00
☛1st Kirk Manhunter
53-59 .... 1,450.00
60 .... 2,500.00
61 .... 10,750.00
☛1st Starman
62-65 .... 1,300.00
66 .... 1,800.00
67-68 .... 1,300.00
69 .... 1,650.00
70-71 .... 1,275.00
72 .... 13,200.00
☛1st Kirby Sandman
73 .... 11,500.00
☛1st Kirby Manhunter
74-80 .... 1,500.00
81-91 .... 925.00
92-99 .... 700.00
100 .... 800.00
101-102 .... 700.00
103 .... 2,400.00
☛Super-heroes start
104 .... 850.00
105-110 .... 525.00
111-120 .... 450.00
121-126 .... 390.00
127 .... 450.00
128 .... 400.00
129-130 .... 375.00
131-149 .... 340.00
150-151 .... 425.00
152 .... 310.00
153 .... 425.00
154 .... 310.00
155 .... 425.00
156 .... 310.00
157 .... 425.00
158 .... 310.00
159 .... 425.00
160 .... 310.00
161 .... 425.00
162 .... 310.00
163 .... 425.00
164-169 .... 310.00
170-180 .... 255.00
181-199 .... 235.00
200 .... 350.00
201-209 .... 260.00
210 .... 2,400.00
☛1st Krypto
211-220 .... 200.00
221-246 .... 170.00
247 .... 4,400.00
☛1st Legion

248-255.............................130.00
256.....................................525.00
257-259.............................125.00
260.....................................500.00
☛Aquaman origin
261-266...............................80.00
267.....................................740.00
☛2nd Legion
268.......................................80.00
269.....................................225.00
☛1st Aqualad
270.......................................80.00
271.....................................225.00
☛Lex Luthor origin
272-274...............................65.00
275.....................................145.00
276-280...............................65.00
281.......................................60.00
282.......................................95.00
283.....................................100.00
284.......................................60.00
285-286.............................110.00
287-289...............................60.00
290.....................................100.00
291-292...............................45.00
293.....................................100.00
294.......................................90.00
☛1st Mon-El Legion
295-298...............................45.00
299.......................................55.00
300.....................................200.00
☛Legion
301.......................................70.00
302-305...............................55.00
306-323...............................45.00
324-339...............................40.00
340.......................................45.00
341-345...............................40.00
346.......................................60.00
347-350...............................40.00
☛1st White Witch
351-352...............................50.00
353-355...............................35.00
356.......................................30.00
357.......................................60.00
358-366...............................30.00
367-372...............................25.00
373.......................................22.00
374.......................................30.00
375-377...............................22.00
378.......................................45.00
379-380...............................22.00
381.......................................60.00

☛Supergirl starts
382-389..............................22.00
390.....................................30.00
391-400..............................22.00
401-402..............................21.00
403.....................................50.00
404-415..............................20.00
416.....................................18.00
417-427..............................13.00
428.....................................28.00
☛1st Black Orchid
429-430..............................15.00
431.....................................28.00
☛Aparo Spectre
432-433..............................15.00
434-435..............................12.00
436-441..............................10.00
442-447................................6.00
448-458................................5.00
459-460................................4.00
461..6.00
462..7.00
463-479................................4.00
480-503................................3.00

Adventure Comics (2nd Series)
DC, 1998

1...2.00
GS 1....................................5.00

Adventure Into Mystery
Atlas, 1956

1......................................160.00
2......................................115.00
3..95.00
4-6......................................85.00
7-8......................................75.00

Adventure is My Career
Street & Smith, 1945

1..60.00

Adventure of the Copper Beeches
Tome

1..3.00

Adventure of the Naval Treaty
Caliber

1..4.00

Adventurers (Aircel)
Aircel

1-2.......................................2.00

Adventurers (Book 1)
Adventure, 1986

0-10.....................................2.00

Adventurers (Book 2)
Adventure, 1987

0-10.....................................2.00

Adventurers (Book 3)
Adventure, 1989

1-6.......................................2.00

Adventures
St. John, 1949

1......................................130.00
2......................................100.00

Adventures of Bio Boy
Speakeasy Comics, 2005

1..3.00

Adventures of Ozzie and Harriet
DC, 1949

1......................................600.00
2......................................285.00
3-5....................................230.00

Adventures @ eBay
eBay, 2000

1..1.00

Adventures for Boys
Bailey, 1955

1..28.00

Adventures in Reading Starring: The Amazing Spider-Man
Marvel, 1990

1..1.00

Adventures in the DC Universe
DC, 1997

1..3.00
2-19.....................................2.00
Ann 1...................................4.00

Adventures in the Mystwood
Blackthorne, 1986

Adventures in the Mystwood is a beautiful black-and-white fairy tale by John Arthur Williams. It is the story of Zara, a young princess who lost both her parents and her prince in "a war between rival kingdoms." Wandering through the woods after the war was over, Zara grew weary and fell asleep at the base of a tree. She awoke and found herself in the Mystwood, a magical land populated by "dwelfs" (dwarves and elves) and fairies. Zara soon began to leave behind her sorrows, but her dreams were still haunted by her lost prince, and her nightmares were riddled with monsters. With the dwelfs' instruction, Zara takes her first steps into the Somewhen, where she will confront her nightmares, and there her real journey begins. Without a doubt, this is an enchanting story that unfolds as delicately and beautifully as its pictures are rendered.

1 ....2.00

Adventures in the Rifle Brigade
DC, 2000

1-3...3.00

Adventures in the Rifle Brigade: Operation Bollock
DC, 2001

1-3...3.00

Adventures in 3-D
Harvey, 1953

1 ....55.00
2 ....38.00

Adventures Into Darkness
Standard, 1952

5...215.00

6-9 .... 130.00
10-12 .... 110.00
13 .... 125.00
14 .... 100.00

Adventures Into Terror
Atlas, 1950

1 (#43)............................... 400.00
2 (#44)............................... 240.00
3-4 .... 160.00
5 .... 165.00
6 .... 145.00
7 .... 300.00
8 .... 145.00
9-10 .... 125.00
11-20 .... 110.00
21-31 .... 90.00

Adventures into the Unknown
ACG, 1948

During the twilight of super-heroes in the early 1950s, science-fiction and horror comics were the hottest thing on the newsstands, and this title was one of the pioneers of the genre. Each issue served up three or four short stories featuring alien attacks, post-atomic nightmares, bug-eyed monsters, unexplained phenomena, and other meat-and-potatoes 1950s science-fantasy themes. Adventures into the Unknown was broad enough in format to allow straight mystery and suspense stories side by side with hardcore science fiction, horror, and monsters.

The ACG art and writing staff lacked the talent of such bigger publishers as E.C., Atlas (Marvel), and DC, but managed to produce clean, workmanlike art and entertaining stories.

-- Rob Salkowitz

1 .... 1,400.00
2 .... 600.00
3 .... 580.00
4-5 .... 350.00
6-7 .... 225.00

8-10 .... 175.00
11-15 .... 140.00
16-26 .... 120.00
27 .... 135.00
28-30 .... 120.00
31-40 .... 90.00
41-50 .... 80.00
51 .... 225.00
☛3-D covers start
52-58 .... 190.00
59 .... 85.00
60-62 .... 70.00
63-70 .... 45.00
71-90 .... 38.00
91-99 .... 32.00
100 .... 36.00
101-120 .... 28.00
121-140 .... 26.00
141-160 .... 24.00
161-174 .... 18.00

Adventures into the Unknown
A-Plus, 1990

1-4 .... 3.00

Adventures Into Weird Worlds
Atlas, 1952

1 .... 285.00
2 .... 175.00
3-5 .... 140.00
6-10 .... 125.00
11-20 .... 100.00
21-30 .... 85.00

Adventures in Wonderland
Lev Gleason, 1955

1 .... 140.00
2 .... 100.00
3-5 .... 65.00

Adventures Made in America
Rip Off

0-6 .... 3.00

Adventures of Aaron
Chiasmus, 1995

1-2 .... 3.00

Adventures of Aaron (2nd Series)
Image, 1997

1-100 .... 3.00

Adventures of Adam & Bryon
American Mule, 1998

1 .... 3.00

Adventures of Alan Ladd
DC, 1949

1 .... 450.00
2 .... 325.00
3-5 .... 235.00
6-9 .... 180.00

Adventures of a Lesbian College School Girl
NBM
1 ....9.00

Adventures of Alice
Pentagon, 1945
1 ....40.00
2-3 ....28.00

Adventures of Bagboy and Checkout Girl
Acetelyne, 2002
Ashcan 1 ....1.00

Adventures of Baron Munchausen
Now, 1989
1-4 ....2.00

Adventures of Barry Ween, Boy Genius
Image, 1999
1-3 ....3.00

Adventures of Barry Ween, Boy Genius 2.0
Oni, 2000
1-3 ....3.00

Adventures of Barry Ween, Boy Genius 3: Monkey Tales
Oni, 2001
1-6 ....3.00

Adventures of Bayou Billy
Archie, 1989
1-5 ....1.00

Adventures of Bob Hope
DC, 1950
1 ....900.00
2 ....500.00
3-4 ....450.00
5-6 ....250.00
7-8 ....200.00
9-10 ....150.00
11-15 ....125.00
16-20 ....90.00
21-31 ....85.00
32 ....70.00
33-50 ....55.00
51-60 ....40.00
61-70 ....35.00
71-80 ....30.00
81-90 ....25.00
91-105 ....15.00
106-109 ....25.00

Adventures of B.O.C.
Invasion, 1986
1-3 ....2.00

Adventures of Browser & Sequoia
SaberCat, 1999
1 ....3.00
2 ....2.00

Adventures of Captain America
Marvel, 1991

In the midst of World War II, Project Rebirth, with its Super Soldier Serum, transformed skinny Steve Rogers into the powerhouse known as Captain America. Deciding that he must be kept a secret, the people in charge of Project Rebirth assigned Private Rogers to duty on an army base. Even then Rogers found excitement and adventure, foiling Nazi saboteurs who were stealing ordinance from the base.

This four-issue series relives the early adventures of Captain America. It includes his creation, his introduction to future sidekick, James Buchanan (Bucky) Barnes, and his first battle with his arch-nemesis, the Red Skull.

1-4 .... 5.00

Adventures of Captain Jack
Fantagraphics, 1986
1-12 .... 2.00

Adventures of Captain Nemo
Rip Off
1 .... 3.00

Adventures of Chrissie Claus
Hero, 1991
1-2 .... 3.00

Adventures of Chuk the Barbaric
White Wolf, 1987
1-2 .... 2.00

Adventures of Cyclops and Phoenix
Marvel, 1994
1-4 .... 3.00

Adventures of Dean Martin & Jerry Lewis
DC, 1952
1 .... 550.00
2 .... 275.00
3-10 .... 140.00
11-19 .... 90.00
20-30 .... 75.00
31-40 .... 55.00

Adventures of Dr. Graves
A-Plus
1 .... 3.00

Adventures of Dolo Romy
Dùlo Blue
1 .... 3.00

Adventures of Doris Nelson, Atomic Housewife
Jake Comics, 1996
1 .... 3.00

Adventures of Edgar Mudd and Elaine
Wet Earth
1 .... 4.00

Adventures of Evil & Malice
Image, 1999
1-3 .... 4.00

Adventures of Felix the Cat
Harvey, 1992
1 .... 2.00

Adventures of Ford Fairlane
DC, 1990
1-4 .... 2.00

Adventures of Homer Ghost
Atlas, 1957
1 .... 35.00
2 .... 30.00

Adventures of Jerry Lewis
DC, 1957
41 .... 40.00
42-50 .... 36.00
51-60 .... 34.00
61-80 .... 28.00
81-91 .... 25.00
92 .... 30.00
93-96 .... 25.00
97 .... 35.00
98-100 .... 25.00
101 .... 32.00
102 .... 55.00
☛Beatles app.
103-104 .... 32.00
105 .... 40.00
106-116 .... 14.00

117	20.00
118-119	14.00
120-124	12.00

Adventures of Jo-Joy
W.T. Grant, 1945

1	12.00
2-9	10.00

Adventures of Kelly Belle: Peril on the High Seas
Atlantis, 1996

1	3.00

Adventures of Kool-Aid Man
Marvel, 1983

1	1.00
5	1.00

Adventures of Liberal Man
Political, 1996

1-7	3.00

Adventures of Luther Arkwright (Valkyrie)
Valkyrie, 1987

1-10	3.00

Adventures of Luther Arkwright
Dark Horse, 1990

1	3.00
2-9	2.00

Adventures of Mark Tyme
John Spencer & Co.

1-2	2.00

Adventures of MGM's Lassie
Western Publishing, 1949

1	200.00

Adventures of Mighty Mouse (1st Series)
St. John, 1952

2	125.00
3	85.00
4-5	65.00
6-10	52.00
11-18	38.00

Adventures of Mighty Mouse (2nd Series)
Literary Enterprises, 1955

126	40.00
127-130	34.00
131-140	32.00
141-150	30.00
151-160	26.00

Adventures of Mighty Mouse
Gold Key, 1979

166-172	4.00

Adventures of Mr. Pyridine
Fantagraphics

1	3.00

Adventures of Misty
Forbidden Fruit, 1991

1-12	3.00

Adventures of Monkey
Womp, 1995

1-4	2.00

Adventures of Oat Willie
Austintatious Comics, 1987

1	3.00

Adventures of Pinky Lee
Atlas, 1955

1	145.00
2-5	85.00

Adventures of Pioneer Pete
Pioneer Chicken

1	2.00

Adventures of Quik Bunny
Marvel, 1984

1	3.00

Adventures of Rex the Wonder Dog
DC, 1952

1	675.00
2	350.00
3	275.00
4-5	235.00
6-10	175.00
11	190.00
12-15	115.00
16-20	100.00
21-30	70.00
31-40	42.00
41-46	34.00

Adventures of Rheumy Peepers & Chunky Highlights
Oni, 1999

1	3.00

Adventures of Rick Raygun
Stop Dragon, 1986

1-5	2.00

Adventures of Riggin' Bill
Remington Morse

1	35.00

Adventures of Mighty Mouse
Gold Key, 1979

Adventures of Robin Hood
Gold Key, 1974

1	8.00
2	5.00
3-7	4.00

Adventures of Roma
Forbidden Fruit, 1993

1	4.00

Adventures of Snake Plissken
Marvel, 1997

Paramount Comics paired up with Marvel Comics in the late 1990s to produce comics of movie properties. Snake Plissken is the hero from the movie "Escape From New York." This series relates the exploits of Snake, an outlaw and bounty hunter, in a mad future America. The action-filled stories juxtapose robots and high-tech weapons with clever comments on modern-day obsessions. As with most media tie-ins, there is a certain value for fans of the movie.

1	3.00

Adventures of Spencer Spook
Ace, 1986

1-6	2.00

Adventures of Spider-Man
Marvel, 1996

1-12	2.00

Adventures of Stickboy
Stinky Armadillo

1	1.00

Adventures of Superboy
DC, 1991

19-22	2.00

Adventures of Superman
DC, 1987

It's a bird...it's a plane...it's... Superman, of course, DC's greatest super-hero, and one of the world's best-known characters. With his super-strength, ability to fly, invulnerability, X-ray vision, and other super-powers, he's easily one of the mightiest characters ever created. The challenge is to make such a legendary character come across as fresh and believable to what is now its third or fourth generation of readers. As this title shows, DC is more than up to the job.

In 1987, Superman's character was modified, altering his origin and powers, as well as the backgrounds of his supporting cast. As part of that Superman rebirth, DC switched around its various Superman titles, renaming their old Superman series "The Adventures of Superman" and creating a new, second series of Superman.

0	2.00
424	3.00
425	4.00
426	3.00
427-443	2.00
444-462	2.00
463	3.00
464-465	2.00
466	3.00
467-479	2.00
480	3.00
481-495	2.00
496	3.00
496/2nd	2.00
497	3.00
497/2nd	2.00
498	3.00
498/2nd	2.00
499	5.00
500	3.00
500/CS	4.00
500/Silver	10.00
501-505	2.00
505/Variant	3.00
506-549	2.00
550	4.00
551-599	2.00
600	4.00
601-623	2.00
624	5.00
625	4.00
625/2nd	3.00
626	2.00
627	3.00
628-635	3.00
636	5.00
☛Identity Crisis tie	
637	4.00
638	3.00
639	5.00
640-641	4.00
642	6.00
643	12.00
643/2nd-648	3.00
649	10.00
1000000	2.00
Ann 1	4.00
Ann 2-6	3.00
Ann 7	4.00
Ann 8	3.00
Ann 9	4.00

Adventures of Superman (Magazine)
DC

1-3	2.00

Adventures of Tad Martin
Caliber

1	3.00

Adventures of the Big Boy
WEBS Group, 1956

Created for the Elias Brothers chain of restaurants, Big Boy remains the most recognizable giveaway comics star of all time. Developed by advertising guru Manfred Bernhard, the early issues featuring the amiable (if a bit too well-fed) kid were farmed out to Timely, where Stan Lee and Bill Everett worked on them.

In the late 1970s, Bernhard's WEBS Advertising Group arranged for special issues featuring Superman, Battlestar Galactica, and other media favorites. In 1996, the Elias chain dropped Bernhard's production company after 466 issues. Craig Yoe's Yoe Studios revamped the series, with slicker paper and even more media guests -- and, surprisingly, an issue drawn by Steve Ditko.

Since different parts of the Elias chain had different names, the same issue may be found with many different regional variants. While those only usually have varying labels, an interesting group of variants have alternate art, with Big Boy appearing as a more slender strawberry blond. A "blond" variant existed for #1 and many later issues, with one having been observed as late in the series as #152. They originated from eastern chains such as Frisch's, and are labelled below as "East" variants where we have located them; more certainly exist. We have noticed no difference in price in any of these variants.

A separate series with different content and numbering came from the Shoney's chain in the late 1970s and early 1980s following its separation from the Elias chain; it ran 75 issues.

-- John Jackson Miller

1-1/East	750.00
2-2/East	295.00
3-3/East	125.00
4-4/East	90.00
5-5/East	75.00
6-7	50.00
8-10/East	45.00
11-15	30.00
16-20	24.00
21-25	16.00
26-30/East	12.00
31-40	10.00
41-50/East	6.00
51	5.00
52	8.00
53-100	5.00
101-150/East	4.00
151-300	3.00
301-500	2.00
501-521	1.00

Adventures of the Big Boy (Paragon)
Paragon, 1976

1-34	2.00
35-75	1.00

Adventures of the Fly
Archie, 1959

As super-heroes regained popularity in the late 1950s and early 1960s, the beginning of the Silver Age of Comics, the folks at Archie dusted off some of their Golden Age heroes from the 1940s and offered up new ones. One of those is the Fly, who first appeared in The Double Life of Private Strong #1 in 1959.

The Fly is secretly lawyer Thomas Troy; when the need arises, he touches his magic ring and transforms into his super-powered alter ego. Adventures of the Fly offers up standard super-hero fare, but the run is notable for the work of comics legends Joe Simon and Jack Kirby in early issues.

1	220.00
2	140.00
3	100.00
4-5	80.00
6-17	70.00
18-26	40.00
27-31	30.00

Adventures of the Jaguar
Archie, 1961

1	125.00
2	75.00
3	50.00
4-5	40.00
6-10	30.00
11-15	22.00

Adventures of the Little Green Dinosaur
Last Gasp

1-2	5.00

Adventures of the Mad Hunda Day Day
Thaumaturge, 1995

1	2.00

Adventures of the Mask
Dark Horse, 1996

1-12	3.00
Special 1	1.00

Adventures of the Outsiders
DC, 1986

33-46	1.00

Adventures of Theown
Pyramid, 1986

1-3	2.00

Adventures of the Screamer Brothers
Superstar, 1990

1-3	2.00

Adventures of the Screamer Brothers (Vol. 2)
Superstar, 1991

1-3	2.00

Adventures of the Super Mario Bros.
Valiant, 1991

1	4.00
2-9	3.00

Adventures of the Thing
Marvel, 1992

1-4	2.00

Adventures of the Vital-Man
Budgie, 1991

1-4	2.00

Adventures of the X-Men
Marvel, 1996

1-12	2.00

Adventures of Tintin
Mammoth

1	10.00
1/2nd-22	9.00

Adventures on Space Station Freedom
Tadcorps

1	3.00

Adventures on the Fringe
Fantagraphics, 1992

1-5	2.00

Adventures On the Planet of the Apes
Marvel, 1975

Astronauts Taylor, Stewart, Landon, and Dodge have been away for a while-and while it only seems like 18 months to them, they've been traveling near the speed of light all that time. According to Hasslein's theory, to the world outside, they've been gone for almost 2,000 years. When they return, things will have become very different on Mother Earth.

While they were away, apes had risen in a great rebellion to become masters of the planet. In doing so, they have built great civilizations, and treat humans as no more than pets. The returning astronauts face a world turned upside down-a Planet of the Apes.

An incredibly popular series of movies, this title presents the earlier Planet of the Apes comic for the first time in color.

1	9.00
2-5	4.00
5/30¢	20.00
6	4.00
6/30¢	20.00
7	4.00
7/30¢	20.00
8-11	4.00

Adventure Strip Digest
WCG, 1994

1-4	3.00

Adventurous Uncle Scrooge McDuck
Gladstone, 1998

1-2	3.00

Aeon Flux
Dark Horse, 2005

1-4	3.00

Aeon Focus
Aeon, 1994

1-5	3.00

A

Aertimisan: War of Souls
Almagest, 1997
1-2..3.00

Aesop's Desecrated Morals
Magnecom
1..3.00

Aesop's Fables
Fantagraphics, 1991
1-3..3.00

Aeternus
Brick, 1997
1..3.00

Aetos the Eagle
Orphan Underground, 1994
1-2..3.00

Aetos the Eagle (Vol. 2)
Ground Zero, 1997
1-3..3.00

Affable Tales for Your Imaginaton
Lee Roy Brown, 1987
1..3.00

After Apocalypse
Paragraphics, 1987
1..2.00

After Dark
Millennium
1..3.00

Aftermath
Pinnacle, 1986
1..2.00

Aftermath (Chaos)
Chaos, 2000
1..3.00
1/A-Ash 1 ....2.00

After/Shock: Bulletins from Ground Zero
Last Gasp
1..2.00

After the Rain
NBM, 1999
1..13.00

Against Blackshard: 3-D: The Saga of Sketch, the Royal Artist
Sirius
1..2.00

Agency
Image, 2001
Ashcan 1 ....3.00
Ashcan 1/Gold 5.00
1/A-5 ....3.00
6..5.00

Agent
Marvel
1..10.00

Agent "00" Soul
Twist Records
1 .... 5.00

Agent America
Awesome
Ashcan 1 .... 5.00

Agent Liberty Special
DC, 1991
1 .... 2.00

Agents
Image, 2003
1-6... 3.00

Agents of Atlas
Marvel, 2006
1-6... 3.00

Agents of Law
Dark Horse, 1995

Keith Giffen dramatically revamps 1994's Catalyst: Agents of Change, bringing a mysterious stranger known only as Law to the utopian city-state of Golden City. After seemingly rescuing Grace, Golden City's founder Law becomes a popular favorite amongst the citizens of the city and is appointed its figurehead ruler after her death. Through a combination of Machiavellian trickery and brute force, Law parlays this position into one of power.

In the meantime, the growing tent city beyond the city's walls is becoming a very real threat to public health and safety, and the circumstances surrounding Grace's death cause the remaining members of Catalyst (Mecha, Rebel, Ruby, and Warmaker) to wonder about the true motives of their new leader.

Agents of Law is part of the Dark Horse Heroes line, formerly known as Comics' Greatest World.

1-6... 3.00

Agent 13: The Midnight Avenger
TSR
1 .... 8.00

Agent Three Zero
Galaxinovels
1 .... 4.00

Agent Three Zero: The Blue Sultan's Quest/Blue Sultan- Galaxi Fact Files
Galaxinovels
1-4... 3.00

Agent Unknown
Renegade, 1987
1-3... 2.00

Agent X
Marvel, 2002
1-6... 2.00
7-15....................................... 3.00

Age of Apocalypse: The Chosen
Marvel
1 .... 3.00

Age of Bronze
Image, 1998

Talk about your noble missions! This series from the talented Eric Shanower (The Enchanted Apples of Oz, The Elsewhere Prince) has as its goal retelling the complete story of the Trojan War, from young Paris' idyllic days on Mount Ida and his relationship with the beautiful Oenone to the heroes' departure for the homelands at the war's end. As is typical of Shanower's work, the art here is gorgeous -- even in black and white -- and the script is flawless. There is a sense of drama, as Oenone warns Paris of his death in her dreams, and readers know only too well what lies ahead, as Paris heads to Troy to win back a cow his family had intended as a sacrifice to the gods.

```
1 ............................................... 4.00
2-7 .......................................... 3.00
8-25 ......................................... 4.00
Special 1 ................................. 3.00
Special 2 ................................. 4.00
```

Age of Heroes
Halloween, 1996

```
1-4 .......................................... 3.00
5 ............................................... 4.00
Special 1 ................................. 5.00
Special 2 ................................. 7.00
```

Age of Heroes: Wex
Image, 1998

```
1 ............................................... 3.00
```

Age of Innocence:
The Rebirth of Iron Man
Marvel

```
1 ............................................... 3.00
```

Age of Reptiles
Dark Horse, 1993

```
1-4 .......................................... 3.00
```

Age of Reptiles:
The Hunt
Dark Horse, 1996

```
1-5 .......................................... 3.00
```

Aggie Mack
Superior, 1948

```
1 ........................................... 165.00
2-3 ......................................... 85.00
4 ............................................. 95.00
5-8 ......................................... 85.00
```

Agony Acres
AA2, 1995

```
1-5 .......................................... 3.00
```

Ahlea
Radio, 1997

Ahlea is surprised to discover that her imaginary childhood friend is-apparently-a flesh-and-blood human being and forcing her to look objectively at her life and what she has-and hasn't-done with it.

But there's more to the story than meets the eye in this black-and-white title from Radio Comix and writer/artist Lazarus Berry (Ninja High School).

```
1-2 ......................................... 3.00
```

Aida-Zee
Nate Butler

```
1 ............................................... 2.00
```

Aiden McKain
Chronicles:
Battle for Earth
Digital Webbing, 2005

```
1 ............................................... 3.00
1/Incentive ........................... 10.00
```

AIDS Awareness
Chaos City, 1993

```
1 ............................................... 3.00
```

Aim (Vol. 2)
Cryptic

```
1 ............................................... 2.00
```

Air Ace (Vol. 2)
Street & Smith, 1944

```
1-6 ....................................... 60.00
7 ......................................... 110.00
8 ........................................... 65.00
9-12 ..................................... 60.00
```

Air Ace (Vol. 3)
Street & Smith, 1946

```
1 ......................................... 50.00
```

Airboy
Eclipse, 1986

Airboy combines cutting-edge style and social commentary of the likes of a golden age comic strip.

Featuring characters such as Iron Ace, Skywolf, Misery, and Wolfmark, Airboy has the action and style of an old Buck Rogers serial. At the same time it goes places that Buck would never have gone, such as to Bogantilla, a dictatorship strikingly familiar to certain Central American countries. In this and other adventures, Airboy faces not only the traditional super-bad guys, but also the more down-to-earth evils of civil war, corrupt and oppressive governments, and the cold-war clashing of third-world armies used as pawns by the world's super-powers.

-- George Haberberger

```
1-9 ......................................... 2.00
10-32 ..................................... 1.00
33-49 ..................................... 2.00
50 ........................................... 5.00
```

Airboy Comics (Vol. 2)
Hillman, 1945

```
11 ....................................... 400.00
12 ....................................... 275.00
```

Airboy Comics (Vol. 3)
Hillman, 1946

```
1-8 ....................................... 225.00
9 ......................................... 250.00
10-12 ................................... 225.00
```

Airboy Comics (Vol. 4)
Hillman, 1947

```
1-11 ..................................... 175.00
12 ....................................... 160.00
```

Airboy Comics (Vol. 5)
Hillman, 1948

```
1-9 ....................................... 125.00
10 ....................................... 150.00
11-12 ................................... 125.00
```

Airboy Comics (Vol. 6)
Hillman, 1949

```
1-12 ..................................... 100.00
```

Airboy Comics (Vol. 7)
Hillman, 1950

```
1-12 ....................................... 90.00
```

Airboy Comics (Vol. 8)
Hillman, 1951

```
1 ........................................... 90.00
2-12 ....................................... 85.00
```

Airboy Comics (Vol. 9)
Hillman, 1952

```
1-12 ....................................... 80.00
```

Airboy Comics (Vol. 10)
Hillman, 1953

```
1-4 ....................................... 80.00
```

Airboy
Meets the Prowler
Eclipse, 1987

```
1 ............................................... 2.00
```

Airboy-
Mr. Monster Special
Eclipse, 1987

```
1 ............................................... 2.00
```

Airboy versus
the Airmaidens
Eclipse, 1988

```
1 ............................................... 2.00
```

Air Fighters Classics
Eclipse, 1987

1-7 .... 4.00

Air Fighters Comics (Vol. 1)
Hillman, 1941

1	1,500.00
2	2,200.00
3	1,100.00
4	700.00
5	600.00
6	685.00
7	640.00
8-12	500.00

Air Fighters Comics (Vol. 2)
Hillman, 1943

1	500.00
2	650.00
3-9	425.00
10	450.00

Airfighters Meet Sgt. Strike Special
Eclipse, 1988

1 .... 2.00

Airlock
Eclectus, 1990

1-3 .... 3.00

Airmaidens Special
Eclipse, 1987

1 .... 2.00

Airman
Malibu, 1993

1 .... 2.00

Airmen
Mansion, 1995

1 .... 3.00

Air Raiders
Marvel, 1987

On a far-off, technologically advanced world called Airlandia, air is more precious than gold. A ruthless ruler, Aerozar, and his Tyrants of the Wind control it all. The subjects of Airlandia have to give much of their air in tribute to Aerozar, and whatever surplus air they may have, they can only sell to the government-controlled air distributors at a price that barely covers its cost.

The only opposition the government faces, the only hope the Airlandians have of breathing their own air for free comes from a daring leader named Rokk and his rebels, the Air Raiders. From their free air farm they take air to the impoverished and thwart the Tyrants of the Wind at almost every turn.

1-5 .... 1.00

Airshell
-Ism, 2005

1 .... 4.00

Airtight Garage
Marvel, 1993

1-4 .... 3.00

Air War Stories
Dell, 1964

1	22.00
2-8	14.00

Airwaves
Caliber, 1991

-4 .... 3.00

Ai Yori Aoshi
Tokyopop, 2004

1-11 .... 10.00

A.K.A. Goldfish
Caliber, 1994

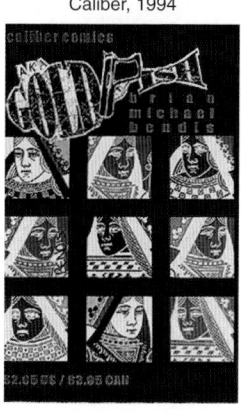

Brian Michael Bendis wrote and drew the noir crime graphic novel, starting with a rough short version in 1988 and eventually developing the story into an attention-grabbing, award-winning dark adventure.

The Image paperback collection (titled, simply, Goldfish) says, "Goldfish is the story of an enigmatic grifter with a heart of gold, who returns to his old haunts to find his old flame, Lauren, practically running the city's underbelly, and his oldest friend and ex-partner in crime, Izzy, a police detective. But Goldfish has come back for one reason, and one reason only, his son."

-- Maggie

1-3	4.00
4	3.00
5	4.00

Akiko
Sirius, 1996

1	6.00
2	5.00
3-10	4.00
11-49	3.00
50	4.00
51-Ash 1	3.00

Akiko on the Planet Smoo
Sirius, 1995

1	5.00
1/HC	20.00
1/2nd	4.00
Fan ed. 1/A	3.00

Akiko on the Planet Smoo: The Color Edition
Sirius, 2000

1 .... 5.00

Akira
Marvel, 1988

Akira - worshiped by some as a god, feared as a weapon of destruction more powerful than a nuclear bomb - is just a boy. After 38 years of cryogenic sleep, his name has passed into legend.

Tetsuo is the latest child captured by the secret government experiment that created Akira. He is the perfect test subject: an orphan and a member of a local gang. But the experiment unhinges his mind. When Tetsuo discovers that Akira may be more powerful, Tetsuo is enraged and goes in search of the sleeping boy, destroying everything in his path.

Kaneda is the leader of the gang from which Tetsuo was abducted. Searching for his missing friend, he becomes enamored of the girl Kay and follows her into a world of intrigue and rebels. The rebels, the government, Kaneda, and Tetsuo come together to witness the awakening of a legend. Nothing will ever be the same.

1	8.00
1/2nd	4.00
2	5.00
2/2nd	4.00
3	5.00
4-33	4.00
34-38	7.00

A*K*Q*J
Fantagraphics, 1991

1	3.00

Aladdin (Conquest)
Conquest, 1993

0	3.00

Aladdin (Disney's...)
Marvel, 1994

1-11	2.00

Alamo
Antarctic, 2004

1	5.00

Alarming Adventures
Harvey, 1962

1	40.00
2	25.00
3	20.00

Alarming Tales
Harvey, 1957

1	110.00
2	65.00
3-4	50.00
5-6	40.00

Albedo (1st Series)
Thoughts & Images, 1984

0	8.00
0/A	30.00
0/B	15.00
0/2nd	5.00
0/3rd-0/4th	3.00
1	14.00
1/A-1/2nd	10.00
2	250.00
☞1st Usagi Yojimbo	
3	10.00
4-5	4.00
6-8	3.00
9-14	2.00

Albedo (2nd Series)
Antarctic, 1991

1	4.00
2-10	3.00
Special 1	4.00

Albedo (3rd Series)
Antarctic, 1994

1-4	3.00

Albedo (4th Series)
Antarctic, 1996

1-2	3.00

Albedo (5th Series)
Antarctic, 2002

1	5.00

Albino Spider of Dajette
Verotik, 1997

1	3.00
2-0	3.00

Albion
DC, 2005

1-6	3.00

Alec Dear
Mediocre Concepts, 1996

1	2.00

Alec:
Love and Beerglasses
Escape

1	4.00

Aleister Arcane
Idea & Design Works, 2004

1-3	4.00

Alex
Fantagraphics, 1994

1-6	3.00

Alexis (Vol. 2)
Fantagraphics, 1995

1-5	3.00

Alf
Marvel, 1988

ALF (Alien Life Form) is an alien from the planet Melmac.

While traveling through space, his craft develops problems and he crashes on Earth, eventually winding up in the Tanner family's garage. Young Brian Tanner immediately takes a liking to ALF and introduces him to the others: sister Lynn and parents Kate and Willie. All of them eventually get used to having a wisecracking alien who looks a bit like an ugly teddy bear. All of them, that is, except Lucky, the family cat. Cats, it seems, were something of a delicacy on Melmac, and ALF is continually chasing Lucky with dinner in mind.

A goofy, popular television show, which ran from 1986 to 1990, ALF also enjoyed a respectable run as a comic book. It ran 50 issues from 1988 to 1992, along with numerous special editions.

1	2.00
2-49	1.00
50-Spring 1	2.00

Alf Comics Magazine
Marvel, 1988

1-2	2.00

Alias:
Now, 1990

1-5	2.00

Alias
Marvel, 2001

1	4.00
2-28	3.00

Ali-Baba:
Scourge of the Desert
Gauntlet

1	4.00

Alice
Ziff-Davis, 1951

10	125.00
11	75.00

Alice and the Engine
Straw Dog

1-3	3.00

Alice in Blunderland
Industrial Services

1	100.00

Alice in Lost World
Radio, 2001

1-4	3.00

Alien 3
Dark Horse, 1992

Alien Fire
Kitchen Sink, 1987

Alien Legion: Binary Deep
Marvel, 1993

At the end of a doomed rescue mission witnessed in the movie Aliens, the few survivors have set their craft on a course toward Earth. They have entombed themselves in the cold embrace of hypersleep, awaiting their eventual arrival. But something, has gone tragically wrong with the ship's guidance system. The ship crashes on a desolate planet housing a penal colony. When the ship is retrieved, the only survivors are Lieutenant Ripley...and an unseen fellow passenger.

In investigating the ship's records, Ripley finds the horrible cause of the crash: a nascent Alien had been aboard the ship all along, and now it's loose in the colony. Trapped on a planet with no weapons, where her only allies are murderers and rapists, Ripley must fight the alien killers once again. But Ripley, who has discovered an even greater terror living within her, knows that whether or not she can stop this Alien, this battle will be her last.

1-3..3.00

Alien Ducklings
Blackthorne, 1986
1-4...2.00

Alien Encounters (Fantaco)
Fantaco, 1980
1...2.00

Alien Encounters (Eclipse)
Eclipse, 1965
1-14...2.00

In the 21st century, the ruin of Earth has become a boon to the interplanetary black market for Earth popular culture. An archivist named Ed joins up with a roving band of traders, who are crossing the galaxy and dealing in pop artifacts from Earth. Along the way he gets involved with the fighting against the lizardous Bahktians, while dealing with the bureaucratic opposition and amorous advances of the government official Chia X. Hong. Written by Anthony Smith and drawn by Eric Vincent, Alien Fire is an action-filled, science fiction, adventure comic.

1-3.. 2.00

Alien Fire: Pass in Thunder
Kitchen Sink, 1995
1 .... 7.00

Alien Hero
Zen, 1999
1 .... 9.00

Alien Legion (Vol. 1)
Marvel, 1984
1-20....................................... 2.00

Alien Legion (Vol. 2)
Marvel, 1987
1-18....................................... 2.00

Alien Legion: A Grey Day to Die
Marvel
1 .... 7.00

A motly crew of roughnecks and soldiers of fortune, killers, and misfits, who hail from any number of races, cultures, and species comprise the Alien Legion. Together, they form a swift, decisive force that takes on the jobs that are too big for more ordinary teams to handle.

In this installment of the Alien Legion legends, legionnaire Torie Montroc needs help of a most dangerous kind, and he knows just whom to recruit: rough-and-ready Jugger Grimrod and the hauntingly beautiful techno-thief Nakhira Doomhar. The mission in question involves defying the inhabitants of a civilization he helped destroy in order to uncover the one bit of evidence that remains of his father's life. Will our heroes make it out alive?

1 .... 4.00

Alien Legion: Jugger Grimrod
Marvel, 1992
1 .... 6.00

Alien Legion: One Planet at a Time
Marvel, 1993
1-3.. 5.00

Alien Legion: On the Edge
Marvel, 1990
1-3.. 5.00

Alien Legion: Tenants of Hell
Marvel, 1991
1-2.. 5.00

Alien Nation
DC, 1988

Alien Nation:
The Lost Episode
Malibu, 1992

Alien Resurrection
Dark Horse, 1997

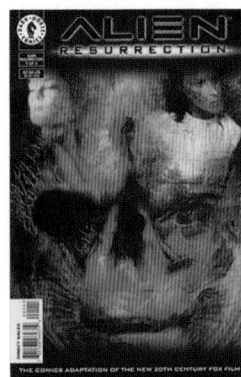

DC's Alien Nation is based on the 1988 motion picture that helped spawn a successful television science fiction series (1989-1991). In it, a ship of alien "Newcomers" from the planet Tencton lands on Earth. The extraterrestrial immigrants soon find themselves a despised underclass in American society. One alien, George Francisco, decides to help his people by joining the police force, and is soon teamed with a hard-edged, embittered cop named Matthew Sikes. Together, the two root out the intrigues and secrecy that form around the edges where human and alien society meet.

The comic-book adaptation by Martin Pasko and Jerry Bingham closely followed Rockne S. O'Bannon's script for the movie and captured the characterizations and social commentary that helped lift the Alien Nation television show above the level of much comic-book science-fiction.

-- Rob Salkowitz

1 ....3.00

Alien Nation:
A Breed Apart
Adventure, 1990
1-4..3.00

Alien Nation:
The Firstcomers
Adventure, 1991
1-4..3.00

It's a lost episode all right, in the sense that the television series was cancelled before the series episode adapted here could ever even film, let alone air. But the show in which an alien race crashed on Earth and lived quite openly among humans did attract a small cult following, and its fans will no doubt be glad to see how the second season, had there been one, would have started. This adventure involves a plot to kill the aliens, known as "newcomers," with a deadly bacteria. The detective team of alien George Francisco and human Matthew Sikes investigates; other characters from the series are on hand as well.

The script this one-shot is based on was called "Soul Train," and for the series' fans it's a chance to see in what direction their favorite characters might have traveled. In black-and-white.

1 .... 5.00

Alien Nation:
The Public Enemy
Adventure, 1991
1-4... 3.00

Alien Nation:
The Skin Trade
Adventure, 1991
1-4... 3.00

Alien Nation:
The Spartans
Adventure, 1990
1-4... 3.00

This two-issue adaptation from Dark Horse of the fourth Aliens movie features story and art by Jim Vance and Eduardo Risso respectively. Ripley, who sacrificed herself to prevent the birth of another Alien in Alien 3, returns, albeit as a clone in this tale. She again finds herself leading a hapless group of would-be victims, but this time against an alien hybrid. It is Ripley's status as a clone that is significant to the existence of the hybrid, making this confrontation more personal than ever. So personal in fact that it could almost be called...maternal.

-- George Haberberger

1-2 .... 3.00

Aliens
Gold Key, 1982
1 .... 12.00
2 .... 5.00

Aliens (Vol. 1)
Dark Horse, 1988
1 .... 5.00
1/2nd 3.00
1/3rd-1/5th............................ 2.00
1/6th 2.00
2 .... 4.00
2/2nd 3.00
2/3rd-2/4th............................ 2.00
3 .... 3.00
3/2nd-3/3rd........................... 2.00
4 .... 3.00
4/2nd 2.00
5 .... 3.00
5/2nd 2.00
6 .... 3.00
6/2nd 2.00

Aliens (Vol. 2)
Dark Horse, 1989
1-4 .... 3.00

Aliens: Alchemy
Dark Horse, 1997
1-3..3.00

Aliens: Apocalypse: The Destroying Angels
Dark Horse, 1999
1-4..3.00

Aliens: Berserker
Dark Horse, 1995
1-4..3.00

Aliens: Colonial Marines
Dark Horse, 1993
1-10..3.00

Aliens: Earth Angel
Dark Horse, 1994
1 ....3.00

Aliens: Earth War
Dark Horse, 1990

Journeying homeward after the disastrous events of the movie Aliens, Lt. Ripley is awakened from hypersleep. The Company, apparently, had sent a second ship after the Sulaku in order to capture an Alien specimen for their weapons labs. Now the commander of that ship wants Ripley to lead them back to the nest. If she refuses, they threaten to take the girl Newt with them instead...

So the soldiers went-and of course the Aliens killed most of them. But The Company never gave up, and eventually succeeded in bringing an Alien to Earth. Not long afterward, Earth itself was overrun by Aliens.

As their home planet turns into a new nesting ground, Ripley and Newt form a desperate plan to stop the Aliens once and for all. It means traveling back to Acheron, where Ripley first met the Aliens, and facing the very source of the Aliens' evil.

1-4..3.00

Alien Sex/Monster Lust
Fantagraphics, 1992
1 .... 3.00

Aliens: Genocide
Dark Horse, 1991
1-4... 3.00

Aliens: Glass Corridor
Dark Horse, 1998
1 .... 3.00

Aliens: Havoc
Dark Horse, 1997
1 .... 3.00
2 .... 4.00

Aliens: Hive
Dark Horse, 1992

A survey mission lands on a strange planet, ready to carry out a suicidal mission. The group is armed with a synthetic jelly which makes them undetectable to the Aliens' sense of smell. With it, they plan to venture deep into the heart of an Alien hive and extract the queen. The money they stand to make for a successful capture is enough reason, it seems, to venture into Hell itself...

1-4... 3.00

Aliens: Kidnapped
Dark Horse, 1997
1-3... 3.00

Aliens: Labyrinth
Dark Horse, 1993
1-4... 3.00

Aliens: Lovesick
Dark Horse, 1996
1 .... 3.00

Aliens (Magazine) (Vol. 1)
Dark Horse, 1991
1-5... 4.00
6-17....................................... 3.00

Aliens (Magazine) (Vol. 2)
Dark Horse, 1992
1-22....................................... 3.00

Aliens: Mondo Heat
Dark Horse, 1996
1 .... 3.00

Aliens: Mondo Pest
Dark Horse, 1995

Some Aliens stories are horrific. Some are politically pointed. This one-shot special may be the first of the bunch that's downright ridiculous.

Mondo Pest is a rough-and-tumble exterminator of the voracious Aliens. In this tale, he's called to the Oryza colony to save the colonists from a rather nasty bug problem. No sooner does he enter their airspace, however, than a surface-to-air missile takes out his ship. Further investigation reveals a human hand in creating the alien monsters who have been overrunning the colony. Nevertheless, Mondo cheerfully wades into the fray, with ridiculously oversized guns blazing.

This story originally appeared in serial form in Dark Horse Comics #22-24. It was written by Henry Gilroy, whose credits include stints on TV shows The Tick and Batman: The Animated Series.

1 .... 3.00

Aliens: Music of the Spears
Dark Horse, 1994
1-4... 3.00

Aliens: Newt's Tale
Dark Horse, 1992
1-2... 5.00

Aliens: Pig
Dark Horse, 1997
1 .... 3.00

Aliens/Predator: The Deadliest of the Species
Dark Horse, 1993

1	3.00
1/Ltd.	4.00
2-12	3.00

Aliens: Purge
Dark Horse, 1997

1	3.00

Aliens: Rogue
Dark Horse, 1993

1-4	3.00

Aliens: Sacrifice
Dark Horse, 1993

1	5.00

Aliens: Salvation
Dark Horse, 1993

1	5.00

Aliens: Salvation and Sacrifice
Dark Horse, 2001

1	13.00

Aliens: Special
Dark Horse, 1997

This one-shot contained two rather nicely done Aliens stories. The first, "45 seconds" is told with pictures only, portraying the final horrific moments as a soldier sets an explosive timer to destroy an Alien egg bed, and then runs headlong into a very nasty surprise.

The second, longer story is "Elder Gods." On the Omni-Tech colony of Mira Ceti 4, tensions are running high between the administration and the various labor groups. One such group, the Esoterics, is assigned quarry detail, a task they fear, given the likely presence of aliens there. Not surprisingly, they uncover an Alien spaceship full of eggs. These eggs, the Esoterics lead themselves to believe, are the very method by which their elder god Tulitu would live again. In a terrifying display of fanaticism, and a turn on fear, the cultists launch a plot to bring these "gods" to life again.

1	3.00

Aliens: Stalker
Dark Horse, 1998

1	3.00

Aliens: Stronghold
Dark Horse, 1994

Philip and Joy Strunk have been sent to investigate alleged misdeeds on the part of Dr. Nordling, chief researcher at an orbital lab studying the Aliens. Nordling's specialty is creating custom viruses and has been chartered by Grant Corp. to develop one that could wipe out the deadly Aliens. On the side, however, Nordling has been illicitly selling Alien embryos, spreading their plague further into the galaxy.

Philip and Joy's investigation was meant to be an undercover affair, but they are quickly unmasked by the deranged Nordling. Trapped on a floating base with a mad doctor and hundreds of his Alien "pets," they find their only friend is an Alien "synthetic" (robot) named Jeri.

This four-issue mini-series is a harrowing tale of madness and horror set in far reaches of space.

1-4	3.00

Aliens: Survival
Dark Horse, 1998

1-3	3.00

Aliens vs. Predator
Dark Horse, 1990

0	5.00
1	4.00
1/2nd	3.00
2	4.00
2/2nd-4/2nd	3.00
Ann 1	5.00

Aliens vs. Predator: Booty
Dark Horse, 1996

1	3.00

Aliens vs. Predator: Duel
Dark Horse, 1995

1-2	3.00

Aliens vs. Predator: Eternal
Dark Horse, 1998

1-4	3.00

Aliens vs. Predator vs. The Terminator
Dark Horse, 2000

1-4	3.00

Aliens vs. Predator: War
Dark Horse, 1995

0-4	3.00

Aliens vs. Predator: Xenogenesis
Dark Horse, 1999

1-4	3.00

Aliens: Wraith
Dark Horse, 1998

1	3.00

Aliens: Xenogenesis
Dark Horse, 1999

Be forewarned, as the title literally means "alien beginning." In the distant future, the existence of the hideous Aliens is no longer a secret. Advanced weaponry has tipped the scales in favor of humanity. The mysterious Company has formed a strike force to take the offensive against the creatures scattered throughout the galaxy. The mission and goal are simple: dispatch soldiers to space colony Salazar VII and obliterate

the Aliens. The mission, some think, is a game. Some think it's a chance for redemption, and others have personal agendas, but none have any idea of the true objective. Acting akin to a faceless dictator, the all-powerful Company has supplanted the government, the military, and the non-secular institutions, and ingrained itself into every aspect of human society in the galaxy. And for that intimacy there will be hell to pay.

1-4 .... 3.00

Alien: The Illustrated Story
HM Communications

1 .... 5.00

Alien Worlds
Pacific, 1982

Alien Worlds is a collection of science-fiction stories by such famous authors as William F. Nolan and Richard Corben. In this series, readers will find post-nuclear worlds inhabited by a race of murderous children; playground hucksters who employ miniature aliens to help them scam their playmates; robots in love; and much, much more.
Following in the tradition of the pre-Code E.C. comics of the '50s, Alien Worlds is a must-read for fans of science-fiction. Sadly, this series ran only seven issues before publisher Pacific Comics went out of business. It then ran two final issues under the Eclipse Comics label before its cancellation.

1 .... 3.00
2-3D 1 .... 2.00

Alien Worlds (Blackthorne)
Blackthorne

1 .... 6.00

Alison Dare, Little Miss Adventures
Oni, 2000

1 .... 5.00

Alister the Slayer
Midnight, 1995

1 .... 3.00

Alizarin's Journal
Avatar, 1999

1 .... 4.00

Allagash Incident
Tundra, 1993

1 .... 3.00

All-American Comics
DC, 1939

1	5,700.00
2	2,000.00
3	1,400.00
4-5	1,250.00
6-7	980.00
8	1,800.00
9-10	950.00
11	1,025.00
12-15	950.00
16	72,000.00

☛1st Green Lantern

17	15,600.00

☛2nd Green Lantern

18	8,800.00
19	13,800.00

☛1st Atom

20	4,850.00
21-23	2,000.00
24	2,200.00

☛1st Mid-Nite, Sargon

25	8,300.00

☛Dr. Mid-Nite origin

26	3,000.00

☛Sargon origin

27	3,500.00
28-30	1,250.00
31-40	1,040.00
41-50	785.00
51-60	675.00
61	4,400.00

☛1st Solomon Grundy

62-70	600.00
71-88	550.00
89	1,200.00

☛1st Harlequin

90	775.00
91-99	525.00
100	850.00
101	1,000.00

☛Scarce

102	1,650.00

☛Scarce

All-American Comics (2nd Series)
DC, 1999

1 .... 2.00

All-American Men of War
DC, 1952

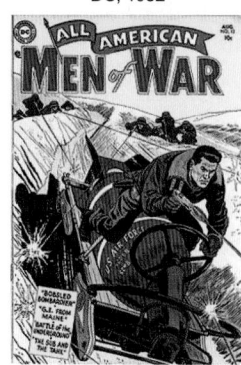

The title began as a general war comic book, with cover stories like "Lifenet to Beach Red!" and the cover description "Fighting actions on every front." Soon, cover copy evolved to showing a cover title and the words "and other stories of blazing action in hand-to-hand combat!" Nevertheless, some of the story titles indicated less than hand-to-hand action ("Diary of a Fighter Pilot"), and eventually the focus of the action was the sky.
Eventually, Johnny Cloud, the Navajo Ace, took the cover spot, and the stories involved fighter pilots, though some of the action could still take place on the ground. Stories shifted to covering "three wars," and finally in #112 (Dec 75) Lt. Steve Savage, "The Balloon Buster" appeared - which didn't mean Johnny Cloud was out of the action. In #115, readers found the issue was "Special: The scorching return of Navajo Ace Johnny Cloud! in the startling mission ... 'Killer Ace - Handle with Care!'"

- Maggie

0 (127)	900.00
1 (128)	500.00
2	360.00
3	295.00
4-5	260.00
6-10	235.00
11-18	210.00
19-28	165.00
29	190.00
30	165.00
31-40	130.00
41-50	100.00
51-60	80.00
61-65	70.00
66	80.00
67	130.00
68-80	70.00
81	50.00
82	135.00

83-90	50.00
91-100	35.00
101-110	24.00
111-117	20.00

All-American Western
DC, 1948

103	375.00
104	265.00
105-110	225.00
111-120	165.00
121-126	110.00

All Detective
Avalon

1	3.00

Allegra
Image, 1996

1-4	3.00

Alley Cat
Image, 1999

1-1/B	3.00
2-Ashcan 1/E	3.00

Alley Cat
Lingerie Edition
Image, 1999

1	5.00

Alley Cat vs.
Lady Pendragon
Image, 2000

1-1/A	3.00

Alley Oop (Standard)
Standard, 1947

10	135.00
11-18	110.00

Alley Oop (Argo)
Argo, 1955

1	125.00
2-3	85.00

Alley Oop
Dell, 1962

1	40.00
2	26.00

Alley Oop
(Dragon Lady)
Dragon Lady

1	6.00
2	7.00
3	8.00

Alley Oop Adventures
Antarctic, 1998

1-3	3.00

Alley Oop Quarterly
Antarctic, 1999

1-3	3.00

All-Famous Crime
Star Publications, 1950

4	185.00

5	135.00
8	125.00
9	175.00
10	115.00

All Famous
Crime Stories
Fox, 1949

1	300.00

All-Famous
Police Cases
Star Publications, 1952

6	100.00
7-8	85.00
9-16	75.00

All-Flash
DC, 1941

In part because of the size of Golden Age comics, it was common for characters that are icons today to begin their careers in anthology comics. So it was that, while The Flash was introduced in Flash Comics #1, that comic book also introduced Hawkman and Johnny Thunder in stories starring them.

It took more than a year to establish that Harry Lampert's character could carry his own title - but, since Flash Comics was still running as an anthology comic book, this different name was chosen for the solo series. The first issue began with a fast recap of the origin story and then filled the rest of the issue almost entirely with Flash episodes. (As with many comics of the era, the series contained occasional comedy fillers with other characters.)

-- Maggie

1	12,500.00
☛Flash origin	
2	2,400.00
3-4	1,600.00
5-10	1,100.00
11-15	850.00
16-20	800.00
21-32	625.00

All for Love (Vol. 1)
Prize, 1957

1	40.00
2	25.00
3-6	20.00

All for Love (Vol. 2)
Prize, 1958

1	28.00
2-5/A	18.00

All for Love (Vol. 3)
Prize, 1959

1	20.00
1/A-4	16.00

All Funny Comics
DC, 1943

1	275.00
2	125.00
3-10	80.00
11-13	70.00
14	55.00
15	70.00
16	175.00
17	55.00
18-19	70.00
20-23	55.00

All Girls School
Meets All Boys School
Angel

1	3.00

All Good Comics
Fox, 1946

1	120.00

All Good
St. John, 1949

1	475.00

All Great
Jungle Adventures
Fox, 1949

1	350.00

All Hallow's Eve
Innovation

1	5.00

All Hero Comics
Fawcett, 1943

1	1,050.00

All Hitler Comics
Paragon

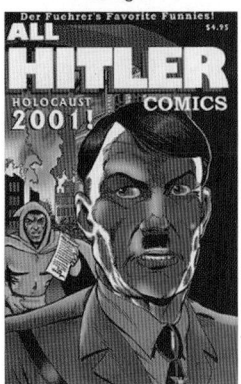

What if the "Man of Hate," Adolf Hitler did not die in his bunker in World War II? What if instead his persona were trapped in cyberspace? And what if he escaped back to our modern world?

With the help of the villainous Lady Luger, it appears that Hitler may again walk the Earth. Can even the mystical powers of the Green Lama stop the cybernetic madman before it is too late?

This issue also contains a reprint of a backup story from the Golden Age comic "Daredevil Battles Hitler" which provides an illustrated account of the dictator's rise to power in Germany.

1 ....5.00

All Humor Comics
Quality, 1946

1	130.00
2	70.00
3	40.00
4-5	34.00
6-10	26.00
11-17	22.00

Alliance
Image, 1995

1-3/A 3.00

All New Adventures of the Mighty Crusaders
Archie, 1983

1-3...1.00

All-New Atom
DC, 2006

1-24.......................................3.00

All New Collectors' Edition
DC, 1977

C-53	26.00
☛Rudolph	
C-54	12.00
☛Supes v. Wonder Woman	
C-55	15.00
☛Legion	
C-56	40.00
☛Superman vs. Ali	
C-56/Whitman	35.00
C-58	12.00
☛Supes vs. Shazam	
C-60	20.00
☛Rudolph's Summer	
C-62	12.00
☛Superman movie	

All-New Comics
Harvey, 1943

1	2,200.00
2	750.00
3	550.00
4	425.00
5-11	485.00
12-14	385.00
15	540.00

All New Exiles
Malibu, 1995

0	2.00
0/Variant-1	2.00
2-4	2.00
5	3.00
6-11	2.00

All New Official Handbook of the Marvel Universe A to Z
Marvel, 2006

1-12.......................................4.00

All-New Tenchi Muyo Part 1
Viz, 2002

1-5...3.00

All-New Tenchi Muyo Part 2
Viz, 2002

1-5...3.00

All New Underground Comix
Last Gasp, 1973

This black-and-white underground goes by a number of titles-those of its various features.

One such feature is "High School Funnies," a strip that stars a teacher in a fox costume who goes by the name "Little Ned." His students have absolutely no interest in education and only seem to come to life when they escape the confines of the classroom. Another feature, "The Mountain," is a rant against everything perceived as being "establishment"-the police, television, politicians, etc., etc. This is fairly typical stuff for the early 1970s.

1	5.00
2-5	3.00

All-Out War
DC, 1979

1-6 .... 3.00

All Picture Adventures
St. John, 1952

1	175.00
2	250.00

All-Select Comics
Timely, 1943

1	11,000.00
2	3,300.00
3	1,750.00
4-5	1,400.00
6-10	1,250.00
11	1,650.00

All Shook Up
Rip Off, 1990

1 .... 4.00

All Star Batman and Robin, The Boy Wonder
DC, 2005

1/Batman-1/Robin	5.00
1/Special	4.00
1/RRP	150.00
2/Miller-2/Lee	4.00
3-10	3.00

All-Star Comics
DC, 1940

All-Star Comics was one of the key titles in DC history. Beginning with a collection of stories featuring such Golden Age heroes as the Flash, Green Lantern, and Hawkman, it moved on with #3 to introduce the world to its first super-hero group, The Justice Society of America. This historic team consisted of Batman, Green Lantern, Doctor Fate, the Atom, the Flash, Hawkman, The Spectre, Hourman, Superman, and The Sandman.

All-Star struck gold again with #8, with the introduction of Diana Prince, Wonder Woman. It continued to feature The JSA, Wonder Woman, and other characters until the series faded from view in 1951 with #57. A quarter of a century later, the series was revived briefly, featuring a variety of DC super-heroes. However, this renaissance was short-lived, and two years later this legendary series seemed to have once again run its course, ending with 1978's #68.

1	10,000.00
2	3,500.00
3	25,000.00

☞1st JSA

4	3,000.00
5	2,800.00

☞1st Hawkgirl

6-7	1,800.00
8	16,000.00

☞1st Wonder Woman

9-11	1,600.00
12-15	1,400.00
16-25	1,200.00
26-32	900.00
33	1,800.00

☞Grundy appearance

34-35	900.00
36	1,300.00

☞Batman, Supes app.

37	900.00
38	975.00

☞Black Canary starts

39-49	900.00
50	975.00

☞Frazetta art

51-56	900.00
57	1,200.00

☞25-year hiatus starts

58	12.00

☞1st Power Girl

59-61	6.00
62	8.00
63	6.00
64-65	7.00
66	8.00
67-68	6.00
69	10.00
70-73	6.00
74	8.00

All Star Comics
(2nd series)
DC, 1999

1	3.00
2	3.00
GS 1	5.00

All-Star Index
Eclipse, 1987

1	2.00

All-Star Squadron
DC, 1981

1	4.00
2-10	2.00
11-14	1.00
15-46	1.00
47	3.00
48-67	1.00
Ann 1	2.00

All-Star Superman
DC, 2006

1-10	3.00

All-Star Western
(1st Series)
DC, 1951

58	325.00
59-60	150.00
61-63	160.00
64-66	125.00
67	170.00

☞Johnny Thunder starts

68-70	125.00
71-80	85.00
81-98	60.00
99	65.00
100	60.00
101-107	50.00
108	100.00
109-119	50.00

All-Star Western
(2nd Series)
DC, 1970

1	30.00
2-3	15.00
4-5	14.00
6-9	9.00
10	260.00

☞1st Jonah Hex

11	75.00

All Surprise
Timely, 1943

1	150.00
2	80.00
3-5	60.00
6-12	48.00

All Suspense
Avalon, 1998

1	3.00

All Teen
Timely, 1947

20	200.00

All the Rules
Have Changed
Rip Off

1	10.00

All the Wrong Places
Laszlo

1	3.00

All-Thrill Comics
Mansion

845	3.00

All-Time
Sports Comics
Hillman, 1949

4	125.00
5-7	90.00

All Top Comics
Fox, 1946

1	110.00
2	60.00
3-7	45.00
8	1,550.00
9-10	800.00
11-13	700.00
14	825.00
15-17	700.00
18	450.00

All True Crime
Leading, 1948

Formerly known as Official True Crime Cases, this series ran under the name All True Crime from 1948 until 1952. During its run, it turned out a respectable collection of crime stories claiming simultaneously to be "all true" yet carrying this disclaimer: "All names and places in these true-to-life stories are fictitious. Any similarity between actual persons or places and those used in these stories in purely coincidental." Which was a comic-book reader to believe?

Regardless of their basis in actual life, the stories were full of the sort of ruthless gangster action and criminal cunning that made crime comics such a hit in the early 1950s. Here, doctors swindle money from widows and murder the people who might expose them; gunmen engage in an endless series of double crosses; and nervous hoods continually outsmart themselves by pulling stunts such as hiding their loot in self-destructing places or unwittingly murdering the people meant to be their alibi.

26	125.00
27-29	85.00
30-40	60.00
41-51	48.00
52	55.00

All Western Winners
Timely, 1948

2	450.00
3	250.00
4	225.00

All-Winners Comics (1st series)
Timely, 1941

1	16,000.00
☛Cap America starts	
2	5,200.00
3	3,150.00
4	3,100.00
5-6	2,300.00
7-10	1,950.00
11-18	1,350.00
19	3,350.00
☛All-Winner Squad org.	
21	3,500.00
☛Scarce	

All-Winners Comics (2nd Series)
Timely, 1948

1	2,150.00

Ally
Ally-Winsor, 1995

Ally is the name David Cruz uses when he wears a fantastic suit with built-in lasers, shields, and a holographic projector that enables him to go undercover by altering his appearance. From drive-by shootings and street-gang warfare to drug-running and fine art heists, Ally confronts whatever may come his way. The suit was developed by Cruz with his friend Jerry, whose death he is attempting to avenge. Cruz' girlfriend, Karina, was Jerry's sister, and David's activities are a constant reminder of her brother's tragic end.

The black-and-white art is stylized and employs unusual diamond-shaped word and thought balloons for Ally. This series has a decidedly Latin beat in portraying the gritty violence of the L.A. streets.

-- George Haberberger

1-3	3.00

Almuric
Dark Horse, 1991

1	11.00

Alone in the Dark
Image, 2002

1-2	5.00

Alone in the Shade Special
Alchemy

1	2.00

Alpha and Omega
Spire, 1978

1	5.00

Alphabet
Dark Visions, 1993

1	3.00

Alpha Centurion Special
DC, 1996

1	3.00

Alpha Flight (1st Series)
Marvel, 1983

1	5.00
☛1st Marrina, Puck	
2-10	4.00
11-19	3.00
20-24	2.00
25-27	1.00
28	3.00
29-32	2.00
33	6.00
☛Wolverine appears	
34	3.00
35-45	2.00
46	3.00
47	4.00
☛1st Jim Lee at Marvel	
48-53	2.00
54	3.00
55-56	2.00
57-74	1.00
75-105	2.00
106	3.00
☛Northstar outed	
106/2nd-130	2.00
Ann 1	4.00
Ann 2	1.00
Special 1	3.00

Alpha Flight (2nd Series)
Marvel, 1997

1	3.00
2-20	2.00
Ann 1998	4.00

Alpha Flight (3rd Series)
Marvel, 2004

1-12	3.00

Alpha Flight: In the Beginning
Marvel, 1997

-1	2.00

Alpha Flight Special
Marvel, 1991

1-4	2.00

Alpha Illustrated
Alpha Productions, 1994

0	1.00
1	4.00

Alpha Korps
Diversity, 1996

1	3.00
Ashcan 1	1.00

Alpha Team Omega
Fantasy Graphics, 1983

1	1.00

Alpha Track
Fantasy General, 1985

1-2	2.00

Alpha Wave
Darkline

1	2.00

Altered Image
Image, 1998

Altered Image is a fun idea that just doesn't seem to work out as well as it should. The three-issue mini-series begins when Maxx wakes up and finds that reality has changed around him. In rapid order, he rounds up Majestic, Spawn, the Savage Dragon, ShadowHawk, and Witchblade to join with him in a quest to find out what the heck's going on. Faster than you can yell "Amalgam Universe," they are blipped through another dimensional portal where the characters become combined versions of one another (along with other Image characters).

Although Jim Valentino writes and draws the series, he doesn't really hit on the idiosyncrasies of each of the characters, and as a result misses out on a great deal of the comic potential this situation gives.

1-3 ....3.00

Altered Realities
Altered Reality
1 ....2.00

Alter Ego
First, 1986
1-4 ....2.00

Alternate Existance
Dragonmaster, 1982
1-2 ....2.00

Alternate Heroes
Prelude
1 ....2.00

Alternating Crimes
Alternating Crimes, 1996
1-2 ....3.00

Alternation
Image, 2004
1-4 ....3.00

Alternative Comics
Revolutionary, 1994
1 ....3.00

Alternity
Navigator, 1992
1 ....3.00

Alvar Mayor: Death and Silver
4Winds
1 ....9.00

Alvin
Dell, 1962
1 ....25.00
2 ....18.00
3-10 ....15.00
11-20 ....12.00
21-28 ....8.00

Alvin and the Chipmunks
Harvey, 1992
1-5 ....2.00

A Man Called Kev
DC, 2006
1-5 ....3.00

Amanda and Gunn
Image, 1997

Part of Image's defunct "non-line," this four-issue, black-and-white mini-series was created by Jamie Robinson, who began his comic book career in 1994 with the self published sci-fi series Cyberzone.

Billed as a mix of Blade Runner and Twin Peaks, this series, set in the year 2036, introduces Amanda Shane, a retired bounty hunter who has moved far away from the city and the life she once lead five years earlier. When a series of murders by a machine called the Organ Snatcher occurs near her town, she teams with her partner, a sentient weapon named Gunn, to solve the mystery.

The book is carried by the fully fleshed-out characters, but falls tremendously short in the resolution-perhaps Robinson had a sequel in mind...?

1-4 ....3.00

Amazing Adult Fantasy
Marvel, 1961

The series changed title twice and is best-remembered for its final issue under an evolved title. Under any name, it was introduced by Editor Stan Lee as an anthology series of fantasy stories. It began as Amazing Adventures. Then, it was Amazing Adult Fantasy, probably as an attempt to reach older consumers. But the last issue of Amazing Adult fantasy preceded a historic key comic book of the Silver Age.

Following Amazing Adult Fantasy #14, the series' final issue, #15, was retitled simply Amazing Fantasy. That was, of course, the comic book that introduced Stan Lee and Steve Ditko's Amazing Spider-Man to comics fans.

-- Maggie

7 .... 600.00
8 .... 475.00
9-13 .... 425.00
13/2nd 3.00
14 .... 525.00

Amazing Adventure
Marvel, 1988
1 .... 5.00

Amazing Adventure Funnies
Centaur, 1940
1 .... 1,200.00
2 .... 750.00

Amazing Adventures (1st series)
Ziff-Davis, 1950
1 .... 450.00
2-6 .... 225.00

Amazing Adventures (2nd Series)
Marvel, 1961
1 .... 900.00
2 .... 525.00
3-6 .... 425.00

Amazing Adventures (3rd Series)
Marvel, 1970

1	30.00
2-3	20.00
4-5	14.00
6	20.00
7	14.00
8	22.00
9-10	20.00
11	150.00

☛1st blue Beast

12-13	30.00
14	25.00
15-17	20.00
18	14.00
19-25	5.00
26-28	4.00
29	5.00
30-36	3.00
36/30¢	20.00
37-37/30¢	8.00
38-39	3.00

Amazing Adventures (4th Series)
Marvel, 1979

1	3.00
2-14	2.00

Amazing Adventures of Ace International
Starhead, 1993

1	3.00

Amazing Adventures of Frank and Jolly (Alan Groening's...)
Press This

1-10	2.00

Amazing Adventures of Professor Jones
Antarctic, 1996

1-4	3.00

Amazing Adventures of The Escapist (Michael Chabon Presents The)
Dark Horse, 2004

1-6	9.00
7	10.00
8	9.00

Amazing Adventures of the JLA
DC, 2006

1	4.00

Amazing Chan and the Chan Clan
Gold Key, 1973

1	14.00
2-4	9.00

Amazing Comics (Timely)
Timely, 1944

1	1,600.00

Amazing Comics (Avalon)
Avalon

1-3	3.00

Amazing Comics Premieres
Amazing, 1987

1-5	2.00

Amazing Cynicalman
Eclipse

1	3.00

Amazing Detective Cases
Atlas, 1950

3	145.00
4-6	85.00
7-10	75.00
11	120.00
12-14	90.00

Amazing Fantasy
Marvel, 1962

During the '50s, Marvel was largely a publisher of monster and science-fiction stories. Super-heroes had largely been a phenomenon of World War II years and had since fallen into disuse. The early '60s saw them beginning to make a comeback. Companies began mass-producing gimmick super-heroes based on animals: apes, cheetahs, flies - whatever hadn't been done already.

In 1961, Stan Lee and Steve Ditko decided to make the company's next super-hero a shy teen who lived with his aunt and was targeted by bullies at school. They figured that readers would identify more with such a character than with stereotypically perfect heroes. Since Amazing Fantasy (formerly Amazing Adult Fantasy) had already been slated for cancellation, there was no risk in using it to introduce the character. That character was Peter Parker, the Amazing Spider-Man. When sales results came in months later, it was clear they had a hit. Today, Spider-Man is Marvel's most popular character.

15	32,000.00

☛1st Spider-Man

15/2nd	5.00
16-18	5.00

Amazing Fantasy (2nd Series)
Marvel, 2004

1	4.00
2-14	3.00
15	4.00
16-20	3.00

Amazing Heroes Swimsuit Special
Fantagraphics, 1990

Ann 1990	6.00
Ann 1991	8.00
Ann 1992	10.00
4	4.00
5	5.00

Amazing High Adventure
Marvel, 1984

1-5	3.00

Amazing Joy Buzzards
Image, 2005

1-4	3.00

Amazing Joy Buzzards (Volume 2)
Image, 2005

1-5	3.00

Amazing-Man Comics
Centaur, 1939

5	11,000.00
6	2,200.00
7	1,425.00
8-9	1,100.00
10-11	950.00
12-13	900.00
14	850.00
15-20	800.00
21-24	750.00
25-26	800.00

Amazing Mysteries
Atlas, 1949

32	500.00
33	210.00
34-35	105.00

Amazing Mystery Funnies
Centaur, 1938

1	2,400.00
2	1,250.00
3	700.00
4	575.00
5-10	525.00
11	2,200.00
12	850.00
13-15	500.00
16	1,000.00

17-18.....................................500.00
19..600.00
20..500.00
21-24.....................................600.00

Amazing Scarlet Spider
Marvel, 1995
1-2...2.00

Amazing Screw-On Head
Dark Horse, 2002
1-1/2nd....................................3.00

Amazing Spider-Girl
Marvel, 2006
0..2.00
1-4...3.00

Amazing Spider-Man
Marvel, 1963

After being bitten by a radioactive spider, Peter Parker, a shy high school student, suddenly finds himself with the ability to sense danger, stick to walls, and possessed of the proportional strength of a spider. When his uncle is killed by a burglar, Peter resolves to use his new powers to fight crime. Thus is born the Amazing Spider-Man, Marvel's most popular character of all time.

The Amazing Spider-Man is the flagship of the Spider-Man titles - a list which has included Marvel Team-Up, Spectacular Spider-Man, Spidey Super Stories, Web of Spider-Man, and (just plain old) Spider-Man. Since its first issue in 1963, it has featured the wisecracking arachnid in many of his greatest adventures and has introduced such famous super-villains as the Green Goblin, Doctor Octopus, The Kingpin, The Vulture, and Venom.

Years later, Marvel restarted the series at #1, hungry for first-issue orders but irritating many long-time collectors. After a few years, the publisher reinstated the long-running numbering of the first series, before embarking on a publication scheduled to three times a month, which quickly took the title to its 600th issue and beyond.

-1 .... 3.00
1 .... 27,000.00
☞1st Chameleon
1/Golden............................ 200.00
2 .... 3,400.00
☞1st Vulture
3 .... 4,600.00
☞1st Dr. Octopus
4 .... 2,300.00
☞1st Sandman
5 .... 2,500.00
☞Dr. Doom app.
6 .... 1,650.00
☞1st Lizard
7 .... 1,100.00
8 .... 800.00
9 .... 1,025.00
☞1st Electro
10 .... 990.00
11 .... 1,900.00
12 .... 825.00
13 .... 1,200.00
☞1st Mysterio
14 .... 2,050.00
☞1st Green Goblin
15 .... 1,800.00
☞1st Kraven
16-17 .... 800.00
☞2nd Green Goblin
18 .... 510.00
☞1st Ned Leeds
19 .... 460.00
20-21 .... 510.00
22 .... 425.00
23 .... 510.00
24-25 .... 500.00
26 .... 550.00
27 .... 500.00
28 .... 450.00
29-30 .... 240.00
31 .... 325.00
32 .... 175.00
33 .... 140.00
34 .... 240.00
35-36 .... 225.00
37 .... 250.00
38 .... 195.00
39 .... 350.00
☞1st Romita Spidey
40 .... 375.00
☞Goblin origin
41 .... 300.00
☞1st Rhino
42 .... 185.00
☞1st view of MJ
43 .... 120.00
44 .... 175.00
45 .... 115.00
46 .... 250.00
☞1st Shocker
47 .... 105.00
48 .... 120.00

49 .... 125.00
50 .... 625.00
☞Spidey quits
51 .... 200.00
52 .... 150.00
53 .... 105.00
54-55 .... 110.00
56 .... 90.00
57 .... 80.00
58 .... 100.00
59 .... 70.00
60 .... 105.00
61 .... 72.00
62 .... 75.00
63 .... 160.00
☞vs. both Vultures
64 .... 60.00
65 .... 55.00
66 .... 80.00
☞1st Randy
67-68 .... 60.00
69 .... 75.00
70-71 .... 70.00
72 .... 85.00
73 .... 50.00
74 .... 80.00
75-77 .... 65.00
78 .... 70.00
79-80 .... 60.00
81 .... 55.00
82-83 .... 50.00
84-85 .... 55.00
86 .... 60.00
87 .... 75.00
88 .... 60.00
89 .... 70.00
90 .... 75.00
91 .... 50.00
92 .... 62.00
93 .... 80.00
94 .... 65.00
95 .... 52.00
96 .... 85.00
97 .... 72.00
98 .... 80.00
99 .... 60.00
100 .... 100.00
101 .... 130.00
101/2nd 3.00
102 .... 105.00
☞Morbius origin
103 .... 50.00
104 .... 90.00
105 .... 25.00
106 .... 40.00
107-108 .... 27.00
109-110 .... 30.00
111 .... 34.00
112 .... 30.00
113 .... 35.00
114 .... 50.00
115 .... 33.00
116 .... 22.00
117 .... 25.00
118 .... 22.00
☞vs. Hulk
119-120 .... 50.00
☞vs. Hulk
121 .... 150.00

☛Gwen Stacy dies
122 ....150.00
☛Green Goblin dies
123 ....35.00
124 ....42.00
125 ....30.00
126 ....18.00
127 ....25.00
128 ....20.00
129 ....225.00
☛1st Punisher
130 ....20.00
131 ....25.00
☛Uncle Doc Ock
132 ....22.00
133 ....16.00
134 ....28.00
☛2nd Punisher
135 ....45.00
136 ....60.00
☛Harry as Goblin II
137 ....25.00
138 ....15.00
139 ....19.00
140 ....17.00
141 ....15.00
142 ....18.00
143 ....15.00
144 ....17.00
145-146 ....15.00
147 ....14.00
148 ....25.00
149 ....27.00
☛Spider-clone dies
150 ....16.00
151 ....24.00
152 ....11.00
153-154 ....10.00
155 ....12.00
155/30¢ 20.00
156 ....12.00
156/30¢ 20.00
157 ....12.00
157/30¢ 40.00
158 ....10.00
158/30¢ 20.00
159 ....11.00
☛vs. Doc Ock
159/30¢ 20.00
160 ....9.00
161 ....12.00
162 ....11.00
163 ....10.00

164 ....12.00
165-166/Whitman.................. 9.00
167-168/Whitman.................. 7.00
169-169/Whitman................ 10.00
169/35¢ 15.00
170-170/Whitman.................. 7.00
170/35¢ 15.00
171-171/Whitman.................. 7.00
171/35¢ 15.00
172-172/Whitman.................. 8.00
172/35¢ 15.00
173 .... 25.00
173/Whitman 18.00
173/35¢ 25.00
174-175/Whitman................ 10.00
176-177 .... 12.00
☛1st Hamilton Goblin
178-180/Whitman................ 11.00
181-181/Whitman.................. 9.00
182 .... 8.00
183-183/Whitman.................. 7.00
184 .... 8.00
184/Whitman 6.00
185-185/Whitman.................. 7.00
186-187/Whitman.................. 8.00
188-188/Whitman.................. 7.00
189-189/Whitman.................. 6.00
190 .... 7.00
191-193 .... 6.00
194 .... 21.00
☛1st Black Cat
195 .... 10.00
196-198 .... 6.00
199 .... 6.00
200 .... 10.00
201 .... 9.00
202 .... 7.00
203 .... 6.00
204 .... 8.00
205-206 .... 6.00
207 .... 5.00
208-211 .... 6.00
212-218 .... 5.00
219-220 .... 6.00
221-222 .... 4.00
223 .... 5.00
224-225 .... 4.00
226 .... 7.00
227 .... 6.00
228 .... 4.00
229 .... 11.00
230-232 .... 6.00
233 .... 4.00
234 .... 6.00

235 .... 4.00
236-237 .... 5.00
238 .... 22.00
☛1st Hobgoblin
239 .... 10.00
240 .... 5.00
241 .... 4.00
242 .... 5.00
243 .... 6.00
244-245 .... 5.00
246-248 .... 4.00
249 .... 5.00
250-251 .... 6.00
252 .... 10.00
☛1st black costume
253-254 .... 5.00
255-258 .... 4.00
259-263 .... 5.00
264-265 .... 4.00
265/2nd 2.00
266-267 .... 3.00
268-270 .... 6.00
271 .... 5.00
272-273 .... 4.00
274-276 .... 5.00
277-279 .... 4.00
280-284 .... 5.00
285 .... 6.00
286 .... 4.00
287 .... 5.00
288-289 .... 6.00
290-293 .... 5.00
294-295 .... 6.00
296 .... 5.00
300/A-300-2 .... 6.00
297 .... 6.00
301-2 .... 4.00
298 .... 16.00
☛McFarlane starts
299 .... 9.00
☛Venom cameo
300 .... 35.00
☛1st Venom
301 .... 6.00
302 .... 4.00
303 .... 5.00
304-307 .... 4.00
308 .... 5.00
309 .... 4.00
310-313 .... 5.00
314 .... 4.00
315-316 .... 5.00
317-318 .... 6.00
319 .... 5.00

320 .... 3.00	434/A-434/B 3.00	553 .... 3.00
321 .... 4.00	422-424 .... 2.00	553/A 4.00
322 .... 5.00	437-2 .... 3.00	554-555 .... 3.00
323 .... 3.00	425-432 .... 2.00	554/A-554/B 4.00
324 .... 5.00	432/Variant 5.00	556-560 .... 3.00
325-327 .... 4.00	433-441 .... 2.00	561-587 .... 4.00
328 .... 5.00	500 .... 5.00	Aim Giveaway 1 .... 4.00
329 .... 4.00	501 .... 4.00	Aim Giveaway 2 .... 2.00
330-343 .... 3.00	502 .... 3.00	Ann 1 .... 700.00
344 .... 4.00	503-509 .... 2.00	☛1st Sinister Six
☛1st Cletus Kassidy	509/DirCut 7.00	Ann 2 .... 550.00
345-347 .... 3.00	☛Director's Cut	Ann 3 .... 140.00
348-353 .... 2.00	510 .... 4.00	Ann 4 .... 90.00
354 .... 3.00	511 .... 3.00	Ann 5 .... 75.00
355-357 .... 2.00	512 .... 5.00	Ann 5/2nd 3.00
358 .... 6.00	513 .... 3.00	Ann 6-7 .... 35.00
359 .... 2.00	514-520 .... 2.00	Ann 8-9 .... 22.00
360 .... 3.00	521-525 .... 3.00	Ann 10-12 .... 8.00
361 .... 6.00	525/A 4.00	Ann 13 .... 7.00
☛1st Carnage	526 .... 3.00	Ann 14 .... 6.00
361/2nd 2.00	526/A 4.00	Ann 15 .... 7.00
362 .... 25.00	527 .... 3.00	Ann 16 .... 5.00
☛2nd Carnage	527/A 4.00	Ann 17-21 .... 4.00
362/2nd 2.00	528 .... 3.00	☛Spidey marries
363 .... 4.00	528/A-528/B 4.00	Ann 21/Direc-22 .... 5.00
364 .... 3.00	529 .... 20.00	Ann 23-25 .... 3.00
365 .... 4.00	529/2nd 6.00	Ann 26 .... 4.00
366-369 .... 2.00	529/3rd 5.00	Ann 27-28 .... 3.00
370 .... 3.00	530 .... 8.00	Ann 1996 .... 4.00
371-373 .... 2.00	531-532 .... 6.00	Ann 1997 .... 3.00
374 .... 3.00	532-2 .... 5.00	Ashcan 1 .... 1.00
375 .... 5.00	533 .... 4.00	Anl 1998 .... 4.00
376 .... 4.00	533/A 5.00	
377 .... 3.00	534-536 .... 4.00	**Amazing Spider-Man**
378 .... 4.00	537 .... 3.00	**(Vol. 2)**
379 .... 5.00	537-2 .... 4.00	Marvel, 1999
380 .... 3.00	538 .... 6.00	1 (442) 7.00
381 .... 4.00	538/A-538/B 5.00	1/DF Romita 12.00
382-388 .... 3.00	539 .... 10.00	1/DF Lee 35.00
388/Variant 2.00	539/A-530-2 .... 8.00	1/Dynamic 5.00
389-394 .... 3.00	540-541 .... 5.00	1/Autographed 10.00
394/Variant 4.00	542-544 .... 3.00	1/Authentix 8.00
395-397 .... 3.00	544/A 5.00	1/Sunburst 18.00
408/A 4.00	545 .... 4.00	2 (443)-2/Kubert 3.00
398-399 .... 3.00	545/A 5.00	3 (444) 2.00
400 .... 5.00	546 .... 4.00	4 (445)-11 (452) 2.00
☛no overlay	546/A-546/B 5.00	12 (453) 3.00
☛gray overlay	547-549 .... 3.00	13 (454)-17 (458) 2.00
400/Gray-400/White 30.00	549/A-549/B 4.00	18 (459)-19 (460) 3.00
☛white overlay	550 .... 3.00	20 (461) 5.00
401-418 .... 2.00	550/A 4.00	21 (462)-24 (465) 2.00
431/A 3.00	551 .... 3.00	25 (466) 3.00
419 .... 2.00	551/A 4.00	25/Speckle 4.00
432/A 3.00	552 .... 3.00	26 (467)-29 (470) 2.00
420-421 .... 2.00	552/A-552/B 4.00	30 (471) 5.00

☞Straczynski starts

31 (472)	3.00
32 (473)-33 (474)	4.00
34 (475)	5.00
35 (476)	4.00
36 (477)	9.00

☞9/11 issue

37 (478)-39 (480)	3.00
40 (481)	2.00
41 (482)	4.00
42 (483)-43 (484)	3.00
44 (485)-45 (486)	2.00
46 (487)-49 (490)	2.00
50 (491)	6.00
51 (492)-56 (497)	2.00
57 (498)-58 (499)	3.00
Ann 1999-2000	4.00
Ann 2001	3.00

Amazing Spider-Man 30th Anniversary Poster Magazine
Marvel

1	4.00

Amazing Spider-Man Giveaways
Marvel, 1977

1	4.00
2-3	4.00
4	6.00
5-11	4.00

Amazing Spider-Man: Hooky
Marvel

1	9.00

Amazing Spider-Man (Public Service Series)
Marvel, 1990

1	3.00
1/2nd	2.00
2	3.00
2/2nd	2.00
3	3.00
3/2nd	2.00
4	3.00
4/2nd	2.00

Amazing Spider-Man: Soul of the Hunter
Marvel, 1992

1	6.00

Amazing Spider-Man Super Special
Marvel, 1995

1	4.00

Amazing Spider-Man: The Birth of a Super Hero!
Marvel, 1969

1	2.00

Amazing Strip
Antarctic, 1994

1-10	3.00

Amazing Wahzoo
Solson, 1986

1	2.00

Amazing Willie Mays
Famous Funnies, 1954

1	500.00

Amazing World of Superman
DC, 1973

1	4.00

Amazing X-Men
Marvel, 1995

Charles Xavier devoted his life to bridging the gap of fear between humans and mutants. Himself a powerful telepath, he trained other mutants in the use of their powers, instilling in them a love for all people. For years, his X-Men have protected innocents from evil, mutant or not.

In this late 1990s revamping of the X-Men, the twisted child called Legion uses his awesome powers to travel back in time and kill the young Xavier, and thus he completely changes the course of world history. A man who should have been a strong leader is now only a memory, and his dream of peaceful coexistence is all but forgotten. The powerful Apocalypse controls most of the world, and imposes his brutal version of Darwinism on humans and mutants alike.

But dreams, unlike men, are hard to kill, and mutants still fight for freedom in Xavier's name. Led by the enigmatic Magneto, once Charles' greatest friend, this alternate version of the Uncanny X-Men struggle to defeat the ultimate evil mutant and end the Age of Apocalypse forever.

1-4	2.00

Amazon
DC, 1996

1	2.00

Amazon
Comico, 1989

1-3	2.00

Amazon Attack 3-D
3-D Zone, 1990

1	4.00

Amazons
Fantagraphics

1	3.00

Amazon Tales
Fantaco

1-3	3.00

Amazon Warriors
AC, 1989

1	3.00

Amazon Woman (1st Series)
Fantaco, 1994

1-2	3.00

Amazon Woman (2nd Series)
Fantaco, 1994

1-4	3.00

Amber: Nine Princes in Amber (Roger Zelazny's...)
DC, 1996

1-3	7.00

Amber: The Guns of Avalon (Roger Zelazny's...)
DC, 1996

1-3	7.00

Ambush Bug
DC, 1985

1-4	1.00

Ambush Bug Nothing Special
DC, 1992

1	3.00

Ambush Bug Stocking Stuffer
DC, 1986

1	1.00

Amelia Rules
Renaissance, 2001

When her parents divorce, Amelia's entire life is uprooted, and she and her mom move in with Amelia's aunt. Luckily, Aunt Tanner is pretty cool, and seems a lot more understanding of Amelia than mom does. Plus, Amelia has managed to make some friends in her new neighborhood. Reggie, a boy Amelia won't admit she "likes," is obsessed with super-heroes and usually makes Amelia and the rest of the gang wear homemade costumes. Rhonda, known as The Mouth, also has a crush on the boy, and has quickly become Amelia's "arch enemy." Reggie, of course, is too busy swooning over Tanner to notice the girls' attentions.

Even though it portrays some of the serious aspects of divorce, this is a fun, lighthearted comic, with the pace and feel of an animated cartoon show. The creator, Jimmy Gownley, has also produced Shades of Gray.

1-11 ....3.00

America's Greatest Comics (AC)
AC, 2005

1-13...7.00

America in Action
Dell, 1942

1 ....100.00
2 ....75.00

America Menaced!
Vital, 1950

1 ....175.00

American
Dark Horse, 1987

1-8...2.00
Special 1 ....2.00

American Air Forces
Wise, 1944

1 .... 100.00
2 .... 115.00
3-4 .... 60.00

American Book
Dark Horse, 1988

1 .... 6.00

American Century
DC, 2001

1-27 .... 3.00

American Flagg
First, 1983

It's 2076, and the world is falling apart. America has become a mass-media ghetto where the very idea of morality seems charmingly old-fashioned. Daily, the great television networks broadcast a steady diet of sex and violence to a nation of depraved viewers. Someone's got to put it back together, and that someone seems to be Reuben Flagg.

Told in a style which mimics the quick edits of a music video, American Flagg! was hailed as a revolutionary series which brought the world of comics up to the level of adults. Created by Howard Chaykin (Black Kiss, Midnight Men), this extraordinary series won seven Eagle awards for comic-book excellence in its first year of publication alone.

1 .... 3.00
2-13 .... 2.00
14-45 .... 1.00
46-Special 1 .... 2.00

American Flagg (Howard Chaykin's...)
First, 1988

1-12 .... 2.00

American Flyer
Last Gasp

1-2 .... 4.00

American Freak: A Tale of the Un-Men
DC, 1994

1-5 .... 2.00

American Heroes
Personality

1 .... 3.00

American Library
David McKay, 1944

1 .... 160.00
2 .... 125.00
3-6 .... 60.00

American: Lost in America
Dark Horse, 1992

1-4 .... 3.00

American Primitive
3-D Zone

1 .... 3.00

American Splendor
DC, 2006

1-2 .... 3.00
3-4 .... 20.00

American Splendor
Pekar, 1976

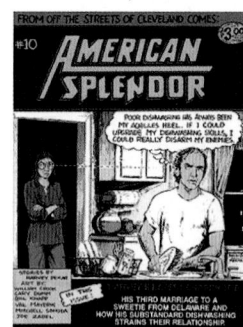

The spirit of independent publishing is alive and well, deep within the pages of American Splendor. Written by Cleveland-based author Harvey Pekar, American Splendor turns the "simple" complexities of everyday life into highly addictive, hard-to-put-down short stories.

Ethical issues such as social prejudice, personal insecurities, and street violence are at the core of every self-contained story - each reading more like a "day in the life" journal entry rather than standard comic-book fare. But perhaps the most personal tales, the ones most likely to have caught the attention of comic-book publisher Dark Horse Comics, are the ones relating to Pekar's bout with cancer. So touching are these stories, in fact, that they act as the

precursor to the writer's graphic non-novel, co-written with Joyce Brabner, Our Cancer Year.

1	65.00
2	30.00
3-5	20.00
6-10	15.00
11-13	10.00
14	18.00
15	8.00
16	4.00
17	8.00

American Splendor: Bedtime Stories
Dark Horse, 2000

1 ....4.00

American Splendor: Comic-Con Comics
Dark Horse, 1996

1 ....3.00

American Splendor: Music Comics
Dark Horse, 1997

1 ....3.00

American Splendor: Odds & Ends
Dark Horse, 1997

1 ....3.00

American Splendor: On the Job
Dark Horse, 1997

1 ....3.00

American Splendor: Portrait of the Author in his Declining Years
Dark Horse, 2001

1 ....4.00

American Splendor: Terminal
Dark Horse, 1999

This black-and-white one-shot is yet another installment in the continuing adventures of

Cleveland hospital file clerk and freelance writer Harvey Pekar, probably the most prominent proponent of autobiographical comics--what Dark Horse Comics refers to as "neo-realism." There are several short stories in this collection: Pekar instructs younger readers ("Most of you are younger than me") on how to handle money worries, jazz, Jewish-American writers, blues, bank-related red tape, etc.--life's details and distractions.

1 .... 3.00

American Splendor: Transatlantic Comics
Dark Horse, 1998

1 .... 3.00

American Splendor: Unsung Hero
Dark Horse, 2002

1-3... 4.00

American Splendor: Windfall
Dark Horse, 1995

1-2... 4.00

American Splendor Special: A Step Out of the Nest
Dark Horse, 1994

1 .... 3.00

American Tail, An: Fievel Goes West
Marvel, 1992

1-3... 1.00

American Virgin
DC, 2006

1-15... 3.00

American Way
DC, 2006

1-8... 3.00

American Woman
Antarctic, 1998

1-2... 3.00

America's Best Comics
America's Best, 2001

Special 1 .... 7.00

America's Best Comics
Nedor, 1942

1	1,600.00
2	850.00
3	600.00
4-6	440.00
7	575.00
8-10	400.00
11-20	360.00
21-24	325.00
25-31	265.00

America's Best Comics Preview
America's Best, 1999

1 .... 2.00

America's Best Comics Sketchbook
DC

1 .... 6.00

America's Best TV Comics
ABC TV, 1967

1 .... 95.00

America's Biggest Comics Book
Wise, 1944

1 .... 275.00

America's Greatest Comics
Fawcett, 1941

1	1,900.00
2	900.00
3	675.00
4-5	500.00
6-8	450.00

America vs. the Justice Society
DC, 1985

1	2.00
2-4	1.00

Americomics
AC, 1983

April 1983 saw the debut of Americomics (AC), along with the premiere issue of this, their vanguard title. The first issue introduced Roger Brant, a man who has learned to unleash an astral projection of himself known as Shade to fight evil. Shade continued through the series, along with such characters as the Slayer, the Messenger, and Captain Freedom & the Liberty Corps.

AC also picked up the rights to reprint several unpublished stories from the defunct Charlton

Bullseye. AC began running these with Americomics #3. AC also rescued Charlton characters Captain Atom, Blue Beetle, Nightshade, and the Question from obscurity, bringing them together in a special edition of Americomics. Several of these characters were later acquired by DC.

1-Special 1 ....2.00

Amethyst
DC, 1985

1-Special 1 ....1.00

Amethyst
DC, 1987

1-4...1.00

Amethyst, Princess of Gemworld
DC, 1983

Amy Winston was just a normal girl on the eve of her 13th birthday. There would be many presents given to her the next day, but one would be very different from the normal dolls and costume jewelry. A strange creature has put a gem among the presents -- a gem that changes 13-year-old Amy Winston into the woman Amethyst, lost princess of Gemworld.

Amethyst, Princess of Gemworld is a tale of magic and fantasy meant to appeal to young women as well as young men. The 12-issue maxi-series is an epic adventure, as Amy/Amethyst seeks to regain her lost heritage and save the Violet Realm from the dark lord, Opal.

1 ....1.00
1/75 cent 5.00
2 ....1.00
2/75 cent 5.00
3 ....1.00
4 ....1.00
5 ....1.00
6 ....1.00

7 ....1.00
8-10 ....1.00
11 ....1.00
12 ....1.00
Ann 1 ....1.00

A Midnight Opera
Tokyopop, 2005

1 ....10.00

Ammo Armageddon
Atomeka

1 ....5.00

Amnesia
NBM

1 ....10.00

Amora (Gray Morrow's...)
Fantagraphics, 1991

1 ....3.00

Amusing Stories
Renegade, 1987

1 ....2.00

Amy Papuda
Northstar

1-2 ....3.00

Amy Racecar Color Special
El Capitan, 1997

1 ....3.00
2 ....4.00

Anal Intruders from Uranus
Fantagraphics, 2005

1-2 ....4.00

Anarchy Comics
Last Gasp

1-4 ....3.00

Anarky
DC, 1997

1-4 ....3.00

Anarky
DC, 1999

Anarky is a curious super-villain. He's a teenage computer

hacker with an ideological bent, determined to thumb his nose at society's elite. Although he got his start as a minor nuisance to Batman, this mini-series sees the teen summoning demons, traveling to far-off worlds, and even facing down Apokolips himself in order to gain the power for a unique invention he's designed.

And what does this ingenious device do? Nothing less than raise the consciousness of the world. With it, Anarky hopes to topple society as we know it, and pave way for what he sees as the only valid government: the rule of anarchy.

1-8 ....3.00

Anchors Andrews
St. John, 1953

1 ....85.00
2-4 ....40.00

Ancient Joe
Dark Horse, 2001

1-3 ....4.00

Andromeda (Andromeda)
Andromeda, 1995

1-2 ....3.00

Andromeda (Silver Snail)
Silver Snail, 1977

1-6 ....2.00

Andy Devine Western
Fawcett, 1950

Fawcett's line of Western comic books was apparently so successful it even spun off titles featuring comedy relief characters. This brief run featured Andy Devine (1905-1977), best known for his heft and distinctive rasping voice, which took him through such films as Stagecoach (1939, he drove the team himself, no small feat) and TV

shows Adventures of Wild Bill Hickok (1951-8), Andy's Gang (1957-8), and Flipper (1964-5).
-- Maggie

1 ....325.00
2 ....225.00

Andy Panda
(Walter Lantz...)
Dell, 1952

16-20.....................................13.00
21-30.....................................11.00
31-56......................................9.00

Andy Panda
Gold Key, 1973

1 ....4.00
2-4...3.00
5-23...2.00

A-Next
Marvel, 1998

1-12..2.00

Angel (1st series)
Dell, 1955

2-16..9.00

Angel (2nd series)
Dark Horse, 1999

1-17/Variant.............................3.00

Angel (3rd series)
Dark Horse, 2001

1-4/Variant...............................3.00

Angela
Image, 1994

1-1/B 4.00
2-3...3.00

Angel: After the Fall
Idea & Design Works, 2007

1 ....12.00
2 ....5.00

Angela/Glory:
Rage of Angels
Image, 1996

1/A-1/B 3.00

Angel and the Ape
DC, 1968

1 ....40.00
2 ....20.00
3-7...15.00

Angel and the Ape
DC, 1991

1-4...1.00

Angel and the Ape
DC, 2001

1-4...3.00

Angel: Auld Lang Syne
Idea & Design Works, 2006

1 ....4.00
2 ....4.00

Angel Dust
Neo Manga One Shot
ADV Manga, 2007

1 ....11.00

Angel Fire
Crusade, 1997

Anastasia Pizer is no ordinary spy. After she was injected with microscopic nanites, she developed enhanced strength, remarkable healing ability and an array of largely unexplained energy powers, all of which made her a valuable if unpredictable asset to her company. In this series, she's helping a renegade Russian agent recover a doomsday weapon-- codenamed Angel Fire--before it falls into the wrong hands (although it's not entirely clear which hands those are). Since this is a Crusade Comic, it's practically a requirement that this series feature a guest appearance by Shi, the crown jewel (perhaps the only jewel?) in Bill Tucci's minor comics empire. The series is scripted by veteran writer Dan Mishkin, with art by Roberto Flores.
-- Stephen C. George

1/A-1/C 3.00
2-3.. 3.00

Angel Girl
Angel, 1997

0 .... 3.00
0/Nude.................................... 5.00

Angel Girl:
Before the Wings
Angel, 1997

1 .... 3.00

Angel Girl Vs.
Vampire Girls
Angel

1 .... 3.00
1/Nude.................................. 10.00

Angelic Layer
Tokyopop, 2002

1 .... 10.00

Angel Love
DC, 1986

1-Special 1 .... 1.00

Angel:
Masks
Idea & Design Works, 2006

1 .... 7.00

Angel of Death
Innovation

1-4 .... 2.00

Angel:
Old Friends
Idea & Design Works, 2005

1-5 .... 4.00

Angel:
Old Friends Cover Gallery
Idea & Design Works, 2006

1 .... 4.00

Angels 750
Antarctic, 2004

1-5 .... 3.00

Angel Sanctuary
Tokyopop, 2004

1-10 .... 10.00

Angel Scriptbook
Idea & Design Works, 2006

1-7 .... 4.00

Angels of Destruction
Malibu, 1996

1 .... 3.00

Angel Spotlight:
Connor
Idea & Design Works, 2006

1 .... 4.00

Angel Spotlight:
Doyle
Idea & Design Works, 2006

1 .... 4.00

Angel Spotlight:
Gunn
Idea & Design Works, 2006

1 .... 4.00

Angel Spotlight:
Illyria
Idea & Design Works, 2006

1 .... 4.00

Angel Spotlight:
Wesley
Idea & Design Works, 2006

1 .... 4.00

Angel Stomp Future (Warren Ellis'...)
Avatar, 2005

1 ....4.00

Angel: The Curse
Idea & Design Works, 2005

1-5..4.00

Angel: The Curse Cover Gallery
Idea & Design Works, 2006

1 ....4.00

Angeltown
DC, 2005

1-5..3.00

Anger Grrrl
Blatant, 1999

1 ....3.00

Angryman
Caliber

1-3...3.00

Angryman (2nd Series)
Iconografix

1-3...3.00

Angry Shadows
Innovation, 1989

1 ....5.00

Anima
DC, 1994

0-15..2.00

Animal Antics (Movietown's...)
DC, 1946

1	350.00
2	175.00
3-4	120.00
5-10	100.00
11-20	80.00
21-30	58.00
31-40	46.00
41-51	40.00

Animal Comics
Dell, 1942

1	900.00
2	450.00
3	340.00
4	150.00
5	300.00
6-7	135.00
☛War bonds cover	
8-10	225.00
11-15	170.00
16-20	130.00
21-25	105.00
26-30	80.00

Animal Confidential
Dark Horse, 1992

1 .... 2.00

Animal Fables
E.C., 1946

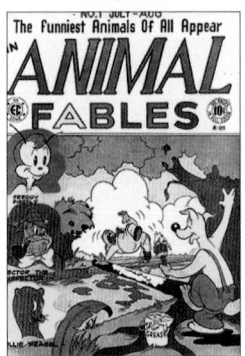

Face it, fans who think of E.C. do not initially conjure up an image of funny animal titles. But, as the publisher sought to find its niche in its earliest days, it tried a number of genres before striking the successful field of fantastic horror, striking art, and satire.

The series' primary continuing character was Human Torch imitation Freddy Firefly; other characters included Hector the Inspector and Korky Kangaroo. In addition, several of the stories were modernizations of the anthropomorphic stories of Aesop. Two issues carried work by Minute Movies creator Ed Wheelan, and the final issue promoted Moon Girl and the Prince, a title that seemed to be aimed at a more mature audience.

-- Maggie

1	250.00
2	175.00
3-7	150.00

Animal Fair
Fawcett, 1946

1	200.00
2-9	100.00

Animal Man
DC, 1988

1	4.00
2	3.00
3-49	2.00
50	3.00
51-55	2.00
56	4.00
57-89	2.00
Ann 1	4.00

Animal Mystic
Cry for Dawn, 1994

1	10.00
1/Ltd.	10.00
1/2nd	5.00
2	7.00
2/2nd	4.00
3	5.00
3/2nd	3.00
4-4/Ltd.	5.00
4/2nd	4.00

Animal Mystic Water Wars
Sirius, 1996

Dragons that are more cuddly than threatening, martial arts expertise, and lesbian insinuations are the elements in the popular fantasy world of Queen Jatarri, the Animal Mystic. This title picks up the exploits of Queen Jatarri after her adventures on the world of Praktill. A mystical dragon-like messenger known as Mota transports Queen Jatarri and her paramour Ryntha, the sensuous feline creature from Praktill, to the faraway planet of Antakia. There she becomes embroiled in a dispute caused by the pollution being generated by the fortress of the dictator, Lord Multa, and the underwater city of Marinopolis that is threatened with destruction because of it.

Water Wars features full-color artwork which serves to give this series a lighter tone than its precursor, Animal Mystic.

-- George Haberberger

1-4 .... 3.00

Animal Rights Comics
Stabur

1 .... 3.00

Animal Weirdness
Cozmic

1 .... 3.00

Animaniacs
DC, 1994

Warner Bros., best known for cartoon characters like Bugs Bunny and Porky Pig, introduced this series in 1995 in conjunction with a popular afternoon television show. Its stars are - you guessed it - the Warner Brothers (and a Warner sister), also known as The Animaniacs. This trio of cartoon troublemakers is known for their zany, over-the-top antics which never fail to reel in the laughs.

Although Animaniacs are aimed squarely at the pre-teen crowd, their occasional co-stars Pinky and the Brain have a more devilishly adult sensibility. Pinky is a punked-out goofball of a mouse, but his partner, the Brain, has a definite goal for life: to take over the world. To that end, he puts his incredible brain power to work to launch scheme after scheme. He's a megalomaniac, but endearing in his own way.

1	3.00
2-59	2.00
Holiday 1	3.00

Animated Comics
E.C., 1947

1	400.00

Animated Funny Comic Tunes
U.S.A., 1944

16	75.00
17	60.00
18-23	55.00

Animated Movie-Tunes
Margood, 1945

1-2	130.00

Animation Comics
Viz

1-4	4.00

Animax
Marvel, 1986

1-4	1.00

Animerica Extra
Viz, 1998

1-2	5.00

Animerica Extra (Vol. 2)
Viz, 1999

1-12	5.00

Animerica Extra (Vol. 3)
Viz, 2000

1-12	5.00

Animerica Extra (Vol. 4)
Viz, 2001

1-12	5.00

Animerica Extra (Vol. 5)
Viz, 2002

1-12	5.00

Animerica Extra (Vol. 6)
Viz, 2003

1	5.00

Animism
Centurion, 1987

1	2.00

Anita Blake: Vampire Hunter: Guilty Pleasures
Marvel, 2006

1	12.00
2	7.00
3	5.00

Aniverse
Weebee, 1987

1-2	2.00

Annex
Marvel, 1994

1-4	2.00

Annex
Chalk Outlines Studios, 1999

1	4.00

Annie
Marvel, 1982

1	1.00
1/Special	5.00
2	1.00

Annie Oakley
Timely, 1948

1	300.00
2	165.00
3-4	125.00
5	90.00
6-9	65.00
10-11	60.00

Annie Oakley and Tagg
Dell, 1955

Annie Oakley (1860-1926) was, of course, a real person, called by many the greatest sharpshooter of all time. She joined Buffalo Bill's Wild West Show in 1885; while there, Sioux Chief Sitting Bull adopted her as his daughter into the Sioux nation and gave her the name "Little Sureshot."

In one of her fictional incarnations (never forgetting that she was the female lead in the Broadway show and film Annie Get Your Gun), she shared the title with her kid brother, Tagg. That incarnation was a daytime syndicated TV show that was broadcast from 1954 to 1956 (and in reruns later) and starred trick shot artist Gail Davis as Annie. The era of the show's stories preceded Annie's Wild West Show adventures, and the comic-book version was based on the TV show, photo covers and all.

-- Maggie

4-10	60.00
11-18	45.00

Annie Oakley and Tagg (2nd series)
Gold Key, 1965

1	40.00

Annie Sprinkle Is Miss Timed
Rip Off, 1991

1-4	3.00

Annihilation
Marvel, 2006

1	3.00
2	3.00
4-5	3.00

Annihilation: Nova
Marvel, 2006

1-4	3.00

Annihilation Prologue
Marvel, 2006
1 ....4.00

Annihilation:
Ronan the Accuser
Marvel, 2006
3-85 ....3.00

Annihilation:
Silver Surfer
Marvel, 2006
1-4 ....3.00

Annihilation:
Super-Skrull
Marvel, 2006
1-4 ....3.00

Annihilation:
The Nova Corps Files
Marvel, 2006
1 ....4.00

Anomalies
Abnormal Fun, 2000
1 ....3.00

Anomaly
Bud Plant, 1972
1 ....8.00
2-4 ....5.00

Anomaly
(Brass Ring)
Brass Ring, 2000
1-2 ....4.00

Another Day
Raised Brow, 1995
1-2 ....3.00

Ant
Arcana, 2004
1 ....10.00
1/Red foil 35.00
2 ....5.00
3 ....5.00
3/Variant...............................6.00

Ant
(Vol. 2)
Image, 2005
1 ....5.00
1/Sketch 3.00
1/RRP 20.00
1/Conv..................................15.00
2-9 ....3.00

Antabuse
High Drive

Antabuse is distributed by High Drive Publications, whose motto is "Subversion and sexuality through micropublishing." This title, the work of San Francisco artist Matthew Zodrow and writer Kathleen Hanna, fits that offbeat category nicely.

Presented in two oversized black-and-white issues, Antabuse is a dark look at sex, abortion, and the perils of growing up. The first issue is an almost brutally frank depiction of a fifteen year-old girl's trip to the abortion clinic after "a little accident" with her boyfriend. Disturbing in its very casualness, the storyline alternates panels between the events leading to the girl's situation, and the details of her current plan for dealing with it.

It's very thought-provoking reading, but recommended for mature audiences only.

1-2 .... 3.00

Antarctic Press Jam
1996
Antarctic, 1996
1 .... 3.00

Antares Circle
Antarctic
1-2 .... 2.00

Ant Boy
Steeldragon, 1988
1-2 .... 2.00

Ant Farm
Gallant, 1998
1-2 .... 3.00

Anthro
DC, 1968

Anthro lives at the dawn of human history. His father is chief of the bear people, and his destiny is one day to become a chief himself. In the meanwhile, his abilities as a hunter makes him well-loved by his people.

In this prehistoric adventure series, Anthro battles for survival in a hostile world. Using brains, brawn, and skill he takes on all manner of huge beasts and engages in the ages-old battle of the heart, as he attempts to win a beautiful woman from another tribe as his wife.

Following a debut in Showcase #74, Anthro was featured in this 1968 solo series. Although it lasted only six issues, the character survived far longer as DC's "oldest," including an appearance in DC's Crisis on Infinite Earths.

1 .... 50.00
2-6 .... 20.00

Anticipator
Fantasy, 1996
1 .... 2.00

Antietam: The Fiery Trail
Heritage Collection, 1997
1 .... 4.00

Anti-Hitler Comics
New England
1-2 .... 3.00

Anti-Social
Helpless Anger
1 .... 2.00
2-4 .... 3.00

Anti Social
for the Disabled
Helpless Anger
1 .... 5.00

Anti Social Jr.
Helpless Anger
1 ....2.00

Ant-Man's Big Christmas
Marvel, 2000
1 ....6.00

Anton's Drekbook
Fantagraphics, 1991
1 ....3.00

Anubis
Super Crew
1 ....3.00

Anubis (2nd Series)
Super Crew
1 ....3.00

Anything but Monday
Anything But Monday, 1988
1-2 ....2.00

Anything Goes!
Fantagraphics, 1986
1-6 ....2.00

A-OK
Antarctic, 1992
1-4 ....3.00

Apache Dick
Eternity, 1990
1-4 ....2.00

Apache Kid
Atlas, 1950
53 (1)...................................200.00
2..100.00
3-5..65.00
6-10...55.00
11-19..45.00

Apache Skies
Marvel, 2002
1-4 ....3.00

Apache Trail
Steinway, 1957

Apache Trail was a standard Western series from Steinway in the late 1950s. The main stories in each issue were focused primarily on conflicts between Indian tribes and the US Army, reflecting a slightly higher level of sophistication than many comic books from the time. Indians were depicted not as a unified block of "savages," but as a diverse culture containing both good and bad. Once this fact was established, however, the stories proceeded with the same rifle-shooting, fort-burning, scalp-hunting abandon as most action-oriented Westerns. Apache Trail also included filler stories of the usual Western variety about outlaws, settler families and farmers vs. cattlemen.

1 .... 58.00
2-4 .... 36.00

Apathy Kat
Express, 1995
1-4 .... 3.00

Ape
Catalan
1 .... 11.00

Ape City
Adventure, 1990
1-4 .... 3.00

Ape Nation
Adventure, 1991
1 .... 3.00
1/Ltd. 4.00
2-4 .... 2.00

Ape Omnibus
Ape Entertainment, 2004
1-2 .... 6.00

Apex
Aztec
1 .... 2.00

Apex Project
Stellar, 1990
1-2 .... 1.00

Aphrodisia
Fantagraphics, 1995
1-2 .... 3.00

Aphrodite IX
Image, 2000

She is a beautiful woman with green hair. She is also Aphrodite IX, a purely synthetic being created in a lab and trained to be a killer. Too bad no one told her. Now she is beginning to question her existence, but it's difficult for someone to remember her past when her memory is erased 15 minutes after every mission. Her only hope is a mysterious man named Burch who may be able to provide her with answers. In a futuristic world in which humans have begun to alter their bodies with synthetics, Aphrodite IX must follow orders, relentlessly carrying out her duties as a trained assassin, yet unable to recall her past. Top Cow adds another buxom beauty to its line-up in this series written by Dave Finch (Batman/Darkness) and illustrated by David Wohl (Witchblade).

0 .... 2.00
0/2nd 6.00
0/A-0/B 9.00
0/C-0/F 4.00
1/A 4.00
1/B-1/D 3.00
1/E-1/F 5.00
1/G-1/H..................................... 4.00
1/I 5.00
2 .... 2.00
2/A-2/K 3.00
3 .... 2.00
4 .... 4.00
4/A 5.00
Ashcan 1 .... 6.00
Ashcan 1/Ltd. 5.00

Apocalypse Nerd
Dark Horse, 2005
1-5 .... 3.00

Apollo Smile
Mixx, 1998
1 .... 4.00
2 .... 3.00

Apparition
Caliber, 1996

1-5 ....3.00

Apparition: Abandoned
Caliber, 1995

1 ....4.00

Apparition: Visitations
Caliber, 1995

1 ....4.00

Apple, P.I.
Parrot Communications, 1996

1 ....1.00

Appleseed Book 1
Eclipse, 1988

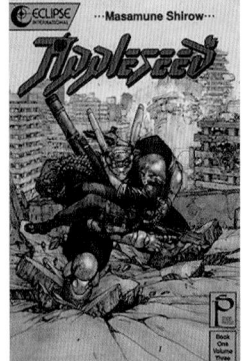

Masamune Shirow's Appleseed is an influential Japanese manga series, as well as a series of anime films. The futuristic tale takes place after World War III, when society looks for new ideas, as it begins rebuilding its cities. The city of Olympus is meant to be the perfect place to live: a shining example to the world around it. In Olympus, there is almost no crime or homelessness, and the residents lack for nothing. In order to create the perfect city, however, perfect citizens are required. Olympus' builders supplied these, using genetic engineering to create a population suited for life in paradise. In total, some 80% of Olympus' population have been bio-engineered for life there.

Among the few that were not are Deunan Knute, a hard-fighting leader of the city's S.W.A.T. unit. Her job is to keep the peace, even as paradise begins to show signs of cracking under the strain of perfection.

1 ....7.00
2-3 ....5.00
4-5 ....4.00

Appleseed Book 2
Eclipse, 1989

1 .... 5.00
2-5 .... 4.00

Appleseed Book 3
Eclipse, 1989

1-5 .... 4.00

Appleseed Book 4
Eclipse, 1991

1-4 .... 4.00

Appleseed Databook
Dark Horse, 1994

1-2 .... 4.00

Approved Comics
St. John, 1954

1 .... 60.00
2 .... 90.00
3-4 .... 58.00
5 .... 60.00
6 .... 65.00
7 .... 60.00
8 .... 58.00
9 .... 65.00
10-12 .... 75.00

April Horrors
Rip Off, 1993

1 .... 3.00

Aquablue
Dark Horse, 1989

1 .... 7.00

Aquablue: The Blue Planet
Dark Horse, 1990

1 .... 9.00

Aqua Knight
Viz, 2000

1 .... 3.00
2-6 .... 4.00

Aqua Knight Part 2
Viz, 2000

1-5 .... 4.00

Aqua Knight Part 3
Viz, 2001

1-5 .... 4.00

Aquaman (1st Series)
DC, 1962

1 .... 900.00
2 .... 275.00
3-5 .... 150.00
6-10 .... 90.00
11 .... 125.00
☞1st Mera
12-17 .... 75.00
18 .... 90.00
☞Weds Mera
19-28 .... 60.00
29 .... 75.00

☞1st Ocean Master
30 .... 50.00
31 .... 45.00
32 .... 50.00
33-34 .... 45.00
35-41 .... 40.00
42-43 .... 30.00
44-46 .... 25.00
47 .... 40.00
48-49 .... 25.00
50 .... 75.00
51 .... 50.00
52 .... 40.00
53-58 .... 20.00
59-60 .... 10.00
61-62 .... 10.00
63 .... 10.00

Aquaman (2nd Series)
DC, 1986

1 .... 3.00
2 .... 3.00
3 .... 3.00
4 .... 3.00
Special 1 .... 2.00

Aquaman (3rd Series)
DC, 1989

1-5 .... 1.00
Special 1 .... 2.00

Aquaman (4th Series)
DC, 1991

1 .... 2.00
2-13 .... 1.00

Aquaman (5th Series)
DC, 1994

0-2 .... 3.00
3-70 .... 2.00
71-75 .... 3.00
1000000 .... 2.00
Ann 1 .... 4.00
Ann 2 .... 3.00
Ann 3 .... 4.00
Ann 4-5 .... 3.00

Aquaman (6th series)
DC, 2003

1-14 .... 3.00
15 .... 12.00
☞Old costume back
16-17 .... 6.00
18-47 .... 3.00

Aquaman Secret Files
DC, 1998

Aquaman's variety of origins and complex history made him a natural for a Secret Files title. Like others of this type, this title retells Aquaman's origin. All of Aquaman's disparate history has been woven into a complex tapestry; from being Arthur Curry, the son of a lighthouse keeper to Prince Orin, son of the immortal warrior, Atlan. A timeline detailing significant events and concise biographies of Aquaman's friends and family are featured.
-- George Haberberger

1-2...5.00

Aquaman:
Time and Tide
DC, 1993
1-4...2.00

Aquarium
CPM Manga, 2000
1/A-6.......................................3.00

Arabian Nights on the World of Magic: The Gathering
Acclaim, 1995
1-2...3.00

Arachnophobia
Disney
1..3.00

Aragonés 3-D
3-D Zone

Sergio Aragonés is a talented, witty, and extremely prolific cartoonist. Best known for his comical squigglings in the margins of Mad, he also co-created and drew Groo the Wanderer, as well as contributing gags to everything from Plop! to The Mighty Magnor.

In 1989, 3-D Zone converted a number of his cartoons using their very effective 3-D process. Although the effect is not as stunning as in some of the Blackthorne 3-D comics, it still forces the reader to slow down to both enjoy the 3-D visuals, and to drink in the almost unbelievably detailed sketches that are an Aragonés trademark.

1 .... 5.00

Araknis
Mushroom, 1995
0-6..3.00

Arak Son of Thunder
DC, 1981

On a Viking expedition in ages past, Norsemen come across a sinking boat. The sole passenger turns out to be a boy with skin the color of fire. Taken in by the Vikings, the boy is called "Eric," which he interprets as "Arak." He soon grows into a man and proves a naturally skilled warrior.

Years later, Arak accompanies the Vikings on a raid in which the party is destroyed by mystical forces. Arak is the sole survivor. He then sets out on a path of adventure in an age of swords and sorcery, becoming a legend in an age of legends.

First appearing in Warlord #48, Arak is one of a number of epic fantasy titles tied into the Warlord world, including Arion, Lord of Atlantis, and Conqueror of the Barren Earth.

1	1.00
2-50	1.00
Ann 1	2.00

Aramis
Comics Interview
1-3 .... 2.00

Arana:
Heart of the Spider
Marvel, 2005

1	3.00
1/Incentive	7.00
2-12	3.00

Arc
(Vol. 2)
Arts Industria, 1994
1 .... 3.00

Arcade
Print Mint, 1975

1	10.00
2-3	8.00
4-6	7.00
7	5.00

Arcana
DC, 1994
Ann 1.................................... 4.00

Arcana
Tokyopop, 2005
1-3 .... 10.00

Arcana
(Wells & Clark)
Wells & Clark, 1995

1-3	3.00
4-10	2.00

Arcane
Arcane

1	2.00
2	10.00

Arcane
(2nd Series)
Graphik
1 .... 1.00

Arcanum
Image, 1997

1/2	3.00
1/2/Gold	5.00
1-8	3.00

Archaic
Fenickx Productions, 2003
1-5 .... 3.00

Archangel
Marvel, 1996
1 .... 3.00

Archangels:
The Saga
Eternal, 1996
1-8 .... 3.00

Archard's Agents
CrossGen, 2003
1 .... 3.00

Archenemies
Dark Horse, 2006

1-4 .... 3.00

Archer & Armstrong
Valiant, 1992

0 .... 4.00
0/Gold 25.00
1 .... 4.00
2 .... 3.00
3-7 .... 2.00
8 .... 3.00
9 .... 2.00
10-21 .... 1.00
22 .... 2.00
23-25 .... 1.00
26 .... 5.00

Archie
Archie, 1942

Archie Andrews is an American icon. For more than 50 years, he and his perpetually teen-aged supporting cast have been entertaining children of all ages. Created by Bob Montana on assignment, Archie was introduced in Pep #22 in 1941. He received his own series shortly after. After more than 400 issues, Archie, blonde Betty, rich Veronica, dense-but-lovable Jughead, oxlike Moose, and the crafty Reggie are still getting into trouble and having laughs at Riverdale High School.

Naturally, a series with this sort of long-term appeal was bound to result in numerous spinoff titles. Among them are Betty and Veronica, Archie and Me, Archie Digest Magazine, Archie's Date Book, Reggie, and even The Punisher Meets Archie. All feature the Riverdale teens in adventures suitable for young readers.

1992 marked Archie's 50th year in comics.

1 .... 12,200.00
2 .... 3,325.00

3 .... 2,175.00
4 .... 1,100.00
5 .... 1,000.00
6 .... 740.00
7-9 .... 660.00
10 .... 585.00
11-15 .... 475.00
16-20 .... 400.00
21-24 .... 325.00
25-30 .... 275.00
31-35 .... 220.00
36-40 .... 175.00
41-50 .... 125.00
51-60 .... 110.00
61-70 .... 70.00
71-80 .... 56.00
81-90 .... 44.00
91-99 .... 34.00
100 .... 55.00
101-120 .... 22.00
121-140 .... 16.00
141-150 .... 13.00
151-180 .... 9.00
181-200 .... 5.00
201-250 .... 3.00
251-599 .... 2.00
Ann 1 .... 1,350.00
Ann 2 .... 660.00
Ann 3 .... 475.00
Ann 4 .... 345.00
Ann 5 .... 285.00
Ann 6 .... 180.00
Ann 7 .... 160.00
Ann 8 .... 135.00
Ann 9 .... 120.00
Ann 10 .... 110.00
Ann 11 .... 70.00
Ann 12 .... 60.00
Ann 13 .... 58.00
Ann 14-15 .... 50.00
Ann 16-17 .... 26.00
Ann 18-19 .... 22.00
Ann 20 .... 14.00
Ann 21-22 .... 9.00
Ann 23-26 .... 8.00

Archie All Canadian Digest
Archie, 1996

1 .... 2.00

Archie and Friends
Archie, 1992

1 .... 3.00
2-129 .... 2.00

Archie and Me
Archie, 1964

1 .... 125.00
2 .... 75.00
3 .... 45.00
4-5 .... 34.00
6-10 .... 20.00
11-20 .... 12.00
21-30 .... 8.00
31-40 .... 6.00
41-50 .... 4.00
51-80 .... 3.00
81-100 .... 2.00
101-161 .... 1.00

Archie Annual Digest Magazine
Archie, 1995

66-68 .... 2.00

Archie... Archie Andrews, Where Are You? Digest Magazine
Archie, 1977

1 .... 5.00
2-10 .... 3.00
11-117 .... 2.00

Archie As Pureheart the Powerful
Archie, 1966

As the campy Batman TV series gained massive popularity in 1966, the Archie line tried to jump on the bandwagon by transforming Archie Andrews into a super-hero satire called Captain Pureheart. Captain Pureheart wore a costume similar to Superman's, reversing the colors: Pureheart's cape was blue and the rest of his outfit was dominated by red.

The title didn't spoof specific super-hero titles or stories; the series mainly offered the usual lighthearted Archie fare, except that Archie spent more time fighting crime than choosing between Betty and Veronica. Archie's high-school rival Reggie also donned spandex, becoming Evilheart. Low on violence, high on silliness, Archie as Captain Pureheart was eventually seen as a dated curio, a time capsule of '60s pop-culture cheese.

1 .... 55.00
2 .... 35.00
3-6 .... 25.00

Archie at Riverdale High
Archie, 1972

1 .... 42.00
2 .... 22.00
3-5 .... 16.00

6-10	11.00
11-20	8.00
21-30	5.00
31-40	4.00
41-60	3.00
61-100	2.00
101-114	1.00

Archie Comics Presents the Love Showdown Collection
Archie, 1994

1	5.00

Archie Digest Magazine
Archie, 1973

1	26.00
2	10.00
3-5	6.00
6-10	4.00
11-20	3.00
21-244	2.00

Archie Giant Series Magazine
Archie, 1954

Perhaps the most remarkable thing about the Archie Giant Series Magazine is its weird penchant for discontiguous issue numbering and alternate names. Basically, it's an umbrella title for various Archie family stories, virtually indistinguishable from numerous other Archie magazines. Each issue, however, nominally features a different Archie character, calling itself "World of Jughead," "World of Archie," etc. on the cover, in rotating fashion. Adding to this complication are strange gaps in issue numbering: The issue immediately following #35 was #136. Later, an even bigger chasm opened in the issue numbering sequence, when issue #251 was followed by #452. Whether these gaps were meant to make the series seem more long-lived or whether they were merely the case of typographical errors gone uncorrected is anyone's guess.

1	750.00
2	475.00
3-4	325.00
5-6	275.00
7-8	200.00
9-10	185.00
11	140.00
12	125.00
13	140.00
14-15	110.00
16	125.00
17	110.00
18	125.00
19	110.00
20	100.00
21	85.00
22	60.00
23	80.00
24-25	60.00
26	80.00
27	60.00
28	80.00
29-30	60.00
31-141	40.00
142	45.00
143-160	20.00
161-180	12.00
181-200	10.00
201-220	8.00
221-250	6.00
251	4.00
452-550	3.00
551-632	2.00

Archie Meets the Punisher
Marvel, 1994

1	3.00

Archie's Christmas Stocking (2nd Series)
Archie, 1994

1	3.00
2-7	2.00

Archie's Date Book
Spire

1	4.00

Archie's Double Digest Magazine
Archie, 1982

1	6.00
2-10	4.00
11-138	3.00
139-196	4.00

Archie's Family Album
Spire, 1978

1	4.00

Archie's Girls Betty & Veronica
Archie, 1950

1	1,400.00
2	675.00
3	485.00
4-5	375.00
6-10	285.00
11-19	225.00

20-29	165.00
30-39	115.00
40-50	85.00
51-60	55.00
61-70	45.00
71-90	32.00
91-110	24.00
111-140	16.00
141-160	13.00
161-180	10.00
181-200	7.00
201-250	5.00
251-319	3.00
320	8.00
321	4.00
322-347	3.00
Ann 1	525.00
Ann 2	325.00
Ann 3-4	265.00
Ann 5	250.00
Ann 6	175.00
Ann 7	150.00
Ann 8	100.00

Archie's Holiday Fun Digest Magazine
Archie, 1997

1-10	2.00
11-12	3.00

Archie's Jokebook Magazine
Archie, 1953

nn	600.00
2	375.00
3	275.00
15	165.00
16-20	135.00
21-30	100.00
31-40	75.00
41	135.00
42-43	65.00
44-48	70.00
49-60	35.00
61-70	24.00
71-80	16.00
81-90	12.00
91-100	8.00
101-120	5.00
121-150	3.00
151-200	2.00
201-288	1.00

Archie's Love Scene
Spire, 1973

1	5.00

Archie's Madhouse
Archie, 1959

1	175.00
2	95.00
3	68.00
4-5	50.00
6-10	38.00
11-15	26.00
16-20	23.00
21	18.00
22	100.00
23-25	18.00
26-30	14.00

31-40......................................9.00
41-50......................................6.00
51-66......................................4.00
Ann 1.....................................65.00
Ann 2.....................................25.00
Ann 3.....................................15.00
Ann 4-10 ....10.00

Archie's Mechanics
Archie, 1954

1..45.00
2..35.00
3..30.00

Archie's Mysteries
Archie, 2003

25-34......................................2.00

Archie's Pal Jughead
Archie, 1949

1....................................2,000.00
2..675.00
3..350.00
4-5......................................230.00
6-10.....................................150.00
11-15.....................................95.00
16-20.....................................85.00
21-30.....................................55.00
31-40.....................................38.00
41-60.....................................22.00
61-80.....................................16.00
81-100...................................10.00
101-120...................................7.00
121-126...................................5.00
Ann 1....................................650.00
Ann 2....................................350.00
Ann 3....................................145.00
Ann 4.....................................85.00
Ann 5.....................................65.00
Ann 6-8 ....45.00

Archie's Pal Jughead Comics
Archie, 1993

46-193....................................2.00

Archie's Pals 'n' Gals
Archie, 1952

1..575.00
2..290.00
3..215.00
4-5......................................185.00
6-7......................................135.00
8-10.....................................80.00
11-20.....................................45.00
21-28.....................................22.00
29..45.00
30..22.00
31-40.....................................13.00
41-50......................................9.00
51-70......................................7.00
71-81......................................5.00
82-100....................................4.00
101-150...................................3.00
151-224...................................2.00

Archie's Pals 'n' Gals Double Digest
Archie, 1995

1..4.00

2-76......................................3.00
77-129....................................4.00

Archie's R/C Racers
Archie, 1989

1-10......................................2.00

Archie's Rival Reggie
Archie, 1950

1.......................................740.00
2.......................................375.00
3.......................................225.00
4.......................................200.00
5.......................................175.00
6-7.....................................140.00
8-10....................................125.00
11-12....................................85.00
13-14....................................80.00

Archie's Spring Break
Archie, 1996

1-5......................................3.00

Archie's Story & Game Digest Magazine
Archie, 1995

32-39....................................2.00

Archie's Super-Hero Special
Archie, 1979

1-2......................................3.00

Archie's Super Teens
Archie, 1994

1-4......................................3.00

Archie's TV Laugh-Out
Archie, 1969

1.......................................42.00
2.......................................24.00
3-5.....................................16.00
6.......................................12.00
7.......................................22.00
8-10....................................12.00
11-20....................................9.00
21-30....................................7.00
31-40....................................6.00
41-60....................................4.00
61-106...................................3.00

Archie's Vacation Special
Archie, 1994

1-8......................................3.00

Archie's Weird Mysteries
Archie, 2000

1-24.....................................2.00
Ashcan 1 ....1.00

Archie 3000
Archie, 1989

1..3.00
2-5......................................2.00
6-16.....................................1.00

Arcomics Premiere
Arcomics, 1993

1..3.00

Arctic Comics
Nick Burns

The lure of the frozen North has long fascinated us, with the endless miles of tundra, the months-long nights, and the mystical quality of the Aurora Borealis.

Author Nick Burns combines tales of myth and legend with realistic present-day adventures, and even looks to the future, where the Arctic is the last bastion of human freedom.

He is able to relate stories of Inuit hunters and city-born tourists with the same veracity, while breaking down the stereotypical views of "Eskimos" and Alaskan life. Mixed among the short tales are informational pages providing information on wildlife, Inuit language, and native folklore.

1..1.00

Area 52
Image, 2001

1-4......................................3.00

Area 88
Eclipse, 1987

Comics in Japan run from science-fiction to adult fiction, and are read by millions of Japanese. According to its editors, Area 88 was the first large scale attempt to bring Japanese comics ("manga") to the U.S. in a traditional comic book form. In doing so, it helped open the U.S. comic marketplace to the amazing variety of Japanese comic storytelling.

The Area 88 of this series is a battleground in North Africa, right at the front lines of the war between Asran and its enemy. Asran employs a force of mercenaries to do their dirty work, running their air force much like a taxi company. The pilots provide their own planes, pay for their own ammunition and fuel, then receive payment for the kills they make. To survive at this game takes both skill and cunning, a combination which is best found in Shin Kazama, a blonde, Japanese mercenary, and the hero of the series.

1	4.00
1/2nd	2.00
2	3.00
2/2nd-42	2.00

Areala: Angel of War
Antarctic, 1998

1-4	3.00

Arena
Alchemy

1	2.00

Ares
Marvel, 2006

1-5	3.00

Argonauts
Eternity, 1988

1-4	2.00

Argonauts: System Crash
Alpha Productions

1-2	3.00

Argon Zark!
Arclight, 1997

1	7.00

Argus
DC, 1995

1-6	2.00

Aria
Image, 1998

This series began with a predominantly black-and-white preview edition of writer Brian Holguin and artist Jay Anacelto's Aria that is simply beautiful; it's a quick look at the characters who will populate an intriguing new series from Image Comics and Avalon Studios. In Aria, myth mixes with reality; gods and Faeries walk the streets of contemporary Manhattan, and a 900-year-old expatriate Faerie princess named Kildare operates a bookstore called Otherworld in Greenwich Village.

Anacelto's art is haunting and lovely, and Brian Holguin's excellent writing is showcased in an engaging short story starring Kildare and other creatures from the "[other] side of the metaphysical fence."

1-7	3.00
Ashcan 1	4.00

Aria: A Midwinter's Dream
Image, 2002

1	5.00

Aria Angela
Image, 2000

1-2	3.00

Aria Angela Blanc & Noir
Image, 2000

1	3.00

Aria Blanc & Noir
Image, 1999

1-2	3.00

Aria (Manga)
ADV Manga, 2004

1	10.00

Ariane & Bluebeard
Eclipse, 1989

1	4.00

Arianne
Slave Labor, 1991

1	5.00
2	3.00

Arianne (Moonstone)
Moonstone, 1995

1	5.00

Aria Summer's Spell
Image, 2002

1-2	3.00

Aria: The Soul Market
Image, 2001

1-6	3.00

Aria: The Uses of Enchantment
Image, 2003

1-4	3.00

Arik Khan (A+)
A-Plus

1-2	3.00

Arik Khan (Andromeda)
Andromeda, 1977

1-3	2.00

Arion, Lord of Atlantis
DC, 1982

Like Arak, Son of Thunder, and Conqueror of the Barren Earth, Arion has its origins in the pages of Warlord. First appearing in Warlord #55, Arion is a young mage, created out of cosmic forces. He is part human, part cosmic matter, and a force to be contended with by any reckoning.

Arion owes his allegiance to Atlantis, which he must save from the mortal and mystical forces that imperil it. 45,000 years before the birth of Christ, Atlantis was a world of magic and marvel, swords and sorcery. Aided by his friends Wyynde, Chian, and Mara, Arion battles everything from cyborg jackal-warriors to cosmic witches to save Atlantis.

1-3..1.00

Arion the Immortal
DC, 1992

1-6..2.00

Aristocats
Gold Key, 1971

1..4.00

Aristocratic X-Traterrestrial Time-Traveling Thieves
Comics Interview, 1987

1-12..2.00

Aristocratic X-Traterrestrial Time-Traveling Thieves Micro-Series
Comics Interview, 1986

1-1/2nd......................................2.00

Aristokittens
Gold Key, 1973

1..16.00
2..10.00
3-5..8.00
6-9..6.00

Arizona: A Simple Horror
London Night, 1998

1-3..3.00

Arizona Kid
Atlas, 1951

1..100.00
2-4..60.00
5-6..50.00

Arizona: Wild at Heart
London Night, 1998

1..3.00

Arkaga
Image, 1997

1-2..3.00

Ark Angels
Tokyopop, 2005

1..10.00

Arkanium
Dreamwave, 2002

1-5..3.00

Arkeology
Valkyrie, 1989

1..2.00

Arkham Asylum Living Hell
DC, 2003

1-6..3.00

Arlington Hammer in: Get Me to the Church on Time
One Shot

1 .... 3.00

A.R.M.
Adventure, 1990

1-3 .... 3.00

Armadillo Comics
Rip Off, 1969

Texan Jim Franklin managed to get his work published by Rip Off Press in the early 70s. The series was a showcase for Franklin's short pieces, which were mostly surreal comics and pictures of armadillos. The armadillo is Franklin's central icon, and he uses it as a symbol for everything. The pieces are bizarre and nonlinear, and expertly drawn in a confident hatching style. A forgotten underground, Jim Franklin's Armadillo Comics are a good example of the unique expression of one artist.

1-2 .... 3.00

Armageddon
Last Gasp

1-2 .... 3.00

Armageddon (Chaos)
Chaos, 1999

1-4 .... 3.00

Armageddon 2001
DC, 1991

1-2 .... 2.00

Armageddon: Inferno
DC, 1992

1-4 .... 1.00

Armageddon: The Alien Agenda
DC, 1991

1-4 .... 1.00

Armageddon Factor
AC, 1987

1-3 .... 2.00

Armageddon Factor: The Conclusion
AC, 1990

1 .... 4.00

Armageddon Patrol: The Shot
Alchemy Texts, 1998

1 .... 3.00

Armageddonquest
Starhead, 1984

1-2 .... 4.00

Armageddon Rising
Millennium, 1997

1 .... 5.00

Armageddon Squad
Haze

1 .... 2.00

Armature
Olyoptics, 1996

1-2 .... 3.00

Armed and Dangerous (Acclaim)
Acclaim, 1996

1-4 .... 3.00
Special 1 .... 3.00

Armed & Dangerous: Hell's Slaughterhouse
Acclaim, 1996

1-4 .... 3.00

Armed & Dangerous
Kitchen Sink, 1995

1 .... 10.00

Armen Deep & Bug Boy
Dilemma, 1995

2 .... 3.00

Armitage
Fleetway-Quality

1-2 .... 3.00

Arm of Kannon
Tokyopop, 2004

1-7 .... 10.00

Armor
Continuity, 1985

4-13 .... 2.00

Armor (2nd Series)
Continuity, 1993

1-6 .... 3.00

Armored Trooper Votoms
CPM, 1996

1-2 .... 3.00

Armorines
Valiant, 1993

The Armorines are a special strike force of marines clad in high-tech armor developed by copying features of the X-O Manowar suit worn by Aric Dacia. Although their armor doesn't allow them to fly like the Manowar suit, it does provide them with strength and near-invulnerability. Moreover, their suits are armed with ion and laser weapons, as well as an awesomely destructive particle beam cannon. To command all this, the marines are paired up with remote "co-pilots" who help them analyze the battlefield and prepare strategy. (In this, the Armorines resemble the members of H.A.R.D. Corps who rely on a remote command center to switch their powers.)

This title premiered in X-O Manowar #25, in a bound-in Armorines #0 comic. That issue also showed that even though the Armorines are fundamentally good men, there is always the chance that they, or those that command them will abuse their great powers.

0/Gold	25.00
0	1.00
0/StandAlone	30.00
1/VVSS	40.00
1-8	1.00
9-11	2.00
12	4.00

Armorines (Vol. 2)
Acclaim, 1999

1-4	4.00

Armorquest
Alias, 2005

0-2	3.00

Armor X
Image, 2005

1-4	3.00

Arm's Length
Third Wind, 2000

1	4.00

Army and Navy Comics
Street & Smith, 1941

1	325.00
2	175.00
3-4	125.00
5	275.00

Army Ants
Michael T. Desing

8	3.00

Army Attack
Charlton, 1964

1	20.00
2-47	15.00

Army at War
DC, 1978

1	10.00

Army of Darkness
Dark Horse, 1992

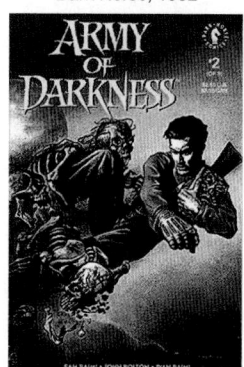

Army of Darkness was the big-budget sequel to cult video releases Evil Dead and Evil Dead II. Its story begins when a man named Ash finds the Necronomicon at a remote cabin he had rented with his wife Linda. The book, a leftover from Evil Dead was an unspeakably evil artifact bound in human flesh and written in blood. When Ash began reading it, a demonic force was unleashed that stole his wife. Then it got into Ash's body through his hand. To stop it, he had to lop the hand off. Ash tried reading a different passage of the book which was meant to open a hole in time that would send the evil back. Unfortunately, it ended up sending Ash back into a dark age of sorcery in approximately 1130 A.D.

This two-issue movie adaptation features dark painted art by John Bolton (Black Dragon).

1	12.00
2-3	9.00

Army of Darkness: Ashes 2 Ashes
Devil's Due, 2004

1	10.00
1/Incentive	5.00
1/Photo	4.00
1/Silvestri	3.00
1/Sketch	11.00
1/DirCut	7.00
1/Templesmith	3.00
2	4.00
2/B&W	5.00
2/Photo	3.00
2/Land	3.00
2/Isanove	4.00
3	3.00
4	4.00
4/Garza	3.00

Army of Darkness: Shop Til You Drop (Dead)
Devil's Due, 2005

1	3.00
1/Ebas	4.00
1/Isanove	3.00
1/Lee	4.00
1/Rivera	3.00
1/Glow	35.00
2	3.00
2/Variant	8.00
2/DF	15.00
3-4	3.00

Army Surplus Komikz Featuring: Cutey Bunny
Quagmire, 1985

1-5	3.00

Army War Heroes
Charlton, 1963

1	20.00
2	10.00
3-5	8.00
6-19	6.00
20-21	4.00
22	6.00
23-38	4.00

Aromatic Bitters
Tokyopop, 2004

1	10.00

Around the World Under the Sea
Dell, 1966

1	20.00

Arrgh!
Marvel, 1974

Over the years, Marvel has created a huge number of gag magazines such as Not Brand Echh, Spoof, and Crazy, to name just a few. This series took a slightly different approach and specialized in the forgotten art of "genre spoofing." Instead of making fun of a particular story or film, Arrgh! took aim at the entire field of horror. Its tales were filled with monsters, vampires, and werewolves and usually ended on an ironic note. On the way, however, they were filled with humor, gags, and ridiculous situations.

```
1 .............................................15.00
2 ...............................................4.00
3-5 ............................................3.00
```

Arrow
Centaur, 1940

```
1 .......................................2,000.00
2 ..........................................950.00
3 ..........................................800.00
```

Arrow
Malibu, 1992

```
1 ...............................................2.00
```

Arrow Anthology
Arrow, 1997

```
1-5 ............................................4.00
```

Arrowhead
Atlas, 1954

```
1 .............................................100.00
2-4 ...........................................60.00
```

Arrowman
Parody

```
1 ...............................................3.00
```

Arrowsmith
DC, 2003

```
1-6 ............................................3.00
```

Arrowsmith/Astro City
DC, 2004

```
1 ..............................................3.00
```

Arrow Spotlight
Arrow, 1998

```
1 ..............................................3.00
```

Arsenal
DC, 1998

```
1-4 ............................................3.00
```

Arsenal Special
DC, 1996

```
1 ..............................................3.00
```

Arsenic Lullaby
A. Silent, 1998

A one-man show created by writer/artist Douglas Paszkiewicz, this anthology presents six stories distinguished from each other only in the details.

A pair of U.S. Census Bureau workers go to murderous extremes to keep the numbers accurate; a snowman refuses to give way to the reality of spring; a winged demon somehow ends up in a television commercial; a bodiless head is envious of his wife; and a cook must deal with finicky customers.

There's not a lot of story in any of the shorts, and none contain enough depth to even pass as weak satire. In all, the book reads like one bleak bar story after another, which when combined with the raw art, grows tiresome. Paszkiewicz' decision to take two of the stories and split them in half, with part one early on and part two later, is inexplicable and distracting.

```
1-20 ......................................... 3.00
```

Arsinoe
Fantagraphics, 2005

```
1-4 ............................................. 4.00
```

Art & Beauty Magazine
Kitchen Sink, 2003

```
1-2 ......................................... 5.00
```

Artbabe (Vol. 2)
Fantagraphics, 1997

```
1-4 ......................................... 3.00
```

Art D'Ecco
Fantagraphics, 1990

```
1-4 ......................................... 3.00
```

Artemis: Requiem
DC, 1996

```
1-6 ......................................... 2.00
```

Artesia
Sirius, 1999

Artesia is not a place. It is a woman. A beautiful woman. A woman who is at once warrior, priestess, concubine, and spiritwalker. The goddesses smile upon her.

The story begins in battle. Artesia leads her lord's troops into battle against a rival noble house. Though the field is hers, something is not quite right. In religious ecstasy, she witnesses spirits guiding the dead to the underworld. Though Geniche, Dark Queen of the Underworld, assures Artesia that they do not come for her, the Dark Queen kisses Artesia, and that cannot be an omen of peace and contentment. The portents warn also that Geniche will walk the Earth again and Artesia's lord plans to betray her to the witch hunters. If Artesia is to survive, the goddesses must indeed be with her.

```
1-6 ......................................... 3.00
```

Artesia Afield
Sirius, 2000

```
1-6 ......................................... 3.00
```

Artesia Afire
Archaia Studios Press, 2003

```
1-6 ......................................... 4.00
```

Arthur King of Britain
Tome, 1993
1-4 ....3.00
5 ....4.00

Arthur Sex
Aircel, 1991
1-8 ....3.00

Artillery One-Shot
Red Bullet, 1995
1 ....3.00

Art in Shambles
Max Hopper
1 ....3.00

Artistic Comics
Golden Gate, 1973
0 ....10.00

Artistic Comics
Kitchen Sink, 1995
1-1/2nd....................................3.00

Artistic Licentiousness
Starhead, 1994
1-3...3.00

Art of Abrams
Lightning, 1996
1 ....4.00

Art of Aubrey Beardsley
Tome
1 ....3.00

Art of Heath Robinson
Tome
1 ....3.00

Art of Homage Studios
Image, 1993
1 ....6.00

Art of Jay Anacleto
Image, 2002
1 ....6.00

Art of Marvel Comics
Marvel, 2004
1-2..30.00

Art of Moebius
Marvel
1 ....15.00

Art of Mucha
Tome, 1992
1 ....3.00

Art of Pulp Fiction
A-List, 1998
1 ....3.00

Art of Spanking
NBM
1 ....18.00

Art of the Witchblade
Image, 2006
1 .... 3.00

Art of Usagi Yojimbo
Radio, 1997
1-2... 4.00

Art of Walter Simonson
DC
1 .... 20.00

Art of Wrightson
Side Show, 1996
1 .... 10.00

Art School Superstars
Fantagraphics
1 .... 3.00

Artxilla Tasty Treats 2005
Image, 2005
0 .... 7.00

Ascension
Image, 1997

Two thousand years ago two tribes-the Mineans, a race of angelic, winged people, and the Dayaks, blue skinned and demonic -- existed as one. To the Dayaks a child named Viovodul was born. So strong was his evil that scientists from both sides imprisoned him in a realm between their world and ours.

The pages containing the full formula to free him were scattered to both realms, coming into the possession of Lucien and Andromeda, who have been given fantastic powers and whose destiny it is to stop Viovodul from being released.

Originally a tale of heaven and hell, centering on the war between the tribes, the series spun into a new direction after Batt, one of the co-creators and owners, departed

after issue #7 due to creative differences.

0	3.00
0/Gold	4.00
0/Ltd.	6.00
1/2	4.00
1-1/A	3.00
1/B-1/D	4.00
2	3.00
2/A-2/Gold	4.00
3-22	3.00
Ashcan 1	4.00

Ash

Event, 1994
0-0/C	4.00
1/2	3.00
1/2/Ltd.-1/2/Platinum	4.00
1	3.00
1/A	4.00
1/B-6/A	3.00

Ash/22 Brides
Event, 1996
1-2 .... 3.00

Ash: Cinder & Smoke
Event, 1997
1 .... 3.00

Ashen Victor
Viz, 1997
1-4 .... 3.00

Ashes
Caliber
1-5 .... 3.00

Ash Files
Event, 1997
1 .... 3.00

Ash: Fire and Crossfire
Event, 1999

Veterans Jimmy Palmiotti and Joe Quesada, creators of the first Ash series, return with the help of Starman (2nd Series) writer James

Robinson for another go-round with their flame-retardant super-hero.

Things are turning personal for Ashley Quinn, mild-mannered firefighter for Ladder Company #2. While trying to quell gang upheaval so normal people can live out their lives in peace, some unknown evildoer plants a bomb in his mother's house. As luck would have it, Ashley's mother wanders out to hang the laundry just before the house explodes. Though his mother is still alive, it seems doubtful that she will survive. Ashley becomes Ash and tracks down the sinister Actor who has been blowing up warehouses in order to put the Russian mob out of business and take over the entire city. When confronted, however, the Actor denies any involvement. Who then is this malefluent presence seeking revenge on Ash and his family?

1	3.00
1/A	5.00
2	3.00

Ashley Dust
Knight, 1994
1-3	3.00

Ashpile
Side Show
1	9.00

Ash: The Fire Within
Event, 1996
1-2	3.00

Askani'son
Marvel, 1996
1-4	3.00

Sort of Homecoming, A
Alternative, 2004
1-3	4.00

Aspen Extended Edition
Aspen, 2004
1	8.00
1/Conv	15.00

Aspen
Aspen, 2003
1	7.00
1/Variant	12.00
1/Conv	10.00
2	4.00
2/Variant	6.00
2/Conv	10.00
3	6.00
3/Variant	8.00
3/Conv	10.00

Aspen Seasons: Spring 2005
Aspen, 2005
0	3.00

Aspen Sketchbook
Aspen, 2003
1	3.00

Asrial vs. Cheetah
Antarctic, 1996
1-2	3.00

Assassin
Arcana, 2003
1	3.00

Assassination of Malcolm X
Zone
1	3.00

Assassinette
Pocket Change, 1994
1-7	3.00

Assassinette Hardcore!
Pocket Change, 1995
1-2	3.00

Assassins
DC, 1996

Assassins was one of twelve titles DC and Marvel published jointly under the Amalgam masthead. Early in 1996, the two companies united to produce a four-issue series in which their characters encountered and were forced to fight each other. Between the third and final issue the two universes merged, resulting in character fusions heretofore unimagined.

Assassins features Dare and Catsai on a mission to kill Enigma Fisk, the corrupt and sadistic mayor of Gotham City. Combining elements of Elektra, Catwoman, Daredevil, and Deathstroke,

Assassins was the "bad girl" entry of the Amalgam line, specializing in provocative poses of the title characters. Since this title is meant to see part of a larger history in the Amalgam comic universe, references are made to "previous issues," and letters of comment on the mocked-up letters page make great play of discussing "previous stories" that were never printed.

-- *George Haberberger*

1	2.00

Assassin School
APComics, 2003
0-1	3.00

Assassin School (Vol. 2)
APComics, 2003
1	5.00
2-6	4.00

Assassins Inc.
Silverline

One of the first titles published by the fledgling Silverline Comics in 1987, Assassins Inc. is short on big names but dreams large nonetheless. Similar in tone to many Hollywood films, the title follows the mercenary career of John Dowan and his band of ex-military friends, teamed up for high-caliber adventure, at the will of the highest bidder.

With art help from Silverline's largest name (Rich Buckler), the quality of Assassins Inc. belies its freshmen talent.

1-2	2.00

Assembly
Antarctic, 2003
1	3.00
2	4.00
3-4	3.00

Aster
Express, 1994

Aster, the last Celestial Knight, plummeted from the sky in a fiery plume and was found and cared for by the Mountsmen. In his confused and weakened state he is educated in the legend that the Mountsmen have inherited from their ancestors. He is told of Lord Dessa, the rogue Celestial Guardian, and his imprisonment in the heart of the world.

With the necessary exposition taken care of, Aster begins his quest for the Gem of Saghal which is inhibiting his ability to absorb cosmic energy, and also insures Lord Dessa's captivity. Along the way he becomes a zealous champion of the Mountsmen against Lord Dessa's minions, the Groggs.

This mini-series picks up from the Harriers mini-series.

0-4	3.00
Ashcan 1	1.00

Aster:
The Last Celestial Knight
Express, 1995

1	4.00

Astonish!
Wehner

1	2.00

Astonishing
Atlas, 1951

3	675.00
4-6	465.00
7-10	225.00
11-20	200.00
21-24	160.00
25-29	135.00
30	175.00
31-40	125.00
41-63	85.00

Astonishing Excitement
All-Jonh

This series features anthology stories of action-packed adventures, angst-ridden romances, and pulse-pounding drama--with a few cheap gags for good measure. This black-and-white anthology is published by All-Jonh Comics, a comic book company based in Canada. In it, a wide variety of writer/artist teams contribute satires of sci-fi comics, superheroes, even teen angst. No concept is too high to mock, no gag too low. Done mostly in cartoony styles, the series is chock full of super-heroes and soft sandwiches that speak like men.

501-502	3.00
503	4.00

Astonishing Spider-Man
Marvel

1-32	4.00

Astonishing Tales
Marvel, 1970

Although it began as a rather nondescript collection of Dr. Doom/Ka-Zar stories, Astonishing Tales struck gold when it introduced the

character of Deathlok in issue #25. Since then Deathlok has gone on to become one of the hottest characters in comics.

Deathlok's story begins in the near future. The U.S. has been at war for years, and the military is desperate for some new weapon to turn the tide. When Luther Manning, a great military strategist, is killed a decision is made to transplant his brain into a robotic body. Thus Luther lives again as Deathlok, a cyborg killing-machine. However, when Luther realizes what has happened to him, he rebels against his creators and escapes. Unable even to end his own existence (the computer built into him prevents this), Deathlok goes on the run but has nowhere to hide.

1	40.00
2-5	20.00
6	12.00
7-8	15.00
9	10.00
10	20.00
11	10.00
12	30.00
☛Man-Thing story	
13-20	10.00
21	25.00
22	10.00
23	15.00
24	10.00
25	25.00
☛1st Deathlok	
26	10.00
27-29	7.00
30-32	5.00
33	10.00
34	6.00
35	7.00
☛Low distribution	
35/30¢	20.00
☛Low distribution	
36-36/30¢	10.00

Astonishing X-Men
Marvel, 1995

1-3	6.00
4	8.00

Astonishing X-Men
Marvel, 1999

1	5.00
2-3	3.00

Astonishing X-Men
Marvel, 2004

1	8.00
☛Whedon starts	
1/Cassaday-1/DirCut	45.00
1/Dynamic	8.00
2	16.00
3	4.00

4	8.00
4/Variant	25.00
☛Colossus cover	
5	8.00
6	5.00
7	4.00
8-10	3.00
10/Variant	5.00
11-19	3.00

Astounding Space Thrills
Day 1, 1998

1-3	3.00

Astounding Space Thrills: The Comic Book
Image, 2000

Savvy collectors knew it would be a matter of time before the Internet and the world of comics came crashing together. The result: no, not ComicBase! It's Astounding Space Thrills from Image Comics. With benefits for both the publisher and strip creators, the World Wide Web offers a unique form of marketing and yet another means by which to attract more readers.

Starting with the book's title story, Steve Conley has adapted his popular cyber-strip for the printed page, continuing the 21st century adventures of Argosy Smith and crew as they fight evil capitalists after the time and space altering "Shift." The book's backup story, The Crater Kid, is another popular Internet comic that tells the story of a 1950s retro-futuristic boy hero, protecting the universe from robots, aliens, and every other form of space bad guy imaginable.

Weaving self-contained stories independent of their cyber brethren, both features manage to refer back to their corresponding websites as a resource for story

elaboration, marrying both the virtual and printed worlds.

1-4	3.00
GS 1	5.00

Astrider Hugo
Radio, 2000

1-2	4.00

Astro Boy
Gold Key, 1965

1	265.00

Astro Boy
Dark Horse, 2002

1-23	10.00

Astro City: A Visitor's Guide
DC, 2004

1	6.00

Astro City Local Heroes
DC, 2003

1-5	3.00

Astro City: Samaritan Special
DC, 2006

1	4.00

Astro City Special
DC, 2004

1	4.00

Astro City: The Dark Age
DC, 2005

1-4	3.00

Astro City
Image, 1995

1	5.00
2-6	3.00

Astro City
Image, 1996

1/2-1/2/Direct	3.00
1	4.00
1/3D	5.00
2-22	3.00

AstroComics
Harvey

1	3.00

Astronauts in Trouble: Space 1959
AiT, 2000

1	3.00

Astrothrill
Cheeky, 1999

1	13.00

Asylum
Maximum, 1995

1-13	3.00

Asylum
Millennium

1-2	3.00
3	5.00

Asylum
New Comics

1-2	2.00

Atari Force
DC, 1984

Officially it's an acronym for the Advanced Technology And Research Institute, but this comic book, focusing on a team of rebels and renegades, originated from the comics shipped with Atari home computer games. Don't let that fool you. The characters have personality and motivation that belies their arcade game origins.

The first five adventures of the Atari force were included as mini-comics in several of Atari's most popular home videogames, such as Defender and Phoenix. This series, written by Gerry Conway, marks their debut in mainstream comics.

1-20	1.00
Special 1	2.00

A-Team
Marvel, 1984

1	2.00
2	2.00
3	2.00

Atheist
Image, 206

1-3	4.00

Athena
Antarctic, 1995

Athena seems like your average, cigarette-smoking, guitar-playing, leather jacket-wearing musician. She's the new guitarist in a band called Serpenteena. She and her fellow bandmates Kallie and Jay have been hitting the clubs around Crete, playing music and getting into fights. All just business as usual for a struggling rock band.

Still, there's something strange about Athena. For one, she can take on the biggest lugs in the bar, and seems to heal instantly from any cuts and scrapes. Then there are her friends: the horned bar owner Dionysus, and even the man/woman stripper called Herma (short for "Hermaphrodite"). In case it's not blatantly obvious, this aspiring rocker is actually the Athena of Greek myth. And Serpenteena's road tours are going to get interesting.

Dean Hsieh created Athena for Antarctic's Absolute Zero, then self-published the first series under A.M. Works.

0-14 ....3.00

Athena Inc.
Agents Roster
Image, 2002
1 ....6.00

Athena Inc.
The Beginning
Image, 2001
1 ....6.00

Athena Inc. The
Manhunter Project
Image, 2002
1-1/A 3.00
2/A-5/B 3.00
6/A-6/B 5.00
Ashcan 1 ....1.00

Atlantis Chronicles
DC, 1990
1-7 .... 3.00

@Large
Tokyopop, 2003
1-3 .... 10.00

Atlas
Dark Horse, 1994
1-4 .... 3.00

Atlas (Avatar)
Avatar, 2002
1/A-1/F 4.00
1/G 6.00

Atom
DC, 1962
1 .... 750.00
2 .... 300.00
3 .... 225.00
4-5 .... 175.00
6 .... 125.00
7 .... 250.00
☞Hawkman app.
8 .... 125.00
9 .... 90.00
10-13 .... 85.00
14 .... 95.00
☞Hawkman app.
15 .... 85.00
16-17 .... 45.00
18 .... 50.00
19 .... 45.00
20 .... 60.00
21-23 .... 35.00
24 .... 40.00
25 .... 50.00
26-28 .... 35.00
29 .... 100.00
30 .... 55.00
31 .... 48.00
32 .... 35.00
33 .... 40.00
34-35 .... 35.00
36-37 .... 45.00
38 .... 30.00
Special 1-2 .... 3.00

Atom-Age Combat
St. John, 1952
1 .... 225.00
2 .... 140.00
3 .... 100.00
4 .... 125.00
5 .... 100.00

Atom-Age Combat
St. John, 1958
1 .... 85.00
2-3 .... 60.00

Atoman
Spark, 1946
1 .... 265.00
2 .... 175.00

Atom and Hawkman
DC, 1968
39-41 .... 30.00

42 .... 35.00
43-45 .... 30.00

Atom Ant
Gold Key, 1966
1 .... 85.00

Atomic Age
Marvel, 1990
1-4 .... 5.00

Atomic Age
Truckstop Waitress
Fantagraphics, 1991
1 .... 2.00

Atomic Bomb
Jay Burtis, 1945
1 .... 750.00

Atomic City Tales
Kitchen Sink, 1996
1-3 .... 3.00
Special 1 .... 3.00

Atomic Comics
Green, 1946
1 .... 750.00
2 .... 400.00
3-4 .... 275.00

Atomic Man
Blackthorne, 1986
1-3 .... 2.00

Atomic Mouse
Charlton, 1953

Atomic Mouse, a funny animal super-hero, enjoyed a 10-year run as a comic book, television, and movie character during the 1950s and 1960s. Atomic Mouse helps keep the world safe from fiendish (and generally feline) menaces to the funny animal community, using his atomically-enhanced powers, which include super strength and flight, to foil their schemes.

Illustrated with insane energy by Al Fago, one of the true masters of the funny animal style, Atomic Mouse provided fun, entertaining, and "wholesome" reading (it even says so on the cover!) for younger fans. Atomic Mouse made an encore appearance in the 1980s, courtesy of Charlton Comics.

1	150.00
2	75.00
3-5	50.00
6-10	35.00
11-20	25.00
21-25	18.00
26	45.00
27-29	18.00
30-50	15.00
51-54	13.00

Atomic Mouse
Charlton, 1984

10	5.00
11-13	3.00

Atomic Mouse
A+, 1990

1-3	3.00

Atomicow
Vision, 1990

1	3.00

Atomic Rabbit & Friends
Avalon

1	3.00

Atomics
AAA Pop, 2000

1-11	3.00
12-15	4.00

Atomic Spy Cases
Avon, 1950

1	175.00

Atomic Thunderbolt
Regor, 1946

1	325.00

Atomic Toybox
Image, 1999

1-1/B	3.00

Atomic War!
Ace, 1952

1	600.00
2-4	375.00

Atomika
Speakeasy Comics, 2005

1-3	3.00
4/Turner	5.00
4/Buzz	3.00
4/Jay	4.00
4/Rupps	3.00

Atomik Angels
Crusade, 1996

1	3.00
1/Variant	4.00
2-3	3.00
3/Variant	4.00
4-Special 1	3.00

Atom the Atomic Cat
Avalon

1	3.00

Atomz Man and Super Seeker
Atomz

1	1.00

Attack
Youthful, 1952

1	165.00
2-4	85.00
5	65.00
6-9	55.00

Attack
Trojan, 1953

5	35.00

Attack
Charlton, 1958

54	24.00
55-60	10.00
1	25.00
2	15.00
3-4	12.00

Attack
Charlton, 1971

1	7.00
2-3	4.00
4-30	3.00
31-48	2.00

Attack!
Spire, 1975

1	5.00

Attack of the Amazon Girls
Fantaco

1	5.00

Attack of the Mutant Monsters
A-Plus

A giant monster is captured and then taken back to civilization to be put on display as the Eighth Wonder of the World. If you're thinking King Kong, think again. The monster is an enormous lizard named Kegor whose similar appearance to Godzilla must be one more coincidence. In another story, a tyrannical dictator believes he can use Kegor as an offensive weapon to conquer his neighbors.

This title, published in 1991, reprints stories from the late 1950s and contains no mutants. The popularity of the X-Men and other mutants of the time, must have been the impetus for including the somewhat misleading word "mutant" in the title. Although the stories are predictable and formulaic, the classic artwork by Steve Dikto should be enough reason to not resort to a deceptive title.

-- George Haberberger

1	3.00

Attack on Planet Mars
Avon, 1951

1	750.00

At the Seams
Alternative, 1997

1	3.00

Attitude
NBM, 2004

1-3	14.00

Attitude Lad
Slave Labor

1	3.00

Attractive Forces
NBM

1	10.00

Attu
4Winds, 1989

This black-and-white graphic novel series from artist/storyteller Sam Glanzman (G.I. Combat, Weird War Tales) opens in 137 million B.C. in the land of Gondwana, where caveman Attu comes face-to-face with his destiny. In the Forbidden Cave, he discovers a spaceship and a woman frozen in suspended animation and is bombarded with images of his future-fantastic

visions of eras far beyond 137 million B.C. This is wonderful, imaginative stuff from one of the comic industry's finest, whose style here is reminiscent of the legendary Joe Kubert's work on Tarzan and Tor.

1-2 ....10.00

Augie Doggie
Gold Key, 1963
1 ....45.00

August
Arrow
1-3 ....3.00

Aurora Comic Scenes
Aurora, 1974
181 ....30.00
☛Tarzan minicomic
182 ....28.00
☛Spider-Man mini
183 ....27.00
☛Tonto minicomic
184 ....30.00
☛Hulk minicomic
185 ....28.00
☛Superman mini
186 ....27.00
☛Superboy mini
187 ....26.00
☛Batman minicomic
188 ....25.00
☛Lone Ranger mini
192 ....27.00
☛Capt. America mini
193 ....30.00
☛Robin minicomic

Authentic Police Cases
St. John, 1948
1 ....285.00
2 ....165.00
3 ....290.00
4-5 ....165.00
6 ....300.00
7-15 ....135.00
16-23 ....85.00
24-28 ....175.00
29-30 ....75.00
31-32 ....60.00
33-38 ....65.00

Authority
DC, 1999
1 ....5.00
2-3 ....4.00
4-29 ....3.00
Ann 2000...................................4.00
1/HC-2/HC 50.00

Authority
DC, 2003
0-14 ....3.00

Authority
DC, 2006
1-1/2nd variant 3.00

Authority: Kev
DC, 2002
nn 5.00

Authority/Lobo Christmas Special
DC, 2003
1 .... 5.00

Authority/Lobo: Spring Break Massacre
DC, 2005
0 .... 5.00

Authority: The Magnificent Kevin
DC, 2005
1-5 .... 3.00

Authority: More Kev
DC, 2004
1-4 .... 3.00

Authority: Revolution
DC, 2004
1-12 .... 3.00

Authority: Scorched Earth
DC, 2003
1 .... 5.00

Automatic Kafka
WildStorm, 2002
1-9 .... 3.00

Automaton
Image, 1998

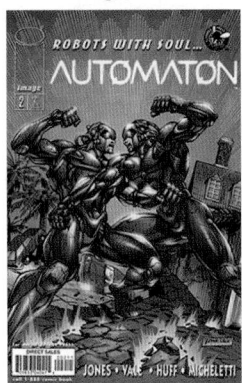

There is life on Mars. It had remained undetected because the Martians are beings of pure energy. At least they were until they possessed the metal constructs, called automatons, developed by Dr. Brad Shekter to explore the planet. Inhabiting these energy creatures, Sherzad, Bront and Konak, traveled to Earth to make first contact. The long months of confinement and the

bizarre experience of being physical for the first time in their existence drove Konak insane. He now believes his mission of exploration is to be one of destruction. Since he can interface with computer systems, including the systems that control the nuclear arsenal, he is capable of destruction on a global scale.

The definition of humanity is challenged when Dr. Shekter teams with the other automatons to stop Konak while Shekter's supervisor attempts to eliminate all of the automatons, regardless of their actions.

-- George Haberberger

1-3 .... 3.00

Autumn
Caliber, 1995
1-3 .... 3.00

Autumn Adventures
Disney
1 .... 3.00

Autumn...Earth
Acid Rain
1 .... 3.00

Avalon
Harrier, 1986

Avalon is an anthology series published by Britain's Harrier Comics. It served as a tryout book for new artists, so quality varies, although some is quite good.

Leading off the first issue was "Diana is...The Power" by Ron Sharp and Staz Johnson. This is a rather dark story of a woman with multiple personality disorder. One half of Diana's personality is a shy and conservative police officer. The other, more dominant side is "Janet," a sexy seductress with little regard for the law. When Janet takes over control of the mind, she does everything she can to screw up Diana's life. Other stories in the debut issue included "Mutant Love," a surrealistic story of doomed love by Dave Thorpe & Phil Elliott; "Grun," a lighthearted look at terrorism; and "The Alchemist" by Howard Stangroom and Peter Martin. Most of the stories in this series are of an adult nature and should be read by mature audiences only.

1-14 ....2.00

Avant Guard: Heroes at the Future's Edge
Day One, 1994
1-3 ....3.00

Avataars: Covenant of the Shield
Marvel, 2000
1-3 ....3.00

Avatar
DC
1-3 ....4.00

Avelon
Drawbridge, 1997
1-11 ....3.00

Avengeblade
Maximum, 96
1-2 ....3.00

Avengelyne
Maximum, 1995
1-1/A 3.00
1/Gold-1/Variant 4.00
2-3/B 3.00
Ashcan 1 ....4.00

Avengelyne
Maximum, 1996
0-1/2 ....3.00
1/2/Platinum 4.00
1-1/Variant 3.00
2-2/A 4.00
2/B 5.00
3-15 ....3.00

Avengelyne
Awesome, 1999
1 ....3.00

Avengelyne Armageddon
Maximum, 1996
1-3 ....3.00

Avengelyne Bible
Maximum, 1996
1 ....4.00

Avengelyne: Dark Depths
Avatar, 2001
1/2-1/2/B 5.00
1/291/C 3.00
1-1/D 4.00
1/E 6.00
2-2/C 4.00

Avengelyne: Deadly Sins
Maximum, 1996

The fallen angel, Avengelyne, was one of the foremost "bad girl" characters that populated the comic racks in the mid-1990s. In this mini-series, she confronts seven demons in Las Vegas.

Avengelyne has more than just her pinup figure going for her in this series. The seven deadly sins, Wrath, Envy, Greed, Lust, Sloth, Gluttony, and Pride are anthropomorphically depicted as demons from hell. Designed by penciler John Stinsman, these embodiments of intangible concepts have a supernatural demeanor that is reminiscent of the representations of the Endless from Sandman. The seven wreak havoc in Las Vegas by influencing and awakening their aspects in humans. Only Avengelyne can stop them before they utterly destroy the city and its people.

-- George Haberberger

1 .... 3.00
1/Variant 4.00
2 .... 3.00

Avengelyne/Glory
Maximum, 1995
1-1/Variant 4.00

Avengelyne/Glory: The Godyssey
Maximum, 1996
1-1/Variant 3.00

Avengelyne: Power
Maximum, 1995
1/A-3 .... 3.00

Avengelyne-Prophet
Maximum, 1996
1-2 .... 3.00

Avengelyne Swimsuit
Maximum, 1995
1-1/D 3.00

Avengelyne/ Warrior Nun Areala
Maximum, 1996
1/A-1/B 3.00

Avenger
AC, 1996
Ashcan 0 .... 6.00

Avengers
Marvel, 1963

September 1963 gave birth to two of Marvel's greatest super-groups: The Uncanny X-Men and the Avengers, "Earth's Mightiest Heroes." Originally consisting of Thor, Iron Man, Ant-Man, Wasp, and The Incredible Hulk, the team was soon joined by Captain America (in issue #4). Since then, it seems that virtually every Marvel super-hero has served as a one-time Avenger. Even such famous loners as Spider-Man have briefly served with this legendary fighting team.

Like a large corporation, The Avengers have even divisionalized, giving birth to the Great Lakes Avengers and the more famous West Coast Avengers. These teams operated independently, although they occasionally combined forces, as in the Infinity Gauntlet series, to fight a great enemy.

1 .... 4,200.00
☛1st Avengers
1.5 .... 3.00
2 .... 935.00
3 .... 750.00
4 .... 1,450.00
☛Cap. America joins
4/Golden 40.00
5 .... 350.00
6 .... 390.00
7 .... 460.00
8 .... 275.00
9 .... 225.00
☛1st Wonder Man
10 .... 180.00

1st Hercules
11 .... 275.00
Spider-Man app.
12 .... 115.00
13-14 .... 150.00
15 .... 100.00
16 .... 125.00
17 .... 115.00
18 .... 100.00
19 .... 150.00
20 .... 80.00
21-22 .... 70.00
23 .... 75.00
24 .... 70.00
25 .... 95.00
26 .... 65.00
27 .... 70.00
28-30 .... 50.00
31 .... 43.00
32 .... 37.00
33 .... 50.00
34 .... 55.00
35 .... 50.00
36 .... 35.00
37 .... 40.00
38 .... 43.00
39-41 .... 40.00
42 .... 50.00
43 .... 45.00
44 .... 40.00
45 .... 50.00
46 .... 30.00
47-48 .... 37.00
49 .... 32.00
50 .... 30.00
51 .... 40.00
52 .... 41.00
53 .... 60.00
X-Men app.
54-55 .... 30.00
56 .... 50.00
57 .... 110.00
1st Vision
58 .... 65.00
59-60 .... 40.00
61-66 .... 30.00
67 .... 45.00
68 .... 27.00
69-70 .... 30.00
71 .... 50.00
1st Invaders
72-73 .... 30.00
74-76 .... 25.00
77 .... 20.00
78 .... 25.00
79-81 .... 23.00
82 .... 26.00
83 .... 36.00
1st Valkyrie
84 .... 23.00
85-86 .... 25.00
87 .... 40.00
88 .... 25.00
88/2nd 2.00
89 .... 20.00
90-91 .... 22.00
92 .... 26.00
93 .... 120.00

Double-size
94 .... 35.00
95 .... 38.00
96 .... 35.00
97-98 .... 26.00
99 .... 30.00
100 .... 55.00
Knight gets sword
101 .... 18.00
102 .... 16.00
103 .... 40.00
Sentinels
104 .... 20.00
105 .... 18.00
106 .... 17.00
107 .... 20.00
108 .... 12.00
109 .... 18.00
110 .... 25.00
111 .... 22.00
112 .... 25.00
113 .... 11.00
114 .... 15.00
115 .... 13.00
116 .... 27.00
Defenders War
117 .... 20.00
118 .... 24.00
119 .... 15.00
120 .... 14.00
121 .... 10.00
122 .... 13.00
123 .... 9.00
124 .... 12.00
125 .... 20.00
126 .... 18.00
127-129 .... 12.00
130 .... 15.00
131 .... 12.00
132 .... 10.00
133 .... 8.00
134-135 .... 10.00
136-137 .... 8.00
138-140 .... 7.00
141 .... 10.00
142-145 .... 8.00
146 .... 10.00
146/30¢ 18.00
147 .... 7.00
147/30¢ 15.00
148 .... 12.00
148/30¢ 18.00
149 .... 6.00
149/30¢ 15.00
150 .... 7.00
150/30¢ 15.00
151 .... 7.00
152-155 .... 6.00
156 .... 9.00
156/Whitman 8.00
157-157/Whitman 6.00
158 .... 8.00
158/Whitman 6.00
159 .... 8.00
159/Whitman-160/Whitman 6.00
160/35¢ 15.00
161 .... 7.00
161/Whitman 6.00

161/35¢ 15.00
162-162/Whitman 8.00
162/35¢-163 .... 15.00
163/Whitman 6.00
163/35¢-164 .... 15.00
164/Whitman 6.00
164/35¢ 15.00
165-166/Whitman 6.00
167 .... 5.00
168 .... 7.00
169-170 .... 4.00
171 .... 6.00
171/Whitman-174/Whitman 4.00
175 .... 5.00
175/Whitman-180/Whitman 4.00
181 .... 5.00
182 .... 4.00
183 .... 6.00
183/Whitman 6.00
184 .... 6.00
185 .... 7.00
186 .... 5.00
187-189 .... 6.00
190 .... 4.00
191-195 .... 5.00
196 .... 7.00
197-199 .... 5.00
200 .... 9.00
Double-size
201-218 .... 3.00
219-224 .... 2.00
225 .... 3.00
226-249 .... 2.00
250 .... 3.00
251-262 .... 2.00
263 .... 3.00
264-349 .... 2.00
350 .... 3.00
351-359 .... 1.00
360 .... 3.00
361-362 .... 1.00
363 .... 3.00
364-365 .... 1.00
366 .... 4.00
Foil cover
367-368 .... 1.00
369 .... 3.00
370-374 .... 1.00
375 .... 2.00
375/Collector's 3.00
376-379 .... 2.00
379/Double 3.00
380 .... 2.00
380/Double 3.00
381 .... 2.00
381/Double 3.00
382 .... 2.00
382/Double 3.00
383-399 .... 2.00
400 .... 4.00
401-402 .... 3.00
Ann 1 .... 125.00
Ann 2 .... 120.00
Ann 3-4 .... 22.00
Ann 5 .... 25.00
Ann 6 .... 7.00
Ann 7 .... 12.00
Ann 8-9 .... 8.00

Avengers Infinity
Marvel, 2000

Six of the Avengers' mightiest members travel across the galaxy to answer a distress call from a former teammate, the Jack of Hearts. Among their number is Thor, a mythological God, and Quasar, the cosmic-powered Protector of the Universe. The rest possess powers that set them apart from even Earth's many other super-heroes. The combined might of this group should be enough to tackle any problem, but when they join their erstwhile friend, they find more than a ravaged planet in need of rescue. A race of cosmic beings, whose vastness and powers could dwarf Gods, is busy harvesting entire

galaxies, reshaping the universe to their own whims.

Thor, Photon, Quasar, Moondragon, Starfox, Tigra, and Jack must somehow stand against creatures who consider a star a marble, solar systems mere toys. What hope do they have, especially when they don't even trust one of their own?

Avengers Spotlight
Marvel, 1989

Whereas Solo Avengers brought readers the exploits of individual Avengers, the title's change to Avengers Spotlight meant a metamorphosis to stories featuring sub-groups of The Avengers working in teams.

Over the years, the ranks of active and reserve Avengers have swelled to include a huge number of characters. With two storylines running in each issue, Avengers Spotlight had the opportunity to give such lesser-known Marvel characters as Starfox, Swordsman, and Vision a chance to grab the spotlight, with a team-up focus on The Avengers' member Hawkeye, the archer.

21-40......................................1.00

Avengers Strike File
Marvel, 1994

1 ....2.00

Avengers: The Crossing
Marvel, 1995

1 ....5.00

Avengers: The Terminatrix Objective
Marvel, 1993

1 ....3.00
2-4...1.00

Avengers: The Ultron Imperative
Marvel, 2001

1 ....6.00

Avengers/Thunderbolts
Marvel, 2004

1-6...3.00

Avengers: Timeslide
Marvel, 1996

1 ....5.00

Avengers Two: Wonder Man & Beast
Marvel, 2000

1-3...3.00

Avengers/Ultraforce
Marvel, 1995

1 ....4.00

Avengers: Ultron Unleashed
Marvel, 1999

1 ....4.00

Avengers: United They Stand
Marvel, 1999

1 ....3.00
2-7...2.00

Avengers Universe
Marvel, 2000

1-6...3.00

Avengers Unplugged
Marvel, 1995

1-6...1.00

Avengers West Coast
Marvel, 1989

Within the space of a year, Marvel took a look at the sales figures for two of its titles -- West Coast Avengers and Classic X-Men -- and decided that they'd be better off if retailers who sorted comics alphabetically racked them with their "parent" titles. As such, West Coast Avengers became Avengers West Coast, significant in that it's something no character would likely say. One can visualize the conversation: "Hi! We're the Avengers West Coast!" "Glad to meet you! We're the Cheerleaders Dallas Cowboy!"

Ahem. Well, anyway, this series continued the adventures of the Californian offshoot of Earth's Mightiest Heroes. It was cancelled just as the bubble market of the early 1990s burst, levelling many of the Marvel spinoffs.

-- John Jackson Miller

47-55 .... 1.00
56 .... 8.00
☛Psycho Scarlet Witch
57-74 .... 1.00
75 .... 2.00
76-102 .... 1.00
Ann 4-7 .... 2.00
Ann 8 .... 3.00

Avengers/X-Men: Bloodties
Marvel, 1995

1 .... 16.00

Avenue D
Fantagraphics

1 .... 4.00

Avenue X
Purple Spiral, 1992

1-3 .... 3.00

Aviation Cadets
Street & Smith

1 .... 125.00

Avigon
Image, 2000

1 .... 6.00

A-V in 3-D
Aardvark-Vanaheim, 1984

A-V in 3-D was a one-shot special designed to introduce new readers to Aardvark Vanaheim's 1984 lineup. Aardvark-Vanaheim's founder, Dave Sim, is the creator of the highly successful comic book series Cerebus the Aardvark. Among A-V's other offerings were such worthwhile titles as Ms. Tree from Max Collins, Bob Burden's Flaming Carrot, Valentino's Normalman, Bill Messner-Loebs' Journey, and Arn Saba's Neil the Horse.

This special is an oddity for Aardvark-Vanaheim, which is known for their straightforward "no gimmicks" approach to comics publishing. In an attempt to boost sales and bring more readers into the Aardvark-Vanaheim stable, Publishers Deni Loubert and Sim made an exception and printed this special with a 3-D process. The effect (which was used in a similar line of books by Pacific Comics) can be quite striking at times, such as when illustrating the dream sequence found in the issue's Cerebus story.

1 .... 3.00

Awakening
Image, 1997

1-4 .... 3.00

Awakening Comics
Awakening Comics, 1997

1-2 .... 4.00
3-4 .... 3.00

Awakening Comics 1999
Awakening Comics, 1999

1 .... 4.00

Awesome Adventures
Awesome, 1999
1/A-1/B 3.00

Awesome Holiday Special
Awesome, 1997
1 ....3.00

Awesome Man
Astonish, 2002
1 ....3.00
2 ....4.00

Awesome Preview
Awesome, 1997
1 ....1.00

Awful Oscar
Timely, 1949
11-12 ....40.00

Awkward
Slave Labor
1 ....5.00

Awkward Universe
Slave Labor, 1995
1 ....10.00

Axa
Eclipse, 1987
1-2 ....2.00

Axa
Ken Pierce, 1981
1-GN 1 ....6.00

Axed Files
Express, 1995
1 ....3.00

Axel Pressbutton
Eclipse, 1984
1-6 ....2.00

Axiom
Icon Creations, 94
1 ....3.00

Axis Alpha
Axis, 1994
1 ....3.00

Axis Mundi
Amaze Ink, 1996
2 ....3.00

Az
Comico, 1983
1-2 ....2.00

Azrach
Dark Horse, 1996
nn 7.00

Azrael
DC, 1995

In 1992, the editors of DC were already planning the 71-part Knightfall saga which would result in Bruce Wayne being crippled, replaced, then eventually returned to the role of Batman. To pull it off, they needed a character who would fill in as Batman, before being driven over the edge and requiring Wayne to wrest the mantle of Batman from him. That character was to be John Paul Valley: Azrael.

Valley was an unassuming computer science student whose father had been the latest in a line of holy assassins for the secret Order of Saint Dumas. The Order's assassin was called Azrael -- the angel of death -- and had passed its role from father to son for generations. Unwittingly, Jean Paul had already been trained to assume the role through a subconscious sort of training called "The System." When his father died, the shy computer scientist suddenly discovered within himself a knowledge of advanced martial techniques -- and a violent destiny as the new Azrael.

1	3.00
2-46	2.00
47	4.00
47/Ltd.	6.00
48-68	2.00
69-74	3.00
75	4.00
76-100	3.00
1000000	3.00
Ann 1	4.00
Ann 2	3.00
Ann 3	4.00

Azrael/Ash
DC, 1997
1 ....5.00

Azrael Plus
DC, 1996
1 ....3.00

Aztec Ace
Eclipse, 1984

Aztec Ace is a defender of time itself. Hailing from a time 400 years in our future, he uses advanced technology to allow him to slip in and out of the timestream, making small but vital changes along the way.

As it turns out, he is not alone in his ability to alter history. A group known as the Ebonites has made it their business to disrupt history for their own ends. Merely by preventing Ben Franklin from flying his kite that fateful day, or by disrupting the events of a German beer hall in 1923, they could profoundly change the course of world events.

Ace's job is to stop them, but it's a lot more complicated than it might seem. For even the slightest misstep could cause an anomaly which could destroy history as we know it.

1 .... 3.00
2-15 .... 2.00

Aztec Anthropomorphic Amazons
Antarctic, 1994
1 .... 3.00

Aztec of the City
El Salto, 1993
1 .... 2.00

Aztec of the City
El Salto, 1996
1-2 .... 3.00

Aztek: The Ultimate Man
DC, 1996
1-10 .... 2.00

Azumanga Daioh
ADV Manga, 2003
1-4 .... 10.00

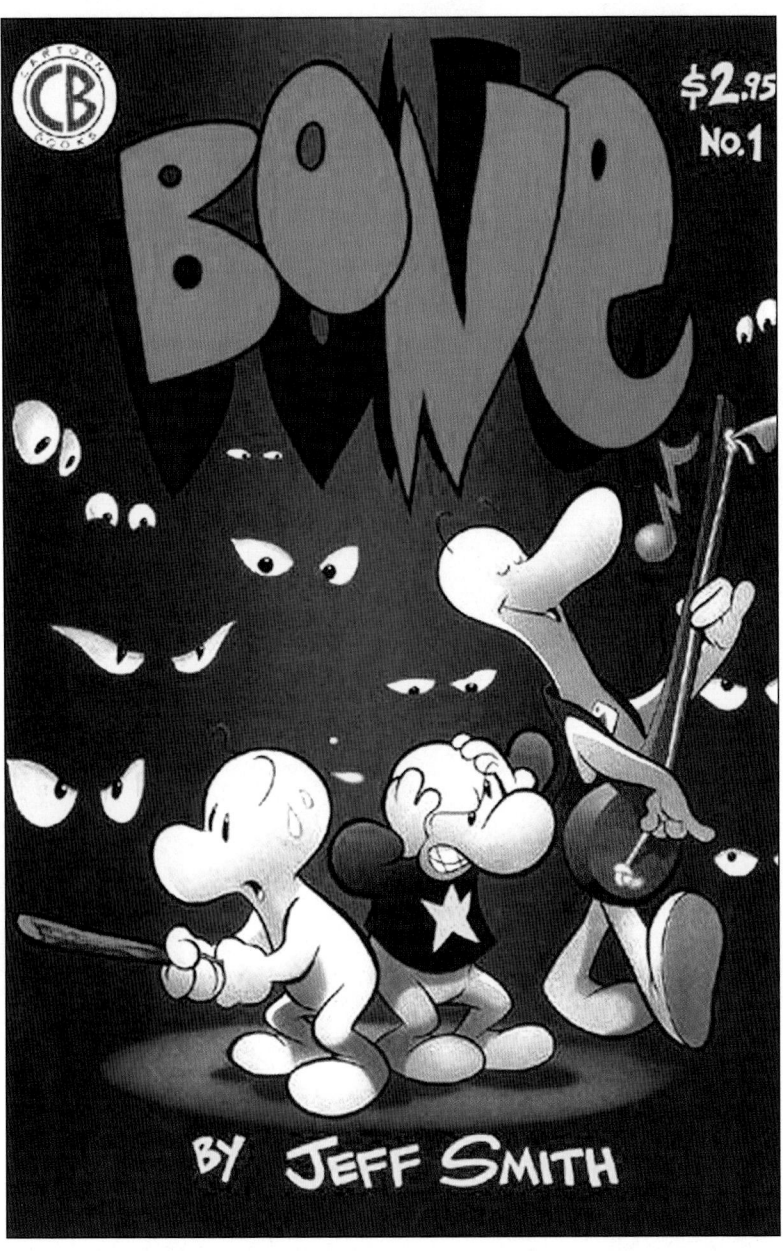

Jeff Smith's fantasy adventure series, featuring the three Bone cousins' journey through a lost valley, is popular with adults and children.

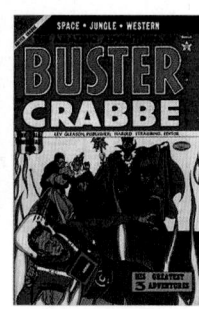

Babewatch
Express, 1995

1-1/A 3.00

Baby Angel X
Brainstorm, 1995

1 .... 3.00

Baby Huey Digest
Harvey, 1992

1 .... 2.00

Baby Huey in 3-D
Blackthorne, 1998

1 .... 3.00

Baby Huey
The Baby Giant
Harvey, 1956

1 .... 175.00
2 .... 90.00
3 .... 50.00
4-5 .... 36.00
6-10 .... 20.00
11-20 .... 15.00
21-30 .... 12.00
31-40 .... 9.00
41-50 .... 6.00
51-70 .... 4.00
71-99 .... 3.00
100-102 .... 1.00

Baby Huey
Harvey, 1991

1-9 .... 1.00

Babylon 5
DC, 1995

Babe
Dark Horse, 1994

1-4 .... 3.00

Babe 2
Dark Horse, 1995

1-2 .... 3.00

Babe,
Darling of the Hills
Feature Publications, 1948

Enjoy homespun humor with Babe, Darling of the Hills, as the Appalachian Apollonia discovers new friends and new fun. A certified country girl, Babe finds mirth and mischief around every corner of the globe. Often her down-home country cousins join Babe on her wacky travels, as the beautiful Southern supergal takes on every adventure that comes her way.

The book is similar to Li'l Abner with its cartoonish stories and barefoot, backwoods characters. The book is light in tone and features a variety of events and world calamities to challenge the enthusiastic Babe. But no matter how big the situation, Babe never forgets her rural roots in this funny, entertaining title by Sparky Watts artist-writer Boody Rogers.

1 .... 85.00
2 .... 60.00
3-11 .... 50.00

Babe Ruth
Sports Comics
Harvey, 1949

1 .... 240.00
2 .... 150.00
3 .... 125.00
4-11 .... 120.00

Babes of Broadway
Broadway, 1996

1 .... 3.00

In the 23rd century, Earth reached for the stars, but initial alien contacts resulted in devastating wars. After Earth's almost total defeat, the quest for peace finally began, with the creation of a vast space station to function as neutral territory.

Administered by Earthforce, Babylon 5 soon becomes the focal point for almost all interstellar activity. Which, of course, makes it an exciting, and dangerous, place. Earth, Minbar, and Centauri Prime become the mainstays in the conflict between the enigmatic Vorlons and the deadly Shadows.

TV series creator J. Michael Straczynski participated in stories for this series. It may be considered unusual for a television dramatist to involve himself in a comic book spinoff of his work, but he maintains strict and loving control over the franchise. He also went on to write Marvel's Amazing Spider-Man.

1	5.00
2-4	4.00
5-11	3.00

Babylon 5: In Valen's Name
DC, 1998

1	4.00
2-3	3.00

Babylon Crush
Boneyard, 1995

1-Xmas 1	3.00

Baby's First Deadpool Book
Marvel, 1998

1	3.00

Baby Snoots
Gold Key, 1970

1	12.00
2	10.00
3	8.00
4-12	6.00
13-22	5.00

Baby, You're Really Something!
Fantagraphics, 1990

1	3.00

Bacchus
Harrier, 1988

1	5.00
2	4.00

Bacchus
Eddie Campbell, 1995

1	6.00
1/2nd	3.00
2-5	4.00
6-60	3.00

Bacchus Color Special
Dark Horse, 1995

1	3.00

Bachelor Father
Dell, 1962

2	50.00

Back Down the Line
Eclipse

1	9.00

Backlash
Image, 1994

Backlash is Marc Slayton, one of the core members of the U.N. troubleshooting team StormWatch. Slayton is a skilled fighter armed with an energy whip and with the ability to turn incorporeal.

As this solo series begins, he'll need all his abilities to save the life of his lady love Diane LaSalle. LaSalle has been possessed by a Daemonite, one of the dread elder beings which the WildC.A.T.s were founded to stop. Under Daemonite control, LaSalle is about to destroy StormWatch's orbital station, when Backlash is forced to battle her. He succeeds in forcing the Daemonite out of LaSalle's body, but, in leaving, the Daemonite rips away part of her mind. Backlash will do anything to save her - even if that means breaking into an ultra-security prison to enlist a dangerous super-villain's help.

1-32	3.00

Backlash & Taboo's African Holiday
DC, 1999

1	6.00

Backlash/Spider-Man
Image, 1996

1-2	3.00

Backpack Marvels: Avengers
Marvel, 2001

1	7.00

Backpack Marvels: Spider-Man
Marvel, 2000

1	7.00

Backpack Marvels: X-Men
Marvel, 2000

1-2	7.00

Back-To-Back Horror Special
Timbuktu, 1989

1	2.00

Back to the Future
Harvey, 1991

1-4	2.00
Special 1	1.00

Back to the Future: Forward to the Future
Harvey, 1992

1-3	2.00

Bad Apples
High Impact, 1997

1-2	3.00

Bad Art Collection
Slave Labor, 1996

1	2.00

Badaxe
Adventure

On the mythical world of Pangea, the people worship a pantheon of gods, the most fearsome of which is Badaxe. Badaxe is a bloodthirsty and ruthless god. He occasionally visits his supplicants in the form of a wrathful skeleton, usually ripped by Badaxe himself out of the body of a human who had been sacrificed to him.

Badaxe has ordered his human minions to slay all the young boys in the towns and posts in the area and to catalog their hands. Meanwhile, in the same town a demon called Horse has sent his servant to find a boy-a nearly impossible task due to Badaxe's pogrom.

Blissfully unaware of this horror, a girl, raised by wolves and called Tanree comes frighteningly close to the core of the madness when she has her first encounter with civilization.

1-3 .... 1.00

Bad Boy
Oni, 1997

1 .... 5.00

Bad Comics
Cat-Head

1 .... 3.00

Bad Company
Fleetway-Quality

1-19 .... 2.00

Bade Biker & Orson
Mirage, 1986

1-4 .... 2.00

Bad Eggs
Acclaim, 1996

1-8 .... 3.00

Badge
Vanguard, 1981

1 .... 3.00

Badger
Capital, 1983

Badger gives Madison, Wis., a super-hero to call its own. OK, so this particular super-hero is a little unhinged, suffers from multiple personality disorder, and sometimes lets murderers get away so he can devote his energies to brutalizing litterbugs. He may not be the ideal super-hero, but, heck, Madison's gotta start somewhere. By the way, Badger is hooked up with a powerful druid-wizard named Ham, making for a dangerous combination, indeed.

Brought to you by writer Mike Baron (the same writer who co-

created Nexus with Steve Rude), Badger is an offbeat, but extremely enjoyable, title. In the world of comics, it's a fine antidote for super-hero burnout.

1	5.00
2-5	3.00
6-49	2.00
50	4.00
51	2.00
52-54	3.00
55-70	2.00

Badger
First, 1991

1 .... 5.00

Badger
Image, 1997

1-11 .... 3.00

Badger Goes Berserk
First, 1989

1-4 .... 2.00

Badger: Shattered Mirror
Dark Horse, 1994

1-4 .... 3.00

Badger: Zen Pop Funny-Animal Version
Dark Horse, 1994

1-2 .... 3.00

Bad Girls
DC, 2003

1-6 .... 3.00

Bad Girls (Bill Ward's...)
Forbidden Fruit

1 .... 2.00

Bad Girls of Blackout
Blackout, 1995

0-Ann 1 .... 4.00

Bad Hair Day
Slab-O-Concrete

1 .... 1.00

Bad Ideas
Image, 2004

1-2 .... 6.00

Bad Kitty
Chaos, 2001

1-3 .... 3.00

Bad Kitty: Mischief Night
Chaos, 2001

1-3 .... 3.00

Badlands
Dark Horse, 1991

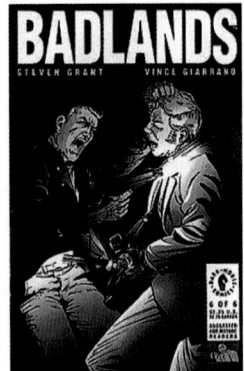

It's 1963 and, shortly after his release from jail, small-time crook and full-time patsy Connie Bremen is contacted by a former cellmate with an offer of work. He has moved to Texas and has been given a job guarding the promiscuous daughter of a local businessman. It gradually dawns on Bremen that he's there for a reason. Yup, it's Kennedy shooting time in Dallas. Considering that the assassination shaped the American psyche, astonishingly few comic stories have used it, even as a touchstone for the times. Steven Grant and Vince Giarrano weave a compelling story around a man no longer in control of his destiny, but about to change the destiny of a nation.

~WJ

1-6 .... 3.00

Bad Luck
Hero

1 .... 4.00

Bad Luck and Rick Dees Sentinel of Justice
King Comics, 1994

1 .... 3.00

Bad Meat
Fantagraphics, 1991

1-2 .... 2.00

Bad News
Fantagraphics

3 .... 4.00

Bad Planet
Image, 2005

1 .... 3.00

Badrock
Image, 1995

1-3 .... 2.00
Ann 1 .... 3.00

Badrock & Company
Image, 1994
1-Special 1 ....3.00

Badrock/Wolverine
Image, 1996
1/A-1/D....................................5.00

Baffling Mysteries
Ace, 1951
5	225.00
6-15	165.00
16-19	150.00
20	165.00
21-24	150.00
25-26	135.00

Bakers
Kyle Baker Publishing, 2005
1 ....3.00

Bakersfield Kountry Comics
Last Gasp, 1973
1 ....2.00

Bakers Meet Jingle Belle
Dark Horse, 2007
1 ....3.00

Baker Street
Caliber, 1989
1-10..3.00

Baker Street Graffiti
Caliber
1 ....3.00

Baker Street Sketchbook
Caliber
1 ....4.00

Balance of Power
Mu, 1990
1-4..3.00

Balder the Brave
Marvel, 1985

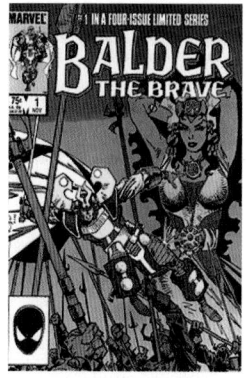

With Thor returning to popularity under the guidance of Walter Simonson, Marvel launched this spinoff limited series to further explore Thor's world.

Thor's friend, Balder, was the bravest of warriors, a skilled fighter that could be touched by no weapon unless he allowed it. He had only two weaknesses: Mistletoe, and his love for Karnilla, the Norn Queen. The first of these had caused his death once, but in the world of Asgard, death is not always forever. Balder returned from Hela's realm, and lives with Karnilla in Nornkeep as the series begins.

When a rider comes to ask Balder to join Thor's quest to save mortal souls unjustly trapped in Hela's realm, the proud and jealous Karnilla has the rider imprisoned before his message can be delivered. In time, however, Balder discovered her deception, and resolved to take up Thor's quest. Balder, who knew its terrors firsthand, was about to venture back into Hel...

1-4.. 1.00

Ballad of Halo Jones
Fleetway-Quality, 1987
1-12.. 2.00

Ballad Of Utopia
Black Daze, 2000
1-8.. 3.00

Ball and Chain
DC, 1999
1-4.. 3.00

Ballast
Active Images, 2005
0 .... 4.00

Ballistic
Image, 1995
1-3.. 3.00

Ballistic Action
Image, 1996
1 .... 3.00

Ballistic Imagery
Image, 1996
1-2.. 3.00

Ballistic Studios Swimsuit Special
Image, 1995
1 .... 3.00

Ballistic/Wolverine
Top Cow, 1997
1 .... 4.00

Balloonatiks
Best, 1991
1 .... 3.00

Balloon Vendor Comix
Rip Off, 1971

Awash in psychedelic art, Balloon Vendor Comix is typical of the underground titles that appeared in the late ë60s and early ë70s. Although low on the sexual content that often saturated these books, Balloon Vendor Comix is nevertheless high on hallucinogenic imagery. The first story, "The Time Machine," epitomizes the drug-laced, irreverent style of underground comix, featuring a scientist who visits different periods in history until he reaches the birth of the universe, a chaotic landscape of floating pigs, singing vegetables, and flowers blooming out of nothingness.

1 .... 4.00

Baloo & Little Britches
Gold Key, 1968
1 .... 25.00

Bambeano Boy
Moordam, 1998
1 .... 3.00

Bambi
Dell, 1956
3	30.00
3/A	50.00

Bambi
Whitman
1 .... 3.00

Bambi and Her Friends
Friendly, 1991
1-9	3.00
SE 1	4.00

Bambi in Heat
Friendly
1-3.. 3.00

Bambi the Hunter
Friendly, 1992
1-5.. 3.00

Bamm-Bamm and Pebbles Flintstone
Gold Key, 1964
1 ....75.00

Banana Fish
Tokyopop, 2004
1-7..16.00
8-10......................................10.00

Banana Splits (Hanna Barbera...)
Gold Key, 1969
1 ....30.00
2..18.00
3-5...14.00
6-8...12.00

Banana Sundays
Oni, 2005
1-4..3.00

Bandy Man
Caliber, 1996
1-3..3.00

Bang Gang
Fantagraphics
1 ....3.00

Bangs and the Gang
Shhwinng, 1994
1 ....3.00

Banished Knights
Image, 2001
1 ....7.00
1/A-2/B 3.00

Banzai Girl
Sirius, 2002
1-4..3.00
Ann 1..4.00

Baobab
Fantagraphics, 2005
1-2..8.00

Baoh
Viz, 1995
1 ....4.00
2-8...3.00

Barabbas
Slave Labor, 1985

After the mayor of the mouse

village is brutally killed by the leader of a group of gorillas who have come to extort tribute from the citizenry, Rizby, the mayor's son, seeks help from a famed warrior named Barabbas. No problem, right? Barabbas should take out the gorilla-guy in no time. Unfortunately, Barabbas, a muscle-bound boar (literally!), is a drunk, passed out in a low-rent tavern. Will Barabbas wake up and become the hero he's reputed to be? Will Rizby's father be avenged? Dan Vado (Justice League America, Extreme Justice) is the plotter of this amusing fantasy parody, while the fairly amateurish artwork is provided by Gino Attanasio.

1-2.. 2.00

Barbarian Comics
California, 1972
1-3.. 3.00

Barbarians
Atlas-Seaboard, 1975
1 .... 8.00

Barbarians
Avalon
1-2.. 3.00

Barbarians and Beauties
AC, 1990

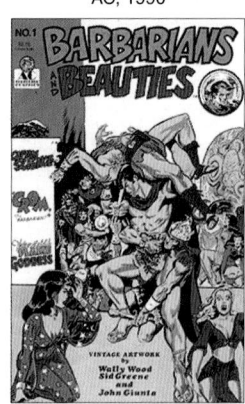

In the early 1950s, in the waning years of the Golden Age and well before the advent of the Silver Age, a wide variety of genres filled the comics racks. Bill Black of AC Comics endeavored to expose these long-neglected stories to a new generation. As he had done with lost western stories (Great American Western), Black collected tales of lost civilizations and cultures in this title that certainly contained beauties, though the barbarians were often

modern men in savage surroundings. The artwork, by such luminaries as Wally Wood, Sid Greene and Joe Orlando, is the real attraction. Sadly the stories are little more than bare bones plots with standard iconic heroes and damsels in distress.
-- George Haberberger

1 .... 3.00

Barbaric Tales
Pyramid
1-2.. 2.00

Barbarienne
Fantagraphics, 1992
1-3.. 3.00
4-10 .... 4.00

Barbarienne
Harrier, 1987
1-8.. 2.00

Barbie
Marvel, 1991

Mattel's Barbie remains one of the most recognizable toy properties, and it was only natural that Marvel, during its "mini-Disney" stage (in which it sought to become a broad "youth entertainment company")would seek out the venerable-yet-always-young Barbie's fans.

One of the few comic books aimed at girls by Marvel in the 1990s, Barbie (and its sister title, Barbie Fashion), delivered lighthearted adventures with Barbie participating in various sports and school events.

The Barbie titles were unusual in the portion of their sales that came from subscriptions -- far, far above what's typical for comics. That's, in part, due to the marketing of then-Marvel exec Jerry Calabrese, who built huge mailing lists of children for the company and worked subscription promotions involving many other properties, including Barbie. That's why there seem to be more Barbie copies around that one would have guessed from the small numbers ordered by retailers at the time; they went by mail.(Calabrese would, in 1994, get in trouble with comics retailers for trying to launch Marvel Mart, a mail-order service for Marvel.)

-- John Jackson Miller

1-1/A	3.00
2-63	2.00

Barbie & Baby Sister Kelly
Marvel, 1995

1	8.00

Barbie and Ken
Dell, 1962

1	200.00
2-4	150.00
5	165.00

Barbie Fashion
Marvel, 1991

1-1/A	3.00
2-55	2.00

Barbi Twins Adventures
Topps, 1995

1	3.00

Barb Wire
Dark Horse, 1994

1-9	3.00

Barb Wire: Ace of Spades
Dark Horse, 1996

1-4	3.00

Barb Wire Comics Magazine Special
Dark Horse, 1996

1	4.00

Barb Wire Movie Special
Dark Horse, 1996

Barb Wire proved to be one of the more successful characters to come out of Dark Horse's Comics' Greatest World titles. In 1996, Barb Wire made it to the big screen starring Pamela Anderson in the title role.

The movie itself is essentially a futuristic remake of Casablanca. After the fascistic Congressional Directorate decided to throw out the Constitution, America broke out in a second American Civil War. Barb runs the Hammerhead bar in Steel Harbor, a shady crossroads of characters from both sides of the war (think: Rick's All American). Barb had been a freedom fighter long ago, but has since decided to avoid politics and concentrate on running the bar. All was business as usual until an old flame appeared in the Hammerhead asking for Barb's help in smuggling a fugitive freedom fighter out of town. While the resulting story has far more action than Casablanca, it lacks the romantic appeal of that classic movie.

1	4.00

Bar Crawl of the Damned
Mortco, 1997

1	3.00

Barefootz Funnies
Kitchen Sink, 1975

1	3.00
2-3	2.00

Barefootz The Comix Book Stories
Renegade

1	3.00

Barf
Revolutionary, 1990

1	2.00
2-3	3.00

Barker
Quality, 1946

1	125.00
2-10	75.00
11-15	50.00

Barney and Betty Rubble
Charlton, 1973

1	15.00
2	10.00
3-11	6.00
12-23	5.00

Barney Bear Home Plate
Barbour

Barney Bear Home Plate, by Al Hartley, is a Kiddies Christian Comic-an illustrated story used to teach children about the Bible. The colorful drawings and light hearted story of a family of bears living all too human lives masks a greater message of family values and respecting one's parents.

Barney Bear is your average cub. He plays on a Little League baseball team, hates broccoli and leaves his room a mess. When he tells his father that his friends think his parents are too strict, the loving papa bear goes about showing his son why they do the things they do-only he uses a garden as his analogy. As the father and son tend to the garden, seeing that it receives all the TLC necessary to grow strong roots, the cub comes to realize that he too needs strong roots to survive in the real world. As the story states, the family is God's garden and He wants to grow beautiful, healthy fruit.

1	2.00

Barney Bear Lost and Found
Spire

1	2.00

Barney the Invisible Turtle
Amazing

1	2.00

Barnyard Comics
Animated, 1944

If Barney Rooster, Snooze the dog, Hucky Duck, Professor Bacon, Robin Hood Robin, and Francois Feline aren't the household names that some of the other funny animals of the comics and movies have become, it isn't for lack of wacky mishaps, goofy humor, and zany merriment produced in the pages of their series, Barnyard Comics, during the 1940s.

Issues featured each of the characters in their own eight-page adventure, often with a guest appearance from one or more of the others. And readers could enjoy a couple of text stories between comics sections. Some of the spot illustrations for these stories were provided by a young Frank Frazetta, who went on to become a hugely successful fantasy illustrator and painter. Barnyard Comics was also specifically cited as an influence by underground comics pioneer Robert Crumb.

-- Rob Salkowitz

1	125.00
2	65.00
3-5	42.00
6-10	32.00
11-12	24.00
13-15	42.00
16	24.00
17	42.00
18-20	75.00
21	42.00
22	75.00
23	42.00
24-25	75.00
26-27	42.00
28	24.00
29	42.00
30-31	22.00

Barr Girls
Antarctic

1	3.00

Barron Storey's Watch Annual
Vanguard

1	6.00

Barry Windsor-Smith: Storyteller
Dark Horse, 1996

Barry Windsor-Smith spun three separate serials in this short-lived oversized anthology series published in 1996 and 1997 by Dark Horse.

The Freebooters featured the drunken barbarian Axus the Great and his misadventures; The Paradoxman starred a time-traveler whose main mode of transportation was a motorcycle that could break the time barrier; and Young Gods was a tribute to Jack Kirby's New Gods.

While the stories were engaging and, as with all of Windsor-Smith's work, well-drawn, it was the packaging that drew the most attention to the series. The oversized comics, much larger than a regular comic book or magazine, although smaller than the mid-1970 treasury-sized comics, proved difficult to store and display and fans let their displeasure be known. A slipcase was produced and marked to hold the first 12 issues, but only nine were ever produced.

Adastra, the heroine of Young Gods, did reappear in the Fantagraphics hardcover Adastra in Africa, which recycled an unused X-Men story.

-- Brent

1-9	5.00

Bar Sinister
Windjammer, 1995

1-4	3.00

Bartman
Bongo, 1993

1	4.00
2-6	3.00

Basara
Viz, 2003

1-27	10.00

Baseball Classics
Personality

1-3	3.00

Baseball Comics
Kitchen Sink, 1991

In 1948, Will Eisner tried to expand out from his successful newspaper section, The Spirit, to publish comic books for newsstand distribution. One of these efforts was Baseball Comics, featuring the exploits of the talented but none-too-bright phenom, Rube Rooky. Despite the excellent art by Eisner and his studio (Tex Blaisdell, Jerry Grandenetti and Jules Feiffer) and the storytelling power of Eisner at his late 40s peak, the market reacted with indifference to the concept and Baseball Comics was sent to the showers after the first issue. The 1991 reprint is a facsimile of the original issue, with superb reproduction, slick paper and an introductory essay by David Schreiner. As a bonus, there's a tip-in set of baseball cards drawn by Eisner, featuring rookie players from the 1948 baseball season.

1	4.00
2	3.00

Baseball Comics
Personality
1-2..3.00

Baseball Greats
Dark Horse, 1992
1-3..3.00

Baseball Hall of Shame in 3-D
Blackthorne
1..3.00

Baseball Heroes
Fawcett, 1952
1..500.00

Baseball Legends
Revolutionary, 1992
1-19..3.00

Baseball's Greatest Heroes
Magnum, 1991
1-2..3.00

Baseball Sluggers
Personality
1-4..3.00

Baseball Superstars Comics
Revolutionary, 1991
1-20..3.00

Baseball Thrills 3-D
3-D Zone
1..3.00

Basically Strange
John C., 1982
1..4.00

Bastard
Viz, 2001
1-15..4.00

Bastard Samurai
Image, 2002
1-3..3.00

Bastard Tales
Baboon Books, 1998
1-2..3.00

Bat
Apple, 1994
1..3.00

Batbabe
Spoof
2..3.00

Batch
Caliber
1..3.00

Batgirl
DC, 2000

Since the crippling of Barbara Gordon in Batman: The Killing Joke, fans had been clamoring for a new Batgirl - or for the miraculous return of the Commissioner's daughter to the cape-and-cowl business. But with Barbara firmly established as Oracle - the DC universe's hacker supreme and an integral part of the Birds of Prey - a new Batgirl arose from the ashes of the Bat-titles' No Man's Land storyline. She is the non-speaking daughter of Cain, the world's deadliest assassin, and she has been trained by her father to be a living weapon. Now, under the tutelage of both Batman and Oracle, she is learning to use her skills in the war against crime as one of Gotham City's many costumed protectors. This ain't your daddy's Batgirl by any stretch of the imagination, but she's definitely worth a look.

1 .... 4.00
1/2nd 3.00
2-5 .... 4.00
6-73 .... 3.00
Ann 1 .... 4.00

Batgirl Adventures
DC, 1998
1 .... 4.00

Batgirl Secret Files and Origins
DC, 2002
1 .... 5.00

Batgirl Special
DC, 1988
1 .... 3.00

Batgirl: Year One
DC, 2003
1-9 .... 3.00

Bathing Machine
C&T, 1987
1 .... 3.00
2-3 .... 2.00

Bathroom Girls
Modern, 1997
1-2 .... 3.00

Bat Lash
DC, 1968
1 .... 25.00
2-7 .... 15.00

Batman
DC, 1940

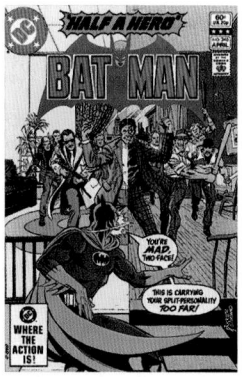

Since his debut in Detective Comics #27 (May 39), Batman has become one of the best-known comics heroes of all time. Created by the legendary Bob Kane, Batman is one of the rare characters that have transcended comics to become cultural icons.

Batman (aka Bruce Wayne) protects the citizens of Gotham City from a never-ending array of criminals. Over the years, his foes have included such famous villains as The Joker, The Penguin, and Catwoman.

Where once he was a fairly straightforward super-hero (complete with Robin, the boy sidekick), Batman has been transformed over time into an increasingly complex character. Now he is The Dark Knight, an avenger of evil who also must face up to the darkness within his own soul.

0 .... 3.00
1 .... 80,000.00
☛1st Catwoman
2 .... 15,000.00
3 .... 9,750.00
4 .... 7,500.00
5 .... 5,500.00
☛1st Batmobile
6-7 .... 4,500.00

8 ....4,000.00	84 .... 485.00	182-185 .... 60.00
9 ....3,750.00	85-90 .... 435.00	186 .... 70.00
10 ....7,500.00	91-99 .... 400.00	187 .... 65.00
11 ....4,750.00	100 .... 2,000.00	188 .... 40.00
12 ....2,900.00	☛Anniversary issue	189 .... 250.00
☛1st Batcave	101-104 .... 400.00	☛1st SA Scarecrow
13-14 ....2,775.00	105 .... 490.00	190 .... 45.00
15 ....2,625.00	106-109 .... 400.00	191 .... 40.00
16 ....4,600.00	110 .... 425.00	192 .... 60.00
☛1st Alfred	111-120 .... 290.00	193 .... 70.00
17-20 ....1,650.00	121 .... 375.00	194 .... 80.00
21-22 ....1,275.00	☛1st Mr. Freeze	195-196 .... 40.00
23 ....2,000.00	122 .... 225.00	197 .... 100.00
24 ....1,275.00	123 .... 220.00	☛Catwoman app.
25 ....2,050.00	124-126 .... 195.00	198 .... 85.00
26-30 ....1,275.00	127 .... 240.00	199 .... 40.00
31-36 ....950.00	☛vs. Joker	200 .... 100.00
37 ....1,200.00	128 .... 195.00	☛Robin origin
38 ....1,000.00	129 .... 250.00	201-202 .... 35.00
39 ....950.00	☛Robin origin	203-204 .... 30.00
40 ....1,140.00	130 .... 195.00	205 .... 40.00
41-43 ....760.00	131 .... 145.00	206 .... 30.00
44 ....1,080.00	132-135 .... 130.00	207-208 .... 50.00
45-46 ....760.00	136 .... 215.00	209-212 .... 30.00
47 ....3,000.00	☛vs. Joker	213 .... 45.00
☛Batman origin	137-145 .... 140.00	214-217 .... 30.00
48 ....965.00	146-147 .... 110.00	218 .... 70.00
49 ....1,350.00	148 .... 140.00	☛Giant-size
☛1st Mad Hatter	☛vs. Joker	219 .... 50.00
50-51 ....690.00	149-150 .... 110.00	220-221 .... 30.00
52 ....850.00	151 .... 90.00	222 .... 75.00
53-54 ....690.00	152 .... 100.00	223 .... 40.00
55 ....850.00	153 .... 125.00	224-226 .... 30.00
56-57 ....690.00	154 .... 85.00	227 .... 50.00
58 ....750.00	155 .... 300.00	228 .... 40.00
59-61 ....690.00	☛1st SA Penguin	229-231 .... 30.00
62 ....1,250.00	156-164 .... 85.00	232 .... 350.00
☛Catwoman origin	165 .... 130.00	☛1st Ra's al Ghul
63 ....575.00	166-168 .... 85.00	233 .... 30.00
64 ....515.00	169 .... 90.00	234 .... 115.00
65 ....575.00	170 .... 85.00	☛1st SA Two-Face
66 ....660.00	171 .... 450.00	235 .... 17.00
☛vs. Joker	☛1st SA Riddler	236 .... 25.00
67-68 ....515.00	172 .... 125.00	237 .... 75.00
69 ....575.00	173-175 .... 75.00	☛1st Reaper
70-72 ....515.00	176 .... 85.00	238 .... 65.00
73 ....660.00	177 .... 75.00	☛100 pages
74 ....550.00	178 .... 85.00	239-240 .... 17.00
75-77 ....500.00	179 .... 120.00	241 .... 30.00
78 ....585.00	☛vs. Riddler	242 .... 17.00
79-80 ....500.00	180 .... 60.00	243 .... 70.00
81 ....485.00	181 .... 175.00	☛vs. Ra's al Ghul
82-83 ....435.00	☛1st Poison Ivy	244 .... 65.00

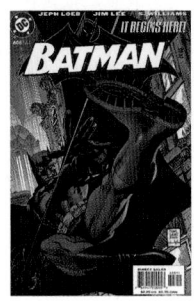

☞vs. Ra's al Ghul
245 ....70.00
246-247 ....15.00
248 ....20.00
249-250 ....15.00
251 ....60.00
☞vs. Joker
252 ....14.00
253 ....26.00
254-255 ....32.00
256-258 ....35.00
259-261 ....32.00
262-263 ....15.00
264-266 ....9.00
267-285 ....8.00
286 ....12.00
☞vs. Joker
287-290 ....9.00
291 ....12.00
292-294 ....9.00
295-299 ....8.00
300 ....15.00
301-306 ....7.00
306/Whitman 14.00
307 ....7.00
307/Whitman 14.00
308 ....7.00
308/Whitman 14.00
309-311 ....7.00
311/Whitman 20.00
312 ....7.00
312/Whitman 14.00
313 ....7.00
313/Whitman 14.00
314 ....7.00
314/Whitman 14.00
315 ....7.00
315/Whitman 14.00
316 ....7.00
316/Whitman 14.00
317 ....7.00
317/Whitman 17.00
318 ....7.00
318/Whitman 17.00
319 ....7.00
319/Whitman 17.00
320 ....7.00
320/Whitman 14.00
321-331 ....7.00
332 ....8.00
333-352 ....7.00
353 ....5.00
354-356 ....7.00

357 ....9.00
358-367 ....7.00
368 ....8.00
369-370 ....6.00
371-399 ....5.00
400 ....10.00
401-403 ....4.00
404 ....5.00
405 ....6.00
406-408 ....5.00
409-416 ....3.00
417 ....5.00
418-420 ....4.00
421-425 ....3.00
426-427 ....6.00
427/Direct 4.00
428 ....6.00
429 ....4.00
430 ....3.00
431-435 ....2.00
436 ....3.00
436/2nd 1.00
437-441 ....2.00
442 ....3.00
443-456 ....2.00
457 ....3.00
457/Direct 4.00
457/2nd-486 ....2.00
487 ....1.00
488-492 ....3.00
492/Silver 5.00
492/2nd 2.00
493 ....3.00
494-496 ....2.00
497 ....3.00
497/2nd-500 ....2.00
500/CS 4.00
501-515 ....2.00
515/Variant 4.00
516-530 ....2.00
530/Variant 3.00
531 ....2.00
531/Variant 3.00
532 ....2.00
532/Variant 3.00
533-535 ....2.00
535/Variant 4.00
536-549 ....2.00
550 ....3.00
550/Variant 4.00
551-562 ....2.00
563-564 ....3.00
565-599 ....2.00

600 ....4.00
601-607 ....2.00
608 ....5.00
☞Jim Lee begins
608/2nd 2.00
608/Dynamic 25.00
608/Retailer ed 500.00
608/NYPost 5.00
609 ....4.00
☞vs. Superman
610-619/2nd 3.00
620-629 ....2.00
630 ....3.00
631-632 ....2.00
633 ....3.00
634 ....6.00
635 ....15.00
☞Red Hood
636-637 ....12.00
638 ....11.00
638/2nd 6.00
639 ....16.00
640-641 ....6.00
642-650 ....3.00
651 ....6.00
652-671 ....3.00
1000000 ....4.00
Ann 1 ....540.00
Ann 1/2nd 6.00
Ann 2 ....275.00
Ann 3 ....215.00
Ann 4-5 ....110.00
Ann 6-7 ....85.00
Ann 8 ....7.00
Ann 9-11 ....6.00
Ann 12-13 ....5.00
Ann 14-15 ....3.00
Ann 15/2nd 2.00
Ann 15/Silver/3 ....4.00
Ann 16-18 ....3.00
Ann 19 ....4.00
Ann 20 ....3.00
Ann 21 ....4.00
Ann 22-23 ....3.00
Ann 24 ....4.00
Ann 25 ....12.00
GS 1-GS 2 ....5.00

Batman Adventures
DC, 1992
1 ....3.00
1/Silver 4.00
2-7 ....2.00

7/CS 3.00
8-24......................................2.00
25..3.00
26-36....................................2.00
Ann 1.....................................3.00
Ann 2.....................................4.00
Holiday 1 ....3.00

Batman Adventures
DC, 2003

1-17......................................2.00

Batman Adventures, The: Mad Love
DC, 1994

1 ....8.00
1/2nd....................................6.00

Batman Adventures, The: The Lost Years
DC, 1998

1-5..2.00

Batman/Aliens
Dark Horse, 1997

1-2..5.00

Batman/Aliens II TP
DC, 2003

1 ....15.00

Batman/Aliens II
DC-Dark Horse, 2003

1-3..6.00

Batman Allies Secret Files 2005
DC, 2005

0 ....5.00

Batman and Other DC Classics
DC, 1989

1 ....2.00

Batman and Robin Adventures
DC, 1995

1 ....3.00
2-24......................................2.00
25..3.00
Ann 1-2 ....4.00

Batman and Robin Adventures, The: Sub-Zero
DC, 1998

1 ....4.00

Batman and Robin: The Official Adaptation of the Warner Bros. Motion Picture
DC, 1997

Batman & Robin adapts the 1997 feature film, in which Batman, Robin, and Batgirl attempt to thwart the latest diabolical villains to hit Gotham City. The villains are Mr. Freeze, a Nobel Prize-winning scientist who turns to crime to help save his wife from a terminal illness, and Poison Ivy, a scientist who wants to make the Earth safe for plant life, even if at the expense of humanity. With the aid of drug-powered arch-nemesis Bane, they join forces to destroy Gotham City. Only with the help of Robin and Batgirl can Batman hope to stop their evil plans.

1 .... 6.00

Batman & Superman Adventures: World's Finest
DC, 1997

1 .... 7.00

Batman and Superman: World's Finest
DC, 1999

1 .... 3.00
2-10..................................... 2.00

Batman and the Mad Monk
DC, 2006

1-5.. 4.00

Batman and the Monster Men
DC, 2006

1-5.. 3.00
6 .... 4.00

Batman and the Outsiders
DC, 1983

1 .... 3.00
2-32..................................... 2.00
Ann 1.................................... 3.00
Ann 2.................................... 2.00

Batman: Arkham Asylum - Tales of Madness
DC, 1998

1 .... 3.00

Batman: Arrow, Ring and Bat
DC, 2003

1 .... 20.00

Batman: A Word to the Wise
DC

1 .... 1.00

Batman: Bane
DC, 1997

1 .... 5.00

Batman: Bane of the Demon
DC, 1998

1-4.. 2.00

Batman: Batgirl
DC, 1997

Barbara Gordon is the beautiful, vivacious daughter of Jim Gordon, commissioner of the Gotham City Police Department. She's also Batgirl, female sidekick to Batman and a menace to the evil that stalks the night. Or at least she'd like to be. For now she'll have to settle for riding around with cops and waiting for the right moment to assume her alter ego. But her chance comes quickly after the Joker escapes from Arkham asylum, ready to spread his own brand of hilarious horror on the unwitting citizens of Gotham.

Tracking the Joker to his lair, Barbara finds the Clown Prince of Crime to be more than she bargained for, and discovers there's more to police work than guns and glory.

1 ....5.00

Batman: Batgirl
DC, 1998
1 ....2.00

Batman Begins
Movie Adaptation
DC, 2005
0 ....7.00

Batman Beyond
DC, 1999
1 ....3.00
2-6 ....2.00

Batman Beyond
DC, 1999

Like The Batman Adventures and Batman: Gotham Adventures, Batman Beyond is a monthly series based on an animated television series. Here, the high-tech Batman of the future has further adventures in a vice-ridden Gotham City. Under the guidance of an aging and bitter Bruce Wayne, the original Batman, young Terry McGinnis learns what it means to wear the mantle of the Bat, avenges the death of his father, and faces such foes as the Jokerz, Inque, and The Splicers. The future is now-and pretty darned intriguing-in Batman Beyond.

1 ....3.00
2-24 ....2.00

Batman Beyond:
Return of the Joker
DC, 2001
1 .... 3.00

Batman Beyond
Special Origin Issue
DC, 1999
1 .... 1.00

Batman Black and White
DC, 1996

This anthology was designed to get attention and to provide a showcase for writers and (especially) artists who would find storytelling without color a challenge. Some of the contributions to the unusual (for a major publisher) project are outstanding and compelling.

Writers involved in the four-issue mini-series included Neil Gaiman, Brian Bolland, Howard Chaykin, Archie Goodwin, Joe Kubert, Ted McKeever, Bill Sienkiewicz, Walter Simonson, and Bruce Timm, while artists included Jim Lee, Simon Bisley, Bolland, Chaykin, Gary Gianni, Sienkiewicz, Simonson, Brian Stelfreeze, and Kent Williams. Covers were by Jim Lee and Scott Williams, Frank Miller, Barry Windsor-Smith, and Alex Toth.
-- Maggie

1 .... 4.00
2-4 .... 3.00

Batman: Blackgate
DC, 1997
1 .... 4.00

Batman:
Blackgate, Isle of Men
DC, 1998
1 .... 3.00

Batman: Bloodstorm
DC, 1994

In the Elseworlds tale Batman and Dracula: Red Rain, Batman paid a terrible price to save Gotham from Dracula and his vampiric horde. Now writer Doug Moench (Batman, The Spectre, Moon Knight, The Fantastic Four) and Kelley Jones (Sandman, Swamp Thing, Aliens) reunite for the terrifying sequel.

It seems not all of Gotham's children of the night have been vanquished, and now with the Joker as the vampires' leader, the city's streets once again flow with the blood of innocents. To save his city, Batman-battling his own growing hunger for human blood-must enter into an alliance with Selina Kyle who is experiencing unusual feline, lunar transformations. While the red rain falls from the sky, The Dark Knight faces his darkest foe yet, himself. But as Commissioner Gordon says, "Vampires are real, but thank God not all of them are evil."

Bloodstorm is followed by Crimson Mist, the final chapter in this haunting trilogy.

1 .... 13.00
1/HC 25.00

Batman:
Book of the Dead
DC, 1999
1-2 .... 5.00

Batman: Bullock's Law
DC, 1999
1 .... 5.00

Batman/
Captain America
DC, 1996
1 .... 6.00

Batman: Castle of the Bat
DC, 1994
1 ....6.00

Batman: Catwoman Defiant
DC, 1992
1 ....5.00

Batman/Catwoman: Trail of the Gun
DC, 2004
1-2...6.00

Batman Chronicles
DC, 1995
1-12.......................................4.00
13-23.....................................3.00

Batman Chronicles Gallery
DC, 1997
1 ....4.00

Batman Chronicles: The Gauntlet
DC, 1997
1 ....5.00

Batman: City of Light
DC, 2003
1-8...3.00

Batman Confidential
DC, 2007
1-30.......................................3.00

Batman/Danger Girl
DC, 2005
1 ....5.00

Batman/Daredevil
DC, 2000
1 ....6.00

Batman: Dark Allegiances
DC, 1996
1 ....6.00

Batman: Dark Detective
DC, 2005
1-6...3.00

Batman: The Dark Knight Adventures
DC
1 ....8.00

Batman: Dark Knight Gallery
DC, 1996
1 ....4.00

Batman: Dark Knight of the Round Table
DC, 1999
1-2 .... 5.00

Batman: Dark Victory
DC, 1999

Published jointly by DC Comics and Wizard Press, the one-shot zero issue leads into the regular Dark Victory limited series. The story is early in Batman's career, immediately following the events of The Long Halloween.

The serial killer known as Holiday has finally been captured, and Jim Gordon is Gotham's new Police Commissioner. But District Attorney Harvey Dent, one of Gordon and Bruce Wayne's closest friends, was horribly disfigured and driven insane in the process. Dent's transformation into the demented Two-Face pushes even Batman's cold, emotionally detached demeanor beyond its limits. The efforts of the new DA to free Holiday from Arkham Asylum only increases the pressure on Gordon and the Dark Knight.

The introduction of an orphaned 10-year-old boy may be the key to surviving the latest trial. With the optimistic, innocent Robin at his side, it may be possible for Batman to achieve victory without sacrificing the last of his humanity.

0 .... 1.00
1 .... 5.00
2-13....................................... 3.00

Batman: Day of Judgment
DC, 1999
1 .... 4.00

Batman: Death and the Maidens
DC, 2003
1-9 .... 3.00

Batman/Deathblow: After the Fire
DC, 2002
1-3 .... 6.00

Batman: Death of Innocents
DC, 1996
1 .... 4.00

Batman/Demon
DC, 1996
1 .... 5.00

Batman/Demon: A Tragedy
DC, 2000
1 .... 6.00

Batman: DOA
DC, 2000
1 .... 7.00

Batman: Dreamland
DC, 2000
1 .... 6.00

Batman: Ego
DC, 2000
1 .... 7.00

Batman Family
DC, 1975
1 .... 16.00
2 .... 10.00
3-6 .... 8.00
7-8 .... 6.00
9-12 .... 7.00
13-16 .... 5.00
17-19 .... 7.00
20 .... 8.00

Batman: Family
DC, 2002
1-8 .... 3.00

Batman Forever: The Official Comic Adaptation of the Warner Bros. Motion Picture
DC, 1995
1 .... 4.00
1/Prestige 6.00

Batman: Fortunate Son
DC

This 1999 graphic novel finds the Batman and Robin at odds: the Dark Knight believes that cult-status rock star Izaak Crowe is a manipulative mastermind empowering his legion of teenage followers to commit crimes and riot in his name. Meanwhile, the Boy Wonder-who is among the performer's many fans-insists that Crowe is just misunderstood, something of a tortured genius. Certainly a mystery worth solving, and one that finds the Dynamic Duo following separate paths as Batman vows to bring Crowe down and Robin works to exonerate his rocker-hero.

Beautifully illustrated by Gene Ha (Starman) and compellingly written by Gerard Jones (Green Lantern), Batman: Fortunate Son, a tale set in the early days of Batman and Robin's partnership, is a treasure.

1 ....25.00

Batman: Full Circle
DC, 1991

Once upon a time, a petty stick-up man named Joe Chill robbed

Bruce Wayne's parents on their way out of a theatre. The robbery ended in tragedy, with Chill shooting both of Bruce's parents to death. The bitterness over their murder was what led Bruce to become the Batman.

Years later, Batman tracked down Chill and held a gun to his head. He might even have pulled the trigger then had not a costume-clad killer named Reaper appeared and shot Chill first. Later, Batman would battle the Reaper, and watch as he fell forty stories to his apparent death. With that, Bruce Wayne had thought a chapter of his life forever closed.

But unknown to the two costumed characters, Joe Chill's murder had been observed by an unseen party-a person who now has donned the costume of the Reaper in order to gain a very personal revenge upon Batman.

1 .... 6.00

Batman Gallery
DC

1 .... 3.00

Batman: GCPD
DC, 1996

1-4 .... 2.00

Batman: Ghosts
DC, 1995

1 .... 5.00

Batman: Gordon of Gotham
DC, 1998

1-4 .... 2.00

Batman: Gordon's Law
DC, 1996

1-4 .... 2.00

Batman: Gotham Adventures
DC, 1998

1-10 .... 3.00
11-60 .... 2.00

Batman: Gotham By Gaslight
DC, 1989

What if Batman had been active in the late 19th Century? That's the question asked by Gotham by Gaslight, the first installation in DC's Elseworlds line.

An arch-criminal, broadly suggested to be Jack the Ripper, travels to Gotham City from London. Unfortunately for him (and fortunately for Gotham's residents), there's a crazy millionaire in town who's been dressing up as a bat at night.

This is an interesting and stylish interpretation, but its success is to blame for what followed: what, to some, seemed an interminable number of unimaginative historical Elseworlds one-shots, with Superman fighting in the Civil War, etc.

-- John Jackson Miller

1 .... 4.00

Batman Gotham City Secret Files
DC, 2000

1 .... 5.00

Batman: Gotham County Line
DC, 2005

1-3 .... 6.00

Batman: Gotham Knights
DC, 2000

1 .... 4.00
2-54 .... 3.00
55 .... 4.00
56-74 .... 3.00

Batman: Gotham Noir
DC, 2001

1 .... 7.00

Batman/Green Arrow: The Poison Tomorrow
DC, 1992
1 ....6.00

Batman/Grendel
DC, 1993
1-2 ....6.00

Batman/Grendel
DC, 1996
1-2 ....5.00

Batman: Harley & Ivy
DC, 2004
1-3 ....3.00

Batman: Harley Quinn
DC, 1999

DC finally brings a popular character created for the animated Batman television series into the official DC universe.

When it was discovered that Doctor Quinzel was falling in love with her patient, the Joker, and had helped him escape, her license was revoked, and she was committed on the spot. She awoke one morning to discover her cell door unlocked and Arkham Asylum deserted. Finding a suitable costume to blend in with the gang, she searched the streets of earthquake-ravaged Gotham City and finding her lover in the midst of some delicate supply negotiations with the Penguin. Eventually, the Joker grew tired of her and attempted to blast her out of his existence. Harley is rescued by Poison Ivy, whose antitoxins increase her natural agility and strength. And she has a score to settle with her old boss...

1 ....12.00
1/2nd 6.00

Batman: Haunted Gotham
DC, 2000
1-4 .... 5.00

Batman: Haunted Knight
DC
1 .... 13.00
1/2nd 15.00

Batman/Hellboy/ Starman
DC, 1999
1 .... 3.00
2 .... 3.00

Batman: Hollywood Knight
DC, 2001
1-3 .... 3.00

Batman: Holy Terror
DC, 1991
1 .... 5.00

Batman/Houdini: The Devil's Workshop
DC
1 .... 5.00

Batman/Huntress: Cry for Blood
DC, 2000
1-6 .... 3.00

Batman: Hush Double Feature
DC, 2003
1 .... 5.00

Batman: I, Joker
DC, 1998
1 .... 5.00

Batman: In Darkest Knight
DC, 1994
1 .... 5.00

Batman: Jekyll and Hyde
DC, 2005
1-5 .... 3.00

Batman: Joker's Apprentice
DC, 1999
1 .... 4.00

Batman/Joker: Switch
DC, 2003
1 .... 13.00

Batman: Joker Time
DC, 2000
1-3 .... 5.00

Batman: Journey into Knight
DC, 2005
1-12 .... 3.00

Batman/Judge Dredd: Die Laughing
DC, 1998
1-2 .... 5.00

Batman/Judge Dredd: Judgment on Gotham
DC
1 .... 6.00

Batman/Judge Dredd: The Ultimate Riddle
DC
1 .... 5.00

Batman/Judge Dredd: Vendetta in Gotham
DC, 1993
1 .... 6.00

Batman: League of Batmen
DC, 2001
1-2 .... 6.00

Batman: Legends of the Dark Knight
DC, 1989

Although it eventually became just another of the many Batman titles, Legends of the Dark Knight began by telling stories of Batman's earliest adventures, reinventing the legend in the process. With dark, impressionistic art and multi-issue storylines by such greats as Matt Wagner and Grant Morrison, Legends of the Dark Knight raises Batman from a costumed crime fighter to a mythic figure. He's the lone savior of Gotham, a city whose heart seems as dark as a cave; and, when he battles a villain such as Two-Face, he seems to be fighting, not just another bad-guy, but a symptom of the disease that has infected the city.

1-15	3.00
16	4.00
17-20	3.00
21-26	2.00
27	3.00
28-49	2.00
50	4.00
51-64	2.00
0	3.00
65-99	2.00
100	5.00
101-119	2.00
120	4.00
121-157	2.00
158-198	3.00
200	5.00
201-213	3.00
Ann 1	5.00
Ann 2-5	4.00
Ann 6	3.00
Ann 7	4.00
Special 1	7.00

Batman: Legends of the Dark Knight: Jazz
DC, 1995

1-3 .... 3.00

Batman: Madness a Legends of the Dark Knight Halloween Special
DC, 1994

Jervis Tetch, aka The Mad Hatter, has never been nearly as murderous or as effective a foe for Batman as The Joker or Ra's Al Ghul. Yet, in this one-shot special by the superb team of Jeph Loeb and Tim Sale, Tetch's Alice in Wonderland fetish is warped into something chilling. A young Barbara Gordon finds herself in the clutches of the demented Hatter, sparking a psychological battle of wills that not only tests her policeman father, but The Batman, as well. As often as extraneous details are grafted onto the night Bruce Wayne lost his parents, Loeb's addition is a moving footnote about Wayne's mother and the time they spent reading Alice together just before that fateful evening in Gotham City. Everyone faces their demons by story's end, and Wayne comes to terms with his loss in a novel way.

1 .... 5.00

Batman: Manbat
DC, 1995

1-3 .... 5.00

Batman: Mask of the Phantasm- The Animated Movie
DC, 1993

1 .... 3.00
1/Prestige-1/Video 5.00

Batman: Masque
DC, 1997

1 .... 7.00

Batman: Master of the Future
DC, 1991

1 .... 6.00

Batman: Mr. Freeze
DC, 1997

1 .... 5.00

Batman: Mitefall
DC, 1995

1 .... 5.00

Batman: Nevermore
DC, 2003

1-5 .... 3.00

Batman/Nightwing: Bloodborne
DC, 2002

1 .... 6.00

Batman: No Law and a New Order
DC

1 .... 6.00

Batman: No Man's Land
DC, 1999

0	5.00
1	3.00
1/Variant	4.00
2-4	3.00

Batman: No Man's Land Gallery
DC, 1999

1 .... 4.00

Batman: No Man's Land Secret Files
DC, 1999

1 .... 5.00

Batman: Nosferatu
DC, 1999

This sequel to Superman's Metropolis is the second in a proposed trilogy of one-shots based on the great German expressionist films of the early twentieth century. As the story opens, the idle rich of Metropolis are under the spell of "The Cabinet of Dr. Arkham," whose main attraction, "The Laughing Man," predicts the violent deaths of his wealthy audience members. Only one who operates in the shadows beneath the city-Nosferatu the Bat-Man-seems capable of halting the murder spree, but what happens when the mysterious Bat-Man runs afoul of the glorious Super-Man, the savior of Metropolis? Find out in this tale that draws its inspiration from F.W. Murnau's "Nosferatu: A Symphony of Horrors" and Robert Weine's "The Cabinet of Dr. Caligari." Also look for Wonder Woman: The Blue Amazon-based on Josef Von Sternberg's "The Blue Angel" and Fritz Lang's "Doctor Mabuse: The Gambler.

1 .... 6.00

Batman of Arkham
DC

1 .... 6.00

Batman: Order of the Beasts
DC, 2004

1 .... 6.00

Batman: Orpheus Rising
DC, 2001

1-5 .... 3.00

Batman: Our Worlds at War
DC, 2001

This issue is part of the planet-spanning summer crossover, Our Worlds at War, in which the DC Universe super-heroes must face the would-be world conqueror known as Imperiex.

In this special "Prelude to War" issue, Batman's attention is drawn to the site of a mysterious explosion when federal authorities, acting at the behest of President Lex Luthor, cordon off the decimated construction site.

Why would NASA scientists and Army generals be sent to investigate an alleged terrorist attack? Could it have anything to do with the crash-landing of a space ship with an alien inside?

Before it is all over, Batman will have to travel straight to Metropolis and face down Lex Luthor for the answers he seeks.

1 ....3.00

Batman: Outlaws
DC, 2000
1-3...5.00

Batman: Penguin Triumphant
DC, 1992
1 ....5.00

Batman/Phantom Stranger
DC, 1997
1 ....5.00

Batman Plus
DC, 1997
1 ....3.00

Batman: Poison Ivy
DC, 1997
1 ....5.00

Batman/Poison Ivy: Cast Shadows
DC, 2004
1 .... 7.00

Batman/Predator III
DC, 1997
1-4.. 2.00

Batman: Prodigal
DC
1 .... 15.00

Batman/Punisher: Lake of Fire
DC, 1994
1 .... 5.00

Batman: Reign of Terror
DC, 1999
1 .... 5.00

Batman Returns: The Official Comic Adaptation of the Warner Bros. Motion Picture
DC, 1992
1 .... 4.00
1/Prestige.............................. 6.00

Batman: Riddler: The Riddle Factory
DC

Hitting the stands at the same time "Batman Forever"-featuring Jim Carrey as the Riddler-hit the multiplexes, Batman: The Riddle Factory is a Prestige Format one-shot. Here, we find the King of Conundrums pirating Gotham's airwaves to broadcast a rapid-fire game show that tests the wits of its contestants and slings a bit of mud at the city's social elite. But the Dark Knight is convinced that there's more to the Riddler's antics than a desire to be the next Alex Trebek. But what? Find out in this excellent detective story from

writer Matt Wagner (Grendel) and artist Dave Taylor (Batman & Superman: World's Finest).

1 .... 5.00

Batman: Roomful of Strangers
DC, 2004
1 .... 6.00

Batman: Run, Riddler, Run
DC, 1992
1-3... 5.00

Batman/Scarecrow 3-D
DC, 1998
1 .... 4.00
1/Variant 8.00

Batman/Scarface: A Psychodrama
DC, 2001
1 .... 6.00

Batman: Scar of the Bat
DC
1 .... 5.00

Batman: Scottish Connection
DC, 1998
1 .... 6.00

Batman Secret Files
DC, 1997
1 .... 5.00

Batman: Secrets
DC, 2006
1-5... 3.00

Batman: Seduction of the Gun
DC, 1993
1 .... 4.00

Batman: Shadow of the Bat
DC, 1992

This brilliant series begins with a bang. Arkham Asylum, that home of lunatics, paranoids, and the murderously insane, is being torn down and rebuilt. The son of the original architect, Jeremiah Arkham, is the new chief administrator, and he's ripping out the old and bringing in the new. Now, instead of the dark Victorian corridors and dank cells, there are shiny new fluorescent lights illuminating a floor plan laid out like a labyrinth - all of this, of course, in the name of progress.

But in the new asylum are the same old inmates: Cornelius Stirk, the murderously insane night-dweller; Scarecrow, whose greatest joy is to bring fear to others; and Mr. Zsasz, the serial killer who has laid waste to more than 100 lives -

- as well as one other, very special guest of Arkham Asylum: Batman.

0-1	3.00
2-34	3.00
35	4.00
35/Variant	3.00
36-79	2.00
80-80/Ltd.	5.00
81-82	2.00
83	9.00
84-93	2.00
1000000	3.00
94	2.00
Ann 1-3	4.00
Ann 4	3.00
Ann 5	4.00

Batman-Spawn: War Devil
DC, 1994

1	5.00

Batman Special
DC, 1984

1	3.00

Batman/Spider-Man
DC, 1997

1	5.00

Batman: Spoiler/Huntress: Blunt Trauma
DC, 1998

1-4	3.00

Batman Strikes
DC, 2004

1-29	2.00

Batman/Superman/ Wonder Woman Trinity
DC, 2003

1	9.00
2	8.00
3	7.00

Batman/Superman World's Finest TP
DC, 2003

1	20.00

Batman: Sword of Azrael
DC, 1992

For centuries, the secret order of St. Dumas has chosen one of its members to become Azrael, the angel of death. Azrael's purpose: to exact deadly vengeance on those who spread the evils of crime and corruption. When the current Azrael encounters arms merchant Carlton LeHah, however, he finds that his armor is no match for the arms dealer's Teflon bullets. Azrael falls, mortally wounded, into the midst of a parade in Gotham City, escaping only to die at the house of his young son.

The son, discovering that he is heir to a terrible legacy, travels to Switzerland to assume the role of the new Azrael. Meanwhile, Batman's investigation of the strange disturbance at the parade leads him to uncover Azrael's secret. He follows the boy to Switzerland, only to find himself in the midst of a war of vengeance.

1	4.00
1/Silver	2.00
2	3.00
2/Silver	2.00
3	3.00
3/Silver	2.00
4	3.00
4/Silver	2.00

Batman/Tarzan: Claws Of The Cat-Woman
Dark Horse, 1999

1-4	3.00

Batman: Tenses
DC, 2003

1-2	7.00

Batman: Terror
DC, 2003

1	13.00

Batman: The Abduction
DC, 1998

1	6.00

Batman: The Ankh
DC, 2002

1-2	6.00

Batman: The Blue, the Grey, and the Bat
DC, 1992

1	6.00

Batman: The Book of Shadows
DC

1	6.00

Batman: The Cult
DC, 1988

1	5.00
2-4	4.00

Batman: The Dark Knight
DC, 1986

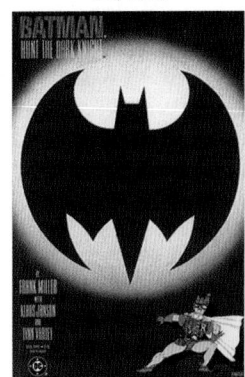

The super-heroes have been persecuted, then regulated. Wonder Woman has gone back to her people; Green Lantern has left for the stars; and Superman is an agent for the government, quietly fighting its dirty little wars for it. Only Batman - that aging legend - dares laugh in their faces.

The world is poised on the brink of nuclear war; Batman has been declared an outlaw; and Commissioner Gordon has been replaced by a woman whose dearest desire is to see Batman dead or behind bars.

And The Joker is guest-starring on late-night TV.

This four-issue series by Frank Miller changed the legend of the Batman forever and introduced a new format for comics. Before, he was just a crimefighter. When it's over, he'll have truly become The Dark Knight.

1	25.00

☞Frank Miller series

1/2nd	7.00
1/3rd	5.00
2	9.00
2/2nd-2/3rd	3.00
3	6.00
3/2nd	3.00
4	5.00

Batman: The Doom that Came to Gotham
DC, 2000

1-3	5.00

Batman: The Hill
DC, 2000

1	3.00

Batman: The Killing Joke
DC, 1988

1	7.00

☞Alan Moore, Brian Bolland

1/2nd	6.00
1/3rd-1/8th	5.00

Batman: The Long Halloween
DC, 1996

1	9.00
2	7.00
3	6.00
4-6	5.00
7-12	4.00
13	6.00

Batman: The Man Who Laughs
DC, 2005

1	7.00

Batman: The Official Comic Adaptation of the Warner Bros. Motion Picture
DC, 1989

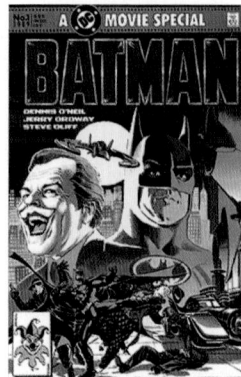

The 1989 release of Batman was a huge hit, breaking box office records and successfully transferring the mystique of the Dark Knight to the silver screen. This was a marked contrast to the campy Batman of 1960s television, and the little-noticed movie it had spawned.

Released in both regular and prestige formats, this comic adapted the 1989 blockbuster in comic book form. It told how a mobster named Jack Napier was set up by his boss and cornered by police at the Axis Chemical plant. During flight, he was across the face by a face by a bullet and fell into a vat of chemicals. He survived-barely-but the chemicals had bleached his skin white and turned his hair a bright green. Moreover, the bullet had severed muscled in his face, leaving him with a ghastly perpetual smile. When he resurfaced, Jack Napier was no more-instead, he was the Joker, a mad killer whom only Batman could stop.

1	3.00
1/Prestige	5.00

Batman/The Spirit
DC, 2007

1	5.00

Batman: The 10-Cent Adventure
DC, 2002

1	1.00

Batman: The Ultimate Evil
DC

1-2	6.00

Batman 3-D
DC, 1990

1	10.00

Batman: Thrillkiller
DC

1	13.00

Batman: Toyman
DC, 1998

1-4	2.00

Batman: Turning Points
DC, 2001

1-5	3.00

Batman: Two-Face: Crime and Punishment
DC

1	5.00

Batman: Two Faces
DC, 1998

1	5.00
1/Ltd.	10.00

Batman: Two-Face Strikes Twice
DC, 1993

Harvey Dent was a rising young district attorney, until "Boss" Moron threw acid in his face during a trial. Dent, who had been handsome, was suddenly cursed by a face whose entire left side was greenish and twisted. The shock of this drove him over the edge of sanity, and he became the criminal Two-Face, obsessed with the number 2 and habitually flipping a two-headed coin to decide his next action. One side of the coin is "scarred" by marks etched into it. If that side comes up, his next act will be evil. If the other side came up, he will act for the cause of goodness.

Two-Face Strikes Back epitomizes this Batman villain's character in its very format. It's a set of two graphic novels, published as a flip-book. One side gives a classic Two-Face story drawn in the style of the Golden Age. The other is a more contemporary tale featuring modern, painted art.

1-2 ....5.00

Batman: Vengeance of Bane II
DC

1 ....4.00

Batman: Vengeance of Bane Special
DC, 1993

1 ....4.00

Batman Versus Predator
DC, 1991

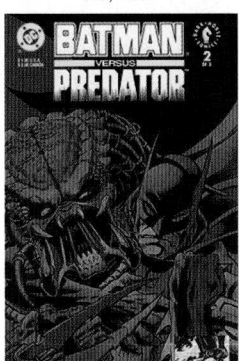

There are all kinds of killers. Some, like Gotham City's Leo Brodin and Alex Yeager, are the "hands-off" type, mob bosses who order others to do their dirty work. Others, like the thugs they hire, have no such qualms and blindly follow their violent orders. Batman is used to dealing with all of these, but now he's up against something new: a killer of astonishing strength and savagery who hunts humans for the sheer joy of the blood sport.

Gotham's mob rivalries had been intensifying for some time, with Brodin and Yeager eager to divide the town between them. But now this new player -- a Predator from another world -- has begun hunting Gotham's power players. How can even Batman hope to stop a killer who is stronger than any man, kills using alien technology, and who can not even be seen with the naked eye?

1 ....3.00

1/Prestige Batm-1/Prestige
  Pred 5.00
2 .... 3.00
2/Prestige 5.00
3 .... 3.00
3/Prestige 5.00

Batman versus Predator II: Bloodmatch
DC, 1994

1-4 .... 3.00

Batman vs. the Incredible Hulk
DC, 1981

1 .... 3.00
1/2nd 4.00

Batman Villains Secret Files
DC, 1998

1 .... 5.00

Batman Villains Secret Files 2005
DC, 2005

0 .... 5.00

Batman: War On Crime
DC, 1999

1 .... 10.00

Batman/Wildcat
DC, 1997

1-3 .... 2.00

Batman: Year 100
DC, 2006

1-4 .... 6.00

Bat
Adventure, 1992

1 .... 3.00

Bat Masterson
Dell, 1960

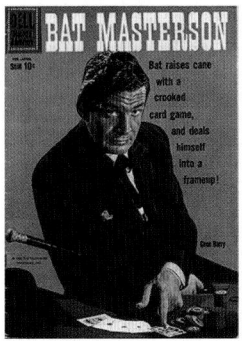

Masterson was a real person (1853-1921), but this series was based on the Gene Barry TV series (1959-61) and featured photo covers of Barry. The real Masterson served as a Dodge City sheriff, and his appearance was set off by a derby and cane - which Barry's costuming

echoed. The comic book's run did not continue long beyond the airing of the TV show.

-- Maggie

B

2 .... 55.00
3-9 .... 40.00

Bat Men
Avalon

1 .... 3.00

Bats, Cats & Cadillacs
Now, 1990

1-2 .... 2.00

Bat-Thing
DC, 1997

1 .... 2.00

Battle
Atlas, 1951

"Hi-ya-a! This will be our last retreat comrades! I have just thought of a cunning plan ... which will destroy the Yankee Fox company!"

Ok, it wasn't exactly literature, and the plan in question (to let the company of brave Americans capture a hill, then use what looks like a couple of regiments to surround them) wasn't so hot, either. Still, Battle was escapist reading for the 1950s.

Like many, many comics starting in the early 1950s, it tended to feature at least a couple of Korean War stories per issue, wherein the hard-fighting Americans would stop hordes of Asian soldiers from trampling over life, liberty, and the inevitable innocents in harm's way.

On what seemed like a lighter note, it also included war features dating back to the American Civil War or earlier, lending a period-piece feel to what were some of the least believable -- but fun -- war stories published during the era.

1 .... 175.00
2 .... 100.00

3..75.00
4-10..54.00
11-20..45.00
21...58.00
22...42.00
23...58.00
24-30..42.00
31-50..32.00
51-63..26.00
64-66..45.00
67-68..55.00
69-70..45.00

Battle Action
Atlas, 1952

1..150.00
2..80.00
3-10..48.00
11-15..44.00
16-30..40.00

Battle Angel Alita Part 1
Viz, 1992

Scavenging in the junkyard, Doctor Daisuke discovers the head of a cyborg girl. She has lost her memory, so he names her Alita. As he tries to find parts to rebuild her, he discovers that she may not be the angel he had sought to create. His dreams of tranquility are replaced by his recognition of the incredible martial skills she instinctively possesses, and they are drawn into the consequences that having such power can bring.

Creator Yukito Kishiro was inspired to create Alita by the toys he'd played with when young. The world is one in which the garbage of a beautiful floating island provides the source of material for the poor - and in which cyborg gladiators compete.

1-3..4.00
4-9..3.00

Battle Angel Alita Part 2
Viz, 1993

1-7..3.00

Battle Angel Alita Part 3
Viz, 1993

1-13...3.00

Battle Angel Alita Part 4
Viz, 1994

1-7..3.00

Battle Angel Alita Part 5
Viz, 1995

1-7..3.00

Battle Angel Alita Part 6
Viz, 1996

1-8..3.00

Battle Angel Alita Part 7
Viz, 1996

1-8..3.00

Battle Angel Alita Part 8
Viz, 1997

1-9..3.00

Battle Angel Alita: Last Order Part 1
Viz, 2002

1-6..3.00

Battle Armor
Eternity, 1988

1-3..2.00

Battle Attack
Stanmor, 1954

1... 60.00
2... 50.00
3... 40.00
4-8... 30.00

Battle Axe
Comics Interview

1... 3.00

Battleaxes
DC, 2000

1-4.. 3.00

Battle Axis
Intrepid, 1993

1... 3.00

Battle Beasts
Blackthorne, 1988

1-4.. 2.00

Battle Binder Plus
Antarctic, 1994

1-6.. 3.00

Battle Chasers
Image, 1998

1-1/Wraparound 5.00
1/Holochrome...................... 17.00
1/Gold................................ 14.00
1/2nd................................. 3.00
2 .... 4.00
2/Dynamic 5.00
2/B 6.00
3 .... 4.00
4/A-8.................................. 3.00
9 .... 4.00

Ashcan 1 .... 5.00
Ashcan 1/Gold...................... 7.00
Deluxe 1 .... 25.00

Battle Classics
DC, 1978

1 .... 4.00

Battle Cry
Stanmor, 1952

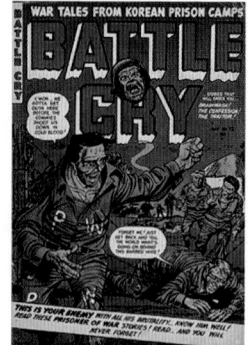

In the early 1950s, E.C. Comics revolutionized the war-comics genre with Two-Fisted Tales and Frontline Combat, two titles that set an unmatched standard for stylish storytelling and literate treatment of the grim details of warfare. Someone at Stanmor Publications was paying attention: Battle Cry looked as if the layouts had been picked out of Harvey Kurtzman's trashcan, right down to the pages loaded with text captions. The covers were reminiscent of E.C.'s recognizable designs.

Inside, the art is swiped from a gallery of impressive sources, from Wally Wood to Alex Toth to Milton Caniff. Unfortunately, the resemblance stopped there. Instead of E.C.'s thoughtful analysis of the horrors of war, Battle Cry substituted the shallow jingoism and stereotypes of Korean War-era propaganda.

1 .... 65.00
2 .... 42.00
3-10 .... 28.00
11-20 .... 24.00

Battlefield
Atlas, 1952

1 .... 110.00
2 .... 60.00
3-5 .... 58.00
6-11 .... 44.00

Battlefield Action
Charlton, 1957

16 .... 28.00
17 .... 13.00

18-20	10.00
21-30	9.00
31-40	7.00
41-50	6.00
51-62	5.00
63-89	3.00

Battle for a Three Dimensional World
3-D Cosmic, 1982

1	3.00

Battleforce
Blackthorne, 1987

1-2	2.00

Battlefront
Marvel, 1952

Pack up your mess kit and join the patrol with the soldiers of Battlefront! This war series ran from 1952 to 1957 and covered most of the wars in which Americans have fought. In both text stories and regular comic-book tales, the heroism of American forces is extolled, while readers are repeatedly told just why the Communist menace is something worth fighting. Typical stories might include the saga of a soldier escaping from an enemy prison or the difficulties encountered by a young man assigned to a unit commanded by his father. Battlefront isn't just an entertaining collection of war stories; it's also a glimpse into the way the world was perceived during many of the early years of the Cold War era.

1	130.00
2	75.00
3-5	55.00
6-10	42.00
11-20	34.00
21-30	28.00
31-48	22.00

Battle Girlz
Antarctic, 2002

1-2	3.00

Battle Gods: Warriors of the Chaak
Dark Horse, 1990

1-4	3.00

Battleground
Marvel, 1954

1	90.00
2	50.00
3-5	35.00
6-8	24.00
9	32.00
10	24.00
11-12	20.00
13	32.00
14	35.00
15-17	20.00
18	32.00
19-20	20.00

Battleground Earth
Best

1-4	3.00

Battle Group Peiper
Tome

1	3.00

Battle Hymn
Image, 2005

1-5	3.00

Battle of the Planets
Gold Key, 1979

One of the better early anime adaptations, Battle of the Planets follows the adventures of a group of children known, in the Sandy Frank U.S. version, as G-Force. (It's Gatchaman in Japan.) The kids defend Earth against alien aggressors and, when put to great challenge, call upon a fiery bird effect to surround their ship. (It may call Marvel's Phoenix to mind, but the Gatchaman series premiered in Japan in 1972.)

Costume coloring helps readers tell the G-Force characters apart, a trick that would later prove helpful to readers of the various Mighty Morphin Power Rangers comics series.

Notable for being among the earlier comics adaptations of a Japanese comics series - if only via its U.S. syndicated version - Battle of the Planets enjoyed a revival in 2002, with a new Image series in the works.

- John Jackson Miller

1	20.00
2	15.00
3-6	12.00
7	30.00
8-10	20.00

Battle of the Planets Artbook
Image, 2003

1	5.00

☛Alex Ross art

Battle of the Planets
Image, 2002

1/2	3.00
1/2/Gold	5.00
1/A-7	3.00
7/A	5.00
8-11	3.00
12	5.00

Battle of the Planets: Jason
Image, 2003

1	5.00

Battle of the Planets: Manga
Image, 2003

1-3	3.00

Battle of the Planets: Mark
Image, 2003

1	5.00

Battle of the Planets: Princess
Image, 2004

1-6	3.00

Battle of the Planets/ Thundercats
Image, 2003

1-1/A	5.00

Battle of the Planets/ Witchblade
Image, 2003

1	6.00

Battle of the Ultra-Brothers
Viz

1-5	5.00

BattlePope
Funk-O-Tron, 2000

1	3.00

8-9	3.00
10	5.00
11-13	4.00

BattlePope
Funk-O-Tron, 2000

2	3.00

BattlePope
Funk-O-Tron, 2000

3-4	3.00

BattlePope
Funk-O-Tron, 2000

5	5.00

BattlePope
Funk-O-Tron, 2000

6-7	3.00

Battle Pope
Funk-O-Tron, 2006

1	5.00

Battle Pope
Funk-O-Tron, 2006

2-3	4.00

Battle Pope
Funk-O-Tron, 2006

5	3.00

Battle Pope
Funk-O-Tron, 2006

6	3.00

Battle Pope
Funk-O-Tron, 2006

7-9	3.00
11	5.00

Battle Pope Color
Image, 2005

1-8	3.00
9-12	4.00

Battler Britton
DC, 2006

1-5	3.00

Battle Report
Farrell, 1952

1	54.00

Battle Royale
Tokyopop, 2003

1	16.00
2-14	10.00

Battlestar Galactica 1999 Tour Book
Realm, 1999

1/A-1/B	3.00
1/C	7.00

Battlestar Galactica: Apollo's Journey
Maximum, 1996

1-3	3.00

Battlestar Galactica: Eve of Destruction Prelude
Realm, 1999

nn	4.00

Battlestar Galactica: Journey's End
Maximum, 1996

1-4	3.00

Battlestar Galactica
Marvel, 1979

1-1/Whitman	4.00
1/2nd	5.00
2-10	3.00

Battlestar Galactica
Maximum, 1995

1-Special 1	3.00

Battlestar Galactica
Realm, 1997

1/A-5	3.00

Battlestar Galactica: Search for Sanctuary
Realm, 1998

The never-ending quest of the Galactica fleet for the planet Earth was relegated to a subplot in this two-issue series. An attempt by an extra-dimensional race called the Somnians to escape their homeworld resulted in the presumed loss of Apollo to an unknown planet. The remaining warriors mounted a desperate search for him, ignoring for the moment their ever-present enemy, the Cylons.

The lush artwork of Chris Scalf is the primary enticement of this title. His airbrush paintings have a warm, soft-focus appearance that, although enthralling, possess a static, posed aspect. A gallery of his artwork fills out the issue. -- Stephen C. George

-- George Haberberger

1	3.00

Special 1	4.00

Battlestar Galactica: Season III
Realm, 1999

1	3.00
1/A-3/A	5.00
3/B	3.00
3/Conv	5.00

Battlestar Galactica: Starbuck
Maximum, 1995

1-3	3.00

Battlestar Galactica: The Compendium
Maximum, 1997

1	3.00

Battlestar Galactica: The Enemy Within
Maximum, 1995

1-3/Variant	3.00

Battlestone
Image, 1994

1-2	3.00

Battle Stories
Fawcett, 1952

1	75.00
2	45.00
3-11	24.00

BattleTech
Malibu, 1995

For centuries of interstellar warfare and political intrigue, powerful dynastic leaders have pitted their military forces against each other in a seemingly endless quest for control of the known universe. But the real combat, as always, is fought by the men and women in the midst of the brutal battles on the front lines.

BattleTech started as a role-playing game that featured powerful humanoid fighting machines, called Mechs, and their human pilots; since then, it's also been showcased in an animated series, several novels, and comic series from Blackthorne and Malibu.

This special edition is introduces the BattleTech storyline to new readers. It features three short stories, a brief history of the political/military situation, and short bios of some of the characters involved, as well as the specs on some of the powerful Mechs used by the invading Clans.

0 .... 3.00

Battletech
Blackthorne, 1988
1-6 .... 2.00

BattleTech: Fallout
Malibu, 1994
1-4 .... 3.00

Battletech in 3-D
Blackthorne, 1988
1 .... 3.00

Battletide
Marvel, 1992

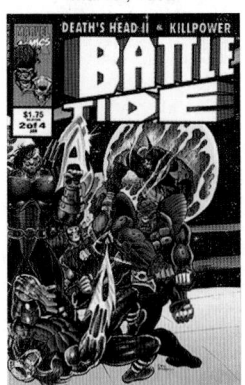

Merging characters from the successful Death's Head II and Motormouth (Motormouth is Harley Davis, able to phase across myriad dimensions of the universe) titles, BattleTide pits the over-brawned, under-brained Killpower against the schizoid killing machine, Death's Head II. The two are brought together by the inhabitants of Colosseum, a planetoid dedicated to bloody gladiatorial battle. To complicate things, several more of Earth's heroes -- including Dark Angel, Motormouth, and the X-Men's Wolverine and Psylocke -- are also captured.

Colosseum's goal is to use these heroes as competitors in an intergalactic battle royal.

1-4 .... 2.00

Battletide II
Marvel, 1993
1 .... 3.00
2-4 .... 2.00

Battle to the Death
Imperial, 1987
1-3 .... 2.00

Battle Vixens
Tokyopop, 2004
1 .... 10.00

Battlezones: Dream Team 2
Malibu, 1996
1 .... 4.00

Battron
NEC, 1992
1-2 .... 3.00

Battron's 4 Queens: Guns, Babes & Intrigue
Commode
1 .... 4.00

Bay City Jive
DC, 2001
1-3 .... 3.00

Baywatch Comic Stories
Acclaim
1-4 .... 5.00

Bazooka Jules
Com.x, 2001
1- SE2 .... 3.00

Beach High
Big, 1997
1 .... 3.00

Beach Party
Eternity
1 .... 3.00

Beagle Boys
Gold Key, 1964
1 .... 22.00
2-5 .... 16.00
6-10 .... 12.00
11-20 .... 8.00
21-30 .... 6.00
31-40 .... 4.00
41-47 .... 3.00

Beagle Boys versus Uncle Scrooge
Whitman, 1979
1 .... 6.00
2 .... 5.00
3-7 .... 4.00
8-12 .... 3.00

Beany and Cecil
Dell, 1962
1 .... 75.00
2-5 .... 60.00

Bear
Slave Labor, 2003
1-10 .... 3.00

Bearers of the Blade Special
Image, 2006
1 .... 3.00

Bearfax Funnies
Treasure
1 .... 3.00

Bearskin: A Grimm Tale
Thecomic.Com
1 .... 2.00

Beast
Marvel, 1997
1-3 .... 3.00

Beast Boy
DC, 2000

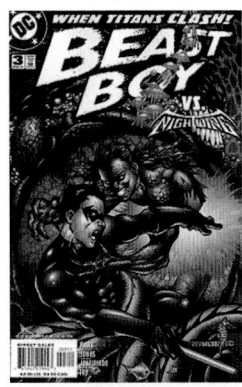

Having served as a member of both the original Doom Patrol and The New Teen Titans, Garfield Logan-a.k.a. Beast Boy a.k.a. Changeling-is no stranger to trouble. However, when it looks as though he's responsible for a gruesome murder, Gar doesn't know where to turn in this limited series from writers Geoff Johns (JSA, Stars and S.T.R.I.P.E.) and Ben Raab (Union Jack) and artist Justiano (Titans). Will Gar stay ahead of the cops and bring the real killer to justice? Will his former teammates Nightwing and Flamebird be forced to bring him down? There's action a-plenty and a mystery to be solved in this one!

1-4 .... 3.00

B.E.A.S.T.I.E.S.
Axis, 1994
1 .... 2.00

Beast Warriors of Shaolin
Pied Piper, 1987
1-3..2.00

Beatles
Dell, 1964
1...440.00

Beatles Experience
Revolutionary, 1991
1-8...3.00

Beatles
Personality
1...5.00
1/Ltd. 8.00
2...4.00

Beatles vs. The Rolling Stones
Celebrity, 1992
1...3.00

Beatrix
Vision, 1997
1-2...3.00

Beauties & Barbarians
AC
1...2.00

Beautiful People
Slave Labor, 1994
1...5.00

Beautiful Stories for Ugly Children
DC, 1989

Those who like slightly off-kilter fairy tales should take a look at this series. As the title indicates, the writer and artist take beautiful stories but add a bizarre twist throughout, juxtaposing classic storylines with the grotesque, the impossible, and the downright weird. It's a treat for the twisted mind.

All the stories and illustrations come from writer Dave Louapre and artist Dan Sweetman, who seem to be the sort of folks who spend their time worrying about whether the Andy Griffith Show's "Opie" is stalking them and what would happen if smog were blue. That should be a clear indication of the approach of this series.

1-30......................................3.00

Beauty and the Beast
Disney
1...3.00
1/Direct....................................5.00

Beauty and the Beast
Disney, 1994
1-13...2.00
Holiday 1 ....5.00

Beauty and the Beast
Innovation, 1993
1...3.00
1/CS 4.00
2-6...3.00

Beauty and the Beast
Marvel, 1984
1...3.00
2-4...2.00

Beauty and the Beast: Night of Beauty
First, 1990
1...6.00

Beauty and the Beast: Portrait of Love
First, 1989
1...6.00

Beauty and the Beast
Dark Horse
1...5.00

Beauty Is the Beast
Viz, 2005
1...9.00

Beauty of the Beasts
Mu, 1991
1-3...3.00

Beavis & Butt-Head
Marvel, 1994
1...3.00
1/2nd 2.00
2-5...3.00
6-28...2.00

Beck & Caul Investigations
Caliber, 1994
1-5...3.00
Ann 1.......................................4.00

Beck: Mongolian Chop Squad
Tokyopop, 2005
1-10 ....10.00

Bedlam!
Eclipse, 1985
1-2...2.00

Bedlam
Image, 2006
1...5.00

Bedlam
Chaos, 2000
1-1/Variant.............................3.00

Beelzelvis
Slave Labor, 1994

What if an oxymoron was one of the great mysteries of the universe? One answer could be a jumpsuit-attired demon with a perverse sense of justice. This demon might appear and behave something like this: cursed with obesity that causes profuse sweating, exhibits a fondness of eating and displays a healthy devotion to Mama. The low notes far outnumber the humorous ones and it's worse than a certain rock and roll hillbilly's acting abilities: it is like watching cement dry in the dark. Slave Labor Graphics usually can be counted on as a publisher of provocative or interesting material, but this is not one of its finer moments.

1...3.00

Beep Beep
Dell, 1960
4-9...24.00
10-14 ....16.00

Beep Beep, The Road Runner
Gold Key, 1966

1	50.00
2-5	30.00
6-15	15.00
16-40	10.00
41-59	8.00
60-79	6.00
80-90	3.00
91-92	12.00
93	17.00
94-101	3.00
102-105	12.00

Beer & Roaming in Las Vegas
Slave Labor, 1998

1	3.00
Ashcan 1	1.00

Beer Nutz
Tundra

1	3.00
2-3	2.00

Beethoven
Harvey, 1994

1-3	2.00

Beetle Bailey
Dell, 1956

5-10	24.00
11-20	18.00
21-30	14.00
31-40	10.00
41-50	8.00
51-60	7.00
61-70	6.00
71-100	4.00
101-132	3.00

Beetle Bailey
Harvey, 1992

1-GS 2	2.00

Beetle Bailey Big Book
Harvey, 1992

2	2.00

Beetlejuice
Harvey, 1991

1-2	2.00

Beetlejuice: Elliot Mess and the Unwashables
Harvey, 1992

1-3	2.00

Beetlejuice Holiday Special
Harvey, 1992

1	2.00

Beetlejuice in the Neitherworld
Harvey, 1991

1-2	2.00

Beet the Vandel Buster
Viz, 2004

1-10	8.00

Before the Fantastic Four: Ben Grimm and Logan
Marvel, 2000

To be more accurate, this four-issue limited series should be entitled Before the Fantastic Four: Ben Grimm, Logan, Tony Stark, and Carol Danvers, as it features several key players in the modern Marvel Universe in their early days. Test pilot Ben Grimm (aka the ever-lovin', blue-eyed Thing), Canadian secret agent Logan (aka the claw-wielding Wolverine), and Department of Defense operative Carol Danvers (aka the mighty Avengers' Warbird) take an experimental spy plane into Russian airspace to get the skinny on some mysterious Soviet technology. Espionage at its finest from the House of Ideas.

For more fun in the same vein, check out Before the FF: The Adventures of Reed Richards and Before the FF: The Storms.

1-3	3.00

Before the FF: Reed Richards
Marvel, 2000

1-3	3.00

Before the FF: The Storms
Marvel, 2000

1-3	3.00

Behold 3-D
Edge Group

1	4.00

Believe in Yourself Productions
Believe in Yourself Productions

1/Ashcan-1/Ltd.	1.00

Belladonna
Avatar, 2004

0/Preview	6.00
0/Conv	5.00
1	4.00
1/Foil	8.00
1/Platinum	10.00
1/Wraparound	5.00
2	4.00
2/Platinum	10.00
2/Premium	8.00
2/Wraparound	5.00
3	4.00
3/Platinum	10.00
3/Premium	8.00
3/Wraparound	5.00
4	4.00

Bella Donna
Pinnacle

1	2.00

Belly Button
Fantagraphics, 2004

1-2	5.00

Ben Casey Film Stories
Gold Key, 1962

1	55.00

Beneath the Planet of the Apes
Gold Key, 1970

1	35.00

Benzango Obscuro
Starhead

1	3.00

Benzine
Antarctic, 2000

1-7	5.00

Beowulf
DC, 1975

In medieval times, Beowulf hunted down a grim murderer,

Grendel, who senselessly killed his men. For this he was immortalized in the oldest existing English saga. Now the classic story has been updated into a set of adventures. Beowulf does much more than just slay dragons. Eternal arch-nemesis Grendel has made a deal with Satan and now has supernatural powers which he uses to try to kill Beowulf and his friends.

Beowulf's a powerful warrior, but he gets some legendary help from his historic comrades, Hondscio and Wiglaf; and some new heroes, Nan-Zee the Amazon, and Shaper, the story-teller and magician in the group.

1 ....5.00
2 ....3.00
3-6 ....2.00

Beowulf
Comic.Com, 1999
1-3..5.00

Beowulf
Speakeasy Comics, 2005
1-4..3.00

Berlin
Drawn & Quarterly, 1996
1-8..3.00
10-12..4.00

Bernie Wrightson, Master of the Macabre
Pacific, 1983
1-5..3.00

Berserk
Dark Horse, 2003
1-10..14.00

Berzerker
Gauntlet, 1993
1-6..3.00

Berzerkers
Image, 1995
1-3..3.00

Best Cellars
Out of the Cellar

This showcase issue from Out of the Cellar Comics has Monster Boy, Krystal Kalisto and the Committed as its featured characters is intended for mature readers only.

Half man, half ogre and full of malice, Mog AKA Monster Boy is not a happy camper. He's been arrested and convicted in a kangaroo court. His punishment? To be banished to Earth, where he has been ordered to destroy renegade monster terrorists.

Krystal Kalisto steps into action when the women of Dalworth City are threatened. Her vengeance is driven by an intense dislike of men.

Perhaps the strangest story of all is the Committed. John Wright believes that he has been wrongly imprisoned. He assembles a rag-tag group whose only goal is escaping. There is one small problem though--John Wright is an inmate at a mental hospital!

1 .... 3.00

Best from Boys' Life Comics
Gilberton, 1957
1 .... 60.00
2 .... 40.00
3 .... 35.00
4 .... 40.00
5-6 .... 35.00

Best of Barron Storey's W.A.T.C.H. Magazine
Vanguard, 1993
1 .... 3.00

Best of Dark Horse Presents
Dark Horse, 1989
1 .... 6.00
2-3 .... 9.00

Best of DC
DC, 1979
1 .... 5.00
2-70 .... 4.00

Best of Dennis the Menace
Hallden Publications, 1959
1 .... 100.00
2-5 .... 65.00

Best of Donald Duck and Uncle Scrooge
Gold Key, 1964
1-2 .... 50.00

Best of Dork Tower
Dork Storm, 2001
1 .... 2.00

Best of Furrlough
Antarctic, 1995
1-2 .... 4.00

Best of Gold Digger
Antarctic, 1999
Ann 1 .... 3.00

Best of Horror and Science Fiction
Webster

E.C. Comics may have received much of the negative publicity during the anti-comic-book backlash of the ë50s, but E.C. had numerous imitators and not all of them were awash in sex and violence. The Best of Horror and Science Fiction Comics compiles some of the more notable tales from E.C.'s competition. Included are early work by legendary artists such as Basil Wolverton, Steve Ditko, Bob Powell, and Frank Frazetta. As with E.C.'s books the stories have "shock" endings. The tales are not as gory as one would expect from the time period but the third panel of "Mother's Advice," featuring a close-up of a woman's cleavage with the text "...with plenty to offer," probably wouldn't have passed the Comics Code decades later, even after it became less strict.

1 .... 2.00

Best of Marvel Comics
Marvel, 1987

1 .... 20.00

Best of Northstar
Northstar, 1992

1 .... 2.00

Best of the Brave and the Bold
DC, 1988

1-6 .... 3.00

Best of the British Invasion
Revolutionary, 1993

1-2 .... 3.00

Best of the West
Magazine Enterprises, 1951

1 .... 265.00
2 .... 125.00
3-5 .... 110.00
6-12 .... 85.00

Best of the West
AC, 2005

1 .... 7.00
2-3 .... 5.00
4-32 .... 6.00
33-69 .... 7.00

Best of Tribune Co.
Dragon Lady, 1985

1-4 .... 3.00

Best of 2000 A.D.
Fleetway-Quality, 1985

1 .... 5.00
2-5 .... 4.00
6-20 .... 3.00
21-119 .... 2.00
Special 1-2 .... 4.00

Best of Uncle Scrooge & Donald Duck
Gold Key, 1968

1 .... 45.00

Best of Walt Disney Comics
Western, 1974

1 .... 15.00
2-4 .... 12.00

Best Romance
Standard, 1952

5-7 .... 50.00

Beta Sexus
Fantagraphics, 1994

1-2 .... 3.00

Betta: Time Warrior
Immortal

1-3 .... 3.00

Betti Cozmo
Antarctic, 1999

1-2 .... 3.00

Bettie Page Comics
Dark Horse, 1996

1 .... 4.00

Bettie Page Comics: Spicy Adventure
Dark Horse, 1997

1 .... 3.00

Bettie Page: Queen of the Nile
Dark Horse, 1999

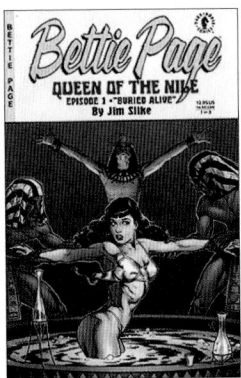

There's nothing wrong with a little bit of silly cheesecake. This latest tribute to a woman who is arguably the most beloved and rendered pinup girl in history is just that.

Bettie finds herself abducted from New York City and taken to a planet in the far future, where she is more valuable than gold. Here, a crazy computer has created a world based on the pulp adventures of the 1920s and 1930s, with Bettie its principal goddess: the sort of goddess tribes tie up and sell to the highest bidder.

There are white slavers, Egyptian priests, a randy mummy, and many more annoyances Bettie handles, all the while posing in her underwear and tossing off saucy comments. All she really wants to do is get back home, where a modeling contract awaits.

This limited series was created by Jim Silke and has the bonus of some cover art from Dave Stevens, creator of The Rocketeer.

1-3 .... 3.00

Betty
Archie, 1992

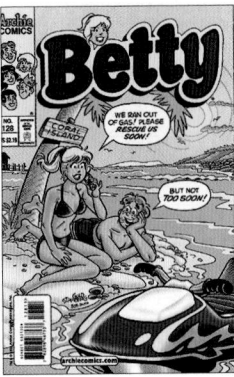

The blonde, all-American girl Betty Cooper got the jump on rival Veronica Lodge, appearing with Archie right from the beginning, in Pep #22 (Dec 41). When Archie Comics relaunched its comic lines almost 50 years later, it was Veronica who went first, getting her solo series in 1989. This new Betty title didn't start until 1992.

Although Veronica Lodge may be the richest girl in town, Betty Cooper uses her down-home good looks to her advantage when competing for the affection of Archie Andrews. Betty tends to be straightforward and good-natured, leaving her the victor more often than not, when Veronica's own schemes to attract Archie's attention backfire. However, when the notoriously undecided Archie finally was forced to choose in the well-publicized "Love Showdown," the winner was the little-known Cheryl Blossom. As could be expected, Betty and Veronica were not long in returning to the picture.

1 .... 4.00
2-161 .... 2.00
162-178 .... 3.00

Betty & Me
Archie, 1965

1 .... 65.00
2 .... 40.00
3-5 .... 24.00
6-10 .... 15.00
11-20 .... 10.00
21-30 .... 7.00
31-40 .... 6.00
41-50 .... 5.00
51-60 .... 4.00
61-70 .... 3.00
71-200 .... 2.00

Betty and Veronica
Archie, 1987
1 ....6.00
2-3 ....4.00
4-20 ....3.00
21-223 ....2.00

Betty & Veronica
Annual Digest Magazine
Archie, 1995
12-16 ....2.00

Betty and Veronica
Comics Digest
Archie, 1982
1 ....9.00
2-3 ....5.00
4-10 ....4.00
11-43 ....3.00

Betty and Veronica
Digest Magazine
Archie, 1990
44-50 ....3.00
51-192 ....2.00

Betty and Veronica
Double Digest
Archie, 1987
1 ....8.00
2-3 ....5.00
4-10 ....4.00
11-108 ....3.00
109-168 ....4.00

Betty and Veronica
Spectacular
Archie, 1992
1 ....4.00
2-5 ....3.00
6-87 ....2.00

Betty & Veronica
Summer Fun
Archie, 1994
1-4 ....3.00
5-6 ....2.00

Betty Boop 3-D
Blackthorne, 1986
1 ....3.00

Betty Boop's Big Break
First, 1990
1 ....6.00

Betty in Bondage:
Betty Mae
Shunga
1 ....7.00

Betty in Bondage
Shunga, 1994
1-8 .... 3.00
Ann 1-3 .... 6.00

Betty Page 3-D Comics
3-D Zone
1 .... 4.00

Betty Page
3-D Picture Book
3-D Zone
1 .... 4.00

Betty Page
Captured Jungle Girl 3-D
3-D Zone, 1990
1 .... 4.00

Betty Pages
Pure Imagination, 1989
1 .... 6.00
1/2nd-9 .... 5.00

Betty Page:
The 50's Rage
Illustration, 1993
1/A-2/B 3.00

Betty's Diary
Archie, 1986
1 .... 4.00
2-5 .... 3.00
6-40 .... 2.00

Betty's Digest Magazine
Archie, 1996
1-2 .... 2.00

Between the Sheets
Tokyopop, 2003
1 .... 10.00

Beverly Hillbillies
Dell, 1963
1 .... 60.00
2 .... 38.00
3 .... 28.00
4-5 .... 24.00
6-10 .... 18.00
11-17 .... 15.00
18-21 .... 12.00

Beware
Youthful, 1952
10 .... 180.00
11-12 .... 90.00

Beware
Trojan, 1953
13 (1) 400.00
14 (2) 250.00
15 (3)-16 (4) 200.00
5-13 .... 175.00
14-15 .... 150.00

Beware
Marvel, 1973
1 .... 8.00
2-8 .... 5.00

Beware Terror Tales
Fawcett, 1952
1 .... 350.00
2 .... 220.00
3-7 .... 165.00
8 .... 175.00

Beware the Creeper
DC, 1968
1 .... 45.00
2-5 .... 32.00
6 .... 55.00

Beware the Creeper
DC, 2003
1-5 .... 3.00

Bewitched
Dell, 1965
1 .... 85.00
2 .... 50.00
3-10 .... 40.00
11-14 .... 30.00

Beyblade
Viz, 2004
1-10 .... 8.00

Beyond (Ace)
Ace, 1950
1 .... 265.00
2 .... 175.00
3 .... 120.00
4-10 .... 110.00
11-20 .... 85.00
21-30 .... 80.00

Beyond!
Marvel, 2006
1-6 .... 3.00

Beyond
Blue, 1996
1 .... 3.00

Beyond Avalon
Image, 2005
1 .... 3.00
2-3 .... 4.00

Beyond Communion
Caliber
1 .... 3.00

Beyond Mars
Blackthorne, 1989
1-5 .... 2.00

Beyond the Grave
Charlton, 1975

Ghosts, witches, and demons dominate the pages of this series. Its stories are quite charming and usually ironic. For instance, a coven of witches and warlocks finds out that there is more to their sacrificial victim than they bargained for. A sickly old man finds the ideal place to die, and an overly curious writer discovers that a creepy castle is not abandoned after all. Though many of the tales may seem clichTd, the stories are always entertaining, classic, and in a horrifying sort of way, wholesome.

1	7.00
2-3	4.00
4-17	3.00

Bicentennial Gross-Outs
Yentzer and Gonif, 1976

1	3.00

Biff Bang Pow!
Paisano, 1992

1-2	3.00

Big
Dark Horse, 1989

1	3.00

Big All-American Comic Book
DC, 1944

1	6,500.00

Big Ass Comics
Rip Off, 1969

1	50.00
1/2nd	24.00
1/3rd-1/4th	10.00
1/5th-1/6th	6.00
2	25.00
2/2nd	15.00

Big Bad Blood of Dracula
Apple

1-2	3.00

Big Bang Comics: Round Table of America
Image, 2004

1	4.00

Big Bang Comics
Caliber, 1994

0	4.00
1-4	3.00

Big Bang Comics
Image, 1996

1-22	3.00
23	4.00
24-26	3.00
27-35	4.00

Big Bang Presents: Ultiman Family
Image, 2005

1	4.00

Big Bang
Zoo Arsonist

1	3.00

Big Bang Summer Special
Image, 2003

1	5.00

Big Black Kiss
Vortex, 1989

1-3	4.00

Big Black Thing
Upton

1	3.00

Big Blown Baby
Dark Horse, 1996

1-4	3.00

Big Blue Couch Comix
Couch

1	2.00

Big Boob Bondage
Antarctic, 1997

1	3.00

Big Bruisers
Image, 1996

1	4.00

Big Chief Wahoo
Eastern Color, 1942

This series stemmed from one of the most-metamorphosed newspaper strips in the field. It began in 1936 with The Great Gusto by Elmer Woggon. The medicine-show windbag had Big Chief Wahoo as a sidekick - and Wahoo took over the strip and its title, by now written by Allen Saunders. While seemingly packed with stereotypes, the strip's title character is far from typical: He's rich and kind, and the usual plot consists of crooks who think they can put one over on him. Other characters include Wahoo's sweetheart Minnie Ha Cha (who, by the way, has entertained in night clubs). Of note is the fact that a character introduced to the strip's continuity in 1940 was Steve Roper, who took over the strip from Wahoo in the late 1940s - only to be replaced in turn by Mike Nomad. This Wahoo-focused comic-book series ran seven issues from 1942 until 1944 and featured gag continuity.

1	230.00
2	125.00
3-5	95.00
6-7	65.00

Big Crap Scare
Fireman

1	3.00

Big Daddy Danger
DC, 2002

1-9	3.00

Big Dog Funnies
Rip Off, 1992

1	3.00

Big Edsel Band
Ace

1	2.00

Bigfoot
Idea & Design Works, 2005
1-4..4.00

Big Funnies
Radio, 2001
1-8..4.00

Bigger
Free Lunch, 1998
1 ....4.00

Bigger: Will Rison & the Devil's Concubine
Free Lunch, 1998
1-4..3.00

Bigg Time
DC
1 ....15.00

Big Guy and Rusty the Boy Robot
Dark Horse, 1995
☞Miller, Darrow series
1-2..10.00

Big Hair Productions
Image, 2000
1-2..4.00

Big Lou
Side Show
1 ....3.00

Big Monster Fight
Kidgang Comics
0-1..3.00

Big Mouth
Starhead, 1996
1-7..3.00

Big Numbers
Mad Love, 1990

Talented artist Bill Sienkiewicz and ace writer Alan Moore teamed up in 1990 to produce Big Numbers, meant as a twelve issue tour-de-force. Unfortunately, the project fell apart and only two issues were ever published before the series went on indefinite hiatus.

Although it's difficult to tell where the series was meant to end up, it begins with a homecoming. Author Christine Gathercole had left Hampton when she had gotten pregnant, but a little operation took care of that problem. Later, she had found success as a writer in London, but peace continued to elude her. But if peace was what she searched for upon returning home to Hampton, it was going to be an uphill struggle. Hampton was a city in decay where cutbacks were forcing the psych wards to release inmates, and the ghosts of the past were everywhere. And now, Hampton had been chosen as the site for a huge and bizarre development project.

1-2.. 6.00

Big 0 Part 1
Viz, 2002
1-5.. 4.00

Big 0 Part 2
Viz, 2002
1-4.. 4.00

Big 0 Part 3
Viz, 2002
1-4.. 4.00

Big 0 Part 4
Viz, 2003
1-4.. 4.00

Big Prize
Eternity, 1985
1-2.. 2.00

Big Questions
Drawn & Quarterly, 2005
7 .... 5.00

Big Shot
Columbia, 1940

Started in 1940, Big Shot Comics was a wide-ranging

compendium of humor and adventure strips, many in reprint form.

Newspaper-strip reprints of such features as J.P. McEvoy and John H. Strieble's Dixie Dugan, Ham Fisher's Joe Palooka, Lank Leonard's Mickey Finn, and Harry Tuthill's The Bungle Family appeared alongside such characters as Ogden Whitney's heroic Skyman, Captain Devildog of the U.S. Marines, Boody Rogers' Sparky Watts, and the startling character The Face (aka Tony Trent). A solid middle player in the comics scene, Big Shot ran until 1949.

1	1,000.00
2	475.00
3	385.00
4-5	335.00
6-10	275.00
11-13	225.00
14	300.00
15	340.00
16-20	160.00
21-27	135.00
28	185.00
29-30	135.00
31-40	110.00
41-49	95.00
50-60	85.00
61-70	65.00
71-80	55.00
81-104	48.00

Big 3
Fox, 1940
1	1,400.00
2	650.00
3-5	450.00
6-7	375.00

Big Time
Delta, 1996
1-3 .... 2.00

Big Top
Toby, 1951
1	50.00
2	36.00

Big Top Bondage
Fantagraphics
1 .... 3.00

Big Town
DC, 1951
1	500.00
2	250.00
3	185.00
4-5	140.00
6-10	110.00
11-20	75.00
21-30	65.00
31-50	50.00

Big Town
Marvel, 2001

1-4..4.00

Big Valley
Dell, 1966

1..40.00
2-6..25.00

Bijou Funnies
Kitchen Sink, 1968

The anthology series Bijou offers many of the most notable examples of talent and stories that the underground comix genre has to offer, and full-color #8 featured its creators providing spoofs of the comix genre. Among the creators whose work appears in Bijou are Roger Brand, Robert Crumb, Justin Green, Kim Deitch, (Editor) Jay Lynch, Jim Osborne, Gilbert Shelton, Art Spiegelman, and Skip Williamson. Each issue running from the late 1960s to the mid-1970s had more than one printing, and the press runs on those printings could be as high as 10,000 -- or more. Such characters as Nard n' Pat were featured.

1..85.00
1/2nd-2....................................30.00
3..25.00
3/2nd.......................................15.00
3/3rd.......................................10.00
4..25.00
5..20.00
6-8..18.00
8/2nd..4.00

Biker Mice from Mars
Marvel, 1993

1-3..2.00

Bikini Assassin Team
Catfish

1..3.00

Bikini Battle 3-D
3-D Zone

1..4.00

Bill & Ted's Bogus Journey
Marvel, 1991

1..3.00

Bill & Ted's Excellent Adventure Movie Adaptation
DC

1..2.00

Bill & Ted's Excellent Comic Book
Marvel, 1991

1-12..2.00

Bill Barnes Comics
Street & Smith, 1940

1..525.00
2..275.00
3-5..200.00
6-12...175.00

Bill Battle, The One-Man Army
Fawcett, 1952

1-4..80.00

Bill Boyd Western
Fawcett, 1950

1..250.00
2-6..200.00
7-23...100.00

Bill, the Galactic Hero
Topps, 1994

1-3..5.00

Billi 99
Dark Horse

The rich minority gets richer, while the poor majority sinks further into despair. It is an old story, one that too closely resembles that of our time. But the masses have always held onto belief in a champion, someone who will fight for those that can't:

Robin Hood, Zorro, and in bleak, dismal Sulter City-the Toleado.

Born into a wealthy 'risto family, young Billi has abandoned her family and lifestyle. Her father also chose the plight of the lower classes over his own comfort, fighting back in the guise of the Toleado. But Billi's father lost his life in his crusade. As Billi searches for her father's killers, the conflicts between the 'risto families increases, gang violence continues to grow, and a new killer stalks the impoverished streets. Billi realizes that although her father is dead, the Toleado must live again!

1-4..4.00

Bill the Bull: Burnt Cain
Boneyard, 1992

1-3..5.00

Bill the Bull: One Shot, One Bourbon, One Beer
Boneyard, 1994

1-2..3.00

Bill the Clown
Slave Labor, 1992

1-1/2nd.......................................3.00

Bill the Clown: Comedy Isn't Pretty
Slave Labor, 1992

1..3.00

Bill the Clown: Death & Clown White
Slave Labor, 1993

1..3.00

Billy Boy The Sick Little Fat Kid
Asylum, 2001

1..3.00

Billy Buckskin
Atlas, 1955

1..85.00
2..55.00
3..60.00

Billy Cole
Cult, 1994

Billy Cole is an infant with an attitude, a baby with the strength of an adult. Wasting no time, Cole crawls out of his mother's womb, tears off the umbilical cord, and fights crime. "I'll be right back, mom. I've got to stop evil from destroying the world," he vows in the first issue as he ventures into the city to fight brain-eating zombies. Ted Seko writes an allegorical tale wherein evil is pumped into the air like pollution and workers are living zombies.

1-4..3.00

Billy Dogma
Modern, 1997
1-3..3.00

Billy Joe Van Helsing: Redneck Vampire Hunter
Alpha
1...3.00

Billy Nguyen, Private Eye
Attitude, 1988
1-3..2.00

Billy Nguyen, Private Eye
Caliber
1...3.00

Billy Ray Cyrus
Marvel Music
1...6.00

Billy the Kid
Charlton, 1957

A villain in real life, this legendary figure of the old West gets a facelift in this Charlton series. William Bonney, aka Billy the Kid, was actually a hot-tempered gunslinger who once was said to have killed a man for snoring too loudly. In this title, however, he becomes a dashing and heroic figure, helping homesteaders defend their land from greedy cattle ranchers and forcing con men and gamblers to hightail it out of town. And in a final contrast to reality, any money that falls into The Kid's hands is usually turned over to the less fortunate or the local church.

9 .... 58.00
10 .... 35.00
11 .... 40.00
12 .... 30.00
13 .... 40.00
14 .... 30.00
15-16 .... 40.00
17-19 .... 30.00
20-22 .... 35.00
23 .... 20.00
24-26 .... 35.00
27-30 .... 20.00
31-40 .... 14.00
41-50 .... 8.00
51-60 .... 7.00
61-70 .... 5.00
71-100 .... 4.00
101-153 .... 3.00

Billy the Kid Adventure Magazine
Toby, 1950
1 .... 175.00
2 .... 80.00
3-10 .... 75.00
11-20 .... 48.00
21-30 .... 36.00

Billy the Kid and Oscar
Fawcett, 1945
1 .... 75.00
2-3 .... 55.00

Billy the Kid's Old-Timey Oddities
Dark Horse, 2005
1-4 .... 3.00

Billy West
Standard, 1949
1 .... 60.00
2 .... 40.00
3-6 .... 28.00
7-8 .... 30.00
9 .... 28.00

B1N4RY
APComics, 2004
0-2 .... 4.00
3 .... 5.00
3/Sketch 6.00
4 .... 4.00

Binky
DC, 1970

Binky is a lovable, but unlucky teen-ager whose efforts to impress girls, act chivalrous, or lend a helping hand almost always end in disaster. Binky is joined in his misadventures by his girlfriend, Peggy, and a collection of their teen pals.

This series bears an uncanny resemblance to the Archie comics. Note that the title is a continuation of Leave It to Binky, and by this time in the series, Binky is making an obvious, and often clumsy, effort to be "hip." In Binky, the "chicks" are really "groovy," and the "cats" are "terrif!" The gags are often based on this generational lingo: "Someone stole my old bag!" - "You mean someone stole your mother?!" - "No, my purse!" However the funniest aspect of the series comes when DC's editors try to use the same "with it"

language to explain how they need to "rap" with their fans about needing to raise the price of their comics, etc.

72-75	7.00
76-81	6.00
82	3.00

Binky's Buddies
DC, 1969

1	26.00
2	16.00
3	12.00
4-12	10.00

Bio 90
Bullet, 1992

A sort of modern vampire retelling, Bio 90 owes much to the strong storytelling of writer/creator Peter Koch. While the story of biological experimentation gone awry is not new, the energy invested in this story is. When professor Lorus Prine and Guillermo Garcia discover a cure for AIDS, their lives seem destined for greatness. But professor Prine's dreams edge into madness and after injecting himself, he injects Garcia. What follows is a race to find a cure for the dangerous and uncharted side effects while also racing to contain the destructive urges of Prine.

With art assists from Trevor Von Eeden (Green Arrow, Batman) and Mark Beachum (Vampirella, Spiderman), Bio 90 is cleverly written and smartly drawn with an eye for shadows and an ear for realism.

1	3.00

Bio-Booster Armor Guyver
Viz, 1993

1-5	4.00
6-12	3.00

Bio-Booster Armor Guyver Part 2
Viz, 1994

1-6	3.00

Bio-Booster Armor Guyver Part 3
Viz, 1995

1-7	3.00

Bio-Booster Armor Guyver Part 4
Viz, 1995

1-6	3.00

Bio-Booster Armor Guyver Part 5
Viz, 1996

1-7	3.00

Bio-Booster Armor Guyver Part 6
Viz, 1996

1-6	3.00

Biologic Show
Fantagraphics, 1994

0-1	3.00

Bioneers
Mirage, 1994

Team Dragonfighters is a training cadre flying state of the art "Hornet" fighters. The real story lies in their affiliation with the top-secret "Bioneers" project. That project, led by the genetically mutated telepath Cypher Cray and bionics genius Dr. Janus Kowalski, is involved with expanding the boundaries of both biology and robotics.

So far, the project had two major creations. The first is the Bioneers themselves, a pair of genetic hybrids crossing human genes with those of a lion and amphibian (a.k.a. Garth Felis and Carmilla O'Reilly). The second is a group of "Protozoid" cyborgs named "Fearless," "Firebrand,"

"Forward Alert Recon," and "Fumigator" (they answer to "Fe," "Fi," "Fo," and "Fum" respectively). These were giant cyborgs designed to carry out lifesaving missions. These were joined by a fifth member when Jean "Bandit" Flint, a Dragonfighter pilot, was transferred into one to save her life after a terrible crash.

1-3	3.00

Bionic Dog
Hugo Rex

1	3.00

Bionicle
DC, 2001

1-9	2.00

Bionic Woman
Charlton, 1977

1	14.00
2-5	6.00

Bionix
Maximum, 1996

1	3.00

Bird
Entertainment, 1987

1	2.00

Birdland
Fantagraphics, 1990

1-3	2.00

Birdland (Vol. 2)
Fantagraphics, 1994

1	3.00

Birds of Prey
DC, 1999

Following a series of Birds of Prey mini-series and one-shots, writer Chuck Dixon and artists Greg Land and Drew Geraci put the duo of Oracle and Black Canary into their own ongoing series.

Oracle is Barbara Gordon, the former Batgirl, now a wheelchair-bound paraplegic computer whiz who provides information to many heroes in the DC universe. Black Canary is an independent woman who works with Oracle to put the kibosh to various nefarious schemes around the globe. Using her natural beauty and crimefighting skills, The Canary is aided in her missions by Oracle who communicates via a pair of earrings and a necklace.

While the two may have their differences from time to time, they do make an effective team.

-- Brent

1	4.00
2-7	3.00
8	12.00

☛Nightwing app.

9-75	3.00
76	15.00

☛1st Black Alice

77-99	3.00
100	4.00
101	3.00

Birds of Prey: Batgirl
DC, 1998

1	3.00

Birds of Prey: Catwoman
DC, 2003

1-2	6.00

Birds of Prey: Manhunt
DC, 1996

1-4	2.00

Birds of Prey: Revolution
DC, 1997

Barbara Gordon (Batgirl before her tragic shooting by The Joker in Batman: The Killing Joke left her a paraplegic) is now known as Oracle, and is tapped into vast amounts of information thanks to her consummate skill with computers. Dinah Lance, a.k.a. vigilante crimefighter Black

Canary, best known for her fishnets (now sadly missing) and former paramour of Green Arrow, is the "leg man." Together they are Birds of Prey.

In this mini-series, Black Canary travels to the Caribbean island of Santa Prisca (where Batman-nemesis Bane was spawned) to break up a slavery ring that operates from that corrupt, isolated dictatorship. Along the way Black Canary impetuously involves herself in a number of harrowing situations which serve to reveal some of her best attributes, while Oracle is left to worry and wonder through the communication satellite uplink.

-- George Haberberger

1	3.00

Birds of Prey: Secret Files 2003
DC, 2003

1	5.00

Birds of Prey: The Ravens
DC, 1998

1	2.00

Birds of Prey: Wolves
DC, 1997

1	3.00

Birth Caul
Eddie Campbell, 1999

1	6.00

Birthday Boy
Beetlebomb

1-4	3.00

Birthday Boy
Beetlebomb

1	3.00

Birthday Riots
NBM

1	15.00

Birthright
Fantagraphics, 1990

1-3	3.00

Birthright
TSR

1	2.00

Birth Rite
Congress

The street war began as a lark, really. A couple of skinhead punks saw a homeless bum in an alley and decided to have some fun before they went 'round and got themselves a beer. So the big one, a sadistic fellow named Brick, decided to kill the bum. No big deal. After all, life was cheap in Any City, year 2038.

Only the bum wasn't really a bum. He was an undercover cop. His murder set off a chain of events that had a police department in the hands of the mob thinking that their competition was doing battle. So they decided to launch a few strikes of their own...

Birth Rite is a striking, if somewhat abstract piece of work by Patrick Farncombe and Scott Blatchley of London's Congress Press. Farncombe's work in black-and-white mixed media is here reminiscent of Bill Sienkiewicz (Stray Toasters), giving this series a tense, off-kilter feel.

1-4	3.00

Bishop
Marvel, 1994

1	4.00
2-4	3.00

Bishop The Last X-Man
Marvel, 1999

Bishop, the time-traveling mutant from the future, finds himself troubled by dreams from his the world he left behind. He sets out from the safety of the Xavier Institute to pursue his destiny and take care of unfinished business -- and promptly finds himself in a Road Warrior type future world in pursuit of his mortal foe, the energy vampire Fitzroy.

Bishop is a solid stand-alone series from writer Joseph Harris, penciller Georges Jeanty, and inker Art Thibert. It appears designed for readers unfamiliar with the twists and turns of X-universe continuity and simply in search of an intelligent, well-drawn contemporary science-fiction series with a strong lead character.

1	3.00
2-11	2.00
12	3.00
13-16	2.00

Bishop: Xse
Marvel, 1998

1-3	3.00

Bisley's Scrapbook
Atomeka

1	3.00

Bitch in Heat
Fantagraphics, 1997

1-14	3.00

Bite Club
DC, 2004

1	3.00
2	4.00
3-6	3.00

Bite Club:
Vampire Crime Unit
DC, 2006

1-5	3.00

Bits and Pieces
Mortified, 1994

1	3.00

Bitter Cake
Tin Cup

1	2.00

Bizarre 3-D Zone
Blackthorne, 1986

1-5	2.00

Bizarre Adventures
Marvel, 1981

Bizarre Adventures (formerly Marvel Preview) was one of Marvel's more adventurous magazine undertakings. It let Marvel present some of its more offbeat characters in a different, more adult context than comics usually allow. Included were such new stars as The Unlikely Heroes & Hangman, as well as new takes on old favorites such as King Kull and The Uncanny X-Men.

To read a story featuring a familiar character in Bizarre Adventures was like meeting that character for the first time again. Bizarre Adventures used its black-and-white magazine format to the fullest, concentrating on stark imagery and detailed storytelling- and it never shied away from the offbeat. Its final issue, #34, bade farewell in style, featuring a holiday send-up, "Son of Santa," and a Howard the Duck feature by Paul Smith.

25-26	3.00
27	4.00
28	5.00
29-34	3.00

Bizarre Fantasy
Flashback, 1995

0	3.00
1-2	3.00

Bizarre Heroes
Kitchen Sink, 1990

1	3.00

Bizarre Heroes
Fiasco, 1994

0-17	3.00

Bizarre Sex
Kitchen Sink, 1972

1	15.00
2	9.00
3	7.00
4	5.00
4/2nd-4/3rd	4.00
5-8	5.00
9	18.00

Bizzarian
Ironcat, 2000

1-8	3.00

B. Krigstein Sampler, A
Independent

1	3.00

Blab!
Kitchen Sink, 1995

8	17.00
9	19.00
10-16	20.00

Black & White
Image, 1994

1-3	2.00

Black & White
Image, 1996

1	3.00
Ashcan 1	1.00

Black & White
Viz, 1999

1-3	3.00

Black and White Bondage
Verotik

1	5.00

Black and White Comics
Apex Novelties

Robert Crumb has shocked, entertained, titillated, and challenged the imaginations of comic book fans the world over. His voluptuous, acid-inspired romps of the1960s gave way to comparatively sober, introspective dialogues and biting indictments of American culture. As is typical of Crumb, this title is unflinchingly honest, regardless of how unsympathetic he or anyone else appears. Very few artists would risk depicting--ëan urge to return to the womb' as Crumb does in one story. Nonetheless Crumb's stories are effective satire as his message is delivered throughout the body of the narrative in a perfectly unabashed, undisguised and undaunted manner. All of this gooey and unpleasant stuff is deeply embedded in our culture and our collective subconscious. It simmers under pressure and the next moment it erupts like a geyser. Hallucinogenic drugs are not required for reading.

1 ....4.00

Black and White Theater
Double M, 1996
1-2..3.00

Black Angel
Verotik, 1996
1 ....10.00

Black Axe
Marvel, 1993
1-7..2.00

Blackball Comics
Blackball, 1994
1 ....3.00

Black Book
Eclipse, 1985
1 .... 2.00

Black Bow
Artline
1 .... 3.00

Blackburne Covenant
Dark Horse, 2003
1-4.. 3.00

Black Canary
DC, 1991
1-4... 3.00

Black Canary
DC, 1993

Known to readers of the Green Arrow series as the Arrow's love interest, Black Canary gets a chance to strike out on her own in this new series.

The Canary's sole super-power was her sonic scream (a la the Uncanny X-Men's Banshee), a power she lost for good in Green Arrow: The Longbow Hunters. Luckily, she learned early on never to rely upon her super-power as her only weapon, and she trains hard to become an accomplished martial artist. She uses these talents to fight crime on an up-close and personal level.

The Black Canary has garnered praise for its portrayal of a strong female character, and she went on to more adventures in later stories.

1-12...................................... 2.00

Black Canary/Oracle: Birds of Prey
DC, 1996
1 .... 4.00

Black Cat Comics
Harvey, 1946

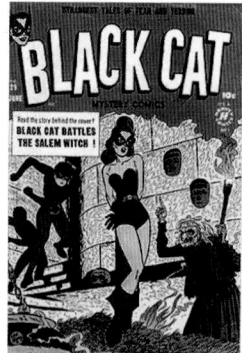

Imagine it's the late 1940s. Imagine Elizabeth Taylor is not only one of the most gorgeous young women in Hollywood, but in her spare time she dons a disguise (complete with fishnet stockings) and careens around town on her motorcycle, fighting crime. That's pretty much the premise of Black Cat Comics. The Black Cat is gorgeous movie star Linda Turner: not only a popular actress but a woman trained in the martial arts.

She had starred in short comics stories in Speed Comics but finally got her own title. Artist Lee Elias drew her with verve, including illustrations for several how-to judo features.

-- Maggie

1	450.00
2	275.00
3-5	220.00
6-8	175.00
9	225.00
10-20	135.00
21-29	100.00
30	150.00
31	130.00
32-42	125.00
43	75.00
44-50	125.00
51	165.00
52-62	54.00
63	80.00
64-65	75.00

Black Cat
Lorne-Harvey
1 .... 4.00

Black Cat The War Years
Recollections
1 .... 1.00

Black Cauldron
Scholastic
1 .... 4.00

Black Cobra
Ajax, 1954

1	185.00
2	120.00
3	100.00

Black Condor
DC, 1992

1	2.00
2-12	1.00

Black Cross: Dirty Work
Dark Horse, 1997

1	3.00

Black Cross Special
Dark Horse, 1988

1	3.00
1/2nd	2.00

Black Diamond
AC, 1983

1-5	2.00

Black Diamond Effect
Black Diamond Effect, 1991

1-7	3.00

Black Diamond Western
Lev Gleason, 1949

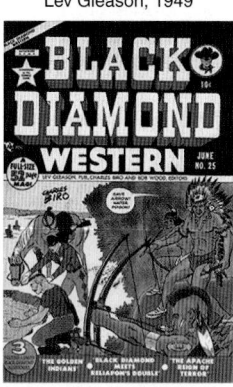

In the mold of The Lone Ranger or Zorro, The Black Diamond is a masked Western character. Clad in a red shirt, black hat, and mask which wraps around his head like Zorro's, Black Diamond roams the West securing justice for settlers and thwarting the schemes of outlaws. But, unlike the vigilante Lone Ranger, Black Diamond has legal standing as a badge-carrying Federal marshal. His territory is uncommonly vast, as he is involved locales as widespread as Montana and Arizona.

In place of Tonto, The Black Diamond's companion is a man named Bumper, whose handlebar mustache gives him the appearance of boxer John L. Sullivan. His tan Palomino, Reliapon, is a magnificent horse in keeping with the tradition of The Lone Ranger's Silver, Roy Roger's Trigger, and Hopalong Cassidy's Topper.

-- George Haberberger

9	100.00
10	70.00
11-12	58.00
13-15	45.00
16-28	50.00
29-50	30.00
51-52	65.00
53-60	24.00

Black Dragon
Marvel, 1985

1-4	3.00
5-6	2.00

Black Flag
Image, 1994

1	2.00

Black Flag
Maximum, 1995

0-4/B	3.00

Black Forest
Image, 2003

1	10.00

Black Fury
Charlton, 1955

1	36.00
2	18.00
3	14.00
4-5	10.00
6-15	9.00
16-18	30.00
19-30	6.00
31-57	5.00

Black Goliath
Marvel, 1976

Long before Icon, Hardware, or Shadowman, this 15-foot-tall black super-hero was thwarting criminals-white, brown, and black, as well as extraterrestrial-in his own series. It began when Bill Foster helped Avenger Henry Pym, the original Goliath, fight the side-effects of his super-powers. In doing so, Foster learned and perfected the ability to grow 15feet in an instant.

But being a super-hero wasn't all it was cracked up to be, as Black Goliath discovered when he lost his girlfriend and realized that the public cared less about his true exploits than about gossip and rumor.

This series, which only had a five-issue run, may simply have been before its time.

1	11.00
2	5.00
2/30¢	20.00
3	4.00
3/30¢	20.00
4	4.00
4/30¢	20.00
5	4.00

Black Harvest
Devil's Due, 2005

1-6	3.00

Blackhawk
DC, 1944

9	2,600.00
10	1,100.00
11	900.00
12-15	800.00
16-20	525.00
21-25	460.00
26-30	400.00
31-35	350.00
36-40	300.00
41-49	225.00
50	200.00
51-60	165.00
61-70	145.00
71	200.00
☞Blackhawk origin	
72-80	130.00
81-86	125.00
87-92	120.00
93	135.00
94-99	110.00
100	140.00
101-107	105.00
108	325.00
☞1st DC issue	
109	130.00
110-117	110.00
118	135.00
119-130	85.00
131-140	65.00
141-149	50.00
150-163	48.00
164	60.00
165-166	48.00
167-180	22.00
181-200	16.00
201-227	15.00
228	30.00
229-243	15.00
244-260	4.00
261-273	3.00

Blackhawk
DC, 1988

1-3...4.00

Blackhawk
DC, 1989

1-6..2.00
7...3.00
8-16..2.00
Ann 1.......................................3.00
Special 1 ....4.00

Black Heart: Assassin
Iguana

Black Heart: Assassin is the second title from independent publisher Iguana Comics (the first being Heretics). Its star is the greatest warrior of the Kuryu Clan that once held great power on Mars. The Kuryu Clan were loyal servants of their emperor and became renowned both as warriors and assassins. However, when the Emperor no longer needed them to fight his wars for him, he betrayed them, fearing their increasing power.

The Emperor ordered his armies to attack their ancestral home with a force of warriors and dragons. The Kuryu were overwhelmed, but in a final act of defiance, the head of the clan passed the planet's greatest weapon, the Soul Blade to Black Heart. Black Heart would wield that blade to gain revenge for his fallen comrades, but at the same time, others would try to use him in their own schemes for power.

1 ....3.00

Black Heart Billy
Slave Labor, 2000

1-2..3.00

Black Hole
Kitchen Sink, 1995

1-5 .... 4.00
6-10 .... 5.00

Black Hole
Whitman, 1980

1-4 .... 2.00

Black Hood
M.L.J., 1943

9 .... 650.00
10 .... 375.00
11 .... 275.00
12-18 .... 240.00
19 .... 315.00

Black Hood
DC, 1991

1-12 .... 1.00
Ann 1 .... 2.00

Black Hood
Archie, 1983

1 .... 3.00
2-3 .... 2.00

Blackjack
Dark Angel, 1996

1-4 .... 3.00
Special 1 .... 4.00

Blackjack
Dark Angel, 1997

1-2... 3.00

Black Jack
Charlton, 1957

20 .... 40.00
21 .... 25.00
22-23 .... 35.00
24-26 .... 45.00
27 .... 25.00
28 .... 45.00
29-30 .... 25.00

Black Jack
Viz, 1999

Special 1 .... 3.00

Black Kiss
Vortex, 1988

1 .... 3.00
1/2nd-1/3rd............................. 2.00
2 .... 3.00
2/2nd-12 .... 2.00

Black Knight
Toby, 1953

1 .... 150.00

Black Knight
Atlas, 1955

1 .... 575.00
2 .... 375.00
3-5 .... 285.00

Black Knight
Marvel, 1990

1-4 .... 2.00

Black Knight: Exodus
Marvel, 1996

1 .... 3.00

Black Lamb
DC, 1996

1-6 .... 3.00

Blacklight
Image, 2005

1-2 .... 3.00

Black Lightning
DC, 1977

1 .... 10.00
2-11 .... 5.00

Black Lightning
DC, 1995

1 .... 3.00
2-5 .... 2.00
6 .... 3.00
7-13 .... 2.00

Black Lion
The Bantu Warrior
Heroes from the Hood, 1997

1 .... 3.00

Black Magic
Prize, 1950

1 .... 640.00
2 .... 340.00
3 .... 250.00
4-6 .... 200.00

Black Magic
Prize, 1951

1 .... 165.00
2-12 .... 140.00

Black Magic
Prize, 1952

1-6 .... 125.00

Black Magic
Prize, 1953

1-2 .... 140.00
3 .... 300.00
4 .... 200.00
5 .... 160.00
6 .... 50.00

Black Magic
Prize, 1954

1 .... 50.00
2-3 .... 45.00

Black Magic
Prize, 1957

1-6 .... 36.00

Black Magic
Prize, 1958
1-6...32.00

Black Magic
Prize, 1961
1-5...30.00

Black Magic
DC, 1973
1..15.00
2-9..7.00

Black Magic
Eclipse, 1990
1..4.00
2-4..3.00

Blackmask
DC, 2000

Dan Cady had returned home from a long and exceedingly unpleasant stay in Korea. The North Koreans had taken him as a prisoner of war, and an overenthusiastic torturer had taken a "personal interest" in Dan. The torturer wore a black mask.

After far too long, the war finally ended and Dan went home to Iroquois Falls. But he didn't find peace there-instead, he found war of a different sort, with crime and corruption tearing apart the city. Only this time, Dan didn't have to just sit there and take it. He donned the mask of his former torturer and found it gave him power. Now, as Blackmask, he was ready to fight back.

1-3..5.00

Blackmask
Eastern, 1988
1-3..2.00

Black Mist
Caliber, 1994
1-4... 3.00

Black Mist:
Blood of Kali
Caliber, 1998
1-3... 3.00

Blackmoon
U.S.Comics, 1985
1-3... 2.00

Black Ops
Image, 1996
1-5/B....................................... 3.00

Black Orchid
DC, 1993

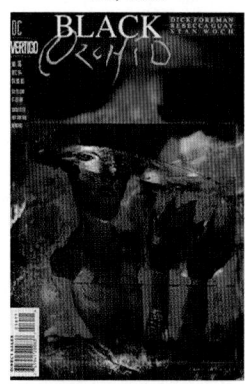

Once, Black Orchid was a super-hero. Of course, that was before the Black Orchid mini-series, when she died - and was reborn as something else. She is beyond human now, ethereal and celestial, though she masquerades as a woman when the mood suits her. As a model, an escort, or even as a campaign worker, she wields a strange power of enchantment. To look in her eyes is to lose yourself in them.

But wherever such a thing of beauty exists, men will seek to hunt it down and possess it. In her own way, Black Orchid inspires obsession - even murder.

1... 3.00
1/Platinum 5.00
2-22.. 2.00
Ann 1.................................... 4.00

Black Orchid
DC, 1988
1 .... 6.00
☛1st U.S. Gaiman
2-3... 5.00

Black Panther
Marvel, 1977

T'Challa is the son of T'Chaka, ruler of the African kingdom of Wakanda. Educated in the U.S., he is forced to return home when his father is killed by perennial Spider-Man villain Klaw. As the new ruler of Wakanda, T'Challa has to undergo a strange initiation rite which leads to his gaining great strength and agility - and taking on the role of Wakanda's protector, The Black Panther.

Black Panther had long been a member of The Avengers, but only in 1977 did he appear in a series of his own. This title pits the Panther against a variety of foes, both in his native Wakanda and abroad.

1 .... 12.00
2 .... 7.00
3-4 .... 5.00
4/35¢ 15.00
5 .... 5.00
5/35¢ 15.00
6-10 .... 5.00
11-15 .... 4.00

Black Panther
Marvel, 1998
1 .... 5.00
1/Variant................................. 7.00
2/A-2/B 4.00
3-62 .... 3.00

Black Panther
Marvel, 1988
1-4 .... 2.00

Black Panther
Marvel, 2005
1 .... 6.00
1/2nd 4.00
1/Ribic 20.00
2-17 .... 3.00
18 .... 4.00
19-20 .... 3.00
21 .... 14.00
22 .... 6.00
23-41 .... 5.00

Black Panther: Panther's Prey
Marvel, 1991
1-4 .... 5.00

Black Pearl
Dark Horse, 1996
1 .... 4.00
2-5 .... 3.00

Black Phantom
AC
1-3 .... 3.00

Black Phantom
Magazine Enterprises, 1954
1 .... 250.00

Black Raven
ArtEffect Entertainment, 1998
1 .... 3.00

Black Rider
Atlas, 1950
8 .... 260.00
9 .... 125.00
10 .... 155.00
11-14 .... 95.00
15-19 .... 80.00
20 .... 90.00
21-27 .... 75.00

Black Rider Rides Again!
Atlas, 1957
1 .... 70.00

Black Sabbath
Rock-It, 1994
1 .... 4.00

Black Scorpion
Special Studio
1-3 .... 3.00

Black September
Malibu, 1993
Infinity 2.00

Blackstar
Imperial, 1987
1-2 .... 2.00

Blackstone, the Magician Detective Fights Crime
EC, 1947
1 .... 440.00

Blackstone, Master Magician Comics
Vital, 1946
1 .... 250.00
2-3 .... 175.00

Black Sun
WildStorm, 2002
1-6 .... 3.00

Black Sun: X-Men
Marvel, 2000

To celebrate the 25th anniversary of the "all-new, all-different" X-Men, Marvel offers this five-issue limited series that features the return of the other-dimensional demon Belasco and Illyana Rasputin, mystic warrior and former member of The New Mutants. Belasco prepares to take over the world, and Marvel's merry mutants stand ready to stop him. Unfortunately, they're going to have to go through each other to get at him - not willingly, of course. That demon-possession'll get you every time. To make this anniversary event even more special, writer Chris Claremont (Fantastic Four) is joined by former X-writers Len Wein (The Incredible Hulk), Roy Thomas (The Avengers), and Louise Simonson (Power Pack).

1 .... 3.00
1/A 6.00
2-5 .... 3.00

Black Swan Comics
M.L.J., 1945
1 .... 450.00

Black Terror
Visual Editions, 1942
1 .... 1,850.00
2 .... 725.00
3 .... 500.00
4-5 .... 425.00
6-10 .... 365.00
11-20 .... 300.00
21 .... 315.00
22-27 .... 275.00

Black Terror
Eclipse, 1989
1 .... 5.00
2 .... 5.00
3 .... 5.00

Blackthorne's 3 in 1
Blackthorne, 1986
1-2 .... 2.00

Blackthorne's Harvey Flip Book
Blackthorne
1 .... 2.00

Black Tide
Image, 2001
1/A-4 .... 3.00

Black Tide
Avatar, 2003
1-10 .... 3.00

Black Web
Inks
1-2 .... 3.00

Black Widow
Marvel, 1999
1 .... 4.00
2-3 .... 3.00

Black Widow
Marvel, 2001
1-3 .... 3.00

Black Widow
Marvel, 2004
1-6 .... 3.00

Black Widow: Pale Little Spider
Marvel, 2002
1-3 .... 3.00

Black Widow: Things They Say About Her
Marvel, 2005
1-2 .... 3.00

Black Widow 2
Marvel, 2005
1-6 .... 3.00

Black Widow: Web of Intrigue
Marvel, 1999
1 .... 4.00

Blackwulf
Marvel, 1994
1 .... 3.00
2-10 .... 2.00

Black Zeppelin
Renegade, 1985
1-5 .... 2.00

Blade
Buccaneer, 1989
1-2 .... 2.00

Blade
Marvel, 1997
1 .... 2.00

Blade
Marvel, 1998
1 ....4.00

Blade
Marvel, 1998
1-4 ....3.00

Blade
Marvel, 1998
1-6 ....4.00

Blade
Marvel, 2006
1-4 ....3.00

Blade of Heaven
Tokyopop, 2005
1-8 ....10.00

Blade of Kumori
Devil's Due, 2005
1-5 ....3.00

Blade of Shuriken
Eternity, 1987
1-5 ....2.00

Blade of the Immortal
Dark Horse, 1996

Blade of the Immortal tells the story of Manji, a swordsman who was cursed with immortality by another immortal. His escape from immortality - his release from the curse - will be his, if he manages to kill 1,000 evil men. Hiroaki Samura's comic book, influenced by Osamu Tezuka's Dororo (1967 manga, eventual 1969 anime), was one of the best-selling manga in Japan in the 1990s and is faithfully reprinted for the American audience.

The series is fast-paced and well-written and is a fine example of the raw energy manga can transmit.

1 ....4.00
2-8 ....3.00
9-11 ....4.00
12-33 ....3.00
34 ....4.00

35 ....3.00
36-38 ....4.00
39-99 ....3.00
100 ....6.00
101-121 ....3.00

Blade Runner
Marvel, 1982
1 ....2.00
2 ....1.00

Blade: Sins of the Father
Marvel, 1998

Blade's mother was murdered during her son's birth by the vampire Deacon Frost, leaving our hero a human-vampire hybrid and a vampire hunter with the goal of eradicating the "leeches" (as he calls them) from the face of the earth. This Prestige Format one-shot deals with a vampire gang war that has its roots in the gangster-ridden Chicago of the 1920s: Cordelia Passolini, the daughter of a mob boss, was made a vampire by her father, and her first victim was her fiancè, Roberto Strati. As a result, Ms. Passolini despises vampires and, like Blade, wants to see them destroyed. She lets our hero know that something big is about to go down between two rival vampire gangs and vows to help him. But can she be trusted? Is there more to her story than meets the eye? Find out in this one-shot tie-in with the 1998 film "Blade."

1 ....6.00

Bladesmen
Blue Comet
0-2 ....2.00

Blade:
The Vampire-Hunter
Marvel, 1994
1 ....3.00
2-10 ....2.00

Blade: Vampire Hunter
Marvel, 1999
1 ....4.00
2-6 ....3.00

Blade 2:
Movie Adaptation
Marvel, 2002
1 ....6.00

Blair Which?
Dark Horse, 1999
1 ....3.00

Blair Witch Chronicles
Oni, 2000
1-4 ....3.00

Blair Witch:
Dark Testaments
Image, 2000
1 ....3.00

Blair Witch Project
Oni, 1999
1 ....5.00
1/2nd 3.00

Blame!
Tokyopop, 2005
1-10 ....10.00

Blanche
Goes to Hollywood
Dark Horse
1 ....3.00

Blanche
Goes to New York
Dark Horse, 1992

Blanche Goes to New York is a delightfully genteel combination of piano lessons and demonic invasion. The one-shot special begins when Blanche arrives in 1900s New York to study piano at the home of Professor Pellegrini. The professor is a former intimate of some of the more "radical" composers, such as Debussy, Schoenberg, and Mahler.

As exotic as these piano compositions might sound to the gentle Blanche's ears, it is nothing compared to the strange sounds that sometimes emanate from the lower levels of the house. When Blanche investigates, she finds that the wondrous city of New York harbors some very old secrets.

1 ....3.00

Blarney
Discovery

1 ....3.00

Blast Corps
Dark Horse, 1998

1 ....3.00

Blasters Special
DC, 1989

1 ....2.00

Blast-Off
Harvey, 1965

Harvey Comics, famous for Richie Rich and Casper, is not the first name that comes to mind when listing the premier publishers of science-fiction comics. However, the evidence indicates that when they did decide to publish one, such as the one-shot Blast-Off from 1965, they assembled some top-drawer comics talent on the project.

The lead story features the "Three Rocketeers," a team of astronauts tangling with deadly alien menaces, illustrated in absolutely classic style by Jack Kirby. Other stories in the issue include a two-page Simon & Kirby fable, "Caution! Atoms!," and two superbly drawn backups in the style of EC titles such as Weird Science, by EC veterans Al Williamson and Reed Crandall.
-- Rob Salkowitz

1 ....28.00

Blaze
Marvel, 1994

1 .... 3.00
2-12 .... 2.00

Blaze Carson
Marvel, 1948

1 .... 125.00
2 .... 90.00
3-5 .... 85.00

Blaze: Legacy of Blood
Marvel, 1993

1-4 .... 2.00

Blaze of Glory
Marvel, 2000

1-4 .... 3.00

Blaze The Wonder Collie
Marvel, 1949

2-3 .... 100.00

Blazin' Barrels
Tokyopop, 2005

1-3 .... 10.00

Blazing Battle Tales
Seaboard, 1975

1 .... 3.00

Blazing Combat
Warren, 1965

1 .... 90.00
2-3 .... 30.00
4 .... 40.00
Ann 1 .... 45.00

Blazing Combat
Apple, 1993

1-2 .... 5.00

Blazing Combat: World War I and World War II
Apple, 1994

1-2 .... 4.00

Blazing Comics
Enwil, 1944

1 .... 300.00
2-5 .... 150.00

Blazing Comics
Enwil, 1955

5-6 .... 100.00

Blazing Foxholes
Fantagraphics, 1994

1-3 .... 3.00

Blazing Sixguns
Avon, 1952

1 .... 100.00

Blazing West
ACG, 1948

American Comics Group published primarily non-super-hero titles from 1943 to 1967. Although it did venture into super-heroes with Magicman and Nemesis - and super-hero parody with Herbie, the Fat Fury - during the craze inspired by the Batman TV series of the mid-1960s, ACG stayed the course with funny animal, teen humor, horror, science fiction, adventure, and war comics. ACG's Western offerings were The Hooded Horseman and Blazing West.

Blazing West was an anthology title that ran for 22 issues, from 1948 to 1952, and featured such gun-toting stalwarts as "Injun" Jones, a white man who was a friend to the Apache tribe; Bantam Buckaroo, a boy billed as "90 pounds of pure TNT"; Buffalo Belle, a fiery female gunfighter; and The Hooded Horseman, a mysterious, Lone Ranger-type hero who was introduced in #14.

1 .... 85.00
2 .... 48.00
3-5 .... 36.00
6-10 .... 30.00
11-13 .... 24.00
14 .... 58.00
15 .... 30.00
16-17 .... 24.00
18-20 .... 22.00
21-22 .... 20.00

Blazing Western
AC

1 .... 3.00

Blazing Western
Avalon, 1997

1 .... 3.00

Bleach
Viz, 2004

1-26 .... 8.00

Bleat
Slave Labor, 1995
1 ....3.00

Bleeding Heart
Fantagraphics, 1991
1-5...3.00

Blessed Pope Pius X and the Confraternity of Christian Doctrine
George A. Pflaum
1 ....3.00

Blindside
Image, 1996
1 ....1.00
1/A-1/B 3.00
2-7..1.00

Blink
Marvel, 2001
1-4...3.00

Blip
Marvel, 1983
1-7...1.00

Blip
Bardic, 1998
1 ....1.00

Blip and the C.C.A.D.S.
Amazing
1-2..2.00

Bliss Alley
Image, 1997
1-2..3.00

Blite
Fantagraphics
1 ....2.00

Blitz
Nightwynd

By the year 2010, the process to clone a human body had been perfected. Moreover, there existed the capability to transplant a human brain into a younger, cloned body. For those who were rich enough to afford the operation, virtual immortality was assured. The rich grew progressively richer, moving into elite residences away from the common folk. After a series of cloning-rights riots, the rich eventually left the commoners behind altogether, setting off for one of the paradise moons recently discovered around Jupiter.

Meanwhile, those who couldn't afford the cloning procedure were condemned to life in the rapidly decaying cities. Just when it seemed things couldn't get any worse, they do. A group of terrorists demanding cloning rights has stolen a neutra-cosma bomb. Unless Blood, a renegade clone/private investigator and his partner, the furry B-Wang can stop them, they'll level the entire city with it.

1-4.. 3.00

Blitzkrieg
DC, 1976
1 .... 16.00
2 .... 8.00
3-5... 6.00

Blockade
Heritage Collection
1 .... 10.00

Blokhedz
Image, 2003
1-2.. 3.00

Blonde
Fantagraphics
1-3.. 3.00

Blonde Addiction
Blitzweasel
1-4.. 3.00

Blonde Avenger
Blitz Weasel, 1993
1-8.. 4.00

Blonde Avenger: Crossover Crazzeee
Blitzweasel
1 .... 4.00

Blonde Avenger
Fantagraphics, 1993
1-4.. 3.00

Blonde Avenger Monthly
Blitzweasel, 1996
1 .... 4.00
2-6.. 3.00

Blonde Avenger One-Shot Special: The Spying Game
Blitzweasel, 1996
1 .... 3.00

Blonde, The: Bondage Palace
Fantagraphics, 1994
1-5.. 3.00

Blonde Phantom
Timely, 1946
12 .... 1,075.00
13 .... 665.00
14-15 .... 590.00
16 .... 700.00
17-22 .... 500.00

Blondie Comics
David McKay, 1947

The Blondie strip created by Chic Young (1901-1973) has been a part of the American consciousness since it was introduced in 1930. It began as a gag strip about Blondie as a pert flapper, surrounded by suitors - but she married Dagwood Bumstead in 1933, and the strip turned into a family comedy gag-a-day.

Dagwood works for Mr. Dithers, an old blowhard who chews out Dagwood with legendary frequency. Other regular characters include Dagwood and Blondie's children and even their pet dogs. Comic-book appearances included strip reprints and stand-alone stories produced specifically for the comic books.

Originally published by McKay, this series moved first to Harvey, then over to Charlton from #177 on.

-- Rob Salkowitz

1 .... 245.00
2 .... 100.00
3-5 .... 75.00
6-10 .... 45.00
11-16 .... 30.00
17-20 .... 22.00
21-50 .... 16.00
51-80 .... 12.00
81-99 .... 9.00
100 .... 10.00
101-124 .... 8.00

125	9.00
126-130	8.00
131-140	7.00
141-167	8.00
168-180	5.00
181-200	4.00
201-222	3.00

Blood
Fantaco
1	4.00

Blood and Glory
Marvel
1-3	6.00

Blood & Kisses
Fantaco
1	3.00
2	4.00

Blood & Roses Adventures
Knight, 1995
1	3.00

Blood & Roses: Future Past Tense
Sky, 1993
1	2.00
1/Ashcan-1/Gold	3.00
2	2.00

Blood & Roses: Search for the Time-Stone
Sky, 1994
1-2	3.00

Blood & Roses Special
Knight, 1996
1	3.00

Blood and Shadows
DC
1-4	6.00

Blood and Thunder
Conquest
1	3.00

Blood & Water
Slave Labor, 1991
1	3.00

Blood and Water
DC, 2003
1-5	3.00

Blood: A Tale
Marvel, 1987

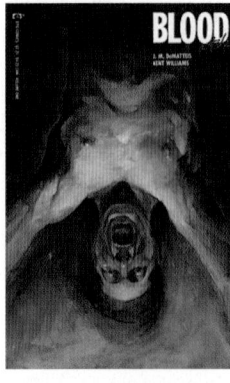

Epic Comics is known for its mature reader format and Blood: A Tale is no exception. The story of the life of a vampire that discovers the secret of life is violent, bloody, and extremely touching. People are born, people live, and people die. JM DeMatteis and Kent Williams have put together an incredible story, which is well worth the reading.

1-4	3.00

Blood: A Tale
DC, 1996
1-4	3.00

Bloodbath
DC, 1993
1-2	4.00

Blood Bounty
Highland
1	2.00

Bloodbrothers
Eternity
1-4	2.00

Bloodchilde
Millennium, 1994

In this urban vampire tale, Childe Benington is a brooding creature fond of internal monologue desperate for a life of normalcy. But his need to feed is growing greater, and instead of taking it to the anonymity of the streets, he feeds on his artist wife, who sadly had no idea of his true nature. Then he broods about killing her and how he'll hate himself forever. Afterwards, he yells at an ethereal woman in white who always shows up to claim the souls of those he loves and kills.

Meanwhile, an FBI agent hot on his trail goes to a gypsy psychic, tells her he's with the FBI and that he's hunting a vampire, and orders her to read the Tarot cards to give him insight into the case. Which she does.

The series is written by Faye Perozich with art by O.J. Cariello.

1-4	3.00

Blood Club
Kitchen Sink
2	6.00

Bloodfang
Epitaph, 1996
0-1	3.00

Blood Feast
Eternity
1-2/Variant	3.00

Blood Feast: The Screenplay
Eternity
1	5.00

Bloodfire
Lightning, 1993
0-1/Variant	4.00
2-12	3.00

Bloodfire/Hellina
Lightning, 1995
1	3.00
1/Nude	4.00
1/Platinum	3.00

Blood Gothic
Fantaco
1-2	5.00

Bloodhound
DC, 2004
1-10	3.00

Bloodhunter
Brainstorm, 1996
1	3.00

Blood is the Harvest
Catechetical Guild, 1950
1	750.00

Blood Is the Harvest
Eclipse, 1992
1-4	3.00

Blood Junkies
Eternity
1-2...3.00

Blood Legacy:
The Story of Ryan
Image, 2000

Ryan Alexander began her life as a peasant in the 14th century. She is raised as a boy in a harsh, medieval world, but that life changes forever when she is attacked by a dark stranger, Victor, and reborn into the world of the Others. Fast-forward to present day, when geneticist Dr. Susan Ryerson finds Ryan's 600 year-old body in the morgue-then watches in amazement as she comes back to life. The more Susan learns about the mysterious woman, the more she begins to suspect that Ryan and her "Kind" are really vampires. But Ryan is not telling her everything. A limited series that is equal parts soap opera, historical romance and action-adventure, the ambitious and somewhat convoluted story by first-timer Kerri Hawkins is aided in grand fashion by the gorgeous art of Mark Pajarillo (JLA, Warcry).
-- *Stephen C. George*

1-4...3.00

Blood Legacy/
Young Ones One Shot
Image, 2003
1 ....5.00

Bloodletting
Fantaco
1 ....3.00

Bloodletting
Fantaco
1-2...4.00

Bloodlines
Aircel
1-7...3.00

Bloodlines
Moonstone
1 .... 4.00

Bloodlines: A Tale from
the Heart of Africa
Marvel, 1992
1 .... 6.00

Bloodlust
Slave Labor, 1990
1 .... 2.00

Blood 'n' Guts
Aircel, 1990
1-4... 3.00

Blood of Dracula
Apple, 1987

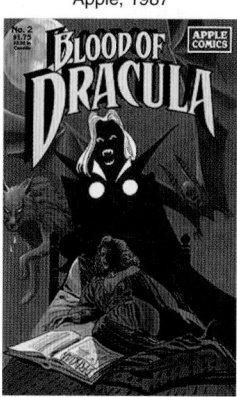

Ever since Bram Stoker, the vampire known as Dracula has been haunting the world's dreams. The subject of countless books, movies, and comics, it would seem that there would be little that could be added to his legend. Still, Apple Comics does just that in Blood of Dracula.

The series runs as a serial anthology, featuring three stories in each issue. Dracula is shown throughout the ages: hunting for blood in his native land and stalking the streets of America. In one story set in the 1930s, he comes across a moonshiner who is actually a werewolf and who has been creating other werewolves by putting filings from his teeth into the libations he distributes. The wildest concept is Dracula in 2199, where The Lord of the Vampires awakens after a long sleep to find himself in a world ruled by cold, hard science and populated by advanced robots. That world has forgotten the mystical -but Dracula is determined to show them fear.

1-14....................................... 2.00
15 .... 4.00
16-20 .... 2.00

Blood of the Demon
DC, 2005
1 .... 4.00
2-17 .... 3.00

Blood of the Innocent
Warp, 1986
1-4 .... 2.00

Blood Pack
DC, 1995
1-4 .... 2.00

Bloodpool
Image, 1995
1-4 .... 3.00
Special 1 .... 4.00

Blood Reign
Fathom, 1991

Horror and science fiction come together in this splatterpunk comic pairing two stories.

In the first, a ghoul slayer with a penchant for introspection avenges his way through a graveyard, while a human survivor of one of his attacks is guarded by an alleged police detective in a tight shirt and high heels. In the second story, an elite commando unit in the far future discovers their rescue mission takes place on a planet full of zombies.

Neither is pretty. One of them almost makes sense. This book was created by cartoonist Tim Tyler.

1-8 .... 3.00

Bloodscent
Comico, 1988
1 .... 2.00

Bloodseed
Marvel, 1993
1-2 .... 2.00

Bloodshed
Damage!, 1994
1-3 .... 3.00
Ashcan 1 .... 2.00

Bloodshot
Valiant, 1993

He is a fierce warrior with enhanced reactions, computerized nano-machines in his bloodstream, and a burning need to avenge himself on those who took away his former life. A creation of "Project Rising Spirit," the American branch of Musashi Labs, he was one of a line of enhanced humans being built to serve as weapons of the corporation. His case file bore the name "Bloodshot."

Bloodshot's fate changes, when a boy (who will look familiar to fans of Eternal Warrior) appears and alters the shape of the experiment. When Bloodshot wakes up, he breaks free from Project Rising Spirit. He is now a renegade, an altered human with a shrouded past that apparently involved organized crime. And he's a very, very dangerous person to tangle with.

0/VVSS	25.00
0/PlatError	750.00
0	3.00
0/Gold	25.00
1	2.00
2-6	1.00
6/VVSS	50.00
7-15	1.00
16	2.00
17-24	1.00
25-37	2.00
38-43	3.00
44-47	4.00
48-49	5.00
50	6.00
51	10.00
YB 1-2	5.00

Bloodshot
Acclaim, 1997

1-16	3.00
Ashcan 1	1.00

Bloodstone
Marvel, 2001

1-4	3.00

Bloodstream
Image, 2004

1-4	3.00

Bloodstrike
Image, 1993

Created by Rob Liefeld, Bloodstrike is an elite strike force of super-humans. It consists of Fourplay, a four-armed avenger; Tag, a lithe martial artist whose touch causes people to freeze in their tracks; Shogun, a heavily armored walking arsenal; and Deadlock, a Wolverine-like fighter with deadly claws.

The leader of the powerful team is Col. Cabbot, a perfect combination of firepower and strategic thinking. Cabbot is also the brother of the leader of Brigade, another Liefeld-created team - a team that does not always work cooperatively with Bloodstrike, to say the least.

1	3.00
2-12	2.00
13-24	3.00
25	2.00

Bloodstrike Assassin
Image, 1995

0-4	3.00

Bloodsucker
Fantagraphics

1	3.00

Blood Sword
Jademan, 1988

1-51	2.00

Blood Sword Dynasty
Jademan, 1989

1-29	1.00

Blood Syndicate
DC, 1993

1	2.00
1/CS	3.00
2-9	2.00
10	3.00
11-24	2.00
25	3.00
26-27	2.00
28	3.00
29	1.00
30-32	3.00
33	1.00
34	3.00
35	4.00

Bloodthirst: Terminus Option
Alpha Productions

1-2	3.00

Bloodthirst: The Nightfall Conspiracy
Alpha

1-2	3.00

Bloodthirsty Pirate Tales
Black Swan, 1995

Not every character in comics is a tights-wearing super-hero or mutant monster bent on destroying the universe as we know it. Some guys just want to have fun, raping and pillaging while sailing the seven seas in search of treasure and adventure. Black Swan Press brings us a little bit of history thrown in with tales of adventure, Long John Silver-style. Not since the days of Piracy, Buccaneers, and Seven Seas Comics have we been exposed to these bloodthirsty cutthroats and their wenching ways.

Bloodthirsty Pirate Tales also included a continuing biography of Blackbeard, the notorious Edward Teach himself, as well as smaller articles ranging from the true story of rum to the history of pirate comics through the years.

1-8	3.00

Blood Ties
Full Moon, 1991
1 .... 2.00

Bloodwing
Eternity, 1988
1-6 .... 2.00

Bloodwulf
Image, 1995

Bloodwulf is ultra-violence with a smile on its face - death with a sense of humor. The character was introduced in Image Comics' Darker Image #1 in 1992, although little background was given until this 1995 series was introduced.

Very much like DC Comics' Lobo, Bloodwulf is an intergalactic bad boy, causing a commotion everywhere he goes. This four-issue mini-series opens with a disgruntled Bloodwulf. He hasn't indulged in senseless violence for a while. His wife has him go find someone to beat up, because he is driving her crazy by loitering around the house. The rest of the series chronicles Bloodwulf's adventures, as he drives around the galaxy on his galactic gun-starship.

1-Summer 1 .... 3.00

Bloody Bones & Blackeyed Peas
Galaxy
1 .... 1.00

Bloodyhot
Parody
1 .... 3.00

Bloody Mary
DC, 1996
1-4 .... 2.00

Bloody Mary: Lady Liberty
DC, 1997
1-4 .... 3.00

Bloody School
Curtis Comic
1 .... 3.00

Blowjob
Fantagraphics, 2001
1 .... 10.00
2-5 .... 7.00
6-10 .... 5.00
11-23 .... 4.00

Blue
Image, 1999
1-2 .... 3.00

Bluebeard
Slave Labor, 1993
1-3 .... 3.00

Blue Beetle
Fox, 1939
1 .... 2,750.00
2 .... 950.00
3 .... 700.00
4 .... 475.00
5 .... 425.00
6 .... 390.00
7-8 .... 350.00
9-15 .... 325.00
16-20 .... 275.00
21-27 .... 200.00
28-30 .... 175.00
31-40 .... 165.00
41-45 .... 140.00
46 .... 150.00
47 .... 800.00
48-50 .... 625.00
51-54 .... 510.00
55-57 .... 485.00
58-60 .... 100.00

Blue Beetle
Charlton, 1964
1 .... 45.00
2 .... 30.00
3-5 .... 20.00

Blue Beetle
Charlton, 1965
50-54 .... 27.00
1 .... 60.00
2 .... 40.00
3-5 .... 27.00

Blue Beetle
Modern, 1977
1-3 .... 5.00

Blue Beetle
DC, 1986
1-24 .... 1.00

Blue Beetle
DC, 2006
1 .... 6.00
1/2nd 4.00
2-10 .... 3.00

Blue Block
Kitchen Sink
1 .... 3.00

Blue Bolt
Novelty, 1940
1 .... 2,900.00
2 .... 1,400.00
3 .... 1,100.00
4 .... 805.00
5 .... 950.00
6-12 .... 800.00

Blue Bolt
Novelty, 1941
1 .... 250.00
2 .... 180.00
3-6 .... 150.00
7-12 .... 115.00

Blue Bolt
Novelty, 1942
1 .... 100.00
2-12 .... 85.00

Blue Bolt
Novelty, 1943
1 .... 90.00
2-12 .... 60.00

Blue Bolt
Novelty, 1944
1-8 .... 45.00

Blue Bolt
Novelty, 1945
1-10 .... 38.00

Blue Bolt
Novelty, 1946
1-12 .... 32.00

Blue Bolt
Premium, 1947
1-12 .... 32.00

Blue Bolt
Premium, 1948
1-9 .... 32.00

Blue Bolt
Premium, 1949
1-2 .... 32.00

Blue Bolt
Star Publications, 1949
102-104 .... 160.00
105 .... 325.00
106-119 .... 250.00

Blue Bulleteer
AC, 1989
1 .... 3.00

Blue Circle
REWL Publications, 1944
1 .... 160.00
2 .... 105.00
3 .... 130.00
4-6 .... 85.00

Blue Devil
DC, 1984

Whiz kid Dan Cassidy creates a blue devil costume with a tough exoskeleton, inner motors that give him great strength, and pyrotechnics for effect. The costume gets him a starring roll in a horror film -- but not, unfortunately, the girl he's in love with. When a bumbling actor unleashes a real demon, it is Dan, with the powers his costume gives him, who is the only one who can save cast and crew.

However, the battle with the real demon has one devastating side effect. When Dan gets home, he finds out he has become one with the suit. Though initially horrified, he eventually comes to enjoy his new situation and becomes skilled in use of his rocket-trident weapon.

1-31 ....1.00
Ann 1 ....2.00

Blue Hole
Christine Shields
1 ....3.00

Blue Ice
Martyr, 1992
1-2 ....3.00

Blue Lily
Dark Horse, 1993
1-4 ....4.00

Blue Loco
Kitchen Sink, 1997
1 ....6.00

Blue Monday: Absolute Beginners
Oni, 2001
1-4 ....3.00

Blue Monday: Lovecats
Oni, 2002
1 ....3.00

Blue Monday: Painted Moon
Oni, 2004
1-4 .... 3.00

Blue Monday: The Kids Are Alright
Oni, 2000
1-3 .... 3.00

Blue Moon
Mu, 1992
1-5 .... 3.00

Blue Moon
Aeon, 1994
1 .... 3.00

Blue Notebook
NBM
1 .... 14.00

Blue Ribbon Comics
M.L.J., 1939
1 .... 2,200.00
2 .... 900.00
3-4 .... 600.00
5-8 .... 440.00
9 .... 1,850.00
10-13 .... 650.00
14-22 .... 550.00

Blue Ribbon Comics
Archie, 1983
1 .... 3.00
2-14 .... 2.00

B-Movie Presents
B-Movie
1-4 .... 2.00

BMW Films: The Hire
Dark Horse, 2004
1-4 .... 3.00

Board of Superheros
Not Available
1 .... 1.00

Bobby Benson's B-Bar-B Riders
Magazine Enterprises, 1950
1 .... 250.00
2 .... 95.00
3-5 .... 75.00
6-8 .... 65.00
9 .... 90.00
10 .... 65.00
11 .... 90.00
12 .... 60.00
13 .... 90.00
14-15 .... 75.00
16 .... 70.00
17-19 .... 60.00
20 .... 75.00

Bobby Benson's B-Bar-B Riders
AC, 1990
1 .... 3.00

Bobby Ruckers
Art

Bebe Williams originally created this surrealistic photo-comic for the magazine "Performance Art Funnies." It uses the unusual technique of combining photographs of various actors with drawn backgrounds and captions, producing an effect that is not quite fumetti, but very different than a traditional comic book.

Of course, Bobby Ruckers would have been different from a traditional comic book even if it had been drawn like one. The title character is a balding businessman whose super-powers include a never-empty wallet and who thinks nothing of taking dates out to dinner in a flying Cadillac. When a date makes the mistake of opening the window to escape Ruckers' cigar smoke, she is sucked out into space where Ruckers has to employ his time-travel telephone to retroactively break the date and save her. Such surrealism continues in his other adventures, making this an engaging, yet slightly bizarre, reading experience.

1 .... 3.00

Bobby Sherman
Charlton, 1972
1 .... 15.00
2-7 .... 10.00

Bob Colt
Fawcett, 1950
1 .... 225.00
2 .... 150.00
3-5 .... 110.00
6-10 .... 90.00

Bob, the Galactic Bum
DC, 1995
1-4 .... 2.00

**Bob Marley,
Tale of the Tuff Gong**
Marvel
1-3...6.00

Bobobo-bo Bo-bobo
Viz, 2005
1 ....8.00

"Bob's" Favorite Comics
Rip Off
1-1/3rd.....................................3.00

Bob Steele Western
Fawcett, 1950
1..400.00
2-10....................................200.00

Bob Steele Western
AC, 1990
1 ....3.00

Bob Swift
Fawcett, 1951
1...30.00
2-5..20.00

Body Bags
Dark Horse, 1996

It's only natural for a daughter to look up to her father. Perhaps she even wants to grow up to be like him, to make him proud of her. Maybe that's why fourteen-year-old Panda Carmen Maria Delgado is so desperate to become a body bagger.

Panda's father is Clownface, a mountain of a man who makes his living as a "body bagger"-a bounty hunter-living in the tough town of Terminus Georgia. His partner is "Pops," a shrewd operator whose headgear is actually a concussion cap screwed to his skull. The two have been making a good living in their chosen trade by being smarter and meaner than both their quarry and their competitors. Only now do they find out that their newest competitor is none other than Clownface's barely teenage

daughter. She's got attitude, panache, and uncanny ability with firearms. And the only way to get her off their backs is for Clownface and Pops to let her join the family business.

1 .... 4.00
2-Ashcan 1 .... 3.00

Body Bags: Father's Day
Image, 2005
1-2... 6.00

Body Count
Aircel
1-4... 2.00

Bodycount
Image, 1996
1-4... 3.00

Body Doubles
DC, 1999
1-4... 3.00

Body Doubles (Villains)
DC, 1998
1 .... 2.00

Bodyguard
Aircel, 1990
1-3... 3.00

Body Heat
NBM
1 .... 12.00

Body Paint
Fantagraphics, 1995
1-4... 3.00

Body Swap
Roger Mason
1 .... 3.00

Boffo in Hell
Neatly Chiseled Features

Mr. Boffo and his wonder dog, Weederman, have been entertaining newspaper strip fans for many years. In that time, "hell jokes" had been slowly creeping

into the strip like a virus. In 1995 Mr. Boffo's creator, Joe Martin decided to gather the various "Boffo in Hell" strips, along with new material, into a comic book-length collection.

In this comic book debut, the lovable fat man Mr. Boffo and his dog are transformed into heroes that save a town from three mass-murderers. They receive their power from a ring that was sent to Earth by a philandering alien god. Mr. Boffo and Weederman believe they've finally hit the big time and start planning for a future as masked heroes. There is only one problem: the ring's owner has been forgiven by his wife on the condition that he retrieve the ring-and kill anyone who touched it. Meanwhile, the three dead killers go to Hell and cause the Devil to wish that he'd picked a different profession.

1 .... 3.00

Boffo Laffs
Paragraphics
1 .... 3.00
2-5... 2.00

Boffy the Vampire Layer
Fantagraphics, 2000
1-3... 3.00

Bogie Man
Fat Man, 1989
1-4... 3.00

**Bogie Man, The:
Chinatoon**
Atomeka
1-4... 3.00

**Bogie Man, The:
The Manhattan Project**
Tundra, 1992
1 .... 5.00

Bog Swamp Demon
Hall of Heroes, 1996
1-1/Variant............................. 3.00
1/Commem............................. 5.00
2-4... 3.00

Bohos
Image, 1998
1-3... 3.00

**Bo Jackson vs.
Michael Jordan**
Celebrity
1-2... 3.00

Bold Adventure
Pacific, 1983
1-3... 2.00

Bolt and Starforce Six
AC, 1984

1 ....2.00

Bolt Special
AC

1 ....2.00

Bomarc
Nightwynd

In the aftermath of devastating nuclear war, Earth's survivors created a Utopian society, snuggled safely beneath city-sized, inter-connected domes. But the idyllic world is rotting from within, soured by corrupt politicians and threatened by savage mutants. Even Bomarc, their protector, has been declared an outlaw for daring to defy the cities' power-mad rulers. But when a powerful psionic thwarts a mutant terrorist attack by absorbing the energy of their detonated nuclear bomb, only Bomarc is able to offer any resistance to the God-like being she becomes. Although the transformed Cassandra purifies the air and environment, freeing the populace from the domes, she also decides mankind itself needs to be purified, and goes on a deadly "cleansing" spree. Given Mankind's propensity for war and destruction, even Bomarc wonders if stopping Cassandra is really the right thing to do.

1-3..3.00

Bomba The Jungle Boy
DC, 1967

1 ....16.00
2-7..8.00

Bombast
Topps, 1993

1 ....3.00

Bombastic
Screaming Dodo, 1996

1-5...3.00

Bomber Comics
Elliott, 1944

1 .... 400.00
2 .... 275.00
3 .... 225.00
4 .... 250.00

Bomb Queen
Image, 2006

1-4... 4.00

Bomb Queen (Vol. 2)
Image, 2006

1-3... 4.00

Bomb Queen vs. Blacklight
Image, 2006

1 .... 4.00

Bonafide
Bonafide, 1994

0-0/2nd................................... 4.00

Bonanza
Gold Key, 1962

The Cartwright clan - Pa and his sons, half-brothers Adam, Hoss, and Little Joe - helped keep their Nevada ranch safe from cattle rustlers and natural forces on the popular television show that ran from 1959 to 1973. The show was the first Western televised in color and starred Lorne Greene, Pernell Roberts, Dan Blocker, and Michael Landon as a family of men coping with their personal problems and the problems of coordinating the business of ranching and dealing with other ranchers and mining interests in the area. It was one of the most successful TV Westerns.

The comic-book adaptation offered the typical slick Gold Key packaging, with photo covers and stories featuring father and sons facing familiar Western situations.

-- Rob Salkowitz

1	110.00

1 .... 110.00
2 .... 75.00
3-5 .... 50.00
6-10 .... 32.00
11-20 .... 22.00
21-30 .... 15.00
31-37 .... 12.00

Bondage Confessions
Fantagraphics, 1998

1-4 .... 3.00

Bondage Fairies
Antarctic, 1994

1 .... 4.00
1/2nd-1/4th 3.00
2 .... 4.00
2/2nd-6/2nd 3.00

Bondage Fairies Extreme
Fantagraphics, 1999

1-15 .... 4.00

Bondage Girls at War
Fantagraphics, 1996

1-6 .... 3.00

Bone
Cartoon Books, 1991

Jeff Smith created a classic funnybook for the 1990s, combining Walt Disney-style art with strong storytelling and characterization. Bone is the story of a little character called Fone Bone. Originally from Boneville, he finds himself, along with other Bone characters Phoney Bone and Smiley Bone, in a village a long way from home. In the course of settling into village life, they discover there are more forces at work than would seem usual in a rural town. Eventually, they come to learn about Stupid, Stupid Rat Creatures, a gigantic dragon, and more. The beautiful village girl Thorn quickly wins Fone Bone's adoration - but she is more than she seems, and so is her grandmother.

Winner of numerous awards, including the 1994 Eisner for Best New Series and the 1995 Eisner for Best Continuing Series, Bone has appeal for young and old alike.

1	80.00
1/2nd	8.00
1/3rd-1/9th	3.00
2	45.00
2/2nd	6.00
2/3rd-2/8th	3.00
3	25.00
3/2nd-3/8th	3.00
4	16.00
4/2nd-4/6th	3.00
5	12.00
5/2nd-5/7th	3.00
6	7.00
6/2nd-6/6th	3.00
7	7.00
7/2nd-7/5th	3.00
8	7.00
8/2nd-8/7th	3.00
9	4.00
9/2nd-9/4th	3.00
10	4.00
10/2nd-10/3rd	3.00
11	4.00
11/2nd	3.00
12	4.00
12/2nd-12/3rd	3.00
13	4.00
13/2nd	3.00
13.5-13.5/Gold	4.00
14-55	3.00
Special 1	2.00

Bone
Image, 1993
1-20 .... 3.00

Bone Sourcebook
Image, 1995
1/A-1/B 2.00

Bonerest
Image, 2005
1-8 .... 3.00

Bones
Malibu, 1987
1-4 .... 2.00

Bone Saw
Tundra
1 .... 15.00

Boneshaker
Caliber, 1994
1 .... 4.00

Boneyard
NBM, 2001
1-28 .... 3.00

Boneyard Press 1993 Tourbook
Boneyard
1 .... 2.00

Bongo Special Edition
Bongo
1 .... 20.00

Boof
Iconografix
1 .... 3.00

Boof
Image, 1994
1-6 .... 2.00

Boof and the Bruise Crew
Image, 1994
1-6 .... 2.00

Boogeyman
Dark Horse, 1998
1-4 .... 3.00

Boogieman
Rion
1 .... 2.00

Book
Dreamsmith, 1998
1-2 .... 4.00

Book of Angels
Caliber, 1997
1 .... 4.00

Book of Ballads and Sagas
Green Man, 1996
1-2 .... 3.00
3-4 .... 4.00

Book of Fate
DC, 1997
1-9 .... 2.00
10-12 .... 3.00

Book of Lost Souls
Marvel, 2005
1-6 .... 3.00

Book of Night
Dark Horse, 1987
1 .... 3.00
2-3 .... 2.00

Book of Shadows
Image, 2006
1-2 .... 4.00

Book of Spells
Double Edge, 1994
1-4 .... 2.00

Book of the Damned: A Hellraiser Companion
Marvel, 1991
1-4 .... 5.00

Book of the Dead
Marvel, 1993

After many years in decline, horror comics enjoyed a resurgence in popularity in the early '90s. Accordingly, Marvel took the opportunity to republish the adventures of some of its creepier characters from the '70s in this "Book of the Dead" series.

Among its features, the Book of the Dead reprints the first Marvel appearance of the Frankenstein monster, as well as the origin and first appearance of the shambling swamp creature known as Man-Thing (from the hard-to-find Savage Tales #1). For variety, Marvel also threw in various and sundry horror stories from Chamber of Darkness and other obscure scare titles.

1-4 .... 2.00

Book of the SubGenius
Simon & Schuster
1 .... 11.00

Book of the Tarot
Caliber
1 .... 4.00

Book of Thoth
Circle, 1995
1 .... 3.00

Book on the Edge of Forever
Fantagraphics, 1994
1 .... 7.00

Books of Doom
Marvel, 2006
1-6 .... 3.00

Books of Faerie
DC, 1997
1-3 .... 3.00

Books of Faerie, The: Auberon's Tale
DC, 1998
1-3...3.00

Books of Faerie, The: Molly's Story
DC, 1999
1-4...3.00

Books of Lore: Special Edition
Peregrine Entertainment, 1997
1...3.00
1/Ltd. 5.00
2...3.00

Books of Lore: Storyteller
Peregrine Entertainment
1...3.00

Books of Lore: The Kaynin Gambit
Peregrine Entertainment, 1998
0-Ashcan 1 ....3.00

Books of Magic
DC, 1990
1-4...4.00

Books of Magic
DC, 1993
1...3.00
1/Silver 4.00
2-75..3.00
Ann 1-3 ....4.00

Books of Magick: Life During Wartime
DC, 2004
1-15.......................................3.00

Boom Boom
Aeon, 1994
1-4...3.00

Boondoggle
Knight, 1995

Boondoggle is the mythical town created by cartoonist Steve

Steglin to house a collection of humorous characters. Chief among the bunch is Beauregard McGillicuddy (a.k.a. "Bumper"), an effervescent orphan with attention deficit disorder and an appreciation for the finer points of junk food. He is accompanied on his adventures by a collection of anthropomorphic animals including the slacker bunny Aristotle, pig Potpie, and dog Flea.

This humorous cast first appeared in college papers at the University of Cincinnati and Northern Kentucky University. Steglin also created the spinoff strip "Quish Quosh" for the UC News-Record's Entertainment supplement "Panorama," episodes of which are reprinted here.

1-Special 1 .... 3.00

Boondoggle
Caliber, 1997
1-2... 3.00

Booster Gold
DC, 1986
1 .... 3.00
2-25... 1.00

Booster Gold
DC, 2007
0... 3.00
1 .... 6.00
2-27... 3.00

Boots of the Oppressor
Northstar, 1993
1 .... 3.00

Borderguard
Eternity, 1987
1-2... 2.00

Borderline
Kardia, 1992
1 .... 2.00

Border Patrol
P.L., 1951
1 .... 50.00

Border Worlds
Kitchen Sink, 1986
1-7/A....................................... 2.00

Border Worlds
Kitchen Sink
1 .... 2.00

Boris' Adventure Magazine
Nicotat, 1988
1 .... 2.00
2-4... 3.00

Boris Karloff Tales of Mystery
Gold Key, 1962

Like many of the best of the Gold Key comics, this title featured suspenseful stories with clever twists that provide comeuppance to the bad guys. In one such tale, thieves are hypnotized by a swamp monster that cons them into giving it their entire take and eventually lures them into its quicksand home. In another story, members of two feuding families set aside their animosity toward each other to fight a monster together -- with unexpected results.

Those who enjoy such other fantasy titles like Gold Key's Twilight Zone or DC's Unexpected will appreciate Boris Karloff's Tales of Mystery.

3 .... 27.00
4-5 .... 25.00
6-8 .... 20.00
9 .... 25.00
☞Wood art
10 .... 15.00
11 .... 22.00
12 .... 15.00
13-14 .... 12.00
15 .... 15.00
16-20 .... 12.00
21 .... 18.00
22-30 .... 10.00
31-40 .... 9.00
41-50 .... 8.00
51-59 .... 6.00
60-74 .... 5.00
75-79 .... 3.00
80 .... 7.00
☞Giant ish; scarce
81 .... 6.00
☞Giant ish; scarce
82 .... 5.00
☞Giant ish; scarce
83 .... 6.00
☞Giant ish; scarce
84 .... 5.00
☞Giant ish; scarce

85 ....6.00
☛Giant ish; scarce
86-97 ....3.00

Boris Karloff Thriller
Gold Key, 1962
1 ....75.00
2 ....55.00

Boris the Bear
Dark Horse, 1986

Boris is a comics-collecting teddy bear who lives in a tree fort in his boy, David's, back yard. But this cute little animal isn't like all the others in the funny books: He's got an attitude - and an Uzi.

Once upon a time, critters like the Teenage Mutant Ninja Turtles were recognized as satirical; now, these mutant funny animals have become a genre unto themselves. Boris decides it's time to put things straight - with as much violence as possible.

James Dean Smith's Boris the Bear (with writing assists from Mike Richardson and Randy Stradley) is hilarious, self-effacing, and (of course) more than a little twisted. Those who have become numbed from comic book overload may find this title will sensitize them again. This was one of Dark Horse's earliest titles.

1 ....3.00
1/2nd-2 ....2.00
3-6 ....3.00
7-29 ....2.00
30-34 ....3.00

Boris the Bear
Instant Color Classics
Dark Horse, 1987
1-3 ....2.00

Born
Marvel, 2003
1 ....5.00
2-4 ....4.00

Born Again
Spire
1 .... 4.00

Born to Kill
Aircel, 1991
1-3 .... 3.00

Boston Blackie:
Blackout
Moonstone
0 .... 6.00

Boston Bombers
Caliber, 1990
1-6 .... 3.00
Special 1 .... 4.00

Boudoir
Akbar
1 .... 3.00

Boulevard of
Broken Dreams
Fantagraphics
1 .... 4.00

Bouncer
Fox, 1944
10 .... 165.00
11 .... 140.00
12-14 .... 110.00

Bound and Gagged
Iconografix
1 .... 3.00

Bound in Darkness:
Infinity Issue
CFD
1 .... 3.00

Bounty
Caliber, 1991
1-3 .... 3.00

Bounty of Zone-Z
Sunset Strips
1 .... 3.00

Bowie Butane
Mike Murdock, 1995
1 .... 2.00

Box
Fantagraphics, 1991
1-6 .... 2.00

Boxboy
Slave Labor, 1993
1-2 .... 1.00

Box Office Poison
Antarctic, 1996

Alex Robinson's Box Office Poison is a slice-of-life series featuring characters that many readers will identify with: Sherman, the bookstore clerk; Ed, the struggling cartoonist; Stephen, the history teacher; Dorothy, Sherman's manipulative girlfriend; and Irving Flavor, an elderly cartoonist who created a Batman-like character and was cheated out of the rights and profits.

The long-running story features Sherman's ongoing love-hate relationship with both his job and Dorothy, both of which are cutting into his writing and free time. Meanwhile, Ed tries to help Irving gain some of the recognition he feels the old artist is due for his creation. The soap-opera aspects of the strip are what kept readers coming back for more than four years and more than 20 issues.

- Brent

0 .... 4.00
1 .... 8.00
2 .... 5.00
3-4 .... 4.00
5-20 .... 3.00
SS 1 .... 5.00

Box Office Poison:
Kolor Karnival
Antarctic, 1999
1 .... 4.00

Boy and His 'Bot, A
Now, 1987
1 .... 2.00

Boy Comics
Lev Gleason, 1942

Product of quality-conscious Lev Gleason Publications and a classic "sleeper" title from the Golden Age, Boy Comics featured the storytelling skills of Charles Biro and the adventures of Crimebuster, a charismatic and interesting boy hero. For the first several issues of Boy Comics, Crimebuster was locked in battle with the terrifying Nazi villain Iron Jaw, perhaps the most evil and hateful character of the entire Golden Age. Young Crimebuster and his pet monkey, Squeeks, often suffered horribly at the hands of Iron Jaw before eventually prevailing. (Iron Jaw kept being killed and then recovering.) Boy Comics eventually lost some of its edge, but CB and Squeeks soldiered on against the minions of the underworld into the 1950s. Backup features included Dilly Duncan, Rocky X, Young Robin Hood, and Bombshell.

3	1,500.00
4	1,100.00
5	575.00
6	950.00
✏Iron Jaw origin	
7	620.00
8	515.00
9	450.00
10	615.00
11-14	350.00
15	400.00
16	225.00
17	250.00
18-20	200.00
21-25	140.00
26-29	130.00
30	200.00
✏Crimebuster origin	
31-40	58.00
41-50	42.00
51-62	30.00
63-80	27.00
81-100	24.00
101-119	22.00

Boy Commandos
DC, 1942

1	4,500.00
2	1,500.00
3	1,000.00
4-6	500.00
7-10	275.00
11-22	190.00
23	220.00
24-30	150.00
31-35	135.00
36	195.00

Boy Commandos
DC, 1973

1	8.00
2	5.00

Boy Explorers Comics
Harvey, 1946

1	350.00
2	250.00

Boy Loves Girl
Lev Gleason, 1952

25	40.00
26-33	30.00
34-42	25.00
43	40.00
44-50	20.00
51-57	15.00

Boy Meets Girl
Lev Gleason, 1950

1	150.00
2-6	100.00
7-18	80.00
19-24	60.00

Boys
DC, 2006

1-6	3.00

Boys
Dynomite, 2007

7-40	3.00

Boys Be ...
Tokyopop, 2004

1-7	10.00

Boys Over Flowers
Viz, 2003

1-34	10.00

Boys' Ranch
Harvey, 1950

1	385.00
2	260.00
3	230.00
4	200.00
5-6	110.00

Bozo
Dell, 1951

2	85.00
3	45.00
4-7	38.00

Bozo
Dell, 1962

1	60.00
2-3	35.00
4	28.00

Bozo the Clown in 3-D
Blackthorne

1-2	3.00

Bozo: The World's Most Famous Clown
Innovation

1	6.00

Bozz Chronicles
Marvel, 1985

1-6	2.00

BPRD: A Plague of Frogs
Dark Horse, 2004

1-5	3.00

BPRD: Dark Waters
Dark Horse, 2003

1	3.00

BPRD: Hollow Earth
Dark Horse, 2002

For years, the demonic, heroic Hellboy has been a faithful agent for the Bureau for Paranormal Research and Defense. But when he goes on sabbatical (in a tale related in Hellboy: The Third Wish), he leaves behind a disenfranchised Abe Sapien (a bizarre amphibian) and the homunculus Roger. They too want a life beyond the Bureau. But where would they go? They hardly get a moment to explore that question when Abe gets a visitation from an old colleague who is under attack at the monastery where she has taken refuge. Abe, Roger and new recruit Johann Kraus (a spirit medium who lost his body, but whose essence lives on in a shell the BPRD created for him) go to investigate and find themselves fending off a supernatural invasion. Great storytelling from Hellboy creator Mike Mignola, with deliciously moody art from Ryan Sook.

-- Stephen C. George

1-3...3.00

BPRD: Night Train
Dark Horse, 2003
1 ....3.00

BPRD: Soul of Venice
Dark Horse, 2003
1 ....3.00

BPRD: The Black Flame
Dark Horse, 2005
1-6...3.00

BPRD: The Dead
Dark Horse, 2004
1-5...3.00

BPRD: There's Something Under my Bed
Dark Horse, 2003
1 ....3.00

BPRD: The Universal Machine
Dark Horse, 2006
1-5...3.00

Bradleys
Fantagraphics, 1999
1-4...3.00

Brady Bunch
Dell, 1970
1 ....45.00
2 ....30.00

Bragade
Parody, 1993
1 ....3.00

Brainbanx
DC, 1997
1-6...3.00

Brain Bat 3-D
3-D Zone, 1992
1 ....4.00

Brain Boy
Dell, 1962
2 ....65.00
3 ....50.00
4-6...45.00

Brain Capers
Fantagraphics
1 ....4.00

Brainchild
Minneapolis College of Art and Design
2 ....1.00

Brain Fantasy
Last Gasp, 1972
1 .... 3.00

Brainglo
Psi Comics
1 .... 2.00

Brain
Magazine Enterprises, 1956
1 .... 45.00
2-3...................................... 30.00
4-7...................................... 26.00

Brain
I.W., 1958
1 .... 12.00
2-10...................................... 9.00
11-18...................................... 8.00

Braintrust Komicks
Spoon, 1993
1 .... 3.00

Brand New York
Mean, 1997
1-2.. 4.00

Brass
Image, 1996
1 .... 3.00
1/Deluxe 5.00
2-3.. 3.00

Brass
DC, 2000
1-6.. 3.00

Brath
CrossGen, 2003
1-14...................................... 3.00

Bratpack
King Hell, 1990

In the city of Slumberg, the masked avengers are lowlifes who terrorize the population and make a mockery of civil rights. But even more despised are their irresponsible teen sidekicks: a "Brat Pack" of bullies and drug abusers who use their "super" status to get their kicks. That is,

until leather-masked Doctor Blasphemy decides to wipe them out with a car bomb.

From the acid-tipped pen of Rick Veitch comes this dark, five-part mini-series published by King Hell, told with verve and energy in a dramatic palette of gray wash tones. Brutal, compelling, and darkly humorous, the Brat Pack practices its credo: "Live fast, love hard, and die with your mask on."

-- Rob Salkowitz

1-5 .... 3.00

Brat Pack/Maximortal Super Special
King Hell, 1996
1 .... 3.00

Brats Bizarre
Marvel, 1994
1-4.. 3.00

Brave and the Bold
DC, 1955
1	3,000.00
2	1,500.00
3	700.00
4-5	650.00
6-10	500.00
11-22	400.00
23	500.00
☞Vik. Prince origin	
24	350.00
25	500.00
☞1st Suicide Squad	
26	325.00
27	330.00
28	5,000.00
☞1st JLA	
29	2,000.00
30	1,750.00
31	350.00
32-33	200.00
34	1,750.00
☞1st SA Hawkman	
35-36	400.00
37	250.00
38-39	225.00
40-41	140.00
42	300.00
43	350.00
☞Hawkman origin	
44	260.00
45-49	60.00
50	175.00
51	225.00
52	125.00
53	75.00
54	350.00
☞1st Teen Titans	
55-56	45.00
57	150.00
☞1st Metamorpho	
58	65.00
59	80.00
60	100.00
☞1st Wonder Girl	

61	125.00
☞Starman origin	
62	100.00
☞1st SA Wildcat	
63	40.00
64	60.00
65-66	22.00
67	65.00
☞Batman starts	
68	80.00
☞Batman Hulk parody	
69-73	50.00
74	40.00
75	60.00
76	50.00
77-78	40.00
79	75.00
☞Batman, Deadman	
80-82	50.00
83	60.00
84	50.00
85	60.00
☞N. Adams GA	
86	50.00
87	26.00
88-90	20.00
91-92	18.00
93	30.00
94	18.00
95	24.00
96-98	15.00
99	22.00
100	30.00
101-102	15.00
103-110	12.00
111-114	18.00
115	22.00
116-118	18.00
119-126	7.00
127-128	6.00
129-130	11.00
131	6.00
132	4.00
133	5.00
134-140	4.00
141	10.00
142-145	4.00
145/Whitman	8.00
146	4.00
146/Whitman	8.00
147	4.00
147/Whitman	8.00
148-149	4.00
149/Whitman	8.00
150	4.00
150/Whitman	12.00
151	4.00
151/Whitman	8.00
152	4.00
152/Whitman	8.00
153	4.00
153/Whitman	20.00
154	4.00
154/Whitman	8.00
155	4.00
155/Whitman	8.00
156	4.00
156/Whitman	8.00
157	4.00

157/Whitman	8.00
158	4.00
158/Whitman	8.00
159	4.00
159/Whitman	8.00
160	4.00
160/Whitman	8.00
161	4.00
161/Whitman	8.00
162	4.00
162/Whitman	8.00
163	4.00
163/Whitman	8.00
164	4.00
164/Whitman	8.00
165	4.00
165/Whitman	8.00
166-179	4.00
180-190	3.00
191	8.00
192-196	3.00
197	4.00
198-199	3.00
200	7.00
Ann 1	6.00

Brave and the Bold
DC, 1991

1	3.00
2-6	2.00

Brave and the Bold
DC, 1996

1-35	3.00

Brave Old World
DC, 2000

1-4	3.00

Bravestarr in 3-D
Blackthorne

1-2	3.00

Bravo for Adventure
Dragon Lady

1	6.00

Bravura Preview Book
Malibu, 1993

0	3.00
1-2	2.00

Breach
DC, 2005

1-2	3.00
3	5.00
☞Inf. Crisis tie	
4-11	3.00

Bread & Circuses
Moe, 1995

1	3.00

Breakdown
Devil's Due, 2004

1	4.00
1/Variant	5.00
2	4.00
2/Variant	5.00
3-6	3.00

Breakdowns
Infinity, 1986

1	2.00

Breakfast After Noon
Oni, 2000

Lost your job? Planning a wedding at the same time? Staring at the mounting bills and pondering the future? Rob and Louise are, and things are far from easy. To make matters worse, many of their friends are in the same boat. So what do you do in this situation? Simple: you never give up.

Andi Watson's signature woodcut-like style art and believable characters breath life into this all-too-real storyline. A good book for fans of realism titles like Love & Rockets and Strangers in Paradise.

1-6	3.00

Breakneck Blvd.
Motion, 1994

0-2	3.00

Breakneck Blvd.
Slave Labor, 1995

1-6	3.00

Break the Chain
Marvel Music

1	7.00

Break-Thru
Malibu, 1993

1	3.00
1/Ltd.	4.00
2	3.00

Breathtaker
DC, 1990

1-4	5.00

'Breed
Malibu, 1994

1-6	3.00

'Breed II
Malibu, 1994

1-6	3.00

Breeder// certain.revolutions
Visceral
1 ....1.00

Brenda Lee's Life Story
Dell, 1962
1 ....50.00

Brenda Starr
Superior, 1947
13 ....550.00
14 ....500.00
3-4 ....425.00
5-12 ....350.00

Brenda Starr
Charlton, 1955
13-15 ....85.00

Brenda Starr
Avalon
1-2 ....3.00

Brenda Starr Cut-Outs and Coloring Book
Blackthorne
1 ....7.00

Brenda Starr Reporter
Dell, 1963
1 ....150.00

Brick Bradford
Standard, 1948

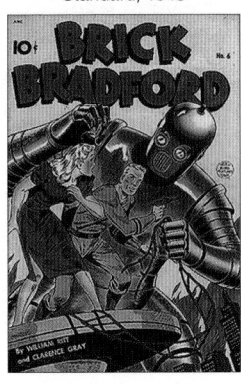

The character began in newspaper comic strips in 1933, written by William Ritt and drawn by Clarence Gray and featured a combination of all sorts of traditional pulp adventures. The main gimmick was Brick's "Time Top," used to get his buddies and him "safely" out of one era's dangers (and into those of another).

Dressed in what critic Coulton Waugh termed a "specially designed cosmosuit, a startling compromise between riding breeches and bell-bottomed

trousers, the dynamic adventurer faced crises with aplomb. His prowess, however, didn't extend to long-term support of his own comic-book series.
-- *Maggie*

5-6 .... 120.00
7-8 .... 75.00

Brickman
Harrier
1 .... 2.00

Bride's Diary
Ajax, 1955
4 .... 18.00
5-7 .... 15.00
8-10 .... 12.00

Brides in Love
Charlton, 1956
1 .... 60.00
2 .... 35.00
3-10 .... 24.00
11-30 .... 18.00
31-45 .... 12.00

Bride's Secrets
Ajax, 1954
1 .... 48.00
2 .... 28.00
3-6 .... 18.00
7-10 .... 12.00
11-19 .... 10.00

Bridgman's Constructive Anatomy
A-List, 1998
1-4 .... 3.00

Brigade
Image, 1992
1-1/Gold 2.00
2-2/Gold 4.00
3-4 .... 2.00

Brigade
Image, 1993
0-2 .... 2.00
2/A 3.00
3-11 .... 2.00
12-22 .... 3.00
25-26 .... 2.00
27 .... 3.00

Brigade
Awesome, 2000
1 .... 3.00

Brigade Sourcebook
Image, 1994
1 .... 3.00

Brik Hauss
Blackthorne, 1987
1 .... 2.00

Brilliant Boy
Circus, 1997
1-5 .... 3.00

Brinke of Destruction
High-Top, 1995
1 .... 3.00
1/CS 7.00
2-3 .... 3.00
Special 1 .... 7.00

Brinke of Destruction
BV Books
1 .... 3.00

Brinke of Disaster
High-Top, 1996
1 .... 2.00

Brinke of Eternity
Chaos, 1994
1 .... 3.00

Brit
Image, 2003
1-2 .... 5.00

Brit-Cit Babes
Fleetway-Quality
1 .... 6.00

Brit/Cold Death One Shot
Image, 2004
1 .... 5.00

Brit: Red, White, Black & Blue One-Shot
Image, 2004
1 .... 5.00

Broadway Babes
Avalon

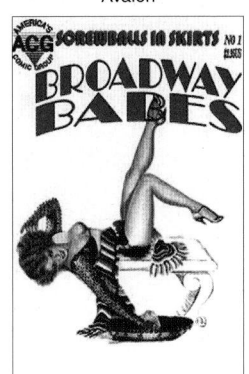

The inane adventures of Moronica are detailed in this black-and-white collection reprinting stories dating from 1950 to 1954. Moronica, a simple-minded young woman, wanders through her life, vexing and perplexing all who are unlucky enough to experience a conversation with her. When she's running a dog laundry, she tosses a live beagle and a stuffed eagle into a washing machine, resulting in a unique kind of "bird dog." At the circus, she gets into a fight with a balloon vendor who won't sell his hat even though it carries a sign that reads "5 cents." No matter what kind of foolish trouble Moronica gets into, her dumb luck always ensure that she lands on her feet, looking like the only one who really understands her wacky situations. It's all extremely reminiscent of the classic "My Friend Irma."

1 ....3.00

Broadway Video Special Collectors Edition
Broadway, 1995
1 ....1.00

Brodie's Law
Studio G, 2004
1-5 ....3.00

Broid
Eternity, 1990
1 ....3.00
2-4 ....2.00

Broken Axis
Antarctic
1 ....3.00

Broken Fender
Top Shelf Productions, 1997
1-2 ....3.00

Broken Halo: Is There Nothing Sacred?
Broken Halos, 1998
2 ....3.00
2/Nude 5.00

Broken Heroes
Sirius, 1998
1-12 ....3.00

Broncho Bill
Standard, 1948
5 ....135.00
6 ....85.00
7-16 ....50.00

Bronte's Infernal Angria
Headless Shakespeare Press, 2005
1 ....4.00

Bronx
Eternity
1-3 ....3.00

Brood Trouble in the Big Easy
Marvel, 1993
1 ....7.00

Brooklyn Dreams
DC, 1994
1-4 ....5.00

Brother Billy The Pain From Plains
Marvel, 1979
1 ....20.00

Brother Destiny
Mecca, 2004
1-3 ....3.00

Brotherhood
Marvel, 2001
1-9 ....2.00

Brotherman
Big City
1-8 ....2.00

Brother Man: Dictator of Discipline
Big City, 1996
11 ....3.00

Brother Power, the Geek
DC, 1968
1 ....45.00
2 ....20.00

Brothers, Hang in There
Spire
1 ....3.00

Brothers of the Spear
Gold Key, 1972

The Brothers of the Spear originally appeared as a backup feature in the classic Tarzan (Dell) series. The two title characters are Dan-El of Aba-Zulu, a white man, and Natongo of Tungelu, a black man, but the stories in Tarzan began with the two as boys growing up together in Natongo's tribe. By the time of this title, both have become warrior kings in Africa. And the stunning art is by Russ Manning.

Dan-El and Natongo are renowned both for their bravery and for their fighting skills. Unlike so many other action heroes, the two are not only kings (with armies to command, if they wish), but are

also married to equally capable warrior queens.

This series ran from 1972 until 1976 and was revisited for a single new issue in 1982.

1 ....20.00
2 ....10.00
3-5 ....6.00
6-17 ....4.00
18 ....3.00

Bruce Gentry
Superior, 1948
1 ....350.00
2-18 ....180.00

Bruce Lee
Malibu, 1994
1-6 ....3.00

Bruce Wayne: Agent of S.H.I.E.L.D.
Marvel, 1996
1 ....2.00

Bru-Hed
Schism, 1993
1-4 ....3.00

Bru-Hed's Breathtaking Beauties
Schism, 1995
1 ....3.00

Bru-Hed's Bunnies, Baddies & Buddies
Schism
1 ....3.00

Bru-Hed's Guide to Gettin' Girls Now!
Schism
1-2 ....3.00

Bruiser
Anthem, 1994
1 ....2.00

Bruiser
Mythic
1-2 ....3.00

Brunner's Beauties
Fantagraphics
1 ....5.00

Brusel
NBM
1 ....20.00

Brute
Atlas-Seaboard, 1975
1 ....7.00
2-3 ....5.00

Brute Force
Marvel, 1990
1-4 ....1.00

B-Sides
Marvel, 2002

1 ....4.00
2-3..3.00

B-36
Paradise Valley

1-2..3.00

B'Tx
Tokyopop, 2006

1 ....10.00

Bubblegum Crisis: Grand Mal
Dark Horse, 1994

After the Great Kanto Earthquake of 2025, Tokyo rebuilds into a great megalopolis. Explosive growth lends itself to corruption and the Genom Corporation is ready to reap the rewards. They've created the "boomers"-humanoid robots built to withstand industrial and extraterrestrial use. The boomers occasionally go rogue, and not even the specially equipped AD Police can fully contain them. Only a small band of female vigilantes known as the Knight Sabers with their powered-armor "hardsuits" are up to the challenge of stopping Genom and their mad robots.

And now a shadow committee of newly developed intuitive boomers works to further Genom's goals. They lured a former human operative, Peter Vashnevskaya, back to Mega-Tokyo and plan to use his violent delusional psychosis to their advantage. Can the Knight Sabers save Peter from himself?

1-4..3.00

Buccaneers
Quality, 1950

19 ....320.00
20-21 ....240.00
22-23 ....185.00

24-26 .... 160.00
27 .... 180.00

Buce N Gar
Rak

1-3.. 2.00

Buckaroo Banzai
Marvel, 1984

1-2 .... 1.00

Buck Godot, Zap Gun For Hire
Palliard, 1993

1 .... 4.00
2-8 .... 3.00

Buck Jones
Dell, 1951

2 .... 50.00
3-8 .... 35.00

Buck Rogers
Eastern Color, 1940

1 .... 1,950.00
2 .... 850.00
3-4 .... 700.00
5-6 .... 625.00

Buck Rogers
Gold Key, 1964

1 .... 36.00
2 .... 5.00
3-4 .... 4.00
5-16 .... 3.00

Buck Rogers Comics Module
TSR

1-9.. 3.00

Bucky O'Hare
Continuity, 1991

1 .... 3.00
2-5 .... 2.00

Buddha on the Road
Aeon, 1996

1-6 .... 3.00

Buffalo Bill
Youthful, 1950

2 .... 65.00
3-9 .... 50.00

Buffalo Bill Jr.
Dell, 1958

7-13 .... 30.00

Buffalo Bill Jr.
Gold Key, 1965

1 .... 30.00

Buffalo Bill Picture Stories
Street & Smith, 1949

1 .... 75.00
2 .... 60.00

Buffalo Wings
Antarctic, 1993

1-2 .... 3.00

Buffy the Vampire Slayer
Dark Horse, 1998

In 1992, Kristy Swanson played Buffy Summers in a feature film, where creator Joss Whedon introduced the concept of The Slayer, a young woman whose role is to kill vampires. In March 1997, "Welcome to the Hellmouth" introduced the TV audience to Sunnydale High and Sarah Michelle Gellar as Buffy. In addition, the cast expanded to add such characters as "the Scooby Gang" of Xander Harris and Willow Rosenberg, along with Buffy's new Watcher, Rupert Giles.

A little over a year later, Dark Horse began producing new comic-book stories about the team that spends much of its time patrolling Sunnydale and staking newly risen vampires before they can menace the general population. Care is taken to adhere to appearance and mythos of the TV series and the cast and storyline evolve.

-- Maggie

1/2 .... 4.00
1/2/Gold................................ 8.00
1/2/Platinum 10.00
1 .... 5.00
1/A.. 10.00
1/B.. 5.00
1/Gold-1/Variant 10.00
1/2nd-2 .... 4.00
2/Variant-3/Variant................ 5.00
4-20 .... 4.00
20/Variant-49/Variant.............. 3.00
50-50/Variant......................... 4.00
51-63 .... 3.00
Ann 1999.............................. 6.00

Buffy the Vampire Slayer: Angel
Dark Horse, 1999

1-1/Variant............................. 4.00
2-3/Variant............................. 3.00

Buffy the Vampire Slayer: Chaos Bleeds
Dark Horse, 2003
1 ....3.00

Buffy the Vampire Slayer: Food Chain
Dark Horse
1 ....17.00

Buffy the Vampire Slayer: Giles
Dark Horse, 2000
1-1/Variant.................................3.00

Buffy the Vampire Slayer: Haunted
Dark Horse, 2001
1-4.................................3.00

Buffy the Vampire Slayer: Jonathan
Dark Horse, 2001
1/Gold 10.00
1/Platinum 20.00

Buffy The Vampire Slayer: Lost and Found
Dark Horse, 2002
1 ....3.00

Buffy the Vampire Slayer: Lover's Walk
Dark Horse, 2001
1 ....3.00

Buffy The Vampire Slayer: Oz
Dark Horse, 2001
1-3/Variant.................................3.00

Buffy the Vampire Slayer: Reunion
Dark Horse, 2002
1 ....4.00

Buffy the Vampire Slayer: Ring of Fire
Dark Horse, 2000
1 ....10.00

Buffy the Vampire Slayer: Season Eight
Dark Horse, 2007
2.................................6.00
3.................................4.00
4-30.................................3.00

Buffy the Vampire Slayer: Spike and Dru
Dark Horse, 1999
1-3.................................3.00

Buffy the Vampire Slayer, Tales of the Slayers
Dark Horse, 2001
1-1.................................4.00

Buffy The Vampire Slayer: The Dust Waltz
Dark Horse, 1998
1 ....10.00

Buffy the Vampire Slayer: The Origin
Dark Horse, 1999
1 ....4.00
1/Ltd. 15.00
2-3.................................3.00

Buffy the Vampire Slayer: Willow & Tara
Dark Horse, 2001
1 ....5.00

Buffy the Vampire Slayer: Willow & Tara: Wilderness
Dark Horse, 2002
1-2.................................3.00

Bug
Marvel, 1997
1 ....3.00

Bug
Planet-X
1 ....2.00

Bug & Stump
Aaargh!, 1993
1-9.................................3.00

Bugboy
Image, 1998
1 ....4.00

B.U.G.G.'s
Acetylene Comics, 2001
1-2.................................2.00

B.U.G.G.'s (Vol. 2)
Acetylene Comics, 2001
1.................................2.00
1/A.................................3.00
2.................................2.00
3-4.................................3.00

Bughouse
Ajax, 1954
1 ....75.00
2 ....50.00
3-4.................................45.00

Bughouse (Cat-Head)
Cat-Head, 1994
1-5.................................3.00

Bug-Hunters
Trident
1 ....6.00

Bugnut
Comicosley, 1999
1 ....3.00

Bugs Bunny
Dell, 1952
28-40.................................35.00

41-60.................................25.00
61-80.................................20.00
81-85.................................15.00

Bugs Bunny
Gold Key, 1962
86-101.................................7.00
102-150.................................6.00
151-200.................................5.00
201-212.................................3.00
213-245.................................2.00

Bugs Bunny
DC, 1990
1-3.................................2.00

Bugs Bunny and Porky Pig
Dell, 1965
1 ....26.00

Bugs Bunny!
Burghley
1-2.................................3.00

Bugs Bunny Monthly
DC
1-3.................................2.00

Bugs Bunny's Christmas Funnies
Dell, 1950
1 ....115.00
2 ....75.00
3-5.................................65.00
6-9.................................55.00

Bugs Bunny's County Fair
Dell, 1957
1 ....125.00

Bugs Bunny's Halloween Parade
Dell, 1953
1 ....75.00
2 ....65.00

Bugs Bunny's Trick 'n' Treat Halloween Fun
Dell, 1955
3-4.................................65.00

Bugs Bunny's Vacation Funnies
Dell, 1951
1 ....150.00
2 ....120.00
3 ....100.00
4-9.................................80.00

Bugs Bunny Winter Fun
Gold Key, 1967
1 ....30.00

Bug's Gift, A
Discovery
1 ....2.00

Bugtown
Aeon, 2004
1-6 .... 3.00

Bug Wars
Avalon Communications, 1998
1 .... 3.00

Building
DC, 2000
1 .... 10.00

Buja's Diary
NBM, 2005
1 .... 20.00

Bulldog
Five Star
1 .... 3.00

Bulldog Drummond
Moonstone
0 .... 5.00

Bullet Crow, Fowl of Fortune
Eclipse
1-2 .... 2.00

Bulletman
Fawcett, 1941

Bulletman (known as "the flying detective") was one of the stars among Fawcett's universe of super-heroes and appeared, for example, in Master Comics. His adventures began as the cover feature of the biweekly Nickle Comics #1 (May 17 40), and, when that series ended, he quickly moved to Master Comics (in #7, Oct 40). It was there that his companion, Bulletgirl, was introduced. (She joined him in #13, Apr 41).

The couple's headgear consisted of a sort of "shell" hat, they could fly in their fight against evil, and they were joined by Bulletdog in #10 (Dec 42). Note: There was no #13 in the series, probably owing to a change in frequency from monthly to quarterly.

-- *Maggie*

1 .... 2,250.00
2 .... 975.00
3 .... 700.00
4-5 .... 625.00
6-10 .... 500.00
11-16 .... 375.00

Bullet Points
Marvel, 2007
1-4 .... 3.00

Bulletproof
Known Associates
1 .... 4.00

Bulletproof Comics
Wet Paint Graphics, 1999
1-3 .... 2.00

Bulletproof Monk
Image, 1998
1-3 .... 3.00

Bulletproof Monk: Tales of the Bulletproof Monk
Image, 2003
1 .... 3.00

Bullets and Bracelets
Marvel, 1996

Marvel and DC Comics combined their universes and jointly published twelve one-shot "Amalgam" comics which were intended to be issues of the adventures of the various combined characters. A marvel of publicity, it answered super-hero fans' dreams about a Marvel/DC merger.

Bullets and Bracelets is the adventures of the team of Wonder Woman (Diana Prince) and The Punisher (Trevor Castle). The two had apparently been husband and wife in the Amalgam universe, but their union had come to tears after their first child was born. In this adventure, they reunite to find their baby who had been kidnapped by the Hand, although more nefarious forces including the villainous Thanoseid (read: Darkseid + Thanos) are masterminding the abduction. John Ostrander wrote, Gary Frank penciled, and Cam Smith inked.

1 .... 2.00

Bullseye Greatest Hits
Marvel, 2004
1-5 .... 3.00

Bulls-Eye
Mainline, 1954
1 .... 500.00
2 .... 400.00
3 .... 300.00
4-7 .... 250.00

Bullwinkle
Dell, 1962
1 .... 100.00

Bullwinkle and Rocky
Gold Key, 1962
1 .... 90.00
2 .... 68.00
3 .... 45.00
4-5 .... 40.00
6-11 .... 28.00
12 .... 14.00
13 .... 20.00
14 .... 16.00
15-20 .... 10.00
21-25 .... 8.00

Bullwinkle and Rocky
Charlton, 1970
1 .... 30.00
2 .... 18.00
3 .... 15.00
4-7 .... 12.00

Bullwinkle and Rocky
Marvel, 1987
1-9 .... 2.00

Bullwinkle & Rocky
Blackthorne, 1987
1-3D 1 .... 3.00

Bullwinkle for President in 3-D
Blackthorne, 1987
1 .... 3.00

Bullwinkle Mother Moose Nursery Pomes
Dell, 1962
1 .... 85.00

Bumbercomix
Starhead
1 .... 1.00

Bumperboy Loses His Marbles
Adhouse Books, 2005
1 .... 8.00

Bunny
Harvey, 1966

1	50.00
2-20	30.00
21	15.00

Bunny Town
Radio, 2002

1	3.00

Burger Bomb
Funny Book Institute, 1999

1-3	3.00

Burglar Bill
Image, 2005

1-4	3.00

Burglar Bill
Trident

1	2.00

Burial of the Rats
Roger Corman's Cosmic Comics, 1995

1-3	3.00

Buried Terror
NEC, 1995

1	3.00

Buried Treasure
Pure Imagination

1-3	6.00

Buried Treasure
Caliber

1-4	3.00

Burke's Law
Dell, 1964

1	24.00
2-3	20.00

Burrito
Accent!, 1995

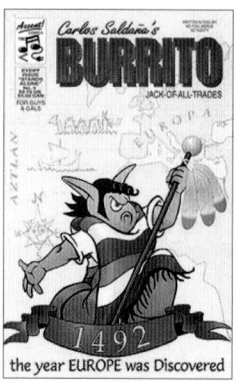

the year EUROPE was Discovered

In this series from Accent! Comics, Burrito-which means "Little Burro"-and his friends, Adelita and Torito, get involved in adventures that are somewhat reminiscent of those of Uncle Scrooge and Donald Duck. For example, one issue finds them tossed about on the ocean until they "discover" Europe, which Burrito dubs "New Tijuana." In this strange new land, Burrito, Adelita, and Torito learn about books, astronomy, knights, and violent inquisitions. This is excellent-and funny-stuff!

1-5	3.00

Bushido
Eternity, 1988

1-4	2.00

Bushido Blade of Zatoichi Walrus
Solson, 1987

1-2	2.00

Bushwhacked
Fantagraphics

1	3.00

Buster
Crisis

1-2	3.00

Buster Brown Comic Book
Buster Brown

Buster Brown is one of the oldest characters in American comics, dating from 1902, the creation of Yellow Kid pioneer Richard Outcault (1863-1928). While The Yellow Kid was a slum character, Buster was clearly wealthy -- but the child of privilege was, nevertheless, naughty. And that's what each strip was built on: the disaster caused by Buster, followed by his promise to be good from that point on.

Outcault had considerable success licensing The Yellow Kid for a number of products, but with Buster Brown he outdid his previous efforts. The best-known of his licenses is one that continues to this day: Buster Brown shoes, where the symbol includes Buster's dog, Tige. The shoe company used this comic book as an additional promotional tool, but its stories did not contain the antics of boy and dog; it was simply an anthology giveaway comic book available in stores selling Buster Brown shoes. The adventure stories were entertaining, and the art was often excellent.

-- Maggie

1	115.00
2	80.00
3-5	55.00
6-10	36.00
11-20	26.00
21-24	20.00
25	35.00
26-28	20.00
29-37	35.00
38-39	16.00
40-41	35.00
42-43	20.00

Buster Brown of the Safety Patrol
Custom

1	22.00

Buster Bunny
Standard, 1949

1	40.00
2	22.00
3-5	16.00
6-16	15.00

Buster Crabbe
Lev Gleason, 1953

1	125.00
2-4	110.00

Buster Crabbe
Famous Funnies, 1951

1	250.00
2-3	210.00
4	150.00
5-8	105.00
9	90.00
10-12	60.00

Buster the Amazing Bear
Ursus, 1992

1-5	3.00

Bustline Combat
Fantagraphics, 1999

1	3.00

Butcher
DC, 1990

1	3.00
2-5	2.00

Butcher Knight
Image, 2000
1-4..3.00

Butt Biscuit
Fantagraphics, 1992
1-3..2.00

Butterscotch
Fantagraphics
1-3..3.00

Button Man:
The Killing Game
Kitchen Sink, 1995
1...16.00

Buz Sawyer
Standard, 1948

The Buz Sawyer adventure comic strip was created by Roy Crane (1901-1977), following his work on NEA's Wash Tubbs and Captain Easy. The new strip began in 1943, starring a Navy pilot and his gunner buddy, Roscoe Sweeny -- and featuring the stylish art of Crane, who used screening to great effect in the black-and-white daily strips. The strip long outlived Crane, but the comic book had only a short run.

He told members of The National Cartoonists Society, "If I had it to do over, I'd never do a Sunday. It's the straw that breaks backs." Nevertheless, Crane was an artist's artist (as witness the number of Crane panels that found their way into other artist's swipe files.

-- Maggie

1..125.00
2..75.00
3..50.00

Buz Sawyer Quarterly
Dragon Lady, 1986
1-3....................................... 6.00

Buzz
Kitchen Sink, 1990
1-3....................................... 3.00

Buzz
Marvel, 2000
1-3....................................... 3.00

Buzz and Colonel Toad
Belmont, 1998
1-3....................................... 3.00

Buzzard
Cat-Head, 1990
1-11...................................... 3.00
12-20.................................... 4.00

Buzzboy
Skydog, 1998
1-4....................................... 3.00

Buzz Buzz
Comics Magazine
Horse
1... 5.00

Buzzy
DC, 1944

When Archie proved the viability of teen humor in comics during World War II, DC was quick to come out with its own competing title, Buzzy. "America's Favorite Teen-Ager" is a good-looking, blond, high-school student facing the hassles of pleasing his girlfriend Suzy and fending off his high-handed rival Wolfie.

Each issue features three or four short vignettes centered on such familiar teen-humor plot devices as Suzie's ill-tempered father, foiling the school principal, Wolfie's schemes to get girls, and so on.

Both the art and writing heavily mine the vein made popular by Archie, which was enough to keep the series going into the mid-1950s.

-- Rob Salkowitz

1.. 125.00
2.. 65.00
3.. 48.00
4-5.. 40.00
6-10...................................... 35.00
11-20.................................... 30.00
21-30.................................... 22.00
31-40.................................... 16.00
41-50.................................... 13.00
51-77...................................... 9.00

By Bizarre Hands
Dark Horse, 1994
1-3....................................... 3.00

By Bizarre Hands
Avatar, 2004
1... 4.00
1/Red foil............................. 10.00
1/Wraparound 5.00
2... 4.00
2/Red foil............................... 8.00
2/Wraparound 5.00
3... 4.00
3/Red foil............................... 8.00
3/Wraparound 5.00
4... 4.00
4/Red foil............................... 8.00
4/Wraparound 5.00
5... 4.00
5/Red foil............................... 8.00
5/Wraparound 5.00
6... 4.00
6/Red foil............................... 8.00
6/Wraparound 5.00

By the Time I Get to
Wagga Wagga
Harrier
1... 2.00

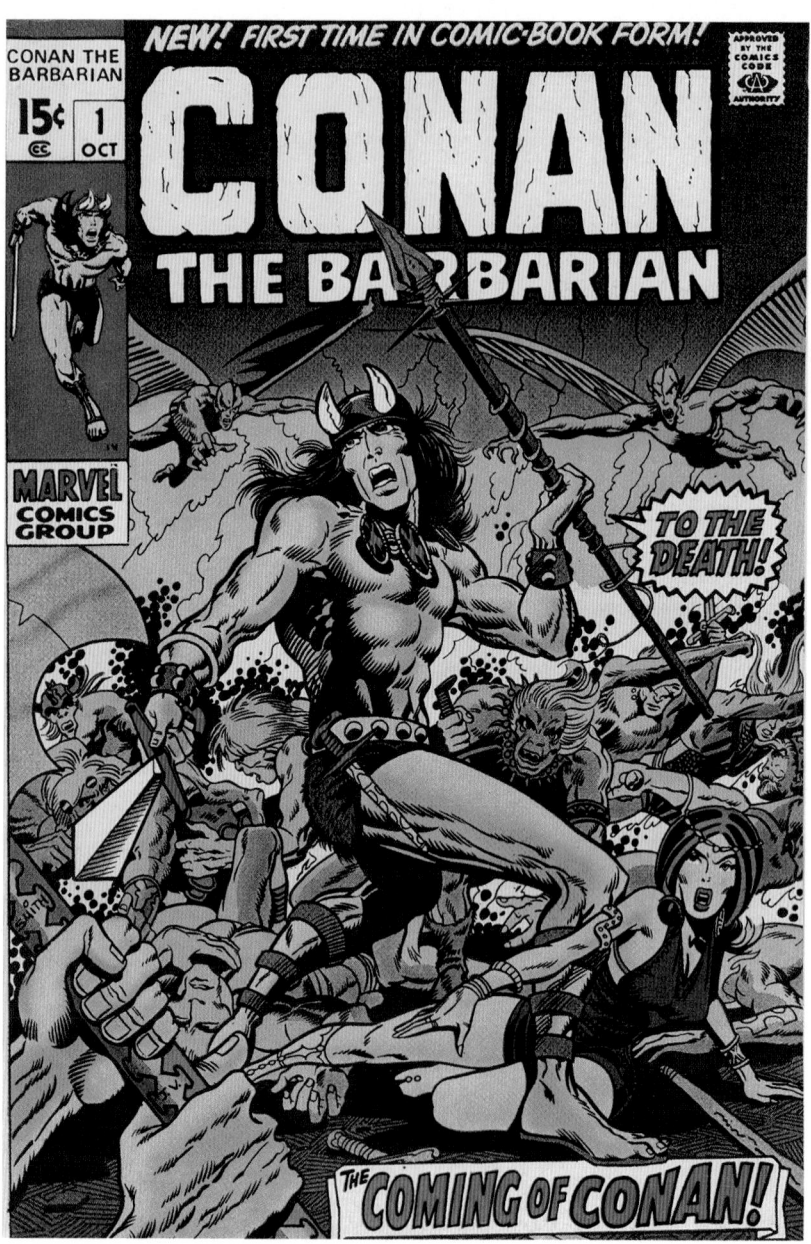

Writer Roy Thomas convinced Marvel Editor in Chief Stan Lee to take a chance and obtain the comics license for Robert E. Howard's barbarian hero.

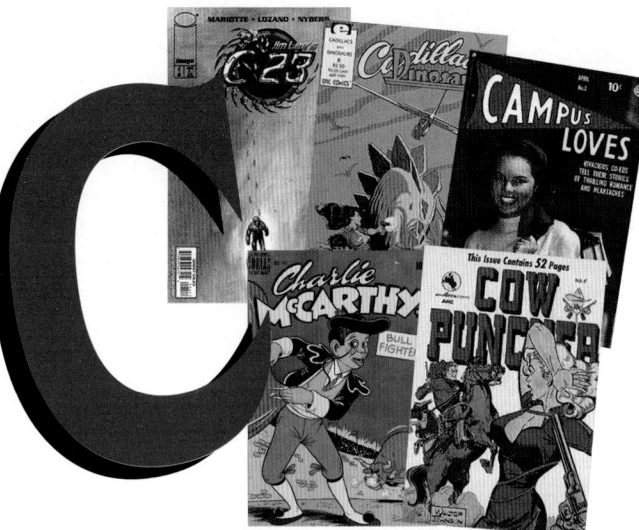

C•23
Image, 1998

1	5.00
1/Ashcan	4.00
2	3.00
2/Variant	2.00
3-8	3.00
8/Variant	4.00

Cabbot: Bloodhunter
Maximum, 1997

1	3.00

Cabinet of Dr. Caligari
Monster, 1992

1-3	2.00

Cable
Marvel, 1993

He first was seen in our timeline in The New Mutants #87 (Mar 90), but, although he has had remarkable influence on the various mutant teams in the Marvel Universe, readers have only relatively recently begun to discover much about him. They now know that the man known as Cable has another name, Nathan Dayspring, and that he hails from a dark, totalitarian version of our world, centuries in the future. Thanks to the technology of that period, he has the ability to transport himself back in time. He uses that ability to wage a war in time and space, with the ultimate goal of preventing that dark future from occurring.

An immensely popular character since he first appeared, Cable was featured in the two-issue Cable: Blood and Metal, then in 1993 was given this, his first ongoing series. In it readers finally learn many of the answers to the questions they have been asking about this mysterious warrior.

-1	2.00
1	4.00
2-10	3.00
11-16	2.00
16/Variant	4.00
17-24	2.00
25	4.00
26-49	2.00
50	3.00
51-74	2.00
75	5.00
76-99	2.00
100	4.00
101-107	2.00
Ann 1998	3.00
Ann 1999	4.00

Cable: Blood and Metal
Marvel, 1992

1	4.00
2	3.00

Cable/Deadpool
Marvel, 2004

1	4.00
2-50	3.00

Cable: Second Genesis
Marvel, 1999

1	4.00

Cable TV
Parody

1	3.00

Cadavera
Monster

1-2	2.00

Cadence of the Dirge
Gothic

1	3.00

Cadet Gray of West Point
Dell, 1958

1	75.00

Cadillacs & Dinosaurs
Marvel, 1990

1-6	3.00
3D 1	4.00

Cadillacs & Dinosaurs
Kitchen Sink, 1993

1	4.00

Cadillacs & Dinosaurs
Topps, 1994

1-10	3.00

Caffeine
Slave Labor, 1996

Caffeine is a humorous showcase for the work of cartoonist Jim Hill. Hill brings an edgy, angry feel to his work, which here centers around a crew of amusingly dysfunctional twenty-somethings. Included is a nymphomaniac with a psychotic husband, a pair of road-tripping buddies discussing chicken-fried steak on their way to a trip with destiny, and the incredibly hostile, but oh-so-hip Alice Armour.

In addition to these misfits, Hill also includes prize rant pieces like, "I'm so Pissed!" which tear into everything from hippies to karaoke. Finally, there's the adventures of Disco Mail Man, whose urge to "lighten up" and "let the good vibes flow" is curbed by a truncheon-wielding cop, out for blood in enforcing the "no disco zone."

1-10 ....3.00

Cage
Marvel, 1992

1 ....3.00
2-20 ....1.00

Cage
Marvel, 2002

1 ....4.00
2-5 ....3.00

Caged Heat 3000
Roger Corman's Cosmic Comics, 1996

1-3 ....3.00

Cages
Tundra, 1993

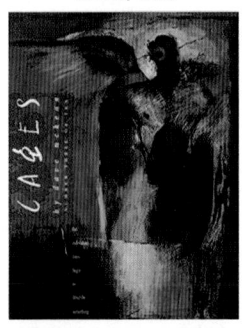

Dave McKean is well-known as the talented artist whose work includes Batman: Arkham Asylum and Sandman. In Cages, McKean handles not only the art, but the story as well. The result is an intense, brilliant story in 10 parts.

In some ways, this series is about the cages we build for ourselves, as seen in the lives of the people who occupy a city apartment building. One man in particular, a reclusive writer who lives upstairs, has built the tightest cage of them all. Two years ago, he

channeled all the pain and grief in his life into a book critical of religion and its effect on people. That book was "Cages," and the author was Jonathan Rush. Much like real-life author Salmon Rushdie, he was attacked by religious zealots. To this day, book-burnings of "Cages" are still held, and Rush is forced to live his life as a fugitive. But just as the caged bird is said to sing the most sweetly, his pain (and that of the other residents) is seen here with a certain poignant beauty.

1 .... 5.00
2-9 .... 4.00
10 .... 5.00

Cain
Harris, 1993

1-2 .... 3.00

Calculated Risk
Genesis, 1990

1 .... 2.00

Caliber Christmas, A
Caliber

1 .... 4.00

Caliber Christmas, A
Caliber, 1998

1 .... 6.00

Caliber Core
Caliber

0 .... 3.00
Ashcan 1 .... 1.00

Caliber Presents
Caliber, 1989

1 .... 15.00
☞1st Crow
2-7 .... 3.00
8 .... 2.00
9-24 .... 3.00

Caliber Presents: Cinderella on Fire
Caliber, 1994

1 .... 3.00

Caliber Presents: Generator Comics
Caliber

1 .... 3.00

Caliber Presents: Hybrid Stories
Caliber

1 .... 3.00

Caliber Presents: Petit Mal
Caliber

1 .... 3.00

Caliber Presents: Romantic Tales
Caliber, 1995

1 .... 3.00

Caliber Presents: Sepulcher Opus
Caliber, 1993

1 .... 3.00

Caliber Presents: Something Inside
Caliber

1 .... 4.00

Caliber Presents: Sub-Atomic Shock
Caliber

1 .... 3.00

Caliber Spotlight
Caliber, 1995

Caliber Spotlight is a giant one-shot that previews the publisher's new offerings for 1995. The weighty volume includes sneak previews at Unleashed (by Joe Sinn's Brooks Hagen), Gabriel, and Nowheresville, along with "New Worlds" titles Raven Chronicles, Inferno, Underside, and The Searchers. The last has a particularly interesting premise: Its stars are a team of researchers descended from the key characters in such H.G. Wells and Jules Verne novels as The Island of Doctor Moreau and 20,000 Leagues under the Sea.

With these previews are short stories featuring Caliber's leading characters: A.K.A. Goldfish, Kabuki, Kilroy, and Oz. Altogether, it's an impressive introduction to a publisher regarded as a bright light in black-and-white comics.

1 .... 3.00

Calibrations
Caliber
1-5 .... 1.00

Calibrations
Caliber, 1996
1-5 .... 1.00

California Comics
California, 1977
1 .... 5.00
2-3 .... 4.00

California Girls
Eclipse, 1987
1-8 .... 2.00

California Raisins in 3-D
Blackthorne, 1987
1-5 .... 3.00

Caligari 2050
Monster, 1992
1-3 .... 2.00

Caligari 2050: Another Sleepless Night
Caliber, 1993
1 .... 4.00

Call
Marvel, 2003
1-4 .... 2.00

Called From Darkness
Anarchy
1-1/2nd 3.00

Calling All Boys
Parents' Magazine Institute, 1946

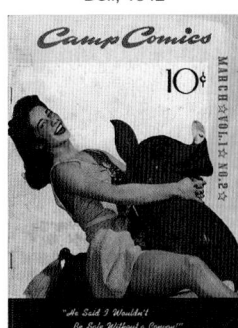

Drawing on the success of the earlier Calling All Girls and Calling All Kids, the publishers of Parents Magazine launched this, the logical extension of the series, in 1946.

Each giant-sized issue brought numerous stories, including the comical exploits of Hector, sports comics featuring Streaky Smith, and the super-smart adventures of "Big Brain Billy." In an unusual move for a comics magazine, it

also includes numerous multi-page text stories. Wrapping things up, a "Coach's Corner," written by such sports legends as Joe DiMaggio gave kids tips for improving their playing abilities.

After 17 issues under the Calling All Boys name, the title became known as Tex Granger, after the title's popular Western feature.

1	60.00
2	28.00
3	18.00
4-9	15.00
10	30.00
11	15.00
12	35.00
13	30.00
14-17	. 15.00

Calling All Girls
Parents' Magazine Institute, 1941

1	100.00
2	95.00
3	90.00
4	85.00
5	80.00
6	75.00
7	70.00
8	65.00
9	60.00
10-13	50.00
14-16	45.00
17-19	40.00
20-22	35.00
23-26	30.00
27-39	25.00
40-43	20.00

Calling All Kids
Parents' Magazine Institute, 1946

1	55.00
2	25.00
3	18.00
4-10	14.00
11-26	12.00

Call Me Princess
CPM, 1999
1-6 .... 3.00

Call of Duty: The Brotherhood
Marvel, 2002
1-6 .... 2.00

Call of Duty: The Precinct
Marvel, 2002
1-5 .... 2.00

Call of Duty: The Wagon
Marvel, 2002
1-4 .... 2.00

Calvin and the Colonel
Dell, 1962
2 .... 25.00

Cambion
Slave Labor, 1995
1-3 .... 3.00

Cambion
Moonstone
3-5 .... 3.00

Camelot Eternal
Caliber
1-8 .... 3.00

Camelot 3000
DC, 1982
1 .... 3.00
2-12 .... 2.00

Camera Comics
U.S. Camera, 1944

1	250.00
2	140.00
3	125.00
4-6	100.00
7-11	90.00

Camp Candy
Marvel, 1990
1-7 .... 1.00

Camp Comics
Dell, 1942

When World War II broke out, Dell -- noted for its comics dedicated for young readers -- tried out a title to be distributed to the Armed Forces. The stories were clearly aimed at adult males and carried advertising (something else that was not a feature of Dell comics of the day) for cigarettes and shaving gear.

The anthology title featured pin-up photo covers, straight adventure strips, and slapstick comedy, one of the latter features being "Seaman Sy Wheeler" written and drawn by Walt Kelly. It's not clear today what forces led to the cancellation of the title; what is clear is that the war lasted longer than Camp Comics did.

-- Maggie

1	500.00
2	450.00
3	400.00

Campfire Stories
Global, 1992

1	2.00

Camping with Bigfoot
Slave Labor, 1995

1	3.00

Camp Runamuck
Dell, 1966

1	40.00

Campus Loves
Quality, 1949

1	300.00
2	165.00
3-4	125.00
5	100.00

Campus Romances
Avon, 1949

1	120.00
2-3	85.00

Canadian Comics Cavalcade
Artworx

1	2.00

Canadian Ninja
Quebec

1	2.00

Canadian Rock Special
Revolutionary, 1994

This black-and-white special from Revolutionary Comics chronicles the - unauthorized - story of Canadian rockers Rush. The art is a bit simple, but the story is the stuff of "VH1: Legends" or "Behind the Music." It begins with early attempts by Geddy Lee, Alex Lifeson, and Neil Peart to form a band, as well as the impact of Led Zeppelin's first album on that band's sound. Rush gained recognition opening for such established acts as Blue Oyster Cult and Nazareth and appearing on "In Concert" and "Don Kirshner's Rock Concert." Of course, the band hit its zenith in the late 1970s and the early 1980s, but it has continued to produce music that gets air-time.

1	3.00

Cancer: The Crab Boy
Sabre's Edge

1-5	3.00

Candidate Goddess
Tokyopop, 2004

1-2	10.00

Candide Revealed
Fantagraphics

1	2.00

Candy
Quality, 1944

1	340.00
2	215.00
3	185.00

Candy
Comic Magazines, 1947

1	100.00
2	55.00
3-5	36.00
6-10	26.00
11-20	22.00
21-30	18.00
31-39	15.00
40-50	14.00
51-64	12.00

Candyappleblack
Good Intentions Paving, 2004

1-5	4.00

Cannibalis
Raging Rhino

1	3.00

Cannon
Fantagraphics, 1991

1-8	3.00

Cannon Busters
Devil's Due, 2004

0	15.00
1	3.00
1/Variant	4.00
2	3.00
2/Variant	4.00

Cannon God Exaxxion
Dark Horse, 2001

1-8	3.00
9-14	4.00
15-20	3.00

Cannon Hawke: Dawn of War (Michael Turner's)
Aspen, 2004

1	6.00

Canteen Kate
St. John, 1952

1	350.00
2-3	300.00

Canyon Comics Presents
Grand Canyon Association, 1995

1-2	2.00

Cape City
Dimension X

1-3	3.00

Caper
DC, 2003

1-12	3.00

Capes
Image, 2003

1-3	4.00

Capital Capers Presents
BLT, 1994

1-2	3.00

Cap'n Oatmeal
All American

1	2.00

Cap'n Quick & a Foozle
Eclipse, 1984

1-3	2.00

Captain Action
Karl Art

0	2.00

Captain Action
DC, 1968

1	45.00
2-4	35.00
5	20.00

Captain Aero Comics
Continental, 1941

1	1,600.00
2	850.00
3-5	725.00
6-7	675.00
8	325.00
9-10	265.00
11-13	225.00
14-17	190.00
21-26	165.00

Captain Africa
African Prince Productions, 1992

1	3.00

Captain America
Marvel, 1968

When World War II began, Steve Rogers attempted to enlist in the army, but was turned away because he was considered too frail. Wanting to help any way he could, he offered to serve as a human guinea pig for the experimental Super Soldier Serum. The formula worked, transforming this former 98-pound weakling into the powerhouse known as Captain America.

A star of the Golden Age of comics, Captain America joined the Silver Age when he was revived in The Avengers #4. He soon became the leader of that team, as well as co-starring with Iron Man in Tales of Suspense. Following issue #99, Tales of Suspense spun Iron Man off into a new title, and changed its name to Captain America.

The series ran uninterrupted for years, with writer Mark Gruenwald redefining the series in the 1980s and early 1990s. Writer Mark Waid was returning attention to the title when Marvel booted him off and ended the series to make way for Rob Liefeld's "Heroes Reborn" version. Several series restarts have occurred since.

100	210.00
101	55.00
102-108	35.00
109	45.00
☛Origin retold	
109/2nd	3.00
110	75.00
☛Steranko begins	
111	65.00
112	50.00
113	60.00
☛Avengers app.	
114-116	30.00
117	95.00
☛1st Falcon	

118-124	25.00
125-127	20.00
128-130	15.00
131-132	18.00
133	15.00
134-136	18.00
137	35.00
138	30.00
139-146	25.00
147	18.00
148	16.00
149	15.00
150	25.00
151-153	15.00
154-155	25.00
156	20.00
157-162	10.00
163-164	12.00
165-167	10.00
168	15.00
169	10.00
170	12.00
171-172	10.00
173	15.00
174	12.00
175-176	10.00
177-183	8.00
184-187	5.00
188	8.00
189-196	6.00
196/30¢	20.00
197	5.00
197/30¢	20.00
198	6.00
198/30¢	20.00
199	5.00
199/30¢	20.00
200	6.00
200/30¢	20.00
201	6.00
202	4.00
203	5.00
204-205	4.00
206-206/Whitman	5.00
207-207/Whitman	4.00
208-209/Whitman	5.00
210-210/Whitman	4.00
210/35¢	15.00
211-211/Whitman	4.00
211/35¢	15.00
212-212/Whitman	4.00
212/35¢	15.00
213-213/Whitman	4.00
213/35¢	15.00
214-214/Whitman	4.00
214/35¢	15.00
215-233/Whitman	4.00
234	6.00
235-240	4.00
241	8.00
242-255	4.00
256-271	2.00
272	3.00
273-275	2.00
276	4.00
277-281	2.00
282	3.00
282/2nd-283	2.00
284	3.00
285	2.00

286-288	3.00
289-297	2.00
298	3.00
299-331	2.00
332	3.00
333-349	2.00
350	3.00
351-382	2.00
383	3.00
384-399	2.00
400	3.00
401-420	2.00
420/CS	3.00
421-424	2.00
425	3.00
425/Variant	4.00
426-443	2.00
444	3.00
445-447	2.00
448	3.00
449-454	2.00
Ann 1	35.00
Ann 2	20.00
Ann 3-4	8.00
Ann 5-7	3.00
Ann 8	12.00
☛Wolverine app.	
Ann 9-13	3.00
Ashcan 1	1.00
Special 1-2	4.00

Captain America
Marvel, 1995

1	3.00
1/Flag	4.00
1/Conv	25.00
2-13	2.00
Ashcan 1-Ashcan 1/A	1.00

Captain America
Marvel, 1998

1	4.00
1/Sunburst	5.00
2	3.00
2/Variant	4.00
3-12	2.00
12/Ltd.	6.00
13-17	2.00
18	3.00
19-24	2.00
25	3.00
26-49	2.00
50	6.00
Ann 1998-2000	4.00
Ann 2001	3.00

Captain America
Marvel, 2002

1	4.00
2-32	3.00

Captain America
Marvel, 2005

1	8.00
2-3	5.00
4-5	3.00
6	7.00
6/Variant	5.00
7	3.00

8	5.00
9-21	3.00
22-24	5.00
25-25/Variant	15.00
25/2nd	5.00
26-50	3.00

Captain America and the Campbell Kids
Marvel, 1980

1	3.00

Captain America & The Falcon
Marvel, 2004

1-5	3.00
6	4.00
☛Avengers Disassembled	
7-14	3.00

Captain America Battlebook
Marvel, 1998

1	4.00

Captain America Comics
Marvel, 1941

As war raged across Europe in 1941, America watched the action nervously from the sidelines. There were many, however, who yearned to strike back at Hitler. Among these was Joe Simon, who, along with Jack Kirby, created Captain America as an exercise in patriotic wish-fulfillment. The first-issue cover even features Captain America wading through a legion of Nazis to land a hard right cross on Hitler's chin.

Along with the premiere of Captain America himself, this series introduced young sidekick "Bucky" Barnes, a camp mascot who discovered Captain America's secret identity and decided to join him in his adventures. During the war years of 1941-1945, the pair took on Nazis and fifth columnists, and their fan club, "The Sentinels of Liberty," even turned in

numerous neighbors as suspected saboteurs. Once the war was over, however, Cap faded from sight, to be reawakened later in The Avengers #4.

1	80,000.00
2	20,000.00
3	10,000.00
4	6,500.00
5	5,500.00
6	4,750.00
7	5,500.00
8	4,000.00
9-10	3,600.00
11-12	3,100.00
13	3,275.00
14-15	3,100.00
16	3,600.00
17	2,585.00
18-20	2,075.00
21-22	1,850.00
22/A	12,000.00
☛GS issue	
23-25	1,850.00
26-30	1,650.00
31-35	1,385.00
36	1,650.00
37	1,550.00
38-40	1,285.00
41-58	1,175.00
59	2,650.00
☛Cap origin	
60	1,175.00
61	1,850.00
62-65	1,075.00
66	1,400.00
67-70	1,175.00
71-73	1,025.00
74	4,350.00
☛Cap Weird Tales	
75	2,750.00
76-78	875.00

Captain America: Dead Man Running
Marvel, 2002

1-3	3.00

Captain America: Deathlok Lives!
Marvel

1	5.00

Captain America: Drug War
Marvel, 1993

1	2.00

Captain America Goes to War Against Drugs
Marvel, 1990

1	1.00

Captain America: Medusa Effect
Marvel, 1994

1	3.00

Captain America/ Nick Fury: Blood Truce
Marvel, 1995

1	6.00

Captain America/ Nick Fury: The Otherworld War
Marvel, 2001

1	7.00

Captain America: Sentinel of Liberty
Marvel, 1988

1	2.00
1/Variant	3.00
2-5	2.00
6	3.00
7-11	2.00
12	3.00

Captain America 65th Anniversary Special
Marvel, 2006

1	4.00

Captain America: The Legend
Marvel, 1996

1	4.00

Captain America: The Movie Special
Marvel, 1992

1	4.00

Captain America: What Price Glory
Marvel, 2003

1-4	3.00

Captain & The Kids
United Feature, 1947

1	100.00
2	75.00
3	50.00
4-6	45.00
7-9	40.00
10-12	35.00
13-16	30.00
17-19	25.00
20-24	20.00
25-29	15.00
30-32	12.00

Captain Armadillo: The Adventure Begins
Staton Graphics, 1989

1	2.00

Captain Atom
Nationwide, 1950

1	325.00
2	165.00
3-5	150.00
6-7	125.00

Captain Atom
Charlton, 1965

78	40.00
79-85	25.00
86-89	20.00

Captain Atom
Modern, 1977

83-85	5.00

Captain Atom
DC, 1987

1-49	1.00
50	2.00
51-57	1.00
Ann 1-2	2.00

Captain Atom: Armageddon
DC, 2005

1-9	3.00

Captain Awareness: Assault on Campus
2-D Graphics

1	4.00

Captain Battle
Picture Scoop, 1942

3	550.00
4-5	450.00

Captain Battle Comics
New Friday, 1941

1	1,250.00
2	750.00

Captain Battle Jr.
Lev Gleason, 1943

1	925.00
2	700.00

Captain Britain
Marvel UK, 1985

1	3.00
2-14	2.00

Captain Canuck
Comely, 1975

Canada has had a lively comics publishing industry since the 1940s, but the first visible product of it in the United States was Captain Canuck, a super-hero popular during the 1970s. Dressed in a patriotic red and white costume with a maple leaf insignia on his mask, Captain Canuck kept the Great White North safe from criminals, terrorists, and other bad-guys with his super-human strength, speed, and agility.

Artist Jean-Claude St. Aubin synthesized the styles of several popular artists into a fun, decorative, and colorful look for the Captain, as well as for the fantasy-based backup story "Beyond."

-- Rob Salkowitz

1	3.00
2-14	2.00

Captain Canuck First Summer Special
Comely, 1980

1	2.00

Captain Canuck Reborn
Semple, 1993

0	2.00
1-3	3.00

Captain Carrot and His Amazing Zoo Crew
DC, 1982

1	2.00
2-20	1.00

Captain Confederacy
Steeldragon, 1987

1-Special 2	2.00

Captain Confederacy
Marvel, 1991

1-4	2.00

Captain Cosmos, the Last Starveyor
Ybor City

1	3.00

Captain Crafty
Conception, 1994

1	3.00
2-14	2.00

He is the Archangel of Art, the Baron of Baroque, and has the ability to make or create anything. Wrongdoers beware! Captain Crafty is on the prowl, and he may turn you into a really ugly-looking Picasso painting.

Working from his secret headquarters in the Kraft mansion, and accompanied by his faithful butler Frank, Crafty cruises the city streets at high speed, at least until the Crafty Car runs out of gas.

Captain Crafty must live up to the heroic tradition set by his deceased father. Luckily, with his floppy hat and his extradimensional cape, he has all the crayons, hot glue guns, and other art supplies he needs to paint the bad guys into a corner.

1-2	3.00
2.5	1.00

Captain Crafty Color Spectacular
Conception, 1996

1-2	3.00

Captain Crusader
TPI, 1990

1	1.00

Captain Cult
Hammac

1	2.00

Captain Dingleberry
Slave Labor, 1998

1-6	3.00

Captain D's Adventure Magazine
Paragon, 1983

1-6	1.00

Captain Easy
Standard, 1947
10	160.00
11	125.00
12-14	100.00
15-17	90.00

Captain Electron
BCSI
1	2.00

Captain Eo 3-D
Eclipse, 1987
1	5.00

Captain Fearless Comics
Holyoke, 1941
1	475.00
2	300.00

Captain Flight Comics
Four Star, 1944
1	2,000.00
2	1,650.00
3	1,400.00
4	1,250.00
5	1,500.00
6	1,100.00
7-10	1,500.00
11	1,800.00

Captain Fortune
Rip Off
1-4	3.00

Captain Gallant
Charlton, 1955
1	11.00
1/A-3	8.00
4	5.00

Captain Glory
Topps, 1993
0-1	3.00

Captain Gravity
Penny-Farthing, 1998

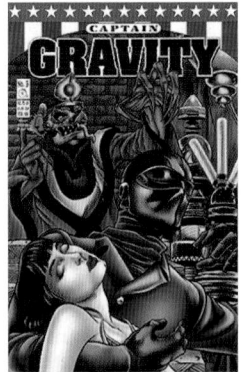

On location among the historic ruins of Chichen Itza, Mexico, a movie crew is attempting to shoot the debut of the newest serial sensation, Captain Gravity. Unfortunately, the film is just a front for a group of Nazis who seek a legendary extraterrestrial artifact known only as Element 115.

Tricked into betraying his friends and the artifact to the Germans, young Joshua Jones seems to be the only one left to foil the Nazis' evil scheme. Gambling everything on the unknown effects of his exposure to Element 115, Jones hopes the appearance of the supposedly fictional Captain Gravity will save the day.

This four-issue mini-series combines the campiness of Golden Age stories with the melodrama of B-grade movies but also provides solid storytelling with realistic characters. The story also confronts the issue of racism head-on, comparing Hitler's campaign against the Jews to America's treatment of blacks and other minorities during the same time period.

1	3.00
2-4	3.00

Captain Gravity and the Power of the Vril
Penny-Farthing, 2004
1-6	3.00

Captain Gravity: One True Hero
Penny-Farthing, 1999
1	3.00

Captain Harlock
Eternity, 1989
1-13	3.00
Holiday 1	3.00

Captain Harlock: Deathshadow Rising
Eternity
1-6	2.00

Captain Harlock: The Fall of the Empire
Eternity, 1992
1-4	3.00

Captain Harlock: The Machine People
Eternity

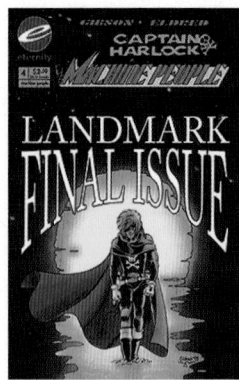

Created by Japanese animator Leiji Matsumoto, space pirate Captain Harlock and the crew of the Arcadia debuted in American comics in 1989, setting sales records at the time for a black-and-white comic. In this final four-issue series, Harlock and his friends are swept up in the rebellion against the Illuminadas and the Machine People, the android aristocracy that now controls Earth. It is a desperate time for Harlock and the others, their battles brutal and deadly, and many do not survive to see the outcome of their struggle. At what point does the price of victory become too high, the cost of freedom too much bear?

1-4	3.00

Capt. Holo and His Adventures in the Holographic Dimension in 3-D
Blackthorne
1	3.00

Captain Jet
Farrell, 1952
1	125.00
2	85.00
3	60.00
4-5	40.00

Captain Johner & the Aliens
Valiant, 1995
1-2	6.00

Captain Justice
Marvel, 1988
1-2	1.00

Captain Kidd
Fox, 1949
24-25 .... 100.00

Captain Marvel
M.F., 1966
1 .... 40.00
2-4 .... 25.00

Captain Marvel
Marvel, 1968
1 .... 60.00
2-3 .... 18.00
4 .... 24.00
5 .... 15.00
6 .... 30.00
7-8 .... 15.00
9 .... 25.00
10-15 .... 15.00
16 .... 25.00
17-24 .... 22.00
☛Thanos War starts
25-27 .... 25.00
28 .... 30.00
29 .... 16.00
30 .... 12.00
31 .... 16.00
32-33 .... 12.00
34 .... 6.00
35-37 .... 3.00
38 .... 5.00
39-44 .... 3.00
44/30¢ 20.00
45 .... 3.00
45/30¢ 20.00
46-47 .... 3.00
48 .... 9.00
49 .... 3.00
50 .... 10.00
51-52 .... 4.00
52/35¢ 15.00
53-54 .... 3.00
55 .... 5.00
56 .... 3.00
57 .... 6.00
58-62 .... 3.00

Captain Marvel
Marvel, 1989
1 .... 2.00

Captain Marvel
Marvel, 1994
1-2 .... 2.00

Captain Marvel
Marvel, 1995
1 .... 3.00
2-6 .... 2.00

Captain Marvel
Marvel, 1999
0-1 .... 3.00
1/A 4.00
2-35 .... 3.00

Captain Marvel
Marvel, 2002
1-4 .... 2.00
5-25 .... 3.00

Captain Marvel Adventures
Fawcett, 1941

An ancient Egyptian wizard gives newsboy Billy Batson the power to transform himself into the world's mightiest mortal by uttering his magical name, Shazam! As Captain Marvel, he has a hugely successful career during comics' Golden Age and helps keep the world safe from villains like the evil scientist Dr. Sivana and the evil mastermind, Mr. Mind.

The good-humored Captain, co-created by C.C. Beck, made his debut in the first issue of Whiz Comics (numbered #2) in 1940 and quickly added his own series in 1941. Loose, funny, and filled with memorable characters and great stories, Captain Marvel was one of the most significant comic-book series ever created. During the 1940s, his popularity rivaled that of Superman, which prompted a lawsuit claiming that Captain Marvel had infringed on Superman's copyright. In 1953, a consent decree finally put Captain Marvel out of action until DC arranged with Fawcett that DC would publish new stories about The Big Red Cheese.

-- Rob Salkowitz

1 .... 27,500.00
2 .... 3,500.00
3 .... 1,800.00
4 .... 1,200.00
5 .... 1,050.00
6-7 .... 750.00
8-10 .... 675.00
11-15 .... 590.00
16-17 .... 550.00
18 .... 1,800.00

☛1st Mary Marvel
19-20 .... 500.00
21-22 .... 400.00
23 .... 610.00
☛1st Mr. Mind
24-40 .... 225.00
41 .... 190.00
42 .... 163.00
43-109 .... 125.00
110-120 .... 80.00
121 .... 115.00
☛Cap Marvel origin
122-150 .... 80.00

Captain Marvel Jr.
Fawcett, 1942
1 .... 4,000.00
2 .... 1,500.00
3 .... 865.00
4 .... 915.00
5 .... 735.00
6-8 .... 545.00
9-10 .... 500.00
11-15 .... 390.00
16-20 .... 340.00
21-25 .... 275.00
26-30 .... 235.00
31-40 .... 205.00
41-50 .... 180.00
51-70 .... 155.00
71-80 .... 135.00
81-119 .... 120.00

Captain Marvel Presents The Terrible Five
M.F., 1967
1 .... 18.00

Captain Marvel Storybook
Fawcett, 1947
1 .... 450.00
2 .... 310.00
3-4 .... 300.00

Captain Marvel Thrill Book
Fawcett
1 .... 5,000.00

Captain Midnight
Fawcett, 1942
1 .... 2,400.00
2 .... 1,050.00
3-5 .... 750.00
6-10 .... 585.00
11-15 .... 400.00
16-20 .... 375.00
21-30 .... 285.00
31-40 .... 225.00
41-50 .... 200.00
51-60 .... 175.00
61-67 .... 160.00

Captain Nauticus & the Ocean Force
Express, 1994
1-2 .... 3.00

Captain Nice
Gold Key, 1967

The television series starring William Daniels as the titular captain ran only 15 episodes from January to May 1967, wrapping up before the Gold Key issue hit the stands -- which may account for its one-shot status. Starting with the episode "The Man Who Flies like a Pigeon," the comedy TV series featured a super-hero whose civilian identity was "mild, meek, mother's boy" Carter Nash but who was also "the super-human protector of Big Town."

The show's theme carried the line, "Look, it's some nut who walks around in pajamas. That's no nut boy! It's Captain Nice!" -- which conveys much of the feel of the show, plugging into the campy world super-heroes inhabited in the era following the success of the Batman TV show.

-- Maggie

1 ....35.00

Captain N:
the Game Master
Valiant, 1990
1-6...2.00

Captain Oblivion
Harrier, 1987
1 ....2.00

Captain Paragon
AC, 1983
1-4...2.00

Captain Paragon and
the Sentinels of Justice
AC
1-6...2.00

Captain Phil
Steeldragon
1 ....2.00

Captain Planet and
the Planeteers
Marvel, 1991

Captain Planet and the Planeteers was adapted almost verbatim from the Saturday morning cartoon series by the same name. Its stars are five kids from around the globe who are given power rings by Gaia ("Mother Earth" herself) so that they can defend the planet from polluters.

Each ring gives its bearer control of one of the classic elements of earth, air, water, and fire. The last ring, given to the Indian boy Ma-Ti, has the power of "heart," linking the others through telepathy. When the rings are used together, they also have the power to summon Captain Planet, a super-hero for the planet. Together, Captain Planet and the young "Planeteers" fight to save the Earth from such villains as the pig-like "Hoggish Greedly" whose schemes have included strip-mining wildlife sanctuaries and shooting trash into space.

1-12.. 1.00

Captain Power and the
Soldiers of the Future
Continuity, 1988
1-2... 2.00

Captain Rocket
P.L., 1951
1 .... 300.00

Captain Salvation
Streetlight
1 .... 2.00

Captain Satan
Millennium
1-2.. 3.00

Capt. Savage and
His Leatherneck Raiders
Marvel, 1968
1 .... 35.00
2 .... 25.00
3-11 .... 15.00
12-19 .... 10.00

Captain Science
Youthful, 1950
1 .... 800.00
2 .... 450.00
3-4 .... 350.00
5-6 .... 300.00
7 .... 275.00

Captain's Jolting Tales
One Shot, 1991
1 .... 3.00
2-4 .... 4.00

Captain Sternn:
Running Out of Time
Kitchen Sink, 1993

16-year-old Paul Fremont undertook a journey to find the father who abandoned him and his mother 12 years ago. Known to the world as Captain Thunder, his father could fly and fire blasts of electrical energy from his hands. Then there was a scandal, and Captain Thunder found himself in contempt of Congress. Rather than bring disgrace and exposure to his family, Mike Fremont fled to solitary isolation on the top of Walakima Peak where his powers had originated years before. After a reunion that is something less than a Hallmark moment, Paul found himself trapped in the same abandoned copper mine where it all began for his father. Incredibly, Paul became imbued with the same powers as his father, paving the way for the debut of Blue Bolt.

The precise cause of the powers and the nature of the scandal that drove Mike Fremont

into hiding are just two of the mysteries creators Roy and Dann Thomas employ to entice readers.
-- George Haberberger

1	6.00
2-5	5.00

Captain Steve Savage
Avon, 1951

1	120.00
2	85.00
3-13	55.00

Capt. Storm
DC, 1964

1	28.00
2-5	18.00
6	14.00
7-15	12.00
16-18	9.00

Captain Tax Time
Paul Haynes Comics

1	4.00

Captain 3-D
Harvey, 1953

1	75.00

Captain Thunder and Blue Bolt
Hero, 0

1-10	2.00

Captain Thunder and Blue Bolt
Hero, 1992

1-2	4.00

Captain Universe/ Daredevil
Marvel, 2006

1	3.00

Captain Universe/ Invisible Woman
Marvel, 2006

1	3.00

Captain Universe/ Silver Surfer
Marvel, 2006

1	3.00

Captain Universe/ The Incredible Hulk
Marvel, 2006

1	3.00

Captain Universe/X-23
Marvel, 2006

1	3.00

Captain Venture and the Land Beneath the Sea
Gold Key, 1968

1	26.00
2	18.00

Captain Victory and the Galactic Rangers
Pacific, 1981

Jack Kirby, the artist who created or co-created Captain America, The Fantastic Four, The Incredible Hulk, Thor, and countless others, brings yet another hero into the world with Captain Victory and the Galactic Rangers. "King" Kirby's style shows throughout in the futuristic bent and fantastic weaponry and gadgetry of this series.

Captain Victory, an intergalactic policeman, is always on the lookout for the thieves, criminals, and rogues who roam through outer space. And, once he finds them, he doesn't give up -- he always brings them to justice, no matter how, even if it means having his body replaced, if he gets badly hurt in battle.

1-12	1.00
13-Special 1	2.00

Captain Victory and the Galactic Rangers
Jack Kirby, 2000

1-3	3.00

Captain Video
Fawcett, 1951

1	425.00
2	350.00
3-6	225.00

Captain Wings Compact Comics
AC

1-2	4.00

Captain Zephyr and the Tiger Woman
Millennium

1	3.00

Caravan Kidd
Dark Horse, 1992

Dark Horse Comics is one of the leading American publishers of manga comics. In 1992, it added to its already impressive list of Japanese titles by releasing an English translation of Johji Manabe's Caravan Kidd.

The series is set on a post-apocalyptic Earth where resources are so scarce that traders can charge incredibly high amounts of money for anything. Two of these traders -- Babo, a weird little creature, and Wataru, a human boy -- are a couple of the best. They make a good living from the needs of others, although Wataru seems to feel a little more sympathy for the needy people who cannot afford their goods. Even Babo becomes strangely likable, however, when they are tricked into following a mysterious woman into the Wastelands. This woman is Mian Toris, an accomplished warrior who is being chased by what seems like the entire Helgebard Empire. As for Babo and Wataru, their troubles are only beginning.

1-10	3.00

Caravan Kidd Part 2
Dark Horse, 1993

1-10	3.00

Caravan Kidd Part 3
Dark Horse, 1994

1-8	3.00

Carbon Knight
Lunar, 1997

1-4	3.00

Cardcaptor Sakura Comic
Mixx, 2000

1-34	3.00

Cardcaptor Sakura: Master of the Clow
Tokyopop, 2002
1-6...10.00

Care Bears
Marvel, 1985
1-20..1.00

Career Girl Romances
Charlton, 1964

The 1960s saw women making prominent places for themselves in the work-force. Remember, TV gave us a situation comedy, "That Girl," based on that very "career girl" concept. So, it only seems fitting that there would have been a comic book devoted to romances on the job, and Charlton's Career Girl Romances was that comic book. Like most titles in this genre, this one is high on melodrama, but the women at the center of the stories are high-profile artists, executive assistants, and professional photographers...an idea that was just beginning to catch on at the time.

24-31.......................................4.00
32...40.00
33-78.......................................3.00

Car 54 Where Are You?
Dell, 1962
2..75.00
3..45.00
4-5...40.00
6-7...35.00

Carl and Larry Christmas Special
Comics Interview
1..2.00

Carmen
NBM
1..11.00

Carmilla
Aircel, 1991
1-6... 3.00

Carnage
Eternity

An American military re-con team and a group of American passengers from a hijacked airliner are being held hostage in the Middle East. If the President of the United States chooses to launch an all-out rescue mission, he will surely forfeit the lives of the hostages. He doesn't know what to do...until a mercenary called Carnage shows up and volunteers to get the Americans out of Beirut. For a price. This interesting tale of political intrigue and search-and-rescue comes from Richard Kane Fergueson and Eternity Comics; while the black-and-white artwork is somewhat murky, it certainly gets the job done.

1 .... 2.00

Carnage: It's a Wonderful Life
Marvel, 1996
1 .... 2.00

Carnage: Mindbomb
Marvel, 1996
1 .... 3.00

Carnal Comics: Anna Malle
Re-Visionary, 1996
1 .... 3.00

Carnal Comics: Brittany O'Connell
Re-Visionary, 1996
1 .... 3.00

Carnal Comics: Bunny Bleu
Revisionary, 1996
1 .... 3.00

Carnal Comics: Christi Lake
Re-Visionary, 1998
1 .... 4.00

Carnal Comics: Jeanna Fine
Re-Visionary, 1995
1 .... 3.00

Carnal Comics: Jenna Jameson
Re-Visionary, 1995
1 .... 3.00

Carnal Comics: Jill Kelly
Re-Visionary, 1997
1 .... 4.00

Carnal Comics: Julia Ann
Re-Visionary, 1995
1 .... 3.00

Carnal Comics: Legends of Porn
Re-Visionary, 1998
1 .... 4.00

Carnal Comics: Lisa Ann
Re-Visionary, 1996
1 .... 3.00

Carnal Comics: Nici Sterling
Re-Visionary, 1996
1 .... 3.00

Carnal Comics: Porsche Lynn
Re-Visionary, 1996
1 .... 3.00

Carnal Comics Presents Deja Sin: Fallen Angel
Revolutionary, 1999
1-1/B..................................... 4.00

Carnal Comics Presents Demi's Wild Kingdom Adventure
Revisionary, 1999
1 .... 4.00

Carnal Comics Presents Ginger Lynn is Torn
Revisionary, 1999
1-1/A..................................... 4.00

Carnal Comics Presents Marilyn Chambers Is Still Insatiable
Revisionary, 1999
1-1/A..................................... 4.00

Carnal Comics Presents Porn Star Fantasies
Re-Visionary, 1995
1-10..3.00

Carnal Comics Presents Wicked Weapon: Official Film Adaptation
Revisionary
1-1/Ashcan..............................4.00

Carnal Comics: Rebecca Bardoux
Re-Visionary, 1994
1 ....3.00

Carnal Comics: Rebecca Lord
Re-Visionary, 1998
1-1/Nude 4.00

Carnal Comics: Sarah-Jane Hamilton
Revolutionary, 1994
1-3...3.00

Carnal Comics: Summer Cummings & Skye Blue
Re-Visionary, 1998
1 ....4.00

Carnal Comics: Taylor Wane
Re-Visionary, 1995
1 ....3.00

Carnal Comics: Zo"
Revisionary, 1998
1-1/Nude 4.00

Carneys
Archie, 1994
1 ....2.00

Carnosaur Carnage
Atomeka
1 ....5.00

Cartoon Cartoons
DC, 2001

Following in the popularity of other animated television shows turned into comic books like The Powerpuff Girls and Dexter's Laboratory, Cartoon Network: Cartoon Cartoons follows the antics and adventures of many of the network's other well-liked characters. Cartoon Network: Cartoon Cartoons is an entertaining comic book adaptation of such animation shorts as the strange sibling relationship of "Cow and Chicken," the bumbling schemes of "Ed, Edd, and Eddy," and the relationship-impaired "Johnny Bravo." Geared primarily at a younger audience, aficionados of all ages of such comics as Loony Tunes and Animaniacs will enjoy the fast paced, slapstick tales in Cartoon Network: Cartoon Cartoons.

1-33.. 2.00

Cartoon History of the Universe
Rip Off, 1990
1 .... 5.00
2-5 .... 4.00
6-9 .... 3.00

Cartoonist
Sirius, 1997
1 .... 3.00

Cartoon Network
DC
1 .... 1.00

Cartoon Network Action Pack
DC, 2006
1-45 .... 2.00

Cartoon Network Block Party
DC, 2004
1-2 .... 2.00
3 .... 3.00
4-55 .... 2.00

Cartoon Network Christmas Spectacular
Archie
1 .... 2.00

Cartoon Network Presents
DC, 1997
1-24 .... 2.00

Cartoon Network Presents Space Ghost
Archie, 1997
1 .... 2.00

Cartoon Network Starring
DC, 1999
1-2 .... 3.00
3-18 .... 2.00

Cartoon Quarterly
Gladstone
1 .... 5.00

Cartoon Tales (Disney's...)
Disney, 1992
1-4 .... 3.00

Cartune Land
Magic Carpet, 1987
1-4 .... 2.00

Carvers
Image, 1998

"Carve or starve." "Shreddin' like he's pulling a trailer." Hardly dialogue you'd normally read in a comic book, but it happened, all because of snowboarding. Snowboarders have a new vernacular, a hip attitude, baggy pants, and an assortment of colors of hair and goatees. The culture is one of free spirits, a fulfilling lifestyle, and a real individual expression; about being "stoked and amped," which is jargon for thrilled to death and ready to go. Five snowboarders travel through a dimensional portal and are transported to a frozen wasteland. But rise up, crew! They're attacked by spear-carrying, nuclear-bomb-holding Yetis preparing to invade our dimension. Grab some air with the "carvers," as they embark on a mission to save the world in "phat" style!

1-3 .... 3.00

Car Warriors
Marvel, 1991
1-4 .... 2.00

Casa Howhard
NBM
1-4 ....11.00

Casanova
Aircel, 1991
1-10 ....3.00

Casanova
Image, 1991
1-3 ....3.00
4 ....2.00
5-6 ....3.00

Casefiles: Sam & Twitch
Image, 2003
1-25 ....3.00

Case Morgan, Gumshoe Private Eye
Forbidden Fruit, 1991
1-10 ....3.00
11 ....4.00

Case of Blind Fear, A
Eternity, 1989
1-4 ....2.00

Case of the Wasted Water
Rheem, 1972
1 ....5.00

Cases of Sherlock Holmes
Renegade, 1986
1-24 ....2.00

Casey, Crime Photographer
Marvel, 1949
1-4 ....125.00

Casey Jones & Raphael
Mirage, 1994
1 ....3.00

Casey Jones: North By Downeast
Mirage, 1994

This mini-series stars Casey Jones, the masked vigilante of Teenage Mutant Ninja Turtles fame. Casey is a determined, if slightly simple Ninja in training. He would probably be a great crimefighter if he weren't being constantly distracted by things like needing to know what's on TV while he's in the midst of a fight.

When he does fight, it's no holds barred, using all sorts of makeshift weapons from hockey sticks to golf clubs. In this adventure he battles the Malacostra, a race of lobsters from the planet Neptune. Yes, lobsters. The Malacostra were mutated into human form by their former ruler and are searching for his descendant so they can return to their normal bodies. Unfortunately, in doing so, they run into Casey. As a result, they're discovering that the only thing worse than being condemned to a life on land, is a life on land where a guy in a hockey mask chases after you with a golf club.

1-2 .... 3.00

Casper Adventure Digest
Harvey, 1992
1-8 .... 2.00

Casper and Friends
Harvey, 1991
1-5 .... 2.00

Casper and Friends Magazine
Marvel, 1997
1-3 .... 4.00

Casper and Nightmare
Harvey, 1964
6 .... 35.00
7-10 .... 24.00
11-20 .... 16.00
21-35 .... 14.00
36-46 .... 10.00

Casper and Spooky
Harvey, 1972
1 .... 5.00
2-7 .... 3.00

Casper and the Ghostly Trio
Harvey, 1972
1 .... 20.00
2-4 .... 15.00
5-7 .... 12.00
8-10 .... 2.00

Casper & Wendy
Harvey, 1972
1 .... 9.00
2 .... 5.00
3-5 .... 4.00
6-8 .... 3.00

Casper Digest Magazine
Harvey, 1986
1 .... 3.00
2-13 .... 2.00

Casper Digest Magazine
Harvey, 1991
1-14 .... 2.00

Casper Enchanted Tales Digest
Harvey, 1992
1-10 .... 2.00

Casper Ghostland
Harvey, 1992
1 .... 2.00

Casper Giant Size
Harvey
1-4 .... 2.00

Casper in 3-D
Blackthorne, 1988

Casper the Friendly Ghost is back, and this time he's leapin' right off the page at ya! But so are such luminaries as Sheena, Queen of the Jungle; Dick Tracy; Bullwinkle and Rocky; Underdog; G.I. Joe; Laurel and Hardy; and - hold onto your seats - the California Raisins. This Casper in 3-D special was part of a larger Blackthorne line of 3-D specials, reprinting the adventures of several classic Harvey Comics characters in their own 3-D titles, including Baby Huey, Little Dot, Playful Little Audrey, and Wendy, the Good Little Witch, as well as movie adaptations for Star Wars, Red Heat, Waxworks, and Moonwalker. There were also issues devoted to horror and science-fiction stories.

1 .... 3.00

Casper's Ghostland
Harvey, 1958

1	175.00
2	75.00
3-5	50.00
6-10	40.00
11-20	25.00
21-30	20.00
31-40	15.00
41-60	10.00
61-81	5.00
82-98	4.00

Casper Space Ship
Harvey, 1972

1	16.00
2-3	13.00
4-5	10.00

Casper, The Friendly Ghost
Harvey, 1949

1	2,100.00
2	675.00
3	455.00
4	350.00
5	275.00
7	225.00
8-10	125.00
11-12	90.00
13	90.00
14-15	90.00
16-17	90.00
18	90.00
19	90.00
20	150.00
21	80.00
22	80.00
23	80.00
24-25	80.00
26	80.00
27	80.00
28-30	80.00
31-40	55.00
41-50	40.00
51-70	30.00

Casper, The Friendly Ghost
Harvey, 1952

7	300.00
8	200.00
9-19	100.00
20	500.00
21-39	100.00
40-51	75.00
52-63	60.00
64-70	55.00

Casper, The Friendly Ghost
Harvey, 1990

254-260	2.00

Casper, The Friendly Ghost
Harvey, 1991

1-GS 4	2.00

Casper, The Friendly Ghost Big Book
Harvey, 1992

1-3	2.00

Cast
Nautilus Comics, 2005

1-2	3.00

Castlevania: The Belmont Legacy
Idea & Design Works, 2005

1-5	4.00

Castle Waiting
Olio, 1997

Linda Medley's black-and-white series takes place in a medieval fantasyland in which human characters interact with fantasy characters, yet stories frequently involve historical elements. Clear, confident, excellent line art combine with topnotch fantasy storytelling; the focal storyline features a young woman looking for a place to have her baby -- then meeting other characters and learning more about the people and places around her. Medley excels at depicting the unusual plot element of sheer friendliness.

-- Maggie

1	5.00
1/2nd-1/3rd	4.00
2-16	3.00
Ashcan 1	10.00

Castle Waiting
Cartoon Books, 2000

1-4	3.00

Casual Heroes
Image, 1996

1	2.00

Cat
Marvel, 1972

1	35.00

2	15.00
3	12.00
4	10.00

Cat
Aircel, 1991

1-2	3.00

Catalyst: Agents of Change
Dark Horse, 1994

1-7	2.00

Cat & Mouse
EF Graphics, 1989

1-1/2nd	2.00

Cat & Mouse
Aircel, 1990

1-18	2.00

Cat Claw
Eternity, 1990

1-9	3.00

Catfight
Insomnia, 1995

1-1/Gold	3.00

Catfight: Dream into Action
Lightning, 1996

1	3.00

Catfight: Dream Warrior
Lightning, 1995

1	3.00

Catfight: Escape from Limbo
Lightning, 1996

1	3.00

Catfight: Sweet Revenge
Lightning, 1997

1	3.00

Catharsis
Being, 1994

1	3.00

Cathexis
NBM

1	14.00

Catholic Comics
Catholic, 1946

1	40.00
2-10	36.00

Catholic Pictorial
Catholic Guild, 1947

1	35.00

Catman
AC, 1995

1-2	6.00

Catman Comics
Continental, 1941

1	3,500.00
2	1,650.00
3	1,400.00
4	1,200.00
5-6	875.00
7-9	800.00
10-14	700.00
15-17	650.00
18-20	590.00
21-22	540.00
23-25	485.00
25/2nd	500.00
25/A	550.00
26-29	440.00
30-32	375.00

Catnip
Side Show

1	3.00

Catseye
Manic, 1998

1-8	3.00

Catseye Agency
Rip Off, 1992

1-2	3.00

Cat Tales
Eternity

1	3.00

Cat, T.H.E.
Dell, 1967

1	18.00
2-4	12.00

Cattle Brain
Itchy Eyeball

1-3	3.00

Catwoman
DC, 1989

1-2	3.00
3-4	2.00

Catwoman
DC, 1993

0	2.00
1-10	3.00
11-50	2.00
50/A-50/B	3.00
51-94	2.00
1000000	3.00
Ann 1-2	4.00
Ann 3	3.00
Ann 4	4.00

Catwoman
DC, 2002

1	4.00
2-62	3.00

Catwoman:
Crooked Little Town
DC, 2003

1	15.00

Catwoman:
Guardian of Gotham
DC, 1999

After an evening at the cinema, young Selina Kyle witnesses the murder of her parents at the hand of a common thug on the streets of Gotham City. Over her parents' graves, her eyes brimming with tears, Selina swears to avenge their deaths, and when a cat perches atop the tombstone, Selina knows what she must become to inspire fear in the superstitious and cowardly lot of criminals who prey on the innocent.

This Elseworlds project from Doug Moench (Master of Kung Fu) and Jim Balent (Catwoman) turns the tables on the Batman concept, as Catwoman assumes the role of Gotham City's resident protector and takes on the likes of the maniacal Joker, the raging Killer Croc, the horribly scarred Two-Face, and the murderous...Batman. An intriguing-if somewhat cheesecakey-piece of work from the former Catwoman creative team.

1-2	6.00

Catwoman Plus
DC, 1997

1	3.00

Catwoman
Secret Files and Origins
DC, 2002

1	5.00

Catwoman The Movie
DC, 2004

1	5.00

Catwoman/Vampirella:
The Furies
DC, 1997

1	5.00

Catwoman:
When in Rome
DC, 2004

1-6	4.00

Catwoman/Wildcat
DC, 1998

1-4	3.00

Cave Bang
Fantagraphics, 1996

1-4	3.00

Cave Girl
AC

1	3.00

Cave Girl
Magazine Enterprises, 1954

1	3.00
12-14	185.00

Cave Kids
Gold Key, 1963

1	35.00
2	18.00
3-5	15.00
6-12	12.00
13-16	9.00

Caveman
Caveman, 1998

1-4	4.00
GN 1	10.00

Cavewoman
Basement, 1994

1	26.00
2	20.00
3	15.00
4	12.00
5-6	10.00

Cavewoman
Color Special
Avatar, 1999

1	4.00

Cavewoman:
Missing Link
Basement, 1997

1-2	3.00

Cavewoman: Odyssey
Caliber

1-5	3.00

Cavewoman One-Shot
Basement, 2001

1	4.00

Cavewoman:
Pangaean Sea
Avatar, 1999

0-SE	4.00
Ashcan 1	5.00

Cavewoman: Rain
Basement, 1996

A series that is much better than it might appear at first glance, Cavewoman seems at times part Wonder Woman, part Jurassic Park, and part Night of the Living Dead.

As the second series begins, the town of Marshville has been transported back in time to the age of the dinosaurs. Meriem Cooper (aka Cavewoman) was transported to this age when she was a young girl by her grandfather, using a time machine he'd invented. The idea was to let her escape her abusive mother, but, when her grandfather dies, she is stuck in the prehistoric era for years. When she is 19, however, the entire town of Marshville is transported back to join her. Unfortunately, the townspeople are not nearly as adept at survival in the wilds of prehistory as Meriem and find themselves being picked off, one-by-one, by packs of roving dinosaurs. Luckily, the problem isn't too bad in the heat of summer -- but the rainy season is just about to begin.

1-1/3rd	3.00
2	4.00
2/2nd-2/3rd	3.00
3	4.00
3/2nd-8	3.00

Cavewoman: Raptor
Basement, 2002

1	3.00

Cecil Kunkle
Darkline

1-2	4.00
3	2.00

Cecil Kunkle
Renegade, 1986

1	2.00

Celebrity
Horizontal

1	3.00

Celestial Mechanics: The Adventures of Widget Wilhelmina Jones
Innovation, 1990

Widget Wilhelmina Jones is a charming rogue and space mechanic who has just done the impossible. By studying the remains of a wrecked spaceship, extrapolating from her own mechanical knowledge, and using imagination, she has managed to duplicate a semantic loophole space drive. This drive is the key to interstellar travel -- and a closely guarded trade secret of the Halplex corporation. The way she figures it, she has three choices: use it to break up Halplex's monopoly on space travel; offer to sell it back to Halplex so the secret can remain safe; or go into business for herself. She chooses the last option.

To help her in her scheme, she has enlisted the aid of: her little sister Terebinthia, a cadet in the Halplex-owned Space Patrol; Flange, a gorgeous computer hacker; and Quarkstomper, a fellow rogue who once was the object of Terebinthia's crush. With them, Jones sets out for adventure -- with Halplex assassins close behind.

1-3	2.00

Celestine
Image, 1996

1-2	3.00

Cell
Antarctic, 1996

1-3	3.00

Cement Shooz
Horse Feathers, 1991

1-2	3.00

Cenotaph
Northstar

1	4.00

Centerfield
Alternative, 2005

1	4.00

Centrifugal Bumble-Puppy
Fantagraphics

1-7	2.00
8	3.00

Centurions
DC, 1987

1-4	1.00

Century: Distant Sons
Marvel, 1996

1	3.00

Cereal Killings
Fantagraphics, 1992

1-8	3.00

Cerebus Bi-Weekly
Aardvark-Vanaheim, 1988

1-16	2.00
17	4.00
18-19	2.00
20	6.00
21-26	2.00

Cerebus: Church & State
Aardvark-Vanaheim, 1991

1-30	2.00

Cerebus Companion
Win-Mill, 1993

1-2	4.00

Cerebus Guide to Self Publishing
Aardvark-Vanaheim, 1997

1	4.00

Cerebus: Guys Party Pack
Aardvark-Vanaheim

1	4.00

Cerebus High Society
Aardvark-Vanaheim, 1990

1-25	2.00

Cerebus Jam
Aardvark-Vanaheim, 1985

1	3.00

Cerebus the Aardvark
Aardvark-Vanaheim, 1977

Cerebus, who "stood only five hands high, had a lengthy snout, a long tail and was covered with short gray fur," might seem an unlikely candidate to star in the longest-running independent comic book published today. But since 1977, creator and publisher Dave Sim has put the title character, an aardvark in a fantasy setting that often seemed contemporary, through a dizzying series of career changes: from barbarian to bodyguard, from prime minister to pope, from bum to messiah wanna-be. Sim has, in the course of his nearly finished "300-issue limited series" provided laughter and wrestled with larger dramatic and philosophical themes.

A counterfeit version of #1 exists; it has glossy stock on the inside cover. It still has a significant market value as a historical conversation piece and thus has a listing below.

-- John Jackson Miller

0	4.00
0/Gold	6.00
1	700.00
1/Counterfeit	60.00
2	150.00
3	90.00
4	75.00
5	50.00
6	35.00
7	20.00
8-10	15.00
11	12.00
12-22	10.00
23-31	6.00
32-40	5.00
41-50	4.00
51	6.00
52-57	4.00
58-60	3.00
61-62	4.00
63-100	3.00
101-299	2.00
300	4.00

Cerebus World Tour Book
Aardvark-Vanaheim

1	3.00

Ceres Celestial Legend Part 1
Viz, 2001

1-6	3.00

Ceres Celestial Legend Part 2
Viz, 2001

1-5	3.00
6	4.00

Ceres Celestial Legend Part 3
Viz, 2002

1	3.00
2-4	4.00

Ceres Celestial Legend Part 4
Viz, 2002

1-4	4.00

Ceres Celestial Legend Part 5
Viz, 2003

1	4.00

Chadz Frendz
Smiling Face, 1998

1	2.00

Chaingang
Northstar

1-2	3.00

Chain Gang War
DC, 1993

1-1/Silver	3.00
2-4	2.00
5	3.00
6-12	2.00

Chainsaw Vigilante
NEC

New England Comics Press, publishers of The Tick, also published spinoff titles about characters who originated in that series. Among these was the Chainsaw Vigilante, a warped individual who attacks super-heroes in an effort to make them stop intruding on normal people's lives. For his own part, when he's not being the Chainsaw Vigilante, he's just an average guy named Henry. However, when Henry feels the need, he dons a black leather jacket and "happy face" mask, grabs his chainsaw, and patrols the streets. To complicate matters, his girlfriend Karen, like most of the people in town, is also a super-hero -- in this case, a heroine known as Athena.

Chainsaw Vigilante was a brief, black-and-white comedy series that kicked off in 1993. The title was written and illustrated by Zander Cannon, who went on to write and draw The Replacement God.

1	4.00
1/A	5.00
1/B-1/C	6.00
2-3	3.00

Chains of Chaos
Harris, 1994

1-3	3.00

Chakan
Rak, 1994

1	5.00

Challenge of the Unknown
Ace, 1950

6	225.00

Challengers of the Fantastic
Marvel, 1997

The Amalgam experiment in 1996 proved so successful that Marvel and DC undertook another batch of titles in 1997 featuring character conglomerations, but decided to forego any contrivance to account for the presence of these titles, like the 4-issue mini-series Marvel Versus DC/DC Versus Marvel of the previous year.

There has long been speculation that the Fantastic Four was inspired by artist Jack Kirby's previous work on the Challengers of the Unknown, so the two titles were a natural for this Amalgam pairing. Challengers of the Fantastic featured the notion of "living on borrowed time" from the Challengers and paired it with the close-knit "family of adventurers" aspect of the Fantastic Four. This title was supervised by Marvel and is more heavily influenced by the Fantastic Four than the Challengers. The story featured the group battling the world devourer, Galactiac, which mirrored the FF's encounter with Galactus.

-- George Haberberger

1 ....2.00

Challengers of the Unknown
DC, 1958

1	1,450.00
2	375.00
3-8	220.00
9-10	140.00
11-15	90.00
16-23	52.00
24-31	25.00
32-49	20.00
50-56	15.00
57-69	11.00
70-73	7.00
74	14.00
☞Adams art; Deadman	
75-80	7.00
81	6.00
82-87	5.00

Challengers of the Unknown
DC, 1997

1-17	2.00
18	3.00

Challengers of the Unknown
DC, 1991

1-8	2.00

Challengers of the Unknown
DC, 2004

1-6	3.00

Chamber
Marvel, 2002

1-4	3.00

Chamber of Chills
Harvey, 1951

1	350.00
2-4	275.00
5-9	250.00
10-19	225.00
20-25	200.00
26	175.00

Chamber of Chills
Marvel, 1972

1	25.00
2-10	15.00
11-22	12.00
22/30¢	20.00
23	12.00
23/30¢	20.00
24-25	12.00

Chamber of Clues
Harvey, 1955

27	30.00
28	25.00

Chamber of Darkness
Marvel, 1968

Inspired by the success of the Joe Orlando-edited "mystery" titles at DC in the early 1970s, Marvel launched its own horror and suspense anthology titles like Chamber of Darkness, Tower of Shadows, and others. Many of the chilling stories followed the classic horror comic formulas laid down by E.C. in titles like Tales rom the Crypt (sanitized for the Comics Code, of course) and were illustrated with gusto by some of Marvel's top talents of the time, including John Severin, Gil Kane, John Buscema, and Bernie Wrightson. The Marvel series also mined a richer source for story inspiration, adapting tales from such fantasy and horror pulps of the 1930s as Weird Tales.

-- Rob Salkowitz

1	60.00
2	35.00
3	30.00

4	60.00
☞BWS Conan tryout	
5-7	30.00
8-1/Special	20.00

Chamber of Evil
Comax

1	3.00

Champ Comics
Harvey, 1940

11	850.00
12-13	750.00
14-15	700.00
16-18	650.00
19-21	600.00
22-25	550.00

Champion
Special Studio

1	3.00

Champion Comics
Harvey, 1939

2	950.00
3-4	700.00
5-7	600.00
8-10	475.00

Champion of Katara
Mu, 1992

1-2	3.00

Champion of Katara: Dum-Dums & Dragons
Mu, 1995

1-3	3.00

Champions
Eclipse, 1986

1-6	1.00

Champions
Hero, 1987

1-14	2.00
15	4.00
Ann 1	3.00
Ann 2	4.00

Champions
Marvel, 1975

1	15.00
2-3	6.00
4-5	5.00
5/30¢	20.00
6	4.00
6/30¢	20.00
7	4.00
7/30¢	20.00
8-14	4.00
14/35¢	15.00
15	4.00
15/35¢	15.00
16-17	4.00

Champions Classics
Hero, 1993

1	1.00
13-14	4.00

Champions Classics/ Flare Adventures
Hero, 1993
2-3..3.00
4-7..4.00

Champion Sports
DC, 1973
1...5.00
2-3..4.00

Change Commander Goku
Antarctic, 1993
1-5..3.00

Change Commander Goku 2
Antarctic, 1996
1-4..3.00

Changes
Tundra
1...8.00

Channel Zero
Image, 1998
1-6..3.00

Channel Zero: Dupe
Image, 1999

If you can get past the premise, the Christian right and angry mothers forced Congress to suspend free speech, granting absolute control of the press to the government. If you can also get past the preachiness that bloats word and image, this book offers a fabulous sense of design and compelling art. There's little else.

Dupe contains short comic stories and problematic, unfocused prose. It's center: an information terrorist works to free the minds of the masses. She encourages people to organize using her website, because the establishment can't track you there. Thing is, the establishment can track you over the Internet now, so what's to stop them when they've got complete control? It's a small thing, but this book's chronic failure to attempt substance while championing style cripples the entire work. Instead of extrapolating to create a fresh dystopian universe, Dupe offers every single cliché you've seen before.

Channel Zero was created by artist/writer Brian Wood.

1.. 3.00

Chaos! Bible
Chaos, 1995
1.. 4.00

Chaos! Chronicles
Chaos, 2000
1.. 4.00

Chaos Effect, The: Alpha
Valiant, 1994
1.. 3.00
1/Red foil.............................. 90.00

Chaos Effect, The: Epilogue
Valiant, 1994
1-2.. 2.00

Chaos Effect, The: Omega
Valiant, 1994
1.. 2.00
1/Gold................................... 20.00

Chaos Effect, The: Beta
Valiant
1.. 2.00

Chaos! Gallery
Chaos!, 1997
1.. 3.00

Chaos! Presents Jade
Chaos, 2001
1-4.. 3.00

Chaos! Quarterly
Chaos, 1995
1-2.. 5.00
3.. 4.00

Chapel
Image, 1995

As a member of the elite paramilitary unit known as Knightstrike, Chapel had more than earned his reputation as the CIA's most ruthless and efficient assassin, even before he became a Youngblood operative. His ghoulish appearance, intimidating size, and seemingly limitless knowledge of weaponry and hand-to-hand combat techniques give him the distinction of being one of the government's most feared assassins. This gory book from Awesome Entertainment largely showcases Chapel's numerous methods for killing human beings.

1-2.. 3.00
2/Variant................................ 4.00

Chapel
Image, 1995
1-2.. 3.00

Chapel
Image, 1995
1-7.. 3.00

Chapel
Awesome, 1997
1.. 3.00

Charlemagne
Defiant, 1994
0.. 1.00
1-8.. 3.00

Charles Burns' Modern Horror Sketchbook
Kitchen Sink
1.. 7.00

Charlie Chan
Crestwood, 1948
1.. 550.00
2.. 340.00
3.. 250.00
4-5.. 175.00
6-9.. 140.00

Charlie Chan
Dell, 1965

1 ....35.00
2 ....25.00

Charlie Chan
Eternity, 1989

1-6 ....2.00

Charlie McCarthy
Dell, 1949

1 ....125.00
2 ....75.00
3-5 ....50.00
6-9 ....45.00

Charlie the Caveman
Fantasy General

1 ....2.00

Charlton Action Featuring Static
Charlton, 1985

11-12 ....2.00

Charlton Bullseye
Charlton, 1981

1 ....7.00
2-10 ....2.00

Charlton Classics
Charlton, 1980

1 ....3.00
2-9 ....2.00

Charlton Premiere
Charlton, 1967

19 ....20.00

Charlton Premiere
Charlton, 1967

1 ....6.00
2-4 ....4.00

Charlton Sport Library: Professional Football
Charlton, 1969

1 ....35.00

Charm School
Slave Labor, 2000

1-3 ....3.00

Chase
DC, 1998

1-9 ....3.00
1000000 ....2.00

Chase
APComics, 2004

1 ....4.00
1/Sketch 5.00
2-4 ....4.00

Chaser Platoon
Aircel, 1991

1-6 ....2.00

Chasing Dogma
Image

1 .... 15.00

Chassis
Millennium, 1996

1-3 .... 3.00

Chassis
Hurricane, 1998

0-3 .... 3.00

Chassis
Image, 1999

0-5 .... 3.00

Chastity
Chaos!, 2001

1/2 .... 3.00

Chastity: Lust for Life
Chaos!, 1999

1 .... 4.00
1/Dynamic 5.00
1/Ltd. 20.00
2-3 .... 3.00

Chastity: Reign of Terror
Chaos!, 2000

1 .... 3.00

Chastity: Rocked
Chaos!, 1998

Teenage wanna-be actress turned vampire, Chastity Marks foils an assassination in the midst of the commotion of a punk revival concert in present-day Los Angeles. During the attack, she recognizes an assailant's tattoo as the kanji of an ancient Oriental vampire named Jade. This powerful vampire-sorceress has vowed to destroy her should they meet again. As painful memories of her first encounter with Jade flood her mind she realizes her very existence is threatened. To ensure her survival, Chastity must relive her traumatic battles with Jade to unearth the secret that will defeat her nemesis, but the truth is she would rather be acting. Primarily set in 1980, this mini-series is a wild ride through the New York City punk scene filled with rock, spiked hair, troubled romance, and the problem of auditioning for Broadway when supernatural Yakuza want blood!

1-4 .... 3.00

Chastity: Theatre of Pain
Chaos!, 1997

1 .... 3.00
1/Variant 4.00
2-3 .... 3.00
3/Variant 4.00

Cheapskin
Fantagraphics

1 .... 3.00

Checkmate
DC, 2006

1-30 .... 3.00

Checkmate
Gold Key, 1962

1 .... 30.00
2 .... 20.00

Checkmate
DC, 1988

1 .... 3.00
2-12 .... 1.00
13-33 .... 2.00

Check-Up
Fantagraphics

1 .... 3.00

Cheech Wizard
Last Gasp

1 .... 3.00

Cheeky Angel
Viz, 2004

1-8 .... 10.00

Cheerleaders from Hell
Caliber, 1988

1 .... 3.00

Cheese Heads
Tragedy Strikes

1-5 .... 3.00

Cheese Weasel
Side Show

1-7 .... 3.00

Cheese Weasel: Innocent Until Proven Guilty
Side Show

Innocent Until Proven Guilty is a staple-bound compilation of Jim Ridings' Cheese Weasel strips from 1994 and 1995. The lead character has always been a sleazy lawyer with absolutely no conscience, one who would do anything for money. In this collection, however, he becomes a member of the "ACLUnatics" (a slam at the American Civil Liberties Union), an organization which has taken heat for its firm "no public religion" stance, and for aggressively defending the free speech rights of even such unsavory groups as the KKK.

Ridings uses his strips to poke fun at the entire liberal agenda, from abortion rights to environmental protection. Sometimes the jokes come off with a well-deserved zing; mostly, however, they concentrate on political satire, expressing Ridings' staunchly conservative viewpoint.

1 .... 10.00

Cheeta Pop
Fantagraphics, 1996
1-3 .... 3.00

Cheeta Pop Scream Queen
Antarctic, 1994
1-5 .... 3.00

Chemical Warfare
Checker Comics, 1998
1-3 .... 3.00

Chen -n- Solly
Thwack! Pow!, 1997
1-2 .... 1.00

Cheque, Mate
Fantagraphics
1 .... 4.00

Cherry
Last Gasp, 1982
1 .... 8.00
1/2nd-11/2nd 4.00
12-20 .... 3.00

Cherry Deluxe
Cherry, 1998
1 .... 4.00

Cherry's Jubilee
Tundra, 1994
1-4 .... 3.00

Cheryl Blossom
Archie, 1995
1 .... 3.00
2-3 .... 2.00

Cheryl Blossom
Archie, 1996
1-3 .... 2.00

Cheryl Blossom
Archie, 1997
1-37 .... 2.00

Cheryl Blossom Goes Hollywood
Archie, 1996
1-3 .... 2.00

Cheryl Blossom Special
Archie
1-4 .... 2.00

Chesty Sanchez
Antarctic, 1995
1-3 .... 3.00
Special 1 .... 6.00

Cheval Noir
Dark Horse, 1989

Cheval Noir is an import-oriented black-and-white collection

from top-drawer publisher Dark Horse. "Cheval" means "horse"; "noir" means "black" in French. The anthology features short stories from some of the best comic talents in the world, including Moebius, Daniel Torres, Dave Stevens, and Michael Kaluta. The material is translated and re-lettered (when necessary) for the benefit of an English-speaking audience.

Before it ended its run, the series had encompassed 48 issues in a variety of formats, ranging from standard size (32 pages) to GS (72 pages) issues.

1-19 .... 4.00
20 .... 5.00
21 .... 4.00
22 .... 5.00
23-26 .... 4.00
27-50 .... 3.00

Cheyenne
Dell, 1957
4-5 .... 35.00
6-10 .... 25.00
11-25 .... 20.00

Cheyenne Kid
Charlton, 1957
8 .... 30.00
9 .... 20.00
10 .... 35.00
11 .... 30.00
12-15 .... 20.00
16-20 .... 16.00
21-30 .... 14.00
31-40 .... 10.00
41-50 .... 8.00
51-70 .... 6.00
71-87 .... 4.00
87/2nd 2.00
88-89 .... 4.00
89/2nd 2.00
90 .... 4.00
91-99 .... 3.00

Chiaroscuro
DC, 1995
1-10 .... 3.00

Chicanos
Idea & Design Works, 2005
1-8 .... 4.00

Chi Chian
Sirius, 1997
1-6 .... 3.00

Chick Magnet
Voluptuous

The Chick Magnet is Moriarty Carbunkle, a down-on-his luck, late-night talk show host who has been reduced to spewing bad poetry on open-mike nights. His former on-air sidekick, Caffeine Boy, murdered one of his guests and has vowed to escape from prison and kill the Chick Magnet. Tough life, eh? Different, to be sure. In the middle of all of this, Boo Atticus-an amalgamation of names from Harper Lee's To Kill a Mockingbird-comes back into Carbunkle's life, still garbed in extraordinarily tight Catholic schoolgirl attire and seeking sexual gratification. "Dedicated to Catholic schoolgirls all around this beautiful world," Chick Magnet is the brainchild of Anthony Jukovavich, whose artwork is somewhat reminiscent of the underground comics of the 1960s and 1970s; it is definitely for mature readers.

1 .,...3.00

Chief Victorio's Apache Massacre
Avon, 1951
1 ....275.00

Childhood's End
Image, 1997
1 ....3.00

Children of Fire
Fantagor
1-3..2.00

Children of the Fallen Angel
Ace, 1997
1 ....3.00

Children of the Night
Nightwynd
1-4..3.00

Children of the Voyager
Marvel, 1993
1 .... 3.00
2-4 .... 2.00

Children's Crusade
DC, 1993
1 .... 5.00
2 .... 4.00

Child's Play 2: The Official Movie Adaptation
Innovation
1-3... 3.00

Child's Play 3
Innovation, 1992
1-4... 3.00

Child's Play: The Series
Innovation
1-5... 3.00

Chili
Marvel, 1969

Chili, red-headed rival to Marvel's teen-fashion mainstay Millie the Model, got her own title in 1967 as Marvel, drowning in super-hero titles, tried to keep its female reader base from taking off.

Vain, flighty Chili largely avoids the Archie-like quality inherent in practically all American teen humor comics, offering more witty banter, an element of high-fashion and plain old late-1960s weirdness)

Writer Stan Lee is at his campiest in the scripts for these issues, which sometimes read like Stan's take on a Marx Brothers routine, if you can imagine that!

1 .... 22.00
2 .... 14.00
3-5.. 10.00
6-10 .... 8.00
11-26....................................... 6.00
Special 1 .... 14.00

Chiller
Marvel, 1993
1-2.. 3.00

Chilling Adventures in Sorcery
Archie, 1972
1 .... 42.00
2 .... 25.00
3-5 .... 15.00
☛Becomes Red Circle Sorcery

Chilling Tales
Youthful, 1952
13 .... 450.00
14-15 .... 300.00
16-17 .... 250.00

Chilling Tales of Horror
Stanley, 1969
1 .... 12.00
2-7 .... 10.00

Chilling Tales of Horror
Stanley, 1971
1 .... 9.00
2/A-2/B 8.00
3-5 .... 6.00

Chillins
Moonstone
0 .... 3.00

Chimera
CrossGen, 2003
1-4... 3.00

Chinago and Other Stories
Tome
1 .... 3.00

China Sea
Nightwynd
1-4.. 3.00

Chipmunks & Squirrels
Original Syndicate, 1994
1 .... 6.00

Chip 'n' Dale
Dell, 1955
4-5 .... 35.00
6-10 .... 30.00
11-14 .... 24.00
14/A 30.00
15-20 .... 24.00
21-30 .... 20.00

Chip 'n' Dale
Gold Key, 1967
1 .... 20.00
2 .... 12.00
3-5 .... 8.00
6-20 .... 5.00
21-64 .... 3.00
65-66 .... 5.00

67 ....20.00
68-69..................................17.00
70-77....................................3.00
78-83..................................10.00

Chip 'n' Dale
Disney
1 ....4.00

Chip 'n' Dale Rescue Rangers
Disney, 1990
1-19......................................2.00

Chips and Vanilla
Kitchen Sink, 1988
1 ....2.00

Chirality
CPM, 1997
1-18......................................3.00

Chirôn
Hammac
1-3..2.00

Chisuji
Antarctic, 2004
1-4..3.00

Chitty Chitty Bang Bang
Gold Key, 1969
1 ....35.00

C.H.I.X.
Image, 1998
1-1/Variant..............................3.00

C.H.I.X. that Time Forgot
Image, 1998

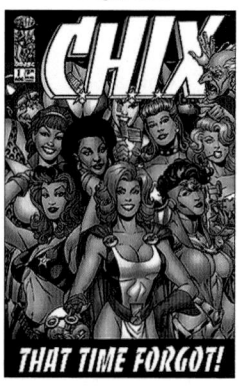

This one-shot is a hilarious follow-up to Aaron Lopresti's C.H.I.X. When last we left our heroine, Good Girl, she had been tricked by her former sidekick, Piguana, into destroying Silicon City. In order to fix the mess, she enlisted the aid of her curmudgeonly mentor, Charles Ruffage. Their plan was to send Good Girl back in time 24 hours to (a) prevent the destruction of Silicon City, and (b) pick up a can of Bran Blast from the store-after all, the sale ended yesterday.

Unfortunately, Ruffage's simian assistant messed up the controls of the time machine, sending Good Girl flitting randomly across time. Along the way, she meets an outlandish assortment of female heroines-all of which wind up getting brought back with her when she is finally scooped back into her own time period!

1 .... 3.00

Chobits
Tokyopop, 2002
1-8.. 10.00

Choice Comics
Great Comics, 1941
1 .... 950.00
2 .... 650.00
3 .... 485.00

Choices
Angry Isis
1 .... 4.00

Choke
Anubis, 1993
1-Ann 1................................. 3.00

Cholly & Flytrap
Image, 2004
1-4 .... 5.00

Choo-Choo Charlie
Gold Key, 1969
1 .... 60.00

Chopper: Earth, Wind & Fire
Fleetway-Quality
1-2 .... 3.00

Chopper: Song of the Surfer
Fleetway-Quality
1 .... 10.00

Chosen
Martinez, 1995
1 .... 3.00

Chosen
Dark Horse, 2004
1-3 .... 3.00

Christian Comics & Games Magazine
Aida-Zee
0-1 .... 4.00

Christina Winters: Agent of Death
Fantagraphics, 1995
1-3 .... 3.00

Christmas Classics (Walt Kelly's...)
Eclipse, 1987
1 .... 2.00

Christmas Treasury, A
Dell, 1954
1 .... 50.00

Christmas with Superswine
Fantagraphics
1 .... 2.00

Christmas with the Super-Heroes
DC, 1988

One of the longest-running traditions in comics is the holiday story. These might feature Superman being saved by Santa Claus, Batman discovering the spirit of Christmas, or a minor crook being set on the straight and narrow by some holiday act of kindness.

In 1988, DC put out Christmas with the Super-Heroes, a 100-page special collecting some of their favorite Christmas stories. Featured were stories from Superman, the Legion of Super-Heroes, Batman, the Justice League of America, and the Teen Titans. 1989 brought up a follow-up issue. Somehow, these tales managed to be schmaltzy and heartwarming at the same time. In any case, they were a welcome addition to the holiday season.

1-2 .... 3.00

Chroma-Tick
New England, 1992
1-9.. 4.00

Chrome
Hot Comics, 1986
1-3 .... 2.00

Chromium Man
Triumphant, 1994
0-15...3.00

Chromium Man: Violent Past
Triumphant
1-2...3.00

Chronic Apathy
Illiterature, 1995
1-4...3.00

Chronic Idiocy
Caliber
1-3...3.00

Chronicles of Corum
First, 1987
1-12.......................................2.00

Chronicles of Crime and Mystery: Sherlock Holmes
Northstar
1..2.00

Chronicles of Panda Khan
Abacus, 1987
1-4...2.00

Chronicles of the Cursed Sword
Tokyopop, 2003
1-20.......................................10.00

Chrono Code
Tokyopop, 2005
1-2...10.00

Chrono Crusade
ADV Manga, 2004
1-6...10.00

Chronos
DC, 1998

Walker Gabriel struggles with a killer, as an energy portal surrounds them and suddenly he finds himself in Smallville, Kansas, in the 1800s

catching a ride on a horse-drawn wagon with a man named Kent. So begins the time-travelling adventures of the new Chronos.

One of The Atom's foes during the Silver Age was the time-traveling villain, Chronos. In 1998, a new character, Walker Gabriel, appropriates the name with the approval of the original Chronos. In addition to moving through time to satisfy himself (like seeing the Beatles in Hamburg in 1960), Gabriel is making a tidy profit as a high-tech thief, until his employer attempts to make him the fall guy in the murder of a Linear Man. The concept of affecting history has made the time traveler a venerable character type in comics, and this series involves itself intricately in DC's past.

-- George Haberberger

1-11 .... 3.00
1000000 .... 4.00

Chronowar
Dark Horse, 1996
1-9...3.00

Chuck Norris
Marvel, 1987
1 .... 2.00
2-5.. 1.00

Chuk the Barbaric
Avatar
1-3.. 1.00

Chyna
Chaos!, 2000
1-1/Variant............................ 3.00

Cinderalla
Viz, 2002
1 .... 16.00

Cinder and Ashe
DC, 1988

Cinder and Ashe was a four-issue mini-series by Gerry Conway

and Jose L. Garcia Lopez. Cinder is a red-headed woman of mixed heritage who grew up in war-torn Vietnam. Jake Ashe is a Cajun who served in that war in hopes of finding his real father. Instead, he met Cinder, his future partner.

Today, Cinder and Ashe are investigators working out of New Orleans, but their latest case feels a bit like going back to war. A farmer named Wilson Starger hires them to find his missing daughter, Jennifer. However, the more they look into the case, the stranger things become. Their employer turns out to be a cipher -- a man without a credit record, driver's license, or official presence of any kind. Moreover, the people they contact regarding the case exhibit a nasty tendency to turn up dead.

1-4 .... 2.00

Cinderella
Gold Key, 1965
1 .... 24.00

Cinderella Love
Ziff-Davis, 1950
1 .... 85.00
2 .... 48.00
3 .... 40.00
4-10 .... 35.00
11-29 .... 28.00

Cindy
Timely, 1947
27 .... 75.00
28-40 .... 50.00

Cinnamon El Ciclo
DC, 2003
1-5 .... 3.00

Circle Unleashed
Epoch, 1995
1 .... 3.00

Circle Weave: Apprentice to a God
Abalone
1-4 .... 2.00

Circus the Comic Riot
Globe, 1938
1-3 .... 6,500.00

Circus World
Hammac
1-3 .... 3.00

Cisco Kid
Dell, 1951
2 .... 100.00
3 .... 85.00
4-5 .... 80.00
6-10 .... 75.00
11-20 .... 55.00

21-30 ....45.00
31-36 ....30.00
37-41 ....60.00

Citizen V and the V-Battalion
Marvel, 2001
1-3 ....3.00

Citizen V and the V Battalion: The Everlasting
Marvel, 2002
1-4 ....3.00

Citizen V Battlebook
Marvel, 1998
1 ....4.00

City of Heroes
Blue King Studios, 2004
1-12 ....3.00

City of Heroes
Image, 2005
1 ....3.00
1/Keown 5.00
1/Perez...................................4.00
2-17 ....3.00

City of Silence
Image, 2000

"The future is bad for you." These are the opening lines of Warren Ellis' three issue futuristic romp. The city Stealth is anything but normal. It is a city ruled by ideas and overrun with mad technology. If anyone's ideas and inventions pose a threat, then it is the Silencers who are ordered to wipe out the problem. When a mysterious silicon pentagram is discovered on the body of a corpse, the deadly trio of Litany, Frost, and Gitane are sent to investigate, and if necessary, "silence" anyone who gets in their way. What they discover is a frightening conspiracy involving satanic occult programmers,

voltage monks stealing public electricity, and a mysterious figure known only as Metalghost who may be responsible for the most dangerous idea of all time.

Originally commissioned by Epic Comics in the mid-nineties, Image Comics eventually published this story in 2000 giving readers a chance to see some of Ellis' early work which foreshadowed his critically acclaimed titles such as Transmetropolitan and Planetary.

1-3 .... 3.00

City of the Living Dead
Avon, 1952
1 .... 300.00

City of Tomorrow
DC, 2005
1 .... 5.00
2-6 .... 3.00

City People Notebook
DC, 2000
1 .... 10.00

City Surgeon
Gold Key, 1963
1 .... 18.00

Civil War
Marvel, 2006
1 .... 5.00
2 .... 7.00
2/Variant 8.00
3 .... 5.00
3/2nd 3.00
4 .... 5.00
4/Variant 3.00
5 .... 4.00
5/Variant 3.00
6 .... 4.00

Civil War: Choosing Sides
Marvel, 2007
1 .... 4.00

Civil War Files
Marvel, 2006
1 .... 4.00

Civil War: Front Line
Marvel, 2006
1-10 .... 3.00

Civil War: The Confession
Marvel, 2007
1 .... 8.00

Civil War: The Initiative
Marvel, 2007
1 .... 6.00

Civil War: War Crimes One-Shot
Marvel, 2007
1 .... 4.00

Civil War: X-Men
Marvel, 2006
1-4 .... 3.00

Civil War: Young Avengers & Runaways
Marvel, 2006
1-4 .... 3.00

Claire Voyant
Leader, 1946

The newspaper strip by Jack Sparling began in 1943 and ran until 1948, featuring the adventures of a young woman first introducedsuffering from amnesia in a lifeboat . The strip outlived the comic book.

-- Maggie

1 .... 375.00
2 .... 225.00
3-4 .... 165.00

Clair Voyant
Lightning, 1996
1 .... 4.00

Clan Apis
Active Synapse, 1998
1-4 .... 3.00
5 .... 4.00

Clandestine
Marvel, 1994
1-12 .... 3.00
Ashcan 1 .... 2.00

Claritin Syrup Presents Looney Tunes
DC, 1998
1 .... 3.00

Clash
DC, 1991

It is impossible not to compare Joe McClash to Indiana Jones. Both brave danger in exotic locales for the sake of ancient artifacts. Both had fathers who neglected them, so involved were they in their own quest for ancient treasure. Both had a way with women.

But there the comparisons stop. Joe McClash ("Clash" to his friends) is callous and uncaring, willing to sacrifice anyone or anything in his quest for power. He uses people and he takes what he wants. Someday, he swears, he'll be king of the world.

Now Clash might just get the chance. A rare architectural find in Afghanistan reveals a vast underground city, and a source of awesome power. Under the dead eyes of the city's inhabitants, Clash uses ancient machinery to imbue himself with super-human power. When he emerges from the ruins, this young man will make the world tremble.

1-3...5.00

Classic Adventure Strips
Dragon Lady, 1985
1-12..4.00

Classic Alex Toth Zorro
Image, 1998
1-2..16.00

Classic Girls
Eternity, 1991
1-4..3.00

Classic Jonny Quest: Skull & Double Crossbones
Illustrated Productions, 1996
1...1.00

Classic Jonny Quest: The Quetong Missile Mystery
Illustrated Productions, 1996
1 .... 1.00

Classic Judge Dredd
Fleetway-Quality
1-15....................................... 3.00

Classic Punisher
Marvel, 1989
1 .... 5.00

Classics Desecrated
NBM
1 .... 9.00

Classics Illustrated
Gilberton, 1941

In 1941, Albert E. Kanter introduced Classic Comics, later renamed Classics Illustrated. Kanter's idea was to use the comic-book form to make great literature accessible to readers who might never otherwise make the effort. Whether his idea represented a watering-down of the classics, as some critics claimed, it was an amazingly popular move. Most of the 169 comics in this series were reprinted numerous times, with 23rd printings being relatively common. Their popularity even extended to schools, where the colorful, well-written adaptations must have seemed a welcome alternative to reading lengthy texts.

Kanter later introduced Classics Illustrated Junior, adapting children's literature for younger readers. The series also gave rise to numerous imitations over the years.

For collectors, their popularity is particularly problematic, since various reprintings were not clearly marked. The best clue to figuring out which printing a given issue is lies in the highest reorder number

(HRN) from the series order form on the back of each copy.

We extend our thanks to Classics Illustrated authority Dan Malan, who has painstakingly determined the distinguishing characteristics of each printing and who has generously allowed us to use this information here. If you'd like to learn more about this remarkable series, we would encourage you to refer to his definitive "The Complete Guide to Classics Collectibles," available in four volumes from: Malan Classical Enterprises, 7519 Lindbergh Dr., St. Louis, MO 63117 (314) 781-2319. In later years, other publishers reprinted issues, usually with new covers or coloring.

1 The Three Musketeers .	4400.00
1/2nd HRN #10	325.00
1/3rd HRN #15	135.00
1/4th HRN #18	100.00
1/5th HRN #21	90.00
1/6th HRN #28	75.00
1/7th HRN #36	35.00
1/8th HRN #60	24.00
1/9th HRN #64	20.00
1/10th-11th	18.00
1/12th-13th	15.00
1/13th-15th	15.00
1/16th-24th	10.00
2 Ivanhoe	1750.00
2/2nd HRN #10	250.00
2/3rd HRN #15	130.00
2/4th HRN #18	100.00
2/5th HRN #21	90.00
2/6th HRN #28	75.00
2/7th HRN #36	35.00
2/8th HRN #60	24.00
2/9th HRN #64	20.00
2/10th HRN #78	18.00
2/11th HRN #89	16.00
2/12th-14th	15.00
2/15th-22nd/A	10.00
2/22nd/B HRN #166; Variation: Center ad for Children's Digest & Young Miss	35.00
2/23rd-25th	10.00
3 The Count of Monte Cristo	1250.00
3/2nd HRN #10	240.00
3/3rd HRN #15	125.00
3/4th HRN #18	100.00
3/5th HRN #20	90.00
3/6th HRN #21	85.00
3/7th HRN #28	75.00
3/8th HRN #36	40.00
3/9th HRN #60	24.00
3/10th HRN #62	20.00
3/11th HRN #71	18.00
3/12th HRN #87	16.00
3/13th-15th	15.00
3/16th-23rd	10.00
4 The Last of the Mohicans	1050.00
4/2nd HRN #12	240.00
4/3rd HRN #15	125.00

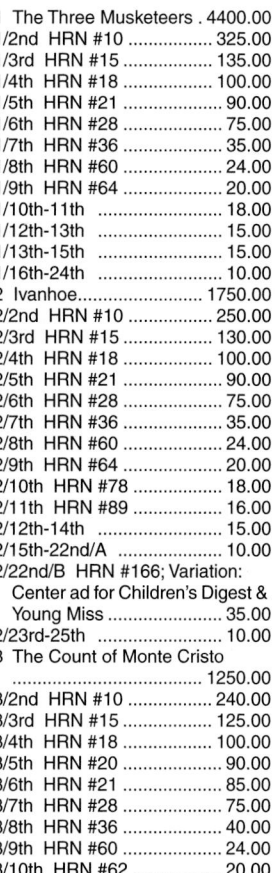

4/4th HRN #20 ....100.00
4/5th HRN #21 ....90.00
4/6th HRN #28 ....75.00
4/7th HRN #36 ....40.00
4/8th HRN #60 ....24.00
4/9th HRN #64 ....20.00
4/10th HRN #78 ....18.00
4/11th HRN #89 ....16.00
4/12th-13th 15.00
4/14th-15th 12.00
4/16th-23rd 10.00
5 Moby Dick 1150.00
5/A Rare variation, free promo
 ....1900.00
5/2nd HRN #10 ....235.00
5/3rd HRN #15 ....175.00
5/4th HRN #18 ....160.00
5/5th HRN #20 ....125.00
5/6th HRN #21 ....100.00
5/7th HRN #28 ....90.00
5/8th HRN #36 ....45.00
5/9th HRN #60 ....30.00
5/10th-11th 24.00
5/12th-14th 15.00
5/15th-25th 10.00
6 A Tale of Two Cities 1050.00
6/2nd HRN #14 ....240.00
6/3rd HRN #18 ....185.00
6/4th HRN #20 ....135.00
6/5th HRN #28 ....80.00
6/6th HRN #51 ....45.00
6/7th HRN #64 ....30.00
6/8th HRN #78 ....25.00
6/9th-11th 15.00
6/12th-23rd 10.00
7 Robin Hood.....................800.00
7/2nd HRN #12 ....225.00
7/3rd HRN #18 ....165.00
7/4th HRN #20 ....130.00
7/5th HRN #22 ....100.00
7/6th HRN #28 ....90.00
7/7th HRN #51 ....45.00
7/8th HRN #64 ....28.00
7/9th-10th 25.00
7/11th-12th 18.00
7/13th-14th 15.00
7/15th-23rd 10.00
8 Arabian Nights 1550.00
8/2nd HRN #17 ....525.00
8/3rd HRN #20 ....425.00
8/A/4th HRN #28 ....350.00
8/B/4th Has stiff cover 350.00
8/5th HRN #51 ....185.00
8/6th HRN #64 ....135.00

8/7th HRN #78 .... 120.00
8/8th HRN #164 .... 110.00
9 Slick & Glossy Cover;
 Les Miserables 750.00
9/A Rough & Pulpy cover .. 800.00
9/2nd HRN #14 .... 185.00
9/3rd HRN #18 .... 165.00
9/4th HRN #20 .... 135.00
9/5th HRN #28 .... 100.00
9/6th HRN #51 .... 45.00
9/7th-8th 28.00
9/9th HRN #161 .... 25.00
9/10th-12th 15.00
10/A Violet/Purple cover;
 Robinson Crusoe........... 675.00
10/B Blue/Gray cover 700.00
10/A/2nd Violet/Purple cover
 .... 235.00
10/B/2nd Blue/Gray cover . 200.00
10/3rd HRN #18 .... 125.00
10/4th HRN #20 .... 110.00
10/5th HRN #28 .... 85.00
10/6th HRN #51 .... 45.00
10/7th HRN #64 .... 28.00
10/8th HRN #78 .... 24.00
10/9th HRN #97 .... 18.00
10/10th-12th 15.00
10/13th-21st 10.00
11 Don Quixote 750.00
11/2nd HRN #18 .... 225.00
11/3rd HRN #21 .... 135.00
11/4th HRN #28 .... 100.00
11/5th HRN #110 .... 25.00
11/6th HRN #156 .... 15.00
11/7th-10th 10.00
12 Rip Van Winkle and the
 Headless Horseman....... 750.00
12/2nd HRN #15 .... 225.00
12/3rd HRN #20 .... 135.00
12/4th HRN #22 .... 110.00
12/5th HRN #28 .... 90.00
12/6th HRN #60 .... 45.00
12/7th HRN #62 .... 25.00
12/8th-9th 18.00
12/10th-12th 15.00
12/13th-19th 10.00
13 Dr. Jekyll and Mr. Hyde. 985.00
13/2nd HRN #15 .... 240.00
13/3rd HRN #20 .... 185.00
13/4th HRN #28 .... 125.00
13/5th HRN #60 .... 45.00
13/6th HRN #62 .... 28.00
13/7th-9th 20.00
13/10th-16th 10.00

14 Westward Ho! 1600.00
14/2nd HRN #15 .... 525.00
14/3rd HRN #21 .... 400.00
14/4th HRN #28 .... 325.00
14/5th HRN #53 .... 260.00
15 Uncle Tom's Cabin........ 575.00
15/2nd HRN #15 .... 215.00
15/3rd HRN #21 .... 135.00
15/4th HRN #28 .... 85.00
15/5th HRN #53 .... 40.00
15/6th HRN #71 .... 28.00
15/7th HRN #89 .... 24.00
15/8th HRN #117 .... 18.00
15/9th HRN #128 .... 15.00
15/10th-19th 10.00
16 Gulliver's Travels........... 575.00
16/2nd HRN #18 .... 185.00
16/3rd HRN #22 .... 135.00
16/4th HRN #28 .... 80.00
16/5th HRN #60 .... 35.00
16/6th HRN #62 .... 24.00
16/7th HRN #78 .... 20.00
16/8th-9th 15.00
16/10th-15th 10.00
17 The Deerslayer 575.00
17/A/2nd Published by
 Queens Home News 185.00
17/B/2nd Published by
 Gilberton Co. 135.00
17/3rd Published by Queens
 Home News 80.00
17/4th HRN #28 .... 28.00
17/5th HRN #60 .... 24.00
17/6th-7th 20.00
17/8th-10th 15.00
17/11th-12th 12.00
18/A Published by Gilberton Co.;
 The Hunchback of Notre
 Dame............................... 675.00
18/B Published by Island
 Publishers....................... 675.00
18/2nd Published by Queens
 Home News 225.00
18/3rd Published by Queens
 Home News 135.00
18/4th HRN #28 .... 110.00
18/5th HRN #60 .... 40.00
18/6th HRN #62 .... 28.00
18/7th HRN #78 .... 24.00
18/A/8th HRN #89; Henry C.
 Kiefer artist listed on lower
 right cover 18.00
18/B/8th Artist name on
 lower right cover omitted... 18.00

18/9th-12th 18.00
18/13th-18th 10.00
19/A Published by Gilberton Co.;
   Huckleberry Finn 450.00
19/B Published by Island
   Publishers.......................450.00
19/2nd Published by Nassau
   Bulletin 200.00
19/3rd Published by Queens
   Home News....................135.00
19/4th HRN #28 ....85.00
19/5th HRN #60 ....35.00
19/6th HRN #62 ....28.00
19/7th-8th 18.00
19/9th-10th 15.00
19/11th-22nd 10.00
20/A Published by Gilberton Co.;
   The Corsican Brothers 425.00
20/B Published by The Courie
   r...425.00
20/C Published by Long Island
   Independent 425.00
20/D Published by Gilberton
   Co. & Long Island Independent,
   Rare 425.00
20/2nd HRN #22 ....165.00
20/3rd HRN #28 ....140.00
20/4th HRN #60 ....85.00
20/A/5th Classics III logo at top
   of pages 65.00
20/B/5th No logo on top of
   pages 65.00
20/6th HRN #78 ....55.00
20/7th HRN #97 ....40.00
21/A Published by Gilberton Co.;
   3 Famous Mysteries 825.00
21/B Published by Island
   Publishers.......................825.00
21/C Published by The Courier
   ....825.00
21/2nd Published by Nassau
   Bulletin 265.00
21/3rd HRN #30 ....200.00
21/4th HRN #62 ....150.00
21/5th HRN #70 ....130.00
21/6th-7th 110.00
22/A Published by Gilberton Co.;
   The Pathfinder.................365.00
22/B Published by Island
   Publishers.......................335.00
22/C Published by Queens
   Home News....................335.00
22/2nd HRN #30 ....28.00
22/3rd HRN #60 ....24.00

22/4th HRN #70 .... 20.00
22/5th HRN #85 .... 16.00
22/6th-11th 15.00
23 Oliver Twist 340.00
23/A/2nd Printers Union logo on
   bottom left front cover..... 140.00
23/B/2nd Logo omitted...... 100.00
23/3rd HRN #60 .... 35.00
23/4th HRN #62 .... 28.00
23/5th HRN #71 .... 24.00
23/6th HRN #85 .... 18.00
23/7th-9th 15.00
23/10th HRN #150 .... 12.00
23/11th-17th 10.00
24 A Connecticut Yankee in
   King Arthur's Court......... 325.00
24/2nd HRN #30 .... 85.00
24/3rd HRN #60 .... 28.00
24/4th HRN #62 .... 26.00
24/5th-8th 18.00
24/9th HRN #153 .... 14.00
24/10th-15th 10.00
25 Two Years Before the Mast
   .... 325.00
25/2nd HRN #30 .... 95.00
25/3rd HRN #60 .... 35.00
25/4th HRN #62 .... 28.00
25/5th-6th 18.00
25/7th HRN #114 .... 16.00
25/8th HRN #156 .... 15.00
25/9th-12th 10.00
26 Frankenstein................. 800.00
26/A/2nd No Indicia at the
   bottom of page one 265.00
26/B/2nd With Indicia 265.00
26/3rd-4th HRN #60 & 62.... 65.00
26/5th HRN #71 .... 35.00
26/A/6th HRN #82.............. 30.00
26/B/6th Stiff cover............. 35.00
26/7th-8th 24.00
26/9th Scarcer.................... 30.00
26/10th-20th 10.00
27 The Adventures of Marco
   Polo 325.00
27/2nd HRN #30 .... 100.00
27/3rd HRN #70 .... 28.00
27/4th HRN #87 .... 20.00
27/5th-6th 15.00
27/7th-10th 10.00
28 Michael Strogoff 325.00
28/2nd HRN #51 .... 95.00
28/3rd HRN #115 .... 20.00
28/4th-5th 15.00
28/6th-7th 12.00

29 The Prince and the Pauper
   .... 465.00
29/2nd HRN #60 .... 28.00
29/3rd HRN #62 .... 24.00
29/4th-5th 20.00
29/6th-7th 15.00
29/8th-15th 10.00
30 The Moonstone 300.00
30/2nd HRN #60 .... 36.00
30/3rd-4th 32.00
30/5th HRN #165 .... 20.00
30/6th-8th 10.00
31 The Black Arrow 265.00
31/2nd HRN #51 .... 35.00
31/3rd HRN #64 .... 20.00
31/4th HRN #87 .... 16.00
31/5th-7th 15.00
31/8th-14th 10.00
32 Lorna Doone 300.00
32/2nd HRN #53 .... 45.00
32/3rd HRN #85 .... 28.00
32/4th-5th 20.00
32/6th-10th 10.00
33 The Adventures of Sherlock
   Holmes 1025.00
33/2nd HRN #53 .... 385.00
33/3rd HRN #71 .... 295.00
33/4th HRN #89 .... 240.00
34 Mysterious Island 285.00
34/2nd HRN #60 .... 32.00
34/3rd HRN #62 .... 28.00
34/4th-5th 24.00
34/6th HRN #92 .... 18.00
34/7th-8th 15.00
34/9th-13th 10.00
35 The Last Days of Pompeii
   .... 325.00
35/2nd HRN #161 .... 32.00
35/3rd-5th 12.00
36 Typee............................ 215.00
36/2nd HRN #64 .... 40.00
36/3rd HRN #155 .... 20.00
36/4th HRN #167 .... 14.00
36/5th-6th 10.00
37 The Pioneers................ 165.00
37/A/2nd Price circle left blank
   .... 28.00
37/B/2nd 10¢ written on cover,
   very rare written on cover,
   very rare 55.00
37/3rd HRN #70 .... 20.00
37/4th-5th 15.00
37/6th-8th 12.00
37/9th-11th 10.00

38 Adventures of Cellini 185.00
38/2nd-3rd HRN #164 & 167
....24.00
38/4th-5th 18.00
39 Jane Eyre.....................215.00
39/2nd HRN #60 ....28.00
39/3rd-5th............................24.00
39/6th-10th 18.00
39/11th-13th 15.00
40 Mysteries......................585.00
40/2nd HRN #62 ....250.00
40/3rd HRN #75 ....175.00
40/4th HRN #92 ....130.00
41 Twenty Years After........365.00
41/2nd HRN #62 ....28.00
41/3rd HRN #78 ....22.00
41/4th-7th 10.00
42 Swiss Family Robinson .175.00
42/2nd/A Outside back cover:
   CI Gift Box Ad....................38.00
42/2nd/B Outside back cover:
   CI Reorder list 45.00
42/3rd HRN #75 ....24.00
42/4th-5th..............................18.00
42/6th-9th 15.00
42/10th-17th 10.00
43 Great Expectations 675.00
43/2nd Great Expectations
....450.00
44/A Printed on newsprint;
   Mysteries of Paris............550.00
44/B Printed on white, heavier
   paper 550.00
44/2nd/A CI Gift box ad on outside
   back cover......................225.00
44/2nd/B CI Reorder list on
   outside back cover 225.00
44/3rd 135.00
45 Tom Brown's School Days
....95.00
45/2nd HRN #64 ....35.00
45/3rd HRN #161 ....16.00
45/4th-6th 10.00
46 Kidnapped....................110.00
46/2nd/A Front cover price
   circle is blank....................35.00
46/2nd/B 10¢ listed as price
   on front cover....................60.00
46/3rd HRN #78 ....20.00
46/4th 18.00
46/5th-6th 15.00
46/7th-17th 10.00
47 Twenty Thousand Leagues
   Under The Sea 100.00

47/2nd HRN #64 .... 35.00
47/3rd HRN #78 .... 18.00
47/4th HRN #94 .... 16.00
47/5th-7th 15.00
47/8th-17th 10.00
48 David Copperfield........... 90.00
48/2nd HRN #64 .... 35.00
48/3rd HRN #87 .... 18.00
48/4th-15th 15.00
49 Alice in Wonderland 185.00
49/2nd HRN #64 .... 45.00
49/3rd/A Regular cover paper,
   slick & glossy 35.00
49/3rd/B Rough, thick, pulpy
   cover paper (scarce)......... 35.00
49/4th HRN #155 .... 28.00
49/5th-6th............................ 24.00
49/7th-8th 15.00
50/A Date: August, 1948
   (Correct date); Adventures
   of Tom Sawyer............... 110.00
50/B Date: September, 1948
   (Printing error) 110.00
50/C Outside back cover is blue &
   yellow (very rare); Date:
   September, 1948
   (Printing error) 110.00
50/2nd HRN #64 .... 24.00
50/3rd HRN #78 .... 18.00
50/4th-9th 15.00
50/10th-15th 10.00
51/A Christmas Carol illustration
   on inside back cover; The Spy
   .... 85.00
51/B Man In The Iron Mask
   illustration on inside back
   cover................................. 85.00
51/C August, 1948 (printing
   error)................................. 85.00
51/D Outside back cover -
   blue & yellow 100.00
51/2nd HRN #89 .... 26.00
51/3rd HRN #121 .... 20.00
51/4th HRN #139 .... 16.00
51/5th HRN #156 .... 15.00
51/6th HRN #167 .... 12.00
51/7th-8th 10.00
52 The House of Seven Gables
   .... 80.00
52/2nd HRN #89 .... 24.00
52/3rd-4th 18.00
52/5th-10th 10.00
53 A Christmas Carol........ 125.00
54 Man in the Iron Mask.... 110.00

54/2nd HRN #93 .... 40.00
54/3rd/A Regular LDC logo
   lettering............................ 32.00
54/3rd/B Changed to PC-type
   lettering (scarce).............. 32.00
54/4th HRN #142 .... 20.00
54/5th-9th 12.00
55 Silas Marner.................. 80.00
55/2nd HRN #75 .... 28.00
55/3rd-4th 15.00
55/5th-12th 10.00
56 The Toilers of the Sea... 135.00
56/2nd HRN #165 .... 28.00
56/3rd HRN #167 .... 24.00
56/4th HRN #167 .... 20.00
57 The Song of Hiawatha 85.00
57/2nd HRN #75 .... 28.00
57/3rd-4th 20.00
57/5th-7th 15.00
57/8th-11th 10.00
58 The Prairie..................... 85.00
58/A/2nd No "Coming Next"
   ad...................................... 38.00
58/B/2nd HRN #62; Includes
   "Coming Next" ad.............. 38.00
58/3rd HRN #78 .... 18.00
58/4th-7th 15.00
58/8th-11th 10.00
59 Wuthering Heights........ 110.00
59/2nd HRN #85 .... 38.00
59/3rd HRN #156 .... 15.00
59/4th-6th 10.00
60 Black Beauty 95.00
60/2nd No cover price 35.00
60/3rd HRN #85 .... 24.00
60/4th-5th 15.00
60/6th-7th 12.00
60/8th .... No HRN; ca. 2008
   .... 10.00
61/A Top front cover - deep purple;
   The Woman in White 90.00
61/B Top Front cover - pink.. 90.00
61/2nd HRN #156 .... 20.00
61/3rd-4th 18.00
62 Western Stories.............. 80.00
62/2nd HRN #89 .... 28.00
62/3rd HRN #121 .... 20.00
62/4th HRN #137 .... 15.00
62/5th-9th 10.00
63 The Man Without A Country
   .... 90.00
63/2nd HRN #78 .... 28.00
63/3rd HRN #156 .... 20.00
63/4th HRN #165 .... 14.00

111/3rd-4th 10.00
112 Adventures of Kit Carson
....30.00
112/2nd-9th 10.00
113 The Forty-Five Guardsmen
....60.00
113/2nd HRN #166 ....35.00
114 The Red Rover.............55.00
114/2nd HRN #166 ....35.00
115 How I Found Livingstone
....55.00
115/2nd HRN #167 ....28.00
116 The Bottle Imp..............60.00
116/2nd HRN #167 ....28.00
117 Captains Courageous ...55.00
117/2nd HRN #167 ....25.00
117/3rd HRN #169; Fall 1970
....20.00
118 Rob Roy 55.00
118/2nd HRN #167 ....28.00
119 Soldiers of Fortune........55.00
119/2nd HRN #166 ....20.00
119/3rd HRN #169; Spring
1970 ....15.00
120 The Hurricane 50.00
120/2nd HRN #166 ....25.00
121 Wild Bill Hickok.............26.00
121/2nd-8th 10.00
122 The Mutineers 25.00
122/2nd-7th 10.00
123 Fang and Claw 25.00
123/2nd-6th 10.00
124 The War of the Worlds...45.00
124/2nd HRN #131 ....16.00
124/3rd-4th 12.00
124/5th-12th 10.00
125 The Ox Bow Incident.....24.00
125/2nd-8th 10.00
126 The Downfall 25.00
126/2nd-3rd 10.00
127 The King of the Mountains
....24.00
127/2nd-3rd 10.00
128 Macbeth 28.00
128/2nd-8th 10.00
129 Davy Crockett...............65.00
129/2nd HRN #167 ....40.00
130 Caesar's Conquests......30.00
130/2nd-7th 10.00
131 The Covered Wagon 24.00
131/2nd-8th 10.00
132 The Dark Frigate 28.00
132/2nd-4th 10.00
133 The Time Machine.........40.00
133/2nd The Time Machine..16.00
133/3rd-5th 12.00
133/6th-10th 10.00
134 Romeo & Juliet.............32.00
134/2nd-7th 10.00
135 Waterloo.......................24.00
135/2nd-5th 10.00
136 Lord Jim 24.00
136/2nd-5th 10.00
137 The Little Savage 24.00
137/2nd-7th 10.00
138 A Journey to the Center
of the Earth........................40.00
138/2nd-9th 10.00
139 In the Reign of Terror 24.00
139/2nd-5th 10.00

140 On Jungle Trails............ 24.00
140/2nd-5th 10.00
141 Castle Dangerous 30.00
141/2nd-4th 10.00
142 Abraham Lincoln 30.00
142/2nd HRN #154 .... 14.00
142/3rd-7th 10.00
143 Kim 24.00
143/2nd-5th 10.00
144 The First Men in the Moon
.... 35.00
144/2nd HRN #153 .... 12.00
144/3rd-7th 10.00
145 The Crisis 26.00
145/2nd-5th 10.00
146 With Fire and Sword..... 26.00
146/2nd-4th 10.00
147 Ben-Hur....................... 26.00
147/2nd-8th 10.00
148 The Buccaneer............. 26.00
148/2nd-5th 10.00
149 Off on a Comet............. 26.00
149/2nd-7th 10.00
150 The Virginian 45.00
150/2nd-3rd 15.00
150/4th HRN #167 .... 12.00
151 Won By the Sword........ 45.00
151/2nd-3rd 15.00
151/4th HRN #166 .... 12.00
152 Wild Animals I Have
Known 40.00
152/2nd HRN #149 .... 15.00
152/3rd-5th 10.00
153 The Invisible Man 45.00
153/2nd/A HRN #149.......... 15.00
153/2nd/B HRN #149.......... 12.00
153/3rd-7th 10.00
154 The Conspiracy Of Pontiac
.... 10.00
154/2nd-3rd 10.00
154/4th December 1967...... 12.00
155 The Lion of the North ... 28.00
155/2nd-3rd 10.00
156 The Conquest of Mexico
.... 28.00
156/2nd-4th 10.00
157 Lives of the Hunted 38.00
157/2nd-3rd 15.00
158 The Conspirators.......... 38.00
158/2nd-3rd 18.00
159 The Octopus................. 38.00
159/2nd-3rd 15.00
160/A HRN #159; The Food
of the Gods 40.00
160/B HRN #160 .... 40.00
160/2nd-3rd 15.00
161 Cleopatra..................... 40.00
161/2nd-3rd 15.00
162 Robur the Conqueror ... 40.00
162/2nd-3rd 16.00
163 Master of the World...... 40.00
163/2nd-3rd 15.00
164 The Cossack Chief....... 40.00
164/2nd-3rd 15.00
165 The Queen's Necklace . 40.00
165/2nd-3rd 15.00
166 Tigers and Traitors........ 65.00
166/2nd HRN #167 .... 20.00
166/3rd HRN #167 .... 16.00
167 Faust 75.00

167/2nd HRN #167 .... 35.00
167/3rd HRN #166 .... 25.00
168 In Freedom's Cause 80.00
169 Negro Americans:
The Early Years................. 75.00
169/2nd HRN #169 .... 30.00

Classics Illustrated
First, 1990
1-27 .... 4.00

Classics Illustrated Junior
Famous Authors, 1953

Following the success of Classics Illustrated, the publisher decided to broaden the line in 1953 by launching a series based on popular fairy tales. Alice's Adventures in Wonderland had been tried in the earlier Classics Illustrated series, but the somewhat older readers of that line did not receive it well. The new series of Classics Illustrated Junior editions proved popular, however, and soon was reprinted to almost the same extent that the main series had been.

Among the (public domain) stories adapted were The Little Mermaid, The Frog Prince, Rapunzel, Jack and the Beanstalk, Cinderella, and Pinocchio. From a collector's point of view, the Junior editions are a bargain, with almost all later printings selling for just a few dollars, in comparison to the princely prices that issues of Classics Illustrated often command.

501 Snow White and the Seven
Dwarves.......................... 75.00
501/2nd HRN #524 .... 12.00
501/3rd-9th 10.00
501/10th HRN #577 .... 4.00
502 The Ugly Duckling 44.00
502/2nd HRN #524 .... 12.00
502/3rd-9th 10.00
503 Cinderella 28.00
503/2nd HRN #524 .... 12.00

503/3rd-11th 10.00
504 The Pied Piper 20.00
504/2nd-9th 10.00
505 Sleeping Beauty..........20.00
505/2nd-9th 10.00
505/10th ca. 2008 ....6.00
506 The Three Little Pigs 18.00
506/2nd-8th 10.00
506/9th ca. 2008 ....6.00
507 Jack and the Beanstalk 18.00
507/2nd-8th 10.00
507/9th ca. 2008 ....6.00
508 Goldilocks and the Three
Bears.......................18.00
508/2nd-7th 10.00
508/8th ca. 2002 ....6.00
509 Beauty and the Beast...18.00
509/2nd-8th 10.00
509/9th...............................6.00
510 Little Red Riding Hood .18.00
510/2nd-7th 10.00
510/8th ca. 2008 ....6.00
511 Puss in Boots..............18.00
511/2nd HRN #526 ....18.00
511/3rd-7th 10.00
512 Rumpelstiltskin.............18.00
512/2nd-3rd 18.00
512/4th HRN #161 (CI) 15.00
512/5th-7th 12.00
512/8th ca. 2004 ....4.00
513 Pinocchio 28.00
513/2nd HRN #530 ....12.00
513/3rd-9th 10.00
513/10th HRN #576; ca. 2002
....6.00
514 The Steadfast Tin Soldier
.....................................24.00
514/2nd-5th 10.00
514/6th 6th printing 4.00
515 Johnny Appleseed 18.00
515/2nd-7th 10.00
515/8th ca. 2004 ....4.00
516 Aladdin and his Lamp ..28.00
516/2nd-7th 10.00
517 The Emperor's New
Clothes 18.00
517/2nd-6th 10.00
518 The Golden Goose.......18.00
518/2nd-5th 10.00
519 Paul Bunyan................24.00
519/2nd-11th 10.00
519/12th HRN #577 ....4.00
520 Thumbelina 24.00
520/2nd-7th 10.00
520/8th ca. 2004 ....4.00

521 The King of the Golden
River 15.00
521/2nd-6th 10.00
522 The Nightingale 18.00
522/2nd-5th 10.00
523 The Gallant Tailor 15.00
523/2nd-5th 10.00
524 The Wild Swans 15.00
524/2nd-6th 10.00
525 The Little Mermaid 22.00
525/2nd-6th 10.00
526 The Frog Prince...........15.00
526/2nd-6th 10.00
527 The Golden-Haired Giant
....15.00
527/2nd-6th 10.00
528 The Penny Prince........15.00
528/2nd-6th 10.00
529 The Magic Servants 15.00
529/2nd-4th 10.00
530 The Golden Bird 15.00
530/2nd-5th 10.00
530/6th HRN #577 ....4.00
531 Rapunzel.....................15.00
531/2nd-6th 10.00
532 The Dancing Princess . 18.00
532/2nd-7th 10.00
533 The Magic Fountain.....15.00
533/2nd-5th 10.00
534 The Golden Touch 15.00
534/2nd-5th 10.00
535 The Wizard of Oz 30.00
535/2nd HRN #557 ....15.00
535/3rd-7th 10.00
536 The Chimney Sweep 15.00
536/2nd-6th 10.00
536/7th HRN #577; ca. 2003
....4.00
537 The Three Fairies 15.00
537/2nd-5th 10.00
538 Silly Hans 15.00
538/2nd-5th 10.00
539 The Enchanted Fish 15.00
539/2nd-6th 10.00
539/7th HRN #576 ....4.00
540 The Tinder-Box............15.00
540/2nd-6th......................10.00
540/7th 7th printing 4.00
541 Snow White and Rose Red
....20.00
541/2nd-5th 10.00
542 The Donkey's Tale 16.00
542/2nd-5th 10.00
543 The House in the Woods
....15.00

543/2nd-5th 10.00
544 The Golden Fleece......26.00
544/2nd HRN #556 ....15.00
544/3rd-6th 12.00
545 The Glass Mountain 15.00
545/2nd-5th 10.00
546 The Elves and the
Shoemaker 15.00
546/2nd-5th 10.00
546/6th HRN #577; ca. 2003
....4.00
547 The Wishing Table 15.00
547/2nd-5th 10.00
548 The Magic Pitcher 15.00
548/2nd-6th 10.00
548/7th ca. 2005..................6.00
549 Simple Kate.................15.00
549/2nd-6th 10.00
550 The Singing Donkey 15.00
550/2nd-5th 10.00
551 The Queen Bee...........15.00
551/2nd-5th 10.00
552 The Three Little Dwarfs;
Aesop's Fables: The
Woodcutters and the Ax .. 15.00
552/2nd-5th 10.00
553 King Thrushbeard........15.00
553/2nd-6th 10.00
554 The Enchanted Deer ... 15.00
554/2nd-6th 10.00
555 The 3 Golden Apples... 15.00
555/2nd-4th 10.00
556 The Elf Mound.............15.00
556/2nd-5th 10.00
557 Silly Willy 15.00
557/2nd-5th 10.00
558 The Magic Dish 15.00
558/2nd-4th 10.00
559 The Japanese Lantern 15.00
559/2nd-4th 10.00
560 The Doll Princess 15.00
560/2nd-4th 10.00
561 Hans Humdrum...........15.00
561/2nd-4th 10.00
562 The Enchanted Pony ... 15.00
562/2nd-4th 10.00
563 The Wishing Well........15.00
563/2nd-4th 10.00
563/5th 5th printing 4.00
564 The Salt Mountain 15.00
564/2nd-4th 10.00
564/5th 5th printing 4.00
565 The Silly Princess........15.00
565/2nd-4th 10.00
565/5th 4.00

566 Clumsy Hans................15.00
566/2nd-4th 10.00
567 The Bearskin Soldier....15.00
567/2nd-5th 10.00
568 The Happy Hedgehog ..15.00
568/2nd-4th 10.00
569 The Three Giants 15.00
569/2nd-4th 10.00
570 The Pearl Princess.......15.00
570/2nd-4th 10.00
570/5th HRN #577; ca. 2003
....4.00
571 How Fire Came to the
  Indians..............................15.00
571/2nd-4th 10.00
571/5th HRN #577; ca. 2004...6.00
572 The Drummer Boy........15.00
572/2nd-3rd 10.00
573 The Crystal Ball............15.00
573/2nd-3rd 10.00
574 Brightboots...................15.00
574/2nd-3rd 10.00
575 The Fearless Prince 15.00
575/2nd-3rd 10.00
576 The Princess Who Saw
  Everything 15.00
576/2nd-3rd 10.00
577 The Runaway Dumpling 18.00

Classics Illustrated
Special Issue
Gilberton, 1955

129 ....50.00
132 ....45.00
135-138................................35.00
138/2nd................................25.00
138/3rd.................................35.00
141-159................................40.00
162 ....75.00
165 ....45.00
166-167................................50.00

Classics Illustrated
Study Guide
Acclaim, 1997

1-38..5.00

Classic Star Wars
Dark Horse, 1992

Among the adaptations
spawned by Star Wars, one of the
overlooked greats is a daily

newspaper strip that continued the
adventures of Luke Skywalker, Han
Solo, and the rest of the characters
seeking to save the galaxy from the
tyranny of the Empire.

More than a decade later, Dark
Horse Comics brought the Archie
Goodwin/Al Williamson run on that
strip back in comic-book form as
Classic Star Wars. Dark Horse
does a reasonably good job of
converting the newspaper strip into
comic book form, removing
redundant panels and coloring the
artwork (with Williamson's
participation).

Strip enthusiasts will still long
for a reprint work that preserves
the original form, but this will do in
the meantime. A later Dark Horse
series, Classic Star Wars: The
Early Adventures, reprinted Russ
Manning's strips.

1-3.. 4.00
4-19 .... 3.00
20 .... 4.00

Classic Star Wars:
A Long Time Ago
Dark Horse, 1999
1-6 .... 13.00

Classic Star Wars:
A New Hope
Dark Horse, 1994
1-2 .... 4.00

Classic Star Wars:
Devilworlds
Dark Horse, 1996
1-2 .... 3.00

Classic Star Wars:
Han Solo at Stars' End
Dark Horse, 1997
1-3 .... 3.00

Classic Star Wars:
Return of the Jedi
Dark Horse, 1994
1-2 .... 4.00

Classic Star Wars:
The Early Adventures
Dark Horse, 1994
1-9 .... 3.00

Classic Star Wars:
The Empire Strikes Back
Dark Horse, 1994
1-2 .... 4.00

Classic Star Wars:
The Vandelhelm Mission
Dark Horse, 1995
1 .... 3.00

Classic Terry &
the Pirates
Avalon
1-5 .... 3.00

Classic 2000 A.D.
Fleetway-Quality
1 .... 4.00
2-12 .... 3.00

Classic X-Men
Marvel, 1986
1 .... 6.00
2 .... 4.00
3-29 .... 3.00
30-45 .... 2.00

Claus
Draco, 1997
1-2 .... 3.00

Claws
Conquest, 2006

Claws
Marvel, 2006
1-3 .... 4.00

Claw
the Unconquered
DC, 1975

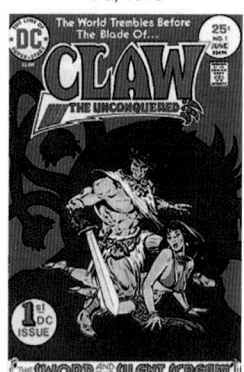

Years ago, an evil prince
conspired to be king. Yet even
though he was assured of his
destiny, it was foretold that a man
with a hideously deformed hand
would one day challenge his rule.
Accordingly, he hatched a plot to
have the kingdom searched and to
have any such man killed. So it
was that a loyal farmer named
Kregar was unjustly put to death.
Years later, thanks to a deadly
poison in the King's cup, the prince
achieved his destiny, becoming
King Occulus the First.

But he did not know that poor
Kregar had left an heir with a
similar deformity. Known
throughout the land as Claw, the
heir had become a mighty

swordsman. And though the prince would try to stop him with soldiers, magic, and summoned demons, nothing could long stand between Claw and his revenge.

1	7.00
2	4.00
3	3.00
4-6	2.00
7	4.00
8-12	2.00

Claw the Unconquered
DC, 2006

1-6	3.00

Clay Cody, Gunslinger
Pines, 1957

1	25.00

Clem: Mall Security
Spit Take, 1997

0	2.00

Cleopatra
Rip Off, 1992

1	3.00

Clerks: The Comic Book
Oni, 1998

1	5.00
1/2nd-2	3.00
Holiday 1	4.00

Cletus and Floyd Show
Asylum, 2002

1	3.00

CLF: Cybernetic Liberation Front
Anubis

1	3.00

Click!
NBM

1	11.00
2-3	13.00
4	11.00

Cliffhanger!
Image, 1997

1	3.00

Cliffhanger Comics
AC, 1989

1-2	3.00

Cliffhanger Comics
AC, 1990

1/A-2/A	3.00

Climax
Gillmor, 1955

1	85.00
2	65.00

Climaxxx
Aircel, 1991

1-4	4.00

Clint
Trigon, 1986

1-2	2.00

Clint: The Hamster Triumphant
Eclipse

1-2	2.00

Clive Barker's The Great and Secret Show
Idea & Design Works, 2006

1-8	4.00

Cloak and Dagger
Ziff-Davis, 1952

1	100.00

Cloak & Dagger
Marvel, 1983

1-2	3.00
3-4	2.00
5-10	1.00
11	2.00

Cloak and Dagger in Predator and Prey
Marvel

1	7.00

Clock!
Top Shelf

3	3.00

Clockmaker
Image, 2003

1-4	3.00

Clockmaker Act 2
Image, 2003

1-2	5.00

Clockwork Angels
Image

1	11.00

Clonezone Special
Dark Horse, 1989

Clonezone is an intergalactic comedic celebrity who is picked to

be the Master of Ceremonies for the annual, Back-Pimple telethon. It's a star-studded event that lasts forty-eight continuous hours-all to raise funds for research into a cure for that most heartbreaking of ailments. Among the guests slated to appear are Judah Maccabee ("The Hammer of God"), aging comedian Ribeye (whose jokes are old enough to draw pensions), and the McJaggerz, the hottest (and most obnoxious) band in the galaxy. The real star of the show is the obnoxious reptilian comedian Clonezone, who manages to offend virtually everyone during the course of the telethon.

Dark Horse Comics and First Comics teamed up to publish this "Clonezone Special" in 1989. The black-and-white, one-shot story was written by Mike Baron (Badger, Nexus),with illustrations by Neil Vokes.

1	2.00

Close Shaves of Pauline Peril
Gold Key, 1970

1	20.00
2-4	14.00

Cloudfall
Image, 2003

1	5.00

Clown Figure
Image, 1994

1	1.00

Clown: Nobody's Laughing Now
Fleetway-Quality

1	5.00

Clowns
Dark Horse, 1998

1	3.00

Clowns
Yahoo Pro

1	3.00

Clue Comics
Hillman, 1943

1	530.00
2-3	360.00
4-6	225.00
7-9	260.00
10-12	155.00

Clue Comics
Hillman, 1947

1	530.00
2-3	360.00

Clutching Hand
ACG, 1954
1 ....200.00

Clyde Crashcup
Dell, 1963
1 ....90.00
2 ....65.00
3-5 ....48.00

C-M-O Comics
Chicago Mail Order, 1942
1-2 ....1,000.00

Cobalt 60
Tundra
1-2 ....5.00

Cobalt Blue
Power, 1978
1 ....2.00

Cobalt Blue
Innovation, 1989
1-2 ....2.00
GN 1 ....6.00

Cobalt Warrior Angel
Mindchyld Comics, 2005
0 ....4.00

Cobbler's Monster
Image, 2006
1 ....15.00

Cobb: Off the Leash
Idea & Design Works, 2006
1-3 ....4.00

Cobra
Viz, 1990
1-12 ....3.00

Cocomalt
Big Book of Comics
Harry A. Chesler, 1938
1 ....1,000.00

Cocopiazo
Slave Labor, 2004
1-4 ....3.00

Coda
Coda
1-4 ....2.00

Code Blue
Image, 1998
1 ....3.00

Codename: Danger
Lodestone, 1985
1-4 ....2.00

Codename: Firearm
Malibu, 1995

Written by James Robinson, Firearm was one of the best of Malibu's Ultraverse titles in the initial run. In late 1995, Malibu relaunched its universe, eventually reincarnating Firearm in this new "Codename: Firearm" series.

Alec Swann, the original Firearm, appears in issues #0-2 as part of a backup story, but, otherwise, the series is devoted to the adventures of Jimmy Hitch. Jimmy is a covert agent and sniper working in the service of the Lodge, just one of those average, everyday secret organizations.

0-5 .... 3.00

Codename: Genetix
Marvel, 1993
1-4 .... 2.00

Codename: Knockout
DC, 2001
0-23 .... 3.00

Code Name Ninja
Solson
1 .... 2.00

Codename: Scorpio
Antarctic, 1996
1-4 .... 3.00

Codename: Spitfire
Marvel, 1987
10-13 .... 1.00

Codename: Strikeforce
Spectrum, 1984
1 .... 2.00

Codename: Stryke Force
Image, 1994

Marc Silvestri's Cyberforce is back in action in this hard-hitting title. It begins when a demonic being leads a high-tech attack against the shipyards of Sebastopol, Ukraine. There, world leaders have gathered to witness the disarming of what was considered the most powerful nuclear submarine the world has ever seen. But what should have been a moment of hope for the world turns into a bloodbath, as heavily armed attackers swarm over the proceedings, hijack the sub, and take several world leaders hostage.

Luckily, the four-armed mutant named Stryker is working security for the American president, and he manages to prevent the president from being captured. The only question now is: Can Stryke Force find the sub and save the world from nuclear devastation?

0-1/Variant 3.00
2-14 .... 2.00

Code of Honor
Marvel, 1997
1-4 .... 6.00

Code XIII
Comcat, 1989
1-5 .... 7.00

Cody of the Pony Express
Charlton, 1955
8-10 .... 35.00

Cody Starbuck
Star*Reach, 1978
1 .... 2.00

Co-Ed Sexxtasy
Fantagraphics, 1999
1-11 ....4.00

Coexisting
Alternative, 2005
1 ....3.00

Coffee World
World

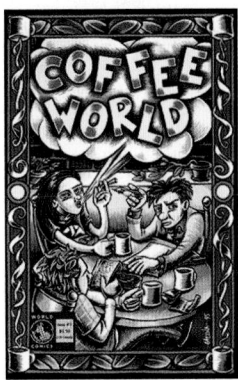

Yes, it's a comic featuring stories about, singing the praises of, and paid for by ads about...coffee.

Whereas other generations have socialized over chocolate malts, cocktails, or a bottle of suds, the 90s are all about coffee. But while Starbucks and Co. have made a killing selling triple-decaf-skinny-lattes (hold the foam!) to the nouveau caffeinated, this special is more about the simple joys of a straight "cuppa joe."

Ian Smith's story by that very name sets a humorous, surreal tone for the rest of the first issue. This is followed by the infamous Too Much Coffee Man, a very nicely done bit of comic storytelling by Gheena called "A Saving Grace," and several other coffee-related tales. Unusual in most indie comics, the whole effort is financed by several pages of-what else-coffee ads in the back.

1 ....2.00

Coffin
Oni, 2000
1 ....6.00
2-4 ....4.00

Coffin Blood
Monster
1 ....4.00

Cold Blooded
Northstar, 1993
1-2 ....3.00

3 .... 5.00

Cold-Blooded Chameleon Commandos
Blackthorne, 1986
1-5 .... 2.00

Cold Blooded: The Burning Kiss
Northstar, 1993
1 .... 5.00

Cold Eden
Legacy, 1995
4 .... 2.00

Cole Black
Rocky Hartberg
1-6 .... 2.00

Cole Black
Hartberg, 2007
1-5 .... 2.00

Collection
Eternity
1 .... 3.00

Collector's Dracula
Millennium
1-2 .... 4.00

Collectors Guide to the Ultraverse
Malibu, 1994
1 .... 1.00

Collier's
Fantagraphics
1-2 .... 3.00

Colonia
Colonia, 1998

Young Jack and his two uncles find themselves cast adrift after a mysterious storm sinks their boat off the coast of Massachusetts. They're quite happy when they're rescued, until they realize they have been saved by what appears to be a group of pirates in an ancient galleon. Their escape from the privateers is only the beginning of their adventures, however. While his uncles seem oblivious to the unusual circumstances of their situation, Jack slowly adjusts to the notion that they may have been somehow cast back in time, to the era of Columbus. But after encounters with a talking duck, a strange fish-man, and Spanish Conquistadors with removable heads, Jack soon realizes that time travel is the least of their problems.

Jeff Nicholson provides some interesting fantasy tales here in a series marred only by its irregular schedule of release.

1-10 .... 3.00
11 .... 4.00

Colors in Black
Dark Horse, 1995

This four-issue anthology mini-series, part of Spike Lee's "Comics from Spike" line, explores the issue of race in America, and makes clear that the "issue" is actually many issues, separate but intertwined.

In the first issue, "The Introduction an' S*** or The Bad Rap Song" takes a semi-humorous look at black stereotypes and those who perpetuate them. "The Life That Jack Built" tells of a hard-working black man whose struggle for acceptance in mainstream America has blinded him to the toll it has taken. "The Red Hot Pizza Girls" is a Love and Rockets-like tale of interracial attraction and the misunderstandings and strong reactions it produces. "Passion Play" contrasts a college professor's "expert" opinion on race relations with a brutal, and much more plausible, example of the same.

1-4 .... 3.00

Colossal Show
Gold Key, 1969
1 ....25.00

Colossus
Marvel, 1997
1 ....3.00

Colossus Battlebook
Marvel
1 ....4.00

Colossus Comics
Sun, 1940
1 ....2,700.00

Colossus: God's Country
Marvel
1 ....7.00

Colour of Magic
(Terry Pratchett's...)
Innovation
1-4..3.00

Colt
Kz Comics, 1986
1-4..1.00

Colt .45
Dell, 1960
4-5...35.00
6 ....30.00
7-9...20.00

Colt Special
AC, 1985
1 ....2.00

Columbus
Dark Horse
1 ....3.00

Colville
King Ink, 1997
1 ....3.00

Combat
Atlas, 1952
1 ....135.00
2 ....80.00
3 ....75.00
4-5...65.00
6-11...55.00

Combat
Dell, 1961
1 ....10.00
2 ....20.00
3 ....18.00
4 ....25.00
☛JFK story
5 ....16.00
6-9...12.00
10-20...9.00
21-27...8.00
28-40...6.00

Combat
Image, 1996
1-2 .... 3.00

Combat Casey
Sports Action, 1953

Formerly War Combat, Combat Casey was a rather crude and violent war comic set during the Korean War, churned out by Atlas during the 1950s under their "Sports Action" imprint. Casey is a rough-and-ready fighting machine with a fierce red goatee. With no fear and even less doubt, he leads his squad into blistering fire fights behind enemy lines. Casey's bravado is counterbalanced by his compatriot Penny P. Pennington, an intellectual (how do we know? It's the glasses, of course!) private who uses his smarts to get himself and Casey out of tough spots. Each issue of Combat Casey features two bloody bust-em-up stories of Casey and his crew, and a filler story highlighting some aspect of life in the military.

6 .... 40.00
7 .... 34.00
8-10................................. 26.00
11-34................................ 20.00

Combat Kelly
Marvel, 1951
1 .... 175.00
2 .... 85.00
3-11 .... 70.00
12-28 .... 65.00
29-38 .... 45.00
39-44 .... 30.00

Combat Kelly
Marvel, 1972
1 .... 10.00
2-3 .... 6.00
4-9 .... 4.00

Combat Zone
Avalon
1 .... 3.00

Come Again
Fantagraphics, 1997
1-2 .... 3.00

Comedy Comics
Timely, 1942
9 .... 2,200.00
10 .... 1,600.00
11-13 .... 525.00
14-16 .... 400.00
17-20 .... 300.00
21-24 .... 200.00
25-27 .... 150.00
28-31 .... 100.00
32-34 .... 75.00

Comet
Archie, 1983
1-2 .... 1.00

Comet
DC, 1991
1-18 .... 1.00
Ann 1 .... 2.00

Comet Man
Marvel, 1987
1-6 .... 1.00

Comet Tales
Rocket, 1983
1-3 .... 1.00

Comic Album
Dell, 1958
1 .... 100.00
2 .... 50.00
3 .... 75.00
4-6 .... 30.00
7 .... 40.00
8-10 .... 30.00
11 .... 40.00
12-14 .... 30.00
15 .... 40.00
16 .... 80.00
17 .... 40.00
18 .... 80.00

Comicana
-Ism, 2005
1-3 .... 4.00

Comic Book
Marvel, 1996
1-2 .... 7.00

Comic Book Confidential
Sphinx, 1988
1 ....2.00

Comic Book Heaven
Slave Labor, 2000
1-9...2.00

Comic Book Talent Search
Silverwolf, 1987
1 ....2.00

Comic Capers
Timely, 1944
1 ....120.00
2 ....85.00
3-4 ....65.00
5-6 ....50.00

Comic Cavalcade
DC, 1942

The anthology title began as self-contained stories of a number of DC's super-heroes in something of a companion anthology to the World's Finest Comics' assemblage of Superman, Batman, and Robin. Flash, Green Lantern, and Wonder Woman initially starred in the 15-cent giant Comic Cavalcade - but the popularity of those characters wasn't enough to support the series. Also, much like World's Finest, while the three heroes would appear together on the cover, they had separate adventures inside.

At the end of 1948, funny animals took it over, and Fox, Crow, Dodo, Frog, and Nutsy Squirrel romped where heroes had once fought evil.

-- Maggie

1 ....7,000.00
2 ....2,400.00
3 ....1,650.00
4-5 ....100.00
6-10 ....875.00

11-12 .... 750.00
13 .... 950.00
☛Sol. Grundy app.
14-20 .... 750.00
21-29 .... 650.00
30 .... 275.00
31-40 .... 150.00
41-50 .... 100.00
51-62 .... 90.00
63 .... 150.00

Comic Clock (Oscar and Friday's...)
Fawcett
1 .... 15.00

Comic Comics
Fawcett, 1946
1 .... 100.00
2-10 .... 75.00

Comic Land
Fact and Fiction, 1946
1 .... 80.00

Comico Black Book
Comico, 1987
1 .... 2.00

Comico Christmas Special
Comico, 1988
1 .... 3.00

Comico Collection
Comico
1 .... 10.00

Comic Party
Tokyopop, 2004
1-5 .... 10.00

Comics
Dell, 1937
1 .... 1,500.00
2 .... 750.00
3 .... 600.00
4-5 .... 575.00
6-8 .... 500.00
9-11 .... 425.00

Comics and Stories
Dark Horse, 1996
1-4 .... 3.00

Comics Are Dead
Slap Happy, 1999
1 .... 5.00

Comics Artist Showcase
Showcase
1 .... 1.00

Comics for Stoners
Jason Neuman
1 .... 1.00

Comics' Greatest World
Dark Horse, 1993
1 .... 1.00

Comics' Greatest World: Arcadia
Dark Horse, 1993
1 .... 2.00
1/Ltd. 3.00
2 .... 1.00
3 .... 3.00
4 .... 1.00

Comics' Greatest World: Cinnabar Flats
Dark Horse, 1993
1 .... 1.00
1/A-1/Ltd................................ 3.00
2-4 .... 1.00

Comics' Greatest World: Golden City
Dark Horse, 1993
1 .... 1.00
1/Ltd. 3.00
2-4 .... 1.00

Comics' Greatest World: Out of the Vortex
Dark Horse, 1993
1-4 .... 2.00

Comics' Greatest World Sourcebook
Dark Horse, 1993
1 .... 1.00

Comics' Greatest World: Steel Harbor
Dark Horse, 1993
1 .... 3.00
2-4 .... 1.00

Comics Magazine
Comics Magazine, 1936
1 .... 8,200.00
2 .... 2,650.00
3 .... 1,500.00
4 .... 1,200.00
5 .... 1,100.00

Comics 101 Presents
Cheap Thrills, 1994
1 .... 2.00

Comics on Parade
United Features, 1938

Comics on Parade was one of the very first comic books to reach the newsstands, making its debut in 1938. Published by United Features Syndicate, Comics on Parade focused on a different comic strip character each issue, reprinting 64 pages worth of color Sundays and dailies.

Among the features were Tarzan by Hal Foster and Burne Hogarth; The Captain and the Kids; Little Mary Mixup; Dynamite Dunn; Tailspin Tommy; Nancy and Fritzi Ritz; and Li'l Abner. All came from the United Features stable, and several made the successful transition to titles of their own.

-- Rob Salkowitz

1	2,800.00
2	1,050.00
3	775.00
4-5	600.00
6-8	420.00
9-10	325.00
11-15	285.00
16-20	260.00
21-25	230.00
26-30	210.00
31-35	135.00
36-40	100.00
41-50	75.00
51-60	60.00
61-80	50.00
81-Special 1	36.00

Comics Reading Libraries
King, 1973

1	10.00
2-5	8.00
6	12.00
7	8.00
8	12.00
9-16	8.00

ComicsTrips (Peter Kuper's...)
Tundra

1	7.00

Coming of Aphrodite
Hero

1	4.00

Comix Book
Marvel, 1974

1	10.00
2-3	8.00
4-5	5.00

Comix International
Warren, 1974

1	125.00
☞Scarce	
2	90.00
☞Dracula story	
3-5	75.00
☞Spirit story	

Commander Battle and the Atomic Sub
ACG, 1954

1	225.00
2	125.00
3-4	100.00
5-7	70.00

Command Review
Thoughts & Images, 1986

1-2	4.00
3-4	5.00

Commies From Mars
Last Gasp

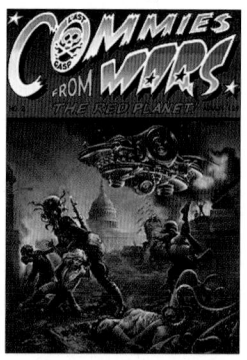

You didn't think they called it "the red planet" because of the color of its soil, did you?

Begun in the late 1970s and published sporadically until the mid-1980s, Commies from Mars is an unusual, funny comic book. It combines a fondness for alien invader science-fiction with good, old-fashioned anti-Communist paranoia and a hippie's love of sex, jokes, and sly humor.

Ted Boxell was the organizing force behind this anthology series, and he invited a collection of underground comix artists to contribute short stories to each issue. Although all submissions were based on the theme of Communist invaders from Mars, each has its own take on the subject. Expect to see everything from depictions of President Reagan as a Martian lizard creature to lowbrow alien sex strips to devilish tales of Martians using our own stupidity to help them destroy our world.

1-5	2.00
6	3.00

Common Foe
Image, 2005

1-4	4.00

Common Grounds
Image, 2004

1-6	3.00

Communion
Fantagraphics, 1991

1	3.00

Complete Cheech Wizard
Rip Off, 1986

1-2	2.00
3-4	3.00

Complete Comics
Timely, 1944

2	1,500.00

Completely Bad Boys
Fantagraphics

1	3.00

Complete Mystery
Marvel, 1948

1	300.00
2	240.00
3-4	200.00

Complete Rog 2000
Pacific, 1982

1	3.00

Complex City
Better, 2000

1-4	3.00

Compost Comics
Gasparotti

1	3.00

Compu-M.E.C.H.
Monolith, 1999

1-2	3.00
3-10	8.00

Comrades of War
Dead Air
1-2..2.00

Conan
Marvel, 1995

Robert E. Howard's Conan the Barbarian, first brought to comics in the early 1970s, has an updated look-and-attitude-in this series.

Slashing and hacking at his targets, whether they're fellow gladiators or giant spiders, is just the natural course of action for this Cimmerian, who has much more cunning and intelligence than the corrupt, corpulent despots who think he serves them. Though he appears to be nothing more than an ignorant barbarian, he has plans and schemes that belie his unrefined appearance. In addition to his strength and skill with a sword, this muscular hero has a sense of humor that serves him as well.

-- George Haberberger

1-12..3.00
32..3.00

Conan
Dark Horse, 2004
0...4.00
1...10.00
1/2nd..3.00
2...5.00
2/2nd-50....................................3.00

Conan Classic
Marvel, 1994
1-11..2.00

Conan and the Daughters of Midora
Dark Horse, 2004
1...5.00

Conan and the Demons of Khitai
Dark Horse, 2005
1-4..3.00

Conan and the Songs of the Dead
Dark Horse, 2006
1-5.. 3.00

Conan: Book of Thoth
Dark Horse, 2006
1-4.. 5.00

Conan and the Jewels of Gwahlur
Dark Horse, 2005
1-3.. 3.00

Conan: Death Covered In Gold
Marvel, 1999
1-3.. 3.00

Conan: Flame and the Fiend
Marvel, 2000
1-3.. 3.00

Conan: Return of Styrm
Marvel, 1998
1-3.. 3.00

Conan: River of Blood
Marvel, 1998
1-3.. 3.00

Conan Saga
Marvel, 1987
1-74...................................... 3.00
75.. 4.00
76-97...................................... 2.00

Conan: Scarlet Sword
Marvel, 1998
1-3.. 3.00

Conan the Adventurer
Marvel, 1994
1-14...................................... 2.00

Conan the Barbarian
Marvel, 1970

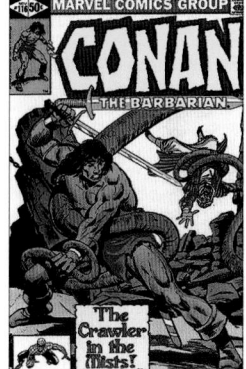

Known variously as "Conan of Cimmeria," "Amra" (the Lion), or

merely "Conan," his sword and skills are the stuff of legends. In his adventures, first written for the pulps by Robert E. Howard, he has fought gods and devils, monsters and men. He has led armies and sailed the seas as a pirate captain with the beautiful Belit at his side. He has fought with, and beside, fellow Howard creations the legendary Kull of Atlantis and the she-devil with a sword Red Sonja. In the end, he became King Conan, as he always knew he would.

With his popularity revived by a series of paperbacks collecting the pulp adventures, Conan the Barbarian is one of the best-known sword-and-sorcery characters of all time. The popularity of the Marvel comics series led to other media outlets, including a pair of motion pictures starring Arnold Schwarzenegger.

1	160.00
☛1st comics Conan	
2	55.00
3	72.00
4	26.00
5	30.00
6-7	26.00
8	30.00
9	20.00
☛Giant-size	
10-11	35.00
☛Giant-size	
12	15.00
13-14	20.00
15	17.00
16	20.00
17	17.00
18	20.00
19	17.00
20	27.00
☛1st Red Sonja	
21-24	20.00
25	10.00
26-30	8.00
31-35	7.00
36-38	9.00
39-47	7.00
48-50	6.00
51-61	5.00
61/30¢	20.00
62	5.00
62/30¢	20.00
63	5.00
63/30¢	20.00
64	5.00
64/30¢	20.00
65	5.00
65/30¢	20.00
66-75/Whitman	5.00
75/35¢	15.00
76-76/Whitman	5.00
76/35¢	15.00
77-77/Whitman	5.00
77/35¢	15.00
78-78/Whitman	5.00

78/35¢-79	15.00
79/Whitman	5.00
79/35¢	15.00
80-93/Whitman	5.00
94-99	4.00
100	6.00
101-274	2.00
275	3.00
Ann 1	10.00
Ann 2-3	6.00
Ann 4-12	2.00
Special 1	3.00

Conan the Barbarian
Marvel, 1997

1-3	3.00

Conan the Barbarian Movie Special
Marvel, 1982

1-2	1.00

Conan the Barbarian: The Usurper
Marvel, 1997

1-3	3.00

Conan the Destroyer
Marvel, 1985

1-2	1.00

Conan the King
Marvel, 1984

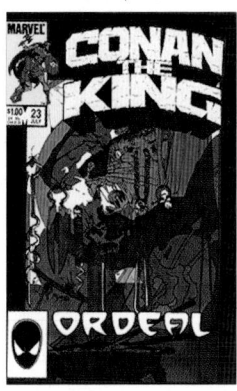

Beginning with issue #20, and continuing until its conclusion with issue #55, King Conan ran under the new title Conan the King. It continued the adventures of the former barbarian, now having risen to become the lord of Aquilonia.

This second phase of the series concentrated more heavily on the conflict between Conan's two sons, Conn and Taurus. Taurus was second-born, less courageous, and athletically inferior to his brother, and was accordingly less favored by his father. This embittered him, and he turned to dark magicks in order to gain a measure of revenge. He

even went so far as to ally himself with a sorcerer who sought to slay his father and older brother. Ultimately, his treachery was revealed and he was defeated, but not before bringing untold woe to his family.

20-55	2.00

Conan: The Lord of the Spiders
Marvel, 1998

1-3	3.00

Conan the Savage
Marvel, 1995

1-12	3.00

Conan vs. Rune
Marvel, 1995

1	3.00

Concrete
Dark Horse, 1985

When Ronald Lithgow's brain was transplanted into its new, rocky body, he was on his way to instant stardom. As Concrete, he has become the talk of the town, and is taking to his newfound fame like a duck to water.

He may look like the Thing, but the lovable Concrete is no brawler. Instead, he tries his hand at more "normal" pursuits, such as rescuing mine workers and trying to swim the Atlantic Ocean. Since Concrete is also a writer, he records these experiences on paper, eventually turning them into books. These pursuits, combined with his penchant for publicity, would seem to almost guarantee the books to be best-sellers.

A well-written and intelligent character, Concrete first appeared in the pages of Dark Horse Presents #1. This first solo book continues that tradition of fine storytelling and exquisitely detailed art.

1	3.00
1/2nd-10	2.00
Hero ed. 1	1.00

Concrete: A New Life
Dark Horse, 1989

1	3.00

Concrete Celebrates Earth Day
Dark Horse, 1990

1	4.00

Concrete Color Special
Dark Horse, 1989

1	3.00

Concrete: Eclectica
Dark Horse, 1993

1-2	3.00

Concrete: Fragile Creature
Dark Horse, 1991

1-4	3.00

Concrete Jungle: The Legend of the Black Lion
Acclaim, 1998

1	3.00

Concrete: Killer Smile
Dark Horse, 1994

1-4	3.00

Concrete: Land & Sea
Dark Horse, 1989

1	3.00

Concrete: Odd Jobs
Dark Horse, 1990

1	4.00

Concrete: Strange Armor
Dark Horse, 1997

1-5	3.00

Concrete: The Human Dilemma
Dark Horse, 2005

1-6	4.00

Concrete: Think Like a Mountain
Dark Horse, 1996

1-6	3.00
Ashcan 1	1.00

Condom-Man
Aaaahh!!

1	4.00

Condorman
Whitman, 1981

1-3	2.00

Coneheads
Marvel, 1994
1-4 .... 2.00

Confessions of a Cereal Eater
NBM, 2000

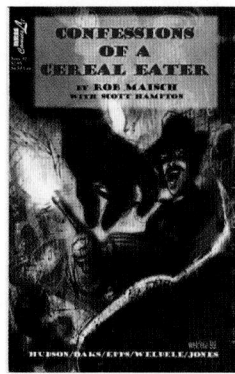

Rob "Rocco" Maisch has lived an average life. But it's rather amazing how vividly he remembers it. This series provides true stories from his life, arranged in random order over roughly 30 years.

As examples of the tales, in "Daniel's Den" Rob and his friends experience all the trials and tribulations of attending a rock show at a club. In "Movin' In" the author tells the story of the rivalry and hi-jinks between two adjacent college dorms. And in "Scott's Jock," he experiences the joys and embarrassment of purchasing his first jock strap with his father.

As the author states in his introduction, "Some are a bit nostalgic while others hold the grim fascination of a really outstanding train wreck. Hopefully, they are all funny to various twisted degrees."

1-4 .... 3.00

Confessions of a Teenage Vampire: The Turning
Scholastic, 1997
1 .... 5.00

Confessions of a Teenage Vampire: Zombie Saturday Night
Scholastic, 1997
1 .... 5.00

Confessions of Romance
Star, 1953
7 .... 60.00
8 .... 45.00
9-11 .... 40.00

Confessions of the Lovelorn
ACG, 1954
52-114 .... 20.00

Confessor (Demonicus Ex Deo)
Dark Matter
1 .... 3.00

Confidential Confessions
Tokyopop, 2003
1-6 .... 10.00

Confrontation
Sacred Origin, 1997
1-4 .... 3.00
Special 1 .... 5.00

Congo Bill
DC, 1954
1 .... 1,100.00
2 .... 650.00
3 .... 500.00
4-6 .... 325.00
7 .... 450.00

Congo Bill
DC, 1999
1-4 .... 3.00

Congorilla
DC, 1992
1-4 .... 2.00

Conjurors
DC, 1999
1-3 .... 3.00

Connor Hawke: Dragon's Blood
DC, 2007
1-2 .... 3.00

Conqueror
Harrier, 1984
1-Special 1 .... 2.00

Conqueror of the Barren Earth
DC, 1983

Thousands of years in the future, Earth's sun has become a red giant, laying waste to the planet it once warmed. Long before, most of mankind had departed for other worlds, leaving the dying world to be fought over by the savage forces that remained behind.

In conquering the stars, mankind had found new friends and a terrible new enemy, the Qlov. The warring between the Qlov and the Confederation had spanned the galaxy, until finally mankind was back where it had begun- trying to reclaim its homeworld, Earth. Sadly, as the spaceship Renewal approached Earth orbit, it was attacked by Qlov forces. Only one escape craft from each ship survived.

Light-years from her countrymen, the warrior Jinal now leads the five other Confederation survivors in a quest in which she is determined to succeed: to become the conqueror of the barren Earth.

1-4 .... 1.00

Conqueror Universe
Harrier
1 .... 3.00

Conservation Corps
Archie, 1993
1-3 .... 1.00

Conspiracy
Marvel, 1998

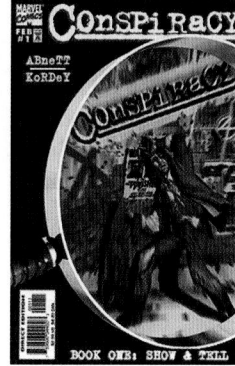

Yet another super-villain crashes through the Daily Bugle offices, leaving behind the usual path of destruction. But as reporter Mark Ewing picked up the pieces of his desk, he noticed an envelope hidden inside part of a destroyed wall. Inside were the notes left behind by Cliff Garner, a crusading reporter who had disappeared years earlier after an altercation with Bugle publisher J. Jonah Jameson. Before Garner stormed out the door, he ranted about a huge story he had been working on involving a vast conspiracy to control superhuman activities throughout the world. But Garner couldn't name his source, and the story was killed. Garner then left the offices and was never seen again.

Now Ewing is picking up the pieces of what could be the biggest conspiracy theory of them all. All he has are fragments and clues-and the sure knowledge that someone is trying to kill him!

1-2...3.00

Conspiracy Comics
Revolutionary, 1991
1-3...3.00

Constantine Movie Adaptation
DC, 2005
0...7.00

Constellation Graphics
Stages
1-2...2.00

Construct
Caliber
1-6...3.00

Contact Comics
Aviation, 1944
1...550.00
2...425.00
3...400.00
4-6...350.00
7-8...300.00
9...275.00
10-11...350.00
12...1,100.00

Containment (Eric Red's)
Idea & Design Works, 2004
1-4...4.00

Contaminated Zone
Brave New Words, 1991
1-3...3.00

Contemporary Bio-Graphics
Revolutionary, 1991
1-8...3.00

Contender Comics Special
Contender
1...1.00

Contest of Champions II
Marvel, 1999

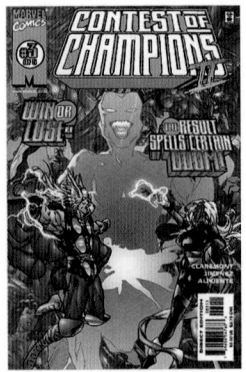

Reprising the classic 1980s three-issue limited series, with a five-issue one, Chris Claremont and Oscar Jiminez introduce the Coterie, a space-faring race of gamemasters that values physical competition, who transport most of the Marvel super-heroes from the Earth to their ship to test their skills against one another. In exchange for providing this entertaining display for the Coterie, the heroes will earn for the Earth the accumulated knowledge the aliens have gathered in their travels. On the surface, it sound like a good deal, but is something more sinister going on behind the scenes? Iron Man certainly believes so, when he finds the entire place crawling with "nanites" and the Coterie's offer too good to be true. Before he gets the opportunity to investigate, he's forced to fight the X-Men's Psylocke and the members of X-Force.

An early dose of 1980s nostalgia here that, while interesting, doesn't quite have the simple charm of the original.

1-5... 3.00

Continuum
Continuity, 1988
1... 3.00

Continuum Presents
Continuum, 1988
1-2... 2.00

Contractors
Eclipse, 1987
1... 2.00

Contract With God, A
DC, 2000
1... 13.00

Convent of Hell
NBM
1... 13.00

Convocations: A Magic: The Gathering Gallery
Acclaim, 1995
1... 3.00

Coochy Cooty Men's Comics
Print Mint
1... 3.00

Coo Coo Comics
Animated, 1942
1... 175.00
2... 80.00
3-5... 45.00
6-10... 38.00
11-20... 32.00
21-30... 28.00
31-33... 24.00
34-40... 35.00
41... 85.00
42... 75.00
43-46... 40.00
47... 75.00
48... 40.00
49... 60.00
50-51... 50.00
52-62... 20.00

Cookie
ACG, 1946
1... 90.00
2... 55.00
3-5... 38.00
6-10... 28.00
11-20... 24.00
21-40... 20.00
41-55... 18.00

Cool World
DC, 1992
1-4... 2.00

Cool World Movie Adaptation
DC

The 1992 film by Ralph Bakshi (1938-) focused on a comic-book artist whose cartoons, rather than being simply his own imagined world, actually exist. His sexy "Holli" crosses over to the artist's world, and the film evoked comparisons to 1988's Who Framed Roger Rabbit.

-- Maggie

1 ....4.00

Cop Called Tracy, A
Avalon
1-22..3.00

COPS
DC, 1988

In the future, criminals have turned to high technology to commit their dastardly deeds. The evil Dr. Kranial, for instance, supposedly makes construction robots. In reality, he designs automatons which can pull off bank jobs and destroy buildings. This made him a shoo-in when he tried out for The Big Boss's criminal gang, which includes similar high-tech heavies.

To combat the rising crime wave, the police have turned to the Central Organization of Police Specialists. This group of highly talented hotshots resembles nothing so much as a police version of the G.I. Joes. The members each have special talents and equipment along with a colorful codenames like Bulletproof, Barricade, Sundown, Highway, Blitz, and Bullseye. This dedicated crew is more than a match for any bad guy.

Cops is adapted from a TV show and line of Hasbro toys.

1-15...1.00

Cops: The Job
Marvel, 1992
1-4..1.00

Copybook Tales
Slave Labor, 1996
1-6... 3.00

Corban the Barbearian
Me Comix
1-2... 2.00

Corben Special, A
Pacific, 1984
1 .... 2.00

Corbo
Sword in Stone
1 .... 2.00

Cormac Mac Art
Dark Horse, 1989
1-4.. 2.00

Corny's Fetish
Dark Horse, 1998
1 .... 5.00

Corporate Crime Comics
Kitchen Sink, 1977
1-2... 3.00

Corporate Ninja
Slave Labor, 2005
1 .... 3.00

Cortez and the Fall of the Aztecs
Tome
1-2... 3.00

Corto Maltese: Ballad of the Salt Sea
NBM
1-4.. 3.00

Corum: The Bull and the Spear
First
1-4.. 2.00

Corvus Rex: A Legacy of Shadows
Crow, 1996
1 .... 2.00

Cosmic Book
Ace
1 .... 2.00

Cosmic Boy
DC, 1986

Rokk Krinn is a member of the Legionnaires, a team of super-heroes in the far-distant future. As the story begins, he is stalked, not by some cosmic super-villain, but by a mere mortal named Lydda Jath. Lydda has developed a crush on Rokk and has persuaded her bio-engineer father to scrape up limited super-powers for her so she can join the Legionnaires. After a few months, in a new identity as Night Girl, she can't compete and the Legionnaires reject her -- but she has what she wanted: Rokk, aka Cosmic Boy.

When the Time Institute borrows a time bubble, Cosmic Boy and Night Girl decide to vacation in the 20th century together. Unfortunately, something goes terribly wrong during the trip, and they end up on an Earth where super-heroes like themselves are almost universally despised.

1-4 .... 1.00

Cosmic Guard
Devil's Due, 2004
1 .... 5.00
2 .... 4.00
3-6 .... 3.00

Cosmic Heroes
Eternity
1-8 .... 2.00
9 .... 3.00
10-11 .... 4.00

Cosmic Kliti
Fantagraphics, 1991
1 .... 2.00

Cosmic Odyssey
DC, 1988

For lack of a better name, it's called "Anti-Life": the very force of death and destruction. In normal times, this force exists within its own realm, but to the universe's horror, it has somehow managed to break into our world. Inhabiting the bodies of dead creatures, it has divided into parts and spread across the galaxy. Its mission: to destroy all life.

The Demon, Batman, The Martian Manhunter, Superman, Green Lantern, and the New Gods find themselves united, even with the malevolent Darkseid, in order to stop the Anti-Life. If they fail, it will trigger doomsday weapons that it has scattered across different worlds.

When it comes to star-spanning fiction, few writers can compare to Jim Starlin. Creator of outstanding titles such as Dreadstar and Warlock, he returns again to script this cosmic saga.

1	4.00
2-4	4.00

Cosmic Powers
Marvel, 1994

1-6	3.00

Cosmic Powers Unlimited
Marvel, 1995

1-5	4.00

Cosmic Ray
Image, 1999

1/A-3	3.00

Cosmic Steller Rebellers
Hammac

1-2	2.00

Cosmic Waves
AmF, 1994

1-3	3.00

Cosmo Cat
Fox, 1946

1	110.00
2-5	85.00

Cosmos
Micmac

1	2.00

Cosmo the Merry Martian
Archie, 1958

1	75.00
2-6	50.00

Cougar
Atlas-Seaboard, 1975

1	5.00
2	3.00

Countdown
DC, 2000

The "countdown" of the title is a serious one: it's until the total destruction of the Earth. Alien creatures are determined to obliterate it, and they're not even necessarily evil themselves-but the criminals they are pursuing are so unspeakably horrible that they can justify their actions. That explanation doesn't sit well with a team of powerful heroes who mean to put an end to the aliens' scheme. They'd better hurry, though: the Earth is being cooked, humans are being herded into mountainous hideaways, and now the heroes themselves are beginning to feel and behave strangely...

It's apocalypse on a global scale, with only a somewhat flawed-seeming team of heroes standing in its way. By Jeff Mariotte and Aaron Lopresti, published by Wildstorm.

1-8	3.00

Count Duckula
Marvel, 1989

1-15	1.00

Counter Ops
Antarctic, 2003

1-4	4.00

Counterparts
Tundra, 1993

1-3	3.00

Coup D'Etat: Afterword
DC, 2004

1	3.00

Coup D'Etat: The Authority
DC, 2004

1	4.00

Coup D'Etat: Sleeper
DC, 2004

1	6.00
1/Variant	10.00

Coup D'Etat: Stormwatch
DC, 2004

1	5.00
1/Variant	7.00

Coup D'Etat: Wildcats Version 3.0
DC, 2004

1	5.00
1/Variant	6.00

Couple of Winos, A
Fantagraphics, 1991

1	2.00

Courage Comics
J. Edward, 1945

1-3	75.00

Courageous Man Adventures
Moordam, 1998

1-3	3.00

Courageous Princess
Antarctic, 2000

1	12.00

Courtney Crumrin & The Night Things
Oni, 2002

1-4	3.00

Courtney Crumrin Tales
Oni, 2005

1	6.00

Courtship of Eddie's Father
Dell, 1970
1 ....30.00
2 ....24.00

Courtyard
Avatar, 2003
1-2/A 4.00

Coutoo
Dark Horse
1 ....4.00

Coven
Awesome, 1997
1/A..5.00
1/B..3.00
1/C 4.00
1/D-6 ....3.00

Coven
Awesome, 1999
1-4...3.00

Coven Black and White
Awesome, 1998
1 ....3.00

Coven: Dark Origins
Awesome, 1999
1 ....3.00

Coven, The: Fantom
Awesome, 1998
1-1/Gold 3.00

Coven 13
No Mercy, 1997
1 ....3.00

Coven, The: Tooth and Nail
Avatar, 2002
1 ....3.00
1/Ltd. 30.00

Coventry
Fantagraphics, 1996
1-3...4.00

Covert Vampiric Operations
Idea & Design Works, 2003
1 ....6.00

Covert Vampiric Operations: Artifact
Idea & Design Works, 2003
1-3...4.00

Cow
MonsterPants
1-3...2.00

Cow-Boy
Ogre, 1997

Clan Apis' creator Jay Hosler did a comic strip which appeared for some time in Comics Buyer's Guide. It featured the comedy adventures of a costumed hero who wore the mask of a cow's head and used spray from udders dangling from the costume's front. Only one issue starring Cow-Boy as its title character appeared and focused on the character's origin, but keep in mind that the writer-artist did win a Xeric Grant (for Clan Apis). Hosler's cruder style in Cow-Boy is appropriate to the parodies he writes.

-- Maggie

1 .... 4.00

Cowboy Action
Atlas, 1955
5 .... 120.00
6-11 .... 100.00

Cowboy in Africa
Gold Key, 1968
1 .... 40.00

Cowboy Love
Fawcett, 1949
1 .... 100.00
2 .... 75.00
3-11 .... 60.00

Cowboy Love
Avalon
1 .... 3.00

Cowboy Romances
Atlas, 1949
1-2 .... 140.00
3 .... 100.00

Cowboy Western
Charlton, 1948
17 .... 125.00
18-21 .... 100.00

22-25 .... 90.00
26-30 .... 85.00
31-35 .... 80.00
36-39 .... 68.00
46-49 .... 55.00
50-57 .... 42.00
58 .... 68.00
59-60 .... 42.00
61-66 .... 36.00
67 .... 68.00

Cowgirl Romances
Fiction House, 1950
1 .... 225.00
2 .... 150.00
3 .... 125.00
4-6 .... 100.00
7-9 .... 75.00
10-12 .... 50.00

Cowgirl Romances
Marvel, 1950
28 .... 250.00

Cow Puncher
Avon, 1947
1 .... 185.00
2 .... 140.00
2/2nd 50.00
3 .... 90.00
4-5 .... 80.00
6 .... 110.00
7 .... 70.00

Cow Special
Image, 2001
1 .... 3.00

Coyote
Marvel, 1983
1 .... 3.00
2-10 .... 2.00
11 .... 3.00
12-16 .... 2.00

Crabbs
Cat-Head
1 .... 4.00

Crackajack Funnies
Dell, 1938
1 .... 1,800.00
2 .... 900.00
3 .... 650.00
4-5 .... 500.00
6-9 .... 450.00
10-19 .... 350.00
20-25 .... 250.00
26-29 .... 200.00
30-39 .... 175.00
40-43 .... 150.00

CrackBrained Comix
Crackbrained

This black-and-white mini-comic pokes a lot of fun at consumerism, particularly the products that we buy to enhance our lives. The humor is baudy and the artwork is sketchy, but the analysis is dead-on-something of a hallmark of underground comix.

1-3..2.00

Crack Busters
Showcase, 1986

1-2...2.00

Crack Comics
Quality, 1940

1	3,850.00
2	1,785.00
3	1,200.00
4	1,000.00
5-10	850.00
11-20	650.00
21-24	475.00
25-26	425.00
27	600.00
28-30	350.00
31-40	200.00
41-51	165.00
52-62	145.00

Cracked
Globe, 1958

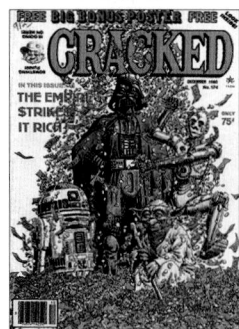

Not long after Mad paved the way for an irreverent humor magazine, a host of imitators appeared. Although comics like Eh!, Nuts, and Whack are long gone, Cracked held on for more than 40 years.

Perhaps the main reason for its success was that Cracked captures the true essence of Mad more effectively than its ham-handed competition. Cracked doesn't talk down to its readers, and its parodies -- although often outrageous -- speak of a sharp wit, with a decidedly naughty bent. Although it never became the cultural icon that Mad is, Cracked remains a schoolyard favorite and a source of amusement for kids of all ages.

1	125.00
2	60.00
3-5	35.00
6-10	20.00
11-20	12.00
21-30	10.00
31-50	8.00
51-100	5.00
101-145	4.00
146	8.00
147-149	5.00
150	4.00
151-156	3.00
157	6.00
158-163	3.00
164	4.00
165-168	3.00
169	4.00
170-181	3.00
182	4.00
183-250	3.00
251-350	2.00
351-354	3.00
Ann 1	7.00
Ann 2-3	5.00
Ann 4-19	4.00

Cracked Collectors' Edition
Globe, 1973

4	10.00
5	8.00
6-10	6.00
11-nn (30)	5.00
nn (31)-nn (50)	4.00
nn (51)-125	3.00

Cracked Guide to the Movies
NBM

1...9.00

Crack Western Comics
Quality, 1949

63	120.00
64-65	85.00
66	75.00
67	85.00
68-70	75.00
71	85.00

72	75.00
73	45.00
74-76	60.00
77	45.00
78-79	60.00
80	45.00
81	60.00
82	45.00
83	60.00
84	65.00

Crap
Fantagraphics, 1993

1-7...3.00

Crash Comics
Tem, 1940

1	2,100.00
2	1,000.00
3	800.00
4	1,650.00
5	750.00

Crash Dummies
Harvey, 1994

1-3...2.00

Crash Metro & the Star Squad
Oni, 1999

1...3.00

Crash Ryan
Marvel, 1984

Christopher C. "Crash" Ryan was once a respected airline pilot, until the day his engine caught fire and he had to land in a windswept field. Despite his courageous struggle to control his failing plane, it struck hard and burned, killing many of the passengers. Crash's license was revoked, and the only job he could get was ferrying air mail in the jungles of Central America.

Then one day, making a routine run, Crash sees two strange planes chasing a third. All three look like something out of a science-fiction novel, with propulsion systems unlike anything he's ever seen. The attacking planes force their quarry down, before turning on Crash, who manages to outmaneuver them, even in his old biplane. Investigating the downed plane, Crash encounters an old friend and is drawn into a jet-age struggle...

1-4...2.00

Crash Test Dummies
Harvey
1-3...2.00

Cray Baby
Adventures Special
Electric Milk
1...3.00

Cray-Baby
Adventures, The:
Wrath of the Pediddlers
Destination Entertainment, 1998
1-3...3.00

Crazy
Atlas, 1953
1...225.00
2...165.00
3...125.00
4-7...95.00

Crazy
Marvel, 1973
1...16.00
2-3...10.00

Crazy (Magazine)
Marvel, 1973
1...16.00
2-3...10.00
4-5...5.00
6-15...3.00
16-94.......................................2.00

Crazy Bob
Blackbird
1...3.00
2...2.00

Crazyfish Preview
Crazyfish
1-2...1.00

Crazy Love Story
Tokyopop, 2004
1-5...10.00

Crazyman
Continuity, 1992
1...4.00
2-3...3.00

Crazyman
Continuity, 1993
1...4.00
2-4...3.00

Crazy, Man, Crazy
Charlton, 1956
1...60.00
2...45.00

Creature
Antarctic, 1997
1-2...3.00

Creature Commandos
DC, 2000
1-8...3.00

Creature Features
Mojo
1...5.00

Creature Features
(Art Adams'...)
Dark Horse, 1996
1...14.00

Creatures of the Id
Caliber, 1990
1...11.00

Creatures on the Loose
Marvel, 1971

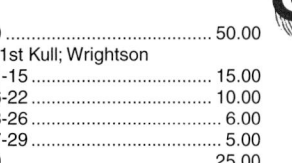

Beginning with issue #10, the series, "Tower of Shadows" became "Creatures on the Loose," trading in its stock of science-fiction/horror stories for sword and sorcery. Its first issue brought us a new character, King Kull featuring the art of Bernie Wrightson. Kull, a barbarian warrior from the lost continent of Atlantis, was very popular and later appeared in a number of series bearing his name.

Back at Creatures on the Loose, the sword and sorcery storylines continued. Issue #16 introduced us to Gulliver Jones, Warrior of Mars. In an action-filled storyline based very loosely on Edward L. Arnold's Lieut. Gulliver Jones: His Vacation (1905) and reminiscent of Edgar Rice Burroughs, Gullivar fought a host of otherworldly menaces, saving

alien women from the jaws of certain death.

Later experiments at COTL included Thongor, and lastly, Manwolf. Unfortunately, neither of these caught on, and Creatures on the Loose ceased with issue #37.

10...50.00
☛1st Kull; Wrightson
11-15.......................................15.00
16-22.......................................10.00
23-26...6.00
27-29...5.00
30...25.00
☛Man-Wolf
31...12.00
32-36...8.00
37...12.00
King Size 1...............................10.00

Creech
Image, 1997
1-1/A...2.00
2-3...3.00

Creech, The:
Out for Blood
Image, 2001
1-2...5.00

CreeD
Hall of Heroes, 1994
1...4.00
2...3.00

CreeD
Lightning, 1995
1-2...3.00
2/Platinum.................................4.00
3-3/Platinum..............................3.00

CreeD: Apple Tree
Gearbox, 2000
1...3.00

CreeD: Cranial Disorder
Lightning, 1996
1-3...3.00

CreeD:
Mechanical Evolution
Gearbox, 2000
1-2...3.00

CreeD/Teenage Mutant
Ninja Turtles
Lightning, 1996
1...3.00

CreeD:
The Good Ship and the
New Journey Home
Lightning, 1997
1...3.00

CreeD Use Your Delusion
Avatar, 1998
1-2...3.00

CreeD: Utopiate
Image, 2002

1-4..3.00

Creeper
DC, 1997

1-11..3.00
1000000......................................2.00

Creeper (2nd series)
DC, 2006

1-5..3.00

Creeps
Image, 2001

Here's one of those titles that you have to look harder at--no matter how frightening the images are--because there is something important being said. It is a simple message--you'll find it spoken in a dialogue balloon in the very first issue. But how many readers will catch it...?

Not many perhaps. Just as most of us tend to skip by those people who are always there--that homeless man in the alley, that bag lady who always speaks to herself...

Well, as the blurb printed on the back cover suggests, it is time to stop...look...and acknowledge. The Creeps are real. The Creeps are not going away. The Creeps are tired of all the crap. And the Creeps are going to do something about it!

This is a story about the users and the used. The Creeps actually represent a much larger demographic. But how many readers will catch it...?

1-4..3.00

Creepsville
Go-Go

1-5..3.00

Creepy
Warren, 1964

1...160.00
2...50.00

3	25.00
4	35.00
5	18.00
6	15.00
7-8	24.00
9	45.00
10	20.00
11-13	15.00
14	22.00
15	25.00
16-17	30.00
18	25.00
19-20	15.00
21-22	12.00
23-25	11.00
26-31	10.00
32	35.00
33-35	10.00
36	15.00
37-38	10.00
39-40	7.00
41	10.00
42-47	6.00
48	9.00
49	6.00
50	12.00
51-54	6.00
55	9.00
56-64	5.00
65	8.00
66-73	5.00
74	10.00
75-76	5.00
77	10.00
78-82	5.00
83	6.00
84	5.00
85-87	6.00
88-90	5.00
91	6.00
92-94	5.00
95	6.00
96-100	5.00
101-102	4.00
103	6.00
104-112	4.00
113	7.00
114-140	4.00
141	5.00
142	6.00
143-144	5.00
145	6.00
146	22.00
Ann 1971-1972	15.00
YB 1968-1970	18.00

Creepy Tales
Pinnacle, 1975

1..2.00

Creepy: The Limited Series
Dark Horse, 1992

1-4..4.00
FB 1993......................................12.00

Creepy Things
Charlton, 1975

1..5.00
2-6..3.00

Cremator
Chaos, 1998

1-5..3.00

Crescent
B-Line, 1996

0..1.00

Crescent Moon
Tokyopop, 2004

1-6..10.00

Crew
Marvel, 2003

1-7..3.00

Crime & Justice
Charlton, 1951

1...240.00
2...125.00
3-5...100.00
6-10...80.00
11-19...65.00
20-23...50.00

Crime & Justice
Avalon, 1998

1..3.00

Crime and Punishment
Lev Gleason, 1948

The crime comics of the late 1940s were the stage for intense, complex, and disturbing stories told in comic-book form. Possibly the greatest of all the crime comics publishers was Lev Gleason, who pioneered the genre with the ground-breaking Crime Does Not Pay and other titles, including Crime and Punishment.

Like their counterparts in film noir movies of the period, comic-book criminals rarely, if ever, escape ultimate punishment for their misdeeds. Nevertheless, the emphasis on their activities and personalities make the criminals into the focal point of many stories. Editor-artist Charles Biro had a real feel for the moral geography of the criminal classes, and his stories in

Gleason's magazines had an authenticity and sociological rigor that others often lacked. The Comics Code obliterated much of the ambiguity (and drama) of crime comics and doomed the genre in the mid-1950s.

-- Rob Salkowitz

1	185.00
2	100.00
3-5	60.00
6-10	55.00
11-20	42.00
21-30	38.00
31-38	32.00
39	55.00
40-58	30.00
59	85.00
60-65	28.00
66	175.00
67-68	135.00
69	55.00
70-74	28.00

Crime and Punishment Marshal Law Takes Manhattan
Marvel, 1989
1	5.00

Crimebuster
AC
0	3.00

Crimebuster
Avalon
1	3.00

Crimebuster Classics
AC
1	4.00

Crime Can't Win
Marvel, 1950
1	115.00
2	85.00
3	75.00
4-10	55.00
11-12	48.00

Crime Classics
Eternity, 1988
1-13	2.00

Crime Clinic
Ziff-Davis, 1951
1	225.00
2	165.00
3-5	150.00

Crime Clinic
Slave Labor, 1995
1-2	3.00

Crime Detective Comics (Vol. 1)
Hillman, 1948
1	155.00
2	75.00

3-4	55.00
5	60.00
6-8	55.00
9	125.00
10-12	48.00

Crime Detective Comics (Vol. 2)
Hillman, 1950
1	50.00
2-3	36.00
4	40.00
5-6	30.00
7	45.00
8-12	30.00

Crime Detective Comics (Vol. 3)
Hillman, 1952
1-8	30.00

Crime Detector
Timor, 1954
1	150.00
2	75.00
3	50.00
4	30.00
5	150.00

Crime Does Not Pay
Lev Gleason, 1942

This is the comic book that got the entire crime comics genre rolling -- and may have unwittingly contributed to the formation of the Comics Code years later. It began when Bob Wood and Charles Biro were swapping yarns in a bar and decided that gangsters and criminals would provide a neverending flow of new stories for a comic book. Grabbing the name from a popular series of MGM live-action shorts of the 1930s, the pair conspired to rename Silver Streak to Crime Does Not Pay, one of the earliest, and most lurid, crime comics of all time.

The allure of the series was in its graphic and violent stories, drawing material from sources as far back as the middle ages, but concentrating mostly on gangsters of the 1930s.

Biro's ghostly "Mr. Crime" narrated many early episodes. This character was a duplicitous advisor to criminals, egging on the thugs -- until their inevitable comeuppance in the final page.

22	800.00
23	525.00
24	375.00
25-30	225.00
31-41	115.00
42	110.00
43-50	90.00
51-60	65.00
61-70	60.00
71-80	50.00
81-90	42.00
91-100	35.00
101-110	32.00
111-130	30.00
131-146	26.00
Ann 1944	700.00
Ann 1945	600.00
Ann 1946-1949	500.00
Ann 1950-1953	400.00

Crime Exposed
Marvel, 1950
1	165.00
2	100.00
3	80.00
4-9	70.00
10-14	60.00

Crimefighters
Marvel, 1948
1	120.00
2-10	80.00

Crime Files
Standard, 1952
5	175.00
6	100.00

Crime Must Lose
Timely, 1950
4	185.00
5-6	150.00
7-10	120.00
11-12	100.00

Crime Must Pay the Penalty
Current, 1948
1	165.00
2	100.00
3-4	85.00
5-7	55.00
8	70.00
9-10	55.00
11-20	45.00
21-30	40.00
31-40	32.00
41	55.00
42-46	32.00

Crime Mysteries
Ribage, 1952

1	450.00
2-3	300.00
4	400.00
5-10	200.00
11-15	175.00

Crime on the Waterfront
Realistic Comics, 1952

4	210.00

Crime Patrol
E.C., 1948

7	600.00
8-9	575.00
10	550.00
11-14	500.00
15	2,200.00

☛1st Cryptkeeper

16	1,500.00

Crime Patrol
Gemstone, 2000

1-5	3.00
Ann 1	14.00

Crime Pays
Boneyard, 1996

1-2	3.00

Crime Reporter
St. John, 1948

1	225.00
2	345.00
3-4	165.00

Crimes by Women
Fox, 1948

Violence, vice, and really tight dresses -- it didn't take the geniuses at Fox Features Syndicate long to discover the winning formula for Crimes by Women, a notable contribution to both the crime comics and cheesecake genres popular in the late 1940s and 1950s. Purporting to detail "true crime cases," Crimes by Women spotlighted the careers of notorious femmes fatales like Bonnie Parker (of "and Clyde" fame) plus assorted gun molls, fast women, black widow killers, and good girls gone wrong. Crimes by Women adopted the characteristic crime comics' tone that all these crimes were "so very, very wrong," while the art lavished detail on every feminine curve and blood-spattered massacre. Unfortunately, the same qualities that made Crimes by Women a hit also ran it afoul of the Comics Code, and the title was among those swept from the stands in 1954.

-- *Rob Salkowitz*

1	1,100.00
2	550.00
3	450.00
4-5	375.00
6-10	325.00
11-15	265.00
54	165.00

Crime Smasher
Fawcett, 1949

1	275.00

Crime-Smasher
Blue Comet, 1987

Special 1	2.00

Crime Smashers
Ribage, 1950

1	275.00
2	145.00
3-4	125.00
5	165.00
6-10	90.00
11-12	85.00
13	110.00
14-15	85.00

Crime SuspenStories
E.C., 1950

1	800.00
1/A	1,000.00

☛#1 marked out

2	475.00
3-5	315.00
6-10	235.00
11-12	185.00
13	210.00
14-15	185.00
16	190.00
17	235.00

☛Frazetta art

18-19	170.00
20	215.00
21	115.00
22-23	145.00
24-27	115.00

Crime SuspenStories
Gemstone, 1992

1-15	2.00
16-27	3.00
Ann 1	9.00
Ann 2-3	10.00
Ann 4-6	11.00

Criminal
Marvel, 2006

1-3	3.00

Criminal Macabre
Dark Horse, 2003

1-5	3.00

Criminal Macabre: Feat of Clay
Dark Horse, 2006

1	3.00

Criminal Macabre: Two Red Eyes
Dark Horse, 2007

1	3.00

Criminals on the Run
Premium, 1948

1	285.00
2	220.00
3-4	200.00
5-7	165.00
8	175.00
9-10	165.00

Crimson
Image, 1998

Crimson is a vampire tale that rises against the odds to give a very cool, contemporary spin on the old vampire legends.

The story features young Alex Elder, a teenager who had been going through a dark period leading up to the fateful night when he and three friends were ambushed in Central Park by a group of vampires. Alex was saved from complete dismemberment by the intervention of Ekimus, a creature almost as old as the world itself. Although Ekimus had saved Alex from extinction, he could not prevent Alex from being turned into a vampire. Raging with denial at his new state, Alex ran off into the night, where he discovered that the world had a whole new dark side that he had never dreamed of before.

1-1/A	4.00
1/B-1/C	6.00
2	3.00
2/A-2/B	6.00
3	3.00
3/A	4.00
4-7	3.00
7/A	15.00
7/B-24	3.00

Crimson Avenger
DC, 1988

1-4	2.00

Crimson Dreams
Crimson, 1985

1-11	2.00

Crimson Dynamo
Marvel, 2003

1-6	3.00

Crimson Letters
Adventure, 1990

1	2.00

Crimson Nun
Antarctic, 1997

1-4	3.00

Crimson Plague
Event, 1997

1	3.00
1/Ltd.	5.00

Crimson Plague
(George Pèrez's...)
Image, 2000

1-2	3.00

Crimson: Scarlet X
Blood on the Moon
DC, 1999

1	4.00

Crimson Sourcebook
WildStorm, 1999

1	3.00

Crisis Aftermath:
The Spectre
DC, 2006

1-3	3.00

Crisis on
Infinite Earths
DC, 1985

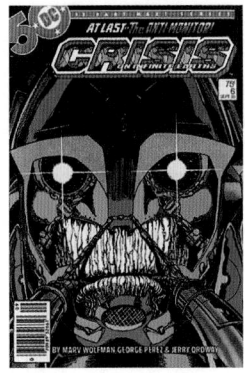

BY MARV WOLFMAN, GEORGE PEREZ & JERRY ORDWAY

This 12-issue maxi-series brought together almost every DC character ever created and destroyed most of the alternate Earths. A must-have for serious fans, this title attempted to clear up inconsistencies in DC continuity and provided an epic, bitter-sweet story to boot. Among the heroes who came to their final end were Supergirl, Dove, the Barry Allen Flash, the Crime Syndicate of Earth-3, and Immortal Man. The heroes and villains left after the Crisis settled in one merged Earth, allowing for more interaction between DC heroes in the future.

Unfortunately, the destruction of the alternate Earths created several new problems for DC, since the old stories that took place on them had to be explained or "retconned" ("retroactive continuity") away. To this day, fans have trouble making sense of the post-Crisis timelines of star-spanning DC groups like The Legion of Super-Heroes. This eventually necessitated DC's Zero Hour series, meant to clean up their continuity for good.

1	5.00
2-3	4.00
4	3.00
5	5.00
6	3.00
7-8	5.00
9-12	3.00

Crisp
Crisp Biscuit, 1997

1-2	3.00

Crisp Biscuit
Crisp Biscuit, 1991

1	2.00

Criss Cross
(Doug Mier's ...)
Arcana, 2005

1	4.00

Cristian Dark
Darque, 1993

1-3	3.00

Critical Error
Dark Horse, 1992

1	3.00

Critical Mass
Marvel, 1989

1-7	5.00

Critters
Fantagraphics, 1986

The popularity of the funny-animal adventure comic book Albedo from Thoughts and Images suggested to many that the "anthropomorhic" genre didn't have to be solely about humor. Many creators in the mid-1980s placed funny-animal characters in a variety of situations, and Fantagraphics provided one of the major showcases with Critters.

The anthology contains stories by such noted writer-artists as Joshua Quagmire, Stan Sakai, and Arn Saba, among many more. Cutey Bunny, Usagi Yojimbo, and Neil the Horse completists will need to add the series to their wantlists.

-- Maggie

1	10.00
2	3.00
3	8.00
4-5	3.00
6-7	5.00
8-9	3.00
10	4.00
11-22	3.00
23	4.00
24-40	3.00
41-49	2.00
50	5.00
Special 1	2.00

Critturs
Mu, 1992

0 ....3.00

Cromartie High School
ADV Manga, 2005

1 ....10.00
2-4 ....11.00

Cromwell Stone
Dark Horse

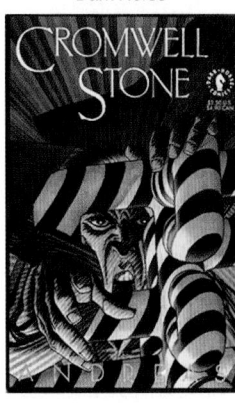

Creator, writer, and artist, Andreas spins an eerie tale about thirteen survivors of a doomed sea voyage. Every year, the survivors meet to celebrate. However, every year another member of the party dies. This goes on for 10 years until only four remain. Cromwell Stone is one of the four. It seems that one of the members possesses a rare "key" to another dimension. The owner of the key wants it back, at all costs. Cromwell escapes every attempt on his life and somehow makes it to the home of Houston Crown, the keeper of the key. When the two meet, it becomes a battle to the death with the dimensional key as the prize.

This one-shot special was published in 1992.

1 ....4.00

Cross
Dark Horse, 1995

0-1 ....3.00
2 ....10.00
3 ....3.00
4-5 ....10.00
6 ....3.00

Cross
Tokyopop, 2004

1-5 ....10.00

Cross and the Switchblade
Spire, 1972

1 .... 3.00
1/2nd 2.00
1/Barbour 1.00

Cross Bronx
Image, 2006

1-4 .... 3.00

Crossed Swords
K-Z, 1986

1 .... 1.00

Crossfire
Eclipse, 1984

by Mark Evanier and Dan Spiegle

Jeff Baker, the first Crossfire could go anywhere and find out anything in his fantastic flying costume-and would do so for anyone, if the price was right. Unfortunately, he found out too much about the wrong people and ended up dead.

His bail bondsman, Jay Endicott, has seen the legal system from the inside out and despite seeing criminals with an expensive lawyer go free while the innocent with public defenders get incarcerated, he has not lost his idealism. When he finds the Crossfire costume, he puts it on in order to uncover information about crime. An associate of the DNAgents, this Crossfire works for justice, not money; nonetheless, the stakes are just as high. Written by Mark Evanier (a television and screen writer), this series is set within the movie industry and has more action and intrigue than a made-for-TV mystery-of-the-week.

1 .... 5.00
2-26 .... 2.00

Crossfire and Rainbow
Eclipse, 1986

1-4 .... 1.00

CrossGen Chronicles
CrossGen, 2000

The series provides freestanding stories of the CrossGeneration universe, usually set before the action of the ongoing titles. The first issue gives brief glimpses into each series at that point (Jun 00) and background on the publishing company itself. After that, however, issues are more focused. For example, #2 is set in the past of Scion; #3 shows how relationships developed leading up to the ongoing series of Meridian; #4 features the first meeting of Samandahl Rey and Tchlusarud of Sigil; #5 takes place on Mystic's Ciress; and #6 is a story from the past of Elysia of The First.

-- Maggie

1-7 .... 4.00

Crossgenesis
CrossGen, 2000

1 .... 5.00

CrossGen Sampler
CrossGen, 2000

1 .... 1.00

Crossing Midnight
DC, 2007

1-2 .... 3.00

Crossovers
CrossGen, 2003

1-9 .... 3.00

Crossroads
First, 1988

1-5 .... 4.00

Crow
Caliber, 1989

1	22.00
☞Crow origin	
1/2nd	4.00
1/3rd	3.00
2	12.00
2/2nd	4.00
2/3rd	3.00
3	10.00
3/2nd	4.00
4	10.00

Crow
Tundra, 1992

1-4	5.00

Crow
Image, 1999

1-10	3.00

Crow, The: City of Angels
Kitchen Sink, 1996

1-3	3.00

Crow, The: Dead Time
Kitchen Sink, 1996

1-3	3.00

Crow, The: Flesh & Blood
Kitchen Sink, 1996

1-3	3.00

Crown Comics
Golfing, 1944

1	450.00
2	300.00
3-5	265.00
6	200.00
7-8	175.00
9-10	150.00
11-14	125.00
15-19	100.00

Crow of the Bearclan
Blackthorne, 1986

1-6	2.00

Crow, The: Waking Nightmares
Kitchen Sink, 1997

1-4	3.00

Crow, The: Wild Justice
Kitchen Sink, 1996

1-3	3.00

Crozonia
Image

1	3.00

Crucial Fiction
Fantagraphics, 1992

1	3.00
2-3	2.00

Crucible
DC, 1993

1	2.00
2-6	1.00

Cruel and Unusual
DC, 1999

Bobbie Flint has been given the dirtiest job in the world. After a scandal, she was forced to leave her job at the Salvation Channel. Marion Meach, her obese and filthy-minded boss, has blackmailed her into becoming the warden of his god-forsaken prison in the Everglades.

The for-profit prison is automated and has almost no staff, but thanks to government regulation and fines, it's sinking into the red. The "ratburner" electric chair sets two out of three death-row inmates on fire, and the main prison industry consists of raising and skinning alligators, but Bobbie somehow has to make the place turn a profit.

Bobbie may not know anything about prisons, but she knows all about the power of television. Now if she can only survive, she's going to turn things around, and at the same time pay back Marion Meach in spades.

1-4	3.00

Cruel & Unusual Punishment
Starhead, 1993

1-2	3.00

Cruel World
Fantagraphics

1	4.00

Crusader from Mars
Ziff-Davis, 1952

1	550.00
2	325.00

Crusaders
Guild

1	1.00

Crusaders
Chick, 1974

1-16	2.00

Crusaders
DC, 1992

1-8	1.00

Crusades
DC, 2001

1-20	3.00

Crusades, The: Urban Decree
DC, 2001

1	4.00

Crush
Aeon, 1995

1-4	3.00

Crush
Dark Horse, 2003

1-4	3.00

Crush
Image, 1996

1-5	2.00

Crusher Joe
Ironcat, 1999

1-3	2.00

Crust
Top Shelf

1	3.00

Crux
CrossGen, 2001

1-33	3.00

Cry for Dawn
Cry for Dawn, 1989

1	45.00
1/A	15.00
1/Counterfeit	2.00
1/2nd	20.00
1/3rd	18.00
2	30.00
2/2nd	15.00
3	25.00
4	15.00
5	15.00
5/2nd	8.00
6	15.00
8	10.00
9	10.00

Crying Freeman
Part 1
Viz, 1989

Yo Hinomura was a brilliant young potter, Emu Hino was a beautiful, lonely painter. Their lives were forever changed by the Chinese Mafia known as the 108 Dragons. He was unwillingly recruited to be their premier assassin, Crying Freeman. She witnessed one of his murders. Now she knows she is next!

This story is a compelling tale of crime and police politics, double crosses, deals with the devil, and a young couple who must determine what the price is of their love.

Ryoichi Ikegami is known for his lifelike style of drawing. He has also worked on Sanctuary, and Mai: The Psychic Girl, among others. Writer Kazuo Koike has produced many other works, including Lone Wolf and Cub. He also has a renowned manga artist school which produced Lum: Urusei Yatsura creator Rumiko Takahashi and Fist of the North Star artist Tetsuo Hara.

1-8 .... 4.00

Crying Freeman
Part 2
Viz, 1990

1-9 .... 4.00

Crying Freeman
Part 3
Viz, 1991

1 .... 6.00
2-10 .... 5.00

Crying Freeman
Part 4
Viz, 1994

1-3 .... 5.00
4-8 .... 3.00

Crying Freeman
Part 5
Viz

1-11 .... 3.00

Crypt
Aaaargh!

1 .... 2.00

Crypt
Image, 1995

1-2 .... 3.00

Cryptics
Image, 2006

1 .... 4.00

Cryptic Tales
Showcase

1 .... 2.00

Cryptic Writings
of Megadeth
Chaos!, 1997

1-4 .... 3.00

Crypt of C*m
Fantagraphics, 1999

1 .... 3.00

Crypt of Dawn
Sirius, 1996

1 .... 4.00
1/Ltd. 6.00
2-6 .... 3.00

Crypt of Shadows
Marvel, 1973

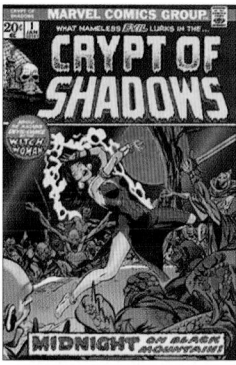

Crypt of Shadows was one of the many horror titles Marvel published in the early 1970s. The Comics Code had relaxed its earlier prohibitions against depicting monsters and ghouls, giving Marvel a chance to reprint reams of material which had lain fallow for years.

The series started out on a strong note, reprinting the classic "Midnight on Black Mountain" from Adventures into Terror #7. Unfortunately, the stories that followed were not compelling enough to win the necessary readers away from DC. The 1970s were tough times in the horror comic business, and Crypt of Shadows fell victim to the inevitable shake-out.

1 .... 35.00
2 .... 16.00
3 .... 15.00
4-5 .... 12.00
6-14 .... 10.00
15-21 .... 8.00

Crypt of Terror
E.C., 1950

17 .... 1,000.00
18 .... 800.00
19 .... 750.00

Cryptozoo Crew
NBM, 2005

1-2 .... 3.00

Crystal Balls
Fantagraphics, 1995

1-3 .... 3.00

Crystal Breeze
Unleashed
High Impact, 1996

1-3 .... 3.00

Crystal Skull Files
Ink & Feathers

1 .... 12.00

Crystal War
Atlantis

1 .... 4.00

CSI: Bad Rap
Idea & Design Works, 2003

1 .... 6.00
2-5 .... 4.00

CSI: Crime Scene
Investigation
Idea & Design Works, 2003

1-5 .... 3.00

CSI: Demon House
Idea & Design Works, 2004

1 .... 5.00
2-5 .... 4.00

CSI:
Dying in the Gutters
Idea & Design Works, 2006

1-5 .... 4.00

CSI Miami: Smoking Gun
Idea & Design Works, 2003
1 ....7.00

CSI Miami: Thou Shalt Not
Idea & Design Works, 2004
1 ....7.00

CSI: New York Bloody Murder
Idea & Design Works, 2005
1-5...4.00

CSI: Secret Identity
Idea & Design Works, 2005
1-5...4.00

CSI: Serial
Idea & Design Works, 2003
1 ....20.00

CSI: Thicker Than Blood
Idea & Design Works, 2003
1 ....7.00

Cthulhu (H.P. Lovecraft's...)
Millennium
1 ....3.00
1/CS 4.00
2-3...3.00

Cthulhu: The Whisper In Darkness (H.P. Lovecraft's...)
Millennium
1 ....7.00

Cuckoo
Green Door, 1996
1-5...3.00

Cud
Fantagraphics, 1993
1-8...3.00

Cuda
Avatar, 1998
1-1/A 4.00
1/B..6.00
1/C 4.00

Cuda B.C.
Rebel
1 ....2.00

Cud Comics
Dark Horse, 1995

Cud Comics is a humor title that features the adventures of Eno and Plum, a young couple facing all the trials and dilemmas that other couples deal with when one of them has no life and likes it that way. Cud Comics is drawn by Terry LaBan in the big-foot style of underground comics like The Fabulous Furry Freak Brothers.

The comedy relies on the risque and scatological subject matter common to underground comics from the 1970s. For example, Eno finds fortune and prosperity by becoming an amazingly successful sperm donor - because it's based on an activity at which he excels.

The series also features backup stories about Eno and Plum's friends, including expletive-wielding, thoroughly pierced friend, Angie O'Plastey.

-- George Haberberger

1-8.. 3.00
Ashcan 1 .... 1.00

Cuirass
Harrier
1 .... 2.00

Cult Television
Zone, 1992
1 .... 3.00

Cultural Jet Lag
Fantagraphics, 1991
1 .... 3.00

Culture Vultures
Iconografix
1 .... 3.00

Cupid's Revenge
Fantagraphics
1-2.. 3.00

Curio Shoppe
Phoenix, 1995
1 .... 3.00

Cursed
Image, 2003
1-4 .... 3.00

Cursed Worlds Source Book
Blue Comet
1 .... 3.00

Curse of Dracula
Dark Horse, 1998
1-3 .... 3.00

Curse of Dreadwolf
Lightning, 1994
1 .... 3.00

Curse of Rune
Malibu, 1995
1-4 .... 3.00

Curse of the Molemen
Kitchen Sink
1 .... 5.00

Curse of the She-Cat
AC, 1989
1 .... 3.00

Curse of the Spawn
Image, 1996

The spinoff to Image's popular Spawn series attempts to marry the Spawn legend with futuristic Gothic horror.

As the legend goes, every 400 years, a new Hellspawn arises. In this future, "a time of damnation given form" also known as the "Antithesis," the few remaining humans flee from zombie soldiers and a variety of other random horrors. One such is the Dessicator, a creature which sucks all cellular moisture from the living. There's also a living-dead Catholic cardinal.

Former human soldier Daniel Llanso comes back to life as

Hellspawn, a skeleton (with the odd bit of muscle) that wreaks vengeance and has to suffer about his existence and memories. The end effect is a grudge-fest among skeletons with claws and machine guns, interspersed with occasional agonized-skull close-ups.

1	3.00
1/A	4.00
2-15	3.00
16-29	2.00

Curse of the Weird
Marvel, 1993

1-4	2.00

Curse of the Zombie
Marvel

4	1.00

CuteGirl
Not Available

1-2	1.00

Cutie Pie
Junior Readers' Guild, 1955

1	24.00
2-5	14.00

Cutting Class
B Comics, 1995

1	2.00

Cutting Edge
Marvel, 1995

1	3.00

CVO: African Blood
Idea & Design Works, 2006

1	4.00

CVO: Covert Vampiric Operations Rogue State
Idea & Design Works, 2004

1-5	4.00

Cyber 7
Eclipse, 1989

Cyber 7 is a black-and-white manga series which was created by Shuho Itahashi and translated into English by David Lewis and Toren Smith. The series is a science-fiction tale about seven cyborgs who actually need to be talked into tasks because they are self-aware.

14 years ago, a young scientist was involved in a terrible automobile accident. He was saved by the seven cyborgs. The picture was kept secret because the cyborgs were supposed to stay secret. However, an evil gang leader, who happens to be a rabbit, wants the picture. A young boy named Tatsuki finds the photograph and sells it to a tabloid newspaper. His life is now in danger. Two children are in the picture, as well. They are now teen-agers who act in a traveling acting troupe. Unknown to them, they, too, are in danger.

1-7	2.00

Cyber 7 Book Two
Eclipse, 1989

1-10	2.00

Cyber City: Part 1
CPM, 1995

1-2	3.00

Cyber City: Part 2
CPM, 1995

1-2	3.00

Cyber City: Part 3
CPM, 1995

1-2	3.00

Cybercom, Heart of the Blue Mesa
Matrix, 1987

1	2.00

Cyber Crush: Robots in Revolt
Fleetway-Quality, 1991

1-14	2.00

Cyberella
DC, 1996

Cyberella is, in the words of creator Howard Chaykin, "about a lot of things I consider pretty important: television, advertising, capitalism run rampant, image over substance, and, let's not forget, the ever-popular personal betrayal." That's basically the essence of DC's free-wheeling, near-future, corporate hellworld satire.

Cyberella began as the fictional creation of entertainment conglomerate Macrocorp: a 1920s cartoon character called Li'l Ella who morphed, over the years into a net-based role-playing game used for behavioral control in the 21st century. Enter Sunny Winston, a feisty young woman with an unusual gift for strategy and connections to the evil head of Macrocorp. Add a well-timed freak power surge, and suddenly Macrocorp's got a whole lot of trouble.

This was part of Helix, DC's attempt to launch a science-fiction comics line. Unfortunately, the cyberpunk-dominated line didn't snag enough traditional SF fans to keep it going.

-- Rob Salkowitz

1-6	2.00
7-12	3.00

Cyberfarce
Parody

1	3.00

Cyber Femmes
Spoof, 1992

1	3.00

Cyberforce (Vol. 1)
Image, 1992

1-2	3.00
3-4	2.00

Cyberforce (Vol. 2)
Image, 1993
0-1/Gold	3.00
1/2nd	1.00
2-5	3.00
6-7	2.00
8-10/Variant	3.00
11-12	2.00
13-16	3.00
17	2.00
18-24	3.00
25	4.00
26-35	3.00
Ann 1	4.00
Ann 2	3.00

Cyberforce (Vol. 3)
Image, 2006
0-6	3.00

Cyberforce Origins
Image, 1995
1-1/Gold	3.00
1/2nd	1.00
2-3	3.00

Cyberforce, Stryke Force: Opposing Forces
Image, 1995
1-2	3.00

Cyberforce Universe Sourcebook
Image, 1994
1-2	3.00

Cyberforce/X-Men
Image, 2007
1-1/Variant	4.00

CyberFrog
Harris, 1996
0-4	3.00

Cyberfrog: Reservoir Frog
Harris, 1996

Ethan Van Sciver's sociopathic cybernetic amphibian returns in a new series which promises to be even more violent than its predecessors (yeah, like that's possible!). Froggie and his sidekick/best friend Heather Swain face a terrifying new set of enemies, not the least of which is the insectoid cybernetic horrors of the Swarm. Ben Riley, formerly Deathfly, passes the myriad amulet to a new host, unleashing the deadly menace of Dragonfly. And the lethal Skorpeone launches a one-monster war on Traffik's cryptogenetics laboratories.

But perhaps the most important event in this series is issue #2's dramatic cliffhanger (Cyberfrog has a mom?!), which leads directly into Cyberfrog #0 and the long-awaited, never-before-revealed origin of... Damn, you guessed!

1-2/A	3.00

CyberFrog: 3rd Anniversary Special
Harris, 1997
1-2	3.00

Cyberfrog vs CreeD
Harris, 1997
1	3.00

Cybergen
CFD, 1996
1	3.00

Cyberhawks
Pyramid, 1987
1-2	2.00

Cyberlust
Aircel, 1991
1-3	3.00

Cybernary
Image, 1995
1-5	3.00

Cybernary 2.0
DC, 2001
1-6	3.00

Cyberpunk (Book 1)
Innovation
1-2	2.00

Cyberpunk (Book 2)
Innovation
1-2	2.00

Cyberpunk Graphic Novel
Innovation
1	7.00

Cyberpunk: The Seraphim Files
Innovation
1-2	3.00

Cyberpunx
Image, 1996
1/A-1/D	3.00

CyberRad
Continuity, 1991
1-7	2.00

Cyberrad
Continuity, 1992
1	3.00
1/A	2.00

CyberRad Deathwatch 2000
Continuity, 1993
1-2	3.00

Cyber Reality Comix
Wonder Comix, 1994

Nils Osmar created this series on a computer (yes, it's a Macintosh!), promising the graphics will "melt your brain". Although the finished product is pretty good, don't expect to need emergency medical help. The character illustrations are exceptional, more like color photographs than drawings, but the background detail is often inconsistent or absent.

The series begins with three multi-part science-fiction stories. "Game Guys" involves a virtual reality game, where the human players experience the game's events as if they were really happening. Unfortunately, though the game is computer-generated, the monster inside is all too real. In "Remyoz", a man follows his former lover to a distant star system on a mission of vengeance, and in "Four of the Fury", the members of a futuristic rock band become cosmic castaways after a meteor wrecks their ship.

Wonder Comics, based in Seattle, also operates a correspondence school for cartoon illustration.

1-2...4.00

Cybersexation
Antarctic, 1997

1 :...3.00

Cyberspace 3000
Marvel, 1993

1...3.00
2-8...2.00

Cybersuit Arkadyne
Ianus, 1992

1-6...3.00

Cybertrash and the Dog
Silverline, 1998

1...3.00

Cyberzone
Jet-Black Grafiks, 1994

1-8...3.00

Cyblade/Ghost Rider
Marvel, 1997

1...3.00

Cyblade/Shi: The Battle for Independents
Image, 1995

1-1/B...6.00
1/CS...10.00
Ashcan 1...3.00

Cyboars
Vintage, 1996

1-1/A...2.00

Cyborg, the Comic Book
Cannon, 1989

1...1.00

Cybrid
Maximum, 1995

1...3.00

Cyclone Comics
Bilbara, 1940

1...1,300.00
2-3...1,000.00
4-5...800.00

Cyclops
Marvel, 2000

Part of Marvel's series of mini-series called X-Men: Icons, Cyclops is a weak attempt to give the leader of The X-Men something to do away from the rest of the team and to better define his character. Scott Summers, otherwise known as Cyclops (the mutant who can fire concussive blasts from his eyes), is stalked and finally kidnapped by a mutant-hating soldier named Ulysses.

Ulysses wants to transport Cyc to The Savage Land for a fight to the death. The trouble is, Ulysses only appears in #2 and #4 of the story, leaving Cyclops time to have issue-long fights with old enemies Juggernaut and Black Tom Cassidy and inhabitants of The Savage Land. The end finds Cyclops just as we found him, with a hollow victory and little or no character growth. The art by Mark Texeira is not his usual tight pencil line but is still powerful and action-packed.

1-4...3.00

Cycops
Comics Interview, 1988

1-3...2.00

Cygnus X-1
Twisted Pearl Press, 1994

1-2...3.00

Cy-Gor
Image, 1999

1-5...3.00

Cylinderhead
Slave Labor, 1989

1...2.00

Cynder
Immortelle, 1996

When Cindy's father died, he left the family fortune to Cindy's stepmother, with the condition that she raise Cindy until she turned twenty-one. Cindy knew, however, that her stepmother had slowly poisoned her father, and she could expect nothing but slow torture at her stepmother's hands. Night after night, she was locked in a room with nothing but a fire for comfort. One night, she stole a knife from her cruel stepmother and swore she would use it on herself if only to prevent her stepmother from inheriting her father's fortune.

But before she could act, the fire seemed to speak to her, giving her power over heat and flame. When her stepmother next tried to beat her, Cindy retaliated with scorching and deadly force. Cindy then began a new life, using her powers to avenge those who had been preyed upon by criminals and other abusers.

1-Ann 1...3.00

Cynder/Hellina Special
Immortelle, 1996

1...3.00

Cynosure
Cynosure, 1994

1...2.00

Cyntherita
Side Show

1...3.00

Czar Chasm
C&T

1-2...2.00

After more than two dozen issues of standard crimefighter stories,
Detective Comics #27 introduced Batman to readers in 1939.

comical, insulting sketches of Qaddafi and the inventive use of Daffy as the omnipotent voice of reason makes for a historically appealing and amusing comic.

1 .... 2.00

Dagar, Desert Hawk
Fox, 1948

14 .... 475.00
15 .... 400.00
16-23 .... 300.00

Dagar the Invincible (Tales of Sword and Sorcery...)
Gold Key, 1972

1 .... 16.00
2 .... 11.00
3-11 .... 7.00
12-14 .... 5.00
15-18 .... 3.00
19 .... 2.00

Dagwood Comics
Harvey, 1950

1 .... 80.00
2 .... 42.00
3-5 .... 32.00
6-10 .... 26.00
11-20 .... 22.00
21-30 .... 18.00
31-50 .... 15.00
51-70 .... 13.00
71-80 .... 10.00
81-100 .... 8.00
101-120 .... 7.00
121-140 .... 6.00

Dahmer's Zombie Squad
Boneyard, 1993

1 .... 4.00

Dai Kamikaze!
Now, 1987

1-12 .... 2.00

Daikazu
Ground Zero, 1988

1-8 .... 2.00

Daily Bugle
Marvel, 1996

1-3 .... 3.00

Daily Bugle: Civil War Special Edition
Marvel, 2006

1 .... 1.00

Daily Planet Invasion! Extra
DC

1 .... 2.00

Daimons
Cry for Dawn

1 .... 3.00

Dadaville
Caliber

1 .... 3.00

Daemonifuge: The Screaming Cage
Black Library, 2002

1-3 .... 3.00

Daemon Mask
Amazing

1 .... 2.00

Daemonstorm
Caliber, 1997

1 .... 4.00
Ashcan 1 .... 1.00

Daffy Duck
Dell, 1956

4-10 .... 18.00
11-20 .... 10.00
21-40 .... 7.00
41-60 .... 5.00
61-80 .... 4.00
81-100 .... 3.00
101-128 .... 2.00
129 .... 18.00
130 .... 25.00
131-134 .... 15.00
135-137 .... 5.00
138 .... 2.00
139-141 .... 5.00
142-144 .... 15.00
145 .... 7.00

Daffy Qaddafi
Comics Unlimited, 1986

This scathing political satire stars Moammar Qaddafi, the mad dog of the Middle East, as his dreams are invaded by a politically correct Daffy Duck. Daffy becomes a biting commentator intent on tearing down the illusions Qaddafi has built to fool his people and himself. Defeated by Reagan, small children, and by his own words, Qaddafi shows his true face, that of a foolish zealot and a mad-dog terrorist.

This is a one-shot book, published at the height of American anger over Qaddafi and his regime in Libya. The book is well researched, often drawing on news reports and making light of Qaddafi's "Green Book." The

Daisy and Donald
Gold Key, 1973

Filled with stories featuring the relationships between Donald and Daisy Duck, the series occasionally provided reprints of stories by writer-artist Carl Barks. Much of the emphasis was on Daisy and her romantic intentions regarding Donald, but many stories also dealt with the difficulties in being Donald's girlfriend -- which are plenty, if you know Donald.

Women's Lib even filters into some of their disagreements, although the Duckburg brand is decidedly tame. In one story reflective of the times, Donald gets caught up in the Citizen's Band radio fad, driving Daisy to distraction as he drives her around, trying to lend traffic tips to truckers and help the police chase criminals. As usual, Donald winds up in jail, which means that Daisy, the empowered 1970s woman, can use his CB to tell her friends about the latest dress sales!

-- John Jackson Miller

1	25.00
2-4	15.00
5-7	10.00
8-10	4.00
11-44	3.00
45-46	25.00
47	60.00
49-54	10.00
55-59	15.00

Daisy and Her Pups Comics
Harvey, 1951

21 (1)	15.00
22 (2)-10	10.00
11-18	7.00

Daisy Kutter: The Last Train
Viper, 2004

1	5.00

1/Conv	6.00
2-4	4.00

Dakkon Blackblade
Acclaim

1	6.00

Dakota North
Marvel, 1986

1-5	2.00

Daktari
Dell, 1967

1	35.00
2-4	30.00

Dale Evans Comics
DC, 1948

1	825.00
2	600.00
3	485.00
4-5	285.00
6-10	250.00
11-20	135.00
21-24	100.00

Dale Kuper's Sketchbook
Green Bay

1	2.00

Dalgoda
Fantagraphics, 1984

1-8	2.00

Dalkiel: The Prophecy
Verotik, 1998

1	4.00

Dalton Boys
Avon, 1951

1	80.00

Dam
Dam

1	3.00

Damage
DC, 1994

Grant Emerson was always the new kid on the block. In the last four years of his life, his family had to move eight times due to his father's job at Solinex. Grant had gotten used to fitting in wherever his family went. Still, the latest school was proving to be something of a problem. Grant had made the mistake of being liked by an over-muscled athlete's girlfriend. As a result, the aforementioned caveman attempted to push Grant's head through the pavement. A coach stopped the fight before it could go anywhere and the thug stormed off. In frustration, Grant slammed on the hood of a car...a slam which demolished the car!

It was then that Grant's superhuman ability to store and use kinetic energy first revealed itself: when you hit him, he could hit back. Harder. Suddenly Grant knew he wasn't going to be fitting in with the other kids...and he would discover that his parents weren't exactly ordinary either!

0-20	2.00

Damage Control (Vol. 1)
Marvel, 1989

1	2.00
2-4	1.00

Damage Control (Vol. 2)
Marvel, 1989

1	2.00
2-4	1.00

Damage Control (Vol. 3)
Marvel, 1991

1	2.00
2-4	1.00

Dame Patrol
Spoof

1	3.00

Damlog
Pyramid

1	2.00

Damnation
Fantagraphics, 1994

1	3.00

Damned
Image, 1997

1-4	3.00

Damn Nation
Dark Horse, 2005

1-3	3.00

Damonstreik
Imperial

1-2	2.00

Dampyr
Idea & Design Works, 2005
1-8 .... 8.00

Damselvis, Daughter of Helvis Supermag
Fantagraphics
1 .... 4.00

Dance of Death
Tome
1 .... 3.00

Dance of Lifey Death
Dark Horse, 1994
1 .... 4.00

Dance Party DOA
Slave Labor, 1993
1 .... 4.00

Dances with Demons
Marvel, 1993
1 .... 3.00
2-4 .... 2.00

Dandy Comics
E.C., 1947

This was a "funny animal" and "bigfoot" title that E.C. produced as an "entertaining comic" in its early days, as the company experimented to find a variety of comic books that would bring readership. "Dandy" is a rabbit, "Tumbles" is a clown, and "Handy Andy" is a bigfoot human. Andy (usually dressed in a sweater with an "H" on the chest) quickly took over the cover spot, which typically showed him getting into some life-threatening situation without realizing the doom that was about to befall him.

Despite its targeting of young readers, Dandy carried ads for such E.C. titles as Picture Stories from the Bible and even Moon Girl.
-- Maggie

1 .... 225.00
2 .... 200.00
3-7 .... 130.00

Danger
Charlton, 1954
1 .... 70.00
2-5 .... 40.00
6-10 .... 30.00
11-14 .... 24.00

Danger
Super, 1964
12-16 .... 14.00

Danger Comics
Danger Comics, 2004
1-2 .... 2.00

Danger Funnies
Cry for Dawn
1 .... 3.00

Danger Girl
Image, 1988

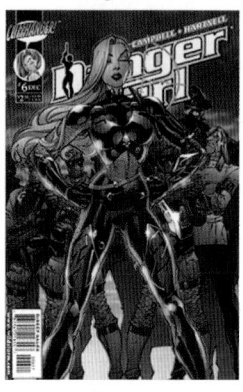

Danger Girl was the first title with the Cliffhanger! imprint, a creator-owned line of books from WildStorm Studios.

An expert marksman and scholar of ancient civilizations, Abbey Chase is recruited into Danger Girl, a team of female operatives from around the world assembled to battle the Fourth Reich, a union of bizarre, yet dangerous, would-be world conquerors.

Chase joins Natalia Kassle, Sydney Savage, and Silicon Valerie, ordinary women with extraordinary skills, and their leader Deuce, an ex-agent for the British secret service.

Renowned for his attractive women and youthful, fun art, J. Scott Campbell depicts the attitude of the action/comedy movie genre on the printed page.

Unfortunately as the delays between each issue's release got longer and longer, reader apathy increased to the point that the release of the final issue was mostly a non-event.

1 .... 5.00
1/Chromium 8.00
1/Mag sized 20.00
1/Tour ed 8.00
1/Go-go cover 31.00
2 .... 3.00
2/Chrome 8.00
2/Gold 6.00
3 .... 3.00
3/A 5.00
3/B-4 .... 3.00
4/A 7.00
5 .... 3.00
6 .... 3.00
6/Gold 5.00
7 .... 6.00
Ashcan 1 .... 5.00
Ashcan 1/Gold 6.00
SP 1 .... 4.00
Deluxe 1 .... 20.00

Danger Girl 3-D
DC, 2003
1 .... 5.00

Danger Girl: Back in Black
DC, 2006
1-4 .... 3.00

Danger Girl: Hawaiian Punch
DC, 2003
1 .... 5.00

Danger Girl Kamikaze
DC, 2001
1-2 .... 3.00

Danger Girls
Animagic
1 .... 3.00

Danger Girl Sketchbook
DC
1 .... 7.00

Danger Girl: Viva Las Danger
DC, 2004
1 .... 5.00

Danger is our Business
Toby, 1953
1 .... 165.00
2 .... 100.00
3-5 .... 75.00
6-10 .... 65.00

Dangerman
Patchwork
1 .... 3.00

Dangerous Times
Evolution
1-6/2nd 2.00

Danger Ranger
Checker, 1998
1-2..2.00

Danger Trail
DC, 1950

This short-lived espionage series has the distinction of being one of the few DC series prior to 1967 to run fewer than six issues. Starring intrepid secret agent King Faraday the 1950-51 series dealt with fairly pedestrian situations and banked on the public's interest with all things spy-related at the time to sell the series. Unfortunately, intrigue and spycraft are difficult to portray on the illustrated page and even art by Alex Toth couldn't help the series, which was canceled after only five issues.

Today, collectors seek it out for its rarity. Several of the stories were later reprinted in Showcase #50 and #51 under the title "I, Spy!"
-- Brent

1..875.00
2..600.00
3..1,250.00
☛Scarce
4-5..385.00

Danger Trail
DC, 1993
1-4..2.00

Danger Unlimited
Dark Horse, 1994
1-4..3.00

Dangle
Cat-Head
1..3.00

Daniel Boone
Gold Key, 1965

At his worst, history tells us that Daniel Boone was a violent, drunken, semiliterate fur trapper, a bigoted Indian-hater, and the cause of a number of avoidable conflicts along the frontier prior to the Civil War. But, thanks to the magic of television, Daniel Boone is best remembered today for those nifty coonskin caps, actor Fess Parker's rugged good looks, and everything that's good, law-abiding, practical, and brave about the mountain folk who expanded west of the Appalachian range.

Gold Key's adaptation of the popular television series featured straight-ahead versions of Daniel Boone and crew taking on outlaws, Indians, and crooks.
-- Rob Salkowitz

1.. 45.00
2.. 28.00
3-5.. 24.00
6-15.. 18.00

Dan'l Boone
Magazine Enterprises, 1955
1.. 70.00
2-8.. 45.00

Danny Blaze
Charlton, 1955
1.. 35.00
2.. 18.00

Dan Panic Funnies
Panic
1.. 2.00

Danse
Blackthorne, 1987
1.. 2.00

Dante's Inferno
Tome
1-2.. 4.00

Dan Turner:
Ace in the Hole
Eternity
1.. 3.00

Dan Turner:
Dark Star of Death
Eternity
1.. 3.00

Dan Turner:
Homicide Hunch
Eternity, 1991
1.. 3.00

Dan Turner:
Star Chamber
Eternity, 1991
1.. 3.00

Dapiek Absaroka:
The Killer of Crows
Tome
1.. 3.00

Darby O'Gill
and the Little People
Gold Key, 1970
1.. 20.00

D'arc Tangent
Ffantasy Ffactory, 1982
1.. 2.00

Dare
Monster, 1991
1-4.. 3.00

Daredevil
Lev Gleason, 1941
1.................................... 11,000.00
2...................................... 2,600.00
3...................................... 1,500.00
4...................................... 1,200.00
5... 975.00
6... 825.00
7... 725.00
8-10...................................... 700.00
11.. 800.00
12...................................... 1,050.00
13.. 925.00
14.. 475.00
15.. 575.00
16-17.................................... 425.00
18.. 950.00
19-20.................................... 350.00
21.. 600.00
22-30.................................... 275.00
31.. 650.00
32-37.................................... 200.00
38.. 350.00
39-41.................................... 200.00
42.. 175.00
43-50.................................... 150.00
51-60.................................... 115.00
61-69...................................... 90.00
70-78...................................... 60.00
79-80...................................... 70.00

81-99	55.00
100	60.00
101-120	45.00
121-134	36.00

Daredevil
Marvel, 1964

Matt Murdock was the son of a second-rate fighter named "Battlin' Jack" Murdock. But although his own life was spent in physical combat, Jack Murdock insisted that Matt avoid fighting, and concentrate instead on his studies. It wasn't easy. The neighborhood kids called him a coward and even nicknamed him "Daredevil" to poke fun at him.

Then fate intervenes in the form of a truck laden with radioactive cargo, headed for an unsuspecting man. Matt runs into the street to save the man, but is hit by the truck himself. Blinded by the accident, he finds his other senses growing far more acute. He even develops a radar sense that lets him "see" objects in the world around him.

When his father was killed for refusing to throw a fight, Matt decides he can hold back no longer — becoming Daredevil, "the Man Without Fear."

Daredevil's record is uneven. Not as popular as some of Stan Lee's other creations, the series has seen many lackluster stretches — including, infamously, a ludicrous storyline involving Matt posing as his own nonexistent, sighted twin brother. But Frank Miller reinvents the character from scratch beginning in #158, generating what is now considered to be the definitive version.

-1	2.00
1	3,000.00
☛1st Daredevil	
2	750.00
3	550.00

4	400.00
5	300.00
6	225.00
7	675.00
☛1st red costume	
8-10	135.00
11-15	85.00
☛Spider-Man app.	
16-17	120.00
☛Spider-Man app.	
18	70.00
☛1st Gladiator	
19	60.00
20	55.00
21-27	50.00
28-30	45.00
31-42	40.00
43	45.00
44-49	30.00
50-52	33.00
53-71	20.00
72-80	17.00
81	25.00
☛Giant-size	
82-83	17.00
84-99	14.00
100	30.00
☛Origin recap	
101-130	8.00
131	75.00
☛1st Bullseye	
132	15.00
132/30¢	20.00
133	6.00
133/30¢	20.00
134	6.00
134/30¢	20.00
135	6.00
135/30¢	20.00
136	6.00
136/30¢	20.00
137-146/Whitman	6.00
146/35¢	15.00
147	6.00
147/35¢	15.00
148	6.00
148/35¢	15.00
149-157	6.00
158	50.00
☛Frank Miller starts	
159	22.00
160-161	17.00
162	9.00
163	18.00
164-167	11.00
168	75.00
☛1st Elektra	
169	16.00
170	10.00
171	12.00
172-177	7.00
178-180	6.00
181	15.00
☛Elektra dies	
182-183	7.00
184	6.00
185	5.00
186	6.00
187-190	5.00
191	6.00

192-195	3.00
196	6.00
197-204	3.00
205	4.00
206-226	3.00
227	4.00
☛ Born Again	
228-247	3.00
248-249	4.00
250	3.00
251	5.00
252	4.00
253	3.00
254	6.00
☛1st Typhoid Mary	
255-257	3.00
258	4.00
259-295	3.00
296-299	2.00
300	3.00
301-303	2.00
304	3.00
305-311	2.00
312	3.00
313-318	2.00
319	5.00
319/2nd-321	2.00
321/Variant	3.00
322-324	2.00
325	3.00
326-349	2.00
350	3.00
350/Variant	4.00
351-374	2.00
375	3.00
376-379	2.00
380	3.00
Ann 1	50.00
Ann 2-3	9.00
Ann 4	8.00
Ann 5	4.00
Ann 6-10	3.00
Ann 1997	4.00

Daredevil
Marvel, 1998

1/2	5.00
1	7.00
1/Ltd.	50.00
1/Variant	9.00
2/A-2/B	5.00
3-5	4.00
5/A	5.00
6	3.00
7	4.00
8-15	3.00
16	5.00
16/Unlimited	6.00
17	3.00
17/Unlimited	5.00
☛Newsstand variant	
18-20	3.00
20/Unlimited	5.00
21	3.00
21/Unlimited	5.00
22	3.00
22/Unlimited	5.00
23	3.00
23/Unlimited	5.00
24-36	3.00

36/No # 5.00
☛Newsstand; no #
37...3.00
37/Unlimited............................5.00
☛Newsstand variant
37/No # 4.00
☛Newsstand; no #
38-56.......................................3.00
57...4.00
58-64.......................................3.00
65...4.00
66-89.......................................3.00
89/Sketch 6.00
90-116.....................................3.00

Daredevil/Batman
Marvel, 1997
1...6.00

Daredevil/Black Widow: Abattoir
Marvel
1...15.00

Daredevil Chronicles
Fantaco, 1982
1...2.00

Daredevil: Father
Marvel, 2004
1...5.00
1/DirCut..................................4.00
2-5...3.00

Daredevil: Ninja
Marvel, 2000
1-3...3.00

Daredevil/Punisher: Child's Play
Marvel
nn..5.00

Daredevil: Redemption
Marvel, 2005
1-6...3.00

Daredevil/Shi
Marvel, 1997
1...3.00

Daredevil/Spider-Man
Marvel, 2000
1-4...3.00

Daredevil The Man without Fear
Marvel, 1993
1-3...4.00
4-5...3.00

Daredevil: The Target
Marvel, 2003
1...4.00

Daredevil vs. Vapora
Marvel, 1996
nn..1.00

Daredevil vs. Punisher
Marvel, 2005
1-6.. 3.00

Daredevil: Yellow
Marvel, 2001

Daredevil's father, Battling Jack Murdock, lived by one rule: "The measure of a man is not in how he gets knocked down to the mat -- it is in how he gets up." Matt Murdock is uncertain about getting up. He has lost control of his life and wonders about the self-doubt slowly creeping into his soul.

Matt vividly remembers the events on that bittersweet night of his father's biggest victory in the ring, but the excitement of the moment clouded the hard scowls of men betrayed. Jack Murdock gave him a prized possession: a robe -- a yellow robe soaked with the essence of a champion. He could feel the reverence and soak up the power within the fabric even without his heightened senses. The power displayed by Murdock in the ring could not prevent his murder from occurring hours later. Murdock raised his son to be a fighter. Now it's time to step into the ring -- and fear be damned.

1-6.. 4.00

Darerat/Tadpole
Mighty Pumpkin, 1987
1... 2.00

Dare the Impossible
Fleetway-Quality, 1990
1-15...................................... 2.00

Daria Jontak
JMJ, 2001
1... 5.00

Daring Adventures
St. John
1.. 200.00

Daring Adventures
I.W., 1963
9-11...................................... 20.00
12... 40.00
13-18.................................... 20.00

Daring Adventures
B Comics, 1993
1-3... 2.00

Daring Comics
Marvel, 1944
9 .... 1,100.00
10 .... 950.00
11-12 .... 875.00

Daring Confessions
Youthful, 1952
4 .... 120.00
5-8 .... 100.00

Daring Escapes
Image, 1998

Instead of arriving at the Great Beyond, Harry Houdini has escaped to a strange dimensional junction known as the Overlap. The Overlap is a populated by extraterrestrial races and historical figures such as Judas Iscariot and Joan of Arc. Another strange fact of the Overlap is an egotistical, pretentious entity known as Nine who performs duties akin to management. One of Houdini's last crusades was exposing fraudulent spiritual mediums, so it's natural that he would be required to prevent any bona fide talismans from falling into the wrong hands. Any Houdini treatise would not be complete without a detailed reenactment of his painfully unorthodox method of escaping from a locked jail cell. The Impossible Possible has returned with his unflagging bravado and sarcastic nature in place. Now, if he could only keep a watchful eye on that damned Judas....

1-4 .... 3.00

Daring Love
Gilmore, 1953
1 ....800.00

Daring Love Stories
Fox, 1950
1 ....250.00

Daring Mystery Comics
Timely, 1940
1 ....14,500.00
2 ....3,500.00
3 ....2,550.00
4 ....2,200.00
5-9 ....2,000.00
10 ....7,000.00
11 ....4,500.00
12 ....2,400.00

Daring New Adventures of Supergirl
DC, 1982
1 ....3.00
2-13 ....2.00

Dark (Vol. 1)
Continuum, 1993
1-7/2nd 2.00

Dark (Vol. 2)
Continuum, 1995
1 ....2.00
1/A 3.00
2 ....2.00
3-4 ....3.00

Dark
August House, 1995
1-2 ....3.00

Dark Adventures
Darkline
1 ....1.00
2-3 ....2.00
4 ....1.00

Dark Ages
Alternate Concepts
1 ....4.00

Dark Angel
Boneyard, 1991
1-3 ....2.00

Dark Angel
Marvel, 1992
6-17 ....2.00

Dark Angel
Boneyard, 1997
1 ....5.00
2-3 ....2.00

Dark Angel
CPM Manga, 1999
1-29 ....3.00

Dark Angel: Death Dreams
Boneyard
1 ....3.00

Dark Angel: Phoenix Resurrection
Image, 2000
1-4 .... 3.00

Dark Assassin
Silverwolf, 1987
1 .... 2.00

Dark Assassin
Greater Mercury, 1989
1-9 .... 2.00

Darkchylde
Maximum, 1996
1-3 .... 3.00

Darkchylde Battlebook
WildStorm
1/A-1/B 4.00

Darkchylde
Image, 1996
0/A-1/2/Variant 3.00
1-1/AmEnt 5.00
1/B 3.00
1/Conv-3 .... 5.00
3/A-5/C 3.00
Ashcan 1 .... 2.00
Ashcan 1/Gold 3.00
Ashcan 1/Ltd. 5.00

Darkchylde/ Painkiller Jane
WildStorm
Ashcan 1 .... 3.00

Darkchylde Remastered
Image, 1997
0-3 .... 3.00

Darkchylde Sketchbook
Image, 1998
1 .... 3.00

Darkchylde Summer Swimsuit Spectacular
DC, 1999

Just in case you didn't see enough of half-demon Ariel Chylde's exposed flesh in the Darkchylde Swimsuit Illustrated special in 1998, Wildstorm offers up this 1999 one-shot featuring more artists' interpretations of our barely dressed heroine. This pinup style book features work from such notables as Jim Lee (X-Men, WildC.A.T.S), Joe Chiodo (Daredevil/Black Widow: Abattoir), J.G. Jones (Black Widow), Mike Wieringo (Flash, Tellos), Randy Green (Witchblade), and Tommy Yune (Speed Racer), as well as Darkchylde's creator, Randy Queen.

1 .... 4.00

Darkchylde Swimsuit Illustrated
Image, 1998
1 .... 4.00
1/Gold 5.00

Darkchylde the Diary
Image, 1997
1/A-1/D 3.00

Darkchylde: The Legacy
Image, 1998
1 .... 3.00
1/A-1/Variant 4.00
2-3 .... 3.00

Dark City Chronicles
Culture
1 .... 4.00

Dark Claw Adventures
DC, 1997
1 .... 2.00

Dark Comics
Imperial
1 .... 2.00

Dark Convention Book
Continuum, 1993
1 .... 2.00

Dark Crossings: Dark Cloud Rising
Image, 2003
1 .... 6.00

Dark Crossings
Image, 2000
1-2 .... 6.00

Dark Crossings: Dark Clouds Overhead
Image, 2000
1 .... 6.00

Dark Crystal
Marvel, 1983
1-2 .... 1.00

Dark Destiny
Alpha, 1994
1 .... 4.00

Darkdevil
Marvel, 2000
1-3...3.00

Dark Dominion
Defiant, 1993
1-13...3.00

Darker Image
Image, 1993

As the name implies, Darker Image is a look into the more shadowy reaches of the Image universe. A sampler series, it showcases some of the top talent at Image.

Included is Jim Lee's Deathblow -- Commander Michael Cray -- a former SEAL and special operative, and easily one of the deadliest men alive.

Rob Liefeld provides a look at the character Bloodwulf, a slightly more literate take on ultraviolence a la Lobo.

Also included is Sam Kieth's Maxx, a strange, purple, toothy behemoth with an odd backstory that was only completely explored in his own title. The point here, however, was to give potential readers a look at some of what Image had to offer at the time.

1 ....3.00
1/Gold-1/Ltd. 4.00

Darker Side of Sex
Fantagraphics
1-3...3.00

Darkewood
Aircel
1-5...2.00

Dark Fantasies
Dark Fantasy
1-3...3.00

Dark Fantasy
Apple, 1992
1 ....3.00

Darkforce
Omega 7
1 .... 3.00
2 .... 4.00

Dark Fringe
Brainstorm, 1996
2 .... 3.00

Dark Fringe, The: Spirits of the Dead
Brainstorm
1-2 .... 3.00

Dark Gauntlet
Tarescent
1-4 .... 2.00

Dark Guard
Marvel, 1993

In a place beyond our space and time is the "No-Space"-a zone of emptiness outside our continuum. Floating in the midst of that blackness is a solitary spacecraft called the Refuge. Motormouth, Killpower, and Ultra-Marine have been brought to the Refuge, and are soon joined by Dark Angel, Death's Head II, Albion (from the Knights of Pendragon), and Col. Liger and Stacey of the Warheads. All of these heroes have been snatched from their own continuum by a being called the Time Guardian, who charges them with a great mission: to stop the sorcerous MyS-TECH corporation.

The Guardian has looked into the future and has seen MyS-TECH controlling the entire world, unless these heroes are able to put an end to its machinations. Thus he has called together Marvel UK's greatest heroes to form a single team-The Dark Guard-to destroy the menace of MyS-TECH before it destroys the future.

1 .... 3.00
2-5 .... 2.00

Darkhawk
Marvel, 1991

It was an ebony amulet of unknown origin. Chris Powell found it in an old amusement park, and it changed his life forever. He found that he could use the amulet to change himself into Darkhawk, a shadowy warrior of tremendous power. Now, Chris has sworn to use that power to fight crime.

Although the origin of the character seems pretty traditional, his super-powers seem less super than many in the field. For example, Darkhawk is anything but bulletproof. When wounded, however, he can heal himself entirely by changing back into Chris, then back again into Darkhawk.

1-14 .... 2.00
15-24 .... 1.00
25 .... 3.00
26-38 .... 1.00
39-49 .... 2.00
50-Ann 3................................ 3.00

Darkhold
Marvel, 1992
1/CS 3.00
2-16 .... 2.00

Dark Horse Classics
Dark Horse
1-2 .... 4.00

Dark Horse Classics: Aliens Versus Predator
Dark Horse, 1997
1-6 .... 3.00

Dark Horse Classics: Godzilla
Dark Horse, 1998
1 .... 3.00

Dark Horse Classics: Godzilla: King of the Monsters
Dark Horse, 1998
1-6...3.00

Dark Horse Classics: Star Wars: Dark Empire
Dark Horse, 1997
1-6...3.00

Dark Horse Classics: Terror of Godzilla
Dark Horse, 1998
1-6...3.00

Dark Horse Comics
Dark Horse, 1992

Dark Horse Comics can be thought of a companion to Dark Horse's popular Dark Horse Presents anthology series. Chiefly featured here are Dark Horse's licensed characters, Predator, Robocop, Timecop, Aliens, and more. The thrills come hard and fast as these sci-fi characters engage in adventure, with each chapter inevitably ending in a cliff-hanger. Each issue features top-notch art and suspenseful writing in the Dark Horse tradition.

1 ....4.00
2-6..3.00
7-8..5.00
9 ....4.00
10-25..3.00

Dark Horse Down Under
Dark Horse, 1994
1-3..3.00

Dark Horse Futures
Dark Horse
1 ....1.00

Dark Horse Maverick: Happy Endings
Dark Horse, 2002
1 ....10.00

Dark Horse Maverick 2000
Dark Horse, 2000
0 ....4.00

Dark Horse Maverick 2001
Dark Horse, 2001
1 ....5.00

Dark Horse Monsters
Dark Horse, 1997
1 ....3.00

Dark Horse Presents
Dark Horse, 1986

Marvel had Marvel Comics Presents; DC had DC Comics Presents; and independent publisher Dark Horse Comics had...well, you can guess.

Dark Horse Presents wasn't just a clone of the big two's try-out books. For one, it was published in a hefty black-and-white format, packing two or three times as many stories into each issue as any of its competitors. Also, the range of stories is, well, frankly amazing! A single issue may start with a terrible spoof of Dark Horse itself, move on to a gritty true-crime drama such as Sin City, switch over to a fairy tale adapted from Oscar Wilde, cut loose with a Predator tale, then return to part two of the spoof.

1 ....4.00
1/2nd Green-1/2nd Silver 2.00
2-4 ....3.00
5-9 ....2.00
10-16 ....3.00
17 ....2.00

18 ....3.00
19-23 ....2.00
24 ....6.00
☞1st comics Aliens
25-27 ....2.00
28 ....3.00
29-31 ....2.00
32 ....4.00
☞Concrete app.
33-35 ....3.00
36 ....4.00
36/A 3.00
37-39 ....2.00
40 ....3.00
41-49 ....2.00
50 ....3.00
51 ....4.00
☞2nd Sin City
52-53 ....3.00
54 ....4.00
55 ....2.00
56-57 ....4.00
58 ....2.00
59-61 ....3.00
62 ....4.00
☞All Sin City
63-66 ....3.00
67 ....4.00
68-134 ....3.00
135 ....4.00
136-149 ....3.00
150 ....5.00
151-157 ....3.00
Ann 1997-2000......................5.00

Dark Horse Presents: Aliens
Dark Horse, 1992
1-1/A.......................................5.00

Dark Horse Twenty Years
Dark Horse, 2006
1 ....1.00

Dark Island
Davdez, 1998
1-3 ....3.00

Dark Knight Strikes Again
DC, 2001
1 ....3.00
1/A..5.00
2 ....3.00
2/A..4.00
3 ....3.00
3/A..4.00

Darklight: Prelude
Sirius, 1994
1-3 ....3.00

Darklon the Mystic
Pacific, 1983
1 ....2.00

Darkman
Marvel, 1990
1-3 ....2.00

Darkman
Marvel, 1993
1	4.00
2-6	3.00

Darkman (Magazine)
Marvel, 1990
1	2.00

Dark Mansion of Forbidden Love
DC, 1971
1	125.00
2-4	50.00

Darkminds
Image, 1998

The city of Macropolis has seven million inhabitants packed into a city that stands five miles high. Here, a killer named Paradox has slain dozens of people -- all in a singularly grisly manner, leaving no clues behind other than a telltale symbol carved into the victims' bodies. Agent Nagawa of the Special Investigations Unit, so far has been unable to stop the killer and has been assigned a new partner as a result: Agent Nakiko, a beautiful level-two cyborg. In addition to stunning physical attributes, Nakiko is an expert in psionic investigation. While her psychic abilities lead to awkward moments (such as noting when her partner is ogling her), it gives her the ability to seek out the killer by reading the minds of his dead victims.

Dreamwave Productions introduced this title in 1998, successfully employing manga stylings in a high-tech, horror thriller.

1/2	3.00
1-1/Variant	4.00
1/2nd-8	3.00

Darkminds
Image, 2000
0-10	3.00

Darkminds: Macropolis
Image, 2002
1/A-2/B	3.00

Darkminds: Macropolis
Dreamwave, 2003
1-4	3.00

Darkminds/Witchblade
Image, 2000
1	6.00

Dark Mists
APComics, 2005
1-2	4.00

Dark Moon Prophesy
Dark Moon Productions, 1995
1	1.00

Dark Mysteries
Master, 1951
1	525.00
2	340.00
3	210.00
4-5	170.00
6-10	140.00
11-20	125.00
21-24	100.00

Dark Nemesis (Villains)
DC, 1998
1	2.00

Darkness
Top Cow, 1996
0-1/Gold	3.00
1/Platinum	8.00
2-10/B	3.00
11/A	8.00
11/B-24	3.00
25	4.00
25/A	20.00
26-28	3.00
28/Graham	5.00
29-Ashcan 1/A	3.00
Deluxe 1	15.00

Darkness
Image, 2002
1	4.00
1/A-24	3.00

Darkness & Tomb Raider
Top Cow, 2005
1	3.00

Darkness/Batman
Image, 1999
1	6.00

Darkness: Black Sails
Image, 2005
0	3.00

Darkness Collected Edition
Image, 2003
1	5.00

Darkness Falls: The Tragic Life of Matilda Dixon
Dark Horse, 2002
1	3.00

Darkness/Hulk
Image, 2004
1	5.00

Darkness Infinity
Image, 1999
1	4.00

Darkness: Level 1
Image, 2007
1-1/2nd variant	3.00

Darkness: Level 0
Image, 2007
1	3.00

Darkness/Painkiller Jane
Image
Ashcan 1-Ashcan 1/A	3.00

Darkness Prelude
Image, 2003
0	4.00
0/A	4.00

Darkness, The: Spear of Destiny
Image, 2000
1	13.00

Darkness/Superman
Image, 2005
1-2	3.00

Darkness: Wanted Dead One Shot
Image, 2003
1	3.00

Darkness/Witchblade Special
Image, 1999
1	4.00

Darkness/Wolverine
Image, 2006
1	3.00

Dark Oz
Arrow, 1997
1-5	3.00

Dark Peril
Quantum
1-4	3.00

Dark Rat
Maverick Pulp Comix, 1997
1	3.00

Dark Realm
Image, 2000

The world of gritty cops, ruthless demons, and scantily clad women come together again in the pages of Dark Realm, a -- you guessed it -- Image Comics book. Perfecting the genre with its numerous Spawn properties, the publisher hopes to make lightning strike again with this copycat release. But are gruesome fight scenes and double-sized splash pages enough to attract buyers?

San Francisco police detective Shannon Davenport has been assigned to one of the most gruesome cases in her career: the murder of 36 women, all in their early 20s. The deeper she gets into her investigation, the more she realizes that her involvement is no accident. The murders are the result of the forces of the Dark Realm: creatures looking for The Chosen One to lead them in their war against humanity. Guess what? Davenport is the Chosen One.

But, as she wages her own war against these demons (turning her back on destiny), she must look for an ally in the most unlikely of places, the Dark Realm itself.

The ensuing demon-bashing will be considered old hat by some, ugly art by others. But as long as there are artists willing to model their careers on the success of Spawn, there may be readers to buy their books.

1-4 .... 3.00

Dark Regions
White Wolf, 1987
1-3 .... 2.00

Darkseed and Other Defamations
Boneyard
1 .... 4.00

Darkseid vs. Galactus: The Hunger
DC, 1995
1 .... 5.00

Darkseid (Villains)
DC, 1998
1 .... 2.00

Dark Shadows
Steinway, 1957
1 .... 70.00
2 .... 40.00
3 .... 36.00

Dark Shadows
Gold Key, 1969
1 .... 175.00
1/A 25.00
2-3 .... 48.00
4-7 .... 25.00
8-16 .... 20.00
17-20 .... 12.00
21-35 .... 10.00

Dark Shadows
Innovation, 1992
1-9 .... 3.00

Dark Shrine
Antarctic, 1999

A war is about to be waged on the demiplane--the place where angels and demons dwell. Aenarion, a sexy fallen angel who once ruled this realm, plots and schemes to overthrow its current lord, Gadrique. With the power of an ancient stone, she manages to transport two young beautiful women from the mortal plane and transforms them into demonic angels like herself, to be her pawns in the great conflict that is to come…which looks like to be just another skirmish in the great battle of the sexes.

Gorgeously rendered babes appear to be the one and only staple that held this black and white series together for as long as it did--a woppin' two issues! Editorial shortcomings, no doubt, help contribute to this title's short life span.

1-2 .... 3.00

Dark Shrine Gallery
Basement
1 .... 3.00

Darkside
Maximum, 1996
1 .... 3.00

Darkside Blues
ADV Manga, 2004
1 .... 15.00

Darkstalkers
Devil's Due, 2004
1 .... 3.00
1/Variant 4.00
2 .... 3.00
2/Variant 4.00
3 .... 3.00
3/Variant 4.00
4 .... 3.00
4/Variant 4.00
4/Foil 3.00
5 .... 4.00
5/Variant 3.00
5/Foil 4.00

Darkstar
Rebel, 1991
1-4 .... 2.00

Darkstars
DC, 1992
0-38 .... 2.00

Dark Tales of Daily Horror
Antarctic, 1994
1 .... 3.00

Dark Tower: The Gunslinger Born
Marvel, 2007
1 .... 5.00
2-3 .... 4.00

Dark Visions
Pyramid, 1986
1-2 .... 2.00

Darkwing Duck
Disney, 1991
1-4 .... 2.00

Dark Wolf
Eternity, 1988
1-Ann 1 ....2.00

Dark Wolf
Malibu, 1987
1-4..2.00

Dark World
Millennium
1 ....3.00

Darling Love
Close-Up, 1949
1 ....100.00
2-5..80.00

Darling Romance
Close-Up, 1949
1 ....350.00
2-7..100.00

Darque Passages
Valiant, 1994
1 ....2.00

Darque Passages
Acclaim, 1998
1-4..3.00

Darque Razor
London Night, 1997
1 ....3.00

Dart
Image, 1996

On the mean streets of Detroit, if you run into trouble, pray that the stunning, silver-clad beauty known as Dart will make an appearance.

Flinging silver, needle-pointed darts, and throwing high-heeled kicks, she'll tear through your average street thugs in seconds flat, while making other Detroit heroes, like Kill-Cat, weak with desire.

But can even Detroit's newest vigilante handle the dangers of this soiled playground of crime and corruption? And when she graduates to super-villains, will she be able to survive facing

evildoers like Mistress Brouhaha, the Carpenter, or the rest of Vogue Attack?

1-3... 3.00

Dartman
Northeastern
1 .... 2.00

Data 6
Artist's Unlimited
1 .... 2.00

Date with Debbi
DC, 1969
1 .... 16.00
2 .... 12.00
3-12 .... 10.00
13-17 .... 12.00
18 .... 10.00

Date With Judy
DC, 1947
1 .... 120.00
2 .... 95.00
3-5 .... 48.00
6-10 .... 34.00
11-20 .... 22.00
21-40 .... 18.00
41-60 .... 15.00
61-79 .... 10.00

Date with Millie
Atlas, 1956
1 .... 100.00
2 .... 75.00
3-7 .... 60.00

Date with Millie
Atlas, 1959
1 .... 75.00
2 .... 50.00
3-7 .... 45.00

Date with Patsy
Atlas, 1957
1 .... 60.00

Daughters of the Dragon
Marvel, 2006
1-6... 3.00

Daughters of the Dragon: Deadly Hands
Marvel, 2006
1 .... 4.00

Daughters of Time 3-D
3-D Zone
1 .... 4.00

David & Goliath
Image, 2003
1-3... 3.00

David Cassidy
Charlton, 1972

Attention, '70s kitsch collectors! Here's a must-have item to go along with your bell-bottoms and Partridge Family lunch box. It's the official David Cassidy comic book, published by Charlton in 1972-1973.

David Cassidy was the young star of the television program The Partridge Family, about a traveling family of pop musicians who always managed to get into trouble. David was the cute teen boy of the group and the biggest teen (and pre-teen) heartthrob of the early '70s. Naturally, he had his own comic book, complete with photo cover, special "inside information," and several stories in each issue about the triumphs and tribulations of being David Cassidy.
-- *Rob Salkowitz*

1 .... 25.00
2-5 .... 16.00
6-9 .... 14.00
10-14 .... 12.00

David Chelsea in Love
Eclipse
1-4 .... 4.00

David Shepherd's Song
Alias, 2005
1-2 .... 3.00

David's Mighty Men
Alias, 2005
1 .... 5.00

Davy Crockett
Gold Key, 1963
1 .... 115.00
2 .... 30.00

Dawn
Sirius Entertainment, 1995

Darrian Ashoka and his friend Jaynis Goldbaum are just a couple of typical New Yorkers. They get up in the morning, put their armor on, grab their swords and battle-axes, and head out to Times Square for a little berserking. It's all part of the weird reality that they live in, where modern neon signs light up scenes that otherwise belong in the age of chivalry.

The real star of this series is the enigmatic Dawn, a red-haired beauty who seems to know the secrets of Heaven and Hell. Darrian follows her advice to leave his "routine" New York existence and strive for the mysteries that lie beyond.

Creator Joseph Michael Linsner split off from his original publishing company and continued Dawn's story with this remarkably beautiful series published by Sirius Entertainment.

1/2	3.00
1/2/Variant	5.00
1	3.00
1/Black	8.00
1/Sharp	6.00
1/Kids	5.00
2	3.00
2/Mystery	6.00
3-6	3.00

Dawn 15th Anniversary Poster Book
Image, 2004

1 .... 5.00

Dawn 2004 Con Sketchbook One-Shot
Image, 2004

1 .... 3.00

Dawn: Convention Sketchbook
Image, 2002

1 .... 3.00

Dawn Convention Sketch Book
Image, 2003

1 .... 3.00

Dawn Hunter
AC

0 .... 3.00

Dawn of the Age of Apocalypse
Marvel

1 .... 9.00

Dawn of the Dead (George Romero's)
Idea & Design Works, 2004

1-3 .... 4.00

Dawn Tenth Anniversary Special
Sirius Entertainment, 1999

1 .... 3.00

Dawn: The Return of the Goddess
Sirius Entertainment, 1999

1	3.00
1/Ltd.	8.00
2-4	3.00

Dawn: Three Tiers
Image, 2003

1-6 .... 3.00

Day Brothers Present
Caliber

1-4 .... 3.00

Daydreamers
Marvel, 1997

1-3 .... 3.00

Day of Judgment
DC, 1999

Asmodel's a fallen angel, condemned to Hell after leading a failed siege on Heaven. That might have been his fate, had not the Demon Etrigan freed him and merged his spirit with the newly soulless Spectre, combining Asmodel's desire for vengeance with the Spectre's righteous judgment. Before long, there are demons running amuck on Earth, and Heaven may have reason to fear Asmodel's assault again, as the powerful being is determined to "destroy everything in God's image," using Earth as a stepping-stone to Heaven. Can The Justice League of America save the day? And, if The JLA fails, will the Sentinels of Magic, including Deadman, Zatanna, and The Phantom Stranger pick up the slack? One thing is clear: any battle that rages across Heaven and Hell is going to feature numerous players, living and dead, including a couple of shocking surprises.

Sharply written by Geoff Johns and dramatically drawn by Matt Smith, this five-issue super-heroes mini-series had lasting implications for a number of DC characters, including The Spectre.

1-5 .... 3.00

Day of Judgment Secret Files
DC, 1999

1 .... 5.00

Day of the Defenders
Marvel, 2001

1 .... 4.00

Day of Vengeance
DC, 2005

1	10.00
1/Variant	5.00

☛2nd printing
1/3rd variant 6.00
2 ....5.00
2/2nd variant 4.00
3-6...3.00

Day of Vengeance: Infinite Crisis Special
DC, 206

1 ....4.00

Days of Darkness
Apple, 1992

1-5...3.00

Days of Wrath
Apple, 1993

1-4...3.00

Daytona 500 Story
Vortex

1 ....2.00

Dazzle
Tokyopop, 2006

1 ....10.00

Dazzler
Marvel, 1981

1 ....5.00
2 ....2.00
3-42...1.00

DC 100-Page Super Spectacular: World's Greatest Super-Heroes
DC, 2004

1 ....7.00

DC Challenge
DC, 1985

1-12...2.00

DC Comics Presents
DC, 1978

This series might have been more aptly named "DC Comics Presents Superman and..." since each issue featured Superman in a new adventure, teamed up with popular DC characters such as Batgirl, Green Lantern, Robin, and Swamp Thing. Over the years, DC used this series to introduce several new characters, including Superwoman, Ambush Bug, and The Global Guardians.

The series also had the distinction of serving as the home for at least two 16-page preview issues of upcoming DC series. A New Teen Titans preview appeared in #26 and an Atari Force preview ran in #53. The series ended just after the events of Crisis on Infinite Earths and prior to the Superman revamp in 1986.

1 .... 9.00
1/Whitman 14.00
2 .... 7.00
2/Whitman 12.00
3 .... 4.00
3/Whitman 8.00
4 .... 2.00
4/Whitman 4.00
5 .... 2.00
6 .... 6.00
7-9 .... 2.00
9/Whitman 6.00
10 .... 2.00
10/Whitman 4.00
11 .... 2.00
11/Whitman 4.00
12 .... 2.00
12/Whitman 4.00
13-14 .... 2.00
14/Whitman 3.00
15 .... 2.00
15/Whitman 3.00
16 .... 2.00
16/Whitman 3.00
17-19 .... 2.00
19/Whitman 3.00
20 .... 2.00
20/Whitman 3.00
21 .... 2.00
21/Whitman 3.00
22 .... 2.00
22/Whitman 3.00
23-25 .... 2.00
26 .... 14.00
☛1st New Teen Titans
27 .... 3.00
28-41 .... 2.00
42-43 .... 1.00
44 .... 2.00
45-46 .... 1.00
47 .... 17.00
☛1st Masters Universe
48-50 .... 1.00
51 .... 6.00
52 .... 3.00
53-71 .... 1.00
72 .... 2.00
73-76 .... 1.00
77-78 .... 3.00
79-84 .... 1.00
85 .... 6.00
☛Moore Swamp Thing
86 .... 4.00
87-92 .... 1.00
93 .... 2.00
94-97 .... 1.00
Ann 1-4................................. 3.00

DC Comics Presents: Batman
DC, 2004

1 .... 3.00

DC Comics Presents: Green Lantern
DC, 2004

1 .... 3.00

DC Comics Presents: Hawkman
DC, 2004

1 .... 3.00

DC Comics Presents: JLA
DC, 2004

1 .... 3.00

DC Comics Presents: Mystery in Space
DC, 2004

1 .... 3.00

DC Comics Presents: Superman
DC, 2004

1 .... 3.00

DC Comics Presents: The Atom
DC, 2004

1 .... 3.00

DC Comics Presents: The Flash
DC, 2004

1 .... 3.00

DC Countdown
DC, 2005

1 .... 6.00
1/2nd 3.00

DC First: Batgirl/Joker
DC, 2002

1 .... 4.00

DC First: Flash/Superman
DC, 2002

1 .... 4.00

DC First: Green Lantern/ Green Lantern
DC, 2002

1 .... 4.00

DC First: Superman/Lobo
DC, 2002

1 .... 4.00

DC Graphic Novel
DC, 1985

1-5	6.00
6	7.00
7	6.00

DC/Marvel: All Access
DC, 1996

1-4	3.00

DC 100 Page
Super Spectacular
DC, 1971

4	175.00
5	350.00
☞Scarce	
5/2nd	7.00
6	150.00
7	60.00
8-9	75.00
10-13	60.00
14-17	45.00
18	30.00
19	24.00
20	35.00
21-22	22.00

DC One Million
DC, 1998

1	3.00
1/Variant	15.00
2-4	2.00
GS 1	5.00

DC Sampler
DC, 1983

1	2.00
2-3	1.00

DC Science Fiction
Graphic Novel
DC

1-7	6.00

DC Silver Age
Classics Action Comics
DC

In the early 1990s, DC reprinted several significant comics from the 1950s and 1960s as part of an overall Silver Age Classics line. The reprint of Action Comics #252 represented Supergirl's first appearance along with text material discussing the character's impact on the DC universe and Superman mythos.

Other reprints in the series included Showcase #4 (the first Silver Age Flash), Showcase #22 (the first Silver Age Green Lantern), Detective Comics #255 (the first Martian Manhunter), and Adventure Comics #247 (first Legion of Super-Heroes). One new issue was published with Sugar & Spike #99, which included text information from CBG Editor Maggie Thompson.

-- Brent

252	1.00

DC Silver Age Classics
Adventure Comics
DC

247	1.00

DC Silver Age Classics
Detective Comics
DC

225-327	1.00

DC Silver Age
Classics Green Lantern
DC

76	1.00

DC Silver Age Classics
House of Secrets
DC

92	1.00

DC Silver Age
Classics Showcase
DC

4-22	1.00

DC Silver Age
Classics Sugar & Spike
DC

99	2.00

DC Silver Age Classics
The Brave and the Bold
DC

28	1.00

DC Sneak Preview
DC

1	1.00

DC Special
DC, 1968

DC Special consisted of a series of double-sized issues spotlighting different parts of the DC universe. One issue, for example, might consist of adventure stories from the early days of The Brave and the Bold, featuring such characters as The Viking Prince, The Silent Knight, and Robin Hood. Other issues focused on topics ranging from strange sports tales to the origins of Golden Age heroes.

Virtually all of this material was reprinted from early DC comics, but at prices ranging from a quarter to 60 cents for many pages of reading, DC Special was a superior reading bargain.

1	60.00
2	50.00
3	35.00
4	25.00
5-14	20.00
15	16.00
16-28	10.00
29	12.00

DC Special
Blue Ribbon Digest
DC, 1980

1	5.00
2-5	4.00
6-17	3.00
18	4.00
19	3.00
20	7.00
21-23	3.00

DC Special Series
DC, 1977

1	10.00
2-5	7.00
6-8	6.00
9	16.00
10-14	6.00
15	8.00
16	20.00

☞Jonah Hex dies
17-18......................................5.00
19-20......................................6.00
21...12.00
☞1st Miller Batman
22-26......................................6.00
27..18.00

DC Special: The Return of Donna Troy
DC, 2005
1..8.00
☞Inf. Crisis tie
2..5.00
3-4..3.00

DC Spotlight
DC, 1985
1..1.00

DC Super-Stars
DC, 1976
1...10.00
2-3..5.00
4..2.00
5...10.00
6-7..2.00
8..4.00
9..2.00
10...5.00
11...7.00
12-13......................................2.00
14-15......................................4.00
16...3.00
17..16.00
☞1st new Huntress
18...2.00

DC: The New Frontier
DC, 2004
1-6..7.00

DC 2000
DC, 2000
1-2..7.00

DCU: Brave New World
DC, 2006
1..1.00

DCU Heroes Secret Files
DC, 1999
1..5.00

DCU Infinite Christmas Special
DC, 2007
1..5.00

DC Universe Christmas, A
DC, 2000
1...20.00

DC Universe Holiday Bash
DC, 1997
1.. 4.00
2-3.. 5.00

DC Universe: Trinity
DC, 1993
1-2.. 3.00

DCU Villains Secret Files
DC, 1999
1.. 5.00

D-Day
Avalon
1.. 3.00

DDP Quarterly
Devil's Due, 2006
1.. 1.00

Dead
Arrow, 1993
1-3.. 3.00

Dead
Arrow
1.. 3.00

Dead Air
Slave Labor
1.. 6.00

Dead@17
Viper, 2003
0.. 27.00
1.. 35.00
2.. 22.00
3.. 10.00
4.. 7.00

Dead@17: Blood of Saints
Viper, 2004
1-4.. 3.00

Dead@17: Protectorate
Viper, 2005
1-3.. 3.00

Dead@17: Revolution
Viper, 2004
1.. 4.00
2-4.. 3.00

Dead@17: Rough Cut
Viper, 2004
1-3.. 3.00

Deadbeats
Claypool, 1992

Deadbeats is a black-and-white vampire soap opera clearly out of the (pardon the expression) mold formed by Dark Shadows. It begins when four teens are found murdered in Mystic Grove, Conn. In time, it becomes clear that a band of vampires who call themselves the Deadbeats are responsible. Not long after the attack, they "recruit" a new member to their band, Michael-Evan Southland ("Southie"), the runaway son of the mayor of Mystic Grove. He, in turn, is made their leader, although it's clear that the original vampire crew has sinister designs that they are not letting him in on.

Opposing the Deadbeats are a motley band of vampire-hunters, including paranormal investigator Dr. V.V. Ralston (the Van Helsing -- or Dr. Julia Hoffman -- of the bunch) and brave-but-foolish kids Kirby Collier and Jo Isles.

The Deadbeats shines, due to its clear art, solid storytelling, and eclectic sensibility.

1.. 4.00
2-82...................................... 3.00

Deadbolt
Hall of Heroes, 1993
1.. 3.00

Dead Boys
London Night, 1996
1.. 4.00

Dead Clown
Malibu, 1993
1-3.. 3.00

Dead Corps(E)
DC, 1998
1-4.. 3.00

Dead End Crime Stories
Kirby Publications, 1949

1 ....180.00

Deadenders
DC, 2000

In a post-apocalyptic future, the citizens of New Bethlehem enjoy a life of luxury, complete with controlled weather, purified air, and artificially generated sunlight. They are the lucky minority, however. Most people are forever exiled behind the electrified fences of the outer sectors, forced to live in the squalor and perpetual darkness called New Bedlam. For them, life cannot get any worse.

But for Beezer, a disenchanted youth involved in minor drug deals and car-jackings, it's as if his whole world has shattered. In addition to the natural hardships of the outer sectors, Beezer gets dumped by his girlfriend and discovers he's adopted, all in the same evening. And, for some reason, he's suddenly wanted by the City Corps, licensed thugs for the inner-city government.

As his life spins out of control, Beezer begins suffering from strange and compelling visions of the world the way it was before the Cataclysm.

1-16...3.00

Dead Eyes Open
Slave Labor, 2005

1-2...3.00

Dead-Eye Western Comics
Hillman, 1948

1 ....85.00
2 ....60.00
3-4...40.00
5-12...30.00

Dead-Eye Western Comics (Vol. 2)
Hillman, 1951

1 .... 85.00
2 .... 60.00
3-4 .... 40.00
5-12 .... 30.00

Dead-Eye Western Comics (Vol. 3)
Hillman, 1953

1 .... 30.00

Deadface
Harrier, 1987

1 .... 5.00
2 .... 4.00
3-8... 3.00

Deadface: Doing the Islands with Bacchus
Dark Horse, 1991

1-3... 3.00

Deadface: Earth, Water, Air, and Fire
Dark Horse, 1992

1-4... 3.00

Deadfish Bedeviled
All American, 1990

1 .... 2.00

Dead Folks (Lansdales & Truman's)
Avatar, 2003

1-3... 4.00

Deadforce
Studio Noir, 1996

1 .... 3.00

Deadforce
Antarctic, 1999

1-2... 3.00
Ashcan 1 .... 1.00

Dead Grrrl: Dead at 21
Boneyard, 1998

So the main character of this series is dead. That doesn't mean she can't have a good time, especially if she happens to be a fun-loving vampire with a penchant for alcohol, drugs, lingerie, and sizable body counts. Thus, the "ultimate party vampire" scores some liquor, screws guys for fun-sometimes leaving them less than fully intact afterwards-and generally drinks, curses, and mutilates her way across the city. Mature readers? You bet. Soft-core eroticism this isn't. Be prepared for a heavy dose of severed and slashed appendages, among other body parts.

Published in black-and-white by Boneyard Press. Various writers and artists here, but it's all overseen by Hart D. Fisher.

1 .... 3.00

Dead Heat
All American

1 .... 2.00

Dead in the West
Dark Horse, 1993

1-2... 4.00

Dead Kid Adventures
Knight, 1998

1 .... 3.00

Dead Killer
Caliber

1 .... 3.00

Dead King: Burnt
Chaos, 1989

In the wake of Evil Ernie's destruction of the nation's capital, several factions are vying for control of the wasteland that was Washington D.C. Now, a ghoul called the Dead King-a creature possessed by the fallen angels of Hell-awakens and seeks the mysterious Mary, creating even more carnage inside the Beltway as he eliminates a military force that would try to control him to achieve their own agenda. This is violent, disturbing stuff, but delivered with a bit of a wink and a nudge from creator Brian Pulido, writer Hart Fisher, and artist David Brewer.

1-4 .... 3.00

Deadliest Creature on Earth...Man
Nicotat, 1989

1 .... 2.00

Deadliest Heroes of Kung Fu
Marvel

1 .... 5.00

Deadline
Deadline, 1988

1-5 .... 6.00
6-58 .... 5.00

Deadline
Marvel, 2002

1-4 .... 3.00

Deadline USA
Dark Horse, 1991

1-8 .... 4.00

Deadly Duo
Image, 1994

1-3 .... 3.00

Deadly Duo
Image, 1995

1-4 .... 3.00

Deadly Foes of Spider-Man
Marvel, 1991

1-4 .... 2.00

Deadly Hands of Kung Fu
Marvel, 1974

1 .... 30.00
2 .... 8.00
3-5 .... 6.00
6-10 .... 5.00
11-19 .... 4.00
20 .... 7.00
21-30 .... 3.00
31 .... 6.00
32-33 .... 3.00
Special 1 .... 4.00

Deadman
DC, 1985

1-7 .... 3.00

Deadman
DC, 1986

1-4 .... 2.00

Deadman
DC, 2002

1-9 .... 3.00

Deadman
DC, 2006

1-5 .... 3.00

Deadman: Dead Again
DC, 2001

1-5 .... 3.00

Deadman: Exorcism
DC

1-2 .... 5.00

Deadman: Love After Death
DC, 1989

1-2 .... 4.00

Dead Man Walking
Boneyard

1 .... 3.00

Dead Meat
Fleetway-Quality

1-3 .... 3.00

Dead Men Tell No Tales
Arcana, 2005

1-3 .... 4.00

Dead Muse
Fantagraphics

1 .... 4.00

Dead of Night
Marvel, 1973

Dead of Night was a deservedly obscure horror/mystery title from Marvel in the mid-1970s. It featured a mix of reprints of old Atlas monster stories from Strange Tales, Tales of Suspense and others, including many by Bill Everett, Steve Ditko, and Dick Ayers, plus new stories by artists and writers Marvel may have been trying out for other, more visible assignments. Issue #11 featured the debut of the Scarecrow, a weird mystery hero who later went on to headline in Marvel Chillers.

-- Rob Salkowitz

1 .... 35.00
2 .... 12.00
3-10 .... 8.00
11 .... 16.00

Dead or Alive: A Cyberpunk Western
Dark Horse, 1998

1-4 .... 3.00

Deadpan
Slave Labor, 2006

1 .... 6.00

Deadpool
Marvel, 1994

1-4 .... 3.00

Deadpool
Marvel, 1988

-1-0 .... 2.00
1 .... 4.00
2-4 .... 3.00
5-10 .... 2.00
11 .... 4.00
12-22 .... 2.00
23 .... 3.00
24 .... 2.00
25 .... 3.00
26-69 .... 2.00
Ann 1998 .... 3.00

Deadpool Team-Up
Marvel, 1998

1 .... 3.00

Deadpool: The Circle Chase
Marvel, 1993

1 .... 3.00
2-4 .... 2.00

Deadshot
DC, 1988

Floyd Lawton, aka Deadshot, first appeared in Batman #59 (Jun 50). Like Bruce Wayne, Lawton is raised in a rich family which is destroyed when his parents are gunned down by criminals. Unlike

Wayne, however, Lawton's rage leads him to a life of crime.

In a story called "The Man Who Replaced Batman," he appears in a black mask and tuxedo and began using his marksmanship skills to round up criminals. He figures if he can upstage and get rid of Batman, he'll then be free to control Gotham City's underworld. Batman stops him, however, and Deadshot disappears until 1977. He then reappears in his current costume, fighting -- and losing to -- Batman several times. In jail he is approached by Amanda Waller and Rick Flag in Legends #2, recruiting Lawton to join The Suicide Squad. But it seems Lawton agreed out of a desire more to get killed than to escape jail. This mini-series finally begins to explain.

1-4..2.00

Deadshot
DC, 2005
1-5..3.00

Deadtime Stories
New Comics, 1987
1...2.00

Deadwalkers
Aircel, 1991
1/A-4 ....3.00

Dead Who Walk
Realistic Comics, 1952
1..180.00

Deadworld
Arrow, 1986
1...6.00
2-26..3.00

Deadworld
Caliber, 1993
1...4.00
2-15..3.00

Deadworld
Image, 2005
1-6...4.00

Deadworld Archives
Caliber
1-3...3.00

Deadworld: Bits and Pieces
Caliber
1...3.00

Deadworld Chronicles: Plague
Caliber
1...3.00

Deadworld: Daemonstorm
Caliber
1 ....4.00

Deadworld: Necropolis
Caliber
1 ....4.00

Deadworld: To Kill a King
Caliber
1 ....3.00
1/Ltd. 6.00
2-3...3.00

Deal with the Devil
Alias, 2005
1-5...3.00

Dear Beatrice Fairfax
Standard, 1950
5-9......................................100.00

Dear Julia
Black Eye, 1997
1-4...4.00

Dear Lonely Heart
Artful, 1951
1 ....70.00
2-5...40.00
6-8...36.00

Dear Lonely Hearts
Comic Media, 1953
1 ....40.00
2-8...25.00

Dearly Beloved
Ziff-Davis, 1952
1 ....75.00

DearS
Tokyopop, 2005
1-6...10.00

Death3
Marvel, 1993

Set in a flawed future, this four-part series exhibits strong parallels

to Mary Shelley's Frankenstein. Just as in that classic, this story is told through the letters and journal of the scientist who creates a half-man, half-monster. There's one chilling difference, however. Whereas Dr. Frankenstein sought to destroy his creation in the name of morality, the doctor in this case, Evelyn Necker, the creator of Death's Head II, has no conscience whatsoever. Instead, she creates cyborgs to perfect her creation, and kills for the needed human parts.

It's yet another Marvel UK title unnecessarily brought over and relabeled for the North American market in the early 1990s glut.

1 ....3.00
2-4..2.00

Death & Candy
Fantagraphics, 1999
1-3..4.00
4..5.00

Death & Taxes: The Real Costs of Living
Parody
1 ....3.00

Deathangel
Lightning, 1997
1/A-1/D 3.00

Death: At Death's Door
DC, 2003
1 ....10.00

Deathblow
Image, 1993

Commander Cray of the S.O.G. (Special Operations Group) is Deathblow. He's one of the deadliest men alive-a virtual killing machine who does America's dirty work at home and abroad.

Many have tried - and failed - to kill him over the years. But now, inoperable cancer of the brain is about to do what no man could. Knowing that his days are numbered brings a new recklessness - and a certain penitence to this dealer of death.

Issues of this title also included a backup book: Cybernary. There, a dark group of man-machines held court in their own shadowy underworld.

0-3	3.00
4-9	2.00
10-15	3.00
16	2.00
16/Variant	4.00
17	3.00
17/A	4.00
18-28	3.00
28/Variant	4.00
29	3.00

Deathblow
DC, 2007

1-2/Variant	3.00

Deathblow: Byblows
WildStorm, 1999

1-3	3.00

Deathblow/Wolverine
Image, 1996

1-2	3.00

Death By Chocolate
Sleeping Giant, 1996

1	3.00

Death By Chocolate: Sir Geoffrey and the Chocolate Car
Sleeping Giant

1	3.00

Death By Chocolate: The Metabolators
Sleeping Giant

1	3.00

Death Crazed Teenage Superheroes
Arf! Arf!

1-2	2.00

Death Dealer
Verotik, 1995

1	6.00
2-4	7.00

Death Dreams of Dracula
Apple

1-4	3.00

Death Gallery, A
DC

1	3.00

Death Hawk
Adventure, 1988

Death Hawk is a sort of space mercenary who will do jobs for just about anyone, as long as the price is right. To his chagrin, however, he does have something of a conscience that prevents him from helping the wrong people.

He's accompanied on these missions by his constant companion, a symbiotic protoplasm-creature named Cyke (who, despite appearances, often seems to possess more good sense than Hawk). As this series begins, Death Hawk is sent to retrieve an ancient artifact of unknown power. Unfortunately, he's far from the only one interested in this artifact, and his competition includes everything from crooked thugs to a dangerous beauty armed with a nerve blaster.

This black-and-white series was created by Mark Ellis and Adam Hughes, with painted covers by Dave Dorman (who would later become famous for his work on Aliens).

1-3	2.00

Death Hunt
Eternity

1	2.00

Death Jr.
Image, 2005

1-3	5.00

Death Jr.
Image, 2006

1-2	5.00

Deathlok
Marvel, 1990

1-4	4.00

Deathlok
Marvel, 1991

1	3.00
2-34	2.00
Ann 1-2	3.00
Special 1-4	2.00

Deathlok
Marvel, 1999

1-5	2.00

Deathmark
Lightning, 1994

1	3.00

Deathmask
Future, 2003

1-3	3.00

Deathmate
Image, 1993

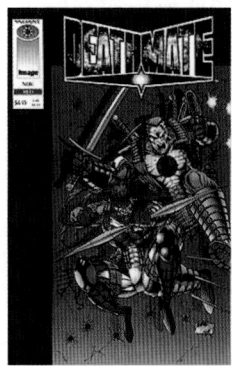

Deathmate combines the talents and comics universes of Image and Valiant for the first time. The origin of this great crossover begins in 2062. Solar, Man of the Atom, had long been keeping his lover, Gayle, young and alive using his powers. He finally agrees to let her die, but in his grief over the loss he suffers a schizoid episode, actually splitting into two separate beings. He then enters the place called Unreality where he encounters WildC.A.T.s' Void. Living vessels of the energy from two different worlds, the two are drawn to each other - even though joining together might spell doom for the entire universe.

Back in 1993, the Geomancer Geoff awakes from a dream to find the world changed. Valiant characters such as Bloodshot and Shadowman exist side by side with Youngblood. But this new world has no future - it will be destroyed by the deadly mating of Solar and Void, 70 years from now...

In addition to its use of colors to denote issues rather than numbers, the series is also noteworthy for the first appearance of Gen13.

1	3.00
1/Gold	4.00
2	3.00
2/Gold	6.00
3	5.00
3/Gold	6.00
4	5.00
4/Gold	6.00
5	5.00
5/Gold	6.00
6	3.00
6/Gold	4.00
Ashcan 1	1.00

Death Metal
Marvel, 1994

1-4	2.00

Death Metal vs. Genetix
Marvel, 1993

1-2	3.00

Death Note
Viz, 2005

1-2	8.00

Death of Angel Girl
Angel

1	3.00

Death of Antisocialman
Not Available

1-10	1.00

Death of Hari Kari
Blackout, 1997

0	3.00

Death of Lady Vamprè
Blackout

1	3.00

Death of Stupidman
Parody

1	4.00

Death of Superbabe
Spoof, 1993

1	4.00

Death of Vampirella
Harris, 1997

1-1/Variant	15.00

Death Race 2020
Cosmic, 1995

1-5	3.00

Death Rattle
Kitchen Sink, 1985

1-18	2.00

Death Rattle
Kitchen Sink, 1995

1/2-6	3.00

Deathrow
Heroic, 1993

Recent years have seen an explosion in the number of "heroes" whose names begin with "Death," "Dead," or "Blood": Death's Head II, Deathblow, Deadpool, Bloodshot, Bloodfire...the list goes on and on ad nauseum. Independent publisher Blue Comet Press had a great chance to parody this trend with Deathrow, but instead chose to play it seriously.

As a result, Deathrow is pretty much what you'd expect: lots of big guns, "bitchin'" cyborg killing machines, and nonstop, shameless violence. Deathrow is a British cyborg assassin who had built a big reputation for himself overseas. L.A. drug lords had recently brought him over to the states to help them secure their territory, and Deathrow had done a shockingly effective job of wiping out the competition. But the other drug dealers weren't about to sit still and be wiped out. Instead, they constructed their own cyborg, named X-187 to take on Deathrow.

1	3.00

Death's-Head
Crystal, 1987

1	2.00

Death's Head
Marvel, 1988

1-10	2.00

Death's Head II (Vol. 1)
Marvel, 1992

1	3.00
1/2nd-4	2.00

Death's Head II (Vol. 2)
Marvel, 1992

1-13	2.00
14	3.00
15-16	2.00

Death's Head II & the Origin of Die-Cut
Marvel, 1993

1	3.00
2	2.00

Death's Head II Gold
Marvel

1	4.00

Death Shrike
Brainstorm, 1993

1	3.00

Deathsnake
Fantagraphics, 1994

1-2	3.00

Deathstroke the Terminator
DC, 1991

Trained as a soldier, Slade Wilson volunteered to imbibe an experimental formula designed to help resist enemy truth serums. That formula, a derivative of A.C.T.H., sent Slade into a screaming rampage, snapping steel bonds that held him into place. He was soon sedated, however, and lapsed into a coma that lasted months. When he awoke again, he had the powers, agility, and healing factor that make him Deathstroke the Terminator.

First appearing in the pages of the New Teen Titans, Deathstroke eventually crossed over into this, his first solo series.

0	2.00
1	3.00
1/2nd-49	2.00
50	4.00
51-60	2.00
Ann 1-4	4.00

Death Talks About Life
DC

1	2.00

Death:
The High Cost of Living
DC, 1993
1	3.00
1/Platinum	6.00
2-3	3.00
3/A	4.00

Death:
The Time of Your Life
DC, 1996
1	4.00
2-3	3.00

Death Valley
Charlton, 1953
1	40.00
2-14	20.00

Death Warmed Over
Cat-Head
1	3.00

Deathwatch
Harrier, 1987
1	2.00

Deathwind
Artline
1	3.00

Deathwish
Milestone, 1994
1-4	3.00

Deathworld
Adventure, 1990

Imagine a planet where every living creature is trying to kill you. A planet with twice Earth's gravity where the climate goes from arctic to tropical in a single day and the beaches offer 30-foot tides and volcanic activity. A planet where plants and animals are armor-plated, poisonous, and fang-mouthed. This is the planet Pyrrus, also known as Deathworld.

Now the man who can't lose, a psionic gambler named Jason dinAlt, has taken the ultimate roll of the dice. He has traveled to Pyrrus to experience Deathworld firsthand. If he can survive the trip from the ship to the adaptation clinic, he'll be gambling with his life every minute of the day.

This mini-series is adapted from the novel by Harry Harrison.
1-4	3.00

Deathworld Book II
Adventure, 1991
1-4	3.00

Deathworld Book III
Adventure, 1991
1-4	3.00

Death Wreck
Marvel, 1994
1-4	2.00

Debbie Dean, Career Girl
Civil Service, 1945
1	60.00

Debbie Does Comics
Aircel, 1992
1	3.00

Debbie Does Dallas
Aircel, 1991
1	3.00
1/3D	4.00
1/2nd-18	3.00

Debbi's Dates
DC, 1969
1	30.00
2-5	18.00
6	30.00
7-11	18.00

Decade
Dark Horse
1	13.00

Decade of Dark Horse, A
Dark Horse, 1996
1-4	3.00

Decapitator
(Randy Bowen's...)
Dark Horse, 1998
1-4	3.00

Deception
Image, 1999
1-3	3.00

Decimation: House of M
- The Day After
Marvel, 2006
1	4.00

Decorator
Fantagraphics
1	3.00

Decoy
Penny-Farthing, 1999

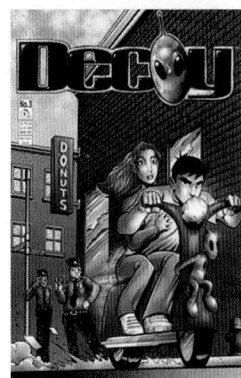

Bobby Luck is a rookie cop trying to make a name for himself, but despite his best efforts, he's got a lot to learn. He might learn it from his tough-as-nails female partner, Tessa Moreno, if he weren't such a natural loner. But, just as Bobby is about to die as the victim of a solo bust-gone-wrong, he's saved by a new partner: one from another planet. Now, they need each other to survive.

Decoy -- a cute, pudgy, green alien -- is stranded on Earth, when his disapproving and more aggressive brethren abandon him. Decoy is not completely helpless in this new world -- he's a shapeshifter -- and, whether he's morphing into a bouncing deer or turning his hand into a gun, he's going to be just the sort of partner Bobby Luck needs, whether Luck likes it or not.

1-4	3.00

Decoy:
Storm of the Century
Penny-Farthing, 2002
1-4	3.00

Dee Dee
Fantagraphics, 1996
1-7	3.00

Deep
Marvel, 1977
1	2.00

Deep 3D Comix
Kitchen Sink
1	3.00

Deep Black
Chaos!, 1997
1/A-1/B	2.00

Deep Dimension Horror
AC
1 ....3.00

Deepest Dimension
Revolutionary, 1993
1-2 ....3.00

Deep Girl
Ariel Bordeaux
1-2 ....3.00
3 ....2.00
4-5 ....3.00

Deep Sleeper
Oni, 2004
1-2 ....4.00

Deep Sleeper
Image, 2004
3-4 ....3.00

Deep Terror
Avalon

This anthology of seafaring horror stories sets sail with a classic horror-comics feel, as the tales are introduced and narrated by an array of creepy characters. The sense of foreboding is compounded by the stark and moody black-and-white art, heavy with shadows. Whether it's a yarn about a man who managed to die on both the Titanic and the Lusitania, or about the supernatural link between a pirate and his treasure -- one that calls him from beyond the grave -- this comic book shows that ghosts, and the evil that drives them on, are not things solely locked to the shore.

1 ....3.00

Dee Vee
Dee Vee, 1997
1-7 ....3.00

DefCon 4
Image, 1996
1/A-5 .... 3.00

Defenders
Dell, 1962
1 .... 26.00
2 .... 16.00

Defenders
Marvel, 1972
1 .... 90.00
2 .... 35.00
3 .... 30.00
4-5 .... 26.00
6-7 .... 16.00
8 .... 25.00
9 .... 16.00
10 .... 55.00
☛Avengers War
11 .... 15.00
12-13 .... 9.00
14-16 .... 10.00
17-20 .... 7.00
21-24 .... 6.00
25-29 .... 7.00
30-33 .... 4.00
34 .... 5.00
34/30¢ 20.00
35 .... 5.00
35/30¢ 20.00
36 .... 5.00
36/30¢ 20.00
37 .... 5.00
37/30¢ 20.00
38-38/30¢ 5.00
39-47/Whitman 4.00
48 .... 15.00
48/Whitman 5.00
48/35¢-49 .... 4.00
49/35¢ 15.00
50-50/Whitman 4.00
50/35¢ 15.00
51-51/Whitman 4.00
51/35¢ 15.00
52-52/Whitman 4.00
52/35¢ 15.00
53-62/Whitman 4.00
63-63/Whitman 5.00
64-92 .... 4.00
93-100 .... 3.00
101-152 .... 2.00
Ann 1 .... 12.00

Defenders
Marvel, 2001
1 .... 3.00
2-11 .... 2.00
12 .... 4.00

Defenders
Marvel, 2005
1 .... 5.00
2-5 .... 3.00

Defenders of Dynatron City
Marvel, 1992

From the creative minds behind Lucasarts comes the super-hero team of the future-Marvel Comics' Defenders of Dynatron City. Revolving around bizarre, otherworldly characters, the Star Wars guru's venture into comics takes a stab at the often "hit and miss" market of all ages humor.

Set in the futuristic Dynatron City -- "proud symbol of the atomic age where mutation is a way of life" -- six oddball heroes battle to keep their metropolis safe from the bumbling clutches of evil. Ms. Megawatt, Jet Headstrong, Buzzsaw Girl, Monkey-Kid, Toolbox, and Radium Dog (brought into "super-herodom" by mutagenic elements found in the popular Proto Cola soft drink) battle not-so-scary villains issue after issue in a series of self-contained stories. Injected with more slapstick comedy than action, each issue's conclusion can be compared to one of two classic Scooby Doo endings: a) the villain is caught after a fortunate mishap, or b) after being caught, the Defenders befriend the villain because -- he's not such a bad guy, after all.

1-6 .... 1.00

Defenders of the Earth
Marvel, 1987
1-4 .... 1.00

Defenseless Dead
Adventure, 1991
1-3 .... 3.00

Defex
Devil's Due, 2004
1 .... 5.00
1/Variant 1.00
2-6 .... 3.00

Defiance
Image, 2001
1 ....4.00
2-8...3.00

Defiant Genesis
Defiant, 1993
1 ....1.00

Definition
Slave Labor, 1997
1 ....13.00

Deicide
DC, 2004
1 ....15.00

Deity
Image, 1997
0 ....6.00
0/A-3 ....3.00
3/A...4.00
4-6/A 3.00

Deity
Image, 1998
1-Ashcan 1..............................3.00

Deity: Requiem
Image, 2005
1 ....7.00

Deity: Revelations
Image, 1999

In just a few short months, Jamie Chin's life changed dramatically. First of all, she found out that she's Deity, a super-powered cosmic goddess; and then she saved her guardians—Diamond Diaz and Tommy Lone—from enigmatic forces called the Darkness and the Light. Now Jamie works at mastering her formidable powers, but why may her friends and protectors have to kill her? More good times from writer/artist Karl Altstaetter.

1-4...3.00

Deja Vu
Fantaco, 2000
1 .... 3.00

Deja Vu
Radio, 2000
1 .... 3.00

Delia Charm
Red Menace
1-2.. 3.00

Delirium
Metro

Delirium is a hit-and-miss science fiction anthology book. Most stories contain what may pass for humor and at least one science fictional element (however, not one that hasn't been used better the first 300 times). Features include one-page gags, alien abduction stories, prose gag pages, and funny animal stories. The artwork is all over the map, varying from extremely good to impressionistic sketches. Unfortunately, Delirium contains nothing to differentiate it from hundreds of better anthology comics.

1 .... 2.00

Deliverer
Zion, 1994
1 .... 3.00

Della Vision
Atlas, 1955
1 .... 50.00
2-3... 40.00

Dell Giants
Dell, 1959
21 .... 105.00
22 .... 80.00
23 .... 90.00
24-25 .... 75.00
26 .... 140.00
☞Carl Barks art
27-28 .... 75.00

29 .... 90.00
30 .... 75.00
31 .... 90.00
32 .... 65.00
33 .... 85.00
34 .... 65.00
35 .... 95.00
36-37 .... 80.00
38-39 .... 85.00
40 .... 60.00
41 .... 85.00
42 .... 70.00
43 .... 115.00
44 .... 85.00
45-46 .... 55.00
47 .... 60.00
48 .... 125.00
☞1st Flintstones
49 .... 75.00
50 .... 65.00
51-54 .... 40.00
55 .... 60.00

Dell Junior Treasury
Dell, 1955
1 .... 50.00
2-3... 40.00
4 .... 35.00
5 .... 40.00
6-10 .... 35.00

Delta Squadron
Anderpol
1 .... 2.00

Delta Tenn
Entertainment, 1987
1-10 .... 2.00

Delta, the Ultimate Difference
Apex One, 1997
1 .... 2.00
2 .... 3.00

Delta-Wave
Miller, 1992
1 .... 3.00

Demented Pervert
Print Mint
1-2 .... 3.00

Demented: Scorpion Child
DMF, 2000
1-5 .... 3.00

Demi's Wild Kingdom Adventure
Opus, 2000
1 .... 10.00

Demi the Demoness
Rip Off, 1993
1-5 .... 3.00
6-Special 1 .... 6.00

Demolition Man
DC, 1993

1-4..2.00

Demon
DC, 1972

1	30.00
2	12.00
3-4	10.00
5-9	9.00
10-11	7.00
12-13	10.00
14-16	7.00

Demon
DC, 1987

1-4..2.00

Demon
DC, 1990

0	2.00
1	4.00
2-3	3.00
4-10	2.00
11	3.00
12-18	2.00
19	3.00
20-42	2.00
43	4.00
44-45	3.00
46-49	3.00
50	3.00
51	2.00
52-54	3.00
55-58	2.00
Ann 1	3.00
Ann 2	12.00

☛1st Hitman

Demon Beast Invasion
CPM, 1996

1..3.00

Demon Beast Invasion: The Fallen
CPM, 1998

1-2..3.00

Demonblade
New Comics

1..2.00

Demon Dreams
Pacific, 1984

Demon Dreams highlights the work of Arthur Suydam. A veteran of DC's House of Secrets, Suydam later went on to create The New Adventures of Cholly and Flytrap, a story about two wandering adventurers in a post-apocalyptic world. He is, perhaps, best known for his work in Heavy Metal, from which many of these stories are adapted.

Suydam's stories are classic adult horror, vaguely reminiscent of H.P. Lovecraft. Among the best in Demon Dreams is "Bad Breath," the tale of a man with chronic halitosis who finds a cure -- and a sure-fire way to woo women -- when a demon springs to life within him.

1-2.. 2.00

Demon Dreams of Dr. Drew
AC

1.. 3.00

Demon Driven Out
DC, 2003

1-6.. 3.00

Demongate
Sirius, 1996

1-9.. 3.00

Demon Gun
Crusade, 1996

1-3.. 3.00

Demon Hunter
Atlas-Seaboard, 1975

1.. 5.00

Demon-Hunter
Atlas-Seaboard, 1975

1.. 2.00

Demon Hunter
Aircel, 1989

1-4 .... 2.00

Demon Hunter
Davdez, 1998

1 .... 3.00

Demonic Toys
Eternity, 1992

1-4 .... 3.00

Demonique
London Night, 1994

1-4 .... 3.00

Demonique: Angel of Night
London Night, 1997

1 .... 3.00

Demon Ororon
Tokyopop, 2004

1 .... 10.00

Demon Realm
Medeia

Representing yet another example of self-publishing at its finest, Demon Realm, the ongoing series from Medeia Press, bursts onto the scene. Over ten years in the making, the stories that grace the title's black and white pages are the brainchild of series creator and self-proclaimed comic book lover Gregory Skopis.

Beginning nearly 5000 years ago and stretching into the world of today, Demon Realm boasts the story of Earth's unsung defenders. Contrary to what you may have learned while studying mythology, most of the Greek gods lost their lives in a spectacular battle to expel an army of vicious demons from this plane of existence. Left to guard the flame (or doorway into the "demon realm") is Hercules and his heirs-each with double the strength and resilience of their forefather. Using this as its jumping point, the book covers the generation spanning battle of good versus evil, as the half-god's descendants battle to keep this dimension safe from the clutches of darkness.

0 ....3.00

Demons & Dark Elves
Weirdworx

1 ....3.00

Demon's Blood
Odyssey

1 ....2.00

Demonslayer
Image, 1999

1-3...3.00

Demonslayer
Next

0 ....3.00

Demonslayer
Image, 2000

1-3...3.00

Demon's Tails
Adventure, 1993

1-4...3.00

Demon Warrior
Eastern, 1987

1-6...2.00

DemonWars: Eye for an Eye (RA Salvatore's)
CrossGen, 2003

1-5...3.00

DemonWars: Trial by Fire (R.A. Salvatore's...)
CrossGen, 2003

1-5...3.00

Demonwish
Pocket Change, 1995

1 ....3.00

Den
Fantagor

1-10...3.00

Denizens of Deep City
Kitchen Sink, 1988

1-9...2.00

Dennis the Menace
Fawcett, 1953

1	350.00
2	125.00
3	85.00
4-5	70.00
6-10	60.00
11-20	45.00
21-30	35.00
31-40	25.00
41-50	18.00

51-70	14.00
71-90	10.00
91-100	6.00
101-120	4.00
121-140	3.00
141-166	2.00

Dennis the Menace (Giants)
Fawcett, 1955

2-6/A	60.00
7-12	50.00
13-20	35.00
21-29	22.00
30-40	18.00
41-50	15.00
51-60	12.00
61-75	10.00
Special 1	95.00
Special 2	80.00

Dennis the Menace
Marvel, 1981

1-13...2.00

Dennis the Menace and His Dog Ruff
Fawcett, 1961

1 ....22.00

Dennis the Menace and his Friends
Fawcett, 1969

This series reprinted earlier Dennis the Menace adventures, particularly those involving his various friends: his dog Ruff, best pal Joey, arch-nemesis Margaret (she's a girrrrlll!), and his next-door neighbor Mr. Wilson. The strips here were "reprinted by popular demand," a claim which is true, although it stretches things a bit insomuch as it recognizes the immense popularity of the title character.

Near the series' end in the late 1970s, it shrank in size to digest format, but increased the page count to 148 pages.

1-4	12.00
5	8.00
6-10	5.00
11-20	4.00
21-46	3.00

Dennis the Menace and his Pal Joey
Fawcett, 1961

1 ....42.00

Dennis the Menace Big Bonus Series
Fawcett, 1980

10-11 ....3.00

Dennis the Menace Bonus Magazine Series
Fawcett, 1970

76-90	8.00
91-120	7.00
121-150	6.00
151-170	4.00
171-194	3.00

Dennis the Menace Comics Digest
Marvel

1	20.00
2-3	1.00

Dennis the Menace Pocket Full of Fun
Fawcett, 1969

1	25.00
2-10	20.00
11-16	15.00
17-50	10.00

Dental Hygiene Funnies
Slave Labor

In only ten pages this black-and-white mini-comic one-shot shows both the comic and tragic sides of the tooth fairy. The first story recounts the antics of two brothers, one with a loose tooth, the other determined to help pull the tooth so they can split the take from the tooth fairy.

The second story gives a much grimmer view of the "quarters for dentition" concept. A man down on his luck is robbed of the few dollars he had remaining, and the rent is due for his pay-by-the-week apartment.

Haunted by thoughts of winding up on the street he comes to the conclusion that the tooth fairy and a pair of pliers may be his only hope.

1 ....1.00

Depressor
Being
1 ....3.00

Deputy Dawg
Gold Key, 1965
1 ....55.00

Deputy Dawg Presents Dinky Duck and Hashimoto-San
Gold Key, 1965
1 ....30.00

Der Countess
Avalon Communications, 1996
1 ....3.00

Der Vandale
Innervision
1-3 ....3.00

Descendants of Toshin
Arrow, 1999
1 ....3.00

Descending Angels
Millennium
1 ....3.00

Desert Dawn
E.C., 1935
1 ....500.00

Desert Peach
Thoughts & Images, 1988
1 ....10.00
2 ....6.00
3-6 ....4.00
7-16 ....3.00
17 ....4.00
18 ....3.00
19-22 ....5.00
23-30 ....3.00

Desert Storm Journal
Apple, 1991

In the tradition of his Vietnam Journal, writer Don Lomax presents an insider's look at America's 1991 conflict in the Persian Gulf. Mixed with factual accounts of Operation Desert Storm is the story of Scott "Journal" Neithammer, Lomax's fictional journalist, known for his daring reports from the front lines. Neithammer's willingness to put his life on the line in combat situations earned him the respect of the soldiers he wrote about. But Vietnam took its toll on "Journal," just as it did to many veterans of that war. He's been living in seclusion for years, and wants no part of the Iraqi situation, but the discovery that his own daughter is in Israel once again sends Neithammer into the midst of war.

Lomax manages to stuff a veritable encyclopedia of facts about the conflict and the military technology involved into his story without sacrificing readability.

1-8 ....3.00

Desert Storm: Send Hussein to Hell!
Innovation, 1991
1 ....3.00

Desert Streams
DC
1 ....6.00

Desolation Jones
DC, 2005
1-8 ....3.00

Despair
Print Mint, 1969
1 ....10.00

Desperado
Lev Gleason, 1948
1 ....85.00
2 ....45.00
3-8 ....34.00

Desperadoes
Image, 1997
1-5 ....3.00

Desperadoes: Banners of Gold
Idea & Design Works, 2004
1-5 ....4.00

Desperadoes: Epidemic!
DC, 1999
1 ....6.00

Desperadoes: Quiet of the Grave
DC, 2001
1-5 ....3.00

Desperate Times
Aaargh, 2000
1-3 ....3.00
4 ....2.00

Desperate Times
Image, 1998
0 ....4.00
1-4 ....3.00

Desperate Times
Image, 2004
1 ....3.00

Desso-Lette
Follis Brothers, 1997
1 ....3.00

Destination Moon
Export, 1950
1 ....240.00

Destiny: A Chronicle of Deaths Foretold
DC, 1997
1-3 ....6.00

Destiny Angel
Dark Fantasy
1 ....4.00

Destroy!!
Eclipse, 1986
1 ....5.00
1/3D 3.00

Destroy All Comics
Slave Labor, 1994
1-5 ....4.00

Destroyer Duck
Eclipse, 1982

When Steve Gerber set out to regain ownership of his creation, cult hero Howard the Duck, he let loose with -- what else? -- another duck. Destroyer Duck, has mastered the art of warfare, struggled through the ivory towers of academia, and conquered crime in his own neighborhood. And when his best friend -- a familiar duck, horribly abused, used and tortured in our world -- comes back, Destroyer Duck visits us to wreak vengeance on the selfish, money-grubbing corporation that took advantage of his friend.

Eclipse published this series, which also included short satirical pieces by Mark Evanier, Martin Pasko, and Sergio Aragones. Aragones' piece is especially notable for the first appearance of Groo the Wanderer.

1	4.00
2-7	2.00

Destroyer (Magazine)
Marvel, 1989

1-8	3.00

Destroyer
Marvel, 1991

1	2.00

Destroyer
Marvel, 1991

1-4	2.00

Destroyer
Valiant, 1995

0	4.00
0/$2.50	10.00

Destructor
Atlas-Seaboard, 1975

1	10.00
2	7.00
3-4	5.00

Detective
Sunset Strips

1-12	3.00

Detective, The: Chronicles of Max Faccioni
Caliber

1	3.00

Detective Comics
DC, 206

The legend of Batman started in Detective Comics #27 (May 39). It was there that the remarkable young Bruce Wayne, heir to the Wayne fortune, saw his parents gunned down by a mugger. The experience changed him forever, and, when he was grown, he began leading a double life. By day, he is an idle playboy, but by night he patrols Gotham City as Batman, a caped crusader who takes on the aspect of a bat in order to frighten criminals.

In the more than 60 years that have followed, Detective Comics has been the flagship title of DC's comic line. Indeed, it is from Detective Comics that DC (formerly National Periodical Publications) derives its name.

0	3.00
1	80,000.00
2	18,250.00
3	10,800.00
4-5	6,850.00
6-7	4,450.00
8	6,500.00
9-17	4,350.00
18	5,000.00
19	4,150.00
20	6,300.00
21	3,250.00
22	3,950.00
23-26	3,250.00
27	225,000.00

☛1st Batman

27/2nd	9.00
28	25,000.00

☛2nd Batman

29	35,000.00

☛3rd Batman

30	7,500.00
31	27,500.00

☛Batman vs. the Monk

32	6,000.00
33	50,000.00

☛Batman origin

34	7,500.00
35	10,000.00
36-37	6,500.00
38	57,500.00

☛1st Robin

39	6,000.00
40	6,500.00
41	4,000.00
42-45	3,000.00
46-50	2,000.00
51-57	1,750.00
58	4,750.00

☛1st Penguin

59	2,000.00
60	1,750.00
61	1,500.00
62	2,250.00
63	1,750.00
64	5,000.00

☛1st Boy Commandos

65	2,250.00
66	4,000.00

☛1st Two-Face

67	2,000.00
68-69	1,750.00
70-71	1,500.00
72-75	1,250.00
76	1,500.00
77-79	1,000.00
80	1,250.00
81-83	1,000.00
84	900.00
85	1,250.00
86-90	900.00
91	1,000.00
92-98	800.00
99	950.00
100	1,000.00
101	700.00
102	950.00
103-108	625.00
109	850.00
110-113	625.00
114	800.00
115-117	625.00
118	825.00
119	600.00
120	800.00

☛Penguin app.

121	600.00
122	1,225.00
123	600.00
124	800.00
125-127	600.00
128	800.00
129-130	600.00
131-136	525.00
137	675.00
138	925.00

☛Robotman origin

139	500.00
140	4,000.00
☞1st Riddler	
141	575.00
142	1,250.00
☞2nd Riddler	
143-148	575.00
149	675.00
150	550.00
151	600.00
152-155	525.00
156	625.00
157-160	500.00
161-167	525.00
168	3,750.00
☞Joker origin	
169-170	500.00
171	700.00
172-176	500.00
177-179	400.00
180	450.00
181-186	400.00
187	425.00
188-189	400.00
190	600.00
191-192	400.00
193	450.00
194-199	400.00
200	575.00
201-202	400.00
203	450.00
204	400.00
205	575.00
206-210	400.00
211	450.00
212	400.00
213	525.00
214-224	375.00
225	4,500.00
☞1st Manhunter	
226	1,500.00
227-229	500.00
230	550.00
231	400.00
232	300.00
233	1,250.00
☞1st Batwoman	
234	325.00
235	600.00
236	350.00
237-240	300.00
241-260	250.00
261-264	200.00
265	325.00

266	200.00
267	250.00
268-271	200.00
272	175.00
273	200.00
274-280	150.00
281-297	125.00
298	200.00
299-310	100.00
311	200.00
☞1st Catman	
312-326	100.00
327	225.00
☞New Bat symbol	
328	175.00
☞Alfred dies	
329-330	75.00
331	65.00
332	115.00
☞Joker	
333-340	60.00
341	75.00
342-352	60.00
353-358	75.00
359	350.00
☞1st Batgirl	
360-362	65.00
363	100.00
☞2nd Batgirl	
364	60.00
365	90.00
366-368	60.00
369	75.00
370	45.00
371	80.00
☞Batmobile	
372-376	50.00
377	65.00
378-380	50.00
381-386	40.00
387	75.00
388	50.00
389-390	35.00
391-393	25.00
394	35.00
395	125.00
☞N. Adams art	
396-397	35.00
398-399	30.00
400	175.00
☞1st Man-Bat	
401	30.00
402	55.00
403-404	35.00

405-407	30.00
408-410	40.00
411	30.00
☞1st Talia	
412-424	25.00
425-427	20.00
428-436	15.00
437	20.00
☞100-page issue	
438-445	28.00
☞100-page issues	
446	12.00
447-450	8.00
451-455	6.00
456-457	9.00
458-462	6.00
463	45.00
☞1st Calculator	
464	6.00
465-468	9.00
469-470	5.00
471-473	8.00
☞1st new Deadshot	
474-476	15.00
477-479	8.00
480	5.00
481	7.00
482	5.00
483	8.00
484	5.00
485-499	4.00
500	5.00
501-503	4.00
504	6.00
505-523	4.00
524	5.00
525-534	4.00
535	5.00
536-564	4.00
565-568	3.00
569-570	4.00
571	3.00
572	4.00
573-574	3.00
575	4.00
576-577	3.00
578-585	4.00
586-587	3.00
588-590	4.00
591-675	3.00
675/Platinum	5.00
675/Variant	4.00
676	3.00
677-682	2.00

D

682/Variant	3.00
683-699	2.00
700	4.00
700/Variant	5.00
701-718	2.00
719	3.00
720	4.00
721-722	3.00
723-740	2.00
741	3.00
742-746	2.00
747-749	3.00
750	5.00
751	12.00
☞1st Sasha	
752-774	3.00
775	4.00
776-799	3.00
800	4.00
801-816	3.00
817	12.00
818-899	3.00
1000000	4.00
1000000/Variant	15.00
Ann 1	5.00
Ann 2	4.00
Ann 3-7	3.00
Ann 8	4.00
Ann 9	3.00
Ann 10	4.00

Detective Eye
Centaur, 1940

1	1,350.00
2	800.00

Detective Picture Stories
Comics Magazine, 1936

1	3,400.00
2	1,650.00
3-5	850.00

Detectives
Alpha Productions, 1993

1	5.00

Detectives, Inc.: A Terror of Dying Dreams
Eclipse, 1987

1-3	2.00

Detectives Inc. (Micro-Series)
Eclipse, 1980

1-2	2.00

Detention Comics
DC, 1996

1	4.00

Detonator
Image, 2005

1-3	3.00

Detour
Alternative, 1997

1	3.00

Detroit! Murder City Comix
Kent Myers, 1993

1-7	3.00

Devastator
Image, 1998

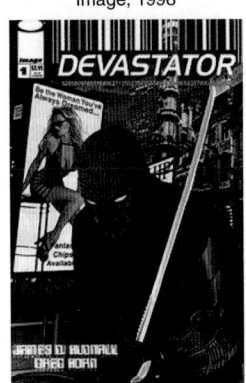

Veteran comics writer James D. Hudnall (ESPers, Chiller) began writing Devastator as a first effort at screenwriting in 1991. It was only much later, in 1997, that the first draft was completed, and was shown to his friend Greg Horn. Together, they agreed to adapt the screenplay to comics form.

The story takes place in the near future, where advances in cyber technology gave rise to the neural interface: a plug-in socket for people's minds, located at the back of their necks. Originally, it was used for medical uses, or to provide instant proficiency in a number of skills. Soon, however, it was used to provide mood-altering experiences, and a trade arose in illicit "E-Drugs." With the police closing in on the dealers, one cartel devised a "Devastator" chip which would turn an innocent-in this case, a former cop named John Blake-into a mindless assassin with super-powers...right before it killed him.

1-3	3.00

Deviant
Antarctic, 1999

1	3.00

Devil Chef
Dark Horse, 1994

1	3.00

Devil Dinosaur
Marvel, 1978

"Moon Boy" is a chimpanzee-like ancestor of man. Unlike most of his kind, he is unafraid of the night, thus earning this peculiar name among his people.

One night while exploring, he comes across a group of larger man-apes who've trapped a mother dinosaur beneath a fiery volcano. The volcano erupts suddenly, scattering the man-apes. However, Moon Boy remains alive and discovers a young offspring of the mother dinosaur. He leads it to safety and tends to its wounds. Soon, they became friends, with Moon Boy using his intelligence, and Devil Dinosaur using its great strength to survive together in a savage world.

One of Jack Kirby's creations for Marvel in 1970s, the series was appreciated by fans of the King and regarded as campy and outdated by others.

1	5.00
2-3	4.00
4	5.00
5	4.00
6-9	3.00

Devil Dinosaur Spring Fling
Marvel, 1997

1	3.00

Devil-Dog Dugan
Atlas, 1956

1	60.00
2	40.00
3	30.00

Devil Dogs
Street & Smith, 1942

1	200.00

Devilina
Atlas-Seaboard, 1975
1	9.00
2	12.00

Devil Jack
Doom Theater, 1995
1-2	3.00

Devil Kids
Harvey, 1962

Casper and Spooky are ghosts; Wendy's a witch. Hot Stuff is a little devil. Fortunately, the Moral Majority never heard of Harvey Comics -- and certainly not the title, Devil Kids, which features the pitchfork-weilding, diaper-wearing devil child and his friends. Of course, premise aside, the comics are otherwise as wholesome as comics come, with Hot Stuff learning patience and other virtues in various stories.

In addition to 19 years in Devil Kids, Hot Stuff's own title saw 177 issues published sporadically over a period of 34 years. Other titles included Hot Stuff Sizzlers and Creepy Caves.

1	150.00
2	75.00
3	50.00
4-5	25.00
6-10	20.00
11-17	15.00
18-20	10.00
21-30	8.00
31-40	5.00
41-60	4.00
61-79	3.00
80-107	2.00

Devilman
Verotik, 1995
1	4.00
2-5	3.00
6	4.00

Devil May Cry
Dreamwave, 2004
1-3	4.00

Devil May Cry 3
Tokyopop, 2005
1	10.00

Devil's Angel
Fantagraphics
1	3.00

Devil's Bite
Boneyard
1-2	3.00

Devil's Brigade
Avalon
1	3.00

Devil's Due Studios Previews 2003
Image, 2003
1	1.00

Devil's Footprints
Dark Horse, 2003
1-4	3.00

Devil's Keeper
Alias, 2005
1	1.00
2	3.00

Devil's Reign
Image, 1996
1/2-1/2/Platinum	3.00

Devil's Rejects
Idea & Design Works, 2005
0/Baby	5.00
0/Otis	6.00
0/Spaulding	5.00
1	4.00

Devlin
Maximum, 1996
1	3.00

Devlin Demon: Not for Normal Children
Dublin
1	3.00

Dewey DeSade
Item
1-2	4.00
Ashcan 1	1.00

Dexter Comics
Dearfield, 1948
1	45.00
2	35.00
3-5	30.00

Dexter's Laboratory
DC, 1999
1	3.00
2-24	2.00
25	1.00
26-34	2.00

Dhampire: Stillborn
DC, 1996

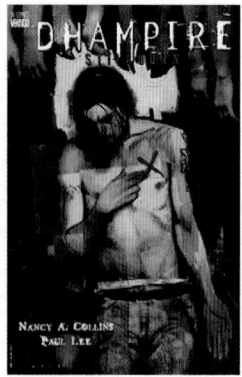

As if in response to Marvels' vampire hero Blade, DC Comics' Dhampire takes an edgier, more gothic approach to the classic horror staple thanks to its "For Mature Readers" imprint Vertigo.

Dhampire tells the story of Nicholas Gaunt, a human/vampire half-breed trying to find his place in the world. With his mother bitten while he was in the womb, Gaunt came into the world a stillborn birth but miraculously regained consciousness a few hours later. Since that day, he has lived his life as an outcast, attempting-but failing-suicide on several occasions. It isn't until he learns the truth about his mother's horrible background that he fully embraces the "dark world," putting into motion a horrific plan to make himself a full-fledged vampire.

A far cry from the typical comic book tale, Dhampire is able to get away with its morbid theme thanks to intelligent storytelling and complimentary art. Known for its plethora of "thinking man" stories, the Vertigo stable of comics makes a perfect home for this gothic graphic novel.

1	6.00

Diablo: Tales of Sanctuary
Dark Horse, 2001
1	6.00

Dia de los Muertos (Sergio Aragonès')
Dark Horse, 1998
nn	3.00

Diary Loves
Quality, 1949
2	60.00

3-15......................................40.00
16-31....................................30.00

Diary of a Dominatrix
Fantagraphics, 1995
1-3...3.00

Diary of Emily K.
Fantagraphics
1...3.00

Diary of Horror
Avon, 1952
1..320.00

Diary Secrets
St. John, 1952
10-30.................................100.00

Diatom
Photographics, 1995
1-3...5.00

Dick Cole
Curtis Publishing, 1948
1......................................240.00
2......................................150.00
3-5....................................125.00
6-10..................................100.00

Dick Danger
Olsen, 1998
1-5...3.00

Dick Hercules of St. Markham's
Sports Cartoons
1...30.00
2...15.00
3-7..8.00

Dickie Dare
Eastern, 1942
1..450.00
2..325.00
3-4....................................275.00

Dicks
Caliber, 1997
1-4..3.00

Dick Tracy
Blackthorne, 1986
1-2...6.00
3-24..7.00

Dick Tracy
Disney, 1990
1...3.00
1/Direct....................................5.00
2...3.00
2/Direct....................................6.00
3...3.00
3/Direct....................................6.00

Dick Tracy 3-D
Blackthorne, 1986
1...3.00

Dick Tracy Adventures
Gladstone, 1991
1 .... 5.00

Dick Tracy Adventures
Hamilton
1 .... 4.00

Dick Tracy Comics Monthly
Harvey, 1950

Harvey picked up the license for a Dick Tracy comic book from the Dell title, continuing its numbering, too. Harvey ran strip reprints, including much classic material.

When the Comics Magazine Association of America began to apply its Comics Code content restrictions to the material by Chester Gould (1900-1985), which had already appeared in family newspapers), its censorship guidelines led to panels in which some of the drawings had simply been removed.

Nevertheless, Harvey continued the title for several years under the restrictions. Later reprints would restore the missing panels.
-- *Maggie*

25 .... 110.00
26-41 .... 85.00
42-50 .... 70.00
51-60 .... 60.00
61-70 .... 52.00
71-80 .... 45.00
81-90 .... 40.00
91-100 .... 32.00
101-110 .... 28.00
111-120 .... 26.00
121-130 .... 24.00
131-140 .... 22.00
141-145 .... 28.00
Giveaway 1 .... 15.00

Dick Tracy Crimebuster
Avalon
1-4 .... 3.00

Dick Tracy Detective
Avalon
1-4 .... 3.00

Dick Tracy Monthly
Dell, 1948
1 .... 365.00
2 .... 250.00
3-5 .... 220.00
6-10 .... 200.00
11-24 .... 140.00

Dick Tracy Monthly
Blackthorne, 1986
1 .... 3.00
2-25 .... 2.00

Dick Tracy Special
Blackthorne, 1988
1-3 .... 3.00

Dick Tracy: The Early Years
Blackthorne, 1987
1-3 .... 7.00
4 .... 3.00

Dick Tracy "Unprinted Stories"
Blackthorne, 1987
1-4 .... 3.00

Dick Tracy Weekly
Blackthorne, 1988
26-99 .... 2.00

Dick Wad
Slave Labor, 1993
1 .... 3.00

Dick Wingate of the United States Navy
Toby, 1953
1 .... 50.00

Dictators of the Twentieth Century: Hitler
Antarctic, 2004
1-4 .... 3.00

Dictators of the Twentieth Century: Saddam Hussein
Antarctic, 2004
1-2 .... 4.00

Didymous: The Night and Day Worlds
Ironhorse, 1999
1-2 .... 3.00

Diebold
Silent Partners, 1996
1-2 .... 3.00

Die-Cut
Marvel, 1993

Die Cut was once a cyborg named Czorn Yson, expert with blades of all kinds. Then another cyborg, Death's Head II, absorbed his consciousness into his own sea of personalities. It was only later (in Death's Head II & The Origin of Die Cut) that he was once again freed, taking on a new body which included the most deadly blade of all.

Now featured in his own series, Die Cut is a violent powerhouse. Angered by his previous entrapment, he has vowed never to let a machine rule his destiny again.

1 ....3.00
2-4..2.00

Die-Cut vs. G-Force
Marvel, 1993

1-2...3.00

Diesel
Antarctic, 1997

1 ....3.00

Different Beat Comics
Fantagraphics

1 ....4.00

Diggers
C&T

1 ....2.00

Digimon Digital Monsters
Dark Horse, 2000

With weather patterns askew and giant monsters ravaging the world, maybe it is a good thing that Tai and his friends inherit their own personal digital monsters. Their evolution powers may be the only thing to help restore the planet!

Adapted from the Saturday morning cartoon, Digimon is similar to the mega-popular Pokemon cartoon in both tone and style. Like the Pocket Monsters, the Digimon morph into larger and more powerful appearances when danger strikes.

Also, as was the case with most Pokemon merchandise, anything Digimon has the power to morph your wallet into its empty form. Be warned!

1-12 .... 3.00

Digimon Tamers
Tokyopop, 2004

1 .... 10.00

Digital Dragon
Peregrine Entertainment, 1999

1-2 .... 3.00

Digital Webbing Presents
Digital Webbing, 2001

1-18... 3.00
19-20 .... 4.00

Digitek
Marvel, 1992

1-4 .... 2.00

Dik Skycap
Rip Off, 1991

1-2 .... 3.00

Dildo
Fantagraphics, 2003

1 .... 6.00
2-10....................................... 4.00

Dilemma Presents
Dilemma, 1994

1-4 .... 3.00

Dilly
Lev Gleason, 1953

1 .... 20.00
2-3... 15.00

Dilton's Strange Science
Archie, 1989

1-5 .... 2.00

Dime Comics
Newsbook, 1945

1 .... 375.00

Dimension 5
Edge, 1995

1 .... 4.00

Dimension X
Karl Art

This large format title brings readers the sort of high quality, end-of-the-world science-fiction that has seldom been seen since the 1950s. In many ways, it's reminiscent of such classic titles as Weird Fantasy and Weird Science.

The series starts off with "The Blood of the Universe," in which a doctor treats a patient who has been experiencing mental flashes from other worlds. A childhood car accident seems to have unlocked some sort of mental door in the man, exposing his mind to another realm of existence. As the doctor continues her examination, she finds her own mind affected in a similar manner. When she finally learns the terrible secret at the heart of the universe, she is driven to commit murder in order to protect the sanity of every person on Earth.

1 .... 4.00

Dimension Z
Pyramid

1-2 .... 2.00

Dimm Comics Presents
Dimm, 1996
Ashcan 0-1 ....1.00

Dim-Witted Darryl
Slave Labor, 1998

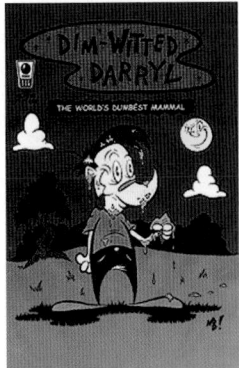

Written and illustrated by
Michael Bresnahan, this black-
and-white mature-readers
funnybook consists of short stories
about Darryl, the "world's dumbest
mammal." This 28-year-old fourth-
grader has plenty of
misadventures, and the series
delivers a boatload of dim-witted
hijinks and slapstick tomfoolery.
    Much of the humor centers on
Darryl's inability to understand
adult subject matter such as sex
and death. Readers can peer in on
Darryl's home life and see how his
friends and neighbors react to his
stupidity. The results are
occasionally very funny.

1-3...3.00

Ding Dong
Compix, 1946
1 ....150.00
2..75.00
3-5...55.00

Dingledorfs
Skylight
1 ....3.00

Dinky Duck
St. John, 1951
1 ....70.00
2..55.00
3-5...40.00
6-8...24.00
9-12..18.00
13-15...15.00
16-19...10.00

Dinky on the Road
Blind Bat, 1994
1 ....2.00

Dino Island
Mirage, 1993
1-2...3.00

Dino-Riders
Marvel, 1989
1-3...2.00

Dinosaur Bop
Monster
1-2...3.00

Dinosaur Island
Monster
1 ....3.00

Dinosaur Mansion
Edge
1 ....3.00

Dinosaur Rex
Upshot
1-3...2.00

Dinosaurs
Hollywood, 1991
1-2...3.00

Dinosaurs: An Illustrated Guide
Caliber, 1991
1 ....3.00

Dinosaurs Attack!
Eclipse

This three-part series features
prehistoric villains in the
contemporary world. A brilliant
scientist has created a device that
scans time on temporal planes, in
effect unfreezing history so it can be
seen as if it were currently
happening. But there are many
protesters against the experiment,
including the scientist's ex-wife, who
manages to get the testing delayed.
    The objections become moot,
when the system "accidentally"
starts. Contrary to the common
belief that scanning time would be
harmless, dinosaurs materialize in

the present and quickly go on a
rampage, eating people,
destroying bridges, and anything
else in their path.
    Readers of this series may also
want to check out the Topps card
series of the same name.

1-3 ....4.00

Dinosaurs, A Celebration
Marvel, 1992
1-4 ....5.00

Dinosaurs For Hire
Eternity, 1988
1 ....2.00
1/3D...3.00
1/2nd-9 ....2.00

Dinosaurs For Hire
Malibu, 1993
1-4 ....2.00
5-12 ....3.00

Dinosaurs for Hire: Dinosaurs Rule!
Eternity
1 ....6.00

Dinosaurs For Hire Fall Classic
Eternity, 1988
1 ....2.00

Dinosaurs for Hire: Guns 'n' Lizards
Eternity
1 ....6.00

Dioramas: Love Story
Image, 2004
1 ....13.00

Dippy Duck
Atlas, 1957
1 ....30.00

Directory to a Nonexistent Universe
Eclipse, 1987

In the late 1980s, amidst the wave of multi-volume super-hero directories, indexes and Who's-Who's came this lighthearted spoof from ICG, an imprint of Eclipse. Comics humorist Kerry Callen provides a glimpse of a whole new absurd universe in this one-shot directory spoof. Featured here are such laugh-out-loud creations as the Black-n-Blue Panther (so named for his tendency to get beat up a lot), Pete Moss (a Swamp Thing-style character) and Pull-Yourself-Together-Man, among many others. A "bonus" story at the end puts some of these characters to good use in the first and only story to come from the "Nonexistent Universe." Although it's a bit dated, any fan who carefully collected the DC and Marvel character directories will smile more than a few times at this arch piece of satire.

-- *Stephen C. George*

1 ....2.00

Dire Wolves: A Chronicle of the Deadworld
Caliber
1 ....4.00

Dirtbag
Twist N Shout, 1993
1-7 ....3.00

Dirty Dozen
Dell, 1967
1 ....25.00

Dirty Pair
Eclipse, 1988

Kei and Yuri are the "trouble consultants" for the Worlds Welfare Work Association, or WWWA. Traveling across the galaxy in their ship The Lovely Angel, they have solved some of the toughest crimes around. Officially, their codename is "the Lovely Angels" after their ship;

after a few destructive mishaps, people call them the Dirty Pair, a name they despise.

They have been called to planet Pacifica to find the clone and brainchip of Kelvin O'Donnell, the famous scientist and to solve his murder. They expected to find an old codger playing with test tubes, not a gorgeous, young CEO involved in a deadly rivalry between biochemical companies.

1 .... 4.00
2-4 .... 3.00

Dirty Pair II
Eclipse, 1989
1-5 .... 3.00

Dirty Pair III
Eclipse, 1990
1-5 .... 2.00

Dirty Pair (4th Series)
Viz, 1993
1-5 .... 5.00

Dirty Pair: Dangerous Acquaintances
Dark Horse, 1997
1-5 .... 3.00

Dirty Pair, The: Fatal but Not Serious
Dark Horse, 1995
1-5 .... 3.00

Dirty Pair, The: Run from the Future
Dark Horse, 2000
1-4 .... 3.00

Dirty Pair, The: Sim Hell
Dark Horse, 1993
1-5 .... 3.00

Dirty Pair, The: Sim Hell Remastered
Dark Horse, 1996
1-4 .... 3.00

Dirty Pair, The: Start The Violence
Dark Horse, 1999
1/A-1/B 3.00

Dirty Pictures
Aircel, 1991
1-3 .... 3.00

Dirty Plotte
Drawn and Quarterly, 1996
1-9 .... 3.00
10 .... 4.00

Disasters of War
Caliber
1 .... 4.00

Disavowed
DC, 2000
1-6 .... 3.00

Disciples
Image, 2001
1-2 .... 3.00

Dishman
Eclipse, 1988
1 .... 3.00

Disney Afternoon
Marvel, 1994
1-10 .... 2.00

Disney Comic Hits
Marvel, 1995

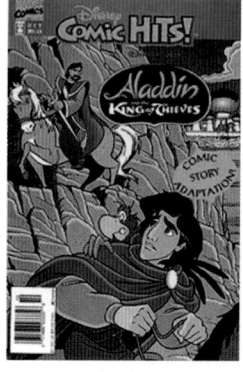

This anthology title, licensed by Marvel Comics, features the continuing adventures of the popular characters from Disney's animated movies: Beauty and the Beast; Timon and Pumbaa from The Lion King; Aladdin; Pocahontas; The Little Mermaid; and Woody and Buzz from Toy Story. This comic replaces the individual titles that each of the featured players had had.

In general, the art correlates well to the movie that inspired it, and the writers do an admirable job of finding new tales about characters that had come to a denouement. Although primarily aimed at children, this can be enjoyed by all ages, much like the movies that fostered it.

-- *George Haberberger*

1-16 .... 2.00

Disneyland Birthday Party
Dell, 1958
1 .... 440.00

Disneyland Birthday Party
Gladstone, 1985
1-1/A 10.00

Disney Movie Book
Disney
1 ....8.00

Disney's Action Club
Acclaim, 1997
1-7..5.00

Disney's Colossal Comics
Disney
1 ....2.00

Disney's Colossal Comics Collection
Disney
1-10..2.00

Disney's Comics in 3-D
Disney
1 ....3.00

Disney's Enchanting Stories
Acclaim
1-4..5.00

Disobedient Daisy
Fantagraphics, 1995
1-2..3.00

Distant Soil, A
Warp, 1983
1 ....8.00
2 ....5.00
3-5...4.00
6-9...3.00

Distant Soil, A
Aria, 1991
1 ....5.00
1/2nd 3.00
1/3rd-1/4th...............................2.00
2 ....3.00
2/2nd 2.00
3 ....3.00
3/2nd-8 ....2.00
9-24...3.00
25..4.00
25/Ltd. 8.00
26-27...3.00
28-31...4.00
38..5.00
32-33...4.00
34..5.00
35..4.00
36..5.00

District X
Marvel, 2004
1 ....4.00
2-13...3.00

Ditko Package
Ditko, 2000
1 .... 9.00

Diva Grafix & Stories
Starhead, 1993
1-2 .... 4.00

Divas
Caliber
1-4 .... 3.00

Divine Intervention/ Gen13
DC, 1999
1 .... 3.00

Divine Intervention/ Wildcats
DC, 1999
1 .... 3.00

Divine Right
Image, 1997
1-Ashcan 1/A.......................... 3.00

Division 13
Dark Horse, 1994
1-4 .... 3.00

Dixie Dugan
Columbia, 1942

The character of Dixie was introduced in a novel by J.P. McEvoy (1897-1958) in 1928. Her character was spun into a movie and a Broadway play, and she appeared in her own newspaper strip by the end of the following year. The strip ran for more than 30 years.

Her comic-book appearances didn't last nearly that long, the Columbia version running from 1942 to around the end of the decade. While the stories were basically innocent, they were suggestive for the era; several cover gags depict men falling all over themselves to get a better look at

Dixie. The first issue features a crossover with Joe Palooka.

A handful of later issues from Prize are believed to exist, but were still being tracked down at press time.

-- Maggie

1 .... 90.00
2 .... 60.00
3-6 .... 45.00
7-10 .... 40.00
11-13 .... 35.00

Dixie Road
NBM
1-2 .... 11.00

Dizzy Dames
ACG, 1952
1 .... 90.00
2 .... 65.00
3-6 .... 40.00

Dizzy Dames Special Edition
Avalon
1 .... 3.00

Dizzy Don Comics
F.E. Howard, 1942
1 .... 75.00
2 .... 40.00
4-19 .... 30.00
20-22 .... 20.00

Dizzy Don Comics
F.E. Howard, 1947
3 .... 40.00

Dizzy Duck
Standard, 1950
32-39 .... 40.00

Django and Angel
Caliber
1-5 .... 3.00

DMZ
DC, 2006
1-14 .... 3.00

DNAgents
Eclipse, 1983

Matrix, Inc. had long wanted to own everything, including its employees. Five years after the project began, the company was about to get its wish. They were called the DNAgents, a unique group of people whose DNA had been subtly altered by the company, and "grown" from scratch. These alterations gave them special powers-powers that Matrix intended to use to their fullest.

Created by Mark Evanier and Will Meugniot, the DNAgents are a new group of super-heroes from one of the most innovative companies in the business.

1	3.00
2-24	2.00
3D 1	3.00

DNAgents Super Special
Antarctic, 1994
1	4.00

D-N-Angel
Tokyopop, 2004
1-10	10.00

D.O.A.
Saving Grace
1	1.00

Doc Carter VD Comics
Health, 1949
1	125.00

Doc Chaos:
The Strange Attractor
Vortex, 1990
1-3	3.00

Doc Frankenstein
Burlyman, 2004
1	7.00
1/Darrow	10.00
2	4.00

2/Sketch	5.00
3	4.00
3/Variant	5.00

Doc Samson
Marvel, 1996
1-4	2.00

Doc Samson
Marvel, 2006
1-5	3.00

Doc Savage
Gold Key, 1966
1	38.00

Doc Savage
Marvel, 1972
1	20.00
2	5.00
3-8	3.00

Doc Savage
Marvel, 1975
1	9.00
2-5	4.00
6-8	3.00

Doc Savage
DC, 1987
1-4	2.00

Doc Savage
DC, 1988
1-24	2.00
Ann 1	4.00

Doc Savage Comics
(Vol. 1)
Street & Smith, 1940
1	3,600.00
2	950.00
3	700.00
4-5	465.00
6-7	340.00
8-11	250.00
12	190.00

Doc Savage Comics
(Vol. 2)
Street & Smith, 1943
1-2	190.00
3-8	145.00

Doc Savage:
Curse of the Fire God
Dark Horse, 1995
1-4	3.00

Doc Savage:
Devil's Thoughts
Millennium
1-3	3.00

Doc Savage:
Doom Dynasty
Millennium
1-2	2.00

Doc Savage:
Manual of Bronze
Millennium, 1992
1	3.00

Doc Savage: Repel
Millennium
1	3.00

Doc Savage:
The Man of Bronze
Millennium, 1991

Doc Savage, "the Man of Bronze" was created in 1933 by Lester Dent, writing under the name of Kenneth Robeson. Savage was arguably one of the two most important characters of the 1930s pulps (the other was The Shadow), serving as the inspiration to countless characters which followed. These include Superman, Batman, Indiana Jones, Buckaroo Banzai, and countless others.

After 182 novels published in the 1930s and 1940s, Savage fell from popularity, and the magazine that spawned him ceased publishing in 1949. Marvel picked up the character for a 1972 color, and a 1975 black-and-white series, with mixed results. The rights then moved over to DC in the 1980s, which tried to place the hero in the modern world, again with unsatisfying results. Millennium's treatment in Doc Savage: The Man of Bronze seems to come closest to the original, capturing all the action, humanity, and humor of the original novels.

1-4	3.00

Dr. Andy
Alliance, 1994
1 ....3.00

Dr. Anthony King, Hollywood Love Doctor
Minoan, 1952
1 ....60.00
2-4 ....35.00

Dr. Atomic
Last Gasp
1 ....5.00
2-3 ....4.00
4-6 ....3.00

Doctor Bang
Rip Off, 1992
1 ....3.00

Doctor Boogie
Media Arts
1 ....2.00

Doctor Chaos
Triumphant, 1993

Doctor Chaos is, "Supreme diviner of all events...strategist unparalleled...shaper of destiny...the seer, the shaper, the molder, the stirrer of the cosmic pot stew." Like DC's Sandman, Doctor Chaos lives in the portion of the universe where immortals walk incarnate. Death, Faith, War, Sex...all of these have gathered at Chaos' palace for dinner parties.

And, like all gods, these seem to enjoy playing tricks on each other and vying for power. This is especially the case between Chaos and Death. As this series begins, Death has just scored a victory, damaging Chaos' thousand year plan. But Chaos, ever the gamer, is more than prepared to up the ante.

1-12 ....3.00

Doctor Cyborg
Attention!
1 .... 3.00
1/Ashcan 1.00
2-3 .... 3.00

Doctor Doom's Revenge
Marvel, 1989
1 .... 1.00

Doctor Fate
DC, 1987
1-4 .... 2.00

Doctor Fate
DC, 2003
1-5 .... 3.00

Doctor Fate
DC, 1988
1 .... 2.00
2-5 .... 1.00
6-41 .... 2.00
Ann 1 .... 3.00

Doctor Faustus
Anarchy, 1994
1-2 .... 3.00
Ashcan 1 .... 2.00

Doctor Frankenstein's House of 3-D
3-D Zone, 1992
1 .... 4.00

Dr. Fu Manchu
I.W., 1964
1 .... 45.00

Dr. Giggles
Dark Horse, 1992
1-2 .... 3.00

Doctor Gorpon
Eternity, 1991
1-3 .... 3.00

Dr. Goyle Special
Arrow
1 .... 3.00

Doctor! I'm Too Big!
NBM
1 .... 11.00

Dr. Jekyll and Mr. Hyde
NBM
1 .... 16.00

Dr. Kildare
Dell, 1962
2 .... 50.00
3-9 .... 40.00

Doctor Mid-Nite
DC, 1999
1-3 .... 6.00

Dr. Radium and the Gizmos of Boola-Boola
Slave Labor, 1992
1 .... 5.00

Dr. Radium, Man of Science
Slave Labor, 1992
1-5 .... 3.00

Dr. Robot Special
Dark Horse, 2000
1 .... 3.00

Dr. Slump
Viz, 2005
1-4 .... 8.00

Doctor Solar, Man of the Atom
Gold Key, 1962

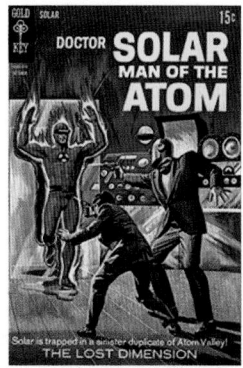

Working in a research laboratory in Atom Valley, Doctor Solar was caught in a premature atomic explosion. The blast had the effect of converting his body into pure energy. At the same time, he retained his consciousness. Later, he would learn to reform his body, and use a special cadmium-lined suit to control the radiation it emitted.

As an energy being, Solar had an awesome range of abilities. He could fly, transmute matter, and unleash atomic blasts of heat or cold. He used these new abilities to fight a variety of would-be world conquerors, including Nuro and King Cybernoid.

Doctor Solar, Man of the Atom was Gold Key's first comics title. Originally published from the early 1960s to the early 1980s, it enjoyed a renaissance in the early '90s when new publisher Valiant licensed the character. Updated, Solar, Man of the Atom became a cornerstone of the Valiant universe.

1	150.00
2	80.00
3	50.00
4	60.00
5	30.00
6-10	25.00
11-14	16.00
15	20.00
16-20	16.00
21-27	12.00
28-31	4.00

Dr. Speck
Bug Books

1-4	3.00

Doctor Spectrum
Marvel, 2004

1-6	3.00

Doctor Strange
Marvel, 1968

169	75.00
170-171	30.00
172-173	27.00
174	20.00
175	35.00
176-183	27.00

Doctor Strange
Marvel, 1974

1	25.00
2	18.00
3-4	10.00
5-6	8.00
7	7.00
8-9	4.00
10	7.00
11	6.00
12-13	4.00
13/30¢	20.00
14	3.00
14/30¢	20.00
15	3.00
15/30¢	20.00
16	3.00
16/30¢	20.00
17	3.00
17/30¢	20.00
18-23	3.00
23/35¢	15.00
24	3.00
24/35¢	15.00
25	3.00
25/35¢	15.00
26-81	2.00
Ann 1	6.00
Special 1	3.00

Doctor Strange
Marvel, 1999

1-4	3.00

Doctor Strange and Doctor Doom: Triumph and Torment
Marvel, 1989

1	10.00
1/HC	18.00

Doctor Strange Classics
Marvel, 1984

1-4	2.00

Doctor Strange/ Ghost Rider Special
Marvel, 1991

1	2.00

Dr. Strange: Oath
Marvel, 2006

1-3	3.00

Doctor Strange: Shamballa
Marvel, 1986

1	7.00

Doctor Strange: Sorcerer Supreme
Marvel, 1988

Doctor Strange is a great character, and just about everybody thinks he ought to have an ongoing series. He gets them, but they just never tend to last very long. After his original series, borne out of Strange Tales, went bimonthly and then folded, Marvel dropped a bit of indignity on the Doc by restarting Strange Tales and sticking him with 1980s hit characters (but now mostly forgotten) Cloak & Dagger as co-stars -- hardly Nick Fury! As times improved, Marvel restored Doc to his own private practice in Doctor Strange, Sorceror Supreme.

The series, most notable editorially for Strange's extended war with vampires, is actually most famous for a lawsuit. The cover to #15 depicts a young woman, who, it turns out, was really gospel singer Amy Grant -- who wasn't thrilled at appearing in "The Vampiric Verses."

Late issues in the series are completely off the wall, as Marvel tried to make Doc more hip and Sandman-like. It didn't work.
-- John Jackson Miller

1	3.00
2-14	2.00
15	3.00
16-49	2.00
50	3.00
51-74	2.00
75	3.00
75/Holo-grafix	4.00
76-90	2.00
Ann 1	3.00
Ann 2	2.00
Ann 3-4	3.00
Ashcan 1	1.00

Dr. Strange vs. Dracula
Marvel, 1994

1	2.00

Doctor Strange: What is it That Disturbs You Stephen?
Marvel, 1997

1	6.00

Doctor Strangefate
DC, 1996

1	2.00

Doctor Tom Brent, Young Intern
Charlton, 1963

1	15.00
2-5	10.00

Dr. Tomorrow
Acclaim, 1997

1-12	3.00

Doctor Weird
Caliber, 1994

1-2	3.00
Special 1	4.00

Dr. Weird
October, 1997

1-2	3.00

Doctor Who
Marvel, 1984

Inspired by the longest-running science-fiction show in television history, Doctor Who reprints tales of the world's favorite Time Lord from Britain's Doctor Who Magazine.

Traveling across time in his slightly-malfunctioning TARDIS (a time machine that looks, in the Doctor's case, like a blue police box), the Doctor constantly finds himself pitted against evil monsters of all shapes and sizes. These have included the infamous Daleks, evil robot-like creatures whose shrill mechanical cries of "EX-TER-MIN-ATE!" are silenced only by the ingenuity of the Doctor.

Intelligent and eccentric, this series mirrors the personality of the Doctor himself. It's a must for any fan of either the Tom Baker Doctor, or the Peter Davison version, which begins appearing partway through this series.

1	3.00
2-23	2.00

Dr. Who and the Daleks
Dell

1	50.00

Dr. Wirtham's Comix & Stories
Clifford Neal, 1987

1-2	2.00
3	5.00
4-6	2.00
7-8	3.00

Dr. Wonder
Old Town, 1996

1-5	3.00

Doctor Zero
Marvel, 1988

1-8	2.00

Dr. Zomb's House of Freaks
Starhead

1	3.00

Doc Weird's Thrill Book
Pure Imagination

1-3	2.00

Dodekain
Antarctic, 1994

1-8	3.00

Dodges Bullets
Image, 2004

1	10.00

Do-Do
Nationwide, 1950

1	65.00
2-5	45.00
6-7	38.00

Do-Do Man
Edge

1	3.00

Dog
Rebel, 1991

1-2	2.00

Dog Boy
Fantagraphics, 1987

1-9	2.00

Dog Moon
DC

1	7.00

Dogpatch Comics (Al Capp's...)
Toby, 1949

1	90.00
2	70.00
3-4	50.00

Dogs of War
Defiant, 1994

1-8	3.00

Dog Soup
Dog Soup

1	3.00

Dogs-O-War
Crusade, 1996

1-3	3.00

Dog T.A.G.S.: Trained Animal Gun Squadron
Bugged Out, 1993

1	2.00

Dogwitch
Sirius, 2003

1	6.00
2-6	4.00
7-17	3.00

Doin' Time with OJ
Boneyard, 1994

1	4.00

Dojinshi
Antarctic, 1992

1-4	3.00

Doll
Rip Off, 1989

1-8	3.00

Doll and Creature
Image, 2006

1	13.00
2-4	3.00

Doll Man
Quality, 1941

17-19	200.00
20-25	150.00
26-30	130.00
31-36	120.00
37	130.00
38-43	120.00
44-47	100.00

Dollman
Eternity, 1991

1-4	3.00

Doll Man Quarterly
Quality, 1941

When the Silver Age Atom was created, it reminded many long-time comics collectors of this Golden Age super-hero. Doll Man came out of the Will Eisner studio, drawn at first by Lou Fine. The costumed crime-fighter shrank from his civilian identity as Darrel Dane to combat the crooks as The Doll Man and was introduced in Feature Comics #27 (Dec 39), where he appeared in (appropriately) short stories (starting as four-pagers, the length slowly growing over the months to nine-pagers, then 11-pagers, then 13, eventually shrinking back to 11-pagers by the time of the series'

end in 1950). But he was given his own title, initially a quarterly, in Fall 1941, and he'd starred in 47 issues by the end of 1953.

-- Maggie

1	1,600.00
2	1,000.00
3	680.00
4-5	400.00
6-7	365.00
8	1,000.00
9	365.00
10-16	240.00

Doll Parts
Sirius, 2000

This black-and-white title from writer Mike L. Taylor and artist Shawn Pacheco traces a cute li'l doll's journey from a sunny land of childhood imagination to a dingy little toy shop, where her maker donned a dress and fishnet stockings and hanged himself. Without a maker, she and a fellow toy make their way into the big, decadent city and discover that the world is darker than they could have guessed. Who will take them in? Find out as the story of their quest unfolds.

1 .... 3.00

Dolls
Sirius, 1996

1 .... 3.00

Doll
Tokyopop, 2004

1-6 .... 10.00

Dolly
Approved, 1951

1 .... 25.00

Dolly Dill
Marvel, 1945

1 .... 55.00

Dollz
Image, 2001

1/A-2 .... 3.00

Dome: Ground Zero
DC

1 .... 8.00

Domination Factor: Avengers
Marvel, 1999

1-2 .... 3.00

Domination Factor: Fantastic Four
Marvel, 1999

1-2 .... 3.00

Dominion
Eclipse, 1990

Earth has become a sewer. Most plant life has died, the atmosphere has become a poisonous bacterial soup, and people cannot walk out of doors without wearing oxygen masks. The population is restive and crime has grown rampant. Who is there to restore order? The Tank Police.

The Tank Police's orders are to capture the Super Criminal Buaku and his gang, which includes the sensual cat sisters Annapuma and Unipuma. Can they stop Buaku and restore the planet to health?

Masamune Shirow displays his concern for the environment in this lively series. He is also the creator of Appleseed and Orion.

1-3	3.00
4-6	2.00

Dominion
Image, 2003

1-2 .... 3.00

Dominion: Conflict 1
Dark Horse, 1996

1-6 .... 3.00

Dominion: Phantom of the Audience
Dark Horse, 1994

1 .... 3.00

Dominique: Family Matters
Caliber

1 .... 3.00

Dominique: Killzone
Caliber, 1995

1 .... 3.00

Dominique: Protect and Serve
Caliber, 1995

1 .... 3.00

Dominique: White Knuckle Drive
Caliber

1 .... 3.00

Domino
Marvel, 1997

1-3 .... 2.00

Domino
Marvel, 2003

1-4 .... 3.00

Domino Chance
Chance, 1982

Domino Chance and Arnie Zoots are space cockroaches with enough charisma to charm a beautiful alien government agent named "Trouble" Galore into working with them.

They're also daring enough to steal priceless technology, swindle away the ownership of the largest conglomerate in known space, and turn a game of Grav-Ball into a clever trap for a corporate criminal.

Follow the adventures of these irrepressible cockroach buddies, as they wheel and deal their way into, and out of, loads of trouble.

1	3.00
1/2nd-9	2.00

Domino Chance:
Roach Extraordinaire
Amazing

1	2.00

Domino Lady
Fantagraphics, 1990

1-3	2.00

Domino Lady's Jungle
Adventure
Fantagraphics, 1992

1-3	3.00

Domu: A Child's Dream
Dark Horse, 1995

1-3	6.00

Donald and Mickey
Gladstone, 1993

19	2.00
20	3.00
21-24	2.00
25	3.00
26-30	2.00

Donald and Mickey in
Disneyland
Dell, 1958

1	105.00

Donald and Scrooge
Disney, 1992

1-3	2.00

Donald Duck
Dell, 1952

26	350.00
27-29	100.00
30-44	65.00
45	125.00
☛Barks art	
46	175.00
☛Barks "Secret"	
47-51	65.00
52	150.00
☛Barks "Lost"	
53	65.00
54	125.00
☛Barks Forbid. Valley	
55-58	50.00
59-60	125.00
☛Barks "Ants"	
61-67	40.00
68	100.00
☛Barks art	
69-70	40.00
71-84	30.00
85-120	25.00
121-135	20.00
136-150	15.00
151-190	10.00
191-210	5.00
211-216	3.00
217	5.00
218-219	10.00
220-228	15.00
229-240	8.00
241-245	15.00
246	17.00
247-249	5.00
250	8.00
251-260	4.00
261-279	3.00
280-285	2.00
286	3.00
287-307	2.00

Donald Duck and Friends
Gemstone, 2003

308-335	3.00

Donald Duck Adventures
Gemstone, 2003

1-14	8.00

Donald Duck Adventures
Disney, 1990

1	3.00
2-38	2.00

Donald Duck Adventures
Gladstone, 1987

1	3.00
2-25	2.00
26	3.00
27-29	2.00
30	3.00
31-48	2.00

Donald Duck Album
Gold Key, 1963

1	50.00
2	40.00

Donald Duck &
Mickey Mouse
Gladstone, 1995

1-7	2.00

Donald Duck
Beach Party
Gold Key, 1965

1	40.00

Donald Duck
Beach Party
Dell, 1954

1	100.00
2	65.00
3-6	55.00

Donald Duck Digest
Gladstone, 1986

1	4.00
2-5	3.00

Donald Duck Fun Book
Dell, 1953

1	320.00
2	240.00

Donald Duck in
Disneyland
Dell, 1955

1	110.00

Donald Duck
(Whitman storybook)
Whitman, 1935

978	2,000.00
☛First Whitman	

Donatello Teenage
Mutant Ninja Turtle
Mirage, 1986

1	2.00

Don Fortune Magazine
Don Fortune, 1946

1	120.00
2	100.00
3-6	80.00

Donielle:
Enslaved at Sea
Raging Rhino, 1993

1-9	3.00

Don Martin Magazine
Welsh

1-3	3.00

Donna Matrix
Reactor, 1993

1	4.00

Donna Mia
Avatar, 1996

1-3	3.00

Donna's Day
Slab-O-Concrete

1	1.00

Don Newcombe
Fawcett, 1950

1	145.00

Don Winslow
of the Navy
Merwil, 1937

1	1,850.00

Don Winslow
of the Navy
Fawcett, 1943

1	750.00
2	360.00
3	225.00
4-6	185.00
7-10	140.00
11-20	100.00
21-30	75.00
31-40	60.00
41-60	46.00
61-73	38.00

Don Winslow Trouble Shooter
AC
1 ....3.00

Doofer
Fantagraphics
1 ....3.00

Doofus
Fantagraphics, 1994
1-2...3.00

Doom
Marvel, 2000

Trapped on the far side of the sun, Dr. Doom fights for his life in a strange and hostile environment. Although originally designed as a duplicate of our world, Counter-Earth's history has taken vastly different paths. Stripped of the legendary armor that has made him a match for the Fantastic Four and the Avengers, Doom finds himself fighting desert slavers and amphibious armies to regain the power he's always craved. But this time victory means more than Doom's own survival. On Earth, Doom is a dictator used to imposing his own will on others. Now, he could be the last hope of freedom for the surviving humans of Counter-Earth. Centering his power-base in New York's Baxter Building (the home of his greatest enemies on his own planet), Doom struggles to conquer the many forces arrayed against him, while secretly planning his return home.

1-3...3.00

Doom Force Special
DC, 1992
1 ....3.00

Doom Patrol
DC, 1964
86 ....135.00

87 .... 70.00
88-90 .... 50.00
91-98 .... 40.00
99 .... 60.00
100 .... 75.00
101-120 .... 25.00
121 .... 45.00
☞Doom Patrol dies
122-124 .... 2.00

Doom Patrol
DC, 1987
1 .... 3.00
2-18 .... 2.00
19 .... 3.00
20-49 .... 2.00
50 .... 3.00
51-56 .... 2.00
57 .... 3.00
58-87 .... 2.00
Ann 1.................................... 1.00
Ann 2.................................... 4.00

Doom Patrol
DC, 2001
1-22 .... 3.00

Doom Patrol
DC, 2004
1-18...................................... 3.00

Doom Patrol and Suicide Squad Special
DC, 1988
1 .... 2.00

Doomsday + 1
Charlton, 1975
1 .... 8.00
2 .... 5.00
3-6... 4.00
7-12...................................... 3.00

Doomsday + 1
Avalon
1-2... 3.00

Doomsday Annual
DC, 1995
1 .... 4.00

Doomsday Squad
Fantagraphics, 1986
1-2... 2.00
3 .... 3.00
4-7... 2.00

Doom's IV
Image, 1994
1/2-4..................................... 3.00

Doom: The Emperor Returns
Marvel, 2002
1-3... 3.00

Doom 2099
Marvel, 1993
1 .... 3.00
2-10...................................... 2.00

11-17 .... 1.00
18-25 .... 2.00
25/Variant 3.00
26-29 .... 2.00
29/Variant 4.00
30-39 .... 2.00
39/Variant 4.00
40-44 .... 2.00

Doorman
Caliber
1 .... 3.00

DoorMan (Cult)
Cult, 1993
1-4... 3.00
Ashcan 1 .... 1.00

Doorman: Family Secrets
Caliber
1 .... 3.00

Doorway to Nightmare
DC, 1978

This supernatural series had a unique advantage over other titles in the same genre: a compelling main character, Madame Xanadu, who pulled all the other characters into a vortex of her own design. The Gypsy fortune teller has set up her own shop in New York City, and she does a lot more on the other characters' behalf than simply reading their tarot cards. In her own way, she acts as a guardian against the mystical forces which imperil her clients' lives.

An interesting, if short-lived title, this 1978 series lasted just five issues.

1 .... 7.00
2-5... 3.00

Dope Comix
Kitchen Sink
1 .... 5.00
2-5... 3.00

Dopey Duck
Timely, 1945
1 ....68.00
2 ....55.00

Dopin' Dan
Last Gasp, 1972
1 ....5.00
2-3 ....3.00

Doris Nelson:
Atomic Housewife
Jake Comics, 1995
1 ....3.00

Dork
Slave Labor, 1993

Without a doubt, Evan Dorkin is one of the funniest alternative cartoonists working in comics today. This series is a showcase for his hilarious work.

Leading off the pack is the Murder Family, a devilishly black situation comedy starring a family of serial killers. While slicing up a meter reader, they remark, "Damn! The knife snapped. Must've hit the breastbone...Aw Matt, your mother gave us that knife. I loved that knife!" Next is a collection of rock review comics Dorkin did with Kyle Baker for a defunct music magazine. Their comments on the crowds at alternative shows were dead-on funny. (A huge person is seen thinking, "I am much taller than Kyle, so I must stand directly in front of him at all times!") Rounding out the bunch are musings on Fisher-Price peg people, the infamous "Baby in the Microwave" story, and episodes from his hilarious Milk & Cheese series ("Dairy Products Gone Bad!").

1-7..3.00
8 ....4.00
9 ....3.00

Dork House Comics
Parody
1 ....3.00

Dorkier Images
Parody, 1993
1-1/Variant.............................3.00

Dork Tower
Dork Storm, 1998
1 ....4.00
2-31 ....3.00

Dothenridge: Tales of the Vampire Monarchy
Dothenridge
1/2 ....2.00

Dotty Dripple Comics
Harvey, 1946

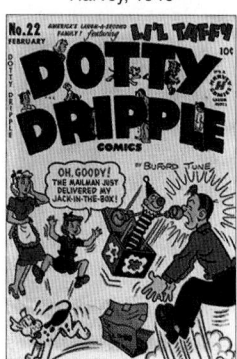

Dotty Dripple was a domestic comedy strip from the mid-1940s, credited to "Buford Tune." It was, to say the least, strongly inspired in both art and writing by the more famous and long-lived Blondie and Dagwood. Horace Dripple is a put-upon family man who just wants to be left alone to nap on the couch. His bubble-brained, blond wife, Dotty, always has a project in the works to disrupt his tranquil life, and, of course, his irritable boss never leaves him alone either. Then there's the troublesome kids, teen-aged son Wilbur and young daughter L'il Taffy. Even the family dog Pepper gets into the act. By the last pages of Dotty Dripple, it's very easy to wonder if the Blondie strips that Buford Tune traced aren't still attached somewhere underneath.
-- Rob Salkowitz

1 ....22.00
2 ....14.00
3-5 ....9.00
6-10 ....8.00
11-24 ....6.00

Double Action Comics
DC, 1940
2 .... 10,000.00

Double Comics
Elliott
1 .... 925.00
2 .... 700.00
3 .... 500.00

Double-Dare Adventures
Harvey, 1966
1 .... 20.00
2 .... 16.00

Double Dragon
Marvel, 1991
1-6 .... 1.00

Double Edge: Alpha
Marvel, 1995
1 .... 5.00

Double Edge: Omega
Marvel, 1995
1 .... 5.00

Double Image
Image, 2001
1-5 .... 3.00

Double Impact
High Impact, 1995
1-1/Ltd. 4.00
2-5 .... 3.00

Double Impact
High Impact, 1996
0 .... 3.00
1 .... 4.00
2-7 .... 3.00

Double Impact: Art Attack
ABC
1 .... 3.00
1/A-1/B 4.00

Double Impact: Assassins for Hire
High Impact, 1997
1 .... 3.00

Double Impact Bikini Special
High Impact, 1998
1 .... 3.00

Double Impact: From the Ashes
High Impact
1 .... 3.00
2 .... 6.00

Double Impact/Hellina
ABC, 1996
1 .... 3.00
1/Gold...................................... 5.00
1/Nude-1/Variant 3.00

Double Impact: One Step Beyond
High Impact, 1998
1 ....3.00
1/Variant.............................20.00

Double Impact: Raising Hell
ABC, 1997
1 ....3.00
1/Nude 4.00

Double Impact: Raw
ABC, 1997
1 ....3.00
1/A-1/2nd 4.00
2-3.................................3.00

Double Impact: Raw
ABC, 1998
1/Nude 3.00

Double Impact: Suicide Run
High Impact, 1997
1 ....3.00
1/A-1/Nude............................4.00

Double Impact: Trigger Happy
High Impact, 1997
1-1/B 3.00
1/Ltd. 4.00

Double Life of Private Strong
Archie, 1959
1 ....340.00
2 ....160.00

Double Talk
Feature, 1962
1 ....85.00

Double Trouble
St. John, 1957
1 ....20.00

Double Up
Eliot, 1941
1 ....450.00

Dover the Bird
Famous Funnies, 1955
1 ....30.00

Down
Image, 2006
1-4.................................3.00

Down with Crime
Fawcett, 1951
1 ....180.00
2 ....95.00
3-7.................................80.00

Do You Believe In Nightmares
St. John, 1957
1 ....290.00
2 ....170.00

D.P.7
Marvel, 1986

Randy O'Brian is working in the emergency room when David Landers, a normal guy who had gained two hundred pounds of muscle in a week, is rushed in. When the wild Landers breaks his restraints, O'Brian is shocked to find a ghostly form rising from his own body.

Seeking help, O'Brian and Landers go to the Institute for Paranormal Research, where they meet other people with unusual powers. The Institute is a front for an agency that wants to use them as operatives, though, and the group flees, becoming known as D.P.7, or "seven displaced paranormals."

One of the better New Universe titles from Marvel (which isn't saying much), this X-Men analog lasted a little longer than the rest.

1-32 .... 1.00
Ann 1-2................................. 1.00

Dracula
Dell, 1962
2 .... 20.00
3-4...................................... 12.00
6-8...................................... 7.00

Dracula
Eternity
1-4...................................... 3.00

Dracula (Bram Stoker's...)
Topps, 1992
1 .... 3.00
1/Variant................................. 4.00
2-4...................................... 3.00

Dracula 3-D
3-D Zone
1 .... 4.00

Dracula Chronicles
Topps
1-3.. 3.00

Dracula in Hell
Apple, 1992
1-2....................................... 3.00

Dracula Lives! (Magazine)
Marvel, 1973
1 .... 5.00
2 .... 4.00
3-13 .... 3.00
Ann 1..................................... 25.00

Dracula: Lord of the Undead
Marvel, 1998
1-3.. 3.00

Dracula: Return of the Impaler
Slave Labor, 1993
1-4.. 3.00

Dracula's Daughter
Fantagraphics, 1991
1 .... 3.00

Dracula's Revenge
Idea & Design Works, 2004
1-2...................................... 4.00

Dracula: The Lady in the Tomb
Eternity
1 .... 3.00

Dracula: The Suicide Club
Adventure, 1992
1-4....................................... 3.00

Dracula Versus Zorro
Topps, 1993
1-2....................................... 4.00

Dracula versus Zorro (Vol. 2)
Topps, 1994
1 .... 6.00

Dracula versus Zorro (Vol. 3)
Image, 1998
1-2.. 3.00

Dracula:
Vlad the Impaler
Topps, 1993

Dracula is one of the most horrifying and enduring figures in all of fiction. Created by novelist Bram Stoker, his legend has been expanded in countless books and films (and yes, comics as well).

But there was also a real Dracula, a prince of Wallachia and son of Vlad Dracul ("The Dragon"). His father was a tyrant, ambitiously seeking to wrest power from the struggle of East against West in the time of the Crusades. When his father was killed, Vlad Dracul the Younger ("Vlad Dracula") proved even more merciless. When he assumed power in Wallachia, he sought out the traitorous boyars who led to his parents' death. On Easter Sunday, he invited them to his palace for a feast, then had his guards arrest them. They marched the boyars for days, then forced them to build castle Dracula. The weak who could not make the journey were impaled on stakes, giving him the name Vlad the Impaler. And the terror had only begun!

1-3...3.00

Draculina
Draculina
1...3.00

Draculina's Cozy Coffin
Draculina, 1994
1-2...3.00

Draft
Marvel, 1988
1...2.00

Drag Comics
(Pete Millar's...)
Sham
1... 6.00
2... 5.00
3-4... 4.00

Drag 'n' Wheels
Charlton, 1968
30-35.................................. 12.00
36-59.................................. 10.00

Dragon
Comics Interview, 1987
1-4... 2.00

Dragon
Image, 1996
1-5... 2.00

Dragon Arms
Antarctic, 2002
1-6... 4.00

Dragon Arms:
Chaos Blade
Antarctic, 2004
1-6... 3.00

Dragon Arms
Stand Alone
Antarctic, 2005
1... 3.00

Dragonball
Viz, 1998

The seven Dragonballs are scattered all over the Earth. Should someone collect all seven, the Eternal Dragon will grant one wish.

World-wise teenager, Bulma, convinces the naive, but powerful boy Goku to accompany her on her search for the dragon balls. Bulma and Goku make friends and enemies on their journey. Both have hardships to overcome, but Goku welcomes most challenges.

Bulma isn't the only person seeking the Dragonballs. Despotical Emperor Pilaf knows the legend, too. His aids seek the dragonballs for the glory of their emperor. Then he will have the power to rule the world.

There are plenty of laughs, although the humor is often juvenile. The eventual wish will astonish you. Goku's adventures continue in Dragonball Part 2.

1-7... 4.00
8-12....................................... 3.00

Dragonball Part 2
Viz, 1999
1... 4.00
2-15....................................... 3.00

Dragonball Part 3
Viz, 2000
1-14....................................... 3.00

Dragonball Part 4
Viz, 2001
1-10....................................... 3.00

Dragonball Part 5
Viz, 2002
1-7... 3.00

Dragonball Part 6
Viz, 2003
1-2... 4.00

Dragonball Z
Viz, 1998
1-5... 4.00
6-10....................................... 3.00

Dragonball Z Part 2
Viz, 1998
1... 4.00
2-14....................................... 3.00

Dragonball Z Part 3
Viz, 2000
1-10....................................... 3.00

Dragonball Z Part 4
Viz, 2000
1-13....................................... 3.00

Dragonball Z Part 5
Viz, 2002
1-12....................................... 3.00

Dragon, The:
Blood & Guts
Image, 1995
1-3... 3.00

Dragon Chiang
Eclipse, 1991

In a dystopian future, a supertough Chinese truck driver who listens to Merle Haggard and Elvis Presley, goes after the bandits who have stolen his high-tech rig. Think "Mad Max Meets Cannonball Run." Throughout this black-and-white adventure, Chiang shows us what happens to men without honor, and waxes philosophic about the politics of a world where America is no longer the land of opportunity. This is cool stuff from the mind of Timothy Truman (The Spider, Grimjack, Hawkworld).

Dragon Chiang originally appeared in short installments in European comics and was collected and published in America by Eclipse Books.

1 ....4.00

Dragonfire
Nightwynd
1-4 ....3.00

Dragonfire
Nightwynd, 1992
1-4 ....3.00

Dragonfire:
The Classified Files
Nightwynd
1-4 ....3.00

Dragonfire:
The Early Years
Night Wynd
1-8 ....3.00

Dragonfire: UFO Wars
Nightwynd
1-3 ....3.00

Dragonflight
Eclipse, 1991

In the past 450 years, Pern has not experienced the deadly rain of Threads. Only dragons and their riders were able to burn them before they ravished the land. Now the Threads have passed into legend and the people of Pern are unhappy that they must keep these obsolete protectors of the land fed and sheltered.

Only the new weyrleader F'lar, his brother F'nor and his new weyrwoman Lessa believe that the Threads will fall once again. They must convince a planet that the danger is real and somehow find enough dragons to protect the planet once again...

Anne McCaffrey has made something of a career of dragon-based fantasy, ever since her classic "Dragonriders of Pern." This three-issue series is an adaptation of McCaffrey's "Dragonflight" novel.

1-3 .... 5.00

Dragon Flux
Antarctic, 1996
2-3 .... 3.00

Dragonfly
AC, 1985
1-8 .... 2.00

Dragonforce
Aircel, 1988
1-13 .... 2.00

Dragonforce Chronicles
Aircel, 1989
1-5 .... 3.00

Dragon Head
Tokyopop, 2006
1 .... 10.00

Dragonheart
Topps, 1996

1	3.00
2	5.00

Dragon Hunter
Tokyopop, 2003
1-13 .... 10.00

Dragon Knights
Slave Labor, 1998
1-3 .... 2.00

Dragon Knights
Tokyopop, 2002
1-21 .... 10.00

Dragon Lady
Dragon Lady, 1985

1-2	7.00
3-8	6.00

Dragonlance
DC, 1988

The Dragonlance world was developed by TSR for its role-playing game, Dungeons & Dragons, in the 1980s to provide gamers with an element they'd never really had: an official storyline with characters from the game manufacturer. It was very popular, leading to a revival not simply in the game, but in instilling an emphasis on storytelling in other role-playing games.

Dragonlance prose novels were very popular, and it's not surprising that comic books came along as well. The DC series, running side-by-side with its Advanced Dungeons & Dragons series, follows the surviving Solamnic Knights in their struggle against the Lord Soth and his Deathknights.

While comics about gamers would grow in popularity in the late 1990s, comics about gaming worlds tended to struggle, and DC ended this series after three years.
-- John Jackson Miller

1-2	2.00
3-5	1.00
6-34	2.00

Dragonlance Chronicles: Dragons of Autumn Twilight
Devil's Due, 2005

1-2	3.00
2/Special	6.00
3	3.00
3/Special	6.00
4	3.00
4/Special	6.00
5	3.00
5/Special	6.00
6	3.00
6/Special	6.00
7	3.00
7/Special	6.00
8	3.00
8/Variant	6.00

Dragonlance Chronicles: Dragons of Winter Night
Devil's Due, 2006

1	5.00
1/Special	9.00
2	5.00
2/Special	9.00
3	5.00
3/Special	9.00

Dragonlance Comic Book
TSR

1	1.00

Dragonlance Saga
TSR, 1987

1-5	10.00

Dragon Lines
Marvel, 1993

1	3.00
2-4	2.00

Dragon Lines: Way of the Warrior
Marvel, 1993

1-2	2.00

Dragon of the Valkyr
Rak, 1989

1-3	2.00

Dragon Quest
Silverwolf, 1986

1-2	2.00

Dragonring
Aircel, 1986

1-6	2.00

Dragonring
Aircel, 1986

1-15	2.00

Dragonrok Saga
Hanthercraft

1-10	3.00

Dragon's Bane
Hall of Heroes

1	3.00
Ashcan 1	5.00

Dragon's Claws
Marvel, 1988

1-10	2.00

Dragons in the Moon
Aircel, 1990

1-4	3.00

Dragon's Lair: Singe's Revenge
CrossGen, 2003

1-3	3.00

Dragonslayer
Marvel, 1981

It's the sixth century, and it's not a pleasant place to be. Here, a kingdom lives in terror of a powerful dragon, and only the sacrifice of a villager's daughter each year keeps the dragon's wrath at bay.

Tired of living in fear, the villagers seek out a magician to aid them, but few true magicians are left. Ulrich, master of all magic, is one of the few that remain-but he is killed by the king's warriors when the villagers go to him for aid. It's up to Ulrich's apprentice, the brave, but highly unqualified Galen Bradwardyn, to finish his master's last task. He must slay the dragon and save the village.

This two-issue story was based on the Paramount movie of the same name.

1-2	2.00

Dragon's Star
Matrix, 1986

1-3	2.00

Dragon's Star 2
Caliber, 1994

1-3	3.00

Dragon's Teeth
Dragon's Teeth

1	3.00

Dragon Strike
Marvel, 1994

1	2.00

Dragonstrike Prime
Illusion, 1996

2	2.00

Dragon Voice
Tokyopop, 2004

1-6	10.00

Dragon Wars
Ironcat, 1998

1-7	3.00

Drag-Strip Hotrodders
Charlton, 1963

1	40.00
2-16	25.00

Drain
Image, 2006

1-1/Variant	3.00

Drake: Demon Box
Image, 2003

1	3.00

Drakkon Wars
Realm, 1997

0	3.00

Drakuun
Dark Horse, 1997

The king of Ledomiam and Princess Rosalia have been captured by the emperor of Romunilia, and Princess Karula goes on a quest to rescue them.

Along the way, she is assisted and has romantic entanglements with Dard, the commander of the Royal Border Guard, and Arl, a retainer.

Written and drawn by Johji Manabe (Outlanders), this Dark Horse series juxtaposes heavy action sequences with stylish humor, while playing loose with fantasy and science fiction conventions.

1-24 ....3.00

Drama
Sirius Entertainment, 1994
1 ....4.00
1/Ltd. 12.00

Dramacon
Tokyopop, 2005
1 ....10.00

Drawing on your Nightmares: Halloween 2003 Special
Dark Horse, 2003
1 ....3.00

Drawn & Quarterly
Drawn & Quarterly, 1990
1-2 ....3.00
3-8 ....4.00

Drax the Destroyer
Marvel, 2005
1-4 ....3.00

Dr. Blink, Super-Hero Shrink
Dork Storm, 2005
1-2 ....3.00

Dreadlands
Marvel, 1992
1-4 ....4.00

Dread of Night
Hamilton, 1991
1-2 ....4.00

Dreadstar
Marvel, 1982

The first -- and, most would agree, the best -- series to come from Marvel's Epic line, Dreadstar follows Vanth Dreadstar as he leads an interstellar rebellion against the Instrumentality, a powerful religious order in service of the Twelve Gods.

First appearing in Epic Magazine, Jim Starlin's Dreadstar is joined by Syzygy Darklock (from the Eclipse graphic album "The Price"), Oedi the catman, Willow the psychic, and others as he works to stay one step ahead of his enemies. It's some of the best original space fantasy work to come from comics.

Starlin moved Dreadstar from Epic to First right at the culmination of the Instrumentality War, and he left the series at #40. Peter David took over the writing reins until the series' end.
-- John Jackson Miller

1 .... 3.00
2-49 .... 2.00
50 .... 3.00
51-64 .... 2.00
Ann 1 .... 3.00

Dreadstar
Malibu, 1994
1/2 .... 2.00
1/Gold-6 .... 3.00

Dreadstar & Co.
Marvel, 1985
1-6 .... 1.00

Dream Angel
Angel Entertainment, 1996
0 .... 3.00

Dream Angel and Angel Girl
Angel
1 .... 3.00

Dream Angel: The Quantum Dreamer
Angel
0-2 .... 3.00

Dream Book of Love
Magazine Enterprises, 1954
1-2 .... 50.00
3 .... 40.00

Dream Corridor (Harlan Ellison's...)
Dark Horse, 1995
1 .... 4.00
2-5 .... 3.00
Special 1 .... 5.00

Dream Corridor Quarterly (Harlan Ellison's...)
Dark Horse, 1996
1 .... 6.00

Dreamer
DC, 2000
1 .... 8.00

Dreamery
Eclipse, 1986
1-14 .... 2.00

Dreaming
DC, 1996
1-60 .... 3.00
Special 1 .... 6.00

Dreaming
Tokyopop, 2005
1 .... 10.00

Dreamland Chronicles
Astonish, 2004
1/Kunkel-1/Yeagle 4.00
2-3 .... 5.00

Dream Police
Marvel, 2005
1 .... 4.00
➥Straczynski series

Dream-Quest of Unknown Kadath (H.P. Lovecraft's...)
Mock Man, 1998
1-5 .... 3.00

Dreams Cannot Die!
Mark's Giant Economy Size, 1996
1 .... 18.00

Dreams 'n' Schemes of Col. Kilgore
Special Studio, 1991
1-2...3.00

Dreams of a Dog
Rip Off, 1990
1...2.00
2...3.00

Dreams of Everyman
Rip Off, 1992
1...3.00

Dreams of the Darkchylde
Darkchylde, 2000
1-1/A 4.00
1/B...10.00
1/C 6.00
1/D...10.00
1/E...15.00
1/F...5.00
2-6...3.00

Dream Team
Malibu, 1995
1...5.00

Dreamtime
Blind Bat, 1995
1-2...3.00

Dreamwalker
Dreamwalker, 1996
1-5...3.00

Dreamwalker
Caliber, 1996
1-6...3.00

Dreamwalker
Avatar, 1998
0...3.00

Dreamwalker
Marvel
1...7.00

Dreamwalker: Autumn Leaves
Avatar, 1999
1-2...3.00

Dreamwalker: Carousel
Avatar, 1999
1-2...3.00

Dreamwalker: Summer Rain
Avatar, 1999
1...3.00

Dream Weaver
Robert Lankford, 1987
1...2.00

Dream Weavers
Golden Realm Unlimited
1-2.............................. 2.00

Dream Wolves
Dramenon, 1994
1-4.............................. 3.00

Dream Wolves Swimsuit Bizarre
Gothic, 1995
0.............................. 3.00

Dredd By Bisley
Fleetway-Quality
1.............................. 6.00

Dredd Rules!
Fleetway-Quality

Dredd Rules! appeared as part of a revival of the Fleetway/Quality line in America in the early 1990s. It recolored and repackaged stories which originally ran in Britain's 2000 AD, and presented them in a glossy format which was miles better than 2000 AD's low-budget newsprint.

The stories all featured Judge Dredd, a tough future cop who worked to keep society under control in the sprawling Mega-City One. For this series, Fleetway picked the best of Dredd's more than 1,000 stories, including works by John Wagner and Simon Bisley.

1.............................. 4.00
2-20.............................. 3.00

Drifter
Brainstorm
1.............................. 3.00

Drifters
Cornerstone
1.............................. 2.00

Drifters
Infinity, 1986
1.............................. 2.00

Drive-In (Joe Lansdale's)
Avatar, 2003
1-4.............................. 4.00

Droids
Marvel, 1986

Unless you've been gone for a long, long time to a galaxy far, far away, you're probably familiar with R2-D2 and C3PO, the two lovable "droids" from George Lucas's Star Wars trilogy. The squat, vaguely sarcastic squeaking of R2-D2 and the hopelessly pompous English-butler mannerisms of C3PO provided comic relief to the cosmic space opera and made for such great merchandise tie-ins as toys and action figures.

Marvel's comic-book adventures of the two droids, based on a short-lived Saturday morning cartoon series, is pitched squarely at young readers, with a light cartoony style, easy-to-read stories, and lots of kid-oriented humor. Dark Horse later put out its own version of the title (Star Wars: Droids) when it acquired the rights to the Star Wars franchise in the 1990s.

1.............................. 3.00
2-8.............................. 2.00

Drool Magazine
Co. & Sons
1.............................. 3.00

Droopy
Dark Horse, 1995
1-3.............................. 3.00

Dropsie Avenue: The Neighborhood
Kitchen Sink, 1995
1.............................. 16.00

Drug Wars
Pioneer
1 .... 2.00

Druid
Marvel, 1995
1 .... 3.00
2-4 .... 2.00

Drunken Fist
Jademan, 1988

The Drunken Fist is a gentle form of Chinese martial arts capable of overcoming other harder styles. Mike Baron and Tony Wong introduce the form to an American audience in this series.

In the first issue, the living reincarnation of the Buddha Dalai Lama is born and, after being hunted by several villains, taken captive by the evil Indian Lama. Wong Mo Gei, Chek Fai and Drunken Kid fail in their mission to protect the Spiritual Child and set out to redeem themselves. Six years later, the child runs away from his captor, but seems to find greater trouble -- he stumbles across the ruthless soldiers of the Eternal Clan. Luckily, Chek Fai appears to challenge the would-be kidnappers.

Attempting to capitalize on what was then a red-hot martial arts market, Drunken Fist misses the mark. While the fight sequences are illustrated so as to accentuate the action, flow through the story's panels is illogical and confusing, leaving readers with the sense that something was lost in the translation.

1-54 .... 2.00

Dry Rot
Zolton
1 .... 3.00

Duck and Cover
Cat-Head
1-2 .... 2.00

Duckbots
Blackthorne, 1987
1-2 .... 2.00

Duckman
Dark Horse, 1990
1-Special 1 .... 2.00

Duckman
Topps, 1994
1-6 .... 3.00

Duckman:
The Mob Frog Saga
Topps, 1994
1-3 .... 3.00

DuckTales
Gladstone, 1988
1-13 .... 2.00

DuckTales (Disney's...)
Disney, 1990
1-18 .... 2.00

Ducktales: The Movie
Disney
1 .... 6.00

Dudley
Prize, 1949
1 .... 70.00
2-3 .... 60.00

Dudley Do-Right
Charlton, 1970

Rocky and Bullwinkle TV appearances, courtesy of Jay Ward (1920-1989) and Bill Scott (1920-1985), in the early 1960s were accompanied by other features. The moronic Dudley (voiced by Scott) was a Canadian Mountie ever on the trail of the villainous Snidely Whiplash, who was often after Inspector Fenwick's daughter Nell (who yearned, in turn, for Dudley). Even Dudley's horse, Horse, was smarter than the bumbling Mountie. Eventually, Dudley got a show with his name in the title (1969-1970), The Dudley Do-Right Show. The comic book's run in 1970 and 1971 is a testimonial to the character.

-- Maggie

1 .... 45.00
2 .... 18.00
3 .... 12.00
4-7 .... 10.00

Duel
Antarctic, 2005
0-1 .... 3.00

Duel Masters
Dreamwave, 2003
1 .... 3.00
1/Dynamic 6.00
1/A 3.00
1/B 6.00
2-4 .... 3.00
5 .... 4.00
6-8 .... 3.00

Dumb-Ass Express
McMann & Tate
1 .... 3.00

Dumm $2099
Parody
1 .... 3.00

Dunc and Loo
Dell, 1961
1 .... 50.00
2 .... 40.00
3-5 .... 35.00
6-8 .... 25.00

Dune
Marvel, 1985
1-3 .... 2.00

Dung Boys
Kitchen Sink, 1996
1-3 .... 3.00

Dungeon
NBM, 2002
1 .... 3.00

Dungeoneers
Silverwolf, 1986
1-4 .... 2.00

Dungeons and Dragons: In the Shadow of Dragons
Kenzer and Company, 2001

One of a slew of comics based on the granddaddy of all role-playing games, In the Shadow of Dragons is set in the Dungeons and Dragons realm of Greyhawk, which is being terrorized by three powerful dragons. They have set their fiery sights on the city of Rel Astra, demanding a strange and mysterious ransom--the remains of one of the dragon's fathers. If their demands are not met, the city and its inhabitants will die by fire. Four heroes rise up to seek what the dragons want, even as they look for a way to defeat the beasts and keep their city safe. Gifre the apprentice wizard, Evina, the swordswoman, Lucien the paladin, and bounty hunter Kiernan Ornarus make new friends and new enemies on their quest. But then, that's what D&D is all about, whether it's played out on a table or in a comic book. RPG fans will enjoy this effort by writer Jay Donovan and penciller Tyler Walpole.

-- Stephen C. George

1-8 .... 3.00

Dungeons & Dragons: Where Shadows Fall
Kenzer and Company, 2003
1-5 .... 4.00

Duplex Planet Illustrated
Fantagraphics, 1993
1-14 .... 3.00
15 .... 5.00

Durango Kid
Magazine Enterprises, 1949
1 .... 300.00
2 .... 200.00
3 .... 165.00

4-5 .... 100.00
6-10 .... 50.00
11-30 .... 40.00
31-41 .... 35.00

Durango Kid
AC
1-2 .... 3.00
3 .... 5.00

Dusk
Deadwood
1 .... 3.00

Dusty Star
Image, 1997
0-1 .... 3.00
2 .... 4.00

Dutch Decker and the Voodoo Queen
Caliber
1 .... 3.00

DV8
DC, 1996
0-14/B 3.00
14/C 5.00
15-Ann 1 .... 3.00
Ann 1999 .... 4.00

DV8 Rave
Image, 1996
1 .... 2.00

DV8 vs. Black Ops
Image, 1997
1-3 .... 3.00

Dyke's Delight
Fanny
1-2 .... 3.00

Dylan Dog
Dark Horse, 1999
1-6 .... 5.00

Dynamic Classics
DC, 1978
1 .... 4.00

Dynamic Comics
Harry A. Chesler, 1941
11 .... 875.00
12 .... 450.00
13 .... 400.00
14-15 .... 300.00
16-17 .... 275.00
18-24 .... 200.00

Dynamite
Comic Media, 1953
1 .... 48.00
2 .... 40.00
3-5 .... 36.00
6-9 .... 30.00

Dynamo
Tower, 1966

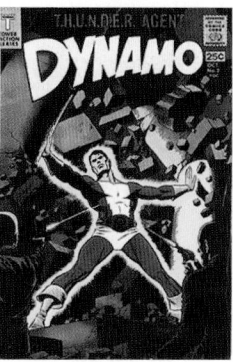

The Tower line of comics is ideal for collectors: there aren't that many of them to find, and they're generally very good. The line is primarily populated by charming, well-drawn, wittily written super-heroes allied with the crime-fighting team called T.H.U.N.D.E.R. Agents.

Dynamo is one of the T.H.U.N.D.E.R. Agents, a powerful (but not too bright) foe of evil who gets his powers from a super-belt.

The four issues feature classic work by artist Wally Wood; other artists involved in the series include Spider-Man co-creator Steve Ditko and Reed Crandall.

-- Maggie

1 .... 35.00
2-3 .... 25.00
4 .... 40.00

Dynamo Joe
First, 1986
1 .... 2.00
2-11 .... 1.00
12-15 .... 2.00
Special 1 .... 1.00

Dynomutt
Marvel, 1977
1 .... 10.00
2 .... 5.00
3-6 .... 3.00

Dystopik Snomen
Slave Labor, 1994
1 .... 5.00

Dystopik Snomen
Slave Labor, 1995
1-2 .... 2.00

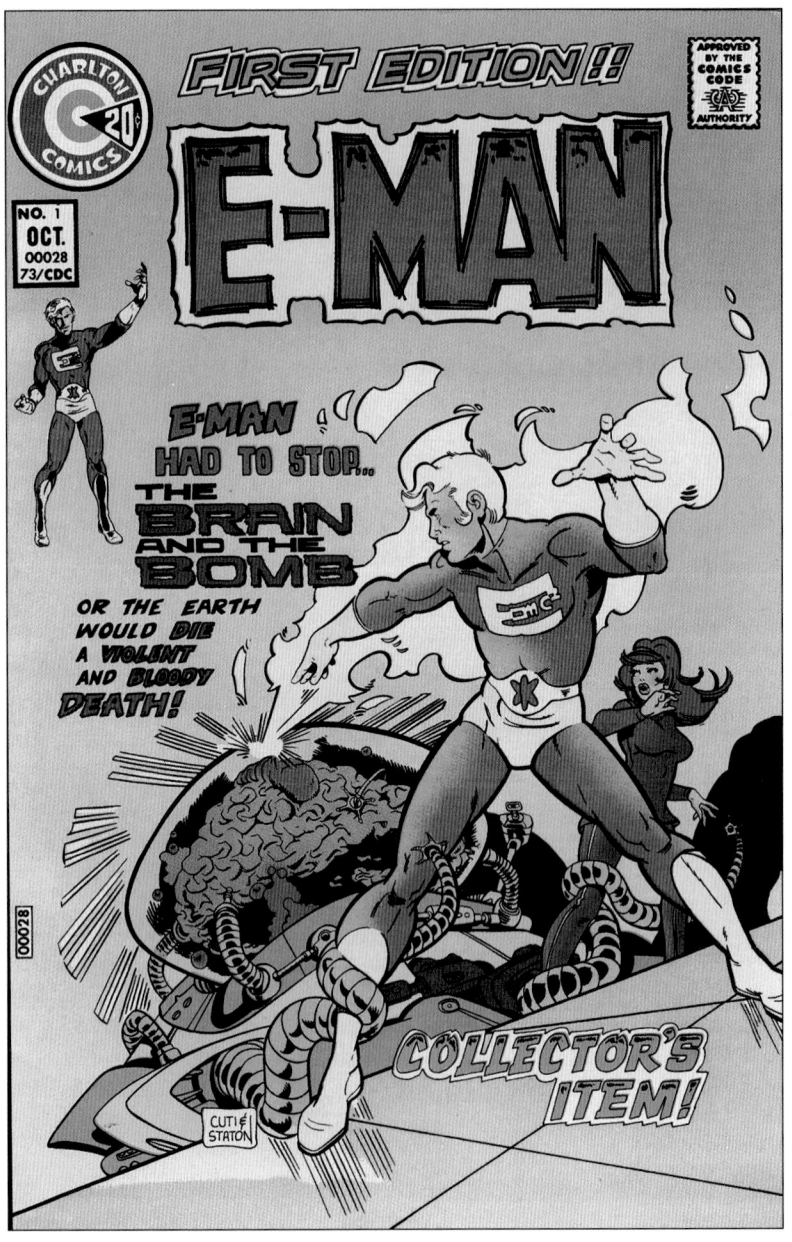

Nicola Cuti and Joe Staton's energy-based hero began his adventures in the early 1970s.

virus now infects nearly all of humanity (Except Tony Stark, who is now a recluse: the likes of Howard Hughes). This virus gives super powers to the entire populace of Earth X.

Old heroes are twisted, new heroes have only the barest resemblance to their former namesakes, sort of a Marvel version of Kingdom Come. This is a world created by Alex Ross (Superman: Peace on Earth, Astro City). Though Earth X is a fully painted story by Ross, the first glimpse of this strange world was seen in a small comics insert to Wizard magazine. It merely contained the basic premise and some of Alex's concept sketches. These were later reprinted in a special edition to this series with a more complete set of sketches.

0	4.00
0/A	5.00
0/B	4.00
0/C	5.00
1	3.00
1/A	5.00
1/B	30.00
1/C	70.00
2-12	3.00
13	4.00

Earth X Sketchbook
Marvel, 1999

1	5.00

East Meets West
Innovation, 1990

1	3.00

Easy Way
Idea & Design Works, 2005

1-4	4.00

Eating Raoul
Kim Deitch, 1982

1	2.00

Eat-Man
Viz, 1997

1-6	3.00

Eat-Man Second Course
Viz, 1998

1	3.00
2-3	4.00
4-5	3.00

Eberron: Eye of the Wolf
Devil's Due, 2006

1	5.00
1/Special	9.00

Eb'nn
Now, 1986

3-6	2.00

Eagle
Fox, 1941

1	1,600.00
2	650.00
3-4	450.00

Eagle
Rural Home, 1945

1	325.00
2	165.00

Eagle
Crystal, 1986

1-23	2.00

Eagle
Comic Zone, 1992

1-3	3.00

Eagles Dare
Aager, 1994

1-2	2.00

Eagle: The Dark Mirror Saga
Comic Zone, 1992

1-3	3.00

Early Days of the Southern Knights
Comics Interview, 1986

1-4	5.00
5	6.00
6-8	7.00

Earth C.O.R.E.
Independent

1	2.00

Earth 4 (Vol. 2)
Continuity, 1993

1-4	3.00

Earth 4 Deathwatch 2000
Continuity, 1993

0-3	3.00

Earthlore
Eternity

1-2	2.00

Earth Man on Venus, An
Avon, 1951

1	875.00

Earthworm Jim
Marvel, 1995

1-4	2.00

Earth X
Marvel, 1999

In the near future, an experiment performed by Reed Richards will go horribly wrong. Richards manipulates the unstable substance vibranium and accidentally creates a virus. This

Eb'nn the Raven
Crowquill
1-2 .... 3.00

Ebony Warrior
Africa Rising, 1993
1 .... 2.00

E.C. Classic Reprints
East Coast Comix, 1973

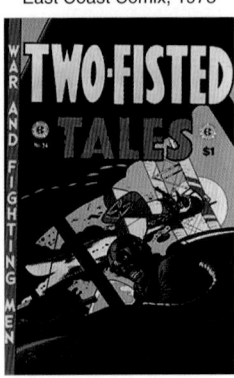

The "other" E.C. - East Coast Comix - reprinted some of the greatest works of the William Gaines' E.C. comics in this 1970s series. Exceptionally faithful to the originals, this series reprinted, in their entirety, issues of Two-Fisted Tales, Haunt of Fear, Weird Science, Crime SuspenStories, and other great E.C. comics from the 1950s.

These comics represent the greatest moments in "comics noir," dark tales of fantasy and suspense which thrilled readers in the days before the Comics Code.

Covers carried the original issue's numbering, leaving the indicia as the only source of this reprint series chronology.

1 .... 4.00
2-12 .... 3.00

EC Classics
Cochran
1-6 .... 5.00

Echo
Image, 2000
0-5 .... 3.00

Echo of Futurepast
Continuity, 1984
1-9 .... 3.00

Eclipse
Graphic Album Series
Eclipse, 1978
1 .... 7.00
1/2nd-1/3rd 6.00
2 .... 5.00
3 .... 7.00
4 .... 6.00
5 .... 7.00
6 .... 6.00
7 .... 8.00
7/HC 20.00
7/2nd 8.00
7/3rd 9.00
8 .... 6.00
9-10 .... 14.00
10/HC-11 .... 25.00
12 .... 8.00
12/HC 15.00
12/Ltd. 25.00
13 .... 9.00
14 .... 5.00
15 .... 4.00
16 .... 5.00
17 .... 7.00
18 .... 5.00
19 .... 15.00
20 .... 5.00
21 .... 4.00
22-24 .... 5.00
25-26 .... 9.00
27 .... 6.00
28 .... 9.00
29 .... 15.00
30 .... 9.00
30/HC 30.00
31 .... 7.00
31/Ltd. 30.00
32-33 .... 10.00
34 .... 4.00
35 .... 8.00
36 .... 5.00
37 .... 4.00
38 .... 9.00
39-41 .... 5.00
42 .... 9.00
43 .... 8.00
44 .... 6.00
45 .... 11.00
46 .... 8.00
47 .... 15.00
48 .... 10.00
49 .... 7.00
50 .... 13.00
51 .... 8.00
52 .... 5.00

Eclipse Magazine
Eclipse, 1981

This black-and-white magazine from the early 1980s featured a couple of strips that earned their own color titles from Eclipse Comics. Steve Englehart (Avengers) and Marshall Rogers (Detective Comics) offered up Coyote, a dimension-hopping mystic, while Max Collins and Terry Beatty delivered another installment in the adventures of P.I. supreme Ms. Tree. The magazine also showcased work from Don McGregor (Detectives, Inc.) and Gene Colan (Tomb of Dracula), Steve Gerber (Howard the Duck) and Val Mayerick (Savage Sword of Conan), Charles Vess (Stardust), and Trina Robbins (Go Girl!).

1-8 .... 3.00

Eclipse Monthly
Eclipse, 1983
1-10 .... 2.00

Eclipso
DC, 1992
1-5 .... 2.00
6-14 .... 1.00
15-18 .... 2.00
Ann 1 .... 3.00

Eclipso:
The Darkness Within
DC, 1992
1-2 .... 3.00

Ectokid
Marvel, 1993

Ectokid is a creation of horror writer Clive Barker. Set in New Orleans, a city known equally for jazz and voodoo, it stars Dex Mungo, a young boy and petty thief.

While ripping off tourists one day at a local hotel, he was invited into a room by three gorgeous women. Dex fell under their spell and into their embrace. When he opened his eyes, however, he saw them as ghastly supernatural creatures. The vision cleared, but Dex fled, hotly pursued by others who appeared alternately as men and demons.

This is how Dex came to discover both his heritage and his own special ability. Dex's mother, it seems, had mated with a ghost to produce Dex. As a result, Dex has ties to both our world and the world beyond. Through his right eye, he sees the world as we know it, but through his left, he sees the parallel ghost world of spirits and demons.

1 ....3.00
2-9 ....2.00

Ectokid Unleashed!
Marvel, 1994

1 ....3.00

Ed
3CG Comics, 1997

1 ....3.00

Eddie Stanky Baseball Hero
Fawcett, 1951

1 ....200.00

Eddy Current
Mad Dog, 1987

1-12 ....3.00

Eden Descendants
Quester Entertainment

1 ....4.00

Eden Matrix
Adhesive

1/A-1/B 3.00

Eden's Trail
Marvel, 2003

1-5 .... 3.00

Edgar Allan Poe
Eternity, 1988

1-5 .... 2.00

Edge
Silverwolf, 1987

1-2 .... 2.00

Edge
Greater Mercury, 1989

1-11 .... 2.00

Edge
Malibu, 1994

1-3 .... 3.00

Edge of Chaos
Pacific, 1983

1-3 .... 1.00

Ed the Happy Clown
Drawn & Quarterly, 2005

1-3 .... 3.00

Eek! the Cat
Hamilton, 1994

1-3 .... 2.00

Eerie
Avon, 1947

1 .... 850.00
1/2nd 400.00
2 .... 500.00
3 .... 400.00
4-6 .... 350.00
7-8 .... 285.00
9-10 .... 240.00
11-13 .... 200.00
14-17 .... 165.00

Eerie
Warren, 1965

1 .... 175.00
1/2nd 35.00
2 .... 100.00
3 .... 40.00
4-6 .... 30.00
7-10 .... 28.00
11-16 .... 18.00
17 .... 60.00
☛Scarce
18-39 .... 18.00
40 .... 6.00
41-60 .... 12.00
61-70 .... 10.00
71-80 .... 9.00
81 .... 70.00
☛Frazetta cover
82-100 .... 9.00
101-139 .... 8.00
YB 1970 .... 36.00
YB 1971 .... 25.00
YB 1972 .... 18.00

Eerie
I.W.

1 .... 24.00
2 .... 17.00

Eerie Adventures
Ziff-Davis, 1951

1 .... 150.00

Eerie Queerie!
Tokyopop, 2004

1-4 .... 10.00

Eerie Tales
Super

12 .... 15.00

Egon
Dark Horse, 1998

Egon is an enigma--the brainchild of a group of Italian creators who share a passion for B-movies and a desire to produce a very new, nontraditional kind of comic.

Egon is a supranatural--a singular individual with the ability to not feel pain and the gift (either a permanent or temporary gift) of immortality.

Egon is a killer--a crusader for the weak and weary whose remedy (to the weak and weary) for a cruel life is a swift death.

Egon is a man--one of very complex values and emotions that an outside observer (such as you, gentle reader) should not try and get too close to.

Egon is Egon--a two issue effort. Take him or leave him (all at a safe distance).

1-2 .... 3.00

Egypt
DC, 1995

1-7 .... 3.00

Eh!
Charlton, 1953

1 .... 150.00
2 .... 90.00

3-4 ....75.00
5 ....60.00
6-7 ....50.00

Ehlissa
Highland Graphics, 1992
1-33 ....2.00

Eightball
Fantagraphics, 1993

Eightball is perhaps the most famous work by alternative comics guru Dan Clowes. Clowes brings a shaky, claustrophobic feel to each of these stories, a mood that is reflected in everything from the perpetually furrowed brows of the characters to the surreal nature of situations they find themselves in. A good example of this is the series' lead story, "Like a Velvet Glove Cast in Iron." Here a man finds an all-knowing oracle in the bathroom of a movie theater and all he can think to ask is whether or not the oracle knew anything about the strange film he just watched. The images from that film reappear again when the man meets a person with fish in his eye sockets, an insane street bum, and a three-eyed prostitute.

Eightball is reminiscent of William S. Burroughs' "Naked Lunch," particularly in how the painfully dull lives of the characters are transformed to take on nightmarish dimensions.

1 ....10.00
1/2nd 5.00
1/3rd 4.00
1/4th 3.00
2 ....6.00
3-4 ....5.00
5-8 ....4.00
9-15 ....3.00
16 ....4.00
17-18 ....3.00
19 ....4.00
20-21 ....5.00
22-23 ....3.00

Eighth Wonder
Dark Horse, 1997
1 .... 3.00

Eight Legged Freaks
WildStorm, 2002
1 .... 7.00

80 Page Giant Magazine
DC, 1964
1 .... 295.00
2 .... 150.00
3-6 .... 125.00
7 .... 150.00
8 .... 265.00
☞Secret Origins
9-11 .... 125.00
12-15 .... 80.00

86 Voltz: Dead Girl One-Shot
Image, 2005
1 .... 6.00

Ekos Preview
Aspen, 2003
1 .... 8.00

El Arsenal Unknown Enemy
Arcana, 2005
1-2 .... 3.00

El Cazador
CrossGen, 2003
1-6 .... 3.00

El Cazador: Blackjack Tom
CrossGen, 2004
1 .... 3.00

El Condün Asesino (Ralf König's...)
Vibora
1-2 .... 2.00

El Diablo
DC, 1989
1 .... 3.00
2-16 .... 2.00

El Diablo
DC, 2001
1-4 .... 3.00

Electric Fear
Sparks, 1984
1-2 .... 2.00

Electric Girl
Mighty Gremlin, 1998
1 .... 4.00
2-3 .... 3.00

Electric Warrior
DC, 1986
1-18 .... 2.00

Electropolis
Image, 2001
1-3 .... 3.00

Elektra (1st Series)
Marvel, 1995
1 .... 4.00
2-4 .... 3.00

Elektra (2nd series)
Marvel, 1996
-1 .... 2.00
1 .... 4.00
1/A-3 .... 3.00
4-19 .... 2.00

Elektra (3rd series)
Marvel, 2001
1 .... 4.00
2-2/A 3.00
3-3/Nude 10.00
4-35 .... 3.00

Elektra & Wolverine: The Redeemer
Marvel, 2002
1-3 .... 6.00

Elektra: Assassin
Marvel, 1986

Elektra was easily one of Marvel's greatest characters, a female assassin that lit up the pages of Daredevil from her first appearance in issue #168 to her death in issue #181. Although her origin was sketched out in Daredevil, this series goes far deeper, delving into her own psyche to show how an innocent girl became transformed into an instrument of death.

Elektra: Assassin was written by Elektra's creator, Frank Miller, and painted by Bill Sienkiewicz. The result is a comic-book tour de force that's almost impossible to put down.

1-8 .... 3.00

Elektra Battlebook
Marvel, 1998
1 .... 4.00

Elektra/Cyblade
Image, 1997
1-1/A 3.00

Elektra: Glimpse & Echo
Marvel, 2002
1-4...3.00

Elektra Lives Again
Marvel, 1991
1..25.00

Elektra Megazine
Marvel, 1996
1-2..4.00

Elektra Saga
Marvel, 1984
1-4..4.00

Elektra: The Hand
Marvel, 2004
1-5..3.00

Elektra: The Movie
Marvel, 2005
1..6.00

Elementals
Comico, 1984
1...3.00
2-29.......................................2.00
Special 1 ....3.00
Special 2 ....2.00

Elementals
Comico, 1989
1...3.00
2-3...2.00
4-41.......................................3.00

Elementals
Comico, 1995
1-3..3.00

Elementals:
Ghost of a Chance
Comico, 1995
1..6.00

Elementals:
How the War Was Won
Comico, 1996
1-2..3.00

Elementals Lingerie
Comico, 1996
1..3.00

Elementals Sex Special
Comico, 1991
1/Gold 5.00
1-4..3.00

Elementals Sex Special
Comico, 1997
1..3.00

Elemental's
Sexy Lingerie Special
Comico, 1993
1/A...3.00
1/B...6.00

Elementals Swimsuit Spectacular 1996
Comico, 1996
1/Gold................................... 4.00
1 .... 3.00

Elementals:
The Vampires' Revenge
Comico, 1996
1-2 .... 3.00

Elephantmen
Image, 2006
0-5 .... 3.00

Eleven or One
Sirius Entertainment, 1995

Joseph Michael Linsner, best known for his work on Dawn, here tells the story of Laddie Lopez, a New York City artist with a unique talent: he actually gets paid for his work. Laddie received countless telephone calls from agents who wanted to represent him, including his ex-wife. Of course, he turned them all down and decided to represent himself.

The stress of taking the lone route seems to have taken its toll on the young artist. Then one morning, Laddie woke with a second middle finger on his right hand. After convincing himself that he was not dreaming, he talked with all of his friends, one by one. None of them noticed his abnormality, even when he flashed his hand right in front of them. Laddie was inspired by this bizarre turn of events and decided to paint a series of paintings which he titled, Eleven or One. It asked the question: "Eleven parts or one whole?" It became a metaphor for Laddie's own search for meaning in his life.

1 .... 4.00
1/2nd 3.00

Elfheim
Nightwynd, 1991
1-4 .... 3.00

Elfheim (Vol. 2)
Nightwynd
1-4 .... 3.00

Elfheim (Vol. 3)
Nightwynd
1-4 .... 3.00

Elfheim (Vol. 4)
Nightwynd
1-2 .... 3.00

Elfheim: Dragon Dream
Night Wynd, 1993
1-4 .... 3.00

Elfin Romance
Mt. Wilson, 1994
1-6 .... 2.00
7 .... 3.00

Elflord
Aircel, 1986
1-8 .... 2.00

Elflord (2nd Series)
Aircel, 1986
1-20 .... 2.00
21 .... 5.00
22-31 .... 2.00

Elflord (3rd Series)
Night Wynd
1-4 .... 3.00

Elflord (4th Series)
Warp, 1997
1-4 .... 3.00

Elflord (5th Series)
Warp, 1997
1-7 .... 3.00

Elflord Chronicles
Aircel, 1990
1-12 .... 3.00

Elflord: Dragon's Eye
Night Wynd, 1993
1-3 .... 3.00

Elflord the Return
Mad Monkey, 1996
1 .... 7.00

Elflord:
The Return of the King
Night Wynd
1-4 .... 3.00

Elflore
Nightwynd
1-4 .... 3.00

Elflore (Vol. 2)
Nightwynd
1-4 .... 3.00

Elflore (Vol. 3)
Nightwynd

1-4 .... 3.00

Elflore: High Seas
Night Wynd, 1993

1-3 .... 3.00

Elfquest
Warp, 1978

Elfquest is a labor of love by husband-and-wife team, Wendy and Richard Pini. They described themselves as "two people who share a too-crowded apartment with elves, wolves, trolls, and lots of drawing paper!" From that environment, they wrote, drew, published, and distributed the comic magazine that would become a cult phenomenon.

Elfquest is the story of Cutter, a young elf, and his Wolfriders as they are driven from their forest home by humans and must travel far in search of a new one. With courage and steadfastness, Cutter leads his clan through all manner of danger and adversity, in an epic tale of fantasy.

1	32.00
1/2nd	12.00
1/3rd	8.00
1/4th	5.00
2	18.00
2/2nd	6.00
2/3rd	4.00
2/4th	3.00
3	18.00
3/2nd-3/4th	3.00
4	16.00
4/2nd	5.00
4/3rd	4.00
4/4th	3.00
5	16.00
5/2nd-5/3rd	3.00
6	13.00
6/2nd	4.00
6/3rd	3.00
7	10.00
7/2nd	4.00
7/3rd	3.00
8	10.00
8/2nd	4.00

8/3rd	3.00
9	10.00
9/2nd	4.00
9/3rd	3.00
10-15	8.00
16	10.00
17-21	7.00

Elfquest
Marvel, 1985

1	4.00
2-5	3.00
6-32	2.00

Elfquest
Warp, 1996

1	6.00
2-31	5.00
32-33	3.00

Elfquest (Warp Reprints)
Warp, 1989

1-4 .... 2.00

Elfquest 25th Anniversary Edition
DC, 2003

1 .... 3.00

Elfquest: Blood of Ten Chiefs
Warp, 1993

1-20 .... 3.00

Elfquest: Hidden Years
Warp, 1992

1-29 .... 3.00

Elfquest: Jink
Warp, 1994

1-12 .... 3.00

Elfquest: Kahvi
Warp, 1995

1-6 .... 2.00

Elfquest: Kings Cross
Warp, 1997

1-2 .... 3.00

Elfquest: Kings of the Broken Wheel
Warp, 1990

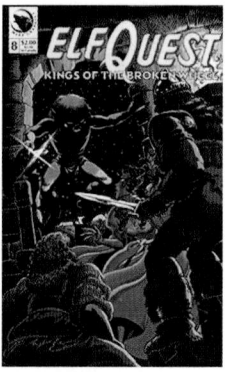

The elves' story began with an accident. The High Ones had been traveling through time from the medieval age and had missed their mark, ending up in an age where men were still basically savages. Instead of being welcomed with open arms, the High Ones found themselves subject to brutal attack by the humans. Disoriented, the High Ones fled their palace and sought refuge in this new world. They and their children eventually became the ancestors of the Cutter and the rest of the Elfquest elves.

Then Rayek, one of Cutter's kinsmen took it into his head to play god. He kidnapped Cutter's family and invaded the palace of the High Ones. Rayek was determined to travel back to the point of the original accident and "correct" it. He sought power, but it's doubtful that he understood the full implications of correcting a mistake that gave birth to his entire species. The elves' history was a broken wheel in time - and by repairing it, Rayek could destroy them all!

1	3.00
2-9	2.00

Elfquest: Metamorphosis
Warp, 1996

1 .... 3.00

Elfquest: New Blood
Warp, 1992

1	5.00
2-10	3.00
11-26	2.00
27-33	3.00
34-35	2.00
Special 1	4.00

Elfquest: Recognition Summer 2001 Special
Warp, 2001

2 .... 3.00

Elfquest: Shards
Warp, 1994

1-5	3.00
6-8	2.00
9-12	3.00
13-16	2.00
Ashcan 1	1.00

Elfquest: Siege at Blue Mountain
Warp, 1987

1-2	3.00
2/2nd	2.00
2/3rd-3	3.00
3/2nd	2.00
4-8	3.00

Elfquest: The Discovery
DC, 2006
1-4 .... 4.00

Elfquest: The Grand Quest
DC, 2004
1-4 .... 10.00

Elfquest: The Rebels
Warp, 1994
1 .... 3.00
2-12 .... 2.00

Elfquest: Two-Spear
Warp, 1995
1-5 .... 2.00

Elfquest: Wavedancers
Warp, 1993
1-8 .... 2.00
Special 1 .... 3.00

Elfquest: Wolfrider
DC, 2003
1 .... 10.00

Elfquest: Wolfshadow Summer 2001 Special
Warp, 2001
1 .... 4.00

Elfquest: Worldpool
Warp, 1997
1 .... 3.00

Elf-Thing
Eclipse, 1987
1 .... 2.00

Elftrek
Dimension, 1986
1-2 .... 2.00

Elf Warrior
Adventure, 1987
1-4 .... 2.00

El Gato Negro
Azteca, 1993
1-3 .... 2.00
4 .... 3.00

El Gaucho
NBM
1 .... 21.00

El-Hazard
Viz, 1997

El Hazard: The Magnificent World is a beautiful fantasy tale. Three students and a teacher are transported to a magical world from a modern Japanese high school. In the realm of El-Hazard, they become entangled in a giant war between the human inhabitants of Roshtaria, the insect drones of Bugrom, and the mysterious Shadow People, all of which are struggling to obtain the immense power of a weapon - the Eye of God. This is the realm of El-Hazard, the land of never-ending adventures. As long as there is a challenging spirit and a readiness to fly into infinity, its gate shall be forever open. The events of the series are loosely based on the El-Hazard, the Magnificent World OAV (Original Animated Video) series.

1 .... 3.00

El Hazard: The Magnificent World Part 1
Viz, 2000
1-5 .... 3.00

El Hazard: The Magnificent World Part 2
Viz, 2001
1-5 .... 3.00

El Hazard: The Magnificent World Part 3
Viz, 2001
1-6 .... 3.00

Eliminator
Malibu, 1995
0-1 .... 3.00
1/Variant 4.00
2-3 .... 3.00

Eliminator
Eternity, 1991
1-3 .... 3.00

Eliminator Full Color Special
Eternity, 1991
1 .... 3.00

Elk's Run
Hoarse and Buggy, 2005
1-3 .... 3.00

Ellery Queen Comics
Superior, 1949
1 .... 440.00
2 .... 260.00
3-4 .... 185.00

Ellery Queen
Ziff-Davis, 1952
1 .... 325.00
2 .... 200.00

Elmo Comics
St. John, 1948
1 .... 50.00

Elongated Man
DC, 1992

Elongated Man first came onto the scene in Flash #112 in the 1960s. His real name is Ralph Dibney, a man who had long dreamed of becoming a contortionist. After years of frustration, he tried drinking a brew of "Gingold," a brand of soda water extracted from a rubber plant. Combined with his unique metabolism, it gave him the ability to stretch and contort himself into any shape he wished.

A former member of The Justice League of America, Ralph now travels the world with his wife, the wealthy Sue Dearborn. When there's mystery in the air, Ralph's nose twitches, and he's off to investigate as the Elongated Man. And, as he says at the beginning of this mini-series, "When a lone wolf

assassin starts working with a
French super-criminal ... I smell a
mystery!"

1-4...1.00

El Perfecto Comics
Print Mint

1..4.00

Elric
Pacific, 1983

Michael Moorcock's Elric has
become one of the most important
figures of the sword and sorcery
genre. The albino king of the
magical land of MelnibonT, Elric is
a legend of furrowed brow and
wizardly power. Son of Sadric
LXXXVI, he was a sickly child,
dependent upon magical potions
to maintain his strength. As it turns
out, he'll need great strength
indeed if he is to forestall the doom
that threatens his kingdom.

Elric's adventures have been
chronicled in a series of popular
paperbacks. Finally, this great
character comes to the realm of
comics.

1-6...2.00

Elric
Topps, 1996

0..4.00
1-4...3.00

Elric: Sailor on the Seas of Fate
First, 1985

1-7...2.00

Elric: Stormbringer
Dark Horse, 1997

1-7...3.00

Elric: The Bane of the Black Sword
First, 1988

1-6...2.00

Elric: The Making of a Sorcerer
DC, 2004

1-4.............................. 6.00

Elric: The Vanishing Tower
First, 1987

1-6... 2.00

Elric: Weird of the White Wolf
First, 1986

1-5... 2.00

El Salvador: A House Divided
Eclipse

1 .... 3.00

Elsewhere Prince
Marvel, 1990

1-6... 2.00

Elseworlds 80-Page Giant
DC, 1999

1 .... 110.00

Elseworld's Finest
DC, 1997

1-2... 5.00

Elseworld's Finest: Supergirl & Batgirl
DC, 1998

1 .... 6.00
1/Ltd. 19.00

Elsinore
Alias, 2005

1-7... 3.00

Elsinore
Devil's Due, 2005

4-5... 3.00

Elven
Malibu, 1994

Little Elvia was the daughter of
a Mexican woman and her abusive
American husband. When her

father would beat up her mother,
Elvia would escape into the world
of fantasy found in books like Lord
of the Rings. Mercifully, her mother
eventually found the courage to
leave, taking refuge in the women's
shelter, Halo House. It was there
that Elvia's Ultra powers
manifested themselves, letting her
transform from a scared little girl
into an fierce woman avenger
named Elven.

In effect, Elven was similar to
Prime in that behind their super-
powerful adult bodies are
frightened children. The two
shared a common origin in the
experiments of Doctor Gross, and
their "Ultra bodies" disintegrate
when they're worn out, fading into
a pool of ooze. In a way, Elven is
the closest thing Prime ever had to
a little sister, although Elven's
childhood was far more traumatic
than Prime's.

0 .... 3.00
1 .... 2.00
1/Ltd. 3.00
2-4 .... 2.00

Elvira, Mistress of the Dark
Marvel, 1988

1 .... 4.00

Elvira, Mistress of the Dark
Claypool, 1993

1 .... 4.00
2-166 .... 3.00

Elvira's House of Mystery
DC, 1986

1 .... 3.00
2-10 .... 2.00
11 .... 3.00
Special 1 .... 2.00

Elvis Mandible
DC, 1990

1 .... 4.00

Elvis Presley Experience
Revolutionary, 1992

1-7... 3.00

Elvis Shrugged
Revolutionary, 1992

1-2... 3.00
3 .... 4.00

El Zombo
Dark Horse, 2004

1-3... 3.00

E-Man
Charlton, 1973

1 .... 4.00
2-10 .... 3.00

E-Man
First, 1983
1-5 .... 2.00
6-25 .... 1.00

E-Man
Comico, 1989
1 .... 3.00

E-Man
Comico, 1990
1-3 .... 3.00

E-Man
Alpha, 1993
1 .... 3.00

E-Man Returns
Alpha Productions, 1994
1 .... 3.00

Emblem
Antarctic, 1994
1 .... 4.00
2-8 .... 3.00

Embrace
London Night, 1997
1 .... 5.00
1/Ltd. 10.00

Emeraldas
Eternity, 1990
1-4 .... 2.00

Emergency!
Charlton, 1976

![Emergency! comic cover]

Emergency was a popular 1970s television show that followed the non-stop rescue adventures of Los Angeles paramedics John Gage and Roy Desoto. The brave paramedics do everything from saving the proverbial trapped pets to treating burn victims at a fire. With all the lives they're saving, it's amazing Gage and Desoto have time for recreation. Even then, free time is often taken up with minor rescues, such as performing the Heimlich maneuver on a choking party guest.

1 .... 20.00
2 .... 16.00
3 .... 14.00
4 .... 16.00

Emergency!
Charlton, 1976
1 .... 30.00
2 .... 25.00
3-4 .... 22.00

Emil and the Detectives
Gold Key, 1964
1 .... 25.00

Emily the Strange
Dark Horse, 2005
1-3 .... 8.00

Emissary
Strateia, 1998
1 .... 4.00

Emma Davenport
Lohman Hills, 1995
1-8 .... 3.00

Emma Frost
Marvel, 2003
1 .... 4.00
2-18 .... 3.00

Emo Boy
Slave Labor, 2005
1-4 .... 3.00

Empire
Eternity, 1988
1-4 .... 2.00

Empire
Image, 2000
1-2 .... 3.00

Empire
DC, 2003
0 .... 5.00
1-6 .... 3.00

Empire Lanes
Northern Lights, 1986
1-4 .... 2.00

Empire Lanes
Keyline
1 .... 2.00

Empire Lanes
Keyline, 1989
1 .... 3.00

Empires of Night
Rebel, 1993
1-4 .... 2.00

Empty Love Stories
Slave Labor, 1994
1-2 .... 3.00

Empty Love Stories
Funny Valentine, 1998
1-Special 1 .... 3.00

Empty Love Stories: 1999
Funny Valentine, 1999
1 .... 3.00

Empty Skull Comics
Fantagraphics, 1996
1 .... 5.00

Empty Zone
Sirius
1-4 .... 3.00

Empty Zone
Sirius, 1998
1-8 .... 3.00

Empty Zone: Trancemissions
Sirius
1 .... 3.00

Enchanted
Sirius, 1997

On one level, this series is a simple story of a young woman's attempt to make a successful musical career for herself, and the elements-including her diverse group of friends, the demanding owner of the bar she plays at, and her nervous steps toward a relationship with the nice yet complex guy her friends introduce her to-that make up her life. But there's more going on here than just that. For one thing, it's also about her letting go of her fears, and being the musician, and person, she is capable of becoming. And for another, the new man in her life has a few disturbing secrets, involving mystical conjuring with mysterious associates, death (murder?), and inhuman creatures coming after him from another dimension.

Written and drawn by Robert Chang, this unusual and multi-faceted series is published in black-and-white by Sirius Entertainment.

1-3..3.00

Enchanted (Vol. 2)
Sirius

1-3..3.00

Enchanted Valley
Blackthorne, 1987

1-2..2.00

Enchanted Worlds
Blackmore

1...3.00

Enchanter
Eclipse, 1985

1-8..2.00

Enchanter: Apocalypse Moon
Express

1...3.00

Enchanter: Prelude to Apocalypse
Express

1-3..3.00

Enchanters
Hidden Poet, 1996

1...3.00

Enchanting Love
Kirby Publications, 1949

1-3......................................75.00

Encyclopêdia Deadpoolica
Marvel, 1998

1...3.00

End, The: In the Beginning
AFC, 2000

1...3.00

Endless Gallery
DC

1...4.00

Enemy
Dark Horse, 1994

1-5..3.00

Enemy Ace Special
DC, 1990

1...3.00

Enemy Ace: War in Heaven
DC, 2001

World War One fighter ace Baron Hans Von Hammer is called from his family's ancestral castle to once again take up the cause of the Fatherland. He returns to the skies and once again is taking out the enemies of Germany, this time over the skies of the Russian front. Yet even in the heat of battle, he still muses on the uselessness of not only this war, but of most wars in general. He battles on against valiant foes in the air and back stabbing fellow officers on the ground. But can even an older and wiser "Hammer of Hell" stand up to the madness of war and the mentality of the Third Reich?

Von Hammer first appeared in Our Army At War #151, continued on in Showcase #57 and #58, then carried a successful run in Star-Spangled War Stories (#138-161).

1-2 .... 6.00

EnForce
Reoccurring Images

1 .... 3.00

Enginehead
DC, 2004

1-6.. 3.00

Enigma
DC, 1993

1-8.. 3.00

Enigma!
Hector Tellez

1 .... 3.00

Eno & Plum
Oni, 1998

1 .... 3.00

Ensign O'Toole
Dell, 1963

1 .... 30.00

Entropy Tales
Entropy

1-4 .... 2.00

Ents
Manic

1-3 .... 3.00

Eo
Rebel

1-4 .... 3.00

Epic
Marvel, 1992

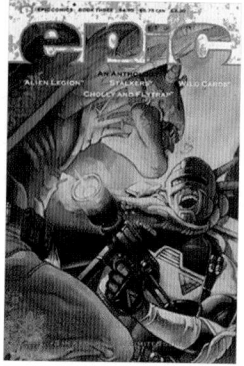

Epic is a full-color anthology series from Marvel Comics' creator-owned Epic imprint. Edited by Atomeka's Dave Elliott (A1), it served as a showcase for some of Epic's many great titles. The series was printed in a deluxe style format, which does a beautiful job of showing off the artistic talents from the various creators.

The four issues of this series featured stories ranging from horror to action-adventure. The first begins with Hellraiser: Birth Rite, wherein Dan Chichester writes of a young couple who try unsuccessfully to conceive a baby. They decide to conjure a demon who is said to aid in conception. The demon does exactly that, just not in the way the couple had pictured. Mark Verheiden's Stalkers follows with a tense tale of the mercenary police force. These tales are followed by the dinosaur-science-fiction of Dreadlands and a new adventure featuring Epic's popular adaptation of the Wildcards characters.

1-4 .... 5.00

Epic Anthology
Marvel, 2004

1 .... 6.00

Esc
Comico, 1996

In rapidly-decaying Los Angeles of 2002, Detective Sara Kelly is seeking a mysterious vigilante calling himself Zamindar. Muggers and other unsavory types are being blown up, apparently by someone who blows up himself and suffers no ill effects from it! Detective Kelly's investigations will lead her to high-ranking officials in the intelligence community, reveal the existence of Cybernormal, and the truth about Zamindar. But as the tag line for this four-issue limited series states: "The Truth Can Get You Killed."

This science-fiction/detective story is based on a screenplay by writer/producer/director Clyde Ware and is something of a departure for Comico. The painted artwork by Marc CaribT is suitably expressionistic and reminiscent of Bill Sienkiewicz.

-- *George Haberberger*

Escape to the Stars
Solson
1 ....2.00

Escape Velocity
Escape Velocity
1-2...2.00

Escapists
Dark Horse, 2006
1 ....1.00
2-6...3.00

Espers
Eclipse, 1986
1 ....3.00
2-5...2.00

Espers
Halloween, 1996
1-6...3.00

Espers
Image, 1997
1 ....4.00
2-9...3.00
Book 1 ....15.00

Espionage
Dell
1 ....18.00
2 ....15.00

Essential Elfquest
Warp, 1995
1 ....2.00

Essential Vertigo: Swamp Thing
DC, 1996
1-5...3.00
6-24...2.00

Essential Vertigo: The Sandman
DC, 1996

Reprinting the groundbreaking Sandman series from Neil Gaiman, Essential Vertigo: The Sandman provides readers unfamiliar with the award winning series an opportunity to catch it a second time around -- much like a re-release of a famous movie.

The Sandman tells the story of the Lord of Dreams' return to power after being held captive by a human sorcerer for over half a century. After freeing himself from a 72-year imprisonment and discovering the deterioration of his realm, the Dreaming, Morpheus sets about recovering his tools of power-a pouch of sand, a sacred amulet and his helm of office. Not only does his quest take him to the seedy streets of mortal men, but it also drops him within the deepest recesses of hell itself.

1-5.. 3.00
6-31 .... 2.00
32 .... 5.00

Essential X-Men
Marvel
1 .... 5.00
2-5 .... 4.00
6-32 .... 3.00

Establishment
DC, 2001
1-13.. 3.00

Etc
DC
1-5... 5.00

Et Cetera
Tokyopop, 2004
1-6....................................... 10.00

Eternal
Marvel, 2003
1-6... 3.00

Eternal Romance
Best Destiny, 1997
1-4.. 3.00

Eternal Romance Labor of Love Sketchbook
Best Destiny
1 .... 3.00

Eternals
Marvel, 1976
1 .... 10.00
1/30¢ 25.00
2 .... 5.00
2/30¢ 15.00
3-5 .... 3.00
6-12/Whitman........................ 2.00
12/35¢ 15.00
13-13/Whitman...................... 2.00
13/35¢ 15.00
14-14/Whitman...................... 2.00
14/35¢ 15.00
15-15/Whitman...................... 2.00
15/35¢ 15.00
16-16/Whitman...................... 2.00
16/35¢ 15.00
17-19 .... 2.00
Ann 1 .... 7.00

Eternals
Marvel, 1985
1 .... 2.00
2-12 .... 1.00

Eternals
Marvel, 2006
1 .... 4.00
1/Variant-1/2nd variant 5.00
2-5/Variant............................. 4.00

Eternals Sketchbook
Marvel, 2006
1 .... 2.00

Eternals: The Herod Factor
Marvel, 1991
1 .... 3.00

Eternal Thirst
Alpha Productions
3-5 .... 2.00

Eternal Warrior
Valiant, 1992

In a time before history, two brothers, Aram and Gilad, were fierce warriors of a nomadic tribe. As the years passed, they began to realize that they were not like others. It was next to impossible to seriously wound them, and they never seemed to grow old. In time, the brothers had to adopt different names and move from place to place to prevent others from discovering their true nature.

Occasionally, the brothers would come into contact with geomancers: mystics to whom the Earth itself told its secrets. "The end of all things is coming," they were warned, and those whose lives burned strong would be called on to save the world. Now Aram is known as "Armstrong" (of Archer & Armstrong fame), and Gilad - often accompanied by a young geomancer named Geoff - is the Eternal Warrior. Each must work, in his own way, to save the world from the evils that imperil it.

1	4.00
1/GoldEmboss	25.00
1/Gold	10.00
2	3.00
3	2.00
4	5.00
5-7	2.00
8	3.00
9-21	1.00
22	2.00
23-25	1.00
26	4.00
27	1.00
27/VVSS	125.00
28-29	1.00
30-40	2.00
41-45	3.00
46-49	4.00
50	7.00
Special 1	4.00
YB 1-2	5.00

Eternal Warrior: Fist and Steel
Acclaim, 1996

1	5.00
2	6.00

Eternal Warriors
Acclaim, 1997

1-1/Variant	4.00
Ashcan 1	1.00

Eternal Warriors: Archer & Armstrong
Acclaim, 1997

1	4.00

Eternal Warriors Blackworks
Acclaim, 1998

1	4.00

Eternal Warriors: Digital Alchemy
Acclaim, 1997

1	4.00

Eternal Warriors: Mog
Acclaim, 1998

1	4.00

Eternal Warrior Special
Acclaim, 1996

1	3.00

Eternal Warriors: The Immortal Enemy
Acclaim, 1998

1	4.00

Eternal Warriors: Time and Treachery
Acclaim, 1997

1	4.00

Eternity Smith
Renegade, 1986

1-5	2.00

Eternity Smith
Hero, 1987

1-9	2.00

Eternity Triple Action
Eternity

1-4	3.00

Eudaemon
Dark Horse, 1993

1-3	3.00

Eugenus
Eugenus

1-2	4.00
3	3.00

Eureka
Radio, 2000

1-3	3.00

Europa and the Pirate Twins
Powder Monkey, 1996

1-1/A	3.00
Ashcan 1	1.00

Evangeline Special
Lodestone, 1986

1	2.00

Evangeline
Comico, 1984

1	3.00
2	2.00

Evangeline
First, 1987

1	3.00
2-12	2.00

Evel Knievel
Marvel

The motorcycle rider got national publicity -- and his own one-shot Marvel comic book. His stunting career was best known for his attempts to jump an assortment of hurdles -- trucks, cars, rattlesnakes, the Caesar's Palace fountains, buses, the Snake River, and the Grand Canyon -- on his motorcycle. There was an Evel Knievel movie in 1971 and Viva Knievel in 1976. The Marvel comic book was done in conjunction with toymaker Ideal, which had the toy license in 1974. Strangely enough, all the action in the story was performed using equipment that was also available as part of the toy line. In the late 1990s, Playing Mantis reissued the Evel Knievel stunt cycle, but not the other toys.
-- Maggie

1	10.00

Evenfall
Slave Labor, 2003

1-7	3.00

Even More Secret Origins 80-Page Giant
DC, 2003

1	7.00

E.V.E. Protomecha
Image, 2000

1-6	3.00

Everquest: The Ruins of Kunark
DC, 2002

1	6.00

Everquest: Transformation
DC, 2002

1	6.00

Everwinds
Slave Labor, 1997

1-4	3.00

Every Dog Has His Day
Shiga

1	2.00

Everyman
Marvel, 1991

1	5.00

Everything's Archie
Archie, 1969

1	48.00
2	26.00
3-5	20.00
6-10	12.00
11-20	7.00
21-40	4.00
41-60	3.00
61-157	2.00

Evil Ernie
Eternity, 1991

1	35.00
1/Ltd.	6.00
2	5.00
3-5	4.00

Evil Ernie (Chaos!)
Chaos!, 1997

0	3.00
0/Platinum	5.00
1-10	3.00

Evil Ernie:
Baddest Battles
Chaos, 1997

1-1/Variant	2.00

Evil Ernie: Depraved
Chaos!, 1999

1-3	3.00

Evil Ernie: Destroyer
Chaos!, 1997

1-Ashcan 1	3.00

Evil Ernie in Santa Fe
Devil's Due, 2005

1-4	3.00

Evil Ernie:
New Year's Evil
Chaos!, 1993

1	5.00

Evil Ernie: Pieces of Me
Chaos!, 2000

1-1/Variant	3.00

Evil Ernie: Revenge
Chaos!, 1993

Ernest Fairchild had been abused as a child, but as a member of the undead, he's getting his revenge. Thanks to a scientific experiment gone awry and an encounter with Lady Death, Ernest is now Evil Ernie, an unstoppable monster whose goal is to murder the world.

As this series begins, Ernie's old psycho-therapist, Dr. Price, hit upon an idea to end Ernie's rampage once and for all. Ernie's leather jacket is adorned with a smiley-face button which in some manner embodies Ernie's childhood imaginary friend. It is through this button that Ernie receives his power, and by separating him from it, Dr. Price manages to incapacitate Ernie. But as anyone can tell you, it's hard to keep a bad man down.

0-1	3.00
1/Deluxe-1/Ltd.	4.00
2-4	3.00

Evil Ernie:
Straight to Hell
Chaos!, 1995

1	3.00
1/A	4.00
2-5	3.00

Evil Ernie:
The Lost Sketches
Chaos, 2001

Ashcan 1	1.00

Evil Ernie:
The Resurrection
Chaos!, 1993

1	4.00
1/Gold	5.00
2-3	4.00
4	3.00
Ashcan 1	5.00

Evil Ernie vs. the
Movie Monsters
Chaos!, 1997

1-1/A	3.00

Evil Ernie vs. the
Super Heroes
Chaos!, 1995

1-2	3.00

Evil Ernie:
War Of The Dead
Chaos!, 1999

1-3	3.00

Evil Ernie:
Youth Gone Wild
Chaos!, 1996

1-5	2.00

Evil Eye
Fantagraphics, 1998

1-3	3.00

Evilman Saves the World
Moonstone, 1996

1	3.00

Evil's Return
Tokyopop, 2004

1-4	10.00

Evo
Image, 2003

1	3.00

Ewoks
Marvel, 1985

1	3.00
2-8	2.00
9	4.00
10-14	2.00

Excalibur
Marvel, 1988

Drawn together by a common menace in the heart of England, the former X-Men Kitty Pryde, Nightcrawler, and Rachel Summers as Phoenix join forces with Captain Britain, shapeshifter Meggan, dragon Lockheed, and a robotic thing called Widget to become Excalibur.

Making its home in a haunted lighthouse, the team is called upon to battle everything from evil wraiths to necromancers bent on destroying the world. The members also travel been back and forth to Limbo enough times to merit frequent-teleport discounts.

Sort of X-Men writer Chris Claremont's pet series, Excalibur is distinguished from some of the other X-titles by its often whimsical bent. The series survived long past Claremont's departure, running exactly 10 years.

-1	2.00
1	3.00
2-49	2.00
50	3.00
51-70	2.00
71	4.00
☛Hologram cover	
72-75	2.00
75/Variant	4.00
76-81	2.00
82	3.00
82/Variant	4.00
83-99	2.00
100	3.00
101-124	2.00
125	3.00
Ann 1	4.00
Ann 2	3.00

Excalibur
Marvel, 2001
1-4..3.00

Excalibur
Marvel, 2004
1-13..3.00

Excalibur: Air Apparent
Marvel, 1991
1..5.00

Excalibur: Mojo Mayhem
Marvel, 1989
1..5.00

Excalibur: Sword of Power
Marvel, 2002
1-4..3.00

Excalibur: The Possession
Marvel, 1991
1..3.00

Excalibur: The Sword Is Drawn
Marvel, 1987
1-1/3rd......................................4.00

Excalibur: Weird War III
Marvel, 1990
1..10.00

Excalibur: XX Crossing
Marvel, 1992
1..3.00

Exciting Comics
Nedor, 1940

The anthology title featured a mix of stories, but the costumed hero The Black Terror (and sidekick Tim) was not only a focal character but also the cover feature for much of his run (#9 until the end of the series). Jungle-dwelling damsels Kara (the Jungle Empress) and Judy (of the Jungle) showed a bit of leg and provided a counterpoint to the Terror, but other features ranged from teen humor to detective to military stories.

The Terror and Tim, along with other characters from their universe, returned for an adventure in Alan Moore's Tom Strong in 2001.

-- Maggie

1 .... 2,400.00
2 .... 1,450.00
3 .... 1,000.00
4-6...................................... 650.00
7-10.................................... 600.00
11-20................................... 465.00
21-30................................... 340.00
31-40................................... 300.00
41-51................................... 240.00
52-60................................... 210.00
61-66................................... 165.00
67-69................................... 100.00

Exciting Romances
Fawcett, 1949
1 .... 50.00
2-12.................................... 25.00

Exciting War
Standard, 1952
5 .... 44.00
6-9....................................... 32.00

Exciting X-Patrol
Marvel, 1997
1 .... 2.00

Exec
Comics Conspiracy, 2001
1 .... 4.00

Executioner, The: Death Squad (Don Pendleton's...)
Vivid, 1996
1 .... 13.00

Exhibitionist
Fantagraphics, 1994
1-2... 3.00

Exile
Eyeball Soup Designs, 1996
1-2... 3.00

Exiled
Exiled, 1998
1-3... 3.00

Exile Earth
River City, 1994

Exile Earth served as the premiere for its publisher, Bloomington, Indiana-based River City Comics. It's an ambitious story which reaches from the dying days of an alien planet to touch the lives of two men in our world: one a slave living in the mid 1800s, and another a modern record store clerk. Both of these men were haunted by visions of a distant planet and found themselves changed by the experience. The slave found the means to escape his bondage, and the record store clerk discovered he possessed the power of flight. But even as each delighted in his newfound freedom, these men had yet to comprehend the nature of the force that had transformed their lives.

1-2 .... 2.00

Exiles
Malibu, 1993
1 .... 2.00
1/Variant................................ 5.00
2 .... 2.00
3 .... 3.00
4 .... 2.00

Exiles
Marvel, 2001
1 .... 4.00
2-24 .... 2.00
25-59 .... 3.00
60 .... 5.00
☛Age of Apoc.
61 .... 4.00
☛Age of Apoc.
62-89 .... 3.00
Ann 1 .... 4.00

Exiles
Alpha Productions
1 .... 2.00

Existing Earth
Windwolf Graphics, 1987

1 ....2.00

Exit
Caliber

1-5...3.00
Book 1 ....15.00

Exit 6
Plastic Spoon, 1998

1-3/Ashcan..............................3.00

Exit from Shadow
Bronze Man

4 ....3.00

Ex-Libris Eroticis
NBM

1 ....10.00

Ex Machina
DC, 2004

1 ....8.00
2 ....4.00
3-25...3.00

Ex Machina Special
DC, 2006

1-2...3.00

Ex-Mutants
Pied Piper, 1987

1-Special 1 ....2.00

Ex-Mutants
Eternity, 1986

1-Ann 1 ....2.00

Ex-Mutants
Malibu, 1992

1 ....2.00
1/Variant...................................3.00
2-16...2.00
17-18...3.00

Ex-Mutants Microseries: Erin
(Lawrence & Lim's...)
Pied Piper

1 ....2.00

Ex-Mutants Pin-Up Book
Eternity, 1988

1 ....2.00

Ex-Mutants Special Consumer Electronics Show Edition
Malibu, 1992

1 ....3.00

Exodus Revelation
Exodus, 1994

1 ....1.00

Exosquad
Topps, 1994

0 .... 1.00

Exotica
Cry for Dawn, 1993

1 .... 4.00
2 .... 3.00

Exotic Fantasy
Fantagraphics, 1992

1-3... 5.00

Exotic Romances
Comic Magazines, 1955

Formerly running as True War Romances, this series became Exotic Romances with issue #22 in 1955. Full of short vignettes that always lead to happiness and matrimony for its "good girl" protagonists, Exotic Romances is typical of the "Horatio Alger romance" comics aimed at 1950s teenage girls. Sometimes the girls in the stories go through heartbreak in the midst of their tales as they realize they're engaged to cads ("I'll never forget the horror and the humiliation I felt when I went to the Paris Club to surprise him!"). Still, there's no need for fear, as the simple buy sweet heroines always find equally simple but sweet boys to wipe away their tears and get happily hitched by the end of the eight page ("Suddenly I saw Chet not as a boy who needed my help, but as a man...a man I needed and loved!")

Despite its title, the stories' settings were, generally, as domestic as the characters.

22-29 .... 26.00
30-31 .... 22.00

Expatriate
Image, 2005

1-4... 3.00

Experience
Aircel

1 .... 3.00

Exploits of Daniel Boone
Quality, 1955

1 .... 185.00
2 .... 115.00
3-6 .... 80.00

Explorers
Explorer, 1996

1-3 .... 3.00

Explorers
Caliber, 1996

1-3 .... 3.00

Explorers of the Unknown
Archie, 1990

1-6 .... 1.00

Expose
Cracked Pepper, 1993

1 .... 3.00

Exposed
D.S., 1948

1 .... 110.00
2 .... 100.00
3 .... 85.00
4-5 .... 65.00
6 .... 125.00
7 .... 95.00
8-9 .... 55.00

Exposure
Image, 1999

1-4 .... 3.00
5-6 .... 4.00

Exquisite Corpse
Dark Horse

1-3 .... 3.00

Exterminators
DC, 2006

1-13 .... 3.00

Extinct!
New England

1-2 .... 4.00

Extinctioners
Shanda Fantasy Arts, 1999

1-2 .... 3.00

Extinction Event
DC, 2003

1-5 .... 3.00

Extra!
E.C., 1955

1 .... 150.00
2-5 .... 100.00

Extra!
Gemstone, 2000

1-5 .... 3.00
Ann 1 .... 14.00

Extra Terrestrial Trio
Smiling Face, 1995
1 ....3.00

Extreme
Image, 1993
0-0/Gold 3.00
Holiday 1 ....1.00

Extreme
Curtis
1 ....3.00

Extreme Destroyer Epilogue
Image, 1996
1 ....3.00

Extreme Destroyer Prologue
Image, 1996
1 ....3.00

Extreme Hero
Image, 1994
1 ....1.00

Extreme Justice
DC, 1995

Five former members of The Justice League have banded together to form a new version of the team, aka Extreme Justice. The new team includes Captain Atom, Blue Beetle, Booster Gold, and Maxima. They have left the Wonder Woman-led Justice League and taken up residence in Mount Thunder, an abandoned silver mine and secret military installation in Nevada.

Captain Atom is the leader of the crew, as they take on their first enemy, a secret program with operations deep in the heart of Mount Thunder. Five different presidents have approved the project's budget without ever seeing its true goal. Now Synge, the power behind the project,

wants to put a stop to Captain Atom before he can expose their plans.

0-18 .... 2.00

Extremely Silly
Antarctic
1 .... 3.00

Extremely Silly (Vol. 2)
Antarctic, 1996
1 .... 1.00

Extremely Youngblood
Image, 1996
1 .... 4.00

Extreme Prejudice
Image, 1994
0 .... 3.00

Extreme Previews
Image, 1996
1 .... 1.00

Extreme Previews 1997
Image
1 .... 1.00

Extreme Sacrifice
Image, 1995

A battle rages in Hell as a dead renegade of the super-team Youngblood overthrows Satan and plots dominion of the entire universe. Only the mysterious Order of the Knight (with the aid of the New Men, Prophet, and the rest of the Image Universe of heroes) stands in the way of absolute annihilation.

Such is the over-the-top premise of this kick-off to Image's 1995 crossover event, with plot and primary art by Image founder Rob Liefeld. The Extreme Sacrifice storyline continued in most of the Image titles, including Supreme, Bloodstrike, and Brigade, before

concluding in the "Epilogue" issue of this series.
-- Stephen C. George

1-2 .... 3.00

Extremes of Violet
Blackout, 1995
0-2 .... 3.00

Extreme Super Christmas Special
Image, 1994
1 .... 3.00

Extreme Super Tour Book
Image
1 .... 1.00
1/Gold....................................... 2.00

Extreme Tour Book
Image
1-1/Gold 3.00

Extremist
DC, 1993
1 .... 3.00
1/Platinum 4.00
2-4 .... 3.00

Eye
Hamster, 1999
Special 1 .... 3.00

Eyeball Kid
Dark Horse
1-3 .... 3.00

Eyebeam
Adhesive, 1994
1-5 .... 3.00

Eye of Mongombo
Fantagraphics, 1991
1-7 .... 2.00

Eye of the Beholder
NBM
1 .... 11.00

Eye of the Storm
Rival, 1994
1 .... 3.00

Eye of the Storm Annual
DC, 2003
1 .... 5.00

Eyeshield 21
Viz, 2005
1-4 .... 8.00

Eyes of Asia
Digital Webbing, 2004
1-2 .... 4.00

The Marvel Age of Comics began in late 1961 with this team of four adventurers.

Comics Shop

Faans
Six Handed
1 .... 3.00

Fables
DC, 2002

Creator Bill Willingham (of Elementals fame) weaves a tale of murder and mayhem that reads a little like a cross between a fairytale and a prime-time soap opera. Deputy Mayor Snow White and Chief of Security Bigby Wolf head the cast of characters of Fabletown, a secret society of fairy-tale and nursery-rhyme creatures, cast out of their homelands ages ago by a mysterious adversary. Now, the creatures are just trying to live their semi-immortal lives in peace.

Of course, it's not always easy for supposedly make-believe characters -- especially non-human ones -- to blend into 21st-century America, hence the structured organization led by Snow, Bigby, and their boss, King Cole. But the Fables' carefully maintained lives among the mundanes are in danger of changing forever, when Snow's sister, Rose Red, vanishes, an apparent victim of a bloody crime.

That's only the first story arc in the ongoing fantasy series, which goes on to deal with such topics as unrest among the sequestered non-human-looking characters.

1 .... 4.00
2-5 .... 3.00
6-6/Retailer ed. 15.00
7-49 .... 3.00
50 .... 4.00
51-55 .... 3.00
56-80 .... 4.00

Fables By the Brothers Dimm
Dimm, 1995
1 .... 2.00

Fables: Last Castle
DC, 2003
1 .... 5.00

Fabulous Furry Freak Brothers
Rip Off, 1975
0 .... 6.00
1 .... 55.00
1/2nd 30.00
1/3rd 28.00
2 .... 35.00

2 .... 365.00
3 .... 225.00
4-5 .... 160.00
6-9 .... 125.00

Fairy Tales of the Brothers Grimm
NBM

1 .... 16.00

Fairy Tales
Ziff-Davis, 1951

10-11 .... 165.00

Faith
Lightning, 1997

1/A 3.00

Faith
DC, 1999

1-5 .... 3.00

Faith: A Fable
Carbon-Based Books, 2000

1 .... 9.00

Faithful
Marvel, 1949

1 .... 55.00
2 .... 42.00

Faith of the Foe
Fandom House

1 .... 5.00

Fake
Tokyopop, 2003

1 .... 10.00

Falcon
Marvel, 1983

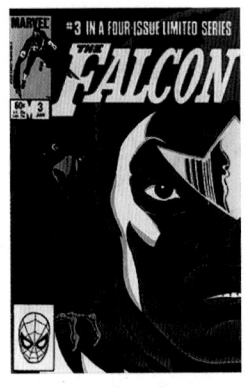

Possessing no super-powers except the ability to fly through a set of advanced-technology wings, Sam Wilson fights crime as the Falcon. First appearing in Captain America #117, he became Cap's partner, and continued in that role until issue #223.

This mini-series finally gives the Falcon a chance to leave the nest and spread his wings, so to speak, as he fights to foil a plot against the President. Paul Smith, a little-known artist before taking on Uncanny X-Men in late 1982, drew the series, rendering the Falcon with his characteristic flair and attention to detail.

1-4 .... 2.00

Fall
Big Bad World

1 .... 3.00

Fall
Caliber

1 .... 3.00

Fallen
NBM

1 .... 9.00

Fallen Angel
DC, 2003

1-20 .... 3.00

Fallen Angel
Idea & Design Works, 2006

1-11 .... 4.00

Fallen Angel on the World of Magic: The Gathering
Acclaim, 1996

1 .... 6.00

Fallen Angels
Marvel, 1987

1-8 .... 2.00

Fallen Empires on the World of Magic: The Gathering
Acclaim, 1995

1-2 .... 3.00

Falling in Love
DC, 1955

1 .... 275.00
2 .... 145.00
3 .... 95.00
4-5 .... 65.00
6-10 .... 60.00
11-20 .... 40.00
21-40 .... 28.00
41-59 .... 20.00
60-80 .... 16.00
81-100 .... 14.00
101-120 .... 12.00
121-143 .... 9.00

Falling Man
Image, 1998

1 .... 3.00

Fall of the Roman Empire
Gold Key, 1964

1 .... 25.00

Fallout 3000 (Mike Deodato's...)
Caliber, 1996

1 .... 3.00

Falls The Gotham Rain
Comico

1 .... 5.00

Family Affair
Gold Key, 1970

Family Affair, a TV series starring Brian Keith (1921-1997) and Sebastian Cabot (1918-1977) as caretakers of three orphans, ran from 1966 to 1971. The show, featuring a bachelor who adopts his nephew and two nieces after the death of his brother, spawned a licensing phenomenon in which girls wanted their own Mrs. Beasley doll.

The comic book, one of Gold Key's many titles adapting 1960s situation comedies, met with less success and had a shorter run. The first issue is notable for the inclusion of a poster; copies without the poster today go for about half the value of copies with the poster.

-- Maggie

1 .... 24.00
2 .... 20.00
3-4 .... 14.00

Family Funnies
Harvey, 1950

1 .... 40.00
2 .... 30.00
3-5 .... 25.00
6-8 .... 22.00

Family Guy
Devil's Due, 2006
1-2 .... 7.00

Family Man
DC
1-3 .... 5.00

Famous Comics
King, 1934
1 .... 150.00
2-3 .... 120.00

Famous Crimes
Fox, 1948
1 .... 210.00
2 .... 185.00
3 .... 225.00
4-5 .... 130.00
6 .... 110.00
7 .... 165.00
8-10 .... 110.00
11-15 .... 75.00
16-20 .... 60.00
51-52 .... 38.00

Famous Fairy Tales
K.K., 1942
1 .... 250.00
2-3 .... 165.00

Famous Features
(Jerry Iger's...)
Pacific, 1984
1 .... 3.00

Famous Feature Stories
Dell, 1938
1 .... 450.00

Famous First Edition
DC, 1974
F-4 .... 15.00
☛Whiz #2
F-5 .... 13.00
☛Batman #1
F-6 .... 10.00
☛W. Woman #1
F-7 .... 12.00
☛All-Star #3
F-8 .... 9.00
☛Flash #1
C-26 .... 10.00
☛Action #1
C-28 .... 9.00
☛Detective #27
C-30 .... 10.00
☛Sensation #1
C-61 .... 9.00
☛Superman #1
C-61/Whitman 18.00

Famous Funnies
Famous Funnies, 1934

Many consider this to be the first modern comic book. After all, it was circulated via newsstand sales. It was a four-color magazine of roughly the same size as the comics that followed it. It carried a cover price of a dime. And early issues kicked off a monthly publication schedule, which lasted for years and years for Famous Funnies and became the industry standard (though, of course, not all ongoing series are published monthly.

Created as a way to keep printing presses going at Eastern Color Printing in New York, its contents initially consisted of newspaper strip reprints. Such strips as Toonerville Folks, Mutt and Jeff, Connie, Tailspin Tommy, and The Nebbs provided content for the first issue, and later additions Buck Rogers and Invisible Scarlet O'Neil are among reasons it's collected today.

-- Maggie

1 .... 16,400.00
2 .... 3,850.00
3 .... 4,200.00
4 .... 1,450.00
5 .... 1,100.00
6-10 .... 825.00
11-12 .... 665.00
13-17 .... 415.00
18 .... 625.00
19-20 .... 415.00
21-22 .... 365.00
23-30 .... 350.00
31-38 .... 235.00
39-40 .... 215.00
41-50 .... 180.00
51-60 .... 165.00
61-70 .... 145.00
71-80 .... 100.00
81 .... 85.00
82 .... 105.00
83-90 .... 85.00
91-99 .... 70.00

100 .... 75.00
101-110 .... 60.00
111-130 .... 50.00
131-150 .... 38.00
151-190 .... 28.00
191-208 .... 25.00
209-216 .... 550.00
☛Frazetta art
217-218 .... 25.00

Famous Funnies: A Carnival of Comics
Eastern Color, 1933
1 .... 10,800.00

Famous Gangsters
Avon, 1951
1 .... 250.00
2-3 .... 190.00

Famous Stars
Ziff-Davis, 1950
1 .... 165.00
2-3 .... 90.00
4 .... 100.00
5-6 .... 75.00

Famous Stories
Dell
1 .... 165.00
2 .... 150.00

Famous Western Badmen
Youthful
13 .... 75.00
14-15 .... 50.00

Fana
Comax
1 .... 3.00

Fana the Jungle Girl
Comax
1 .... 3.00

Fanboy
DC, 1999
1-6 .... 3.00

Fandom Confidential
Kitchen Sink
1 .... 3.00

Fang
Sirius Entertainment, 1995
1-3 .... 3.00

Fang
Conquest
1 .... 3.00

Fang (Tangram)
Tangram
1 .... 3.00

Fang: Testament
Sirius Entertainment
1-4 .... 3.00

Fangraphix
Fangraphix
1-3 .... 2.00

Fangs of the Cobra
Mythic, 1996
1 ....3.00

Fanny
Fanny
1-2 ....3.00
3 ....4.00

Fanny Hill
Shunga
1 ....3.00

Fantaco's Chronicles Series
Fantaco, 1982
1 ....2.00

Fantaescape
Zinzinnati, 1988
1 ....2.00

Fantagor
Last Gasp, 1972
1-3 ....3.00

FantaSci
Apple, 1988
1-9 ....2.00

Fantastic
Youthful, 1952
8 ....165.00
9 ....120.00

Fantastic Adventures
Super, 1963
10 ....25.00
11-18 ....20.00

Fantastic Adventures
Ace, 1987
1-3 ....2.00

Fantastic Comics
Fox, 1939
1 ....3,100.00
2 ....2,000.00
3 ....6,600.00
4-5 ....1,600.00
6-9 ....1,000.00
10-15 ....800.00
16-23 ....650.00

Fantastic Comics
Farrell, 1954
10 ....135.00
11 ....110.00

Fantastic Fables (Basil Wolverton's...)
Dark Horse, 1993
1-2 ....3.00

Fantastic Fanzine
Arrow
1-3 ....2.00

Fantastic Fears
Farrell, 1953
1 ....265.00
2 ....185.00

3-5 ....140.00
6 ....400.00
7 ....140.00
8-9 ....100.00

Fantastic Five
Marvel, 1999
1-3 ....2.00

Fantastic Force
Marvel, 1994
1 ....3.00
2-18 ....2.00

Fantastic Four (Vol. 1)
Marvel, 1961

The 1961 premiere of this self-proclaimed "World's Greatest Comic Magazine" ushered in the Marvel Age of Comics. It all starts when Reed Richards, Susan Storm, Johnny Storm, and Ben Grimm take part in a space shot. Everything goes perfectly until they are bombarded with cosmic rays. Their inadequately shielded spaceship does not protect them, and suddenly the four find themselves altered by the radiation. Reed's body becomes elastic; Susan finds herself able to turn invisible at will; Ben becomes mutated into The Thing; and Johnny becomes a Human Torch. Together, they become The Fantastic Four.

In the decades that followed, The FF has saved the world more times than can be counted and introduced readers to such legendary characters as The Inhumans, The Silver Surfer, Galactus, and Doctor Doom. They're Marvel's longest-running title and a pivotal force in the Marvel universe.

1 ....20,000.00
1st Fantastic Four
1st Skull.....................70.00
2 ....4,500.00
1st Skrull

3 ....3,000.00
4 ....3,500.00
5 ....5,000.00
☛1st Dr. Doom
6 ....2,000.00
7 ....1,250.00
8 ....1,200.00
9-10 ....1,150.00
11 ....1,000.00
12 ....2,700.00
☛Thing vs. Hulk
13 ....600.00
14 ....500.00
15 ....700.00
16-19 ....500.00
20 ....600.00
21 ....450.00
22-23 ....250.00
24 ....240.00
25 ....550.00
☛Avengers app.
26 ....600.00
☛Avengers app.
27 ....300.00
28 ....500.00
☛X-Men app.
29-31 ....260.00
32-34 ....250.00
35-40 ....165.00
41-43 ....110.00
44 ....85.00
45 ....325.00
☛1st Inhumans
46 ....150.00
47 ....100.00
48 ....460.00
☛1st Silver Surfer
49 ....350.00
50 ....400.00
51 ....150.00
52 ....300.00
☛1st Black Panther
53 ....140.00
54 ....105.00
55 ....210.00
☛Thing vs. Surfer
56 ....100.00
57 ....115.00
58 ....90.00
59 ....60.00
60 ....65.00
61 ....70.00
62-63 ....60.00
64 ....50.00
65 ....55.00
66 ....115.00
☛1st Warlock
66/2nd 2.00
67 ....105.00
67/2nd 2.00
68-69 ....60.00
70 ....55.00
71 ....45.00
72 ....100.00
☛Silver Surfer app.
73 ....80.00
74 ....85.00
75 ....55.00
76 ....45.00
77 ....50.00

78	35.00	173	6.00	388-394	2.00

78 ....35.00
79 ....50.00
80-85 ....40.00
86 ....50.00
87 ....40.00
88-89 ....35.00
90-93 ....30.00
94 ....40.00
95-96 ....30.00
97-98 ....25.00
99 ....30.00
100 ....70.00
101-105 ....30.00
106 ....22.00
107 ....30.00
108 ....22.00
109-111 ....20.00
112 ....175.00
☛Thing vs. Hulk
113 ....25.00
114 ....27.00
115 ....25.00
116 ....65.00
☛52 pages
117-120 ....15.00
121 ....30.00
☛Galactus app.
122 ....45.00
123 ....27.00
124-125 ....20.00
126 ....30.00
127 ....35.00
128 ....30.00
129 ....25.00
130-132 ....15.00
133-145 ....12.00
146 ....10.00
147 ....15.00
148-154 ....10.00
155 ....15.00
156-158 ....12.00
159-163 ....10.00
164 ....9.00
165 ....7.00
166 ....10.00
167 ....15.00
168-169 ....10.00
169/30¢ 20.00
170 ....10.00
170/30¢ 20.00
171 ....6.00
171/30¢ 20.00
172 ....6.00
172/30¢ 20.00

173 ....6.00
173/30¢ 20.00
174-183/Whitman 6.00
183/35¢ 15.00
184-184/Whitman 6.00
184/35¢ 15.00
185-185/Whitman 5.00
185/35¢ 15.00
186-186/Whitman 5.00
186/35¢ 15.00
187-187/Whitman 5.00
187/35¢ 15.00
188-200 ....5.00
☛Byrne script/art begins
201-239 ....4.00
240-248 ....3.00
249 ....4.00
250 ....5.00
251 ....4.00
252-255 ....3.00
256 ....4.00
257-259 ....3.00
260 ....5.00
261 ....4.00
262-268 ....3.00
269 ....4.00
270 ....3.00
271 ....4.00
272 ....5.00
273-286 ....3.00
287-295 ....2.00
296 ....3.00
297-299 ....2.00
300 ....3.00
301-318 ....2.00
319 ....3.00
320-346 ....2.00
347 ....3.00
347/2nd 2.00
348 ....3.00
348/2nd 2.00
349-350 ....3.00
351-357 ....2.00
358 ....3.00
359-370 ....2.00
371-371/2nd 3.00
372-374 ....2.00
375 ....2.00
376-378 ....1.00
379-380 ....2.00
381 ....3.00
382 ....3.00
383-387 ....1.00
387/Variant 3.00

388-394 ....2.00
394/CS 3.00
395-398 ....2.00
398/Variant 3.00
399 ....2.00
399/Variant 3.00
400 ....4.00
401-415 ....2.00
416-500 ....4.00
500 ....45.00
500/CS 4.00
501 ....2.00
501 ....100.00
502-503 ....2.00
503 ....85.00
504 ....2.00
504 ....55.00
505 ....2.00
505 ....45.00
506-507 ....2.00
507 ....35.00
508 ....2.00
508 ....50.00
509 ....2.00
509 ....40.00
510 ....2.00
510 ....40.00
511 ....2.00
512-513 ....3.00
514-516 ....2.00
517-526 ....3.00
527 ....7.00
☛Straczynski starts
527/Variant 4.00
527/DirCut 5.00
527/Conv 7.00
528-535 ....3.00
536 ....10.00
537 ....7.00
537/2nd-565 ....3.00
Ann 1 ....900.00
Ann 2 ....500.00
Ann 3 ....175.00
Ann 4 ....90.00
Ann 5 ....60.00
Ann 6 ....40.00
Ann 7-Ann 8 ....18.00
Ann 9 ....10.00
Ann 10-11 ....8.00
Ann 12-14 ....5.00
Ann 15-27 ....3.00
Special 1 ....2.00
Ashcan 1 ....1.00

Fantastic Four
Marvel, 1996
1 (417)	4.00
1/Variant	50.00
1/Gold	4.00
2 (418)-11 (427)	2.00
12 (428)	3.00
13 (429)	2.00

Fantastic Four
Marvel, 1998
1 (430)	3.00
1/A	4.00
2 (431)-5 (434)	3.00
6 (435)-24 (453)	2.00
25 (454)	3.00
26 (455)-34 (463)	2.00
35 (464)	3.00
36 (465)-49 (478)	2.00
50 (479)-51 (480)	4.00
52 (481)	2.00
53 (482)	3.00
54 (483)	4.00
55 (484)-59 (488)	2.00
60 (489)	1.00
61 (490)-70 (499)	2.00
Ann 1998	5.00
Ann 1999	4.00
Ann 2001	3.00

Fantastic Four:
A Death in the Family
Marvel, 2006
1	4.00

Fantastic Four:
Atlantis Rising
Marvel, 1995
1-2	4.00
Ashcan 1	2.00

Fantastic Four:
Fireworks
Marvel, 1999
1-3	3.00

Fantastic Four:
First Family
Marvel, 2006
1-6	3.00

Fantastic Four: Foes
Marvel, 2005
1-6	3.00

Fantastic Four:
Franklin's Adventures
Marvel, 1998
1	2.00

Fantastic Four:
House of M
Marvel, 2005
1	5.00
1/Variant	4.00
☛2nd print	
2-3	3.00

Fantastic Four/Iron Man:
Big in Japan
Marvel, 2006
1-4	4.00

Fantastic Four Legends
Marvel, 2003
1	14.00

Fantastic Four: 1 2 3 4
Marvel, 2001
1-4	3.00

Fantastic Four Roast
Marvel, 1982

One of the three or four funniest comic books ever to come from Marvel, Fantastic Four Roast celebrates the 20th anniversary of the super-team with an all-star comics banquet hosted by funnyman Fred Hembeck and drawn by many different Marvel artists.

It's a four-color Dean Martin Roast, as super-heroes truck to the stage and lob silly remarks at the foursome. Sight gags abound, with all of Marvel's bald characters seated at the same table. And, of course, some sinister agent is out to kill the Fantastic Four, by means of exploding soup and a living ice cream sundae.

Funny bits and trivia from one of the great satirists of comics, and still a wonderful value today.
-- *John Jackson Miller*

1	2.00

Fantastic Four Special
Marvel, 1984
1	3.00

Fantastic Four Special
Marvel, 2006
1	3.00

Fantastic Four: The End
Marvel, 2007
1	3.00
1/RoughCut	4.00
2-4	3.00

Fantastic Four:
The Legend
Marvel, 1996
1	4.00

Fantastic Four:
The Movie
Marvel, 2005
1	5.00

Fantastic Four:
The Wedding Special
Marvel, 2006
1	5.00

Fantastic Four:
The World's Greatest
Comics Magazine
Marvel, 2001
1-12	3.00

Fantastic Four 2099
Marvel, 1996
1	4.00
2-8	2.00

Fantastic Four Unlimited
Marvel, 1993
1	5.00
2-12	4.00

Fantastic Four
Unplugged
Marvel, 1995
1-6	1.00

Fantastic Four:
Unstable Molecules
Marvel, 2003
1-4	3.00

Fantastic Four vs. X-Men
Marvel, 1987
1-4	3.00

Fantastic Giants
Charlton, 1966
24	35.00

Fantastic Panic
Antarctic, 1993
1-8	3.00
Book 1	11.00

Fantastic Panic
Antarctic, 1995
1-8	3.00

Fantastic Tales
I.W.

This one-shot title from I.W. Enterprises reprints the contents of Avon Periodicals' 1952 one-shot City of the Living Dead, an anthology of horror stories that pales in comparison to such E.C. titles as Tales from the Crypt and The Haunt of Fear.

This collection is notable for its art by Mart Nodell, cocreator of the original Green Lantern.

Between 1958 and 1964, I.W. Enterprises reprinted a number of horror, Western, war, romance, jungle, and super-hero comics from the late 1940s and early 1950s, all with new covers that had little or nothing to do with the contents of the comics themselves.

1 ....26.00

Fantastic Voyage (Movie)
Gold Key, 1967

1 ....40.00

Fantastic Voyage (TV)
Gold Key, 1969

1 ....25.00
2 ....16.00

Fantastic Voyages of Sindbad
Gold Key, 1965

1 ....18.00
2 ....12.00

Fantastic Worlds
Standard, 1952

5 ....75.00
6-7 ....60.00

Fantastic Worlds
Flashback Comics, 1995

1 ....3.00

Fantasy Features
AC, 1987

1-2 ....2.00

Fantasy Girls
Comax

1 .... 3.00

Fantasy Masterpieces
Marvel, 1966

1 .... 75.00
2 .... 35.00
3 .... 30.00
4-8 .... 18.00
9 .... 30.00
☛Torch origin
10 .... 10.00
11 .... 15.00

Fantasy Masterpieces
Marvel, 1979

1 .... 6.00
2 .... 4.00
3-10 .... 3.00
11-14 .... 2.00

Fantasy Quarterly
Independent Pub. Synd., 1978

1 .... 55.00

Faraway Looks
Faraway Press, 2002

nn 10.00

Farewell, Moonshadow
DC, 1997

This sequel to J.M. DeMatteis and Jon J. Muth's limited series about a starry-eyed, romantic traveler finds an elderly Moonshadow reflecting on his experiences in "a town built of Memory, Innocence, and a Joy infrequently glimpsed in long years of wandering." Readers learn of a time when he settled down, opened a tinker's shop, married the beautiful Bettina, fathered four children -- Mia, Charles, Charlotte, and Katherine -- found himself occasionally tortured by dreams, and yearned at times for the secrets that the fat, silver moon seemed to keep from him.

Farewell, Moonshadow is a beautiful graphic novel: a worthy sequel to the original series. DeMatteis's prose is as gorgeous and haunting as Muth's painted art.

1 .... 8.00

Farewell to Weapons
Marvel

1 .... 2.00

Fargo Kid
Prize

3 .... 75.00
4-5 .... 60.00

Farmer's Daughter
Stanhall, 1954

1 .... 110.00
2 .... 85.00
3-4 .... 70.00

Farscape: War Torn
DC, 2002

1-2 .... 5.00

Far West
Antarctic, 1998

1-4 .... 3.00

Fashion in Action
Eclipse, 1986

Summer 1-WS 1 .... 2.00

Fashion Police
Bryce Alan

1 .... 3.00

Fast Fiction
Seaboard, 1949

1 .... 125.00
2-4 .... 100.00
5 .... 60.00

Fast Forward
DC

1-3 .... 5.00

Fastlane Illustrated
Fastlane, 1994

1/2 .... 2.00
1-3 .... 3.00

Fast Willie Jackson
Fitzgerald Periodicals, 1976

1 .... 24.00
2-7 .... 16.00

Fatal Beauty
Illustration, 1996

Ashcan 1/A 4.00

Fat Albert
Gold Key, 1974

1 .... 12.00
2 .... 8.00
3-5 .... 7.00
6-10 .... 6.00
11-29 .... 4.00

Fatale
Broadway, 1995

1-6 .... 3.00
Ashcan 1 .... 1.00

Fat and Slat
E.C., 1947

Fat and Slat were the "stage" names of two characters newspaper-comic-strip artist Ed Wheelan had created for his Minute Movies strip, which ran in the 1920s and 1930s -- though the "actors" Fuller Phun and Archibald Clubb didn't appear as Fat and Slat until the Golden Age Flash comic book ran a Wheelan strip. The Minute Movies strip imitated movie types of the day, with feature films followed by short subjects, and its "cast" of actors (Hazel Dearie, Ralph McSneer, and the like) were cast in a variety of roles. The first issue Wheelan did for comic books appeared from DC's AA arm in 1944.

When the E.C. imprint was begun, Wheelan continued the comic book for that company, with the characters continuing in "bigfoot" comedy routines. In the morphing world that E.C. developed, the title turned into Gunfighter with the fifth issue.
-- *Maggie*

1	165.00
2	110.00
3-4	85.00

Fat and Slat Joke Book
Wise, 1944

1	160.00

Fat Dog Mendoza
Dark Horse, 1992

1	3.00

Fate
DC, 1994

Doctor Fate was one of the casualties of Zero Hour. That crisis in time results in the mystical trio, consisting of Doctor Fate and Kent and Inza Nelson, aging terribly as a result.

With their life forces ebbing away by the moment, they travel to the ruined temple in Egypt where the Doctor Fate arcana has returned. But a thief named Jared Stevens gets there first, stealing the artifacts, then heading back to the U.S., where he plans to fence them. Before he can cash in his ill-gotten gains, however, Fate catches up to him.

Kent and Inza use the last of their powers to locate Stevens and the arcana. They manage to subdue Stevens but are, in turn, killed by demons sent by arch-enemy Kingdom. Then, in a flash of light, the mystical relics of Doctor Fate choose a new champion. Stevens, a former thief, is literally branded -- as the new Doctor Fate.

0-1	3.00
2-22	2.00

Fate of the Blade
Dreamwave, 2002

1-5	3.00

Fate's Five
Innervision

1-4	3.00

Fat Freddy's Comics & Stories
Rip Off, 1983

1-2	3.00

Fat Fury Special
Avalon

1	3.00

Father & Son
Kitchen Sink, 1995

1-4	3.00
Ashcan 1	2.00
Special 1	4.00

Fathom (Michael Turner's ...)
Aspen, 2005

1	5.00
1/A cover	4.00
1/B cover	5.00
2-3	3.00

Fathom
Comico, 1987

1-3	2.00

Fathom
Comico, 1992

1-3	3.00

Fathom
Image, 1998

0/Dynamic	15.00
0/Conv	10.00
0-0/B	5.00
1/2	3.00
1/2/A	4.00
1/A	6.00
1/B-1/C	3.00
1/D	115.00
2	3.00
2/A	100.00
3-8	3.00
9	5.00
9/A	8.00
9/B	7.00
9/C	5.00
9/D	9.00
10	3.00
10/A	4.00
10/B	5.00
11	3.00
12-12/B	6.00
12/C	5.00
12/D	8.00
13	3.00
13/A	5.00
13/B-13/C	15.00
14	3.00
14/A	6.00
Deluxe 1	25.00

Fathom: Beginnings
Aspen, 2003

1	5.00
1/Conv	6.00

Fathom: Cannon Hawke
Aspen, 2004

0	6.00
0/Dynamic	15.00
0/Conv	10.00

Fathom: Cannon Hawke: Beginnings
Aspen, 2004

1 ....5.00
1/Conv...................................10.00

Fathom: Dawn of War
Aspen, 2004

0...5.00
1...7.00
1/Jay.....................................10.00
2...4.00
2/Conv..................................10.00
3...4.00

Fathom: East & West Coast Tour Books
Image, 2004

1 ....3.00

Fathom (Michael Turner's...): Killian's Tide
Image, 2001

1-4/B 3.00

Fathom Preview Special
Image, 1998

1 ....3.00

Fathom Swimsuit Special
Image, 1999

1 ....3.00
2000.......................................4.00
2002.......................................8.00

Fatman, the Human Flying Saucer
Lightning, 1967

1 ....35.00
2-3...25.00

Fat Ninja
Silverwolf, 1986

1-5...2.00

Fatt Family
Side Show

1 ....3.00

Faultlines
DC, 1997

1-6...3.00

Fauna Rebellion
Fantagraphics, 1990

1-3...2.00

Fauntleroy Comics
Archie, 1950

1 ....38.00
2-3...24.00

Faust
Northstar, 1988

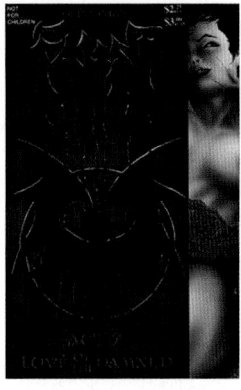

Few comics have had the nerve to balance as far out on the edge as Faust. The series was created by David Quinn and artist Tim Vigil as a sort of Hell set in comic-book New York City. Its cast is a collection of nymphomaniacs, demons, serial killers, and warlocks. These form a potent mix of sex, blood, and utter depravity, as the players vie for power.

The stuff contained here is pure, high-octane horror. It's not suitable for many readers (and it's certainly not meant for children). Nevertheless, Faust found a devoted following and has had to be reprinted in its entirety to meet demand.

1 .... 8.00
1/2nd 4.00
1/3rd 3.00
2 .... 6.00
2/2nd 4.00
2/3rd....................................... 3.00
3 .... 5.00
3/2nd 3.00
4 .... 4.00
4/2nd 3.00
5 .... 4.00
5/2nd 3.00
6 .... 4.00
6/2nd 3.00
7 .... 4.00
7/2nd 3.00
8 .... 4.00
8/2nd-11 .... 3.00
Special 1 .... 10.00

Faust 777: The Wrath
Avatar, 1998

0-1 .... 3.00
1/A 4.00
2-3... 3.00

Faust: The Book of M
Avatar, 1999

1 .... 3.00

Fawcett Miniatures
Fawcett

1-3 .... 60.00
4 .... 100.00
5-10 .... 90.00
11 .... 100.00

Fawcett Movie Comic
Fawcett, 1949

0 .... 165.00
1 .... 125.00
2 .... 275.00
3-9 .... 110.00
10-14 .... 80.00
15 .... 750.00
16-20 .... 80.00

Fawcett's Funny Animals
Fawcett, 1942

1 .... 240.00
2 .... 125.00
3 .... 90.00
4-5 .... 65.00
6-10 .... 52.00
11-20 .... 40.00
21-40 .... 32.00
41-60 .... 24.00
61-91 .... 20.00

Fax from Sarajevo
Dark Horse, 1996

1 .... 17.00
1/HC 25.00
Ash 1 .... 5.00

Faze One Fazers
AC

1-4 .... 2.00

Fazers Sketchbook (Vic Bridges'...)
AC

1 .... 2.00

F.B.I.
Dell, 1965

1 .... 60.00

Fear
Marvel, 1970

This quarterly series from the 1970s featured tales of horror involving both science and the supernatural. These short stories specialized in horrifying monster tales with ironic endings. Whether it was the cruel butterfly collector who found himself stranded on a world of giant butterflies or the brilliant scientist whose time-travel experiments were, literally, all in his mind, the moral of the story was often the saying, "Be careful what you wish for." The characters learn the hard way that expectations are not always the same as reality.

Like so many 1970s Marvel monster comics, Fear had its origin in a loosening of the boundaries of the Comics Code. Formerly, it had banned depictions of "the walking dead, torture, vampires, cannibalism, and werewolfism." When that stricture was loosened, Marvel was free to reprint stories from its inventory of horror tales from the 1950s and 1960s.

1	95.00
2	30.00
3-4	15.00
5	20.00
6-9	15.00
10	35.00

☞Man-Thing starts

11	18.00
12	12.00
13-14	9.00
15-17	12.00
18	9.00
19	25.00

☞1st Howard Duck

20	20.00

☞Morbius begins

21	9.00
22	7.00
23	8.00
24	12.00

☞Blade app.

25	8.00
26-29	7.00
30	12.00
31	7.00

Fear Agent
Image, 2005

1-10	3.00

Fear Book
Eclipse, 1986

1	2.00

Fear Effect: Retro Helix
Image, 2002

1-1/Gold	3.00

Fear Effect Special
Image, 2000

1	3.00

Fear Is Hell
C&T

1	2.00

Fearless Fosdick
Kitchen Sink

1	12.00
1/2nd-1/3rd	10.00

Feather
Image, 2003

1-4	3.00
5	6.00

Feature Book
David McKay, 1936

Early issues of the series, sometimes calling itself "Feature Books" and sometimes "Feature Book" on the cover, were oversized, with heavy covers and black-and-white interiors, almost looking as though they were aimed at children looking for coloring books. They often featured adaptations of material that had appeared elsewhere, primarily strip reprints. (Gangbusters, #17, for example, was "adapted from the popular radio program.") Characters like Dick Tracy, Little Orphan Annie, Popeye, The Phantom, and Mandrake were featured; many of the covers featured new art, obviously not drawn by the popular artists of the strips inside. These command high prices for their age, their historical importance, and the popularity of the strips. Color was introduced with #26, featuring Hal Foster's Prince Valiant.

-- Maggie

1	1,150.00
2	965.00
3	8,000.00
3/2nd	875.00
4	2,500.00
4/2nd	640.00
5-7	425.00
8	450.00
9	425.00
10-12	310.00
13	250.00
14-15	255.00
16-19	300.00
20-24	260.00
25-26	350.00

27	175.00
28-29	155.00
30	100.00
31	125.00
32	105.00
33	200.00
34	125.00
35	100.00
36	125.00
37	85.00
38	100.00
39	140.00
40	100.00
41-45	85.00
46	135.00
47	85.00
48-49	185.00
50	165.00
51	150.00
52	125.00
53	120.00
54-57	125.00

Feature Comics
Quality, 1939

Feature Comics was the continuation of Feature Funnies. Starting as primarily a compilation of strip reprints of such features as Joe Palooka and Mickey Finn, the series began to add features. Moreover, those features tended toward the action-adventure strip that was becoming so popular with comic-book readership. Charlie Chan was introduced in #23 (Aug 39), and the Will Eisner-Lou Fine creation Doll Man began in #27 (Dec 39). Though there were still many gag covers in the series, Doll Man took the cover as often as not, and covers became more and more action-packed and appealing.

-- Maggie

21	425.00
22-26	340.00
27	2,750.00
28	1,400.00
29	850.00
30	900.00
31	650.00
32-37	485.00

38-39	350.00
40-50	275.00
51-59	200.00
60-70	140.00
71-80	100.00
81-99	90.00
100	100.00
101-144	60.00

Feature Films
DC, 1950

1	250.00
2	185.00
3-4	150.00

Feature Funnies
Harry A. Chesler, 1937

1	1,500.00
2	800.00
3	550.00
4-5	425.00
6-10	285.00
11-20	200.00

Feature Presentation
Fox, 1950

5	225.00
6	165.00

Federal Men Comics
Gerard, 1945

2	225.00

Feds 'n' Heads
Print Mint

1	8.00

Feeders
Dark Horse, 1999

1	3.00

Feelgood Funnies
Rip Off, 1972

1	3.00

Felicia Hardy: The Black Cat
Marvel, 1994

This mini-series kicks off immediately after the events of Spectacular Spider-Man #210.

There, Felicia Hardy (a.k.a the Black Cat) broke up with longtime boyfriend Flash Thompson. Before that relationship, she had carried a torch for Peter Parker (Spider-Man), who has since married.

Still torn by her romantic problems, Felicia sought out Peter for counsel. She found him in his Spider-Man identity, battling the self-righteous vigilante Cardiac. Cardiac had been trashing Morelle Pharmaceuticals, which he had believed to be in violation of ethical standards. Felicia joined Peter in stopping Cardiac, and afterward was offered a commission by Morelle Pharmaceutical's owner. She was to find a person named Chimera, whose real name was to be a secret even to her. In taking this assignment, however, Chimera's identity was far from the only surprise in store for her.

1-4	2.00

Felix the Cat Silly Stories
Felix, 2005

1	3.00

Felix and His Friends
Toby, 1954

1	250.00
2-3	125.00

Felix's Nephews Inky and Dinky
Harvey, 1957

1	45.00
2-7	24.00

Felix the Cat (Pat Sullivan's...)
Dell, 1948

1	315.00
2	145.00
3	100.00
4-5	85.00
6-10	70.00
11-20	60.00
21-30	85.00
31	45.00
32-33	75.00
34-35	45.00
36	75.00
37	225.00
38-40	75.00
41	60.00
42-51	55.00
52-61	48.00
Ann 1	200.00
Ann 2	165.00

Felix the Cat (1st series)
Harvey, 1955

62-70	32.00
71-80	26.00
81-90	22.00
91-118	18.00

Felix the Cat (2nd series)
Dell, 1962

1	35.00
2-12	24.00

Felix the Cat (3rd series)
Harvey, 1991

1	2.00
2-7	1.00

Felix the Cat and Friends
Felix, 1994

1-5	2.00

Felix the Cat Big Book
Harvey, 1992

1	2.00

Felix the Cat Black & White
Felix

1-8	2.00

Felix the Cat Digest Magazine
Harvey, 1992

1	2.00

Fell
Image, 2005

1	4.00

☛Ellis, Templesmith series
2-4	2.00

Felon
Image, 2001

1-4	3.00

Felt: True Tales of Underground Hip Hop
Image, 2005

1	3.00

Fem 5
Express

1/A-2	3.00

Female Sex Pirates
Friendly

1	3.00

Fem Fantastique
AC, 1988

1	2.00

Femforce
AC, 1984

The American government has decided it wants an all-woman team of super-heroes, and that team is Femforce

Led by Ms. Victory, the team's key members include Nightveil, Dragonfly, She-Cat, Synn, and Stardust, with frequent additions of other super-characters. Many of the cast have origins in the 1940s and occasionally end up facing modernized foes from that era; fans of the Golden Age will find many tributes to its characters.

The stories are often more meaningful than usual super-hero bash-em-ups, with insights into the different characters' personalities, their families, and their pasts.

1-2	4.00
3-86	3.00
87	4.00
88-99	3.00
100	4.00
100/CS	7.00
101-109	5.00
110/A-114	3.00
115-123	6.00
122-133	7.00
Special 1	2.00

Femforce Frightbook
AC
1	3.00

Femforce in the House of Horror
AC, 1989
1	3.00

Femforce: Night of the Demon
AC, 1990
1	3.00

Femforce: Out of the Asylum Special
AC, 1987
1	3.00

Femforce Pin Up Portfolio
AC, 1991
1-3	3.00
4-5	5.00

Femforce: To Die For
AC, 2005
1	16.00

Femforce Uncut
AC
1	10.00

Femforce Up Close
AC, 1992
1-11	3.00

Femforce Victory Reborn
AC, 2005
1	16.00

Femme Macabre
London Night
1	3.00

Femme Noire
Cat-Head
1-2	2.00

Fenry
Raven
1	7.00

Ferret
Malibu, 1992
1	2.00

Ferret
Malibu, 1993
1	2.00
1/Variant-4	3.00
5-10	2.00

Ferro City
Image, 2005
1-4	3.00

Feud
Marvel, 1993
1	3.00
2-4	2.00

Fever
Wonder Comix
1	2.00

Fever Dreams
Kitchen Sink, 1972
1	3.00

Fever in Urbicand
NBM
1	13.00

F5
Image, 2000
1-Ashcan 1	3.00

F5 Origin
Dark Horse, 2001
1	3.00

Fierce
Dark Horse, 2004
1-4	3.00

15 Minutes
Slave Labor, 2004
1-3	4.00

Fifth Force Featuring Hawk and Animal
Antarctic, 1999
1	2.00
2	3.00

Fifties Terror
Eternity, 1988
1-6	2.00

52
DC, 2006
1	4.00
2-6	3.00
7	4.00
8-36	3.00

Fight Against Crime
Story, 1951
1	240.00
2	185.00
3-5	145.00
6-9	125.00
10-15	175.00
16-21	165.00

Fight Against The Guilty
Story, 1954
22-23	150.00

Fight Comics
Fiction House, 1940
1	3,500.00
2	1,250.00
3	650.00
4	600.00
5	500.00
6-10	450.00
11-14	425.00
15-16	500.00
17-18	425.00
19	450.00
20-30	350.00
31-40	200.00
41-50	175.00
51-60	125.00
61-86	100.00

Fight For Love
United Feature, 1952
1	45.00

Fight for Tomorrow
DC, 2002
1-6	3.00

Fightin' 5
Charlton, 1964
28	20.00
29-30	10.00

31-39	9.00
40	18.00

☛1st Peacemaker

41	10.00
42-49	3.00

Fightin' Air Force
Charlton, 1956

3	32.00
4-5	20.00
6-10	15.00
11-20	12.00
21-53	8.00

Fightin' Army
Charlton, 1956

16	24.00
17-20	18.00
21-30	15.00
31-40	12.00
41-50	10.00
51-75	8.00
76	10.00

☛Willy Schultz

77-100	6.00
101-120	5.00
121-172	4.00

Fighting American
Headline, 1954

1	850.00
2	525.00
3-5	400.00
6-7	285.00

Fighting American
Harvey, 1966

1	20.00

Fighting American
DC, 1994

1-6	2.00

Fighting American
Awesome, 1997

1/A-1/C	3.00
1/D	16.00
2-3	3.00

Fighting American:
Dogs of War
Awesome, 1998

In a Baltimore warehouse,
Fighting American breaks up a

deadly transaction between expatriate Russians and Iranian terrorists with deadly measures of his own. Figures hiding in the shadows wait to play their part in this bloody tableau. In another reality, one could be Sharon Carter and the other Nick Fury. This version of the Captain America substitute, (written by Jim Starlin) is more than ready to use deadly force, which sets him far afield from his template.

This is the third mini-series featuring Rob Liefeld's version of an obscure character originally intended as a humor title. The sales strategy of publishing a number of short series rather than one ongoing title may prompt extra sales due to continual "first issue" enthusiasm, but for indexers, it is another item to catalogue that is not substantially different from its predecessor.

-- George Haberberger

1-3	3.00

Fighting American:
Rules of the Game
Awesome, 1997

1-3	3.00

Fighting American
Special Comicon Edition
Awesome, 1997

1	1.00

Fighting Daniel Boone
Avon, 1953

1	70.00

Fighting Fem Classics
Forbidden Fruit, 1993

1	4.00

Fighting Fems
Forbidden Fruit

1-2	4.00

Fighting Fronts
Harvey, 1952

1	52.00
2-5	40.00

Fighting Indians
of the Wild West
Avon, 1952

1	95.00
2	65.00

Fighting Leathernecks
Toby, 1952

1	85.00
2	50.00
3-6	40.00

Fighting Man
Ajax, 1952

1	42.00
2	26.00

3	22.00
4-8	20.00

Fighting Undersea
Commandos
Avon, 1952

1	75.00
2	50.00
3	42.00
4-5	38.00

Fighting Yank
Nedor, 1942

1	3,450.00
2	1,400.00
3	800.00
4	725.00
5-10	600.00
11-15	465.00
16-20	385.00
21-26	325.00
27-29	270.00

Fightin' Marines
Charlton, 1951

1	200.00
2	145.00
3	140.00
4-6	110.00
7-9	90.00
10	34.00
11-13	22.00
14	75.00
15	30.00
16	22.00
17	55.00
18-24	16.00
25	36.00
26	40.00
27-29	16.00
30-39	13.00
40-50	10.00
51-70	7.00
71-74	6.00
75-81	4.00
82	6.00
83-100	4.00
101-120	3.00
120/2nd	2.00
121-150	3.00
151-176	2.00

Fightin' Navy
Charlton, 1956

74	24.00
75-80	18.00
81-90	15.00
91-100	12.00
101-120	8.00
121-125	5.00
126-133	2.00

Fightin' Texan
St. John, 1952

16-17	55.00

Fight Man
Marvel, 1993

Perhaps the biggest clichT of the modern super-hero comic is the Obligatory Fight Scene. Whether it's the heroes beating up the bad guys, the bad guys beating up the heroes, or two heroes mistrusting the other's motives and beating themselves up-somehow the writers inevitably manage to fill several pages with mindless mayhem.

Marvel, one of the most notorious practitioners of this, manages to spoof itself in this well-placed special. The "star" is Fight Man, an unimaginative loser whose solution to every problem is to pulverize it. This is only a one-shot special, but for Fight Man, one shot is all he needs.

1 ....2.00

Fight the Enemy
Tower, 1966
1 ....22.00
2-3 ....16.00

Figments
Blackthorne
1-2 ....2.00

Figments Unlimited
Graphik
1-3 ....1.00

Files of Ms. Tree
Renegade, 1984
1-3 ....6.00

Filibusting Comics
Fantagraphics, 1995
1 ....3.00

Film Funnies
Marvel, 1949
1 ....85.00
2 ....55.00

Film Stars Romances
Star Publications, 1950
1 ....250.00
2 ....165.00
3 ....140.00

Filth
DC, 2002
1-13 ....3.00

Filthy Animals
Radio, 1997
1-4 ....3.00

Filthy Habits
Aeon, 1996
1-3 ....3.00

Final Cycle
Dragon's Teeth, 1987
1-4 ....2.00

Final Man
C&T
1 ....2.00

Final Night
DC, 1996
1 ....6.00
2-4 ....4.00
Ash 1 ....1.00

Final Taboo
Aircel, 1991
1-2 ....3.00

Finals
DC, 1999
1-4 ....3.00

Finder
Lightspeed, 1996

Jaeger Ayers is a Finder, a person talented in tracking people and things. He's a free spirit, a member of a native tribe more at home in the badlands or desert than in the city. Yet Jaeger is periodically drawn to the mega-city of Anvard and his friends who reside there.

The characters in Finder live in a setting that meshes science fiction and fantasy -- lion creatures guard bookstores, museums of pain pay for memories, virtual-reality personalities run households and vie for favors, and the crumbling dome covering the crowded city is a mystery even to its residents.

Finder is a complex, mature story which follows Jaeger and the many lives he touches. It delivers an intense and compelling character study set in a strange and imaginative setting. In the issues, creator Carla Speed McNeil has provided extensive notes on the world she has created.

1-14 ....4.00
15-35 ....3.00
Ashchan 1 ....1.00

Finder Footnotes
Lightspeed
1 ....6.00

Finieous Treasury
TSR
1 ....3.00

Fink, Inc.
Fink, Inc.
1 ....4.00

Finn
Fleetway-Quality
1-4 ....3.00

Fire
Caliber
1-2 ....3.00

Firearm
Malibu, 1993

Alec Swan is the hardboiled star of the series. He's a former secret agent from England, now living in Southern California. While in England, he was a member of a covert bureau of the government called "The Lodge." They were the ones who gave him the nickname "Firearm," with reference to his expertise with a custom gun which fires everything from bullets to explosive charges.

Nowadays, he makes his living as a private detective. Swan charges $2,000 per day plus expenses, but for that he's willing to take on all manner of bad guys -- including not a few ultra-powered criminals -- in order to solve his case. He's not pretty, but he's very good at what he does.

0	15.00
1	2.00
1/Ltd.-2	3.00
3-9	2.00
10	4.00
11-19	2.00

Firebirds One Shot
Image
1	6.00

Firebrand
DC, 1996
1-9	2.00

Firebreather
Image, 2003
1-4	3.00

Firebreather: Iron Saint One-Shot
Image, 2005
1	7.00

Fire from Heaven
Image, 1996
1/2	1.00
1-2	3.00

Firehair
Fiction House, 1948
1	400.00
2	200.00
7-9	100.00
10-11	90.00

Fires
Catalan
1	13.00

Fire Sale
Rip Off, 1989
1	3.00

Firestar
Marvel, 1986

Angelica Jones is thirteen. It's an awkward age for anyone, but it's been especially difficult for her. Her mother died, and her father's job kept her constantly on the move. Today she would start at her new school, where she would once more desperately try to fit in.

But today would be different. Today she would discover that she is a mutant, possessing the ability to emit incredible amounts of heat simply by thinking. Suddenly, she would be sought out by two powerful forces-the X-Men would try to teach her to use her power for the good of mankind, but the evil Hellfire Club would do everything in its power to add her to its arsenal.

This mini-series tells the tale of Firestar before she first appeared in the Uncanny X-Men #193. Angelica has a lot of problems at thirteen...the chief one being survival!

1-2	2.00
3-4	1.00

Firestorm
DC, 1978
1	8.00
2	2.00
3	3.00
4-5	2.00

Firestorm
DC, 2004
1	3.00
1	8.00
2-5	3.00
6	5.00
☞Identity Crisis tie	
7-29	3.00

Firestorm, the Nuclear Man
DC, 1987
65-93	1.00

30	3.00
94	1.00
31	3.00
95	1.00
32	3.00
96-99	1.00
100	3.00
Ann 5	1.00

Fire Team
Aircel, 1990
1-6	3.00

Firkin
Knockabout
1-6	3.00

First
CrossGen, 2000
1	4.00
2-37	3.00

First Adventures
First, 1985
1-5	1.00

First Deterrent
Devious Drawings, 1996
1	3.00

1st Folio
Pacific, 1984
1	2.00

First Graphic Novel
First, 1984
1-2	6.00
3	12.00
4-5	6.00
6	15.00
7-8	8.00
9-10	10.00
11	15.00
12	8.00
13	12.00
14	8.00
15	10.00
16-17	9.00
18	10.00
19	9.00
20	13.00
21	10.00
22	20.00
23	12.00
24	9.00
25	15.00

1st Issue Special
DC, 1975
1	7.00
2	5.00
3-6	4.00
7	5.00
8	15.00
☞Warlord	
9-12	4.00
13	5.00

First King Adventure
ADV Manga, 2005
1-2	10.00

First Kingdom
Bud Plant, 1978

1-5 ....3.00
6-24 ....2.00

First Kiss
Charlton, 1957

Another of Charlton's romance titles, First Kiss ran from 1957 to 1965 and featured work by Dick Giordano, Charles Nicholas, Vince Alascia, the Vince Colletta Studio, Luis Dominguez, and Sal Trapani.

The stories ran to typical romance fare, from jilted brides to heart-broken lovers to the inevitable summer romance to the girl who spent her entire life caring for a sick relative only to find love when that relative finally kicked the bucket. No deep literary content here, just some fun cliches of a simpler era.

In the 1990s, artist and writer John Lustig acquired the original art to the series and began tinkering with the panels and covers, creating his own "Last Kiss" feature which appears in Comics Buyer's Guide and as its own comic-book series with longer stories.

-- Brent

1 ....45.00
2 ....28.00
3 ....22.00
4-5 ....18.00
6-10 ....13.00
11-20 ....12.00
21-40 ....8.00

First Love Illustrated
Harvey, 1949

1 ....100.00
2 ....65.00
3 ....45.00
4-10 ....35.00
11-20 ....30.00
21-30 ....28.00
31-40 ....22.00
41-50 ....20.00
51-89 ....16.00

First Man
Image, 1997

1 .... 3.00

First Romance Magazine
Harvey, 1949

1 .... 85.00
2 .... 55.00
3 .... 45.00
4-5 .... 38.00
6-10 .... 32.00
11-20 .... 26.00
21-30 .... 22.00
31-40 .... 18.00
41-52 .... 15.00

First Six Pack
First, 1987

First Comics was one of the most fresh and innovative publishers in the independent comics boom of the mid-1980s. Among its offerings were such favorites as American Flagg, Jon Sable, Freelance, Dreadstar, and Nexus.

The First Six Pack previewed upcoming storylines for six of their current and upcoming titles. Costing just 50¢ each, this "six pack" was an excellent and inexpensive way to keep First fans updated on what was going on with this spirited company.

1-2 .... 1.00

First Trip to the Moon
Avalon

1 .... 3.00

First Wave
Andromeda, 2000

1 .... 3.00

Fishmasters
Slave Labor, 1994

1 .... 3.00

Fish Police
Fishwrap, 1985

1-3 .... 1.00
4-11 .... 2.00

Fish Police
Comico, 1987

5-16 .... 2.00
17 .... 3.00
18-Special 1 .... 2.00

Fish Police
Marvel, 1992

1-6 .... 1.00

Fish Shticks
Apple, 1991

1-6 .... 2.00

Fission Chicken
Fantagraphics, 1990

1-4 .... 2.00

Fission Chicken: Plan Nine from Vortox
Mu, 1994

1 .... 4.00

Fist of God
Eternity, 1988

1-4 .... 2.00

Fist of the North Star
Viz, 1989

1-8 .... 3.00

Fist of the North Star Part 2
Viz

This violent manga series is based on an equally violent anime series about a warrior named Ken who comes back from the dead and seeks his lost love in a post-apocalyptic future. Ken is the true Fist of the North Star, which allows him to punch through his adversaries and make them explode, but this is something he must prove over and over again as new would-be overlords oppress the weak and get in the way of Ken and the object of his quest.

1-8 .... 3.00

Fist of the North Star Part 3
Viz, 1996
1-5 ....3.00

Fist of the North Star Part 4
Viz, 1996
1-7 ....3.00

5-Cent Comics
Fawcett, 1940
1 ....10,000.00

Five Fists of Science
Image, 2006
1 ....13.00

Five Little Comics
Scott McCloud
1 ....4.00

Five Years of Pain
Boneyard, 1997
1 ....4.00

Flag Fighters
Ironcat, 1997
1-5 ....3.00

Flame
Fox, 1940
1 ....1,800.00
2 ....1,200.00
3 ....775.00
4 ....525.00
5 ....450.00
6-8 ....340.00

Flamehead
JNCO, 1998
0 ....1.00

Flame of Recca
Viz, 2003
1-14 ....10.00

Flame (Ajax)
Ajax
1 ....285.00
2 ....165.00
3 ....150.00

Flame Twisters
Brown Study, 1994
1-2 ....3.00

Flaming Carrot
Kilian, 1981
1 ....35.00

Flaming Carrot
Image, 2004
1 .... 3.00
2-4 .... 4.00

Flaming Carrot Comics
Aardvark-Vanaheim, 1984
1 .... 26.00
2 .... 15.00
3 .... 12.00
4 .... 10.00
5-6 .... 8.00
7 .... 7.00
8-9 .... 5.00
10-12 .... 4.00
13-15 .... 3.00
15/A-16 .... 4.00
17-24 .... 3.00
25 .... 4.00
26-30/A 3.00
32 .... 4.00
31 .... 3.00
Ann 1 .... 5.00

Flaming Carrot Stories
Dark Horse
1 .... 5.00

Flaming Love
Quality, 1949
1 .... 225.00
2 .... 125.00
3 .... 85.00
4-6 .... 65.00

Flaming Western Romances
Star Publications, 1950
3 .... 200.00

Flare
Hero, 1988
1-3 .... 3.00

Flare
Hero, 1989
1-16 .... 3.00
Ann 1 .... 5.00

Flare
Heroic
1-29 .... 3.00

Flare Adventures
Heroic, 1992
1 .... 1.00
2-3 .... 3.00
4-14 .... 4.00

Flare First Edition
Hero, 1993
1-3 .... 4.00
4-5 .... 5.00
6-11 .... 4.00

Flash
DC, 1959

Picking up the numbering from Flash Comics, this series featured Barry Allen as the red-garbed speedster and Justice League member. Allen was the second person to take on the role of Flash, replacing Jay Garrick, the Flash of the Golden Age.

During the run of this series, Allen squared off against countless colorful villains, including Professor Zoom, Gorilla Grodd, and the Trickster. The series is also notable for the introduction of the hero, Elongated Man, as well as later witnessing EM's marriage to Sue Dearborn.

As can be expected by adventures of The Fastest Man Alive, most of the plots revolved around super-speed antics, including time travel, running across water, vibrating through walls, and creating mini-tornadoes by The Flash whirling his arms at super-speed.

The series ended in the early 1980s when Allen was put on trial for the murder of Zoom, and Allen later gave his life to save the universe in Crisis on Infinite Earths.

105 .... 6,500.00
106 .... 2,000.00
107 .... 1,000.00
108 .... 850.00
109 .... 650.00
110 .... 1,500.00
☛1st Kid Flash
111 .... 450.00
112 .... 600.00
☛1st Elong. Man
113 .... 550.00
114 .... 275.00
115 .... 350.00
116 .... 250.00
117 .... 300.00
118-120 .... 250.00
121-122 .... 200.00

123 ....1,500.00
☛1st Earth-2
124-128 ....150.00
129 ....325.00
☛GA Flash app.
130 ....150.00
131-136 ....125.00
137 ....475.00
☛GA Flash app.
138-140 ....125.00
141-142 ....150.00
143 ....125.00
144-150 ....100.00
151 ....80.00
152-153 ....65.00
154-158 ....60.00
159 ....75.00
160 ....90.00
☛Giant-size
161-164 ....50.00
165 ....70.00
166-167 ....50.00
168 ....95.00
169 ....70.00
☛Origin of Flash
170-174 ....50.00
175 ....175.00
☛Race w/Superman
176-179 ....40.00
180 ....50.00
181-183 ....35.00
184 ....50.00
185-186 ....35.00
187 ....65.00
188-191 ....35.00
192-193 ....25.00
194 ....40.00
195 ....25.00
196 ....40.00
197-200 ....25.00
201-202 ....20.00
203 ....25.00
204 ....20.00
205 ....35.00
206 ....20.00
207-212 ....17.00
213 ....25.00
214 ....40.00
215 ....35.00
216-219 ....17.00
220-228 ....15.00
229 ....30.00
230-231 ....15.00
232 ....30.00
☛100-page issue
233-237 ....10.00
238-245 ....7.00
246 ....12.00
247-262 ....7.00
263-268 ....4.00
268/Whitman 12.00
269-273 ....4.00
273/Whitman 7.00
274 ....5.00
274/Whitman-275/Whitman 7.00
276 ....4.00
276/Whitman 7.00
277-278 ....4.00
278/Whitman 7.00
279-283 ....4.00

283/Whitman 7.00
284-286 .... 4.00
286/Whitman 7.00
287-288 .... 4.00
289 .... 5.00
290-299 .... 3.00
300 .... 5.00
301-304 .... 3.00
305-306 .... 4.00
307-349 .... 3.00
350 .... 7.00
Ann 1 .... 400.00
Ann 1/2nd.............................. 7.00

Flash
DC, 1987
0 .... 4.00
1 .... 5.00
2-20 .... 3.00
21-49 .... 2.00
50 .... 3.00
51-78 .... 2.00
79 .... 3.00
80 .... 2.00
80/Variant.............................. 3.00
81-90 .... 2.00
91 .... 4.00
92 .... 8.00
☛1st Impulse
93 .... 5.00
94-95 .... 3.00
96-99 .... 2.00
100 .... 3.00
100/Variant............................ 4.00
101-149 .... 2.00
150 .... 3.00
151-187 .... 2.00
188 .... 3.00
189-199 .... 2.00
200 .... 4.00
201-205 .... 2.00
206 .... 6.00
207 .... 2.00
208 .... 5.00
209 .... 4.00
210 .... 3.00
210/2nd 2.00
211 .... 4.00
212-213 .... 2.00
214 .... 6.00
☛Identity Crisis tie
215 .... 5.00
☛Identity Crisis tie
216 .... 6.00
☛Identity Crisis tie
217 .... 5.00
☛Identity Crisis tie
218 .... 4.00
219 .... 9.00
☛Inf. Crisis tie
220 .... 6.00
221 .... 5.00
222-223 .... 4.00
224-1000000 .... 3.00
Ann 1 .... 5.00
Ann 2-4.................................. 2.00
Ann 5-7.................................. 3.00
Ann 8..................................... 4.00
Ann 9..................................... 3.00
Ann 10-11.............................. 4.00

Ann 12................................... 3.00
Ann 13................................... 4.00
GS 1-2 .... 5.00
Special 1 .... 4.00
TV 1....................................... 4.00

Flash & Green Lantern: The Brave and the Bold
DC, 1999
1-6 .... 3.00

Flashback
Special, 1974
1-27 .... 3.00

Flash Comics
DC, 1940

Flash Comics began in 1939 and soon became a mainstay of DC's super-hero line. In issue #1, the world met Jay Garrick, a chemistry student who accidentally broke a container filled with hard (or heavy) water gases he had been experimenting on. The room filled with the strange vapors and Garrick barely managed to escape before losing consciousness. When he awoke, however, he found his body chemistry altered by the gas he had inhaled, and became transformed into The Flash, the fastest man alive.

In addition to its title character, Flash Comics introduced the world to Hawkman, Black Canary, and Johnny Thunder (a boy who could summon a "pet thunderbolt" by calling out the magic words "Cei-U" ["Say you!"]). The series ran successfully until 1949 when it fell, a victim of the declining sales of super-hero titles. The Golden Age Flash appeared as a Justice Society member in All-Star Comics for a few more years, then vanished for more than a decade.

1 .... 70,000.00
☛1st Flash, Hawkman
2 .... 8,000.00
3 .... 5,500.00
4 .... 4,500.00
5 .... 3,500.00

6	5,000.00
7	4,500.00
8	3,000.00
9-10	3,250.00
11-20	2,000.00
21-24	1,600.00
25-40	1,000.00
41-50	800.00
51-61	600.00
62	1,000.00

☛Kubert Hawkman

63-69	600.00
70-85	550.00
86	2,250.00

☛1st Black Canary

87	875.00
88-91	900.00
92	3,000.00

☛1st solo Black Canary

93	700.00
94-99	1,000.00
100	2,500.00

☛Scarce

101-102	2,250.00

☛Scarce

103	2,500.00

☛Scarce

104	7,000.00

☛Flash origin recap

Flash Gordon
Gold Key, 1965

1	26.00

Flash Gordon
King, 1966

1	25.00
2-7	20.00
8-14	10.00
15-19	8.00
20-23	6.00
24	5.00
25-29	4.00
30	8.00
30/50¢	4.00
31-37	3.00

Flash Gordon
DC, 1988

1-9	2.00

Flash Gordon
Marvel, 1995

1-2	3.00

Flash Gordon Comics
Harvey, 1950

1	225.00
2	145.00
3-5	110.00

Flash Gordon: The Movie
Golden Press

1	3.00

Flash/Green Lantern: Faster Friends
DC

1	5.00

Flash: Our Worlds at War
DC, 2001

1	3.00

Flash Plus
DC, 1997

1	3.00

Flash Secret Files
DC, 1997

1-3	5.00

Flash: The Fastest Man Alive
DC, 2006

1	6.00
2-7	3.00

Flash, The: Iron Heights
DC, 2001

1	6.00

Flash: Time Flies
DC, 2002

nn	6.00

Flashmarks
Fantagraphics

1	3.00

Flashpoint
DC, 1999

1-3	3.00

Flatline Comics Presents...
Flatline, 1993

1	3.00

Flat Top
Harvey, 1953

1	28.00
2	16.00
3	12.00
4-7	10.00

Flaxen
Dark Horse

Flaxen is a rather odd one-shot celebrating real-life model Susie "Flaxen" Owens. It begins with a comic story starring a golden-haired super-heroine whose powers stem from her incredible self-confidence. In that story, she inspires a depressed and overweight woman to stand up to her corrupt boss. The boss had been using the woman in order to get access to her computer. He then used the information to steal security information on the local nuclear power plant. After consoling the woman, Flaxen must stop the boss from extorting money by planting a bomb at the plant.

The rest of the special is divided between pinup pages of Owens (including a rather funny entry by Sergio AragonTs) and a text piece telling her real-life story. Owens, it turns out, was once an overweight dental assistant who mustered the willpower to turn herself into a knockout. Her story is held up as an inspiration to others.

1	3.00

Flaxen: Alter Ego
Caliber, 1995

1	3.00

Fleener
Zongo, 1996

1-3	3.00

Flesh
Fleetway-Quality

1-4	3.00

Flesh & Blood
Brainstorm, 1996

1	3.00
1/Ashcan	1.00

Flesh & Blood: Pre-Existing Conditions
Blindwolf

1	3.00

Flesh and Bones
Upshot

1-4	2.00

Flesh Crawlers
Kitchen Sink, 1994

1-3	3.00

Flesh Gordon
Aircel, 1992

1-4	3.00

Fleshpot
Fantagraphics, 1997

1	3.00

Flex Mentallo
DC, 1996

1	10.00
2-4	8.00

Flickering Flesh
Boneyard, 1993

1	3.00

Flicker's Fleas
Fifth Wheel

1 .... 3.00

Flinch
DC, 1999

DC once again takes on the horror anthology field with these tales of terror and shock written and drawn by current writers and artists. Under the Vertigo line, these adult stories are scary and frightening, with just a little humor and satire thrown in every now and then to keep the reader from becoming completely terrified and insane. With an average of three stories per issue, the reader doesn't have to worry about long-drawn-out plots or continuing characters, just good storytelling with some interesting twists throughout that make you think for a change.

1-16 .... 3.00

Flint Armbuster Jr. Special
Alchemy

1 .... 3.00

Flintstone Kids
Marvel, 1987

1-11 .... 2.00

Flintstones (Dell/Gold Key)
Dell, 1961

1 .... 55.00
2 .... 38.00
3-5 .... 30.00
6-7 .... 24.00
8-10 .... 20.00
11-20 .... 18.00
21-30 .... 15.00
31-40 .... 12.00
41-60 .... 9.00

Flintstones
Charlton, 1970

1 .... 36.00
2 .... 22.00
3-5 .... 14.00
6-10 .... 9.00
11-20 .... 7.00
21-30 .... 5.00
31-50 .... 4.00

Flintstones 3-D
Blackthorne, 1987

1-4 .... 3.00

Flintstones
Marvel, 1977

1 .... 5.00
2-9 .... 3.00

Flintstones
Harvey, 1992

1 .... 3.00
2-13 .... 2.00

Flintstones
Archie, 1995

1-22 .... 2.00

Flintstones and the Jetsons
DC, 1997

1-21 .... 2.00

Flintstones at the New York World's Fair
Dell, 1964

1 .... 48.00

Flintstones Big Book
Harvey, 1992

1-2 .... 2.00

Flintstones Bigger and Boulder
Gold Key, 1962

1 .... 65.00
2 .... 45.00

Flintstones Doublevision
Harvey, 1994

1 .... 3.00

Flintstones GS
Harvey, 1992

2-3 .... 3.00

Flintstones with Pebbles and Bamm-Bamm
Gold Key, 1965

1 .... 50.00

Flip
Harvey, 1954

1 .... 90.00
2 .... 65.00

Flipper
Gold Key, 1966

1 .... 25.00
2-3 .... 18.00

Flippity and Flop
DC, 1951

Following the decline of most of its super-hero titles in the late 1940s and early 1950s (only comics featuring Superman, Batman, and Wonder Woman survived), DC (then National Periodical Publications) experimented with other genres, including war, espionage, Westerns, crime, and funny animals.

While some series, such as Leading Comics, added funny animals to a previously super-hero title, others, such as Real Screen Comics, introduced new characters such as The Fox and the Crow, Tito and His Burrito, and Flippity and Flop.

This latter anthropomorphic duo was, respectively, a cat and a canary, who were joined in their misadventures by Sam, the dog. The stories proved popular enough to spin off into this long-running series that was published throughout the 1950s.

-- Brent

1 .... 140.00
2 .... 85.00
3 .... 60.00
4-5 .... 45.00
6-10 .... 40.00
11-20 .... 36.00
21-30 .... 30.00
31-40 .... 26.00
41-47 .... 24.00

Floaters
Dark Horse, 1993

1-5 .... 3.00

Flock of Dreamers
Kitchen Sink, 1997

1 .... 13.00

Flood Relief
Malibu, 1994

1 .... 5.00

Flowers
Drawn and Quarterly
1 ....3.00

Flowers on the Razorwire
Boneyard, 1994
1-10......................................3.00

Fly
Archie, 1983
1 ....3.00
2-9..2.00

Fly
DC, 1991
1-17..1.00
Ann 1..2.00

Fly Man
Archie, 1965
32 ....32.00
33-34......................................20.00
35-39......................................16.00

Flyboy
Ziff-Davis, 1952
1 ....90.00
2-4..68.00
5..44.00

Flying Aces
Key, 1955
1 ....35.00
2-5..20.00

Flying A's Range Rider
Dell, 1953
2..60.00
3..45.00
4-5..40.00
6-10..35.00
11-24..28.00

Flying Cadet
Flying Cadet, 1943
1 ....80.00
2..50.00
3-5..40.00
6-10..35.00
11-17..28.00

Flying Colors 10th Anniversary Special
Flying Colors, 1998
1 ....3.00

Flying Models
Health, 1954
3..36.00

Flying Nun
Dell, 1968
1..32.00
2-4..20.00

Flying Saucers
Avon, 1950
1..560.00
2..295.00
2/2nd 165.00

Flying Saucers
Dell, 1967
1 ....26.00
2-5......................................15.00

Flyin' Jenny
Pentagon, 1946
1 ....80.00
2 ....70.00

Focus
DC, 1987
1 ....1.00

Foes
Ram
1 ....2.00

Fog City Comics
Stampart
1 ....1.00

Foodang
Continu.m, 1994
1 ....2.00
Ashcan 1 ....1.00

Foodang
August House, 1995
1-2......................................3.00

Food First Comics
IFDP
1-1/3rd.................................3.00

Foodini
Continental, 1950
1 ....110.00
2 ....75.00
3 ....50.00
4 ....45.00

Foofur
Marvel, 1987
1-6..1.00

Foolkiller
Marvel, 1990

Kurt Gerhardt's life was falling apart. His father had just been murdered by a gang of muggers who decided to kill him when they found he had only six dollars to steal. Still reeling from that loss, Kurt lost his job when his bank was declared insolvent. Then his wife left him. Kurt was forced to take a job at a fast-food restaurant, only to have the place robbed. And he got a crack on the head when he tried to stop the robbers.

Kurt is "born again" when he sees Greg Salinger, the Foolkiller (first seen in The Defenders), on a TV broadcast. Salinger inspires Kurt to stop the criminals, the thugs, the junkies -- the "fools" of the world. Kurt soon takes on the costume, weapons, and mission of the FoolKiller. That mission was to eradicate fools, permanently.

FoolKiller is a haunting story of flawed justice and the penalties it exacts.

1-10 ....2.00

FOOM Magazine
Marvel, 1973
1 ....45.00
2 ....30.00
3-4 ....25.00
5-20 ....20.00
21 ....25.00
22 ....40.00

Football Heroes
Personality
1-2 ....3.00

Football Thrills
Ziff-Davis, 1951
1 ....165.00
2 ....110.00

Foot Soldiers
Dark Horse, 1996
1-4 ....3.00

Foot Soldiers
Image, 1997
1-5 ....3.00

Foozle
Eclipse, 1985
1-3 ....2.00

Forbidden 3-D
3-D Zone
1-1/3D 4.00

Forbidden Frankenstein
Fantagraphics, 1991
1 ....2.00
2 ....3.00

Forbidden Kingdom
Eastern, 1987
1-8 ....2.00

Forbidden Knowledge
Last Gasp, 1975
1 ....4.00

Forbidden Knowledge: Adventure Beyond the Doorway to Souls with Radical Dreamer
Mark's Giant Economy Size
1 ....4.00

Forbidden Love
Quality, 1950

1 ....325.00
2 ....225.00
3-4 ....200.00

Forbidden Planet
Innovation, 1992

1-4 ....3.00

Forbidden Subjects
Angel

0 ....3.00
0/A-0/B 4.00

Forbidden Subjects: Candy Kisses
Angel

1-1/B 3.00

Forbidden Tales of Dark Mansion
DC, 1972

Ghosts, ghouls, and reincarnations haunt the dark mansion, though the stories take place in different locations and times. Formerly known as Dark Mansion of Forbidden Love, this series turned from romance to mystery tales using the supernatural, science-fiction, or weird mystery with an often ironic ending. In one story, reminiscent of television shows such as the Twilight Zone, a boy is captured by insect-like invaders who plan to study him to learn the secrets of humans in order that they might take over Earth. Only an attack by the "soil-dwellers" allowed him to escape...and regain his natural, much larger size. As it turned out, the boy had been captured by termites in a tree in his own backyard; the soil-dwellers are merely ants.

5 ....35.00
6-7 ....17.00
8-9 ....12.00
10-14 ....10.00
15 ....15.00

Forbidden Vampire
Angel

0 ....3.00

Forbidden Worlds
ACG, 1951

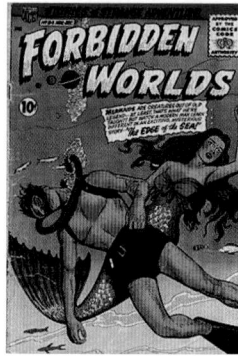

ACG's Forbidden Worlds was another of the original science-fiction/horror titles of the early 1950s. The first several years of Forbidden Worlds featured stories with a horror theme. Toward the middle of the run, around the advent of the Comics Code, the focus shifted toward straight science fiction, with the usual space wars, giant robots, and dinosaur planets common to the stories of that time. In later issues, around the dawning of the Silver Age, Forbidden Worlds featured a science-fiction super-hero called Magicman. But the real hit was Ogden Whitney's kid-humor/super-hero spoof series, Herbie, the Fat Fury, which appeared several times in the unlikely pages of Forbidden Worlds before graduating to his own series.

ACG drew on some of the better comics talent of the day, with early issues featuring art by Al Williamson, Frank Frazetta, and Joe Orlando.

-- Rob Salkowitz

1 .... 875.00
2 .... 500.00
3 .... 465.00
4 .... 270.00
5-6 .... 290.00
7-10 .... 190.00
11-15 .... 135.00

16-20 .... 100.00
21-30 .... 85.00
31-40 .... 75.00
41-50 .... 54.00
51-60 .... 45.00
61-70 .... 40.00
71-72 .... 35.00
73 .... 275.00
☞1st Herbie
74-80 .... 35.00
81-85 .... 24.00
86 .... 30.00
87-90 .... 24.00
91-93 .... 20.00
94 .... 55.00
☞Herbie app.
95-100 .... 20.00
101-109 .... 16.00
110 .... 35.00
☞Herbie app.
111-113 .... 16.00
114 .... 35.00
115 .... 16.00
116 .... 30.00
☞Herbie app.
117-120 .... 16.00
121-124 .... 12.00
125 .... 25.00
☞1st Magicman
126-127 .... 12.00
128 .... 14.00
129 .... 12.00
130 .... 14.00
131-140 .... 12.00
141-145 .... 10.00

Forbidden Worlds (A+)
A-Plus

1 .... 3.00

Forbidden Worlds (Avalon)
Avalon

1 .... 3.00

Forbidden X Angel
Angel, 1997

1 .... 3.00

Forbidden Zone
Galaxy Entertainment

1 .... 6.00

Force 10
Crow

1-1/Ashcan 3.00

Force Majeure: Prairie Bay
Little Rocket, 2002

1 .... 3.00

Force of Buddha's Palm
Jademan, 1988

1-55 .... 2.00

Force Seven
Lone Star, 1999

1-3 .... 3.00

Force Works
Marvel, 1994

1	4.00
2-5	2.00
5/CS	3.00
6-11	2.00
12	3.00
13-22	2.00
Ashcan 1	1.00

Foreplay
NBM

1	19.00

Fore/Punk
Parody

1/A-1/B	3.00

Foreternity
Antarctic, 1997

1-4	3.00

Forever Amber
Image, 1999

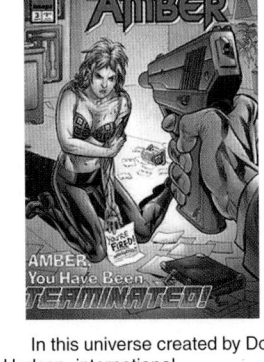

In this universe created by Don Hudson, international governments sold out to international corporations, which used their collective might to create a society where crime and hunger have been virtually eliminated, and everyone has a job. But there is a catch: Try to quit before the corporation is willing to see you go, and they'll send a bounty hunter to hunt you down.

Amber 12, bubbly, dangerous, and with a wardrobe of bikinis and body armor, is a bounty hunter for the First World Corporation. When a high-ranking scientist vanishes from the company dole, Amber is sent to fetch him. But when things go awry and the company turns on her, as well, she's on the run and out for revenge.

The first Amber series from Image, filled with detailed and expertly rendered black-and-white art and nuanced characterizations, ran four issues.

1/A-4	3.00

Forever Eve
Shadow Song, 1997

1-4	3.00

Forever Maelstrom
DC, 2003

1-6	3.00

Forever Now
Entertainment

1-2	2.00

Forever People
DC, 1971

1	35.00
2	20.00
3-5	18.00
6-11	14.00

Forever People
DC, 1988

1-6	2.00

Forever Warriors
CFD, 1997

1	3.00

Forge
CrossGen, 2002

1-3	10.00
4-7	12.00
8-13	8.00

Forgotten Realms
DC, 1989

1	2.00
2-25	1.00
Ann 1	2.00

Forgotten Realms: Exile
Devil's Due, 2005

1	5.00
1/Special	9.00
2	5.00
2/Special	9.00
3	5.00
3/Special	9.00

Forgotten Realms: Homeland
Devil's Due, 2005

1	5.00
1/Variant	9.00
1/Conv	10.00
2	5.00
2/Variant	9.00
3	5.00
3/Variant	9.00

Forgotten Realms: Sojourn
Devil's Due, 2006

1	5.00
1/Variant	9.00
2	5.00
2/Special	9.00
3	5.00
3/Special	9.00

Forgotten Realms: The Crystal Shard
Devil's Due, 2006

1	5.00
1/Special	9.00
2	5.00
2/Variant	9.00
3	5.00
3/Silver	9.00

Forgotten Realms: The Grand Tour
TSR

1	1.00

For Lovers Only
Charlton, 1971

60	20.00
61-87	10.00

Formerly Known as the Justice League
DC, 2003

1-6	3.00

Forsaken
Image, 2004

1-3	3.00

Fort: Prophet of the Unexplained
Dark Horse, 2002

1-4	3.00

Fortune and Glory
Oni, 1999

Ever wonder how comics make it from the printed page to the big screen? Eisner Award winner Brian Michael Bendis (Goldfish, Jinx, Sam and Twitch, Powers) learns the hard way in what is deemed "A True Hollywood Comic Book Story."

When an article in Spin Magazine launches Bendis from the world of black-and-white alternative comics into Hollywood, he discovers that acquiring hot property is more important than actually knowing who or what that property is. From Cleveland to Hollywood, witness Bendis' adventures as he tries to get his comic books made into movies. His humor and crisp art create a hilarious tale of high hopes and heartbreak.

Generate buzz. Discover what feature film packaging is. Learn why a writer needs heat. Take meetings. Meet-and-greet shallow, self-absorbed execs, producers, and agents. Enter the realms of development hell. As Bendis writes, "Showbiz, baby, ain't nothing but smoke and mirrors."

1-3...5.00

Fortune's Fool, The Story of Jinxer
Cranium, 1999
0...3.00

Fortune's Friends: Hell Week
Aria
1...7.00

Forty Winks
Odd Jobs Limited, 1997
1-4...3.00

Forty Winks Christmas Special
Peregrine Entertainment, 1998
1...3.00

Forty Winks S uper Special Edition: TV Party Tonite!
Peregrine Entertainment, 1999
1...3.00

Foton Effect
Aced, 1986
1-3...2.00

Foul!
Traitors Gait
1...3.00

4
Marvel, 2000
1...4.00

Four Color Comics (1st Series)
Dell, 1939
1 Dick Tracy......................7,250.00
2 Don Winslow 1,500.00
3 Myra North 750.00
4 Donald Duck 9,000.00
5 Smilin' Jack 650.00
6 Dick Tracy.....................1,500.00
7 Gang Busters 425.00
8 Dick Tracy........................750.00
9 Terry and the Pirates.......630.00
10 Smilin' Jack 425.00
11 Smitty.............................385.00
12 Little Orphan Annie 550.00
13 Walt Disney's Reluctant
    Dragon 1,500.00

14 Moon Mullins 400.00
15 Tillie the Toiler............... 400.00
16 Mickey Mouse Outwits the
    Phantom Blot.............. 9,800.00
17 Dumbo....................... 2,000.00
18 Jiggs and Maggie 400.00
19 "Four Color Comics" begins on
    covers; Barney Google and
    Snuffy Smith 400.00
20 Tiny Tim........................ 300.00
21 Dick Tracy..................... 675.00
22 Don Winslow of the Navy
    .... 325.00
23 Gang Busters 325.00
24 Captain Easy................ 400.00
25 Popeye 750.00

Four Color Comics (2nd series)
Dell, 1942

Published from 1941 until 1962, Dell's Four Color Comics series had more issues published than any other American comic, although not the full 1,354 its final number would indicate, since some numbers were not published. During its run of more than two decades, it featured dozens of comics icons including Uncle Scrooge, Prince Valiant, Bozo the Clown, Bugs Bunny, Tarzan, and Flash Gordon.

Despite its singular place in comics history, many comics readers have never heard the name "Four Color Comics." Why? Because virtually every issue ran under the name of the main character — the inscription "Four Color Comics" only appearing in the title's indicia and that only in some cases. This was doubly confusing to readers. A cover reading, say "Popeye" with an issue number of #145, naturally left readers wondering where Popeye #1-144 had gone.

The complete list of Four Color Comics that appears here was generously donated by Maggie

Thompson of Comics Buyer's Guide.

1 Little Joe......................... 550.00
2 Harold Teen 275.00
3 Alley Oop........................ 500.00
4 Smilin' Jack.................... 465.00
5 Raggedy Ann and Andy
    .... 465.00
6 Smitty 235.00
7 Smokey Stover 325.00
8 Tillie the Toiler............... 225.00
9 Donald Duck............... 9,000.00
10 Flash Gordon 800.00
11 Wash Tubbs 310.00
12 Bambi (Disney)............. 585.00
13 Mr. District Attorney 340.00
14 Smilin' Jack 350.00
15 Felix the Cat 650.00
16 Porky Pig 725.00
17 Popeye and Wimpy....... 525.00
18 Little Orphan Annie 435.00
19 Thumper Meets the Seven
    Dwarfs 635.00
20 Barney Baxter 235.00
21 Oswald the Rabbit........ 450.00
22 Tillie the Toiler.............. 200.00
23 Raggedy Ann and Andy
    .... 380.00
24 Gang Busters 335.00
25 Andy Panda.................. 460.00
26 Popeye 475.00
27 Mickey Mouse 950.00
28 Wash Tubbs 220.00
29 Donald Duck............. 6,200.00
30 Bambi's Children (Disney)
    .... 575.00
31 Moon Mullins 200.00
32 Smittys 170.00
33 Bugs Bunny 775.00
34 Dick Tracy.................... 475.00
35 Smokey Stovers 165.00
36 Smilin' Jack 210.00
37 Bringing Up Father 200.00
38 Roy Rogers 1,440.00
39 Oswald the Rabbit........ 350.00
40 Barney Google and Snuffy
    Smith 230.00
41 Mother Goose and Nursery
    Rhyme Comics 235.00
42 Tiny Tim 190.00
43 Popeye 350.00
44 Terry and the Pirates 450.00
45 Raggedy Ann and Andy
    .... 450.00
46 Felix the Cat 450.00
47 Gene Autry 450.00
48 Porky Pig 450.00
49 Snow White and the Seven
    Dwarfs 450.00
50 Fairy Tale Parade.......... 450.00
51 Bugs Bunny 385.00
52 Little Orphan Annie 310.00
53 Wash Tubbs 170.00
54 Andy Panda.................. 310.00
55 Tillie the Toiler.............. 150.00
56 Dick Tracy.................... 365.00
57 Gene Autry 445.00
58 Smilin' Jack.................. 210.00

   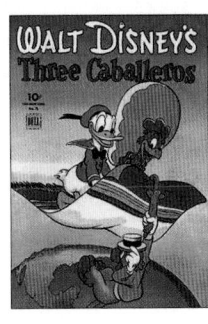

59 Mother Goose and Nursery
    Rhyme Comics 220.00
60 Tiny Folks Funnies 160.00
61 Santa Claus Funnies.....275.00
62 Donald Duck 2,550.00
63 Roy Rogers 575.00
64 Smokey Stovers 125.00
65 Smitty 125.00
66 Gene Autry 395.00
67 Oswald the Rabbit 190.00
68 Mother Goose and Nursery
    Rhyme Comics 210.00
69 Fairy Tale Parade 265.00
70 Popeye and Wimpy 300.00
71 The Three Caballeros....870.00
72 Raggedy Ann and Andy
    ....285.00
73 The Gumps 125.00
74 Little Lulu...................1,100.00
75 Gene Autry....................360.00
76 Little Orphan Annie 285.00
77 Felix the Cat 360.00
78 Porky Pig......................250.00
79 Mickey Mouse 1,150.00
80 Smilin' Jack 160.00
81 Moon Mullins.................100.00
82 Lone Ranger 500.00
83 Gene Autry....................345.00
84 Flash Gordon 460.00
85 Andy Panda 165.00
86 Roy Rogers 405.00
87 Fairy Tale Parade 235.00
88 Bugs Bunny...................225.00
89 Tillie the Toiler 135.00
90 Christmas with Mother
    Goose...........................200.00
91 Santa Claus Funnies.....220.00
92 Pinocchio (Disney) 770.00
93 Gene Autry....................305.00
94 Winnie Winkle 115.00
95 Roy Rogers 395.00
96 Dick Tracy.....................275.00
97 Little Lulu......................495.00
98 Lone Ranger 360.00
99 Smitty 100.00
100 Gene Autry....................300.00
101 Terry and the Piratess
    ....300.00
102 Oswald the Rabbit.......140.00
103 Easter With Mother Goose
    ....200.00
104 Fairy Tale Parade 205.00
105 Albert the Alligator and
    Pogo Possum 740.00

106 Tillie the Toiler............. 100.00
107 Little Orphan Annie 235.00
108 Donald Duck............ 1,650.00
109 Roy Rogers 305.00
110 Little Lulu 275.00
111 Captain Easy.............. 135.00
112 Porky Pig.................... 155.00
113 Popeye 130.00
114 Fairy Tale Parade 195.00
115 Little Lulu 375.00
116 Mickey Mouse 265.00
117 Roy Rogers 245.00
118 Lone Ranger 335.00
119 Felix the Cat 315.00
120 Little Lulu 325.00
121 Fairy Tale Parade 125.00
122 Henry 120.00
123 Bugs Bunny 170.00
124 Roy Rogers 225.00
125 Lone Ranger 255.00
126 Christmas with Mother
    Goose 155.00
127 Popeye 130.00
128 Santa Claus Funnies ... 170.00
129 Uncle Remus and His Tales
    of Brer Rabbit 285.00
130 Andy Panda................. 85.00
131 Little Lulu 300.00
132 Tillie the Toiler............. 100.00
133 Dick Tracy 260.00
134 Tarzan and the Devil Ogre
    .... 625.00
135 Felix the Cat 240.00
136 Lone Ranger 250.00
137 Roy Rogers 200.00
138 Smitty 90.00
139 Little Lulu 285.00
140 Easter With Mother Goose
    .... 165.00
141 Mickey Mouse 230.00
142 Bugs Bunny 145.00
143 Oswald the Rabbit........ 90.00
144/A Fairy Tale Parade;
    there were two #144s 165.00
144/B Roy Rogers; there were
    two #144s 225.00
145 Popeye 125.00
146 Little Lulu 175.00
147 Donald Duck 770.00
148 Albert the Alligator and
    Pogo Possum 640.00
149 Smilin' Jack 100.00
150 Tillie the Toiler............. 85.00
151 Lone Ranger 225.00

152 Little Orphan Annie 165.00
153 Roy Rogers 185.00
154 Andy Panda................ 100.00
155 Henry........................... 75.00
156 Porky Pig.................... 110.00
157 Mickey Mouse 240.00
158 Little Lulu 260.00
159 Donald Duck............... 800.00
160 Roy Rogers 190.00
161 Tarzan and the Fields
    of Tohr............................ 475.00
162 Felix the Cat 200.00
163 Dick Tracy 190.00
164 Bugs Bunny 140.00
165 Little Lulu 245.00
166 Roy Rogers 175.00
167 Lone Ranger 195.00
168 Popeye 135.00
169 Woody Woodpecker ... 135.00
170 Mickey Mouse 180.00
171 Charlie McCarthy 225.00
172 Christmas with Mother
    Goose 145.00
173 Flash Gordon 170.00
174 Winnie Winkle.............. 80.00
175 Santa Claus Funnies....155.00
176 Tillie the Toiler.............. 85.00
177 Roy Rogers 140.00
178 Donald Duck............ 2,875.00
179 Uncle Wiggily.............. 160.00
180 Ozark Ike 90.00
181 Mickey Mouse 180.00
182 Porky Pig.................... 100.00
183 Oswald the Rabbit........ 85.00
184 Tillie the Toiler.............. 80.00
185 Easter with Mother Goose
    .... 140.00
186 Bambi (Disney)........... 195.00
187 Bugs Bunny 120.00
188 Woody Woodpecker ... 120.00
189 Donald Duck.............. 800.00
190 Flash Gordon 180.00
191 Porky Pig.................... 100.00
192 Brownies..................... 130.00
193 Tom and Jerry............. 155.00
194 Mickey Mouse 180.00
195 Tillie the Toiler.............. 65.00
196 Charlie McCarthy 175.00
197 Spirit of the Border 130.00
198 Andy Panda................ 100.00
199 Donald Duck.............. 775.00
200 Bugs Bunny 105.00

201 Christmas with Mother Goose.............................135.00
202 Woody Woodpecker 75.00
203 Donald Duck 675.00
204 Flash Gordon 155.00
205 Santa Claus Funnies ... 150.00
206 Little Orphan Annie.......85.00
207 King of the Royal Mounted 185.00
208 Brer Rabbit Does it Again! (Disney) 140.00
209 Harold Teen...................50.00
210 Tippie and Cap Stubbs 45.00
211 Little Beaver 80.00
212 Doctor Bobbs 50.00
213 Tillie the Toiler 60.00
214 Mickey Mouse 170.00
215 Dick Tracy...................105.00
216 Andy Panda..................65.00
217 Bugs Bunny.................100.00
218 The Three Little Pigs.... 130.00
219 Swee'pea 90.00
220 Easter with Mother Goose 120.00
221 Uncle Wiggily 105.00
222 West of the Pecos 100.00
223 Donald Duck 930.00
224 Little Iodine...................80.00
225 Oswald the Rabbit.........80.00
226 Porky Pig......................80.00
227 The Seven Dwarfs (Disney) 160.00
228 Mark of Zorro 260.00
229 Smokey Stover..............50.00
230 Sunset Pass..................85.00
231 Mickey Mouse 150.00
232 Woody Woodpecker 65.00
233 Bugs Bunny.................100.00
234 Dumbo 100.00
235 Tiny Tim.........................55.00
236 Heritage of the Desert...85.00
237 Tillie the Toiler 55.00
238 Donald Duck 710.00
239 Adventure Bound 60.00
240 Andy Panda..................60.00
241 Porky Pig......................70.00
242 Tippie and Cap Stubbs .. 40.00
243 Thumper.......................115.00
244 Brownies.......................120.00
245 Dick's Adventures in Dreamland........................55.00
246 Thunder Mountain 55.00

247 Flash Gordon 130.00
248 Mickey Mouse 165.00
249 Woody Woodpecker 60.00
250 Bugs Bunny............... 110.00
251 Hubert at Camp Moonbeam 45.00
252 Pinocchio................... 120.00
253 Christmas with Mother Goose........................... 125.00
254 Santa Claus Funnies.... 125.00
255 The Ranger 65.00
256 Donald Duck............... 485.00
257 Little Iodine................. 60.00
258 Andy Panda................. 55.00
259 Santa and the Angel 50.00
260 Porky Pig..................... 65.00
261 Mickey Mouse 145.00
262 Raggedy Ann and Andy 75.00
263 Donald Duck............... 435.00
264 Woody Woodpecker 55.00
265 King of the Royal Mounted 80.00
266 Bugs Bunny................. 95.00
267 Little Beaver 40.00
268 Mickey Mouse 140.00
269 Johnny Mack Brown... 125.00
270 Drift Fence (Zane Grey) 55.00
271 Porky Pig..................... 65.00
272 Cinderella (Disney)..... 120.00
273 Oswald the Rabbit........ 50.00
274 Bugs Bunny................. 100.00
275 Donald Duck............... 415.00
276 Uncle Wiggily 85.00
277 Porky Pig..................... 65.00
278 Wild Bill Elliott............. 135.00
279 Mickey Mouse 150.00
280 Andy Panda................. 55.00
281 Bugs Bunny................. 95.00
282 Donald Duck............... 400.00
283 King of the Royal Mounted 90.00
284 Porky Pig..................... 65.00
285 Bozo 200.00
286 Mickey Mouse 125.00
287 Gene Autry's Champion 125.00
288 Woody Woodpecker 55.00
289 Bugs Bunny................. 95.00
290 The Chief.................... 52.00
291 Donald Duck............... 375.00
292 The Cisco Kid 260.00

293 Brownies..................... 110.00
294 Little Beaver 40.00
295 Porky Pig..................... 65.00
296 Mickey Mouse 125.00
297 Andy Panda................. 50.00
298 Bugs Bunny................. 90.00
299 Buck Jones................. 120.00
300 Donald Duck............... 375.00
301 The Mysterious Rider....55.00
302 Santa Claus Funnies.... 52.00
303 Porky Pig..................... 50.00
304 Mickey Mouse 95.00
305 Woody Woodpecker 40.00
306 Raggedy Ann and Andy 50.00
307 Bugs Bunny................. 75.00
308 Donald Duck............... 335.00
309 Dollface and Her Gang (Betty Betz)..................... 55.00
310 King of the Royal Mounted 75.00
311 Porky Pig..................... 45.00
312 Tonto 135.00
313 Mickey Mouse 90.00
314 Ambush 55.00
315 Oswald the Rabbit 40.00
316 Rex Allen 135.00
317 Bugs Bunny................. 70.00
318 Donald Duck............... 335.00
319 Gene Autry's Champion 62.00
320 Uncle Wiggily................ 70.00
321 Little Scouts................. 38.00
322 Porky Pig..................... 40.00
323 Susie Q. Smith 40.00
324 I Met a Handsome Cowboy 75.00
325 Mickey Mouse 90.00
326 Andy Panda................. 35.00
327 Bugs Bunny................. 65.00
328 Donald Duck............... 335.00
329 Trigger (Roy Rogers) .. 100.00
330 Porky Pig..................... 40.00
331 Alice in Wonderland (Disney) 155.00
332 Little Beaver 40.00
333 Wilderness Trek 48.00
334 Mickey Mouse 90.00
335 Francis, the Famous Talking Mule.......................... 85.00
336 Woody Woodpecker 32.00
337 Brownies..................... 40.00
338 Bugs Bunny................. 65.00

334

339 Donald Duck 85.00
340 King of the Royal Mounted
....70.00
341 Alice in Wonderland (Disney)
......................................150.00
342 Porky Pig.......................35.00
343 Mickey Mouse 80.00
344 Sgt. Preston of the Yukon
......................................135.00
345 Andy Panda...................32.00
346 Hideout..........................52.00
347 Bugs Bunny....................65.00
348 Donald Duck 140.00
349 Uncle Wiggily 65.00
350 Woody Woodpecker 32.00
351 Porky Pig.......................35.00
352 Mickey Mouse 70.00
353 Duck Album (Disney) 85.00
354 Raggedy Ann and Andy
....45.00
355 Bugs Bunny....................65.00
356 Donald Duck 135.00
357 Comeback......................45.00
358 Andy Panda...................32.00
359 Frosty the Snowman 85.00
360 Porky Pig.......................35.00
361 Santa Claus Funnies.....52.00
362 Mickey Mouse 75.00
363 King of the Royal Mounted
....60.00
364 Woody Woodpecker 28.00
365 Brownies 40.00
366 Bugs Bunny...................65.00
367 Donald Duck 330.00
368 Beany and Cecil..........250.00
369 Lone Ranger's Famous
Horse Hi-Yo Silver 100.00
370 Porky Pig.......................32.00
371 Mickey Mouse 65.00
372 Riders of the Purple Sage
....45.00
373 Sgt. Preston of the Yukon
....70.00
374 Woody Woodpecker 28.00
375 John Carter of Mars (Edgar
Rice Burroughs) 260.00
376 Bugs Bunny...................60.00
377 Suzie Q. Smith 35.00
378 Tom Corbett, Space Cadet
......................................220.00
379 Donald Duck 80.00
380 Raggedy Ann and Andy
....45.00

381 Tubby.......................... 185.00
382 Snow White and the Seven
Dwarfs (Disney) 145.00
383 Andy Panda.................. 28.00
384 King of the Royal Mounted
.... 55.00
385 Porky Pig...................... 32.00
386 Uncle Scrooge......... 1,050.00
387 Mickey Mouse 65.00
388 Oswald the Rabbit........ 40.00
389 Andy Hardy 35.00
390 Woody Woodpecker 28.00
391 Uncle Wiggily 50.00
392 Lone Ranger's Famous
Horse Hi-Yo Silver 65.00
393 Bugs Bunny.................. 60.00
394 Donald Duck............... 155.00
395 Forlorn River 42.00
396 Tales of the Texas Rangers
.... 110.00
397 Sgt. Preston of the Yukon
.... 65.00
398 Brownies 35.00
399 Porky Pig...................... 32.00
400 Tom Corbett, Space Cadet
.... 165.00
401 Mickey Mouse 50.00
402 Mary Jane and Sniffles
.... 80.00
403 Li'l Bad Wolf (Disney) ... 65.00
404 Range Rider.............. 100.00
405 Woody Woodpecker 28.00
406 Tweety and Sylvester ... 65.00
407 Bugs Bunny.................. 55.00
408 Donald Duck............... 350.00
409 Andy Panda.................. 28.00
410 Porky Pig...................... 32.00
411 Mickey Mouse 50.00
412 Nevada 35.00
413 Robin Hood 135.00
414 Beany and Cecil 175.00
415 Rootie Kazootie.......... 130.00
416 Woody Woodpecker 28.00
417 Double Trouble with Goober
.... 30.00
418 Rusty Riley: A Boy, a Horse,
and a Dog........................ 48.00
419 Sgt. Preston of the Yukon
.... 70.00
420 Bugs Bunny................. 50.00
421 Tom Corbett, Space Cadet
.... 145.00
422 Donald Duck............... 335.00

423 Rhubarb, the Millionaire Cat
.... 40.00
424 Flash Gordon 120.00
425 Return of Zorro........... 175.00
426 Porky Pig..................... 32.00
427 Mickey Mouse 45.00
428 Uncle Wiggily............... 45.00
429 Pluto (Disney)............... 75.00
430 Tubby.......................... 115.00
431 Woody Woodpecker 28.00
432 Bugs Bunny................. 45.00
433 Wildfire 40.00
434 Rin Tin Tin 200.00
435 Frosty the Snowman 50.00
436 Brownies...................... 35.00
437 John Carter of Mars (Edgar
Rice Burroughs).............. 175.00
438 Annie Oakley............. 150.00
439 Little Hiawatha (Disney)
.... 68.00
440 Black Beauty 42.00
441 Fearless Fagan 38.00
442 Peter Pan (Disney) 115.00
443 Ben Bowie and His Mountain
Men.................................. 64.00
444 Tubby.......................... 110.00
445 Charlie McCarthy 58.00
446 Captain Hook and Peter
Pan (Disney) 95.00
447 Andy Hardy 30.00
448 Beany and Cecil 165.00
449 Tappan's Burro 38.00
450 Duck Album (Disney).... 65.00
451 Rusty Riley: A Boy, a Horse,
and a Dog......................... 42.00
452 Raggedy Ann and Andy
.... 40.00
453 Susie Q. Smith 40.00
454 Krazy Kat..................... 40.00
455 Johnny Mack Brown 65.00
456 Uncle Scrooge............ 650.00
457 Daffy 90.00
458 Oswald the Rabbit........ 30.00
459 Rootie Kazootie 90.00
460 Buck Jones.................. 60.00
461 Tubby.......................... 100.00
462 Little Scouts................. 28.00
463 Petunia 30.00
464 Bozo 100.00
465 Francis, the Famous Talking
Mule................................. 48.00
466 Rhubarb, the Millionaire Cat
.... 34.00

467 Desert Gold...................35.00
468 Goofy (Disney)............125.00
469 Beetle Bailey..............100.00
470 Elmer Fudd 36.00
471 Double Trouble with Goober
..............................25.00
472 Wild Bill Elliott...............54.00
473 Li'l Bad Wolf (Disney)....48.00
474 Mary Jane and Sniffles
..............................70.00
475 Two Mouseketeers 65.00
476 Rin Tin Tin 85.00
477 Beany and Cecil..........145.00
478 Charlie McCarthy 50.00
479 Dale Evans.................200.00
480 Andy Hardy 25.00
481 Annie Oakley.................85.00
482 Brownies 30.00
483 Little Beaver 30.00
484 River Feud....................32.00
485 Little People (Walt Scott's...)
..............................65.00
486 Rusty Riley: A Boy, a Horse,
and a Dog.........................40.00
487 Mowgli Jungle Book 65.00
488 John Carter of Mars (Edgar
Rice Burroughs) 165.00
489 Tweety and Sylvester 35.00
490 Jungle Jim.....................75.00
491 Silvertip 80.00
492 Duck Album (Disney) 58.00
493 Johnny Mack Brown......58.00
494 Little King 90.00
495 Uncle Scrooge 515.00
496 Green Hornet 300.00
497 The Sword of Zorro 180.00
498 Bugs Bunny's Album 42.00
499 Spike and Tyke 42.00
500 Buck Jones 42.00
501 Francis, the Famous
Talking Mule 55.00
502 Rootie Kazootie............80.00
503 Uncle Wiggily 45.00
504 Krazy Kat 40.00
505 The Sword and the Rose
..............................80.00
506 Little Scouts 24.00
507 Oswald the Rabbit........30.00
508 Bozo.............................90.00
509 Pluto (Disney) 60.00
510 Son of Black Beauty......40.00
511 Outlaw Trail 32.00
512 Flash Gordon 65.00

513 Ben Bowie and His Mountain
Men 38.00
514 Frosty the Snowman 40.00
515 Andy Hardy 25.00
516 Double Trouble with Goober
.... 25.00
517 Chip 'n' Dale (Disney)... 70.00
518 Rivets 30.00
519 Steve Canyon............... 80.00
520 Wild Bill Elliott.............. 45.00
521 Beetle Bailey 48.00
522 Brownies 30.00
523 Rin Tin Tin 80.00
524 Tweety and Sylvester ... 30.00
525 Santa Claus Funnies.... 44.00
526 Napoleon (and Uncle Elby)
.... 26.00
527 Charlie McCarthy 45.00
528 Dale Evans................. 110.00
529 Little Beaver 30.00
530 Beany and Cecil......... 145.00
531 Duck Album (Disney).... 48.00
532 The Rustlers................ 32.00
533 Raggedy Ann and Andy
.... 35.00
534 Western Marshal 55.00
535 I Love Lucy 470.00
536 Daffy............................ 45.00
537 Stormy, The Thoroughbred
with an Inferiority Complex
.... 40.00
538 Mask of Zorro 165.00
539 Ben and Me (Disney) ... 35.00
540 Knights of the Round Table
.... 75.00
541 Johnny Mack Brown..... 50.00
542 Super Circus 65.00
543 Uncle Wiggily 40.00
544 Rob Roy 95.00
545 The Wonderful Adventures of
Pinocchio (Disney) 80.00
546 Buck Jones.................. 48.00
547 Francis, the Famous Talking
Mule.................................. 48.00
548 Krazy Kat..................... 30.00
549 Oswald the Rabbit........ 30.00
550 Little Scouts................. 22.00
551 Bozo 85.00
552 Beetle Bailey 45.00
553 Susie Q. Smith 25.00
554 Rusty Riley: A Boy, a Horse,
and a Dog......................... 30.00
555 Range War 32.00

556 Double Trouble with Goober
.... 20.00
557 Ben Bowie and His Mountain
Men................................... 40.00
558 Elmer Fudd.................. 30.00
559 I Love Lucy 340.00
560 Duck Album (Disney)... 48.00
561 The Nearsighted Mr. Magoo
and Gerald McBoing Boing
.... 125.00
562 Goofy (Disney) 70.00
563 Rhubarb, the Millionaire Cat
.... 36.00
564 Li'l Bad Wolf (Disney) ... 40.00
565 Jungle Jim 48.00
566 Son of Black Beauty 35.00
567 Prince Valiant 125.00
568 Gypsy Colt................... 45.00
569 Priscilla's Pop 28.00
570 Beany and Cecil 145.00
571 Charlie McCarthy 45.00
572 Silvertip 42.00
573 Little People (Walt Scott's...)
.... 32.00
574 The Hand of Zorro 165.00
575 Annie Oakley and Tagg
.... 85.00
576 Angel 30.00
577 Spike and Tyke 25.00
578 Steve Canyon 55.00
579 Francis, the Famous Talking
Mule.................................. 40.00
580 Six Gun Ranch 36.00
581 Chip 'n' Dale (Disney)... 50.00
582 Mowgli Jungle Book 45.00
583 The Lost Wagon Train... 32.00
584 Johnny Mack Brown 50.00
585 Bugs Bunny's Album (1954)
.... 36.00
586 Duck Album (Disney).... 45.00
587 Little Scouts................. 22.00
588 King Richard and the
Crusaders......................... 110.00
589 Buck Jones.................. 45.00
590 Hansel and Gretel 65.00
591 Western Marshal 60.00
592 Super Circus 50.00
593 Oswald the Rabbit........ 30.00
594 Bozo 85.00
595 Pluto (Disney).............. 40.00
596 Turok, Son of Stone.... 375.00
597 Little King 55.00
598 Captain Davy Jones 40.00

 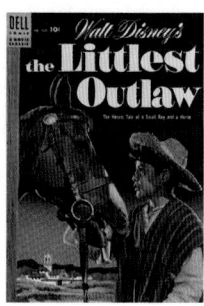  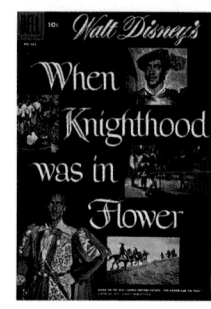

599 Ben Bowie and His Mountain
  Men 35.00
600 Daisy Duck's Diary (Disney)
  ....65.00
601 Frosty the Snowman 35.00
602 The Nearsighted Mr. Magoo
  and Gerald McBoing Boing
  ....135.00
603 Two Mouseketeers 45.00
604 Super Circus 45.00
605 Brownies 30.00
606 Sir Lancelot 90.00
607 Santa Claus Funnies.....40.00
608 Silvertip 45.00
609 The Littlest Outlaw 65.00
610 Drum Beat...................100.00
611 Duck Album (Disney) 50.00
612 Little Beaver 32.00
613 Western Marshal 52.00
614 20,000 Leagues Under the
  Sea 100.00
615 Daffy 45.00
616 To the Last Man.............32.00
617 Quest of Zorro 155.00
618 Johnny Mack Brown 50.00
619 Krazy Kat 40.00
620 Mowgli Jungle Book 48.00
621 Francis, the Famous Talking
  Mule 36.00
622 Beetle Bailey 35.00
623 Oswald the Rabbit 25.00
624 Treasure Island 80.00
625 True-Life Adventure Beaver
  Valley (Walt Disney's ...) 50.00
626 Ben Bowie and His Mountain
  Men 35.00
627 Goofy (Disney) 65.00
628 Elmer Fudd 28.00
629 Lady and the Tramp with
  Jock 65.00
630 Priscilla's Pop 30.00
631 Davy Crockett, Indian Fighter
  (Disney) 165.00
632 Fighting Caravans 34.00
633 Little People (Walt Scott's...)
  ....30.00
634 Lady and the Tramp Album
  (Disney) 55.00
635 Beany and Cecil 145.00
636 Chip 'n' Dale (Disney)....40.00
637 Silvertip 40.00
638 Spike and Tyke 25.00

639 Davy Crockett at the Alamo
  (Walt Disney's) 145.00
640 Western Marshal 45.00
641 Steve Canyon 50.00
642 Two Mouseketeers 45.00
643 Wild Bill Elliott 35.00
644 Sir Walter Raleigh 70.00
645 Johnny Mack Brown 50.00
646 Dotty Dripple and Taffy . 35.00
647 Bugs Bunny's Album 40.00
648 Jace Pearson's Tales of the
  Texas Rangers 55.00
649 Duck Album (Disney).... 50.00
650 Prince Valiant 80.00
651 King Colt....................... 35.00
652 Buck Jones................... 30.00
653 Smokey the Bear.......... 10.00
654 Pluto (Disney).............. 35.00
655 Francis, the Famous Talking
  Mule................................ 30.00
656 Turok, Son of Stone.... 200.00
657 Ben Bowie and His Mountain
  Men 35.00
658 Goofy (Disney) 6.00
659 Daisy Duck's Diary (Disney)
  .... 45.00
660 Little Beaver 30.00
661 Frosty the Snowman 35.00
662 Zoo Parade (Marlin Perkins...)
  .... 50.00
663 Winky Dink 60.00
664 Davy Crockett and the Great
  Keelboat Race (Disney)
  .... 145.00
665 The African Lion 52.00
666 Santa Claus Funnies.... 44.00
667 Silvertip 40.00
668 Dumbo (Disney) 75.00
669 Robin Hood 65.00
670 Mouse Musketeers 36.00
671 Davy Crockett and the River
  Pirates (Disney) 145.00
672 Quentin Durward 65.00
673 Buffalo Bill Jr. 60.00
674 Little Rascals 85.00
675 Steve Donovan, Western
  Marshal 65.00
676 Will-yum! 25.00
677 Little King 60.00
678 The Last Hunt 65.00
679 Gunsmoke 135.00
680 Out Our Way with the Worry
  Wart................................ 32.00

681 Forever, Darling 105.00
682 When Knighthood Was in
  Flower.............................. 75.00
683 Hi and Lois 28.00
684 Helen of Troy 100.00
685 Johnny Mack Brown 50.00
686 Duck Album (Disney).... 50.00
687 The Indian Fighter 60.00
689 Elmer Fudd................... 30.00
688 Alexander the Great 75.00
690 The Conqueror 140.00
691 Dotty Dripple and Taffy
  .... 25.00
692 Little People (Walt Scott's...)
  .... 30.00
693 Song of the South 85.00
694 Super Circus 55.00
695 Little Beaver 30.00
696 Krazy Kat...................... 35.00
697 Oswald the Rabbit 25.00
698 Francis, the Famous Talking
  Mule................................ 32.00
699 Prince Valiant 68.00
700 Water Birds and the Olympic
  Elk.................................. 55.00
701 Jiminy Cricket (Disney). 90.00
702 Goofy (Disney) 75.00
703 Scamp 85.00
704 Priscilla's Pop 30.00
705 Brave Eagle 55.00
706 Bongo and Lumpjaw
  (Disney) 45.00
707 Corky and White Shadow
  (Walt Disney's) 70.00
708 Smokey the Bear.......... 65.00
709 The Searchers........... 225.00
710 Francis, the Famous Talking
  Mule................................ 32.00
711 Mouse Musketeers 26.00
712 Great Locomotive Chase
  .... 65.00
713 The Animal World 55.00
714 Spin and Marty............. 90.00
715 Timmy 35.00
716 Man in Space 90.00
717 Moby Dick..................... 90.00
718 Dotty Dripple and Taffy...25.00
719 Prince Valiant 70.00
720 Gunsmoke 75.00
721 Captain Kangaroo 165.00
722 Johnny Mack Brown 50.00
723 Santiago 110.00
724 Bugs Bunny's Album 40.00

 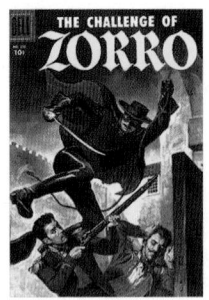  

725 Elmer Fudd 25.00
726 Duck Album (Disney) 40.00
727 The Nature of Things.....25.00
728 Mouse Musketeers........25.00
729 Bob, Son of Battle 35.00
730 Smokey Stover..............30.00
731 Silvertip 40.00
732 Challenge of Zorro
    (not Walt Disney's)..........150.00
733 Buck Jones 35.00
734 Cheyenne..................135.00
735 Crusader Rabbit..........200.00
736 Pluto (Disney) 40.00
737 Steve Canyon...............55.00
738 Westward Ho, the Wagons
    ....75.00
739 Bounty Guns 40.00
740 Chilly Willy....................45.00
741 The Fastest Gun Alive....75.00
742 Buffalo Bill Jr. 40.00
743 Daisy Duck's Diary (Disney)
    ....40.00
744 Little Beaver 30.00
745 Francis, the Famous Talking
    Mule..................................32.00
746 Dotty Dripple and Taffy .. 25.00
747 Goofy (Disney) 60.00
748 Frosty the Snowman 35.00
749 Secrets of Life 60.00
750 Great Cat Family 65.00
751 Our Miss Brooks 80.00
752 Mandrake the Magician
    ....115.00
753 Little People (Walt Scott's...)
    ....30.00
754 Smokey the Bear..........55.00
755 Littlest Snowman..........40.00
756 Santa Claus Funnies.....34.00
757 The True Story of Jesse
    James................................90.00
758 Bear Country................70.00
759 Circus Boy..................100.00
760 Hardy Boys 135.00
761 Howdy Doody..............115.00
762 The Sharkfighters..........90.00
763 Grandma Duck's Farm
    Friends (Disney) 60.00
764 Mouse Musketeers........26.00
765 Will-yum! 25.00
766 Buffalo Bill Jr. 40.00
767 Spin and Marty.............75.00
768 Steve Donovan, Western
    Marshal 50.00

769 Gunsmoke................... 75.00
770 Brave Eagle................. 35.00
771 Brand of Empire 35.00
772 Cheyenne.................... 65.00
773 The Brave One 50.00
774 Hi and Lois 25.00
775 Sir Lancelot and Brian.. 95.00
776 Johnny Mack Brown..... 50.00
777 Scamp.......................... 65.00
778 Little Rascals............... 55.00
779 Lee Hunter, Indian Fighter
    .... 45.00
780 Captain Kangaroo 145.00
781 Fury............................. 90.00
782 Duck Album (Disney).... 45.00
783 Elmer Fudd.................. 25.00
784 Around the World in 80
    Days 75.00
785 Circus Boy................... 95.00
786 Cinderella (Disney)....... 65.00
787 Little Hiawatha (Disney)
    .... 42.00
788 Prince Valiant 70.00
789 Silvertip; based on Max
    Brand novels.................. 45.00
790 The Wings of Eagles ... 175.00
791 The 77th Bengal Lancers
    .... 80.00
792 Oswald the Rabbit........ 25.00
793 Morty Meekle 30.00
794 The Count of Monte Cristo
    .... 100.00
795 Jiminy Cricket (Disney)
    .... 75.00
796 Ludwig Bemelman's
    Madeleine and Genevieve
    .... 45.00
797 Gunsmoke.................... 65.00
798 Buffalo Bill Jr. 45.00
799 Priscilla's Pop 30.00
800 The Buccaneers 65.00
801 Dotty Dripple and Taffy
    .... 25.00
802 Goofy (Disney) 70.00
803 Cheyenne.................... 55.00
804 Steve Canyon.............. 55.00
805 Crusader Rabbit......... 140.00
806 Scamp 60.00
807 Savage Range 35.00
808 Spin and Marty............ 80.00
809 Little People (Walt Scott's...)
    .... 32.00

810 Francis, the Famous Talking
    Mule................................. 32.00
811 Howdy Doody............. 115.00
812 The Big Land 85.00
813 Circus Boy................... 95.00
814 Covered Wagons, Ho!
    (Disney) 55.00
815 Dragoon Wells Massacre
    .... 75.00
816 Brave Eagle................. 95.00
817 Little Beaver 25.00
818 Smokey the Bear.......... 55.00
819 Mickey Mouse in Magic Land
    .... 40.00
820 The Oklahoman............ 70.00
821 Wringle Wrangle 80.00
822 Paul Revere's Ride with
    Johnny Tremain 115.00
823 Timmy.......................... 25.00
824 The Pride and the Passion
    .... 9.00
825 Little Rascals................ 45.00
826 Spin and Marty and Annette
    .... 225.00
827 Smokey Stover 30.00
828 Buffalo Bill Jr............... 35.00
829 Tales of the Pony Express
    .... 55.00
830 Hardy Boys 95.00
831 No Sleep 'Til Dawn....... 65.00
832 Lolly and Pepper 40.00
833 Scamp 60.00
834 Johnny Mack Brown..... 45.00
835 Silvertip 40.00
836 Man in Flight................. 75.00
837 All-American Athlete Cotton
    Woods 60.00
838 Bugs Bunny's Life Story
    Album 50.00
839 The Vigilantes............... 75.00
840 Duck Album (Disney).... 45.00
841 Elmer Fudd.................. 25.00
842 The Nature of Things.... 64.00
843 The First Americans
    (Disney) 75.00
844 Gunsmoke.................... 65.00
845 The Land Unknown 125.00
846 Gun Glory................... 115.00
847 Perri............................. 45.00
848 Marauder's Moon 40.00
849 Prince Valiant 65.00
850 Buck Jones.................. 35.00
851 The Story of Mankind ... 75.00

 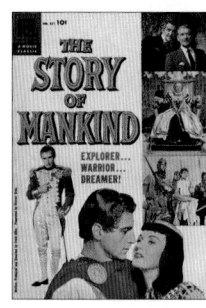  

852 Chilly Willy.....................25.00
853 Pluto (Disney) 45.00
854 The Hunchback of Notre
   Dame...............................135.00
855 Broken Arrow 45.00
856 Buffalo Bill Jr. 40.00
857 Goofy (Disney) 65.00
858 Daisy Duck's Diary
   (Disney) 45.00
858/A Daisy Duck's Diary (Disney);
   Cover price variant 75.00
859 Topper and Neil.............45.00
860 Wyatt Earp 115.00
861 Frosty the Snowman 35.00
862 The Truth About Mother
   Goose...............................75.00
863 Francis, the Famous Talking
   Mule 30.00
864 Littlest Snowman Rescues
   Christmas 44.00
865 Andy Burnett (Disney)...85.00
866 Mars and Beyond..........70.00
867 Santa Claus Funnies.....44.00
868 Little People (Walt Scott's...)
   ....30.00
869 Old Yeller.......................75.00
870 Little Beaver 30.00
871 Curly Kayoe vs. the Barefoot
   Blockbuster........................32.00
872 Captain Kangaroo.......125.00
873 Grandma Duck's Farm
   Friends (Disney) 45.00
874 Old Ironsides with Johnny
   Tremain 75.00
875 Trumpets West 30.00
876 Tales of Wells Fargo 95.00
877 Frontier Doctor 100.00
878 Peanuts........................225.00
879 Brave Eagle...................35.00
880 Steve Donovan, Western
   Marshal 40.00
881 Captain and the Kids.....35.00
882 Zorro (Disney) 165.00
883 Little Rascals.................40.00
884 Hawkeye and the Last of
   the Mohicans.....................80.00
885 Fury................................85.00
886 Bongo and Lumpjaw
   (Disney) 35.00
887 Hardy Boys 110.00
888 Elmer Fudd 25.00
889 Clint and Mac (Disney)
   ....110.00

890 Wyatt Earp 70.00
891 Light in the Forest 75.00
892 Maverick...................... 200.00
893 Jim Bowie..................... 55.00
894 Oswald the Rabbit........ 25.00
895 Wagon Train 105.00
896 The Adventures of Tinker Bell
   (Disney) 85.00
897 Jiminy Cricket (Disney)
   .... 65.00
898 Silvertip 40.00
899 Goofy (Disney) 45.00
900 Prince Valiant 65.00
901 Little Hiawatha (Disney)
   .... 45.00
902 Will-yum! 26.00
903 Dotty Dripple and Taffy
   .... 25.00
904 Lee Hunter, Indian Fighter
   .... 34.00
905 Annette (Disney) 200.00
906 Francis, the Famous Talking
   Mule................................. 30.00
907 Sugarfoot..................... 125.00
908 Little People (Walt Scott's...)
   .... 32.00
909 Smitty and Herby.......... 25.00
910 The Vikings.................. 95.00
911 The Gray Ghost............ 85.00
912 Leave It to Beaver 190.00
913 The Left-Handed Gun
   .... 100.00
914 No Time for Sergeants
   .... 110.00
915 Casey Jones 68.00
916 Red Ryder Ranch Comics
   .... 45.00
917 The Life of Riley 130.00
918 Beep Beep the Road Runner
   .... 75.00
919 Boots and Saddles....... 75.00
920 Zorro (Disney) 160.00
921 Wyatt Earp 65.00
922 Johnny Mack Brown..... 50.00
923 Timmy........................... 25.00
924 Colt .45......................... 95.00
925 Last of the Fast Guns... 65.00
926 Peter Pan (Disney) 60.00
927 Top Gun........................ 35.00
928 Sea Hunt 135.00
929 Brave Eagle.................. 30.00
930 Maverick..................... 115.00
931 Have Gun, Will Travel . 120.00

932 Smokey the Bear: His Life
   Story 60.00
933 Zorro (Disney) 145.00
934 Restless Gun................ 95.00
935 King of the Royal Mounted
   .... 45.00
936 Little Rascals................ 40.00
937 Ruff and Reddy 115.00
938 Elmer Fudd................... 25.00
939 Steve Canyon 45.00
940 Lolly and Pepper 35.00
941 Pluto (Disney).............. 35.00
942 Tales of the Pony Express
   .... 55.00
943 White Wilderness 60.00
944 The 7th Voyage of Sinbad
   .... 165.00
945 Maverick 95.00
946 The Big Country 75.00
947 Broken Arrow 48.00
948 Daisy Duck's Diary
   (Disney) 45.00
949 Lowell Thomas' High
   Adventure 58.00
950 Frosty the Snowman 40.00
951 The Lennon Sisters Life
   Story 110.00
952 Goofy (Disney) 40.00
953 Francis, the Famous Talking
   Mule................................. 36.00
954 Man in Space: Satellites
   .... 80.00
955 Hi and Lois 25.00
956 Ricky Nelson 180.00
957 Buffalo Bee................... 90.00
958 Santa Claus Funnies.... 44.00
959 Walt Scott's Christmas
   Stories 40.00
960 Zorro (Disney) 140.00
961 Jace Pearson's Tales of the
   Texas Rangers.................. 55.00
962 Maverick 95.00
963 Johnny Mack Brown..... 45.00
964 Hardy Boys................. 105.00
965 Grandma Duck's Farm
   Friends (Disney) 50.00
966 Tonka........................... 70.00
967 Chilly Willy 36.00
968 Tales of Wells Fargo 80.00
969 Peanuts 165.00
970 Lawman........................ 90.00
971 Wagon Train................. 55.00
972 Tom Thumb................. 120.00

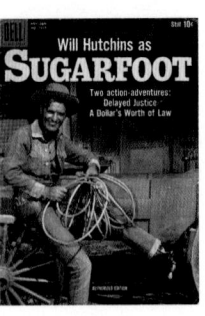

973 Sleeping Beauty and the Prince 110.00
974 Little Rascals (Spanky and Alfalfa...) 40.00
975 Fury..............................65.00
976 Zorro (Disney) 140.00
977 Elmer Fudd 25.00
978 Lolly and Pepper 25.00
979 Oswald the Rabbit.........25.00
980 Maverick........................95.00
981 Ruff and Reddy 70.00
982 The New Adventures of Tinker Bell (Disney) 70.00
983 Have Gun, Will Travel 70.00
984 Sleeping Beauty's Fairy Godmothers 100.00
985 Shaggy Dog 65.00
986 Restless Gun 70.00
987 Goofy (Disney) 45.00
988 Little Hiawatha (Disney) 40.00
989 Jiminy Cricket (Disney) 60.00
990 Huckleberry Hound 90.00
991 Francis, the Famous Talking Mule 30.00
992 Sugarfoot 90.00
993 Jim Bowie......................55.00
994 Sea Hunt.....................110.00
995 Duck Album (Disney) 45.00
996 Nevada..........................32.00
997 Nine Lives of Elfego Baca; Tales of Texas John Slaughter 70.00
998 Ricky Nelson 175.00
999 Leave It to Beaver 160.00
1000 The Gray Ghost...........85.00
1001 Lowell Thomas' High Adventure 48.00
1002 Buffalo Bee 60.00
1003 Zorro (Disney) 145.00
1004 Colt .45.......................70.00
1005 Maverick......................90.00
1006 Hercules....................105.00
1007 John Paul Jones..........75.00
1008 Beep Beep the Road Runner 60.00
1009 The Rifleman.............160.00
1010 Grandma Duck's Farm Friends (Disney) 100.00
1011 Buckskin......................80.00
1012 Last Train from Gun Hill 70.00

1013 Bat Masterson............ 95.00
1014 The Lennon Sisters ... 100.00
1015 Peanuts 150.00
1016 Smokey the Bear Nature Stories 45.00
1017 Chilly Willy 30.00
1018 Rio Bravo................. 200.00
1019 Wagon Train 55.00
1020 Jungle Jim 40.00
1021 Jace Pearson's Tales of the Texas Rangers................. 55.00
1022 Timmy........................ 25.00
1023 Tales of Wells Fargo ... 85.00
1024 Darby O'Gill and the Little People 90.00
1025 Vacation in Disneyland 225.00
1026 Spin and Marty........... 85.00
1027 The Texan................... 75.00
1028 Rawhide................... 225.00
1029 Boots and Saddles..... 50.00
1030 Little Rascals (Spanky and Alfalfa...) 50.00
1031 Fury........................... 60.00
1032 Elmer Fudd................ 25.00
1033 Steve Canyon............. 45.00
1034 Nancy and Sluggo: Summer Camp 35.00
1035 Lawman...................... 58.00
1036 The Big Circus............ 55.00
1037 Zorro (Disney) 145.00
1038 Ruff and Reddy 60.00
1039 Pluto (Disney)............. 40.00
1040 Quick Draw McGraw 120.00
1041 Sea Hunt 110.00
1042 Three Chipmunks (Alvin) 45.00
1043 The Three Stooges... 130.00
1044 Have Gun, Will Travel .. 75.00
1045 Restless Gun.............. 60.00
1046 Beep Beep the Road Runner 45.00
1047 Gyro Gearloose (Disney) 185.00
1048 The Horse Soldiers .. 165.00
1049 Don't Give Up the Ship 75.00
1050 Huckleberry Hound 65.00
1051 Donald in Mathmagic Land (Disney) 120.00
1052 Ben-Hur (adapting 1959 film)................................ 120.00

1053 Goofy (Disney) 45.00
1054 Huckleberry Hound Winter Fun 65.00
1055 Daisy Duck's Diary (Disney) 100.00
1056 Yellowstone Kelly 52.00
1057 Mickey Mouse Album (1959) 45.00
1058 Colt .45...................... 70.00
1059 Sugarfoot 75.00
1060 Journey to the Center of the Earth.................... 140.00
1061 Buffalo Bee................ 55.00
1062 Walt Scott's Christmas Stories 42.00
1063 Santa Claus Funnies.. 44.00
1064 Bugs Bunny's Merry Christmas 45.00
1065 Frosty the Snowman .. 40.00
1066 77 Sunset Strip......... 125.00
1067 Yogi Bear 115.00
1068 Francis, the Famous Talking Mule.................... 32.00
1069 The FBI Story 115.00
1070 Solomon and Sheba 110.00
1071 The Real McCoys..... 100.00
1072 Blythe 48.00
1073 Grandma Duck's Farm Friends (Disney) 125.00
1074 Chilly Willy 30.00
1075 Tales of Wells Fargo ... 75.00
1076 The Rebel.................. 90.00
1077 The Deputy.............. 110.00
1078 The Three Stooges..... 90.00
1079 Little Rascals (Spanky and Alfalfa...)..................... 45.00
1080 Fury........................... 60.00
1081 Elmer Fudd................ 25.00
1082 Spin and Marty.......... 75.00
1083 Men Into Space 70.00
1084 Speedy Gonzales 35.00
1085 The Time Machine.... 175.00
1086 Lolly and Pepper 25.00
1087 Peter Gunn 120.00
1088 A Dog of Flanders 48.00
1089 Restless Gun............. 65.00
1090 Francis, the Famous Talking Mule.................................. 26.00
1091 Jacky's Diary 50.00
1092 Toby Tyler (Disney) 70.00
1093 Mackenzie's Raiders .. 65.00
1094 Goofy (Disney) 40.00

1095 Gyro Gearloose (Disney)
....120.00
1096 The Texan....................65.00
1097 Rawhide 160.00
1098 Sugarfoot...................70.00
1099 Donald Duck Album
(Disney) 45.00
1100 Annette's Life Story
(Disney) 220.00
1101 Kidnapped....................70.00
1102 Wanted: Dead or Alive!
....95.00
1103 Leave It to Beaver 160.00
1104 Yogi Bear 70.00
1105 Oh! Susanna: Gale
Storm...............................95.00
1106 77 Sunset Strip 100.00
1107 Buckskin......................65.00
1108 The Troubleshooters....65.00
1109 This Is Your Life, Donald
Duck 215.00
1110 Bonanza....................295.00
1111 Shotgun Slade 55.00
1112 Pixie and Dixie and
Mr. Jinks 55.00
1113 Tales of Wells Fargo 80.00
1114 Huck Finn....................65.00
1115 Ricky Nelson 160.00
1116 Boots and Saddles......55.00
1117 The Boy and the Pirates
....75.00
1118 The Sword and the Dragon
....85.00
1119 Smokey the Bear Nature
Stories 45.00
1120 Dinosaurus!................75.00
1121 Hercules Unchained
....105.00
1122 Chilly Willy...................30.00
1123 Tombstone Territory.....85.00
1124 Whirlybirds 85.00
1125 Laramie 80.00
1126 Sundance....................65.00
1127 The Three Stooges......85.00
1128 Rocky and His Friends
....400.00
1129 Pollyanna 90.00
1130 The Deputy..................85.00
1131 Elmer Fudd 25.00
1132 Space Mouse 50.00
1133 Fury.............................60.00
1134 The Real McCoys......100.00
1135 Mouse Musketeers......30.00

1136 Jungle Cat.................60.00
1137 Little Rascals (Spanky and
Alfalfa...) 45.00
1138 The Rebel..................75.00
1139 Spartacus................165.00
1140 Donald Duck Album
(Disney) 45.00
1141 Huckleberry Hound for
President 70.00
1142 Johnny Ringo 70.00
1143 Pluto (Disney)..............40.00
1144 The Story of Ruth 85.00
1145 The Lost World 130.00
1146 Restless Gun..............65.00
1147 Sugarfoot....................65.00
1148 I Aim at the Stars: The
Werner von Braun Story
....100.00
1149 Goofy (Disney) 40.00
1150 Daisy Duck's Diary
(Disney) 100.00
1151 Mickey Mouse Album
(1960) 40.00
1152 Rocky and His Friends
....265.00
1153 Frosty the Snowman .. 40.00
1154 Santa Claus Funnies
....440.00
1155 North to Alaska 165.00
1156 Swiss Family Robinson
....95.00
1157 Master of the World 70.00
1158 The 3 Worlds of Gulliver
....85.00
1159 77 Sunset Strip 90.00
1160 Rawhide 165.00
1161 Grandma Duck's Farm
Friends (Disney) 95.00
1162 Yogi Bear 75.00
1163 Daniel Boone.............70.00
1164 Wanted: Dead or Alive!
....75.00
1165 Ellery Queen, Detective
....120.00
1166 Rocky and His Friends
....235.00
1167 Tales of Wells Fargo .. 75.00
1168 The Detectives 95.00
1169 The New Adventures of
Sherlock Holmes 165.00
1170 The Three Stooges..... 85.00
1171 Elmer Fudd................25.00
1172 Fury............................55.00

1173 Twilight Zone 240.00
1174 Little Rascals (Spanky and
Alfalfa...)..........................35.00
1175 Mouse Musketeers.....26.00
1176 Dondi.........................45.00
1177 Chilly Willy 30.00
1178 Ten Who Dared...........60.00
1179 The Swamp Fox 75.00
1180 Danny Thomas Show
....140.00
1181 Texas John Slaughter
....55.00
1182 Donald Duck Album
(Disney) 45.00
1183 101 Dalmatians 110.00
1184 Gyro Gearloose (Disney)
....125.00
1185 Sweetie Pie 35.00
1186 Yak Yak: A Pathology of
Humor...............................85.00
1187 The Three Stooges.....80.00
1188 Atlantis: The Lost Continent
....120.00
1189 Greyfriars Bobby 65.00
1190 Donald and the Wheel
(Disney) 70.00
1191 Leave It to Beaver 165.00
1192 Ricky Nelson 140.00
1193 The Real McCoys.......85.00
1194 Pepe 40.00
1195 National Velvet...........70.00
1196 Pixie and Dixie and
Mr. Jinks.........................45.00
1197 The Aquanauts 65.00
1198 Donald in Mathmagic Land
(Disney) 75.00
1199 The Absent-Minded
Professor 80.00
1200 Hennessey 65.00
1201 Goofy (Disney) 40.00
1202 Rawhide 150.00
1203 The Wonderful Adventures
of Pinocchio (Disney)........60.00
1204 Scamp 40.00
1205 David and Goliath.......70.00
1206 Lolly and Pepper 25.00
1207 The Rebel...................80.00
1208 Rocky and His Friends
....225.00
1209 Sugarfoot...................65.00
1210 The Parent Trap 85.00
1211 77 Sunset Strip...........80.00
1212 Chilly Willy 30.00

Four Color Comics (2nd series)

1213 Mysterious Island......100.00
1214 Smokey the Bear Nature
Stories................................45.00
1215 Tales of Wells Fargo 70.00
1216 Whirlybirds 80.00
1218 Fury.............................55.00
1219 The Detectives 75.00
1220 Gunslinger...................75.00
1221 Bonanza...................180.00
1222 Elmer Fudd 25.00
1223 Laramie 55.00
1224 Little Rascals (Spanky and
Alfalfa...) 40.00
1225 The Deputy.................85.00
1226 Nikki, Wild Dog of the
North..............................55.00
1227 Morgan the Pirate 85.00
1229 Thief of Baghdad.......115.00
1230 Voyage to the Bottom
of the Sea.....................120.00
1231 Danger Man 130.00
1232 On the Double.............50.00
1233 Tammy, Tell Me True 65.00
1234 The Phantom Planet ...70.00
1235 Mister Magoo 100.00
1236 King of Kings..............85.00
1237 The Untouchables 200.00
1238 Deputy Dawg 90.00
1239 Donald Duck Album
(Disney).............................45.00
1240 The Detectives 75.00
1241 Sweetie Pie 30.00
1242 King Leonardo and His
Short Subjects.................115.00
1243 Ellery Queen, Detective
....115.00
1244 Space Mouse 48.00
1245 The New Adventures of
Sherlock Holmes 150.00
1246 Mickey Mouse Album
(1961).................................35.00
1247 Daisy Duck's Diary
(Disney)...............................40.00
1248 Pluto Joins the Circus
(Disney)...............................40.00
1249 Danny Thomas Show
....135.00
1250 The 4 Horsemen of the
Apocalypse.........................90.00
1251 Everything's Ducky......48.00
1252 Andy Griffith 240.00
1253 Spaceman...................85.00
1254 Diver Dan 60.00
1255 The Wonders of Aladdin
....80.00
1256 Kona, Monarch of Monster
Isle.....................................65.00
1257 Car 54, Where Are You?
....80.00
1258 The Frogmen...............75.00
1259 El Cid; says 1251 in indicia,
1259 on cover; no publication
date 70.00
1260 The Horsemasters.....100.00
1261 Rawhide 140.00
1262 The Rebel...................70.00
1263 77 Sunset Strip 80.00

1264 Pixie and Dixie and
Mr. Jinks 40.00
1265 The Real McCoys.......75.00
1266 Spike and Tyke 26.00
1267 Gyro Gearloose
(Disney) 85.00
1268 Oswald the Rabbit 25.00
1269 Rawhide 140.00
1270 Bullwinkle and Rocky
....200.00
1271 Yogi Bear Birthday Party
....60.00
1272 Frosty the Snowman .. 35.00
1273 Hans Brinker 65.00
1274 Santa Claus Funnies... 36.00
1275 Rocky and His Friends
....200.00
1276 Dondi.........................32.00
1278 King Leonardo and His
Short Subjects 110.00
1279 Grandma Duck's Farm
Friends (Disney) 45.00
1280 Hennessey 55.00
1281 Chilly Willy 28.00
1282 Babes in Toyland (Disney)
....135.00
1283 Bonanza...................175.00
1284 Laramie 55.00
1285 Leave It to Beaver 140.00
1286 The Untouchables 170.00
1287 Man from Wells Fargo
....60.00
1288 Twilight Zone 150.00
1289 Ellery Queen, Detective
....100.00
1290 Mouse Musketeers.....25.00
1291 77 Sunset Strip 70.00
1293 Elmer Fudd.................25.00
1294 Ripcord......................65.00
1295 Mister Ed the Talking
Horse..............................140.00
1296 Fury............................50.00
1297 Little Rascals (Spanky
and Alfalfa...) 35.00
1298 The Hathaways...........48.00
1299 Deputy Dawg............110.00
1300 The Comancheros.....150.00
1301 Adventures in Paradise
....48.00
1302 Johnny Jason, Teen
Reporter 38.00
1303 Lad: A Dog 40.00
1304 Nellie the Nurse..........80.00
1305 Mister Magoo 100.00
1306 Target: The Corruptors
....65.00
1307 Margie 42.00
1308 Tales of the Wizard of Oz
....125.00
1309 87th Precinct 95.00
1310 Huck and Yogi Winter
Sports..............................65.00
1311 Rocky and His Friends
....200.00
1312 National Velvet 55.00
1313 Moon Pilot 80.00
1328 The Underwater City .. 80.00
1330 Brain Boy..................135.00

1332 Bachelor Father..........80.00
1333 Short Ribs 58.00
1335 Aggie Mack.................35.00
1336 On Stage 48.00
1337 Doctor Kildare 90.00
1341 Andy Griffith 210.00
1348 Yak Yak......................75.00
1349 Yogi Bear Visits the UN
....110.00
1350 Comanche (Disney)....55.00
1354 Calvin and the Colonel
....70.00

4-D Monkey
Dr. Leung's, 1988

1-12 .... 2.00

Four Favorites
Ace, 1941

1 .... 1,150.00
2 .... 575.00
3 .... 360.00
4-5 .... 285.00
6-9 .... 250.00
10 .... 300.00
11-12 .... 325.00
13-20 .... 185.00
21-26 .... 125.00
27-32 .... 95.00

Four Horsemen
DC, 2000

The legendary Four Horsemen of the Apocalypse have landed in New York City's equally legendary Times Square at midnight Jan. 1, 2000. Let the mayhem that marks the beginning of the end of time commence, right?

Wrong.

The fabled chaos-bringers are actually welcomed by a crowd that feels that the world is rotten: full of dangers and evils far worse than any the Horsemen can unleash upon it. After taking refuge in a bar to mull this turn of events, Famine learns of the political and personal minefield that is reproductive rights; War hears of the bloody battles that take place in corporate boardrooms; Pestilence is exposed to constant invasions of privacy that plague contemporary society; and Death -- well, that would be telling. This intriguing four-parter gives readers much to consider; it was released as a part of Vertigo's "Y2K" event.

1-4 ....3.00

Four Kunoichi, The: Bloodlust
Lightning, 1996

1 ....3.00
1/Nude-1/Platinum 10.00
1/Platinum Nude 4.00

Four Kunoichi: Enter the Sinja
Lightning, 1997

1 ....3.00

4Most
Premium, 1942

1 ....700.00
2 ....325.00
3 ....275.00
4 ....240.00
5 ....90.00
6-7 ....80.00
8 ....100.00
9 ....60.00
10-13 ....45.00
14-16 ....32.00
17 ....35.00
18-24 ....30.00
25 ....40.00
26 ....30.00
27 ....100.00
28 ....30.00
29-31 ....100.00
32 ....30.00
33-34 ....110.00
35 ....30.00
36 ....110.00
37 ....30.00
38-40 ....35.00

411
Marvel, 2003

1-2 ....4.00

Four-Star Battle Tales
DC, 1973

1 ....20.00
2 ....7.00
3-5 ....6.00

Four Star Spectacular
DC, 1976

1 ....12.00
2-6 ....7.00

Four Teeners
A.A. Wyn, 1948

34 ....26.00

Fourth World (Jack Kirby's...)
DC, 1997

1 ....3.00
2-20 ....2.00

Fourth World Gallery
DC, 1996

1 ....4.00

Four Women
DC, 2001

1-5 ....3.00

Fox and the Crow
DC, 1951

Creator James F. Davis produced many, many short stories in which the crow works to outwit the relatively simple fox. As Crow says in Real Screen Comics #42, "If dey gave da Nobel Prize for bein' a great chiseler, I'd win every year!" This series from the late 1950s and 1960s pits the crow against the fox in stories reminiscent of Aesop's fables. However, in this series, the clever crow is also sometimes too clever for his own good. Moreover, he's unabashedly nasty. As a result, the simple fox comes off as more lovable than foolish.

Fox and the Crow also featured a series of backup stories such as Hare and Hound. These were eventually usurped by Stanley and His Monster, a feature which proved so popular that Fox and the Crow later changed its name to Stanley and His Monster.

1 ....775.00
2 ....400.00
3-5 ....285.00
6-10 ....195.00
11-15 ....135.00
16-20 ....120.00
21-30 ....90.00
31-40 ....85.00
41-61 ....60.00
62-80 ....42.00

81-94 ....26.00
☛1st Stanley
95 ....50.00
96-100 ....22.00
101-108 ....18.00

Fox Comics
Fantagraphics

24-Special 1 ....3.00

Fox Comics Legends Series
Fantagraphics, 1992

1-2 ....3.00

Foxfire
Malibu, 1996

1/A-1/GO 0.00
1-4 ....2.00

Foxfire
Nightwynd, 1992

1-3 ....3.00

Foxhole
Mainline, 1954

1 ....225.00
2 ....170.00
3-5 ....125.00
6 ....100.00
7 ....125.00

Foxhole (Super)
Super

10-18 ....14.00

Fox Kids Funhouse
Acclaim

1-2 ....5.00

Foxy Fagan Comics
Dearfield, 1946

1 ....60.00
2 ....40.00
3-5 ....30.00
6-7 ....24.00
Ashcan 1-Ashcan 1/2nd 6.00

Fraction
DC, 2004

1-6 ....3.00

Fractured Fairy Tales
Gold Key, 1962

1 ....75.00

Fraggle Rock
Marvel, 1985

1 ....2.00
2-8 ....1.00

Fraggle Rock
Marvel, 1988

1 ....2.00
2-5 ....1.00

Fragile Prophet
Lost in the Dark, 2005

1 ....3.00

Fragments
Screaming Cat

When Doctor Alyk Elstrom acquired the power of molecular fragmentation, (through a rather arcane, mystical and incredible set of circumstances), his life as an accepted member of the aristocracy was no more. He became a dreaded "non-com" (non-conformist), in this convoluted tale of social disenfranchisement. Now he and Augustus, (a native from the unspecified country where Elstrom's life was extraordinarily altered) are on the run from those who are after the secret of his fragmentation power.

Artist and writer Gregg Hinlicky attempts to get things going quickly by starting in the middle and telling the back-story at the same time. The story confusingly switches between the present and flashbacks using only rounded panel borders to indicate the time shift.

1 ....3.00

Francis,
Brother of the Universe
Marvel
1 ....2.00

Frank
Nemesis, 1994
1 ....2.00
1/Direct....................................3.00
2 ....2.00
2/Direct....................................3.00
3 ....2.00
3/Direct....................................3.00
4 ....2.00
4/Direct....................................3.00

Frank
Fantagraphics, 1996
1 ....3.00
2 ....4.00

Frank Frazetta
Fantasy Illustrated
Frank Frazetta Fantasy Illustrated, 1998
1-1/Variant.............................. 7.00
2-5... 6.00
5/Variant................................. 8.00
6-7/Variant.............................. 6.00

Frank in the River
Tundra
1 .... 3.00

Frank Buck
Fox, 1950
70 .... 165.00
71 .... 90.00
3 .... 80.00

Frank Luther's
Silly Pilly Comics
Children Comics, 1949
1 .... 35.00

Frank Merriwell at Yale
Charlton, 1955
1 .... 35.00
2 .... 25.00
3-4 .... 16.00

Frank the Unicorn
Fragments West, 1986
1-9... 2.00

Frank Zappa:
Viva La Bizarre
Revolutionary, 1994
1 .... 3.00

Frankenstein
Prize, 1945
1 .... 1,025.00
2 .... 650.00
3-5 .... 340.00
6-10 .... 275.00
11-20 .... 200.00
21-33 .... 165.00

Frankenstein
Dell, 1963
1 .... 35.00
2 .... 25.00
3-4 .... 15.00

Frankenstein
(The Monster of...)
Marvel, 1973
1 .... 40.00
2 .... 15.00
3-5 .... 9.00
6-7 .... 7.00
8 .... 18.00
9 .... 20.00
10 .... 6.00
11-18 .... 5.00

Frankenstein
Eternity, 1989
1 .... 2.00

Frankenstein
(Mary Shelley's...)
Topps, 1984
1-4 .... 3.00

Frankenstein/
Dracula War
Topps, 1995
1-3 .... 3.00

Frankenstein Jr.
Gold Key, 1967
1 .... 55.00

Frankenstein Mobster
Image, 2003
0-7/B...................................... 3.00

Frankenstein: Or the
Modern Prometheus
Caliber

This color one-shot from Caliber Press is a faithful adaptation of Mary Wollstonecraft Shelley's 1818 novel. Consumed with discovering the secret of life, young Victor Frankenstein cobbles together a creature from dead bodies; but once it has been brought to life, the obsessed scientist rejects it as a thing of evil. This rejections sets in motion all the events of the remainder of the story: every tragedy that befalls Victor, his friends, and his family stems from his refusal to take responsibility for his creation.

1 .... 3.00

Frankie Comics
Margood, 1946
4 .... 35.00
5 .... 25.00
6-10 .... 22.00
11-15 .... 18.00

Frank Ironwine
(Warren Ellis')
Avatar
1 .... 4.00
1/Foil..................................... 20.00

Franklin Richards:
Happy Franksgiving
Marvel, 2007
1..3.00

Franklin Richards, Son
of a Genius - Everybody
Loves Franklin
Marvel, 2006
1..3.00

Franklin Richards:
Son of a Genius Super
Summer Spectacular
Marvel, 2006
1..3.00

Fray
Dark Horse, 2001

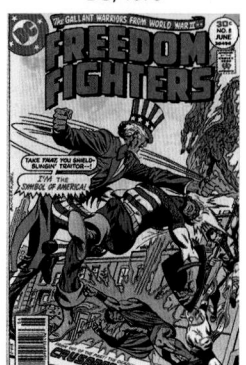

To every generation, a slayer is born, but for two hundred years no one has been called. Now in a dystopian future, Meleka Fray is informed of her destiny, via a self-immolating watcher. Far from an innocent high school girl like Buffy Summers, Mekela is a thief and enforcer for a mutant gang boss. Her job on the shady side of society is a sore point for her sister, a police sergeant, and her residence in the slum called Versi is far removed from Sunnydale.

Joss Whedon, the writer/creator of the television series, Buffy the Vampire Slayer, has brought the latest iteration of his popular concept to comics in this eight-issue series from Dark Horse.
-- George Haberberger

1-8...3.00

Freak Force
Image, 1993
1-7...2.00
8-18...3.00

Freak Force
Image, 1997
1-3...3.00

Freak Out on
Infant Earths
Blackthorne, 1987
1-2... 2.00

Freaks
Fantagraphics, 1992
1-3... 2.00

Freaks' Amour
Dark Horse, 1992
1-3... 4.00

Freaks of the Heartland
Dark Horse, 2004
1-6... 3.00

Freckles and His Friends
Standard, 1947
1 .... 30.00
2-4... 20.00
5-12... 20.00

Fred & Bianca
Censorship Sucks
Special
Comics Interview, 1989
1 .... 2.00

Fred & Bianca
Mother's Day Massacre
Comics Interview
1 .... 2.00

Fred & Bianca
Valentine's Day
Massacre
Comics Interview
1 .... 2.00

Fred the Clown
Hotel Fred, 2001
1-2... 3.00

Freddy
Dell, 1964
1 .... 26.00
2-3... 18.00

Freddy Krueger's
Nightmare
on Elm Street
Marvel, 1989
1 .... 5.00
2 .... 4.00

Freddy's Dead:
The Final Nightmare
Innovation
1-3/3D 3.00

Freddy vs. Jason vs. Ash
DC, 2007
1 .... 12.00
2 .... 6.00
3-4 .... 4.00

Frederic Remington:
The Man Who
Painted the West
Tome
1 .... 3.00

Fred Hembeck Destroys
the Marvel Universe
Marvel, 1989
1 .... 2.00

Fred Hembeck Sells the
Marvel Universe
Marvel, 1990
1 .... 2.00

Fred the
Possessed Flower
Happy Predator
1-6 .... 3.00

Free Cerebus
Aardvark-Vanaheim
1 .... 1.00

Free Laughs
Deschaine
1 .... 1.00

Free Speeches
Oni, 1998
1 .... 3.00

Free-View
Acclaim, 1993
1 .... 1.00

Freebooters/
Young Gods/
Paradoxman Preview
Dark Horse
1 .... 1.00

Freedom Agent
Gold Key, 1963
1 .... 45.00

Freedom Fighters
DC, 1976

The Freedom Fighters first banded together in their own dimension, Earth-X, to fight the tyrants in a world where the Nazis had won World War II. The team includes Uncle Sam, who has super strength and can see for brief periods into the future; The Ray, a solar-powered being who can turn himself into pure light; The Human Bomb, who can blast through anything by simply removing his glove; Phantom Lady, who can turn everything into night with her blackout ray; Doll Man, who can shrink himself to a diminutive size; and Black Condor, who can fly like a bird. Eventually, the super team decimated the Nazi leadership with the help of the JLA and JSA and, later, teleported itself to Earth-1 where the Freedom Fighters' adventures continued.

The characters' Golden Age adventures were originally published by Quality, later acquired by DC.

1	12.00
2-3	5.00
4-15	4.00

Freedom Force
Image, 2005

1-6	3.00

Freedom Train
Street & Smith, 1948

1	125.00

Freeflight
Thinkblots, 1994

1	3.00

Freejack
Now, 1992

1	2.00
1/Direct	3.00
2	2.00
2/Direct	3.00
3	2.00
3/Direct	3.00

Freemind
Future, 2002

1-6	4.00
7	3.00

Freeway Ninja Hanzo
SleepyHouse

1	4.00

Freex
Malibu, 1993

Super-powers are not always a blessing. Lewis was a high-school football star until he was hit so hard in a game that he temporarily lost consciousness and his body went into its ultra-powered, but liquid, state. Val's power to burn things led her to prison, where she was abused by the guards. And Ray's parents were so shocked by his rock-like appearance that they kept him locked in the basement for years. These are just some of the hapless teen-agers who become outcasts due to the same sorts of ultra-powers that made others (like The Strangers) into heroes.

Then, these "freaks" receive a reprieve of sorts in the form of a mysterious message that calls them together. In doing so, they discover that they are not alone. They become a gang of sorts, the Freex, leaning on each other in order to survive.

1	2.00
1/Hologram	5.00
2-3	2.00
4	3.00
5-14	2.00
15	4.00
16	2.00
17-GS 1	3.00

French Ice
Renegade, 1987

1-13	2.00

French Ticklers
Kitchen Sink, 1989

1-3	2.00

Frenzy
Independent

1-1/A	1.00

Frescazizis
Last Gasp

1	1.00

Fresh Blood Funny Book
Last Gasp

1	1.00

Freshmen
Image, 2005

1/Preview	7.00

☛Seth Green series

1/Linsner	4.00
1/Migliari	3.00
1/Perez	4.00
2-6	3.00

Freshmen II
Image, 2006

1-2	3.00

Freshmen Yearbook One Shot
Image, 2006

1	3.00

Friday Foster
Dell, 1972

1	25.00

Friday the 13th
DC, 2007

1-2	3.00

Friendly Ghost, Casper
Harvey, 1958

1	190.00
2	100.00
3	85.00
4-5	55.00
6-10	46.00
11-20	36.00
21-30	25.00
31-40	18.00
41-50	15.00
51-60	12.00
61-70	10.00
71-80	8.00
81-89	7.00
90-100	6.00
101-120	5.00
121-140	4.00
141-169	3.00
170-253	2.00

Friendly Neighborhood Spider-Man
Marvel, 2005

1	10.00
2-3	6.00
4-16	3.00
17	6.00
18	4.00
19-24	3.00

Friends
Renegade, 1987

1-3	2.00

Friends of Maxx
Image, 1996
1-3...3.00

Fright
Atlas-Seaboard, 1975
1..6.00

Fright
Eternity, 1989
1-12..2.00

Fright Night
Now, 1988
1..3.00
2-22...2.00

Fright Night
1993 Halloween Annual
Now, 1993
1..3.00

Fright Night 3-D
Now, 1992
1-2...3.00

Fright Night
3-D Winter Special
Now, 1993
1..3.00

Fright Night II
Graphic Novel
Now
1..4.00

Fringe
Caliber
1-8...3.00

Frisky Animals
Star Publications, 1951
44-55...................................125.00

Frisky Animals
on Parade
Ajax, 1957
1...100.00
2...36.00
3...70.00

Frisky Fables
Premium, 1945
1...110.00
2...56.00
3...38.00
4-5..32.00
6-10...26.00
11-20..24.00
21-30..20.00
31-43..16.00

Fritzi Ritz
St. John, 1953
3...45.00
4-7..40.00
27-37..25.00
38...35.00
39-49..25.00
50-59..20.00

Frogman Comics
Hillman, 1952

Frogman Comics featured one of the more innovative, not to say offbeat, premises for a comics series: underwater exploits through history.

Issues featured several different stories focusing on the theme of underwater adventurers, from wartime frogmen out to sink enemy ships, to treasure hunters in the Caribbean, to "pirate frogmen" of the 18th century in full period costume. The stories were generally action-oriented yarns of courage and daring illustrated in workmanlike style, but occasionally graced by the pens of luminaries like Bernie Krigstein and Mort Meskin.

1 .... 60.00
2 .... 38.00
3-5 .... 28.00
6-11 .... 24.00

Frogmen
Dell, 1962
2 .... 34.00
3 .... 26.00
4 .... 20.00
5 .... 22.00
6 .... 20.00
7-11 .... 18.00

From Beyonde
Studio Insidio, 1991
1 .... 2.00

From Beyond
the Unknown
DC, 1969
1 .... 45.00
2 .... 20.00
3-6 .... 15.00
7-10 .... 12.00
11-17 .... 10.00
18-25 .... 8.00

From Dusk Till Dawn
Big
1 .... 5.00
1/Deluxe 10.00

From Far Away
Viz, 2004
1-7 .... 10.00

From Heaven to Hell
Dead Dog Comics, 2005
1 .... 5.00

From Hell
Tundra, 1991

Artist Eddie Campbell and writer Alan Moore teamed to tell this ambitious story of the Whitechapel Murderer -- better known as Jack the Ripper. "Jack" stalked London in the years just prior to the turn of the century, killing and then anatomizing a number of women with surgical precision.

Despite a massive police investigation, the murders were never solved. In the years that followed, countless theories have been offered, with suggestions being made concerning possible involvement of Freemasons and even the royal family. Moore and Campbell's version draws from a variety of sources to offer a chilling, historical account of the most notorious serial killer of all time.

Alan Moore won the 1995 Best Writer Eisner award for his work on this series, and the film version was released in 2001, starring Johnny Depp, Heather Graham, Ian Holm, Robbie Coltrane, and Ian Richardson.

1 .... 6.00
☛Alan Moore series
1/2nd-10 .... 5.00

From Hell: Dance
of the Gull Catchers
Kitchen Sink, 1998
1 .... 7.00
☛Alan Moore

From Here to Insanity
Charlton, 1955
8-12 .... 45.00
1 .... 125.00

From the Darkness
Adventure, 1990
1-4 .... 3.00

From the Darkness Book II: Blood Vows
Cry for Dawn
1-3..............................3.00

Front Page Comic Book
Harvey
1...............................250.00

Frontier
Slave Labor, 1994
1...................................3.00

Frontier Fighters
DC, 1955
1.................................220.00
2-3..............................165.00
4-8..............................120.00

Frontier Romances
Avon, 1949
1.................................425.00
2.................................240.00

Frontiers '86 Presents
Frontiers
1-2...................................2.00

Frontier Scout, Dan'l Boone
Charlton, 1956
10..................................60.00
11-13.............................35.00
14..................................22.00

Frontier Western
Atlas, 1956
1.................................125.00
2-3..............................100.00
4-10..............................50.00

Frontline Combat
E.C., 1951
1.................................535.00
2.................................340.00
3.................................250.00
4-5..............................200.00
6-10..............................150.00
11-15............................120.00

Frontline Combat
Gemstone, 1995
1-4...................................2.00
5-15..................................3.00
Ann 1..............................11.00
Ann 2..............................13.00

Frost
Caliber
1...................................2.00

Frostbiter: Wrath of the Wendigo
Caliber

In a cabin in the woods, on a remote island, a mysterious old man stands guard over a terrible secret. A thousand miles away, a young woman leads a normal, quiet life. And then a pair of drunken hunters looking for a good time stumble upon the old man's cabin, and all hell breaks loose. For that man and his magics are all that keep a terrible evil spirit creature, the Wendigo, from crossing over to our world. And once it's here, thanks to the foolishness of the aforementioned hunters, only one person on earth can possibly stop it. And she has no idea how...

This creepy mystical adventure is published by Caliber Press, in black-and-white, through an agreement with Troma Films. That's right, it's based on a B-movie screenplay. Check your video store.

1-3.......................... 3.00

Frost: The Dying Breed
Caliber
1-3.......................... 3.00

Frozen Embryo
Slave Labor, 1992
1............................ 3.00

Fruits Basket
Tokyopop, 2004
1-12....................... 10.00

F-3 Bandit
Antarctic, 1995
1-10......................... 3.00

F-Troop
Gold Key, 1966
1............................ 50.00
2............................ 40.00
3-5.......................... 36.00
6-7.......................... 32.00

Fugitive
Caliber, 1989
1............................. 3.00

Fugitives from Justice
St. John, 1952
1............................ 185.00
2............................ 100.00
3............................. 80.00
4-5.......................... 60.00

Fugitoid
Mirage, 1985
1............................. 3.00

Full Frontal Nerdity
Dork Storm, 2004
Ann 1....................... 3.00

Full Metal Fiction
London Night, 1997
1............................. 4.00

Full Metal Panic
ADV Manga, 2003
1-2......................... 10.00

Full Metal Panic!
ADV Manga, 2005
1............................ 10.00
2-8......................... 10.00

Full Metal Panic: Overload
ADV Manga, 2005
1-2......................... 10.00

Full Moon
Viz, 2005
1-3........................... 9.00

Full of Fun
Decker, 1957
1............................ 40.00
2............................ 25.00

Full Throttle
Aircel
1-2........................... 3.00

Fun and Games Magazine
Marvel, 1979
1............................. 4.00
2-13.......................... 3.00

Fun Boys Spring Special
Tundra
1............................. 2.00

Fun Comics
Star Publications, 1953
9............................ 110.00
10-12........................ 85.00

Fun Comics (Bill Black's...)
AC, 1983
1-4........................... 2.00

Fun House
MN Design
1............................. 7.00

Fun House
(J.R. Williams'...)
Starhead, 1993
1 ....4.00

Fun-In
Gold Key, 1970
1 ....16.00
2 ....10.00
3-4 ....9.00
5-6 ....8.00
7-10 ....6.00
11-15 ....5.00

Funky Phantom
Gold Key, 1972

The Funky Phantom cartoon may not be everyone's cup of tea, but the comic-book version -- thankfully minus the Hanna-Barbera laugh track -- is a lot more palatable. Muddles, a revolutionary war figure, helps a a group of teen-agers fight crime along with his ghostly cat. (It's amazing anyone pays for a police force at all in the Funtastic World of Hanna-Barbera with all these kid detectives running around.

Formulaic as the source material may be, some of the longer mystery stories from this series do show some imagination and invention on the part of the creators. If it's a choice between watching the cartoon and reading the comic book, though, take the comic book.
-- *JJM*

1 ....24.00
2 ....15.00
3-5 ....10.00
6-10 ....8.00
11-13 ....6.00

Funland
Ziff-Davis, 1949
1 ....120.00

Funland Comics
Croyden, 1945
1 ....100.00

Funnies
Dell, 1936
1 .... 1,950.00
2 .... 925.00
3 .... 675.00
4-5 .... 540.00
6-10 .... 425.00
11-20 .... 340.00
21-29 .... 265.00
30 .... 800.00
31 .... 575.00
32-35 .... 500.00
36-44 .... 465.00
45-51 .... 475.00
52-56 .... 460.00
57 .... 3,400.00
58 .... 1,175.00
59-63 .... 575.00
64 .... 600.00

Funnies Annual
Avon, 1959
1 .... 350.00

Funnies on Parade
Eastern Color, 1933
1 .... 14,600.00

Funny Animals
Charlton, 1984
1 .... 450.00
2 .... 250.00

Funnybone
LaSalle, 1943
1 .... 200.00

Funny Book
Parents' Magazine Institute, 1942
1 .... 85.00
2 .... 50.00
3-4 .... 40.00
5-8 .... 35.00

Funny Fables
Decker, 1957
1 .... 28.00
2 .... 20.00

Funny Films
ACG, 1949
1 .... 70.00
2 .... 40.00
3-5 .... 32.00
6-10 .... 26.00
11-20 .... 20.00
21-29 .... 16.00

Funny Folks
DC, 1946
1 .... 225.00
2 .... 90.00
3-5 .... 65.00
6-10 .... 50.00
11-20 .... 38.00
21-26 .... 28.00

Funny Frolics
Marvel, 1945
1 .... 110.00
2 .... 60.00
3-4 .... 45.00
5 .... 35.00

Funny Funnies
Nedor
1 .... 90.00

Funnyman
Magazine Enterprises, 1948

The popular TV series "Smallville" features an innocuous line in the opening credits-- "Superman created by Jerry Siegel and Joe Shuster." To comic fans who understand how long and hard those two men--and later their estates--fought for recognition from the company that published their creation, those few words are a poignant and welcome sight. In 1948, after losing a lawsuit against DC over the rights to Superboy, Siegel and Shuster tried again to capture lightning in a bottle with a new creation for Magazine Enterprises. The result was Funnyman--a "super-hero" based on vaudeville stage humor. It was the start of a long, steep decline for the creative team that eventually resulted in Siegel returning to DC as a freelance writer and Shuster sinking into illness and obscurity. Funnyman #1 incidentally features the first published work by future Marvel Bullpen stalwart Dick Ayers.

1 .... 185.00
2 .... 140.00
3 .... 125.00
4-6 .... 110.00

Funny Pages
Centaur, 1936
6 .... 1,650.00
7 .... 900.00
8 .... 800.00
9-11 .... 650.00
12-16 .... 540.00

17	600.00
18-20	450.00
21	2,400.00
22	1,450.00
23	885.00
24-29	665.00
30	1,350.00
31-32	665.00
33	1,850.00
34	2,100.00
35	1,350.00
36-38	875.00
39-42	1,000.00

Funny Picture Stories
Comics Magazine, 1936

1	2,650.00
2	1,150.00
3	775.00
4-5	650.00
6-7	485.00

Funny Picture Stories
Centaur, 1937

1	485.00
2-3	365.00
4-5	325.00
6-11	300.00

Funny Picture Stories
Centaur, 1939

1	300.00
2-3	285.00

Funny Stuff
DC, 1944

Though best known for practically every other genre of comics it published, DC did produce a few funny-animal titles aimed at beginning readers. Funny Stuff, along with The Fox and the Crow, later issues of Leading Comics, Comics Cavalcade, and Peter Porkchops, featured loony-style animal capers throughout the mid-1940s and 1950s. Funny Stuff offered a cornucopia of the animal kingdom, including the stars, The Dodo and the Frog, with backup from Blabber Mouse, J. Rufus Lion, Blackie Bear, and Bernard the Brave (a hound dog). Hard to imagine any kid passing up Uncle Scrooge or Animal Comics to grab a copy of Funny Stuff, but someone must have bought, it because it ran more than 80 issues before changing to Dodo and the Frog for the last year or so.
-- Rob Salkowitz

1	550.00
2	275.00
3-4	150.00
5	140.00
6-10	100.00
11-20	80.00
21	60.00
22	100.00
23-30	60.00
31-40	40.00
41-50	32.00
51-59	26.00
60-70	20.00
71-79	16.00

Funny Stuff Stocking Stuffer
DC, 1985

1	1.00

Funny 3-D
Harvey, 1953

1	75.00

Funnytime Features
Eenieweenie, 1994

1-8	3.00

Funny Tunes
U.S.A., 1944

16	80.00
17	54.00
18-23	38.00

Funny World
Marbak, 1947

1	40.00
2-3	28.00

Funtastic World of Hanna-Barbera
Marvel, 1977

1	13.00
2	9.00
3	6.00

Fun Time
Ace, 1953

1	85.00
2-4	50.00

Furies
Avatar, 1997

0-0/Nude	3.00

Furies
Carbon-Based, 1996

1-8	3.00

Furkindred
Mu, 1991

1	7.00
2	8.00

Furrlough
Antarctic, 1991

Furrlough is one of the the longest-running anthologies of anthropomorphic characters. (Anthropomorphics are animal characters with human attributes and attitudes. The genre is wide enough to range from talking cartoon mice to the decidedly adult antics of Omaha the Cat Dancer.) What distinguishes "furries" like the ones in Furrlough from the cartoons of old is the general willingness of their creators to cast the characters in complex roles and situations.

Furrlough is a military- and action-oriented anthology series with a surprising range of content. Stories like "Ninjara" star catlike Ninjas. "Viva la Revolution" is a space war story. Others, like Scotty Arsenault's "Heebas" with its mice swashbucklers, strike an almost Disney-like sword-and-sorcery note.

1-3	4.00
4-22	3.00
23	4.00
24-34	3.00
35	4.00
36-49	3.00
50	4.00
51-139	3.00
140-144	4.00

Further Adventures of Cyclops and Phoenix
Marvel, 1996

1-4	2.00

Further Adventures of Indiana Jones
Marvel, 1983

1	3.00
2-34	2.00

Further Adventures of Nyoka the Jungle Girl
AC, 2005

1-4	2.00

5..3.00
6-7...7.00

Further Adventures of Young Jeffy Dahmer
Boneyard

1..3.00

Further Fattening Adventures of Pudge, Girl Blimp
Star*Reach

1..4.00
1/A...5.00
2-3..4.00

Fury
Dell, 1962

1..25.00

Fury
Marvel, 1994

1..3.00

Fury
Marvel, 2001

1..4.00
2-6..3.00

Fury/Agent 13
Marvel, 1998

1-2..3.00

Fury/Black Widow: Death Duty
Marvel, 1995

1..6.00

Fury of Firestorm
DC, 1982

1..6.00
2-10...2.00
11-61..1.00
61/A..10.00
62-64..1.00
Ann 1-4 ....2.00

Fury of Hellina
Lightning, 1995

1..3.00

Fury of S.H.I.E.L.D.
Marvel, 1995

1..3.00
2-3..2.00
4..3.00

Fused
Image, 2002

1-4..3.00

Fused
Dark Horse, 2004

1-4..3.00

Fushigi Yugi
Viz, 2002

1-16..10.00

Fusion
Eclipse, 1987

1-17..2.00

Futaba-kun Change
Ironcat

1-3 .... 3.00

Futaba-kun Change
Ironcat, 1999

1-4... 3.00

Futurama
Slave Labor, 1989

1-3... 2.00

Futurama
Bongo, 2000

1 .... 7.00

Futurama/Simpsons Infinitely Secret Crossover Crisis
Bongo, 2002

1-2... 3.00

Future Beat
Oasis, 1986

This black-and-white science-fiction series from Oasis Comics featured two unrelated stories in its tone-setting first issue. The lead feature was the story of a future cop trying to take down a criminal organization and deal with a serial killer. The backup story, "The Exodus," focused on the political and sociological struggles that take place on a spaceship containing what was once the population of Earth. Interesting stuff-especially the insightful, semi-Orwellian commentary of the backup feature-but, by and large, it was sketchily rendered with little attention given to background details.

1-2... 2.00

Future Comics
David McKay, 1940

1 .... 1,800.00
2 .... 1,100.00
3-4 .... 885.00

Future Cop: L.A.P.D.
DC, 1998

1 .... 5.00
Ashcan 1 .... 1.00

Future Course
Reoccurring Images, 1993

1 .... 3.00

Futuretech
Mushroom, 1995

1 .... 4.00

Future World Comics
George W. Dougherty, 1946

1 .... 200.00
2 .... 160.00

Future World Comix
Warren, 1978

1 .... 4.00

Futurians by Dave Cockrum
Lodestone, 1985

1-3... 2.00

Futurians
Aardwolf, 1995

1 .... 3.00

Fuzzy Buzzard and Friends
Hall of Heroes, 1995

This black-and-white funny animal comic from writer Mister Tom and artist Ethan Van Sciver (Impulse) packs some old-fashioned punch, echoing such luminaries as Fox and Crow and Wacky Squirrel. Aimed at kids under twelve years of age, the stories focus on Fuzzy Buzzard, Queen Fussy, Gilly Goose, Messycat, and the super-heroic Froggy Wonder as they get into one mess after another. Who says there aren't good comics for kids out there?!?

1 .... 3.00

Gene Autry, "The Singing Cowboy," parlayed his fame into a long-running Dell comics series.

G-8 and His Battle Aces
Blazing, 1966
1 .... 2.00

Gabby
Quality, 1953

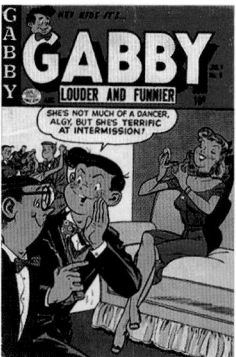

A teen humor offering from the mid-1950s, Gabby was one of the final titles released by the Quality Comics group.

Issues of Gabby provide the standard teen laughs, with the standard cast of characters: Gabby, the luckless "average teen;" his high-handed rival Smedley; fickle girlfriend Taffy; and the supporting cast of the "brain;" the dumb, buzz-cut jock; and a generous measure of hopelessly square authoritarian adults.

Each issue features a variety of stories focusing on different members of the cast, plus a few single-page gag strips.

Gabby folded in 1954 when the Quality Comics line sputtered out.
-- Rob Salkowitz

1 .... 32.00
2 .... 20.00
3 .... 16.00
4-9 .... 12.00

Gabby Hayes Western
Fawcett, 1948
1 .... 315.00
2 .... 160.00
3-5 .... 125.00
6-10 .... 110.00
11-20 .... 80.00
21-30 .... 65.00
31-40 .... 45.00

41-50 .... 36.00
51-59 .... 32.00

Gabriel
Caliber, 1995
1 .... 4.00

!Gag!
Harrier, 1987
1 .... 4.00
2-7 .... 3.00

Gag Reflex
(Skip Williamsons...)
Williamson, 1994
1 .... 3.00

Gaijin (Matrix)
Matrix, 1987
1 .... 2.00

Gaijin
Caliber
1 .... 4.00

Gajit Gang
Amazing
1 .... 2.00

Galactic
Dark Horse, 2003
1-3 .... 3.00

Galactica:
The New Millennium
Realm, 1999

Fleeing the Cylon tyranny, the last Battlestar, Galactica, leads a rag-tag fugitive fleet on a lonely quest for a bright shining planet known as…Earth.

The Universal one-season wonder of 1978 to 1979 was, for its time, the most expensive television program ever produced. Many have tried to carry on Glen Larson's tale but many have fallen along the way. Marvel's Battlestar Galactica lasted around three years before going away. Maximum chose the more cautious approach of incredible stories in four-or-so

issue mini-series such as Battlestar Galacticia, Battlestar Galactica : Apollo's Journey, Battlestar Galactica : Journey's End, and Battlestar Galactica: Starbuck, as well as one shots such as Battlestar Galactica : The Compendium. During the late 1990s, Realm managed to take a shot at telling the stories that were no longer being filmed as the remnants of the Colonial Empire seek out the sanctuary of their long-lost thirteenth tribe.

1 .... 3.00
1/Conv 5.00

Galactic Gladiators
Playdigm, 2001
1-4 .... 3.00

Galactic Guardians
Marvel, 1994
1-4 .... 2.00

Galactic Patrol
Eternity, 1990

Following rapidly on the heels of Eternity's first Lensman mini-series, this is a slight improvement by virtue of not having to reconcile inconsistencies between novel and manga movie. Tim Eldred is also now a more experienced penciller, as displayed by improved layouts and storytelling. The plot, though, is still very much reliant on space warfare. Comics might be a cheap way of presenting such material, but pages of space fights don't make for an enthralling read.

1-5 .... 2.00

Galactus the Devourer
Marvel, 1999
1-6 .... 4.00

Galaxina
Aircel, 1991
1-4 .... 3.00

Galaxion
Helikon, 1997

1-11 ....3.00
Special 1 ....1.00

Galaxy Girl
Dynamic

1 ....3.00

Gallegher Boy Reporter
Gold Key, 1965

1 ....15.00

Gall Force: Eternal Story
CPM, 1995

1-4 ....3.00

Gambit
Oracle, 1986

1 ....3.00
2 ....2.00

Gambit
Eternity, 1988

1 ....4.00

Gambit
Marvel, 1993

1 ....3.00
1/Gold 4.00
2-4 ....3.00

Gambit
Marvel, 1997

1-4 ....3.00

Gambit
Marvel, 1998

1 ....3.00
1/A-1/B 4.00
1/C 6.00
1/D 4.00
2-4 ....3.00
5-24 ....2.00
25 ....3.00
Ann 1999-2000 ....4.00
GS 1 ....5.00

Gambit
Marvel, 2004

1-12 ....3.00

Gambit and Associates
Eclectic

1-3 ....2.00

Gambit and Bishop
Marvel, 2001

This six-issue limited series
from writer Scott Lobdell (Wildcats)
and artists Georges Jeanty (Green
Lantern) stars the Marvel
Universe's resident Cajun thief and
time-traveling conductor of energy-
Gambit and Bishop, respectively.
But why are their comrades in the
ever-uncanny X-Men attacking
these mutants-in-good-standing?
Could it have something to do with
armored-to-the-nines super-villain
and long-time X-foe Stryfe? It
could, but find out for certain as
this "buddy-movie-in-comic-book-
form" unfolds. It's a winner from
beginning to end!

1-6 .... 2.00

Gambit and
Bishop Alpha
Marvel, 2001

1 .... 2.00

Gambit and
Bishop Genesis
Marvel, 2001

1 .... 4.00

Gambit & the X-Ternals
Marvel, 1995

1-4 .... 2.00

Gambit Battlebook
Marvel, 1998

1 .... 4.00

Game Boy
Valiant, 1990

1-4 .... 2.00

Game Guys!
Wonder

1 .... 3.00

Gamera
Dark Horse, 1996

1-4 .... 3.00

Gammarauders
DC, 1989

1-6 .... 1.00
7-10 .... 2.00

Gamorra
Swimsuit Special
Image, 1996

1 .... 3.00

Gandy Goose
St. John, 1953

1 .... 40.00
2 .... 26.00
3 .... 20.00
4 .... 16.00
5-6 .... 14.00

Gangbang Girls: All Wet
Angel

1 .... 3.00

Gangbusters
DC, 1947

Although Westerns were big in
comics in the 1950s, true-to-life
crime dramas had their own
successful niche. One of DC's
better enrties in this genre is
Gangbusters, based in part on the
radio and TV series of the same
name, which was a peer with such
classics as Dragnet and Highway
Patrol. While nowhere near as
edgy or innovative as, say, EC's
Crime SuspensStories or the
seminal Crime Does Not Pay,
Gangbusters has its own appeal,
full of relatively nonviolent crime
stories with clever twists.

Like many DC comics of the
era, however, plots also tended to
rely on unlikely gimmicks and
premises, such as "Indian
Detective," the tale of a
plainclothes Native American cop
who uses stereotypical devices like
smoke signals, and bows and
arrows to help stop the bad guys.

Many of the top comics artists
of the era, including Frank
Frazetta, Jack Kirby and even

Mad's Mort Drucker, contributed to the short stories of this title, which enjoyed a modest run.

-- Stephen C. George

1	565.00
2	300.00
3	200.00
4-5	175.00
☛Lady Cop	
6-10	140.00
11-13	110.00
14	150.00
15-16	85.00
17	150.00
18-20	85.00
21-30	70.00
31-51	54.00
52-67	44.00

Gangland
DC, 1998

1-4 ....3.00

Gangsters and Gun Molls
Realistic Comics, 1951

1	240.00
2	185.00
3	155.00
4	135.00

Gangsters Can't Win
D.S., 1948

1	145.00
2	90.00
3	75.00
4-9	58.00

Gantar: The Last Nabu
Target, 1986

1-7 ....2.00

Gargoyle
Marvel, 1985

Isaac Christians was an old man whose beloved town was headed into ruin. To save it, Isaac made a deal with a demon named Avarish, who agreed to help him ... under certain conditions. Avarish placed Isaac in the body of a stone gargoyle, which he imbued with sorcerous power.

Needless to say, Isaac began having second thoughts about the deal, and when the Defenders battled Avarish, Isaac took their side. Avarish was defeated, but Isaac remained trapped in the stone body of the Gargoyle.

This series begins when Isaac decides to make a visit to his old town of Christiansboro. To his horror, he discovers that his old body is very much alive, but is inhabited by the evil spirit of the original Gargoyle. What follows is a supernatural conflict which changes the way readers view this star-crossed member of the Defenders.

1-4 .... 2.00

Gargoyles
Marvel, 1995

1	3.00
2-11	2.00

Garou: The Lone Wolf
Bare Bones, 1999

1 .... 2.00

Garrison's Gorillas
Dell, 1968

1	21.00
2-4	14.00
5	12.00

Gasp!
Quebecor, 1994

1 .... 1.00

Gatecrasher: Ring of Fire
Black Bull, 2000

1-4/A.. 3.00

Gatekeeper
Gatekeeper

This black-and-white title from storytellers Susan Van Camp and Mark Harmon is part comic book-- along the lines of Conan the Barbarian or Swords of Swashbucklers--and part-role-playing game--much like Dungeons & Dragons. A graphic

story makes readers aware of the world of Delicar, a place where good and evil clash on a regular basis; and a text section provides a danger-filled scenario for a role-playing adventure, complete with maps and background information.

1 .... 3.00

Gate Manga
ADV Manga, 2005

1 .... 10.00

Gates of Eden
Fantaco, 1982

1 .... 4.00

Gates of Pandragon
Ianus

1 .... 2.00

Gatesville Company
Speakeasy Comics, 2005

1 .... 3.00

Gateway to Horror (Basil Wolverton's...)
Dark Horse, 1987

1 .... 2.00

Gathering of Tribes
KC Arts

1 .... 1.00

Gauntlet
Aircel, 1992

1-8 .... 3.00

Gay Comics
U.S.A., 1944

A deceptively simple humor anthology title from the 1940s, Gay Comics didn't feature many regular strips and characters per se. Rather, it served as an outlet for the talents of two of the most wildly funny and creative cartoonists in comics history: Harvey Kurtzman (whose insane genius later helped spawn the groundbreaking Mad title for EC), and Basil Wolverton (the inspiration for an entire generation of underground comix artists in the 1960s).

Kurtzman was just beginning to explore his style and develop his early signature strip, "Hey Look!" but Wolverton's mastery of grotesque caricature and mind-numbing detail were at their full peak, producing some beautiful and hilarious three-to-four page gems. Issues were filled out with romantic, slapstick, and military-service comedy strips by other inspired lunatics.

1	375.00
18	220.00
19	185.00
20-25	150.00
26-29	125.00
30-31	65.00
32	45.00
33-34	65.00
35	45.00
36-37	65.00
38-40	45.00

Gay Comics (Bob Ross)
Bob Ross, 1980

1	13.00
2	8.00
3-5	6.00
6-9	5.00
10-16	4.00
17-21	3.00
22-24	5.00
25	4.00
Special 1	3.00

Gazillion
Image, 1998

1-1/Variant	3.00

GD Minus 18
Antarctic, 1998

1	3.00

Gear
Fireman, 1998

1-6	3.00

Gear Station
Image, 2000

1-5	3.00

Geeksville
3 Finger Prints, 1999

1-3	3.00

Geeksville (Vol. 2)
Image, 2000

0-6	3.00

Geisha
Oni, 1998

1-4	3.00

Gem Comics
Spotlight, 1945

1	165.00

Geminar
Image, 2000

Special 1	5.00

Gemini Blood
DC, 1996

It's 2094, the Age of Options. Thanks to advances in genetic technology coupled with good old fashioned greed, the world has gone to heck in a handbasket. The elite control most of the world's resources, amusing themselves with singing dogs and robotic courtesans. The poor, meanwhile, are starving, as usual.

Then there are the Paratwa: pairs of human fetuses genetically altered to hhave telepathic links. With the ability to act as one, these twins grow to become more than a match for any human. Unfortunately, these "beings of Gemini Blood" are bred from birth to hunt humans.

Part of DC's unsuccessful attempt at a science-fiction imprint, this nine-issue series explores this bleak future world, and the lives of four people who dared to go up against the Paratwa.

1-9	2.00

Gen-Active
WildStorm, 2000

1-6	4.00

Gene Autry and Champion
Dell, 1955

102-121	20.00

Gene Autry Comics
Fawcett, 1942

1	4,500.00
2	1,100.00
3	1,000.00
4-5	875.00
6-10	775.00
11-12	660.00

Gene Autry Comics
Dell, 1946

1	475.00
2	265.00
3	200.00
4-5	145.00
6-10	125.00
11-20	85.00
21-40	60.00
41-60	45.00
61-80	38.00
81-90	30.00
91-100	28.00
101	20.00

Gene Autry's Champion
Dell, 1951

3-19	22.00

Gene Dogs
Marvel, 1993

1	3.00
2-4	2.00

Gene Pool
Idea & Design Works, 2003

1	7.00

Generation Hex
DC, 1997

1	2.00

Generation M
Marvel, 2006

1-5	3.00

Generation Next
Marvel, 1995

1-4	2.00

Generation X
Marvel, 1994

Taking as its own the title of a popular work of pop-culture non-fiction, Generation X can be considered sort of the "New" New Mutants. Another class of mutants arrives for training at Professor Xavier's School for Gifted Youngsters, and they're hipper and more diverse than the X-Men and the New Mutants who came before them. Among the most interesting are: Jubilation Lee, a pyrokinetic who was adopted by the X-Men and took part in their adventures before honing her talents formally at the school; ambitious Paige Guthrie, whose ability to shed her skin, damaged or not, has given her the super-hero name, Husk; British Jonothan Starsmore, who wants to be able to harness the powers of the bio-psionic field within him; and a Samoan called Mondo who can absorb others' physical mass, but has yet to develop a battle instinct.

Although guided by telekinetic Emma Frost and Sean Cassidy (Banshee), as well as a mysterious being known only as Gateway, these teenagers are see more live super-hero action than formal schooling.

-1	2.00
1/2-1/2/Ltd.	3.00
1	4.00
2-24	2.00
25	3.00
26-49	2.00
50-50/Autographed	3.00
51-56	2.00
57	3.00
58-74	2.00
75	3.00
Ann 1995	4.00
Ann 1996-1997	3.00
Ann 1998-1999	4.00
Ashcan 1	2.00
Holiday 1	4.00

Generation X/Gen13
Marvel, 1997

1-1/A	4.00

Generation X Underground
Marvel, 1998

1	3.00

Generic Comic
Marvel, 1984

1	3.00

Generic Comic
Comics Conspiracy, 2001

1-5	2.00
5/Variant	6.00
6-9	2.00

Genesis
Malibu, 1993

0	4.00

Genesis
DC, 1997

1-4	2.00

Genesis: The #1 Collection
Image

1	10.00

Genetix
Marvel, 1993

1	3.00
2-6	2.00

Genie
Fc9 Publishing, 2005

1-2	3.00

Genocide
Renegade Tribe, 1994

1-1/2nd	3.00

Genocyber
Viz, 1993

1-5	3.00

Gen of Hiroshima
Educomics, 1980

1-2	2.00

Gensaga
Express

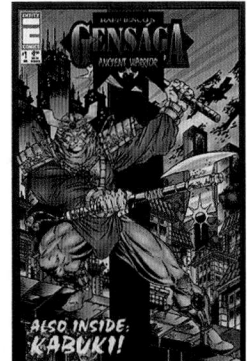

Melding medieval Japanese settings and Wildstorm-eque art, Raff Ienco's Gensaga is the story of a young samurai's battle with evil in both his and our worlds. Can he trust the masterful warrior Threshold and the lovely Daisi? Will he help or hinder the struggle to overthrow the dark Lord Abyss? How is disgraced basketball star Jordan Phillips involved?

While not a Wildstorm title, Gensaga takes a definite bow to the Jim Lee style of art with larger-than-life heroes, lovelier-than-life heroines and extravagant villains evil enough to evoke the four-color comic strips of the 1940s. Raff Ienco's Gensaga is a nice compliment to early Stormwatch or Gen 13 issues.

1	3.00

Gen12
Image, 1998

1-5	3.00

Gen13
Image, 1994

0	4.00
1/2	2.00
1/2/A	5.00
1	4.00
1/A-1/B	5.00
1/C	4.00
1/2nd-5/A	3.00
Ashcan 1	4.00

Gen13
Image, 1994

-1-0	3.00
1/3D	5.00
1/A-1/F	3.00
1/G-1/H	4.00
1/I-1/M	3.00
1/N	40.00
1/2nd-10	3.00
11-11/A	5.00
12	3.00
13/A-13/C	2.00
13/CS-13/D	7.00
14-24	3.00
25-25/CS	4.00
26-49	3.00
50	4.00
51-77	3.00
3D 1	6.00
3D 1/A	5.00
Ann 1	3.00
Ann 1999-2000	4.00

Gen13
WildStorm, 2002

0-0/Variant	1.00
1-16	3.00

Gen13
DC, 2006

1-4/Variant	3.00

Gen13: A Christmas Caper
WildStorm, 2000

1	6.00

Gen13: Backlist
Image, 1996

1	3.00

Gen13 Bikini Pin-Up Special
Image

1	5.00

Gen13 Bootleg
Image, 1996

1-17	3.00
Ann 1	4.00

Gen13: Carny Folk
WildStorm, 2000

1	4.00

Gen13/Fantastic Four
WildStorm, 2001

1	6.00

Gen13/Generation X
Image, 1997

1/A-1/B	3.00
1/C-1/D	5.00
1/E-1/G	4.00

Gen13: Going West
DC, 1999

1	3.00

Gen13: Grunge Saves the World
DC, 1999

1	6.00

Gen13 Interactive
Image, 1997

1-3	3.00

Gen13: London, New York, Hell
DC, 2001

1	7.00

Gen13: Magical Drama Queen Roxy
Image, 1998

1-3/A	4.00

Gen13/Maxx
Image, 1995

1	4.00

Gen13: Medicine Song
WildStorm

1	6.00

Gen13/ Monkeyman & O'Brien
Image, 1998

1-2/A	3.00

Gen13: Ordinary Heroes
Image, 1996

1-2	3.00

Gen13 Rave
Image, 1995

1	3.00

Gen13: Science Friction
WildStorm, 2001

1	6.00

Gen13: The Unreal World
Image, 1996

1	3.00

Gen13: Wired
DC, 1999

1	3.00

Gen13 Yearbook '97
Image, 1997

1	3.00

Gen13 'Zine
Image, 1996

1	2.00

Gentle Ben
Dell, 1968

1	30.00
2-5	20.00

Genus
Antarctic, 1993

1	4.00
2-57	3.00
58-89	4.00

Genus Greatest Hits
Antarctic, 1996

1-4	5.00

Genus Spotlight
Radio, 1998

1-2	3.00

Geobreeders
CPM Manga, 1999

1-31	3.00

Geomancer
Valiant, 1994

Throughout history, certain people have been called to represent the earth itself. The earth spoke to these people, whispered its secrets to them. And in turn, these Geomancers spoke for the earth. Protected both by their magic and their champion, Gilad Anni-Padda (the Eternal Warrior), their line has continued throughout history.

The most recent Geomancer was Geoff McHenry, a young boy who helped protect Earth during the Unity crisis, and also served as a catalyst to usher in such heroes as Bloodshot. In the end, he apparently sacrificed himself during the Chaos Effect crisis.

Earth needed a new Geomancer and the Eternal Warrior chose Clay McHenry, a crooked cop who lost his vision during an illegal "transaction." Now he has the chance to become a hero...if he lives that long!

1	2.00
1/VVSS	40.00
2-3	1.00
4-7	2.00
8	4.00

George of the Jungle
Gold Key, 1969

1	35.00
2	24.00

George Romero's Land of the Dead
Idea & Design Works, 2005

1-5	4.00

Georgie Comics
Timely, 1945

1	90.00
2	60.00
3-5	50.00
6-10	40.00
11-20	36.00
21-39	32.00

Gepetto Files
Quick to Fly, 1998

1	3.00

Gerald McBoing Boing and the Nearsighted Mr. Magoo
Dell, 1952

1	85.00
2-6	55.00

Geriatric Gangrene Jujitsu Gerbils
Planet-X

With a ridiculous name like the above, what else could this be but yet another totally offbeat spoof of the wildly successful Teenage Mutant Ninja Turtles. Perhaps the biggest difference is that these are not teenagers, but rather elderly nursing home residents, called back into action when the life of the scientist who created them, Dr. Milton Meltdown, is threatened. In fact, all life is threatened by the Dr.'s new experiment, a mutated genetic lifeform (like the gerbils) that the government forced him to create. Unfortunately, this one is a god-like super-being that can't be controlled.

Throw a hulking Samurai warrior, a lovely female assistant to Dr. Meltdown, and a host of predictable jokes involving old age and the like, and you've got this black-and-white Planet-X-Productions title written and drawn, somewhat crudely, by Tony Basilicato.

1-2 ....2.00

Geriatricman
C&T
1 ....2.00

ge rouge
Verotik, 1997
1/2-3 ....3.00

Gertie the Dinosaur Comics
Gertie the Dinosaur, 2000
1 ....3.00

Gestalt
New England, 1993
1-2 ....2.00

Gestalt
Caliber
0 ....3.00

Get Along Gang
Marvel, 1985
1-6 ....1.00

GetBackers
Tokyopop, 2004
1-12 ....10.00

Get Bent!
Ben T. Steckler, 1998
1-6 ....3.00
7 ....2.00
8-9 ....3.00

Get Lost
Mikeross, 1954
1 ....145.00
2 ....90.00

Get Lost
New Comics, 1987
1-3 ....2.00

Get Real Comics
Tides Center
1 ....2.00

Get Smart
Dell, 1966
1 ....45.00
2 ....30.00
3-5 ....22.00
6-8 ....20.00

Ghetto Bitch
Fantagraphics
1 ....3.00

Ghetto Blasters
Whiplash, 1997
1 ....3.00

Ghost
Dark Horse, 1994

Corrupted by organized crime, corporate robber barons, and dishonest leaders, Arcadia is a film-noir-style city with an eclectic cast of characters, including men in fedora hats and extraterrestrials with psionic powers. And inn Arcadia, reporter Elisa Cameron follows her leads to uncover an amazing news story -- and pays for it with her life.

She becomes Ghost, a vigilante spectre who spares Arcadia's criminals no kindness, as she tries to figure out why, how, and by whom she was killed. Ironically, this ghost is herself haunted, though not by the dead, but by the living: her alcoholic parents, who are addled by years of alcohol abuse, and her emotionally unstable sister, who has slipped into Arcadia's sleazy underground.

One of Dark Horse's more durable original characters, Ghost has appeared in several other titles.

1-24 .... 3.00
25 .... 4.00
26-36 .... 3.00
Special 1-Special 3 .... 4.00

Ghost
Dark Horse, 1998
1 .... 4.00
2-22 .... 3.00

Ghost and the Shadow
Dark Horse, 1995
1 .... 3.00

Ghost/Batgirl
Dark Horse, 2000
1-4 .... 3.00

Ghostbusters
First, 1986
1-6 .... 2.00

Ghostbusters II
Now, 1989
1-3 .... 2.00

Ghost Comics
Fiction House, 1951
1 .... 485.00
2 .... 365.00
3-5 .... 285.00
6-11 .... 220.00

Ghostdancing
DC, 1995
1-2 .... 2.00
3-6 .... 3.00

Ghost Handbook
Dark Horse, 1999
1 .... 3.00

Ghost/Hellboy Special
Dark Horse, 1996
1-2 .... 3.00

Ghost in the Shell
Dark Horse, 1995

In the future, technology and information access has become ever more important. Perhaps it was inevitable that human beings would find their own bodies wedded to cybertechnology. Ultimately, "cyberbrain" technology allows for the transplanting of human consciousness into mechanical bodies. Such beings became little more than human minds -- "ghosts" -- in mechanical shells.

Creator Matsamunu Shirow created a startling vision of the future with his movie Ghost in the Shell, on which this comics series is based. Nominally, it's a crime drama wherein a futuristic cyborg police officer searches for the killer

Ghost in the Shell

of a prominent businessman. Below the surface, however, it's a story of alienation and the search for identity in a world where technology strips the individual of the very things which make them human.

1-8 .... 4.00

Ghost in the Shell 2: Man/Machine Interface
Dark Horse, 2003

1 .... 4.00
1/Hologram 10.00
2-11 .... 4.00

Ghost in the Shell 1.5: Human Error Processor
Dark Horse, 2006

1-9 .... 3.00

Ghostly Haunts
Charlton, 1971

20 .... 6.00
21-30 .... 5.00
31-40 .... 4.00
41-58 .... 3.00

Ghostly Tales
Charlton, 1966

55 .... 16.00
56-59 .... 7.00
60-70 .... 5.00
71-100 .... 4.00
101-169 .... 3.00

Ghostly Weird Stories
Star Publications, 1953

120 .... 170.00
121-124 .... 125.00

Ghost Manor
Charlton, 1968

1 .... 12.00
2-5 .... 7.00
6-10 .... 6.00
11-19 .... 5.00

Ghost Manor
Charlton, 1971

1 .... 10.00
2-7 .... 6.00
8 .... 8.00
9-10 .... 5.00
11-30 .... 4.00
31-77 .... 3.00

Ghost Rider
Magazine Enterprises, 1950

1 .... 400.00
2-5 .... 285.00
6-10 .... 175.00
11 .... 200.00
12-14 .... 135.00

Ghost Rider
Marvel, 1967

1 .... 28.00
2-3 .... 20.00
4-7 .... 13.00

Ghost Rider
Marvel, 1973

1 .... 130.00
2 .... 37.00
3-4 .... 25.00
5 .... 23.00
6-14 .... 15.00
15-16 .... 12.00
17 .... 10.00
17/30¢ 20.00
18 .... 10.00
18/30¢ 20.00
19 .... 10.00
19/30¢ 20.00
20 .... 10.00
21-23 .... 7.00
24-26/35¢ 15.00
27-30 .... 7.00
31-49 .... 6.00
50 .... 12.00
51-68 .... 5.00
69-80 .... 4.00
81 .... 10.00

Ghost Rider
Marvel, 1990

-1 .... 2.00
1 .... 4.00
1/2nd 2.00
2-5/Variant 3.00
5/2nd 2.00
6 .... 3.00
7-14 .... 2.00
15 .... 5.00
15/2nd-27 .... 2.00
28 .... 3.00
29-30 .... 2.00
31 .... 3.00
32-49 .... 2.00
50 .... 3.00
50/Variant 4.00
51-60 .... 2.00
61 .... 3.00
62-92 .... 2.00
93 .... 3.00
Ann 1 .... 4.00
Ann 2 .... 3.00

Ghost Rider
Marvel, 2001

1/2 .... 4.00
1-6 .... 3.00

Ghost Rider
Marvel, 2005

1 .... 6.00
1/Ribic 18.00
1/DirCut 4.00
1/RRP 45.00
2-6 .... 3.00

Ghost Rider (Vol. 5)
Marvel, 2006

1-6 .... 3.00

Ghost Rider & Cable: Servants of the Dead
Marvel, 1991

1 .... 4.00

Ghost Rider and the Midnight Sons Magazine
Marvel

1 .... 4.00

Ghost Rider/Ballistic
Marvel, 1997

1 .... 3.00

Ghost Rider/Blaze: Spirits of Vengeance
Marvel, 1992

1 .... 2.00
1/CS 3.00
2-11 .... 2.00
12 .... 3.00
13-23 .... 2.00

Ghost Rider/ Captain America: Fear
Marvel, 1992

1 .... 6.00

Ghost Rider: Crossroads
Marvel, 1995

1 .... 4.00

Ghost Rider: Highway to Hell
Marvel, 2001

1 .... 4.00

Ghost Rider Poster Magazine
Marvel, 1992

1 .... 5.00

Ghost Rider: The Hammer Lane
Marvel, 2001

1-6 .... 3.00

Ghost Rider 2099
Marvel, 1994

1 .... 2.00
1/CS 3.00
2-24 .... 2.00
25 .... 3.00

Ghost Rider; Wolverine; Punisher: The Dark Design
Marvel, 1991

1 .... 6.00

Ghosts
DC, 1971

1 .... 100.00
2 .... 35.00
3-5 .... 17.00
6-10 .... 12.00
11-20 .... 10.00
21-30 .... 6.00
31-39 .... 5.00
40 .... 6.00
41-50 .... 5.00
51-70 .... 4.00
71-112 .... 3.00

Ghost Ship
Slave Labor, 1996
1 ....4.00
2-3..3.00

Ghosts of Dracula
Eternity, 1991
1-5..3.00

Ghost Spy
Image, 2004
1-5..3.00

Ghost Stories
Dell, 1962

The horror-story anthology title is an oddity, introduced (with a few others) into a line that for years had carried as its slogan, "Dell Comics are good comics!" accompanying a pledge to parents that there the contents would contain nothing inappropriate for young readers. However, while other ongoing comics titles of its day had carried the Comics Magazine Association of America stamp for six years and were subjected to careful content control, the Codeless Ghost Stories offered at least one memorably horrifying tale.

The first issue carried the cover text "Stories to shock you! Ghostly tales of suspense and terror!" And many of those who read it as children remember it to this day. Written by John Stanley, the opening story -- "The Monster of Dresd End ..." -- gave many young readers nightmares. It featured a monsterous hand on the end of a tentacle -- a hand that sucked out the contents of a person's body, leaving behind only the skin. Brrr. Not all the stories were that memorable, but it was successful enough as a title that it continued for years.

-- Maggie

1 ....36.00

---

2 .... 20.00
3-5... 14.00
6-10 .... 10.00
11-16 .... 7.00
17-20 .... 6.00
21-37 .... 5.00

Ghost Stories
Dark Horse
1 .... 9.00

Ghouls
Eternity
1 .... 2.00

Giant Comics Editions
St. John, 1948
1 .... 575.00
2 .... 340.00
3 .... 425.00
4 .... 1,100.00
5 .... 1,200.00
5/A 500.00
6 .... 675.00
7 .... 525.00
8 .... 485.00
9 .... 650.00
10 .... 525.00
11 .... 650.00
12 .... 1,700.00
13 .... 600.00
14 .... 450.00
15 .... 770.00
16 .... 625.00
17 .... 450.00

Giantkiller
DC, 1999
1-6 .... 3.00

Giantkiller A to Z
DC, 1999
1 .... 3.00

Giant-Size Amazing Spider-Man
Marvel, 1999
1 .... 5.00

Giant-Size Avengers
Marvel, 1974
1 .... 30.00
2 .... 25.00
3-4 .... 20.00
5 .... 15.00

Giant-Size Captain America
Marvel
1 .... 20.00

Giant-Size Captain Marvel
Marvel

In the 1970s, Marvel produced a series of giant-size specials titled -- appropriately enough -- Giant-Size Avengers, Giant-Size Spider-Man, Giant-Size Defenders, etc. Some of these extra-thick titles featured new stories, while others were composed of reprints.

The first and only issue of Giant-Size Captain Marvel reprints #17, #20, and #21 of the Kree warrior's title, which features scripts by Roy Thomas (All-Star Squadron) and Gil Kane (Green Lantern). Here, Marvel's space-born super-hero bonds with perennial sidekick Rick Jones -- the stereotypical teen-ager who palled around with Captain America and the Avengers -- and frees himself from the Negative Zone. This bond allows the Captain and Rick to switch places, when one or the other is needed, making their relationship similar to the one between a certain Billy Batson and another Captain Marvel. This reprint collection also features a battle royal between Captain Marvel and The Hulk, another of Rick Jones' former partners.

1 .... 16.00

Giant-Size Chillers
Marvel, 1974
1 .... 25.00
☛1st Lilith

Giant-Size Chillers
Marvel, 1975
1 .... 20.00
2-3 .... 15.00

Giant-Size Conan
Marvel, 1974
1 .... 16.00
2 .... 10.00
3 .... 7.00
4-5 .... 6.00

Giant-Size Creatures
Marvel, 1974

1 ....25.00

Giant-Size Daredevil
Marvel, 1975

1 ....15.00

Giant-Size Defenders
Marvel, 1974

1 ....20.00
2-3 ....10.00
4-5 ....7.00

Giant-Size Doc Savage
Marvel, 1975

1 ....10.00

Giant-Size Doctor Strange
Marvel, 1975

1 ....15.00

Giant-Size Dracula
Marvel, 1974

This title continues from Giant-Size Chillers and interweaves around plot lines from Tomb of Dracula.

During the 1970s, Marvel attempted to pick up where Bram Stoker's Dracula left off. Quincy Harker, son of Jonathan and Mina Harker carried on the fight begun by his parents and their friends in an attempt to destroy the undead creature known as Dracula. This most famous of vampires was portrayed as a blood-sucking fiend but with a strange warped sense of honor that kept him one of those villains you love to hate. Eventually the horror craze of the seventies died out but Dracula keeps returning with new artists, new writers, and old plots.

2 ....22.00
☞was GS Chillers
3-4 ....15.00
5 ....20.00
☞1st Marvel Byrne

Giant-Size Fantastic Four
Marvel, 1974

1 .... 20.00
2 .... 12.00
3 .... 10.00
4 .... 12.00
5-6 .... 10.00

Giant-Size Hulk
Marvel, 1975

1 .... 23.00

Giant-Size Hulk
Marvel, 2006

1 .... 8.00

Giant-Size Invaders
Marvel, 1975

1 .... 15.00
☞G.A. Subby origin

Giant-Size Iron Man
Marvel, 1975

1 .... 17.00

Giant-Size Kid Colt
Marvel, 1975

1 .... 27.00
2-3 .... 20.00

Giant-Size Man-Thing
Marvel, 1974

1 .... 15.00
2 .... 9.00
3 .... 12.00
4 .... 10.00
5 .... 12.00

Giant-Size Marvel Triple Action
Marvel, 1975

1 .... 15.00
2 .... 12.00

Giant-Size Master of Kung Fu
Marvel, 1974

1 .... 17.00
2 .... 12.00
3-4 .... 10.00

Giant-Size Mini Comics
Eclipse, 1986

1-4 .... 2.00

Giant-Size Mini-Marvels: Starring Spidey
Marvel, 2002

1 .... 4.00

Giant-Size Ms. Marvel
Marvel, 2006

1 .... 5.00

Giant-Size Official Prince Valiant
Pioneer

1 .... 4.00

Giant-Size Power Man
Marvel, 1975

1 .... 20.00

Giant-Size Spider-Man
Marvel, 1974

1 .... 35.00
2-3 .... 12.00
4 .... 45.00
☞Punisher app.
5 .... 12.00
6 .... 15.00

Giant-Size Spider-Man
Marvel, 1998

1 .... 4.00

Giant-Size Spider-Woman
Marvel, 2005

1 .... 5.00

Giant-Size Super-Heroes
Marvel, 1974

1 .... 25.00

Giant-Size Super-Stars
Marvel, 1974

1 .... 20.00

Giant-Size Super-Villain Team-Up
Marvel, 1975

1 .... 17.00
2 .... 10.00

Giant-Size Thor
Marvel, 1975

1 .... 20.00

Giant-Size Werewolf By Night
Marvel, 1974

2 .... 20.00
3-5 .... 15.00

Giant-Size Wolverine
Marvel, 2006

1 .... 5.00

Giant-Size X-Men
Marvel, 1975

1 .... 800.00
☞1st new X-Men
2 .... 80.00
3-4 .... 5.00

Giant THB Parade
Horse

1 .... 5.00

G.I. Combat
Quality, 1952

1 .... 440.00
2 .... 210.00
3-5 .... 150.00
6-9 .... 125.00
10 .... 135.00
11-20 .... 90.00
21-31 .... 75.00
32 .... 110.00
33-43 .... 75.00

G.I. Combat
DC, 1953

44	500.00
45	300.00
46	250.00
47	225.00
48-50	100.00
51-54	85.00
55	125.00
56-60	85.00
61-66	70.00
67	125.00

☞1st Tank Killer

68	400.00
69-86	70.00
87	300.00

☞1st Haunted Tank

88-100	55.00
101-110	45.00
111-113	38.00
114	75.00

☞Haunted Tank origin

115-120	28.00
121-140	22.00
141-145	8.00
146-150	10.00
151-160	8.00
161-180	7.00
181-200	5.00
201-250	4.00
251-288	3.00

Gideon Hawk
Big Shot, 1994

This black-and-white series from Big Shot Comics and creator Steve Brooks features a high-tech bounty hunter in far-flung outer space. As the series opens, Gideon Hawk is not asked to bring back a criminal, but a mystically empowered stone called the Jewel of Shambali. If this precious and powerful stone should fall into the wrong hands, its possessor could wreak havoc the likes of which the universe has never seen. Money, of course, encourages Hawk to take the job, but his innate heroism will seem him through. Unlike a number of black-and-white independents,

Gideon Hawk boasts crisp, clean artwork, and Brooks' story is energetic and entertaining.

1-3	2.00

Gidget
Dell, 1966

1	100.00

Gift
Image, 2004

1	3.00
1/DirCut	4.00
2-14	3.00

Gift, The: A First Publishing Holiday Special
First, 1990

1	6.00

Gifts of the Night
DC, 1999

It is the time of medieval kingdoms in Europe. Reyes is the tutor of Prince Magdin, the innocent, simple, slow-witted son of the king. Reyes himself has no political ambition, content to pass his time among the texts of the library, absorbing the wisdom of ancient scholars. He sees his role as the Prince's teacher as an obligatory-if futile task-since someone so mentally challenged will not be allowed to inherit the throne.

But when a difficult military impasse is solved by the prince's description of a story from history, (related as a vision, but actually told to him by Reyes), Prince Magdin earns some appreciation from his father. Consequently Reyes, as Magdin's tutor is elevated to a position of power he finds uncomfortable...at least initially.

This thoughtful, moving story is written by Paul Chadwick, (renowned as the creator of Concrete) and painted by John Bolton.

1-4	3.00

Gigantor
Antarctic, 2000

1	3.00

Giggle Comics
ACG, 1943

1	125.00
2	75.00
3-5	60.00
6-10	45.00
11-20	30.00
21-30	22.00
31-50	20.00
51-70	16.00
71-99	14.00

Gigolo
Fantagraphics, 1995

1-2	3.00

G.I. Government Issued
Paranoid, 1994

1-2	2.00

G.I. in Battle
Four Star, 1952

War comics from the early 1950s generally trade in a pretty narrow range, content-wise. At best, they're recycled stories of glory and valor from the freshly won World War II. At worst, they're hysterical, bloodthirsty, and ideologically shrill anticommunist propaganda based on the then-current Korean conflict. G-I In Battle, a quick-and-dirty little war book from Ajax Publishing, probes the bottom reaches of the low register, combining crude racism ("Hurry up! We'll have the whole gook army on us in no time") as a central plot device with artwork that looks as if it were drawn with an entrenchment tool. G-I in Battle is remarkably bad stuff even for a period and a genre noted for low standards.

-- Rob Salkowitz

1	48.00
2	26.00

3-5	20.00
6-9	18.00
Ann 1	38.00
Ann 1/A	115.00
Ann 2-3	24.00
Ann 4-6	20.00

G.I. in Battle
Four Star, 1957

1	55.00
2-6	35.00

G.I. Jackrabbits
Excalibur, 1986

There's only one thing worse than superbly rendered anthropomorphic critters spoofin' a popular licensed property like G.I. Joe and that's poorly rendered anthropomorphic critters spoofin' a popular licensed property like G. I. Joe. But this title is a child of the 1980s Teenage Mutant Ninja Turtles wanna-be glut so you can't expect much.

A handful of specially trained rabbits plus a few other special ops personnel (a walrus, a fish and a crow) battle it out with…COWBRA, an evil herd of cows bent on being bad. Watch the G. I. Jackrabbits set out to turn them all into hamburger!

1	2.00

G.I. Jane
Stanhall, 1953

1	75.00
2-6	45.00
7-10	35.00

G.I. Joe
Ziff-Davis, 1950

1	100.00
2-5	60.00
6-10	50.00
11-17	42.00
18	95.00
19-30	36.00
31-40	34.00
41-47	30.00
48	35.00
49-51	30.00

GI Joe
Dark Horse, 1995

1-4	2.00

GI Joe
Dark Horse, 1996

1-4	3.00

G.I. Joe
Image, 2001

1-3	3.00
4	4.00
5-22	3.00
23-25	3.00

G.I. Joe (Devil's Due)
Devil's Due, 2004

26-35	3.00
35/Variant	4.00
36-42	3.00

G.I. Joe: America's Elite
Devil's Due, 2005

0	1.00
1	3.00
1/Conv	10.00
2-4	3.00
5-6	5.00
7-13	3.00
13/Special	6.00
14-18	3.00

G.I. Joe: America's Elite Data Desk Handbook
Devil's Due, 2005

1	3.00

G.I. Joe and the Transformers
Marvel, 1987

1-4	1.00

G.I. Joe: Battle Files
Image, 2002

1-3	6.00

G.I. Joe Comics Magazine
Marvel, 1986

1	3.00
2-13	2.00

G.I. Joe: Declassified
Devil's Due, 2006

1	5.00
1/Spaulding	9.00
2	5.00
2/Special	9.00
3	5.00
3/Special	9.00

G.I. Joe: Dreadnoks Declassified
Devil's Due, 2006

1	5.00
1/Special	9.00

G.I. Joe European Missions
Marvel, 1988

G.I. Joe European Missions reprints the Action Force comic from the United Kingdom. In the U.S., Action Force is more commonly known as the "Joes" (featured in the American series G.I. Joe, a Real American Hero).

The Action Force is a group of elite strike teams located in London, New York, and various other cities around the world. Each member has a codename and a particular specialty. For instance, Sci-fi is an ace marksman who uses his laser rifle to bulls-eye targets from two miles off; Roadblock is a huge, 50-caliber machine gun-toting powerhouse. The Action Force's mission is to safeguard world peace-and to stop the terrorist Cobra Commander and his minions, the Crimson Guard.

The Transformers, that other great Hasbro toy line-turned-comic-book, are featured in backup stories throughout this series.

1-15	2.00

G.I. Joe: Frontline
Image, 2002

1	3.00
1/Platinum	5.00
2-18	3.00

G.I. Joe in 3-D
Blackthorne, 1987

1-6	3.00

G.I. Joe: Master & Apprentice
Devil's Due, 2004

1-4	3.00

G.I. Joe: Master & Apprentice Vol. II
Devil's Due, 2005

1	3.00

1/Variant	4.00
2	3.00
2/Variant	4.00
3	3.00
3/Variant	4.00

G.I. Joe Order of Battle
Marvel, 1986

1-4	1.00

G.I. Joe,
A Real American Hero
Marvel, 1982

1	14.00
2	8.00
2/2nd	2.00
3	4.00
3/2nd	2.00
4	4.00
4/2nd	2.00
5	4.00
5/2nd	2.00
6	4.00
6/2nd	1.00
7	4.00
7/2nd	1.00
8	4.00
8/2nd	1.00
9	4.00
9/2nd	1.00
10	6.00
10/2nd	1.00
11	4.00
11/2nd	1.00
12	4.00
12/2nd	1.00
13	4.00
13/2nd	1.00
14	5.00
14/2nd	1.00
15	4.00
15/2nd	1.00
16	4.00
16/2nd	1.00
17	4.00
17/2nd	1.00
18	4.00
18/2nd	1.00
19	6.00
19/2nd	1.00
20	4.00
20/2nd	1.00
21	15.00

☛Silent issue

21/2nd	1.00
22	4.00
22/2nd	1.00
23	4.00
23/2nd	1.00
24	4.00
24/2nd	1.00
25	4.00
25/2nd	1.00
26	4.00
26/2nd	1.00
27	4.00
27/2nd	1.00
28	4.00
28/2nd	1.00
29	4.00

29/2nd	1.00
30	4.00
30/2nd	1.00
31	4.00
31/2nd	1.00
32	4.00
32/2nd	1.00
33	4.00
33/2nd	1.00
34	4.00
34/2nd	1.00
35	4.00
35/2nd	1.00
36	4.00
36/2nd	1.00
37-55	4.00
56	5.00
57	3.00
58	4.00
59-151	3.00
152-154	7.00
155	16.00

☛Low circulation

YB 1	3.00
YB 2-4	2.00
Special 1	20.00

G.I. Joe: Reloaded
Devil's Due, 2004

1	5.00
2-14	3.00

G.I. Joe:
Scarlett Declassified
Devil's Due, 2006

1	5.00

G.I. Joe: Sigma 6
Devil's Due, 2006

1-6	3.00

G.I. Joe:
Snake Eyes Declassified
Devil's Due, 2005

1-6	3.00

G.I. Joe Special Missions
Marvel, 1986

1	2.00
2-28	1.00

G.I. Joe Special
Missions: Antarctica
Devil's Due, 2006

1	5.00

G.I. Joe Special
Missions: Manhattan
Devil's Due, 2006

1	5.00

G.I. Joe: Special
Missions - Manhattan
Devil's Due, 2006

1	5.00

G.I. Joe:
Special Missions - Tokyo
Devil's Due, 2006

1	5.00

G.I. Joe vs.
Transformers:
The Art of War
Devil's Due, 206

1-4/Variant	3.00

G.I. Joe/Transformers
Image, 2003

1	4.00
1/Campbell	3.00
1/Foil	9.00
1/Graham	4.00
1/Graham foil	6.00
1/Miller-2	3.00
2/Sketch	12.00
3	3.00
3/Conv	4.00
3/Variant	3.00
4	2.00
4/Variant	3.00
5	2.00
5/Variant	3.00
6	2.00

G.I. Joe vs.
The Transformers
Devil's Due, 2004

1-1/Variant	4.00
2-4/Variant	3.00

Gilgamesh II
DC, 1989

The story began Aug. 17, 1987. Around the world, people were gearing up for the Harmonic Convergence, a rare astronomical event that is predicted to bring about cosmic changes on Earth. As things turn out, that's exactly what happens. Circling around its atmosphere is an alien craft carrying the last survivors of a race in search of a new home. Bad luck has brought it, badly damaged, to Earth. Only Earth is already inhabited.

The captain of the ship decides that there is no other choice but to land. The ship is picked up on U.S. radar and immediately shot down. Only the two infants escape, having been placed in escape pods earlier. Landing on Earth, one infant is found by a hippie couple and raised as their son. When Earth falls into cataclysmic wars, the infant, known as Gilgamesh, will become a hero and later become a world leader. Not until much later will the world learn of their leader's brother.

1-4 ....4.00

Gimme
Head Imports

1 ....3.00

Gimoles
Alias, 2005

1 ....1.00
2-4 ....3.00

G.I.M.P.:
The Monkey Boy and
The Short Order Dwarf
Wasteland

1 ....3.00

G.I. Mutants
Eternity, 1987

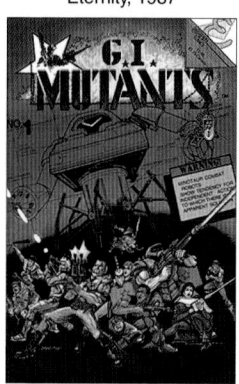

"The government made them mutants. Can they also make them soldiers?" That's the premise, and indeed pretty much the entire story, of this series featuring a bunch of immature young mutants and the military's efforts to turn them into a well-oiled fighting machine. Their various powers-Flyboy can fly, while Flaw can find the hidden flaws in anything-make them useful to the military, but can tough-as-nails Sargent Rushmore train their minds, teaching them both discipline and teamwork? He may not have as much time as he'd like, for another military project has unleashed a squad of killer robots on the world, and the powers of the G.I. Mutants are required, ready or not.

This series from Eternity Comics is written and drawn by

Martin Berkenwald and published in black-and-white.

1-4 .... 2.00

Ginger
Archie, 1951

1 .... 45.00
2 .... 28.00
3-6 .... 20.00
7-10 .... 30.00

Ginger Fox
Comico, 1988

1-4 .... 2.00

Gin-Ryu
Believe in Yourself, 1995

1-3 .... 3.00
3/Ashcan 1.00
4 .... 3.00

Gipsy
NBM

1-2 .... 11.00

G.I. R.A.M.B.O.T.
Wonder Color, 1987

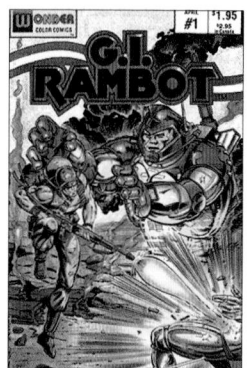

In the future, war hasn't disappeared from the world, it's just gotten more high-tech. Machines battle against other machines, and no one ever really wins these bloodless battles, for victory would end the war-and the all-important corporate profits. Such insanity compels a throwback warrior named "Ram" Stewart, a man who used to live for the honor of the battlefield, to take up arms again, and remind the world that man is still better than machine. Before long he's stealing an experimental robot, the G.I. Rambot, and changing the entire face of the unending war. With any luck he might just end it altogether.

Published by the Wonder Color Comics, the series is notable for featuring early art by Tom Lyle, who went on to bigger and better things at Marvel Comics a few years later.

1 .... 2.00

Girl
Rip Off, 1991

1-4 .... 3.00

Girl
NBM

1 .... 16.00

Girl
DC, 1996

1-3 .... 3.00

Girl Called...Willow!, A
Angel, 1996

1 .... 3.00

Girl Called...Willow!
Sketchbook, A
Angel

1 .... 3.00

Girl Comics
Marvel, 1949

1 .... 100.00
2 .... 75.00
3 .... 100.00
4-12 .... 75.00

Girl Confessions
Marvel, 1952

13-35 .... 50.00

Girl Crazy
Dark Horse, 1996

1-3 .... 3.00

Girl Fight Comics
Print Mint

1 .... 3.00

Girl from U.N.C.L.E.
Gold Key, 1967

1 .... 36.00
2 .... 24.00
3 .... 20.00
4-5 .... 15.00

Girl Genius
Studio Foglio, 2000

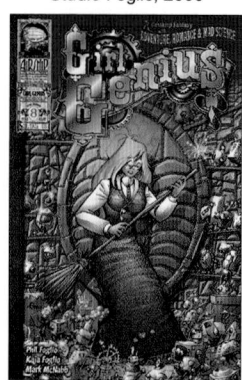

Written by Phil and Kaja Foglio and drawn by Phil (Funny Stuff Stocking Stuffer), Girl Genius is the story of Agatha Clay, a bespectacled student and lab assistant at Transylvania Polygnostic University in a world where the Industrial Revolution went out of control and left the world at the mercy of Mad Science. Agatha bumbles and fumbles, but her saga is just beginning, as this black-and-white series from StudioFoglio gets under way. She is destined for greatness in a universe rife with pneumatic robots, bizarre dirigibles, and scientists committed to discovery.

Ashcan 1	1.00
1-3	3.00
4-12	4.00

Girlhero
High Drive, 1993

1-3	3.00

Girl on Girl College Kink: New Year's Babes
Angel

1	3.00

Girl on Girl: Feedin' Time
Angel

1	3.00

Girl on Girl: Ticklish
Angel

1	3.00

Girls
Image, 2005

1	7.00
1/Variant	5.00
1/Sketch	6.00
2	4.00
2/Variant	5.00
3-20	3.00

Girls Bravo
Tokyopop, 2005

1-2	10.00

Girls' Love Stories
DC, 1949

1	325.00
2	165.00
3	130.00
4-11	110.00
12-22	75.00
23-32	48.00
33-49	38.00
50-71	30.00
72-94	25.00
95-105	20.00
106-111	17.00
112-123	15.00
124-143	14.00
144-164	9.00
165-180	7.00

Girls of '95: Good, Bad & Deadly
Lost Cause, 1996

1	4.00

Girls of Ninja High School
Antarctic, 1991

1-4	4.00
5	5.00
6-8/B	4.00
9	3.00

Girl Squad X
Fantaco

1	3.00

Girls' Romances
DC, 1950

1	400.00
2	225.00
3-10	115.00
11-20	80.00
21-30	50.00
31-70	40.00
71-90	26.00
91-100	22.00
101-108	18.00
109	65.00
110-120	15.00
121-140	13.00
141-160	8.00

Girl Talk
Fantagraphics, 1996

4	4.00

Girl: The Rule of Darkness
Cry for Dawn

1	3.00

Girl: The Second Coming
NBM

1	11.00

Girl Who Would Be Death
DC, 1998

1-4	3.00

Give It Up! and Other Short Stories
NBM, 1995

1	15.00

Give Me Liberty! (Rip Off)
Rip Off, 1976

1	4.00

Give Me Liberty
Dark Horse, 1990

1-4	5.00

G.I. War Tales
DC, 1973

DC attempted to revive the war comic craze of the sixties by putting reprints of Star Spangled War Stories, the successor of Star Spangled Comics of the forties, and other tales out under the title G.I. War Tales.

After four issues, they gave up. Without strong, continuing central characters such as Enemy Ace or The Unknown Soldier, no one was interested in seeing World War Two soldiers and sailors battling dinosaurs on forgotten islands, especially if they had been done before.

1	12.00
2	7.00
3-4	6.00

Gizmo
Mirage, 1986

1-6	2.00

Gizmo
Chance

1	3.00

Gizmo and the Fugitoid
Mirage, 1989

1-2	2.00

GLA
Marvel, 2005

1	5.00
2-4	3.00

Gladiator/Supreme
Marvel, 1997

1	5.00

Glamorous Graphix Presents
Glamorous Graphix, 1996

1	4.00

Glass Jaw
Clay Heeled

1	3.00

Global Force
Silverline
1-2 ....2.00

Global Frequency
DC, 2002
1-12 ....3.00

GloomCookie
Slave Labor, 1999
1-2 ....4.00
3-25 ....3.00

Gloom
APComics, 2005
1-2 ....4.00

Glorianna
Press This
1 ....4.00

Glory
Image, 1995

Glory was created by comics industry legend and one of the founders of Image Comics Rob Liefeld. This mini-series began in 1995.

Like DC's Wonder Woman, Glory is an Amazon who traces her history back to World War II. Her real name is Gloriana, and she is the daughter of the legendary Lady Demeter. In this series, she teams up with friends named Vandal and Rumble. In a story called, "Who Wrote the Book of Love?" Glory is framed for multiple murders, and the three friends have to find out who caused the frame-up and why. In doing so, they must also unravel the mystery behind a demonic "Book of Love" and a strange symbol that shows up at the murder scenes.

Mike Deodato handles the pencilling with scripts by Jo Duffy.

0-11 ....3.00
12 ....4.00
12/A 5.00
13-23 ....3.00

Glory & Friends Bikini Fest
Image, 1995
1-1/Variant 3.00

Glory & Friends Christmas Special
Image, 1995
1 .... 3.00

Glory & Friends Lingerie Special
Image, 1995
1-1/Variant 3.00

Glory/Angela: Angels in Hell
Image, 1996
1 .... 3.00

Glory/Avengelyne
Image, 1995
1/A-1/B 4.00

Glory/Celestine: Dark Angel
Image, 1996
1-2 .... 3.00

GLX-Mas Special
Marvel, 2006
1 .... 4.00

Glyph
Labor of Love
1-3 .... 5.00

G-Man
Image, 2005
1 .... 6.00

G-Men
Caliber
1 .... 3.00

Gnatrat: The Dark Gnat Returns
Prelude, 1986
1 .... 2.00

Gnatrat: The Movie
Innovation
1 .... 2.00

Gnome-Mobile
Gold Key, 1967
1 .... 25.00

Gnomes, Fairies, and Sex Kittens
Fantagraphics, 2006
1 .... 4.00

G'n'R's Greatest Hits
Revolutionary, 1993
1 .... 3.00

Go-Go
Charlton, 1966
1 .... 40.00
2-9 .... 30.00

Gobbledygook
Mirage
1 .... 110.00
2 .... 70.00

Gobbledygook
Mirage, 1986
1 .... 5.00

Goblin Lord
Goblin, 1996
1-6 .... 3.00

Goblin Magazine
Warren, 1982
1 .... 9.00
2-4 .... 5.00

Goblin Market
Tome
1 .... 3.00

Goblin Studios
Goblin, 1995
1-5 .... 2.00

Go Boy 7 Human Action Machine
Dark Horse, 2003
1-5 .... 3.00

Goddess
DC, 1995

Mudhawk is a borderline psychotic who believes in animal rights so fervently that he's been known to dangle shark hunters from fishing lines until they become shark food themselves. Jeff is a loser who decides to throw himself to the zoo lions when his girlfriend moves out. And Rosie -- Rosie has just gained psychic powers which result in geographically dislocating Scotland from the rest of the British Isles.

The lives of these three collide, when the CIA tries to kidnap Rosie for use in one of its secret projects. Perhaps not surprisingly, Rosie retaliates by psychically separating the agents' heads from their shoulders. In the course of the eight issues of this mini-series (scripted by Garth Ennis and drawn by Phil Winslade), Rosie and her friends must escape from the law, resolve old problems, and figure out why the universe has chosen the otherwise normal Rose Nolan to become a goddess.

1-8 ....3.00

Goddess
Twilight Twins

1 ....2.00

Godhead
Anubis

1-1/Ltd. 4.00
2-3 ....6.00

Godland
Image, 2005

1-14 ....3.00

Gods & Tulips
Westhampton

1 ....3.00

Godsent
Lock Graphic Publications, 1994

1 ....2.00

Gods for Hire
Hot, 1986

1-2 ....2.00

God's Hammer
Caliber, 1990

1-3 ....3.00

God's Smuggler
Spire

1 ....6.00

Godwheel
Malibu, 1995

0-3 ....3.00

Godzilla
Marvel, 1977

Gojira was released in Japan in 1954; with a name-change, cuts,

and additional scenes, Godzilla, King of the Monsters stomped into U.S. theaters the same year. Marvel imported Japanese cinema's favorite grumpy lizard in this 1970s series.

Eons ago, Godzilla, a hybrid of land and sea reptiles, was trapped in a state of suspended animation. Awakened by an undersea nuclear test, he rose again. Now, with fiery breath and awesome, city-smashing strength, Godzilla shows the world how much he hates having his sleep interrupted.

Fearsome but not evil, Godzilla is befriended by a young man, Rob Takiguchi. Rob has his hands full, however, trying to keep this giant friend out of trouble and out of the hands of those who want to control him.

1 .... 12.00
1/35¢ 15.00
2 .... 6.00
2/35¢ 15.00
3-3/Whitman 5.00
3/35¢ 15.00
4-5 .... 5.00
6-10 .... 4.00
11-24 .... 3.00

Godzilla
Dark Horse, 1987

1 .... 4.00
2-6 .... 3.00

Godzilla
Dark Horse, 1995

0 .... 4.00
1-16 .... 3.00

Godzilla Color Special
Dark Horse, 1992

1 .... 4.00

Godzilla, King of the Monsters Special
Dark Horse, 1987

1/A-1/B 3.00

Godzilla vs. Barkley
Dark Horse, 1993

1 .... 3.00

Godzilla Versus Hero Zero
Dark Horse, 1995

1 .... 3.00

Go Girl!
Image, 2000

1-5 .... 4.00

Go-Go Boy Ashcan
Mermaid

Ashcan 1 .... 1.00

Gog (Villains)
DC, 1998

1 .... 2.00

Going Home
Aardvark-Vanaheim

1 .... 2.00

Gojin
Antarctic, 1995

1-8 .... 3.00

Gold Digger
Antarctic, 1992

1 .... 35.00
2 .... 20.00
3 .... 15.00
4 .... 13.00
5 .... 3.00
6 .... 3.00
7-22 .... 3.00
24-70 .... 3.00

Gold Digger
Antarctic, 1993

1 .... 5.00
2-50 .... 4.00
50/CS 6.00
Ann 1-5 .... 4.00
Special 1 .... 3.00

Gold Digger
Antarctic, 1999

1 .... 4.00
2-38 .... 3.00
39-44 .... 4.00
45-110 .... 3.00
Ann 4 .... 5.00

Gold Digger Annual 2005
Antarctic, 2005

1 .... 5.00

Gold Digger: Beta
Antarctic, 1998

Whether it takes its major inspiration from Indiana Jones or Tomb Raider's Lara Croft, or both, those influences are on display here in this manga-style comic. Two pairs of rival explorer-adventurers, all female, do heated battle in their respective quests to uncover earth's greatest archaeological secrets wherever they might be and no matter how great the danger. On one side, the cool and confident Penny Pincer and her somewhat cowardly, genetically engineered companion. On the other, envious and competitive Gina and her sister, the were-cheetah Britanny. Sometimes working against each other, sometimes forced to work together, the rivalry persists across this lighthearted series. The obstacles can be anything from each other to a strange alien creature (the "Beta" of the title) made of silver-a special problem, of course, for the otherwise powerful were-cheetah.

Full-color from Antarctic Press, the title is created, written, and drawn by Fred Perry.

1 ....3.00

Gold Digger: Edge Guard
Radio, 2000

1-5..3.00

Gold Digger Halloween Special
Antarctic, 2005

1 ....3.00

Gold Digger Mangazine
Antarctic, 1994

1-1/2nd....................................3.00

Gold Digger Perfect Memory
Antarctic, 1996

1 ....5.00
2-4..7.00

Gold Digger Swimsuit End of Summer Special
Antarctic, 2003

1 ....5.00

Gold Digger: Swimsuit End of Summer Special 2005
Antarctic, 2005

0 ....5.00

Gold Digger Swimsuit Special
Antarctic, 2000

1-4..5.00

Golden Age
DC, 1993

1-4..6.00

Golden Age Of Triple-X
Revisionary, 1997

1 ....4.00

Golden Age of Triple-X: John Holmes Special "Johnny Does Paris"
Re-Visionary

1 .... 3.00

Golden Age Secret Files
DC, 2001

1 .... 5.00

Golden Age Sheena
AC

1 .... 10.00

Golden Arrow
Fawcett, 1942

1 .... 900.00
2 .... 365.00
3-5 .... 250.00
6 .... 235.00

Golden Comics Digest
Gold Key, 1969

1-30 .... 20.00
31-48 .... 15.00

Golden Dragon
Synchronicity, 1987

1 .... 2.00

Golden Features (Jerry Iger's...)
Blackthorne, 1986

1-6 .... 2.00

Golden Lad
Fact and Fiction, 1945

1 .... 650.00
2 .... 375.00
3-4 .... 285.00
5 .... 250.00

Golden Plates
AAA Pop, 2004

1-3 .... 8.00

Golden Warrior
Industrial Design, 1997

1 .... 3.00

Golden Warrior Iczer One
Antarctic, 1994

1-5 .... 3.00

Golden West Rodeo Treasury
Dell, 1957

1 .... 65.00

Goldfish
Image

1 .... 17.00
1/Deluxe 20.00

Gold Key Spotlight
Gold Key, 1976

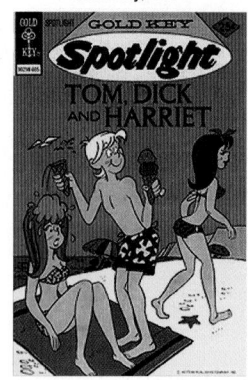

Gold Key Spotlight was a showcase for a variety of Gold Key comics features. In its 11 issues that ran for nearly two years, it spanned the whole range of genres, from the lighthearted high school comedy of Tom, Dick and Harriet to the far-off science-fiction of Tragg and the Sky Gods. Other Gold Key features such as O.G. Whiz, Cracky, Dagar, Wacky Witch, and Dr. Spektor (the latter from Spine-Tingling Tales) also put in appearances in their own issues of this series.

The series provides another opportunity for fans to pick up stories of their favorite characters.

1 .... 6.00
2-11 .... 4.00

Gold Medal Comics
Cambridge, 1945

1 .... 175.00

Goldyn 3-D
Blackthorne

1 .... 2.00

Golgothika
Caliber, 1996

1-4 .... 3.00

Golgo 13
Lead

1 .... 1.00
2 .... 2.00

Golgo 13
Viz

1-3 .... 5.00

Go-Man!
Caliber, 1989

1-4 .... 3.00

Gomer Pyle
Gold Key, 1966

1 .... 40.00
2-3 .... 25.00

Gon
DC, 1996
1-4 ....6.00
5 ....7.00

Gonad the Barbarian
Eternity
1 ....2.00

Gon Color Spectacular
DC
1 ....6.00

Gon on Safari
DC, 2000

Writer/artist Masashi Tanaka's poignant tales of world's smallest and fiercest dinosaur are wordless, but speak volumes. In this collection of stories from DC's Paradox Press imprint, Gon befriends a dying elephant and aids him in his journey to the sacred elephant graveyard, where he will find his final rest. Another tale finds Gon exploring his paternal feelings for a net of eagle-chicks that has landed on his head. The third tale in this paperback collection finds littlest dino and his friends making an incredible journey in spite of impossible odds, while the final story speaks to Gon's endurance-both physical and spiritual-as he makes his way to the top of a mountain.

Tanaka's stories are wonderful-simple, but powerful in terms of their characterization and their universal truths; and his artwork is drop-dead gorgeous. If you haven't yet discovered Gon, you must.

1 ....8.00

Gon Underground
DC
1 ....8.00

Good-Bye, Chunky Rice
Top Shelf, 1999
1 ....15.00

Good Girl Art Quarterly
AC, 1990
1-18 .... 4.00
19 .... 7.00

Good Girls
Fantagraphics, 1987
1-6 .... 2.00

Good Guys
Defiant, 1993
1-12 .... 3.00

Goody Good Comics
Fantagraphics, 2000
1 .... 3.00

Goofy
Dell, 1962
-211 .... 40.00

Goofy Adventures
Disney, 1990
1 .... 3.00
2-17 .... 2.00

Goofy Comics
Nedor, 1943
1 .... 125.00
2 .... 60.00
3-5 .... 45.00
6-10 .... 38.00
11-19 .... 32.00
20-29 .... 45.00
30-35 .... 38.00
36-48 .... 24.00

Goon
Avatar, 1999
1 .... 15.00
2-3 .... 10.00

Goon
Albatross Exploding, 2002
1-1/Variant............................ 10.00
2-4 .... 5.00

Goon
Dark Horse, 2003
1-30 .... 3.00

Goon Noir
Dark Horse, 2006
1-2 .... 3.00

Goon Patrol
Pinnacle
1 .... 2.00

Gordon Yamamoto and the King of the Geeks
Humble, 1997

by Gene Yang

Gordon Yamamoto and his friend Devon delighted each year in picking one kid to terrorize in school. They would appoint their victim "king of the geeks" and rough him up, lob "not-water balloons" at him, and generally make his life miserable.

Gordon was about to learn a hard lesson this year. He's been having strange dreams involving foreign objects in his nose. In time, he discovered that Cuticle-3, a microdroid of the San Peligran Order of galactic peacekeepers was using his brain as excess data storage. The San Peligran Order looks for individuals who either have superior brain capacity, or don't use much of what they have. Gordon (who fell into the latter category) had to make contact with the other local San Peligran Order victim, who as it turned out, was the very geek he had been victimizing. All in all, it's a strange, but worthy story by Gene Yang.

1 .... 3.00

Gore Shriek
Fantaco, 1986
1-4 .... 3.00
5-6 .... 4.00
Ann 1 .... 5.00

Gore Shriek
Fantaco
1-3 .... 3.00

Gore Shriek Delectus
Fantaco
1 .... 9.00

Gorgana's Ghoul Gallery
AC
1-2 .... 3.00

Gorgo
Charlton, 1961

1	200.00
2-3	100.00
4	75.00
5	50.00
6-10	40.00
11-16	30.00
17-23	20.00

Gorgon
Venus, 1996

1-5 .... 3.00

Gorilla Gunslinger
Mojo

0 .... 1.00

Gotcha!
Rip Off, 1991

1 .... 3.00

G.O.T.H.
Verotik, 1996

1-3 .... 3.00

Gotham Central
DC, 2003

1-40 .... 3.00

Gotham Girls
DC, 2002

1-5 .... 2.00

Gotham Nights
DC, 1992

A desperate man who turns to crime to support his family becomes convinced that his wife is cheating on him.

An attractive woman who has her heart broken going from bed to bed ignores the longtime friend who could give her the love she needs.

An old man, loved by his wife, but dying of disease and high medical bills, looks for a way out for both of them.

A train-station doughnut-seller is bored with life. She's convinced that the man who comes by for breakfast every day is really Batman and is sure that he secretly loves her. One day, she climbs to a rooftop with a hunting rifle in order to force his hand.

In a city built for giants, the streets are filled with regular people. Gotham Nights is their story.

1-4 .... 2.00

Gotham Nights II
DC, 1995

1-4 .... 2.00

Gothic
5th Panel, 1997

1-2 .... 3.00

Gothic Moon
Anarchy Bridgeworks

1 .... 6.00

Gothic Nights
Rebel

1-2 .... 2.00

Gothic Red
Boneyard, 1997

1-3 .... 3.00

Gothic Scrolls, The: Drayven
Davdez, 1997

1-3	3.00
Ashcan 1	2.00

Grackle
Acclaim, 1997

1-4 .... 3.00

Graffiti Kitchen
Tundra

1 .... 3.00

Grafik Muzik
Caliber, 1990

1	15.00
2	10.00
3-4	6.00

Grammar Patrol
Castel

1 .... 2.00

Grand Prix
Charlton, 1967

Porsches, Lotuses, Ferraris, and other formula cars are the real stars of this series, which features the European style of cross-country auto racing. Although the cars are the hook, for plot purposes, the stories pivot on the drivers, who race for reasons ranging from familial duty to proving self-worth to greed. Artists like Don Perlin (who drew The Defenders) and Jack Keller (who filled in on Kid Colt Outlaw for Marvel) contributed art.

Like romance comics and military titles, comics for racing enthusiasts are a branch of the industry that has withered and died for lack of enthusiasm. This title from Charlton was one of a stable of four comics relating to auto sports. Hot Rods and Racing Cars, Worlds of Wheels, and Drag n' Wheels populated the comics racks along side Grand Prix in the late 1960s.

-- *George Haberberger*

16	14.00
17-20	8.00
21-31	5.00

Grand Slam Comics
Double A Comics, 1943

51-53 .... 45.00

Graphic
Fantaco

1 .... 4.00

Graphic Heroes in House of Cards
Graphic Staffing

1 .... 1.00

Graphic Story Monthly
Fantagraphics

1-7 .... 4.00

Graphique Musique
Slave Labor, 1989

1-3 .... 8.00

Grasa Del Sol
Estatua, 1998

1 .... 3.00

Grateful Dead Comix
Kitchen Sink, 1992

1	6.00
2-7	5.00

Grateful Dead Comix
Kitchen Sink, 1994

1-2 .... 4.00

Gravediggers
Acclaim, 1996

1-4 .... 3.00

Gravedigger Tales
Avalon

1 .... 3.00

Grave Grrrls: Destroyers of the Dead
Moonstone, 2005
1 ....4.00

Gravestone
Malibu, 1993
1-7..2.00

Gravestown
Ariel, 1997
1 ....3.00

Grave Tales
Hamilton, 1991
1-3..4.00

Gravity
Marvel, 2005
1-5..3.00

Gray Area
Image, 2004
1 ....7.00
1/Incentive.................................8.00
1/SigSeries.............................20.00
1/Conv....................................15.00
2-3..6.00

Grease Monkey
Kitchen Sink, 1995
1-2..4.00

Grease Monkey
Image, 1998
1-2..3.00

Great Action Comics
I.W.
8-9..70.00

Great American Western
AC, 1988
1 ....2.00
2-3..3.00
4 ....4.00
5 ....5.00

Great Big Beef
ERR, 1996
97-99..2.00

Great Comics
Great Comics, 1941
1 ....500.00
2 ....285.00
3 ....660.00
☛Hitler story

Great Comics
Novack, 1945
1 ....165.00
1/A..200.00
1/B..140.00
1/C 85.00

Great Detective
Avalon
1-7.. 3.00

Greater Mercury Comics Action
Greater Mercury, 1990
5-9.. 2.00

Greatest American Comic Book
Ocean, 1992
1 .... 3.00

Greatest Diggs of All Time!
Rip Off, 1991
1 .... 2.00

Greatest Stars of the NBA: Allen Iverson
Tokyopop, 2005
1 .... 8.00

Greatest Stars of the NBA: Future Greats
Tokyopop, 2005
1 .... 8.00

Great Exploits
Decker, 1957
1 .... 25.00

Great Galaxies
Zub
0-5.. 3.00
6/Ashcan 1.00

Great Gazoo
Charlton, 1973
1 .... 20.00
2 .... 12.00
3-20 .... 10.00

Great Morons in History
Revolutionary, 1993
1 .... 3.00

Great Society Comic Book
Parallax
1 .... 16.00
2 .... 12.00

Greeenlock
Aircel
1 .... 3.00

Green Arrow
DC, 1983
1-2.. 3.00
3-4.. 2.00

Green Arrow
DC, 1988

Originally introduced in More Fun Comics #73 (Nov 1941), Oliver Queen was a millionaire, who fell overboard off a yacht one night at sea. Washed up on a deserted island, Queen found himself with time on his hands and learned to wield a bow and arrow to survive with. He eventually devised trick arrows to help catch small game and, when a group of criminal invaded the island, he captured them and returned home, turning his new-found skills into a crime-fighting career that closely paralleled Batman's with a young sidekick (Speedy), an Arrowcave, Arrowcar, and Arrowplane.

After losing his fortune and fancier gadgets due to an unscrupulous partner's dealings, Queen took a more simplistic approach to crimefighting in Green Arrow: The Longbow Hunters by Mike Grell, eschewing the trick arrows for more traditional ones.

This series continued the adventures from that prestige format mini-series, with Queen's illegitimate son, Connor, taking on the title role near the series' end.
- Brent

0 .... 3.00
1 .... 4.00
2-20 .... 2.00
21 .... 3.00
22-49 .... 2.00
50 .... 3.00
51-74 .... 2.00
75 .... 3.00
76-95 .... 2.00
96-99 .... 3.00
100 .... 7.00
101 .... 18.00
☛Death of O. Queen
102-124 .... 2.00
125 .... 4.00
126-136 .... 3.00

137 ....4.00
1000000 ....3.00
Ann 1 ....4.00
Ann 2-5 ....3.00
Ann 6-7 ....4.00

Green Arrow
DC, 1998

1-2 ....6.00
3-42 ....3.00
43 ....7.00
☞Speedy HIV
44 ....4.00
45-49 ....3.00
50 ....4.00
51-70 ....3.00

Green Arrow:
Archer's Quest
DC, 2003

1 ....20.00
1/2nd 15.00

Green Arrow
by Jack Kirby
DC, 2001

nn 6.00

Green Arrow:
The Longbow Hunters
DC, 1987

1 ....4.00
1/2nd-3 ....3.00

Green Arrow:
The Wonder Year
DC, 1993

1-4 ....2.00

Green Candles
DC, 1995

1-3 ....6.00

Greener Pastures
Kronos, 1994

1-4 ....3.00
4.5 ....2.00
5-7 ....3.00

Green Giant Comics
Pelican, 1940

1 ....6,000.00

Green Goblin
Marvel, 1995

Long-time readers of Marvel comics will recognize the Green Goblin as the arch-nemesis of Spider-Man. In this series, the Green Goblin's mantle has passed to Philip Urich, nephew of veteran Daily Bugle reporter Ben Urich. Even more interestingly, this Green Goblin was not a villain.

This series portrays a young man who has acquired an assortment of weapons and paraphernalia and who tries to do the right thing without placing himself in danger. The tried-and-true Marvel tactic of depicting ordinary people dealing with extraordinary situations is much in evidence here, and evokes the feel of early Spider-Man stories. But can the super-villain legacy of Green Goblin be overcome? Though Philip Urich revels in the excitement, he may not have the devotion necessary to be accepted as a hero.

-- George Haberberger

1 .... 3.00
2-13 .... 2.00

Green-Grey Sponge-Suit
Sushi Turtles
Mirage

1 .... 4.00

Greenhaven
Aircel

1-3 .... 2.00

Green Hornet
Gold Key, 1967

1 .... 120.00
2-3 .... 80.00

Green Hornet
Now, 1989

1-1/2nd 4.00
2 .... 3.00
3-14 .... 2.00

Green Hornet
Now, 1991

1-11 .... 2.00
12 .... 3.00
13-21 .... 2.00
22-23 .... 3.00
24-26 .... 2.00
27 .... 3.00
28-37 .... 2.00
38 .... 3.00
39 .... 2.00
40-Ann 1994 .... 3.00

Green Hornet
Anniversary Special
Now, 1992

1 .... 3.00
2-3 .... 2.00

Green Hornet Comics
Harvey, 1940

Frustrated with the slow speed of justice and the corruption of the police, newspaper publisher Brit Reid donned a green hat, coat, and mask to fight denizens of the underworld as the Green Hornet. Alongside his Asian servant Kato, the Green Hornet made life tough for racketeers and crooks on his famous radio show during the 1930s and 40s, and inevitably made the jump to comics early in the Golden Age. First published by Holyoke, The Green Hornet was taken over by Harvey, which continued the run through the late 1940s. The Hornet has made several comebacks, including a notable television series in the 1960s featuring the young Bruce Lee as Kato.

1 .... 4,500.00
2 .... 1,500.00
3 .... 1,250.00
4-6 .... 1,000.00
7 .... 900.00
8 .... 750.00
9 .... 900.00
10 .... 650.00
11-19 .... 600.00
20 .... 700.00

21-31	400.00
32-38	300.00
39	350.00
40-47	250.00

Green Hornet, The: Dark Tomorrow
Now, 1993

1-3	3.00

Green Hornet, The: Solitary Sentinel
Now, 1992

1-3	3.00

Green Lama
Spark, 1944

1	750.00
2	475.00
3	340.00
4-5	240.00
6-8	180.00

Green Lantern
DC, 1941

1	37,500.00

☞Green Lantern origin

2	7,500.00
3	5,500.00
4	4,000.00
5	2,750.00
6	2,250.00
7-10	2,000.00
11-20	1,500.00
21-30	1,250.00
31-34	1,000.00
35-38	1,250.00

Green Lantern
DC, 1960

In Showcase #22, test pilot Hal Jordan encountered a dying alien who gave Hal his power ring. Upon wearing that ring, Hal became Earth¬s new Green Lantern (the Golden Age version, Alan Scott, operated on an alternate Earth). Hal¬s power ring gave him almost unlimited powers, but the ring needed to be recharged from a special battery every 24 hours. He also had a weakness to anything yellow. For instance, bullets would bounce off the energy field created by his ring, but Hal could still be knocked out by a club painted yellow.

1	4,500.00

☞1st Guardians

2	1,000.00
3	600.00
4-5	450.00
6	400.00
7-10	300.00
11-12	200.00
13	250.00
14-16	175.00
17-20	150.00
21-27	125.00
28-30	100.00
31-39	75.00
40	350.00

☞GA Lantern app.

41-49	75.00
50-51	60.00
52	80.00
53-58	55.00
59	125.00

☞1st Guy Gardner

60-75	50.00
76	375.00

☞Green Arrow starts

77-78	75.00
79-84	60.00
85	50.00
86	60.00

☞Drug issue

87	50.00
88	30.00
89	45.00
90-92	10.00
93-99	9.00
100	10.00
101	9.00
102-111	4.00
112	8.00
113-115	3.00
116	8.00
116/Whitman	16.00
117	3.00
117/Whitman	6.00
118	3.00
118/Whitman	6.00
119	3.00
119/Whitman	5.00
120	3.00
120/Whitman	5.00
121	3.00
121/Whitman	5.00
122	4.00
123	6.00
124-130	3.00
131-135	2.00
136-139	3.00
140	2.00
141	5.00

☞1st Omega Men

142-144	3.00
145-149	2.00
150	5.00
151-173	2.00
174	3.00
175-178	2.00
179	3.00
180-193	2.00
194	3.00
195	4.00
196-205	2.00
Special 1-2	3.00

Green Lantern
DC, 1990

0	4.00
1	7.00
2	3.00
3-26	2.00
27-45	1.00
46	4.00
47	2.00
48-50	5.00
51	3.00
52-80	2.00
81	3.00
81/Variant	4.00
82-99	2.00
100/A	5.00
100/B	3.00
101-149	2.00
150	4.00
151-174	2.00
175	4.00
176	8.00
177	4.00
178-181	2.00
1000000	3.00
Ann 1	4.00
Ann 2-3	3.00
Ann 4	4.00
Ann 5	3.00
Ann 6	4.00
Ann 7-8	3.00
Ann 9	4.00
Ann 1963	6.00
GS 1-2	5.00
GS 3	6.00
3D 1	5.00
3D 1/Ltd.	17.00

Green Lantern
DC, 2005

1	6.00
2	4.00
3-24	3.00
25	5.00
26-40	3.00

Green Lantern/ Adam Strange
DC, 2000

1	3.00

Green Lantern/Atom
DC, 2000

1	3.00

Green Lantern: Brightest Day, Blackest Night
DC, 2002

1	6.00

Green Lantern: Circle of Fire
DC, 2000
1-2 .... 5.00

Green Lantern Corps
DC, 1985
206-224 .... 2.00
Ann 1 .... 3.00
Ann 2-3 .... 2.00

Green Lantern Corps Quarterly
DC, 1992
1-8 .... 3.00

Green Lantern Corps: Recharge
DC, 2005
1 .... 4.00
2-5 .... 3.00

Green Lantern Corps
DC, 2006
1-40 .... 3.00

Green Lantern: Dragon Lord
DC, 2001
1-3 .... 5.00

Green Lantern: Emerald Allies
DC, 2000
1 .... 15.00

Green Lantern: Emerald Dawn
DC, 1989

Long a stalwart yet undeveloped character, Hal Jordan (aka Green Lantern) has long been one of the cornerstones of DC's modern era. However, his personal legend underwent a fairly major revision in this 1989 mini-series.

As a boy, Hal had worshipped his father, Lt. Martin Jordan, Ferris Aircraft's test pilot. Then, on a fateful day, Lt. Jordan's craft crashed in the desert, killing him in the resultant fireball. Since that day, Hal had always tried to live up to his father's reputation -- and had always come up short. He was kept on at Ferris Aircraft only out respect for his father -- and the fact that he was dating the boss' daughter. Still, this somewhat cowardly loser dreamed of flying. As it turned out, his dream came true when he met a dying member of the Green Lantern Corps who gave him his ring and battery. Now, Hal had the power to be a hero -- if he could find the courage.

1-6 .... 2.00

Green Lantern: Emerald Dawn II
DC, 1991
1 .... 2.00
2-6 .... 1.00

Green Lantern: Emerald Twilight New Dawn
DC, 2003
1 .... 20.00

Green Lantern: Evil's Might
DC, 2002
1-3 .... 6.00

Green Lantern/Firestorm
DC, 2000
1 .... 3.00

Green Lantern/Flash: Faster Friends
DC
1 .... 5.00

Green Lantern Gallery
DC, 1996
1 .... 4.00

Green Lantern: Ganthet's Tale
DC, 1992
1 .... 6.00

Green Lantern/ Green Arrow
DC, 1983
1-7 .... 4.00

Green Lantern/ Green Lantern
DC, 2000
1 .... 3.00

Green Lantern-Legacy: The Last Will & Testament of Hal Jordan
DC, 2002
1 .... 25.00

Green Lantern: Mosaic
DC, 1992
1-18 .... 1.00

Green Lantern: 1001 Emerald Nights
DC, 2001
1 .... 7.00

Green Lantern: Our Worlds At War
DC, 2001
1 .... 3.00

Green Lantern Plus
DC, 1996
1 .... 3.00

Green Lantern/ Power Girl
DC, 2000
1 .... 3.00

Green Lantern: Rebirth
DC, 2004
1 .... 10.00
1/2nd 12.00
1/3rd 5.00
2 .... 6.00
2/2nd 3.00
3 .... 4.00
4-6 .... 3.00

Green Lantern Secret Files
DC, 1998
1-3 .... 5.00

Green Lantern/Sentinel: Heart of Darkness
DC, 1998
1-3 .... 2.00

Green Lantern/Silver Surfer: Unholy Alliances
DC, 1995
1 .... 5.00

Green Lantern Sinestro Corps Special
DC, 2007
1 .... 5.00

Green Lantern/ Superman: Legend of the Green Flame
DC, 2000
1 .... 6.00

Green Lantern: The New Corps
DC, 1999
1 .... 5.00
2 .... 5.00

Green Lantern vs. Aliens
DC, 2000
1-4 .... 3.00

Green Lantern: Willworld
DC, 2001

1	25.00
2	18.00

Greenleaf in Exile
Cat's Paw

1-6	3.00

Greenlock
Aircel, 1991

1	3.00

Green Mask
Fox, 1940

In the spirit of many other super-hero adventures of the Golden Age, The Green Mask featured a non-super-powered hero who donned, what else, a Green Mask. Additionally attired in blue tights and a green cape, The Green Mask was accompanied by a young sidekick, Domino (a name taken from the boy's type of mask, although he did occasionally wear a cowl similar to his mentor's).

With Lou Fine covers and art by George Tuska and Bob Powell, the series ran 17 issues from 1940 to 1946. Other features in the series included Rick Evans, Adventurer; Dick Transom, Detective; and One Round Hogan.
- Brent

1	2,850.00
2	1,200.00
3	650.00
4-5	475.00
6	345.00
7-10	250.00
11	185.00
12-17	140.00

Green Planet
Charlton, 1962

1	26.00

Green Skull
Known Associates

1	3.00

Gregory
DC, 2004

1-1/2nd	8.00
2	5.00
3	8.00
3/Gold	9.00
4	5.00

Gremlin Trouble
Anti-Ballistic, 1960

1	4.00
2-29	3.00
29-30	5.00
Special 1-2	3.00

Grendel
Comico, 1983

1	45.00
2	35.00
3	26.00

Grendel
Comico, 1986

1	5.00
1/2nd	3.00
2-5	4.00
6-15	3.00
16	4.00
17-32	3.00
33	4.00
34-39	3.00
40	4.00

Grendel: Black, White, & Red
Dark Horse, 1998

1-4	4.00

Grendel Classics
Dark Horse, 1995

Dark Horse revisits the world of Matt Wagner's original Grendel, Hunter Rose, in this two-issue series that reprints some early Comico material. Grendel has his fingers in a number of illicit pies in these film noir-type stories, but, unlike many costumed characters, he spends more his time as a presence in these atmospheric tales, rather than as an actual player. Grendel Classics finds Matt

Wagner at his best with the character that helped establish his reputation for excellence.

1-2	4.00

Grendel Cycle
Dark Horse, 1995

1	6.00

Grendel: Devil By the Deed
Comico, 1993

1	4.00
1/Ltd.	8.00
1/2nd	4.00

Grendel: Devil Child
Dark Horse, 1999

1-2	3.00

Grendel: Devil Quest
Dark Horse, 1995

1	5.00

Grendel: Devil's Legacy
Comico, 2000

1-12	3.00

Grendel: Devil's Reign
Dark Horse, 2004

1-7	4.00

Grendel: Devil's Vagary
Comico

1	8.00

Grendel: God & the Devil
Dark Horse, 2003

1-9	4.00
10	5.00

Grendel: Past Prime
Dark Horse, 2000

1	15.00

Grendel: Red, White & Black
Dark Horse, 2002

1-4	5.00

Grendel Tales: Devils and Deaths
Dark Horse, 1994

1-2	3.00

Grendel Tales: Devil's Choices
Dark Horse, 1995

1-4	3.00

Grendel Tales: Devil's Hammer
Dark Horse, 1994

1-3	3.00

Grendel Tales: Four Devils, One Hell
Dark Horse, 1993

1-6	3.00

Grendel Tales: Homecoming
Dark Horse, 1994
1-3..3.00

Grendel Tales: The Devil in Our Midst
Dark Horse, 1994

This volume of Grendel Tales is brought to you by Steve Seagle and Paul Grist. It begins with a Grendel being discovered aboard a pirate ship in the area of Cape Horn and then set adrift on a rowboat. Later, the Grendel (a suicidal lad named Jonah) washes up near an Antarctic ice station. The ice station watches over a toxic waste dumping ground which virtually covers the continent. Two months ago, the waste shipments stopped coming...and so did the supplies.

The crew was reluctant to take in the Grendel since one more mouth to feed meant that much less chance of survival for the rest of them. Only minutes after the Grendel arrived at the station, however, a bigger problem materialized: a virus infected one of the crew causing his body to virtually explode from the inside. Is Jonah's presence the crew's doom- or their best chance for survival?

1-5..3.00

Grendel Tales: The Devil May Care
Dark Horse, 1995
1-6..3.00

Grendel Tales: The Devil's Apprentice
Dark Horse, 1997
1-3..3.00

Grendel: The Devil Inside
Comico, 2001
1-3..3.00

Grendel: War Child
Dark Horse, 1992

This series takes place in the post-cataclysmic future, several years after Grendel #40, and the death of ruler Orion Assante. Those trouble-filled times become even more chaotic when the child heir to the throne, Jupiter Assante, is kidnapped. As it turns out, the kidnapper is none other than Grendel Prime.

Grendel is a fierce warrior who will stop at nothing to fulfill his duty to the dead ruler. This time that means saving the child from his demented mother and her cunning accomplices who have taken over control of the government. Thus Grendel spirits the child away for training and safekeeping.

But he'll be back - bringing woe to any who stand against him!

1 .... 4.00
2-9 .... 3.00
10 .... 4.00

Grenuord
Fantagraphics, 2005
1 .... 6.00

Grey
Viz, 1989
1-5.. 4.00
6-9 .... 3.00

Grey Legacy
Fragile Elite
1 .... 3.00

Greylore
Sirius Comics, 1985
1-5 .... 2.00

Greymatter
Alaffinity, 1993
1-11 .... 3.00

Greyshirt: Indigo Sunset
DC, 2001
1-6 .... 4.00

Griffin (Slave Labor)
Slave Labor, 1988
1-3 .... 2.00

Griffin
DC, 1991
1-6 .... 5.00

Griffin
Slave Labor, 1997
1 .... 3.00

Griffith Observatory
Fantagraphics
1 .... 5.00

Grifter and the Mask
Dark Horse, 1996
1-2 .... 3.00

Grifter/Badrock
Image, 1995
1/A-2/B 3.00

Grifter: One Shot
Image, 1995
1 .... 5.00

Grifter/Shi
Image, 1996
1-2 .... 3.00

Grifter
Image, 1995
1 .... 3.00
1/Direct.................................... 4.00
2-10 .... 2.00

Grifter
Image, 1996
1-14 .... 3.00

Grim Ghost
Atlas-Seaboard, 1975
1 .... 10.00
2-3 .... 5.00

Grimjack
First, 1984

Grimjack, together with BlackJacMac, Jericho, Chris

Heyman, and others fight to protect their city from murdering cyborgs, evil gangs, and all the other social ills that plague the world after a series of trade wars has nearly decimated the population. Grimjack works closely with BlackJacMac; together they're almost like a team of contemporary detectives. Jericho is in charge of letting them know the local action. Chris Heyman is one of the few remaining Free Marines in the world, a militaristic band of vigilantes. Each episode has more suspense than action and the cliff-hangers really leave you breathless for more.

Issue #26 of the series was backed with a much less serious story, as the Teenage Mutant Ninja Turtles made one of their first color appearances, visiting a transdimensional bar where they fight sailors, drink illegally (they're underage, after all!), and win a dance contest.

1	3.00
2-25	2.00
26	3.00
27-74	2.00
75	4.00
76-81	2.00

Grimjack Casefiles
First, 1990
1-5	2.00

Grimjack: Killer Instinct
Idea & Design Works, 2004
1-6	4.00

Grimlock
Asylum, 1996
1-3	3.00

Grimmax
Defiant, 1994
0	1.00

Grimm's Ghost Stories
Gold Key, 1972
1	14.00
2-5	8.00
6-10	6.00
11-30	4.00
31-42	3.00
43-44	4.00
45-54	3.00
55-60	5.00

Grimoire
Speakeasy Comics, 2005
1-5	3.00

Gringo
Caliber
1	2.00

Grips
Silverwolf, 1986
1	3.00
1/Ltd.	10.00
2-4	3.00

Grips
Greater Mercury, 1990
1-9	2.00
10-12	3.00

Grips Adventures
Greater Mercury, 1989
1-8	3.00

Grip: The Strange World of Men
DC, 2002
1-5	3.00

Grit Bath
Fantagraphics, 1993
1-3	3.00

Groo
Image, 1994
1	4.00
2-3	3.00
4-12	2.00

Groo
Dark Horse, 1998
1-4	3.00

Groo and Rufferto
(Sergio Aragonès')
Dark Horse, 1998
1-4	3.00

Groo: Death & Taxes
(Sergio Aragonès'...)
Dark Horse, 2001
1-4	3.00

Groo: Mightier than the Sword
(Sergio Aragonès')
Dark Horse, 2000
1-4	3.00

Groo Special
Eclipse, 1984
1	3.00

Groo The Wanderer
(Sergio Aragonès')
Pacific, 1982
1	7.00
2	5.00
3-4	4.00
5-8	3.00

Groo the Wanderer
Marvel, 1985

Epic Comics knew a winner when they saw it -- and peerless barbarian (and klutz) Groo was that winner (as much of a contradiction in terms as this sounds). So when they got the chance, Epic grabbed him.

So it happened that the adventures of Groo were chronicled in this highly popular Marvel series under the Epic imprint.

Nothing had really been changed from the original. Groo was still a likable lummox, addicted to wholesale slaughter and the taste of cheese dip. Disaster still befel all who make the mistake of enlisting his aid. And, yes, it was still one of the funniest magazines around.

1	5.00
2-3	4.00
4-30	3.00
31-49	2.00
50	3.00
51-99	2.00
100	3.00
101-120	2.00

Grootlore
Fantagraphics
1-2	2.00

Grootlore
Fantagraphics, 1991
1-3	2.00

Groovy
Marvel, 1968
1	25.00
2-3	16.00

Gross Point
DC, 1997
1-14	3.00

Grounded
Image, 2005
1	5.00
1/Variant	4.00

☛2nd print

2-5...3.00

16...4.00

Ground Pound! Comix
Blackthorne, 1987

1..2.00

Ground Zero
Eternity, 1991

Led Edwards is the pilot of a mini-submarine used as a sort of tug-boat, pulling vessels between the two islands making up the mining colony called Independence.

Edwards and his colleagues on the sub, Mark and Lynn, lead normal lives, until the day Independence Colony becomes ground zero for an alien invasion. Suddenly, bombs rain down from the sky, and the populace is being imprisoned.

The crew manages to submerge their vessel. They know they have to fight back or at least figure out what is happening. But what can three people on a mini-submarine do to turn back the alien hordes?

1-2...3.00

Group LaRue
(Mike Baron's...)
Innovation, 1989

1-4...2.00

Growing Up Enchanted
Too Hip Gotta Go, 2002

1-3...3.00

Grrl Scouts
(Jim Mahfood's...)
Oni, 1999

1-4...3.00

Grrl Scouts: Work Sucks
Image, 2003

1-4...3.00

Grrrl Squad
Amazing Aaron, 1999

1 .... 3.00

Grumpy Old Monsters
Idea & Design Works, 2003

1-3.. 4.00

Grun
Harrier, 1987

1-4.. 2.00

Grunts
Mirage, 1987

1 .... 2.00

Guano Comix
Print Mint

4 .... 3.00

Guardian
Spectrum, 1984

1-2.. 1.00

Guardian Angel
Image, 2002

1-2.. 3.00

Guardian Knights:
Demon's Knight
Limelight

1-2.. 3.00

Guardians
Marvel, 2004

1-5.. 3.00

Guardians of Metropolis
DC, 1994

1-4.. 2.00

Guardians of the Galaxy
Marvel, 1990

One of Marvel's few series set in the future to gain much traction, Guardians of the Galaxy follows a group of 31st Century refugees from the Badoon invasion of the solar system in their adventures in the cosmos.

Marvel had published appearances of Vance Astro, Charlie-27, Martinex, Yondu, and the others in various titles since the 1970s -- in fact, they probably spent more time visiting the 20th Century than they spent in their own. The team never really caught on until this title, in which writer Jim Valentino sent the Guardians off in search of the artifacts of the Marvel universe. Where did Captain America's shield wind up? Where did all the mutants go? Could there be a civilization based on Iron Man's armor? Great, imaginative stories were the rule for Valentino's tenure -- but the title faded after his departure.

-- John Jackson Miller

1-24 .... 2.00

25-25/Variant........................... 3.00

26-29 .... 2.00

30-35 .... 1.00

35/Variant 3.00

36-38 .... 1.00

39 .... 3.00

40-47 .... 1.00

48-50 .... 2.00

50/Variant 3.00

51-61 .... 2.00

62 .... 3.00

Ann 1....................................... 4.00

Ann 2-4................................... 3.00

Guerrilla Groundhog
Eclipse, 1987

1-2 .... 2.00

Guerrilla War
Dell, 1965

12-14 .... 10.00

Guff!
Dark Horse, 1998

1 .... 2.00

Gullivera
NBM, 1996

1 .... 14.00

Gumbo
Deadline Studios, 1994

1-2 .... 3.00

Gumby 3-D
Blackthorne

1-7 .... 3.00

Gumby's
Summer Fun Special
Comico, 1987

1 .... 3.00

Gumbys
Winter Fun Special
Comico

1 .... 3.00

Gumps
Bridgeport Herald, 1947

1 .... 75.00

2 .... 48.00

3	38.00
4-5	32.00

Guncandy
Image, 2005

1-2	6.00

Gundam Seed Astray R
Tokyopop, 2005

1-4	10.00

Gundam: The Origin
Viz, 2002

1-2	8.00

Gundam Wing: Blind Target
Viz, 2001

1-4	3.00

Gundam Wing: Episode Zero
Viz, 2001

1-8	3.00

Gunfighter
E.C., 1948

5	340.00
6	315.00
7-10	235.00
11-14	190.00

Gunfighters
Charlton, 1966

51-52	6.00
53	4.00
54-85	3.00

Gunfighters
Super

15	8.00

Gun Fighters in Hell
Rebel

1-5	2.00

Gunfire
DC, 1994

0-13	2.00

Gun Fury
Aircel, 1989

1-10	2.00

Gun Fury Returns
Aircel, 1990

1-4	2.00

Gun Fu: Showgirls Are Forever
Image, 2006

1	4.00

Gung Ho
Avalon

1	3.00

Gunhawk
Atlas, 1950

12	95.00
13	70.00
14-18	65.00

Gunhawks
Marvel, 1972

1	50.00
2	18.00
3-7	8.00

Gunhed
Viz

1-3	6.00

Gunner
Gun Dog, 1999

1	3.00

Gunparade March
ADV Manga, 2004

1-3	10.00

Gunpowder Girl & The Outlaw Squaw
Active Images, 2005

1	13.00

Gun Runner
Marvel, 1993

1	3.00
2-6	2.00

Guns Against Gangsters
Novelty, 1948

1	365.00
2	225.00
3-7	180.00

Gunslinger Girl
ADV Manga, 2004

1-3	10.00

Gunslingers
Marvel, 2000

1	3.00

Gunsmith Cats
Dark Horse, 1995

Gunsmith Cats follows two women who work in the traditionally male-dominated professions of bounty-hunting and demolition. Rally Vincent is the brunette gunsmith and sometime bounty hunter. "Minnie" May Hawkins is an ace demolitions expert when she's not busy driving Rally crazy.

An attorney contracts the duo to capture and deliver Dodge, Chicago's most notorious drug dealer. Dodge has more than one enemy, however. John Harper, Dodge's boss is afraid that Dodge will turn stool pigeon if caught by the police, and wants to "whack" him. The series is loaded with action as the two girls go from one problem to another in this black-and-white series.

Created by Kenichi Sonoda, with English translations provided by Studio Proteus and Dark Horse Comics, this was the first of a string of Gunsmith Cats limited series.

1-10	3.00

Gunsmith Cats: Bad Trip
Dark Horse, 1998

1-6	3.00

Gunsmith Cats: Bean Bandit
Dark Horse, 1999

1-9	3.00

Gunsmith Cats: Goldie vs. Misty
Dark Horse, 1997

1-7	3.00

Gunsmith Cats: Kidnapped
Dark Horse, 1999

1-10	3.00

Gunsmith Cats: Mister V
Dark Horse, 2000

1-11	4.00

Gunsmith Cats: Shades of Gray
Dark Horse, 1997

1-5	3.00

Gunsmith Cats Special
Dark Horse, 2001

1	3.00

Gunsmith Cats: The Return of Gray
Dark Horse, 1996

1-7	3.00

Gunsmoke Western
Marvel, 1955

32	90.00
33-35	70.00
36-40	60.00
41-50	52.00
51-60	44.00
61-69	36.00
70	30.00
71	26.00
72	34.00
73-77	26.00

Gunsmoke
Dell, 1957

6-10	35.00
11-20	25.00
21-27	22.00

Gunsmoke
Gold Key, 1969

1	30.00
2-6	20.00

Guns of Shar-Pei
Caliber

1-3	3.00

Guns of the Dragon
DC, 1998

1-4	3.00

Gun That Won the West
Winchester

1	24.00

Gun Theory
Marvel, 2003

1-2	3.00

Gunwitch, The: Outskirts of Doom
Oni, 2001

1	3.00

Gustav P.I.
NBM

1	10.00

Gutwallow
Numbskull, 1998

1-12	3.00

Gutwallow
Numbskull, 2000

1-3	3.00

Guy Gardner
DC, 1992

This is one crass, brash, annoying Guy.

Guy Gardner first appeared in 1968's Green Lantern #59. Even then, it seemed unbelievable that this despicable, self-serving opportunist could ever have been chosen by the Green Lantern Corps to become a Green Lantern. But of course, that's exactly what happened.

Although he was a founding member of the new Justice League, Guy retains a habit of rubbing his compatriots the wrong way. Perhaps it's all for the best that he now stars in a series of his own. Armed with Sinestro's power ring, he's got all of Green Lantern's power, but without the weakness to the color yellow that had traditionally plagued his emerald counterpart.

The series changes its name, partway through, to Guy Gardner, Warrior, to reflect changes in Guy's life.

1-5	2.00
6-14	1.00
15-16	2.00

Guy Gardner: Collateral Damage
DC, 2007

1-2	6.00

Guy Gardner Reborn
DC, 1992

1-3	5.00

Guy Gardner: Warrior
DC, 1994

0-24	2.00
25	3.00
26-29	2.00
29/Variant	3.00
30-44	2.00
Ann 1	4.00
Ann 2	3.00

Guy Pumpkinhead
Saint Gray

1	3.00

Guzzi Lemans
Antarctic, 1996

1-2	3.00

Gyre
Abaculus, 1997

Jacob Guyler's life has taken a strange turn in recent days. His dead father recently appeared before him, rambling incoherently about an ice pick lobotomy he'd been given, and imploring Jake to find the people responsible. Moments later, soldiers under the command of a General Mayhem burst into Jake's mobile home, kidnapped him, drugged him, and locked him into a "psyche-resistant" box. He was in the process of being flown to a secret research base when Jake-with the help of a few dozen lost spirits-shattered the box and freed him. Just then, the plane seemed to crash into a mountain...but luckily the last part, at least, was merely an illusion. The rest of Jake's life, unfortunately, is all too real.

Winner of the British National Comics Award for best new series, Gyre is a bizarre tale of secret government programs, lost souls, psychics, and Hell on Earth. It was created by Six Degrees' Marc Laming and Martin Shipp.

1	4.00
2-3	3.00
Ashcan 1	1.00
Special 1	5.00

Gyre: Traditions & Interruptions
Abaculus

1	1.00

Gyro Comics
Rip Off, 1988

1-3	2.00

Gyro Gearloose
Dell, 1962

-207	50.00

Deriving his powers from a vast store of lollipops,
Herbie Popnecker donned a super-costume and became The Fat Fury.

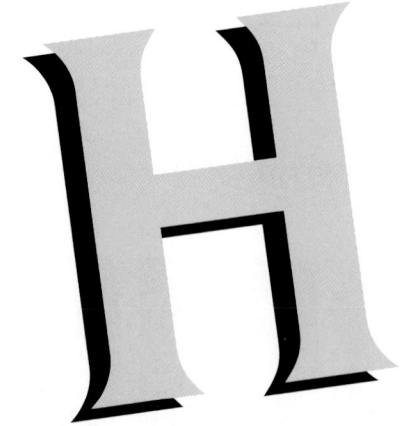

Robespier, a scrappy alley cat; and Daniel Spaniel, who leads a dog's life in the back pages of the comic book. The cast provides satisfactory laughs and entertainment in typical funny-animal style, benefiting from competent drawing and big, bold colorful layouts.

1	150.00
2	85.00
3	65.00
4-5	60.00
6-10	45.00
11-20	35.00
21-30	28.00
31-40	24.00
41-50	20.00
51-70	18.00
71-90	16.00
91-98	13.00
99	55.00

Hairbat
Screaming Rice
1-4 .... 3.00

Hairbat
Slave Labor, 1995
1 .... 3.00

Hair Bear Bunch
Gold Key, 1972
1 .... 10.00
2 .... 7.00
3-5 .... 6.00
6-9 .... 4.00

Hacker Files
DC, 1992
1-12 .... 2.00

Hackmasters of EverKnight
Kenzer and Company, 2000
1 .... 4.00
2-10 .... 3.00

Hack Slash: Land of Lost Toys
Devil's Due, 2005
1-3/Variant 3.00

Hack/Slash: Slice Hard
Devil's Due, 2006
1-1/Variant 5.00

Hack/Slash: Trailers
Devil's Due, 2006
1-1/2nd variant 3.00

Hägar the Horrible
Avalon
0 .... 2.00

Ha Ha Comics
ACG, 1943

Ha Ha Comics is another in the seemingly endless assortment of undistinguished funny-animal comics that brought cheer and good-natured gags to the lives of kids during the Golden Age. The mainstays in Ha Ha were: Izzy and Dizzy, a pair of twin troublemaking mice; the Impulsive Imps, who cavort around an Alice-in-Wonderland fantasy world;

Hairbutt the Hippo
Rat Race, 1992
1-3 .... 3.00

Hairbutt the Hippo Crime Files
Rat Race, 1995
1-6 .... 4.00

Hairbutt the Hippo: Private Eye
Ratrace, 1997
1-3 .... 3.00

Halifax Explosion
Halifax, 1997
1 .... 3.00

Hallelujah Trail
Dell, 1966
1 .... 30.00

Hall of Fame
J.C., 1983
1-3 .... 2.00

Hall of Heroes
Hall of Heroes, 1997
1-3 .... 3.00

Hall of Heroes Halloween Special
Hall of Heroes, 1997

1 ....3.00

Hall of Heroes Presents
Hall of Heroes, 1993

1-3 ....3.00

Hall of Heroes Presents
Hall of Heroes, 1996

0/A-5 ....3.00

Hall of Horrors
Hall of Heroes, 1997

1 ....3.00

Hallowed Knight
Shea, 1997

1-2 ....3.00

Halloween
Chaos, 2000

Fans of the long-running series of Halloween movies should enjoy this effort by British horror novelist Phil Nutman and artist David Brewer (Evil Ernie: Destroyer). In addition to some visceral, visual storytelling, readers get some interesting and thoroughly blood-curdling backstory on the history of Michael Myers, the man behind that freakish white mask.
-- *Stephen C. George*

1 ....3.00

Halloween Horror
Eclipse, 1987

1 ....2.00

Halloween Megazine
Marvel, 1996

1 ....3.00

Halloween Terror
Eternity

1 ....3.00

Halls of Horror (John Bolton's...)
Eclipse, 1985

1-3 .... 2.00

Halo, an Angel's Story
Sirius, 1996

1-4 .... 3.00

Halo Graphic Novel
Marvel, 2006

1 .... 25.00

Halo: Uprising
Marvel, 2007

1-2 .... 4.00

Hammer
Dark Horse, 1997

1-4 .... 3.00

Hammerlocke
DC, 1992

Archer Locke was the greatest scientist of his generation. His was the mind behind the Olympus Starbridge, a tower that stretched 72,000 kilometers into space. Cargo could be affordably transported up the starbridge into space, solving a crucial problem for man as he makes his journey toward the stars. Tragically, in 2025, Locke was caught in an accident during construction of the starbridge, and was critically injured. He survived thanks to an organization called UNICORN: The United Nations Covert Operations and Research Network. They rebuilt him using cyberprosthetics, but Locke put himself in self-imposed exile for seven years rather than be beholden to UNICORN and its director Jacob Kingman Rhee.

After Locke's daughter was kidnapped by a group of post-Luddites led by a lunatic named Tharn, Locke returned to save her, even it if meant playing into the

hands of the ambitious Rhee and selling out his dream.

1-9 .... 2.00

Hammer of God
First, 1990

1-4 .... 2.00

Hammer of God: Butch
Dark Horse, 1994

1-3 .... 3.00

Hammer of God: Pentathlon
Dark Horse

1 .... 3.00

Hammer of God: Sword of Justice
First, 1991

1-2 .... 5.00

Hammer of the Gods
Insight, 2001

1-5 .... 3.00

Hammer of the Gods Color Saga
Insight, 2001

nn 5.00

Hammer of the Gods: Hammer Hits China
Image, 2003

1-3 .... 3.00

Hammer, The: The Outsider
Dark Horse, 1999

1-3 .... 3.00

Hammer, The: Uncle Alex
Dark Horse, 1998

1 .... 3.00

Hamster Vice
Blackthorne, 1986

1-9 .... 2.00
3D 2....................................... 3.00

Hamster Vice
Eternity, 1989

1-2 .... 2.00

Hana-Kimi
Viz, 2004

1-8 .... 10.00

Hand of Fate (Ace)
Ace, 1951

8 .... 200.00
9-10 .... 140.00
11-15 .... 120.00
16-20 .... 100.00
21-23 .... 85.00
24 .... 115.00
25-25/A.................................... 85.00

Hand of Fate
Eclipse, 1988
1-3..2.00

Hand Shadows
Doyan, 1986
1-2..2.00

Hands Off!
Tokyopop, 2004
1-5..10.00

Hands Off!
Ward Sutton
1...3.00

Hands of the Dragon
Atlas-Seaboard, 1975
1...6.00

Hangman Comics
M.L.J., 1942
2......................................1,850.00
3......................................1,300.00
4-8.......................................950.00

Hanna-Barbera All-Stars
Archie, 1995
1-4..2.00

Hanna-Barbera Bandwagon
Gold Key, 1962
1...70.00
2-3...50.00

Hanna-Barbera Big Book
Harvey, 1993
1...2.00
3...3.00

Hanna-Barbera GS
Harvey, 1992
2...2.00

Hanna-Barbera Parade
Charlton, 1971

William Hanna met Joseph Barbera at MGM studios in 1939 and began one of the most prolific partnerships in animation history.

Hanna-Barbera Parade takes some of the animated characters created by the duo and puts them into original stories full of fun and excitement. The Flintstones, Dixie & Pixie, Huckleberry Hound, Yakky Doodle, Fibber Fox & Chopper, Hokey Wolf, Yogi Bear and Boo Boo, Quickdraw McGraw, Snagglepuss, and most of the animal characters created by Hanna and Barbera make appearances in these short, fun stories. Sadly, this particular series only lasted 10 issues.

1 .... 35.00
2 .... 18.00
3 .... 15.00
4 .... 13.00
5 .... 14.00
6-10 .... 12.00

Hanna-Barbera Presents
Archie, 1995
1-8 .... 2.00

Hanna-Barbera Presents All-New Comics
Harvey
1 .... 1.00

Hanna-Barbera Super TV Heroes
Gold Key, 1968
1 .... 58.00
☞Herculoids, Birdman
2-3 .... 36.00
4-5 .... 30.00
6-7 .... 35.00

Hansi, the Girl Who Loved the Swastika
Spire, 1973
1 .... 28.00

Hap Hazard
Fandom House
1 .... 2.00

Hap Hazard Comics
Ace, 1944
1 .... 75.00
2-6 .... 50.00
7-24 .... 40.00

Happenstance Jack, III
-Ism, 1998
1 .... 3.00

Happiest Millionaire
Gold Key, 1968
1 .... 25.00

Happy
Wonder Comics
1 .... 2.00

Happy Birthday Gnatrat!
Dimension
1 .... 2.00

Happy Birthday Martha Washington
Dark Horse, 1995
1 .... 3.00

Happy Comics
Standard, 1943

Like its sister publications Barnyard Comics and Coo Coo Comics, Happy Comics is an inoffensive humor title aimed at young readers. The most notable character is Happy Rabbit, an accident-prone bunny that comes off as a nicer version of the movie star Bugs Bunny. Unlike Bugs, Happy has a girlfriend (the hard-to-please Bonny Bunny) as well as an inventor uncle who can be counted on to provide him with an array of unworkable devices. Other characters featured in this series include Wally Wolf and Dizzy Duck: stock animal comedy characters.

Following #40 of this series, the title was renamed Happy Rabbit.

1 .... 125.00
2 .... 75.00
3-5 .... 45.00
6-10 .... 35.00
11-20 .... 28.00
21-31 .... 35.00
32 .... 90.00
33 .... 125.00
34-37 .... 35.00
38-40 .... 18.00

Happydale: Devils in the Desert
DC
1-2 .... 7.00

Happy Days
Gold Key, 1979
1 .... 20.00
2-6 .... 10.00

Happy Houlihans
E.C., 1947

1	200.00
2	165.00

Happy Rabbit
Standard, 1951

41-48	40.00

Harbinger
Valiant, 1992

Toyo Harada is the powerful head of the Harbinger Foundation. He named the Foundation as such because Harada, a mutant himself, believes other mutants to be the harbingers of a new era for humanity and he wants to gather such mutants to him and to train them as he sees fit.

Many Harbingers have grown to use their powers in Harada's personal service, becoming his "Eggbreakers." Others, fortunately, have rebelled - leaving the Foundation in order to lead lives of their own. This series focuses on these youths as they struggle to make it on their own and to use their powers for good.

0	6.00
0/Pink	65.00
0/2nd	3.00
1	30.00
2-3	8.00
4	11.00
5	10.00
6	9.00
7	7.00
8-10	4.00
11	2.00
12-28	1.00
29	2.00
30-34	1.00
35	2.00
36-38	1.00
39	3.00
40	4.00
41	5.00

Harbinger: Acts of God
Acclaim, 1998

1	4.00

Harbinger Files
Valiant, 1994

1	2.00
2	4.00

Hardball
Aircel, 1991

1-4	3.00

Hard Boiled
Dark Horse, 1990

1	5.00
2-3	6.00

Hardcase
Malibu, 1993

In 1992, Tom Hawke -- Hardcase -- is a member of the super-powered group known as The Squad. As "Ultras," they are used to overwhelming any foe easily. But on March 10, 1992, they fight their first really powerful enemy -- another Ultra. That battle ends in disaster, leaving two Squad members dead and a third crippled. Hardcase is the only one to pull through.

Hardcase gives up crime-fighting after this and uses his abilities to become a famed action movie actor. Once he was a hero, but now he swears to avoid such danger. All that changes, when a super-powered being named Headknocker begins slaughtering innocents in a bank robbery, scarcely a mile from where Hardcase is shooting a movie. Hardcase steps in and stops the carnage, but it is too late for some of Headknocker's victims. This tragedy teaches Hardcase a powerful lesson, and he once again joins the fight against crime.

1	3.00
1/Hologram	5.00

1/Ltd.	3.00
2-15	2.00
16	4.00
17-19	2.00
20-26	3.00

Hardcore Station
DC, 1998

1-6	3.00

H.A.R.D. Corps
Valiant, 1992

1	1.00
1/Gold	12.00
2-5	1.00
6-17	1.00
18	2.00
19-25	1.00
26-28	2.00
29	3.00
30	5.00

Hardkorr
Aircel, 1991

1-4	3.00

Hard Looks
Dark Horse, 1992

1-9	3.00
10	4.00

Hard Rock Comics
Revolutionary, 1992

1	5.00
2	4.00
3	3.00
4	4.00
5	8.00
5/2nd	5.00
6-20	3.00

Hard Time
DC, 2004

1-12	3.00

Hard Time: Season Two
DC, 2006

1-7	3.00

Hardware
DC, 1993

Hardware was one of the premiere titles of DC's ethnically

oriented Milestone line of comics. It featured Curtis Metcalf, a black genius from a working-class neighborhood. After he won a science fair, world-famous inventor Edwin Alva took him under his wing, and eventually gave him a job researching and inventing whatever he wanted, and paying him extremely well, to boot. Metcalf's inventions made millions for Alva's firm, but when Metcalf asked Alva to share some of the profits, all of Metcalf's illusions were shattered as his mentor and boss refuses. Metcalf can't quit, and, as he soon finds out, Alva is deeply involved in organized crime but is so powerful that he's beyond the reach of the law.

But knowledge is power. In his own laboratory, Metcalf creates a suit that gives him fantastic powers. With it, he takes on Alva, as Hardware. Once a cog in the corporate machinery, now he's out to strip some gears.

1	2.00
1/CS-1/Platinum	3.00
2-15	2.00
16	3.00
16/Variant	4.00
17-24	2.00
25	3.00
26-28	2.00
29-49	3.00
50	4.00

Hardwired
Bangtro, 1994

1	2.00

Hardy Boys
Gold Key, 1970

1	28.00
2-4	18.00

Har*Har
Fantagraphics

1-2	2.00

Hari Kari
Black Out

0-1	3.00

Hari Kari: Live & Untamed
Blackout

0	3.00
0/Variant	4.00
1	3.00

Hari Kari Private Gallery
Blackout

0	3.00

Hari Kari: Rebirth
Black Out

1	3.00

Hari Kari Resurrection
Blackout

1	3.00

Hari Kari: The Beginning
Black Out

1	3.00

Hari Kari: The Diary of Kari Sun
Blackout

1/2	3.00

Hari Kari: The Silence of Evil
Black Out

0	3.00

Harlem Globetrotters
Gold Key, 1972

Based on the Hanna-Barbera animated series from the early 1970s, the Harlem Globetrotters comic book ran between 1972 and 1975 and featured The Clown Princes of Basketball in a number of wild adventures, from being trapped in a haunted castle to being the prisoners of a race of abominable snowmen.

Of course, all of these situations can be remedied by a little friendly competition -- namely, a game of hoops in which Meadowlark, Curly, Geese, and the gang can show what they've got.

As the comics feature the most recognizable Globetrotter personalities of all time (and the cartoon is responsible for some part of this), no Globetrotter memorabilia collection should be without them.

1	13.00
2	9.00
3-5	7.00
6-12	5.00

Harlem Heroes
Fleetway-Quality

1-6	2.00

Harlequin
Caliber, 1993

1	3.00

Harley & Ivy: Love on the Lam
DC, 2001

1	6.00

Harley Quinn
DC, 2000

When psychiatrist Harleen Quinzel was assigned to the Joker's case, she never realized she would fall in love, go somewhat insane herself, and enter into a life of crime. But falling for the Clown Prince of Crime is a curse, and Harley soon finds herself out on her own in a one woman crime spree and loving every minute of her new found freedom.

DC finally brought the Harley Quinn character from the popular animated television series into its universe and discovered she was a character with staying power. Her series gives her a chance to interact with the rest of Gotham's best and worst.

1	4.00
2-10	3.00
11	2.00
12	3.00
13-22	2.00
23-38	3.00

Harley Quinn: Our Worlds At War
DC, 2001

1	3.00

Harley Rider
Hungness

1	2.00

Harold Hedd
Last Gasp Eco-Funnies

1	8.00
2	4.00

Harold Hedd in "Hitler's Cocaine"
Kitchen Sink, 1984

1-2 ....40.00

Harpy Pin-Up Special
Peregrine Entertainment, 1998

1 ....3.00

Harpy Preview
Ground Zero, 1996

1 ....3.00

Harpy: Prize of the Overlord
Ground Zero, 1996

1-6 ....3.00

Harrier Preview
Harrier

This book is exactly what the title suggests, an introduction and preview of the stories published by Harrier Comics. Their books cover a wide variety of interests, from the swordplay of Cuirass and the sci-fi pirate action of Nightbird, to the humor of the spoof Moon Fighting and the spy-game adventures of Grun.

Whether you are already a die-hard Harrier fan, or someone looking for something new without having to buy an entire series, Harrier Preview gives you what you want: good stories and interesting characters in a format that lets you complete a collection or just stop and browse.

1 ....1.00

Harriers
Express

1-3 ....3.00

Harrowers (Clive Barker's)
Marvel, 1993

1-6 ....3.00

Harry the Cop
Slave Labor, 1992

1-1/2nd 3.00

Harsh Realm
Harris, 1994

1-6 .... 3.00

Harte of Darkness
Eternity

1-4 .... 3.00

Harvey
Marvel, 1970

1 .... 50.00
2 .... 18.00
3 .... 8.00
4-6 .... 6.00

Harvey Collectors Comics
Harvey, 1975

1 .... 7.00
2 .... 4.00
3-16 .... 3.00

Harvey Comics Hits
Harvey, 1951

51 .... 120.00
52 .... 85.00
53 .... 110.00
54 .... 55.00
55 .... 45.00
56 .... 100.00
57 .... 70.00
58 .... 35.00
59 .... 40.00
60 .... 125.00
61 .... 140.00
62 .... 55.00

Harvey Comics Library
Harvey, 1952

1 .... 650.00
2 .... 140.00

Harvey Hits
Harvey, 1957

In its heyday from the mid-1950s to the late '70s, Harvey was a formidable comic-book presence, with a line-up that included The Friendly Ghost (Casper), Sad Sack, Wendy (the Good Little Witch), Little Dot, and Richie Rich, plus adventure stalwart The Phantom. Harvey Hits provides a rotating showcase for this cavalcade of kiddie faves, with the spotlight often on such backup characters as Casper's horse Nightmare (The Galloping Ghost), Sad Sack's dog (Muttsy), and, early in the run, Richie Rich himself, when the world's poorest little rich kid was second-fiddle to Little Dot. Harvey offered dependable entertainment by rarely straying from the formula of fun, wholesome stories, and simple, friendly-looking characters.

-- Rob Salkowitz

1 .... 165.00
2 .... 24.00
3 .... 550.00
4 .... 105.00
5 .... 18.00
6 .... 115.00
7 .... 120.00
8 .... 35.00
9 .... 315.00
10 .... 85.00
11 .... 55.00
12 .... 100.00
13 .... 65.00
14 .... 16.00
15 .... 100.00
16 .... 80.00
17 .... 34.00
18 .... 16.00
19 .... 36.00
20 .... 45.00
21 .... 48.00
22 .... 26.00
23 .... 40.00
24 .... 50.00
25 .... 14.00
26 .... 75.00
27 .... 40.00
28 .... 20.00
29 .... 24.00
30 .... 40.00
31 .... 12.00
32 .... 15.00
33 .... 32.00
34 .... 18.00
35 .... 12.00
36 .... 65.00
37 .... 30.00
38 .... 16.00
39 .... 12.00
40-41 .... 10.00
42 .... 12.00
43 .... 9.00
44 .... 52.00
45 .... 22.00
46-47 .... 10.00
48 .... 45.00
49 .... 55.00
50-51 .... 8.00
52 .... 20.00
53 .... 8.00

54	40.00
55	8.00
56	18.00
57	30.00
58	8.00
59	18.00
60	26.00
61	6.00
62	15.00
63	24.00
64	6.00
65	15.00
66	24.00
67	6.00
68	15.00
69	24.00
70	5.00
71	12.00
72	20.00
73-74	6.00
75	12.00
76-77	6.00
78	24.00
79-87	6.00
88	15.00
89-90	6.00
91-122	5.00

Harvey Hits Comics
Harvey, 1986

1	2.00
2	2.00
3	2.00
4	2.00
5	2.00
6	2.00

Harvey Spotlite
Harvey, 1987

1	4.00
2-4	3.00

Hate
Fantagraphics, 1990

Hate is the Harvey Award-winning title from Peter Bagge, following up on characters introduced in his previous work, Neat Stuff. Hate is primarily the story of a loser named Buddy Bradley, a man living the slacker equivalent of the good life in a dumpy apartment in Seattle. Buddy works at crummy jobs, watches the neighbors for recreation, and his main cultural aspiration is to become a true beer connoisseur.

His life may be purposeless and depressing, but he's really just an Everyman for the Nineties. Some years after the start of this 1990 series, journalists would give the post-Baby Boom generation the moniker "Generation X." Supposedly, Gen X-ers lived in an era of diminished expectations, condemned to dreary "McJobs" and cynical about what the future holds. If so, Buddy Bradley would make a fine candidate as the Generation-X poster child.

1	8.00
1/2nd	4.00
1/3rd	2.00
2	5.00
2/2nd-2/3rd	3.00
3	4.00
3/2nd-3/3rd	3.00
4	4.00
4/2nd	2.00
5	4.00
5/2nd	2.00
6	4.00
7-30	3.00

Hateball
Fantagraphics

Ann 1-6	5.00

Hate Jamboree!
Fantagraphics, 1998

1	4.00

Haunted
Charlton, 1971

This series was more commonly known by its cover title, "Baron Weirwulf's Haunted Library." Just as DC's Cain and Abel gave readers tours of the House of Mystery and the House of Secrets, Charlton's Baron Weirwulf led readers through his Haunted Library. The mysterious and sinister Weirwulf's whole home, particularly his library, held many a terrifying tale, often with ironic endings. Stories included a peculiar little girl who has found an unusual -- and supernatural -- way to be everywhere at once; a lifelike doll who becomes a cuckolded husband's only faithful companion; and a couple who is mysteriously brought together by death.

1	12.00
2-3	6.00
4-6	5.00
7-10	4.00
11-75	3.00

Haunted
Chaos, 2001

1-4	3.00

Haunted Love
Charlton, 1973

1	10.00
2	6.00
3	5.00
4-11	4.00

Haunted Man
Dark Horse, 2000

1-3	3.00

Haunted Mansion
Slave Labor, 2005

1	3.00

Haunted Thrills
Farrell, 1952

1	300.00
2	220.00
3	165.00
4-5	125.00
6-15	100.00
16-18	85.00

Haunt of Fear
E.C., 1950

1	2,750.00
2-3	1,000.00
4	750.00
5	550.00
6	425.00
7-9	400.00
10	375.00
11-13	300.00
14	450.00
15-18	300.00
19	375.00
20	300.00
21-28	250.00

Haunt of Fear
Gladstone, 1991

1-2	3.00

Haunt of Fear
Cochran, 1991

1-5	2.00

Haunt of Fear
Gemstone, 1992

1-15 ....2.00
16-28 ....3.00
Ann 1 ....9.00
Ann 2 ....10.00
Ann 3-4 ....11.00
Ann 5 ....12.00
Ann 6 ....9.00

Haunt of Horror
Marvel, 1974

1 ....8.00
2 ....6.00
3-5 ....5.00

Haunt of Horror: Edgar Allan Poe
Marvel, 2006

1-3 ....4.00

Have Gun, Will Travel
Dell, 1960

4-5 ....38.00
6-10 ....35.00
11-14 ....28.00

Haven: The Broken City
DC, 2002

1-9 ....3.00

Havoc, Inc.
Radio, 1998

1-9 ....3.00

Havok & Wolverine: Meltdown
Marvel, 1989

1-4 ....4.00

Hawaiian Dick
Image, 2002

1-3 ....3.00

Hawaiian Dick: The Last Resort
Image, 2004

1-2 ....3.00

Hawk
Ziff-Davis, 1951

1 ....145.00
2 ....90.00
3-6 ....60.00
7-12 ....55.00
3D 1 ....250.00

Hawk & the Dove
DC, 1968

1 ....60.00
2-5 ....40.00
6 ....30.00

Hawk and Dove
DC, 1988

1-2 ....3.00
3-5 ....2.00

Hawk and Dove
DC, 1989

1 ....2.00
2-24 ....1.00

25 ....2.00
26-27 ....1.00
28 ....2.00
Ann 1 ....3.00
Ann 2 ....2.00

Hawk and Dove
DC, 1997

1-5 .... 3.00

Hawk & Windblade
Warp, 1997

1-2 .... 3.00

Hawkeye
Marvel, 1983

1 .... 3.00
2-4 .... 2.00

Hawkeye
Marvel, 1994

1-4 .... 2.00

Hawkeye
Marvel, 2003

1-8 .... 3.00

Hawkeye: Earth's Mightiest Marksman
Marvel, 1998

1 .... 3.00

Hawkgirl
DC, 2006

50-59 .... 3.00

Hawkman
DC, 1964

1 .... 475.00
2 .... 200.00
3 .... 75.00
4 .... 200.00
☛1st Zatanna
5-9 .... 65.00
10-12 .... 50.00
13-15 .... 40.00
16-19 .... 36.00
20-27 .... 32.00

Hawkman
DC, 1986

1 .... 3.00
2-17 .... 2.00
Special 1 .... 3.00

Hawkman
DC, 1993

0-1 .... 3.00
2-33 .... 2.00
Ann 1-2 .... 4.00

Hawkman
DC, 2002

1-40 .... 3.00
41 .... 8.00
42 .... 4.00
43-49 .... 3.00

Hawkman Secret Files and Origins
DC, 2002

1 .... 5.00

Hawkmoon: The Jewel in the Skull
First, 1986

Dorian Hawkmoon is another aspect of Michael Moorcock's Eternal Champion character, a single hero destined to decide the fate of his world. This world is an alternate Britain whose expansionist policies are fueled by darkness and degredation, and empowered by sorcery in chivalrous times. Hawkmoon is sent to infiltrate the one European principality honorably resisting Granbretan, his loyalty seemingly insured by the implantation of a jewel on his forehead. Should betrayal be suspected, the jewel will kill him. Gerry Conway and Rafael Kayanan provide a readable outing of one of Moorcock's lesser-known heroes

1-4 .... 2.00

Hawkmoon: The Mad God's Amulet
First, 1987

1-4 .... 2.00

Hawkmoon: The Runestaff
First, 1988

1-4 .... 2.00

Hawkmoon: The Sword of the Dawn
First, 1987

1-4 .... 2.00

Hawkshaws
Image, 2000

1 .... 3.00

Hawk, Street Avenger
Taurus, 1996
1 ....3.00

Hawkworld
DC, 1989
1-3 ....4.00

Hawkworld
DC, 1990
1 ....3.00
2-32 ....2.00
Ann 1-Ann 3 ....3.00

Haywire
DC, 1988

Deep in the heart of a secured facility, a very special armored suit has been developed. Capable of unbelievable, deadly force, the suit is driven by a psionic link with its wearer. Unfortunately that meant that the suit could only be driven to its full potential by a person with a rare kind of highly repressed personality.

Accordingly, "auditions" were held. But although the applicants were screened carefully, an outsider somehow managed to infiltrate the program and proved all too perfect a match for the armored suit. Driving the suit to its full power, he suddenly went "haywire" and began killing the technicians. This stranger managed to steal the suit and is using it to carry out a particularly nasty war against organized crime.

Nobody seems to know who Haywire is - including Haywire himself!

1-13 ....1.00

Hazard
Image, 1996
1-7 ....2.00

Hazard!
Motion
1 ....3.00

Hazard!
Reckless Vision
1 .... 3.00

H-Bomb
Antarctic, 1993
1 .... 3.00

Head
Fantagraphics, 2002
1 .... 7.00
2-13 .... 4.00

Headbanger
Parody
1 .... 3.00

Headbuster
Antarctic, 1998
1 .... 3.00

Headhunters
Image, 1997
1-3 .... 3.00

Headless Horseman
Eternity
1-2 .... 2.00

Headline Comics
Headline, 1943

Headline Comics was a late, and not especially notable, entry into the World War II comic-book boom, featuring patriotic heroes such as Yank and Doodle, The Junior Rangers, and The Blue Streak. Following the atomic bombing of Japan in 1945, a super-hero named Atomic Man made a brief appearance in the pages of Headline but soon faded away along with most of the other super-heroes of the late 1940s.

Headline changed direction with #23 in December 1947, when the creative team of Simon and Kirby introduced a hard-edged true-crime format to the title. From then until its demise in 1956, Headline featured the typically brutal, morally ambiguous, and luridly sensational crime stories that eventually led to the formation of the Comics Code.

1 .... 325.00
2 .... 275.00
3 .... 140.00
4-5 .... 100.00
6-7 .... 85.00
8 .... 110.00
9-10 .... 85.00
11-15 .... 70.00
16 .... 175.00
17-18 .... 65.00
19 .... 175.00
20-22 .... 60.00
23-24 .... 155.00
25-35 .... 120.00
36 .... 100.00
37 .... 58.00
38-44 .... 38.00
45 .... 45.00
46-50 .... 28.00
51-55 .... 26.00
56 .... 60.00
57-60 .... 26.00
61-70 .... 22.00
71-77 .... 18.00

Headman
Innovation
1 .... 3.00

Health
David Tompkins
1 .... 1.00
2-5 .... 2.00
6 .... 5.00

Heap
Skywald, 1971
1 .... 16.00

Heartbreak Comics
Eclipse
1 .... 4.00

Heartbreakers
Dark Horse, 1996
1-4 .... 3.00

Heartbreakers Superdigest: Year Ten
Image, 1999
1 .... 14.00

Heartland
DC, 1997
1 .... 5.00

Heart of Darkness
Hardline
1 .... 3.00

Heart of Empire
Dark Horse, 1999

This sequel to the epic Adventures of Luther Arkwright revolves around an alternate history of Britain, where the Empire never diminished, Queen Anne never died, and Oliver Cromwell's puritanical influence never faded. Unknown to the despotic Queen and her subjects, a catastrophic event is coming, and may focus on her daughter Victoria, who suffers from mysterious migraines and blackouts as well as the shadowy legacy of her missing father Luther Arkwright. There are rumors that the Pope has sent his best assassin to the Imperial Palace in London to commit a dreadful deed, and that Armageddon begins in seven days. Throw in healthy doses of historical reverence, political satire, eroticism, and fart jokes, and add celebrity cameos and you have the makings of a classic in a comic book. From the sublime to the profane, Bryan Talbot has once again woven a remarkably complex tale of politics, personalities, and perverse eccentricities.

1-9 ....3.00

Heart of the Beast
DC
1 ....20.00

Hearts of Africa
Slave Labor
1 ....11.00

Hearts of Darkness
Marvel, 1991
1 ....5.00

Heart Throbs
DC, 1949

DC inherited Heart Throbs from Quality Comics in the 1950s and continued to churn out issues until the market for love comics finally dried up in the early 1970s. The stories and art in Heart Throbs were as stiff and formulaic as the worst of the love comic genre could be, but were burnished with the cool professionalism of the DC house style and packaged as a slick and attractive product for the sisters of the readers of DC's harder-edged super-hero and war comics. The goofy stories and off-the-wall features, including some bizarre fashion tips and love poetry submitted by readers, make Heart Throbs a campy reading experience for modern audiences.

Stories from Heart Throbs and other DC love comics were collected in a "Heart Throbs" trade paperback edition in the late 1970s.

-- Rob Salkowitz

1	240.00
2	135.00
3	65.00
4	85.00
5	50.00
6	80.00
7	48.00
8	80.00
9-10	48.00
11-15	30.00
16-20	26.00
21	45.00
22-23	35.00
24-40	22.00
41-46	18.00
47	125.00
48	65.00
49-50	60.00
51-60	48.00
61-70	38.00
71-80	27.00
81-90	20.00
91-100	16.00
101	60.00
102-110	13.00
111-130	10.00
131-146	9.00

Heartthrobs
DC, 1999
1-4 .... 3.00

Heathcliff
Marvel, 1985

The star of this series is a rather mischievous cat named Heathcliff. Unlike his low-key cartoon contemporary, Garfield, Heathcliff is always up to something or other: usually, getting into trouble. His favorite pastimes include chasing birds and mice; annoying Spike, the huge neighborhood dog; and romancing Sonya, his girlfriend. All of it is done for laughs in high style.

Heathcliff enjoyed long-running popularity as a newspaper cartoon (created by George Gately) before making the transition to comics. This helps account for the relative longevity of Heathcliff as a comic book. Heathcliff ran for more than 50 issues, outlasting the Marvel's Star line of children's comics itself. In contrast, the majority of Star titles ceased publication after less than a dozen issues.

1	2.00
2-49	1.00
50	2.00
51-Ann 1	1.00

Heathcliff's Funhouse
Marvel, 1987
1-10 .... 1.00

Heatseeker
Fantaco
1 .... 6.00

Heaven Above Heaven
Tokyopop, 2005
1-3...10.00

Heaven LLC
Image, 2004
1...13.00

Heaven's Devils
Image, 2003
1...3.00
2-4...4.00

Heaven Sent
Antarctic, 2004
1-11...3.00

Heaven's War
Image, 2003
0...13.00

Heavy Armor
Fantasy General
1-3...2.00

Heavy Hitters
Marvel, 1993
Ann 1.......................................4.00

Heavy Liquid
DC, 1999
1-5...6.00

Heavy Metal
Metal Mammoth, 1977

Heavy Metal is one of the longest-running and most distinguished American comics magazines. From the magazine's inception in 1977, Heavy Metal has made great strides in bringing illustrated comics art to an adult audience. At the same time, it has refined its approach over the years, cutting back on pop culture filler pieces and interviews and adding in new showcases for alternative comic art. Today, it's one of the most accessible (and affordable) ways to see what's best in the world of illustrated fiction.

The list of creators who have contributed work to Heavy Metal is both long and impressive. Among them: Boris Vallejo, Howard Chaykin, Walt Simonson, Harlan Ellison, Moebius, Bernie Wrightson, and even Robert Crumb. Its masthead also reveals a pleasant surprise: the editor in chief (as of 1993) is Kevin Eastman, indie comics pioneer and co-creator of the Teenage Mutant Ninja Turtles.

The Heavy Metal staff provided the Standard Catalog indexers their complete Statement of Ownership files making the process of compiling those figures considerably easier than is normally the case.

1 .... 20.00
2-3..................................... 10.00
4-11...................................... 7.00
12-22.................................... 5.00
23-193................................... 4.00
194 .... 5.00

Heavy Metal Greatest Hits
HM Communications, 1992
1 .... 6.00

Heavy Metal Havoc
HM Communications
1 .... 6.00

Heavy Metal Monsters
Revolutionary, 1992
1 .... 3.00
2 .... 4.00

Heavy Metal War Machine
HM Communications
1 .... 6.00

Heck!
Rip Off
1 .... 8.00

Heckle and Jeckle
Pines, 1952
1.. 140.00
2... 75.00
3... 52.00
4-5... 45.00
6-10.. 32.00
11-20....................................... 28.00
21-34....................................... 20.00

Heckle and Jeckle
Gold Key, 1962
1... 36.00
2... 18.00
3-4... 16.00

Heckle and Jeckle
Dell, 1966
1... 25.00
2-3... 13.00

Heckler
DC, 1992
1-6 .... 1.00

Hector Plasm
Image, 2006
1 .... 6.00

Hector Heathcote
Gold Key, 1964
1 .... 30.00

Hedge Knight
Image, 2003
1-2 .... 3.00
2/A... 6.00
3 .... 3.00

Hedy De Vine Comics
Red Circle, 1947
22 .... 75.00
23-30 .... 60.00
31-40 .... 42.00
41-50 .... 36.00

Hee Haw
Charlton, 1970
1 .... 13.00
2 .... 8.00
3-7 .... 6.00

Heirs of Eternity
Image, 2003
1-5 .... 3.00

He Is Just a Rat
Exclaim! Brand Comics, 1995
1-5 .... 3.00

Hell
Dark Horse, 2003
1-4 .... 3.00

Hellbender
Eternity
1 .... 2.00

Hellblazer
DC, 1988

Hellblazer is the dark story of demon-foiler John Constantine, who first appeared in Saga of the Swamp Thing. Dying of inoperable cancer, he thwarted three demons by selling each of them his soul. Then, he calmly slashed his own wrists. Each demon learned he was about to die, and showed up to claim his prize. Each was shocked, of course, to learn that they had been duped. To keep from sparking a war in Hell, the demons were forced not only to heal Constantine, but to cure his cancer as well. Constantine returned the favor by ever defying them, thumbing his nose at both heaven and hell, and meddling in all manner of celestial affairs.

1	10.00
2	5.00
3-13	4.00
14-26	3.00
27	9.00
☞Gaiman story	
28-39	3.00
40	4.00
41	6.00
☞1st Ennis story	
42-46	4.00
47-49	3.00
50	4.00
51-74	3.00
75	4.00
76-199	3.00
200	5.00
201-260	3.00
Ann 1	6.00
Special 1	5.00

Hellblazer Special: Bad Blood
DC, 2000

1-4 .... 3.00

Hellblazer Special: Lady Constantine
DC, 2003

1-4 .... 3.00

Hellblazer/ The Books of Magic
DC, 1997

1-2 .... 4.00

Hellboy: Almost Colossus
Dark Horse, 1997

1-2 .... 3.00

Hellboy: Art of the Movie
Dark Horse, 2004

1 .... 25.00

Hellboy: Box Full of Evil
Dark Horse, 1999

1-2 .... 3.00

Hellboy Christmas Special
Dark Horse, 1997

1 .... 4.00

Hellboy: Conqueror Worm
Dark Horse, 2001

1-4 .... 3.00

Hellboy, the Corpse and The Iron Shoes
Dark Horse

1 .... 4.00

Hellboy: Makoma
Dark Horse, 2006

1-2 .... 3.00

Hellboy: Seed of Destruction
Dark Horse, 1994

First appearing in Dark Horse Presents (and as a comics character in Next Men), Hellboy now appears in his own multiple Eisner award-winning series. His story begins as the Third Reich began ticking down its final hours. The Nazis made a last, desperate attempt to turn the tide by summoning unearthly powers to come to their rescue. What they got was a strange red child -- Hellboy.

Hellboy fell into the hands of the Allies and has now grown into adulthood. No stranger to weird phenomena, he now makes his living as a paranormal investigator. In "Seed of Destruction," he takes on his strangest case yet -- the murder of his adoptive father. Joined by Elizabeth Sherman, a pyrokinetic, and Abraham Sapien, a genetically engineered man-fish, they'll take on all manner of danger in order to solve the case. And before it's all over, Hellboy will have come face-to-face with the sorcerer who summoned him into this world.

Hellboy: The Island
Dark Horse, 2005

1	6.00
2-4	4.00

1-2 .... 3.00

Hellboy: The Third Wish
Dark Horse, 2002

1-2 .... 3.00

Hellboy: The Wolves of Saint August
Dark Horse

1 .... 5.00

Hellboy: Wake the Devil
Dark Horse, 1996

1-5 .... 4.00

Hellboy: Weird Tales
Dark Horse, 2003

1-8 .... 3.00

Hellboy Jr.
Dark Horse, 1999

1-2 .... 3.00

Hellboy Jr. Halloween Special
Dark Horse, 1997

1 .... 4.00

Hell Car Comix
Alternating Crimes, 1998

1 .... 3.00

Hellcat
Marvel, 2000

One of Marvel Comics' oldest characters still in use, this mini-series was used to reintroduce Patsy Walker, AKA Hellcat, back into the Marvel Universe. The star of serial romance comics from the 1940s through the 1960s such as Patsy Walker Comics and Patsy & Heddy, Walker was modernized for a new generation of readers in the 1970s. Reintroduced to continuity as a confidant of the Beast, Walker convinced the then blue-furred Avenger to help her become a costumed crimefighter. Taking on the masked persona of Hellcat in the Avengers, Walker eventually joined Marvel's "non-team" the Defenders. Suffering from depression, brought on by years of abuse at the hands of her husbands Buzz Baxter and Daimon Hellstrom, alias the Son of Satan, Walker took her own life and was sent to the "Arena of Tainted Souls." Rescued from Hell by the Avengers, Walker has returned to the land of the living with newfound magical powers and a host of new enemies all making her wonder if maybe she would have been better off staying dead.

1-3..3.00

Hell City, Hell
Diablo Musica
1..2.00

Hellcop
Image, 1998
1-4..3.00

Hell Eternal
DC
1..7.00

Hellgate: London
Dark Horse, 2006
1-2..3.00

Hellgirl: Demonseed
Knight, 1995
1..3.00

Hellhole
Image, 1999
1-3..3.00

Hellhounds
Image, 2003
1-4..3.00

Hellhounds: Panzer Corps
Dark Horse, 1994
1-6..3.00

Hellhound: The Redemption Quest
Marvel, 1993
1-4..2.00

Hellina
Lightning, 1994
1..3.00

Hellina 1997 Pin-Up Special
Lightning, 1997
1..4.00

Hellina/Catfight
Lightning, 1995
1-1/2nd...................................3.00

Hellina: Christmas in Hell
Lightning, 1996
1...3.00
1/A-1/C...................................4.00

Hellina/Cynder
Lightning, 1997
1-1/C.......................................3.00

Hellina/Double Impact
Lightning, 1996
1-1/C.......................................3.00
1/Nude.....................................4.00
1/Platinum..............................3.00

Hellina: Genesis
Lightning, 1996
1-1/Nude................................4.00

Hellina: Heart of Thorns
Lightning, 1996
1-2/Nude................................4.00

Hellina: Hellborn
Lightning, 1997
1-2/B.......................................3.00

Hellina: Hell's Angel
Lightning, 1996
1/Nude.....................................3.00

Hellina: in the Flesh
Lightning, 1997
1-1/B.......................................3.00

Hellina: Kiss of Death
Lightning, 1995

Hellina: Kiss of Death is really just the continuation of a battle scene started earlier in Fury of Hellina #1. The cultists known as the 7th Day had joined with Lucifer to turn the dead body of Hellina's old boyfriend into a demonic being called Despair. Hellina, joined by a

"good" demon called Perg, was in mid-battle with Despair; then Perg suggests stabbing Despair through the head with a special dagger Perg carries. This has the effect of filtering out the stab-ee's evil nature and giving them a fresh chance in life. Always a game one for stabbing people, Hellina gives it a shot, but finds out that the "stab through the head/make you into a nice person" trick only works for pure-of-heart folks like Perg. Despair, instead, turned even more evil...

This one-shot was sold in a regular edition, as well as in a "gold" edition for the gullible, and a "nude" edition for the easily amused.

1-1/Gold................................3.00
1/Nude.....................................4.00
1/2nd.......................................3.00

Hellina: Naked Desire
Lightning, 1997
1-1/B.......................................3.00

Hellina/Nira X
Lightning, 1996
1-1/B.......................................3.00

Hellina: Skybolt Toyz Limited Edition
Lightning, 1997
1/A-1/B...................................2.00

Hellina: Taking Back the Night
Lightning, 1995
1-1/A.......................................5.00

Hellina: Wicked Ways
Lightning, 1995
1/A-1/B...................................3.00
1/Nude...................................10.00
1/Silver...................................3.00

Hell Magician
Fc9 Publishing, 2005
1...3.00

Hell Michigan
Fc9 Publishing, 2005
1-2..3.00
1/Ashcan................................4.00

Hello Pal
Harvey, 1943
1-3.......................................400.00

Hellraiser (Clive Barker's)
Marvel, 1989
Holiday 1................................5.00
Summer 1..............................6.00
Spring 1..................................7.00

Hellraiser III: Hell on Earth
Marvel
1 ....5.00

Hellraiser Nightbreed: Jihad
Marvel
1-2 ....5.00

Hellraiser Posterbook (Clive Barker's)
Marvel
1 ....5.00

Hellraiser: Spring Slaughter
Marvel
1 ....7.00

Hellsaint
Black Diamond, 1998

A big, moody, badly drawn guy in black roughs up assorted nasties who are killing priests and robbing the local church. You know these guys are hard because when one of them has his face melted by our hero he doesn't collapse into a grieving heap or dial 911, he runs off vowing revenge. Forget about the comic and go straight to the back inside-cover editorial where the creators give gushing thanks. It's as if they're somehow aware that their paucity of talent will only ever permit them this one shot at a thanks list, and they really go for it.

1 ....3.00

Hell's Angel
Marvel, 1993
1-5 ....2.00

Hellshock
Image, 1994
1-4/B 2.00
Ashcan 1 ....1.00

Hellshock
Image, 1997
1-6 ....3.00
7 ....4.00

Hellspawn
Image, 2000
1-16 ....3.00

Hellspock
Express
1 ....3.00

Hellstalker
Rebel Creations, 1989
1-2 ....2.00

Hellstorm: Prince of Lies
Marvel, 1993
1 ....3.00
2-21 ....2.00

Hellstorm: Son of Satan
Marvel, 2006
1-3 ....4.00

Helm Premiere
Helm, 1995
1 ....3.00

Help
Warren, 1964
1 ....45.00
2 ....28.00
3-12 ....20.00

Help
Warren
1 ....26.00
2-3 ....16.00

Helsing
Caliber, 2008
1-2 ....3.00

Helter Skelter
Antarctic, 1997
0-6 ....3.00

Helyun: Bones of the Backwoods
Slave Labor, 1991
1 ....3.00

Helyun Book 1
Slave Labor, 1990
1 ....7.00

He-Man
Toby, 1954
1 ....85.00
2 ....65.00

Hembeck
Fantaco, 1980

Fred Hembeck, whose Dateline @#&% cartoons had been seen in the precursor to Comics Buyer's Guide, The Buyer's Guide to Comic Fandom in the 1970s and early 1980s, collected them in Hembeck #1 for Fantaco. While harder to read at this smaller size, the zany interviews conducted by Cartoon Fred with Marvel, DC, and other companies' characters are knee-slappers for those in the know. Better still are the original extended stories written for this series taking place in a world where characters from different companies - as well as real-life figures - interact. (Doctor Octopus arrives on scene with eight pies in search of Soupy Sales, for example.

The attention from CBG and this series led to freelance work for Marvel. Hembeck restarted Dateline in Comics Buyer's Guide in the late 1990s, sending up a new generation of comic books.
-- John Jackson Miller

1-2 ....3.00
3-4 ....2.00
5 ....3.00
6-7 ....2.00

Hemp for Victory
Starhead, 1993
1 ....3.00

Henry (Carl Anderson's...)
Dell, 1948
1 ....75.00
2 ....40.00
3 ....30.00
4-5 ....25.00
6-10 ....22.00
11-21 ....18.00
22-30 ....15.00
31-40 ....12.00
41-50 ....10.00
51-65 ....8.00

Henry Aldrich
Dell, 1950
1	50.00
2	25.00
3	18.00
4-10	15.00
11-22	12.00

Henry V
Caliber
1	3.00

Hepcats
Double Diamond, 1989
1	5.00
2	4.00
3-14	3.00
Special 1- 2	4.00

Hepcats
Antarctic, 1996
0	4.00
0/A	6.00
0/Deluxe	10.00
1-2	4.00
3-12	3.00

Herbie
Dark Horse, 1992
1-2	3.00

Herbie (A+)
A-Plus
1-6	3.00

Herbie
ACG, 1964
1	95.00
2	60.00
3-5	48.00
6-7	40.00
8	50.00
9-10	38.00
11-23	30.00

Hercules
Charlton, 1967
1	14.00
2	9.00
3-5	6.00
6-8	5.00
8/A	10.00
9-13	5.00

Hercules
Marvel, 1982
1-4	2.00

Hercules (Vol. 2)
Marvel, 1984
1	2.00
2	1.00
3-4	1.00

Hercules (Vol. 3)
Marvel, 2005
1	3.00
2	3.00
3	3.00
4-5	3.00

Hercules
Avalon, 2002
1-2	6.00

Hercules: Heart of Chaos
Marvel, 1997

Hercules, legendary hero of Greek mythology and longtime member of the Avengers, is at loose ends. Most of his comrades were presumed killed in the final battle against Onslaught, and Hercules himself had been stripped of his immortality by Zeus. Hercules has even begun to question his role as a warrior and a hero.

Meanwhile Ares, Hercules' half-brother and the Olympian god of war, has plans to plunge the entire planet into conflict with his own high-tech organization aptly named the Warhawks. But global warfare isn't enough for Ares: he also wants to crush his hated brother.

Lacking the help of his fellow Avengers, Hercules reluctantly allies himself with the forces of SHIELD. Unfortunately, SHIELD has already been infiltrated by the Warhawks, and Ares has obtained a powerful artifact known only as the Heart of Chaos.

1-3	3.00

Hercules: Official Comics Movie Adaptation
Acclaim
1	5.00

Hercules Project
Monster, 1991
1-2	2.00

Hercules: The Legendary Journeys
Topps, 1996
1-5	3.00

Hercules Unbound
DC, 1975
1	12.00
2	7.00
3	4.00
4-12	3.00

Here Come the Big People
Event, 1997
1-1/A	3.00

Here Come the Lovejoys Again
Fantagraphics, 2005
1-3	4.00

Here Is Greenwood
Viz, 2004
1-9	10.00

Here's Howie
DC, 1952
1	120.00
2	75.00
3-5	60.00
6-10	48.00
11-18	36.00

Heretic
Dark Horse, 1996
1-4	3.00

Heretics
Iguana, 1993
1-3	3.00

Hermes vs. the Eyeball Kid
Dark Horse, 1994
1-3	3.00

Hero
Marvel, 1990

Good and Evil must always remain in balance. When Evil begins to grow too powerful, Good must look for a champion, a hero to restore the balance. When it can't find one, it settles for someone like Cody Pace.

Cody was a loser in all senses of the world. He was a lazy security courier who couldn't understand women and who was several payments late on his Corvette payments.

Then, he lost the big one. He was to deliver a sealed briefcase from a group calling itself the Petroleum Mediation League and deliver it to the U.N. building. Unknown to Pace, the briefcase chained to his wrist contained a bomb. Metal detectors at the U.N. detected it, and he was placed in a bomb-safe room where he waited helplessly for a bomb disposal team. Then, the bomb exploded—and Cody woke up in a new world—a world of fantasy and magic.

1-6..2.00

Hero Alliance
Wonder Color, 1987
1 ....2.00

Hero Alliance
Innovation, 1989
1-16...2.00
17-Special 1 ....3.00

Hero Alliance & Justice Machine: Identity Crisis
Innovation, 1990
1 ....3.00

Hero Alliance: End of the Golden Age
Innovation, 1989
1-3..2.00

Hero Alliance Quarterly
Innovation, 1991
1-4..3.00

Hero at Large
Speakeasy Comics, 2005
1 ....3.00

Herobear And The Kid
Astonish, 1999
1-2/2nd.....................................3.00
3-5..4.00

Herobear and the Kid and Decoy
Astonish, 2002
1-2..3.00

Hero Camp
Image, 2005
1-4..3.00

H-E-R-O
DC, 2003
1 ....3.00
1/2nd..5.00
2-22..3.00

Hero Double Feature
DC, 2003
1 .... 5.00

Heroes
Blackbird, 1985
1 .... 3.00
2-6 .... 2.00

Heroes
DC, 1996
1-6.. 3.00

Heroes
Marvel, 2001
1 .... 7.00
1/2nd 4.00

Heroes Against Hunger
DC, 1986

After Marvel released its Heroes for Hope, DC pulled together the best of its talent to put together its own benefit comic book to relieve hunger in Africa.

In the story, Superman and Batman are doing their best to help Ethiopia, but they're face-to-face with the allegorical Master. The Master finds his strength in places that once supported life but now have died. He would love nothing better than to play a tune and have Ethiopia turn to waste.

The two super-heroes have to turn to science in order to turn things around, finding an unlikely, but excellent, ally in super-villain mastermind Lex Luthor. But even if they defeat the Master, can they save a country which has had its once-rich farmland destroyed by greed and neglect?

1 .... 3.00

Heroes All (Vol. 1)
Heroes All, 1943
1 .... 150.00
2 .... 120.00

Heroes All (Vol. 2)
Heroes All, 1944
1 .... 95.00
2-3 .... 85.00

Heroes All (Vol. 3)
Heroes All, 1945
1-5 .... 80.00
6-10 .... 70.00

Heroes All (Vol. 4)
Heroes All, 1946
1-35 .... 65.00

Heroes All (Vol. 5)
Heroes All, 1947
1-20 .... 60.00

Heroes All (Vol. 6)
Heroes All, 1948
1-10 .... 60.00

Heroes Anonymous
Bongo, 2003
1-6 .... 3.00

Heroes for Hire
Marvel, 1997
1 .... 3.00
2/A-11...................................... 2.00
12 .... 3.00
13-19 .... 2.00
Ann 1998................................... 3.00

Heroes for Hire
Marvel, 2006
1 .... 3.00
2 .... 2.00
3-5 .... 3.00

Heroes for Hope
Marvel, 1985

The mid-1980s were a time of need for many, and the world responded with a number of benefit events, such as Live Aid and Farm Aid, and benefit recordings, such as "We Are the World." Eventually, benevolent intentions began to fade into the background of what became a fad of increasingly silly staged events. (Hands Across America, anyone?)

But Marvel can be said to have reacted rather quickly in putting together its own charity edition for Ethiopian famine relief, well before such efforts began to appear driven by public relations rather than need.

Marvel brought in Steven King, Harlan Ellison, and many of its own top writers and artists to contribute portions of a story about the X-Men battling against the forces of disease and starvation on a fantasy plane. The issue is entertaining in its own right, as well as notable for its historical significance.
-- John Jackson Miller

1 ....5.00

Heroes from Wordsmith
Special Studio
1 ....3.00

Heroes Incorporated
Double Edge, 1995
1 ....3.00

Heroes, Inc. Presents Cannon
Armed Services, 1969

This anthology series was published during the Vietnam War for American soldiers, edited and drawn by comics legend Wally Wood, with work by other famous contributors such as Steve Ditko.

The dubious highlight of the series, Cannon presents the story of an ex-P.O.W., brainwashed by Communists, who after reprogramming is a man with no emotions. The unstoppable Cannon can destroy an entire Communist base single-handedly, while saving a kidnapped woman, and protecting American military secrets.

"The Misfits" tells the tale of three bizarre creatures, a beautiful android woman, a furry telepathic

alien, and a huge, dimwitted mutant, who together turn out to be mankind's only hope against an alien bent on strip-mining the Earth.

Finally, in the humorous "Dragonella," an infant girl is abandoned in the woods and raised by dragons. When she blooms into a young woman, Dragonella and her jealous dragon companion St. George, go in search of a prince.

1 .... 13.00
2 .... 10.00

Heroes of Faith
Coretoons, 1992
1 .... 3.00

Heroes of Rock 'n Fire
Wonder Comix, 1987
1-2 .... 2.00

Heroes of the Equinox
Fantasy Flight
1 .... 9.00

Heroes Reborn
Marvel, 1996
1/2 .... 3.00

Heroes Reborn: Ashema
Marvel, 2000
1 .... 2.00

Heroes Reborn: Doom
Marvel, 2000
1 .... 2.00

Heroes Reborn: Doomsday
Marvel, 2000
1 .... 2.00

Heroes Reborn: Masters Of Evil
Marvel, 1999
1 .... 2.00

Heroes Reborn Mini Comic
Marvel, 1996
1 .... 1.00

Heroes Reborn: Rebel
Marvel, 2000
1 .... 2.00

Heroes Reborn: Remnants
Marvel, 2000
1 .... 2.00

Heroes Reborn: The Return
Marvel, 1997

Faced with sagging sales on its core super-hero titles, Marvel Comics turned over the reins of Fantastic Four, The Avengers, Captain America, and Iron Man to Jim Lee, Rob Liefeld, and other one-time Marvel artists who had since left to form Image Comics. The result was "Heroes Reborn," a revamped Marvel universe that restarted the aforementioned titles at Vol. 2, #1, and updated origins for the characters to reflect modern-day sensibilities.

A little more than a year later (the length of the contracts with the new teams), Marvel undid the whole thing by "returning" the established heroes to their place in the mainstream Marvel universe. The other universe, it seems, was merely a pocket universe created by young Franklin Richards. Credit this series which gives us one of the great lines of dialogue: "Mom! Dad! They told me I gotta wipe out a universe ... and I don't know which one ...! Tell which one I should get ridda ... and promise you won't be mad at me ... ?"

1-4/Variant.............................. 3.00
Ashcan 1 .... 1.00

Heroes Reborn: Young Allies
Marvel, 2000
1 .... 2.00

Hero for Hire
Marvel, 1972

Lucas is a small-time loser, sent to Seagate Prison for a crime he didn't commit. While there, a sadistic prison guard named Rackham makes it his business to make Lucas' life miserable. Lucas' one hope for salvation is to agree to take part in a risky cell-regeneration experiment conducted by Doc Burstein. The experiment proved fatal to all the previous subjects, but, if Lucas survives, he will be granted parole.

Lucas takes the gamble and is locked into a bio-bath full of strange chemicals. Rackham hates Lucas so much that he turns up the electricity flowing to the bio-bath, hoping to electrocute him. The power overloads, but, instead of killing Lucas, it gives him incredible power and steel-hard skin. He breaks out of his tank, then escapes to New York, where he sets up shop as Luke Cage, Hero for Hire. Later, he adopts the moniker Power Man and teams up with Iron Fist in a continuation of this, his first title.

1	125.00
2	30.00
3	14.00
4-6	12.00
7-9	9.00
10	8.00
11-16	9.00

Hero Graphics Super-Spectacular
Hero

1	4.00

Hero Hotline
DC, 1989

1-6	2.00

Heroic
Lightning

1	2.00

Heroic 17
Pennacle, 1993

1	3.00

Heroic Comics
Famous Funnies, 1940

1	850.00
2	475.00
3	375.00
4	340.00
5-6	285.00
7	300.00
8-10	200.00
11-13	185.00
14	200.00
15	210.00
16-20	130.00
21-29	90.00
30	42.00
31-33	44.00
34	32.00
35-42	44.00
43-47	38.00
48	30.00
49-50	38.00
51	42.00
52	38.00
53	32.00
54-55	26.00
56	38.00
57-60	34.00
61-64	24.00
65	60.00
66-67	35.00
68	26.00
69	44.00
70-71	36.00
72	44.00
73	36.00
74	26.00
75	36.00
76-80	18.00
81-82	20.00
83-85	18.00
86-87	25.00
88-97	18.00

Heroic Tales
Lone Star, 1997

1-10	3.00

Heroine
Axess

Gina Ganes a.k.a. Heroine began her career as Omega Girl with Team Omega, a team of U.S. military-sanctioned superhumans genetically engineered by her father, George Ganes. After the death of her father, Team Omega began to drift apart, and her cousin, Mason Ganes a.k.a. Omega Boy left for good and struck out on his own as the Omega, the greatest super-hero of all time. Gina dealt with an untimely pregnancy and eventually established herself as Heroine, the protector of Swan City. This zero-issue by writer/artist Mike Gerardo relates her origin and sets her up for future adventures.

0/A-0/B	3.00

Heroines Inc.
Avatar, 1989

1	2.00

Heroman
Dimension, 1986

1	2.00

Hero on a Stick
Big-Baby

1	3.00

Hero Premiere Edition
Warrior, 1993

1-9	2.00

Heros
OK

1	3.00

Hero Sandwich
Slave Labor, 1987

They're a team of super-hero detectives for hire to whom no case is too unusual -- or too dangerous. If the money is attractive and there are plenty of opportunities to either beat people up or to meet beautiful women, it's bound to entrance at least one member of this irreverent, oft-bickering team.

In one story arc, the group -- including an elastic man; a former spy with some dark secrets; a wisecracking alien; two women who represent the brains, and the "kick-ass" attitude of the group -- is hired by a vampire to capture a killer. In another, they're forced to confront a past that has a reach from beyond the grave. Wherever the case takes them, the adventurers keep their cool, making for a sharp-witted series with a focus on fun. Written by Dan Vado and illustrated by Chuck Austen, Pete Krause, and Aldin Baroza, this black-and-white series helped put Slave Labor Graphics on the map.

1-7 ....2.00
8-9 ....3.00

Hero Squared
Boom Studios, 2005
1-1/Finger...............................4.00

Hero Zero
Dark Horse, 1994
0 ....3.00

Heru, Son of Ausar
Ania, 1993
1 ....2.00

He Said/She Said Comics
First Amendment
1-6 ....3.00

Hex
DC, 1985

When he was last seen at the end of his regular series, bounty hunter Jonah Hex was sitting at a bar in the Old West of 1875. As this series begins, Hex is pulled forward in time to the year 2050. Reinhold Borsten, a megalomaniacal future scientist has kidnapped Hex, along with military men from different time periods, to keep in a sort of collection for his personal amusement.

Hex, however, is not about to let himself be caged. He stages a daring escape and leaves Reinhold's compound. Outside he finds a blasted world, victim of a nuclear holocaust. The skies rain pure acid, and the land is overrun with criminal gangs who fight over the means to purify water from the nuclear radiation. It is a whole new world but, for Hex, it might as well be the Wild West all over again.

1 .... 5.00
2-18 .... 2.00

Hexbreaker: A Badger Graphic Novel
First, 1988
1 .... 9.00

Hex Of The Wicked Witch
Asylum, 1999
0/A 2.00
0/B 4.00

Hey, Boss!
Visionary
1 .... 2.00

Hey, Mister
Insomnia, 1997
1-4 .... 3.00

Hey Mister: After School Special
Top Shelf
1 .... 5.00

Hi-Adventure Heroes
Gold Key, 1969
1 .... 12.00
2 .... 7.00

Hickory
Quality, 1949
1 .... 48.00
2 .... 34.00
3-6 .... 24.00

Hideo Li Files
Raging Rhino
1 .... 3.00

Hideo Li Files Comic Novella
Raging Rhino
1 .... 13.00

Hiding Place
DC
1 .... 13.00

Hiding Place
Spire, 1973
1 .... 5.00

Hieroglyph
Dark Horse, 1999
1-4 .... 3.00

High Adventure
Red Top, 1957
1 .... 40.00

Highbrow Entertainment
Image
Ashcan 1 .... 1.00

High Caliber
Caliber

Caliber Comics' flagship title was a showcase series, highlighting various stories from various authors.

The reoccurring "Ghost Sonata" storyline from Gary Reed (Baker Street) and Andy Bennett (St. Germaine) followed Isaac's dark journey of despair and solitude. Although his psychic powers allow him to sense the thoughts and feelings of others, they are uncontrollable and ultimately unrewarding. Like The Crow, Ghost Sonata" almost drips emotional pain as loss and grief rock Isaac's life.

The second half of High Caliber rotated between "Amongst the Stars" for the first two issues, "Stain" in the third issue and the X-Files-esque "Raven Chronicles" for the fourth.

```
1 ...........................................10.00
2-4.........................................4.00
```

High Chaparral
Gold Key, 1968
```
1 ...........................................40.00
```

High Octane Theatre
Infiniti
```
1 ...........................................3.00
```

High Roads
DC, 2002
```
1-6.........................................3.00
```

High School Agent
Sun
```
1-4.........................................3.00
```

High Shining Brass
Apple, 1990
```
1-4.........................................3.00
```

High Stakes Adventures
Antarctic, 1998
```
1 .............................................3.00
1/Deluxe .................................6.00
```

Hightop Ninja
Authority, 1997
```
1-3...........................................3.00
```

High Voltage
Black Out
```
0 .............................................3.00
```

Highway 61
Vortex
```
1 .............................................12.00
```

Hi Hi Puffy Amiyumi
DC, 2006
```
1-3............................................2.00
```

Hi-Jinx
ACG, 1947
```
1 ...........................................140.00
2-3.........................................100.00
4-7.........................................120.00
```

Hikaru No Go
Viz, 2004
```
1-5..........................................8.00
```

Hilly Rose
Astro, 1995

Hilly is an investigative reporter for Earth's Rocket Times. She has been given the job by her father, Steeltrap Rose, as a means of keeping her busy and close to home. Steeltrap is of the opinion that Hilly can never make it as a reporter on her own, since he thinks her too young and naive for serious sleuthing. This makes it all the more ironic, when Hilly stumbles onto a story involving corruption and murder-for-hire that winds up pointing back to her own father.

Hilly Rose is a wonderful mix of space fantasy and quick humor, propelled by the wonderful writing of creator B.C. Boyer. The characters in the series seem to be aware of their own cartoon existence and acknowledge it with a wink to the reader. The characters poke fun at everything from comic-book storytelling conventions to the art styles in which they are themselves drawn. Boyer even manages to slip in running gags from such sources as TV's Seinfeld.

```
1-1/A..................................... 3.00
2 .......................................... 4.00
3-9......................................... 3.00
```

Hip Flask
Comicraft, 1998
```
1/2 ......................................... 3.00
```

Hip Flask: Elephantmen
Active Images, 2003
```
1/Desert ............................... 6.00
1/Street.................................. 5.00
1/Sushi .................................. 4.00
1/Townhouse ......................... 6.00
```

Hip Flask: Ladronn Sketchbook
Active Images, 2005
```
1-3......................................... 10.00
```

Hip Flask: Mystery City
Active Images, 2005
```
0 ............................................. 5.00
```

Hiroshima: The Atomic Holocaust
Antarctic, 2005
```
1 ........................................... 4.00
```

Hi-School Romance
Home, 1949

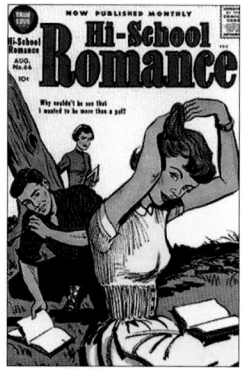

Hi-School Romance was a teen-romance series that ran from 1949 to 1958. The years following World War II saw a continuation of a trend that had begun following World War I -- dating as we know it today, with teen-agers being given a great deal of freedom to meet each other without constant adult supervision. This is a true product of that time, full of malt shops, sock hops, and double-dates. In it, starry-eyed schoolgirls do their best to win the man of their dreams. To accomplish this, however, there is always some obstacle to overcome, whether it means fighting off a rival or merely learning how to play the game of love better.

What may be most remarkable about this series is noting how much has changed between men and women in the last few decades -- as well as how much has stayed the same.

```
1 ............................................. 75.00
2 ............................................. 45.00
3-10 ........................................ 32.00
11-20 ...................................... 20.00
21-31 ...................................... 16.00
32 ............................................ 25.00
33-40 ...................................... 13.00
41-75 ...................................... 10.00
```

His Name Is... Savage
Adventure House
```
1 ............................................. 24.00
```

Hi-Spot Comics
Hawley, 1940
2 ....1,000.00

History of
Marvels Comics
Marvel, 2000
1 ....1.00

History of the
DC Universe
DC, 1986
1-2..3.00

History of Violence
DC
1 ....10.00

Hitchhiker's Guide
to the Galaxy
DC, 1993
1-3..5.00

Hit Comics
Quality, 1940

Early issues of Hit Comics featured such characters as Hercules, The Red Bee, The Strange Twins, and Neon the Unknown, and dynamic covers featured brawny costumed guys (often, Hercules wearing a cape but no shirt) bopping baddies. With #25 (Dec 42), Kid Eternity was introduced and immediately took over the cover spot, was described on the cover as the "most sensational hero ever to appear in print!"

He was killed, but his death had not been supposed to occur. As a result, Mr. Keeper, who was in charge of the list of who was to live and who was to die, was charged with giving the dead lad the remaining 75 years of his life.

Keeper and the resurrected Kit were featured on Hit's covers, often as pictured by Reed Crandall, and the stories featured Kit's ability to change from mortal to spirit and to call on any figure of history or mythology or travel through time

simply by saying the word, "Eternity!"

-- Brent

1	4,550.00
2	2,250.00
3	1,700.00
4	1,500.00
5	2,350.00
6-10	1,300.00
11	1,175.00
12-20	825.00
21-23	700.00
24	1,100.00
25	850.00
26	525.00
27-29	700.00
30-35	500.00
36-39	350.00
40-49	200.00
50-55	165.00
56-65	135.00

Hitman
DC, 1996
1-10 .... 3.00
11-29 .... 2.00
30-1000000 .... 3.00
Ann 1 .... 4.00

Hitman/Lobo:
That Stupid Bastich
DC, 2000
1 .... 4.00

Hitomi 2
Antarctic, 1993

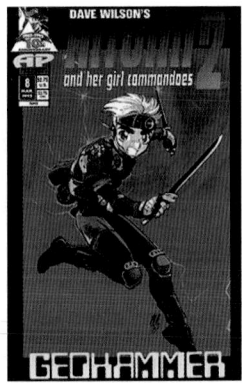

High-tech espionage and combat form the backbone of this manga-style title from Dave Wilson. But it's not all bumps and bruises being a commando; there's heartache and complaint, companionship and romance, and a nasty set of corporate villains.

Wilson's sketchy art is figure-focused, with backgrounds few and far between, but it's good cartooning, and his endearingly wacky footnotes complement a character-based writing style. The

major fault of the title is that there are no concessions to anyone who can't keep up, and a platoon of characters referencing plot twists in previous issues all the time becomes a nuisance. Pity the poor soul who read it during its bimonthly scheduled run.

1-9 .... 3.00
10 .... 4.00

Hitomi and
Her Girl Commandos
Antarctic, 1992
1-4 .... 3.00

Hit the Beach
Antarctic, 1993
1 .... 3.00
1/Gold..................................... 5.00
2-5 .... 3.00
5/CS 5.00
6 .... 4.00

Hobbit
(J.R.R. Tolkie'...)
Eclipse, 1989
1-3 .... 5.00

Hockey Masters
Revolutionary, 1993
1 .... 3.00

Hoe
Thunderball
1 .... 3.00

Hogan's Heroes
Dell, 1966
1 .... 50.00
2 .... 40.00
3-5 .... 32.00
6-9 .... 26.00

Hokum & Hex
Marvel, 1993
1 .... 3.00
2-9 .... 2.00

Holed Up
(Rich Johnson's)
Avatar, 2004
1 .... 4.00

Holiday Comics
Star Publications, 1951
1 .... 165.00
2-4 .... 125.00
5-8 .... 90.00

Holiday for Screams
Malibu
1 .... 5.00

Holiday Out
Renegade, 1987
1-3 .... 2.00

Hollow Earth
Vision, 1996
1-3 .... 3.00

Hollow Grounds
DC, 2000
1 ....20.00

Hollywood Film Stories
Feature Publications, 1950
1 ....120.00
2-4..80.00

Hollywood Funny Folks
DC, 1950
27 ....90.00
28-30.......................................70.00
31-37.......................................50.00
38-49.......................................40.00
50-60.......................................30.00

Hollywood Romances
Charlton, 1966

Hollywood Romances presents a "can't miss" spin on the tried and true romance comics formula, setting the tales of heartbreak against the background of Tinseltown. Here, young ingènues face seduction by lustful producers, diva starlets feud over straight-shooting leading men, and the make-up girl wonders when handsome Rock Chambers will look her way, when in fact it's homely Harry the key grip who's her secret admirer. Hollywood Romances has the makings of a camp classic, right down to the artless, irony-free treatment at the hands of the hapless Charlton production crew.

46 ....35.00
47-49.......................................18.00
50-59.......................................12.00

Hollywood Superstars
Marvel, 1990
1 ....3.00
2-5..2.00

Holo Brothers
Monster, 1988
1-Special 1 ....2.00

Holy Avenger
Slave Labor, 1996
1 .... 5.00

Holy Cross
Fantagraphics, 1994
0 .... 5.00
1-2.. 3.00

Holy Knight
Pocket Change, 1994
1-8.. 3.00

Holy Terror
Image, 2002
1 .... 3.00

Homage Studios Swimsuit Special
Image, 1993
1 .... 2.00

Home Grown Funnies
Kitchen Sink, 1971
1 .... 55.00
1/2nd 22.00
1/3rd...................................... 10.00
1/4th 6.00
1/5th-1/15th........................... 4.00

Homelands on The World of Magic: The Gathering
Acclaim
1 .... 6.00

Homer, The Happy Ghost
Atlas, 1955
1 .... 150.00
2-9...................................... 100.00
10-17.................................... 80.00
18-22.................................... 60.00

Homer, The Happy Ghost
Marvel, 1969
1 .... 40.00
2-4....................................... 30.00

Homicide
Dark Horse, 1990
1 .... 2.00

Homicide: Tears of the Dead
Chaos, 1997
1 .... 3.00

Homo Patrol
Helpless Anger
1 .... 4.00

Honeymoon
Marvel, 1950
41 .... 100.00

Honeymooners
Lodestone, 1986
1 .... 2.00

Honeymooners
Triad, 1987
1-2.. 2.00

3 .... 4.00
4-13 .... 2.00

Honey Mustard
Tokyopop, 2005
1-3 .... 10.00

Honey West
Gold Key, 1966
1 .... 25.00

Hong Kong Phooey
Charlton, 1975
1 .... 40.00
2 .... 20.00
3-9 .... 10.00

Hong on the Range
Image, 1997
1-3 .... 3.00

Honk!
Fantagraphics, 1986
1-5 .... 2.00

Honko the Clown
C&T
1 .... 2.00

Honor Among Thieves
Gateway, 1987

Capturing the feel of a Dungeons & Dragons module, Honor Among Thieves features an ensemble cast that is suited for a role-playing game. Led by lawman Galen, the sorcerer Dar, and the youthful Daven Turdock, they are asked by Korin, a tailor who tried to steal their horses, to overthrow Meggin Jarfys. Jarfys controls Korin's hometown Mir, taking money from frightened people's businesses. Preparing to attend a horse fair, Galen and his companions instead join some of Mir's residents to stop Jarfys.

1 .... 2.00

Honor of the Damned
-Ism, 2005
1 .... 4.00

Hood
South Central

1 ....3.00

Hood
Marvel, 2002

1-6...3.00

Hooded Horseman
ACG, 1952

21-24.....................................20.00
25...25.00
26...30.00
27...20.00

Hooded Horseman
ACG, 1954

18...30.00
19...20.00
20...25.00
21-22.....................................20.00

Hooded Menace
Avon, 1951

1 ....250.00

Hooded Rider Comics
Action

1 ....60.00
2...42.00
3...32.00
4-5...25.00
6-10.......................................18.00
11-20.....................................15.00
21-44.....................................12.00
Special 1 ....20.00

Hood Magazine
Oakland

1-2...3.00

Hoodoo
3-D Zone, 1988

1 ....3.00

Hook
Marvel, 1992

Hook is Marvel's four-issue adaptation of Steven Spielberg's 1991 pirate film starring Robin Williams, Dustin Hoffman, and Julia Roberts. Spielberg updated the classic tale of Peter Pan, with Robin Williams as a corporate take-over artist who must rediscover the innocence of childhood by becoming Peter Pan and rescuing kids from the clutches of the evil pirate Captain Hook.

Marvel's mini-series faithfully follows the script, but has understandable difficulties in capturing the subtleties of a performer like Williams. Charles Vess adapted the script, with art chores handled by an assortment of talents including Dan Panosian and John Ridgway.

1-4 .... 1.00

Hook (Magazine)
Marvel

1 .... 3.00

Hoon
Eenieweenie, 1995

1-6 .... 3.00

Hoon
Caliber, 1996

1-2 .... 3.00

Hopalong Cassidy
Fawcett, 1943

1 .... 4,000.00
2 .... 1,000.00
3 .... 500.00
4-7 .... 400.00
8-11 .... 300.00
12-14 .... 200.00
15-62 .... 100.00
63-74 .... 75.00
75-85 .... 50.00

Hopalong Cassidy
DC, 1954

86 .... 200.00
87-89 .... 150.00
90-96 .... 100.00
97-105 .... 80.00
106-117 .... 60.00
118-135 .... 50.00

Hopeless Savages
Oni, 2001

1-4 .... 3.00

Hopeless Savages: Ground Zero
Oni, 2002

1-4 .... 3.00

Hoppy the Marvel Bunny
Fawcett, 1945

1 .... 150.00
2-15 .... 100.00

Hopster's Tracks
Bongo

1-2 .... 3.00

Horde
Swing Shift

1 .... 2.00

Horde
DC, 2004

1 .... 18.00

Horizontal Lieutenant
Dell, 1962

1 .... 30.00

Horny Biker Sluts
Last Gasp, 1991

1-5 .... 3.00
6-13 .... 4.00

Horny Comix & Stories
Rip Off, 1991

1-4 .... 3.00

Horny Tails
NBM

1 .... 13.00

Horny Toads (Wallace Wood's...)
Fantagraphics

1 .... 3.00

Horobi Part 1
Viz, 1990

1-8 .... 4.00

Horobi Part 2
Viz, 1990

1-7 .... 4.00

Horrible Truth About Comics
Alternative, 1999

1 .... 3.00

Horrific
Comic Media, 1952

1 .... 120.00
2-8 .... 100.00
9-13 .... 80.00

Horror House
AC, 1994

1 .... 3.00

Horror, The Illustrated Book of Fears
Northstar, 1990

1-2 .... 4.00

Horror in the Dark
Fantagor

1-4 .... 2.00

Horrorist
DC, 1995

1-2 .... 6.00

Horror of Collier County
Dark Horse, 1999

1-5 .... 3.00

Horror
(Robert E. Howard's...)
Cross Plains, 2000
nn 6.00

Horrors
Star Publications, 1953
11-15....................................200.00

Horror Show
Caliber, 1991
1 ....4.00

Horror Show
Dead Dog Comics, 2005
1 ....5.00

Horrors of the Haunter
AC
1 ....3.00

Horse
Slave Labor, 1989
1-3..3.00

Horseman
Kevlar, 1996
0-2..3.00

Hosie's Heroines
Slave Labor, 1993
1 ....3.00

Hostile Takeover
Malibu, 1994
Ashcan 1 ....1.00

Hot Comics Premiere
Hot Comics, 1994
1-2..3.00

Hot Dog
Magazine Enterprises

Drawing heavily on funny animal animated shorts for inspiration, Hot Dog's basic premise is familiar. Hot Dog is an irascible type who expends enormous effort on gadgets that fail, and in predictable fashion his plots backfire on him. Blessed with an enormous ego not above underhanded tactics to achieve his aims, there is an obvious resemblance to Donald Duck.

It's not bad reading material, though. The gags work well and can still earn a smile, and the morality of the times always has Hot Dog getting his comeuppance. It's a type of comic book, so prevalent in the 1950s, that is all-too-absent today.

1 .... 28.00
2 .... 20.00
3-4 .... 16.00

Hotel Harbour View
Viz
1 .... 10.00

Hothead Paisan:
Homicidal Lesbian
Terrorist
Giant Ass
1-13....................................... 4.00

Hot Line
Fantagraphics, 1992
1 .... 3.00

Hot Mexican
Love Comics
Hot Mexican Love Comics
1-5... 4.00

Hot N' Cold Heroes
A-Plus, 1991
1-2... 3.00

Hot Nights in Rangoon
Fantagraphics, 1994
1-3... 3.00

Hot Rod and
Speedway Comics
Hillman, 1952
1 .... 150.00
2-5 .... 100.00

Hot Rod Comics
Fawcett, 1951
1 .... 125.00
2-6 .... 100.00
7 .... 80.00

Hot Rod Racers
Charlton, 1965
1 .... 30.00
2-15 .... 20.00

Hot Rods and
Racing Cars
Charlton, 1951

The reader's interest in this series of wild teen-agers, muscle cars, and reckless driving doesn't last long enough to clock a decent time for a quarter mile. Almost every good guy is law-abiding, righteous, and a skillful driver. Almost every bad boy is inexperienced, stubborn, and a reckless driver.

So the formula is simple: bad boy has inflated opinion of his own driving skills, good guy thinks otherwise; then using proper driving techniques, good guy defeats bad boy.

It's hard enough depicting the speed of hurtling cars on the comics page, and it certainly doesn't help that the plots are about as exciting as a school bus drag race. Even the descriptions of the "hot rods" aren't particularly hot.

Auto enthusiasts may be better entertained digging up copies of Car-Toons.

1 .... 135.00
2 .... 90.00
3 .... 58.00
4-10 .... 50.00
11-20 .... 36.00
21-30 .... 28.00
31-50 .... 24.00
51-60 .... 18.00
61-80 .... 13.00
81-100 .... 10.00
101-120 .... 7.00

Hot Shots
Hot, 1987
1 .... 2.00

Hot Shots: Avengers
Marvel, 1995
1 .... 3.00

Hot Shots: Spider-Man
Marvel, 1996

1 ....3.00

Hot Shots: X-Men
Marvel, 1996

1 ....3.00

Hotspur
Eclipse, 1987

1-3...2.00

Hot Stuf'
Sal Quartuccio, 1976

1 ....4.00
2-8...3.00

Hot Stuff
Harvey, 1991

1 ....2.00
2-8...1.00
9-12...2.00

Hot Stuff Big Book
Harvey, 1992

1-2...2.00

Hot Stuff Creepy Caves

1 ....12.00
2 ....8.00
3 ....8.00
4-5...8.00
6 ....8.00
7 ....8.00

Hot Stuff Digest
Harvey, 1992

1-5...2.00

Hot Stuff Giant-Size
Harvey, 1992

1-3...2.00

Hot Stuff, The Little Devil
Harvey, 1957

1 ....450.00
2 ....200.00
3 ....150.00
4-5.......................................100.00
6-10.......................................75.00
11-20.....................................60.00
21-30.....................................40.00
31-40.....................................25.00
41-50.....................................20.00
51-70.....................................15.00
71-100...................................10.00
101-121...................................7.00
122-145...................................5.00
146-177...................................3.00

Hot Stuff Sizzlers
Harvey, 1960

1 ....90.00
2-5...45.00
6-19.......................................25.00
20-44.....................................12.00
45-52.......................................7.00
53-59.......................................5.00

Hot Stuff Sizzlers
Harvey, 1992

1 .... 1.00

Hot Tails
Fantagraphics, 1996

1 .... 4.00

Hot Wheels
DC, 1970

1 .... 45.00
2 .... 30.00
3-5... 24.00
6 .... 30.00

Hourman
DC, 1999

OK, you're an android from the 853rd century, and you're programmed with the memories of Rex Tyler, the Golden Age Hourman. After nearly destroying the universe in the DC One Million limited series, you settle down in your past -- somewhere around the turn of the 21st century -- and give up a good portion of your chronal powers, you decide that you dearly want to be as human as possible. So to whom do you turn for help? Why, former Justice League of America mascot Snapper Carr, that's who! Sure, he's something of a loser, but he needs a purpose in life and it may as well be you.

This was a fun, imaginative super-hero series -- certainly one of the best to come out of the late 1990s. Hourman struggled to gain humanity, and it was a thrill to watch him take on such foes as Amazo, The JLAndroids, Epoch the Lord of Time, and his own makers in the 853rd century.

1 .... 3.00
2-25 .... 3.00

House II The Second Story
Marvel, 1987

1 .... 2.00

House of Frightenstein
AC

1 .... 3.00

House of Java
NBM, 2000

1-4 .... 3.00

House of M
Marvel, 2005

1 .... 4.00
1/Quesada........................... 30.00
1/DirCut................................. 4.00
1/Gatefold............................. 5.00
1/Madurera......................... 12.00
2 .... 3.00
2/Dodson............................ 25.00
3 .... 6.00
☛Hawkeye returns
3/Cassaday 20.00
4 .... 3.00
4/Peterson 15.00
5 .... 5.00
5/McKone 15.00
6 .... 3.00
6/Land 15.00
7 .... 4.00
8 .... 3.00

House of Mystery
DC, 1951

Beginning in 1951, the House of Mystery welcomed its readers into the dark world of the mysterious and macabre. Cain, the caretaker, was the host, as readers reveled in his strange tales of ghosts, witchcraft, demons from beyond the grave, and terror from our own world. No true fear fan dared miss a single issue.

Alas, after 321 issues and more than 30 years, the House had to close its doors. But even in its final issue, the title stayed true to form. In a last story, fictitious DC editors planned to turn the "House of Mystery" into "Condo of Fun." Cain, cantankerous till the end, responded by moving his pet ghouls into the DC publishing offices. Although the strategy failed, it was a fitting send-off to one of the best-loved fright titles of all time.

1	2,000.00
2	850.00
3	600.00
4-5	450.00
6-10	350.00
11-15	300.00
16-25	220.00
26-35	170.00
36-50	140.00
51-61	95.00
62	70.00
63	85.00
64	70.00
65	85.00
66-69	70.00
70	85.00
71-75	65.00
76	85.00
77-79	65.00
80-83	54.00
84-85	85.00
86-99	54.00
100	65.00
101-116	45.00
117-119	35.00
120	45.00
121-130	28.00
131-142	22.00
143	175.00

☞J'onn J'onzz starts

144	75.00
145-155	50.00
156	75.00

☞1st Robby Reed

157-159	50.00
160	90.00

☞1st Silver Age Plastic Man

161	35.00
162-173	32.00
174	50.00
175	45.00
176-177	24.00
178	45.00

☞Neal Adams art

179	60.00

☞1st Wrightson art

180-181	25.00
182	18.00
183	25.00
184	18.00
185	30.00
186	75.00

☞Bernie Wrightson art

187	20.00
188	30.00
189-190	20.00
191	25.00
192	20.00
193	25.00
194	30.00
195	45.00

☞Wrightson swamp man

196-201	20.00
202-203	14.00
204	20.00
205-206	12.00
207	40.00

☞Wrightson art

208	12.00
209-213	10.00
214-220	6.00
221	12.00
222-223	6.00
224	35.00
225-226	18.00
227	27.00
228-229	18.00
230-250	5.00
251-259	4.00
260-321	3.00

House of Secrets
DC, 1956

The House of Mystery's Cain has a kinder, gentler brother, Abel, who hosts this exploration of the weird and the supernatural. Witches, goblins, bogey men, and psychotics roam the pages, and the hapless mortals who get caught in their clutches sometimes thwart them and sometimes don't. Some of DC's best artists, including Steve Ditko, Sheldon Mayer, and of course, that master of the macabre himself, Bernie Wrightson, contributed to this series.

The series' title, but little else, returned in the late 1990s as a Vertigo horror series that was more focused on the house itself, rather than the anthology of horror stories.

1	1,500.00
2	550.00
3	450.00
4	350.00
5-7	200.00
8	230.00
9-12	200.00
13-15	125.00
16-20	110.00
21	85.00
22	80.00
23	100.00

☞1st Mark Merlin

24-30	80.00
31-50	65.00
51-60	52.00
61	125.00

☞1st Eclipso

62	60.00
63-65	50.00
66	65.00

☞Eclipso cover

67	40.00
68-79	36.00
80	45.00
81	55.00

☞1st Abel

82-84	20.00
85	32.00
86	20.00
87	45.00

☞Wrightson art

88-91	40.00
92	450.00

☞1st Swamp Thing

93-99	25.00
100	27.00
101-112	18.00
113-141	10.00
142-154	7.00

House of Secrets
DC, 1996

1-25	3.00

House of Secrets: Facade
DC, 2001

1-2	6.00

House of Yang
Charlton, 1975

1	5.00
2	3.00
3	10.00
4	3.00
5	10.00
6	3.00

House of Yang
Modern, 1978

1-2	2.00

Housewives at Play
Fantagraphics, 1999

1-3	3.00

Howard the Duck
Marvel, 1976

1	5.00
2-3	2.00
3/A-3/30¢	20.00
4	2.00
4/A-4/30¢	20.00
5-11	2.00
12	6.00
13	4.00
13/A	15.00
13/Whitman	5.00
13/35¢	15.00
14	2.00
14/A-14/35¢	15.00
15	2.00
15/A-15/35¢	15.00
16	2.00
16/A-16/35¢	15.00
17	2.00

17/A-17/35¢ 15.00
18-33......................................2.00
Anl 1......................................5.00

Howard the Duck
Marvel, 2002
1-6..3.00

Howard the Duck (Magazine)
Marvel, 1979
1 ....4.00
2-3..3.00
4 ....4.00
5-9..3.00

Howard the Duck Holiday Special
Marvel, 1997
1 ....3.00

Howard the Duck: The Movie
Marvel, 1986
1-3..1.00

Howdy Doody Comics
Dell, 1950
1 ....425.00
2 ....185.00
3 ....125.00
4-5...100.00
6 ....125.00
7-10..75.00
11-20.......................................55.00
21-30.......................................40.00
31-38.......................................36.00

Howl
Eternity, 1989
1-2..2.00

Howl's Moving Castle Film Comics
Viz, 2005
1-4..10.00

How The West Was Won
Gold Key, 1963
1 ....18.00

How To Break Into Comics
Antarctic, 2005
1 ....3.00

How to Draw Comics Comic
Solson, 1985
1 ....2.00

How To Draw Felix The Cat And His Friends
Felix, 1992
1 ....2.00

How to Draw Manga
Antarctic, 2000
1-25...5.00

How to Draw Manga: Next Generation
Antarctic, 2005
1/A-10................................... 5.00

How to Draw Teenage Mutant Ninja Turtles
Solson

This publication teaches readers how to draw the Teenage Mutant Ninja Turtles, using sketches and pinups drawn by Turtle co-creators Kevin B. Eastman and Peter Laird.
Commentary accompanying the sketches introduces each of the turtles and their weapons of choice. In addition, there are separate pieces on the construction of turtle heads, hands, and feet, as well as analysis of action scenes and motion. There is even coverage of turtle expressions and the proper way to draw turtle teeth and shells.
With help from this comic book, anyone can try their hand at drawing Leonardo, Michaelangelo, Raphael, and Donatello in the Eastman and Laird style.

1 .... 2.00

How To Pick Up Girls If You're A Comic Book Geek
3 Finger Prints, 1997
1 .... 4.00

How to Publish Comics
Solson
1 .... 2.00

How to Self-Publish Comics ... Not Just Create Them
Devil's Due, 2006
1-4 .... 5.00

H.R. Pufnstuf
Gold Key, 1970
1 .... 55.00
2-3 .... 40.00
4-6 .... 35.00
7-8 .... 25.00

Hsu and Chan
Slave Labor, 2003
1-7 .... 3.00

Huckleberry Hound
Gold Key, 1960
3-5 .... 35.00
6-10 .... 30.00
11-17 .... 20.00
18-19 .... 26.00
20 .... 20.00
21-30 .... 15.00
31-39 .... 9.00
40-43 .... 6.00

Huckleberry Hound & Quick Draw McGraw Giant-Size Flip Book
Harvey, 1993
1 .... 2.00

Huey, Dewey, and Louie Junior Woodchucks
Gold Key, 1966
1 .... 36.00
2 .... 20.00
3 .... 16.00
4-10 .... 12.00
11-20 .... 10.00
21-40 .... 8.00
41-60 .... 6.00
61-81 .... 4.00

Hugga Bunch
Marvel, 1986
1-6 .... 1.00

Hugo
Fantagraphics, 1985
1-3 .... 2.00

Hulk
Marvel, 1978
☛Magazine
10-21 .... 7.00
22-27 .... 5.00

Hulk
Marvel, 1999
1 .... 4.00
1/A 5.00
2-11 .... 3.00

Hulk
Marvel, 2008
1 .... 6.00
1/2nd 3.00
2 .... 4.00
3-18 .... 3.00

Hulk and Thing: Hard Knocks
Marvel, 2004
1-4 .... 4.00

Hulk: Destruction
Marvel, 2005
1-4 .... 3.00

Hulk: Gamma Games
Marvel, 2004
1-3 .... 3.00

Hulk: Gray
Marvel, 2003
1 .... 5.00
2 .... 4.00
3 .... 5.00
4 .... 4.00
5 .... 5.00
6 .... 4.00

Hulk Legends
Marvel, 2003
1 .... 14.00

Hulk Movie
Marvel, 2003
1 .... 13.00

Hulk/Pitt
Marvel, 1996
1 .... 6.00

Hulk: Project H.I.D.E.
Marvel, 1998
1 .... 2.00

Hulk Smash
Marvel, 2001

Marvel's Green-Skinned Goliath gets knighted-Marvel Knighted, that is-in this two-issue limited series from lauded creators Garth Ennis (Preacher), John McCrea (Hitman), and Klaus Janson (Daredevil). The story is focused on one Lt. Patrick D. Mitchell, a soldier with a lot of potential...who has abandoned his unit in the middle of a confrontation with none other than the ever-incredible Hulk, who is depicted here as nothing short of an incredibly destructive force of nature. Will Mitchell conquer his fears? Will he become a victim of the mindless behemoth's rampage through the Nevada desert? The answers to these questions-and many more-are to be found in this action-packed two-parter from some of comics' greatest craftsmen!

1-2 .... 3.00

Hulk: The Movie Adaptation
Marvel, 2003
1 .... 4.00

Hulk 2099
Marvel, 1994
1 .... 3.00
2-10 .... 2.00

Hulk: Unchained
Marvel, 2004
1-3 .... 3.00

Hulk Versus Thing
Marvel, 1999
1 .... 4.00

Hulk/Wolverine: 6 Hours
Marvel, 2003
1-4 .... 3.00

Human Defense Corps
DC, 2003
1-6 .... 3.00

Human Fly
Marvel, 1977
1 .... 3.00
1/35¢ 15.00
2-2/Whitman 2.00
2/35¢ 15.00
3-19 .... 2.00

Human Gargoyles
Eternity, 1988
1-4 .... 2.00

Human Head Comix
Iconografix
1 .... 3.00

Humankind
Image, 2004
1 .... 4.00
1/A 2.00
2-5 .... 3.00

Human Powerhouse
Pure Imagination
1 .... 2.00

Human Race
DC, 2005
1-7 .... 3.00

Human Remains
Black Eye
1 .... 4.00

Human Target
DC, 1999
1-4 .... 3.00

Human Target
DC, 2003
1-21 .... 3.00

Human Target Special
DC, 1991
1 .... 2.00

Human Target: Strike Zone
DC, 2004
1 .... 10.00

Human Torch
Marvel, 1940
1 .... 32,000.00
2 .... 7,400.00
3 .... 4,800.00
4 .... 3,400.00
5 .... 4,650.00
6-7 .... 2,100.00
8 .... 3,400.00
9 .... 2,100.00
10 .... 2,750.00
11-15 .... 1,850.00
16-20 .... 1,250.00
21-30 .... 1,025.00
31-38 .... 850.00

Human Torch
Marvel, 1974
1 .... 9.00
2 .... 4.00
3-8 .... 3.00

Human Torch
Marvel, 2003
1-12 .... 3.00

Humants
Legacy
1-2 .... 2.00

Humbug
Humbug, 1957

Mad magazine began as a comic book, created by editor-writer-artist Harvey Kurtzman, who oversaw its transition, with #24, to a magazine format. After a falling-out with Publisher William Gaines, Kurtzman created the glossy magazine Trump for Hugh Hefner but eventually tried an evolution of the standard comic-book format again, albeit in black and white, with Humbug.

He added to such of his regular co-conspirators as Jack Davis and Will Elder the cartoonist Arnold Roth and other talented cartoonists, and Humbug was as funny and satire-packed as Kurtzman's Mad had been, though the low-tech production didn't provide much in the way of printing worthy of the content. Like Mad, Humbug changed to a magazine format eventually -- but that wasn't enough to save it.

-- Maggie

1 ....120.00
2-11 ....100.00

Hummingbird
Slave Labor, 1996

1 ....5.00

Humongous Man
Alternative, 1997

1-2 ....2.00

Humor on the Cutting...Edge
Edge

1-4 ....3.00

Humphrey Comics
Harvey, 1948

Ham Fisher's Joe Palooka, the happy-go-lucky hillbilly heavyweight fighter, was such a hit with comic-strip and comic-book readers in the 1940s that even his sidekick Humphrey could support his own title. Humphrey is a great big fella with a soft heart and an even softer head. He lives with his dear old mama and shares his pal Palooka's gentlemanly manners. The problem is, he's such a behemoth that every time he sets foot in the ring, he clobbers his opponents with a single swat ("Aw

shucks, I didn't mean to hit 'em that hard!") while he's pre-occupied with other matters. Humphrey ambled through a series of lighthearted tales from Harvey Comics from the late 1940s through the early 1950s, featuring a kid-friendly mix of humor and adventure.

In addition to the comedic stories in the series, there were activity pages and a tin toy version of the Humphreymobile, a combination of a small woodshed and a large tricycle that Humphrey peddled around the country.

-- Rob Salkowitz

1 .... 50.00
2 .... 30.00
3 .... 22.00
4-10 .... 20.00
11-22 .... 16.00

Hunchback of Notre Dame (Disney's...)
Marvel, 1996

1 .... 5.00

Hunger
Speakeasy Comics, 2005

1-4 .... 3.00

Hunter-Killer
Image, 2004

0 .... 1.00
0/Ltd. 5.00
0/Autographed..................... 20.00
0/Conv.................................... 6.00
1/Campbell 3.00
1/Hairsine 4.00
1/Silvestri............................... 5.00
2/Silvestri............................... 3.00
2/Linsner 4.00
3-10 .... 3.00

Hunter-Killer Dossier
Image, 2005

0 .... 3.00

Hunter's Heart
DC

1-3 .... 6.00

Hunter: The Age of Magic
DC, 2001

This mini-series continues the tale begun in Books of Magic and Names of Magic, as it follows an older, and hopefully wiser, Tim Hunter into realms both known and unknown.

Aided by his owl familiar Yo-Yo, Tim will continue his arcane studies at the White School, if he can manage not to be drawn away into other adventures. But staying focused isn't an easy task when your school is linked to a thousand worlds which you can visit by simply opening another door.

Now Tim has received a mysterious letter, protected by a runic seal which only he can break. Where will the letter lead him? And what can explain his fiery visions, which draw him to the lake outside the White School? Can he be seeing his own funeral?

1 .... 4.00
2-25 .... 3.00

Hunter x Hunter
Viz, 2005

1-5 .... 8.00

Hunt for Black Widow
Fleetway-Quality

1 .... 3.00

Hunting
Northstar, 1993

1 .... 4.00

Huntress
DC, 1989

1 .... 3.00
2-5 .... 2.00
6-19 .... 1.00

Huntress
DC, 1994

1-4 .... 2.00

Hup
Last Gasp, 1986

R. Crumb disappeared from the field of "comix" in 1976, bidding a cheery "So long, folks!" to his fans. Nevertheless, he was back in 1987 with Hup, "The Comic for Modern Guys." Hup was published sporadically, reaching only issue #4 by 1992. It's still an interesting title, however, showing a more mature (if studiously cynical) Crumb. The lighter moments are given to Mr. Natural, allowing the strips in which Crumb draws himself to focus their attention on portraying the apparent misery of modern life.

1-4 .... 3.00

Hurricane Girls
Antarctic, 1995

1-7 .... 4.00

Hurricane LeRoux
Inferno

1 .... 3.00

Hustler Comix
L.F.P., 1997

1-4 .... 5.00

Hustler Comix
L.F.P., 1998

1-5 .... 5.00

Hustler Comix XXX
L.F.P., 1999

1 .... 6.00

Hutch Owen's Working Hard
New Hat

1 .... 4.00

Hy-Breed
Division, 1994

1-3 .... 2.00
4-10 .... 3.00

Hybrid: Etherworlds
Dimension 5

1-3 .... 3.00

Hybrids
Continuity, 1993

0 .... 1.00
1-5 .... 3.00

Hybrids
Continuity, 1994

1 .... 3.00

Hybrids: The Origin
Continuity, 1993

2-5 .... 3.00

Hyde-25
Harris, 1995

0 .... 3.00

Hydrogen Bomb Funnies
Rip Off, 1970

1 .... 5.00

Hydrophidian
NBM

1 .... 11.00

Hyena
Tundra

1-4 .... 4.00

Hyperactives
Alias, 2006

0 .... 1.00

Hyper Comix
Kitchen Sink, 1979

1 .... 5.00

Hyper Dolls
Ironcat, 1998

1-2 .... 3.00

Hyper Dolls
Ironcat, 1998

1-6 .... 3.00

Hyperkind
Marvel, 1993

Clive Barker's Hyperkind tells of how, in years gone by, a group of super-powered heroes known as the Paxis fought a version of World War I against alien invaders. After 75 years had gone by, they would be all but forgotten. But one day, a drunken bum literally drops from the sky -- and is attacked by a giant reptilian creature, Thermakk, Lawgiver of Quo. A woman who helps the bum (who's really the last of an alien race) gets an unhappy reward: Her bones are replaced with metal, and her body is charged with super-human power. She and three others then became the super-team Hyperkind.

Part of Marvel's Razorline, an attempt to create a comics world based on the works of Clive Barker, this and most of the other titles died fast in the glutted environment of the early 1990s.

1 .... 3.00
2-9 .... 2.00

Hyperkind Unleashed!
Marvel, 1994

1 .... 3.00

Hyper Mystery Comics
Hyper, 1940

1 .... 1,500.00
2 .... 1,000.00

Hyper Police
Tokyopop, 2005

1-5 .... 10.00

Hyper Rune
Tokyopop, 2004

1-4 .... 10.00

Hypersonic
Dark Horse, 1997

1-4 .... 3.00

Hyper Violents
CFD, 1996

1 .... 3.00

Hypothetical Lizard (Alan Moore's)
Avatar, 2005

1 .... 4.00
1/Wraparound 5.00
1/Platinum 12.00
1/Tarot-2 .... 4.00
2/Wraparound 5.00
3 .... 4.00
3/Foil...................................... 6.00
3/Wraparound 5.00

Hysteria: One Man Gang
Image, 2006

1-2 .... 3.00

Collectors looking for Incredible Hulk #7 through #101 should know that the series was canceled after #6 and picked up its numbering with #102 from Tales to Astonish.

i 4 N i
Mermaid, 1994
1-2 .... 2.00

I Am Legend
Eclipse
1-4 .... 6.00

I am Legion: Dancing Faun
DC, 2004
1 .... 7.00

I Before E
Fantagraphics, 1994
1-2 .... 4.00

Ibis the Invincible
Fawcett, 1943

Ibis was Fawcett's magic hero, and this sporadically published comic book was packed with his tales. (By the way, while he was on every cover, none of the covers

were actually connected with any of the contents of the issues.) As a bonus, though, Basil Wolverton's zany four-page comedy featurette "Mystic Moot and His Magic Snoot" appeared in the last four issues.

Though there were such other magical characters in comics as the newspaper-strip-featured Mandrake the Magician, Ibis didn't really copy them. A short version of his origin story appeared in Fawcett's Whiz anthology title, but the full version was presented in the initial issue of this series. Ibis' actual name was Amentep, and he was an Egyptian prince 4,000 years earlier. Betrothed to Princess Taia, Ibis was grief-stricken at what appeared to be her violent death. After avenging her, he tried to use his magic wand, the Ibistick, to kill himself. When he found that the Ibistick wouldn't harm him, he used to to put himself into suspended animation and, when he was revived, he revived his beloved, as well. They had numbers of adventures against evil (both fantastic and mundane) in the years that followed.

-- Maggie

1 .... 1,400.00
2 .... 750.00
3 .... 575.00
4-6 .... 400.00

I-Bots (Isaac Asimov's...)
Tekno, 1995
1-7 .... 2.00

I-Bots (Isaac Asimov's...)
Big, 1996
1-9 .... 2.00

iCandy
DC, 2003
1-6 .... 3.00

Icarus
Aircel, 1987
1-5 .... 2.00

Icarus
Kardia, 1992
1 .... 2.00

Ice Age on the World of Magic: The Gathering
Acclaim, 1995
1-4 .... 3.00

Iceman
Marvel, 1984
1 .... 4.00
2-4 .... 3.00

Iceman
Marvel, 2001
1 .... 4.00
2-4 .... 3.00

Icicle
Hero, 1992
1 .... 5.00
2-5 .... 4.00

I Come In Peace
Greater Mercury
1 .... 2.00

Icon
DC, 1993

Icon is one of Milestone's more interesting takes on the subject of racial relations. Its title character, Augustus Freeman, is an alien who crashed on our planet more than 150 years ago, taking the form of a black human baby. Extremely long-lived, he is now a conservative lawyer, living in a suburb of the city of Dakota. Until recently, he had concentrated on his own affairs.

Then a gang of youngsters broke into his house and tried to burglarize it. The would-be thieves were stunned, however, when Freeman took several shots to the chest, only to rise again, and fly after them.

Later, a young girl named Raquel came to visit Freeman. She had been along with the other teens that night, but when she saw what he could do, she had other thoughts. She returned to challenge Freeman to be an icon - a super-powered symbol of hope to his people. And of course, she, a street-smart liberal, would be his sidekick.

1	2.00
1/CS	3.00
2-24	2.00
25	3.00
26	2.00
27-30	3.00
31	1.00
32-42	3.00

Icon Devil
Spider

1-2	2.00

Icon Devil
Spider

2	2.00

Iconografix Special
Iconografix

1	3.00

Iczer 3
CPM, 1996

1-2	3.00

Id
Fantagraphics, 1995

1-3/2nd	3.00

ID4: Independence Day
Marvel, 1996

ID4: Independence Day was without a doubt the science-fiction blockbuster of 1996. Audiences around the world were astonished at the sight of huge alien ships casting shadows over New York, London, Moscow, and other major cities. In the story, the aliens waited just long enough to move all their ships into position, then they began an awesome wave of destruction with the ultimate goal of exterminating humanity.

Within days most of earth's major cities were gone, and even nuclear weapons proved useless against the invaders. The president, having narrowly escaped the destruction of the White House, traveled to Area 51, where an alien craft had been secretly been held since it crashed in the 1950s. From there, he hoped to launch a counterassault against the invaders and win back the planet. The date was July 4th: Independence Day for America-and now hopefully for the world as well.

0	3.00
1-2	2.00

Idaho
Dell, 1963

1	28.00
2-8	18.00

Ideal
Timely, 1948

1	250.00
2	225.00
3-4	200.00
5	150.00

Ideal Comics
Timely, 1944

1	150.00
2	100.00
3-4	75.00

Ideal Romance
Key, 1954

3	50.00
4-8	35.00

Id_entity
Tokyopop, 2005

1-4	10.00

Identity Crisis
DC, 2004

1	15.00
1/2nd	6.00
1/3rd	5.00
1/Sketch	225.00
2	8.00
3	7.00
4	8.00
5	7.00
6	8.00
7	7.00

Identity Disc
Marvel, 2004

1-5	3.00

I Die at Midnight
DC, 2000

1	3.00

Idiotland
Fantagraphics, 1993

1-6	3.00

Idle Worship
Visceral

1	3.00

Idol
Marvel

1-3	3.00

I Dream of Jeannie
Dell, 1966

1	60.00
2	40.00

I Dream of Jeannie
Airwave, 2002

1	3.00
Ann 1	4.00

I Feel Sick
Slave Labor, 1999

Can a Goth comic truly be funny? Jhonen Vasquez's "I Feel Sick" comes awfully close. Vasquez, creator of Johnny the Homicidal Maniac, offers up a morbidly comical tale revolving around Devi, the semi-sane lead character of the book and all her friends (and enemies). Like most young hermits, Devi stays in her apartment, unless dragged out by best pal Tenna. She relives--almost with relish--the dark moments of her past, including a car accident with a horny boyfriend. Oh yeah, and she thinks her painting of a doll is talking to her. Vasquez's story shows deft pacing and some truly funny and touching moments as Devi and Tenna make their way in the world. It's a rather dark world, where one can dine in a restaurant called Eat or Die and hang out in vampire bars where, of course, the music always sucks. But this comic sure doesn't.

-- Stephen C. George

1 ....4.00

If the Devil Would Talk
Catholic Guild, 1950
1 ....850.00

If the Devil Would Talk
Impact, 1958
1 ....450.00

Igrat
Verotik, 1995
1 ....3.00

Igrat Illustrations
Verotik, 1997
1 ....4.00

I Had a Dream
King Ink Empire, 1995
1 ....3.00

I (Heart) Marvel: Marvel AI
Marvel, 2006
1 ....3.00

I (Heart) Marvel: Masked Intentions
Marvel, 2006
1 ....3.00

I (Heart) Marvel: My Mutant Heart
Marvel, 2006
1 ....3.00

I (Heart) Marvel: Outlaw Love
Marvel, 2006
1 ....3.00

I (Heart) Marvel: Web of Romance
Marvel, 2006
1 ....3.00

I Hunt Monsters
Antarctic, 2004
1-9...3.00

I Hunt Monsters
Antarctic, 2005
1-9...3.00

Ike and Kitzi
A Capella
1 ....3.00

Iliad
Slave Labor, 1997

In the futuristic city-state of Krete, ancient tales are given new life in this story of tyranny, betrayal, and monsters. Powerful King Minos rules the known world with bitterness and a brutal hand, backed by the power of the mysterious creature known as the Minotech. But not all are willing to bow before Minos' fist.

Unwilling to be part of the human sacrifice required of all conquered nations, young Prince A'Tum offers to battle the Minotech in exchange for his people's freedom.

Meanwhile, the beautiful Eve discovers the role of Minos and his creature in the death of her mother and in the exile of her father Daedales, Krete's designer and one-time technological wizard. She, too, vows to destroy the fearsome beast, and to make Minos pay for his evil deeds.

Individually, they have no chance for survival, but together they may set in motion the necessary events needed to restore Krete to its former glory.

1-2.. 3.00

Iliad II
Micmac, 1986
1-3... 2.00

Illegal Alien
Kitchen Sink
1 .... 10.00

Illegal Aliens
Eclipse, 1999
1 .... 3.00

Illuminations
Monolith, 1995
1-5.. 3.00

Illuminator
Marvel, 1993

This joint project between Christian publisher Nelson and Marvel Comics stars Andy Prentiss, an average underconfident teen. His parents send him to camp for the summer, where his campmates make fun of him. One night, they trick him into going on a "wampus hunt," and Andy stands in wait for hours in the dark, holding a bag and waiting to trap the mythical "wampus."

Seeing strange lights in the sky, Andy discovers he has great powers, including the ability to fly. But, while the powers gave Andy confidence, he doesn't understand what to do with them until an evil spirit begins terrorizing his hometown. An old church caretaker encourages Andy to find his spiritual faith and to battle evil as the Illuminator.

Part of one of Carol Kalish's many projects to widen Marvel's audience, this series saw far more distribution in religious bookstores than through comics shops.

1-2... 5.00
3 .... 3.00

Illuminatus
Eye-N-Apple
1-2... 2.00

Illuminatus!
Rip Off, 1990
1-3... 3.00

Illustrated Classex
Comic Zone, 1991
1 .... 3.00

Illustrated Dore: Book of Genesis
Tome
1 .... 3.00

Illustrated Dore: Book of the Apocrypha
Tome

1 ....3.00

Illustrated Editions
Thwack! Pow!, 1995

1 ....2.00

Illustrated Kama Sutra
NBM

1 ....13.00

Illustrated Life of Seymour
Sofa Comics

1-4 ....3.00

Illustrated Stories of the Operas
Bailey, 1943

1-4 ....400.00

Illustrated Tales (Jaxon's...)
FTR

1 ....2.00

I Loved
Fox, 1949

29-32 ....75.00

I Love Lucy
Eternity, 1990

1-6 ....3.00

I Love Lucy Book Two
Eternity, 1990

1-6 ....3.00

I Love Lucy Comics
Dell, 1954

I Love Lucy was one of the first indisputable hits of the then-new television medium in the early 1950s. Starring the real-life married couple, Lucille Ball and Desi Arnaz as Lucy and Ricky Ricardo, with perennial sidekicks William Frawley and Vivian Vance as friends and neighbors Fred and Ethel Mertz, this comical battle of the sexes reached immortality through reruns.

Whereas the Dell series tells stories developed specifically for the comic-book format, the later Eternity series reprints the daily comic strip that writer Lawrence Nadel and artist Bob Oksner produced under the name Bob Lawrence.

3	110.00
4	85.00
5	70.00
6-10	55.00
11-20	45.00
21-35	36.00

I Love Lucy in 3-D
Eternity

1 .... 4.00

I Love Lucy in Full Color
Eternity

1 .... 6.00

I Love New York
Linsner.com, 2002

1 .... 10.00

I Love You
Charlton, 1955

7	55.00
8-10	16.00
11-16	14.00
17	18.00
18-20	14.00
21-30	12.00
31-50	10.00
51-59	8.00
60	60.00
61-69	4.00
70-121	3.00
122-130	2.00

I Love You
Avalon

1 .... 3.00

I Love You Special
Avalon

1 .... 3.00

I, Lusiphur
Mulehide

1	20.00
2	12.00
3	15.00
4	12.00
5	10.00
6-7	8.00

I Luv Halloween
Tokyopop, 2005

1 .... 10.00

Image
Image, 1993

In the earliest issues of the various initial Image Comics series, there were coupons for Image #0, an anthology one-shot featuring stories from the Image founding fathers.

Included in this rare issue are Troll by Rob Liefeld and Art Thibert, StormWatch by Jim Lee and Brandon Choi, The Savage Dragon by Erik Larsen, Stryker by Marc Silvestri, ShadowHawk by Jim Valentino, and several pinup-style pages of characters created by Todd McFarlane.

Even though they stand alone, the stories presented here tie into the characters' ongoing adventures while providing insight, however brief, into what each of the heroes (or anti-heroes) is all about.

0 .... 4.00

Image Comics Holiday Special 2005
Image, 2006

1 .... 10.00

Image Introduces... Believer
Image, 2001

1 .... 3.00

Image Introduces... Cryptopia
Image, 2002

1 .... 3.00

Image Introduces... Dog Soldiers
Image, 2002

1 .... 3.00

Image Introduces... Legend of Isis
Image, 2002
1 ....3.00

Image Introduces... Primate
Image, 2001
1/A-1/B 3.00

Image of the Beast
Last Gasp, 1979
1 ....3.00

Image Plus
Image, 1993
1 ....2.00

Images of a Distant Soil
Image, 1997
1 ....3.00

Images of Omaha
Kitchen Sink, 1992
1-2..4.00

Images of Shadowhawk
Image, 1993
1-3..2.00

Image Two-In-One
Image, 2001
1 ....3.00

Imagi-Mation
Imagi-Mation
1-2..2.00

Imaginaries
Image, 2005
1-4..3.00

Imagine
Star*Reach, 1978
1 ....20.00
1/2nd-2 ....10.00
3 ....15.00
4 ....10.00
5-6 ....6.00

I'm Dickens... He's Fenster
Dell, 1963
1 ....25.00
2 ....20.00

Immortal Combat
Express, 1995
1 ....3.00

Immortal Doctor Fate
DC, 1985
1-3..2.00

Immortal II
Image, 1997
1-5..3.00

Immortal Iron Fist
Marvel, 2007
1 ....8.00
2 ....6.00

Immortals
Comics By Day
1 ....1.00

Imp
Slave Labor, 1994
1 ....3.00

Impact
E.C., 1955

There were six E.C. titles in its "New Direction," cover-bannered as "an entirely novel and unique reading experience." The cover of each had a frame with the title on top and an identifying icon down the left side. The "New Direction" was one designed to accommodate the Comics Magazine of America's new Comics Code, though the first issue of each did not carry the Code stamp, and all but one lasted for five issues. The six titles were: Aces High, Extra!, MD, Psychoanalysis, Valor -- and Impact.

Above Impact's title was the line "Tales designed to carry an ..." and the stories were each designed to have a punch ending. The first issue cover-featured the classic Bernie Krigstein-illustrated "Master Race," and for its time, and considering the restrictions, the series was outstanding. In at least one case (the cover story of #4), Code censorship rendered the story incomprehensible. Nevertheless, the anthology series was powerful, illustrated by Jack Davis, Reed Crandall, Graham Ingels, George Evans, Krigstein, Joe Orlando, and Jack Kamen.

-- Maggie

1 .... 225.00
2 .... 125.00
3-4 .... 90.00
5 .... 80.00

Impact
RCP, 1999
1-5... 3.00
Ann 1 .... 14.00

Impact Christmas Special
DC, 1991
1 .... 3.00

Impact Comics Who's Who
DC, 1991
1-3... 5.00

Impaler
Image, 2006
1-2 .... 3.00

Imperial Dragons
Alias, 2005
1 .... 1.00

Imperial Guard
Marvel, 1997
1-3... 2.00

Impossible Man Summer Vacation Spectacular
Marvel, 1990
1-2 .... 2.00

Impulse
DC, 1995

Before Barry Allen -- The Flash -- died in the Crisis on Infinite Earths, he lived for a time in the future of the 30th century with his wife, Iris. There, she gave birth to twins, Don and Dawn, who became known as the Tornado Twins. In turn, Don eventually had a son named Bart who inherited his grandfather's speed.

Unfortunately, Bart's speed came at a price: His metabolism was accelerated so that by the time he was 2 years old he appeared, physically, to be 12. To help match his physical and mental ages, Bart's parents had him educated in a virtual reality environment. In time, however, Bart would have died, if his parents hadn't brought him to this century to have the current Flash,

Wally West, teach him how to control his speed. Today, he lives with Max Mercury, who is trying to teach him wisdom. The lesson is coming hard for Bart, however, who grew up in a world which was all just a big game.

1-2	4.00
3-5	3.00
6-64	2.00
65-89	3.00
1000000	4.00
Ann 1	5.00
Ann 2	4.00

Impulse/Atom Double-Shot
DC, 1998

1	2.00

Impulse: Bart Saves the Universe
DC

1	6.00

Impulse Plus
DC, 1997

1	3.00

Imp-Unity
Spoof

1	3.00

Incomplete Death's Head
Marvel, 1993

1	3.00
2-12	2.00

In-Country Nam
Survival Arts

1-2	2.00

Incredible Drinkin' Buddies
Luxurious

1	3.00

Incredible Hulk
Marvel, 1962

Bruce Banner was a respected scientist who was working for the

military to develop a gamma bomb. Seconds before the gamma bomb was to be tested, he saw a young man driving through the test area. Banner ordered the countdown stopped and raced to save the teen - but a jealous research assistant neglected to stop the countdown, and the bomb was exploded. Although Banner was able to get the boy to safety, he was caught in the gamma radiation released by the bomb. Thereafter, whenever he became angry, he found himself changing into a huge green monster with unbelievable strength. This monster became known as The Incredible Hulk.

In the years since, The Hulk has gone from raging berserker to sharing Banner's intellect and back again.

The Jekyll-and-Hyde-like story has been turned on its ear by Banner's remorse for what his alter-ego does when he's not in control.

-1	2.00
1	13,000.00
☞1st Hulk	
2	3,500.00
3	2,000.00
4-5	1,750.00
6	2,250.00
102	150.00
103	100.00
104	75.00
105	70.00
106-112	50.00
113-115	40.00
116-121	35.00
122	55.00
☞Thing vs. Hulk	
123-125	30.00
126-130	25.00
131	30.00
132	25.00
133	20.00
134-136	16.00
137-140	20.00
☞Harlan Ellison	
140/2nd	3.00
☞1st Doc Samson	
141-151	20.00
152	25.00
153-160	20.00
161	30.00
162	55.00
☞1st Wendigo	
163-171	15.00
172	25.00
☞X-Men app.	
173-176	15.00
177-178	17.00
179	16.00
180	180.00
☞Wolverine cameo	

181	750.00
☞1st Wolverine story	
181/Ace	5.00
182	100.00
☞2nd Wolverine	
183	12.00
184-190	10.00
191-198	8.00
198/30¢	20.00
199	8.00
199/30¢	20.00
200	11.00
200/30¢	30.00
201	7.00
201/30¢	20.00
202	7.00
202/30¢	20.00
203-212/Whitman	7.00
212/35¢	15.00
213-213/Whitman	7.00
213/35¢	15.00
214-214/Whitman	7.00
214/35¢	15.00
215-215/Whitman	7.00
215/35¢	15.00
216-216/Whitman	7.00
216/35¢	15.00
217-218/Whitman	7.00
219-240	5.00
241-249	4.00
250	7.00
251-285	3.00
286	4.00
287-295	3.00
296	5.00
297	4.00
298-299	3.00
300	4.00
301-319	3.00
320-323	2.00
324	5.00
325	3.00
326	4.00
327-328	3.00
329	2.00
☞1st McFarlane	
330-334	5.00
335	2.00
336-339	3.00
340	14.00
☞vs. Wolverine	
341	4.00
342-349	2.00
350	5.00
☞1st Dale Keown	
351-371	2.00
372	3.00
373-376	2.00
377	3.00
377/2nd-377/3rd	2.00
378	3.00
379-384	2.00
385	4.00
386	3.00
387-391	2.00
392	3.00
393	4.00

393/2nd-394............................3.00
395-399..................................2.00
400-400/2nd............................3.00
401-418..................................2.00
418/Variant.............................3.00
419-425..................................2.00
425/Variant.............................4.00
426-448..................................2.00
449..8.00
450..5.00
451-474..................................2.00
Ann 1..................................115.00
Ann 2....................................40.00
Ann 3-4 ....25.00
Ann 5......................................9.00
Ann 6......................................7.00
Ann 7......................................9.00
Ann 8......................................5.00
Ann 9......................................3.00
Ann 10....................................4.00
Ann 11-19 ....3.00
Ann 20....................................4.00
Ann 1997-1998 ....3.00
Ashcan 1 ....1.00

Incredible Hulk
Marvel, 1999
☛Cont'd from Hulk
12-20......................................3.00
21-24......................................2.00
25..3.00
26-33......................................2.00
34..13.00
☛Bruce Jones starts
35..6.00
36-38......................................5.00
39-41......................................4.00
42-46......................................3.00
47-49......................................2.00
50..5.00
51..4.00
52-54......................................3.00
55-63......................................2.00
64..3.00
65-66......................................2.00
67-72......................................3.00
73-74......................................2.00
75-76......................................4.00
77-82......................................3.00
83..5.00
83/Variant..............................4.00
☛2nd print
84..3.00
84/Variant..............................4.00
☛2nd print
85-91......................................3.00
92..25.00
92/2nd....................................6.00
93-99......................................3.00
100-100/Variant......................4.00
101-115..................................3.00
Ann 1999................................5.00
Ann 2000................................4.00
Ann 2001................................3.00

Incredible Hulk and the Thing: The Big Chance
Marvel
1 .... 6.00

Incredible Hulk and Wolverine
Marvel, 1986
1 .... 7.00
1/2nd 4.00

Incredible Hulk, The: Future Imperfect
Marvel, 1993
1-2 .... 6.00

Incredible Hulk: Hercules Unleashed
Marvel, 1996
1 .... 3.00

Incredible Hulk Megazine
Marvel, 1996
1 .... 4.00

Incredible Hulk, The: Nightmerica
Marvel, 2003
1-6 .... 3.00

Incredible Hulk Poster Magazine
Marvel
1/A... 4.00
1/B... 2.00

Incredible Hulk: The End
Marvel, 2002
1 .... 6.00

Incredible Hulk Versus Quasimodo
Marvel, 1983
1 .... 2.00

Incredible Hulk vs. Superman
Marvel, 1999
1 .... 6.00

Incredible Hulk vs. Venom
Marvel, 1994
1 .... 3.00

Incredible Mr. Limpet
Dell, 1964
1 .... 25.00

Incredible Science Fiction
E.C., 1955

The Comics Magazine Association of America's implemented the Comics Code, which forbade "all scenes of horror" in newsstand comics and altered possibly offensive titles. So Weird Science-Fantasy changed its name to Incredible Science Fiction, and each issue carried the Code seal. Famously, one story was challenged because fantastic birds in a jungle-planet setting were called satires on angels. And a reprint of "Judgment Day" was initially rejected because, it was claimed, it would offend black readers. E.C. ran both stories, despite pressures to change them. Incredible Science Fiction #33 (Jan 56) was E.C.'s last publication in color comic-book form.
-- *Maggie*

30-33 .... 250.00

Incredibles
Dark Horse, 2004
1-4 .... 3.00

Incubus
Palliard
1-2 .... 3.00

Independent Publisher's Group Spotlight
Hero, 1993
0 .... 4.00

Independent Voices
Peregrine Entertainment, 1998
1 .... 2.00
2-3 .... 3.00

Indiana Jones and the Arms of Gold
Dark Horse, 1994
1-6 .... 3.00

Indiana Jones and the Fate of Atlantis
Dark Horse, 1991

Dr. "Indiana" Jones, the noted archaeologist and adventurer returns in this limited series. It began when a strange man appeared, inquiring about the origins of an ancient key. Dr. Jones traced the key to a 3,000 year-old archaeological find, and discovered that the key opened a secret compartment in one of the artifacts from that dig.

No sooner had Jones discovered this than the man, revealed as an S.S. colonel, returned and attempted to seize the artifact. The Nazis felt that it held the key to finding Atlantis, and to a source of limitless power - and only Indiana Jones could stop them from getting it.

Lucasfilm Games created the concept for Indiana Jones and the Fate of Atlantis for use in a computer game by the same name.

1-4...3.00

Indiana Jones and the Golden Fleece
Dark Horse, 1994
1-2...3.00

Indiana Jones and the Iron Phoenix
Dark Horse, 1994
1-4...3.00

Indiana Jones and the Last Crusade
Marvel, 1989
1-4...1.00

Indiana Jones and the Last Crusade (Magazine)
Marvel, 1989
1...3.00

Indiana Jones and the Sargasso Pirates
Dark Horse, 1995
1-4...3.00

Indiana Jones and the Shrine of the Sea Devil
Dark Horse, 1994
1...3.00

Indiana Jones and the Spear of Destiny
Dark Horse, 1995

Picking up shortly after the events of Indiana Jones and the Last Crusade, Doctor Henry Jones writes to his son in 1945 that certain parties of Nazi persuasion are interested in another religious artifact that might help them turn the tide in the current World War. The Spear of Longinus, which pierced the side of Jesus Christ at the Crucifixion and was carried away after the Resurrection by Joseph of Aramethea to the Glastonbury area and kept by his descendants in a chapel.

Now the Nazi's are seeking the pieces of the Spear in order to destroy their enemies and lead their armies to victory before it is too late. And the only people standing in their way again are named Jones.

1-4...3.00

Indiana Jones and the Temple of Doom
Marvel, 1984
1-3...2.00

Indiana Jones: Thunder in the Orient
Dark Horse, 1993
1-6...3.00

Indian Chief
Dell, 1951
3...40.00

4-12	30.00
13-29	25.00
30-33	22.00

Indian Fighter
Dell, 1950
1...75.00
2...50.00
3-11...35.00

Indians
Fiction House, 1950
1...200.00
2...135.00
3-5...100.00
6-10...70.00
11-17...48.00

Indians on the Warpath
St. John, 1949
1...200.00

Indian Summer
NBM
1...22.00

Indian Warriors
Star Publications, 1951
7...100.00
8...80.00

Indigo Vertigo One Shot
Image
1...5.00

In Dream World
Tokyopop, 2005
1-3...10.00

Industrial Gothic
DC, 1995

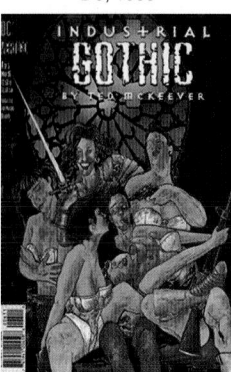

Industrial Gothic is Ted McKeever's (Doom Patrol (2nd Series), Metropol A.D.) allegorical tale of two misfits in a society that eschews handicaps and defects. Together with the stylistic lettering of John Workman, McKeever shows us his personal vision of the self-centered attitude prevalent in today's world of beautiful people. The protagonists, Pencil and Nickel, two escapees from prison,

search for the fabled Aluminum Tower, a quest that they expect to bring them fulfillment in this horrible post-apocalyptic world.
-- George Haberberger

1-5 ....3.00

Industrial Strength Preview
Silver Skull

1 ....2.00

Industry of War One-Shot
Image, 2006

1 ....8.00

Indy Buzz
Blindwolf, 1999

1 ....3.00

Inedible Adventures of Clint the Carrot
Hot Leg, 1994

1 ....3.00

Infantry
Devil's Due, 2004

1 ....3.00
1/Alternative 4.00
2-3 ....3.00

Infectious
Fantaco

1 ....4.00

Inferior Five
DC, 1967

1 ....24.00
2 ....16.00
3-10 ....14.00
11-12 ....10.00

Inferno
Aircel, 1990

1-4 ....3.00

Inferno
Caliber, 1995

1 ....3.00

Inferno
DC, 1997

1-4 ....3.00

Inferno: Hellbound
Image, 2002

0-3 ....3.00

Infinite Crisis
DC, 2005

1/Perez-1/Lee 6.00
1/2nd 4.00
1/RRP 450.00
2/Perez-4/Lee 6.00
5/Perez-7 ....4.00

Infinite Crisis Secret Files 2006
DC, 2006

1 ....12.00

Infinite Kung Fu
Kagan McLeod, 2000

1-1/2nd 5.00

Infinity Abyss
Marvel, 2002

1-5 ....3.00
6 ....4.00

Infinity Charade
Parody

1/A-1/B 3.00
1/Gold 4.00

Infinity Crusade
Marvel, 1993

1 ....4.00
2-6 ....3.00

Infinity Gauntlet
Marvel, 1991

It's the end of the universe. Thanos, the mad god who worships death, has gained control of the Infinity Gauntlet: six gems that give him ultimate power over everything. He exerts power that dwarfs that of Galactus. He possesses ultimate knowledge. And with a single thought, he wipes half the living beings in the galaxy from existence.

In a star-spanning, six-part epic by Jim Starlin, the most powerful beings in the universe unite to try to stop galactic Armageddon. Drawn together by Adam Warlock (who possesses the soul gem -- the only infinity gem not in Thanos' control), Earth's heroes must fight an unwinnable battle against an all-powerful foe.

1-6 ....3.00

Infinity Graphics Presents
Infinity, 1987

1 ....2.00

Infinity, Inc.
DC, 1984

1 ....3.00

2-10 ....2.00
11-13 ....1.00
14 ....4.00
☞McFarlane starts
15-37 ....3.00
38-45 ....1.00
46 ....2.00
47-49 ....1.00
50 ....3.00
51-52 ....1.00
53 ....2.00
Ann 1-2 ....3.00
Special 1 ....2.00

Infinity of Warriors
Ominous, 1994

1 ....2.00

Infinity War
Marvel, 1992

1-6 ....3.00

Infochameleon: Company Cult
Mediawarp, 1997

1 ....5.00

Informer
Feature, 1954

1 ....48.00
2 ....34.00
3-5 ....28.00

In His Steps
Marvel

1 ....10.00

Inhumanoids
Marvel, 1987

1-4 ....1.00

Inhumans
Marvel, 1975

1 ....8.00
2-4 ....4.00
4/30¢ 7.00
5 ....4.00
6 ....3.00
6/30¢ 20.00
7-11 ....3.00
11/35¢ 15.00
12 ....3.00
12/35¢ 15.00
Special 1 ....4.00

Inhumans
Marvel, 1998

1-1/Variant 4.00
2/A-12 ....3.00

Inhumans
Marvel, 2000

1-4 ....3.00

Inhumans
Marvel, 2003

1-12 ....3.00

Inhumans, The: The Great Refuge
Marvel, 1995

1 ....3.00

Inhumans: The Untold Saga
Marvel, 1977

1 .... 4.00

Initial D
Tokyopop, 2002

1-20 .... 10.00

Inkpunks Quarterly
Funk-O-Tron

1-3 .... 3.00

In Love
Mainline, 1954

1 .... 130.00
2 .... 85.00
3-4 .... 70.00
5-6 .... 35.00

Inmates Prisoners Of Society
Delta, 1997

1-4 .... 3.00

Innercircle
Mushroom, 1995

0.1-0.3 .... 3.00

Inner-City Products
Hype

1 .... 2.00

Inner City Romance
Last Gasp, 1972

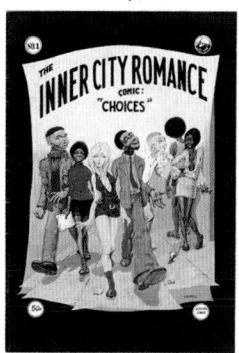

This underground title from writer-artist Guy Colwell explores the politics of sex: the sex between two people who love each other, the sex between two people who simply need someone else, the sex in the criminal act of rape, and so on. There's also commentary on his times and the issue of the environment. The artwork runs the gamut from sketchy and crude to beautiful and expressive.

1 .... 5.00
2-5 .... 3.00

Innocent Bystander
Ollie Ollie! Oxen Free, 1997

1-6 .... 3.00

Innocent Ones
Fantagraphics, 2005

1 .... 8.00

Innocents
Image, 2006

1 .... 3.00

Innovation Preview Special
Innovation, 1989

1 .... 1.00

Innovation Spectacular
Innovation, 1990

1-2 .... 3.00

Innovation Summer Fun Special
Innovation

1 .... 4.00

Inovators
Dark Moon, 1995

Inovators (sic) is one of the first titles from Manchester, Connecticut's Dark Moon Productions. It's the story of an ages-old battle between the primal forces of Good and Evil, a battle which has recently taken a critical turn. The force of Good is called Yang-Ki, and is contained in an energy sphere guarded by an old man named Lao Shan. There is a corresponding force of Evil, served by the dread guardian Balac-Soon and his minions.

The evil orb seemed full of vitality, and had caused most of man's suffering on this planet. At the same time, Lao Shan had grown old and tired and was on the verge of admitting defeat. Then, two teens found themselves attracted to Lao Shan's shop, where they found the orb, Yang-Ki, and were transformed by it. The teens' bodies were left behind, and their souls became the first of the Inovators, new warriors in the battle against evil.

1 .... 3.00

In Rage
CFD, 1994

1 .... 3.00

Insane
Dark Horse, 1988

1-2 .... 2.00

Insane Clown Posse
Chaos!, 1999

1 .... 3.00
1/A 4.00
2 .... 3.00
2/CS 4.00
3 .... 3.00
3/A 4.00
4 .... 3.00
4/CS 4.00
5 .... 3.00
5/CS 4.00
6 .... 3.00
6/CS 4.00
7 .... 3.00
7/CS 4.00
8 .... 3.00
8/CS 4.00
9-11 .... 3.00
11/CS 4.00
12-12/CS 3.00

In Search of Shirley
NBM

1 .... 10.00

In Search of the Castaways
Gold Key, 1963

1 .... 20.00

Insect Man's 25th Anniversary Special
Entertainment, 1991

1 .... 2.00

Inside Crime
Fox, 1950

1 .... 150.00
2-3 .... 140.00

Inside Out King
Free Fall

1-1/2nd 3.00

Insomnia
Fantagraphics, 2005

1 .... 8.00

Insomnia
Fantagraphics, 2005

1 .... 8.00

Inspector
Gold Key, 1974

1 ....20.00
2 ....10.00
3-19 ....5.00

Inspector Gill of the Fish Police
Apple, 1991

0 ....3.00

Instant Piano
Dark Horse, 1994

1-4 ....4.00

Intense!
Pure Imagination

1-3 ....3.00

Interactive Comics
Adventure

1-2 ....5.00

Interface
Marvel, 1989

1 ....3.00
2-8 ....2.00

Internal Fury
Fierce Comics, 2005

1 ....2.00
2 ....2.00
3-4 ....4.00

International Comics
E.C., 1947

Gardner Fox wrote the stories for this E.C. title which began a morphing sequence which ended as The Crypt of Terror. The Pre-Trend title began as a crime comic book and it had adventures of continuing characters Van Manhattan and Madelon. The first morphing occurred with #6, which was retitled International Crime Patrol, introduced in #5 with the cover copy "Introducing the INTERNATIONAL CRIME-BUSTING PATROL … featuring Van Manhattan, Igor, Madelon and the Chessmen … in a thrilling book-length story!"
-- Maggie

1 .... 425.00
2 .... 275.00
3-5 .... 240.00

International Cowgirl Magazine
Iconografix

1-2 .... 3.00

International Crime Patrol
E.C., 1948

6 .... 375.00

International Fallout Shelter Zone
KHB

1-4 .... 1.00

Interplanetary Lizards of the Texas Plains
Leadbelly, 1991

0 .... 3.00
1-7 .... 2.00
8 .... 3.00

Interstellar Overdrive
Leonine, 1990

1-2 .... 1.00

Interview With the Vampire (Anne Rice's...)
Innovation, 1991

1-12 .... 3.00

In the Days of the Ace Rock 'n' Roll Club
Fantagraphics

1 .... 5.00

In The Days of the Mob
DC, 1971

1 .... 50.00

In the Presence of Mine Enemies
Spire

Life for American POWs in Vietnam was often a terrible ordeal, pushing soldiers to their mental and physical limits. No one knows this better than Captain Howard Rutledge who spent seven years in a Hanoi prison after his plane was shot down during the war. Separated from his country, his wife, and his children, Rutledge turns to God and the other American prisoners for support as he endures some of the harshest punishment known to man. And while Rutledge struggles to stay alive, his wife Phyllis endures her own tests of faith on the home front. Published by Spire Christian Comics, this true story of war, suffering, faith and redemption was also published as a book and made into a short film.

1 .... 7.00

In Thin Air
Tome

1/A-1/B 3.00

Intimate Confessions
I.W., 1964

9-10 .... 12.00

Intimate Confessions
Realistic Comics, 1951

1 .... 375.00
2 .... 150.00
3-7 .... 115.00

Intimate Love
Standard, 1950

Standard stories of romantic complications interspersed between single page fashion and beauty tips, as well as the requisite text story and advice column, comprise the bulk of this title. The romantic complications range from simple, immature misunderstandings to memory-suppressed tragedies. Definitely a product of its times, the moral of these stories taught its generally female audience that true love will solve a multitude of life's problems. Regardless of the severity of the dilemma, a happily-ever-after scenario could always be counted on in eight pages or less.

-- George Haberberger

5-10	24.00
11-20	14.00
21-28	10.00

Intimates
DC, 2005

1-12	3.00

Intimate Secrets of Romance
Star Publications, 1953

1	95.00
2	65.00

Intimidators
Image, 2006

1-4	4.00

Intrazone
Brainstorm, 1993

1	3.00
1/Ltd.	6.00
2	3.00
2/Ltd.	6.00

Intrigue
Quality, 1955

1	150.00

Intrigue
Image, 1999

1/A-3	3.00

Intruder Comics Module
TSR

1-9	3.00

Inu-Yasha
Viz, 1997

Ranma 1/2 creator Rumiko Takahashi began this feudal fairy tale in 1996 in the pages of the weekly manga magazine Shonen Sunday. Set in medieval Japan, the series features demons,

monsters, and a modern-day girl who has been transported back in time by an evil monster that was haunting the shrine her family had taken up residence in.

The girl, Kagome, is hailed as the reincarnation of the ancient people's long-dead priestess Kikyo, who had slain the demon Inu-Yasha with a magic arrow before she, herself died. When Kagome faces other monsters, the truth of her reincarnation seems to be revealed.

Later Kagome learns that Kikyo didn't kill Inu-Yasha, merely trapped him. Kagome frees the demon, who becomes her ally.

-- Brent

1-15	3.00

Inu-Yasha Part 2
Viz, 1998

1-9	3.00

Inu-Yasha Part 3
Viz, 1999

1-7	3.00

Inu-Yasha Part 4
Viz, 1999

1-7	3.00

Inu-Yasha Part 5
Viz, 2000

1-11	3.00

Inu-Yasha Part 6
Viz, 2001

1-15	3.00

Inu-Yasha Part 7
Viz, 2002

1-7	3.00

Invaders
Gold Key, 1967

1	40.00
2-4	28.00

Invaders
Marvel, 1975

1	18.00
2	10.00
3-4	6.00
5-6	5.00
6/30¢	20.00
7	5.00
7/30¢	20.00
8-9	5.00
10-17/Whitman	4.00
17/35¢	7.00
18-18/Whitman	4.00
18/35¢	7.00
19-19/Whitman	4.00
19/35¢	7.00
20-20/Whitman	5.00
20/35¢	10.00
21-21/Whitman	3.00
21/35¢	6.00
22-30	4.00
31-32	3.00
33	4.00
34-40	3.00
41	4.00
Ann 1	12.00

Invaders
Marvel, 1993

1-4	2.00

Invaders
Marvel, 2004

0-9	3.00

Invaders from Home
DC

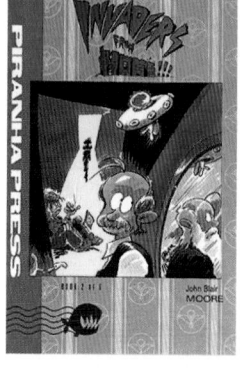

This six-issue mini-series is a whirlwind comedic tour through the mind of a man who is learning to cope with middle-age. Bobby Boomer (a not-so-subtle play on the term, Baby Boomer) is an average man with an average house, wife, and child. This is the way it is and this is the way he likes it.

Boomer's life is turned up-side down when his niece comes to live with them. She is a teenager, which in practical terms means that she might as well be an invader from another planet. Bobby doesn't know how to relate to her. He doesn't like the way she dresses, and talks. He especially doesn't like her choice of boyfriends.

This series is filled with the sort of humor that only comes from real life. All in all, Invaders From Home is a must-read for humor fans.

1-6	3.00

Invaders from Mars
Eternity, 1990

1-3	3.00

Invaders from Mars (Book II)
Eternity, 1990
1-3...3.00

Invasion!
DC, 1989

The Dominators, an alien race, were notorious for their ability to plan and scheme. Recently, they had decided that the greatest threat to their security was the planet Earth. For although the galaxy knows many races, none seem to have Earth's capacity for spawning all manner of super-powered individuals. The Dominators could face any hero whose powers they knew, but there seems to be no predicting the super-powers which manifest themselves in Earth's population. For this reason, the Dominators consider Earth dangerous - and have decided that it must be destroyed.

Accordingly, they have formed an alliance of the galaxy's most warlike races, and have proceeded to invade the Earth. Meanwhile, heroes from the Omega Men to Adam Strange have risen in Earth's defense. This series (which contained the first appearance of L.E.G.I.O.N.) tells of Earth's battle for survival against the alien menace.

1-3...3.00

Invasion
Avalon
1 ....3.00

Invasion '55
Apple, 1990
1-3...2.00

Invasion of the Mind Sappers
Fantagraphics, 1996
1 .... 9.00

Invasion of the Space Amazons from the Purple Planet
Grizmart, 1997
1-3... 2.00

Invert
Caliber
1 .... 3.00

Invincible
Image, 2003
0 .... 1.00
1 .... 25.00
2-4 .... 12.00
5-11 .... 7.00
12-15 .... 5.00
16-24 .... 3.00
25 .... 5.00
26-37 .... 3.00

Invincible Ed
Summertime, 2002
1-2... 4.00

Invincible Ed
Dark Horse, 2003
1-4... 3.00

Invincible Four of Kung Fu & Ninja
Dr. Leung's
1-5... 2.00

Invincible Man
Junko, 1998
1 .... 5.00
1/Ltd. 8.00

Invincibles
CFD, 1997
1 .... 3.00

Invincible Script Book
Image, 2006
1 .... 4.00

Invisible 9
Flypaper, 1998
1 .... 3.00

Invisible Dirty Old Man
Red Giant
1 .... 4.00

Invisible Frontier
NBM
1 .... 16.00

Invisible People
Kitchen Sink

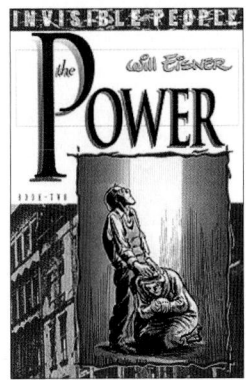

Invisible People is a three-issue series of stories that deals with the themes of alienation and isolation. The first issue, "Sanctum," is about a man who becomes so isolated from the world around him that he is accidentally reported as dead. The second issue, "The Power," relates the story of a faith healer striving for importance. The last issue, "Mortal Combat," is concerned with a man whose life is being controlled by his mother and girlfriend. Will Eisner presents a compelling exploration of city life and modern apathy. Eisner's graphic skill is at the top of its form here, and his cartooning is marvelous. A terrific read, and a great example of the joys a well-crafted comic can bring.

1-3... 3.00

Invisible Scarlet O'Neil
Harvey, 1950
1 .... 165.00
2 .... 90.00
3 .... 75.00

Invisibles
DC, 1994
1 .... 4.00
2-3 .... 3.00
4-8 .... 2.00
9-24 .... 3.00
25 .... 4.00

Invisibles
DC, 1997
1-22... 3.00

Invisibles
DC, 1999
12-1 .... 3.00

Invisoworld
Eternity
1 .... 2.00

I.N.V.U.
Tokyopop, 2003

1-2..10.00

Io
Invictus, 1994

1-3..2.00

Ion
DC, 2006

1-9..3.00

I, Paparazzi
DC

1..30.00

Ironcat
Ironcat, 1999

1-2..3.00

Iron Corporal
Charlton, 1985

23-25..2.00

Iron Corporal
Avalon

1..3.00

Iron Devil
Fantagraphics, 1994

1-3..3.00

Iron Fist
Marvel, 1975

First appearing in Marvel Premiere #15, Iron Fist is really martial artist Daniel Rand. As a child, Daniel had been taken by his parents on an expedition to Tibet, to search for the legendary city of K'un-Lun. His parents were killed in the quest, but Daniel was taken in by the city's inhabitants where he was trained to become a master of the martial arts. Eventually he rose to the ultimate position, received the brand of the dragon on his chest, and learned to focus his chi -- his soul force -- into an awesomely powerful Iron Fist.

Striking with the Iron Fist, however, drained him terribly, leaving him weak for several hours.

In this series, most famous for writer Chris Claremont's introduction of Sabretooth, Iron Fist teams with detectives Colleen Wing and Misty Knight to fight legions of kung-fu-fighting bad guys. He would later join forces with strongman Luke Cage, to form the freelance "Heroes for Hire" service.

1	35.00
2	12.00
3	10.00
4	8.00
4/30¢	20.00
5	8.00
5/30¢	20.00
6	8.00
6/30¢	20.00
7-13	8.00
13/35¢	10.00
14	80.00
☞1st Sabretooth	
14/35¢	150.00
15	27.00
☞X-Men app.	
15/35¢	75.00

Iron Fist
Marvel, 1996

1-2..2.00

Iron Fist
Marvel, 1998

1-3..3.00

Iron Fist
Marvel, 2004

1-6..3.00

Iron Fist: Wolverine
Marvel, 2000

1-4..3.00

Iron Ghost
Image, 2005

1-6..3.00

Ironhand of Almuric
Dark Horse

1-4..2.00

Ironjaw
Atlas-Seaboard, 1975

1	9.00
2-3	6.00
4	8.00

Iron Lantern
Marvel, 1997

1..2.00

Iron Man
Marvel, 1968

A genius with gadgets, industrialist Tony Stark first put on the armor of Iron Man in Tales of Suspense #39. After sharing that title with Captain America, Shellhead finally received his own series in 1968.

While Stark engages in some selfless super-heroing as Iron Man, many of his adventures involve protecting his business interests from super-villains, who seem far more interested in bothering his factories than, say, Ford's. The most highly regarded runs of Iron Man are by writer David Micheline, who added considerably to the supporting cast and gave Stark a dependency on alcohol. "Demon in a Bottle," in #128, could indeed be considered the story Stark's greatest battle. Sandwiched between Michelinie runs, a storyline by Denny O'Neill takes the alcoholism storyline to a greater extreme, with Stark ending up in the gutter while friend Jim Rhodes subs as Iron Man.

This long-running series was abruptly (and, it would turn out, needlessly) ended to give Marvel a chance to restart the series during "Heroes Reborn."

— *John Jackson Miller*

1	275.00
2-4	60.00
5	55.00
6-7	50.00
8	40.00
9	90.00
10	42.00
11-12	35.00
13-17	27.00
18-20	25.00

21-30	20.00
31-40	15.00
41-42	12.00
43	35.00
☛1st Guardsman	
44	12.00
45-46	15.00
47	35.00
☛Barry Smith art	
48-50	12.00
51	17.00
52-53	10.00
54	16.00
55	110.00
☛1st Thanos	
56-67	15.00
68-85	10.00
85/30¢	20.00
86	10.00
86/30¢	20.00
87	10.00
87/30¢	20.00
88	10.00
88/30¢	20.00
89	10.00
89/30¢	20.00
90-95	10.00
95/Whitman	18.00
96	10.00
96/Whitman	18.00
97	10.00
98	8.00
98/Whitman	18.00
99	8.00
99/Whitman	18.00
99/35¢	15.00
100	12.00
100/Whitman	20.00
100/35¢	18.00
101	7.00
101/Whitman	14.00
101/35¢	12.00
102	7.00
102/Whitman	14.00
102/35¢	12.00
103	7.00
103/Whitman	14.00
103/35¢	12.00
104	7.00
104/Whitman	14.00
105-113	7.00
113/Whitman	14.00

114	7.00
114/Whitman	14.00
115	7.00
115/Whitman	14.00
116	7.00
116/Whitman	14.00
117	7.00
117/Whitman	14.00
118	7.00
118/Whitman	14.00
119	7.00
119/Whitman	14.00
120-122	7.00
122/Whitman	14.00
☛Alcoholism issue	
123-129	7.00
130-149	5.00
150	7.00
151-153	5.00
154	7.00
155-159	5.00
160	7.00
161-170	5.00
171-181	3.00
182	4.00
183-185	3.00
186	4.00
187-191	3.00
192	4.00
193-200	3.00
201-224	2.00
225-232/A	3.00
233-243	2.00
244	3.00
245-250	2.00
251-257	1.00
258-280	2.00
281-282	3.00
283-284	2.00
285-287	1.00
288	3.00
289	1.00
290	4.00
291-299	1.00
300	3.00
300/Variant	4.00
301-304	1.00
305-310	2.00
310/CS	3.00
311-316	2.00
317	3.00
318-324	2.00

325	3.00
326-332	2.00
Ann 1	27.00
Ann 2	20.00
Ann 3	10.00
Ann 4	4.00
Ann 5-10	3.00
Ann 11-13	2.00
Ann 14-15	3.00
Ashcan 1	2.00

Iron Man
Marvel, 1996

1-1/A	3.00
2-11	2.00
12	4.00
13	3.00

Iron Man
Marvel, 1998

1-1/A	4.00
2	2.00
2/Variant	3.00
3-12	2.00
13	3.00
14-45	2.00
46	4.00
47-49	2.00
50	3.00
51-66	2.00
67-83	3.00
84	8.00
☛Avengers Disassemble	
85	5.00
86-89	3.00
Ann 1998-2000	4.00
Ann 2001	3.00

Iron Man
Marvel, 2004

1	4.00
2-16	3.00
16/Variant	14.00
17-30	3.00

Iron Man & Sub-Mariner
Marvel, 1968

1	100.00

Iron Man: Bad Blood
Marvel, 2000

1-4	3.00

Iron Man Battlebook
Marvel, 1998

1 ....4.00

Iron Man/ Captain America: Casualties of War
Marvel, 2007

1 ....4.00

Iron Man: House of M
Marvel, 2005

1 ....5.00
1/Variant..................................4.00
☞2nd print
2-3..3.00

Iron Man: Hypervelocity
Marvel, 2007

1 ....3.00

Iron Man: The Inevitable
Marvel, 2006

1-6..3.00

Iron Man: The Iron Age
Marvel, 1998

1-2..6.00

Iron Man: The Legend
Marvel, 1996

1 ....4.00

Iron Man 2020
Marvel, 1994

1 ....6.00

Iron Manual
Marvel, 1993

Iron Manual was released to help commemorate Iron Man's 30th anniversary. Iron Manual gives technical details behind the various suits of armor that Tony Stark has created over the years for his identity of Iron Man. Stark narrates the description of the various armors, much as the Punisher does in The Punisher Armory. Iron Manual also includes "design

sketchbook" pages, and a tour of Stark's armor production facilities.

1 .... 2.00

Iron Man/X-O Manowar: Heavy Metal
Marvel, 1996

1 .... 3.00

Iron Marshal
Jademan, 1990

1-32 .... 2.00

Iron Saga's Anthology
Iron Saga, 1987

1 .... 2.00

Iron West
Image, 2006

1 .... 15.00

Iron Wings
Action, 1999

1 .... 3.00

Iron Wings
Image, 2000

1 .... 3.00

Ironwolf
DC, 1986

1 .... 2.00

Ironwood
Fantagraphics, 1991

1-6 .... 2.00
7-10 .... 3.00

Irredeemable Ant-Man
Marvel, 2006

1-4 .... 3.00

I Saw It
Educomics

Keiji Nakazawa was a six-year-old Japanese boy living in Hiroshima on August 6, 1945. The event of that day influenced the course of his life and forever affected the history of the world.

This incredible true story depicts the horror and misery of surviving the blast of an atomic bomb. Most of his family was killed but Keiji lived to witness the aimless procession of living specters with melting flesh and the eventual mass cremations to hinder the stench.

Nakazawa's narrative is a personal recollection of his experiences as he, his mother and brother struggled to survive in post-war Japan. Eventually, Nakazawa became enthralled with comic books. He left his mother and moved to Tokyo to become a cartoonist. He has achieved a measure of notoriety with "Barefoot Gen," a historical fiction graphic novel based on his own life.

Nakazawa's prose and art are somewhat stilted and stiff but the powerful reality of his story overcomes any technical shortcomings.

-- George Haberberger

1 .... 2.00

Isis
DC, 1976

"Mighty Isis!"
Science teacher Andrea Thomas only had to utter those two words in order to be transformed into an Egyptian goddess during her live-action series every Saturday morning in the mid 1970s. The words work just as well in this eight-issue series adaptation by DC.

While on an archeological expedition in Egypt, Andrea Thomas found a headband which gave her the powers of Isis, including flight, divine strength, powers over the forces of nature and animals, and powers over the mystical regions of the mind. Now whenever disaster strikes, Andrea turns into Isis and saves the day.

For some unspecified reason, commands (except for "Mighty Isis!") need to be spoken in rhyming couplets - perhaps nature only understands rap?

A new, different Isis series was announced for 2002.

1	6.00
2-8	4.00

Island of Dr. Moreau
Marvel, 1977

1	3.00

Ismet
Canis, 1981

1-5	1.00

I Spy
Gold Key, 1966

1	55.00
2	40.00
3-6	33.00

Is This Tomorrow?
Catechetical Guild, 1947

1-1/B	125.00

Itchy & Scratchy Comics
Bongo, 1993

1	3.00
2-Holiday 1	2.00

Itchy Planet
Fantagraphics, 1988

1-3	2.00

It Really Happened
Visual Editions, 1945

It Really Happened, a 1940s title from William Wise/Visual Editions, offered wholesome and generally accurate pictorial biographies of famous figures from history. Each issue featured four to six literate, well-illustrated stories about characters from all walks of life - from industrialists like Henry Ford to pirates like Captain Kidd to explorers, adventurers, and scientists. William Wise took its educational mission seriously and strove for factual accuracy and entertainment in equal measure, to inspire children to strive for greatness in their own lives.

-- Rob Salkowitz

1	85.00
2	60.00
3-5	45.00
6-7	38.00
8	70.00
9	38.00
10	50.00
11	38.00

It's a Bird
DC, 2004

1	25.00

It's About Time
Gold Key, 1967

1	25.00

It's a Duck's Life
Atlas, 1950

1	55.00
2	40.00
3-5	35.00
6-11	26.00

It's Fun to Stay Alive
National Automobile Dealers Association, 1947

1	60.00

It's Game Time
DC, 1955

1	285.00
2-3	190.00
4	165.00

Itsi Kitsi
Funny Book Institute, 2000

1	3.00

It's Love, Love, Love
St. John, 1957

1	30.00
2	26.00

It's Only a Matter of Life and Death
Fantagraphics

1	4.00

It's Science With Dr. Radium
Slave Labor, 1986

1-7	2.00
Special 1	3.00

It! The Terror from Beyond Space
Millennium, 1993

The Challenge 141 had set off toward Mars with high hopes for its crew, led by veteran Mars explorer Colonel Edward Carruthers. Only minutes after planetfall, however, all radio contact was lost with the ship. NASA feared that the crew had been lost, and dispatched a second ship to investigate. Still, nothing could have prepared them for what they found when the rescue ship arrived on Mars.

Carruthers was alive, living in a wrecked spaceship with the rest of his crew buried in the sands around it. Carruthers babbled about a "monster" that had killed his men, but the skull of a crewman with a bullet hole in it seemed to belie the tale. Carruthers was charged with murder and placed in custody as the rescue ship made the long journey toward earth. But as mad as it sounded, Carruthers had been telling the truth-and the very same monster was now lurking within the ship!

1-4	3.00

I Want to Be Your Dog
Fantagraphics, 1990

1-5	2.00

DC teamed its biggest stars in Justice League of America.
To celebrate its 200th issue, the original team faced its later replacements.

J2
Marvel, 1998

One of the more interesting characters to come from the unsuccessful Marvel2 universe, J2 is high-school nebbish Zane Marko, son of X-Men villain Juggernaut (long since vanished from Zane's life; in this story, he's been exiled to another dimension).

But poor Zane hardly seems his father's son. He's a skinny weakling and an easy mark for the school bullies. At least he is until one day, when he's pushed too far and makes a startling transformation into a Gen-Y Juggernaut. In an origin that is lovingly reminiscent of the early Spider-Man stories, Zane chooses to use his powers for good and, thus, dons the mantle of J2. Writer Tom DeFalco brings a good deal of charm to this series, with great art by Ron Lim.

-- *Stephen C. George*

1-12 .... 2.00

Jab
Adhesive, 1993
1-5 .... 3.00

Jab
Cummings Design Group, 1994
3 .... 3.00

Jab
Funny Papers, 1993
1-2 .... 3.00

Jace Pearson
of the Texas Rangers
Dell, 1951
2-9 .... 45.00

Jace Pearson's Tales
of the Texas Rangers
Dell, 1956
11 .... 35.00
12-20 .... 42.00

Jack
Med Systems Company, 1995
1 .... 3.00

Jack Armstrong
Parents' Magazine Institute, 1947
1 .... 225.00
2 .... 95.00
3-5 .... 58.00
6-11 .... 52.00
12 .... 85.00
13 .... 52.00

Jackaroo
Eternity, 1990
1-3 .... 2.00

Jack Cross
DC, 2005
1-4 .... 3.00

Jack Frost
Amazing
1-2 .... 2.00

Jack Hunter
Blackthorne, 1988
1 .... 1.00

Jackie Gleason
St. John, 1955
1 .... 385.00
2 .... 225.00
3-4 .... 185.00

Jackie Gleason
and the Honeymooners
DC, 1956
1 .... 440.00
2 .... 300.00
3-4 .... 220.00
5-6 .... 165.00
7-9 .... 135.00
10-11 .... 125.00
12 .... 250.00

Jackie Jokers
Harvey, 1973
1 .... 12.00
2-4 .... 10.00

Jackie Robinson
Fawcett, 1950
1 .... 400.00
2 .... 225.00
3-5 .... 200.00
6 .... 165.00

Jack in the Box Comics
Charlton, 1946
11 .... 85.00
12 .... 45.00
13 .... 60.00
14-16 .... 45.00

Jack Kirby's Galactic
Bounty Hunters
Marvel, 2006
1 .... 4.00
2-3 .... 3.00

Jack of Fables
DC, 2006
1-35 .... 3.00

Jack of Hearts
Marvel, 1984

The Jack of Hearts limited series begins, interestingly enough, with Jack trying to kill himself. It seems that his immense power has been steadily growing, to the point at which, if he does not release it, he will die. Unfortunately, his supply of stored energy has become so huge that any release will imperil the entire Earth. Jack sees no choice but to end his own life in order to save humanity.

It is at this point that a race of aliens seeks out Jack as a source of energy to revive their dying sun. In the four issues of this limited series, we join our favorite human playing card, as he becomes embroiled in plots and intrigues that will determine the fates of both worlds.

1-4 .... 2.00

Jackpot Comics
Archie, 1941

1 .... 3,000.00
2 .... 1,250.00
3 .... 1,000.00
4 .... 3,850.00
☛Archie starts
5 .... 1,600.00
6 .... 800.00
7-9 .... 450.00

Jack's Luck Runs Out
Beekeeper Cartoon Amusements
1 .... 4.00

Jack Staff
Image, 2003

1-4 .... 3.00
5-12 .... 4.00

Jack the Giant Killer
Dell, 1963

1 .... 32.00

Jack the Ripper
Caliber, 1998

1 .... 3.00

Jack the Ripper
Eternity

1-3 .... 2.00

Jacquelyn the Ripper
Fantagraphics, 1994

1-2 .... 3.00

Jacque's Voice of Doom
Doomed Comics

1 .... 2.00

Jademan Collection
Jademan, 1990

1-3 .... 3.00

Jademan Kung Fu Special
Jademan

Tony Wong began Jademan (Holdings) Limited back in 1971 and finally hit upon a comic book formula that kept gaining popularity all over Hong Kong. They would control every aspect of the comic book production, from writing to actual printing. Jademan Kung Fu Special was designed to introduce English speaking audiences to the Jademan format and characters. Oriental Heroes, The Blood Sword, Drunken Fist, and The Force of Buddha's Palm are all introduced here with a brief description of the stories and characters to help bring new readers up to date. All four titles lasted from 1988 until the early 1990s.

1 .... 2.00

Jade Warriors
Image, 2000

1-2 .... 3.00

J.A.G.
ThwackPow

1-3 .... 2.00

Jaguar
DC, 1991

1-14 .... 1.00
Ann 1 .... 3.00

Jaguar God
Verotik, 1995

0-5 .... 4.00
6-8 .... 3.00

Jaguar God Illustrations
Verotik, 2000

nn 4.00

Jaguar God: Return to Xibalba
Verotik, 2003

1 .... 5.00

Jailbait
Fantagraphics, 1998

1 .... 3.00

Jake Thrash
Aircel

1-2 .... 2.00

Jam
Slave Labor, 1989

1 .... 3.00
2-3 .... 2.00
4-13 .... 3.00

Jamar Chronicles
Sweat Shop

1 .... 2.00

Jamboree Comics
Round, 1946

1 .... 70.00
2-3 .... 35.00

James Bond 007: A Silent Armageddon
Dark Horse, 1993

Ten years ago, James Bond was an observer at a CIA raid on (what was believed to be) a safehouse for stolen military computer software. In reality, the

CIA had been set up. When they entered the safehouse, they triggered an explosive device, killing several agents. The world had just seen the emergence of the terrorist group called Cerberus.

Years later, Cerberus is back, this time working its plans through the world's computers. An intelligent virus called Omega has been unleashed in the world's computers. Adaptive and seemingly unstoppable, there doesn't seem to be a system it can't enter-including nuclear launch computers. If the world's most celebrated secret agent can't find a way to stop it, Omega will soon provide Cerberus with the codes it needs to threaten the world with nuclear annihilation.

1-2..3.00

James Bond 007/ Goldeneye
Topps, 1995

1-3..3.00

James Bond 007: Serpent's Tooth
Dark Horse, 1992

1-3..5.00

James Bond 007: Shattered Helix
Dark Horse, 1994

1-2..3.00

James Bond 007: The Quasimodo Gambit
Dark Horse, 1995

1-3..4.00

James Bond for Your Eyes Only
Marvel, 1981

1-2..2.00

James Bond Jr.
Marvel, 1992

1-12..1.00

James Bond: Permission to Die
Eclipse, 1989

Mike Grell brings back the world's most famous spy in this action-packed two-part series. A reclusive scientist has discovered a means for launching satellites into space for a tiny fraction of the cost of a conventional spaceshot. This method could spell success for the Star Wars defense system, but the inventor has refused to deal with the military. He will, however, give the plans to the British-if they do him one small favor. He wants them to rescue his niece from behind the Iron Curtain.

Naturally, James Bond, agent 007, is called into action. In a story worthy of Ian Fleming, Grell's 007 treks across the world and into the face of incredible danger to complete his mission. As a member of the "00" section, he has been given permission to kill for his country. "But," he is reminded, "nobody gave you permission to die."

1-2.. 4.00
3... 5.00

Jam Quacky
JQ

1... 2.00

Jam Special
Matrix

1... 3.00

Jam Super Cool Color-Injected Turbo Adventure from Hell
Comico, 1988

1... 3.00

Jam Urban Adventure
Tundra, 1992

1-3.. 3.00

Jane Arden
St. John, 1948

1 .... 70.00
2 .... 50.00

Jane Bondage
Fantagraphics, 1992

1-2.. 3.00

Jane Bond: Thunderballs
Fantagraphics, 1992

1 .... 3.00

Jane Doe
Raging Rhino

1-3.. 3.00

Jane's World
Girl Twirl, 2003

1-8.. 3.00
9-16.. 6.00

Jann of the Jungle
Atlas, 1955

8 .... 125.00
9-10....................................... 100.00
11-15 .... 85.00
16-17 .... 90.00

Janx
Es Graphics

1-2.. 1.00

J.A.P.A.N.
Outerealm

1 .... 2.00

Jaq Hammer
Anubis, 1994

0 .... 1.00
1 .... 3.00

Jar of Fools Part One
Penny Dreadful, 1994

1 .... 6.00

Jason and the Argonauts
Tome

This title adapts the classic Greek story of Jason and the Argonauts and their adventures retrieving the legendary Golden Fleece.

Jason's father, King Aeson, is dethroned by Jason's Uncle Pelias, and the boy vows to regain the kingdom. Yet when Jason returns to the kingdom as a young man, he inexplicably finds himself welcomed by his cunning uncle.

Uncle Pelias tricks Jason into undertaking a fool's quest; to locate and return with the Golden Fleece. But a long sea voyage and monsters as well as other obstacles stand in the way. On his side, though, Jason will have the greatest ship in Greek history as well as the best men from throughout the kingdom. Even the half-god Hercules will join the expedition.

But can even this hardy crew survive confrontations with Cyclopses and Gorgons?

1-5...3.00

Jason Goes to Hell: The Final Friday
Topps, 1993
1-3...3.00

Jason Monarch
Oracle, 1979
1 ....2.00

Jason vs. Leatherface
Topps, 1995
1-3...3.00

Java Town
Slave Labor, 1992

In the tradition of Mad Magazine, Scott Saavedra has put together a hilarious black-and-white collection of articles, comics, and advertisements guaranteed to bring a chuckle to any reader. The java theme is throughout much of the series, but not every page is limited to that one specific subject. Java Town employs various art styles with subtle (and not so subtle) humor that's bound to

appeal to most anyone who is or knows a coffee drinker.

1-6... 3.00

Javerts
Firstlight, 1997
1 .... 3.00

Jax and the Hell Hound
Blackthorne, 1986
1-4... 2.00

Jay Anacleto Sketchbook
Image, 1999
1-1/A....................................... 2.00

Jay & Silent Bob
Oni, 1998
1 .... 4.00
1/Variant................................. 5.00
1/2nd-4 .... 3.00

Jazz
High Impact, 1996
1-2... 3.00

Jazz Age Chronicles
EF Graphics, 1989
1-3... 2.00

Jazz Age Chronicles
Caliber, 1990
1-5 .... 3.00

Jazzbo Comics That Swing
Slave Labor, 1994
1-2... 3.00

Jazz: Solitaire
High Impact, 1998
1 .... 3.00
1/A-1/Gold.............................. 4.00
2 .... 3.00
2/A-2/B 5.00
3 .... 3.00
3/A-3/B 5.00

JCP Features
J.C., 1981
1 .... 3.00

Jeanie
Timely, 1947

She's "Queen of the Teens," and the perky brunette was quite a change from #12 of the series -- which had been titled Daring Comics and cover-featured The Sub-Mariner and The Human Torch and Toro attacking thugs apparently trying to take over a pleasure boat filled with people. The shock to the young comics purchaser wouldn't have been too great, since there'd also been more than a year and a half between Daring #12 and Jeanie #13. The war was over, and the focus (at least in Jeanie) was on teens, dating, and long, shapely legs. At first, the covers went for simple depictions of guys drooling at the sight of her. By #17, the cover come-on described the contents as "another romance-packed mirth-filled magazine," and the emphasis on gags was increased.

And then, suddenly, it morphed, ever so briefly, into Cowgirl Romances. Yikes.

-- Maggie

13 .... 145.00
14-17 .... 100.00
18-23 .... 85.00
24-27 .... 65.00

Jeep Comics
R.B. Leffingwell, 1944
1 .... 265.00
2 .... 165.00
3 .... 200.00

Jeff Jordan, U.S. Agent
D.S., 1947
1 .... 90.00

Jeffrey Dahmer: An Unauthorized Biography of a Serial Killer
Boneyard, 1992

1 ....4.00
1/2nd 3.00

Jeffrey Dahmer vs. Jesus Christ
Boneyard, 1993

1 ....4.00

Jemm, Son of Saturn
DC, 1984

1 ....2.00
2-12 ....1.00

Jennifer Daydreamer: Oliver
Top Shelf, 2003

1 ....5.00

Jenny Finn
Oni, 1999

1-4 ....3.00

Jenny Finn: Messiah
Oni

1 ....7.00

Jenny Sparks: The Secret History of the Authority
DC, 2000

1-5 ....3.00

Jeremiah: A Fistful of Sand
Adventure, 1991

1-2 ....3.00

Jeremiah: Birds of Prey
Adventure, 1991

European storytellers have generally done very well in creating exciting romantic tales of the Old West--the dominate feel of this black and white title by Hermann is definitely that of a western. But really it is that classic apocalyptic fantasy--life after nuclear holocaust!

After several generations, clumps of people have scattered across North America rebuilding civilization on top of the ruins of the old. But society is slow to learn the lessons from history--after his village is wiped out by a band of merciless raiders, a young boy named Jeremiah sets out on a quest for vengeance. And thus is the great tragedy destined to be played out all over again!

1-2 .... 3.00

Jeremiah: The Heirs
Adventure

1-2 .... 3.00

Jeremy Brood
Fantagor, 1982

1 .... 6.00
1/2nd 12.00

Jerkbox & Punk'nhead
Jerkbox Studios, 1999

1 .... 3.00

Jerry Drummer
Charlton

10-12 .... 18.00

Jersey Devil
South Jersey Rebellion, 1992

1 .... 2.00
2 .... 3.00
3-7 .... 2.00

Jesse James
Avon, 1950

1 .... 60.00
2 .... 30.00
3-5 .... 40.00
6-9 .... 35.00
15-19 .... 30.00
20-21 .... 28.00
22-29 .... 24.00

Jesse James
AC

1 .... 4.00

Jest
Harry A. Chesler, 1944

10-11 .... 85.00

Jester's Moon
One Shot, 1996

1 .... 1.00

Jesus Comics (Foolbert Sturgeon's...)
Rip Off, 1972

1 .... 5.00
2-3 .... 4.00

Jet
Authority, 1996

1 .... 3.00

Jet
DC, 2000

1-4 .... 3.00

Jet Aces
Fiction House, 1952

1 .... 90.00
2-4 .... 55.00

Jet Black
Monolith, 1997

1 .... 3.00

Jet Comics
Slave Labor, 1997

1-3 .... 3.00

Jet Dream
Gold Key, 1968

1 .... 18.00

Jet Fighters
Standard, 1953

5 .... 80.00
6 .... 50.00
7 .... 80.00

Jet Fury
Herald Gravure

This black-and-white Australian series features the globe-trotting adventures of a costumed air fighter and spy whose alter ego is that of a wealthy socialite who lives in a stylish, uptown penthouse. Taking on racketeers and jetting off to exotic foreign lands, Jet Fury certainly seems to owe a debt to such American series as "Terry and the Pirates" and "Steve Canyon." However, both the stories and the artwork lack the complexity of Milton Caniff's work, leaving Jet Fury as something of a poor relative.

1 .... 20.00
2-24 .... 14.00

Jet Powers
Magazine Enterprises, 1950

1 .... 140.00
2 .... 110.00
3-4 .... 100.00

Jetsons
Gold Key, 1963

1	90.00
2	65.00
3-5	48.00
6-10	40.00
11-20	24.00
21-30	16.00
31-36	14.00

Jetsons
Charlton, 1970

1	35.00
2	22.00
3-5	14.00
6-10	10.00
11-20	7.00

Jetsons
Harvey, 1992

1-5	2.00

Jetsons
Archie, 1995

1-12	2.00

Jetsons Big Book
Harvey, 1992

1-3	2.00

Jetsons GS
Harvey, 1992

1-3	3.00

Jetta of the 21st Century
Standard, 1952

5	110.00
6-7	75.00

Jew in Communist Prague, A
NBM

1-2	12.00

Jezebel Jade
Comico, 1988

1-3	2.00

Jezebelle
WildStorm, 2001

1/A-6	3.00

JFK Assassination
Zone

1	4.00

Jhereg
Marvel

1	9.00

Jigaboo Devil
Millennium

0	3.00

Jiggs & Maggie
Harvey, 1953

11	20.00
12	20.00

13-14	20.00
15-16	20.00
17-18	20.00
19	20.00
20	20.00
21	20.00
22	20.00
23	20.00
24	20.00
25	20.00
26	20.00
27	20.00

Jiggs is Back
Celtic

1	13.00

Jigsaw
Harvey, 1966

Col. Gary Jason is on an orbital mission, photographing stars from space, when his craft is sucked into a strange magnetic vortex. Although he tries to escape, a fossilized tree (yes, a tree) is also caught in the vortex and spears his ship. Jason is pulled out of his ship and flies into the source of the vortex, an alien base on the Moon. The aliens regret their inadvertent capture of Jason, and rebuild his shattered body using special elastic materials to reconnect most of his joints. But the result is uneven, leaving him a virtual jigsaw puzzle.

Jason discovers that these alterations gave him super strength, as well as the ability to stretch his limbs to incredible lengths. These powers let him do everything from rounding up circus animals to saving Earth from aliens. Unfortunately, they can't save this series from its outrageous premise.

1	16.00
2	10.00

Jill: Part-Time Lover
NBM

1	12.00

Jim (Vol. 1)
Fantagraphics

1	8.00
2	6.00
3-4	5.00

Jim (Vol. 2)
Fantagraphics, 1993

1	5.00
2-3	4.00
4-6	3.00
Special 1	4.00

Jimbo
Bongo, 1995

1-7	3.00

Jim Dandy
Lev Gleason, 1956

1	40.00
2-3	25.00

Jim Hardy
United Feature, 1944

1	300.00

Jim Hardy
United Feature, 1947

1	100.00
2	60.00

Jim Lee Sketchbook
WildStorm

1	40.00

Jimmy Durante
Magazine Enterprises, 1948

1	365.00
2	275.00

Jimmy Wakely
DC, 1949

1	850.00
2	525.00
3-4	465.00
5	325.00
6-7	425.00
8-10	275.00
11-18	225.00

Jim Ray's Aviation Sketchbook
Vital, 1946

1	200.00
2	180.00

Jing: King of Bandits
Tokyopop, 2003

1-7	10.00

Jing: King of Bandits - Twilight Tales
Tokyopop, 2004

1-6	10.00

Jingle Belle
Oni, 1999

1-2	3.00

Jingle Belle (Paul Dini's...): The Mighty Elves
Oni, 2001

1 ....3.00

Jingle Belle
Dark Horse, 2004

1-4 ....3.00

Jingle Belle Jubilee
Oni, 2001

nn 3.00

Jingle Belle's All-Star Holiday Hullabaloo
Oni, 2000

1 ....5.00

Jingle Belle: The Fight Before Christmas
Dark Horse, 2006

1 ....3.00

Jingle Belle Winter Wingding
Oni, 2002

nn 3.00

Jingle Jangle Comics
Eastern Color, 1943

Although there were many characters by an assortment of creators (such as Nostalgia Press' Woody Gelman) featured in their own comedy short stories in Jingle Jangle Comics, the reason the series has drawn much attention from collectors is that it contained the off-the-wall cartooning of George Carlson (1887-1962). Although he was also a "serious" artist (he painted the cover for the first book release of Gone with the Wind), Carlson's comic-book work was goofy fantasy. His two classic features for Jingle Jangle Comics (a name he apparently originated) were "Jingle Jangle Tales" and "The

Pie-Face Prince of Old Pretzelburg." He filled his stories to the panel borders and beyond with nutty wordplay and delightful details.

-- *Maggie*

1	225.00
2	200.00
3	175.00
4	150.00
5-6	125.00
7-9	100.00
10-12	80.00
13-15	75.00
16-18	60.00
19-25	50.00
26-29	45.00
30-35	40.00
36-39	35.00
40-42	30.00

Jing Pals
Victory, 1946

1	80.00
2	40.00
3-4	30.00

Jinn
Image, 2000

1-3 ....3.00

Jinx
Caliber, 1996

Brian Michael Bendis has become one of those comic-book creators whose name attached to a project means increased interest and higher pre-orders. Jinx was one of his earliest projects, a series devoted to the title character, Jinx Alameda, a female bounty hunter in Cleveland. She's beautiful, she's tough, and she hunts people for money. Bendis not only wrote Jinx; he drew it, using models and lots of photo reference. Readers will find him experimenting with many story-telling devices to tell a compelling thriller in this early stage of his

career. The series has traditional "noir" overtones and tells a complete story, with beginning, middle, and end. Crime-novel buffs are in for a treat.

-- *Maggie*

1	4.00
2-7	3.00
8-9	5.00
10-11	3.00
12-17	4.00
18-19	3.00
20-21	4.00
Special 1	5.00

Jinx Pop Culture Hoo-Hah
Image

1 ....4.00

Jizz
Fantagraphics

1-7	2.00
8-10	3.00

JLA
DC, 1997

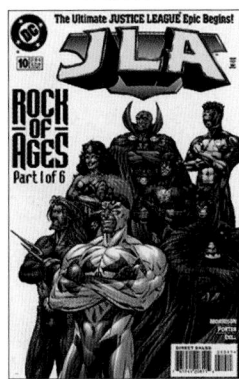

Grant Morrison breathed new life into the Justice League with this acclaimed series. Since their first appearance as a team in The Brave and the Bold #28, the Justice League of America has been the premier group of super-heroes in DC's stable. The team has been through many changes during the years, including a reorganization into several groups, including Justice League Europe and a Justice League Task Force to handle more covert operations.

Legends on their own - heroes like Superman, Wonder Woman, Green Lantern, and others have often recognized the need to band together against forces too powerful for any one super-hero to defeat. But although their names and costumes have been associated with the League for more than 40 years, the current versions of these characters had never appeared together before, thanks to the continuity-altering effects of such series as Crisis On Infinite Earths and Zero Hour.

1	6.00
2-6	4.00
7-15	3.00
16-40	2.00
41	3.00
42-49	2.00
50	4.00
51-74	2.00
75	4.00
76-99	2.00
100	4.00
101-106	2.00
☛Post ID Crisis	
107-108	5.00
☛Post ID Crisis	
109-114	2.00
115	12.00
☛ID Crisis follow-up	
116	5.00
117-125	3.00
1000000	2.00
Ann 1	6.00
Ann 2	5.00
Ann 3	4.00
GS 1-2	5.00
GS 3	6.00

JLA: Act of God
DC, 2001
1-3 ....5.00

JLA: Age of Wonder
DC, 2003
1-2 ....6.00

JLA/Avengers
Marvel, 2003

1	7.00
3	6.00
3/2nd	7.00

JLA: Black Baptism
DC, 2001
1-4 ....3.00

JLA: Classified
DC, 2005

1	6.00
2	4.00
3-31	3.00

JLA Classified: Cold Steel
DC, 2006
1-2 ....6.00

JLA: Created Equal
DC, 2000
1-2 ....6.00

JLA/Cyberforce
DC, 2005
0 ....6.00

JLA: Destiny
DC, 2002
1-4 .... 6.00

JLA: Foreign Bodies
DC, 1999
1 .... 6.00

JLA Gallery
DC, 1997
1 .... 3.00

JLA: Gatekeeper
DC, 2001
1-3... 5.00

JLA: Gods and Monsters
DC, 2001
1 .... 7.00

JLA/Haven: Anathema
DC, 2002
1 .... 6.00

JLA/Haven: Arrival
DC, 2002
1 .... 6.00

JLA: Heaven's Ladder
DC, 2000
1 .... 10.00

JLA: Incarnations
DC, 2001

The enduring popularity of the Justice League spawned another version of the team's history. Each issue of this 7-issue series from John Ostrander and Val Semeiks highlights a different era of the Justice League of America. These heretofore untold tales span the time from the formation of the Silver Age Justice League, when they took over from their Golden Age counterparts, up to the present.

The events acknowledged as worthy of defining an era include the addition of Superman and Batman, the days when the league was based in Detroit and featured the likes of Gypsy and Vibe, and

the lighthearted team by Keith Giffen and J. M. DeMattis.

This time the league has an unabashed cheerleader in the form of Tully Reed, a small cable TV station investigative reporter who functions as a Greek chorus, providing exposition and over-the-top enthusiasm.

-- George Haberberger

1-7 .... 4.00

JLA in Crisis Secret Files
DC, 1998
1 .... 5.00

JLA/JSA: Virtue & Vice
DC, 2003
1 .... 18.00

JLA: Liberty & Justice
DC, 2004
1 .... 10.00

JLA: Obsidian Age
DC, 2003
1-2 .... 13.00

JLA: One Million
DC, 2004
1 .... 20.00

JLA: Our Worlds At War
DC, 2001
1 .... 3.00

JLA: Paradise Lost
DC, 1998
1-3 .... 2.00

JLA: Primeval
DC, 1999
1 .... 6.00

JLA: Scary Monsters
DC, 2003
1-6 .... 3.00

JLA Secret Files
DC, 1997

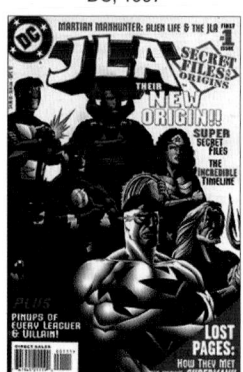

With the publication of JLA, a back-to-the-basics title featuring DC's big guns (Superman, Batman,

Wonder Woman) as the prominent members of the team, DC's editors needed clarify the history of this venerable title. Since the time of the Crisis on Infinite Earths, which essentially rewrote the history of the DC Universe, the status and continuity of the Justice League of America has been in an almost constant state of flux. This Secret Files title attempts to clarify and highlight the most important events of the League's history. Like other books of this sort, it features a series of concise biographies of the members as well as a fresh look at the League's origin with the retelling of their encounter with Starro the Conqueror. Especially significant is a Justice League timeline outlining the various lineups.

-- George Haberberger

1	5.00
2	4.00
3	5.00

JLA Secret Files 2004
DC, 2004

1	5.00

JLA: Secret Society of Super-Heroes
DC, 2000

1-2	6.00

JLA: Seven Caskets
DC

1	6.00

JLA: Shogun of Steel
DC, 2002

1	7.00

JLA Showcase
DC, 2000

GS 1	5.00

JLA/Spectre: Soul War
DC, 2003

1-2	6.00

JLA: Superpower
DC, 1999

1	6.00

JLA: The Island of Dr. Moreau
DC, 2002

1	7.00

JLA: The Nail
DC, 1998

1	6.00
2-3	5.00

JLA/Titans
DC, 1998

1	3.00
1/Ltd.	5.00
2-3	3.00

JLA: Tomorrow Woman
DC, 1998

1	2.00

JLA: Tower of Babel
DC

1	13.00

JLA Versus Predator
DC, 2000

1	6.00

JLA: Welcome to Working Week
DC, 2003

1	7.00

JLA/WildC.A.T.s
DC, 1997

1	6.00

JLA/Witchblade
DC, 2000

1	6.00

JLA: World Without Grown-Ups
DC, 1998

1	6.00
2	5.00

JLA: Year One
DC, 1998

After a title has achieved a certain measure of longevity, inserting retroactive continuity to flesh out situations and foreshadow personality conflicts becomes an attractive option. Readers who were not born when the title started are anxious to read stories that purport to retell the early days, even though older fans may remember things differently.

JLA: Year One is a mini-series featuring characters from the Silver Age with Barry Allen as The Flash, Hal Jordan as Green Lantern, and Black Canary, The Martian Manhunter, and Aquaman rounding out the team. Writer Mark Waid reveals how five disparate strangers mesh to become the Justice League, while, behind the scenes, a mysterious group named Locus exhibits an ominous interest in the fledgling alliance.

-- George Haberberger

1	4.00
2-5	3.00
6-11	2.00
12	3.00

JLA-Z
DC, 2003

1-3	3.00

JLA: Zatanna's Search
DC, 2003

1	13.00

JLX
DC, 1996

1	2.00

JLX Unleashed
DC, 1997

1	2.00

Joan of Arc
Magazine Enterprises, 1949

1	300.00

Joe 90
Fleetway-Quality

1	4.00
2-7	3.00

Joe College
Hillman, 1949

1	50.00
2	38.00

Joe Dimaggio
Celebrity

1	7.00

Joe Louis
Fawcett, 1950

1	385.00
2	225.00

Joe Palooka
Columbia, 1942

1	525.00
2	265.00
3	200.00
4	175.00

Joe Palooka
Harvey, 1945

1	240.00
2	160.00
3-4	90.00
5	135.00
☞Simon/Kirby issue	
6-7	95.00
8-10	75.00
11-14	55.00
15	75.00
☞Humphrey origin	
16-20	55.00
21-30	44.00
31-44	38.00
45-51	32.00
52-60	28.00
61	26.00
62	42.00
63-80	26.00
81-115	24.00
116-118	34.00

Joe Palooka Fights His Way Back
Harvey, 1945

1	100.00

Joe Palooka Hi There
American Red Cross, 1949

1	75.00

Joe Psycho & Moo Frog
Goblin, 1996

1	4.00
2-5	3.00
Ashcan 1	2.00

Joe Psycho Full Color Extravagarbonzo
Goblin, 1998

1	3.00

Joe Sinn
Caliber

1-2	3.00

Joe Yank
Standard, 1952

5	50.00
6	55.00
7	25.00
8	35.00
9-16	18.00

Johan & Peewit: The Black Arrow
Fantasy Flight

1	9.00

John Carter of Mars (Edgar Rice Burroughs'...)
Gold Key, 1964

1	30.00
2-3	16.00

John Carter, Warlord of Mars
Marvel, 1977

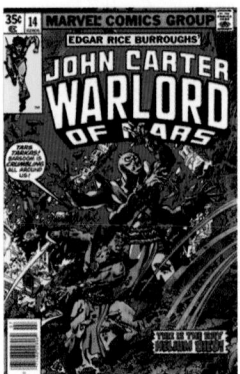

John Carter was an Earthman who ventured into a cave one day and saw a strange light. When the light touched him, his body seemed split into two, with one body staying behind on Earth, and another being transported to Mars. There he discovered strange races, including green, four-armed giants and ancient humanoid warriors. Carter rose to become a prince on this world, leading a swashbuckling life of space adventure. He also found friendship in the alien known as Tars Tarkas, and true love in the beautiful Dejah Thoris.

John Carter, Warlord of Mars was Edgar Rice Burroughs' first hero, predating his work on Korak and Tarzan. Carter made his comics debut in 1939's The Funnies #30. It appeared sporadically under several different publishers, including a 1972 run in DC's Weird Worlds. Marvel's version began in 1977, and presented Carter's sword and fantasy adventures until issue #28 in 1979.

1	8.00
1/35¢	15.00
2	4.00
2/35¢	8.00
2/Whitman	4.00
3-5/35¢	8.00
6-28	3.00
Ann 1-3	2.00

John Constantine - Hellblazer: Papa Midnite
DC, 2005

1-5	3.00

John F. Kennedy
Dell, 1964

1	45.00

1/2nd	30.00
1/3rd	22.00

John Hix Scrapbook
Eastern Color, 1937

1	200.00
2	145.00

John Law Detective
Eclipse, 1983

1	2.00

Johnny Atomic
Eternity

1-3	3.00

Johnny Comet
Avalon, 1999

1-5	3.00

Johnny Cosmic
Thorby

A two-in-one black-and-white flip-over issue.

Johnny Cosmic, former Patrol Force member, who decided he could do more good freelancing and fighting alien invaders on his own, awoke one morning to discover himself in an alternate reality. Earth is a work camp and infested with K'Thal agents only Johnny can see. Working with his side-kick computer N.I.C., Johnny befriends Captain Saffo and works to do what he does best thereby saving the planet and, hopefully, making his way back to his own world.

Gina hailed from a farming community on the planet Lusus. Her brother left home and joined the rebel forces, a drought nearly wiped out the farm, so she decided to go to Darcinia, make it big, and pull her family out of debt. When she was down to her last hunk of change, she met up with Black Hole Joel, a fantastic pilot and lousy card player, and Gina's life was never the same again.

1	3.00

Johnny Danger
Toby, 1954

1 ....90.00

Johnny Dynamite
Dark Horse, 1994

Max Collins and Terry Beatty's Johnny Dynamite is a terrific series which mixes hardboiled detective fiction with a smoldering tale of the occult. Johnny Dynamite was an up-and-coming prizefighter whose career was derailed by a term of duty in Korea which left him with a leg full of shrapnel. He used his reputation to become a police officer, but made the mistake of arresting a powerful mobster. Practically before he could blink, he was left working the worst beat in town with no chance of promotion. That's when he decided to become a private detective. Although another run-in with the mob had cost him an eye, it was a profitable living chasing down adulterous husbands and petty crime...

...until a blonde from his past appeared in his office, asking for protection from the man who had cost Dynamite his career. The next day, the blonde was dead, and Dynamite set off to find her killer in the strangest case of his career.

1-4 ....3.00

Johnny Gambit
Hot, 1987

1 ....2.00

Johnny Hazard
Best, 1948

5 ....90.00
6-7 ....70.00
8 ....55.00

Johnny Hazard
Pioneer, 1988

1 ....2.00

Johnny Hazard Quarterly
Dragon Lady

1-4 ....6.00

Johnny Jason, Teen Reporter
Dell, 1962

2 ....20.00

Johnny Law, Sky Ranger
Good, 1955

1 ....50.00
2-4 ....35.00

Johnny Mack Brown Comics
Dell, 1950

2 ....110.00
3 ....85.00
4-5 ....75.00
6-8 ....60.00
9 ....75.00
10 ....60.00

Johnny Nemo Magazine
Eclipse, 1985

1-6 ....3.00

Johnny the Homicidal Maniac
Slave Labor, 1995

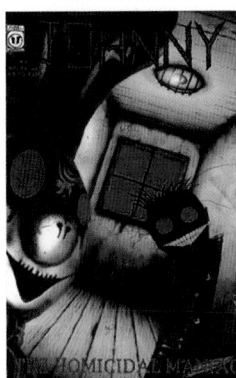

For fans of black humor, Johnny the Homicidal Maniac is about as darkly funny as it gets. Jhonen Vasquez' series reads like a Vincent Price movie -- the sort where the bad guy is having altogether too much fun.

Nobody knows what it was that sent Johnny over the edge, but he's definitely there now. He lives in house #777, decorated with parts of his victims, a bunny nailed to the wall, and even an evil Pillsbury doughboy cookie jar. When none of them are busy talking to Johnny, he raves on to himself, contemplating suicide routinely before being distracted by a really good commercial on television. It's the combination of

murderous intensity and sudden banality that makes for much of this book's humor.

1 .... 13.00
1/2nd 4.00
1/3rd-1/4th............................. 3.00
2 .... 9.00
2/2nd 3.00
3 .... 7.00
3/2nd 3.00
4 .... 6.00
4/2nd 3.00
5 .... 5.00
5/2nd 3.00
6-7 .... 4.00
Special 1 .... 20.00

Johnny Thunder
DC, 1973

1 .... 12.00
2-3 .... 8.00

John Steele, Secret Agent
Gold Key, 1964

1 .... 18.00

John Wayne Adventure Comics
Toby, 1949

With the big-screen popularity of John Wayne already established by the late 1940s, Toby Press brought the actor's likeness to comics with the 31-issue John Wayne Adventure Comics.

Running from 1949 to 1955, the series featured "The Duke" in a variety of situations, many set in the Old West (his most popular genre), with a smattering of war stories (his second most-popular genre) thrown in for good measure. Back-up features included "Genius Jones" and Harvey Kurtzman's "Potshot Pete." While the stories were stiff and uninteresting, Wayne collectors will go for the photo covers featuring their favorite star.
-- Brent

1 .... 1,285.00

2	640.00
3	550.00
4	525.00
5-9	485.00
10-12	425.00
13-16	275.00
17	325.00
18-20	275.00
21-24	240.00
25-31	300.00

Jo-Jo Comics
Fox, 1946

1	125.00
2-3	75.00
4-6	60.00
7	825.00
8	500.00
9-10	375.00
11-20	300.00
21-29	240.00

Joker
DC, 1975

1	16.00
2	12.00
3-5	8.00
6-9	7.00

Joker Comics
Timely, 1942

1	2,000.00
2	775.00
3	400.00
4-5	325.00
6-10	260.00
11-20	205.00
21-27	155.00
28	60.00
29-30	155.00
31	125.00
32	80.00
33	40.00
34-35	80.00
36-42	48.00

Joker: Last Laugh
DC, 2001

1-6	3.00

Joker: Last Laugh Secret Files
DC, 2001

1	6.00

Joker/Mask
Dark Horse, 2000

1-4	3.00

Jolly Jack Starjumper Summer of '92 One-Shot
Conquest

1	3.00

Jolly Jingles
Archie, 1943

10	160.00
11	85.00
12	60.00
13-16	35.00

Jonah Hex
DC, 1977

First introduced in All-Star Western (2nd series) #10 in 1972, bounty hunter and mountain man Jonah Hex would travel the west seeking out criminals and bringing them in to face justice. Dressed in Confederate gray, Hex was also distinguished by an ugly bit of scarring on the right side of his face that pulled his face into a perpetual grimace.

When the series switched titles to Weird Western Tales, Hex came along for the ride and, eventually received his own series. Feared both by criminals and most townspeople due to his violent nature, Hex has trouble finding love, since he carries a torch for his ex-wife, Mei Ling.

In addition to the Old West, Hex's adventures took him to the Orient, the South, and the future (in the short-lived, and shorter-named, Hex). In recent years, Jonah has returned to a combination of supernatural and Western tales with a series of mini-series from DC's Vertigo imprint.

-- Brent

1	28.00
2	10.00
3-5	7.00
6	6.00
7-8	7.00
9-10	5.00
11-20	4.00
21-92	3.00

Jonah Hex
DC, 2006

1	8.00
2-20	2.00
21-50	3.00

Jonah Hex and Other Western Tales
DC, 1979

1-3	7.00

Jonah Hex: Riders of the Worm and Such
DC, 1995

1-5	3.00

Jonah Hex: Shadows West
DC, 1999

1-3	3.00

Jonah Hex: Two-Gun Mojo
DC, 1993

1	4.00
☛Lansdale, Truman series	
1/Silver	6.00
2-5	3.00

Jonas! (Mike Deodato's...)
Caliber

1	3.00

Jonathan Fox
Mariah Graphics

1	2.00

Jones Touch
Fantagraphics, 1993

1	3.00

Jonesy
Quality, 1953

1	40.00
2-4	25.00
5-8	20.00

Jon Juan
Toby, 1950

1	425.00

Jonni Thunder
DC, 1985

1-4	1.00

Jonny Demon
Dark Horse, 1994

1-3	3.00

Jonny Double
DC, 1998

1-4	3.00

Jonny Quest
Gold Key, 1964

1	85.00

Jonny Quest
Comico, 1986

1-5	3.00
6-Special 2	2.00

Jonny Quest Classics
Comico, 1987
1-3...2.00

Jon Sable, Freelance
First, 1983

While living in Africa, a brave man named Jon Sable tried to stop a band of poachers from preying on protected species. In retaliation, the poachers killed his family.

Years later, Jon Sable is living in New York, where, under the assumed name of B.B. Flemm, he is a favorite children's book writer. But as Jon Sable, he is a mercenary-a freelance gun for hire. If the pay is right, no job is considered too dangerous. At the same time, he possesses an inner sense of nobility and fair play.

An excellent action-adventure series, Jon Sable, Freelance was created, written, and illustrated by the great Mike Grell.

1 ....3.00
2-56...2.00

Jon Sable, Freelance: Bloodline
Idea & Design Works, 2005
1-6...4.00

Jontar Returns
Miller
1-4...2.00

Josie
Archie, 1965

Josie, a popular teen-girl backup feature in Archie comic books, received her own title, She's Josie, in 1963. After a short time, the title changed to simply Josie.

Josie began as typical teen-age comic-book fare. Earning a spot on Archie's cartoon show, Josie would later form a rock band and get a show of her own, "Josie and the Pussycats." That concept would take her title over with issue #45 in 1969.

Dan DeCarlo based the character Josie on his wife Josie. When the character appeared to hit it big again with a feature film in 2001, DeCarlo was at legal loggerheads with Archie Comics over ownership of the character. The film proved to be lackluster, however, and DeCarlo died around the same time that the courts were ruling on his claim.

17-20 .... 16.00
21-30 .... 10.00
31-44 .... 8.00

Josie & the Pussycats
Archie, 1969
45 .... 12.00
46-60 .... 6.00
61-70 .... 5.00
71-90 .... 4.00
91-106 .... 3.00

Josie & the Pussycats
Archie, 1993
1-2 .... 2.00

Journey
Aardvark-Vanaheim, 1983
1 .... 4.00
2-10 .... 3.00
11-27 .... 2.00

Journey Into Fear
Superior, 1951
1 .... 400.00
2 .... 240.00
3-5 .... 210.00
6-10 .... 165.00
11-21 .... 125.00

Journey into Mystery
Marvel, 1952
-1 .... 2.00
1 .... 3,100.00
2 .... 950.00
3-4 .... 700.00
5 .... 800.00
6-11 .... 450.00
12-22 .... 350.00
23-32 .... 225.00
33 .... 250.00
34-40 .... 225.00
41-49 .... 200.00
50 .... 160.00
51-61 .... 155.00
62 .... 250.00
63-71 .... 145.00
72 .... 140.00
73 .... 200.00
74-81 .... 140.00
82 .... 160.00
83 .... 4,500.00
☛1st Thor
83/Golden Record 60.00
84 .... 725.00
85 .... 450.00
86 .... 400.00
87 .... 600.00
88 .... 250.00
89 .... 300.00
90 .... 150.00
91-92 .... 130.00
93 .... 160.00
94-96 .... 130.00
97 .... 325.00
98 .... 120.00
99 .... 105.00
100 .... 115.00
101 .... 150.00
102-108 .... 75.00
109 .... 90.00
110-111 .... 75.00
112 .... 210.00
☛Thor vs. Hulk
113-114 .... 75.00
115 .... 90.00
116 .... 75.00
117-125 .... 70.00
503-521 .... 2.00
Ann 1 .... 150.00

Journey into Mystery
Marvel, 1972
1 .... 17.00
2-3 .... 7.00
4-5 .... 6.00
6-19 .... 5.00

Journey Into Unknown Worlds
Atlas, 1950

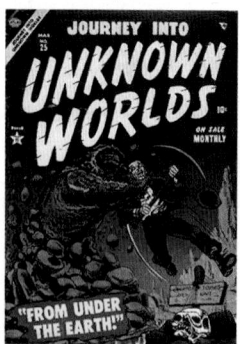

A science-fiction/horror title during the 1950s, Journey Into Unknown Worlds was atypical of Atlas fare of the time in the relative subtlety of its approach. The horror was more of "isn't that strange" flavor than the "eeww! gross!" approach found in such Atlas horror titles as Mystic. And the science fiction was more literary and fantasy-oriented than the bug-eyed monster stories and space operas popular in other titles.

Such top-of-the-line artists as Joe Kubert, Steve Ditko, Al Williamson, Reed Crandall, and the under-rated Angelo Torres all graced its pages with fine, detailed work. Journey Into Unknown Worlds therefore did not seem as likely to suffer when the Comics Code came in during the mid-1950s. But, quality notwithstanding, it did not survive the Atlas implosion of 1957.

-- Rob Salkowitz

1	1,535.00
2	700.00
3	540.00
4-6	400.00
7	560.00
8-10	400.00
11-13	260.00
14-15	445.00
16-20	225.00
21-30	160.00
31-40	110.00
41-54	85.00
55-59	100.00

Journeyman
Image, 1999

1-3	3.00

Journeyman/Dark Ages
Lucid, 1997

1	3.00

Journey: Wardrums
Fantagraphics, 1987

1-2	2.00

Jr. Carrot Patrol
Dark Horse, 1989

1-2	2.00

JSA
DC, 1999

Old and new members of the Justice Society of America are brought together in this story by writers James Robinson and David Goyer, to create the group for a new era.

In the opening story, Scarab, a hero from the early days of the team, emerges from the far past with a warning and a plea: the new Doctor Fate is about to be born, and an evil group is murdering heroes and regular folk alike, trying to get at the child. The group must travel throughout the world, identify which of the three babies is destined for fate, and protect the child. Their quest puts them in touch with the insecure new Hawkgirl, as well as the dark force that might cause the end of them all.

1	5.00
2-36	3.00
37	4.00
38-49	3.00
50	4.00
51-57	3.00
58	4.00
59-66	3.00
67	7.00
☛Identity Crisis tie	
68	5.00
69-70	4.00
71	3.00
72	4.00
73	5.00
☛Infinite Crisis tie	
74	4.00
☛Infinite Crisis tie	
75-87	3.00
Ann 1	5.00

JSA: All Stars
DC, 2003

1-6	3.00
7	4.00
8	3.00

JSA: Classified
DC, 2005

1/Conner	16.00
1/Hughes	24.00
1/Sketch	7.00
☛Hughes, 2nd print	
2	9.00
2/Sketch	4.00
3-4	5.00
5-20	3.00

JSA: Our Worlds At War
DC, 2001

1	3.00

JSA Secret Files
DC, 1999

1-2	5.00

JSA: Strange Adventures
DC, 2004

1-6	4.00

JSA: The Liberty File
DC, 2000

1-2	7.00

JSA: Unholy Three
DC, 2003

1-2	7.00

Jubilee
Marvel, 2004

1-6	3.00

Judge Dredd Versus Aliens: Incubus
Dark Horse, 2003

1-4	3.00

Jude, the Forgotten Saint
Catechetical Guild

1	14.00

Judge Child
Eagle

The Judge Child Quest is a five-issue mini-series which originally ran in 2000 A.D. #156-181. Mega-City One has fallen on hard times, and oracles have predicted the city's destruction would happen in the year 2120. The only hope lies in locating a special child named Owen Krysler, who bears the mark of an eagle on his forehead. Unfortunately, Owen has been taken by mutant slavers into the Cursed Earth, and it's up to Judge Dredd to find him.

Eagle Comics brought the Judge Dredd stories from Great Britain to the United States and presented it to an entirely new audience. Judge Dredd was created for the comic magazine 2000 A.D., which has run weekly since 1977.

With colorful covers by English comic artist Brian Bolland, The Judge Child Quest features artwork by Brian Bolland, Ron Smith, and Mike McMahon. Longtime favorite John Wagner wrote the script.

1-5 .... 2.00

Judge Colt
Gold Key, 1969
1 .... 15.00
2-4 .... 10.00

Judge Dredd
Eagle, 1983
1 .... 4.00
2-10 .... 3.00
11-35 .... 2.00

Judge Dredd
Fleetway-Quality, 1986
1-2 .... 3.00
3-61 .... 2.00
Special 1 .... 3.00

Judge Dredd
DC, 1994
1-3 .... 3.00
4-18 .... 2.00

Judge Dredd: America
Fleetway-Quality
1-2 .... 3.00

Judge Dredd Classics
Fleetway-Quality

Following issue #61 of the second U.S. volume of Judge Dredd, the series changed names to become Judge Dredd Classics. Like its predecessor, it reprinted several Judge Dredd stories per issues. The source for these stories seems to have been the earlier issues of 2000 A.D., a British comics weekly that ran both Judge Dredd and other science-fiction stories as serials.

These early stories captured all the straight-lipped insanity of Dredd's world. Here, almost total unemployment combined with huge overpopulation made for an explosion of crime that not even the Draconian tactics of the police ("Judges") could control. Judge Dredd is a sort of futuristic Joe Friday (from Dragnet) who tirelessly fights for law and order when it's clear that the entire world has gone to the dogs.

62-77 .... 2.00

Judge Dredd: Emerald Isle
Fleetway-Quality, 1991
1 .... 5.00

Judge Dredd: Legends of the Law
DC, 1994
1 .... 3.00
2-13 .... 2.00

Judge Dredd Megazine
Fleetway-Quality
1 .... 8.00
2-5 .... 6.00
6-15 .... 5.00
16-20 .... 4.00
Ann 1986 .... 9.00
Ann 1989 .... 8.00

Judge Dredd Megazine
Fleetway-Quality
1 .... 6.00
2-83 .... 3.00
MS 1988-1994 .... 4.00
YB 1993-1994 .... 8.00

Judge Dredd Megazine
Fleetway-Quality, 2000
1 .... 4.00
2-42 .... 3.00
43-45 .... 4.00
46 .... 7.00
47-80 .... 4.00

Judge Dredd: Raptaur
Fleetway-Quality
1-2 .... 3.00

Judge Dredd's Crime File
Eagle, 1985
1-6 .... 3.00

Judge Dredd's Crime File
Fleetway-Quality
1-4 .... 4.00

Judge Dredd the Early Cases
Eagle, 1986
1-6 .... 3.00

Judge Dredd the Megazine
Fleetway-Quality
1-3 .... 5.00

Judge Dredd: The Official Movie Adaptation
DC
1 .... 6.00

Judge Parker
Argo, 1956
1 .... 35.00
2 .... 25.00

J.U.D.G.E.: Secret Rage
Image, 2000

Victoria Grace was recruited by Thomas Crowell to lead J.U.D.G.E. due to her leadership abilities with a background in psychology and the occult. Together with her team of inexperienced civilians gifted with bizarre abilities thanks to either science or magic, they hunt down and destroy rogue agents and other strange creatures, no matter what the cost.

In J.U.D.G.E.: Secret Rage, Greg Horn combines real life photography and painting to depict one of the most realistic comics to ever hit the stands. It looks like a cross between a full-length motion picture and the ever popular graphic novel. For mature audiences, but worth it.

1 ....3.00

Judgment Day
Lightning, 1993

1/A-1/Platinum 4.00
2-8 ....3.00

Judgment Day
Awesome, 1997

1-3/A 3.00

Judgment Day: Aftermath
Awesome, 1998

1-1/A 4.00

Judgment Day: Final Judgment
Awesome, 1997

3 ....3.00

Judgment Day Sourcebook
Awesome

1 ....1.00

Judgment Pawns
Antarctic, 1997

1-3 ....3.00

Judgments
NBM

1 .... 15.00

Judo Girl
Alias, 2005

0/Conv 8.00
1/Balan 3.00
1/Taylor 4.00
2/Balan 3.00
2/Taylor 4.00
3/Balan 3.00
3/Taylor 4.00
4/Balan 3.00
4/Miller 4.00

Judo Joe
Jay-Jay Corp., 1953

1 .... 30.00
2-3 .... 24.00

Judomaster
Charlton, 1966

The 1960s comics renaissance known as the Silver Age came late to third-string publisher Charlton, and lasted only until the departure of innovative editor Dick Giordano in 1968. But during that brief flicker of creativity, Charlton produced a few titles that are recognizable as credible super-hero efforts.

Judomaster is at the bottom of that list. It's a simple-minded, martial-arts action series set during World War II. Judomaster is an American trained in the martial arts, set against vicious "Japs and Nazis" in flimsy stories designed to showcase plenty of fighting action.

Written and drawn in obvious haste by the otherwise competent Frank McLaughlin, Judomaster folded after only a short run. In the 1980s, DC acquired the Charlton super-hero properties and Judomaster made an unlikely cameo appearance in the multiple-universe-collapsing epic mini-series Crisis On Infinite Earths.

-- *Rob Salkowitz*

89 .... 12.00
90-98 .... 9.00

Judomaster
Modern, 1977

93-98 .... 2.00

Judy Canova
Fox, 1950

1 .... 110.00
2-3 .... 80.00

Juggernaut
Marvel, 1997

1 .... 3.00

Juggernaut
Marvel, 1999

1 .... 3.00

Jughead's Folly
Archie, 1957

1 .... 120.00

Jughead
Archie, 1965

127-130 .... 12.00
131-140 .... 9.00
141-150 .... 8.00
151-171 .... 7.00
172-200 .... 5.00
201-220 .... 4.00
221-240 .... 3.00
241-352 .... 2.00

Jughead
Archie, 1987

1 .... 3.00
2-176 .... 2.00

Jughead and His Friends Digest
Archie, 2005

1-16 .... 2.00

Jughead as Captain Hero
Archie, 1966

1 .... 28.00
2 .... 15.00
3 .... 10.00
4-7 .... 7.00

Jughead Jones Digest Magazine
Archie, 1977

1 .... 16.00
2 .... 12.00
3-6 .... 6.00
7 .... 8.00
8-10 .... 6.00
11-20 .... 5.00
21-30 .... 4.00
31-50 .... 3.00
51-100 .... 2.00

Jughead's Baby Tales
Archie, 1994

1-2 .... 2.00

Jughead's Diner
Archie, 1990

1-7 .... 2.00

Jughead's Double Digest
Archie, 1989

1	6.00
2-5	4.00
6-79	3.00
80-127	4.00

Jughead's Fantasy
Archie, 1960

1	80.00
2-3	55.00

Jughead's Jokes
Archie, 1967

1	60.00
2	35.00
3	25.00
4-5	18.00
6-10	15.00
11-15	12.00
16-20	10.00
21-30	7.00
31-40	5.00
41-60	4.00
61-78	3.00

Jughead's Pal Hot Dog
Archie, 1990

1-5	1.00

Jughead's Time Police
Archie, 1990

1-6	1.00

Jughead with Archie Digest Magazine
Archie, 1974

After some 30 years of Archie comic books, Archie's publishers hit on the idea of repackaging Archies adventures in a series of digest magazines. These digests were smaller than a regular comic book in page size, but much thicker. They were often sold alongside supermarket check-out line pamphlets and TV Guides, and proved the perfect present to quiet fretful children who had been forced to accompany their parents to the store.

Jughead with Archie Digest concentrates a bit more on Archie's best friend Jughead than on the rest of the Riverdale gang. Still, no Archie magazine would be complete without including Betty, Veronica, Archie, Reggie, Moose, and the rest of Jug's friends.

1	12.00
2-10	7.00
11-20	4.00
21-50	3.00
51-199	2.00

Jugular
Black Out

0	3.00

Juke Box Comics
Famous Funnies, 1948

1	185.00
2	125.00
3-6	110.00

Jumbo Comics
Fiction House, 1938

Jumbo Comics was one of the more important titles of comics' Golden Age and the flagship of the Fiction House publishing enterprise, which was also responsible for Planet Comics, The Spirit, and Jungle Comics. In its first (oversized) issue alone, Jumbo introduced the world to some of the earliest work of comic art king Jack Kirby ("The Count of Monte Cristo," his first professional work), master stylist Will Eisner ("Hawk of the Seas"), and Batman creator Bob Kane ("Peter Pupp")! The star was Mort Meskin's Sheena, Queen of the Jungle, the first significant comics heroine, who went on to star in movie serials and television during the 40s and 50s. Sheena continued to anchor the lineup through 160 issues before Jumbo switched over to science fiction and horror at the end of its run.

Early issues of Jumbo Comics were printed in a 10-1/2-inch-by-14-1/2-inch format - large even by Golden Age standards.
-- Rob Salkowitz

1	18,500.00
2	6,000.00
3-4	4,200.00
5	3,300.00
6-7	2,900.00
8	2,975.00
9	2,550.00
10	1,500.00
11-12	1,200.00
13-14	1,100.00
15-20	750.00
21-30	575.00
31-40	475.00
41-50	350.00
51-60	295.00
61-70	220.00
71-80	180.00
81-90	155.00
91-110	135.00
111-120	100.00
121-167	90.00

Jumper
Zav

1-2	3.00

Jun
Disney

1	2.00

Junction 17
Antarctic, 2003

1	4.00
2-4	3.00

Jungle Action
Atlas, 1954

1	240.00
2-6	200.00

Jungle Tales
Atlas, 1954

1	250.00
2	175.00
3-4	145.00
5-7	130.00

Jungle Action
Marvel, 1972

1	15.00
2-4	7.00
5	35.00
☛Black Panther begins	
6	12.00
7	8.00
8	15.00
9	7.00
10-16	6.00
17-21	5.00
21/30¢	20.00
22	5.00
22/30¢	20.00
23-24	5.00

Jungle Adventures
Super, 1963

10-18	28.00

Jungle Adventures
Skywald, 1971

1	10.00
2-3	7.00

Jungle Book
Gold Key, 1968

1	25.00

Jungle Book
Disney, 1990

1/A	3.00
1/B	6.00

Jungle Book
NBM

1	17.00

Jungle Comics
Fiction House, 1940

In the 1940s, long before the founders of Image were twinkles in their parents' eyes, Fiction House made the important discovery that people would buy comics to look at pictures of half-naked women. Jungle Comics was one of its flagship titles, with a format featuring (white) African adventurers (both male and female) wrestling with lions, discovering lost cities and elephant graveyards, hunting down cruel native kings and craven poachers - all while wearing as little clothing as physically possible.

Among the regular features in Jungle Comics were Ka'a'nga, Lord of the Jungle (the obligatory Tarzan clone), Wambi the Jungle Boy, explorer Terry Thunder, and, of course, Camilla, a variation on their own character Sheena, who appeared in Jumbo Comics. Top artists like Lou Fine and Will Eisner worked on early issues of the run, then left the features in the hands of the workman-like Fiction House staff.

1	4,000.00
2	1,500.00
3-4	1,250.00
5	1,500.00
6	650.00
7	600.00
8-10	545.00
11-15	475.00
16-20	425.00
21-25	370.00
26-30	340.00
31-35	290.00
36-40	250.00
41-50	215.00
51-60	200.00
61-70	180.00
71-80	165.00
81-90	150.00
91-97	140.00
98	210.00
99-100	140.00
101-110	130.00
111-130	125.00
131-150	115.00
151-163	100.00

Jungle Comics
A-List, 1997

1-5	3.00

Jungle Fantasy
Avatar, 2002

1-3	4.00

Jungle Girl
Fawcett, 1942

1	975.00

Jungle Girls
AC, 1988

1-2	2.00
3-16	3.00

Jungle Girls!
Eternity

8	3.00

Jungle Jim
Standard, 1949

11	60.00
12-15	40.00
16-20	35.00

Jungle Jim
Dell, 1954

3	30.00
4-9	25.00
10-19	20.00

Jungle Jim
King, 1967

5	9.00

Jungle Jim
Charlton, 1969

22	24.00
23-24	18.00
25-28	16.00

Jungle Jim
Avalon

1	3.00

Jungle Jo
Fox, 1950

0	300.00
1	375.00
2	285.00
3	240.00

Jungle Lil
Fox, 1950

1	325.00

Jungle Love
Aircel

1-3	3.00

Jungle Tales of Cavewoman
Basement

1	3.00

Jungle Tales of Tarzan
Charlton, 1965

1	45.00
2-4	35.00

Jungle Twins
Gold Key, 1972

1	10.00
2	7.00
3-5	4.00
6-17	3.00
18	2.00

Jungle War Stories
Dell, 1962

1	24.00
2-5	16.00
6-11	14.00

Junie Prom
Dearfield, 1947

1	50.00
2	36.00
3-7	30.00

Junior Carrot Patrol
Dark Horse, 1989

1-2	2.00

Junior Comics
Fox, 1947

9	220.00
10	165.00
11-16	125.00

Junior Hopp Comics
Stanmor, 1952

1	40.00
2-3	30.00

Junior Jackalope
Nevada City, 1982

1-2	2.00

Junior Miss
Timely, 1947

24-26	75.00
27-29	65.00
30-33	60.00
34-36	55.00
37-39	50.00

Junior Woodchucks
Disney, 1991
1-4 ....2.00

Junk Culture
DC, 1997
1-2 ....3.00

Junker
Fleetway-Quality
1-4 ....3.00

Junkfood Noir
Oktober Black, 1996
1 ....2.00

Junk Force
ComicsOne, 2004
1 ....10.00

Junkwaffel
Print Mint, 1972
1 ....5.00
2-3 ....3.00

Junkyard Enforcer
Boxcar, 1998
1 ....3.00

Jupiter
Sandberg, 1999
1-3 ....3.00

Jurassic Lark
Deluxe Edition
Parody
1 ....3.00

Jurassic Park
Topps, 1993
0-4/Direct 3.00

Jurassic Park
(Magazine)
Dark Horse
1 ....4.00
2-15 ....3.00

Jurassic Park
Adventures
Topps, 1994

Running some ten issues in all,

this series reprinted the earlier Jurassic Park: Raptor mini-series that had gone before it, beginning with Jurassic Park: Raptors Attack. In it, we see Dr. Alan Grant and Ellie Sattler crashing down in the Amazon jungle with three of the surviving Raptors from Jurassic Park. They were immediately taken in by a drug dealer who trained the Raptors to act as his personal guard dogs and trained assassins. Grant and Nessler do their best not only to escape, but to save the animals from extinction.

1-10 .... 2.00

Jurassic Park: Raptor
Topps, 1993
1-2 .... 3.00

Jurassic Park:
Raptors Attack
Topps, 1994
1-4 .... 3.00

Jurassic Park:
Raptors Hijack
Topps, 1994
1-4 .... 3.00

Just a Pilgrim
Black Bull, 2000

There came a day when the sun cooled and grew larger, swallowing Mercury, burning Venus, and drying Earth's oceans. Those who survived found treasure and weapons in the great ships that had sunk over the years, now lying in the hot light of day. Little Billy Shepherd and his family are being hunted by a pack of "real bad men," when they and their survival group, searching for water in the deep canyons, are saved by a mysterious man who says he's "just a pilgrim."

An expert shot with a cross on his face and the scriptures in his

heart, he saves them time and again. But can even a man of God stand long against Captain Castenado and his deranged crew -- or even those he protects -- when Billy's mom realizes where she's seen this Pilgrim before?

1 .... 4.00
2-5 .... 3.00

Justice
Atlas, 1947
7 (1) 130.00
8 (2) 90.00
9 (3) 75.00
4-5 .... 65.00
6-9 .... 55.00
10-15 .... 65.00
16-20 .... 55.00
21-30 .... 48.00
31-40 .... 42.00
41-52 .... 34.00

Justice
Marvel, 1986
1-25 .... 1.00
26-32 .... 2.00

Justice
Antarctic, 1994
1 .... 4.00

Justice Brigade
TCB Comics
1-8 .... 2.00

Justice
DC, 2005
1/Heroes................................ 5.00
1/Villains-12........................... 4.00

Justice: Four Balance
Marvel, 1994
1-4 .... 2.00

Justice, Inc.
DC, 1975
1 .... 3.00
2-4 .... 2.00

Justice, Inc.
DC, 1989
1-2 .... 4.00

Justice League
DC, 1987

The Justice League of America had once been the premier super-group in the DC universe. Over the years, however, its key members drifted off, leaving the organization weakened. The death knell of the old Justice League came during the Legends storyline, when Darkseid conspired to move public sentiment against super-heroes. The old Justice League of America was dissolved, only to be reformed in Legends #6 as simply The Justice League.

The new team consisted of Doctor Fate, Batman, Shazam, Guy Gardner, The Martian Manhunter, Black Canary, Mister Miracle, and Blue Beetle. The group was sponsored by Maxwell Lord, a multimillionaire who had fallen under the influence of a sentient super-computer. The computer's plan was to organize the Justice League as a force to bring peace to the world. In issue #7, the computer (via Maxwell Lord) would further this plan by arranging for the team's globalization as Justice League International.

1	6.00
2-3	3.00
3/Ltd.	10.00
4	3.00
5-6	2.00
Ann 1	3.00

Justice League Adventures
DC, 2002

1	3.00
2-34	2.00

Justice League America
DC, 1989

0-50	2.00
51-68	1.00

69	3.00
69/2nd-99	2.00
100	3.00
100/Variant	4.00
101-113	2.00
Ann 4-8	3.00
Ann 9	4.00
Ann 10	3.00
Special 1	2.00
Special 2	3.00

Justice League: A Midsummer's Nightmare
DC, 1996

1-3	3.00

Justice League Elite
DC, 2004

1-11	3.00

Justice League Europe
DC, 1989

Justice League International eventually spun off a European branch, sending its Russian member, Rocket Red, to Paris with Animal Man, Captain Atom, Wonder Woman, Power Girl, Elongated Man, Metamorpho, and the new Flash. But teamwork was going to come hard: Captain Atom was a nervous new leader, Flash had his eyes on the female members of the team, and Animal Man's costume went up in flames when it was sent over in the teleporter. Paris didn't exactly seem overjoyed to see them either...

The conflicts between the members gave this spinoff from Justice League International a unique twist as they worked out their problems and become a team.

1-20	2.00
21-49	1.00
50	3.00
Ann 1-2	2.00
Ann 3	3.00

Justice League International
DC, 1987

7-10	2.00
11-23	1.00
24	2.00
25-58	1.00
59-68	2.00
Ann 2-5	3.00
Special 1	2.00
Special 2	3.00

Justice League of America
DC, 1960

After their first appearances in The Brave and The Bold #28-30, DC realized that the Justice League of America was a hit. It seemed that if heroes such as Batman, Superman, Flash, Wonder Woman, Green Lantern, and Aquaman were great on their own, they'd be even better together. Thus The Justice League of America was started, gathering these and other heroes together to fight the sort of foes that only their combined might could challenge.

Among the team's most popular adventures were a series of annual crossovers with The Justice Society of America.

1	5,000.00
2	1,250.00
3	1,000.00
4	700.00
5	600.00
6-8	400.00
9	1,000.00
☞JLA origin	
10	400.00
11-15	250.00
16-20	225.00
21	350.00
☞Earth-2 visit	
22	325.00
23-30	150.00
31	100.00
32-33	90.00

34-36	75.00

☛Supes vs. Cap. Mrv.

37-39	125.00
40-41	75.00
42-45	60.00

☛1st SA Sandman

46	110.00

☛JSA app.

47	95.00
48	140.00

☛Giant issue

49-52	60.00
53-54	55.00
55	115.00

☛JSA team-up

56	100.00

☛JSA team-up

57-62	55.00
63-66	45.00
67	60.00

☛Giant

68	50.00
69-72	45.00

☛Giant

73-81	35.00
82	45.00

☛G.A. Batman app.

83-84	30.00
85	40.00

☛Giant

86-90	25.00
91	35.00
92	32.00
93	25.00

☛Giant

94	60.00

☛Sandman origin

95-99	20.00
100	65.00
101-106	20.00
107-108	25.00
109	20.00
110-116	25.00
117-125	15.00
126-136	10.00
137	20.00
138-150	7.00
151-158	5.00
158/Whitman	10.00
159-160	5.00
160/Whitman	10.00
161	5.00
161/Whitman	10.00
162	5.00
162/Whitman	10.00
163-165	5.00
166	12.00
166/Whitman	25.00
167	12.00
167/Whitman-168	25.00

☛Mindwipe story

168/Whitman	35.00
169	5.00
169/Whitman	10.00
170-171	5.00
171/Whitman	10.00
172	5.00
172/Whitman	10.00
173	5.00
173/Whitman	10.00

174-176	5.00
176/Whitman	10.00
177	5.00
177/Whitman	10.00
178	5.00
178/Whitman	10.00
179	5.00
179/Whitman	10.00
180-181	5.00
181/Whitman	10.00
182-199	5.00
200	7.00
201-217	3.00
218	4.00
219	3.00
220	4.00
221-226	3.00
227	4.00
228-260	3.00
261	4.00
Ann 1	5.00
Ann 2-3	4.00

Justice League of America
DC, 2006

0-1/Variant	6.00
2-2/Variant	4.00
3-38	3.00

Justice League of America: Another Nail
DC, 2004

1-3	6.00

Justice League of America Index
Eclipse, 1986

1-8	2.00

Justice League of America Super Spectacular
DC, 1999

1	6.00

Justice League Quarterly
DC, 1990

1-17	3.00

Justice Leagues: JL?
DC, 2001

1	3.00

Justice Leagues: JLA
DC, 2001

An alien race is planning an invasion of the planet Earth. And the Justice League of America can't stop them- because they no longer exist. After erasing the memory of the JLA's existence from Earth's entire population, the Advance Man begins preparing the way for his employer's assault on the human race. As each member of the JLA attempts to recreate the team from their faintest recollections, the hope of humanity may lie in the hands of the super villain telepath, Hector Hammond. This one-shot comic is the sixth and final part of the "Justice Leagues" crossover event in which members of the team remake the JLA in their own images such as Wonder Woman's Justice League of Amazons and the Martian Manhunter and Superman's Justice League of Aliens. But the strength of the JLA they eventually discover in this battle, just as it always has, comes from the team's diversity.

1	3.00

Justice Leagues: Justice League of Aliens
DC, 2001

1	3.00

Justice Leagues: Justice League of Amazons
DC, 2001

1	3.00

Justice Leagues: Justice League of Arkham
DC, 2001

1	3.00

Justice Leagues: Justice League of Atlantis
DC, 2001

1	3.00

Justice League
Task Force
DC, 1993

0-5	2.00
6	1.00
7-37	2.00

Justice League
Unlimited
DC, 2004

1-29	2.00

Justice Machine (Noble)
Noble, 1981

1-5	3.00
Ann 1	5.00

Justice Machine
Comico, 1987

1	3.00
2-29	2.00
Ann 1	3.00

Justice Machine
Innovation, 1990

1-7	2.00

Justice Machine
Millennium, 1992

1-2	3.00

Justice Machine
Featuring the
Elementals
Comico, 1986

The Justice Machine is a super-powered police force on the world of Georwell. On their world, the Justice Machine are heroes. But the Georwell is a repressive dictatorship of the worst kind, and those who stand against the government are quickly suppressed. Can one truly be a hero if the things that one fights for are repulsive?

The Justice Machine had just put an end to the latest rebellion, but in their haste to get home they did not notice the contingency plan the rebels had put in place. A wizard had been left behind who summoned the super-powered Elementals from Earth to fight on the rebels' behalf. Although he was not able to magically compel them to do his bidding, he was able to convince the Elementals that his cause was just. Before long, the heroes of Earth had come head-to-head with the heroes of Georwell- and both would come out changed by the experience.

1-4	2.00

Justice Machine
Summer Spectacular
Innovation

1	3.00

Justice Riders
DC, 1997

1	6.00

Justice Society
of America
DC, 1991

1-8	2.00

Justice Society
of America
DC, 1992

1-5	2.00
6-10	1.00

Justice Society
of America
DC, 2007

1-1/Variant	6.00
2	4.00
3-30	3.00

Justice Society
of America 100-Page
Super Spectacular
DC

1	7.00

Justice Traps the Guilty
Headline, 1947

One of the pioneering crime comics titles, Justice Traps the Guilty -- sometimes simply known as Guilty -- was a product of the studios of prolific comics masters Joe Simon and Jack Kirby. By the late 1940s, Kirby's style had matured into one of power and depth, bringing a white-hot intensity to Simon's poignant scripts. In the early issues of Justice Traps the Guilty, action and drama simply explode off the pages.

The creators drew from their own experiences growing up in working-class ethnic neighborhoods in the 1920s and 1930s to create complex and convincing portraits of the criminal underworld, melded with an almost Old Testament brand of justice and retribution.

As Simon and Kirby's involvement diminished and imitators flooded the market with crime comics of lesser quality, Justice Traps the Guilty lost much of its edge. It was squashed after the arrival of the Comics Code.
-- Rob Salkowitz

1	350.00
2	210.00
3	175.00
4-6	160.00
7-10	135.00
11-12	85.00
13	90.00
14-20	58.00
21-30	42.00
31-40	28.00
41-50	24.00
51-70	20.00
71-92	18.00

Just Imagine Comics
and Stories
Just Imagine, 1982

1-Special 1	2.00

Just Imagine's Special
Just Imagine, 1986

1	2.00

Just Imagine Stan Lee...
Secret Files and Origins
DC, 2002

1	5.00

Just Imagine Stan Lee With Chris Bachalo Creating Catwoman
DC, 2002

When super-model Joanie Jordan and her cat are struck by a mysterious bolt of green lightning, she gains many of the attributes of her feline pet, including super-human agility and razor-sharp claws. Before long, Joanie, in the guise of Catwoman, is leaping from rooftops and fighting hired thugs and their super-powered masters. But from the shadows, all her actions are carefully monitored by the enigmatic figure known only as Reverend Darrk.

The "Just Imagine…" series teams long-time Marvel Comics icon Stan Lee with various DC artists, to recreate many of DC's most popular characters using only their names as a starting point. Although each book in the series, featuring Lee's versions of characters such as Catwoman, Batman, Superman, Shazam, and Aquaman, stands alone, they are loosely tied together in a story-arc that culminates in Just Imagine Stan Lee With John Cassaday Creating Crisis.

1 .... 6.00

Just Imagine Stan Lee With Dave Gibbons Creating Green Lantern
DC, 2001

1 .... 6.00

Just Imagine Stan Lee With Gary Frank Creating Shazam!
DC, 2002

1 .... 6.00

Just Imagine Stan Lee With Jerry Ordway Creating JLA
DC, 2002

1 .... 6.00

Just Imagine Stan Lee With Jim Lee Creating Wonder Woman
DC, 2001

1 .... 6.00

Just Imagine Stan Lee With Joe Kubert Creating Batman
DC, 2001

1 .... 6.00

Just Imagine Stan Lee With John Buscema Creating Superman
DC, 2001

1 .... 6.00

Just Imagine Stan Lee With John Byrne Creating Robin
DC, 2002

1 .... 6.00

Just Imagine Stan Lee With John Cassaday Creating Crisis
DC, 2002

1 .... 6.00

Just Imagine Stan Lee With Kevin Maguire Creating The Flash
DC, 2002

1 .... 6.00

Just Imagine Stan Lee With Scott McDaniel Creating Aquaman
DC, 2002

1 .... 6.00

Just Imagine Stan Lee with Walter Simonson Creating Sandman
DC, 2002

1 .... 6.00

Just Married
Charlton, 1958

Just Married, one of Charlton's numerous love comics, offered up stories of romance, betrayal, jealousy, heartbreak, and heartwarming sentiment in a glossy, standardized, and highly sanitized style. While the social upheavals of the 1960s proved a fertile source of creative ideas for many types of comics, the genre of love and romance comics remained as formulaic and uninspired as ever, dressing up the conventional morality of the 1950s in the new flashy fashions and jet-set backdrops of the 1960s.

Never a trailblazing publisher under the best of circumstances, Charlton set some new standards for mediocrity with some issues of this series.

-- Rob Salkowitz

1	40.00
2	24.00
3-5	15.00
6-10	10.00
11-20	9.00
21-30	6.00
31-60	5.00
61-80	4.00
81-114	3.00

Just Twisted
Necromics

1 .... 2.00

Justy
Viz, 1988

1-9 .... 2.00

Bill Woggon's pin-up character has been around the Archie universe since 1945.

Ka'a'nga Comics
Fiction House, 1949

1	500.00
2	270.00
3	185.00
4-5	150.00
6-10	125.00
11-20	100.00

Kaboom
Awesome, 1997

1-Ashcan 1/Gold 3.00

Kabuki
Image, 1997

David Mack's impressive series came to Image in 1998, following a legion of one-shots and mini-series at Caliber. Mack uses a multitextured, mixed-media style to illustrate the tale of a girl turned into a weapon of vengeance. It's an intensely psychological series,

which explores the story from the private thoughts of the characters, rather than merely filling time between action sequences.

As the series begins, Kabuki is interned in a secret institution designed to house agents who have run amuck or broken down in some way. There, she exchanges countless messages with a fellow inmate called Akemi, all written on tiny squares of paper folded into origami. Over the course of the first four issues, she meets her friend in person, as well as the other members of her circle. Together, they launch a bold plan to break out of the asylum of spies, all the while playing sly games with the doctors who are trying to unlock their secrets.

1/2	3.00
1/2/A	4.00
1-1/A	5.00
2-4	4.00
5-9	3.00

Kabuki Agents
Image, 1999

1-8 .... 3.00

Kabuki: Circle of Blood
Caliber, 1995

1	4.00
1/Ltd.	5.00
1/2nd-3	4.00
4-6	3.00
6/Ltd.	15.00

Kabuki Classics
Image, 1999

1-2	3.00
3	5.00
4-12	3.00

Kabuki Color Special
Caliber, 1996

1 .... 4.00

Kabuki Compilation
Caliber, 1995

1 .... 8.00

Kabuki: Dance of Death
London Night, 1995

1 .... 4.00

Kabuki Dreams
Image, 1998

nn 5.00

Kabuki: Dreams of the Dead
Caliber, 1996

1 .... 3.00

Kabuki: Fear the Reaper
Caliber, 1994

1 .... 4.00

Kabuki Gallery
Caliber, 1995

1	3.00
1/A	15.00

Kabuki: The Ghost Play
Image, 2002

1 .... 3.00

Kabuki-Images
Image, 1998

1-2 .... 5.00

Kabuki
Marvel, 2004

1	4.00
1/Variant	5.00
2-4	3.00
4/Hughes	4.00
5-7	3.00

Kabuki:
Masks of the Noh
Image, 1996

1-4	3.00

Kabuki Reflections
Image, 1998

1-4	5.00

Kabuki: Reflections
Marvel, 2007

1	6.00

Kabuki: Skin Deep
Caliber, 1996

1	4.00
2-2/A	3.00
2/Ltd.	8.00
3	3.00

Kafka
Renegade, 1987

As writer Steven T. Seagle notes in the afterword, this comic can be read in five minutes or the reader can slow down and admire the way Seagle uses few words and many silent panels to craft an intriguing story. The black-and-white art lends to the desperate mood in the story of a man whose past has finally caught up with him. Calling himself Robert Kafka, he has been in hiding for years giving up everything including his identity and his wife. When several men show up unexpectedly on his doorstep claiming to be CIA, Kafka must run for his life, fleeing into the unknown future while forever craving all that he has left behind.

1-6	3.00

Kafka:
The Execution
Fantagraphics

1	3.00

Kaktus
Fantagraphics

1	3.00

Kalamazoo Comix
Discount Hobby, 1996

1-3	2.00
4-5	3.00

Kalgan the Golden
Harrier, 1988

1	2.00

Kamandi:
At Earth's End
DC, 1993

1-6	2.00

Kamandi,
the Last Boy on Earth
DC, 1972

1	20.00
2	15.00
3	10.00
4-10	8.00
11-19	7.00
20-38	6.00
39-40	5.00
41-54	4.00
55-58	3.00
59	4.00

Kama Sutra
(Manara's...)
NBM

1	13.00

Kama Sutra
(Girl's...)
Black Lace

1	3.00

Kamichama Karin
Tokyopop, 2005

1-2	10.00

Kamikaze
DC, 2003

1-6	3.00

Kamikaze Cat
Pied Piper, 1987

If Howard the Duck had been so successful that Marvel felt the need to change their entire universe over to funny animals, the results might resemble the world of Kamikaze Cat. Written by Mark Hamlin and Roger McKenzie and drawn by Mark Sullivan, this offbeat black-and-white independent from the late 1980s offers a crisp, entertaining, well-told detective story featuring a cast of animals. KC and his girlfriend Boopsie bear some slight resemblance to more famous adult-oriented felines Fritz and Omaha, but the action and attitude keep the premise fresh and original.

-- Rob Salkowitz

1	2.00

Kane
Dancing Elephant, 1998

1-22	4.00
23-26	3.00
27	5.00
28-32	3.00

Kanpai!
Tokyopop, 2005

1-2	10.00

Kansas Thunder
Red Menace

1	3.00

Kaos
Tommy Regalado, 1994

1	2.00

Kaos Moon
Caliber, 1996

1-4 ....3.00

Kaptain Keen & Kompany
Vortex, 1986

1-6 ....2.00

Karas
Dark Horse, 2005

1 ....3.00

Karate Girl
Fantagraphics, 1993

1-2 ....3.00

Karate Girl Tengu Wars
Fantagraphics, 1995

1-3 ....3.00

Karate Kid
DC, 1976

The 30th century's Val Armorr was born the son of a super-villain (The Black Dragon) and raised by The Sensei, the super-hero that defeated that villain. Trained in the martial arts essentially from birth, Armorr mastered every form of hand-to-hand and armed combat known across the galaxy.

Seeing his mastery as its own super-power, The Legion of Super-Heroes inducted the newly named Karate Kid into its ranks in Adventure Comics #346. As a Legionnaire, Karate Kid met and fell in love with Princess Projectra, the heir to the throne of the planet Orando. To prove himself worthy, Karate Kid went on an extended quest, including a time-traveling trip to the 20th century, where these stories take place.

-- Brent

1 ....12.00
2-3 ....7.00
4-15 ....5.00

Karate Kreatures
Ma, 1989

1-2 .... 2.00

Kare Kano
Tokyopop, 2003

1-18 .... 10.00

Karma Incorporated
Viper, 2005

1-2 .... 3.00

Karney
Idea & Design Works, 2005

1-4 .... 4.00

Karza
Image, 2003

1-4 .... 3.00

Kasco Comics
Kasko Grainfeed, 1949

1 .... 55.00
2 .... 48.00

Kathy (Standard)
Standard, 1949

1 .... 70.00
2 .... 48.00
3-4 .... 42.00
5-7 .... 36.00
8-17 .... 32.00

Kathy
Atlas, 1959

1 .... 48.00
2-5 .... 35.00
6-9 .... 30.00
10-27 .... 26.00

Katmandu
Antarctic, 1993

1-7 .... 3.00
8-12 .... 2.00
13-25 .... 3.00
26-Ann 4 .... 5.00

Kato of the Green Hornet
Now, 1991

The Green Hornet's sidekick, Hiyashi Kato, returns to Communist China in this four-part mini-series. His phenomenal ability in the martial arts inspires the Communist government to use Kato as an actor in one of its propaganda films. Of course, Kato wants none of this, but he quickly finds out that he has no other choice but to comply.

Martial arts and mysticism meet as Kato struggles to escape from the reach of the government, free friends from jail, and recover an artifact known as the Demon Sword.

1-4 .... 3.00

Kato of the Green Hornet II
Now, 1992

1-2 .... 3.00

Katy Keene
Archie, 1949

1 .... 650.00
2 .... 375.00
3-5 .... 240.00
6-10 .... 170.00
11-20 .... 125.00
21-30 .... 90.00
31-50 .... 70.00
51-62 .... 55.00
Ann 1 .... 285.00
Ann 2 .... 165.00
3D 1 .... 325.00

Katy Keene
Archie, 1985

8-20 .... 2.00
21-33 .... 1.00

Katy Keene Fashion Book Magazine
Archie, 1955

1 .... 325.00
2 .... 180.00
13-14 .... 140.00
15-16 .... 110.00
17-19 .... 95.00
20-21 .... 85.00
22-23 .... 80.00

Katy Keene Pin Up Parade
Archie, 1955

1 .... 300.00
2 .... 175.00
3 .... 165.00
4-5 .... 145.00
6-8 .... 125.00
9-10 .... 110.00
11-15 .... 80.00

Katy Keene Special
Archie, 1983

Fashion model Katy Keene has been a love comics star since the late 1940s, and has been periodically revived over the past years anytime Archie Publications decided to get back into the romance comics business. This series (known simply as "Katy Keene" beginning with issue #7), presents Katy in a new set of up-to-date adventures, with issue-to-issue plot continuities and dramatic complications worthy of then-current prime time soap operas like Dallas and Dynasty.

Archie's presentation and packaging of love comics has never been anything short of thoroughly professional, and this incarnation of Katy Keene is no exception. Writer Susan Berkley is teamed with venerable love-comic pros Don Sherwood and Vince Colletta to produce enjoyable, fast-paced, competently illustrated fare for (presumably) younger girls.

1	3.00
2-7	2.00

Katzenjammer Kids
David McKay, 1947

1	110.00
2	80.00
3	65.00
4-5	50.00
6-9	42.00
10-16	36.00
17-22	30.00
23-27	24.00

Ka-Zar
Marvel, 1970

1	35.00
2-3	15.00

Ka-Zar
Marvel, 1974

1	17.00
2	7.00

3-7	5.00
8-15	3.00
15/30¢	20.00
16	3.00
16/30¢	20.00
17	3.00
17/30¢	20.00
18-20	3.00

Ka-Zar
Marvel, 1997

-1	2.00
1	3.00
2-20	2.00
Ann 1997	3.00

Kazar of the Savage Land
Marvel, 1997

1	3.00

Ka-Zar the Savage
Marvel, 1981

Like Tarzan, that other great jungle-man, Ka-Zar was once a creature of civilization. Lord Kevin Plunder's father had been a scientist and explorer who discovered the Savage Land-a strange jungle oasis in the heart of the Antarctic. In the Savage Land, his father had discovered a substance known as anti-metal. When outside forces tried to wrest its secrets from him, he sought refuge with his son in the Savage Land. Instead, he was killed by a group of man-apes who were hunting a giant sabre-tooth tiger. The sabre-tooth, a giant cat named Zabu, used that moment to turn on his attackers, slaying them.

The tiger formed an attachment to the now-orphaned boy, and watched over him. The boy then grew up to be Ka-Zar, Lord of the Savage Land.

1	5.00
2-12	2.00
12/2nd	1.00
13-34	2.00

K Chronicles
Keith Knight, 1998

1-9	2.00

Keen Detective Funnies (Vol. 1)
Centaur, 1938

8	1,400.00
9	650.00
10-11	550.00

Keen Detective Funnies (Vol. 2)
Centaur, 1939

1	550.00
2	500.00
3-6	440.00
7	1,650.00
8	585.00
9-11	525.00
12	610.00

Keen Detective Funnies (Vol. 3)
Centaur, 1940

17	475.00
18-19	500.00
20	640.00
21-22	475.00
23-24	625.00

Keen Komics
Centaur, 1939

1	575.00
2	285.00
3	265.00

Keenspot Spotlight
Keenspot, 2002

2002-2003	1.00

Keen Teens
Life's Romances, 1945

1	145.00
2	165.00
3	58.00
4	50.00
5	55.00
6	50.00

Keep
Idea & Design Works, 2005

1-5	4.00

Keif Llama
Oni, 1999

1	3.00

Keif Llama Xeno-Tech
Fantagraphics, 1987

1-6	2.00

Keif Llama: Xenotech
Aeon, 2005

1-2	3.00

Kekkaishi
Viz, 2005

1-3	10.00

Kelly Belle
Police Detective
Newcomers

With a name like Kelly Belle, you just know she's going to be...a top-notch police detective? That's the case here as the buxom blonde is not only beautiful, but also deadly, as her various enemies have come to discover. That doesn't stop fearsome foes like the Scarab Master from capturing and imprisoning her, leaving her associates-the bookish Kitty Smith, and the square-jawed Detective Chen, who just may have feelings for Ms. Belle-to lend a helping hand. Kelly has other foes too, such as curvaceous Princess Zanzibar, but her skills and various charms will usually win out in the end.

Written by James Watson and drawn by Rob Ewing, this black-and-white series offers up another bad girl-or is that good girl?-heroine. Published by Newcomers Publishing.

1-3 .... 3.00

Kelly Green
Dargaud

1-2 .... 15.00

Kelvin Mace
Vortex, 1988

1 .... 3.00
2 .... 2.00

Kendra:
Legacy of the Blood
Perrydog, 1987

1-2 .... 2.00

Ken Maynard Western
Fawcett, 1950

1 .... 375.00
2 .... 265.00
3 .... 185.00
4-5 .... 165.00
6-8 .... 150.00

Ken Shannon
Quality, 1951

1 .... 175.00
2 .... 120.00
3-5 .... 90.00
6-10 .... 75.00

Ken Stuart
Publication Enterprises, 1949

1 .... 38.00

Kent Blake of the
Secret Service
Atlas, 1951

1 .... 150.00
2 .... 90.00
3-5 .... 65.00
6-14 .... 45.00

Kents
DC, 1997

1-12 .... 3.00

Kerry Drake
Blackthorne, 1986

1-5 .... 7.00

Kerry Drake
Detective Cases
Life's Romances, 1944

The Kerry Drake comic strip created by Alfred Andriola (1912-1983) and Allen Saunders (1899-1986) was introduced in 1943 and lasted under Andriola's hand for 40 years, ending with Andriola's death. To begin with, Drake was just one of the many, many private investigators in popular fiction, complete with an office and office staff.

Unusual developments eventually took over, however, as the white-haired Drake assumed a status more involved with actual law enforcement. He became employed by the District Attorney and became engaged to Sandy, who had been his secretary when the strip began. And then -- in a shocking sequence for a newspaper strip -- Sandy was murdered, changing the strip's tone

and direction. Most of the stories used in the comic book, however, are taken from Drake's P.I. days.
-- *Maggie*

1 .... 150.00
2 .... 115.00
3 .... 95.00
4-5 .... 85.00
6-8 .... 65.00
9-10 .... 80.00
11-15 .... 50.00
16-20 .... 42.00
21-30 .... 38.00
31-33 .... 32.00

Kewpies
Will Eisner, 1949

1 .... 125.00

Key Comics
Consolidated, 1944

1 .... 215.00
2 .... 170.00
3-5 .... 150.00

Keyhole
Millennium, 1996

1-5 .... 3.00

Key Ring Comics
Dell, 1941

1-5 .... 45.00

Khan
Moonstone, 2005

1 .... 3.00

Kick Ass
Marvel, 2008

1 .... 8.00
2 .... 4.00

Kickers, Inc.
Marvel, 1986

1-12 .... 1.00

Kid's Joker
ADV Manga, 2005

1 .... 10.00

Kid Anarchy
Fantagraphics, 1990

1-3 .... 3.00

Kid Blastoff
Slave Labor, 1996

1 .... 3.00

Kid Cannibal
Eternity, 1991

1-4 .... 3.00

Kid Carrots
St. John, 1953

1 .... 35.00

Kid Colt Outlaw
Marvel, 1948

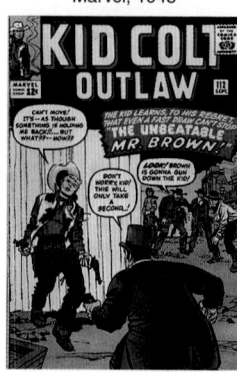

Back when he was young and foolish, Kid Colt killed an outlaw in self-defense. Although innocent, he fled, and has since been hunted as an outlaw. Of course, readers knew that this was no cattle-rustling hombre, but a Robin Hood of the range - a blond knight who came to the aid of ladies, pioneers, and other victims of frontier violence.

A hugely popular series in its heyday, Kid Colt switched to reprints after issue #140, and ran nearly a decade longer, until finally ceasing in 1979.

Colt would later return in Marvel's Blaze of Glory mini-series.

1	665.00
2	335.00
3-5	250.00
6-10	175.00
11	225.00
12-20	150.00
21-30	105.00
31-40	90.00
41-50	80.00
51-60	65.00
61-70	48.00
71-100	40.00
101-110	28.00
111-120	18.00
121-130	14.00
131-139	10.00
140-170	5.00
171-200	4.00
201-205	3.00
205/30¢	20.00
206-219	3.00
219/35¢	15.00
220	3.00
220/35¢	15.00
221-229	3.00

Kid Cowboy
Ziff-Davis, 1950

1	75.00
2	70.00
3	60.00
4	50.00
5-6	45.00

7-9	40.00
10-11	35.00
12-14	30.00

Kid Death & Fluffy: Halloween Special
Event, 1997

1	3.00

Kid Death & Fluffy Spring Break Special
Event, 1996

1	3.00

Kiddie Kapers
Kiddie Kapers

1	40.00
2	30.00

Kiddie Karnival
Ziff-Davis, 1952

1	165.00

Kid Eternity
Quality, 1946

1	560.00
2	290.00
3	250.00
4-5	175.00
6-10	135.00
11-18	105.00

Kid Eternity
DC, 1991

1-3	5.00

Kid Eternity
DC, 1993

1-16	2.00

Kid from Dodge City
Atlas, 1957

1	60.00
2	40.00

Kid from Texas
Atlas, 1957

1	60.00
2	40.00

Kid Komics
Timely, 1943

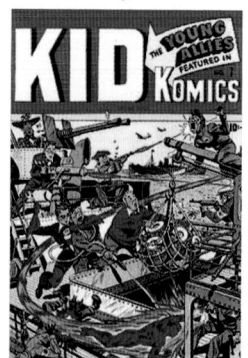

Though the first issue's main figure is yet another costumed

beefy guy punching out Asians in combat, even that cover declares that the issue co-stars kids: Whitewash, Knuckles, Trixie Troubles, Pinto Pete, and Subbie. With the second issue, the line-up at the bottom of the page is identified as The Young Allies, and the lineup now reads: Bucky, Toro, Knuckles, Whitewash, Jeff, and Tubby. From that point on, until it metamorphosed in 1946 to a kids' comic book for one issue before morphing again into a Blondie pastiche called Rusty, it was The Young Allies who took center stage.

Cluttered covers take time to analyze, as in the ninth cover, featuring such details as a bound Tubby suspended over an octopus pit, a hooded villain winching him lower, Bucky aiming an arrow at the octopus, the octopus with an arrow in its head, Toro flamingly separating one of the octopus' tentacles having burned another hooded villain, Jeff in the pit next to the octopus, Knuckles grabbing another hooded villain, and Whitewash preparing to strike with a mallet the winching hooded villain. And, oh, yes, a couple of other hooded types, one brandishing a sword, the other out of commission with one of Bucky's arrows in his back. Classic.

-- Maggie

1	2,800.00
2	1,150.00
3-4	1,000.00
5-7	650.00
8-10	515.00

Kid Montana
Charlton, 1957

9	28.00
10	18.00
11-12	14.00
13	18.00
14-20	14.00
21-30	9.00
31-40	6.00
41-50	4.00

Kid 'n Play
Marvel, 1992

1-9	1.00

Kid Slade, Gunfighter
Atlas, 1957

5	45.00
6-7	40.00

Kid Supreme
Image, 1996

1-3/A	3.00

Kid's WB Jam Packed Action
DC, 2004

1 ....8.00

Kid Terrific
Image, 1998

1 ....3.00

Kidz of the King
King, 1994

This multi-racial super-team is powered by their Christian beliefs, and their adventures offer them opportunities to witness to the power of their faith. Team leader Truth (a.k.a. Joshua Glover) is of African descent, has the strength of ten grown men, and believes in the power of the truth of God. Mercy (a.k.a. Kathi Shidara) is of Asian descent, possesses unbelievable acrobatic skills, and believes in God's mercy in the form of his son, Jesus Christ. Faith (a.k.a. Darah Delgado) is of Hispanic descent, is endowed with the power of flight, and believes in the ability of faith to move mountains. Last but not least, Zeal (a.k.a. Daniel Cassidy) is of Western European descent, runs at speeds of up to 100 mph, and believes in being zealous about your beliefs. Kidz of the King is designed to teach lessons in Christianity.

1-3..3.00

Kid Zoo Comics
Street & Smith, 1948

1 ....130.00

Ki-Gorr the Killer
AC

1 ....4.00

Kiku San
Aircel, 1988

1-6..2.00

Kilgore
Renegade, 1987

1-4 ....2.00

Kill Barny
Express, 1992

1 ....3.00

Kill Barny 3
Express, 1992

1 ....3.00

Killbox
Antarctic, 2002

1-3 ....5.00

Killer Fly
Slave Labor, 1995

Marvin drinks and treats Maria badly. Just another bad relationship? Well, in this case, it's pretty deadly. You see, Marvin is Baron Blade, a knife-throwing circus performer, and Maria is his assistant and often his target. The only one who seems to care for her is the lowly, beleaguered Putt, but she just won't listen to his pleas for her to leave Marvin. Meanwhile, a young boy who can transform into the gigantic Killer Fly is locked in a cage and treated badly by the circus owner; Putt also feels the need to reach out to him. What will become of these three misfits as they head out into the world? Find out in this intriguing series from Slave Labor Graphics.

1-3..3.00

Killer Instinct
Acclaim, 1996

1-6 ....3.00

Killer Instinct Nintendo Power Exclusive Edition
Acclaim

1 ....1.00

Killer Instinct Tour Book
Image

1/A-1/Gold 3.00

Killers
Magazine Enterprises, 1947

1 ....650.00
2 ....575.00

Killer 7
Devil's Due, 2006

1-3 ....3.00
3/Special 6.00
4 ....3.00
4/Special 6.00

Killer Stunts, Inc.
Alias, 2005

1-4 ....3.00

Killer...Tales by Timothy Truman
Eclipse, 1985

1 ....2.00

Kill Image
Boneyard

1 ....4.00

Killing Stroke
Eternity

1-4 ....3.00

Kill Marvel
Boneyard

1/Ltd. 5.00

Killpower: The Early Years
Marvel, 1993

1-4 ....2.00

Killraven
Marvel, 2001

H.G. Wells' War of the Worlds really happened: The Martians really did land on Earth. What's more, they enslaved humans, experimented on them, and turned them into gladiators who killed one another for sport. But one man rose up from the human misery to strike back at the alien oppressors. His name? Killraven.

Written and drawn by Joe Linsner (Dawn), this version doesn't exactly pick up where the 1970s Amazing Adventures series or the 1983 Marvel Graphic Novel left off. But Linsner, a self-professed fan of the original series, nevertheless lovingly captures all the flavor of Marvel's futuristic barbarian, as Killraven blasts the green baddies, saves a buxom beauty, and makes plans to take his war to Mars itself.

-- Stephen C. George

1 ....3.00

Killraven
Marvel, 2002

1-6...3.00

Kill Razor Special
Image, 1995

1 ....3.00

Kill Your Boyfriend
DC, 1995

1 ....5.00
1/2nd 6.00

Kilroy: Daemonstorm
Caliber, 1997

....3.00

Kilroy
Caliber, 1998

1-1/A 3.00

Kilroy Is Here
Caliber, 1994

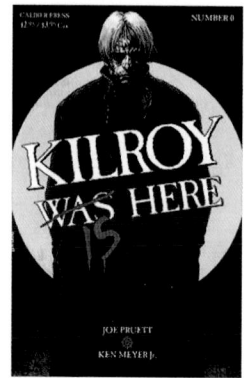

American GI's deployed to the European theater during World War II engaged in the popular practice of scrawling the words "Kilroy was here" on walls and buildings, implying that a single individual was ubiquitously present in a multitude of battles. Joe Pruett used this legend as the inspiration for his

mysterious spirit of vengeance who appears to enact retribution for wronged innocents, leaving an enigmatic "Kilroy is here" written above his victims. The change to present tense is significant since the cover logo displays the word "was" crossed out and "is" apparently written in blood below it.

Kilroy's first appearance (reprinted in #0 of this title), hints at his origin and ties to World War II. "I was an innocent once," he reveals to a Neo-nazi who murdered a foreigner to advance the racial purity of present-day Germany. Kilroy reveals that Hitler did not commit suicide. "It wasn't suicide. It wasn't the Russians. It was me."

Kilroy previously appeared in Calibrations and Negative Burn as well as Kilroy: The Short Stories, all from Caliber.

-- George Haberberger

0-10 .... 3.00

Kilroy: Revelations
Caliber, 1994

1 .... 3.00

Kilroys
ACG, 1947

1 .... 90.00
2 .... 55.00
3-5 .... 38.00
6-10 .... 30.00
11-20 .... 20.00
21-30 .... 16.00
31-40 .... 14.00
41-47 .... 12.00
48-49 .... 40.00
50-54 .... 12.00

Kilroys
Avalon, 2002

1 .... 3.00

Kilroy:
The Short Stories
Caliber, 1995

1 .... 3.00

Kimber,
Prince of the Feylons
Antarctic, 1992

1-2 .... 3.00

Kimera
ADV Manga, 2005

1 .... 10.00

Kimura
Nightwynd, 1991

1-4 .... 3.00

Kin
Image, 1999

1-5 .... 3.00
6 .... 4.00

Kindred
Image, 1994

1 .... 3.00
2-3/A 2.00
4 .... 3.00

Kindred II
DC, 2002

1-4 .... 3.00

Kinetic
DC, 2004

1-8 .... 3.00

King Arthur and the Knights of Justice
Marvel, 1993

1-3 .... 1.00

King Comics
David McKay, 1936

United Features Syndicate had Ace Comics and Sparkler Comics; King Features Syndicate had Magic Comics -- and King Comics. And King Comics featured reprints of its comic strips, noting on early covers that its contents are packed with "laughs and thrills." Strips include Blondie, Brick Bradford, Buz Sawyer, Flash Gordon, G-Man, Henry, Hurricane Yank, King of the Royal Mounted, Little Annie Roonie, The Little King, The Lone Ranger, Mandrake the Magician, The Phantom, and Private Bucks.

Nevertheless, as many of these strip reprints come and go, Popeye and his friends (Olive, Wimpy, and Swee'Pea) continue to star on the cover.

-- Maggie

1 .... 8,000.00
2 .... 2,650.00
3 .... 1,350.00
4 .... 1,100.00
5 .... 850.00
6-10 .... 625.00
11-15 .... 450.00
16-20 .... 390.00
21-30 .... 275.00

31-40	220.00
41-50	175.00
51-60	135.00
61-70	110.00
71-80	95.00
81-90	75.00
91-100	65.00
101-120	50.00
121-140	35.00
141-159	25.00

King Comics Presents
King Comics

1	2.00

King Conan
Marvel, 1980

1	5.00
2-10	2.00
11-19	1.00

King David
DC, 2002

1	20.00

Kingdom
DC, 1999

1	3.00
2	3.00

Kingdom Come
DC, 1996

Mark WAID   Alex ROSS

Kingdom Come is an Elseworlds story of what might happen in a different version of the DC universe. In it we see the world of the near future where super-heroes and super-villains have become largely indistinguishable from each other. Both have grown jaded with power, and even the heroes have lost any regard for the mere humans they are meant to protect. In the end, their ceaseless battles eventually result in blasting Kansas into a radioactive ruin.

It's then that an aging pastor is visited by The Spectre and shown what it is that the world has become. It's a place where super-heroes have taken the place of gods, and where the final battle

between them threatens to usher in Ragnarok - the end of the world.

A four-issue tour de force by writer Mark Waid and painter Alex Ross, Kingdom Come was one of the standout series of 1996.

1-4	5.00

Kingdom Hearts
Tokyopop, 2005

1-4	6.00

Kingdom, The: Kid Flash
DC, 1999

1	2.00

Kingdom, The: Nightstar
DC, 1999

1	2.00

Kingdom, The: Offspring
DC, 1999

1	2.00

Kingdom of the Dwarfs
Comico

1	5.00

Kingdom of the Wicked
Caliber, 1996

1-4	3.00

Kingdom, The: Planet Krypton
DC, 1999

1	2.00

Kingdom, The: Son of the Bat
DC, 1999

1	2.00

King Kong
Gold Key, 1968

1	12.00

King Kong
Monster, 1991

1-6	3.00

King Leonardo and His Short Subjects
Gold Key, 1962

1	35.00
2-4	25.00

King Louie and Mowgli
Gold Key, 1968

1	20.00

King of Diamonds
Dell, 1962

1	30.00

King of Hell
Tokyopop, 2003

1-11	10.00

King of the Dead
Fantaco, 1988

0-3	2.00
4	3.00

King of the Royal Mounted
Dell, 1952

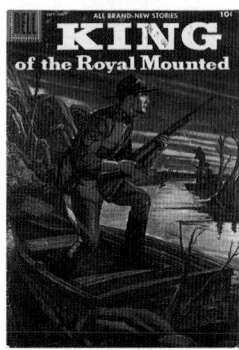

Whereas Sgt. Preston of the Yukon began on radio (as Challenge of the Yukon) in 1938, ran until 1955 there, was transformed into a TV show (1955-1958), and earned a comic-book spin-off in 1951, King of the Royal Mounted preceded it as a popular-fiction look at adventure north of the U.S. border with Canada. King started its existence as a King Features comic strip, beginning in 1935. Though attributed to popular writer Zane Grey, that was apparently simply part of a licensing deal, the character not featured in an inciting Grey novel.

The year Preston left radio for TV was the year King of the Royal Mounted left newspaper pages, but his comic-book adventures continued until Preston went off the air. Coincidence? Well, maybe yes.
-- *Maggie*

8	35.00
9-10	32.00
11-28	28.00

Kingpin
Marvel, 1997

1	6.00

Kingpin
Marvel, 2003

1-7	3.00

Kings in Disguise
Kitchen Sink, 1988

It would be the severest of understatements to say that times were tough in 1932. Still, it was a place where two brothers, Albert and Freddy, could escape to the movies and buy dreams for the price of a dime. Sadly, their father's dream had died when unemployment led to alcoholism. And when, to his shame, he admitted he could no longer support his family, he left Albert to care for his little brother, and went to find work in another town.

For a while, the boys got along all right, but the bad times were relentless. Albert went without food so his brother could eat, and eventually he tried to mug someone. Albert failed and was caught, and Freddy fled the house before he could be thrown into an orphanage. Out on his own, he came into the company of the hoboes: poor bands of people who hitched rides from town to town on passing railway cars. They were thought of as bums, and some deserved the title. But others were more like kings in disguise...

1-6 .... 2.00

Kings of the Night
Dark Horse, 1990

1-2 .... 2.00

King Tiger & Motorhead
Dark Horse, 1996

1-2 .... 3.00

Kinki Klitt Komics
Rip Off, 1992

1-2 .... 3.00

Kinky Hook
Fantagraphics

1 .... 3.00

Kip
Hammer & Anvil

1 .... 3.00

Kirby King of the Serials
Blackthorne, 1989

1 .... 2.00

Kiss
Personality

1 .... 4.00
2-3 .... 3.00

Kiss
Dark Horse, 2002

1-13/Photo 3.00

Kiss & Tell
Patricia Breen, 1995

1 .... 3.00

Kiss & Tell
Sirius, 1996

1 .... 3.00

Kiss Classics
Marvel

Gene Simmons and Paul Stanley wanted more from life than the dull careers in accountancy that the world had planned for them. They got their wish when they came into possession of a mysterious box of Khyscz containing four talismans. These changed Gene into a demonic figure who could spit fire; Paul into a "star child" who could fire blasts of energy from his eye; and friends Peter Chris and Ace Frehley into a feline creature and teleporting "space ace," respectively. Together, they became known as Kiss.

This 1995 special edition reprints Marvel Super Special #1 and #5. These were the first full comic book stories to star the legendary, costumed rock group, Kiss. Well known as masters of theatricality, the group went so far as to mix vials of their own blood into the printer's ink of the original special. Although this edition contains no such additions to the

inks, it uses modern techniques and high-quality paper to bring out more vivid colors than the original.

1 .... 10.00

Kisses
Spoof, 1996

1 .... 3.00

Kissing Canvas
MN Design

1 .... 6.00

Kiss Kiss Bang Bang
CrossGen, 2004

1 .... 4.00
1/2nd-5 .... 3.00

Kissnation
Marvel

1 .... 11.00

Kiss of Death
Acme, 1987

1 .... 2.00

Kiss of the Vampire
Brainstorm, 1996

1 .... 3.00

Kiss Pre-History
Revolutionary, 1993

1-3 .... 3.00

Kiss: Psycho Circus
Image, 1997

1-28 .... 2.00
29-31 .... 3.00
Special 1 .... 2.00

Kiss: Satan's Music?
Celebrity

1 .... 4.00

Kissyfur
DC, 1989

1 .... 2.00

Kiss: You Wanted the Best, You Got the Best
Wizard, 1998

1 .... 1.00

Kit Carson and the Blackfeet Warriors
Realistic Comics, 1953

1 .... 40.00

Kitchen Sink Classics
Kitchen Sink, 1994

1 .... 5.00
2-3 .... 3.00

Kitty
St. John, 1948

1 .... 34.00

Kitty Pryde & Wolverine
Marvel, 1984

1-6 .... 3.00

Kitty Pryde, Agent of Shield
Marvel, 1997

Kitty Pryde has seen and done many amazing things in her short life. She has battled evil mutants, fought interdimensional demons, and traveled to the far ends of the universe. Most recently, she has served alongside the heroes of Excalibur.

Now, Kitty finds herself recruited by the world's ultimate intelligence group, the Strategic Hazard Intervention Espionage Logistic Directorate, more commonly known as SHIELD. SHIELD's mobile base and computer network has been usurped by Ogun, a demonic ninja who has tried to possess Kitty in the past. This time, he has all the power of SHIELD's technology to add to his own mystical force.

Kitty has costarred in several limited series, including Kitty Pryde & Wolverine, and Pryde & Wisdom. This solo adventure has repercussions that will affect Kitty's life in Excalibur.

1-3 .... 3.00

Kitz 'n' Katz Komiks
Phantasy, 1986
1-6 .... 2.00

Kiwanni: Daughter of the Dawn
C&T, 1988
1 .... 2.00

Klor
Sirius, 1998
1-3 .... 3.00

Klownshock
Northstar, 1992
1 .... 3.00

Knewts of the Round Table
Pan, 1998
1-5 .... 3.00

Knight
Bear Claw, 1993
0 .... 3.00

Knightfool: The Fall of the Splatman
Parody
1 .... 3.00

Knighthawk
Acclaim, 1995
1-6 .... 3.00

Knightmare (Antarctic)
Antarctic, 1994
1-6 .... 3.00

Knightmare
Image, 1995
0 .... 4.00
1-8 .... 3.00

Knightshift
London Night, 1996
1-2 .... 3.00

Knights' Kingdom
Lego
1 .... 5.00

Knights of Pendragon
Marvel, 1990
1 .... 3.00
2-18 .... 2.00

Knights of Pendragon
Marvel, 1992
1-15 .... 2.00

Knights of the Dinner Table
Kenzer, 1994

Knights of the Dinner Table began as a series of jokes about gamers (as in Dungeons & Dragons, not Las Vegas) in a gaming magazine. In comic-book form, it probably did more to attract new readers to comic books than any other series in the late 1990s. That may not be saying much, but how many series find the majority of their readership outside of comics shops? It's the case with Knights, which sells about 75% of its copies in game shops.

Jolly Blackburn's art is a triumph of minimalism, basically cut-outs that only move when a mouth requires opening. But we still learn a lot about gamers B.A., Bob, Dave, Sara, and Brian as they sit at the table "adventuring." Brian has to be cured of an imaginary girlfriend in the classic "Great Intervention." And neither Bob nor Dave know what a gazebo is, given how they brutally attack one in one story.

Later years would find the title, which started at Alderac and moved to Kenzer early on, attempting to become first a general gaming magazine and then a support magazine for Kenzer's own game line, with mixed success. The real attraction of Knights remains the Knights.
-- John Jackson Miller

1	150.00
2	45.00
3	25.00
4	30.00
4/2nd-5	25.00
6-10	18.00
11-15	14.00
16-21	10.00
22-30	6.00
31-32	4.00
33-49	3.00
50	5.00
51-69	3.00
70-99	4.00
100	8.00
101-108	4.00
109-155	5.00

Knights of the Dinner Table: Black Hands Gaming Society Special
Kenzer and Company, 2003
1-2 .... 3.00

Knights of the Dinner Table: Everknights
Kenzer and Company, 2002
Special 1 .... 3.00

Knights of the Dinner Table/Faans Crossover Special
Six Handed, 1999
1 .... 3.00

Knights of the Dinner Table Illustrated
Kenzer, 2000
1-41 ....3.00

Knights of the Jaguar Super Limited One Shot
Image, 2004
1 ....3.00

Knights of the Zodiac
Viz, 8
1-12 ....8.00

Knights on Broadway
Broadway, 1996
1-3...3.00

Knight's Round Table
Knight, 1996
1-1/A 3.00

Knightstrike
Image, 1995
1 ....3.00

Knight Watchman
Image, 1998
1-4...3.00

Knight Watchman: Graveyard Shift
Caliber, 1994
1-2...3.00

Knight Wolf
Five Star
1-3...3.00

Knockout Adventures
Fiction House, 1954
1 ....75.00

Knuckles
Archie, 1997

Knuckles is a quick-tempered, gullible Echidna and something of a second banana to Sonic the Hedgehog in assorted Sonic Adventure computer games. He's got red fur, quills, and shoes, a beige muzzle, and a white crescent mark on his upper chest. Oh, yes, and sharp knuckles on his white mitts. In the world of the game, he can use shovel claws, hammer gloves, and special glasses and can teleport. He's the guardian of the Master Emerald on Angel Island.

So, of course, he was a natural to not only appear as one of the gang in Archie's ongoing Sonic the Hedgehog title but also to spin off into his own only four years after Sonic's first comic-book tryout.
-- *Maggie*

1 .... 4.00
2-3.. 3.00
4-29.. 2.00

Knuckles' Chaotix
Archie, 1996
1 .... 3.00

Knuckles the Malevolent Nun
Fantagraphics, 1991
1-2.. 2.00

Kobalt
DC, 1994
1-12.. 2.00
13-16 .... 3.00

Kobier and Oso
Gebhart
1 .... 2.00

Kobra
DC, 1976
1 .... 9.00
2-7.. 3.00

Kodocha: Sana's Stage
Tokyopop, 2002
1-3.. 10.00

Kogaratsu: The Lotus of Blood
Acme
1 .... 6.00

Kokey Koala
Toby, 1952
1 .... 25.00

Koko and Kola
Magazine Enterprises, 1947
1 .... 45.00
2 .... 35.00
3-6.. 25.00

K.O. Komics
Gerona, 1945
1 .... 425.00

Kolchak Tales: Black & White & Red All Over
Moonstone, 2005
1/A cover-1/B cover 5.00

Kolchak: Tales of the Night Stalker
Moonstone, 2004
1/A-6/B 4.00

Kolchak: The Night Stalker: Get of Belial
Moonstone, 2002
1 .... 7.00

Kolchak: The Night Stalker
Moonstone, 2002
1 .... 7.00

Kolynos Presents the White Guard
Whitehall Pharmacal, 1949
1 .... 20.00

Komic Kartoons
Timely, 1945
1 .... 70.00
2 .... 65.00

Komik Pages
Harry A. Chesler, 1945
10 .... 125.00

Komodo and the Defiants
Victory, 1987
1-2.. 2.00

Kona
Dell, 1962
2 .... 18.00
3-5... 15.00
6-14 .... 12.00
15-21 .... 10.00

Konga
Charlton, 1960

Steve Ditko adapted the 1961 Gorgo film to comic-book form; that story features a prehistoric sea monster captured and brought to London with resultant scenes reminiscent of those at the end of King Kong (1933) and of some of the aspects of Godzilla (1956). Though Gorgo was relatively run-of-the-mill (though with a nice plot twist toward the end), the success of the Steve Ditko comic book (where Gorgo's adventures continued long after what happened in the film) led Charlton to go for a Steve Ditko adaptation of Konga (also 1961). In that film, a scientist who's managed to grow plants to a huge size turns a cute chimpanzee into a giant, killer monster. Once again, the series continues long after events that occur in the film. (Note: Not all issues of the comic book contain Ditko art.)

-- Maggie

1	75.00
2	50.00
3-4	35.00
5-10	25.00
11-20	16.00
21-23	14.00

Konga's Revenge
Charlton, 1963

1	10.00
2-3	7.00

Kong, 8th Wonder of the World - Movie Adaptation
Dark Horse, 2006

1	4.00

Kong the Untamed
DC, 1975

1	9.00
2-5	3.00

Konny and Czu
Antarctic, 1994

1-4	3.00

Koolau the Leper (Jack London's...)
Tome

1	3.00

Koosh Kins
Archie, 1991

1-4	1.00

K.O. Punch
E.C., 1948

1	650.00

Korak, Son of Tarzan
Gold Key, 1964

Brave Korak, much like his father, can talk to the animals and is leery of civilization. A more youthful version of Tarzan, with greater appeal to younger readers, Korak frequently traveled beyond the jungle and into the outside world. No matter where he went, adventure was sure to follow.

This series began as a Gold Key title. In 1972, it switched over to DC with issue #46. It then continued until issue #60, when it was retitled The Tarzan Family.

Back-ups included adaptations of Burroughs' Carson of Venus stories and a continuation of his one-shot Beyond the Farthest Star.

1	65.00
2-5	45.00
6-11	30.00
12-18	25.00
19-37	20.00
38-46	17.00
47-51	15.00
52-59	10.00

Kore
Image, 2003

1-5	3.00

Korg: 70,000 B.C.
Charlton, 1975

1	8.00
2-9	5.00

Korvus
Arrow, 1998

0-3	3.00

Korvus
Arrow, 1998

1-2	3.00

Kosmic Kat
Image, 1999

1	3.00

Kosmic Kat Activity Book
Image, 1999

1	3.00

Krazy Kat
Dell, 1951

1	40.00
2-5	25.00

Krazy Kat
Gold Key, 1964

1	15.00

Krazy Komics
Timely, 1942

A spectacularly unappetizing entry in the world of "funny-animal comics" was Krazy Komics, which, for many of the covers of its first several issues featured the exploits of the derby-wearing Toughy Tomcat. He menaced characters like Ziggy Pig and Silly Seal (who would have been of an unidentifiable species had he not been named) with a buzzsaw, a cannon, a hatchet, and so on. Toughy's prey, initially sweating over his desire to eat them, eventually began to turn the tables on him, and the animal world took on a more positive aspect, as characters like Krazy Krow and Super Rabbit joined the mix of characters.

-- Maggie

1	300.00
2	165.00
3	120.00
4-5	95.00
6-9	80.00
10-11	70.00
12	100.00
13-15	65.00
16-19	45.00
20-22	30.00
23-26	25.00

Krazy Krow
Marvel, 1945

1 ....100.00
2 ....65.00
3 ....55.00

Krazy Life
Fox, 1945

1 ....60.00

Kree-Skrull War Starring The Avengers
Marvel, 1983

1-2 ....3.00

Kremen
Grey Productions

1-3 ....3.00

Krey
Gauntlet, 1992

The humans and mutants have waged war on each other for years, but on one fateful day a human infant is claimed as a trophy of war and bestowed with the name Krey which means "battle prize." He is raised by mutants and trained in the art of combat under the watchful eye of his adoptive mutant father. On the day he comes of age, Krey witnesses the ruthless attack by humans on his village. As Krey's adoptive father lays dying from the attack, he gives Krey the sword which belonged to Krey's birth father. Now with his father's sword, Krey must journey into the unknown world of fantasy and adventure forever coping with his losses and his own identity in an attempt to understand his place in the world.

1-3 ....3.00
Special 1 ....4.00

Krofft Supershow
Gold Key, 1978

1 .... 6.00
2-6 .... 4.00

Krull
Marvel, 1983

1-2 .... 1.00

Krusty Comics
Bongo, 1995

1-3 .... 3.00

Krypton Chronicles
DC, 1981

1-3 .... 2.00

Krypto the Super Dog
DC, 2006

1 .... 2.00
2 .... 3.00
3-4 .... 2.00

Kull and the Barbarians
Marvel, 1975

1 .... 16.00
2 .... 4.00
3 .... 5.00

Kull in 3-D
Blackthorne

1-2 .... 3.00

Kull the Conqueror
Marvel, 1971

1 .... 20.00
2 .... 12.00
3-4 .... 8.00
5 .... 7.00
6-10 .... 5.00

Kull the Conqueror
Marvel, 1982

1 .... 5.00
2 .... 3.00

Kull the Conqueror
Marvel, 1983

1-5 .... 2.00
6-10 .... 1.00

Kull the Destroyer
Marvel, 1973

Before Conan the Barbarian, there was Kull. Robert E. Howard's second great barbarian warrior, Kull, wandered the continent of Atlantis in the age preceding Conan's. Through strength of sword, and quickness of wit, Kull became the ruler of Valusia, the greatest kingdom of Atlantis.

In this, his first series, Kull slays a corrupt ruler to win his crown. Life for the new king is far from uneventful, though, as he battles both mortal and supernatural foes.

Previously known as "Kull the Conqueror," this series changed names with issue #11, becoming "Kull the Destroyer." Its flair for great storytelling, however, was unaltered.

11-16 .... 2.00
16/30¢ 20.00
17-21 .... 2.00
21/35¢ 15.00
22 .... 2.00
22/35¢ 15.00
23-23/Whitman 2.00
23/35¢ 15.00
24-29 .... 2.00

Kunoichi
Lightning, 1996

1 .... 3.00

Kwaiden
Dark Horse, 2004

1 .... 15.00

Kyra
Elsewhere, 1985

1-6 .... 2.00

Kyrie
ADV Manga, 2005

1 .... 10.00

K-Z Comics Presents
K-Z, 1985

1 .... 2.00

DC attempted to rewrite the history of their futuristic teen super-team in a two-part story.

Lab
Astonish, 2001

1 .... 4.00
2 .... 3.00

La Blue Girl
CPM, 1996

1-12 .... 3.00

Labman
Image, 1996

Rudy Coby is the self-proclaimed "hippest magician in the world." Certainly, he's one of the more unusual ones. Distinctive in his trademark hairdo and glasses, he takes on the persona of "Labman," a scientific wizard, magician, and crimefighter. His television special, which premiered on the Fox network in 1996, combined stage magic, showbiz razzle-dazzle, and cartoony fun into one entertaining spectacle.

It's only natural that such a comic character would make his way to comic books. In this three-issue series, readers learn how a mild-mannered, licensed scientist discovered a four-legged atomic chicken and stumbled onto the path of super-powered greatness.

1-1/C 4.00
2-3 .... 3.00

Labman Sourcebook
Image, 1996

1 .... 1.00

Labor Force
Blackthorne, 1986

1-8 .... 2.00

Labor is a Partner
Catechetical Guild, 1949

1 .... 120.00

Labours of Hercules
Malan Classical Enterprises

1 .... 3.00

Lab Rats
DC, 2002

1-7 .... 3.00

Labyrinth of Madness
TSR

1 .... 1.00

Labyrinth: The Movie
Marvel, 1986

Sarah was a fifteen-year-old who dearly missed the mother who had left her. Now, she lived with her father and stepmother and seemingly was always left in charge of their baby boy, Toby. Sarah escaped by dreaming she was a beautiful princess, and that the Goblin King would come and spirit away the bratty baby so she could be free.

Then one night, Sarah got her wish. She wished out loud that goblins would take the baby. They appeared out of nowhere to do just that. Sarah begged the Goblin King to give the baby back, but he refused. Instead, he gave Sarah thirteen hours to find the baby, hidden somewhere in the castle beyond Goblin City. To get there, she would have to navigate the Labyrinth, a vast maze full of strange, whimsical creatures.

Labyrinth was a movie starring David Bowie as the Goblin King, and featuring Jim Henson's wonderful Muppets.

1-3 .... 2.00

Lackluster World
Gen: Eric Publishing, 2004

1-3 .... 4.00

L.A. Comics
Los Angeles, 1971

1-2 .... 3.00

La Cosa Nostroid
Fireman, 1996

Set in the world of Scud the Disposable Assassin -- a world in which robot hitmen are available from vending machines -- La Cosa Nostroid focuses on a cybernetic crime family that is run by wiseguy Tony, who deals with the day-to-day business of the family.

Then, there's Doghouse, Tony's right-hand man and his most trusted advisor -- even though they often disagree on how to do things. Meredino is an expert marksman and sandwich-maker. Forehead is the most cybernetic of the lot because of the input-output jacks mounted on his forehead and the computer displays that fill his eyes.

Finally, there is Joe, the late member of the family, who bought it when he put a girl ahead of the business.

1-9..........................3.00

Lad, A Dog
Dell, 1962

2..........................30.00

Lady and the Tramp
Dell, 1955

1..........................25.00

Lady and the Tramp
Gold Key, 1963

1..........................25.00
1 (1973)..........................14.00

Lady and the Vampire
NBM

1..........................11.00

Lady Arcane
Hero Graphics, 1992

1..........................5.00
2-3..........................4.00
4..........................3.00

Lady Crime
AC, 1992

1..........................3.00

Lady Death
10th Anniversary Edition
Avatar, 2004

1..........................4.00
1/Leather..........................30.00
1/Painted..........................4.00
1/Platinum-1/Premium 10.00

Lady Death
Chaos!, 1994

0..........................3.00
1/2..........................4.00
1/2/A..........................6.00
1/2/Gold 5.00
1..........................8.00
1/Ltd...........................12.00
1/2nd..........................3.00
2..........................8.00
3..........................5.00

Lady Death
Chaos!, 1998

1..........................7.00
1/Ltd...........................9.00
2-5..........................3.00
5/Variant..........................4.00
6-16..........................3.00

Lady Death
(Brian Pulidós...):
A Medieval Tale
CrossGen, 2003

1-12..........................3.00

Lady Death: Alive
Chaos, 2001

![Lady Death: Alive comic cover — CHAOS! Lady Death]

During an event called the Tribulation, Lady Death defeated Abaddon and his dark forces, but found herself cast out of the death-realm and into…reality! She is now mortal and feeling emotions that force her to leap into action and answer a desperate cry for help. Her skills prove formidable, but she finds herself at odds with those who dabble in the dark arts to serve their own selfish ambitions. Will the bikini-clad Lady Death survive in the world of flesh and bone? Read this excellent limited series--the first issue of which sports a cool cover by Mike Wieringo (Flash, Fantastic Four)--and find out!

1-4..........................3.00

Lady Death and the
Women of Chaos!
Gallery
Chaos, 1996

1..........................2.00

Lady Death/Bad Kitty
Chaos, 2001

1..........................3.00

Lady Death
(Brian Pulidós...):
Wild Hunt
CrossGen, 2004

1-2..........................3.00

Lady Death:
Dark Millennium
Chaos, 2000

1-2..........................3.00

Lady Death:
Dragon Wars
Chaos, 1998

1..........................3.00

Lady Death IV:
The Crucible
Chaos!, 1996

1/2..........................5.00
1/2/A..........................8.00
1..........................3.00
1/A..........................13.00
1/B..........................16.00
1/Silver..........................4.00
2-5..........................3.00
5/Variant..........................5.00
6..........................3.00

Lady Death:
Heartbreaker
Chaos, 2002

1-4..........................3.00
Ashcan 1..........................1.00

Lady Death in Lingerie
Chaos!, 1995

1..........................3.00
1/Ltd. 10.00

Lady Death:
Judgement War
Chaos!, 1999

1-3..........................3.00

Lady Death:
Judgement War Prelude
Chaos!, 1999

1..........................3.00

Lady Death: Retribution
Chaos!, 1998

1..........................3.00
1/A-1/Ltd...........................4.00

Lady Death Swimsuit
2005
Avatar

0..........................4.00
0/Battle..........................6.00
0/Gold..........................10.00
0/Leather..........................25.00
0/Platinum..........................15.00
0/Wraparound..........................4.00

Lady Death
Swimsuit Special
Chaos!, 1994

1..........................3.00
1/Variant..........................8.00

Lady Death:
The Gauntlet
Chaos, 2002

1-2..........................3.00

Lady Death: The Rapture
Chaos!, 1999

1-4..........................3.00

Lady Death III:
The Odyssey
Chaos!, 1996

-1..........................2.00
1..........................4.00
1/Variant..........................5.00

2-4	3.00
4/A	8.00

Lady Death: Tribulation
Chaos!, 2000

1-2	3.00

Lady Death II:
Between Heaven & Hell
Chaos!, 1995

1-1/A	4.00
1/B-1/Ltd.	5.00
1/2nd-4	3.00
4/Variant	5.00

Lady Death/Vampirella:
Dark Hearts
Chaos!, 1999

1	4.00
1/A	8.00

Lady Death Vs. Purgatori
Chaos!, 1999

1	3.00
1/A	5.00

Lady Death vs. Vampirella
Chaos, 2000

Lady Death, chaos incarnate, and Vampirella, vampire champion of order, generated incredible amounts of energy drawn directly from the Cosmic Balance itself during their last battle. It stands to reason that a rematch could tap into even greater reserves and that power could be used to conquer the Earth. Time and space bend into unimaginable directions during the carnage. Can even this most beautiful pair stand against the most potentient forces of Hell itself when the true goal is their deaths and the destruction of a planet?

Lady Death first appeared in Eternity's Evil Ernie #1, her orgin's were revealed in the Lady Death mini-series. Vampirella first appeared in Warren's Vampirella magazine back in 1969.

Ashcan 1	1.00

Lady Death:
Wicked Ways
Chaos!, 1998

1	3.00
1/Variant	5.00

Lady Dracula
Fantaco

1-2	5.00

Lady Justice (Vol. 1)
(Neil Gaiman's...)
Tekno, 1995

1-11	2.00

Lady Justice (Vol. 2)
(Neil Gaiman's...)
Big, 1996

1-9	2.00

Lady Luck
Quality, 1949

86	550.00
87-88	375.00
89-90	325.00

Lady Pendragon
Maximum, 1996

1-1/A	3.00
1/Autographed	6.00
1/2nd	3.00
Ashcan 1	4.00
Ashcan 1/Autogr	6.00

Lady Pendragon
Image, 1998

0	3.00
0/A	4.00
1-1/2nd	3.00
2	4.00
2/A-3/A	3.00
Ashcan 1	2.00

Lady Pendragon
Image, 1999

1-1/A	3.00
1/B	4.00
2-6	3.00
7	4.00
8-10	3.00

Lady Pendragon
Gallery Edition
Image, 1999

1-1/A	3.00

Lady Pendragon:
Merlin
Image, 2000

1	3.00

Lady Pendragon/
More Than Mortal
Image, 1999

1	3.00
1/A	4.00
1/B	5.00
Ashcan 1	2.00

Lady Rawhide
Topps, 1995

The predominance of "Bad Girl" art in the 1990s introduced this scintillating character to the then-unmined-by-Bad-Girls era of the 1800s. Originating in Zorro #3, Lady Rawhide is Anita Santiago. She adopts this scandalous identity to avenge the blinding of her brother, Ramon. Although her abbreviated, bright, red leather costume could be considered de rigueur for female comics characters in the present, her revealing outfit is daring for the Old West and forms a large part of her offense, since it understandably distracts her male adversaries.

Lady Rawhide stories have more of a storyline than most of the "Bad Girl" ilk, as a testament to its creator, Don McGregor, a writer known for stories with subtext and character motivation. His Black Panther tales in Jungle Action in the early 1970s were prime examples of his talent.

-- George Haberberger

1-5	3.00

Lady Rawhide (Vol. 2)
Topps, 1996

1/2	5.00
1-5	3.00

Lady Rawhide
Mini Comic
Topps, 1995

1	1.00

Lady Rawhide:
Other People's Blood
Image, 1999

1-5	3.00

Lady Rawhide
Special Edition
Topps, 1995
1 ....4.00

Lady Spectra &
Sparky Special
J. Kevin Carrier, 1995
1 ....3.00

Lady Supreme
Image, 1996

An obvious Supergirl… um… homage, Lady Supreme was originally called Probe, a woman from the future possessed of psionic powers and a genetic descendent of Supreme, the Superman clone. When her battles brought her to the present, she was trapped in the form of a man-- that of Supreme himself. Soon, she regained her female body and discovered that she was actually the daughter of Supreme and Glory, the Wonder Woman doppelganger. This series finds Lady Supreme coming to terms with her lineage and establishing herself as a super-hero in her own right by kicking bad-guy butt and taking down names.

1-2..3.00

Lady Vamprè
Black Out
0-1..3.00

Lady Vamprè:
Pleasures of the Flesh
Black Out
1 ....3.00

Lady Vamprè vs.
Black Lace
Black Out, 1996
1 ....3.00

Laff-a-Lympics
Marvel, 1978

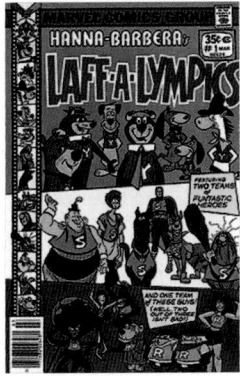

Probably the best title to come from Marvel's largely unsuccessful stint as a Hanna-Barbera licensee, Laff-a-Lympics captured the spirit of its inspiration, an ABC-TV cartoon from the mid-1970s.

With the 1976 Innsbruck and Austria Olympics fresh in viewer's minds, H-B sent all its characters into sports, with the funny animals playing for the Yogi Yahooeys, the crimefighters playing for the Scooby Doobies, and the villains playing for the Really Rottens.

On TV, the sports segments were used as bumpers surrounding other cartoons, but in the comics, the Laff-a-Lympics events were the whole story. Several issues have clever subplots going on in the background involving some Really Rotten plan, making for generally entertaining issues.

The series also includes well-researched text pieces on individual Hanna-Barbera characters.

-- John Jackson Miller

1 .... 18.00
2 .... 10.00
3-5.. 8.00
6-13...................................... 6.00

Laffin' Gas
Blackthorne, 1986
1-12...................................... 2.00

Laffy-Daffy Comics
Rural Home, 1945
1-2.. 40.00

Lagoon Engine Einsatz
ADV Manga, 2005
1 .... 11.00

Lament of the Lamb
Tokyopop, 2004
1 .... 10.00

Lana
Timely, 1948
1 .... 100.00
2 .... 65.00
3-7... 40.00

Lance Barnes:
Post Nuke Dick
Marvel, 1993

Lance Barnes was no stranger to danger. His adventures were chronicled everywhere, and he was a hero to millions...until the day he fell into the villain's trap and wound up accidentally blowing up the world.

Haunted by that rather terrible secret, he prowls post-nuclear society like a latter-day Sam Spade. In this irradiated version of film noir, Barnes runs from mutated attack dogs, is hunted by a femme fatale with one leg (named "Peg," naturally), and is given to narrating his life in a series of thought balloons that read like a bad Hemingway contest. Wonderful stuff.

1-4... 3.00

Lancelot Link,
Secret Chimp
Gold Key, 1971
1 .... 30.00
2 .... 17.00
3-8... 10.00

Lancelot Strong,
the Shield
Archie, 1983
1 .... 2.00

Lance O'Casey
Fawcett, 1946
1 .... 250.00
2 .... 150.00
3-4... 100.00

Lancer
Gold Key, 1969

1	25.00
2-3	20.00

Land of Nod
Dark Horse, 1997

1-4	3.00

Land of Oz
Arrow, 1998

1-9	3.00

Land of the Giants
Gold Key, 1968

1	30.00
2	18.00
3-5	15.00

Land of the Lost Comics
E.C., 1946

The radio show The Land of the Lost ran on and off from 1943 to 1948, created, written and produced by Isabel Manning Hewson. The land was located at the bottom of the sea, where everything that had been lost wound up. Children Isabel and Billy traveled there with Red Lantern, a talking fish. The show motto was "Never say lost."

E.C. licensed the show, and Hewson wrote the series, mostly drawn by Olive Bailey. Intriguingly, the company imprint changed from "An Educational Comic" to "An Entertaining Comic" with #6. This alternating imprint was typical of the company, which continued to use the "E.C." logo for both.

-- Maggie

1	200.00
2	135.00
3	100.00
4-9	85.00

Landra Special
Alchemy

1	2.00

Lands of Prester John
Noble

1	15.00

Lann
Fantagraphics, 1991

1	3.00

La Pacifica
DC

1-3	5.00

L.A. Phoenix
David G. Brown, 1994

1-3	2.00

L.A. Raptor
Morbid, 1995

MATURE READERS

Paleontologist Doctor Webb is very secretive about the experiments he's conducting in an old warehouse. Even the security guards don't really know what Webb is doing, until a blown fuse releases the doctor's little experiment.

Suddenly a vicious, hungry raptor is loose in Los Angeles, eating its way from street to street. Only Doctor Webb and a lone security guard know that the dinosaur is on the loose. And they have only a tranquilizer gun and a forklift at their disposal.

Can the doctor recapture his experiment before it makes a meal of most of Los Angeles? Another security guard, a hooker, a drug dealer, and a wheelchair-bound homeless man already have fallen to the beast. Now the monster has found its way into the sewers.

This comic depicts graphic violence and is intended for mature audiences.

1	3.00

Large Feature Comics
Dell, 1939

1	1,250.00
2	1,100.00
3	1,000.00

4	650.00
5-7	750.00
8-15	600.00
16-19	500.00
20-23	400.00
24-30	350.00

Large Feature Comics
Dell, 1942

1-3	400.00
4	365.00
5	325.00
6	340.00
7	350.00
8	600.00
9	385.00
10	350.00
11	325.00
12	300.00
13	350.00

Larry Doby, Baseball Hero
Fawcett, 1950

1	400.00

Lars of Mars
Ziff-Davis, 1951

10	500.00
11	400.00

Lars of Mars 3-D
Eclipse, 1987

Back in 1951, Superman co-creator Jerry Siegel and future Silver Age artist extraordinaire Murphy Anderson came up with a new super-hero, Lars of Mars. The series was a masterpiece of schlock 1950s sci-fi so perfectly guileless, innocent, and fun that in 1987, Eclipse reprinted every episode- in 3-D, no less-for post-modern audiences to enjoy all over again.

Lars is an interplanetary agent sent to Earth to battle injustice. He's disguised as a television actor portraying an imaginary super-hero-"Lars of Mars!" No one suspects that he really does have super-powers, until he's forced to reveal himself to save his pretty producer from a gang of terrorists that try to take over the TV station.

Lars of Mars comes with a pair of 3-D glasses to help readers enjoy every two-fisted, Commie-bating, jet-streaming panel.

1 ....3.00

Laser Eraser & Pressbutton
Eclipse, 1985
1-6..2.00
3D 1 ....3.00

Laser Quest Comics
Laser Quest
1 ....3.00

Lash LaRue Western
Fawcett, 1949
1 ....625.00
2 ....385.00
3 ....310.00
4-5..270.00
6-10..215.00
11-20...172.00
21-30...130.00
31-40...100.00
41-50...75.00
51-60...65.00
61-70...58.00
71-80...50.00
81-84...42.00

Lash Larue Western
AC
1 ....4.00
Ann 1 ....3.00

Lassie
Dell, 1950
1 ....90.00
2 ....54.00
3-5..38.00
6-10...26.00
11-20..20.00
21-23..18.00
24-50..16.00
51-59..15.00
60-70..13.00

Lassie
Golden Press, 1978
1 ....22.00

Last American
Marvel, 1990
1-4..2.00

Last Avengers
Marvel, 1995

Several years in the future, in a universe parallel to our own, Earth's Mightiest Heroes are about to face their final battle. Most of the old guard are already gone: Thor, Hercules, and The Thing were killed in the Great Cataclysm years before. The Hulk had become utterly evil and attacked his own teammates, killing Tigra and Wonder Man before dying himself. Captain America became president - only to be gunned down in the third year of his office. The rest were gone or retired, and a new group of Avengers took their place. Then someone dropped a bomb on the Avengers' headquarters, slaying the new group.

Afterward, Hank Pym was visited by Ultron-59 and told to warn the surviving heroes. A coalition of villains led by Kang and Ultron-59 were about to wage a final battle against the old Avengers. Pym and the rest were hopelessly outclassed, but it got worse: Kang had already been to the future, read how it would turn out...and was smiling.

The story was based on a script that Peter David originally ran in the pages of Comics Buyer's Guide.

1-2... 6.00

Last Christmas
Image, 2006
1-5... 3.00

Last Dangerous Christmas
Aeon
1 .... 6.00

Last Days of Hollywood, U.S.A.
Morgan
1-5... 3.00

Last Days of the Justice Society Special
DC, 1986
1 .... 3.00

Last Daze of the Bat-Guy
Mythic
1 .... 3.00

Last Defender of Camelot
Zim
1 .... 2.00

Last Ditch
Edge
1 .... 3.00

Last Gasp Comics and Stories
Last Gasp Eco-Funnies, 1994
1-4... 4.00

Last Generation
Black Tie, 1987
1-5... 2.00

Last Hero Standing
Marvel, 2005
1-5... 3.00

Last Kiss
Eclipse, 1990

Last Kiss is a rarity, a thinking man's horror comic. Combining his skills as a professional painter and storyboard artist, John Watkiss takes a fresh look at classics such as Poe's Black Cat and D. H. Lawrence's The Rocking Horse Winner. He also experiments with original wordless tales, such as The Lighthouse, about loneliness, and The Whirlwind, about man fighting nature in the form of a tornado.

The seven stories in this anthology evoke every emotion from terror to absurdity, and Watkiss's dark art is perfect for the mood he wishes to convey.

1 .... 4.00

Last Kiss
Shanda, 2001
1-3 ....5.00

Last Knight
NBM
1 ....16.00

Last Minute
-Ism, 2004
1-6 ....3.00

Last of the Dragons
Marvel
1 ....7.00

Last of the Viking Heroes
Genesis West, 1987
1-10 ....2.00
Summer 3 ....3.00

Last One
DC, 1993
1-6 ....3.00

Last Planet
MBS
1 ....3.00

Last Planet Standing
Marvel, 206
1-5 ....3.00

Last Shot
Image, 2001
1-4 ....3.00

Last Shot: First Draw
Image, 2001
1 ....3.00

Last Starfighter
Marvel, 1984
1-3 ....2.00

Last Temptation
Marvel Music, 1994
1-3 ....5.00

Last Train to Deadsville, The: A Cal McDonald Mystery
Dark Horse, 2004
1-4 ....3.00

Latest Comics
Spotlight, 1945
1 ....80.00
2 ....50.00

Latigo Kid Western
AC
1 ....2.00

Laugh
Archie, 1987
1 ....3.00
2-5 ....2.00
6-29 ....1.00

Laugh Comics
Archie, 1946

One of the major homes of a true cultural icon, Laugh chronicled the adventures of Archie, Jughead, and the rest of the Riverdale gang for almost 40 years. Witness Archie's dating dilemmas: Will he chose the lovely and rich Veronica or the equally fetching Betty? Will either of them give him the time of day, once he does decide? And will Reggie, the perpetual cloud over Archie's parade, ever stop trying to be just a little bit better at everything than his redheaded opponent? Throughout the years, in the pages of Laugh, Archie, his friends, and his adversaries mirrored the fads and fashions that were sweeping the real-world kids who read this classic comic book.

20 ....200.00
21-25 ....160.00
26-30 ....130.00
31-40 ....94.00
41-50 ....62.00
51-60 ....46.00
61-70 ....30.00
71-80 ....25.00
81-90 ....20.00
91-100 ....18.00
101-130 ....15.00
131-170 ....12.00
171-189 ....9.00
190-200 ....8.00
201-250 ....6.00
251-300 ....4.00
301-350 ....3.00
351-400 ....2.00

Laugh Comix
M.L.J., 1944
46 ....115.00
47-48 ....80.00

Laugh Digest Magazine
Archie, 1974
1 ....10.00
2-5 ....8.00

6-10 ....4.00
11-20 ....3.00
21-200 ....2.00

Launch!
Elsewhere
1 ....2.00

Laundryland
Fantagraphics, 1991
1 ....2.00
2-4 ....3.00

Laurel and Hardy
Dell, 1962
-210 ....30.00
2-4 ....20.00

Laurel and Hardy
Gold Key, 1967
1 ....24.00
2 ....18.00

Laurel and Hardy
DC, 1972
1 ....40.00

Laurel & Hardy in 3-D
Blackthorne, 1987
1-2 ....3.00

Lava
Crossbreed
1 ....3.00

Law
Asylum Graphics
1 ....2.00

Law Against Crime
Essenkay, 1948
1 ....625.00
2 ....350.00
3 ....550.00

Law and Order
Maximum, 1995

A government agency is charged with the duty of apprehending two murderous vigilantes, Law and Order. Law is a rough-and-tough cyborg who is killed in the first few pages of the first issue. He was part of a warrior race of aliens who have vowed to keep innocents safe from danger using any means necessary. Upon coming to this planet, Law chose Vanessa Kelly, a young, drug-addicted girl as his partner. He took her in, cleaned her up, and taught her both philosophy and combat. He also gave her a new identity: "Order." After Law is killed, she was captured by a black-ops team, but a female vigilante soon freed her. This new ally had been instructed by Law to take his place should anything ever happen to him. The two females join forces and become the new Law and Order.

Maximum Press introduced this mini-series in 1995. Law and Order first appeared in Extreme #0, with follow-ups in Extreme Hero and Maximum Hero.

1-3	3.00

Lawbreakers Always Lose!
Atlas, 1948

1	235.00
2	160.00
3-5	95.00
6	75.00
7	80.00
8-10	75.00

Lawbreakers Suspense Stories
Charlton, 1953

10	235.00
11	325.00
12-14	145.00
15	275.00

Lawdog
Marvel, 1993

When you travel the highway connecting North Dakota with Hell, you'll want to make darn sure that your van doesn't break down. If it does, pray that the man the demons call "Lawdog" finds you before anyone else does.

Lawdog is a highway patrolman of sorts, but his turf isn't limited to the interstates most people know. He's the man who keeps order, when chaos causes reality to drift.

So, when you've been driving all night, are getting a bit tired, and decide to stop at the town up the road, make sure the exit isn't marked "Gehenna." If it is, you'd better hope that a certain cop is keeping an eye out for you.

1	3.00
2-10	2.00

Lawdog and Grimrod: Terror at the Crossroads
Marvel, 1993

1	4.00

L.A.W. (Living Assault Weapons)
DC, 1999

1-6	3.00

Lawman
Dell, 1960

3-4	30.00
5-11	26.00

Law of Dredd
Fleetway-Quality

1-33	2.00

Lawrence
Dell, 1963

1	14.00

Lazarus Churchyard
Tundra, 2001

1-3	5.00

Lazarus Five
DC, 2000

1-5	3.00

Lazarus Pits
Boneyard, 1993

1	4.00

Leading Comics
DC, 1941

Leading Comics -- which eventually adjusted its title to

Leading Screen Comics -- began just as U.S. involvement in World War II was beginning, and it began with DC costumed heroes Star-Spangled Kid, Crimson Avenger, Green Arrow, Vigilante, and Shining Knight. With the war in full swing and including the Kid's sidekick (Stripesy) and Green Arrow's kid pal (Speedy), they became the Seven Soldiers of Victory, battling to right wrongs (though dealing less with Nazis than with criminals and fantasy foes.

In the mid-1940s, though, the direction changed to feature funny animals, with character Nero Fox ("the jive-jumping emperor of ancient Rome") taking over, only to be replaced by Peter Porkchops, constantly outwitting The Big Bad Wolf.

-- Maggie

1	3,500.00
2	1,100.00
3	850.00
4-5	675.00
6-10	580.00
11-15	440.00
16-22	70.00
23	110.00
24-30	55.00
31-41	40.00

Leading Screen Comics
DC, 1950

42	40.00
43-60	30.00
61-77	24.00

Leaf
Nab

1	2.00
1/Deluxe	5.00
2	2.00

League of Champions
Hero, 1990

1-3	3.00
4-11	4.00
12	3.00

League of Extraordinary Gentlemen
DC, 1999

1	8.00
1/A-2	5.00
3-5	4.00
5/A	65.00
☛Recalled edition	
6	4.00

League of Extraordinary Gentlemen (Vol. 2)
America's Best, 2002

1-6	4.00

League of Justice
DC, 1996

League of Justice finds the heroes of the classic Justice League of America, recast in an Elseworlds universe of sorcery and magic. Aided by four modern-day teenagers, medieval counterparts of The Flash, Green Lantern, the Martian Manhunter, Batman, Wonder Woman, and other classic DC heroes oppose the evil sorcerer Liuthorr and his duped, adopted son, the Sovereign, a familiar figure in knight's armor with a prominent red "S" emblazoned on his chest.

League of Justice is a story of epic proportions in which the teenagers are prompted by a mysterious, phantom Bird Lady to seek champions and make an alliance with a ambivalent hawk-people society. However, to finally thwart the machinations of Liuthorr they must become pivotal proxies for the heroes.

-- George Haberberger

1-2 .... 6.00

League of Rats
Caliber

1 .... 3.00

League of Super Groovy Crimefighters
Ancient, 2000

This brightly colored title from Ancient Studios flashes back to the swinging years of the 1970s and those bizarre ads for lame novelty items that used to litter comic books: bow-and-arrow sets, martial-arts-training-by-mail, mood rings, X-ray spectacles, bodybuilding courses, croquet mallets, electronics-degrees-by-mail, etc. In this hipster universe, those items and offers worked far better than some of their purchasers could have ever dreamed, inspiring them to band together as the League of Super Groovy Crimefighters and rid New York City of injustice. Funny - if somewhat crudely drawn - this title revisits the slang, the fashions, and the blaxploitation of a bygone era.

1-5 .... 3.00

Leather & Lace
Aircel, 1989

1/A	3.00
1/B	2.00
2/A	3.00
2/B	2.00
3/A	3.00
3/B	2.00
4/A	3.00
4/B	2.00
5/A	3.00
5/B	2.00
6/A	3.00
6/B	2.00
7/A	3.00
7/B	2.00
8/A	3.00
8/B	2.00
9-25	3.00

Leather & Lace: Blood, Sex, & Tears
Aircel, 1991

1-4 .... 3.00

Leather & Lace Summer Special
Aircel, 1990

1 .... 3.00

Leatherboy
Fantagraphics, 1994

1-3 .... 3.00

Leatherface
Arpad, 1991

1 .... 3.00

Leather Underwear
Fantagraphics

1 .... 3.00

Leave it to Beaver
Dell, 1962

-207 .... 100.00

Leave It To Binky
DC, 1948

1	200.00
2	175.00
3	110.00
4	80.00
5-6	55.00
7-10	48.00
11-20	35.00
21-30	28.00
31-40	24.00
41-50	18.00
51-60	12.00
61-71	5.00

Leave It to Chance
Image, 1996

Chance is the daughter of renowned occult investigator Lucas Falconer. While dad is out tangling with demons and vampires, Chance is having adventures of her own in enchanted worlds of fairies as well as in a more sinister world of monster gangsters, accompanied by her pet baby dragon. James Robinson and Paul Smith, creators of the memorable Golden Age mini-series for DC, provide the story and art for this well-crafted series that serves up a refreshingly upbeat take on trendy magical-realism and occult themes. One of Robinson's stated objectives is to appeal to female readers and provide a fun alternative to the grim and dark comics of the 1990s.

1-12	3.00
13	5.00

Led Zeppelin
Personality
1-4	3.00

Led Zeppelin Experience
Revolutionary, 1992
1-5	3.00

Left-Field Funnies
Apex Novelties
1	4.00

Legacy
Majestic, 1993
0-2	2.00

Legacy (Fred Perry's...)
Antarctic, 1999
1	3.00

Legacy
Image, 2003
1-4	3.00

Legacy of Kain: Defiance One Shot
Image, 2004
1	3.00

Legacy of Kain: Soul Reaver
Top Cow, 1999
1	2.00

Legend
DC, 2005
1-3	6.00

Legend Lore
Arrow
1-2	2.00

Legendlore
Caliber
1-4	3.00

LegendLore: Wrath of the Dragon
Caliber
1-2	3.00

Legend of Isis
Alias, 2005
1	4.00
1/B cover	3.00
1/C cover	4.00

2	3.00
2/B cover	4.00
3	3.00
3/B cover	4.00
4-7	3.00

Legend of Jedit Ojanen on the World of Magic: The Gathering
Acclaim, 1996

This two-issue mini-series, set in the world of Magic: The Gathering, tells the story of Jedit Ojanen, the Tiger creature born in the isolated jungles of Efrava.

Adventuring in the outside world, Jedit learns that the evil Johan and the armies of Tirras plan to invade Efrava. Jedit and his comrades-in-arms must travel to Efrava to warn the jungle people of the danger and prepare for battle.

Will he be able to save Efrava from the Tirasian Battlenaughts? The conflict will be a hard-fought war of desert worm beasts and granite gargoyles, catapults, and swords, but luckily, Jedit's allies, the Robaran mercenaries led by the beautiful Adira, will join the conflict as well.

In the end, the secret which drives Jedit on his quest to find his father will be revealed. Thus begins...a legend.

1-2	3.00

Legend of Jesse James
Gold Key, 1966
1	24.00

Legend of Kamui
Eclipse, 1987
1	3.00
1/2nd-37	2.00

Legend of Lemnear
CPM, 1998
1-14	3.00

Legend of Lilith
Image
0	5.00

Legend of Mother Sarah
Dark Horse, 1995

Legend of Mother Sarah is an eight-issue mini-series about a post-apocalyptic Earth in which the elite members of society live in off-world colonies because of the Earth's condition. The oceans are now deserts, and civilization has been reduced to piles of rubble.

Seven years after the colonization of space, a scientist shocks society by claiming that he has developed a special bomb capable of tilting the Earth's axis, which will create new climates and allow the elite to live there once more. This announcement causes the remaining populace to splinter into two groups. Progressives believe that the change is a chance for a new life and, with it, a new civilization. Neo-Conservatives feel that the world has had its chance and that continued manipulation of nature can only lead to more turmoil.

Meanwhile, a cloaked woman wanders the barren deserts. She is known only as Mother Sarah, and she holds the key to the future.

1	4.00
2-8	3.00

Legend of Mother Sarah, The: City of the Angels
Dark Horse, 1997
1-9	4.00

Legend of Mother Sarah, The: City of the Children
Dark Horse, 1996
1-7	4.00

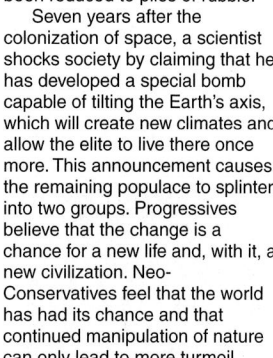

Legend of Sleepy Hollow
Tundra

1 ....7.00

Legend of Supreme
Image, 1994

1-3..3.00

Legend of the Elford
Davdez, 1998

1-3..3.00

Legend of the Hawkman
DC, 2000

1-3..5.00

Legend of the Shield
DC, 1991

1 ....2.00
2-16...1.00
Ann 1...3.00

Legend of Wonder Woman
DC, 1986

1-4..2.00

Legend of Young Dick Turpin
Gold Key, 1966

1 ....16.00

Legend of Zelda
Valiant, 1990

1-5..2.00

Legend of Zelda
Valiant, 1990

1-5..2.00

Legends
DC, 1986

On the cold world of Apokolips, the evil Darkseid had just quashed another rebellion. Still, he felt uneasy. In turning toward Earth, he saw always the same heroes that rose to defeat him time and time again. It was time, he thought, to put an end to them. This time, he would attack not the heroes, but the very ideals - the legends - themselves.

Darkseid sent Doctor Bedlam and Glorious Godfrey to Earth. There, they quickly engineered it so that Billy Batson (aka Shazam) would accidentally murder a super-villain, and accordingly become so ashamed that he would abandon his super-hero identity. At the same time, "Dr. G. Gordon Godfrey" appeared on television to whip the public into an anti-super-hero frenzy.

This series crossed over through countless DC titles in 1986 and served as the birthplace for the new Suicide Squad and the revamped Justice League (which dropped the "of America" from its name).

1-5...2.00
6 ....3.00

Legends and Folklore
Zone, 1992

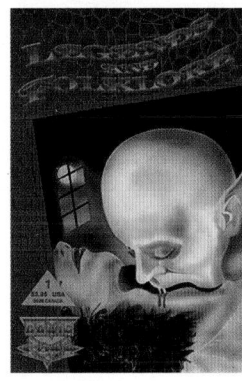

This regrettably short series was a very well done production designed to examine various legends and folklore in a comprehensive text alongside related illustrations by various artists. Issue one covered the existence of vampires throughout history and from all over the world. Issue two delved into the various sorts of werewolves recorded throughout history. The two known issues report not only the legends of various cultures but also mention highlights in fiction where these creatures pop up.

This black-and-white publication that shows research need not be boring.

1 ....4.00
2 ....3.00

Legends from Darkwood
Antarctic, 2003

1-3...4.00

Legends from Darkwood: Summer Fun Special
Antarctic, 2005

0 ....3.00

Legends of Daniel Boone
DC, 1955

1 ....300.00
2 ....135.00
3 ....110.00
4-8..75.00

Legends of Elfinwild
Wehner

1 ....2.00

Legends of Kid Death & Fluffy
Event, 1997

1 ....3.00

Legends of Luxura
Brainstorm, 1996

1 ....3.00
1/Ltd. 4.00

Legends of NASCAR
Vortex

1 ....4.00
1/2nd 2.00
1/3rd 3.00
2 ....2.00
2/Variant 3.00
3-16..2.00

Legends of the Dark Claw
DC, 1996

1 ....2.00

Legends of the DCU: Crisis on Infinite Earths
DC, 1999

1 ....5.00

Legends of the DC Universe
DC, 1998

1-5..3.00
6-30...2.00
31-41..3.00
GS 1-2...5.00

Legends of the DC Universe 3-D Gallery
DC, 1998

1 ....3.00

Legends of the Legion
DC, 1998

1-4..2.00

Legends of the Living Dead
Fantaco

1 ....4.00

Legends of the Stargrazers
Innovation, 1989
1-6 .... 2.00

Legends of the World's Finest
DC, 1994
1 .... 6.00
2-3 .... 5.00

Legendz
Viz, 2005
1-3 .... 8.00

L.E.G.I.O.N.
DC, 1989

A group that traces its origins to the Invasion! mini-series, L.E.G.I.O.N. is the "Licensed Extra-Governmental Interstellar Operatives Network." They are a futuristic fighting force which serves as a peacekeeping force for hire. Unfortunately, they seem to have a talent for getting involved on worlds where the conflicts are not always clear, and where the natives don't always appreciate their intervention.

Led by the hard-nosed Commander Vril Dox II, L.E.G.I.O.N. is remarkable in that its membership includes Lobo, who otherwise would seem to be the ultimate loner. Lobo joined L.E.G.I.O.N. after Dox actually beat him in battle and forced him to make a promise - knowing that Lobo's one virtue is that he always keeps his word.

1 .... 3.00
2-22 .... 2.00
23 .... 3.00
24-49 .... 2.00
50 .... 4.00
51-69 .... 2.00
70 .... 3.00
Ann 1 .... 4.00
Ann 2-3 .... 3.00
Ann 4-5 .... 4.00

Legion
DC, 2001
1-24 .... 3.00
25 .... 4.00
26-38 .... 3.00

Legion Anthology
Limelight
1-2 .... 3.00

Legion Lost
DC, 2000
1-12 .... 3.00

Legion Manga Anthology
Limelight
1-4 .... 3.00

Legionnaires
DC, 1993

The Legionnaires are a group of super-heroes who live in a future 1,000 years from now. By 2995, man destroyed Earth from abuse and neglect, forcing the remaining inhabitants to live in domed cities in space. The Legionnaires protect those cities using their extraordinary powers.

Their ranks include scores of heroes from Cosmic Boy, who fights with magnetic powers, to Brainiac 5, latter-day descendent of the super-genius Brainiac. New characters were constantly added and dropped. Although this could be confusing at times, it gave the title almost infinite possibilities for character development and plot lines.

0 .... 2.00
1 .... 3.00
2-49 .... 2.00
50 .... 4.00
51-64 .... 2.00
65-80 .... 3.00
1000000 .... 4.00
Ann 1 .... 5.00
Ann 2 .... 4.00
Ann 3 .... 3.00

Legionnaires Three
DC, 1986
1-4 .... 1.00

Legion of Monsters
Marvel
1 .... 35.00

Legion of Night
Marvel, 1991
1-2 .... 5.00

Legion of Stupid Heroes
Alternate Concepts, 1997
1-4 .... 3.00

Legion of Stupid Knights
Alternate Concepts, 1998
Special 1 .... 3.00

Legion of Substitute Heroes Special
DC, 1985

Among the coolest aspects of the Silver Age tales of the Legion of Super-Heroes were the occasional "Legionnaire try-outs." Young, would-be heroes from all over the universe would audition for a spot on the future super-team's roster, and, of course, some made it, and some didn't. Five heroes who didn't make the team-Polar Boy, Chlorophyll Kid, Fire Lad, Stone Boy, and Night Girl-formed the Legion of Substitute Heroes. Their mission: to secretly aid the Legion whenever they could. In this 1985 one-shot, writer Paul Levitz and artist Keith Giffen play the Substitute Heroes-who have added Infectious Lass, Porcupine Pete, and Color Kid to their ranks-for a good number of laughs, even as they face a longtime Legion foe, the very deadly Pulsar Stargrave.

1 .... 2.00

Legion of Super-Heroes
DC, 1973

1	15.00
2	8.00
3-4	7.00

Legion of Super-Heroes
DC, 1980

259	4.00
260-261	3.00
261/Whitman	5.00
262	3.00
262/Whitman	5.00
263	3.00
263/Whitman	5.00
264	3.00
264/Whitman	5.00
265	3.00
265/Whitman	5.00
266	3.00
266/Whitman	5.00
267-270	3.00
271-284	2.00
285	3.00
286-296	2.00
297	3.00
298-309	2.00
310	3.00
311-313	2.00
Ann 1	3.00
Ann 2-3	2.00

Legion of Super-Heroes
DC, 1984

1	5.00
2-5	4.00
6-36	2.00
37-38	5.00
39-44	2.00
45	3.00
46-63	2.00
Ann 1	3.00
Ann 2-3	2.00
Ann 4	3.00

Legion of Super-Heroes
DC, 1989

0	2.00
1	3.00
2-37	2.00
38	3.00
39-49	2.00
50	4.00
51-53	2.00
54	3.00
55-99	2.00
100	6.00
101-108	2.00
109-123	3.00
1000000	4.00
Ann 1	5.00
Ann 2-6	4.00
Ann 7	3.00

Legion of Super-Heroes
DC, 2005

1	4.00
2-50	3.00

Legion of Super-Heroes Index
Eclipse, 1987

1-5	2.00

Legion of Super-Heroes Secret Files
DC, 1998

Over the years, DC's futuristic gang of super-teens, the Legion of Super-Heroes, has been one of the most popular, fun, and well-executed titles in its lineup. The Legion features nearly 30 different characters in rotating roles, with a myriad of sub-plots and a truckload of back-issue continuity issues. Legion: Secret Files helps provide readers with a scorecard to keep track of who's who and what happened when.

The one-shot special retells the group's origin and profiles the three original members: the gravity-manipulating Cosmic Boy, lightning master Live Wire, and the telepathic Saturn Girl. Additionally, there's a dossier of info on many of the team's other members and a detailed two-page spread of every Legion hero and villain. Legion: Secret Files is a treat for any fan of the Legion's adventures.

1-2	5.00

Legion of the Stupid-Heroes
Blackthorne

1	2.00

Legion: Science Police
DC, 1998

1-4	2.00

Legion Secret Files 3003
DC, 2004

1	5.00

Legions of Ludicrous Heroes
C&T

1	2.00

Legion Worlds
DC, 2001

The Legion of Super-Heroes is gone. After the Great Rift Disaster, eleven members of the legion were missing and presumed dead. United Planets president, Leland McCauley, decided to disband the Legion in honor of their memory. This perverse "honor" has left M'onel as the sole guardian of Earth on active duty. The first issue of this mini-series illustrates that this will be a monumental task even for someone as powerful and messianic as M'onel.

This mini-series is the lead-in to the next legion book titled simply The Legion and follows the 12-issue maxi-series, Legion Lost, which revealed the fate of the missing Legionnaires and their quest to return home. Legion Worlds, on the other hand, divulges the story of the survivors and how they coped. This is similar to the theme of the Funeral for a Friend story arc that followed the death of Superman in 1993.

-- George Haberberger

1-6	4.00

Legion X-1
Silverwolf, 1987

1-2	2.00

Legion X-1
Greater Mercury, 1989

1-3	2.00

Legion X-2
Greater Mercury, 1989

1-7	2.00

Lejentia
Opus, 1987

1-2...2.00

Lemonade Kid
AC

1...3.00

Lena's Bambinas
Fantagraphics

1...4.00

Lenore
Slave Labor, 1998

1-7...3.00

Lensman
Eternity, 1990

Situated at the furthest reaches of the galactic rim is the lush, green planet called Mqueie -- home to a retired space soldier and his son, Kim, who is now 18 and ready to leave for the stars. But, on the eve of his departure, a war-battered starship appears out of warp space and threatens to crash on the peaceful planet. As the young are apt to do, Kim makes a bold, rash plan -- to take his small flyer to attempt to gain control of the falling ship, thus averting catastrophe.

Making it on board, Kim discovers an injured Lensman at the helm. Just what is the mysterious Lens that grants awesome powers to a select few? Kim's incredible odyssey is about to begin.

This title was published in association with Harmony Gold U.S.A., presenting a new adaptation of the Japanese animated film and television series purporting to feature E. E. "Doc" Smith's concepts. Smith (1890-1965), "The Father of Space Opera," introduced the Lensmen in Skylark of Space, published in a science-fiction magazine in 1928;

there is little connection between his work and that in the anime.

1 .... 2.00
1/Variant................................. 4.00
2-6 .... 2.00

Lensman: War of the Galaxies
Eternity, 1990

1-7 .... 2.00

Leonard Nimoy
Celebrity

1 .... 6.00

Leonardo Teenage Mutant Ninja Turtle
Mirage, 1986

1 .... 4.00

Leopold and Brink
Faultline, 1997

1-3 .... 3.00

Leroy
Standard, 1949

1 .... 30.00
2 .... 25.00
3-6 .... 18.00

Lester Girls: The Lizard's Trail
Eternity

1-3 .... 3.00

Lethal
Image, 1996

1 .... 3.00

Lethal Enforcer
Alias, 2005

1 .... 1.00

Lethal Foes of Spider-Man
Marvel, 1993

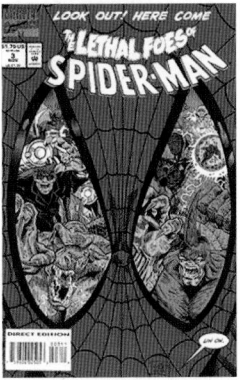

The bad guys are back-in force - in this follow-up to the Deadly Foes of Spider-Man limited series. It begins with the imprisoned Otto Octavius forced to sit helplessly by

as government agents destroy the mechanical arms that had once made him Doctor Octopus. Octavius still shares a bond with the arms, however, and he feels their destruction even though he is physically some 2,000 miles away from them when it happens.

Then, someone - or something - contacts Octavius over the same psychic link that had once connected him to his arms. It turns out that the criminal once known as the Answer has regained an incorporeal awareness after his apparent disintegration in Spectacular Spider-Man #96. Now he seeks Octavius' help in recovering his physical form. Meanwhile, The Vulture, The Rhino, Boomerang, and Hardshell have joined forces...all in order to gain revenge on the friendly neighborhood Spider-Man!

1-4 .... 2.00

Lethal Instinct
Alias, 2005

1-5 .... 3.00

Lethal Orgasm
NBM

1 .... 10.00

Lethal Strike
London Night, 1995

0 .... 6.00
1/2-Ann 1................................ 3.00

Lethal Strike/Double Impact: Lethal Impact
London Night, 1996

1 .... 3.00

Lethargic Comics
Alpha, 1994

1 .... 4.00
2-14 .... 3.00

Lethargic Comics, Weakly
Lethargic, 1991

1 .... 4.00
2-12 .... 3.00

Lethargic Lad
Crusade, 1996

1-3 .... 3.00

Lethargic Lad
Crusade, 1997

1-9 .... 3.00

Let's Pretend
D.S., 1950

1 .... 95.00
2-3 .... 65.00

Let's Take a Trip
Pines, 1958

1 .... 24.00

Level X
Caliber
1-2..4.00

Levi's World
Moordam, 1998
1-4..3.00

Lewd Moana
Fantagraphics
1..3.00

The Lexian Chronicles: Full Circle
APComics, 2005
1/Preview 5.00
1..4.00

Lex Luthor: Man of Steel
DC, 2005
1-5..3.00

Lex Luthor: The Unauthorized Biography
DC, 1989

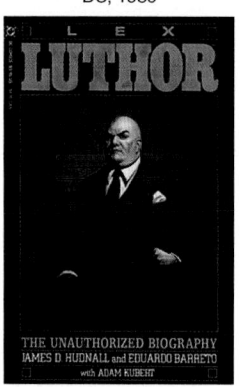

Down-and-out writer Peter Sands desperately needed a big story in order to pay his bills. He thought he had hit the jackpot when a publisher asked him to write the unauthorized biography of Lex Luthor. The ruthless Luthor, however, was sure to object, as the unfortunate Sands quickly discovered. Luthor's rise in the crime world dated back to his childhood, and the few people who knew Luthor's secrets were afraid to reveal them. Sands eventually persuaded them to discuss Luthor's past, but not even Superman could save him when Luthor found out about Sands' investigation.

1..4.00

Lex Talionis: Jungle Tale One Shot
Image, 2004
1..6.00

Liaisons Delicieuses
Fantagraphics, 1990
1-6.. 2.00

Libby Ellis
Eternity, 1988
1-4.. 2.00

Libby Ellis
Malibu
1-4.. 2.00

Liberality For All
-Ism, 2005
1... 3.00

Liberator
Malibu, 1987
1-6.. 2.00

Liberator
Images & Realities
1... 2.00

Libertine
Fantagraphics
1... 2.00
2... 3.00

Liberty Comics
Green, 1945
5-9...................................... 125.00
10-15.................................... 90.00

Liberty Guards
Chicago Mail Order, 1942
1.. 250.00

Liberty Meadows
Insight, 1999

Fans of Frank Cho's newspaper strip had their requests for a collected version answered when Cho's Insight Studios began reprinting the strip in comic-book form in 1999. In addition to strips that appeared in the newspapers, Cho also included unedited strips that had been rejected or changed by his syndicate.

The strip is set at an animal preserve where Frank (no relation or resemblance to Cho) has been hired as the veterinarian. He pines for the voluptuous Brandy who cares for the animals, who include Leslie, a hypochondriac bullfrog; Ralph, a midget circus bear; Dean, a male chauvinist pig (a real swine); and Truman, a baby duckling. The strips deal with the pains of unrequited love, various bits of pop culture, and the strange behavior of the bizarre anthropomorphic animals. Cho occasionally draws himself in the strip as a talking monkey. In late 2001, Cho ended the newspaper strip and moved new adventures to the comic book, which moved to Image in 2002.

-- Brent

1 .... 18.00
1/2nd 3.00
2 .... 10.00
3-4 .... 6.00
5 .... 5.00
6-10 .... 4.00
11-37 .... 3.00

Liberty Meadows Source Book
Image, 2005
1 .... 5.00

Liberty Meadows Wedding Album
Insight, 2001
nn 3.00

Liberty Project
Eclipse, 1987
1-8 .... 2.00

Liberty Scouts
Centaur, 1941
2 .... 775.00
3 .... 550.00

Libra
Eternity, 1987

Libra follows the trials of young Dale Stevens as he tries to assume his father's heroic mantle. The bad news is that his dad doesn't like the idea of his son playing super-hero. Seems Dale doesn't take being a super-hero very seriously. Then again, what teenager does take their job seriously? Look for things to really get interesting once dad's former sidekick steps up to claim the name Libra.

Del Barral, creator, writer and penciller, brings us this black-and-white, anime-inspired, semi-serious Japanese-styled comic.

1 ....2.00

Librarian
Fantagraphics
1 ....3.00

Licensable Bear
About, 2003
1-2 ....3.00

License to Kill
Eclipse

Licence to Kill (with that distinctive British spelling) was the second James Bond movie to star Timothy Dalton, who kept the franchise going until Pierce Brosnan was available. This episode finds Ian Fleming's top British agent on a personal crusade to bring down Franz Sanchez, a drug lord who was responsible for the mutilation of a friend, and the death of that friend's wife. But the British Secret Service has no official interest in Sanchez and demands that Bond let the Americans deal with him. Bond abruptly resigns so M, his director, just as abruptly revokes his famous "licence to kill." Apparently this license is merely a formality since Bond is not the least bit inhibited by its revocation.

Mike Grell (James Bond 007: Permission to Die) did the

breakdowns for this adaptation but a trio of artists finished the pencilling.
-- *George Haberberger*

1 .... 8.00

Lidsville
Gold Key, 1972
1 .... 20.00
2 .... 14.00
3-5 .... 12.00

Lieutenant Blueberry: General Golden Mane
Marvel
1 .... 15.00

Lt. Robin Crusoe, U.S.N.
Gold Key, 1966
1 .... 20.00

Life and Adventures of Santa Clause
Tundra, 1992
nn 25.00

L.I.F.E. Brigade
Blue Comet
1-3 .... 2.00

Life Eaters
DC, 2003
1 .... 30.00

Life Force, A
Kitchen Sink
1-1/2nd 13.00

Life of Captain Marvel
Marvel, 1985
1-5 .... 3.00

Life of Christ
Marvel, 1993
1 .... 3.00

Life of Christ, The: The Easter Story
Marvel
1 .... 3.00

Life of Pope John Paul II
Marvel, 1983
1 .... 3.00

Life on Another Planet
DC, 2000
1 .... 13.00

Lifequest
Caliber, 1997
1-5 .... 3.00

Life Story
Fawcett, 1949
1 .... 60.00
2 .... 45.00
3-9 .... 30.00
10-29 .... 25.00
30-47 .... 20.00

Life Under Sanctions
Fantagraphics, 1994
1 .... 3.00

Life, the Universe and Everything
DC
1-3 .... 7.00

Life with Archie
Archie, 1958

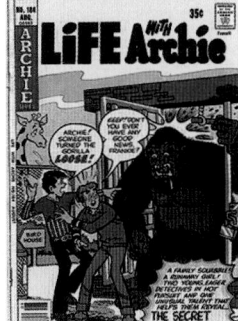

Running from 1958 to 1991, Life With Archie was one of many comics to feature Archie Andrews and the rest of his pals from Riverdale High. Throughout the years, Archie has proved one of the most enduring comics, using good-natured humor and light adventure to draw in its audience of primarily young readers.

There was nothing particularly different to set Life With Archie apart from such other Archie series as Laugh Digest, Archie, or Pep. It focused equally on the entire Riverdale crew, following them on adventures ranging from getting lost on road trips, or even (yes) turning into werewolves. Of course, by issue's end, all problems are resolved, typically in a humorous manner. All in all, it's tame stuff, but the years have proved that it's a perfect way for young readers to discover the joys of comics.

1 .... 225.00
2 .... 110.00
3-5 .... 85.00
6-10 .... 55.00
11-20 .... 32.00
21-31 .... 25.00
32-40 .... 16.00
41-50 .... 12.00
51-60 .... 8.00
61-70 .... 5.00
71-80 .... 4.00
81-120 .... 3.00
121-250 .... 2.00
251-285 .... 1.00

Life with Millie
Atlas, 1960

8	35.00
9-10	28.00
11-20	26.00

Life with Snarky Parker
Fox, 1950

1	145.00

Light and Darkness War
Marvel, 1988

1-6	2.00

Light Brigade
DC, 2004

1-4	6.00

Light Fantastic (Terry Pratchett's...)
Innovation, 1992

0-4	3.00

Lightning Comics
Feature, 1940

4	700.00
5	450.00
6	400.00
7-13	325.00

Lightning Comics Presents
Lightning, 1994

This title introduces War Party and Dreadwolf...in full color! War Party is an ultraviolent, ultracool mercenary-for-hire who, in his debut story, takes down the bad guys and disrupts the performance of an opera. By the way, you know he's ultracool because he ties a strip of red cloth around his head as he jumps into action. Dreadwolf is a werewolf-with-a-heart-of-gold feature; he's savage, but only when pursued by the bad guys. This anthology title introduces the "Lightning Universe," an attempt by Lightning Comics to publish a group of connected titles.

1	4.00

Lights Out
Tokyopop, 2005

1	10.00

Li'l Abner
Harvey, 1947

61	175.00
62	125.00
63	105.00
64-67	85.00
68-71	60.00
72-73	40.00
74-77	35.00
78-82	32.00
83-87	28.00
88-95	25.00
96-97	20.00

Li'l Genius
Charlton, 1955

5-30	10.00
31-54	8.00
55	2.00

Lili
Image, 1999

0	5.00

Liling-Po
Tokyopop, 2005

1-3	10.00

Li'l Jinx
Archie, 1956

11	50.00
12-16	32.00

Li'l Keiki
Kiddieland Books, 2005

1	4.00

Li'l Kids
Marvel, 1970

1	35.00
2-5	22.00
6-12	16.00

Lillith: Demon Princess
Antarctic, 1996

It's the old boy-meets-girl story...sort of.

Once upon a time, there was a great battle between Heaven and Hell. Representing Heaven was an archangel named Azara. Fighting for Hell was the warrior goddess Hexa. The two waged a mighty battle which shook the universe. At the end, Hexa was defeated. But instead of slaying her, Azara looked into her eyes, and she into his, and they fell instantly in love. Azara was later slain through treachery, but not before he gave Hexa a daughter named Lilith. Once grown, Lilith earned a fearsome reputation as the greatest warrior on the Seven Levels. Even though she owed loyalty to Orcus, her mere allegiance was not enough. Through treachery, Orcus framed her for murder (ironically, a crime in Hell). To save her life, Hexa agreed to banishment, and Lillith became his slave.

0	2.00
0/Variant-3	5.00

Li'l Menace
Fago, 1958

1	30.00
2	18.00
3	16.00

Li'l Pals
Marvel, 1972

1	25.00
2-5	20.00

Li'l Pan
Fox, 1946

6	40.00
7-8	30.00

Li'l Rascal Twins
Charlton, 1957

6	20.00
7-10	12.00
11-18	8.00

Li'l Santa
NBM

1	15.00

Li'l Tomboy
Charlton, 1956

92-100	18.00
101-107	15.00

Limited Collectors' Edition
DC, 1973

C-20	32.00
☛Rudolph	
C-21	16.00
C-22	14.00
C-23	16.00
C-24	26.00
☛Rudolph	

C-25 ....28.00
☛Batman
C-27 ....16.00
C-29 ....10.00
C-31 ....15.00
C-32 ....10.00
C-33 ....16.00
C-34 ....12.00
C-35 ....10.00
C-36 ....16.00
C-37 ....20.00
☛Batman
C-38-C-39 ....10.00
C-40 ....12.00
C-41-C-43 ....10.00
C-44 ....12.00
C-45-C-47 ....10.00
C-48 ....12.00
C-49-C-50 ....10.00
C-51 ....12.00
C-52 ....10.00
C-57-C-59 ....14.00

Lincoln-16
Skarwood, 1997
1-2..3.00

Linda
Ajax, 1954
1 ....60.00
2 ....42.00
3-4 ....36.00

Linda Carter, Student Nurse
Atlas, 1961
1 ....60.00
2-5..40.00
6-9..30.00

Linda Lark
Dell, 1961
1 ....15.00
2-8..10.00

Line the Dustbin Funnies
East Willis, 1997
1 ....3.00

Lionheart
Awesome, 1999
1/A..4.00
1/B-Ashcan 1 ....3.00

Lion King (Disney's...)
Marvel, 1994
1 ....3.00

Lions, Tigers & Bears
Image, 2005
1-3..3.00

Lions, Tigers & Bears
Image, 2006
1-3..3.00

Lippy the Lion and Hardy Har Har
Gold Key, 1963
1 ....60.00

Lipstick
Rip Off, 1992
1 ....3.00

Lisa Comics
Bongo

LISA IN WORDLAND!

This one-shot title stars the often overlooked Lisa Simpson, Bart Simpson's younger (and much better behaved) sister.

In the story "Lisa in Wonderland," she falls asleep while writing a letter, and struggling to find just the right words to express her thoughts. Just as she nods off, she is awakened by a Lewis Carroll novel that fell off a bookshelf and bonked her on the head. When she looks around, she discovers she is no longer in Springfield. Like Alice in Wonderland, she's become Lisa in Wordland, a surrealistic place where grammar rules. Consequently, Lisa Simpson feels right at home. She follows the Wordland letter carrier, Ned Flanders, and experiences bizarre occurrences like growing huge as well as shrinking to the size of a bug. Lisa meets a dinosaur called a thesaurus, who takes forever to finish a sentence, and comes across a man who swallowed a dictionary.

1 .... 2.00

Lita Ford: The Queen of Heavy Metal
Rock-It Comics

Rock-It Comix got underway in late 1993, launching rock-star comics featuring Lita Ford, Metallica, Ozzy Osbourne, and World Domination Enterprises. In contrast to the "unauthorized and proud of it" Rock 'n' Roll Comics, the Rock-It titles were all developed with the cooperation of the artists they featured.

Lita Ford: The Queen of Heavy Metal is a rock and roll fantasy starring the ex-Runaways guitarist and enduring rock favorite. Lita is shown here trying to get through another gig, while jousting with Libby Snore (a thinly disguised version of Tipper Gore) and the PMRC (the Parents' Music Resource Center-an organization that promoted the labeling of certain records as containing offensive lyrics). All this was bad enough, then Libby decided to up the stakes and use witchcraft to make Lita out to be a Satan worshiper. As it turns out, Lita has a few surprises of her own...

1 .... 5.00

Little Scrowlie
Slave Labor, 2004
1-12 .... 3.00

Little Al of the FBI
Ziff-Davis, 1950
10 .... 95.00
11 .... 70.00

Little Al of the Secret Service
Ziff-Davis, 1951
1 .... 95.00
2-3 .... 70.00

Little Ambrose
Archie, 1958
1 .... 60.00

Little Angel
Pines, 1954

5 ....24.00
6-9 ....20.00
10-16 ....16.00

Little Annie Rooney
David McKay, 1948

1 ....48.00
2-3 ....35.00

Little Archie
Archie, 1956

1 ....525.00
2 ....210.00
3 ....150.00
4-5 ....115.00
6-10 ....80.00
11-20 ....52.00
21-40 ....32.00
41-60 ....22.00
☛Giant-size
61-80 ....16.00
81-100 ....11.00
101-120 ....6.00
121-140 ....4.00
141-180 ....3.00

Little Archie Digest Magazine
Archie, 1991

1 ....3.00
2-25 ....2.00

Little Archie Mystery
Archie, 1963

1 ....60.00
2 ....42.00

Little Aspirin
Marvel, 1949

1 ....60.00
2 ....45.00
3 ....24.00

Little Audrey
St. John, 1948

2 ....100.00
3-5 ....65.00
6-10 ....48.00
11-21 ....38.00
22-24 ....30.00

Little Audrey
Harvey, 1945

25 ....125.00
26-29 ....75.00
30-40 ....50.00
41-53 ....40.00

Little Audrey
Harvey, 1992

1 ....2.00
2-9 ....1.00

Little Audrey and Melvin
Harvey, 1962

Little Audrey and Melvin are two mischievous kids in the time-honored tradition of Little Lulu. In fact, Little Audrey was created when Paramount's Famous Studios found its Little Lulu cartoons to be doing so well that it could drop her and keep all the money, if it introduced the new character. Cartoon plots featured her in fantasy adventures from which she learned lessons.

In comic books, Audrey is the brains of the operation, frequently foiling her freckle-faced pal Melvin with harmless kid-mischief pranks. The stories cover themes popular with young readers, like dealing with parents who just don't get it, ways to get out of doing chores, the tedium of shopping for clothes, and misunderstandings that crop up when kids play "grown up." Audrey and Melvin stories run about four pages, with frequent gags leading to a punchline or finish.

-- Rob Salkowitz

1 ....45.00
2 ....25.00
3-5 ....18.00
6-10 ....14.00
11-20 ....12.00
21-30 ....9.00
31-40 ....6.00
41-61 ....4.00

Little Audrey TV Funtime
Harvey, 1962

1 ....45.00
2 ....28.00
3 ....24.00
4-5 ....20.00
6-10 ....16.00
11-20 ....12.00
21-33 ....9.00

Little Beaver
Dell, 1951

3 ....24.00
4-8 ....20.00

Little Bit
St. John, 1949

1-2 ....25.00

Little Dot
Harvey, 1953

1 ....1,250.00
2 ....500.00
3 ....400.00
4-5 ....325.00
6 ....400.00
7 ....200.00
8-10 ....125.00
11-20 ....100.00
21-30 ....60.00
31-40 ....45.00
41-50 ....25.00
51-60 ....20.00
61-80 ....15.00
81-100 ....10.00
101-141 ....7.00
142-145 ....10.00
146-164 ....5.00

Little Dot
Harvey, 1992

1-7 ....2.00

Little Dot Dotland
Harvey, 1962

1 ....75.00
2-3 ....40.00
4-5 ....35.00
6-10 ....24.00
11-20 ....20.00
21-29 ....16.00
30-39 ....12.00
40-54 ....10.00
55-61 ....8.00
62-63 ....10.00

Little Dot in 3-D
Blackthorne

1 ....3.00

Little Dot's Uncles and Aunts
Harvey, 1961

1 ....70.00
2-3 ....42.00
4-5 ....36.00
6-10 ....28.00
11-35 ....22.00
36-52 ....14.00

Little Dracula
Harvey, 1992

1-3 ....2.00

Little Ego
NBM

1 ....11.00

Little Endless Storybook
DC, 2001

1 ....6.00

Little Eva 3-D
St. John, 1953

1 ....80.00
2 ....70.00

Little Fir Tree
W.T. Grant, 1943

1 ....40.00

Little Ghost
St. John, 1959

1 ....38.00
2-3 ....25.00

Little Giant Comics
Centaur, 1938

1 ....425.00
2 ....335.00
3-4 ....260.00

Little Giant Detective Funnies
Centaur, 1938

1 ....500.00
2 ....375.00
3-4 ....330.00

Little Giant Movie Funnies
Centaur, 1938

1 ....360.00
2 ....310.00

Little Gloomy
Slave Labor, 1999

Gloomy is a young girl who's afraid of just about everything-too afraid, some days, to even leave the house. And who can blame her? It's not every little girl whose acquaintances are werewolves and Frankenstein monsters, and whose typical experiences include being abducted, hypnotized, or otherwise attacked. More often than not, though, she does go out...because staying home alone in her big old mansion is just as scary. These forays are usually the launching pad to the beginning of yet another spooky adventure that has her wishing she'd stuck to her original plan.

These tales aren't truly spooky, though, in fact, given the generally cute, little-kid styled monsters-think "Family Circus" meets Bram Stoker-they're actually very lighthearted. Clever, funny, and unique, it's a charming little series of chills and jokes, through the eyes of a child in a world of monsters. Published in black-and-white by Slave Labor Graphics.

1 .... 3.00

Little Gloomy's Super Scary Monster Show
Slave Labor, 2005

1-2 .... 3.00

Little Greta Garbage
Rip Off, 1990

1-2 .... 3.00

Little Grey Man
Image

1 .... 7.00

Little Groucho
Reston, 1955

1 .... 35.00
2 .... 25.00

Little Ike
St. John, 1953

1 .... 40.00
2 .... 26.00
3-4 .... 24.00

Little Iodine
Dell, 1950

Jimmy Hatlo (1898-1963) so tapped into the national experience with the title "They'll do it every time" that he was able to cull "you ain't heard nothing yet" experiences from his audience for decades. The King Features newspaper feature began in 1936. The concept was somewhat along the lines of "My mother says I should keep my phone calls short but" (next panel) "When she gets on the phone she doesn't get off for an hour." And it has been so popular that it's still running, now done by Al Scaduto.

The suburban Tremblechin family's red-haired little girl eventually became so popular she earned her own strip, which ran from 1943 to 1986, and Little Iodine starred in her own comic book for some time. Much of the comic-book version was original material, consisting of short stories with beginning, middle, and end.

-- Maggie

1 .... 45.00
2-5 .... 30.00
6-10 .... 25.00
11-19 .... 20.00
20-29 .... 16.00
30-39 .... 13.00
40-56 .... 9.00

Little Italy
Fantagraphics

1 .... 4.00

Little Jack Frost
Avon, 1952

1 .... 38.00

Little Jim-Bob Big Foot
Jump Back, 1998

1-2 .... 3.00

Little Joe
St. John, 1953

1 .... 24.00

Little Lana
Marvel, 1949

8 .... 36.00
9 .... 30.00

Little Lenny
Marvel, 1949

1 .... 50.00
2-3 .... 30.00

Little Lizzie
Marvel, 1949

1 .... 50.00
2-5 .... 28.00

Little Lizzie
Marvel, 1953

1 .... 40.00
2-3 .... 28.00

Little Lotta
Harvey, 1955

1 .... 225.00
2 .... 90.00
3 .... 75.00
4-5 .... 55.00
6-10 .... 40.00
11-20 .... 28.00
21-30 .... 22.00
31-40 .... 18.00

41-50	15.00
51-70	12.00
71-90	8.00
91-98	5.00
99-102	6.00
103-120	3.00

Little Lotta
Harvey, 1992

1-4	2.00

Little Lotta Foodland
Harvey, 1963

1	45.00
2-3	35.00
4-5	30.00
6-10	24.00
11-15	16.00
16-20	12.00
21-29	8.00

Little Lulu
Dell, 1948

1	600.00
2	300.00
3	225.00
4-5	200.00
6-10	165.00
11-20	125.00
21-30	105.00
31-38	90.00
39	125.00
40	90.00
41-50	70.00
51-60	60.00
61-70	55.00
71-80	45.00
81-90	40.00
91-99	35.00
100	50.00
101-120	30.00
121-140	28.00
141-160	25.00
161-164	20.00
☛...in Paris	
165-166	70.00
☛Christmas Diary	
167-180	20.00
181-200	15.00
201-220	9.00
221-240	6.00
241-250	4.00
251-257	3.00
258-259	12.00
260	325.00
☛Sold only in packs	
261	45.00
☛Sold only in packs	
262-265	12.00
☛Sold only in packs	
266-268	15.00
☛Sold only in packs	
Ann 1	225.00
Ann 2	175.00

Little Lulu and
Her Special Friends
Dell, 1955

3-4	125.00

Little Lulu and
Tubby at Summer Camp
Dell, 1957

1	35.00
2	30.00

Little Lulu and
Tubby Halloween Fun
Dell, 1957

1	35.00
2	30.00

Little Lulu and
Tubby in Alaska
Dell, 1959

1	35.00

Little Max Comics
Harvey, 1949

Joe Palooka's mute friend, Max, is the star of this long-running series. The little red-headed boy wore a large straw hat, idolized the boxer, and often tagged along to his matches.

Stories in the series, which ran from 1949 to 1961, featured Max in typical situations a boy of his age would get into, from shining shoes on street corners to playing with the neighborhood dog to pining for a little blonde-haired girl. While he would never speak, Max did have big thoughts, ably captured in thought balloons, often punctuated with images rather than words.

-- Brent

1	85.00
2	60.00
3	50.00
4-5	40.00
6-9	35.00
10-19	30.00
20-39	25.00
40-59	20.00
60-73	15.00

Little Mermaid
(Disney's...)
Marvel, 1994

1	3.00
2-12	2.00

Little Mermaid Limited
Series (Disney's...)
Disney, 1992

1-4	2.00

Little Mermaid
W.D.

1	4.00

Little Mermaid, The:
Underwater
Engagements
(Disney's...)
Acclaim

1	5.00

Little Mermaid
Disney

1	3.00
1/Direct	6.00

Little Miss Muffet
Best, 1948

11	40.00
12-13	28.00

Little Miss Strange
Millennium

1	3.00

Little Miss Sunbeam
Magazine Enterprises, 1950

1	65.00
2-4	40.00

Little Mister Man
Slave Labor, 1995

Remember those sweet, endearing stories of Superman when he was Ma and Pa Kent's Superbaby? Well, forget 'em because Little Mister Man is one superspoiled brat of a super-powered child! When a group of kids refuses to play with him, Little

Mister Man incinerates them with his heat vision! Rocketed to earth as a baby, Little Mister Man was raised by a father who fears his adoptive son's powers, and a mother who feels he will one day be a great hero. Boy, does she have a lot to learn!

1-3 ....3.00

Little Monsters
Gold Key, 1964

1	20.00
2	12.00
3-5	8.00
6-9	6.00
10-20	5.00
21-44	4.00

Little Monsters
Now, 1990

1-6 ....2.00

Little Nemo in Slumberland 3-D
Blackthorne, 1987

1 ....3.00

Little Orphan Annie
David McKay, 1948

1	125.00
2-3	80.00

Little Oz Squad
Patchwork, 1995

1 ....3.00

Little Red Hot: Bound
Image, 2001

This three-issue limited series finds Chane, writer-artist Dawn Brown's soulless bounty hunter, hot on the trail of a missing child…but not necessarily of her own free will. Chane has been abducted by a pair of rookie bounty hunters who need her help in tracking down the boy before he's put on the auction block in India. This is high-octane stuff; Brown's

reluctant heroine just doesn't slow down for a minute!

1-3 .... 3.00

Little Red Hot: Chane of Fools
Image, 1999

1-3 .... 3.00

Little Ronzo in Slumberland
Slave Labor, 1987

1 .... 2.00

Little Roquefort
St. John, 1952

1	40.00
2	30.00
3-10	24.00

Little Sad Sack
Harvey, 1964

George Baker's Sad Sack was a long-running humor strip based on the deathless patriotic premise of making fun of the military. As such, it remained one of Harvey's top features for a long time, but Army life may have seemed somewhat distant from the concerns of Harvey's primary readership, very young kids. The answer? Little Sad Sack, the adventures of the crafty layabout private when he was 5 years old!

What seems like an editorial contrivance actually works, because Sad Sack and his crew are so goofy-looking that the transition from the barracks to the playground is practically seamless from a stylistic point of view. From there, it's child's play to insert the Sad Sack family into the typical domestic-comedy antics of the kid strip.

1	7.00
2-5	4.00
6-19	3.00

Little Scouts
Dell, 1951

2-6 .... 15.00

Little Shop of Horrors
DC, 1987

Seymour was a clumsy loser who worked in a failing flower shop and pined after Audrey, a co-worker with a borderline sadistic boyfriend (not surprisingly, a dentist). Then he brought home a strange plant that appeared after a solar eclipse, and his life was changed. The little plant was so interesting that people started flocking in to the moribund flower shop. His boss suddenly saw him as a hero, and Audrey started taking an interest in him.

But the plant started to die, and nothing Seymour could feed it seemed to make it better. Then Seymour accidentally cut his finger, spilling a few drops of blood onto the new plant. Overnight, it grew enormously. Fed by Seymour's blood, it soon grew into a huge plant. Then one day, it spoke-promising Seymour the object of his heart's desire if only he would feed it something truly nourishing...such as Audrey's boyfriend!

1 .... 2.00

Little Snow Fairy Sugar Manga
ADV Manga, 2006

1-3 .... 10.00

Little Star
Oni, 2005

1-5 .... 3.00

Little Stooges
Gold Key, 1972

1	16.00
2-3	12.00
4-7	9.00

Little White Mouse
Caliber, 1997
1-4.................................3.00

Little White Mouse
Caliber, 1998
1-4.................................3.00

Little White Mouse: Entropy Dreaming
Caliber, 2000
1.................................3.00

Little White Mouse: Open Space
Blue Line, 2002
1-3.................................3.00

Livewires
Marvel, 2005
1-6.................................3.00

Living Bible
Living Bible, 1945
1.................................175.00
2.................................150.00
3.................................140.00

Livingstone Mountain
Adventure, 1991
1-4.................................3.00

Living with Zombies
Frightworld Studios, 2005
1-3.................................3.00

Liz and Beth
Fantagraphics, 1991
1-4.................................3.00

Liz and Beth
Fantagraphics, 1992
1-4.................................3.00

Liz and Beth
Fantagraphics, 1993
1-7.................................3.00

Lizard Lady
Aircel, 1991
1-4.................................3.00

Lizards Summer Fun Special
Caliber
1.................................4.00

Lizzie McGuire Cine-Manga
Tokyopop, 2003
1.................................8.00

Llisica
NBM
1.................................10.00

Lloyd Llewellyn
Fantagraphics, 1986
1-6.......................... 2.00
Special 1-Special 1/2nd 3.00

Loaded
Interplay

Raulf is the barren prison planet used to hold the criminally insane. But the inmates are about to take over. And break out. Terry the Tosser murdered his wife with a shotgun. Cap'n Hands is a space pirate who pillaged his way across seven systems. Fwank is a psychotic who carries balloons that change colors to reflect his murderous moods. Butch likes knives and always "accidentally" dresses in women's clothes. Besides being beautiful, Vox carries a flamethrower and she'll kill you as soon as look at you. Together, these and other murderous lunatics have stolen a spaceship and busted off Raulf. And that's all you need to know to play Loaded.

Serving as a backstory for the Sony Playstation computer game Loaded, this twelve-page one-shot is a prose story by bloody fan-favorite Garth Ennis, with character illustrations by Greg Staples and Les Spink.

1 .... 1.00

Lobo
DC, 1990
1 .... 3.00
1/2nd-4 .... 2.00

Lobo
DC, 1993
0 .... 3.00
1 .... 4.00
2-10 .... 3.00
11-55 .... 2.00
56-64 .... 3.00
1000000 .... 4.00
Ann 1 .... 5.00
Ann 2-3.......................... 4.00

Lobo: A Contract on Gawd
DC, 1994
1-4 .... 2.00

Lobo: Blazing Chain of Love
DC, 1992
1 .... 2.00

Lobo: Bounty Hunting for Fun and Profit
DC
1 .... 5.00

Lobo: Chained
DC, 1997
1 .... 3.00

Lobo Convention Special
DC, 1993
1 .... 2.00

Lobo/Deadman: The Brave and the Bald
DC, 1995
1 .... 4.00

Lobo: Death and Taxes
DC, 1996
1-4 .... 2.00

Lobo/Demon: Helloween
DC, 1996
1 .... 2.00

Lobo: Fragtastic Voyage
DC, 1998
1 .... 6.00

Lobo Gallery, The: Portraits of a Bastich
DC, 1995
1 .... 4.00

Lobo Goes to Hollywood
DC, 1996
1 .... 2.00

Lobo: Infanticide
DC, 1992

Nobody in their right mind would mistake Lobo for a role model. He's the world's foremost practitioner of mindless mayhem, has no regard whatsoever for the sanctity of life, and his moral sense can at best be described as depraved. What's more, he has fathered countless illegitimate children over the years. His offspring are scattered across the galaxy, growing up traumatized, hated by their peers, and unloved by the father.

In this four-part series, the children of Lobo band together, their hearts afire with the spirit of vengeance. They mean to take on the Main Man and make him pay-big time!

1-4 ....2.00

Lobo: in the Chair
DC, 1994

1 ....2.00

Lobo: I Quit
DC, 1995

1 ....3.00

Lobo/Judge Dredd: Psycho-Bikers Vs. The Mutants from Hell
DC

1 ....5.00

Lobo/Mask
DC, 1997

1-2 ....6.00

Lobo Paramilitary Christmas Special
DC, 1991

1 ....3.00

Lobo: Portrait of a Victim
DC, 1993

1 .... 2.00

Lobo's Back
DC, 1992

1-4 .... 2.00

Lobo's Big Babe Spring Break Special
DC, 1995

1 .... 2.00

Lobo the Duck
DC, 1997

1 .... 2.00

Lobo: Un-American Gladiators
DC, 1993

It's called the Maim Game, a popular TV show where the contestants face a variety of lethal challenges (including the other gladiators!) in an attempt to win cash, fame, and prizes.

Of course, anything that promises huge amounts of mayhem and destruction is sure to bring Lobo running. Chain in hand, the Main Man signs up as the star contestant. The contest becomes an interplanetary blood battle with sixteen of the universe's most deadly hombres fighting to the finish.

But is there ever any real doubt who'll be the last one standing?

1-4 .... 2.00

Lobo Unbound
DC, 2003

1-6 .... 3.00

Lobocop
DC, 1994

1 .... 2.00

Local
Oni, 2005

1-2 .... 3.00

Loco vs. Pulverine
Eclipse, 1992

1 .... 3.00

Logan: Path of the Warlord
Marvel, 1996

Before he was a member of the X-Men, before he was Wolverine, before he was Weapon X, he was a man simply called Logan. At least, that's what the cover copy would have us believe, but this scrappy, little fella was involved in all sorts of espionage and leading a life that was anything but simple. Here, we find our hero in Japan, fending off an other-dimensional threat to Earth. Even without the claws, Logan was well on his way to being the best there is at what he does. Good, intriguing stuff from writer Howard Mackie (Peter Parker: Spider-Man) and artist John-Paul Leon (Challengers of the Unknown, Earth X).

1 .... 6.00

Logan: Shadow Society
Marvel, 1996

1 .... 6.00

Logan's Run
Marvel, 1977

1 .... 5.00
2-5 .... 2.00
☞Thanos back-up
6-7 .... 15.00
7/35¢ 5.00

Logan's Run
Adventure, 1990

1-6 .... 3.00

Logan's World
Adventure, 1991
1-6..3.00

Lois Lane
DC, 1986

In many ways, this is Lois Lane's first solo title. Although she starred in the long-running Superman's Girl Friend Lois Lane, her role in that series seemed to revolve around her romantic obsession with Superman. In contrast, this two-issue series relegates Clark Kent to a few panels in the background.

Lois was out on a date when she heard the call of police sirens. Sensing a story, she ended her romantic engagement for the evening and went to investigate. The scene she had chanced upon was enough to horrify even veteran cops, as police divers pulled the waterlogged body of a small child from the South River. Although a hardened reporter, Lois was so affected by the experience that she began a quest to bring the public's attention to the problem of children being kidnapped and murdered. This series does the same, spending most of its time educating the reader about a tragedy that touches thousands of lives every year.

1-2..2.00

Loki
Marvel, 2004
1..12.00
2..6.00
3-4..4.00

Lolita
NBM
1-2..11.00
3-4..10.00

London's Dark
Titan
1 .... 9.00

Lone
Dark Horse, 2003
1-6 .... 3.00

Lone Gunmen
Dark Horse, 2001
Special 1 .... 3.00

Lonely Heart
Ajax, 1955
9 .... 40.00
10-14 .... 35.00

Lonely Nights Comics
Last Gasp
1 .... 2.00

Lonely Tombstone One Shot
Image, 2005
1 .... 6.00

Lonely War of Willy Schultz
Avalon
1-4 .... 3.00

Loner
Fleetway-Quality

One is reminded of the "Mad Max" movies from the 1980s when reading Loner. The title character doesn't trust easily as he roams the wastelands, looking for criminals. He encounters large, mutated animals and monsters along the way, which make for tougher hunts than he usually counts on. This black-and-white series originally appeared in 2000 A.D. and featured stories about the title character. Loner is a bounty hunter in a post-apocalyptic society. His bounties are not so much the story as is his arch-rival bounty hunter, Barquooth, a spike-clad, deranged lunatic who more obsessed with gunning for Loner than in bringing in the criminals.

Fleetway/Quality, famous for its reprints of the popular English comic magazine, 2000 A.D., published "Loner," a seven-issue mini-series, starting in 1990.

1-7 .... 2.00

Lone Ranger
Dell, 1948
1 .... 660.00
2 .... 360.00
3 .... 265.00
4-5 .... 230.00
6-7 .... 195.00
8 .... 275.00
☛Lone Ranger origin
9-10 .... 195.00
11-20 .... 138.00
21-30 .... 100.00
31-40 .... 75.00
41-50 .... 58.00
51-60 .... 50.00
61-70 .... 48.00
71-80 .... 38.00
81-100 .... 34.00
101-111 .... 30.00
112 .... 55.00
113-117 .... 45.00
118 .... 50.00
119-145 .... 45.00

Lone Ranger
Gold Key, 1964
1 .... 35.00
2 .... 18.00
3 .... 14.00
4-6 .... 12.00
7-10 .... 10.00
11-20 .... 9.00
21-28 .... 5.00

Lone Ranger
Pure Imagination, 1996
1 .... 3.00

Lone Ranger and Tonto
Topps, 1994
1 .... 3.00
1/Variant 4.00
2 .... 3.00
2/Variant 4.00
3-4/Variant 3.00

Lone Ranger Comics
Lone Ranger Inc., 1939
1 .... 2,450.00

Lone Ranger Golden West
Gold Key, 1966
1 .... 45.00

Lone Ranger in Milk for Big Mike
Dell, 1955
1 .... 90.00

Lone Ranger Movie Story
Dell, 1956

1 ....285.00

Lone Ranger's Companion Tonto
Dell, 1951

2	50.00
3-5	32.00
6-10	25.00
11-20	22.00
21-33	18.00

Lone Ranger's Famous Horse Hi-Yo Silver
Dell, 1952

3	45.00
4-5	32.00
6-10	25.00
11-20	21.00
21-36	18.00

Lone Ranger's Golden West
Dell, 1955

3 ....50.00

Lone Ranger's Western Treasury
Dell, 1953

1	125.00
2	100.00

Lone Rider
Superior, 1951

1	95.00
2	60.00
3-5	45.00
6-10	36.00
11-20	32.00
21-26	28.00

Lone Wolf 2100: Red Files
Dark Horse, 2003

1 ....3.00

Lone Wolf and Cub
First, 1987

1	6.00
1/2nd-1/3rd	3.00
2	4.00
2/2nd	3.00
3	4.00
3/2nd-38	3.00
39	6.00
☛Giant-size	
40	3.00
41-49	4.00

Lone Wolf and Cub
Dark Horse, 2000

1-28 ....10.00

Lone Wolf 2100
Dark Horse, 2002

1-11 ....3.00

Long Bow
Fiction House, 1951

1	85.00
2	60.00
3	50.00
4-9	40.00

Long, Hot Summer
DC, 1995

1-3 .... 3.00

Longshot
Marvel, 1985

This six-part limited series introduced readers to both Longshot, its tousled namesake, and the entire universe of Mojo-world. Both have become regular features in the X-Men/mutant titles.

Readers first meet Longshot when he crosses from dimension to elude a group of heavily armed pursuers. In crossing, however, he loses his memory and can no longer tell who he is or why he was being chased. He needn't have worried, since his pursuers, the denizens of a twisted world, named "Mojo-world" after its (literally) spineless ruler, catch up to him on Earth. Now, using only his throwing knives and his apparent power to beat impossible odds, Longshot must find a way to regain his identity and save his new world from the menace of his old one.

1	4.00
2-4	3.00
5	2.00
6	3.00

Longshot (2nd Series)
Marvel, 1998

1 .... 4.00

Longshot Comics
Slave Labor, 1995

1-2 .... 3.00

Lookers
Avatar, 1997

1-2 .... 3.00

Lookers: Slaves of Anubis
Avatar, 1998

1 .... 4.00

Looking Glass Wars: Hatter M
Image, 2006

1-4 .... 4.00

Looney Tunes: Back in Action The Movie
DC, 2003

1 .... 4.00

Looney Tunes
Gold Key, 1975

1	12.00
2	7.00
3-5	5.00
6-10	4.00
11-20	3.00
21-32	2.00
33	25.00
34	40.00
35	30.00
36-42	2.00
43-44	15.00
45-47	20.00

Looney Tunes
DC, 1994

1-190 .... 2.00

Looney Tunes and Merrie Melodies Comics
Dell, 1941

The comic book (carrying Producer Leon Schlesinger's credit line, much as Walt Disney's associated comics carried his name as their creator) of Looney Tunes and Merrie Melodies was primarily an anthology of short stories featuring characters introduced in Warner Brothers cartoons. These included Porky Pig and Bugs Bunny, of course. Even Sniffles was a Warner

Brothers character, though the comic-book creators memorably teamed the little mouse with a little girl named Mary Jane. (The idea was that she could magically become as small as the mouse and at first accomplished this by tossing magic sand over herself accompanied by the chant, "Magic sand, magic sand, make me small at my command!" When mothers complained about having to wash sand out of their children's hair, the spell was changed to "Magic words of poof, poof, piffles, make me just as small as Sniffles." It didn't work, either, but it didn't make a mess.)

Not all the characters originated in movies; "Pat, Patsy, and Pete," for example, were only to be found in comic books.

-- Maggie

1	9,500.00
2	1,750.00
3	1,100.00
4-5	850.00
6-10	575.00
11-15	425.00
16-20	350.00
21-29	265.00
30-40	200.00
41-50	140.00
51-60	110.00
61-70	85.00
71-80	60.00
81-90	45.00
91-99	32.00
100	38.00
101-110	22.00
111-120	20.00
121-130	18.00
131-140	15.00
141-150	12.00
151-170	10.00
171-200	8.00
201-221	6.00
222-246	4.00

Looney Tunes Magazine
DC, 1994

1	3.00
2-20	2.00

Loose Cannon
DC, 1995

By day, he's Eddie Walker, a crutch-bound homicide detective for the Metropolis Police Force. What really sets Walker apart, however, is the alien blood which courses through his system (as seen in the Bloodlines crossover storyline, specifically, Action Comics Ann #5). By night, this turns Walker into a gigantic blue behemoth with immense strength. Unfortunately, it also places him squarely in the middle of the battle against the alien trust, which deems him a traitor.

In this, his first mini-series, Loose Cannon must survive a collection of alien killers, while at the same time eluding the super-powered bounty hunters sent by the police, who believe he is responsible for "murdering" his alter-ego, Eddie Walker.

1-4	2.00

Loose Teeth
Fantagraphics

1-3	3.00

Lord Farris: Slavemaster
Fantagraphics, 1996

1-2	3.00

Lord Jim
Gold Key, 1965

1	18.00

Lord of the Dead
Conquest

1	3.00

Lord Pumpkin
Malibu, 1994

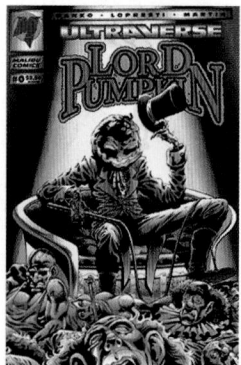

Using his dark magic, the necromancer Lord Pumpkin wreaks havoc on the people of the Godwheel, but what happens when he turns up on Earth as an amnesiac clown in a flea-bitten circus? Well, he gets the stuffing kicked out of him pretty regularly until he is befriended by a boy named Kenny, who is given the means to restore the King of Hate to his former glory. So how will Lord Pumpkin reward his young savior? Find out in this dark offering from Malibu's Ultraverse line.

0-0/A	3.00

Lord Pumpkin/ NecroMantra
Malibu, 1995

1-4	3.00

Lords
Legend (Not Dark Horse Imprint)

1	2.00

Lords of Misrule
Dark Horse, 1997

1-6	3.00

Lords of Misrule
Atomeka

1	7.00

Lords of the Ultra-Realm
DC, 1986

1-Special 1	2.00

Lore
Idea & Design Works, 2003

1	6.00
2-3	4.00
4	6.00

Lorelei
Starwarp, 1994

1	3.00

Lorelei of the Red Mist
Conquest
1-2 .... 3.00

Lori Lovecraft:
My Favorite Redhead
Caliber, 1997
1 .... 4.00

Lori Lovecraft:
Repression
A V, 2002
1 .... 3.00

Lori Lovecraft:
The Big Comeback
Caliber
1 .... 3.00

Lori Lovecraft:
The Dark Lady
Caliber
1 .... 3.00

Lorna the Jungle Girl
Atlas, 1953

Her father is a big-game hunter, now a disabled widower, and Lorna's there to help him, thanks to her expertise in hunting. Oh, yes, and she fights jungle crime and begins her cover credits as "Lorna, the Jungle Queen," soon demoted to "Lorna, the Jungle Girl." The cover of her first issue says it all: "One valiant girl, alone and unafraid, against the savage terrors of the jungle!" It's the usual stuff: headhunters, elephants, gorillas, lions, and similar jungly threats. To equip herself to best jungle mobility, she wears a knife on a belt over a sort of one-piece or two-piece swimsuit outfit that may be made out of tiger and leopard skins. She also wears one of those necklaces made of predator teeth. Oh, yes, and there's a romantic tension between big-game-hunter Greg Knight and Lorna.

-- *Maggie*

1 .... 265.00
2 .... 185.00
3 .... 165.00
4-5 .... 140.00
6-10 .... 110.00
11-14 .... 75.00
15-19 .... 60.00
20-26 .... 50.00

Lortnoc
Radio, 1998
1 .... 3.00

Losers
DC, 2003
1-32 .... 3.00

Losers Special
DC, 1985

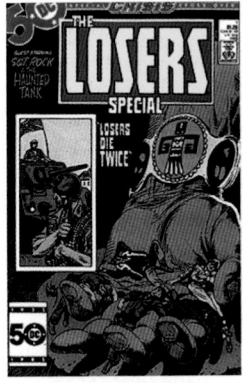

The Losers were some of DC's best-loved war comics characters. First appearing in G.I. Combat #138, their number included Gunner and Sarge, ill-fated P.T. boat commander Capt. Storm, and Native American Johnny Cloud. All of them had seen those they fought with die, while somehow, they survived. But survival never felt like victory when the costs were so high - thus they called themselves "the Losers."

The gang was united for one final special (the first title to bear their name). Unfortunately, this was to be their swan song. After relating the origins of the various team members, the special told the tale of their final battle. The Losers finally met their end, in a special edition that tied in with the Crisis On Infinite Earths, DC's ultimate universe-destroying event.

1 .... 3.00

Lost and Found Season of the Most PopeJoey
Abanne, 2001
1 .... 3.00

Lost Angel
Caliber
1 .... 3.00

Lost
Caliber, 1996
1-2 .... 3.00

Lost
Chaos, 1997
1-3 .... 3.00

Lost Continent
Eclipse, 1990
1-6 .... 4.00

Lost Girl
NBM
1 .... 10.00

Lost Girls
Kitchen Sink, 1995
1-2 .... 6.00

Lost Heroes
Davdez, 1998
0-4 .... 3.00

Lost in Space
Innovation, 1991
1-12 .... 3.00
13 .... 4.00
13/Gold 5.00
14-Ann 2 .... 3.00
Special 1 .... 4.00
Special 2 .... 3.00

Lost in Space
Dark Horse, 1998
1-3 .... 3.00

Lost in Space:
Project Robinson
Innovation, 1993

This two-issue title is a "mini-series-within-a-series," taking place between the events of Lost In Space #12 and #13. The purpose is to give us a retrospective on the lives of Dr. Maureen Robinson and Professor John Robinson. Fans recognize this pair as the married couple who, along with their family, were trapped on an off-course spaceship, becoming "Lost In Space." This series reveals what they were like before the tragedy, including Maureen's love of science and rock and roll music, and telling the story of how John and Maureen met and fell in love.

1 ....3.00

Lost in the Alps
NBM

1 ....14.00

Lost Laughter
Bad Habit, 1994

1-4 ....3.00

Lost Ones
Image, 2000

1 ....3.00

Lost Ones, The: For Your Eyes Only
Image, 2000

1 ....1.00

Lost Planet
Eclipse, 1987

Filled with dragons, pointy-eared forest dwellers, and lots of magic, this intricate fantasy mini-series reads like a well-plotted game of Advanced Dungeons & Dragons.

A wizard, an Air Force pilot, and a young woman on a mysterious quest join forces on a "lost planet" accessible only through magic corridors. As Ambrose Bierce, a self-taught wizard who disappeared from Earth in 1914, tells them, when the evil Zorrin family conquered the planet Iriel, they killed its scientists so it could be dominated by the Zorrins' magic. Before they can return to Earth, the heroes have to destroy the lotus potion which subjugates the world's populace to the Zorrins' will.

1-6 ....2.00

Lost Squad
Devil's Due, 2005

1-5 ....3.00

Lost Universe (Gene Roddenberry's...)
Tekno, 1995

0-7 ....2.00

Lost World
Millennium, 1996

1-2 ....3.00

Lost World, The: Jurassic Park
Topps, 1997

1-3 ....3.00

Lost Worlds
Standard, 1952

5 .... 150.00
6 .... 120.00

Lothar
Powerhouse Graphics, 1995

1 ....3.00

Loud Cannoli
Crazyfish

1 ....3.00

Louder than Words (Sergio Aragonès')
Dark Horse, 1997

1-6 ....3.00

Louie the Rune Soldier
ADV Manga, 2004

1-4 .... 10.00

Louis Riel
Drawn & Quarterly, 2000

1-5 ....3.00

Louis vs. Ali
Revolutionary, 1993

1 ....3.00

Love Adventures
Marvel, 1949

1 .... 90.00
2 .... 70.00
3 .... 60.00
4-5 .... 50.00
6-12 .... 40.00

Love and Marriage
Superior, 1952

1 .... 60.00
2 .... 35.00
3-5 .... 24.00
6-10 .... 20.00
11-16 .... 16.00

Love & Rockets
Fantagraphics, 1982

1 .... 25.00
1/2nd-1/3rd............................. 4.00
1/4th-1/5th............................. 5.00
2 .... 12.00
2/2nd 4.00
2/3rd 5.00

3	9.00
3/2nd	4.00
4	8.00
4/2nd-4/3rd	4.00
5	7.00
5/2nd	3.00
6	5.00
6/2nd	3.00
7	5.00
7/2nd	3.00
8	5.00
8/2nd	3.00
9	5.00
9/2nd	3.00
10	5.00
10/2nd	3.00
11	4.00
11/2nd	3.00
12	4.00
12/2nd	3.00
13	4.00
13/2nd	3.00
14	4.00
14/2nd	3.00
15	4.00
15/2nd-20	3.00
21-27	2.00
28-29	3.00
29/2nd	2.00
30-39	3.00
40	4.00
41-49	3.00
50	5.00

Love & Rockets
Fantagraphics, 2001

1 ....6.00
2-9 ....4.00
10 ....6.00
11-15 ....5.00

Love & Rockets Bonanza
Fantagraphics, 1989

1-1/2nd 3.00

Love and Romance
Charlton, 1971

Love and Romance is a relatively late entry into the romance comics genre, appearing the early 70s when all but a few girl-oriented comics had been crowded off the stands by legions of superheroes. The best that can be said of Love and Romance is that it competently executes the formula of slick, sexless art and cloying sentimentally that typified American romance comics since the 1950s.

1	24.00
2	16.00
3-5	12.00
6-10	8.00
11-20	6.00
21-24	4.00

Love as a Foreign Language
Oni, 2005

1-4	7.00

Love at First Sight
Ace, 1949

1	85.00
2	50.00
3-9	30.00
10-20	25.00
21-35	20.00
36-43	15.00

Love Bites
Fantagraphics, 1991

1-2	2.00

Love Bites
Radio, 2000

1	3.00

Love Bomb
Abaculus

1-2	3.00

Love Bug
Gold Key, 1969

1	15.00

Lovebunny & Mr. Hell: Day in the Love Life
Image, 2003

1	3.00

Lovebunny & Mr. Hell: Savage Love
Image, 2003

1	3.00

Love Classics
Marvel, 1949

1	75.00
2	65.00

Love Confessions
Quality, 1949

"I stole my way into a career! But I couldn't steal romance!" "As I dreamed of Bill's passionate kisses on my lips, my cold selfishness melted away!" (See Princess of the Five and Ten.) "I plunged headlong toward ecstasy -- only to encounter disaster! (Read Torment.) "I had to choose between two ways of life -- work and worry or champagne and mink -- " (Read The man I Choose.)

This was the sort of cover copy typical of newsstand magazines of the day, and Quality happily adopted it for its covers. One intriguing evolution of Love Confession's covers was from line art to photo covers, some featuring such stars of the day as Van Johnson, Jane Russell, and Robert Mitchum.

-- Maggie

1	150.00
2	125.00
3-5	50.00
6-9	35.00
10	50.00
11-20	40.00
21-30	30.00
31-39	25.00
40-54	20.00

Lovecraft
DC, 2004

1	25.00

Lovecraft
Adventure, 1992

1-4	3.00

Love Diary
Our Publishing, 1949

1	90.00
2	60.00
3	50.00
4-5	30.00
6-10	25.00
11-20	22.00
21-30	16.00
31-40	13.00
41-48	10.00

Love Diary
Quality, 1949

1	165.00

Love Diary
Charlton, 1958

1	45.00
2	24.00
3-4	16.00
5	14.00
6	20.00
7-10	14.00
11-15	12.00
16-20	10.00
21-30	7.00
31-40	5.00
41-60	4.00
61-102	3.00

Love Dramas
Marvel, 1949

1	90.00
2	70.00

Love Eternal: A Tortured Soul
Vlad Ent.

1	2.00

Love Experiences
Ace, 1949

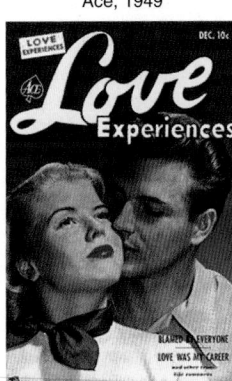

Maudlin, sentimental, and rigorously moralistic, love comics such as Love Experiences helped indoctrinate a generation of young girls with the rigid expectations and narrow sexual roles prescribed for them by mainstream American society during the 1950s.

Stories like "Blamed by Everyone," "I'll Follow My Man," and "Love Was My Career" taught readers that women who were assertive, personally ambitious, intelligent, or aspired to anything beyond suburban housewifedom were doomed to lose the man of their dreams and even wind up as the ultimate social pariah, the "old spinster." Text features like "Help Yourself to Glamour" (featuring "Top Secrets of Popular Girls," and

"Beauty on a Budget") provided guidance on how best to achieve the feminine ideals set forth in the stories.

1	60.00
2	30.00
3-5	22.00
6-10	16.00
11-20	13.00
21-30	11.00
31-38	10.00

Love Fantasy
Renegade

1	2.00

Love Hina
Tokyopop, 2002

1-5	3.00

Love in Tights
Slave Labor, 1998

1	3.00

Love Journal
Our, 1951

10	50.00
11-20	25.00
21-25	20.00

Loveland
Marvel, 1949

1	45.00
2	40.00

Loveless
DC, 2005

1-14	3.00

Love Lessons
Harvey, 1949

1	75.00
2	40.00
3-5	30.00

Love Letters
Quality, 1949

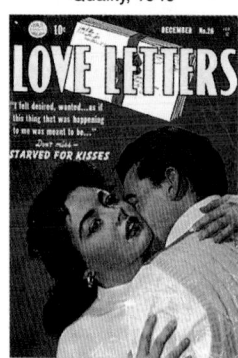

The late 1940s are generally thought of as a low point in comics history because of the demise of the Golden Age super-heroes and funny-animal comics, but in fact comics never before and rarely since enjoyed a larger, more diverse, and more adult readership than in those years. As a result, several genres, including romance, crime, and horror comics, emerged to cater to older readers, with more sophisticated stories and themes and a harder edge to their material. Love Letters, from Quality Comics, came out quickly on the heels of the first romance comics from Simon and Kirby, Young Love and Young Romance. Love Letters took its cue from those pioneering titles, offering bittersweet tales of temptation, betrayal, class conflict, and emotional violence that belied the image of sappy sentimentalism that later overtook the genre. Artists like Bill Ward and Reed Crandall helped lift the standard even higher.

-- Rob Salkowitz

1	110.00
2	85.00
3	60.00
4	80.00
5-11	20.00
12-20	16.00
21-48	12.00
49-50	35.00
51	24.00

Love Letters in the Hand
Fantagraphics, 1991

1-2	2.00
3	3.00

Lovelorn
ACG, 1949

Subtitled "Stirring stories of real romance," the series featured tales of such torment as the heroine's trying to decide which truly pays off, love or money (in "My Heart Went Astray"). Early issues cover-featured major traumas for the characters shown; some later ones were more decoratively devoted to clinches simple (on the Coney Island Ferry) and complex (both kissing while on trapezes).

In the mid-1950s, ACG faced up to the challenge presented by 3-D comics by announcing a "TrueVision" story in the issue. Boasting "Full color!" and "No glasses!" the approach consisted of having characters depicted in front of their panel borders.

-- Maggie

1	65.00
2-3	40.00
4-5	35.00
6-10	30.00
11-20	24.00
21-30	22.00
31-39	18.00
40-51	15.00

Lovely as a Lie
Illustration, 1994

1	3.00

Lovely Ladies
Caliber

1	4.00

Lovely Prudence
All the Rage, 1995

1-3	3.00

Love Memories
Fawcett, 1949

1	70.00
2-4	40.00

Love Me Tenderloin
Dark Horse, 2004

1	3.00

Love Mystery
Fawcett, 1950

1	100.00
2	75.00
3	65.00

Love or Money
Tokyopop, 2004

1-4	10.00

Love Problems
Fox

1	125.00

Love Romances
Timely, 1949

6	100.00
7-10	75.00
11-50	65.00
51-59	60.00
60-70	48.00
71-80	42.00
81-100	36.00
101-106	32.00

Lovers
Marvel, 1949

23	70.00
24-25	40.00
26-40	30.00
41-60	24.00
61-70	20.00
71-86	18.00

Lovers' Lane
Lev Gleason, 1949

1	50.00
2	30.00
3-5	22.00
6-10	16.00
11-20	12.00
21-30	10.00
31-41	8.00

Love Scandals
Quality, 1950

1	175.00
2-5	100.00

Love Secrets
Marvel, 1949

1	75.00
2	50.00

Love Secrets
Quality, 1953

32-56	12.00

Love Stories
DC, 1972

147-152	8.00

Love Stories of Mary Worth
Harvey, 1949

1	40.00
2-5	25.00

Love Sucks
Ace

Created by Kevin Hayes and Jay Juch, and published by Ace Comics, Love Sucks centers its self-contained, black-and-white stories on Nelson, Adrian, and Wendy, three single friends and their relationship woes in New York City.

Each character represents a facet of American dating. Nelson is sensitive and dependent, just coming out of a serious relationship and feeling he will never embrace that love again. Adrian is the self-proclaimed ladies' man, cocky and brash-he

has no trouble meeting the women-it's the part after that scares him to death. The beautiful Wendy can't get a break: every guy who looks like a dream ends up a nightmare.

Funny anecdotes and witty narratives, like how Nelson earned the name "Submarine Boy" in a drunken bar scene, or how Adrian was beaten up by his lover's girlfriend, adds to the realism.

1	3.00

Love Tales
Marvel, 1949

36	75.00
37	50.00
38-40	40.00
41-50	36.00
51-60	32.00
61-70	28.00
71-75	25.00

Love Trails
Marvel, 1949

1	75.00
2	65.00

Lowlife
Caliber, 1994

1-4	3.00

L.T. Caper
Spotlight

Perhaps taking a cue from TV's "Inspector Gadget," Spotlight Comics offers up L.T. Caper, Agent for H.E.R.O. (the Higher Espionage Reinforcement Organization) and his canine assistant Proto. As he matches wits with Dr. Phoenix and the Green Shadow, Caper remains cool, always seeing that justice is done. The title also offers up reprints of Jim Aparo's early 1960s comic strip "Stern Wheeler," which features a hip and swingin' supersleuth.

1	2.00

Luba
Fantagraphics, 1998

1-3	3.00
4-9	4.00

Lucifer
DC, 2000

1	4.00
2-49	3.00
50	4.00
51-74	3.00
75	4.00

Lucifer
Trident, 1990

1-3	2.00

Lucifer: Nirvana
DC, 2002

1	6.00

Lucifer's Hammer
Innovation, 1993

1-6	3.00

Luck of the Draw
Radio, 2000

1	4.00

Lucky
Howard, 1945

1	300.00

Lucky 7
Howard, 1944

1	225.00

Lucky 7
Runaway Graphics, 1993

1	2.00

Lucky Comics
Holyoke, 1944

1	150.00
2	125.00
3-5	75.00

Lucky Duck
Standard, 1953

5	50.00
6-8	35.00

Lucky Fights It Through
E.C., 1949

1	750.00

Lucky Luke: Jesse James
Fantasy Flight

1	9.00

Lucky Luke: The Stage Coach
Fantasy Flight

1	9.00

Lucky Star
Nationwide, 1950

1	60.00
2	45.00
3-5	36.00
6-14	28.00

Lucy Show
Gold Key, 1963
1..65.00
2..40.00
3-5..32.00

Ludwig Von Drake
Dell, 1961
1..16.00
2..10.00
3-4...8.00

Luftwaffe: 1946 Technical Manual
Antarctic, 1998

This nicely illustrated special gives the detailed specifications of the various craft seen in the "Projekt Saucer" storyline that ran through early issues of Luftwaffe: 1946 (Vol. 2). In addition to the technical drawings and descriptions, it includes summaries of "foo fighter" sightings over German airspace which were at first thought to be some sort of strange new German superweapon. Creator Ted Nomura seized on this concept for the Projekt Saucer storyline, incorporating the flying discs into his vision of an alternate world where Germany was victorious in World War II.

1-2...4.00

Luftwaffe: 1946
Antarctic, 1996
1...5.00
2-Ann 1 ....4.00

Luftwaffe: 1946
Antarctic, 1997
1-4..4.00
5...3.00
Special 1- 2 ....4.00

Luftwaffe: 1946
Antarctic, 2002
1-17..6.00

Luftwaffe 1946
Antarctic, 2005
1-3... 6.00

Luger
Eclipse, 1986
1-3... 2.00

Lugh, Lord of Light
Flagship, 1987

In the idyllic land of Tir-Na-Nog, peace is symbolized by a field of contentedly grazing unicorns. So when a ferocious dragon shows up and starts killing the lot of them, it's clear that trouble is coming with it. Lugh and his fellow warriors are determined to meet the challenge, even as it threatens their entire land and forces them each to travel to other dimensions on a mystical quest for the magical, all-protecting heart of Danu, Mother to them all. Their journey will set them at odds with all manners of demons and villains, as well as an unexpected traitor from within. As the most powerful of his brethren, Lugh's quest will take him further than that of anyone else--to America of the late 20th century.

This fast-paced, character-rich, and imaginative adventure is published in black-and-white.

1-4... 2.00

Lugo
Lost Boys
1/2 .... 1.00

Lullaby
Alias, 2005
1... 3.00

Lullaby: Wisdom Seeker
Image, 2005
1 .... 3.00
1/B cover 4.00
2 .... 3.00
2/B cover 4.00
3-4 .... 3.00

Lumenagerie
NBM
1 .... 12.00

Lum Urusei*Yatsura
Viz
1 .... 5.00
2-8 .... 4.00

Lunar Donut
Lunar Donut, 1997
0-6 .... 3.00

Lunatic Binge
Eternity

Sporting a cover by classic Mad and Cracked artist Jack Davis, Lunatic Binge is a horror anthology in the tradition of E.C.'s Tales from the Crypt. There's everything from the frightening (we learn what really leads to finding a single shoe in a public place) to the absurd (a man marries Siamese twins and murders one of them.) It's an interesting bit of weirdness from the folks at Triad Publications.

1-2 .... 4.00

Lunatic Fringe
Innovation, 1989
1-2 .... 2.00

Lunatik
Marvel, 1995
1-3 .... 2.00

Lurid
Idea & Design Works, 2003
1-3 .... 3.00

Lurid Tales
Fantagraphics
1 .... 3.00

Lust
Fantagraphics, 1997
1-6 .... 3.00

Lust for Life
Slave Labor, 1997
-4 .... 3.00

Lust of the Nazi Weasel Women
Fantagraphics, 1991

Fantagraphics continues their publication of off-beat material with this four-issue series featuring famed pilot Crash Callahan. It seems however that Crash is having an identity crisis: at least that's what his ventriloquist buddy with the Italian accent thinks. Insane antics and snappy banter abound in this comic which features a greedy dog who nearly kills his owner and a wooden dummy with a big mouth and an insult for everything. There may even be a few Nazi Weasel Women lurking about.

1-4 .... 2.00

Lux & Alby Sign on and Save the Universe
Dark Horse, 1993
1-9 .... 3.00

Luxura & Vampfire
Brainstorm
1 .... 3.00

Luxura Collection (Kirk Lindo's...)
Brainstorm
1 .... 5.00

Luxura Leather Special
Brainstorm, 1996
1 .... 3.00

Lycanthrope Leo
Viz
1-7 .... 3.00

Lyceum
Hunter, 1996
1-2 .... 3.00

Lycra-Woman and Spandex-Girl
Comic Zone, 1992

Lycra-Woman, the city's greatest super-heroine, sees herself as a symbol of justice and a defender of the innocent. Her new sidekick, Spandex-Girl, just wants to be a sex symbol.

Racing to the scene of the latest crime in their Aerobic Mobile, they'll face down deadly villains like the fashion-conscious Prima Donna, the all male G.Q. Squad, the humorless Madame Adhesive, and the insipid Bell Belle. It's time for action, ladies! Spanderiffic!

This series is co-created and illustrated by Michael Avon Oeming.

1 .... 3.00

Lycra Woman and Spandex Girl Christmas '77 Special
Comic Zone
1 .... 3.00

Lycra Woman and Spandex Girl Halloween Special
Lost Cause
1 .... 3.00

Lycra Woman and Spandex Girl Jurassic Dinosaur Special
Comic Zone
1 .... 3.00

Lycra Woman and Spandex Girl Summer Vacation Special
Comic Zone
1 .... 3.00

Lycra Woman and Spandex Girl Time Travel Special
Comic Zone
1 .... 3.00

Lycra Woman and Spandex Girl Valentine Special
Comic Zone
1 .... 3.00

Lynch
Image, 1997
1 .... 3.00

Lynch Mob
Chaos, 1994

The year is 2048 and the Earth is in ruins. The words "hero" and "villain" are archaic terms from a time long-forgotten. When Ameri-corp, a multinational organization that purchased what was once America, needs to protect their "interests," they call on the Lynch Mob, a team of mechanically and genetically augmented parahumans.

When an organism of pure electrical energy created by Ameri-corp escapes and assumes control of the world's computer net, the Mob is called on to retrieve it. But when the organism decides it must either destroy the already-ruined world or return the world to a simpler time, the Lynch Mob discovers they have to prevent both Armageddon and the unraveling of the time stream.

With the debut of over 50 original superpowered characters, this four-issue mini-series was a pivotal event in the Chaos! universe.

1-4 .... 3.00

Lynx: An Elflord Tale
Peregrine Entertainment, 1999
1 .... 3.00

Alan Moore revived England's version of Captain Marvel as Marvelman,
before Marvel Comics asked for a name change.

M
Eclipse, 1990

Young children are being killed by a brutal murderer. The police can't figure out who it is. Mobsters are perplexed. Unions are in a panic. A chain reaction has begun with desperation and suspicion making an entire city suspicious of every shadow, every person.

Jon Muth has put together a murder mystery of mood and suspense that captures the feel of Fritz Lang's classic 1931 German motion picture.

1-3 .... 5.00
4 .... 6.00

Maburaho
ADV Manga, 2005
1 .... 10.00

Macabre
Lighthouse, 1989

This black-and-white horror anthology title from Lighthouse Publications features some creepy, ultraviolent, overtly sexual tales. For example, a young woman finds that her haunted dreams have become a reality as she becomes a vessel through which a demon's evil spawn can enter the world. In another story, the horrors of war are examined. Definitely for mature readers!

1-6 .... 3.00

Macabre (Vol. 2)
Lighthouse, 1989
1-2 .... 3.00

Macbeth (William Shakespeare's...)
Black Dog & Leventhal, 2006
1 .... 13.00

Mace: Bounty Hunter
Image, 2003
1 .... 3.00

M.A.C.H. 1
Fleetway-Quality
1-9 .... 2.00

Machine
Dark Horse, 1994
1-4 .... 3.00

Machine Man
Marvel, 1978

Springing from the pages of Marvel's bizarre "adaptation" of 2001, Jack Kirby's Machine Man was originally known by his experiment number: X-51. The brainchild of Dr. Abel Stack, Machine Man was the first and only success of an experiment to create robotic life. In all ways that matter, X-51 had become a living, sentient creature

Dr. Stack raised X-51 as if he were his own son. When he was given the order to terminate the experiment, Stack sacrificed his own life to save the life of X-51.

In this series, Steve Ditko follows the robot as he finds refuge with friends Peter Spaulding and Gears Garvin and tries to make a "normal" life for himself.

1 .... 3.00
2-18 .... 2.00
☛Alpha Flight app.
19 .... 13.00
☛1st Jack O'Lantern

Machine Man
Marvel, 1984
1-4 .... 2.00

Machine Man/ Bastion '98
Marvel, 1998

1 ....3.00

Machine Man 2020
Marvel, 1994

1-2..2.00

Machine Teen
Marvel, 2005

1-5..3.00

Mack Bolan: The Executioner (Don Pendleton's...)
Innovation, 1993

1 ....3.00
1/A-1/B 4.00
2-4...3.00

Mackenzie Queen
Matrix

1-5..2.00

Mack the Knife: Monochrome Memories
Caliber

1 ....3.00

Macross II
Viz, 1992

1-10...3.00

Macross II: The Micron Conspiracy
Viz, 1995

1-5..3.00

Mad
E.C., 1952

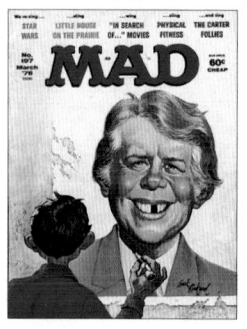

This series, carrying the spine-long text "Humor in a jugular vein" and the top-of-cover lead-in "Tales calculated to drive you," was one of two of Editor Harvey Kurtzman's major projects at E.C. (The other was Frontline Combat.)

Mad began as a color comic book, shifted to black-and-white magazine format with #24. Several of the early covers were by Kurtzman, and the satiric title carried parodies even on many of its covers.

The face of "Alfred E. Neuman" as connected with Mad actually appeared first on a collection of Mad reprints from publisher Ballantine Books (The Mad Reader); the first use of the image in Mad itself appeared on the cover of #21. Issue #23 carried a notification of the upcoming change in format.

The comic book's topics ran from Archie to Gasoline Alley, from Sherlock Holmes to Flash Gordon, from G.I. Joe to Pogo, and from Mickey Mouse to The Shadow. No issue of Mad carried the seal of the Comics Magazine Association of America.

When the shift came to the magazine format, more text was introduced and initial contributions from such mainstream comedy sources as Bob and Ray, Ernie Kovacs, and Tom Lehrer appeared. Kurtzman departed, Al Feldstein took over as editor, and the title continues to this day, with "What -- Me Worry?" kid Neuman as a mascot and satire directed more toward media and society than other comic art staples. Entire books have been devoted to the series.

-- Maggie

1 .... 5,000.00
2 .... 1,250.00
3 .... 725.00
4 .... 700.00
5 .... 1,200.00
☛Low distribution
6-11 .... 525.00
12-19 .... 425.00
20-23 .... 300.00
24 .... 785.00
☛1st magazine issue
25 .... 300.00
26-27 .... 250.00
28-29 .... 225.00
30 .... 350.00
31 .... 200.00
32 .... 175.00
33 .... 165.00
34-35 .... 140.00
36-40 .... 110.00
41-50 .... 80.00
51-60 .... 60.00
61-70 .... 48.00
71-80 .... 36.00
81-100 .... 32.00
101-120 .... 18.00
121 .... 22.00
122 .... 18.00
123-140 .... 15.00
141-150 .... 12.00
151-160 .... 9.00
161-170 .... 8.00

171-189 .... 7.00
190-200 .... 5.00
201-220 .... 4.00
221-260 .... 3.00
261-342 .... 2.00
343-417 .... 3.00
418-501 .... 4.00

Mad 2992
Graphic Image

Ashcan 2 .... 1.00

Mad About Millie
Marvel, 1969

Millie the Model began her long run in 1945, and her "home" series ended in 1973. Marvel published several Millie titles over the years: Life with Millie, A Date with Millie, and this one, Mad about Millie, which ran from 1969 until 1970. Millie is a fashion model who gets into all sorts of Archie Andrews-esque situations, including competitions with her Reggie Mantle-esque rival, Chili. Like Archie comics, the Millie titles are designed to appeal to younger teens, particularly girls, and their emphasis is on lighthearted fun. Because this title's short run fell in the heart of the bell-bottom era, the fashions are indicative of the early 1970s: lots of beads, flared pants legs, and wild prints. And, hey, many of the stories were written by Stan "The Man" Lee himself!

1 .... 50.00
2 .... 35.00
3 .... 30.00
4-5 .... 18.00
6-9 .... 15.00
10-17 .... 14.00
Ann 1 .... 20.00

Madagascar
Tokyopop, 2005

1 .... 8.00

Madame Xanadu
DC, 1981

Mysterious and dark, she inhabits a strange shop in the middle of a small village. To her customers, she is known as Madame Xanadu, reader of the Tarot. Unlike so many charlatans, Madame Xanadu is able to look into the future, and into people's souls by her readings of the cards. She uses this knowledge to help people, although not always in the way they had imagined.

After appearing as a minor character in a number of DC series, this one-shot showcase gave the fortune-teller a chance to shine on her own.

1 ....3.00

Madballs
Marvel, 1986
1-10..1.00

Mad Classics
DC, 2005
1-12..5.00

Mad-Dog
Marvel, 1993
1-6...1.00

Mad Dog Magazine
Blackthorne, 1986
1-3...2.00

Mad Dogs
Eclipse, 1992

Guy Brennen was a burnt-out ex-cop who felt he had nothing left to live for. In his day, he had been one of the good guys who had played the game a little too hard for the department's liking. Then Carla died, and the game didn't seem worth playing at all...

His redemption came when an old friend offered him a new job: heading up a special strike force that would report directly to the district attorney. This strike force would be comprised of other ex-cops like Brennen-rough and tumble types who were good at bringing criminals to justice, but bad at following rules. This crew had each been cops 24 hours a day, and when they were thrown off the force they had no place else to go. Brennen offered them the same deal he had been given: a second chance at being a cop-but this time with no department rules or politics. All they had to do was take on the worst criminal kingpins in the city.

1-3 .... 3.00

Mad Follies
E.C., 1963
1 .... 250.00
2 .... 200.00
3 .... 150.00
4-7 .... 100.00

Mad Hatter
O.W., 1946
1 .... 550.00
2 .... 245.00

Mad House
Red Circle, 1974
95-96.................................... 4.00
97-130.................................. 3.00

Madhouse
Ajax, 1954
1 .... 95.00
2-4 .... 55.00

Madhouse Glads
Archie, 1970
73-77 .... 3.00
78-92 .... 5.00
93-94 .... 3.00

Madhouse Ma-ad Freakout
Archie, 1969
71-72 .... 3.00

Madhouse Ma-ad Jokes
Archie, 1969
66-70 .... 4.00

Mad Kids
DC, 2005
1-5 .... 5.00

Madman
Tundra, 1992

Mike Allred's Madman is one of the strongest and strangest comics of the 1990s. Madman is a disturbed young man who goes around in a baggy costume and a mask with the mouth sewn shut. He has an unusual sensitivity that allows him to sense guilty secrets within people, but his inability to focus and concentrate gets him into all kinds of trouble. Allred's handling of the material maximizes the disturbing qualities of the story, as he abruptly intrudes on an amusing sequence with an intensely violent image or inserts a subversive element that makes the reader doubt the entire sense of reality Allred has created in Madman's world. This psychotic, detached ambiguity is Madman's singular achievement and one which gives it a literary gravity that is impossible to ignore.

-- Rob Salkowitz

1 ....8.00
1/4th-1/2nd 5.00
1/3rd 4.00
2-3 ....6.00

Madman Adventures
Tundra, 1992

1 ....5.00
2-3 ....4.00

Madman Comics
Dark Horse, 1994

1-3 ....4.00
4-20 ....3.00
YB 1995 ....18.00

Madman Picture Exhibition
AAA Pop, 2002

1-4 ....4.00

Madman/The Jam
Dark Horse, 1998

1-2 ....3.00

Mad Monster Party
Dell, 1967

1 ....40.00

Mad Monster Party Adaptation
Black Bear

1-4 ....3.00

Madonna
Personality

1 ....3.00
2 ....3.00

Madonna Sex Goddess
Friendly, 1990

1-3 ....3.00

Madonna Special
Revolutionary, 1993

1 ....3.00

Madonna vs. Marilyn
Celebrity

1 ....3.00

Mad Raccoons
Mu, 1991

1-6 ....3.00

Madraven Halloween Special
Hamilton, 1995

The Madraven Halloween Special is somewhat reminiscent of both E.C.'s Tales from the Crypt and DC's House of Mystery. Marleen, a young woman who is a Silkie (a legendary race of humans who can turn into seals...or seals who can turn into humans), is seeking out the scantily clad, Elvira-esque Madraven, a master of all things paranormal, to help her solve the mystery of her people's demise at the...um... tentacles of the Kraken. Kind of a wonky story, to be sure, but there's some nice artwork from Gray Morrow (Lois Lane, Jonah Hex), Jan Duursema (Incredible Hulk, Professor Xavier and the X-Men), and Batton Lash (Wolff & Byrd: Counselors of the Macabre). Hey, there's even an appearance by Lash's lovable attorneys-at-law!

1 .... 3.00

Madrox
Marvel, 2004

1-5 .... 3.00

Mad Super Special
E.C., 1970

1 .... 90.00
2 .... 54.00
3-5 .... 44.00
6-10 .... 38.00
11-15 .... 26.00
16-20 .... 20.00
21-25 .... 16.00
26-30 .... 12.00
31-40 .... 10.00
41-50 .... 6.00
51-60 .... 5.00
61-135 .... 4.00

Mad TV
E.C., 2000

1 .... 4.00

Mad XL
E.C., 2000

This 100-page series from "the Usual Gang of Idiots" offers up some classic Mad bits, from "Spy Vs. Spy" to the brilliant Don Martin's single page gags, e.g. "One Fine Morning in a Playpen," "One Fine Day Crosstown." Writer/artist Dave Berg's "The Lighter Side of..." series is also represented here, as are Sergio AragonTs' margin doodles. Mad XL also looks at the life of E.C. mastermind William M. Gaines. This is an excellent collection for longtime Mad readers, as well as those wishing to dip a foot in the pool.

1-33 .... 5.00

Mael's Rage
Ominous, 1994

2-2/Variant 3.00

Maelstrom
Aircel, 1987

1-10 .... 2.00

Magdalena
Image, 2000

1-3/A 3.00

Magdalena
Image, 2003

1 .... 3.00
1/A 5.00
2-4 .... 3.00

Magdalena/Angelus
Image, 2001

0-1/2 .... 3.00

Magdalena/Vampirella
Image, 2003

1 .... 3.00

Mage
Comico, 1984

Matt Wagner's Mage is a complex mix of mythology and action-adventure. Its hero is a man named Kevin, who finds himself reluctantly cast as a hero, then discovers he is unable to part with the power once he has it. On the surface, Mage is about Kevin's struggle against shapeshifters called the Gracklefinks. But the true story is played out on many levels, as Kevin discovers his true role as a latter-day King Arthur and realizes that his enemies are agents of a primal evil.

Wagner's Grendel plays a pivotal role in this series (and, indeed, is killed in #13). Fans of the Grendel series would be well advised to check out Mage, as well.

1	5.00
2	4.00
3-5	3.00
6	15.00

☛1st Grendel

7	8.00
8	4.00
9-12	3.00
13	4.00
14	3.00
15	6.00

Mage
Image, 1997

0	3.00
1	4.00
1/3D	5.00
2-3	4.00
4-15	3.00
15/Variant	6.00

Magebook
Comico, 1985

1	9.00
2	8.00

Mage Knight: Stolen Destiny
Idea & Design Works, 2002

1-5 .... 4.00

Mage: The Hero Discovered
Image, 1998

1-8 .... 5.00

Maggie and Hopey Color Special
Fantagraphics, 1997

1 .... 4.00

Maggie the Cat
Image, 1996

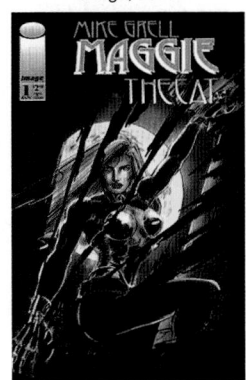

No, this title had nothing to do with Cat on a Hot Tin Roof. Aristocratic Lady Margaret took up cat burglary to retrieve her precious heirloom jewelry, which her profligate and now-dead husband was in the habit of presenting to his mistresses. In this series, her skills have caught the eye of Britain's special services. She's recruited to an anti-terrorist task force and given clever gadgets (think James Bond) to do whatever she needs to do.

Artist-creator Mike Grell (Warlord, Starslayer) first introduced Maggie the Cat in Jon Sable, Freelance in the early 1980s. This is his second title for Image, after the well-received Shaman's Tears.

1-4 .... 3.00

Maggots
Hamilton, 1991

1-3 .... 4.00

Magical Mates
Antarctic, 1996

This manga tale-translated into English-is the story of three unusual girls. Kana Watanabe, a Kokuso Junior High 9th-grader who uses her powerful charms in her battle against evil. Noemi Hi'l, an 11th-grader who is packed with sex appeal and a good bit of magic; and Rinko Miyamoto, another freshman who read the tarot cards to learn the future. This is a cute and entertaining story from Antarctic Press.

1-9 .... 3.00

Magical Nymphini
Rip Off, 1991

1-5/2nd 3.00

Magical Twilight
Graphic Visions

1 .... 3.00

Magic Boy and Girlfriend
Top Shelf, 1998

1 .... 9.00

Magic Boy & the Robot Elf
Slave Labor, 1996

1 .... 10.00

Magic Carpet
Shanda Fantasy Arts, 1999

1 .... 5.00

Magic Comics
David McKay, 1939

1	2,800.00
2	1,150.00
3	685.00
4	415.00
5	330.00
6-11	275.00
12-20	210.00
21-30	130.00
31-40	95.00

41-50	75.00
51-60	58.00
61-80	46.00
81-100	40.00
101-123	34.00

Magic Flute
Eclipse, 1990

1-3 ....5.00

Magicians' Village
Mad Monkey, 1995

1 ....2.00

Magic Inkwell
Comic Strip Theatre
Moordam, 1998

1 ....3.00

Magicman
A-Plus

This black-and-white reprint series from ACG resurrects Magicman, a supernatural crime fighter who was featured in seventeen issues of Forbidden Worlds during the super-hero craze of the mid-1960s. Magicman was the immortal son of a great sorcerer who was arrested for witchcraft in 1789. Vowing never to use magic because of its horrible consequences, Magicman kicked around the world for a few hundred years, doing various odd jobs, until he discovered that his powers could serve to further the cause of justice. Thus, Magicman was born.

1 ....3.00

Magic Pickle
Oni, 2001

1-4 ....3.00

Magic Priest
Antarctic, 1998

1 ....3.00

Magic: The Gathering: Antiquities War
Acclaim, 1995

This four-issue mini-series is set in a time and place which is only now rediscovering the technology that was lost ages before, and exists now only as artifacts. Two brothers, Uzra and Mishra, have discovered the power source for these great relics, and eventually find themselves custodians of two great crystal which together embody this great power. By joining together, they can command the ancient war machines-indeed they could potentially control the planet. But both desire the other's crystal, and if they war against one another, they could destroy the world.

1-4 .... 3.00

Magic: The Gathering: Elder Dragons
Acclaim, 1996

1-2 .... 3.00

Magic: The Gathering: Gerard's Quest
Dark Horse, 1998

1-4 .... 3.00

Magic: The Gathering: Nightmare
Acclaim, 1995

1 .... 3.00

Magic: The Gathering: Shandalar
Acclaim, 1996

1-2 .... 3.00

Magic: The Gathering: The Shadow Mage
Acclaim, 1995

1-4 .... 3.00

Magic: The Gathering: Wayfarer
Acclaim, 1995

1-5 .... 3.00

Magic Whistle
Alternative, 1998

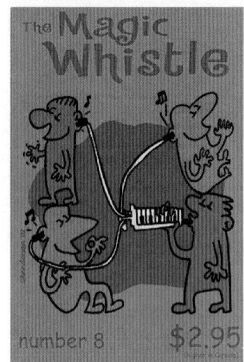

As examples of Henderson's work, the strips cover the joys of cartoonists "selling out;" a duck who speaks only in punctuation and obscenity; the true story of a man wedged in his cat door; another guy named Dirty Dan who can make anything interesting; and an obsessed man who pays more attention to his virtual pet than his real-life girlfriend; as well as an assortment of other strange characters.

1-2 .... 3.00

Magic Words
(Alan Moore's...)
Avatar, 2002

1 .... 7.00

Magik
Marvel, 1983

1-4 .... 2.00

Magik
Marvel, 2000

1-4 .... 3.00

Magilla Gorilla
Gold Key, 1964

1	30.00
2	15.00
3-5	12.00
6-10	10.00

Magna-Man: The Last Superhero
Comics Interview, 1988

1-3 .... 2.00

Magnesium Arc
Iconografix

1 .... 4.00

Magnetic Men
Featuring Magneto
Marvel, 1997
1 ....2.00

Magneto
Marvel, 1993
0 ....3.00

Magneto
Marvel, 1996
1-4 ....2.00

Magneto and the
Magnetic Men
Marvel, 1996

Magneto and the Magnetic Men was one of twelve titles DC and Marvel published jointly under the Amalgam masthead. Early in 1996 the two companies united to produce a four-issue series in which their characters encountered and, of course, were forced to fight each other. Between the third and final issue the two universes merged, resulting in character fusions heretofore unimagined.

Magneto and the Magnetic Men was a combination of Marvel's X-Men villain, Magneto, and the Metal Men from DC. The Magnetic Men were robots created by Magneto to aid mutants against the Sentinels created by his brother, Will Magnus. These robots had the angst-ridden personalities familiar to X-Men readers, combined with the pathos of the Metal Men.
- *George Haberberger*

1 ....2.00

Magneto Ascendant
Marvel, 1999
1 ....4.00

Magneto:
Dark Seduction
Marvel, 2000
1-4 ....3.00

Magneto Rex
Marvel, 1999
1-3 .... 3.00

Magnets:
Robot Dismantler
Parody

Magnets: Robot Dismantler is a Magnus Robot Fighter spoof, brought to you by the fine folks at Parody Press! Here we travel some two thousand years in the future to meet Magnets, a boy raised by a robot to be man's protector. Magnets is great at smashing runaway robots (as well as repairing them again-that's how he pays the bills). Unfortunately, he's thick as the proverbial brick. This leaves him playing the straight man as he fights robots, the dumbest of which have about a thousand times as much as intelligence as he does.

1 .... 3.00

Magnus, Robot Fighter
Gold Key, 1963
1	200.00
2-3	125.00
4-10	60.00
11-20	35.00
21-28	20.00
29-45	10.00
45/Whitman	18.00
46	10.00

Magnus Robot Fighter
Valiant, 1991
0/card	40.00
0/no card	30.00
1	10.00
2	8.00
3-4	5.00
☞Flip-book with Rai #1	
5-6	6.00
7-8	4.00
9-10	3.00
11	6.00
12	20.00

☞1st Valiant Turok
13-16	3.00
17-21	2.00
21/Gold	20.00
22-25	2.00
25/VVSS	15.00
26-35	1.00
36	2.00
37-43	1.00
44	3.00
45-54	2.00
55-57	3.00
57/error	10.00
58-60	3.00
61-62	4.00
63	5.00
64	12.00
YB 1	5.00

Magnus Robot Fighter
Acclaim, 1997
1-18 .... 3.00
Ashcan 1 .... 1.00

Magnus Robot Fighter/
Nexus
Valiant, 1993
0/Preview............................. 10.00
1-2 .... 3.00

Magus
Caliber

Magus is Simon Magus, a sorcerer mentioned in the New Testament. In this series, he is also the father of Lilith (star of another of Caliber's line of Caliber Core comics). Lilith was the onetime companion of St. Germaine, but has since become his enemy. She also had once believed herself to be the original woman (predating Eve), but due to her recent reunification with her father, she has begun to learn the truth about herself.

Both Magus and Lilith are immortal, and Magus had spent much of his neverending life forming his own religion. His small group of followers was wiped out in the opening issue of this series, however, by Beelzebub, another immortal who is better known as the Lord of the Flies. It was he who granted Magus his immortality, but, in return, Magus had promised him the hand of Lilith, his daughter. As the series begins, Beelzebub has decided to use deadly means to collect his bride.

1-2..3.00

Mahoromatic: Automatic Maiden
Tokyopop, 2004

1-7...10.00

Maine Zombie Lobstermen
Maine Stream Comics

1-2..3.00
3..4.00

Mai, the Psychic Girl
Eclipse, 1987

1..4.00
1/2nd...2.00
2...3.00
2/2nd...2.00
3...3.00
4-28...2.00

Maison Ikkoku Part 1
Viz, 1992

Rumiko Takahashi's long-running romance manga mixes slapstick comedy with truly touching moments. The male love-interest is Yusaku Godai, who lives at the boarding house Maison Ikkoku, which has such other tenants as a club hostess. He falls for Kyoko Otonashi, the widowed manager of the establishment, but he's too embarrassed to convey his feelings to her.

This sequence starts a series that actually has a beginning, middle, and end; the art communicates the characters' emotions without getting bogged down in gratuitous detail, and the

manga was adapted as a Japanese TV series and film.

1-7.. 4.00

Maison Ikkoku Part 2
Viz, 1993

1 .... 4.00
2-6... 3.00

Maison Ikkoku Part 3
Viz, 1993

1-6... 3.00

Maison Ikkoku Part 4
Viz, 1994

1-10...................................... 3.00

Maison Ikkoku Part 5
Viz, 1995

1-2 .... 3.00
3-5 .... 4.00
6 .... 3.00
7-8 .... 4.00
9 .... 3.00

Maison Ikkoku Part 6
Viz, 1996

1 .... 4.00
2 .... 3.00
3-4 .... 4.00
5 .... 3.00
6 .... 4.00
7-10 .... 3.00
11 .... 4.00

Maison Ikkoku Part 7
Viz, 1997

1-2 .... 4.00
3-13 .... 3.00

Maison Ikkoku Part 8
Viz, 1998

1 .... 3.00
2 .... 4.00
3 .... 3.00
4-7 .... 4.00
8 .... 3.00

Maison Ikkoku Part 9
Viz, 1999

Artist/writer Rumiko Takahashi throws more curveballs as Maison

Ikkoku nears its conclusion. The still-unconsummated romance between Yusaku Godai and Kyoko Otonashi, the manager of his apartment building, is tested once again as Godai is unable to dump Kozue, a girl he's dated off and on. Frustrated by Godai's indecisiveness and weak-willed nature, Otonashi leaves Maison Ikkoku and lives with her parents. Godai begins visiting Otonashi to bring her back, but she continually ignores him. After Godai is given Otonashi's job at Maison Ikkoku, he suddenly finds himself without the free time to see her, upsetting her even more. The series' eccentric supporting characters continue to provide comic relief, especially the lingerie-clad drunk Akemi, who tricks Godai into getting in bed with her in one issue.

1-10 .... 3.00

Majcans
P.S.

1 .... 1.00

Majestic
DC, 2004

1-5 .... 3.00

Majestic
DC, 2005

1-16 .... 3.00

Major Bummer
DC, 1997

John Arcudi and Doug Mahnke had a 1990s idea for a super-hero with the creation of "Major Bummer." The title character is Lou Martin, the archetypal slacker teen who spent most of his life playing videogames and loafing in front of the TV. Then came the fateful day he opened a strange package that had been left on his doorstep by an unknown party. There was a blinding flash of light, Lou was knocked unconscious ... and, when he woke up, he had been transformed from a gangly teen into a super-heroic hunk.

The next day, Lou was unaware of the changes in him -- even after he zoned out while fixing a VCR and accidentally turned it into a futuristic ray gun. The revelation came when he foiled a holdup at the local convenience store while going on a munchie run to feed his suddenly ravenous appetite. Like so many events in this series, the comedy comes from Lou's utter apathy in the face of extraordinary events.

1-15 ....3.00

Major Damage
Invictus, 1994
1-2 ....2.00

Major Inapak
the Space Ace
Magazine Enterprises, 1952

Major Inapak The Space Ace was a one-shot give-away comic used as a promotional piece for a vitamin fortified chocolate drink called INAPAK. The product derived its name from the "packettes" of product contained in each box.

This 1951 comic tells the story of the first manned landing and discovery of life on the moon by Major Inapak and a stow-away boy in 1984. The moon-landing event takes place just as aliens from the planet Lunrak are planning the destruction of Earth. The very end of the comic features a 3-page science lesson that promotes the virtues of the INAPAK. Startlingly, the benefits not only included strong bones and clear skin, but "good red blood" and "steady nerves." Yes they were serious.

1 ....8.00

Major Power
And Spunky
Fantagraphics, 1994
1 .... 4.00

Major Victory Comics
Harry A. Chesler, 1944
1 .... 400.00
2 .... 255.00
3 .... 220.00

Makebelieve
Liar

Miss Lerty, a teller of fantastic stories who lives in a creepy old house, perishes in a fire, and a group of neighborhood children she entertained with her tales mourn her passing. But what happens when the youngsters sneak into the remains of the mysterious Miss Lerty's home and start investigating the secrets that lie in the basement? Well, to start with, it looks like Miss Lerty's stories were true...!

1 .... 3.00

Malcolm-10
Onli
1 .... 2.00

Malcolm X
Millennium, 1993
1 .... 4.00

Malcolm X, The
Angriest Man in America
London Publishing
1 .... 7.00

Malibu Ashcan:
UltraForce
Malibu, 1994
1 .... 1.00

Malibu Signature Series
Malibu
1993-1994 .... 1.00

Malice in Wonderland
Fantagraphics, 1993
1 .... 3.00

Malinky Robot Bicycle
Slave Labor, 2005
1 .... 3.00

Mallimalou
Chance
1 .... 2.00

Malu in the
Land of Adventure
I.W., 1964
1 .... 50.00

Mammoth Comics
K.K., 1939
1 .... 1,250.00

Man Against Time
Image, 1996
1-6 .... 2.00

Man-Bat
DC, 1975
1 .... 10.00
2 .... 4.00

Man-Bat
DC, 1984
1 .... 3.00

Man-Bat
DC, 1996
1-3 .... 3.00

Man-Bat
DC, 2006
1-5 .... 3.00

Man Called A-X
Malibu, 1994
0-5 .... 3.00

Man Called A-X
DC, 1997
1-8 .... 3.00

Man Called Loco, A
Avalon
1 .... 3.00

Man Comics
Marvel, 1949

One of the early Atlas war comics, Man Comics specialized in tales of combat, courage, and daring in the face of danger. In its early issues, Man Comics was originally a crime and adventure series, but switched to war tales with #9.

Although the stories were not exceptional, Man Comics was lucky to feature early work by several of the medium's legendary artists. Included were #1 and #2's pages by George Tuska, various issues by Gene Colan (Tomb of Dracula), and Bernie Krigstein's unsettling style seen in #22, which became better known at E.C. on such titles as Shock SuspenStories.

1	100.00
2	65.00
3-5	45.00
6-10	38.00
11-20	32.00
21-28	28.00

Mandrake the Magician
King, 1966

1	32.00
2	20.00
3	14.00
4-5	13.00
6-7	10.00
8	16.00
9	9.00
10	24.00

Mandrake the Magician
Marvel, 1995

1-2	3.00

Man-Eating Cow
NEC, 1992

1	5.00
2-4	4.00
5-10	3.00

Man-Frog
Mad Dog, 1987

Although the characters are as bizarre and flamboyant as any super-hero, don't expect any world-saving deeds from Aristotle, the uncanny Man-Frog, or his fellow "freaks" in the traveling circus. But the carnies are a close-knit group, willing to do whatever it takes to watch out for each other. Man-Frog, the werewolf-ish Spider Duvall, the Astonishing Ant, Galley the giant, and "Ears" Phinster often have to deal with prejudice and violence, especially from local townies who think the carnies are easy prey.

1-2	2.00

Man from Atlantis
Marvel, 1978

Fans of so-so science-fiction will recall that, long before Dallas, Patrick Duffy flopped around on the beach with flippers for NBC during the single season of The Man from Atlantis. Well, not flippers, actually, but he did have webbed fingers and the abilities to breathe underwater and communicate with sea animals.

Sensing these talents would come in handy, Foundation for Oceanic Research took in the Atlantean refugee, naming him Mark Harris and sending him out to battle mad scientists and aliens.

Marvel cranked out seven imaginative issues of its adaptation, but by 1978 both it and the TV series were sunk.

-- John Jackson Miller

1	3.00
2-7	2.00

Man from U.N.C.L.E.
Gold Key, 1965

1	150.00
2	75.00
3-5	50.00
6-20	35.00
21-22	25.00

Man from U.N.C.L.E.
Entertainment, 1987

1-11	2.00

Man From U.N.C.L.E., The: The Birds of Prey Affair
Millennium, 1993

1-2	3.00

Manga Caliente
Fantagraphics, 2003

1-3	4.00

Manga Darkchylde
Dark Horse, 2005

1-2	3.00

Manga Horror
Avalon

1	3.00

Mangaphile
Radio, 1999

1-7	3.00

Manga Shi
Crusade, 1996

1	3.00

Manga Shi: Shiseji
Crusade

1	3.00

Manga Shi 2000
Crusade, 1997

1-3	3.00

Manga Surprise!
Morning & Afternoon, Kodansha Ltd., 1996

1	2.00

Manga Vizion
Viz, 1995

This series more resembles a magazine than a comic book. Beginning in 1995, this black-and-white series staked its claim as North America's only manga monthly. Along with entertaining existing fans, the series was dedicated to coax new readers into the world of Japanese comics. Although it was relatively expensive at cover price of $4.95, each issue had almost 100 pages.

Most manga in Japan is published in large anthologies. Viz Communications, Manga Vizion's publisher, saw to it that this tradition would be carried on in the United States. Manga Vizion printed one-shot stories alongside serial manga. Among the artists featured in Manga Vizion are Rumiko Takahashi (Maison Ikkoku, Ranma 1/2, and the Mermaid Saga) Ryoichi Ikegami (Mai, The Psychic Girl), and Kei Kusunoki (Shonen).

1-10 .... 5.00

Manga Vizion (Vol. 2)
Viz, 1996

1-12 .... 5.00

Manga Vizion (Vol. 3)
Viz, 1997

1-8 .... 5.00

Manga Vizion (Vol. 4)
Viz

1-8 .... 5.00

Manga Zen
Zen Comics

1 .... 3.00

Mangazine
Antarctic, 1985

1 .... 4.00
1/2nd 2.00
2 .... 4.00
3 .... 2.00
4-5 .... 4.00

Mangazine (Vol. 2)
Antarctic, 1989

1 .... 4.00
2 .... 3.00
3-5 .... 2.00
6-44 .... 3.00

Mangazine (Vol. 3)
Antarctic, 1999

1-53 .... 9.00
54-71 .... 10.00

Mangle Tangle Tales
Innovation

Once past the tongue-twisting title readers may come to realize that they hold in their hands a tribute to George Carlson's Jingle Jangle Tales. These stories are at once entertaining and incomprehensible or, as Harlan Ellison writes in the book's introduction, the "theater absurd of the 1990s." This collection of wonderfully rendered stories contains such fanciful titles as 'Prepare to Meat Thy Dinner." "Weird Atomic Broccoli," "Harry Hart Farkule Goes to the Pall Mall," and "Cliffed Palate." Each tale is inventive and engaging guaranteed to promote a chuckle.

1 .... 3.00

Manhunt
Print Mint, 1973

1 .... 4.00
2 .... 3.00

Manhunter
DC, 1984

1 .... 3.00

Manhunter
DC, 1988

1 .... 2.00
2-24 .... 1.00

Manhunter
DC, 1994

0-12 .... 2.00

Manhunter
DC, 2004

1-4 .... 3.00
5 .... 4.00
☛Identity Crisis tie
6 .... 8.00
7-27 .... 3.00

Manhunter: The Special Edition
DC, 1999

1 .... 10.00

Manhunt!
Magazine Enterprises, 1947

1 .... 285.00
2 .... 240.00
3 .... 200.00
4-11 .... 165.00

Maniac Chainsaw Weilding Duckbilled Platypus
Duncwadd Comics, 1995

1 .... 1.00

Manic One-Shot
Image, 2004

1 .... 4.00

Manifest Eternity
DC, 2006

1-6 .... 3.00

Manik
Millennium, 1995

1-3 .... 3.00

Manimal
Renegade, 1986

1 .... 2.00

Man in Black
Harvey, 1957

1 .... 110.00
2 .... 75.00
3-4 .... 60.00

Man in Black
Recollections, 1991

1-2 .... 2.00

Mankind
Chaos, 1999

1 .... 3.00

Mann and Superman
DC, 2000

Marty Mann's a loser; his life is pretty much in the dumpster. He's lost his job, his wife, and his son's respect. He would trade his life for almost anyone's-but especially Superman's. Superman has it so easy: he flies around without a care in the world, easily takes down a few criminals here and there, and is idolized by millions. So, Marty steals a priceless amulet from the Metropolis Museum that grants him his deepest, most heartfelt wish: to be Superman. But does Superman really have it as easy as Marty thinks? Find out what happens when everyone starts to tug on Super...er, Marty's cape. This excellent one-shot comes from the imagination of the very talented Michael T. Gilbert (Mr. Monster).

1 ....6.00

Man of Many Faces
Tokyopop, 2003
1 ....10.00

Man of Rust
Blackthorne, 1986
1/A-1/B 2.00

Man of Steel
DC, 1986
1-6/Silver 3.00

Man of the Atom
Acclaim, 1997
1 ....4.00

Man of War
Centaur, 1941
1 ....1,050.00
2 ....775.00

Man of War
Eclipse, 1987
1-5 .... 2.00

Man of War
Malibu, 1993
1 .... 2.00
1/Direct-5................................. 3.00
6-8 .... 2.00

Man O' Mars
Fiction House, 1953
1 .... 275.00
1/2nd 100.00

Manosaurs
Express

Take the best traits of both humans and dinosaurs, and throw in some genetic manipulation to give rise to paranormal powers. Then make these beings the strong arm for a highly advanced force for good, and set them to protect humanity from an equally advanced and far more bloodthirsty force for evil, and you have the Manosaurs. Rapper, whose quips and dialogue have a penchant for rhyme; Rex, level-headed leader; Terry, high-flying hothead; and Tops, the brawn of the group: these four hybrid beings are all that stand between humanity and the might of the M'har. Will humanity accept these monsters as the saviors they are or shun them as freakish outcasts?

1-2 .... 3.00

Mantech Robot Warriors
Archie, 1984

Evil robot warriors fight to take over the planet, Mekka. The inhabitants of the planet had no hope until the planet's leading scientist finds an old spacecraft floating in space. The ship contains the decaying bodies of the earthlings. The men's bodies are beyond help, so the scientist affixes their heads to robotic bodies. After the shock of their situation wears off, the three men decide that they have no choice but to help defend the planet from the attacking robots. They call themselves the Mantech Robot Warriors and take up individual identities derived from each person's unique specialty: Aquatech (water), Lasertech (lasers), and Solartech (sun powers).

Archie Comics, known for-well-Archie Comics, published Mantech warriors as part of an adventure line of comics in 1984.

1-4 .... 1.00

Man-Thing (Vol. 1)
Marvel, 1974
1 .... 30.00
2 .... 14.00
3 .... 10.00
4 .... 8.00
5 .... 10.00
6-10 .... 5.00
11-22 .... 3.00

Man-Thing
Marvel, 1979
1 .... 3.00
2-11 .... 2.00

Man-Thing
Marvel, 1997
1-8 .... 3.00

Man-Thing
Marvel, 2004
1-3 .... 3.00

Mantra
Malibu, 1993

The man known as Lukasz was one of 12 warriors who fight evil throughout the ages. Led by the mystic Archimage, they battle a sorcerous being known as Boneyard and his group of henchmen. Strangely, whenever either Archimage's or Boneyard's soldiers fall in the line of battle, their master mystically reincarnates them in another body to begin the fight anew. Thus, the battle has dragged on over the centuries -- -- until now. A traitor in Archimage's camp has given Boneyard his greatest secret, which has led to Archimage's defeat. In the battle that follows, Lukasz is killed once again, but with Archimage out of the picture, the expected "reincarnation" does not go as smoothly as planned. Lukasz ends up occupying the body of a woman, Eden Blake, and is now known as Mantra. Worse yet, in this story by Mike Barr, transgendered Lukasz finds his only hope for survival lies with Warstrike, the very man who killed him.

1-1/Ltd.	3.00
1/Hologram	6.00
2-3	2.00
4	3.00
5-9	2.00
10	4.00
11-17	2.00
18	3.00
19-20	2.00
21-24	3.00
GS 1	4.00

Mantra
Malibu, 1995

0-7	2.00

Mantra: Spear of Destiny
Malibu, 1995

Mantra is really a centuries-old warrior named Lukasz whose current incarnation resulted in him being trapped in the body of a woman, Eden Blake. To free himself, Mantra sought out the Spear of Destiny, an awesomely powerful artifact which was said to have been used by a Roman soldier to stab Jesus as he was dying on the cross. Its magic might have been enough for Mantra to gain a new body, but others wanted it for their own reasons.

Mantra tried to steal the spear from a local museum display, but she was foiled-not by museum security-but by a rival group of Ultras, called the Herronvolk, who somehow neutralized her powers and made off with the spear. The next day, Mantra returned to work at Aladdin in her identity as Eden Blake, where she was given a new assignment. Her superiors-who had no idea that Eden was really Mantra-sent her on an undercover mission to recover the spear for them!

1-2	3.00

Mantus Files
Eternity

1-4	3.00

Man Who Would Be King
Tome

1	3.00

Man with the Screaming Brain
Dark Horse, 2005

1/A-4/B	3.00

Many Ghosts of Dr. Graves
Charlton, 1967

1	30.00
2	18.00
3	12.00
4-10	10.00
11-20	8.00
21-45	6.00
46-53	4.00
54	6.00
☛Byrne cover	
55-71	4.00
72	5.00

Many Loves of Dobie Gillis
DC, 1960

"My name is Dobie Gillis, and I like girls. What am I saying? I love girls! … I just want one, one beautiful, gorgeous, soft, round, creamy girl for my very own. That's all I want! One lousy girl!" So said the teen (played by Dwayne Hickman) on the sitcom (1959-63) based on the novel of the same name by Max Shulman (1919-1988, author of such other books as Rally Round the Flag Boys! and the film The Tender Trap and the Broadway play How Now, Dow Jones). Gillis' buddy on the TV show, Maynard G. Krebs, was played by Bob Denver.

The comic-book series ran roughly as long as the TV series and featured art by Bob Oksner. DC completists who picked up the short-lived Windy & Willy in the late 1960s were amused to discover that that series consisted of revamps of Dobie and Maynard, complete with new bellbottom trousers.

-- Maggie

1	85.00
2	65.00
3	50.00
4-5	45.00
6-10	35.00

11-20....................................26.00
21-26....................................24.00

Many Reincarnations of Lazarus
Fisher, 1998
1...3.00
Ashcan 1 ....1.00

Many Worlds of Tesla Strong
DC, 2003
1...3.00

Mara
Aircel, 1991
1-4..3.00

Mara Celtic Shamaness
Fantagraphics, 1995

This ongoing series is the third for Mara, who first appeared in Eros Comix Graphic Novel #17, and later in the short-lived Mara of the Celts. The often-naked title character is a beautiful witch who works her magic on behalf of her tribe of Celts. As this latest series begins, she undergoes a "vision quest" through a bizarre dream world, which is her first step toward becoming a full-fledged shamaness.

Created by Dennis Cramer, the Mara books mix their eroticism with ancient Irish lore, making for a combination far more interesting than the average adult comic.

1-6..3.00

Mara of the Celts Book 1
Rip Off, 1993
Special 1 ....3.00

Mara of the Celts Book 2
Fantagraphics, 1995
1...3.00

Marauder
Silverline, 1998
1-4..3.00

March Hare
Lodestone
1 .... 2.00

March of Comics (Boys' and Girls'...)
K.K., 1946

March of Comics was one of the longest-running comic titles, surviving from the mid-1940s all the way into the 80s. Its formula for success was to serve up nothing but favorites issue after issue like newspaper comic strip hits Tarzan, Henry, Krazy Kat and Popeye. Also, blue-chip animation stars like Bugs Bunny, Mickey Mouse, Porky Pig, Woody Woodpecker, Scooby Doo and the Pink Panther; and movie and TV tie-ins like The Three Stooges, Our Gang, Lassie, Gene Autry, and the Lone Ranger. In fact, the titles were those to which Western Printing had access over the years, whether it used Dell or Gold Key or other imprints.

Over the years, the publisher experimented on the giveaway, trying shorter page counts (16 instead of 32), uncoated cover stock (rough, not slick), oblong format, photo covers, full advertiser sponsorships, and more.

1 .... 340.00
2 .... 250.00
3 .... 295.00
4 .... 5,150.00
5 .... 175.00
6 .... 160.00
7 .... 125.00
8 .... 400.00
9-10 .... 75.00
11 .... 60.00
12-14 .... 55.00
15 .... 45.00
16 .... 85.00
17 .... 175.00
18 .... 100.00
19 .... 85.00
20 .... 3,225.00
21 .... 80.00

22 .... 85.00
23 .... 100.00
24 .... 185.00
25 .... 195.00
26 .... 200.00
27 .... 250.00
28 .... 185.00
29-33 .... 40.00
34 .... 70.00
35 .... 165.00
36 .... 140.00
37 .... 110.00
38 .... 45.00
39 .... 165.00
40 .... 60.00
41 .... 2,775.00
42 .... 60.00
43 .... 45.00
44 .... 70.00
45 .... 210.00
46 .... 65.00
47 .... 150.00
48-50 .... 40.00
51 .... 115.00
52 .... 90.00
53 .... 40.00
54 .... 165.00
55 .... 55.00
56 .... 260.00
57 .... 55.00
58 .... 40.00
59 .... 70.00
60 .... 190.00
61 .... 55.00
62 .... 145.00
63-65 .... 35.00
66 .... 80.00
67 .... 30.00
68 .... 115.00
69 .... 190.00
70 .... 45.00
71 .... 50.00
72 .... 60.00
73 .... 110.00
74 .... 175.00
75 .... 45.00
76 .... 50.00
77 .... 110.00
78 .... 90.00
79 .... 30.00
80 .... 65.00
81 .... 25.00
82 .... 90.00
83 .... 40.00
84 .... 35.00
85 .... 30.00
86 .... 120.00
87 .... 55.00
88 .... 45.00
89 .... 30.00
90 .... 120.00
91 .... 115.00
92 .... 28.00
93 .... 20.00
94 .... 55.00
95 .... 25.00
96 .... 50.00
97 .... 35.00
98 .... 85.00

99	25.00	164	18.00	230	30.00
100	80.00	165	60.00	231	10.00
101	20.00	166	20.00	232	55.00
102	110.00	167	55.00	233	50.00
103	25.00	168	20.00	234-235	25.00
104	80.00	169-170	30.00	236-237	30.00
105	65.00	171	18.00	238	40.00
106-108	30.00	172	70.00	239	10.00
109	20.00	173	18.00	240	50.00
110	40.00	174	55.00	241-242	15.00
111	25.00	175	18.00	243	40.00
112-113	20.00	176	50.00	244	35.00
114	75.00	177-179	18.00	245	10.00
115	25.00	180	45.00	246-247	25.00
116	65.00	181-182	15.00	248	50.00
117	50.00	183	18.00	249	10.00
118	75.00	184	15.00	250	30.00
119	20.00	185	65.00	251	85.00
120-121	70.00	186	15.00	252	45.00
122-123	26.00	187	30.00	253	40.00
124	18.00	188-190	15.00	254	30.00
125	75.00	191	45.00	255-256	15.00
126	20.00	192	15.00	257	25.00
127	35.00	193	55.00	258	40.00
128-130	20.00	194	30.00	259	10.00
131	65.00	195	40.00	260	20.00
132	20.00	197-198	18.00	261	10.00
133	70.00	199	40.00	262	40.00
134	40.00	200	25.00	263	45.00
135-136	60.00	201	15.00	264	20.00
137-138	20.00	202	50.00	265	30.00
139	18.00	203	15.00	266	25.00
140	30.00	204	60.00	267	70.00
141	18.00	205	35.00	268	45.00
142	70.00	206	45.00	269-270	15.00
143	18.00	207	15.00	271-272	40.00
144	80.00	208	55.00	273	10.00
145	18.00	209	15.00	274	20.00
146	55.00	210	35.00	275	60.00
147	18.00	212-213	15.00	276	75.00
148	40.00	214	30.00	277	10.00
149	18.00	215	40.00	278	20.00
150-151	60.00	216	50.00	279	25.00
152-153	20.00	217	30.00	280	45.00
154	18.00	218	10.00	281	10.00
155	75.00	219	25.00	282	20.00
156	18.00	220	10.00	283-284	15.00
157	35.00	221	35.00	285	150.00
158	18.00	222	10.00	286	35.00
159	30.00	223	55.00	287-288	10.00
160	18.00	224	10.00	289	35.00
161	50.00	225	45.00	290	15.00
162	18.00	226-228	15.00	291	20.00
163	50.00	229	50.00	292	40.00

M

293	35.00
294	20.00
295	10.00
296-298	15.00
299-300	30.00
301	10.00
302	25.00
303	10.00
304	40.00
305	10.00
306-307	30.00
308	15.00
309	20.00
310	40.00
311-312	15.00
313	10.00
314	25.00
315	10.00
316	35.00
317-318	30.00
319	20.00
320	65.00
321	10.00
322	35.00
323	20.00
324-326	15.00
327	30.00
328	60.00
329	10.00
330	50.00
331	8.00
332	25.00
333	8.00
334	15.00
335	20.00
336	30.00
337	20.00
338	35.00
340	15.00
341-342	25.00
343	8.00
344	15.00
345	8.00
346	15.00
347	8.00
348	40.00
349	20.00
350	30.00
351	10.00
352	50.00
353	8.00
354-355	20.00
356	35.00
357	8.00
358	15.00
359	10.00
360	40.00
361	8.00
362	15.00
363	8.00
364	25.00
365	6.00
366	20.00
367	8.00
368	25.00
369-370	15.00
371	6.00
372	15.00
373	25.00

374-375	6.00
376	10.00
377	6.00
378	50.00
379-380	6.00
381	10.00
382	15.00
383	10.00
384	6.00
385	15.00
386-388	6.00
389	15.00
390	6.00
391	15.00
392-393	5.00
394	10.00
395	8.00
396-398	5.00
399	40.00
400	5.00
401-403	4.00
404	35.00
405	5.00
406	10.00
407	8.00
408	30.00
409-410	4.00
411	10.00
412-413	4.00
414	30.00
415-416	4.00
417	10.00
418-425	4.00
426	15.00
427	6.00
428-437	4.00
438	12.00
439	5.00
440-446	4.00
447	5.00
448-456	4.00
457-458	3.00
459	4.00
460	3.00
461-466	4.00
467	8.00
468-478	4.00
479	6.00
480-488	4.00

March of Crime
Fox, 1950

1	245.00
2	225.00
3	115.00

Marco Polo
Charlton, 1962

1	68.00

Marc Silvestri Sketchbook
Image, 2004

1	3.00

Marc Silvestri Sketchbook
Image, 2006

1	3.00

Marc Spector: Moon Knight
Marvel, 1989

Marc Spector is a cold-hearted mercenary, willing to fight for whatever army pays the most money. All that changes, when he rebels at his commander's wholesale slaughter of a Egyptian village's townsfolk. His commander, a madman named Bushman, knocks Spector unconscious and orders that Marc be dropped in the middle of the desert. Left to die in the blazing heat, Marc crawls across the sand for miles, eventually happening upon an ancient temple of the moon god Khonshu. There, under a statue of Khonshu, "Marc Spector" dies. What emerges later from the temple is a new man -- a Marc Spector who will take on the garb and weapons of Khonshu and use them to fight evil. Marc Spector has become Moon Knight.

In this, the third Moon Knight series, Marc Spector's war rages on.

1	3.00
2-7	2.00
8-9	3.00
10-18	2.00
19-25	3.00
26-31	2.00
32-33	3.00
34-49	2.00
50	3.00
51-54	2.00
55-57	3.00
58-60	2.00
Special 1	3.00

Margie
Dell, 1962

2	25.00

Margie Comics
Marvel, 1946

35	100.00

36-38	50.00
39-41	75.00
42	50.00
43-44	75.00
45	50.00
46	75.00
47-49	50.00

Marginal Prophets
Marginal Prophets

1	1.00

Marie-Gabrielle
NBM

1	16.00

Marilyn Monroe: Suicide or Murder?
Revolutionary, 1993

1	3.00

Marines Attack
Charlton, 1964

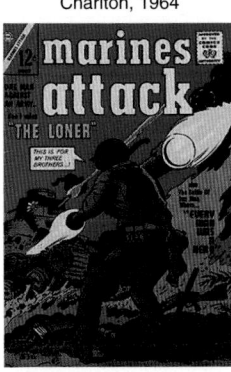

Sam Glanzman, a naval veteran of World War II, brings the perspective of his unique experience and colorful personality to every panel he draws. In the late 60s and 70s, he developed into one of the most reliably enjoyable artists of war and Western comics (mostly for DC), even as those genres were in their dying days. The spark of his talent was obvious even in such a thoroughly undistinguished title as Marines Attack, one of seemingly hundreds of standard-issue war comics brought out by second-tier publishers in the 50s and 60s. Unfortunately, the combination of Glanzman's professional inexperience and the Charlton assembly-line production process put this work squarely in the "diamond in the rough" category. By the time he was tapped for the relatively successful "Private War of Willy Schultz" in Fightin' Army, his chops had matured considerably from this primitive early effort.

1	16.00
2	12.00
3-5	9.00
6-9	6.00

Marines in Action
Atlas, 1955

1	65.00
2-10	42.00
11-14	36.00

Marines in Battle
Marvel, 1954

1	110.00
2	60.00
3-19	45.00
20-25	36.00

Marine War Heroes
Charlton, 1964

War comics, like their polar opposite, romance comics, exist to satisfy a narrow spectrum of fantasies for an audience presumed to despise any variation from tried and true formulas. Some war comics have risen to greater creative heights than love comics, since the male creators may have had more sympathy for and insight into their material, but at their most formulaic -- in comics like Marine War Heroes -- there is little real difference, once you substitute buzz cuts for beehives, green khaki for white lace, and bullets for wedding rings. Marine War Heroes runs grimly through the register of stock plots -- the reluctant soldier, bravery under fire, seeking revenge for a fallen friend, one man against an entire division -- all rendered in the artless, low-budget Charlton house style. It was mustered out of the Charlton lineup in 1967, when the threat of real war dampened the public appetite for war fantasies.

-- Rob Salkowitz

1	15.00
2-3	12.00

4-5	9.00
6-10	7.00
11-18	5.00

Marionette
Alpha Productions

1-3	3.00

Marionette
Raven, 1987

1-3	1.00

Mark
Dark Horse, 1987

1-6	2.00

Mark
Dark Horse, 1993

1-4	3.00

Markam
Gauntlet

Mary Cameron is a fashion model who has a dream about encountering a tall demonic creature while taking a bath. When she wakes up she's in her own tub, her debut on the catwalk merely hours away. However, she never gets the opportunity to fulfill her job as she is suddenly pulled into another world, a medieval kingdom caught in a trade dispute. The nightmarish beast from Mary's imagination turns out to be real and waiting for her.

The first issue includes a two-page filler story about a milk-loving pirate.

1	3.00

Mark Hazzard: Merc
Marvel, 1986

1-Ann 1	1.00

Mark of Charon
CrossGen, 2003

1-5	3.00

Mark of the Succubus
Tokyopop, 2005

1	10.00

Marksman
Hero, 1988

1-5.................................2.00
Ann 1..............................3.00

Mark Trail
Standard, 1955

1...............................35.00
5...............................18.00

Marmaduke Mouse
Quality, 1946

Although sometimes regarded as a rip-off of Tom & Jerry, Marmaduke Mouse had a quirky charm that was its own. Granted, the stories did follow a simple formula: Hapless Marmaduke blunders from adventure to adventure trying to bail his friend (and employer), loony King Louie the lion, out of trouble.

But, like many of the best funny-animal comics and cartoons, Marmaduke Mouse holds a fun-house mirror up to American society in the 1950s. Some stories revolve around a growing obsession with television (and some of the characters featured are thinly disguised representations of many celebrities of the day, including Milton Berle), the rise of suburban sprawl, and even the threat of communism. When Quality Comics folded and DC bought most of its properties, Marmaduke Mouse was canceled and never revived as a comic book.

-- Stephen C. George

1...............................70.00
2...............................40.00
3-5..............................28.00
6-10.............................20.00
11-20............................16.00
21-40............................12.00
41-65.............................9.00

Marmalade Boy
Tokyopop, 2001

1-3..............................3.00

Marooned!
Fantagraphics, 1990

1................................ 2.00

Marquis, The:
Danse Macabre
Oni, 2000

1-3.............................. 3.00

Marquis, The:
Les Preludes
Caliber, 1997

1................................ 3.00

Marriage of
Hercules and Xena
Topps, 1998

1................................ 3.00

Married...With Children
Now, 1990

1................................ 3.00
1/2nd-7 .... 2.00

Married...With Children
Now, 1991

1................................ 3.00
2-7............................... 2.00
Ann 1994......................... 3.00
Special 1 .... 2.00

Married...With Children:
Buck's Tale
Now, 1994

1................................ 2.00

Married...With Children:
Bud Bundy,
Fanboy in Paradise
Now

1................................ 3.00

Married...With Children:
Flashback Special
Now, 1993

1-3.............................. 2.00

Married...With Children:
Kelly Bundy
Now, 1992

Kelly is the beautiful but incredibly stupid daughter in the Bundy family. She's also just a little bit loose with the boys, falling instantly for any motorcycle-riding punk who comes her way. Her only other real vice is that she lives to torture her considerably smarter, but far less sexy younger brother, Bud.

With any other series but television's Married...With Children, Kelly's combination of sleaziness and stupidity would not exactly make for star material. But in the wacky, dysfunctional world of the Bundys, that's exactly what she turned into. At least part of the appeal lies in actress Christina Applegate, who plays the role with a ditzy vampishness that's hilariously over-the-top. Her antics (and those of the rest of the Bundy family) translate very well to comic book form, making this three-issue Married...With Children: Kelly Bundy special one of the funnier comics around.

1-3.............................. 2.00

Married...With Children:
Kelly Goes to Kollege
Now

1-3.............................. 3.00

Married...With Children:
Off Broadway
Now, 1993

1................................ 2.00

Married...With Children:
Quantum Quartet
Now, 1993

1-2.............................. 2.00
3................................ 3.00

Married...With Children
3-D Special
Now, 1993

1................................ 3.00

Married...With Children:
2099
Now, 1993

1-3.............................. 2.00

Mars
First, 1984

1................................ 2.00
2-12 .... 1.00

Mars
Tokyopop, 2002

1-3.............................. 10.00

Mars Attacks
Topps, 1994

1-1/Ltd. 4.00
2-5.............................. 3.00

Mars Attacks
Topps, 1995

1	4.00
2-8	3.00

Mars Attacks Baseball Special
Topps, 1996

1	3.00

Mars Attacks High School
Topps, 1997

In 1996, Tim Burton, (notable to comic fans as the director of the movies Batman and Batman Returns), directed an unusual movie based on a bubblegum card set from the 1960s. Mars Attacks was a high camp send-up of science-fiction movies, and Topps adeptly transferred the fun-filled weirdness to the comic page.

Continued fan support prompted Topps to publish Mars Attacks High School, a two-issue black-and-white mini-series that continues stories interrupted when the full-color Mars Attacks was put on hiatus. The mini-series features a bizarre mix of horror and humor as the invading Martians continue their sometimes-grisly, sometimes-absurd experiments.

-- George Haberberger

1-2	3.00

Mars Attacks Image
Image, 1996

1-4	3.00

Mars Attacks the Savage Dragon
Topps, 1996

1-4	3.00

Marshal Law
Marvel, 1987

1	4.00
2-6	3.00

Marshal Law: Kingdom of the Blind
Apocalypse

1	4.00
1/Direct	6.00

Marshal Law: Secret Tribunal
Dark Horse, 1993

The League of Heroes, home of such "illustrious" members as Biogram Girl, Public Spirit Jr., and Super-Sensitive Girl, is having auditions for new members. For Luminous Lad and Growing Boy to be accepted as members, they were required to spend a night aboard the quarantined ship, "The Cape of Good Hope." The pair accepted the challenge, only to discover that the ship was inhabited-by strange and deadly monsters called Incubi.

The woefully-powered Luminous Lad emitted just one flicker of light before he was killed, and Growing Boy decided that running away was the better part of valor. "Licensed vigilante" Marshal Law was sent in to save the day, along with a collection of misfits known as the secret tribunal. What follows is the equivalent to a teen summer-camp slasher film, with blithering teenage super-heroes as the campers, and Marshal Law as their erstwhile savior.

1-2	3.00

Marshal Law: Super Babylon
Dark Horse, 1992

1	5.00

Marshal Law: The Hateful Dead
Apocalypse

1	6.00

M.A.R.S. Patrol Total War
Gold Key, 1966

The "M.A.R.S." of M.A.R.S. Patrol stands for Marine Attack Rescue Service. At first glance, one might suspect the series to be of a science-fiction origin. However, "M.A.R.S. Patrol" is actually one of many war comic books that saw print in the 1960s. For its first two issues, it was known as Total War.

As with most team war comics, the M.A.R.S. Patrol consisted of a group of individual specialists. Lieutenant Cy Adams was the teams aerial combat man, Sergeant Joe Striker handled communications, Sergeant Ken Hiro specialized in sea warfare, and Corporal Russ Stacey was the weapons wizard. The team was sent on special missions that only they could handle. Most of these missions were secret and not part of any known war.

In formulation and style, M.A.R.S. Patrol was an ancestor of the later G.I. Joe, a Real American Hero.

3	50.00
☛Was Total War	
4-5	35.00
6-10	25.00

Martha Splatterhead's Weirdest Stories Ever Told
Monster

1	4.00

Martha Washington Goes to War
Dark Horse, 1994

Frank Miller and Dave Gibbons' Give Me Liberty was the powerful tale of a young black girl named Martha Washington, who somehow rose out of a life of despair to become a hero in the corporate wars of the next century. In all these situations, she triumphed merely by surviving.

Now, in this mini-series, Martha Washington goes back to war. Once again, she's fighting for the Pax forces, this time in the second American Civil War. Like too many wars, this one is fought for trivialities. Here, the forces of Fat Boy Hamburgers have marshaled the beef-raising state of Texas into a bloody general war.

Grievously wounded in the battle for Texas, Martha finds herself placed in the tender care of the Surgeon General, whom she herself killed in the last series. Other friends, long thought dead, also reappear, followed by a fear that the ghosts of the war dead had returned.

1-5 ....3.00

Martha Washington Saves the World
Dark Horse, 1997
1-3 ....4.00

Martha Washington: Stranded in Space
Dark Horse, 1995
1 ....3.00
☛Reprint from DHP; Miller, Gibbons

Martian Manhunter
DC, 1988
1-4 ....2.00

Martian Manhunter
DC, 1998
0-1 .... 3.00
2-21 .... 2.00
22-36 .... 3.00
1000000 .... 4.00
Ann 1-2................................... 3.00

Martian Manhunter: American Secrets
DC, 1992
1-3 .... 5.00

Martian Manhunter
DC, 2006
1-5 .... 3.00

Martian Manhunter Special
DC, 1996

When J'onn J'onzz travels to the distant planet, Naftali, to seek an ancient cleric who may have information on possible survivors of Mars, he becomes embroiled in a religious war. The holy man, K'rkzar, is rumored to have spent the past several hundred years developing a "one true religion." But the myriad of religious factions on Naftali all fear what K'rkzar may proclaim and so are ready to silence him rather than risk a blasphemy that disagrees with their beliefs.

Rather than a Martian Manhunter special, this title seems more like a team-up book between J'onn J'onzz and The Darkstars, with whom J'onzz allies himself. The Darkstars have been assigned to protect the controversial cleric and keep an interplanetary holy war from erupting so J'onzz volunteers his services in what becomes a "can't we all just get along" morality play.

-- George Haberberger

1 .... 4.00

Martin Kane
Fox, 1949
1 .... 210.00
2 .... 135.00

Martin Mystery
Dark Horse, 1999
1-6 .... 5.00

Martin the Satanic Racoon
Gabe Martinez
1 .... 1.00
2 .... 2.00

Marvel Westerns: Western Legends
Marvel, 2006
1 .... 4.00

Marvel Action Hour, Featuring Iron Man
Marvel, 1994

Encouraged by the success of its X-Men Adventures animated series on Saturday morning television, Marvel relaunched its animated Marvel Action Hour in 1994 with segments featuring Iron Man and the Fantastic Four. Dutifully, Marvel followed with series adapting the TV shows.

The Iron Man segment was actually a team-up between Tony Stark (the original Iron Man) and Force Works, a super-hero group comprising War Machine, the Scarlet Witch, Hawkeye, U.S. Agent, a revamped Spider-Woman, and Century. The comics adaptation finds these heroes battling a cast of classic villains such as the Mandarin, Whirlwind, and Fin Fang Foom. The emphasis is on fast-paced action, dispensing with the angst and complicated subplots characteristic of the regular Iron Man series.

The TV series failed, and both comics adaptations went away.

1	2.00
1/CS	3.00
2-8	2.00

Marvel Action Hour, Featuring the Fantastic Four
Marvel, 1994

1	2.00
1/CS	3.00
2-8	2.00

Marvel Action Universe
Marvel, 1989

1	1.00

Marvel Adventure
Marvel, 1975

Marvel Adventure was a brief, but colorful series. In its six-issue run, it reprinted the classic Daredevil #22-27. These issues, featuring the art of Gene Colan (Tomb of Dracula) pitted the blind super-hero against many of his greatest foes, including the Owl, the Gladiator, and the Masked Marauder.

1	8.00
2-3	5.00
3/30¢	20.00
4	5.00
4/30¢	20.00
5	4.00
5/30¢	20.00
6	4.00

Marvel Adventures
Marvel, 1997

1-18	2.00

Marvel Adventures: Avengers
Marvel, 2006

1-8	3.00

Marvel Adventures: Fantastic Four
Marvel, 2005

0-19	3.00

Marvel Adventures Flip Magazine
Marvel, 2005

1-11	4.00
13-20	5.00

Marvel Adventures: Spider-Man
Marvel, 2005

1-23	3.00

Marvel Adventures: Spider-Man Vol. 1: The Sinister Six Digest
Marvel, 2005

1	7.00

Marvel Adventures: The Thing
Marvel, 2005

1	2.00
2-3	3.00

Marvel Age
Marvel, 1983

Not a comic book but included here because of its massive distribution by the largest comics publisher, Marvel Age served as Marvel's carnival barker in the 1980s and early 1990s, announcing new projects and information from behind-the-scenes. The first 16-page comic-book sized issue was priced to move at 25 cents, with later issues increasing in page count and price.

While a magazine, it was never really perceived as being in competition with the existing magazines about comics, given its status as a house organ. The presence of Fred Hembeck strips (later reprinted in Fred Hembeck Sells the Marvel Universe) and some good background articles explains why the magazine has, itself, become collectible.

1	2.00

2-133	1.00
134	2.00
135-136	1.00
137-138	2.00
139-Ann 4	1.00

Marvel Age: Fantastic Four
Marvel, 2004

1	3.00
2-12	2.00

Marvel Age: Fantastic Four Tales - The Thing
Marvel, 2005

1	2.00

Marvel Age Hulk
Marvel, 2004

1-4	2.00

Marvel Age Preview
Marvel, 1990

1-2	2.00

Marvel Age: Runaways
Marvel, 2004

1	8.00

Marvel Age: Sentinel
Marvel, 2004

1	8.00

Marvel Age: Spider-Girl
Marvel, 2004

1	8.00

Marvel Age: Spider-Man
Marvel, 2004

1	3.00
1/FCBD	2.00
2-4	3.00
5-20	2.00

Marvel Age Spider-Man Team Up
Marvel, 2004

1-5	2.00

Marvel and DC Present
Marvel, 1982

In 1982, crossovers between publishers were rare and special events, and none were as much anticipated as the get-together between Marvel's Uncanny X-Men and DC's New Teen Titans -- the two hottest titles then on the stands. The two super-groups are united, when DC's baddest bad guy, Darkseid of Apokolips, revives the all-powerful Dark Phoenix, who has just met her demise after an action-packed (and top-selling) series in The X-Men. The New Gods' Metron and Titan villain Deathstroke the Terminator make guest appearances.

Len Wein, who had a hand in creating both groups, writes the epic, and artists Walter Simonson and Terry Austin do a good job synthesizing the styles of John Byrne and George Perez to give the crossover an appearance consistent with the art in both series.

-- *Rob Salkowitz*

1 .... 12.00

Marvel Boy
Marvel, 1950

1 .... 875.00
2 .... 610.00

Marvel Boy
Marvel, 2000

1 .... 3.00
1/A 5.00
2-6 .... 3.00

Marvel Chillers
Marvel, 1975

Marvel Chillers was a rather undistinguished (and short-lived) horror title. The highlight of its run was undoubtedly its first issue, where it introduced Modred the Mystic. Modred had been a powerful sorcerer from the time of King Arthur. Bold beyond wisdom, he dared to cast a spell out of the timeless book of evil, the Darkhold. That spell brought

disaster, and Merlin the magician placed Modred's seemingly lifeless body safely in a crypt, knowing that he would once again rise to walk the earth.

That time came eleven centuries later when two adventurers came upon the crypt, disturbing Modred's mystical sleep. Modred has been wandering in the realm of the supernatural ever since, sometimes on the side of good-but just as often pursuing his own designs.

1 .... 12.00
2 .... 7.00
3 .... 10.00
4 .... 7.00
4/30¢ 20.00
5 .... 7.00
5/30¢ 20.00
6 .... 5.00
6/30¢ 20.00
7 .... 5.00

Marvel Chillers: Shades of Green Monsters
Marvel, 1997

1 .... 3.00

Marvel Chillers: The Thing in the Glass Case
Marvel, 1997

1 .... 3.00

Marvel Classics Comics
Marvel, 1976

1 .... 7.00
2-5 .... 5.00
6-27 .... 4.00
28 .... 8.00
☞1st Mike Golden art
29-36 .... 4.00

Marvel Collectible Classics: Amazing Spider-Man
Marvel, 1988

300 .... 14.00

Marvel Collectible Classics: Avengers (Vol. 3)
Marvel, 1998

1 .... 14.00

Marvel Collectible Classics: X-Men
Marvel, 1998

1-GS 1 .... 14.00

Marvel Collectible Classics: X-Men (Vol. 2)
Marvel, 1998

1 .... 14.00

Marvel Collector's Edition
Marvel, 1992

1 .... 3.00

Marvel Collectors' Item Classics
Marvel, 1966

1 .... 125.00
2 .... 70.00
3-4 .... 45.00
5-6 .... 30.00
7-10 .... 15.00
11-20 .... 12.00
21 .... 15.00
22 .... 17.00
23 .... 20.00

Marvel Comics
Marvel, 1939

1 .... 165,000.00
1/A 350,000.00

Marvel Comics Presents
Marvel, 1988

Marvel Comics Presents was a bit like the "chapter plays" of Saturday matinee films. It took four different storylines and presented them as serials, with a new issue every two weeks. This let Marvel experiment with a number of new story ideas while being reasonably sure that, if one didn't appeal to the readers, one of the other three would.

In most issues, at least one of the stories featured The X-Men's Wolverine. The other stories covered diverse characters from Ghost Rider to Nth Man. However, many people will remember the series for the 12-part story titled "Weapon X." This series by Barry Windsor-Smith served as a sort of origin for Wolverine, telling the story of the grisly experiment that laced his bones with adamantium and of the brutal methods by which the experimenters tried to turn him into a human killing machine.

1	4.00
2-5	3.00
6-53	2.00
54-62	3.00
63-71	2.00
72	4.00
73-86	3.00
87-175	2.00

Marvel Comics Presents Spider-Man
Marvel

1	2.00

Marvel Comics Presents the X-Men
Marvel

1	2.00

Marvel Comics: 2001
Marvel, 2001

1	1.00

Marvel Double Feature
Marvel, 1973

Marvel Double Feature reprints many of the classic Iron Man/Captain America stories from Tales of Suspense. Later issues reprinted both Iron Man & Sub-Mariner #1, and Iron Man #1.

1	40.00
2	20.00
3	15.00
4-8	10.00
9-15	8.00
15/30¢	20.00
16	8.00
16/30¢-17/30¢	20.00
18	8.00
19-21	6.00

Marvel Double Shot
Marvel, 2003

1-4	3.00

Marvel Encyclopedia
Marvel, 2003

1-2	30.00
3	20.00
4	25.00
5-6	30.00

Marvel Encyclopedia (Magazine)
Marvel, 2004

1	6.00

Marvel Family
Fawcett, 1945

1	1,100.00
2	525.00
3	425.00
4-5	315.00
6-10	265.00
11-20	200.00
21-30	165.00
31-40	135.00
41-70	100.00
71-81	85.00
82-89	75.00

Marvel Fanfare
Marvel, 1982

A deluxe, bimonthly series, Marvel Fanfare was a way for Marvel to spotlight its artistic rising stars while giving the writers a chance to stretch the bounds of established characters. Indeed, early issues were just that, with Chris Claremont returning The X-Men to the Savage Land to face Sauron in the series opener.

Other guest stars in the series included Iron Man, Moon Knight, and The Black Widow.

While some stories were compelling -- and certainly benefited from the better paper -- eventually some fans regarded the series as a dumping ground for unused file stories. And, if you didn't have a particular interest in a character or characters, an extended story could put you off for good. Such is the life of the anthology.

1	5.00
2-5	3.00
6-50	2.00
51	3.00
52-60	2.00

Marvel Fanfare
Marvel, 1996

1	2.00
2-6	1.00

Marvel Feature
Marvel, 1971

1	125.00
2	60.00
3	30.00
4	25.00
5-10	10.00
11	55.00
☛Thing vs. Hulk	
12	35.00

Marvel Feature
Marvel, 1975

1	10.00
2-4	3.00
4/30¢	35.00
5	3.00
5/30¢	20.00
6-7	3.00

Marvel Frontier Comics Unlimited
Marvel, 1994

1	3.00

Marvel Fumetti Book
Marvel, 1984

1	2.00

Marvel Graphic Novel
Marvel, 1982

The Marvel Graphic Novels feature book-length (OK, short book-length) stories with good writing and are propelled by the visual impact of comics. Freed from poor-quality printing and length restrictions of comic books, the creative teams on a graphic novel can be at their best.

And some of these are impressive. Early issues of The Marvel Graphic Novel series feature The Death of Captain Marvel, the introduction of The New Mutants, and the Holocaust-like cautionary tale "God Loves, Man Kills," starring The Uncanny X-Men. Later issues continue the tradition, demonstrating that comic art need not be limited to the bubble-gum crowd.

```
1 .............................................13.00
1/2nd-1/3rd.............................6.00
2 ...............................................7.00
3 ...............................................8.00
4 .............................................12.00
4/2nd........................................6.00
4/3rd........................................5.00
5 .............................................20.00
5/2nd........................................7.00
5/3rd-8......................................6.00
9 ...............................................7.00
10-11.........................................6.00
12-13.........................................7.00
14-17.........................................6.00
18-21.........................................7.00
22 .............................................9.00
23 .............................................7.00
24 .............................................8.00
25-28.........................................7.00
29 .............................................8.00
30 .............................................6.00
31 .............................................7.00
32 ...........................................10.00
33-34.........................................7.00
35 ...........................................13.00
36-37.........................................7.00
38 ...........................................16.00
```

Marvel Graphic Novel: Arena
Marvel

```
1 ...............................................6.00
```

Marvel Graphic Novel: Cloak and Dagger and Power Pack: Shelter From the Storm
Marvel

When his partner, the luminous Dagger, suffers a head injury and disappears after a tussle with street thugs, the troubled Cloak seeks out the young members of Power Pack to help find her. Their search introduces them to the harsh and dangerous world of teenage runaways, and the Power kids must go undercover in a shelter to rescue the amnesiac Dagger.

This story takes a hard look at the lives of teen runaways, focusing on two kids from very different lifestyles who both end up on the street. But the very real issues that these kids face-physical abuse, sexual assault, drugs, prostitution, suicide-are ultimately trivialized by the introduction of a super-villain who keeps kids from going home by draining their wills and life force.

```
1 .............................................. 8.00
```

Marvel Graphic Novel: Emperor Doom: Starring the Mighty Avengers
Marvel

```
1 .............................................. 6.00
```

Marvel Graphic Novel: Ka-Zar: Guns of the Savage Land
Marvel

```
1 .............................................. 9.00
```

Marvel Graphic Novel: Rick Mason, the Agent
Marvel, 1989

```
1 .......................................... 10.00
```

Marvel Graphic Novel: Roger Rabbit in the Resurrection of Doom
Marvel

Famed toon actor Baron Von Rotten was best known for his portrayal of evil villains in many cartoons until one day an exploding grenade forever changed him into the menace known as Judge Doom. Doom was thought to have perished at the hands of detective Eddie Valiant, but now Doom is back and he is determined to destroy the life and career of Roger Rabbit. Will Eddie and Roger be able to once again defeat the maniacal Doom or will Toontown fall victim to his vile schemes?

Also included in this lively and entertaining graphic novel is an adaptation of the Roger Rabbit cartoon Tummy Trouble.

```
1 ............................................. 9.00
```

Marvel Graphic Novel: The Shadow
Marvel

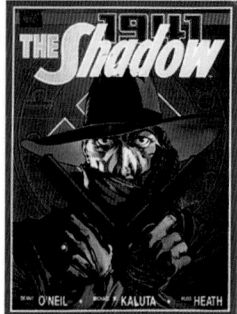

In the late 1980s, many years after their first collaboration on the adventures of the classic pulp hero, Denny O'Neil (Batman, Green Lantern) and Michael W. Kaluta (Starstruck, Time Warp) returned to The Shadow, the.45-toting vigilante "who knows what even lurks in the hearts of men." This tale--entitled "Hitler's Astrologer"--is set in the spring of 1941: Poland, Belgium, Norway, France, and Czechoslovakia have fallen to the Nazis; and the United States of America maintains its neutrality in the affairs of the European nations. There seems to be no stopping the F̦hrer's war machine. Or is there? Hitler's pursuit of the occult is well known; and his star-chart is telling him to honor Germany's non-aggression pact with Russia and to push on toward Great Britain, a defiant--but very vulnerable--nation. Can the Shadow and his elite cadre of operatives find a way to save the United Kingdom and send the Nazis down the path that will eventually lead to their downfall? Well, history tells us the answer, but O'Neil and Kaluta make getting to the inevitable awfully intriguing.

```
1 .......................................... 11.00
```

Marvel Graphic Novel: Who Framed Roger Rabbit?
Marvel

```
1 ............................................. 7.00
```

Marvel Guide to Collecting Comics
Marvel, 1982
1 ....3.00

Marvel Halloween Ashcan 2006
Marvel, 2006
1 ....1.00

Marvel Halloween: Supernaturals Tour Book
Marvel, 1998
1 ....3.00

Marvel: Heroes & Legends
Marvel, 1996
1-2...3.00

Marvel Heroes Flip Magazine
Marvel, 2005
1-11...4.00
13-20...5.00

Marvel Holiday Special
Marvel, 1993

A one-shot for the 1991 Christmas season, this special features many of the most popular Marvel characters in holiday storylines. This is not to say that the stories are all sweetness and light. The Fantastic Four feature is a warm tribute to Charles Dickens' Scrooge, with young Franklin Richards rewarded for donating his last quarter to a needy apparition. On the other hand, the Punisher storyline seems to indicate that his idea of a merry Christmas is a mob deal that goes sour, killing his target for him. Other stories feature the X-Men, Captain America, Ghost Rider, Captain Ultra, and Spider-Man. All are good, some are excellent. Overall, The Marvel Holiday Special, is a great holiday season present from Marvel.

1-1996...3.00

Marvel Holiday Special 2004
Marvel, 2004
1 .... 16.00

Marvel Holiday Special 2005
Marvel, 2006
1 .... 4.00

Marvel Holiday Special 2006
Marvel, 2007
1 .... 4.00

Marvel Illustrated: Swimsuit Issue
Marvel, 1991
1 .... 4.00

Marvel Kids
Marvel
1-4 .... 4.00

Marvel Knights
Marvel, 2000
1 .... 4.00
1/A... 5.00
2/Barreto 4.00
2/Quesada............................... 5.00
3-15 .... 3.00

Marvel Knights
Marvel, 2002
1-6... 3.00

Marvel Knights 4
Marvel, 2004
1 .... 4.00
2-29... 3.00

Marvel Knights Double-Shot
Marvel, 2002
1-4 .... 3.00

Marvel Knights Magazine
Marvel, 2001

For comic lovers who missed the classic, sold-out stories first time around, or perhaps for readers who don't want to be caught reading standard "comics," we have Marvel Knights Magazine, a standard-sized 10X12 magazine that reprints stories from virtually all the Knights books, including Kevin Smith's and Joe Quesada's impossible-to-find inaugural run on Daredevil; Garth Ennis' and Steve Dillon's uproarious and ultra-violent Punisher; an absolutely luscious Black Widow as drawn by J.G. Jones and many others. Magazine-type features and text pieces abound, including short profiles of supporting characters (such as Spacker Dave from Punisher), previews of upcoming Knights books, farcical self-help "tips" from the main characters themselves; and even a sexy pinup or two (suitable for framing!). In all, not a bad way to sample the mature Marvel imprint, and far cheaper in the long run than hunting down and buying the back issues.

-- Stephen C. George

1-6 .... 4.00

Marvel Knights/Marvel Boy Genesis Edition
Marvel, 2000
1 .... 1.00

Marvel Knights: Millennial Visions
Marvel, 2002
1 .... 4.00

Marvel Knights Sketchbook
Marvel
1 .... 1.00

Marvel Knights Spider-Man
Marvel, 2004
1 .... 5.00
2 .... 4.00
3-4 .... 3.00
5 .... 2.00
6-22 .... 3.00

Marvel Knights Tour Book
Marvel, 1998
1 .... 3.00

Marvel Knights 2099: Black Panther
Marvel, 2004
1 .... 4.00

Marvel Knights 2099: Daredevil
Marvel, 2004
1 .... 4.00

Marvel Knights 2099: Inhumans
Marvel, 2004

1 .... 4.00

Marvel Knights 2099: Mutant
Marvel, 2004

1 .... 4.00

Marvel Knights 2099: Punisher
Marvel, 2004

1 .... 4.00

Marvel Knights Wave 2 Sketchbook
Marvel

1 .... 1.00

Marvel Legacy: The 1960s Handbook
Marvel, 2006

1 .... 5.00

Marvel Legends: Thor
Marvel, 2004

1 .... 25.00

Marvel Legends: Wolverine
Marvel, 2003

2 .... 20.00
3 .... 13.00
4-5 .... 14.00
6 .... 20.00

Marvel Legends: X-Men
Marvel, 2003

3 .... 25.00
4 .... 20.00

Marvel Magazine
Marvel, 1998

There are plenty of comic magazines that cover the industry, but when you publish as many books each month as Marvel Comics, all of your titles might not get enough press-unless you publish your own monthly magazine. Jam-packed with previews of upcoming issues, mini-series, and new titles from Marvel, it offers lengthy interviews with creators, overviews of what's coming up in popular titles like the X-Men books, and guides to upcoming chat schedules.

Typical previews include upcoming Marvel Knights mini-series like Doctor Strange, and new creative teams taking over established titles. If it's published by Marvel, you'll find it in here.

1-6 .... 1.00

Marvel Mangaverse
Marvel, 2002

1-6 .... 2.00

Marvel Mangaverse: Avengers Assemble!
Marvel, 2002

1 .... 2.00

Marvel Mangaverse: Eternity Twilight
Marvel, 2002

1 .... 2.00
1/A 4.00

Marvel Mangaverse: Fantastic Four
Marvel, 2002

The revisionist millenium strikes again as the staid cast of Marvel's longest-running title find themselves morphed with the manga style. Reed Richards, Sioux Storm, Ben Grimm and Jonatha Storm are the Earth's premier metatalent response team, dealing with the myriad xenocultures bent on rendering us back to the Stone Age. The four familiar powers still exist but are now channeled through mega-scale exoskeletons, making the team's conflicts echo the Tokyo-flattening battles of Godzilla.

When Annihilus drops into Earth orbit and (ahem) annihilates all opposition, the four leap into action. And while their suits do the big guy some serious damage, he's able to get up after each attack. Just like the other Fantastic Four, it's up to Reed's superior intellect to save the day.

1 .... 2.00

Marvel Mangaverse: Ghost Riders
Marvel, 2002

1 .... 2.00

Marvel Mangaverse: New Dawn
Marvel, 2002

1 .... 4.00

Marvel Mangaverse: Punisher
Marvel, 2002

1 .... 2.00

Marvel Mangaverse: Spider-Man
Marvel, 2002

1 .... 2.00

Marvel Mangaverse: X-Men
Marvel, 2002

1 .... 2.00

Marvelman Special
Fleetway-Quality

1 .... 5.00

Marvel Masterpieces 2 Collection
Marvel, 1994

1-3 .... 3.00

Marvel Masterpieces Collection
Marvel, 1993

This mini-series serves as a portfolio for the renowned artwork of Joe Jusko. Originally presented in a trading card collection of the same name, these four issues collect Jusko's portraits of Marvel's mightiest heroes and villains. Readers are treated to a visual feast as Jusko captures the essence of some of comicdom's most intriguing personalities: the demon Mephisto engulfed in flame, Thor leaving Asgard via the Rainbow bridge, and the Thing and Hulk locked in one of their epic brawls just to name a few. As a special bonus, a total of twenty new paintings are presented for the first time. This is a great collection by one of the most recognizable artists in the business.

1-4...3.00

Marvel Milestone Edition: Amazing Spider-Man
Marvel, 1993
1...3.00
149...3.00

Marvel Milestone Edition: Avengers
Marvel, 1993
1...3.00
16...3.00

Marvel Milestone Edition: Captain America
Marvel, 1995

This replica edition re-presents 46 pages of Joe Simon and Jack Kirby, delivering the first and most successful of their many patriotic heroes for a company then known as Timely Comics. Simon and Kirby were still a decade off their peak in 1941, but even so purveyors of superior action comics. Captain America's often retold origin sequence is but one of four slam-bang stories, one of them introducing the Red Skull, who's

patently not the Red Skull who was feared throughout the Marvel Universe in later years. Simon and Kirby must have been confident they had a winner, as they're offering readers the chance to join the Captain America Sentinels of Liberty from the first issue.

The extra pages common in comics of the 1940s price this Milestone edition at a dollar more than the rest of the line, but it's only the Captain America stories that are reprinted. To see the likes of Hurricane and Tug, also by Simon and Kirby, you'll have to buy the original.

1 .... 4.00

Marvel Milestone Edition: Fantastic Four
Marvel, 1991
1 .... 3.00
5 .... 3.00

Marvel Milestone Edition: Giant-Size X-Men
Marvel, 1991
1 .... 4.00

Marvel Milestone Edition: Incredible Hulk
Marvel, 1991
1 .... 3.00
181 .... 3.00

Marvel Milestone Edition: Iron Fist
Marvel
14 .... 3.00

Marvel Milestone Edition: Iron Man
Marvel, 1992

Otherwise known as Iron Man #55, this is a complete facsimile reprint of the comic that saw the debut of Marvel's cosmic villain Thanos, along with the Destroyer,

Eros, Mentor, and other characters who would play notable parts in an acclaimed Captain Marvel run. Taken in historical context, though, it was a fill-in, and possible tryout, by Jim Starlin during a period when everyone and his mother were producing an issue of Iron Man. It improved on Iron Man #54, but the significance lies in the characters introduced, not the quality.

55 .... 3.00

Marvel Milestone Edition: Iron Man, Ant-Man & Captain America
Marvel, 2005
1 .... 4.00

Marvel Milestone Edition: Tales of Suspense
Marvel, 1994
39 .... 3.00

Marvel Milestone Edition: X-Men
Marvel, 1991

The Marvel Milestone series reprints the most famous stories from the Marvel Comics' early days. With the exception of the front covers, these were exact, page-for-page facsimiles of the original editions, complete with the original ads.

Among the issues reprinted in this series is X-Men (1st Series) #1, the debut of Professor Charles Xavier and his extraordinary students, the X-Men. The original X-Men consisted of five members: the Beast, Iceman, Cyclops, Marvel Girl, and the Angel. The members were teenagers with mutated genes which gave them "X"-tra powers over normal humans. As a rule mutants were not accepted by society. This prejudice turned some mutants against mankind, and so it is that Magneto, the X-Men's first and most powerful enemy, is introduced in the first issue.

1 ....3.00

Marvel Milestones: Beast & Kitty
Marvel, 2006
1 ....4.00

Marvel Milestones: Black Panther, Storm, and Ka-Zar
Marvel, 2006
1 ....4.00

Marvel Milestones: Blade, Man-Thing & Satana
Marvel
1 ....4.00

Marvel Milestones: Captain Britain, Psylocke, and Golden Age Sub-Mariner
Marvel, 2005
1 ....4.00

Marvel Milestones: Dragon Lord, Speedball, and Man in the Sky
Marvel, 2006
1 ....4.00

Marvel Milestones: Dr. Doom, Sub-Mariner, & Red Skull
Marvel, 2005
0 ....4.00

Marvel Milestones: Dr. Strange, Silver Surfer, Sub-Mariner, Hulk
Marvel, 2005
1 ....4.00

Marvel Milestones: Ghost Rider, Black Widow & Iceman
Marvel, 2005
1 ....4.00

Marvel Milestones: Jim Lee and Chris Claremont X-Men and The Starjammers Part #17
Marvel, 2006
1 ....4.00

Marvel Milestones: Legion of Monsters, Spider-Man, and Brother Voodoo
Marvel, 2006
1 .... 4.00

Marvel Milestones: Millie the Model & Patsy Walker
Marvel, 2006
1 .... 4.00

Marvel Milestones: Onslaught
Marvel, 2007
1 .... 4.00

Marvel Milestones: Rawhide Kid and Two-Gun Kid
Marvel, 2006
1 .... 4.00

Marvel Milestones: Star Brand and Quasar
Marvel, 2006
1 .... 4.00

Marvel Milestones: Ultimate Spider-Man, Ultimate X-Men, Microman & Mantor
Marvel, 2006
1 .... 4.00

Marvel Milestones: Venom and Hercules
Marvel, 2005
1 .... 4.00

Marvel Milestones: Wolverine, X-Men, & Tuk: Cave Boy
Marvel, 2005
1 .... 4.00

Marvel Milestones: X-Men & The Starjammers Part 2
Marvel, 2006
1 .... 4.00

Marvel Monsters: Devil Dinosaur
Marvel, 2005
1 .... 4.00

Marvel Monsters Fin Fang Four
Marvel, 2005
1 .... 4.00

Marvel Monsters: From the Files of Ulysses Bloodstone
Marvel, 2006
1 .... 4.00

Marvel Monsters: Monsters On the Prowl
Marvel, 2005
1 .... 4.00

Marvel Monsters: Where Monsters Dwell
Marvel, 2005
1 .... 4.00

Marvel Movie Premiere
Marvel
1 .... 3.00

Marvel Movie Showcase
Marvel, 1982
1-2 .... 1.00

Marvel Movie Spotlight
Marvel, 1982
1 .... 4.00

Marvel Must Haves
Marvel, 2001

After an almost decade-long period of stagnation, Marvel came roaring back in the 21st century with a renewed sense of creativity. Many fans were caught unaware by this unexpected development and missed the start of some excellent new series. Prices for back issues quickly escalated if they were available at all due to Marvel's policy of limiting the press run. Hence the appearance of Mighty Marvel Must Haves, reprinting first issues of the long-awaited origin of Wolverine and Startling Stories: Banner, a brutal look at the consequences of being the Hulk. Also featured was the chilling "Severance Package," from Spider-Man's Tangled Web.

Essentially a "greatest hits" title but with recent stories, this book is similar in concept to Marvel Milestone Edition, which also gave fans the chance to read stories that became significant but were difficult and expensive to obtain.

-- George Haberberger

1-2 ....4.00

Marvel Must Haves: Amazing Spider-Man #30-32
Marvel, 2003

1 ....4.00

Marvel Must Haves: Avengers #500-502
Marvel, 2004

1 ....4.00

Marvel Must Haves: Incredible Hulk #50-52
Marvel, 2003

1 ....4.00

Marvel Must Haves: Incredible Hulk #34-36
Marvel, 2003

1 ....4.00

Marvel Must Haves: New Avengers #1-3
Marvel, 2005

1 ....4.00

Marvel Must Haves: New X-Men #114-116
Marvel, 2003

1 ....4.00

Marvel Must Haves: NYX #4-5
Marvel, 2005

1 ....4.00

Marvel Must Haves: Sentinel #1 & #2 and Runaways #1 & #2
Marvel, 2003

1 ....4.00

Marvel Must Haves: Spider-Man & Black Cat #1-#3
Marvel, 2006

1 ....5.00

Marvel Must Haves: The Ultimates #1-3
Marvel, 2003

1 ....4.00

Marvel Must Haves: Truth: Red, White and Black
Marvel, 2003

1 ....4.00

Marvel Must Haves: Ultimates 2 #1-3
Marvel, 2005

1 .... 5.00

Marvel Must Haves: Ultimate Spider-Man #1-3
Marvel, 2003

1 .... 4.00

Marvel Must Haves: Ultimate Venom
Marvel, 2003

1 .... 4.00

Marvel Must Haves: Ultimate War
Marvel, 2003

1 .... 4.00

Marvel Must Haves: Ultimate X-Men #1-3
Marvel, 2003

1 .... 4.00

Marvel Must Haves: Ultimate X-Men #34 & #35
Marvel, 2003

1 .... 3.00

Marvel Must Haves: Wolverine #1-3
Marvel, 2003

1 .... 4.00

Marvel Mystery Comics
Marvel, 1939

Marvel Comics #1, dated October (with some cover-stamped November) 1939, was the first newsstand comic book from fledgling Marvel Comics. Its inaugural issue introduced newsstand buyers to such characters as the original Human Torch, The Sub-Mariner, and jungle hero Ka-Zar.

With #2, the title changed names to Marvel Mystery Comics. During this time of escalating global tensions, it found a ready audience for such patriotic heroes as The Patriot and Miss America. The Human Torch (with kid sidekick Toro) would soon stop fighting each other and begin battling side by side against Axis forces. Captain America would also make appearances in later issues.

Although these heroes could conquer the Nazis, they eventually fell to the post-war super-hero malaise. With #93, the series dropped its super-hero stories and became Marvel Tales (1st Series).

2	30,000.00
3	15,000.00
4	12,500.00
5	22,500.00
6-7	7,500.00
8	10,000.00
9	25,000.00
10	8,000.00
11	3,800.00
12	4,000.00
13	5,000.00
14-17	2,500.00
18	2,250.00
19-20	2,500.00
21	2,000.00
22-25	1,700.00
26-30	1,475.00
31-41	1,325.00
42-48	1,125.00
49	1,450.00
50	1,125.00
51-67	1,000.00
68-78	860.00
79	810.00
80	1,275.00
81	975.00
82	2,250.00
83	810.00
84	1,250.00
85	810.00
86	890.00
87	785.00
88-91	950.00
92	2,500.00

Marvel Mystery Comics
Marvel, 1999

1 .... 4.00

Marvel Nemesis: The Imperfects
Marvel, 2005

1 .... 4.00
2-6 .... 3.00

Marvel No-Prize Book
Marvel, 1983

1 .... 3.00

Marvelous Adventures of Gus Beezer and Spider-Man
Marvel, 2004

1 ....3.00

Marvelous Adventures of Gus Beezer: Hulk
Marvel, 2003

1 ....3.00

Marvelous Adventures of Gus Beezer: Spider-Man
Marvel, 2003

1 ....3.00

Marvelous Adventures of Gus Beezer: X-Men
Marvel, 2003

1 ....3.00

Marvelous Dragon Clan
Lunar, 1994

1-2..3.00

Marvelous Wizard of Oz (MGM's...)
Marvel

1 ....16.00

Marvel: Portraits of a Universe
Marvel, 1995

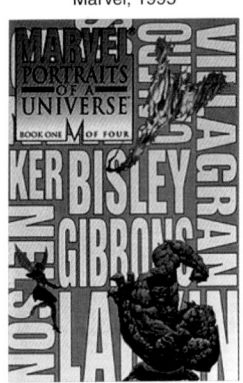

Portraits of a Universe was a four-issue mini-series that tied in with Marvel's line of trading cards. Each issue folded out to show some fourteen scenes from Marvel history, complete with narration. The scenes were chosen not so much for their historical importance as they were for being able to convey a strong image. They include, for instance, Spider-Man versus the Punisher from Amazing Spider-Man #285, or Hobgoblin versus Spider-Man from Spider-Man #6. The scenes were painted by a variety of artists, primarily newcomers, although old favorites like Simon Bisley also appear from time to time.

1-4..3.00

Marvel Poster Book
Marvel, 1991

1 ....3.00

Marvel Poster Magazine
Marvel, 2001

2 ....4.00

Marvel Premiere
Marvel, 1972

In its nearly decade-long run, Marvel Premiere served as a proving ground for a host of new characters. Iron Fist, Woodgod, Caleb Hammer, The Liberty Legion, The 3-D Man, and many others made first appearances in Marvel Premiere. Other characters, like Doctor Strange, The Falcon, Morbius, Ghost Rider, and Jack of Hearts were featured here in their first solo stories. Marvel even tried out its own Elfquest-like series with Weirdworld in #38. And yes, Marvel Premiere was also the venue in which Alice Cooper made his first comic book appearance.

1 ....35.00
2 ....12.00
3 ....30.00
☞Dr. Strange
4 ....10.00
5-6 ....8.00
7 ....15.00
8 ....10.00
9 ....6.00
10 ....9.00
11-12 ....5.00
13 ....8.00
14 ....12.00
15 ....80.00
☞1st Iron Fist
16 ....20.00
☞2nd Iron Fist

17-18 ....12.00
19-24 ....10.00
25 ....15.00
26 ....4.00
27 ....10.00
28 ....13.00
29 ....3.00
29/30¢ 20.00
30 ....3.00
30/30¢ 20.00
31 ....3.00
31/30¢ 20.00
32-36 ....3.00
36/35¢ 15.00
37-37/Whitman..3.00
37/35¢ 15.00
38-38/Whitman..3.00
38/35¢ 15.00
39-49 ....3.00
50 ....13.00
☞1st Alice Cooper
51-56 ....3.00
57 ....5.00
58-61 ....3.00

Marvel Presents
Marvel, 1975

1 ....11.00
2 ....5.00
3 ....10.00
4 ....4.00
4/30¢ 20.00
5 ....4.00
5/30¢ 20.00
6 ....4.00
6/30¢ 20.00
7-10 ....4.00
11 ....15.00
11/35¢-12 ....4.00
12/35¢ 15.00

Marvel Preview
Marvel, 1975

Marvel set out to stretch the bounds of what a comic book could be, when it introduced Marvel Preview, a comics magazine consisting of adult-oriented stories featuring a number of familiar and new characters. In its black-and-white, magazine format, it could reach out to a new group of readers and approach issues that might be too adult for the traditional comic-book medium. As a result, the writers got a chance to create terrific stories.

One of these early stories tells of an ex-marine named Frank Castle, who barely survives when his family is murdered by mobsters. In that origin story (which appeared in Marvel Preview #2), readers see for the first time the origin of the man now known as The Punisher. Marvel Preview also contains the origins or early appearances of such greats as Dominic Fortune, Star-Lord, Kull the Conqueror, and Moon Knight. With #25, Marvel Preview switches names to become Bizarre Adventures.

1 ....15.00
2 ....50.00
☛Punisher origin
3 ....10.00
☛Blade app.
4 ....7.00
☛Blade app.
5-24 ....5.00

Marvel Preview '93
Marvel, 1993
1 ....4.00

Marvel Riot
Marvel, 1995
1 ....2.00

Marvel Romance Redux: But He Said He Loved Me
Marvel, 20006
1 ....3.00

Marvel Romance Redux: Guys & Dolls
Marvel, 2006
1 ....3.00

Marvel Romance Redux: I Should Have Been a Blonde
Marvel, 2006
1 ....3.00

Marvel Romance Redux: Love Is a Four Letter Word
Marvel, 2006
1 ....3.00

Marvel Romance Redux: Restraining Orders Are for Other Girls
Marvel, 2006
1 ....3.00

Marvels
Marvel, 1994

Countless comics readers have grown up in the Marvel universe, where the exploits of Spider-Man, The Fantastic Four, and The X-Men interweave naturally with each other, and with people and events from the real world. Such strong continuity was rare in comic books when Marvel started out, but the creation of coherent "comics universes" has since become almost mandatory for any line of comics.

After 30 years in the Marvel universe, readers take for granted that Norse gods walk the streets of New York alongside winged mutants and human fireballs. This series, however, makes it all seem fresh again, recapturing the wonder of the early days of Marvel. Written by Kurt Busiek, it's told through the eyes of an ace photographer, who recounts the story of when The Marvels first appeared. The fully painted artwork by Alex Ross only adds to the magical feel.

0 .... 4.00
1 .... 6.00
1/2nd 3.00
2 .... 6.00
2/2nd 3.00
3-4 .... 6.00
4/2nd 3.00

Marvel Saga
Marvel, 1985

One of the unusual aspects of The World of Marvel is that there has been created a Marvel universe within our real one -- and the company has taken great pains over the years to be true to it. Marvel Saga traced the evolution of the Marvel universe, beginning with the space shot that created the Fantastic Four, up through the coming of Galactus and the origin of The Silver Surfer.

Marvel Saga presented the origins of every major Marvel character, along with the key elements in each one's lives. What's more, it followed the many crossed paths of these characters, showing readers how things were related to each other at each moment.

1 .... 3.00
2-25 .... 2.00

Marvels Comics: Captain America
Marvel, 2000
1 .... 2.00

Marvels Comics: Daredevil
Marvel, 2000
1 .... 2.00

Marvels Comics: Fantastic Four
Marvel, 2000

Told from the perspective of each of the members, this one-shot pays homage to the Stan Lee and Jack Kirby Fantastic Four classics of the 1960s. Although not part of Marvel Universe continuity--Marvels Comics are a series of fictional titles that exist in the Marvel Universe-- the lineup remains the same: Reed Richards, Mr. Fantastic, a scientific genius with elastic powers; his wife Susan Richards, otherwise known as the Invisible Woman; her brother Johnny Storm, the Human Torch; and Ben Grimm, the Thing, the man with a body of rock and the heart of a teddy bear. A picnic turns into a confrontation with the Fantastic Four's oldest foe, the Mole Man.

1 ....2.00

Marvels Comics: Spider-Man
Marvel, 2000
1 ....2.00

Marvels Comics: Thor
Marvel, 2000

Marvel's version of the Norse

god Thor is given a high-tech makeover in this one-shot, among several titles that would've been published in the Marvel Universe if it was real. In this interpretation, Thor is not a god; instead, he is merely a super-hero identity created by Owen Jolson, a man who acquired powerful extraterrestrial technology when he found the remains of an alien ship and its otherworldly passengers. When he became injured, his son Don inherited the role and the high-tech hammer Mjolnir. As in regular Marvel continuity, Thor's brother--named Leonard instead of Loki--is jealous of his sibling and tries to kill him.

1 .... 2.00

Marvels Comics: X-Men
Marvel, 2000
1 .... 2.00

Marvel Select Flip Magazine
Marvel, 2005
1-11 .... 4.00
12-20 .... 5.00

Marvel Selects: Fantastic Four
Marvel, 2000
1 .... 3.00

Marvel Selects: Spider-Man
Marvel, 2000

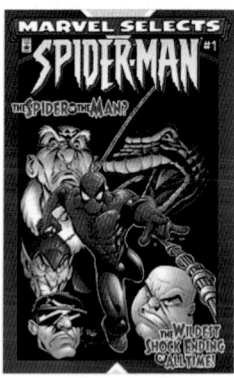

First appearing in 1961's Amazing Fantasy #15, the scrawny, bookish Peter Parker was bitten by a radioactive spider, gaining amazing strength and agility, as well as the ability to sense imminent danger. At first, Peter was only interested in the financial opportunities his new powers could provide. But after the

tragic death of his uncle, a death Spider-Man could have prevented, he vowed to use his abilities to defend the weak and innocent whenever possible.

This series reprints classic stories from the long-running Amazing Spider-Man, focusing on the particularly pivotal and defining moments in Spidey's career. It is similar to 1993's Spider-Man Classics, but that series only reprinted his earliest adventures, in the order that they first appeared.

1-3 .... 3.00

Marvel's Greatest Comics
Marvel, 1969
☛Was Marvel Collector's Item Classics
23-34 .... 15.00
35-37 .... 10.00
38-50 .... 4.00
51-63 .... 3.00
63/30¢ 20.00
64 .... 3.00
64/30¢ 20.00
65-70/Whitman 3.00
71 .... 2.00
71/35¢ 15.00
71/Whitman-72/Whitman........ 2.00
72/35¢ 15.00
73-73/Whitman 2.00
73/35¢ 15.00
74-96 .... 2.00

Marvel's Greatest Comics: Fantastic Four #52
Marvel, 2006
1 .... 3.00

Marvel: Shadows & Light
Marvel, 1997
1 .... 3.00

Marvel 1602
Marvel, 2003
1 .... 6.00
2 .... 5.00
3 .... 6.00
4 .... 5.00
5 .... 6.00
6 .... 5.00
7 .... 4.00
8 .... 5.00

Marvel 1602: New World
Marvel, 2005
1-5 .... 4.00

Marvel 1602: Fantastik Four
Marvel, 2006
1-4 .... 4.00

Marvel 65th Anniversary Special
Marvel, 2004

1 ....5.00

Marvels of Science
Charlton, 1946

1 ....100.00
2 ....55.00
3-4 ....48.00

Marvel Special Edition Featuring Close Encounters of the Third Kind
Marvel, 1978

3 ....9.00

Marvel Special Edition Featuring Spectacular Spider-Man
Marvel, 1975

1 ....12.00

Marvel Special Edition Featuring Star Wars
Marvel, 1977

When the first Star Wars film premiered in 1977, it was not only the most popular movie up to that time, it was also one of Marvel Comics' most successful licensed properties. The original six-issue comic adaptation sold so well, Marvel reprinted it multiple times and also re-released it as a treasury edition and, finally, in this slim paperback by Del Ray. If you want to enjoy Howard Chaykin's (American Flagg) artwork on this groundbreaking series, this is not the best showcase: production values are low, the pages are reprinted in black and white and are reduced from standard comic-page size to fit on a 4X6 page. Still, for those grownups who still don't want to be caught reading comic books, it's certainly a convenient, low-profile format, and still manages to convey some

small slice of the grandeur of the greatest space-fantasy film of all.
-- Stephen C. George

1 .... 14.00
2 .... 12.00
3 .... 14.00

Marvel Spectacular
Marvel, 1973

By the early 1970s, Marvel had created several "Marvel..." titles based on reprints of their work from just a few years past. The Amazing Spider-Man reprints of Marvel Tales and the Fantastic Four reprints of Marvel's Greatest Comics were joined in 1973 by Marvel Spectacular, which reprinted stories from the early days of Thor.

Marvel Spectacular reprised the glory days of Thor, beginning with #1's reprint of Thor #128, and continuing in sequence until issue #19's reprint of Thor #145. These were the classic Jack Kirby issues, showing Thor taking on both gods and men in heroic battle. As an added bonus, early issues contained Tales of Asgard as a backup feature. These stories gave new readers background on the spectacular mythical world that Thor hailed from.

1 .... 5.00
2-19 .... 3.00

Marvel Spotlight: Brian Michael Bendis/ Mark Bagley
Marvel, 2007

1 .... 3.00

Marvel Spotlight: Daniel Way/Oliver Coipel
Marvel, 2006

1 .... 3.00

Marvel Spotlight: David Finch/ Roberto Aguirre-Sacasa
Marvel, 2006

1 .... 3.00

Marvel Spotlight: Ed Brubaker/Billy Tan
Marvel, 2006

1 .... 3.00

Marvel Spotlight: Heroes Reborn/ Onslaught Reborn
Marvel, 2007

1 .... 3.00

Marvel Spotlight: John Cassaday/Sean McKeever
Marvel, 2006

1 .... 3.00

Marvel Spotlight: Joss Whedon/Michael Lark
Marvel, 2006

1 .... 3.00

Marvel Spotlight: Mark Millar/Steve McNiven
Marvel, 2006

1 .... 3.00

Marvel Spotlight: Neil Gaiman/Salvador Larroca
Marvel, 2006

1 .... 3.00

Marvel Spotlight: Robert Kirkman/Greg Land
Marvel, 2006

1 .... 3.00

Marvel Spotlight: Stan Lee/Jack Kirby
Marvel, 2006

1 .... 3.00

Marvel Spotlight
Marvel, 1971

1 .... 25.00
2 .... 130.00
☞1st Werewolf
3-4 .... 30.00
5 .... 275.00
☞1st Ghost Rider
6 .... 45.00
7 .... 35.00
8 .... 25.00
9 .... 30.00
10 .... 35.00
11-12 .... 22.00
13 .... 12.00
14-15 .... 10.00
16-19 .... 7.00
20-21 .... 5.00
22 .... 6.00
23-24 .... 5.00

25-27 ....3.00
27/30¢ 20.00
28 ....10.00
28/30¢ 18.00
29 ....9.00
29/30¢ 15.00
30-31 ....3.00
32 ....50.00
☞1st Spider-Woman
33 ....3.00

Marvel Spotlight
Marvel, 1979

1 ....3.00
2-11 ....2.00

Marvel Spotlight:
Warren Ellis/Jim Cheung
Marvel, 2006

1 ....3.00

Marvel Spring Special
Marvel, 1988

1 ....3.00

Marvel Super Action
Marvel, 1977

1-1/Whitman..............................8.00
2 ....3.00
2/35¢ 15.00
3-3/Whitman..............................3.00
3/35¢ 15.00
4-4/Whitman..............................3.00
5-37 ....2.00

Marvel Super Action
(Magazine)
Marvel, 1976

1 ....35.00

Marvel Super Hero
Contest of Champions
Marvel, 1982

Marvel's first limited series actually announced as such, 1982's Marvel Super Hero Contest of Champions began when every living super-hero was abruptly snatched from Earth and taken to a stadium in space. They had been called there to settle a bet between

a powerful being known as the Grandmaster and a cloaked adversary called "the Unknown." The super-heroes were to divide into teams and search for the four pieces of the Golden Globe of Life, hidden in various places around the planet. If the Grandmaster's team won, the Unknown would be forced to resurrect the Grandmaster's dead brother. If the Grandmaster lost, the Unknown would claim the Grandmaster's life.

This three-issue title was one of Marvel's first limited series. It served as an excuse to introduce several minor super-heroes such as Le Peregrine and Talisman. As a bonus, it included an index to Marvel characters major and minor a la the Marvel Universe handbooks.

1-3 .... 4.00

Marvel Super-Heroes
Marvel, 1966

12 .... 95.00
☞1st Captain Mar-vell; was Fantasy Masterpieces
13 .... 50.00
14 .... 75.00
☞Reprints 1st Kirby
15 .... 42.00
16 .... 25.00
17 .... 30.00
18 .... 40.00
☞1st Guardians
19 .... 20.00
20 .... 35.00
21-27 .... 12.00
28-30 .... 10.00
31 .... 20.00
32 .... 6.00
33-38 .... 5.00
39-45 .... 4.00
46-57 .... 3.00
57/30¢ 20.00
58 .... 3.00
58/30¢ 20.00
59-65/Whitman...................... 3.00
65/35¢ 15.00
66-66/Whitman...................... 3.00
66/35¢ 15.00
67-80/Whitman...................... 3.00
81-105 .... 2.00
Special 1 .... 40.00
☞1966 one-shot

Marvel Super-Heroes
Marvel, 1990

1 .... 4.00
2-15 .... 3.00

Marvel Super-Heroes
Megazine
Marvel, 1994

1-6 .... 3.00

Marvel Super Heroes
Secret Wars
Marvel, 1984

In May, 1984, Marvel editor in chief Jim Shooter decided to shake up the Marvel universe a bit. To do this, the company created the Secret Wars, a 12-issue limited series that involved almost every major Marvel character. In this series, Earth's heroes were kidnapped by an almost omnipotent being known as The Beyonder, and pitted against their deadliest enemies. The members of the winning side were promised their fondest desire - but the losers would be granted no mercy.

The Secret Wars changed the lives of all involved, particularly The Amazing Spider-Man. As part of his involvement, he was given a black alien costume which gave him special powers. Eventually, however, it was revealed that this "costume" was actually a living being - a symbiote. When Spider-Man rejected bonding with it, it found another host and became known as the super-villain Venom.

Like DC's Super Powers line, this series also spawned a companion toy line.

1 .... 4.00
2 .... 2.00
3 .... 3.00
4 .... 4.00
5 .... 3.00
6 .... 4.00
7 .... 3.00
8 .... 15.00
☞1st black costume
9-10 .... 2.00
11 .... 3.00
12 .... 2.00

Marvel Super Hero Island Adventures
Marvel, 1999
1 ....5.00

Marvel Super Special
Marvel, 1977

Marvel Super Special began as a large-format book featuring the first appearance of the rock group Kiss in a comic book. In a publicity stunt, members of the group even arranged to mix drops of their own blood into the ink used in the print run, thus playing up their "Satan-rock" image. Other special issues included a feature on The Beatles and a limited run of the Weirdworld storyline, with each copy signed by the artists.

Most issues, however, were straightforward movie adaptations. The features ranged from Battlestar Galactica to Annie, although science-fiction and fantasy films of one sort or another dominated the series.

The seventh issue, featuring an adaptation of Sgt. Pepper's Lonely Hearts Club Band, was withdrawn from circulation.

1 ....85.00
☛Kiss
2-3 ....8.00
4 ....30.00
☛Beatles
5 ....55.00
☛Kiss
6 ....7.00
8 ....8.00
9 ....7.00
10 ....6.00
11-15 ....5.00
16 ....7.00
17-41 ....4.00

Marvel Swimsuit Special
Marvel, 1992
1 ....4.00
2-4 ....5.00

Marvel Tails
Marvel, 1983
1 .... 2.00

Marvel Tales
Marvel, 1949
93 .... 1,200.00
94 .... 800.00
95 .... 650.00
96 .... 550.00
97 .... 625.00
98-101 .... 550.00
102 .... 660.00
103 .... 500.00
104 .... 575.00
105 .... 445.00
106-108 .... 390.00
109-120 .... 275.00
121-130 .... 225.00
131 .... 200.00
132-133 .... 155.00
134 .... 175.00
135-145 .... 155.00
146-159 .... 125.00

Marvel Tales
Marvel, 1964
1 .... 175.00
2 .... 85.00
3 .... 45.00
4-5 .... 30.00
6-9 .... 25.00
10 .... 30.00
11-16 .... 25.00
17-21 .... 20.00
22-32 .... 15.00
33-44 .... 12.00
45-65 .... 10.00
66-66/30¢ 20.00
67 .... 10.00
67/30¢ 20.00
68 .... 10.00
68/30¢ 20.00
69 .... 10.00
69/30¢ 20.00
70 .... 10.00
70/30¢ 20.00
71 .... 10.00
72-79 .... 7.00
79/Whitman 10.00
80 .... 7.00
80/Whitman 10.00
80/35¢ 18.00
81 .... 7.00
81/Whitman 14.00
81/35¢ 15.00
82 .... 7.00
82/Whitman 14.00
82/35¢ 15.00
83 .... 7.00
83/Whitman 10.00
83/35¢ 15.00
84-84/Whitman 7.00
84/35¢ 15.00
85-85/Whitman 7.00
86-122 .... 5.00
123-136 .... 4.00
137 .... 7.00
138-144 .... 5.00

145-183 .... 4.00
184-191 .... 2.00
192 .... 3.00
193-286 .... 2.00
286/CS-286/2nd 3.00
287-291 .... 2.00

Marvel Tales Flip Magazine
Marvel, 2005
1-10 .... 4.00
11-19 .... 5.00

Marvel Team-Up
Marvel, 1972

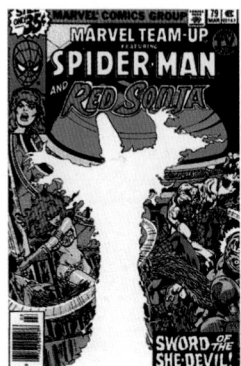

A cynic might call this series, "Trademark Renewal Theater." Here, all Marvel's characters who couldn't support a regular series of their own were given exposure through team-ups with Spider-Man. (There are a few non-Spidey stories in this series' 150-issue run, but they're the exception.) Frog-Man, Valkyrie, Hercules -- even the Not Ready For Prime-Time Players found their logos proudly displayed beneath Spidey's marquee.

Some of the pairings took some creative engineering, such as Chris Claremont's story bringing Spider-Man and Red Sonja (!) together. But as a closer continuity developed between the Spider-Man titles in the early 1980s, Team-Up found itself the "C" book, with writer J.M. DeMatteis only given "charge" of supporting characters Aunt May and the residents of the old folks home. Finally, Marvel replaced Team-Up with a title all Spidey's own, Web of Spider-Man.

-- John Jackson Miller

1 .... 185.00
2 .... 30.00
3 .... 25.00
4 .... 45.00
☛X-Men app.

5 .... 18.00
6-10 .... 16.00
11 .... 13.00
12 .... 18.00
☛Werewolf app.
13-20 .... 13.00
21-31 .... 8.00
32-44 .... 5.00
44/30¢ 20.00
45 .... 5.00
45/30¢ 20.00
46 .... 5.00
46/30¢ 20.00
47 .... 4.00
47/30¢ 20.00
48 .... 4.00
48/30¢ 20.00
49-52 .... 4.00
53 .... 15.00
☛X-Men app.
54-58/Whitman 4.00
58/35¢ 15.00
59-59/Whitman 4.00
59/35¢ 15.00
60-60/Whitman 4.00
60/35¢ 15.00
61-61/Whitman 4.00
61/35¢ 15.00
62-62/Whitman 4.00
62/35¢ 15.00
63-65 .... 4.00
66 .... 7.00
☛Captain Britain app.
67-94 .... 4.00
95-99 .... 3.00
100 .... 6.00
101-136 .... 3.00
137 .... 4.00
138-143 .... 3.00
144 .... 4.00
145-150 .... 3.00
Ann 1 .... 30.00
Ann 2 .... 6.00
Ann 3 .... 4.00
Ann 4-6 .... 3.00
Ann 7 .... 2.00

Marvel Team-Up
Marvel, 1997
1-11 .... 2.00

Marvel Team-Up
Marvel, 2004
1-8 .... 2.00
9-25 .... 3.00

Marvel:
The Lost Generation
Marvel, 2000
12-1 .... 3.00

Marvel Treasury Edition
Marvel, 1974

The Marvel Treasury Edition series stands out (literally) as some of the largest comic books ever printed. Published in the mid-1970s, the series kicked off with a Spider-Man special that reprinted some of his earliest adventures in an enlarged format. This was followed by more than two dozen other specials featuring everyone from Conan the Barbarian to Howard the Duck (in a Defenders issue). Although the oversized format of these specials was a headache for retailers, they were favorites with collectors. As a final send-off to the series, Marvel and DC joined forces to publish a Spider-Man/Superman team-up.

1 .... 15.00
2-25 .... 10.00
26 .... 12.00
27 .... 10.00
28 .... 25.00

Marvel Treasury of Oz
Marvel, 1975
1 .... 15.00

Marvel Treasury Special Featuring
Captain America's Bicentennial Battles
Marvel, 1976
1 .... 16.00

Marvel Treasury Special, Giant Superhero Holiday Grab-Bag
Marvel, 1974
1 .... 10.00

Marvel Triple Action
Marvel, 1972
1 .... 20.00
2-5 .... 12.00
6-29 .... 8.00
29/30¢ 20.00
30 .... 5.00
30/30¢ 20.00

31-36 .... 5.00
36/35¢ 15.00
37 .... 5.00
37/35¢ 15.00
38-47 .... 5.00
GS 1-2 .... 10.00

Marvel Two-In-One
Marvel, 1974

Another "team-up" series, this one featured the Fantastic Four's Thing in a series of adventures involving a wide collection of other characters. Marvel Two-In-One introduced us to a number of new heroes, including Maelstrom and the Impossible Woman. It also told of the demise of at least two characters: Issue #54 brought us the death of Luther Manning, the original Deathlok; and tragedy struck again in issue #93 with the death of Jocasta, a female "living robot" and member of the Avengers. Jocasta was eventually rebuilt, however, and made an appearance in the futuristic Machine Man limited series.

Following #100's tale of an alternate future in which New York had been devastated -- featuring a depiction of a destroyed World Trade Center, spookily enough -- the series was restarted as The Thing.

1 .... 55.00
2 .... 15.00
3 .... 10.00
4 .... 7.00
5-6 .... 8.00
7-10 .... 5.00
11-15 .... 3.00
15/30¢ 30.00
16 .... 3.00
16/30¢ 30.00
17 .... 3.00
17/30¢ 30.00
18 .... 3.00
18/30¢ 30.00
19-25/Whitman 3.00
26-28/Whitman 2.00

28/35¢ 20.00
29-29/Whitman.......................2.00
29/35¢ 20.00
30-30/Whitman.......................2.00
30/35¢ 20.00
31-31/Whitman.......................2.00
31/35¢ 20.00
32-50.....................................2.00
51-51/Whitman.......................3.00
52-53.....................................2.00
54..4.00
55-99.....................................2.00
100...3.00
Ann 1....................................4.00
Ann 2...................................15.00
☛Warlock dies
Ann 3-4 ....2.00
Ann 5.....................................3.00
Ann 6-7 ....2.00

Marvel Universe
Marvel, 1998
1..3.00
2-7...2.00

Marvel Universe: Millennial Visions
Marvel, 2002
1..4.00

Marvel Universe: The End
Marvel, 2003
1-6...4.00

Marvel Valentine Special
Marvel, 1997
1..2.00

Marvel Versus DC/ DC Versus Marvel
DC, 1996
1-4...4.00
Ashcan 1 ....1.00

Marvel Westerns: Outlaw Files
Marvel, 2006
1..4.00

Marvel Westerns: Strange Westerns Starring Black Rider
Marvel, 2006
1..4.00

Marvel Westerns: Two-Gun Kid
Marvel, 2006
1..4.00

Marvel X-Men Collection
Marvel, 1994
1-3...3.00

Marvel Year in Review
Marvel, 1989
1-5...4.00
6..3.00

Marvel Zombies
Marvel, 2006
1 .... 55.00
1/2nd 35.00
1/3rd................................... 12.00
2 .... 16.00
3 .... 6.00
3/2nd 4.00
4-5 .... 3.00

Marvel Zombies vs. Army of Darkness
Marvel, 2007
1 .... 5.00
1/2nd-5 .... 3.00

Marville
Marvel, 2002
1-7 .... 2.00

Marvin Mouse
Atlas, 1957
1 .... 75.00

Mary Jane
Marvel, 2004
1-4 .... 2.00

Mary Jane: Homecoming
Marvel, 2005
1-3 .... 3.00

Mary Marvel
Fawcett, 1945

The third member of Fawcett's burgeoning Marvel Family (which included Captain Marvel, Captain Marvel, Jr. and assorted others), Mary was the long-lost sister of Cap's alter-ego, Billy Batson. She was granted the powers of the goddesses Selena, Hippolyta, Ariadne, Sephyrus, Aurora, and Minerva by the old wizard Shazam and fights evil in the guise of super-heroine Mary Marvel. After some memorable guest appearances in Captain Marvel and Whiz Comics, plus a permanent spot in the team-up feature Marvel Family, Mary got her own book in 1945 where she entertained with lighthearted adventures in the endearing Fawcett style. She was revived along with her super-siblings by DC in the 70s and again in The Power of Shazam.

1 .... 1,450.00
2 .... 650.00
3 .... 450.00
4 .... 400.00
5 .... 275.00
6-10 .... 250.00
11-20 .... 160.00
21-28 .... 135.00

Mary Poppins
Gold Key, 1965
1 .... 28.00

Mary Worth
Argo, 1956
1 .... 35.00

Mask
DC, 1985
1-4 .... 1.00

Mask
DC, 1987
1-9 .... 1.00

Mask
Dark Horse, 1991
0 .... 5.00
1-2 .... 4.00
3-4 .... 3.00

Mask
Dark Horse, 1995
1-17 .... 3.00

Mask, The: Official Movie Adaptation
Dark Horse, 1994
1-2 .... 3.00

Mask Returns
Dark Horse, 1992
1 .... 4.00
2-4 .... 3.00

Mask, The: Toys in the Attic
Dark Horse, 1998
1-4 .... 3.00

Mask, The: Virtual Surreality
Dark Horse, 1997
1 .... 3.00

Mask Comics
Rural Home, 1945
1 .... 2,100.00
2 .... 1,250.00

Mask Conspiracy
Ink & Feathers
1 .... 7.00

Masked Man
Eclipse, 1984

1-12..2.00

Masked Marvel
Centaur, 1940

1 ....1,325.00
2 ....900.00
3 ....800.00

Masked Ranger
Premier, 1954

1 ....175.00
2-3...75.00
4-9...65.00

Masked Rider
Marvel, 1996

On his grandparents' planet Edenoi, Dex Stewart was a prince. Now he's been adopted by an Earth family, and he's a normal teenager. Well, almost normal. He has the transformative power to access armor, weapons, and sentient vehicles to aid him in the battle against the evil Count Dregon. When Dex exclaims "Masked Rider Activate!" he becomes the Masked Rider, a hero who exists in the same continuity as Saban's Mighty Morphin Power Rangers. He's even like a Mighty Morphin Power Ranger, in that he's a teenager who activates and deactivates his heroic persona with a phrase, and his adventures fall in the same vein.

Unlike other Saban-licensed series, however, this book gives you the angst and pathos of typical Marvel characters, since Dex is torn between his adoptive family on Earth and his grandfather on Edenoi.

-- *George Haberberger*

1 ....3.00

Masked Warrior X
Antarctic, 1996

This translated Japanese series only lasted four issues of a planned six, possibly because it's a by-the-numbers manga with no distinguishing features. In a society where athletes are given cybernetic implants and sent to commit crimes, Dan is the invincible Kendo Warrior, the one force for good. Raised from birth to his position, his invincible armor has fused to him, and regenerates from his own body. Sadly the more interesting implications are never explored, pushed out by lengthy combat sequences punctuated by the occasional slapstick gag, usually involving the police, with whom Dan joins in the first issue. The title comes from his kendo mask and his habit of slicing his conquests with an "X" across their torso in Zorro fashion.

1 .... 4.00
2 .... 3.00
3 .... 4.00
4 .... 3.00

Mask/Marshal Law
Dark Horse, 1998

1-2... 3.00

Mask of Dr. Fu Manchu
Avon, 1951

1 .... 385.00

Mask of Zorro
Image, 1998

1-4/Variant.............................. 3.00

Masks: Too Hot for TV
DC, 2003

1 .... 5.00

Masque of the Red Death
Dell, 1964

1 .... 20.00

Masquerade
Mad Monkey

1-2 .... 4.00
Ashcan 1 .... 2.00

Masques
(J.N. Williamson's...)
Innovation, 1992

1-2 .... 5.00

Master
New Comics

1-2 .... 2.00

Master Comics
Fawcett, 1940

Master Comics was one of the cornerstones of the Fawcett lineup during the 1940s. Originally featuring a mix of adventure, Western, and generic super-hero stories - and, for a while, the home of Bulletman, a popular second-string Fawcett hero - Master Comics began featuring the adventures of Captain Marvel, Jr. with issues #21-22 (crossing over into Whiz Comics #25).

Newsboy Freddie Freeman, crippled in a fight against the evil Captain Nazi, was rescued by Captain Marvel and taken to the old wizard, Shazam, who gave him the power to become the world's mightiest boy by uttering the words "Captain Marvel." Junior's adventures were generally grittier than those of the other Marvels, partly due to the superb realistic artwork of Mac Raboy.

This series also introduced Nyoka the Jungle Girl, Tom Mix, and Hopalong Cassidy.

1 .... 8,100.00
2 .... 2,275.00
3 .... 1,550.00

4-5	1,275.00
6	1,200.00
7	2,150.00
8	1,325.00
9-10	1,050.00
11	2,300.00
12	1,150.00
13	1,800.00
14-15	1,000.00
16-20	925.00
21	4,550.00
22	3,925.00
23	2,400.00
24-30	860.00
31-40	625.00
41	525.00
42-47	400.00
48	450.00
49	400.00
50	475.00
51-55	280.00
56-65	230.00
66-80	175.00
81-90	145.00
91-100	125.00
101-132	120.00
133	135.00

Master Darque
Acclaim, 1997

1	6.00
Ash 1	4.00

Master of Kung Fu
Marvel, 1974

17	15.00
18	7.00
19-20	6.00
21-31	5.00
32-39	4.00
39/30¢	20.00
40	3.00
40/30¢	20.00
41	3.00
41/30¢	20.00
42	3.00
42/30¢	20.00
43	3.00
43/30¢	20.00
44-53	3.00
53/35¢	15.00
54	3.00
54/35¢	15.00
55	3.00
55/35¢-57/35¢	15.00
58-99	3.00
100	4.00
101-124	2.00
125	3.00
Ann 1	20.00

Master of Kung Fu: Bleeding Black
Marvel, 1991

1	3.00

Master of Mystics: The Demoncraft
Chakra

A sincere attempt to adapt ancient Indian holy texts as translated by Srila Prabhupada. They concern Krishna, the Supreme Being, and his antics while living on Earth in human guise. If this is to be seen as religious dogma, then seeming inconsistencies must be accepted through faith, but it makes for poor stories. One minute Krishna is as fallible and puzzled as the next human, but is then able to pull the proverbial rabbit from the hat. That he exists in all places at all times further complicates matters. Even readers steeped in super-hero comics might find him a little farfetched. Furthermore, read without faith, the stories have the opposite effect from what's intended. Krishna is portrayed as a capricious despot for whom humanity is but a toy, while the assorted humans seeking revenge have just cause for doing so. One for the converted only.

1-2	2.00

Master of Rampling Gate (Anne Rice's...)
Innovation, 1991

1	7.00

Masters of the Universe: Icons of Evil: Beast Man
Image, 2003

1	5.00

Master of the Void

Iron Hammer, 1993

1	3.00

Masters of Horror
Idea & Design Works, 2005

1	4.00
3-4	4.00

Masters of the Universe
DC, 1982

1	3.00
2-3	2.00

Masters of the Universe
Marvel, 1986

1	4.00
2-13	3.00

Masters of the Universe
Image, 2002

1-1/B	3.00
1/Gold	6.00
2-4/B	3.00

Masters of the Universe
Image, 2003

1	6.00
1/A-4	3.00
4/A-4/C	6.00
5-8	3.00

Master's Series
Avalon

1	3.00

Masterworks Series of Great Comic Book Artists
DC, 1983

1-3	3.00

Matador
DC, 2005

1-5	3.00

Matt Champion
Metro

1	2.00

Matterbaby
Antarctic, 1997

John Marshall's Matterbaby is a very funny set of strips starring a super-powerful hero who needs to pause regularly for naps and diaper changes. When duty calls, it's "Mattah baby whoosh whoosh!" and the little tyke flies off to battle evildoers. The series is very much in the same line as The Tick, with laughs coming from the combination of superstrength and toddler-simple solutions. There's also a good mix of self-referential humor, as well as comedic swipes at the X-Files, Basil Wolverton art, disco, and the purple dinosaur Barney.

1-Ann 1 ....3.00

Matt Slade, Gunflighter
Atlas, 1956
1...90.00
2...60.00
3-4...45.00

Maverick
Dell, 1959
7-10.......................................50.00
11-15......................................40.00
16-19......................................30.00

Maverick
Marvel, 1997
1...3.00

Maverick
Marvel, 1997
1...3.00
2-11...2.00
12...3.00

Maverick Marshal
Charlton, 1957
1...30.00
2...20.00
3-7...16.00

Mavericks
Dagger, 1994
1-5...3.00

Mavericks: The New Wave
Dagger
1-3...3.00

Max Brewster: The Universal Soldier
Fleetway-Quality
1-3...3.00

Max Burger PI
Graphic Image
1...2.00
2...3.00

Max Damage: Panic!
Head, 1995
1...3.00

Maximage
Image, 1995

A movie shoot on Easter Island was rudely interrupted when one of the huge statues fairly exploded, releasing a wizened man who had been trapped inside for millennia. The man was known as The Ancient, and he immediately traveled to Hollywood where he appeared before Robin, a young street urchin. With a wave of his hand, she found herself garbed in a warrior's costume, and had her destiny revealed to her. She had become the Maximage, the most powerful sorcerer on the planet. Of course, the power came with strings attached-the most urgent being the obligation to save the Earth from the ancient space gods who had returned to destroy it.

Maximage is much like a "bad girl" version of the King Arthur legend, with The Ancient substituting for Merlin, and the suddenly buxom Maximage filling the part of King Arthur.

1-10 .... 3.00

Maximo One-Shot
Dreamwave, 2004
1 .... 4.00

Maximortal
Tundra, 1992
1-4 .... 4.00
5-7 .... 3.00

Maximum Security
Marvel, 2000
1-3 .... 3.00

Maximum Security Dangerous Planet
Marvel, 2000
1 .... 3.00

Maximum Security: Thor vs. Ego
Marvel, 2000
1 .... 3.00

Maximum Volume
Kitchen Sink, 1994
1 .... 15.00

Maxion
CPM Manga, 1999
1-20 .... 3.00

Max of the Regulators
Atlantic
1-4 .... 2.00

Max Rep in the Age of the Astrotitans
Dumbbell, 1997
1-2 .... 3.00

Max the Magnificent
Slave Labor, 1987

Before there was Jim Valentino, and before he cofounded Image, the writer/artist was known simply as Valentino, and he enjoyed small-press success in the '80s with such Slave Labor Graphics comics as the hit spoof normalman and this spinoff mini-series, Max the Magnificent. Max-a humanoid frog in a cheap suit with attitude and arrogance to spare-is a TV talk-show host who will gladly insult the Queen herself in the name of ratings. A man (amphibian?) with such a disposition makes a lot of enemies, and it isn't long before Max and his lovely sidekick/protector are on the run from a host of them. Of course, with several normalman regulars on the scene, can Captain Everything be far behind?

Valentino's art style is simple yet effective in this black-and-white tale, and his wit and sense of satire are razor sharp. The mood is irreverent and the pacing really jumps.

1-3 .... 2.00

Maxwell Mouse Follies
Renegade, 1986

1-6..2.00

Maxwell the Magic Cat
Acme

1-3..5.00
4...6.00

Maxx
Image, 1993

Huge. Powerful. Purple. It's that last part about being purple (along with his general confusion about life) that separates The Maxx from the other musclebound mooks you're likely to encounter. Of undetermined origin, The Maxx seems convinced that he's some sort of super-hero, but other than getting beaten up by bad guys, he is not exactly sure of what he's supposed to do. Frankly, he would much rather just go home and watch Cheers.

Created, written, and drawn by Sam Kieth, The Maxx comes off like Image's answer to Groo the Wanderer. Upon further examination, however, it turns out that Kieth has created one of the more complex psychodramas to be seen in comic books. The real story revolves around a girl, Julie, who suffered abuse as a child and has grown into an incredibly shy adult. The Outback is her dreamland, where she appears as a jungle princess. The Maxx is actually just a homeless bum whom Julie took in.

The comics series eventually spawned an MTV animated series of the same name.

1/2	5.00
1/2/Gold	16.00
1	3.00
1/3D	5.00
1/Variant	6.00
2-10	3.00
11-35	2.00

Maxx
DC, 2003

1-3................................ 18.00

Mayhem
Kelva, 1977

1 .... 1.00

Mayhem
Dark Horse, 1989

1-4 .... 4.00

Maze
Metaphrog, 1997

1 .... 4.00

Maze Agency
Idea & Design Works, 2006

1-3.................................... 4.00

Maze Agency
Comico, 1988

1-3	3.00
4-6	2.00
7	3.00
8-15	2.00
16-Ann 1	3.00
Special 1-Xmas 1	3.00

Maze Agency
Caliber, 1997

1-3 .... 3.00

Mazie
Nationwide, 1950

1	85.00
2-3	45.00

Mazie and her Boyfriends
Harvey, 1950

Mazie and her pals at Greenview High School kept teens and their younger siblings entertained throughout the 1950s in a series of innocuous humor stories in the Archie vein. Mazie, the blond flirt, was the titular star of the series, but her suitors Stevie and Flat-Top, rival Jeanie, geekish pal Mortie, and little brother Brod often stole the show with more broad-based gags. The tone of the series was much more hip than

many other teen humor books, with references to jazz, youth-oriented movies like Rebel Without a Cause, and early rock 'n 'roll inserted in the stories and in the text-based features. Mazie disappeared from the stands in 1958.

-- *Rob Salkowitz*

1	26.00
2	13.00
3-10	9.00
11-28	7.00

'Mazing Man
DC, 1986

1-12	1.00
Special 1-3	2.00

McHale's Navy
Dell, 1963

1	40.00
2	32.00
3	26.00

McKeever and The Colonel
Dell, 1963

1	28.00
2-3	20.00

M.D.
E.C., 1955

1	80.00
2-5	65.00

M.D.
Gemstone, 1999

1-5 .... 3.00

M.D. Geist
CPM, 1995

For more than 100 years, the Nexrum Alliance on the planet Jerra has been fighting Earth's loyalists for independence. But Earth's regular army would rather annihilate Jerra completely than give it to the Nexrum Alliance. In its desperation, the regular army unleashes a genetically engineered soldier with supernatural fighting abilities, Most Dangerous (M.D.) Geist. Too late, they find M.D. Geist is a force they can never control, and so lock him away.

Geist has broken loose, and the regular army has all but completely lost ground to the more organized and determined Nexrum Alliance. He quickly becomes the leader of a mercenary group, which includes the calculatingly sly Vaiya. Now only lots of battles in Robotech-style armor will determine whom Geist is fighting for, if he's fighting for anyone at all.

1-3...3.00

M.D. Geist: Ground Zero
CPM, 1996

1-3...3.00

Mea Culpa
Four Walls Eight Windows, 1990

1...13.00

Me-A Day With Elvis
Invincible

1...1.00

Meadowlark
Parody

1...3.00

Me and Her
Fantagraphics, 1991

1-3...2.00
Special 1 ....3.00

Mean, Green Bondo Machine
Mu, 1992

1...3.00

Mean Machine
Fleetway-Quality

1...5.00

Meanwhile...
Crow

1-2...3.00

Measles
Fantagraphics, 1998

1-8...3.00

Meat Cake
Fantagraphics, 1995

1-10...3.00
11...4.00

Meat Cake
Iconografix

1...3.00

Meatface the Amazing Flesh
Monster

1...3.00

Mecha
Dark Horse, 1987

1-6...2.00

Mechanic
Image, 1998

1 .... 6.00

Mechanical Man Blues
Radio, 1998

1 .... 3.00

Mechanics
Fantagraphics, 1985

1-3... 2.00

Mechanimals
Novelle

1 .... 4.00
2... 3.00

Mechanimoids Special X Anniversary
Mu

1 .... 4.00

Mechanoids
Caliber

1-3... 3.00

Mech Destroyer
Image, 2001

Written by Robert Chong and illustrated by Jae Kim, Mech Destroyer is a limited series about a future in which Earth has been overrun by androids led by Kru-Sak, Overlord of the Jadak Empire. The only hope in this dire situation is Reese Taylor and the XR5000, the Mech Destroyer--a gigantic piece of robotic hardware with an arsenal the likes of which the world has never seen. Can Taylor master the XR5000 before it's too late? This exciting thriller keeps readers hooked through the last issue.

1-4 .... 3.00

Mechoverse
Airbrush

1-3... 2.00

Mechthings
Renegade, 1987

1-4 .... 2.00

Medabots Part 1
Viz, 2002

1-4 .... 3.00

Medabots Part 2
Viz, 2002

1-4 .... 3.00

Medabots Part 3
Viz, 2002

1-4 .... 3.00

Medabots Part 4
Viz, 2002

1-4 .... 3.00

Medal of Honor
Dark Horse, 1994

The Congressional Medal of Honor is America's highest military honor, given to those brave few who rise far beyond the call of duty, risking their lives in the service of their country. In 1994, Dark Horse Comics produced this mini-series to tell the real stories of some of the winners of the honor.

Among those was Lt. Charles Q. Williams, who served in the early days of the war in Vietnam. In 1965, Americans were merely advisors in the conflict but, when Williams' base was attacked, they became more than observers. Wounded in the initial skirmish, he led his men through an all-night fire fight, putting back the enemy advance. In the morning, an airstrike leveled the compound, but the helicopters due to evacuate them were ambushed. After several hours of fierce fighting, rescue was finally at hand. Although he had been hit multiple times, Williams insisted that others be evacuated before him.

1-Special 1 .... 3.00

Media*Starr
Innovation, 1989

1-3... 2.00

Medieval Spawn
Image

1-3..2.00

Medieval Spawn/ Witchblade
Image, 1996

1 ....3.00
1/Gold 6.00
1/Platinum 15.00
2...4.00
3...3.00

Medieval Witchblade
Image

1-3..6.00

Medora
Lobster, 1999

1 ....3.00

Medusa Comics
Triangle

1 ....2.00

Meef Comix
Print Mint, 1973

1-2..4.00

Meet Corliss Archer
Fox, 1948

The radio sitcom was another comedy radio show focusing on the goings-on of an irrepressible teen; it aired from 1943 to 1956, first starring Priscilla Lyon, then Janet Waldo as Corliss, 14 going on 15. The characters were created by F. Hugh Herbert in the magazine story "Private Affair," and Shirley Temple starred as Corliss in Kiss and Tell (1945) and A Kiss for Corliss (1949). The TV series ran from 1951 to 1952 with Lugene Sanders as Corliss and from 1954 to 1955 with Ann Baker as Corliss. Other characters were Corliss' parents, Harry and Janet; her boyfriend, Dexter Franklin; brat Raymond Ames; Mildred, Corliss' best friend; and Betty Cameron, Corliss' rival.

In other words, the property was far more successful in media other than comic books, where she was played on covers as a "headlights" character, though the cover also carried the notation "America's favorite teen-age radio and screen star!!!"

-- Maggie

1 .... 475.00
2 .... 350.00
3 .... 270.00

Meet Merton
Toby, 1953

1 .... 40.00
2 .... 22.00
3 .... 20.00

Meet Miss Bliss
Atlas, 1955

1 .... 80.00
2 .... 50.00
3-4 .... 44.00

Meet Miss Pepper
St. John, 1954

5 .... 80.00
6 .... 65.00

Meet the Bank
Custom, 1995

1 .... 1.00

Megacity 909
Devil's Due, 2005

1 ....6.00
1/Variant..................................5.00
2-8/Variant............................. 3.00

Mega Dragon & Tiger
Image, 1999

1-5..3.00

Megahurtz
Image, 1997

1-3..3.00

Megalith
Continuity, 1989

1-4..2.00
5-9..3.00

Megalith
Continuity, 1993

0-0/A......................................1.00
1-7..3.00

Megalomaniacal Spider-Man
Marvel, 2002

1 ....3.00

Megaman
Dreamwave, 2003

1 ....3.00
2-4..3.00

Mega Morphs
Marvel, 2005

1-4 .... 3.00

Megaton
Megaton, 1983

1-2 .... 3.00
3 .... 5.00
4-7 .... 2.00
8 .... 3.00
Holiday 1 .... 4.00

Megaton Man
Kitchen Sink, 1984

In his badly-kept secret identity of Trent Phloog, he's just another hulking, goggled reporter. But as Megaton Man, he's a hulking, goggled super-hero! (You see the difference, right?)

Of course, it's not all fighting super-villains (like the dread "Bad Guy") for our hero. No, he has a sensitive, romantic side as well. For instance, he has an impossible crush on ace reporter Pamela Jointly. Strangely, despite his sensitive cries of "Woo! Pammy Baby!" she is somehow convinced that Trent is a macho jerk. In contrast, the nubile "See-Thru Girl" is dying to do some "patrolling" with him. The only problem: she's married to super-hero Phil Flaccid.

Created by Donald Simpson, Megaton Man is a hilarious send-up of the super-hero genre, poking fun at everyone from Superman to the Fantastic Four.

1 .... 3.00
1/2nd 2.00
2-10 .... 3.00

Megaton Man: Bombshell
Image, 1999

1 .... 3.00

Megaton Man: Hardcopy
Image, 1999
1-2..3.00

Megaton Man Meets the Uncategorizable X+Thems
Kitchen Sink, 1989
1...2.00

Megaton Man vs. Forbidden Frankenstein
Fiasco, 1996
1...3.00

Megazzar Dude
Slave Labor, 1991
Special 1 ....3.00

Mekanix
Marvel, 2002
1-6...3.00

Mel Allen Sports Comics
Standard, 1949

Although super-heroes reign supreme in today's comic books, the Golden Age of comics featured a wider variety of subjects. Mel Allen, the sportscaster for the New York Yankees in the 1940s and 1950s, is featured in this title that uses sports-oriented stories as morality plays to illustrate how organized sports can be an important factor in self-fulfillment. Stories use sports as a vehicle to teach honesty, to illustrate the value of teamwork and to avoid juvenile delinquency.
-- George Haberberger

1...85.00
2...58.00

Melissa Moore: Bodyguard
Draculina
1...3.00

Melody
Kitchen Sink, 1988
1... 3.00
2-8.. 2.00

Melonpool Chronicles
Para-Troop
1... 3.00

Meltdown
Image, 2006
1... 6.00

Melting Pot
Kitchen Sink, 1993
1... 4.00
2-3.. 3.00
4... 4.00

Melty Feeling
Antarctic, 1996
1-4.. 4.00

Melvin Monster
Dell, 1965
1... 60.00
2... 45.00
3... 40.00
4-5.. 32.00
6-10.. 26.00

Melvin the Monster
Atlas, 1956
1... 55.00
2... 40.00
3-5.. 35.00

Melvis
Chameleon, 1994
1-4.. 2.00

Memento Mori
Memento Mori, 1995
1-2.. 2.00

Memories
Marvel, 1992
1... 3.00

Memory
NBM
1... 25.00

Memoryman
David Markoff
1/Ashcan 1.00

Memory Man (Emergency Stop)
Esp
1... 3.00
2-4.. 2.00
5-Ashcan 1 .... 3.00

Menace
Atlas, 1953
1... 400.00
2... 300.00
3... 250.00
4... 215.00
5-6.. 170.00
7-11.. 140.00

Men Against Crime
Ace Magazines, 1951
3... 70.00
4-7.. 50.00

Menagerie
Chrome Tiger, 1987

The stars of this black-and-white anthology title are Scary Cat and Mousekanaut, two mercs-for-hire who take on the jobs that no one else can do-like blowing up a refinery and making it look like an industrial accident. Scary Cat is the flamboyant talker/charmer, while Mousekanaut is the more serious and subdued of the pair. The backup features rotate, but maintain the title's sci-fi theme.

1-2.. 2.00

Mendy and the Golem
Mendy, 1981
1... 3.00
2-19.. 2.00

Men from Earth
Future-Fun
1... 2.00

Men in Action
Marvel, 1952
1... 50.00
2... 36.00
3-6.. 28.00
7... 32.00
8-9.. 28.00

Men in Action
Ajax, 1957
1... 50.00
2... 30.00
3-6.. 25.00

Men in Black
Aircel, 1990
1... 15.00
2... 10.00
3... 8.00

Men in Black
Aircel, 1991

1	14.00
2	10.00
3	8.00

Men in Black: Far Cry
Marvel, 1997

1	4.00

Men in Black: Retribution
Marvel, 1997

1	4.00

Men in Black: The Movie
Marvel, 1997

You probably know the drill: Men in Black agents Jay and Kay are sort of like Immigration and Naturalization officers for the entire planet; they keep track of every extraterrestrial on Earth and make sure humanity is not overrun by the scum of the universe. In this faithful adaptation of the 1997 film, Agent Kay recruits Agent Jay into the MIB organization as a giant alien bug wreaks havoc while trying to locate and steal an entire galaxy. This version of creator and writer Lowell Cunningham's Men in Black veers a bit from the titles original, somewhat darker incarnation, but it's good nonetheless…and a nice souvenir of one of the top films of the 1990s.

1	4.00

Men of Mystery
AC, 2005

1-56	7.00

Men of War
DC, 1977

1	15.00
2-12	6.00
13-26	4.00

Men's Adventure Comix
Penthouse International, 1995

1	6.00
2-7	5.00

Men's Adventures
Atlas, 1950

4	175.00
5	120.00
6-8	100.00
9-20	75.00
21-26	125.00
27-28	675.00

Menthu
Black Inc!, 1998

1-4	3.00

Menz Insana
DC

1	8.00

Mephisto Vs.
Marvel, 1987

In Fantastic Four #277, the devil Mephisto was defeated by Franklin Richards, son of Reed Richards of the Fantastic Four. Of course, the source of evil can never truly be eliminated, only dissipated for a while. And when Mephisto re-formed, he set about planning his revenge on the Fantastic Four.

In the Mephisto Vs...series, he first takes on the Fantastic Four. By dragging them down to Hell, he is able to subject them to any number of delusions. Eventually, he is able to persuade Sue Richards, the Invisible Woman, to trade her soul in return for the release of the others. But while he had no valid claim on the others' souls in the first place, Susan's agreement lets him hold hers. Now the Fantastic Four, and later X-Factor, the Uncanny X-Men, and the Avengers must battle Mephisto to win back the soul of their friend.

1	3.00

2-4	2.00

Mercedes
Angus, 1995

1-12	3.00

Merchants of Death
Eclipse, 1988

1-4	4.00

Merchants of Venus
DC

1	6.00

Mercy
DC

1	6.00

Meridian
CrossGen, 2000

In the interwoven worlds of the CrossGen universe, Demetria is a world that suffered from an ancient cataclysm that led to toxic zones jeopardizing the city-states of the planet. The title island, Meridian, is the first of the cities that survivors created to float in the sky.

The focal character is the Sigil-bearing 16-year-old Sephie, the only daughter of the late Minister of Meridian. Her adventures range from dealing with political intrigue to the physical adventures of visiting other floating islands while coping with inter-city conflicts. Elaborate layouts provide views of the environments of the various city islands and the land below.

-- Maggie

1	4.00
2-44	3.00

Merlin
Adventure, 1990

1-6	3.00

Merlin: Idylls of the King
Adventure, 1992

1-2	3.00

Merlin Jones As The Monkey's Uncle
Gold Key, 1965

1 ....10.00

Merlinrealm 3-D
Blackthorne, 1985

1 ....2.00

Mermaid
Alternative, 1998

1 ....3.00

Mermaid Forest
Viz, 1993

The legend says that if you eat the flesh of a mermaid, you will live forever. Long ago, a member of the Kannagi clan was said to have actually caught a mermaid and buried it somewhere in the forest on their ancestral lands. Nobody seems to know if he ate the mermaid or not, but since then, the place has been known as the Mermaid Forest.

In the here and now, a Doctor Shiina has become fascinated by the old legends and has made it his life's work to find an actual mermaid. His gruesome practice is to perform experiments on his dying patients in the hopes of discovering a real mermaid. But when a young girl named Mana is brought to him, it seems he may have finally found what he sought for so long.

The story of the Mermaid continues after the conclusion of this series in Mermaid's Scar.

1-4 ....3.00

Mermaid's Dream
Viz, 1985

1-3 .... 3.00

Mermaid's Gaze
Viz

1-4 .... 3.00

Mermaid's Mask
Viz

1-4 .... 3.00

Mermaid's Promise
Viz

1-4 .... 3.00

Mermaid's Scar
Viz, 1994

1-4 .... 3.00

Merry Comics
Charlton, 1945

1 .... 95.00

Merry Mouse
Avon, 1953

1 .... 42.00
2 .... 30.00
3-4 .... 24.00

Merton of the Movement
Last Gasp, 1971

1 .... 4.00

Meru Puri
Viz, 2005

1-2 .... 9.00

Merv Pumpkinhead, Agent of D.R.E.A.M.
DC, 2000

nn 6.00

Messenger
Image, 2000

1 .... 6.00

Messenger 29
September, 1989

1 .... 2.00

Messiah
Pinnacle

1 .... 2.00

Messozoic
Kitchen Sink, 1993

1 .... 3.00

Meta-4
First, 1991

Emily Cayce, Allis Krafe, Craig Fallow, and Dirk Penderwhistle are four youthful individuals who were blessed with powers over the four basic elements. In this case, the traditional elements of earth, air, fire, and water, are interpreted rather liberally. Emily controls the "fluid forces that reside within crystals;" Allis can harness emotional and, more interestingly, sexual energy; Craig can change his shape into a creature whose form is based on the surrounding terrain; and Dirk can control the workings of electronic and mechanical systems.

The series by Stefan Petrucha (X-Files) and Ian Gibson chronicles their adventures as they learn how to control their powers in a crazy world where it seems everybody wants to control them. This concept would be revisited in later years in such titles as Gen13.

1 .... 4.00
2-3 .... 2.00

Metabarons
DC, 2004

1 .... 15.00

Metabarons
Humanoids, 2000

1-3 .... 4.00
4-14 .... 3.00

Metacops
Fantagraphics, 1991

1-3 .... 2.00

Metadocs: The Super E.R.
Antarctic, 2005

1 .... 5.00

Metal Bikini
Eternity, 1990

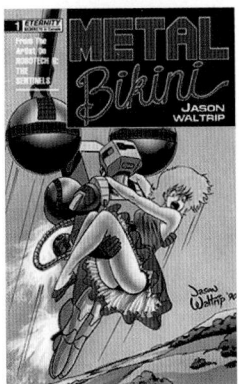

This black-and-white, Manga-inspired title from Eternity and writer/artist Jason Waltrip (Robotech II: The Sentinels) offers up scantily clad, doe-eyed women and lots of heavy-duty machinery. Find out what happens when towel-swathed model-to-be Kenji Kurosawa begins the day in the shower and ends the day by disrupting a military demonstration of a high-tech battlesuit. It's wacky, Manga-style fun, to be sure, but the objective of the story is never really clear.

1-6 ....2.00

Metal Gear Solid
Idea & Design Works, 2004
1	4.00
1/Silver	7.00
1/2nd	4.00
1/Incentive	35.00
2-12	4.00
Ashcan 0	1.00

Metal Gear Solid: Sons of Liberty
Idea & Design Works, 2005
0-8 ....4.00

Metal Guardian Faust
Viz, 1997
1-8 ....3.00

Metal Hurlant
DC, 2002
1-3	8.00
4-6	7.00
7-8	5.00
9-14	4.00

Metallica
Celebrity
1/A	3.00
1/B	7.00

Metallica
Forbidden Fruit, 1992
1-2 ....3.00

Metallica
Rock-It Comics
1 ....5.00

Metallica's Greatest Hits
Revolutionary, 1993
1 ....3.00

Metallix
Future, 2002
0-5	4.00
6	3.00

Metal Men
DC, 1963

The Metal Men were a group of robots created by Dr. Will Magnus. They took their names and their powers from the metals from which they were created. Lead was able to block bullets and radiation; Gold was able to stretch himself to incredible thinness; Iron was super-strong and nearly indestructible; Mercury could turn himself into a collection of liquid globules at room temperature; Tina (Platinum) also had amazing stretching and springing abilities - as well as a schoolgirl crush on Doc Magnus; and Tin, the coward of the bunch, seemed mostly good for laughs.

This strange but lovable bunch debuted in Showcase #37 before beginning this, their first solo series. They appeared regularly throughout the Sixties and Seventies, but seemed to vanish afterward. That changed in 1993, when DC revisited this old favorite in a brand new mini-series.

1	500.00
2	225.00
3-5	150.00
6-10	80.00
11-20	55.00
21-26	45.00
27	80.00
☞Metal Men	
28-30	42.00
31-41	24.00
42-44	12.00
45-56	6.00

Metal Men
DC, 1993
1	3.00
2-4	2.00

Metal Men of Mars & Other Improbable Tales
Slave Labor, 1989
1 ....2.00

Metal Militia
Express, 1995
1/Ashcan	1.00
1	3.00
1/A	7.00
2-3	3.00

Metamorpho
DC, 1965

Originally created in The Brave and the Bold #57 (Jan 1965), archaeologist Rex Mason was tricked into attempting to recover the Orb of Ra, a mystic relic rumored to have great powers.

Millionaire Simon Stagg, whose daughter Sapphire was Mason's fiancee, set Mason on the quest and double-crossed the unsuspecting adventurer when Stagg's henchman, the resurrected Neanderthal Java, trapped Mason in a chamber with the Orb. The object's radiations changed Mason, giving him the ability to transform his body into any combination of the chemical elements and shaping those forms into any shape he pleases. In the years since, Mason has attempted to find a cure for his condition so he can become human once again and marry the girl of his dreams.
-- Brent

1 ....75.00

2	45.00
3	40.00
4-9	30.00
10-17	25.00

Metamorpho
DC, 1993

1-4	2.00

Metaphysique
Malibu, 1995

1-6	3.00
Ashcan 1	1.00

Metaphysique
Eclipse, 1992

1	3.00

Meteor Comics
Baird, 1945

1	265.00

Meteor Man
Marvel, 1993

1-6	1.00

Meteor Man: The Movie
Marvel, 1993

Marvel brings Robert Townsend's movie and super hero of the 1990s into comic book format. Part-time musician, part-time teacher, and full-time inner-city dweller and worrier, Jefferson Reed gets badly burned when a meteor hits him as he hides from ruthless thugs. He recovers quickly, however, and ends up with a wide array of super-powers, including incredible strength, speed, invulnerability, telekinesis and flight-all of which come in handy in defense of himself and others in an area overrun with crime and violence. But more importantly, the new Meteor Man unites the formerly victimized denizens of the area against the criminals and shows them that their own hope and courage can defeat the terror of drugs, violence and vice.

1	2.00

Metropol
(Ted McKeever's...)
Marvel, 1991

1-12	3.00

Metropol A.D.
Marvel, 1992

1-3	4.00

Metropolis S.C.U.
DC, 1994

1-4	2.00

Mez
C.A.P., 1997

1-2	2.00

Mezz:
Galactic Tour 2494
Dark Horse, 1994

1	3.00

M Falling
Vagabond

1	4.00

MFI:
The Ghosts of Christmas
Image, 1999

1	4.00

Miami Mice
Rip Off, 1986

1-3	2.00
3/A	5.00
4	2.00

Michaelangelo
Christmas Special
Mirage, 1990

1	2.00

Michaelangelo Teenage
Mutant Ninja Turtle
Mirage, 1985

1	3.00

Michael Jordan Tribute
Revolutionary

1	3.00

Mickey and Donald
Gladstone, 1988

1-18	2.00

Mickey and Goofy
Explore Energy
Dell, 1976

1	2.00

Mickey & Minnie
W.D.

1	4.00

Mickey Finn
Eastern, 1942

Mickey Finn is an Irish cop on the beat whose humorous adventures focus at least as much on the comic interplay of the stereotyped characters as on the ostensible crime and action storyline. Drawn by Lank Leonard in a goofy, funny-pages style that's one part Dick Tracy and two parts Barney Google, Mickey Finn's crime-busting antics take him to all manner of settings, from the inner city to the rural countryside.

Fast-moving, fun, and innocently unsophisticated, Mickey Finn is nonetheless marred by the gratuitous use of racial and ethnic stereotypes of Irish, Blacks, Jews, and Asians that is conspicuous and notably offensive even for the 1940s. Early issues feature backup stories of "Bo," a saucer-eyed orphan and his dog.

-- Rob Salkowitz

1	85.00
2	45.00
3	32.00
4-5	24.00
6-15	20.00

Mickey Mantle
Magnum, 1991

1-2	2.00

Mickey Mouse
Dell, 1952

28-30	40.00
31-35	30.00
36-40	25.00
41-50	20.00
51-60	16.00
61-70	15.00
71-80	14.00
81-100	12.00
101-120	11.00
121-140	10.00
141-160	8.00
161-180	7.00
181-200	6.00
201-203	5.00

204	8.00
205-206	5.00
207	20.00
208	50.00
209	20.00
210-214	7.00
215-218	10.00
219	12.00
220	4.00
221-240	3.00
241-256	2.00

Mickey Mouse and Friends
Gemstone, 2003

257-295	3.00

Mickey Mouse
Disney

1	4.00

Mickey Mouse Adventures
Disney, 1990

1	3.00
2-18	2.00

Mickey Mouse Album
Gold Key, 1962

-210	25.00
1	20.00

Mickey Mouse and Goofy Explore Energy Conservation
Disney, 1978

1	2.00

Mickey and Goofy Explore the Universe of Energy
Disney, 1985

1	3.00

Mickey Mouse Birthday Party
Dell, 1953

1	365.00

Mickey Mouse Club
Gold Key, 1964

1	25.00

Mickey Mouse Club Parade
Dell, 1955

1	150.00

Mickey Mouse Digest
Gladstone, 1986

1	5.00
2	4.00
3-5	3.00

Mickey Mouse in Fantasyland
Dell, 1957

1	135.00

Mickey Mouse in Frontierland
Dell, 1956

1	125.00

Mickey Mouse Summer Fun
Dell, 1958

1	110.00

Mickey Mouse Surprise Party
Gold Key, 1969

1	18.00

Mickey Rat
Los Angeles Comic Book Co., 1972

1	25.00
2	20.00
3-4	15.00

Micra: Mind Controlled Remote Automaton
Comics Interview, 1986

1-7	2.00

Microbots
Gold Key, 1971

1	10.00

Micronauts
Marvel, 1979

1-1/Whitman	4.00
1/2nd	2.00
2-5/Whitman	3.00
6-58	2.00
59	3.00
Ann 1	4.00
Ann 2	3.00
Special 1-5	2.00

Micronauts
Marvel, 1984

1	3.00
2-20	2.00

Micronauts
Image, 2002

1-11	3.00

Middle Class Fantasies
Cartoonists Co-Op

1-2	3.00

Middleman
Viper, 2005

1-4	3.00

Midget Comics
St. John, 1950

1	80.00
2	55.00

Midnight
Ajax, 1957

This title reads like a poor man's Tales from the Crypt or Vault of Horror. Published by the Farrell Comic Group under the Ajax imprint, Midnight featured material that had been purchased from defunct comic-book publishers and rode the wave of the horror and sci-fi boom of the 1950s. Midnight's horror fare was far from the "strangest tales ever told," as its covers proclaimed; they ranged from mildly interesting to downright silly.

1	54.00
2	38.00
3-6	26.00

Midnight Days (Neil Gaiman's...)
DC, 2000

1	18.00

Midnighter
DC, 2007

1-5	3.00

Midnight Eye Gok
Viz

1-6	5.00

Midnight Kiss
APComics, 2005

1	4.00

Midnight, Mass
DC, 2002

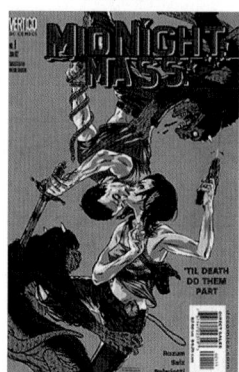

In New England, every quaint little town is haunted to some degree. Just ask the locals. Of course, usually it's just history and good PR, to attract the tourists. But the seemingly sleepy little coastal town of Midnight really is haunted. In fact, it's probably the most haunted place anywhere. But whether that's why, or because, Adam and Julia Kadmon, the world's premier paranormal investigators, make Midnight their home is yet to be decided.

Adam and Julia are just the latest couple in a family business that stretches back several generations. But things are different these days. There's a new generation of monsters out there, not content to lurk in the shadows, on the edge of human awareness. Increasingly, Adam and Julia find themselves functioning less as investigators, and more and more as a supernatural border patrol, protecting an unsuspecting world from the horrors waiting to engulf it.

1-8 .... 3.00

Midnight Mass
DC, 2004

1-6 .... 3.00

Midnight Men
Marvel, 1993

1 .... 3.00
2-4 .... 2.00

Midnight Mystery
ACG, 1961

1 .... 60.00
2 .... 40.00
3 .... 32.00
4-7 .... 30.00

Midnight Nation
Image, 2000

J. Michael Straczynski strikes again. After wowing audiences with his comic-book debut Rising Stars, the writer made famous as the creator of the TV series Babylon 5 launches his own imprint (Joe's Comics) under the Top Cow banner with the flagship title Midnight Nation. Complementing text with imagery that is both attractive and otherworldly, penciller Gary Frank is as much a visual storyteller as Straczynski is a verbal one.

Detective David Grey is trying to solve a murder that no one wants or even cares about helping to solve. In his search for the killer, the detective comes across The Men -- other-worldly beings that kill at will. But David's encounter with them leaves him shouldering a fate worse than death: the loss of his soul. Transported to the "World In-Between" -- an eerie ghost world populated by forgotten souls -- David and his beautiful guide Laurel fight to reclaim the man's soul. If he does not accomplish his mission within 11 months, he will turn into one of The Men and live a life trapped in an eternal Hell.

1/2 .... 5.00
1/2/Gold 9.00
1/A 4.00
1/B 5.00
1/C 8.00
1/D 5.00
2-12 .... 3.00

Midnight Panther
CPM, 1997

1-12 .... 3.00

Midnight Panther: Feudal Fantasy
CPM, 1998

1-2 .... 3.00

Midnight Panther: School Daze
CPM, 1998

1-5 .... 3.00

Midnight Screams
Mystery Graphix, 1992

1-2 .... 3.00

Midnight Sons Unlimited
Marvel, 1993

1-9 .... 4.00
Ashcan 1 .... 1.00

Midnight Tales
Charlton, 1972

In the early 1970s, some Charlton comics were sold in polybagged three-packs at airports, so that Mom and Pop could give junior his comics fix to keep him quiet on the plane ride to visit the grandparents in Florida. This was shrewd marketing, because it assumed that, to parents, a comic book was a comic book ("Spider-Man, E-Man, what's the difference?"), even if every kid knew that Charltons were the airplane food of the comics cafeteria. Midnight Tales is a typical 1970s Charlton horror-mystery anthology title "hosted" by voluptuous young Arachne and her mentor, the Midnight Philosopher. Artist Wayne Howard was clearly imitating the style of comic-art great Wally Wood ,right down to his gothic signature, but at least he aimed high in his tribute. Consequently, Midnight Tales has the look of a seedy, off-register knock-off of an E.C. horror title -- putting it at the top of Charlton's quality spectrum.

-- Rob Salkowitz

1 .... 18.00
2 .... 10.00

3-5	8.00
6-17	6.00
18	8.00

Midnite
Blackthorne, 1986

1-3	2.00

Midnite Skulker
Target, 1986

1-7	2.00

Midnite's Quickies
One Shot, 1997

1	4.00
2-Special 1/B	3.00

Midori Days
Viz, 2005

1-2	10.00

Midvale
Mu, 1990

Underground titles usually never shy away from toilet humor, and Midvale relishes in it. Featuring stories written and drawn by Brad Carlton, Midvale makes no apologies for its gross-outs. In the second issue, a tale called "Midvale Thai" features a man devouring hot, spicy Oriental food and discovers how painful it is to digest as flames erupt from his behind in the bathroom. A Teenage Mutant Ninja Turtle makes an appearance in Midvale # 2's opening tale, "It's a Wonderful Christmas Carol," inspiring one of the series' cleanest jokes: "Please don't sue me…I'm just a poor struggling cartoonist who's trying to eke out a meager living."

1-2	3.00

Mightily Murdered Power Ringers
Express

1	3.00

Mighty Midget Comics: Minute Man
Lowe, 1942

12	100.00

Mighty Ace
Omega 7

1-2	2.00

Mighty Atom
Magazine Enterprises, 1949

6	35.00

Mighty Atom
Magazine Enterprises, 1957

1	22.00
2-6	18.00

Mighty Bomb
Antarctic, 1997

1	3.00

Mighty Bombshells
Antarctic, 1993

1-2	3.00

Mighty Cartoon Heroes
Karl Art

0	3.00

Mighty Comics
Archie, 1966

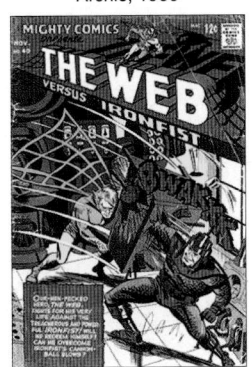

In the early 1940s, MLJ publications produced a number of super-hero comics before stumbling onto a more lucrative formula: the teen humor of Archie and his pals. The reemergence and popularity of super-heroes in the 1960s led MLJ, by then known as Archie Publications, to dust off some of its own Golden Age characters, including The Fly, The Shield, and The Web.

Flyman becomes Mighty Comics with #40 and features new adventures of the patriotic strongman The Shield (aka Private Strong), costumed crusader The Black Hood, and the Spider-Man-influenced Web. Later issues feature The Hangman, a grim vigilante, and Steel Sterling, a

Flash Gordon-style science-fiction adventure strip.

Mighty Comics made an earnest attempt to emulate the art and packaging of 1960s Marvel titles but was retired when the series didn't gain similar reader interest.

-- Rob Salkowitz

40-50	15.00

Mighty Crusaders
Archie, 1965

1	24.00
2	15.00
3	12.00
4-7	10.00

Mighty Crusaders
Archie, 1983

4-13	1.00

Mightyguy
C&T, 1987

Low-grade in just about every measurable way, Mightyguy recounts the highly unlikely (and highly unfunny) adventures of Mike McZiltcho, an unemployed nebbish who finds himself answering a mysterious want ad for a job nobody wants. The job, it turns out, is offered by a comics publisher. The publisher, see, has a magic suit that gives the wearer incredible super powers. So, they want Mike to wear the suit and--here's the brilliant bit--report back on his adventures, which they will then publish in a comic book! Timothy Corrigan's creation, such as it is, strives mightily to be a clever send-up of super-hero comics and comics publishing, but fails as often as its hapless main character.

-- Stephen C. George

1-5	2.00

Mighty Hercules
Gold Key, 1963

1-2	40.00

Mighty Heroes
Dell, 1967

1	125.00
2-4	60.00

Mighty Heroes
Marvel, 1998

1	3.00

Mighty I
Image, 1995

1-2	1.00

Mighty Love
DC, 2004

1	18.00

Mighty Magnor
Malibu, 1993

1	2.00
1/Variant	4.00
2-6	2.00

Mighty Man
Image, 2005

1	8.00

Mighty Marvel Western
Marvel, 1968

1	45.00
2	30.00
3-5	25.00
6-15	20.00
16-21	15.00
22-45	10.00
45/30¢	20.00
46	10.00

Mighty Midget Comics: Captain Marvel Jr.
Lowe, 1942

11	100.00

Mighty Mites
Eternity, 1986

1-3	2.00

Mighty Mites
Eternity, 1987

1-2	2.00

Mighty Morphin Power Rangers (Saban's...)
Marvel, 1995

1	3.00
2-9	2.00

Mighty Morphin Power Rangers: Ninja Rangers/VR Troopers (Saban's...)
Marvel, 1995

1	3.00
2-8	2.00

Mighty Morphin Power Rangers Saga (Saban's...)
Hamilton, 1994

1-3	3.00

Mighty Morphin Power Rangers: The Movie
Marvel, 1995

1	3.00
1/Variant	4.00

Mighty Mouse
Timely, 1946

1	750.00
2	365.00
3-4	200.00

Mighty Mouse
Gold Key, 1964

161-169	15.00

Mighty Mouse
Spotlight, 1987

1-2	2.00

Mighty Mouse
Marvel, 1990

1-10	2.00

Mighty Mouse Adventure Magazine
Spotlight

1	2.00

Mighty Mouse Adventures
St. John, 1951

1	185.00

Mighty Mouse and Friends Holiday Special
Spotlight

1	2.00

Mighty Mouse Comics
St. John, 1947

Aside from giving a new direction to the comic-book industry, the initial popularity of Superman generated characters that were meant to parallel his image. One of these was a mouse. "The Mouse of Tomorrow" was a 1942 animated cartoon from the Terrytoons studio with a character called Super Mouse. He can fly, is invulnerable, and is incredibly strong -- and changes his name to

Mighty Mouse in all the ensuing cartoon shorts, eventually adding the element of a pseudo-operatic style of singing to the mix.

The comic-book stories were funny and lighthearted, consisting of formulaic tales of "good" mice and "bad" cats. Defending Mouseland from the schemes of a band of villains, such as the Sphinx and Oil Can Harry, is a routine task.

In addition to Mighty Mouse, this series from the 1940s and 1950s also featured the misadventures of Heckle and Jeckle, two cunning and crafty crows also from cartoons from the Terrytoons studio.

5	225.00
6-8	145.00
9-10	115.00
11-20	75.00
21-30	50.00
31-36	38.00
37	35.00
38-45	60.00
46-49	28.00
50-70	20.00
71-83	16.00

Mighty Mutanimals
Archie, 1991

1	2.00
2-3	1.00

Mighty Mutanimals
Archie, 1992

1-8	1.00

Mighty Samson
Gold Key, 1964

Nuclear war has laid waste to the world. Those who were not killed immediately fell victim to the radioactive fallout. And the few survivors lived in a world that had literally been bombed into a new Stone Age. Here, technology was lost and strange, mutated plants and animals posed a constant

threat to the humans that remained.

Into this world rose a hero called Samson. Like his world, he is a mix of the old and the new. He wears an eyepatch and the skin of a beast, and possesses strength worthy of his biblical namesake. Along with Mindor, a scientist, and Mindor's daughter Sharmaine, they set out to reclaim this strange new primitive world.

1	75.00
2-4	45.00
5-10	30.00
11-20	20.00
21-31	15.00
32	10.00

Mighty Thor, The: Godstorm
Marvel, 2001
1-3	4.00

Mighty Tiny
Antarctic, 1989
1-4	2.00
5	3.00

Mighty Tiny: The Mouse Marines
Antarctic

The human race destroyed itself with nuclear weapons. Mice and rats have become the dominant life forms and are now at war. The mice have formed a military force which they name, appropriately, the Mouse Marines. This series tells the story of one group of these marines, led by a mouse called Tiny. Tiny fears that there may be dissension in the ranks because he wants to pursue an investigation into the suspicious death of his friend Jerry. To stop him from investigating, Tiny feels that he has been sent on a suicide mission. The series chronicles the adventures of Tiny and his crew as they fight both the rats, and their own population.

This one-shot concludes the Mighty Tiny Mouse Marines storyline that ran as a backup story in Mighty Tiny #1-4.

1	3.00

Mike Barnett, Man Against Crime
Fawcett, 1951
1	125.00
2	85.00
3-6	65.00

Mike Danger (Vol. 1) (Mickey Spillane's...)
Tekno, 1995
1-11	2.00

Mike Danger (Vol. 2) (Mickey Spillane's...)
Big, 1996
1-10	2.00

Mike Mauser Files
Avalon, 1999

This series reprints classic Michael Mauser tales, illustrated by Joe Staton.

His name is Mauser. That's also the name of his pistol. In his profession, it's the only reliable friend he has. He takes care of it and it takes care of him. He's a private eye, and these are his stories.

Short, spike-haired, and bespectacled, wearing his trench coat and hat, Mike Mauser is so tough, his "Indian name" is Iron Shrew. Whether he's bailing out an old friend, solving murders related to an ancient curse, or protecting a tabloid photographer from the mob, he'll have his gun by his side, and he'll get to the bottom of the mystery one way or another.

In addition to Michael Mauser stories, issues may contain other mystery-themed short stories illustrated by Joe Staton.

1	3.00

Mike Mignola's BPRD Collection
Dark Horse, 2004
1	18.00

Mike Mist Minute Mist-Eries
Eclipse, 1981
1	2.00

Mike Regan
Hardboiled
1	3.00

Mike Shayne Private Eye
Dell, 1962
1	16.00
2-3	10.00

Milikardo Knights
Mad Badger, 1997
1-2	3.00

Military Comics
Comic Magazines, 1941

This 1941 series trumpets itself as "stories of military action on land and at sea." It contains an assortment of war strips along those lines, ranging from the naval adventure "PT Boat" to the air/sea flight team of the Atlantic Patrol. A comic piece with the unlikely name of "Death Patrol" paints the Japanese as a collection of goggle-eyed, buck-toothed stooges that are easily routed by a kid-led flight squad. Another long-running feature, The Sniper, is practically a prototype of the later Green Arrow, albeit armed with a rifle instead of a bow and arrow.

The best-known feature of Military Comics is the elite flight squadron known as The Blackhawks. The strip eschews the normal super-heroics and fantasy plots for grim war adventures -- a difference that helps account for its huge and long-running popularity. After running through every issue of Military (later Modern Comics), they star in several incarnations of their own series.

1	9,000.00
2	2,700.00
3	2,150.00
4	1,600.00
5	1,375.00
6-7	1,110.00
8-10	1,000.00
11-12	875.00
13-15	760.00
16-20	650.00
21-22	560.00
23-43	465.00

Milk
Radio, 1997

1-40	3.00
41-43	4.00

Milk & Cheese
Slave Labor, 1991

1	65.00
1/2nd	6.00
1/3rd	5.00
1/4th-1/7th	3.00
2	35.00
2/2nd	5.00
2/3rd	4.00
2/4th-2/5th	3.00
3	28.00
3/2nd	4.00
3/3rd-3/5th	3.00
4	16.00
4/2nd-4/3rd	3.00
5	15.00
5/2nd-5/4th	3.00
6	8.00
6/2nd-7	3.00

Milkman Murders
Dark Horse, 2004

1-4	3.00

Millennium
DC, 1988

Millennium was DC's mega-crossover event of 1988, running for eight weekly issues with dozens of related title crossovers. It was a story which really began billions of years ago, and which would shape the future of Earth for ages to come. Long before intelligent life on Earth, the Oans created a race of androids called the Manhunters to help them enforce order in the universe. After half a billion years, the Manhunters turned on them and the Oans were forced to strip them of power. The Oans tried again, and the result was the Green Lantern Corps.

In the wake of the Crisis on Infinite Earths, the Oans decided the time had come to create the next generation of immortals. They came to Earth intending to choose 10 people for this gift. They needed the aid of Earth's super-heroes to protect the chosen ones from the Manhunters, which had gained new powers and had been living secretly among humans for generations.

1-8	2.00

Millennium 2.5 A.D.
Avalon

1	3.00

Millennium Edition: Action Comics
DC, 2000

As Superman has celebrated his milestone anniversaries in the past, DC has reprinted his first appearance in Action Comics #1 from June 1938. Often, these thin reprints only have that original story and ignore the other material in the issue, which included stories featuring Zatara the magician, adventurer Tex Thomson, rancher Chuck Dawson, and explorer Marco Polo.

In 2000, in anticipation of the new millenium, DC began reprinting significant first issues or first appearances in its Millenium Edition line. Fans were asked to vote for several of their favorites, most of which came from later in DC's history.

The Action #1 reprint included all those early features, giving readers a chance to experience what readers of the late 1930s might have held in their hands at the time.

-- Brent

1	4.00
252	3.00

Millennium Edition: Adventure Comics
DC, 2000

61	4.00
247	3.00

Millennium Edition: All-Star Western
DC, 2000

10	3.00

Millennium Edition: Batman
DC, 2001

1	4.00
1/Chrome	5.00

Millennium Edition: Batman: The Dark Knight Returns
DC, 2000

To celebrate the end of one millennium and the beginning of another, DC Comics published a series of Millennium Editions that reprinted significant books from the Golden, Silver, Bronze, and Modern Ages of Comics. Gotham City is a cesspool of crime. Commissioner Gordon is on the verge of retirement. Bruce Wayne is a middle-aged billionaire with a death wish, and the Batman is considered a myth, for none have seen him in 10 years. But that's about to change as Two-Face escapes, the Joker emerges from a catatonic state, and a dying city's long-lost champion returns for his greatest-and final-battle. Frank Miller's 1986 tale of the Dark Knight presented one of the most startling and realistic visions of Batman ever seen, revitalizing interest in the super-hero genre, and securing Batman's rightful place as the most popular comics hero of the century.

-- Stephen C. George

1 ....6.00

Millennium Edition: Crisis on Infinite Earths
DC, 2000
1 ....3.00
1/Chrome 5.00

Millennium Edition: Detective Comics
DC, 2000
1 ....4.00
38 ....4.00
327 ....3.00
359 ....4.00

Millennium Edition: Flash Comics
DC, 2000
1 .... 4.00

Millennium Edition: Gen13
WildStorm, 2000
1 .... 3.00

Millennium Edition: Green Lantern
DC, 2000
76 .... 3.00

Millennium Edition: Hellblazer
DC, 2000
1 .... 3.00

Millennium Edition: House of Mystery
DC, 2000
1 .... 3.00

Millennium Edition: House of Secrets
DC, 2000
92 .... 3.00

Millennium Edition: JLA
DC, 2000
1 .... 3.00

Millennium Edition: Justice League
DC, 2000
1 .... 3.00
1/Chrome 5.00

Millennium Edition: Kingdom Come
DC, 2000

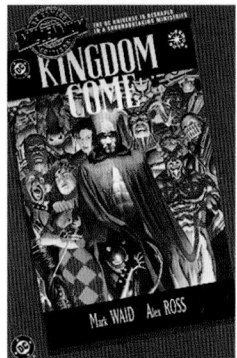

The four-issue Kingdom Come mini-series, written by Mark Waid and lavishly painted by Alex Ross, was the super-hero comic highlight of 1996, if not the entire decade of the 90s. In this Elseworlds (non-continuity) story set 20 years in the future, Superman and the other DC first-generation heroes have retired, leaving crimefighting to a new crew of reckless, irresponsible, and wantonly violent characters. Many readers recognized Waid's plot as a call for a return to the simpler values of the Silver Age, since tarnished by the grim-and-gritty approach of the 80s and 90s. Ross's sumptuous art gave the DC characters an iconic look that meshed perfectly with Waid's grand intentions, to staggering effect. As such, the first issue is a splendid latter-day entry in DC's Millennium series of reprints, though the entire storyline is readily available in graphic novel form.

1 .... 6.00

Millennium Edition: Mad
DC, 2000
1 .... 2.00
1/Recalled 25.00

Millennium Edition: Military Comics
DC, 2000
1 .... 4.00

Millennium Edition: More Fun Comics
DC, 2000
73 .... 4.00
101 .... 3.00

Millennium Edition: Mysterious Suspense
DC, 2000
1 .... 3.00

Millennium Edition: New Gods
DC, 2000
1 .... 3.00

Millennium Edition: Our Army at War
DC, 2000
81 .... 3.00

Millennium Edition: Plop!
DC, 2000
1 .... 3.00

Millennium Edition: Police Comics
DC, 2000
1 .... 4.00

Millennium Edition: Preacher
DC, 2000
1 .... 3.00

Millennium Edition: Sensation Comics
DC, 2000
1..4.00

Millennium Edition: Showcase
DC, 2000
4..3.00
22..3.00

Millennium Edition: Superboy
DC, 2001
.1..3.00

Millennium Edition: Superman
DC, 2000
75..3.00

Millennium Edition: Superman (1st Series)
DC, 2000
233..3.00

Millennium Edition: Superman's Pal Jimmy Olsen
DC, 2000
1..3.00

Millennium Edition: Tales Calculated to Drive You Mad
DC, 2000
1..3.00

Millennium Edition: The Brave and the Bold
DC, 2000

The uninformed might not know The Brave and the Bold #28 would make it into one of DC's special Millennium Editions, but it was here, in 1960, that the legendary Justice League of America debuted. Green Lantern, the Flash, Wonder Woman, Aquaman, and Martian Manhunter (heavy hitters Superman and Batman were too busy to respond to the Justice League summons) unite to battle Starro the Conqueror. This is their first adventure together, and they go on to have several other adventures before moving into their own title. The Brave and the Bold went on to feature such characters as Hawkman, Green Arrow, and others, before spending most of its run as a Batman team-up book, as Batman was joined by Deadman, Green Lantern, and Aquaman (to name but a few).

Besides such historic team-ups, the stories behind the tales in the Millennium Edition's present-day editorial are well worth reading, for information like the fact that Superman and Batman were downplayed, initially, in the League for fear it would take sales away from their own titles. Neal Adams also provided art for quite a few issues of the Batman run.

28 .... 3.00
85 .... 3.00

Millennium Edition: The Flash
DC, 2000
123 .... 3.00

Millennium Edition: The Man of Steel
DC, 2000
1 .... 3.00

Millennium Edition: The New Teen Titans
DC, 2000
1 .... 3.00

Millennium Edition: The Saga of the Swamp Thing
DC, 2000
21 .... 3.00

Millennium Edition: The Sandman
DC, 2000
1 .... 3.00

Millennium Edition: The Shadow
DC, 2001
1 .... 3.00

Millennium Edition: The Spirit
DC, 2000

DC's series of Millennium Edition reprints includes not only comics originally published by DC/National/All-American, but by companies whose properties it subsequently acquired, including Fawcett, Charlton and Quality. Quality's The Spirit (2nd Series) #1 from 1944 is an interesting choice for the lineup. Though it is historically the first appearance of Will Eisner's groundbreaking adventure/mystery hero in his own solo book (The Spirit was distributed in special 8-page newspaper sections in the 1940s and 50s), Quality Spirit #1 contains only one story out of six written and penciled by Eisner himself. Not that the artists who filled in for Eisner while he served in the Army were chopped liver: Lou Fine, Jack Cole and the rest were some of the best storytellers of the Golden Age. It's just that the stories reprinted here are not representative of the pinnacle the character would reach during Eisner's post-war years.

1 .... 3.00

Millennium Edition: Watchmen
DC, 2000
1 .... 3.00

Millennium Edition: Whiz Comics
DC, 2000
2 .... 4.00

Millennium Edition: WildC.A.T.S
DC, 2000
1 .... 3.00

Millennium Edition: Wonder Woman (1st Series)
DC, 2000

1 ....4.00

Millennium Edition: Wonder Woman (2nd Series)
DC, 2000

1 ....3.00

Millennium Edition: World's Finest
DC, 2000

71 ....3.00

Millennium Edition: Young Romance Comics
DC, 2000

1 ....3.00

Millennium Fever
DC, 1995

1-4...3.00
Ashcan 1 ....1.00

Millennium Index
Eclipse, 1988

1-2...2.00

Millie the Lovable Monster
Dell, 1962

1 ....22.00
2-3...18.00
4-6...13.00

Millie the Model Comics
Marvel, 1945

Millie Collins is the good-hearted star of this glamour series. She works as a model at the Hanover Agency with her good friend Toni and the catty Chili. The action in the series revolves around the world of fashion, where the women vie for choice jobs, try out the latest clothes and hairstyles, and struggle with more romantic entanglements than most soap operas.

This series is a rarity among Marvel titles, running without interruption from the end of World War II through 1972. This incredible longevity is, no doubt, due to the remarkable support it enjoyed from its readers, many of whom submitted hairstyles and fashion ideas for Millie. Marvel honored these readers by using many different looks for Millie in each issue, making special note of the names of the readers who had suggested them in a device initiated in this sort of comic book by Bill Woggon with his Katy Keene.

1	500.00
2	300.00
3-8	190.00
9	175.00
10	140.00
11	100.00
12	85.00
13-14	110.00
15	85.00
16	110.00
17-20	85.00
21-30	60.00
31-40	38.00
41-60	35.00
61-70	28.00
71-99	25.00
100	32.00
101-130	15.00
131-154	12.00
155-180	10.00
181-207	9.00
Ann 1	140.00
Ann 2	95.00
Ann 3-4	70.00
Ann 5	65.00
Ann 6-10	45.00
Ann 11-12	25.00

Milton the Monster and Fearless Fly
Gold Key, 1966

1 ....60.00

Mindbenders
MBS

1 ....3.00

Mindgame Gallery
Mindgame

1 ....2.00

Mind Probe
Rip Off

1 ....3.00

Minds' Play
Davan

1 ....3.00

Minerva
NBM

1 ....10.00

Mineshaft
Fantagraphics, 2005

1-16 ....5.00

Minimum Wage
Fantagraphics, 1995

This story features Rob Hoffman, a struggling New York City artist who tries to make a living as a porno-mag comic artist. Hoffman is not exactly thrilled with his current occupation, but it pays the bills and puts food in the fridge. Rob has a roommate named Jack who is steadily filling up the apartment with hundreds of semi-collectible books, which creates a strain in the friendship. Rob does have a saving grace, his sex-crazed girlfriend Sylvia, who is anxious to move out of her home which she shares with her brother and mother. Minimum Wage tells of Rob's efforts to try and keep his sanity between wild parties, underground S&M performances, and maintaining a relationship with his tempestuous girlfriend.

The series was created by Bob Fingerman, a heralded creator in the underground comic ranks. Previous efforts include the critically acclaimed White Like She for Dark Horse.

1-10 ....3.00

Ministry of Space
Image, 2001

1-3 ....3.00

Mink
Tokyopop, 2004

1 ....10.00

Minkenstein
Mu, 2005

0 ....3.00

Minotaur
Labyrinth, 1996

1-4 ....3.00

Minute Man
Fawcett, 1941

1	1,500.00
2	750.00
3	665.00

Minx
DC, 1998

1-8	3.00

Miracle Comics
St. John, 1940

1	1,150.00
2	675.00
3-4	485.00

Miracle Girls
Tokyopop, 2000

1-19	3.00

Miracleman
Eclipse, 1985

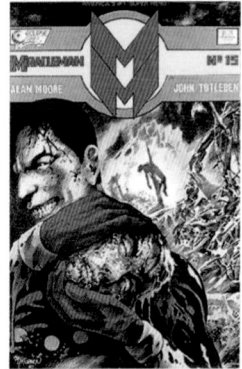

Comic book super-heroes usually do what they do because they think it makes the world a better place. In their darker moments, however, they come to realize the truth: They're simply defending the status quo. They can stop a criminal but can they stop crime? They might save a person from dying in a plane crash but can they stop death itself?

Miracleman (created by Alan Moore as the return of the existing Marvelman character introduced in the UK) is a hero of a different sort. He really can change the world. He's brought about an age of miracles, put an end to poverty and war.

Continuing from a storyline started in the British comic magazine Warrior, later exploits of Miracleman were written by Neil Gaiman (in his pre-Sandman) days. It exhibits the sort of creativity that marks these two writers as among the best in the field.

1	10.00
2-4	8.00
4/Gold	15.00

5	8.00
5/Platinum	15.00
6-8	8.00
8/Gold	15.00
9-10	10.00
11-12	14.00
13	18.00
14	24.00
15	35.00
16	16.00
17	25.00
17/Gold	40.00
18	20.00
19-22	15.00
23	16.00
24	25.00
3D 1	10.00
3D 1/Gold	18.00

Miracleman: Apocrypha
Eclipse, 1991

1-3	3.00

Miracleman Family
Eclipse, 1988

1-2	3.00

Miracle Squad
Upshot

1-4	2.00

Miracle Squad, The: Blood and Dust
Apple, 1989

1-4	2.00

Mirage Mini Comics
Mirage

Those wonderful people at Mirage have brought us an interesting little item. A folder containing thirteen "vest pocket size" black-and-white comics ranging from eight to sixteen pages of art and story that normally wouldn't have fit into one of their regular books. Some stand alone, some seem to be tiny stories that fit into the regular Mirage universe but for one reason or another were left out. Here are stories that make you think, stories that make you worry, stories that will actually have you laughing out loud.

Here you will find Dead Biker and Gutsucker; Melting Pot; and

Atlantic City, Paradise. Also included are Gizmo-Reflections on a Metal Face; The Fraying Weave; The Puma Blues-Mobile; Li'l Comics; Bush Babies; Terrorsaur and Commandosaurs. And, somewhat tied into their most popular series: A Forgotten Teenage Mutant Ninja Turtle Adventure; Casey Jones, Private Eye; and Lasagna Loves.

1	12.00

Mirror Man Comic
Donald F. Peters

21	3.00

Mirrorwalker
Now, 1990

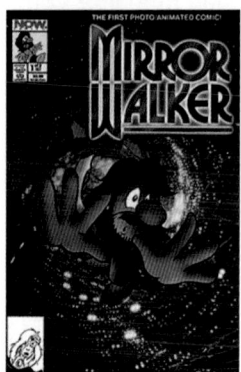

Mirrorwalker is a hilarious series with an odd format: the creators decided to use actual photos for panels. They then illustrated their characters onto the photo prints, creating a surrealistic effect, not unlike that of Who Framed Roger Rabbit?, the Walt Disney movie that merged live action and animation.

The story begins when an inept evil sorcerer accidentally creates a crystal that turns mirrors into doors opening on other dimensions. The sorcerer, Kornephorous, keeps a slave girl who is charged with retrieving a piece of the crystal when it breaks off and fell through a mirror into another dimension, Alan Nonsense's dimension to be exact. Alan is a college student who has never really been able to make it with girls. His luck turned a corner when he found the crystal as he and the slave girl go on wild adventures together.

1-2	3.00

Mirrorworld: Rain
Netco, 1997

0-1	3.00

Misadventures Of Breadman And Doughboy
Hemlock Park, 1999
1-2...3.00

Miseroth: Amok Hell
Northstar
1-3...5.00

Misery
Image, 1995

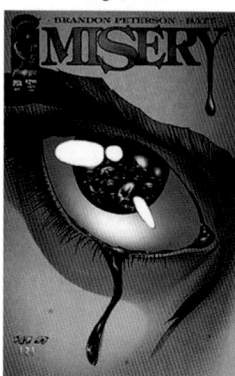

This one-shot chronicles the rise of Lydia O'Rourke from abused teen to superpowered operative of Cyberdata. A latent psychic of great strength, Lydia comes of age in this chilling tale. A controlling father, a married lover, and a case of insurance fraud combine to form a volatile situation. Lydia must come to grips with her power and take charge of her life. The explosive finale leaves one lingering question: Has she truly started steering the course of her own destiny or simply signed on with a different captain?

1...3.00

Misplaced
Image, 2003
1-2...3.00

Miss America (Vol. 1)
Timely, 1944
1...885.00
2...720.00
3-5...300.00
6...70.00

Miss America (Vol. 2)
Timely, 1945
1-6...35.00

Miss America (Vol. 3)
Timely, 1945
1-6...35.00

Miss America (Vol. 4)
Timely, 1946
1-2...35.00

3... 55.00
4-6.. 28.00

Miss America (Vol. 5)
Timely, 1946
1-6... 28.00

Miss America (Vol. 6)
Timely, 1947
1-3... 24.00

Miss America (Vol. 7)
Atlas, 1947
1-9... 24.00
10-24...................................... 20.00
25-93...................................... 16.00

Miss Beverly Hills of Hollywood
DC, 1949
1... 325.00
2... 200.00
3-5... 165.00
6-9... 140.00

Miss Cairo Jones
Croyden, 1945
1................................... 195.00

Miss Fury
Timely, 1942
1...................................... 3,000.00
2...................................... 1,500.00
3...................................... 1,250.00
4...................................... 1,000.00
5-6.. 750.00
7-8.. 700.00

Miss Fury
Adventure, 1991
1.. 3.00
1/Ltd....................................... 5.00
2-4.. 3.00

Miss Fury
Avalon
1-2.. 3.00

Missing Beings Special
Comics Interview

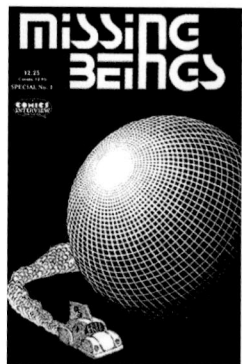

There is both a charm and novelty about this one-shot focusing on the rather too cutely named Tristan Fureel, locator of

missing beings. That the strip is set in the future lends the term "being" a rather cosmopolitan definition. The lesbian computer is probably a first, and her inhabiting a virtual reality world was hardly a threadbare clichT at the time. The change in Bill Neville's art from chapter to chapter is jarring, but it is promising throughout. The material originally appeared as a backup strip in Southern Knights #7-9.

1... 2.00

Mission: Impossible
Dell, 1967
1... 24.00
2-4... 18.00
5... 12.00

Mission Impossible
Marvel, 1996
1.. 3.00

Missions in Tibet
Dimension, 1995
1.. 3.00

Miss Melody Lane of Broadway
DC, 1950
1... 400.00
2... 225.00
3... 185.00

Miss Peach
Dell, 1963
1... 60.00

Misspent Youths
Brave New Words, 1991
1-3.. 3.00

Miss Victory Golden Anniversary Special
AC, 1991
1.. 5.00

Mister America
Endeavor, 1994
1-2.. 3.00

Mr. and Mrs. J. Evil Scientist
Gold Key, 1963
1... 50.00
2... 30.00
3-4... 20.00

Mr. Average
B.S.
1-3.. 2.00

Mr. Beat Adventures
Moordam, 1997
1.. 3.00

Mr. Beat/Craybaby/ Weirdsville Post Halloween Leftover Monster Thanksgiving Special
Blindwolf, 1998
1 ....3.00

Mr. Beat -- Existential Cool
Moordam, 1998
0 ....3.00

Mr. Beat's Babes and Bongos Annual
Moordam, 1998
1/Blue-1/Red 3.00

Mr. Beat's House of Burning Jazz Love
Moordam, 1997
1 ....3.00

Mr. Beat's Two-Fisted Atomic Action Super Special
Moordam, 1997
1 ....3.00

Mr. Beat Superstar
Moordam, 1998
1 ....3.00

Mister Blank
Slave Labor, 1997
0-5 ....3.00

Mr. Cream Puff
Blackthorne, 1987
1 ....2.00

Mr. Day & Mr. Night
Slave Labor, 1993
1 ....4.00

Mr. District Attorney
DC, 1948
1 ....600.00
2 ....265.00
3-5 ....200.00
6-10 ....155.00
11-20 ....110.00
21-30 ....85.00
31-40 ....75.00
41-50 ....60.00
51-67 ....50.00

Mr. Doom
Pied Piper, 1987
1 ....2.00

Mister E
DC, 1991

Since he leapt onto the scene in Secrets of Haunted House #31, Mister E has been just that...a mystery. Although blind, he claims to see the good and evil in men's souls. But though his early adventures portrayed him as a force for good, his later adventures cast him in a different light.

He was last seen as one of the four occult figures whose mission it was to show young Timothy Hunter the aspects of magic in the Books of Magic mini-series. When his turn came, however, he attempted to kill Timothy, mistakenly believing him to be a pawn of the devil. This is when readers first learned that E's blindness was actually brought about by his own father, who gouged out E's eyes when he caught him looking at a dirty magazine. Since then, Mister E has always harbored a secret madness. Timothy escaped Mister E, leaving E stranded at the end of time. Now, in this four-issue mini-series, E is left to find his way back in time and away from his personal demons.

1-4 .... 2.00

Mister Ed, the Talking Horse
Dell, 1962
1 .... 70.00
2 .... 45.00
3-4 .... 40.00
5-6 .... 30.00

Mr. Fixitt
Apple, 1989
1-2 .... 2.00

Mr. Fixitt
Heroic
1 .... 3.00

Mr. Hero-The Newmatic Man (1st Series) (Neil Gaiman's...)
Tekno, 1995
1-17 .... 2.00

Mr. Hero-The Newmatic Man (2nd Series) (Neil Gaiman's...)
Big, 1996
1-4 .... 2.00

Mr. Jigsaw Special
Ocean, 1988
1 .... 2.00

Mr. Lizard 3-D
Now, 1993
1 .... 4.00

Mr. Lizard Annual
Now, 1993
1 .... 3.00

Mr. Majestic
DC, 1999
1-9 .... 3.00

Mister Miracle (1st Series)
DC, 1971
1 .... 50.00
2 .... 25.00
3 .... 20.00
4 .... 25.00
5 .... 30.00
6 .... 22.00
7-8 .... 20.00
9-14 .... 15.00
15-16 .... 12.00
17-18 .... 10.00
19-25 .... 7.00
Special 1 .... 4.00

Mister Miracle (2nd Series)
DC, 1989
1 .... 3.00
2-5 .... 2.00
6-28 .... 1.00

Mister Miracle (3rd Series)
DC, 1996
1-7 .... 2.00

Mr. Monster
Dark Horse, 1988
1-7 .... 2.00
8 .... 5.00

Mr. Monster Attacks!
Tundra, 1992
1-3 .... 4.00

Mr. Monster (Doc Stearn...)
Eclipse, 1985
1 .... 3.00
2-10 .... 2.00

Mr. Monster Presents (Crack-A-Boom!)
Caliber, 1997
1-3...3.00

Mr. Monster's Gal Friday... Kelly!
Image, 2000
1-3...4.00

Mr. Monster's High-Octane Horror
Eclipse, 1986
1...2.00
3D 1 ....3.00

Mr. Monster's Hi-Shock Schlock
Eclipse, 1987
1-2...2.00

Mr. Monster's Hi-Voltage Super Science
Eclipse, 1987
1...2.00

Mr. Monster's Triple Threat 3-D
3-D Zone, 1993
1...4.00

Mr. Monster's True Crime
Eclipse, 1986
1-2...2.00

Mr. Monster's Weird Tales of the Future
Eclipse, 1987
1...2.00

Mr. Monster vs. Gorzilla
Image, 1998
1...3.00

Mr. Mxyzptlk (Villains)
DC, 1998
1...2.00

Mister Mystery
Aragon, 1951

It sounds like a whodunit series, doesn't it? But the covers declared, for the first 18 issues, "Tales of horror and suspense" -- which provides a far more accurate picture of the contents. This pre-Code series came from a small company that had its imprint on only this and two other series: Mutiny ("Stormy Tales of the Seven Seas") and ("Eerie and Startling Adventures into …") Weird Tales of the Future. (There were noticeable similarities, however, between the contents of those and, say, those of Weird Mysteries, released under the Gilmore imprint.)

For such a small company, it produced one of the most-recognized covers in the history of the field with its 12th issue: a "hot poker to the eye" cover that is a classic. The company's timing was impeccable, getting more gross as pressures for comics censorship became more intense.

-- Maggie

1 .... 650.00
2 .... 450.00
3 .... 400.00
4-5 .... 340.00
6 .... 300.00
7 .... 525.00
8-10 .... 300.00
11 .... 385.00
12 .... 550.00
13-18 .... 240.00
19 .... 275.00

Mr. Natural
Kitchen Sink, 1970
1 .... 90.00
1/2nd 75.00
1/3rd 50.00
1/4th 35.00
2 .... 50.00
3 .... 45.00
3/2nd 22.00
3/3rd 10.00
3/4th 5.00
3/5th-3/10th 4.00

Mr. Night
Slave Labor, 2005
1 .... 3.00

Mr. Nightmare's Winter Special
Moonstone, 1995
1 .... 4.00

Mr. Nightmare's Wonderful World
Moonstone, 1995
1-5 .... 3.00

Mister Planet
Mr. Planet
1-2 .... 3.00

Mr. Risk
Humor
1 .... 45.00
2 .... 32.00

Mister Sixx
Imagine Nation

Once a cop, the hero called Mister Sixx has since decided to serve justice (and seek thrills) in his own way. He first breaks onto the scene when he foils a gang of eco-terrorists known as Earth Guard from murdering the heads of several major corporations. Afterward, he learns that one of the men he saved had also been targeted by the Assassin Elite, the world's deadliest man. Never being one who could resist taking the dangerous route, Sixx immediately begins the hunt for this murderer. Unbeknownst to him, his quest would lead him to cross paths with Nguru Dakingari, the feared Nigerian manhunter.

This title marks the start of New Jersey-based publisher Imagine Nation. The creative team of Mark-Wayne Harris and Dennis Morales Francis had previously collaborated on Street Wolf for the now-defunct Blackthorne Publishing. This new title is marked by crisp storytelling and a sense of adventure that sets it apart from the pack.

1 .... 2.00

Mr. T and the T-Force
Now, 1993
1 .... 3.00
1/Gold.................................... 4.00
2-10 .... 2.00

Mister X (Vol. 1)
Vortex, 1984
1 .... 4.00
2-14 .... 3.00

Mister X (Vol. 2)
Vortex
1-5	3.00
6-11	2.00
12	3.00

Mister X (Vol. 3)
Caliber, 1996
1-4	3.00

Mistress of Bondage
Fantagraphics
1-3	3.00

Misty
Marvel, 1985

Many years ago, Millie the Model was Marvel's major comic aimed at girls. By 1985, Millie was far too old for modeling herself, but she passed on hints to her niece Misty, the teenage star of this six-issue limited series. Written and drawn by Trina Robbins (The Legend of Wonder Woman), this title follows Misty and her friends on their various high school adventures.

As with many girls' comics, the editors of Misty invited fans to send in fashion designs for the characters. If chosen, those designs would be worked into the comic, along with credits. About one-quarter of each issue displayed the clothing designs. The letters column answered questions about everything from dating to pimples. Those lucky enough to get their clothing designs published, received a Meet Misty Clothing Design Club card.

1-6	1.00

Misty Girl Extreme
Fantagraphics, 1997
1-2	3.00

Mites
Continuüm
1-2	2.00

Mitzi Comics
Timely, 1948
1	150.00

MixxZine
Mixx, 1997
1-6	5.00

Mnemovore
DC, 2005
1-6	3.00

Mobfire
DC, 1994
1-6	3.00
Ashcan 1	1.00

Mobile Police Patlabor Part 1
Viz, 1997

Officer Noa Izumi is your typical overachiever in this Dirty Dozen-meets-Johnny Socko manga comic. Understaffed and lacking any vehicles, Izumi and her colleagues must suffer under the eccentric command of Goto, Captain of the Special Vehicles Division 2, Section 2. Will they survive long enough for their Patlabors, enormous robotic vehicles designed for heavy construction work, to arrive? Is Goto as incompetent as he seems? And why are all the new Labors malfunctioning? Only time (and the next issue) will answer these questions. Like most modern manga, this title also boasts an anime version of the adventures of Special Vehicles Division 2, Section 2.

1-6	3.00

Mobile Police Patlabor Part 2
Viz, 1998
1-6	3.00

Mobile Suit Gundam 0079
Viz, 1999
1-8	3.00

Mobile Suit Gundam 0083
Viz, 1999
1-13	5.00

Mobile Suit Gundam Seed Astray
Tokyopop, 2004
1	10.00

Mobile Suit Gundam Wing: Ground Zero
Viz, 2000
1-4	3.00

Mobsters and Monsters Magazine
Original Syndicate, 1995
1	3.00

Moby Dick
NBM
1	16.00

Moby Duck
Gold Key, 1967
1	12.00
2	6.00
3-5	5.00
6-10	4.00
11-30	3.00

Mod
Kitchen Sink, 1981
1	5.00

Model
Tokyopop, 2004
1	10.00

Model
NBM, 2002
1	25.00

Model By Day
Rip Off, 1990
1-2	3.00

Modeling with Millie
Marvel, 1963
21	65.00
22-30	48.00
31-40	36.00
41-54	30.00

Modern Comics
Quality, 1945

The title carried the identification "Formerly Military Comics" on its logo for more than two years, but from start (Military Comics #1, Aug 41) to finish (Modern Comics #102, Oct 50) Blackhawk was the focal character. The Blackhawk team (with Blackhawk and his team members Andre, Olaf, Chuck, Hendrickson, Stanislaus, and Chop-Chop) On the other hand, sometimes the focus is on the flying ace and one or another dangerous damsel: Madame Butterfly ("the deadliest of the species"), Tigra ("beautiful and heartless"), Arda Thorn ("gorgeous"), and so on. Much art is outstanding, and Torchy appears in some non-Blackhawk stories.

-- Maggie

44	450.00
45-53	360.00
54-57	250.00
58-80	200.00
81-99	170.00
100	195.00
101	170.00
102	200.00

Modern Grimm
Symptom, 1996

1	3.00

Modern Love
E.C., 1949

1	510.00
2-3	325.00
4-6	450.00
7-8	325.00

Modern Pulp
Special Studio

1	3.00

Modern Romans
Fantagraphics

1-3	2.00

Modest Proposal, A
Tome

1-2	3.00

Modesty Blaise
DC

1	20.00

Modniks
Gold Key, 1967

1	8.00
2	4.00

Mod Squad
Dell, 1969

1	20.00
2-5	12.00
6-8	9.00

Mod Wheels
Gold Key, 1971

This "hip" title from Gold Key is most evocative of the Hot Wheels animated series (1969-1971) and DC comic book (1970-71). Sporting such 1970s accouterments as mutton-chop sideburns and bell-bottom slacks, Wheels and his racing team pals -- Lump, Cube, 'Scot, and Bit -- take on such evils as unethical drivers and rampaging biker gangs. The dialogue is heavy with the perceived teen slang of the day, and the art is vaguely similar to the "heavy" 1970s style Mike Sekowsky was using on DC's Wonder Woman and Supergirl at the time.

1	30.00
2-9	20.00
10-16	15.00
17-19	10.00

Moe & Shmoe Comics
O.S., 1948

1	35.00
2	25.00

Moebius
Marvel

Book 1-Book 2	10.00
Book 3	13.00
Book 4-Book 6	10.00
Book 7	13.00
Book 8	12.00
Book 9	13.00

Moebius Comics
Caliber, 1996

1-6	3.00

Moebius: Exotics
Dark Horse

1	7.00

Moebius: H.P.'s Rock City
Dark Horse, 1996

1	8.00

Moebius: Madwoman of the Sacred Heart
Dark Horse, 1996

1	13.00

Moebius: The Man from the Ciguri
Dark Horse, 1996

1	8.00

Mogobi Desert Rats
Studio 91, 1991

1	2.00

Mojo Action Companion Unit
Exclaim, 1997

1	3.00

Mojo Mechanics
Syndicate

1-2	3.00

Molly Manton's Romances
Marvel, 1949

1	70.00

Molly O' Day
Avon, 1945

1	225.00

Moment of Silence, A
Marvel, 2002

1	4.00

Moment of Freedom, A
Caliber, 1997

nn	5.00

Mona
Kitchen Sink

1	5.00

Monarchy
DC, 2001

1-12	3.00

Mondo 3-D
3-D Zone

1	4.00

Mondo Bondo
LCD

1	3.00

Money Talks
Slave Labor, 1996
1 ....4.00
2-5..3.00

Mongrel
Northstar, 1994
1/A-3 ....4.00

Monica's Story
Alternative, 1999
1 ....4.00

Monkees
Gold Key, 1967
1 ....45.00
2 ....30.00
3 ....24.00
4-5 ....20.00
6-10 ....18.00
11-17 ....12.00

Monkey & The Bear
Avon, 1953
1 ....45.00
2-3 ....28.00

Monkey Business
Parody

Monkey Business consists mainly of reprints of syndicated newspaper cartoon strips, such as Ernie, In the Bleachers, Bizarro, and Mother Goose and Grimm. Good as these features are, the biggest laughs for comic fans come with Parody Press' own stories. Deliciously funny, they succeed in lampooning everything from American consumerism to (the previously believed un-lampoonable) Ren & Stimpy.

1-2 ....3.00

Monkey In A Wagon Vs. Lemur On A Big Wheel
Alias, 2005
1 ....3.00

Monkeyman and O'Brien
Dark Horse, 1996
1 .... 4.00
2-3 .... 3.00
Special 1 .... 3.00

Monkeyshines
Ace, 1944
1 .... 60.00
2 .... 40.00
3-10 .... 30.00
11-15 .... 25.00
16 .... 20.00
17-23 .... 25.00

Monnga
Daikaiju, 1995
1 .... 4.00

Monolith
Comico, 1991
1-4 .... 3.00

Monolith
DC, 2004
1 .... 4.00
2-12 .... 3.00

Monolith
Last Gasp, 1972
1 .... 3.00

Monroe
Conquest
1 .... 5.00

Monster
Fiction House, 1953
1 .... 340.00
2 .... 275.00

Monster (Butler & Hogg's...)
Slave Labor
1 .... 3.00

Monster
Ring
1 .... 2.00

Monster Boy
Monster, 1991
1 .... 3.00

Monster Boy Comics
Slave Labor, 1997
1-3 .... 3.00

Monster Club
APComics, 2002
1 .... 6.00
2 .... 5.00
3-9 .... 4.00

Monster Club
APComics, 2004
0 .... 3.00
1-5 .... 4.00

Monster Crime Comics
Hillman, 1952
1 .... 625.00

Monster Fighters Inc.
Image, 1999

This manga-influenced series mixes in super-heroes, a touch of fantasy, and casual product placement.

The Monster Fighters carry business cards that explain it all: "We kick paranormal butt!" The adventures of the five powerful young people are chronicled by a talking black cat. Tales have included the group trying to figure out who at a comic book convention is an actual monster, as opposed to just being someone in a costume; and the story of a professional wrestler turned really, really bad.

Writer J. Torres wrote Siren and contributed to Love in Tights. Artist Rick Cortes is also creates special effects and his film work includes "The House on Haunted Hill." Co-creator Logan Lubera is a story board artist who has worked for the animated "Beast Wars" on television as well as the X-Men film.

1 .... 4.00

Monster Fighters Inc.: The Black Book
Image, 2000
1 .... 4.00

Monster Fighters Inc.: The Ghosts of Christmas
Image, 1999
1 .... 4.00

Monster Frat House
Eternity, 1989
1 .... 2.00

Monster House
Idea & Design Works, 2006
1 .... 8.00

Monster Hunters
Charlton, 1975
1 .... 6.00

1/2nd......................................3.00
2...4.00
3-18.......................................3.00

Monster in My Pocket
Harvey, 1991

1-4...2.00

Monster Island
Compass, 1998

1...4.00

Monster Love
Kitchen Sink

1...3.00

Monsterman
Image, 1997

1...3.00

Monster Massacre
Atomeka

Monster Massacre packs five bone-crunching tales of weird horror, science fiction, and "carnage-crazed Nordic robo-berzerkers" into a deluxe square-bound anthology, wrapped in a nice painted cover by Simon "Biz" Bisley. Part gonzo Heavy Metal ultra-sex-and-violence, part wacky parody of Jack Kirby-style big bad monster stories, Monster Massacre maintains a consistent level of crazed mayhem from "The Kingdom of Zitturk" to "Headcase" to "Expressway to Your Skull" and all points in between. Bisley, Dougie Braithwaite, Dave Elliott, Simon Furman, Dave Gibbons, James O'Barr, Kevin O'Neill, Peter Snejbjerg, and John Tomlinson all contribute to the full-color volume.
-- Rob Salkowitz

1...8.00

Monster Massacre Special
Blackball

1 .... 3.00

Monster Matinee
Chaos!, 1997

1-3 .... 3.00

Monster Menace
Marvel, 1993

1-4 .... 2.00

MonsterMen (Gary Gianni's...)
Dark Horse, 1999

1 .... 3.00

Monster Posse
Adventure, 1992

1-3 .... 3.00

Monsters Attack!
Globe, 1989

1-5 .... 3.00

Monsters from Outer Space
Adventure, 1992

1-3 .... 3.00

Monsters on the Prowl
Marvel, 1971

Monsters on the Prowl (originally Chamber of Darkness) combined new material and reprints from Marvel's pre-hero Atlas comics (Strange Tales, Tales of Suspense, etc.), a format that Marvel used in a number of its titles during the early 1970s. The new material included stories featuring Kull, a barbarian swordsman created by Robert E. Howard of Conan the Barbarian fame, adapted by Roy Thomas and exquisitely drawn by John Severin. Other fantasy artists of note, including Barry Windsor-Smith and Ralph Reese, also contributed stories to the short-lived series. The back pages of each issue were filled with Atlas monster stories ("I Challenged Groot...Monster from Planet X!") written by Stan Lee and featuring terrific art from Steve Ditko, Jack Kirby, Dick Ayers, and others.
-- Rob Salkowitz

9 .... 25.00
☛Was Chamber of Darkness
10-15 .... 15.00
16 .... 18.00
17-30 .... 12.00

Monsters to Laugh With
Marvel, 1964

1 .... 40.00
2-3 .... 30.00

Monsters Unleashed
Marvel, 1973

1 .... 40.00
2 .... 18.00
3-5 .... 15.00
6-8 .... 10.00
9-11 .... 7.00
Ann 1 .... 12.00

Monster War: Magdalena vs. Dracula
Image, 2005

1 .... 3.00

Monster War: Tomb Raider vs. Wolf Men
Image, 2005

2 .... 3.00

Monster War: Witchblade vs. Frankenstein
Image, 2005

3/A-3/B 3.00

Monster War: Darkness vs. Mr. Hyde
Image, 2005

4/A-4/B 3.00

Monster World
DC, 2001

1-4 .... 3.00

Monstrosity
Slap Happy, 1998

1 .... 5.00

Monte Hale Western
Fawcett, 1948

Monte Hale (1919-) was another singing cowboy, first appearing as a guitar player in The Big Bonanza (1944). Fawcett eventually established an entire line of Western comic books featuring real motion-picture stars such as Tom Mix, Lash LaRue, and Gabby Hayes. Perhaps because of sluggish sales of the Mary Marvel series named for her (and her final cover featuring her in Western garb), Fawcett changed its contents completely and put Hale in the starring role with #29. Cover copy read, "Introducing Monte Hale The Biggest and Boldest Real-Life Cowboy of Them All 6 ft. 5 in. of Solid Muscle." The Hale series had photo covers, and he was also featured in such Fawcett titles as Real Western Hero and Six-Gun Heroes.

-- Maggie

29	200.00
30	100.00
31-36	75.00
37-45	50.00
46-55	45.00
56-70	35.00
71-88	30.00

Monty Hall of the U.S. Marines
Toby, 1951

1	55.00
2	32.00
3-11	24.00

Moon, a Girl ... Romance
E.C., 1949

9	600.00
10-11	500.00
12	600.00

Moon Beast
Avalon

1	3.00

Moonchild
Forbidden Fruit, 1992

1-2	3.00

Moon Child (Vol. 2)
Forbidden Fruit

1-3	4.00

Moondog
Print Mint, 1973

1	4.00
2	3.00

Moonfighting
Harrier, 1988

1	2.00

Moon Girl
E.C., 1947

The first issue's cover copy said, "Featuring America's newest and most exciting characters in four complete and thrilling episodes!" Drawn by Sheldon Moldoff, it was E.C's attempt at creating a sort of super-hero. What happened was a prime example of E.C.'s morphing titles: #2 was simply Moon Girl. With #7 it became Moon Girl Fights Crime! And with #9 it finally angled off 90 degrees to become A Moon, a Girl ... Romance.

E.C. changed gears from the super-heroine Moon Girl to a traditional romance title with cover copy reading, "True stories of young love." The four-issue Pre-Trend experiment then morphed into Weird Fantasy with #13.

-- Maggie

1	765.00
2	400.00
3	325.00
4	300.00
5	665.00
6-8	325.00
9	450.00
10-11	365.00
12	460.00

Moon Knight
Marvel, 1980

1	10.00
2	7.00
3-4	5.00
5-20	3.00
21-24	2.00
25	3.00
26-34	2.00
35	3.00
36-38	2.00

Moon Knight
Marvel, 1985

1	3.00
2-6	2.00

Moon Knight
Marvel, 1998

1-4	3.00

Moon Knight
Marvel, 1999

1-4	3.00

Moon Knight
Marvel, 2006

1-6	3.00

Moon Knight: Divided We Fall
Marvel, 1992

1	5.00

Moon Knight Special
Marvel, 1992

1	3.00

Moon Knight Special Edition
Marvel, 1983

1-3	3.00

Moon Mullins
ACG, 1947

1	80.00
2	50.00
3-6	45.00

Moon Mullins
St. John, 1948

7-8	35.00

Moonshadow
Marvel, 1985

Moonshadow bills itself as "a fairy tale for grown-ups." It's that -- and much more.

It begins in 1968, when a naive young hippie named Sheila Bernbaum is spirited across space by a member of the race of beings called "G'L-Doses" (an anagram for "godless"?). The G'L-Doses' sole purpose is to do whatever strikes their whimsy. This G'L-Dose's whimsy is to father a son, which Sheila names "Moonshadow."

Moonshadow grows up as innocent and starry-eyed as his mother has been, having spent his youth reading tales of romance and derring-do. Eventually, the time comes to leave the outer-space "zoo" he's lived in and set off across the universe. His adventures form a haunting story of his fall from innocence and growth into a man: a moving and beautifully illustrated story.

1	4.00
2-3	3.00
4-12	2.00

Moonshadow
DC, 1994

1-5	3.00
6-11	2.00
12	3.00

Moon Shot, the Flight of Apollo 12
Pepper Pike Graphix, 1994

1	3.00

Moonstone Monsters: Zombies
Moonstone, 2005

1	3.00

Moonstruck
White Wolf, 1987

1	2.00

Moontrap
Caliber

1	2.00

Moonwalker 3-D
Blackthorne

1	3.00

Moordam Christmas Comics
Moordam, 1999

1	3.00

Mopsy
St. John, 1948

1	85.00
2	55.00
3-5	48.00
6-10	40.00
11-15	30.00
16-18	26.00

Mora
Image, 2005

1-4	3.00

Morbid Angel
London Night, 1996

∫-1	3.00

Morbid Angel: Penance
London Night, 1996

1	4.00

Morbius Revisited
Marvel, 1993

1-5	2.00

Morbius: The Living Vampire
Marvel, 1992

Michael Morbius has it all: He is a brilliant scientist, a Nobel prize-winner, and he is engaged to be married. Then he is struck with an incurable blood disease. Rather than give up, he turns his genius to finding a cure. In a secret laboratory, he tries treatment after treatment but always meets with failure. Finally, a bizarre combination of electroshock coupled with serum taken from vampire bats brings the disease to a standstill. But, in its place, a more terrible disease has taken hold. Michael Morbius has become a sort of "living vampire," required to feed on human blood in order to live.

First appearing in Amazing Spider-Man #101, Morbius now stars in this, his first solo series. Launched as part of The Ghost Rider "Rise of the Midnight Sons" epic, the series begins with Morbius on the verge of developing a serum to cure his vampirism. Then the demon Lilith arranges to add a little something extra to the mixture.

1	2.00
1/CS	3.00
2-24	2.00
25	3.00
26-32	2.00

More Fetish
Boneyard, 1993

1	3.00

More Fun Comics
DC, 1936

Continuing from New Fun Comics, More Fun began as a humor comic book before it transformed itself into the breeding ground for many of DC's most stalwart super-heroes.

The heroes began with a costumed appearance by Doctor Occult in issue #14. Various Western and other features followed before the undead super-hero The Spectre made his awe-inspiring first appearance with issues #51-52. Doctor Fate and Congo Bill (the future Congorilla) followed in the next few issues, along with Flash clone Johnny Quick in issue #71. Two issues later, DC cloned Marvel's Namor in a more friendly manner when they introduced Aquaman. In the same issue, archer Green Arrow and his boy sidekick Speedy were also introduced.

Issue #101 saw the debut of Superboy in the title. Unfortunately, it was all downhill from there, as super-heroes - and the title - disappeared over the next few years.

☞Was New Fun Comics

7-8	5,600.00
9	6,500.00
10	3,250.00
11	2,850.00
12-13	2,450.00
14	12,500.00

☞1st Dr. Occult

15-16	5,000.00
17	4,500.00
18-20	2,150.00
21-25	1,950.00
26-29	1,775.00
30-40	1,625.00
41-45	1,325.00
46-50	1,200.00

51	5,000.00

☞Spectre cameo

52	54,000.00

☞1st Spectre story

53	35,000.00
54	9,700.00
55	12,400.00

☞1st Dr. Fate

56	4,400.00
57-59	3,100.00
59/15¢	4,500.00
60	3,100.00
61-64	2,500.00
65-66	2,660.00
67	6,850.00
68-70	2,100.00
71	5,750.00
72	1,725.00
73	12,200.00

☞1st Aquaman, GREEN ARROW

74	2,450.00
75-80	1,725.00
81-88	1,150.00
89	1,325.00
90-99	940.00
100	1,060.00
101	7,850.00

☞1st Superboy

102	1,375.00
103	1,025.00
104-105	760.00
106-107	650.00
108-110	165.00
111-120	140.00
121-124	115.00
125	575.00

☞Superman cover

126	115.00
127	225.00

More Secret Origins
Replica Edition
DC, 1999

1	5.00

More Starlight
To Your Heart
ADV Manga, 2004

1-2	10.00

More Tales
from Gimbley
Harrier, 1988

1	2.00

More Tales From
Sleaze Castle
Gratuitous Bunny, 1990

1	4.00
2-6	3.00

More Than Mortal
Liar, 1997

Deirdre, a lowly maid in an Irish church, has strange dreams: She is Brigid the Protector, a wielder of magic and weapons who protects medieval Ireland from demonic invaders. The only one who gives her dreams any credence is Father Colm, a kind priest, who encourages her to explore her dreams and discover their origins. Strangely, he vanishes and is presumed dead by Deirdre, but his advice is enough to send her on a journey to find out what her dreams of the Protector mean.

Writer Sharon Scott and artist Steve Firchow established a fairly solid foundation in the first issue of More than Mortal, which, apparently, Deirdre is. Questions surround their young Irish heroine, and the reader is compelled to seek the answers along with her. Firchow's art -- while a bit on the cheesecake side -- moves the story along at a nice pace, but it is his work as a colorist that is particularly striking here.

1-6	3.00
Deluxe 1	15.00

More Than Mortal/
Lady Pendragon
Image, 1999

1-1/A	3.00

More Than Mortal:
Otherworlds
Image, 1999

1-4	3.00

More Than Mortal:
Sagas
Liar, 1998

1-3	3.00

More Than Mortal:
Truths & Legends
Liar, 1998

1-1/A	3.00
1/Ltd.	4.00
2-5	3.00

More Trash from Mad
E.C., 1958

1	60.00
2	35.00
3	20.00
4-5	14.00
6-10	10.00
11-12	8.00

Morgana X
Fanatic Press

1	10.00

Morgana X
Sky Comics, 1993

1-SE 1	3.00

Morlocks
Marvel, 2002

1-4	3.00

Morlock 2001
Atlas-Seaboard, 1975

1	9.00
2	6.00
3	8.00

Morning Glory
Radio, 1998

Morning Glory tells the fanciful story of Katherine, a modern-day pagan witch, and her mischievous companion Morning Glory, one of the last faeries left alive. These unlikely partners must face down Goth-girls, naughty cable TV channels, first dates and religious fanatics, not to mention lesbian biker gangs and Zen masters. Add to that the complication that Morning Glory derives sustenance from sexual energy and Katherine is between boyfriends, and much comedy ensues. The manga influenced artwork tells the story in a fun, straightforward manner.

This is pure romantic comedy and adventure, for mature readers.

1-5 ....3.00

Morningstar Special
Comico, 1990

1 ....3.00

Morphing Period
Shanda, 2000

1 ....5.00

Morphos the Shapechanger
Dark Horse, 1996

1 ....5.00

Morphs
Graphxpress, 1987

1-4 ....2.00

Morrigan
Dimension X, 1993

1 ....3.00

Morrigan
Sirius, 1997

1 ....3.00

Mortal Coil Ashcan
Mermaid

Ashcan 1 ....1.00

Mortal Coils: Bloodlines
Red Eye, 2002

1 ....3.00

Mortal Kombat
Malibu, 1994

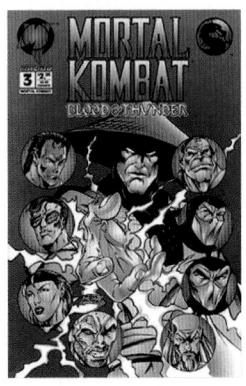

Mortal Kombat became legendary as a video game in the arcades, both for its high-tech kung fu fighting animations and for its grisly "finishing scenes," in which the winning player could literally tear apart his hapless opponent. Hugely popular, it was only a matter of time before the

characters from Mortal Kombat were adapted into comic-book form. In 1994, Malibu did just that in this six-issue mini-series subtitled "Blood & Thunder."

Here are the world's greatest warriors invited to a deadly duel-to-the-death in Hong Kong. A total of 50 are called, including American film star Johnny Cage, who wants to prove his battle skills are not just Hollywood fiction; Liu Kang, a noble warrior from The Order of Light; Sonya Blade, a blonde American Special Forces operative; and Kano, a fighter from the evil Black Dragon organization. All will battle to the death for the honor of fighting Goro, the multi-armed reigning champion.

0-6 .... 3.00

Mortal Kombat: Baraka
Malibu, 1995

1 .... 3.00

Mortal Kombat: Battlewave
Malibu, 1995

1-6 .... 3.00

Mortal Kombat: Goro, Prince of Pain
Malibu, 1994

1-3 .... 3.00

Mortal Kombat: Kitana & Mileena
Malibu, 1995

1 .... 3.00

Mortal Kombat: Kung Lao
Malibu, 1995

1 .... 3.00

Mortal Kombat: Rayden & Kano
Malibu, 1995

1-3 .... 3.00

Mortal Kombat Special Edition
Malibu, 1994

1-2 .... 3.00

Mortal Kombat: Tournament Edition
Malibu, 1994

1-2 .... 4.00

Mortal Kombat U.S. Special Forces
Malibu, 1995

1-2 .... 4.00

Mortal Souls
Avatar, 2002

1/A 4.00

Mortar Man
Marshall Comics, 1993

Daft super-hero comic featuring the explosives-obsessed researcher Cary August and his gung-ho crime-fighting alter ego. A particularly ridiculous creation is the crime organization Apple, permitting all kinds of ludicrous gadgetry and strained metaphors, and there's a full cast of equally stupid villains. Anyone who's read more than a dozen Marvel comics will get most of the jokes, but Mortar Man is just off-center enough to appeal to Flaming Carrot fans. This is particularly the case with the Burdenesque backup strip concerning the misdeeds of the Questionnaire of Crime.

1-3 .... 2.00

Mort Grim
Adhouse Books, 2005

0 .... 5.00

Mortie
Magazine Publications, 1952

1 .... 38.00
2-4 .... 24.00

Mortigan Goth: Immortalis
Marvel, 1993

1 .... 2.00
1/Variant 3.00
2-4 .... 2.00

Mort the Dead Teenager
Marvel, 1992

1-4 .... 2.00

Morty the Dog
Mu, 1991

1-2 .... 4.00

Morty the Dog
Starhead

1 .... 2.00

Mosaic
Sirius, 1999
1/A-5 ....3.00

Mosaic: Hell City Ripper
Sirius, 1999
1-5...3.00

Moses and the Ten Commandments
Dell, 1957
1 ....80.00

Mostly Wanted
WildStorm, 2000

Andromeda Mooncrest, a low-caste member of the galactic ruling body known as the Functionary, has worked hard to get where she is. As a young pilot in government service, Mooncrest is eager to make a name for herself. She does, but not in the way she hoped, when she meets the infamous Sister Crenn-the Functionary's most-wanted criminal-and finds herself a fugitive from the government she's sworn to serve. But Crenn, who is wanted for the murder of 1 trillion beings (a crime she may or may not have committed), is on something of a holy mission, one that may end the rule of the Functionary itself. Will Mooncrest stop Crenn-or join her? Scott Lobdell (Uncanny X-Men) makes a game stab at a sweeping galactic epic, while Roberto Flores is on hand to make sure that, if the story falls flat, at least readers will have some gorgeous women to look at.
-- *Stephen C. George*

1-4...3.00

Moth (Steve Rude's)
Dark Horse, 2004
1-4...3.00

Moth (Steve Rude's) Double-Sized Special
Dark Horse, 2004
1 .... 5.00

Motherless Child
Kitchen Sink

This black-and-white one-shot is a requiem of sorts-a girl now grown remembering her favorite uncle Kenny. Kenny was the sort of person who couldn't live without his mother. He was an ex-marine who was terrified of being alone in the world. The unnamed narrator talks of the good times they'd had together growing up, the girlfriend that Kenny loved for seven years but could never seem to marry, the terrible accident that left him with a brain aneurysm, turning him mean...and the final accident which took him away forever.
Artist/Writer Thom Webb Scott did a fine job of making the characters real and memorable. By story's end you feel as if they were people you knew-which makes it all the sadder when you see them go.

1 .... 3.00

Mother's Oats Comix
Rip Off, 1969
1 .... 5.00
2 .... 3.00

Mother Superion
Antarctic, 1997
1 .... 3.00

Mother Teresa of Calcutta
Marvel, 1984
1 .... 2.00

Motion Picture Comics
Fawcett, 1950

Fawcett Movie Comics changed its name to Motion Picture Comics in 1950, but the concept remained the same: providing comic-book adaptations of popular movies. Motion Picture Comics generally favors war stories and Westerns, including The Vanishing Westerner, Rough Rider of Durango, The Red Badge of Courage, and Code of the Silver Sage. Occasionally a science-fiction title like When Worlds Collide creeps in, as does the odd spy/suspense thriller, like Walk on East Beacon toward the end of the run. Motion Picture Comics all feature photo covers, often taken from the movie theater posters.

101 .... 115.00
102-104 .... 80.00
105 .... 90.00
106-107 .... 75.00
108-109 .... 60.00
110 .... 215.00
111 .... 90.00
112 .... 50.00
113-114 .... 40.00

Motley Stories
Division
1 .... 3.00

Motorbike Puppies
Dark Zulu Lies, 1992
1-2... 3.00

Motorhead
Dark Horse, 1994
1-6... 3.00
Special 1 .... 4.00

Motormouth
Marvel, 1992

Seventeen year-old Harley Davis was a street-punk who ran with a gang on the East End of London. Agile, aggressive, and equipped with a mouth that just won't stop, she could more than hold her own on the streets.

But fate has a way of dealing unexpected hands even to those as savvy as Harley. For when Harley found a pair of abandoned "sneakers" on the streets, she did what came naturally and took them. But these sneakers were actually an experiment in time travel by the MyS-TECH corporation, and were genetically coded for Harley's DNA type. MyS-TECH had hoped to lure Harley into using the sneakers to "digitize" across dimensions in the time-space continuum. Luckily, Harley escaped from both MyS-TECH and the agents of S.H.I.E.L.D. who tried to stop her. Now able to phase across the myriad dimensions of the universe, Harley is out for a good time-no matter what danger she lands in the middle of.

1-12 ....2.00

Mountain
Underground

1 ....3.00

Mountain World
Icicle Ridge

1 ....2.00

Mouse Guard
Archaia Studios Press, 2006

1 ....90.00
1/2nd....................................18.00
2 ....25.00

Mouse Musketeers (M.G.M.'s...)
Dell, 1957

8 .... 35.00
9-21 .... 30.00

Mouse on the Moon
Dell, 1963

1 .... 15.00

Movie Love
Famous Funnies, 1950

1 .... 60.00
2 .... 50.00
3 .... 45.00
4-9 .... 40.00
10 .... 50.00
11-15 .... 35.00
16-22 .... 30.00

Movie Comics
DC, 1939

1 .... 2,450.00
2 .... 1,700.00
3 .... 1,100.00
4-6 .... 950.00

Movie Comics
Fiction House, 1946

1 .... 400.00
2-3 .... 350.00
4 .... 300.00

Movie Star News
Pure Imagination

1 .... 6.00

Movie Thrillers
Magazine Enterprises, 1949

1 .... 160.00

Moxi
Lightning, 1996

1 .... 3.00

Moxi's Friends: Bobby Joe & Nitro
Lightning, 1996

1 .... 3.00

Moxi: Strange Daze
Lightning, 1996

1 .... 3.00

M. Rex
Image, 1999

1-2 .... 3.00
Ashcan 1/A-1/B 5.00

Mr. T
APComics, 2005

1-2 .... 4.00

Ms. Anti-Social
Helpless Anger

1 .... 2.00

Ms. Cyanide & Ice
Black Out

0-1 .... 3.00

Ms. Fantastic
Conquest

1-4 .... 3.00

Ms. Fantastic Classics
Conquest

1 .... 3.00

Ms. Fortune
Image, 1998

1 .... 3.00

Ms. Marvel
Marvel, 1977

Ms. Marvel is Carol Danvers, a former security chief at NASA, who first appeared in Marvel Super-Heroes #13. Later, she would play a supporting role in the Captain Marvel series, although the events of that series would ultimately cause her to lose her job. Before leaving NASA, however, it seems that she had been unknowingly irradiated by the Kree's Psyche-Magnetron - a device which gave her with the powers of Ms. Marvel.

As this series opens, Carol is slowly discovering her new powers and using them to fight crime. In her identity as Carol Danvers, she has become a women's magazine editor and has placed herself at the forefront of the battle for women's rights. That battle plays a strong role in both the plot and the editorial direction of the Ms. Marvel series.

-- Stephen C. George

1 .... 8.00
2-6 .... 3.00
6/35¢ 15.00
7 .... 3.00
7/35¢ 15.00
8 .... 3.00
8/35¢ 15.00
9 .... 3.00
☞1st Mystique
9/35¢ 15.00
10 .... 3.00
10/35¢ 15.00
11-15 .... 2.00

16...15.00
☛Mystique cameo
17...8.00
18..40.00
☛1st Mystique
19...3.00
20-23......................................2.00

Ms. Marvel
Marvel, 2006
1-45..3.00

Ms. Mystic
Pacific, 1982
1..4.00
2..3.00

Ms. Mystic
Continuity, 1988
1-9...2.00

Ms. Mystic
Continuity, 1993
1-4...3.00

Ms. Mystic Deathwatch 2000
Continuity, 1993
1-3...3.00

Ms. PMS
Aaaahh!!, 1992
0-1...3.00

Ms. PMS
Aaaahh!!, 2005
1..4.00

Ms. Quoted Tales
Chance, 1983
1..2.00

Ms. Tree
Eclipse, 1983

Ms. Tree was a popular detective-adventure comic by Max Collins and Terry Beatty. The Collins-Beatty team produced many works, but Ms. Tree was their best-known creation. A popular crime-novel writer, Max Collins, gave the Ms. Tree stories an edge focusing them on real-life issues such as abortion and child molestation.

The stories were always solidly plotted, and often held surprising twists. Running through three different publishers (Eclipse, Aardvark-Vanaheim, and Renegade), this series lasted fifty issues, with assorted specials and spinoffs.

1 .... 4.00
2-5 .... 3.00
6-49.. 2.00
50-3D 2 .... 3.00
Summer 1.............................. 2.00

Ms. Tree Quarterly
DC, 1990
1-10....................................... 4.00

Ms. Victory Special
AC
1 .... 2.00

Mu
Devil's Due, 2004
1 .... 3.00
1/Ropie................................... 4.00
2 .... 3.00
2/Suh...................................... 4.00
3 .... 3.00
3/MLim.................................... 4.00
4 .... 3.00
4/Hyung.................................. 4.00

Mucha Lucha
DC, 2003
1-3 .... 2.00

Muggsy Mouse
Magazine Enterprises, 1951
1 .... 40.00
2 .... 30.00
3-5 .... 24.00

Muggy-Doo Boy Cat
Stanhall, 1953

Although it can't match the sublime weirdness of Herbie, Muggy-Doo Boy Cat rates easily as one of the oddest comics ever published, if only for the name alone.

Of course, like any great oddity, Muggy-Doo's strangeness plays out on several levels. The lead character is a junkyard cat, but in this case, he's a an actual junk peddler as well, who pushes his junk cart through the town in search of someone gullible enough to buy something. Sometimes, he even sings, "Yo-Ho, Yo-Ho! I deal in junk y'know! I'm Muggy-Doo an' warn you, I'm known as a soandso, oh-Yo-Ho, Yo-Ho!"

While stumbling from one misadventure to the next, the wording on Muggy's trademark yellow shirt (sometimes miscolored) changes to comment on the situation. This is a tip of the hat to R.E. Outcault's Yellow Kid, who appeared in the first major American comic strip, "Hogan's Alley."

1 .... 36.00
2-4 .... 25.00

Muktuk Wolfsbreath: Hard-Boiled Shaman
DC, 1998
1-3 .... 3.00

Mullkon Empire (John Jakes'...)
Tekno, 1995
1-6 .... 2.00

Multiverse (Michael Moorcock's...)
DC, 1997
1-12 .... 3.00

Mummy
Monster, 1991
1-4 .... 2.00

Mummy
Dell
1 .... 25.00

Mummy Archives
Millennium, 1992
1 .... 3.00

Mummy or Ramses the Damned (Anne Rice's...)
Millennium, 1990
1-12 .... 3.00

Mummy's Curse
Aircel, 1990
1-4 .... 3.00

Mummy, The: Valley of the Gods
Chaos, 2001
1-3 .... 3.00

Munden's Bar
First, 1988

Ann 1......................................3.00
Ann 2......................................6.00

Munsters
Gold Key, 1965

1..120.00
2..75.00
3-5..48.00
6-10.......................................34.00
11-16......................................30.00

Munsters
TV Comics, 1997

1-Special 1.............................3.00

Muppet Babies
(Star/Marvel)
Marvel, 1985

1...2.00
2-26......................................1.00

Muppet Babies
Harvey, 1993

1-6.......................................2.00

Muppet Babies
Adventures
Harvey, 1992

1...1.00

Muppet Babies
Big Book
Harvey, 1992

1...2.00

Muppets
Take Manhattan
Marvel, 1984

1-3.......................................2.00

Murcièlaga She-Bat
Heroic, 1993

1...2.00
2-3.......................................3.00

Murder
Renegade, 1986

1-2.......................................2.00

Murder Can Be Fun
Slave Labor, 1996

1-4.......................................4.00
5-12......................................3.00

Murder City
Eternity

1...4.00

Murder Incorporated
Fox, 1948

1.......................................400.00
2.......................................300.00
3-6......................................175.00
7-15.....................................150.00

Murder Me Dead
El Capitan, 2000

A beautiful, rich socialite found dead from apparent suicide. Her depressed jazz musician husband who finds comfort in the arms of a long lost high school crush. A seedy private investigator hired to prove foul play is afoot. These are the ingredients that make up David Lapham's comic-book noir, Murder Me Dead. Following the success of his indie title Stray Bullets with Murder Me Dead, Lapham unravels a modern crime thriller. The story follows Steven Russell in the wake of his wife's apparent suicide. Though not considered a suspect by the police, Russell has yet to be exonerated in the eyes of his dead wife's family. As he tries to put his life together, he suddenly finds himself caught in a web of passion, lies, and murder -- wondering whom he can really trust. Fans of crime whodunits with dark overtones and strong characterization, such as Jinx and 100 Bullets, will enjoy Lapham's tale of obsession and betrayal.

1-7... 3.00

Murderous Gangsters
Avon, 1951

1...................................... 300.00
2...................................... 200.00
3-4.................................... 150.00

Music Comics
Personality

2-4...................................... 3.00

Music Comics on Tour
Personality

1... 3.00

Mutant Aliens
NBM

1... 11.00

Mutant
Book of the Dead
Starhead

1... 3.00

Mutant Chronicles
Acclaim, 1996

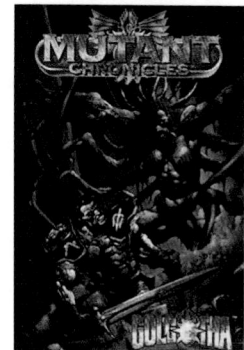

Not so long from now, huge corporations would rise to control most of the world's resources. These megacorporations would stop at nothing in their quest for profit, eventually fouling the Earth so badly that mankind had to seek out life on other planets in order to survive. Eventually the quest for new territories would wind up on Pluto, where explorers would unwittingly unleash a terrible force of darkness upon the universe. In the dark times that followed, mutants, demons, and immense beings known as Nepharites rose against mankind. Only after the greatest of struggles was this darkness defeated and mankind was once again left in peace.

So it seemed at least. Lately, evidence has been mounting that the Dark Legion may not have been defeated, only forced into working by more nefarious means. In this four-issue mini-series (tied to a collectible card game), we discover that true evil is not easily conquered.

1-4... 3.00

Mutant Chronicles
Sourcebook
Acclaim, 1996

1... 3.00

Mutant Earth
Image, 2002

1/A-4/B 3.00

Mutant Misadventures of Cloak & Dagger
Marvel, 1988

1-8	2.00
9	3.00
10-18	2.00
19	3.00

Mutants and Misfits
Silverline, 1987

1	2.00

Mutants vs. Ultras: First Encounters
Malibu, 1995

1	7.00

Mutant, Texas: Tales of Sheriff Ida Red
Oni, 2002

1-4	3.00

Mutant X
Marvel, 1998

1	3.00
1/A	4.00
2-5	3.00
6-11	2.00
12	3.00
13-24	2.00
25	3.00
26-32	2.00
Anl 1999-Anl 2000	3.00
Ann 2001	4.00

Mutant X
Marvel, 2001

1	3.00

Mutant X: Dangerous Decisions
Marvel, 2002

1	4.00

Mutant X: Origin
Marvel, 2002

The television series "Mutant X" has nothing to do with the former Marvel Comics series of the same name, but it is about a team of mutant super-heroes. In this case, the mutants were genetically engineered by a secret government organization that now wants to hunt them down. Led by the mysterious Adam, the members of Mutant X seek out their fellow mutants, help them master their powers and abilities, and protect them from their makers. This one-shot explores the background of the events in the television series; it establishes the mission of the soon-to-be formed Mutant X team.

1	4.00

Mutant Zone
Aircel, 1991

1-3	3.00

Mutation
Speakeasy Comics, 2005

1-2	3.00

Mutatis
Marvel, 1992

1-3	3.00

Mutator
Checker, 1998

1-2	2.00

Muties
Marvel, 2002

Writer Karl Bollers kicked off this series with a controversial tale called "The Changeling" which centered around the all-too-familiar ground of high school bullies and the picked-on kid who decides to get even. Mix in a bit of mutant hatred, and you have the makings of a series which captures the sense of being "different" that drove the early issues of the X-Men.

Muties promises to be a hard-edged look at what it's like for "muties"--children at the age of puberty who are suddenly discovering that their genetic make-up makes them different than everyone else. In time, they might become the sort of flashy, seemingly-all powerful super-heroes that the X-Men are, but for now, they're struggling to adjust to a world which fears the thing they are turning into.

1-6	3.00

Mutiny
Aragon, 1954

1	65.00
2-3	45.00

Mutopia X
Marvel, 2005

1	4.00
☞House of M	
1/Variant-5	3.00

Mutt & Jeff
DC, 1939

1	725.00
2	375.00
3	290.00
4	200.00
5	140.00
6-10	125.00
11-15	90.00
16-20	75.00
21-30	60.00
31-50	40.00
51-70	30.00
71-90	24.00
91-100	18.00
101-120	15.00
121-148	12.00

Muzzle
Dead Fish

1-6	1.00

MX-- The Superhero Series
Radical Comix, 1994

1-2	3.00

My Diary
Marvel, 1949

1	85.00
2	65.00

My Date
Hillman, 1947

1	200.00
2-4	145.00

My Experience
Fox, 1949

19	200.00
20	75.00
21	200.00
22	150.00

My Faith in Frankie
DC, 2004

1-4	3.00

My Favorite Martian
Gold Key, 1964

1	55.00
2	35.00
3-4	30.00
5-9	24.00

My Flesh is Cool (Steven Grant's)
Avatar, 2004

1 ....4.00

My Friend Irma
Marvel, 1950

Did you hear the one about the blond fox that got caught in a trap? Yup, she chewed off three legs and was still stuck (ba-dum-bump!). See, I could have been the writer for My Friend Irma, one long blond joke that ran for nearly 50 issues during the early 1950s, except that the actual writer happened to be one Stan Lee and the artist was teen humor genius Dan DeCarlo (of Archie fame). My Friend Irma was based on a popular radio and TV show featuring the adventures of the air-headed Irma and her pals, young "career girls" whose amazing and incurable dumbness was the root of so much hilarity ("Are you girls amateurs?" asks the art instructor. "No," replies Irma, "we're not even related.") In one memorable sequence, Irma actually complained that Stan and Dan were making her too dumb - then ended up walking out with their paychecks. Excelsior!

-- Rob Salkowitz

3-5..50.00
6-10..40.00
11-19..25.00
20-30..22.00
31-48..18.00

My Girl Pearl
Atlas, 1955

1 ....80.00
2 ....45.00
3-6..30.00
7-11..25.00

My Greatest Adventure
DC, 1955

My Greatest Adventure began its life as an adventure series, quickly switching to a science/fantasy-inspired format. For the first 80 issues of its run it turned in a respectable collection of stories, including several issues featuring the art of Jack Kirby and Alex Toth.

Then, issue #80 introduced the world to the strange crew of characters known as The Doom Patrol. This weird team consisted of ex-racer Cliff Steele, now clad in the metal body of Robotman; the stretchable Elasti-Girl; and the mysterious Negative Man. Like Marvel's X-Men, these oddball heroes were led by a wheelchair-bound scientist ("The Chief"). An offbeat and popular team, the Doom Patrol soon "took over" the series and My Greatest Adventure switched names to The Doom Patrol (1st Series) following issue #85.

1 .... 1,250.00
2 .... 600.00
3-4 .... 425.00
5-10 .... 325.00
11-14 .... 200.00
15-17 .... 250.00
18 .... 300.00
19 .... 200.00
20-21 .... 225.00
22-27 .... 175.00
28 .... 200.00
29-30 .... 150.00
31-40 .... 125.00
41-61 .... 100.00
62-79 .... 75.00
80 .... 425.00
☛1st Doom Patrol
81-85 .... 150.00

My Great Love
Fox, 1949

1 .... 80.00
2 .... 50.00
3-4 .... 40.00

My Intimate Affair
Fox, 1950

1 .... 100.00
2 .... 55.00

My Life
Fox, 1948

"I am in love with a boy who hardly notices me. Will he think I am very bold if I call him?" For the (1940s-style) answer to this and other burning questions, as well as some gritty, emotionally violent, and downright mean confession-oriented tales of love lost and found, turn to Fox Feature Syndicate's series, My Life.

In its short run, My Life managed to draw the attention of comics censor Frederic Wertham, who cited the series for its indecency and poor family values in his book Seduction of the Innocent. My Life's answer to the above question, by the way, is "I've never known a man who liked to be chased by a girl. Men like to do all the chasing." In like fashion, women who strayed outside the lines by displaying initiative, ability, or emotional sophistication were frequently the villains in these stories.

-- Rob Salkowitz

4 .... 155.00
5 .... 80.00
6-7 .... 85.00
8-9 .... 40.00
10 .... 90.00
11-15 .... 40.00

My Life With Eddie Vedder
Chemical Brain Comics, 1998
1-3 .... 4.00

My Little Margie
Charlton, 1954

1 .... 110.00
2 .... 60.00
3-5 .... 35.00
6-10 .... 32.00

11-19	26.00
20	45.00
21-30	20.00
31-39	16.00
40-50	12.00
51-53	9.00
54	40.00

My Little Margie's Boyfriends
Charlton, 1955

1	70.00
2	45.00
3-5	40.00
6-11	30.00

My Love
Marvel, 1949

1	80.00
2	60.00
3-4	40.00

My Love
Marvel, 1969

1	20.00
2	12.00
3	10.00
4-9	8.00
10-20	6.00
21-39	4.00
Special 1	15.00

My Love Affair
Fox, 1949

1	90.00
2	50.00
3-6	60.00

My Love Secret
Fox, 1949

25	50.00
53	25.00

My Love Story
Fox, 1949

1	90.00
2	50.00
3-4	45.00

My Love Story
Atlas, 1956

1	75.00
2-5	40.00
6-9	35.00

My Monkey's Name is Jennifer
Slave Labor, 2002

1	3.00

My Name Is Chaos
DC, 1992

1-4	5.00

My Name Is Holocaust
DC, 1995

1-5	3.00

My Name is Mud
Incognito, 1994

All the credits usually seen on a super-hero comic are replaced here by one name, Brain Denham. This is good for Brian, who has the chance to put his story to the public with no editorial interference, but the flipside is there's no one else to cop the blame for stuff like transposed pages and a bizarre, text-heavy conclusion. Mud is a super-hero working for the police. Big, strong, intelligent and introspective, he's a decent enough chap who regrets having to cancel dates when a supervillain shows up. Denham's drawing isn't bad and will improve once he looks beyond John Byrne, but no one's really going to know because his coloring is so wretched. Remember those "release the rainbow" ads? That's what Denham's done. Every page is a conflicting radiant miasma off-putting to all but the most dedicated.

1	3.00

My Only Love
Charlton, 1975

Ah, True Love! It can mean unlimited happiness for those lucky enough to experience it. But, as many of the stories in this series show, finding it can be pretty tough. Luckily, the stories also always have a happy ending, reinforcing the notion that every woman will eventually find the one man meant for her. But for those girls out there who can't seem to snag the right guy, this series also regularly included an advice column for the love-lorn.

Even though romance comics had their heyday in the 40's and 50's, publishers kept trying for decades. Unfortunately, titles like this one didn't just suffer from a lack of interest in the genre, they also lacked the big-name artists and writers often seen in the early books.

1	10.00
2	4.00
3-9	3.00

My Own Romance
Marvel, 1949

4	100.00
5	60.00
6-18	50.00
19-55	35.00
56-74	20.00
75	25.00
76	20.00

My Personal Problem
Ajax, 1955

1	50.00
2-4	35.00

My Private Life
Fox, 1950

16-17	60.00

My Real Love
Standard, 1952

5	100.00

Myriad
Approbation, 2005

1-6	3.00

Myrmidon
Red Hills, 1998

1	3.00

My Romance
Marvel, 1948

1	95.00
2	60.00
3	50.00

My Romantic Adventures
ACG, 1956

The world of 1950s and 1960s romance comics is one that may be lost to us forever. It was a world of wide-eyed innocence, where pliant young women pined away for dashing, adventurous men, and true love conquered over jealous rivals, personal flaws, family opposition, and harrowing circumstances. The fantasies of chaste, classless romance were rendered in clean lines and rote narrative. By the mid-1950s, the grit and realism of the early romance comics of Simon and Kirby had been burnished to a clean, glossy finish, and the range of products from the different publishers - DC, Charlton, ACG, Marvel - were all stultifyingly similar. My Romantic Adventures fits neatly into this mold, with a tinge of exotic adventure and foreign locales to spice up the usual plot devices.

-- Rob Salkowitz

68	35.00
69-70	28.00
71-80	24.00
81-89	20.00
90-99	16.00
100-110	12.00
111-120	10.00
121-138	8.00

My Romantic Adventures?
Avalon

1	3.00

Myron Moose Funnies
Fantagraphics, 1973

1-3	2.00

My Secret
Superior, 1949

1	75.00
2-3	35.00

My Secret Affair
Fox, 1949

1	125.00
2-3	65.00

My Secret Life
Fox, 1949

22-24	75.00
25-26	60.00

My Secret Life
Charlton, 1957

19	12.00
20-30	6.00
31-47	4.00

My Secret Marriage
Superior, 1953

1	75.00
2	40.00
3-15	30.00
16-24	25.00

My Secret Romance
Fox, 1950

1	100.00
2	85.00

Mysfits
Bon-a-Gram, 1994

1	3.00

Mys-Tech Wars
Marvel, 1993

1-4	2.00

Mysteries
Superior, 1953

1	275.00
2	150.00
3-5	110.00
6-11	85.00

Mysteries of Scotland Yard
Magazine Enterprises, 1954

Inspector Ronald Kirk of the Scotland Yard specializes in solving European mysteries with a supernatural flavor. The tales reprinted in Mysteries of the Scotland Yard, a 1954 one-shot, first appeared in Manhunt. The stories, including "The Stone of the Dying Druid," "The Case of the Perfect Crime," "The Man with the Beast-like Face" and "The Man Who Sold Death" all feature the trench-coated, pipe-smoking Kirk in fast-paced, action-packed pursuit of murderers and menaces against a stylized English-noir setting. Paul Parker's artwork employs the heavy line and cinematic style of Milton Caniff (Terry and the Pirates) to excellent effect in the Kirk adventures.

-- Rob Salkowitz

1	50.00

Mysteries of Unexplored Worlds
Charlton, 1956

1	200.00
2	65.00
3-4	100.00
5-7	135.00
8	100.00
9-10	135.00
11	110.00
12	75.00
13-18	28.00
19	60.00
20	28.00
21-24	60.00
25	20.00
26	55.00
27-30	20.00
31-40	14.00
41-45	10.00
46	22.00
47-48	16.00

Mysterious Adventures
Story, 1951

1	325.00
2	225.00
3-10	175.00
11	200.00
12-13	175.00
14	150.00
15	200.00
16-24	150.00

Mysterious Stories
Premier, 1954

2	300.00
3	200.00
4-7	165.00

Mysterious Suspense
Charlton, 1968

1	35.00

Mysterious Traveler Comics
TransWorld, 1948

1	450.00

Mystery Comics
Wise, 1944

1	725.00
2	585.00
3-4	500.00

Mystery Date
Lightspeed, 1999

1	3.00

Mystery in Space
DC, 1951

Each issue of this series featured adventures in outer space, many with a twist ending. In one story, a human explorer found aliens dividing up the planets of the solar system in a game. But when he thwarted them, he found out they had all bluffed each other.

The series' most popular feature was the adventures of space ranger Adam Strange, drawn by Carmine Infantino. One of the original space heroes, Strange starred in this series for a good part of its run, and even teamed up with Hawkman for a time in order to restore order on his adopted planet, Rann.

1	3,000.00
2	1,250.00
3	900.00
4-5	700.00
6-10	600.00
11-15	400.00
16-25	320.00
26-40	235.00
41-52	195.00
53	1,500.00
☞Adam Strange starts	
54	425.00
55	250.00
56-60	175.00
61-71	125.00
72-74	100.00
75	225.00
☞JLA app.	
76-80	100.00
81-86	75.00
87	175.00
☞Hawkman app.	
88-90	90.00
☞Hawkman app.	
91-93	50.00
94-103	40.00
104-110	30.00
111-117	5.00

Mystery in Space
DC, 2006

1-4	4.00

Mystery Man
Slave Labor, 1988

1-2	2.00

Mystery Men Comics
Fox, 1939

1	10,250.00
2	9,000.00
3	3,250.00
4-5	2,200.00
6	1,700.00
7	1,825.00
8	1,700.00
9	900.00
10-12	850.00
13	550.00
14-19	500.00
20-31	425.00

Mystery Men Movie Adaptation
Dark Horse, 1999

1-2	3.00

Mysterymen Stories
Bob Burden, 1996

1	5.00

Mystery of Woolverine Woo-Bait
Fantagraphics, 2004

1	5.00

Mystery Tales
Marvel, 1952

Mystery Tales was one of many titles Atlas hurried to the stands in the wake of the success of E.C.'s "New Trend" horror comics of the early '50s. Early issues featured Atlas' typical heavy-handed mix of gory and gruesome fare, rendered by a roster of talent including Matt Fox, a young Gene Colan, Bill Everett, and the great Joe Maneely. The arrival of the Comics Code banished the buckets of blood, and the focus shifted to tales of suspense and (as the title says) mystery.

By 1957, Atlas had hit the skids and cut back on all but a few titles. Mystery Tales did not survive the implosion, though stories from its pages have occasionally been reprinted in Marvel horror titles from the '70s such as Dead of Night and Supernatural Tales.

-- Rob Salkowitz

1	400.00
2	250.00
3-5	200.00
6-10	185.00
11-20	150.00
21-30	120.00
31-40	90.00
41-54	65.00

Mystic
Marvel, 1951

1	485.00
2	335.00
3	235.00
4	400.00
5	175.00
6	400.00
7	175.00
8-20	135.00
21-30	105.00
31-36	85.00
37-56	70.00
57	100.00
58-61	70.00

Mystic
CrossGen, 2000

1-43	3.00

Mystic Comics
Timely, 1940

1	11,750.00
2	3,600.00
3-5	2,850.00
6-7	2,650.00
8	1,950.00
9-10	1,700.00

Mystic Comics
Timely, 1944

1	2,000.00
2	1,000.00
3-4	775.00

Mystic Edge
Antarctic, 1998

1	3.00

Mystic Trigger
Maelstrom
1 ....3.00

Mystical Tales
Atlas, 1956
1 ....300.00
2 ....185.00
3-5 ....140.00
6-7 ....125.00

Mystique
Marvel, 2003
1 ....3.00
2-24 ....3.00

Mystique & Sabretooth
Marvel, 1996
1-4 ....2.00

My Story
Fox, 1949
5 ....100.00
6-12 ....80.00

Myst: The Book of the Black Ships
Dark Horse, 1997

Myst, the popular interactive computer game, is translated to the comic book format with this Dark Horse series. The legend of the D'ni inspires Atrus to resist the evil of his father, Gehn. Using magical books that provide links to other worlds, Atrus and his family fights to save his race. Much of the art for the series is taken from the computer graphics of the game.

This title was written by Chris Ulm, and featured art by Doug Wheatley.

0 ....2.00
1-4 ....3.00

My Terrible Romance
NEC, 1994
1-2 .... 3.00

Myth
Fygmok, 1996
1-2 .... 3.00

Mythadventures
Warp, 1984
1-12 .... 2.00

Myth Conceptions
Apple, 1987
1-8 .... 2.00

Mythical Detective Loki
ADV Manga, 2004
1-2 .... 10.00

Mythic Heroes
Chapterhouse, 1996

This series presents several text fiction stories in each issue, containing elements of science fiction, fantasy, adventure, and other genres.

As an example of the stories presented, "FlyByNight" explores how a girl with the power of flight would use her abilities in the real world. J.J. Frost thinks she has found a legitimate job acting as an emergency delivery service, but the work may be more than she bargained for.

"The Hero Who Never Was" tells the story of the Dreadnought, a suit of powered armor that makes its debut during the D-Day invasion. The photographer who first captures the Dreadnought on film is asked by the military to take part in an elaborate ruse to turn the armor into a World War II hero.

Each issue of Mythic Heroes contains the beginning of at least one new story, as well as continuations of other stories from previous issues.

1 .... 3.00

Myth Maker (Robert E. Howard's...)
Cross Plains, 1999
1 .... 7.00

Mythography
Bardic, 1996
1-8 .... 4.00

Mythos
Wonder Comix, 1987
1-3 .... 2.00

Mythos: Hulk
Marvel, 2006
1 .... 4.00

Mythos: The Final Tour
DC, 1996
1-3 .... 6.00

Mythos: X-Men
Marvel, 2006
1 .... 4.00

Mythstalkers
Image, 2003
1-8 .... 3.00

My True Love
Fox, 1949
66 .... 60.00
67-69 .... 50.00

My Uncle Jeff
Origin Comics, 2003
1 .... 4.00

My War With Brian
NBM
1 .... 17.00

Walter Lantz characters, including Andy Panda, Charlie Chicken, and Woody Woodpecker appeared in this long-running anthology.

Names of Magic
DC, 2001

Timothy Hunter is 14 years old. A couple of years ago, a man stepped out of the shadows and asked if he wanted magic in his life. Magic did enter his life-like a hurricane-and swept away everything he ever cared about.

In this five-issue mini-series, Timothy again finds himself on the road, and being pursued by those who want to control his power, or end his life. He will face Faerie warriors and mysterious armed men. And he will follow this path to magic with a man identified only as "A Walker," who seems to know Doctor Occult, John Constantine, and the others that have entered Tim's life.

Continuing the story begun in Books of Magic, Timothy must now find his true name in order to be admitted to the White School and survive the dangers that surround him.

1-5 .... 3.00

'Nam Magazine
Marvel, 1988
1-10 .... 3.00

Namor
Marvel, 2003
1 .... 3.00
2-4 .... 2.00
5-12 .... 3.00

Namora
Timely, 1948
1 .... 2,000.00
2-3 .... 1,200.00

Namor, The Sub-Mariner
Marvel, 1990
1-5 .... 2.00
6-36 .... 1.00
37 .... 2.00
38-49 .... 1.00
50 .... 2.00
50/Variant 3.00

Nadesico
CPM Manga, 1999
1-26 .... 3.00

Nagasaki:
The Forgotten Bomb
Antarctic, 2004
1-2 .... 4.00

Nail
Dark Horse, 2004
1-4 .... 3.00

Naive Inter-Dimensional
Commando Koalas
Eclipse, 1986

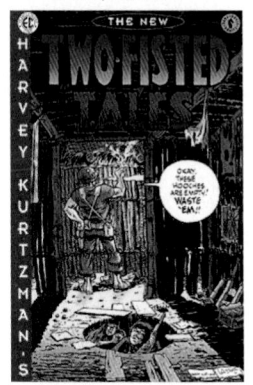

Four marsupials named Bruce front the legendary band from down under known as The Koalas. On the night they plan to play their loudest song ever, to the thrills of fans and record execs alike, a freak occurrence transports the band mates from the upside down world of Australia (literally) to the concrete jungles of New York. There they are recruited by the U.S. government to take down the renegade Sheik Ratal N'Raul who has taken over land of Myopia. Though reluctant to undertake such a dangerous mission, the koalas answer the call. After all this isn't just about protecting the world's oil supply: this is about freedom and justice. Making a cameo appearance in this hilarious comic are the Adolescent Radioactive Black Belt Hamsters.

1 .... 2.00

Naked Angels
Fantagraphics, 1996
1-2 .... 3.00

Naked Eye
(S.A. King's...)
Antarctic, 1994
1-3 .... 3.00

Naked Fangs
Acid Rain, 1994
1-2 .... 3.00

'Nam
Marvel, 1986
1 .... 2.00
1/2nd-25 .... 1.00
26-84 .... 2.00

Nameless
Image, 1997
1-5 .... 3.00

51-62	2.00
Ann 1	3.00
Ann 2	2.00
Ann 3-4	3.00

Nancy and Sluggo
St. John, 1955

121	25.00
122-130	15.00
131-145	12.00

Nancy and Sluggo
Dell, 1957

146	25.00
147-187	10.00

Nancy and Sluggo
Gold Key, 1962

188-192	10.00

Nancy and Sluggo Travel Time
Dell, 1958

1	80.00

Nanny and the Professor
Dell, 1970

1	16.00
2	10.00

Nanosoup
Millennium, 1996

1	3.00

Napoleon & Uncle Elby
Eastern, 1942

1	200.00

Narcolepsy Dreams
Slave Labor, 1995

Narcolepsy Dreams features short stories written and drawn by Jaime Crespo.

As examples of Crespo's work, "Up and Down Career" tells the story of a boy's quest to become a yo-yo champion, until the day he meets the reigning star at the local drugstore.

"Sleepwalk" is told from the point of view of the skull-headed Ruben, a five-dollar-an-hour wage slave who cleans a ratty hotel and its restrooms. When Ruben and his horned partner Ajax must remove a deranged homeless man from the roof of the building, life takes an inexplicable turn.

Finally, in "Hell Bent, Heaven Sent" a mentally retarded man on a playground swing set teaches the artist that angels may turn up in the most unlikely places.

Filled with vignettes from urban life based on adult and childhood experiences, these stories explore the strangeness and poignancy of everyday life in the big city from a surrealistic point of view.

1-2	3.00
4	1.00

Nard n' Pat
Cartoonists Co-Op, 1974

1	3.00

Narrative Illustration
E.C., 1942

1	1,000.00

Nascar Adventures
Vortex, 1992

NASCAR Adventures gives a different race car driver's biography in each issue. In the first issue, readers were told the story of NASCAR legend Fred Lorenzen, who won twenty-six NASCAR races throughout his career. The issue showed how Lorenzen rose in the ranks of drivers until he finally won his first race in 1961. He went on to have an illustrious career in NASCAR.

One of his only setbacks was when his friend and mentor, "Fireball" Roberts, passed away due to injuries sustained in a car crash. This caused Lorenzen to lose concentration and crash too. Fred Lorenzen retired in 1967, having been the first racer ever to earn $100,000 in a single season.

NASCAR Adventures premiered in 1991 and ran just two issues.

1-7	3.00

NASCUB Adventures
Vortex, 1991

1	2.00

Nash
Image, 1999

1-Ashcan 1/Varian	3.00

Nasti: Monster Hunter
Schism

1-3	3.00
Ashcan 1/Ltd.	1.00

Nathaniel Dusk
DC, 1984

1-4	2.00

Nathaniel Dusk II
DC, 1985

1-4	2.00

Nathan Never
Dark Horse, 1999

1-6	5.00

National Comics
Quality, 1940

Begun in 1940, National Comics was published by Quality under its Comic Magazines imprint. Each giant-sized issue packed in a wide variety of features, from gag strips like "Salty Waters" and "Windy Breeze" to crime adventures starring Steve Wood or Sally O'Neil, Policewoman.

National Comics is best remembered today, however, for introducing the comic super-hero Uncle Sam. Looking exactly like the figure in the army recruiting ads, this character had such abilities as super-strength and the power to see into the future. He used these abilities to battle enemies of liberty everywhere, particularly the Axis forces in World War II. Following Quality's demise as a publisher, Uncle Sam would move over to DC where he would eventually become a member of the Freedom Fighters.

1	4,800.00
2	1,800.00
3	1,300.00
4	975.00
5	1,160.00
6-11	1,000.00
12	675.00
13-16	720.00
17	545.00
18	790.00
19-23	545.00
24-30	376.00
31-34	330.00
35-38	250.00
39	275.00
40-50	170.00
51	230.00
52-60	120.00
61-70	100.00
71-75	80.00

National Comics
DC, 1999
1 ....2.00

National Lampoon Presents: French Comics (The Kind Men Like)
National Lampoon
1 ....5.00

National Velvet
Dell, 1962
1-2 ....30.00

National Velvet
Dell, 1962
1 ....12.00
2 ....9.00

Nation of Snitches
DC
1 ....5.00

Nat Turner
Kyle Baker Publishing, 2005
1-2 ....3.00

Natural Inquirer
Fantagraphics, 1989
1 ....2.00

Natural Selection
Atom, 1998
1-2 ....3.00

Nature Boy
Charlton, 1956
3 ....55.00
4-5 ....50.00

Nature of the Beast
Caliber
1-2 ....3.00

Naughty Bits
Fantagraphics, 1991

Cartoonist Roberta Gregory takes on all comers with this daring quarterly. Make no mistake, Naughty Bits can be downright shocking at times. Gregory tackles religion, sex, smut comics, and just about any other controversial topic you can think of. She even takes to task Robert Crumb, grand hero of the underground comix scene, for the role women have played in his comics.

For all this, Naughty Bits can be a very funny book. Particularly humorous are the ongoing escapades of "Bitchy Butch," a super-nasty lesbian who takes negative thinking to the extreme. As much as she tortures other people, it's a riot to watch her contend with dating, disagreeable church services, and other hazards of modern life.

1	7.00
1/2nd	3.00
2	5.00
3-5	4.00
6-38	3.00

Näu Headhunter
Neotek Iconography, 1993
1 ....3.00

Nausicaä of the Valley of Wind Part 1
Viz, 2004
1-7 ....3.00

Nausicaä of the Valley of Wind Part 2
Viz
1-4 ....3.00

Nausicaä of the Valley of Wind Part 3
Viz
1-3 ....4.00

Nausicaä of the Valley of Wind Part 4
Viz, 1995
1-6 ....3.00

Nausicaä of the Valley of Wind Part 5
Viz, 1995
1-8 ....3.00

Nautilus
Shanda Fantasy Arts, 1999
1 ....3.00

Navy Action
Atlas, 1954
1	85.00
2-4	58.00
5-11	45.00
15-18	38.00

Navy Combat
Atlas, 1955

Atlas' war comics were infamous for telling readers exactly what they would get inside with such simple titles as Combat, Battle, and its fleet of naval-related comics, including Navy Action, Navy Tales, and this series, Navy Combat.

Featuring cover art by Joe Maneely and interior art by Don Heck, the series featured World War II-related stories starring such colorful characters as "Torpedo" Taylor and "Battleship" Burke in such simply named stories as "Attack by Sea!" and "Salvo!"

The series ran 20 issues between 1955 and 1958.

-- Brent

1	140.00
2	85.00
3-7	70.00
8-12	62.00
13-20	48.00

Navy Heroes
Almanac, 1955
1 ....75.00

Navy Patrol
Key, 1955
1 ....28.00

Navy Tales
Atlas, 1957
1 ....85.00
2 ....75.00
3-4 ....60.00

Navy Task Force
Stanmor, 1954
1 ....45.00
2 ....25.00
3-8 ....20.00

Navy War Heroes
Charlton, 1964
1 ....12.00
2 ....8.00
3-7 ....6.00

Naza
Dell, 1964
1 ....15.00
2-5 ....8.00
6-9 ....6.00

Nazrat
Imperial, 1986

It's difficult being a rat, particularly when you're wanted by the law for various crimes, when people are out to kill you, and when royalty believes that you are "the key." You never know who your friends are-and who shouldn't be trusted under any circumstances. It's no easier when you're told that the only way to get the help you and your friends (including the kindly Kip) need is to contact "the Underground." What's a rat to do? Throw in the occasional bizarre dream featuring beautiful women and Monty Python characters, and it's easy to see why Naz is confused.

A healthy Dave Sim influence is apparent in this black-and-white series from Eternity Comics. Written and drawn by Jerry Frazee.

1-6 ....2.00

Nazz
DC, 1990
1-4 .... 5.00

NBC Saturday Morning Comics
Harvey, 1991

Bring Harvey Comics and NBC television together, and you get a clever way to preview the network's fall 1991 Saturday morning line-up. The stories are uncredited and the art typical of that era in American animation, but it's still a good idea.

See Macaulay Culkin become Wish Kid, gaining limited super powers from his magic baseball glove! Sports superstars Wayne Gretzky, Bo Jackson and Michael Jordan form the Prostars, called to rescue a rock star and the Amazon rain forest! Atom Ant gets a little help from Yogi Bear and friends when his attempts to defeat a giant cockroach go awry! The Spacecats bumble as they try to capture a jewel thief, while that crazy gang from Saved by the Bell get into mischief!

So what happened next?! Was the rain forest saved? Did Atom Ant get his helmet back? Did the jewel thief get away? Well, that's the thing. You had to tune in to NBC that season to get the rest of the story...

1 .... 2.00

Near Myths
Rip Off, 1978
1 .... 3.00

Near to Now
Fandom House
1-2 .... 2.00

Neat Stuff
Fantagraphics, 1985
1 .... 5.00
1/2nd 3.00

2 .... 4.00
2/2nd 3.00
3 .... 4.00
3/2nd-15 .... 3.00

Nebbs
Dell, 1945
1 .... 75.00

Neck and Neck
Tokyopop, 2004
1-4 .... 10.00

Necromancer
Anarchy
1 .... 3.00
1/Deluxe 4.00
2 .... 3.00
2/Deluxe 4.00
3 .... 3.00
3/Deluxe 4.00
4 .... 3.00
4/Deluxe 4.00

Necromancer
Anarchy
1-4 .... 3.00

Necromancer
Image, 2005
1/Manapul 3.00
1/Horn 4.00
1/Bachalo-6 .... 3.00

Necropolis
Fleetway-Quality
1-9 .... 3.00

Necroscope
Malibu, 1992

Necroscope is the comic adaptation of Brian Lumley's supernatural spy novel of the same name. Martin Powell scripted the series, while Daerick Gr̈ss illustrated. Before the fall of communism, the Soviet Union developed a covert spy group that used ESP-wielding agents as its main weapon. The agents were

"Necroscopes," psychics that could read the memories of the dead.

No other government had a spy unit as developed, until Great Britain began to catch up. Both sides even began employing "spotters," psychics whose gift was to detect other psychics, as a way of ferreting out enemy agents. With these new abilities being employed, the cold war game of cloak-and-dagger was entering a terrifying new age.

This painted, five-issue mini-series began its run in 1992.

1-5 ....3.00

Necroscope Book II: Wamphyri
Malibu, 1994

1-5 ....3.00

Necrowar
Dreamwave, 2003

1-3 ....3.00

Nefarismo
Fantagraphics, 1994

1-8 ....3.00

Negation
CrossGen, 2002

1-27 ....3.00

Negation War
CrossGen, 2004

1-2 ....3.00

Negation Prequel
CrossGen, 2001

1 ....3.00

Negative Burn
Caliber, 1993

1-3 ....6.00
4 ....4.00
5-6 ....6.00
7-12 ....4.00
13 ....7.00
14-47 ....4.00
48-49 ....5.00
50 ....7.00

Negative Burn
Image, 2006

1-7 ....6.00

Negative Burn: Summer Special 2005
Image, 2005

1 ....10.00

Negative One
Eirich Olson, 1999

1 ....3.00

Negro Heroes
Parents' Magazine Institute, 1947

1 ....525.00
2 ....570.00

Negro Romance
Charlton, 1950

1 ....700.00
2-3 ....525.00

Neil & Buzz in Space and Time
Fantagraphics, 1989

1 ....2.00

Neil the Horse Comics and Stories
Aardvark-Vanaheim, 1983

He looks like something out of an early Walt Disney cartoon, but his adventures are not exactly the whimsical, lighthearted fare kids have grown up on. Neil the horse and all of his various friends -- including (for example) Poupee the doll and a clever cat, Soapy (who smokes) -- stumble through adventures including a trip to France, a battle with the villainous Mr. Coffee Nerves, and even full-text adventures in which Neil's innocence gets, all too often, taken advantage of. Still, the happy-go-lucky horse usually comes out OK from his wide-eyed adventuring, just in time for another one.

Making the world safe for musical comedy, the issues typically include several short adventures and cartoons, and even paper doll characters running on the back covers.

1 ....3.00
2-13 ....2.00
14-15 ....3.00

Nellie the Nurse
Atlas, 1945

The late 1940s saw the rise of romance comics, silly situation comedy comics, and comics featuring working women.

Nellie the Nurse was a combination of all three. Featuring cheesecake covers featuring Nellie posing like a model in such incongrous settings as the beach and the hospital ward as well as covers with her out on a date or working the ward, Nellie's antics proved popular enough to sustain the series from 1945 to 1952. The unflappable nurse's stories featured art by Harvey Kurtzman on several issues.

-- Brent

1 ....225.00
2 ....105.00
3-4 ....80.00
5 ....90.00
6-10 ....75.00
11 ....80.00
12 ....75.00
13 ....55.00
14-16 ....80.00
17 ....55.00
18 ....80.00
19-20 ....55.00
21-30 ....50.00
31-36 ....42.00

Nemesis Comics Special
Nemesis

Ashcan 1 ....1.00

Nemesister
Cheeky, 1997

1-3 ....3.00
3/Ashcan 1.00
4-9 ....3.00

Nemesis the Warlock
Eagle, 1984

1-8 ....2.00

Nemesis the Warlock
Fleetway-Quality, 1989
1-19...2.00

Neo
Excalibur
1..2.00

Neomen
Slave Labor, 1987

In this grim future, it is a biological plague run amok, not a war, that has taken its toll on the world, wiping out most of humanity and mutating many of the rest. On the barren surface, pre-technology conditions and savagery exist; but underground, genetic engineers who have survived work feverishly to breed a new mankind, part organic and part steel, that can carry humanity forward. Achieving it with their powerful Neomen, they are faced with new problems. For one thing, not all their creations are as pure of heart as they'd like. Worse still, their entrance into the surface world allows the mutants access to their underground hideout.

Written and drawn by Gary Winnick and Frank Cirocco, this series is published in black-and-white by Slave Labor Graphics.

1-2...2.00

Neon City
Innovation
1..2.00

Neon City: After the Fall
Innovation
1..3.00

Neon Cyber
Image, 1999
1..3.00
1/Variant..................................5.00
2-8..3.00

Neon Genesis Evangelion Book 1
Viz, 1997
1/A-6/B 3.00

Neon Genesis Evangelion Book 2
Viz, 1998
1/A-1/B 4.00
2/A-5/B 3.00

Neon Genesis Evangelion Book 3
Viz, 1998
1/A-6/B 3.00

Neon Genesis Evangelion Book 4
Viz, 1999
1/A-7/B 3.00

Neon Genesis Evangelion Book 5
Viz, 2000
1-7/B... 3.00

Neon Genesis Evangelion Book 6
Viz, 2001
1-4/B... 4.00

Neon Genesis Evangelion Book 7
Viz, 2002
1-5/B... 3.00
6-6/B... 4.00

Neotopia
Antarctic, 2003
1-5 .... 4.00

Neotopia (Vol. 2)
Antarctic, 2003
1-5 .... 3.00

Neotopia (Vol. 3)
Antarctic, 2004
1-4 .... 3.00

Neotopia (Vol. 4)
Antarctic, 2004
1-5 .... 3.00

Nerve
Nerve, 1987
1-7 .... 2.00
8 .... 4.00

Nervous Rex
Blackthorne, 1985
1-10... 2.00

Nestrobber
Blue Sky Blue, 1992

It was a rough mission for the "Birds of Prey" secret military team. Two of their number are dead and another dying, while a madman dictator still has a nuclear device in his possession. And as the surviving members try to hang on and plan another attack, they are reminded grimly of their own mortality-and of the innocents, including their families, that they are fighting to save.

These are the characters in this deeply thoughtful series, written by Jo Duffy and drawn in a manga style by Maya Sakamoto. But that's not all; issues also feature such added elements as a text story from Duffy accompanied by full-page illustrations by Colleen Doran. Published by Duffy's own Blue Sky Blue company.

1-2 .... 2.00

Netherworld
Ambition
1 .... 2.00

Netherworlds
Adventure, 1988

The future world of 1999 is a horrific nightmare. Lee Iacocca is president, the United States is in the midst of a Depression, and cities such as New York are overrun with crime and poverty. Not to mention that an evil demon and his minions, prowling the ruined streets of NetherWorlds, plan to make our reality into the apocalyptic hell that is theirs. And the one man who may be able to stop it is a burnt-out construction worker who drinks away his evenings and doesn't know what to make of the mysterious old guy across the hall who warns him to "watch his back"-up until he himself is attacked by the aforementioned demons.

Despite the dated future-1999 wasn't really all that bad-this 1988 title is compelling and spooky. Published by Adventure Publications, written by Mark Ellis, and drawn by Gabriel Morrissette.

1 ....2.00

Net Prophet: Trouble on Garamond
Penn & Inc.
Ashcan 1 ....1.00

Neuro Jack
Big, 1996
1 ....2.00

Neuromancer: The Graphic Novel
Marvel
1 ....9.00

Neutro
Dell, 1967
1 ....35.00

Nevada
DC, 1998

Writer Steve Gerber was one of comics' angry (and talented) young men of the 1970s, peppering the pages of Howard the Duck, Man-Thing, and The Defenders with barbed wit and

social and political observations. With the Vertigo mini-series Nevada, Gerber may have once again found a suitable platform for his vision: a twisted detective story featuring hardheaded Vegas showgirl Nevada and her loveable pet ostrich Bolero. Nevada was introduced in the pages of the Vertigo: Winter's Edge collection (though the character first appeared nearly 20 years ago in Marvel's Howard the Duck, has now branched out into this mini-series. Deliberately paced, with plenty of shocking mystery, strong art by Phil Winslade and Steve Leialoha, and Gerber's trademark gift for characterization, Nevada is proving to be much more than flash and glitter.

-- Rob Salkowitz

1-6 .... 3.00

Nevermen
Dark Horse, 2000
1-3 .... 3.00

Nevermen: Streets of Blood
Dark Horse, 2003
1-3 .... 3.00

Neverwhere (Neil Gaiman's)
DC, 2005
1-9 .... 3.00

New Adventure Comics
DC, 1937
12 .... 3,400.00
13 .... 3,200.00
14 .... 2,800.00
15-20 .... 1,975.00
21-22 .... 1,750.00
23-31 .... 1,475.00

New Adventures of Abraham Lincoln
Image
1 .... 20.00

New Adventures of Beauty and the Beast (Disney's...)
Disney, 1992
1-2 .... 2.00

New Adventures of Charlie Chan
DC, 1958
1 .... 425.00
2 .... 275.00
3-6 .... 230.00

New Adventures of Cholly and Flytrap, The: Till Death Do Us Part
Marvel, 1990
1-3 .... 5.00

New Adventures of Felix the Cat
Felix, 1992
1-7 .... 2.00

New Adventures of Huck Finn
Gold Key, 1968
1 .... 10.00

New Adventures of Jesus
Rip Off
1 .... 5.00

New Adventures of Judo Joe
Ace, 1987
1 .... 2.00

New Adventures of Pinocchio
Dell, 1962
1 .... 65.00
2-3 .... 50.00

New Adventures of Rick O'Shay and Hipshot
Cottonwood
1-2 .... 5.00

New Adventures of Shaloman
Mark 1
1 .... 2.00
2-Special 1 .... 3.00

New Adventures of Speed Racer
Now, 1993
0 .... 4.00
1-3 .... 2.00

New Adventures of Superboy
DC, 1980
1 .... 4.00
1/Whitman 8.00
2 .... 2.00
2/Whitman 3.00
3-4 .... 2.00
4/Whitman 3.00
5 .... 2.00
5/Whitman 3.00
6 .... 2.00
6/Whitman 3.00
7-8 .... 2.00
8/Whitman 3.00
9-20 .... 2.00
21-54 .... 1.00

New Adventures of Terry & the Pirates
Avalon, 1998
1-6 .... 3.00

New Adventures of the Phantom Blot
Gold Key, 1964
1 ....18.00
2 ....16.00
3 ....12.00
4-7 ....8.00

New Age Comics
Fantagraphics, 1985

In the mid-1980's, the comics world was monopolized by the "Big Two" publishers, DC and Marvel. Alternative story ideas were hard to find, and the ones that did make it to publication often had a very short life span. The long-term success of companies like Dark Horse, Image, and others finally opened the doors for "underground" publishers, greatly increasing the opportunities for new artists and writers, bringing their work to the attention of mainstream readers.

New Age Comics was a cooperative endeavor among several alternative publishers to expose potential new readers to as many of their books as possible. Basically, it was a book-length advertisement, with each company responsible for the production of their own section, which featured art, upcoming storylines, interviews, and other news about their comics.

Some of the more notable companies involved included WaRP Graphics, Kitchen Sink, Blackthorne, Rip-Off Press, and Sirius Comics.

1 ....2.00

New America
Eclipse, 1987

This 1987-1988 mini-series continues the post-apocalyptic saga of the Western U.S., first told in Scout. New America centers around Army Ranger Rosa Winter, a hero from the war in which Mexico invaded the southwestern United States. With national borders changed and political alignments in constant shift, Rosa is called upon to help build a new America.

Her first mission takes her to Baja, Mexico where Japanese business interests are busy trying to buy the entire area from the Communist government of Mexico. Working with a local priest, Rosa must unite the people of Baja to stop this transaction, and begin a war to liberate Mexico from its Communist leaders.

Like the original Scout series, New America features striking art by Timothy Truman.

1-4 .... 2.00

New Archies
Archie, 1987
1 .... 3.00
2-5 .... 2.00
6-22 .... 1.00

New Avengers
Marvel, 2005
0/Military.............................. 10.00
☛Promo for U.S. troops
1 .... 7.00
1/Retailer ed......................... 70.00
☛Spider-Man cover
1/DirCut................................... 5.00
1/Quesada.......................... 12.00
1/Finch 9.00
1/2nd 3.00
2 .... 2.00
2/Hairsine 45.00
3 .... 2.00
3/Wolverine 45.00
4 .... 3.00

4/Cheung............................ 15.00
4/DF 20.00
5 .... 2.00
5/Granov.............................. 15.00
6 .... 2.00
6/Hitch 15.00
7 .... 8.00
7/Adams 25.00
8 .... 3.00
8/Romita 20.00
9 .... 3.00
9/Trimpe 15.00
10-43 .... 3.00
Ann 1 .... 4.00

New Avengers: Illuminati
Marvel, 2007
1 .... 5.00

New Avengers/ Illuminati Special
Marvel, 2006
1 .... 14.00

New Avengers: Most Wanted Files
Marvel, 2006
1 .... 4.00

New Beginning
Unicorn
1-3 .... 2.00

New Bondage Fairies
Fantagraphics, 1996
1-12 .... 3.00

New Book of Comics
DC, 1937
1 .... 13,000.00
2 .... 6,500.00

Newcomers Illustrated
Newcomers
1-6 .... 3.00

Newcomers Showcase
Newcomers
1 .... 3.00

New Comics
DC, 1935
1 .... 16,000.00
2 .... 10,000.00
3-7 .... 3,000.00
8-11 .... 2,750.00

New Crew
Personality, 1991
1-10 .... 3.00

New Crime Files of Michael Mauser, Private Eye
Apple, 1992
1 .... 3.00

New DNAgents
Eclipse, 1985

1	2.00
2-17	1.00

New England Gothic
Visigoth, 1986

For 103 years, the tiny hamlet of Seths Neck, Maine, has existed outside of our reality, victim of an ancient evil that threatens to consume it completely. Only one person has escaped the town's fate, a young man allowed to attend school in the outside world. But Mordred's safe existence comes abruptly to an end when he is summoned home after his father's untimely death. Although ghosts, demons, and other mysterious creatures roam freely throughout Seths Neck, it is a powerful succubus whose evil power lies at the center of the town's distress. It is Mordred's destiny to face, on All Hallows Eve, the creature that killed his father. The fate of the entire village rests on his ability to resist her unholy charms...

1-2	2.00

New Eternals
Marvel, 1999

1	4.00

New Excalibur
Marvel, 2006

1-14	3.00

Newforce
Image, 1996

1-4	3.00

New Frontier
Dark Horse, 1992

1-3	3.00

New Frontiers
Evolution, 1989

The Evolution Comics title New Frontiers truly does live up to its tagline of being a "comic for the highly evolved." While the black and white artwork can be considered "cartoony" and amateurish, the mission of developing highly intelligent yet equally entertaining stories is one that is more than accomplished. With each issue splitting its pages between Action Master and Green Ghost and Lotus, the book puts a new spin on the tired super-hero genre.

Action Master and his work-for-hire teammates at Action Master, Inc. use their alien induced powers to help those in need-much like a super-powered A-Team. Applying an X-Files-type approach to storytelling, the serial tackles such weighty issues as prejudice, drug abuse and top-secret government conspiracies. Green Ghost and Lotus, on the other hand, provide a more lighthearted diversion. The good-looking, Green Ghost-while extremely powerful-lacks the brains necessary to become a well-respected crime fighter. Enter his sidekick/coach Lotus-the real brains of the operation. This unique twist on the super-hero genre provides for intelligent reading, lots of laughs and hours of enjoyment.

1-2	2.00

New Fun Comics
DC, 1935

1	46,000.00
☞Becomes More Fun Comics	
2	21,000.00
3	12,000.00
4-5	9,000.00
6	24,000.00
☞Becomes More Fun	

New Funnies (Walter Lantz...)
Dell, 1942

65	475.00
66-70	255.00
71-75	175.00
76	550.00
77-80	145.00
81-90	115.00
91-100	75.00
101-110	54.00
111-120	42.00
121-130	34.00
131-150	26.00
151-170	18.00
171-190	15.00
191-220	12.00
221-240	10.00
241-260	8.00
272-288	6.00

New Gods
DC, 1971

1	35.00
2	18.00
3-11	12.00
12-19	6.00

New Gods
DC, 1984

1-6	2.00

New Gods
DC, 1989

1-28	2.00

New Gods
DC, 1995

1-11	2.00
12	1.00
13-15	2.00

New Gods Secret Files
DC, 1998

You're probably familiar with some of the generalities. But did you know the whole story behind the formation of New Genesis and Apokalips? The rise to power of mighty Darkseid? The story of Scott Free? The ironically named tyrant "Granny Goodness"? These and other stories can be found in this title that lays the informational groundwork for Walt Simonson's ongoing series that followed it.

This issue also includes a preview of the Simonson series, featuring character bios and sketches; maps of the planets mentioned above; secret information on why Barda and Orion joined the Justice League of America; and more.

1 ....5.00

New Guardians
DC, 1988

1 ....2.00
2-12 ....1.00

New Hat
Black Eye

1 ....1.00

New Hero Comics
Red Spade

1 ....1.00

New Horizons
Shanda Fantasy Arts, 1999

1-5 ....5.00

New Humans
Pied Piper, 1987

1-3 ....2.00

New Humans
Eternity, 1987

1-17 ....2.00
Ann 1 ....3.00

New Justice Machine
Innovation, 1989

1-3 ....2.00

New Kids on the Block, The: Backstage Pass
Harvey, 1991

1 ....1.00

New Kids on the Block: Chillin'
Harvey, 1990

1 ....2.00
2-7 ....1.00

New Kids on the Block Comic Tour '90
Harvey, 1991

1 ....1.00

New Kids on the Block Magic Summer Tour
Harvey, 1991

1 ....1.00
1/Ltd. 4.00

New Kids on the Block, The: NKOTB
Harvey, 1990

1-5 ....1.00
6 ....2.00

New Kids on the Block Step By Step
Harvey, 1991

1 ....1.00

New Kids on the Block: Valentine Girl
Harvey, 1991

1 ....1.00

New Love
Fantagraphics, 1996

1-6 ....3.00

Newman
Image, 1996

1-4 ....3.00

New Mangaverse
Marvel, 2006

1-4 ....3.00

Newmen
Image, 1994

This eleventh title from Rob Liefeld's Extreme Studios brings us a group of super-powered humans who are just now learning to use their powers as a team. These Newmen consist of the bear-like Kodiak, speedstress Dash, winged flyer Byrd, teleporting Exit, and psionic powerhouse Reign. They were gathered together by Proctor in the Extreme Prejudice storyline to battle menaces which threaten our world such as Quantum and the Brotherhood of Man. But if this group of headstrong youngsters can't learn to work together, they'll prove to be their own worst enemies.

1 ....3.00
2-4 ....2.00
5-25 ....3.00

New Mutants
Marvel, 1983

1 ....6.00
2-24 ....2.00
25-26 ....3.00
27-85 ....2.00
86 ....3.00
☛Cable cameo
87 ....6.00
☛1st Cable story
87/2nd 2.00
88 ....3.00
89-97 ....2.00
98 ....5.00
99 ....3.00
100-100/3rd 2.00
Ann 1 ....3.00
Ann 2 ....4.00
Ann 3-5 ....2.00
Ann 6 ....3.00
Ann 7 ....2.00
Book 1 ....9.00
Special 1 ....3.00
Summer 1 ....2.00

New Mutants
Marvel, 2003

1 ....4.00
2-13 ....3.00

New Mutants, The: Truth or Death
Marvel, 1997

1-3 ....3.00

New Night of the Living Dead
Fantaco

0 ....2.00
1-3 ....4.00

New Order
Creative Force, 1994

1 ....3.00

New Paltz Comix
Moods, 1974

1-3 ....2.00

New Partners in Peril
Blue Comet

1 ....2.00

New Partners in Peril
Tami

1 ....2.00

New People
Dell, 1970

1 ....10.00
2 ....8.00

New Power Stars
Blue Comet

1 ....2.00

New Romances
Standard, 1951

5 ....75.00
6-9 ....45.00
10 ....50.00

11	110.00
12-13	40.00
14	50.00
15	40.00
16-17	50.00
18-21	40.00

New Shadowhawk
Image, 1995

1-7	3.00

New Statesmen
Fleetway-Quality

In the 1980s, two scientists successfully cracked the human genetic code. Within ten years they were redesigning physical abilities and attributes. Within ten more years, they tapped the psionic potential of their creations.

America finally had the perfect army, an entire race of super-powered soldiers. For years, the government used these groups of "optimen" to further its political interests, until a mission gone sour brought the project under public scrutiny. Pressured, the national government turned the optimen over to the states. They became official super-heroes, collectively called Statesmen.

But in 2064, America is a lawless, fearful country, and the Statesmen, despite their laboratory origins and genetic enhancements, are still human. They are able to love and hate. And sometimes they make mistakes.

1-5	4.00

Newstime
DC, 1993

1	3.00

Newstralia
Innovation, 1989

1-5	2.00

New Talent Showcase
DC, 1984

One of the dearest dreams of would-be comics writers and artists everywhere is "breaking in." DC's New Talent Showcase provided an avenue for this and gave recent discoveries a chance to strut their stuff.

It may have oversold the series a bit when it billed the artists and writers featured here as "Tomorrow's Superstars." The stories ranged from average to very good, though probably none will ever be hailed as a classic of the art form. Still, stories like "Forever Amber" by Rich Margopoulos and Stan Woch and "Class of 2064" by Todd Klein and Scott Hampton are enjoyable stories that show a great deal of potential.

1-10	2.00
11-19	1.00

New Teen Titans
DC, 1980

1	8.00
2	10.00
☞1st Deathstroke	
3-10	3.00
11-38	2.00
39	3.00
40	2.00
Ann 1	3.00
Ann 2-3	2.00

New Teen Titans
DC, 1984

1-5	3.00
6-49	2.00
Ann 1-4	3.00

New Teen Titans
(Giveaways and Promos)
DC

1-5	1.00

New Teen Titans:
Terror of Trigon
DC, 2003

1	18.00

New Terrytoons
Dell, 1960

1	45.00
2	22.00
3-8	18.00

New Terrytoons
Gold Key, 1962

1	35.00
2	22.00
3	12.00
4-5	8.00
6-10	6.00
11-20	5.00
21-30	4.00
31-40	3.00
41-54	2.00

New Thunderbolts
Marvel, 2004

1-18	3.00

New Titans
DC, 1988

0-59	2.00
60-61	3.00
62-99	2.00
100	3.00
101-124	2.00
125	4.00
126-130	2.00
Ann 5-7	4.00
Ann 8-10	3.00
Ann 11	4.00

New Triumph
Featuring Northguard
Matrix, 1985

When agents of the PACT Corporation kidnap Phillip Wise, he learns he has been chosen to wield an awesome cybernetically controlled weapon system called the UniBand. His brainwave patterns are perfectly suited to control the weapon, and make him the only suitable replacement for the recently murdered agent who was to wear the weapon.

Phillip agrees to submit to the surgery necessary to place the UniBand's control implants into his body, but only if he is allowed to function as a super-hero. Phillip, you see, is a comic book fan.

However, before Phillip can adjust to his new powers, he'll learn his friend is in grave danger, and a group of militants plan to assassinate a Canadian politician. Will Phillip be able to foil the assassination attempt and save his friend? And what will he do when PACT decides they want the technology returned?

1-5 .... 2.00

New Two-Fisted Tales
E.C.

1 .... 6.00

New Two-Fisted Tales
Dark Horse, 1993

1 .... 5.00

newuniversal
Marvel, 2006

1 .... 8.00
2 .... 6.00
3 .... 4.00

New Vampire Miyu (Vol. 1)
Ironcat, 1997

1-6 .... 3.00

New Vampire Miyu (Vol. 2)
Ironcat, 1998

1-6 .... 3.00

New Vampire Miyu (Vol. 3)
Ironcat, 1998

1-7 .... 3.00

New Vampire Miyu (Vol. 4)
Ironcat, 1999

1-6 .... 3.00

New Warriors
Marvel, 1990

1 .... 2.00
1/2nd-24 .... 1.00
25 .... 3.00
26-40 .... 1.00
40/Variant 2.00
41-47 .... 1.00
48-50 .... 2.00
50/Variant 3.00
51-59 .... 2.00
60 .... 3.00
61-75 .... 2.00
Ann 1 .... 3.00
Ann 2 .... 2.00
Ann 3-4 .... 3.00
Ashcan 1 .... 1.00

New Warriors
Marvel, 1999

1-10 .... 3.00

New Warriors
Marvel, 2005

1 .... 4.00
2-6 .... 3.00

New Wave
Eclipse, 1986

1-3 .... 2.00
4-8 .... 1.00
9-13 .... 2.00

New Wave Versus The Volunteers
Eclipse, 1987

1-2 .... 3.00

New World Order
Blazer, 1992

In the modern world, the old gods have been increasingly forgotten, replaced by the gods of technology and science. Then one day, not so far in the future, the old gods would have their revenge. By pooling their energies, they managed to send one of their number-Satan-into our world in corporeal form. Satan quickly raised armies to do his bidding, and killed enemies by the millions in a slaughter that made Hitler's concentration camps look tame by comparison. And this was only the beginning of the Dark Times...and the New World Order.

Daniel Reed scripts and draws New World Order for his own Blazer Studios. Although the covers may not draw the attention of a jaded comic reader, this is one of the most innovative comics available today. Reed creates an entire world while avoiding the same tired stereotypes. In many ways, his ability to create mythologies is reminiscent of the best efforts of the great Jack Kirby himself.

1-8 .... 3.00

New World Order
Pig's Eye

1 .... 1.00

New Worlds Anthology
Caliber, 1996

1 .... 3.00
2-6 .... 4.00

New X-Men (Academy X)
Marvel, 2004

1 .... 4.00
2-16 .... 3.00
☞House of M
16/Variant 4.00
17-43 .... 3.00
44-45 .... 6.00
46 .... 3.00

New X-Men: Academy X Yearbook Special
Marvel, 2005

1 .... 4.00

New X-Men: Hellions
Marvel, 2005

1 .... 4.00
2-4 .... 3.00

New York, the Big City
Kitchen Sink

1 .... 14.00

New York, the Big City
DC, 2000

1 .... 13.00

New York City Outlaws
Outlaw, 1984

1-4 .... 2.00

New York World's Fair Comics
DC, 1939

1939 .... 25,500.00
1940 .... 15,500.00

New York: Year Zero
Eclipse, 1988

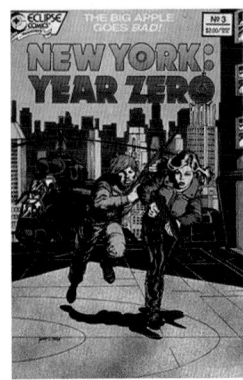

Through a cleverly staged deception, a soldier manages to get on the last flight from Venus after fighting in a disastrous war.

But when he returns home, he finds a war of a different kind. In the year 2015, New York has become the capital of the five United States and has over thirty million inhabitants in its overcrowded streets. Those without money kill and steal in order to survive; those with money buy guns in order to relieve their aggression by randomly shooting people on the street.

The soldier is due $250,000 for his mercenary duties to his country, but after Uncle Sam takes his cut of expenses, the soldier is left with only $16-$7.50 of which goes towards buying shoes to replace the boots he has to turn in. Left with only a few dollars and a bullet-proof vest to his name, the soldier doesn't have much hope. But if he survived Venus, maybe he can survive New York...

1-4 ....2.00

Next
DC, 2006
1-6 ....3.00

Next Exit
Slave Labor, 2004
1-6 ....3.00

Next Man
Comico, 1985

As far as anyone else knows, David Boyd is dead, killed in Vietnam. In truth, he was placed in cold storage for years, then used as the subject of a top-secret military experiment called "Stepping Stone" that made him into a "Next-Generation Man" -- a Next Man. Now, David can move with super-human speed and spontaneously regenerate damage to his body and wears a battle suit that contains sophisticated laser defense systems. Still, David has no urge to be seen as the next

great weapon of war. He rebelled against his creators and has since made it his business to destroy all traces of Project Stepping Stone. At the same time, the military is more than a little interested in regaining control of their prize subject, even if it means clearing towns and kidnapping the ones David holds close.

An interesting, if sporadically published series from Comico, Next Man is unrelated to the similarly titled "Next Men (John Byrne's ...)."

1-5 .... 2.00

Next Men (John Byrne's...)
Dark Horse, 1992
0-20 .... 3.00
21 .... 30.00
☞Hellboy appears
22-30 .... 3.00

Next Nexus
First, 1989
1-4 .... 2.00

Nextwave
Marvel, 2006
1-11 .... 3.00

Next Wave
Overstreet
1 .... 2.00

Nexus
Capital, 1981
1 .... 15.00
2 .... 10.00
3 .... 15.00

Nexus
First, 1983
1 .... 5.00
2 .... 4.00
3-5 .... 3.00
6-49 .... 2.00
50 .... 4.00
51-80 .... 2.00
81-84 .... 4.00
85-98 .... 3.00

Nexus: Alien Justice
Dark Horse, 1992
1-3 .... 4.00

Nexus Legends
First, 1989
1 .... 3.00
2-23 .... 2.00

Nexus Meets Madman
Dark Horse, 1996
1 .... 3.00

Nexus the Liberator
Dark Horse, 1992

Horatio Hellpop is Nexus, a man who received awesome super-powers from an alien intelligence with the condition that he act as an executioner of tyrants. The first to die by his hand was his own father, who previously had destroyed their homeworld. Later, the names of those he was to kill would be sent to Nexus in dreams, by the alien who gave Nexus his powers.

In this four-issue mini-series from Dark Horse (originally begun at ill-fated First Comics), Nexus is sent to kill the Holy Gigo, ruler of the world Uyl. These tyrants have reigned as if by divine right for 3,000 years, tolerating no dissent, and keeping eighty percent of the population in abject poverty. Speaking against them was more than illegal, it was a sin-and a death warrant. And when rebellion did arise, it was put down in the most terrifying way: by contaminating the water supply with a chemical which prevents dreaming and brings on psychosis.

1-4 .... 3.00

Nexus: The Origin
Dark Horse, 1995
1 .... 4.00

Nexus: The Wages of Sin
Dark Horse, 1995
1-4 .... 3.00

NFL Superpro
Marvel, 1991
1-12 .... 1.00
Special 1 .... 2.00
Special 1/Prest 4.00

Nickel Comics
Dell, 1938
1 .... 400.00

Nickel Comics
Fawcett, 1940

1	2,500.00
2	1,000.00
3	850.00
4	625.00
5-7	600.00
8	700.00

Nick Fury, Agent of SHIELD
Marvel, 1968

1	75.00
2-5	40.00
6-8	30.00
9-13	25.00
14	20.00
15	50.00
☛1st Bullseye	
16-18	20.00

Nick Fury, Agent of SHIELD
Marvel, 1983

1-2	3.00

Nick Fury, Agent of S.H.I.E.L.D.
Marvel, 1989

1-47	2.00

Nick Fury's Howling Commandos
Marvel, 2005

1	3.00
1/DirCut	4.00
2-6	3.00

Nick Fury vs. S.H.I.E.L.D.
Marvel, 1988

1-6	4.00

Nick Halliday
Argo, 1955

1	40.00

Nick Hazard
Harrier, 1988

The Golden Age of science-fiction pulp comics is revisited and given a British spin in Harrier Comics' Nick Hazard Interstellar Agent. A modern day recreation of the classic John Russell Fearn/Ron Turner collaboration, contemporary readers are given a glimpse into the past in the way of this 34-page, black and white comics magazine.

With artwork by Turner and scripting by Philip Harbottle (Fearn's biographer), classic Fearn stories, such as "Lords of 9016" and "Planet of Doom," are retold through the eyes of new recurring character Nick Hazard. By throwing him into the thick of the action, the title combines the inventive strengths of the original story-its "sense of wonder"-with a continuing hero. The result: An entertaining adventure that Golden Age fans are sure to love.

1	2.00

Nicki Shadow
Relentless, 1997

0	1.00
1	3.00

Nick Noyz and the Nuisance Tour Book
Red Bullet

1	3.00

Nick Ryan the Skull
Antarctic, 1994

Nick Ryan the Skull is a dose of nostalgia for fans of old pulp heroes like the Shadow. The title character is a rich businessman who feels compelled to battle criminals and gangsters. He does this as his alter ego the Skull, a masked death's-head dressed to the nines in a tuxedo and wielding twin pistols. Accompanied by his faithful, but grumbling servant, Jake, he stalks the night and brings fear into the hearts of evildoers. Sure, it's a bit over the top at times, but that doesn't stop it from being fun.

Issues of this series also include the backup feature El Gato Negro (the Black Cat). This pro wrestler/super-hero mixes humor with adventure as he battles a host of outrageously corny villains.

1-3	3.00

Night
Jester Press, 2005

1	3.00

Night
Slave Labor, 1995

0	2.00

Nightbird
Harrier, 1988

1-2	2.00

Night Breed (Clive Barker's)
Marvel, 1990

1-10	3.00
11-19	2.00
20-25	3.00

Night Brigade
Wonder Comix, 1987

In a dystopian future, rebellious robots meet as part of a secret cabal-the Night Brigade-and plot ways to win emancipation from their creators and enslavers, the human race. This 1987 black-and-white independent, written with some flair by Nils Osmar and drawn by Robin Lefberg is really quite readable. It's also easy on the eyes, thanks in part to some early inking work by Tim Sale (Batman: The Long Halloween, Superman For All Seasons).

-- Stephen C. George

1	2.00

Nightcat
Marvel, 1991

1	4.00

Night City
Thorby

1 ....3.00

Night Club
Image, 2005

1-4..3.00

Nightcrawler (Vol. 1)
Marvel, 1985

1-4..2.00

Nightcrawler (Vol. 2)
Marvel, 2002

1-4..3.00

Nightcrawler (Vol. 3)
Marvel, 2004

1-12..3.00

Nightcry
CFD, 1995

1-6..3.00

Nightfall:
The Black Chronicles
Homage, 1999

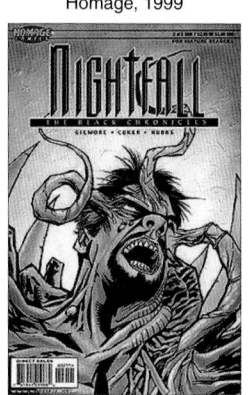

Man shares the City of New Orleans with monsters. That's bad enough, but what's worse is that the monsters are set up like crime families, so people have to worry about not only the monsters themselves but also getting caught in the middle of a clan war. The city's ruling Church finally establishes a kind of peace-but not all the monsters subscribe to it. That's where the Nightwatch comes in: a kind of police force set up to keep the monsters in line. Of course, this police force requires officers with special talents, so demons, wisecracking skeletons, and guys with crucifixes burned into their hand are fairly common. And when the Nightwatch's prodigal son, Proteus, returns with a chip on his shoulder (among other features), all hell just might break loose.

Published by Homage Comics, you might think you're reading a Vertigo book, so dark and spooky is this series. Written with a sharp wit by Ford Lyle Gilmore and drawn in an inky, Mignola-esque style by Tomm Coker.

1-3... 3.00

Night Fisher
Fantagraphics, 2005

1 .... 13.00

Night Force
DC, 1982

Written by Marv Wolfman and drawn by Gene Colan, the team that brought comic-book fans the Tomb of Dracula, this horror series focused on the evil power of the occult.

The Night Force itself was four characters pulled together by circumstance: the magician Baron Winters, down-on-his-luck reporter Jack Gold, parapsychologist Dr. Donovan Caine, and demonically possessed Vanessa Van Helsing. The story began with Dr. Caine's discovery of Vanessa's hidden demon and Jack Gold's interview with the mysterious Baron. From there, strange happenings conspired to force them together in order to save mankind...

A second series followed in the mid-1990s.

1 .... 3.00
2-14....................................... 2.00

Night Force
DC, 1996

1 .... 3.00
2-11....................................... 2.00
12 .... 3.00

Night Glider
Topps, 1993

1 .... 3.00

Nighthawk
Marvel, 1998

Nighthawk was a member of the Defenders who gains increased speed, strength, and agility during the night. In this title, Nighthawk is in a coma. As he hovers between life and death, he is tricked by Mephisto so that he uses his powers against criminals-before they commit their crime. Unfortunately, this has the effect of making Nighthawk look like a brute attacking innocents. This causes Nighthawk to run afoul of Daredevil, who, unaware of Mephisto's machinations, attempts to stop Nighthawk's rampage.

1-3 .... 3.00

Night in a Moorish Harem, A
NBM

1 .... 12.00
2 .... 11.00

Nightjar (Alan Moore's)
Avatar, 2004

1 .... 3.00
☞Alan Moore series
1/Platinum 10.00
1/Wraparound 3.00
1/Tarot 4.00
2 .... 3.00
2/Platinum 10.00
2/Wraparound 4.00
3 .... 3.00
3/Platinum 10.00
3/Wraparound-4 .... 4.00
4/Tarot 5.00

Nightjar: Hollow Bones
Avatar, 2004

1 .... 4.00
1/Platinum 10.00
1/Wraparound 4.00

Night Life
Strawberry Jam, 1987

1-7 .... 2.00
8 .... 3.00

Nightlinger
Gauntlet
1-2..3.00

Nightly News
Image, 2006
1-2..3.00

Night Man
Malibu, 1993
1...3.00
1/Ltd..25.00
2-15..2.00
16...4.00
17-23...3.00
Ann 1...4.00

Night Man
Malibu, 1995
0-4..2.00

Night Man/Gambit
Malibu, 1996
1-3..2.00

Night Man vs. Wolverine
Malibu, 1995
0...5.00

Nightmare
St. John, 1953
10...330.00
11...230.00
12...210.00
13...155.00

Nightmare (Magazine)
Skywald, 1971
1...65.00
2...40.00
3-5...35.00
6...40.00
7...20.00
8-9...35.00
10...40.00
11-19.......................................15.00
20...40.00
21-Ann 1 ....15.00

Nightmare (Alex Niño's...)
Innovation, 1989
1...2.00

Nightmare
Marvel, 1994
1-4..2.00

Nightmare!
Portman
1...5.00
2...4.00

Nightmare & Casper
Harvey, 1963
1...60.00
2-5...35.00

Nightmare on Elm Street
DC, 2006
1-4..3.00

Nightmare on Elm Street, A (Freddy Krueger's...)
Marvel
1...3.00

Nightmare on Elm Street: The Beginning
Innovation
1-2...3.00

Nightmares
Eclipse, 1985

This two-issue series presents two tales of terror, both featuring art by Paul Gulacy and Steve Oliff, with stories by Doug Moench and Don McGregor.

In "Blood on Black Satin," a young man fights for his life and his very soul against a town possessed by a vengeful spirit and its demonic followers. But after a night of horror, the man wakes to find that it was all just a dream -- or perhaps that's just what they want him to believe.

"The Trespasser" involves another young man who witnesses a struggle against forces more man-made, though no less evil. The fear that our own technology will also be our downfall is taken to the extreme in this story of one desperate family. They are as helpless as their hopes and dreams, and their very lives are destroyed by the radioactive waste that permeates the ground beneath their home.

1-2...2.00

Nightmares & Fairy Tales
Slave Labor, 2002
1...8.00
2...6.00
3-6...5.00
7-14...3.00

Nightmares on Elm Street
Innovation, 1991
1-6...3.00

Nightmare Theater
Chaos!, 1997
1-4...3.00

Nightmare Walker
Boneyard, 1996
1...3.00

Nightmark
Alpha Productions
1...2.00

Nightmark: Blood & Honor
Alpha, 1994
1-3...3.00

Nightmark Mystery Special
Alpha
1...3.00

Night Mary
Idea & Design Works, 2005
1-5...4.00

Nightmask
Marvel, 1986

Keith Remsen's parents had been ground-breaking scientists in the field of dream research. Keith, who had often been one of their test subjects, was now about to follow in their footsteps; he prepared to study at the famous Kleinman Institute of dream research in Zurich. But, before he could board the plane, a terrorist's bomb exploded, killing his parents, placing his sister in a wheelchair for life, and leaving Keith in a deep coma.

Then the "White Event" (the strange solar flash that transformed all of Marvel's New Universe super-heroes) happened. Keith arose from his coma, soon discovering that he had the power to enter other people's dreams. With his sister Theodora ("Teddy"), they explore this strange ability, coming face-to-face (in dreams, at least) with their parents' killer.

1-12..1.00

Night Masters
Custom Pic, 1986
1-6...2.00

Night Music
Eclipse, 1984

This seven-issue series featured a collection of tales by master storyteller P. Craig Russell. In these stories, he takes the reader from bright fantasy worlds to the cold night of space. A versatile writer, he also steps into the jungles of Africa for an adaptation of The Jungle Book.

1-7..2.00
8..4.00
9-11...5.00

Night Nurse
Marvel, 1972
1..110.00
2-4...50.00

Night of Mystery
Avon, 1953
1..275.00

Night of the Living Dead
Fantaco, 1991
0..2.00
1-2...5.00
3-4...6.00

Night of the Living Deadline USA
Dark Horse, 1992
1..3.00

Night of the Living Dead: Aftermath
Fantaco
1..2.00

Night of the Living Dead: London
Fantaco
1-2... 6.00

Night of the Living Dead: Prelude
Fantaco, 1991
1 .... 2.00

Night Raven: House of Cards
Marvel, 1991
1 .... 6.00

Night Rider
Marvel, 1974

This title reprints the adventures of the original Ghost Rider -- not the flame-headed spirit of vengeance so familiar to today's comic fans -- but the caped Western adventurer who predated him. Loosely based on legendary figures like The Headless Horseman, this Ghost Rider has no relationship to the current one other than the name. As such, Marvel chose "Night Rider" as the title when it reprinted his original adventures.

The Night Rider in question is Carter Slade, a former school teacher who was shot down by outlaws and left for dead. Luckily, he was saved by a group of Indians who nursed him back to health. It was then that the Great Spirit intervened, giving Slade the tools to become a phantom of the frontier. Clad in a specially blackened cloak, he is able to make parts of his body seem to float in mid-air, terrorizing outlaws, as he makes a stand for justice.

1 .... 25.00
2-6....................................... 10.00

Night's Children
Fantaco
1-4... 4.00

Night's Children: Double Indemnity
Fantaco
1 .... 8.00

Night's Children Erotic Fantasies
Fantaco
1 .... 5.00

Night's Children: Foreplay
Fantaco
1 .... 5.00

Night's Children: The Vampire
Millennium
1-2... 3.00

Night's Children: Vampyr!
Fantaco
1-3... 4.00

Nightshade
No Mercy, 1997
1 .... 3.00

Nightshades
London Night

Make no mistake about it, this comic is definitely not meant for kids. Nightshades is one of the earlier comics from London Night Studios, who later brought out such violent "bad girl" characters as Razor and Stryke. The story is nominally about a woman (Tiffany) who was gang-raped and killed, but who comes back every two weeks in the form of a cat to have an extremely kinky rendezvous with a vampiric exotic dancer (Tori). This 1993 comic is highly reminiscent of Faust, in that it combines bestiality, brutality, mutilation, necrophilia, and just about anything else that could be thought up to shock and/ or titillate readers.

1 .... 3.00

Nightside
Marvel, 2001

-4 ....3.00

Nights into Dreams
Archie, 1998

1-6 ....2.00

Nightstalkers
Marvel, 1992

1 ....1.00
1/CS 3.00
2-18 ....2.00

Nightstreets
Arrow, 1986

1 ....3.00
2-5 ....2.00

Night Terrors
Chanting Monks, 2000

1 ....3.00

Night Thrasher
Marvel, 1993

Dwayne Taylor is the director of the Taylor Foundation, a business left to him by his father. Dwayne is also the vigilante known as Night Thrasher, an armored foe of criminals and head of the New Warriors.

Following a successful try-out in the Night Thrasher: Four Control limited series, Thrash now stars in this ongoing monthly title. Here readers find out more about the man behind the mask, including keeping up on his on-again, off-again relationship with fellow New Warrior Silhouette Chord. We also find out about Bandit - a brother Dwayne never knew he had - and who, jealous of Dwayne's success, threatens to become his greatest enemy.

1 ....3.00
2-21 ....2.00

Night Thrasher: Four Control
Marvel, 1992

1-4 ....2.00

Night Tribes
DC, 1999

1 .... 5.00

Night Trippers
Image, 2006

1 .... 17.00

Nightveil
AC, 1984

1-Special 1 .... 2.00

Nightveil's Cauldron of Horror
AC, 1991

1-3 .... 3.00

Nightvenger
Axis, 1994

Ashcan 1 .... 2.00

Nightvision
Rebel, 1996

David Quinn (Faust) and Hannibal King bring us another of their dark works with this four-issue mini-series. In true Faust fashion, Nightvision mixes shocking horror and cold, seductive sexuality. Here, the star is a woman named Blythe, an ice-maiden in leather who deals in pleasure as well as pain. Also notable are the supporting cast, which includes an actual harpy, a huge, psychic worm-like creature, and Jamaican named Alice James who is stalking Blythe for bounty.

1-4 .... 3.00

Nightvision: All About Eve
London Night, 1996

1 .... 3.00

Nightvision (Atomeka)
Atomeka

1 .... 3.00

Night Vixen
ABC

0/A 3.00
0/B-0/C 4.00

Night Walker
Fleetway-Quality

1-3 .... 3.00

Night Warriors: Darkstalkers' Revenge the Comic Series
Viz, 1998

1-6 .... 3.00

Nightwatch
Marvel, 1994

A decade ago, Doctor Kevin Trench was seeing off his favorite science student, Ashley Croix, as she boarded a flight chartered for Morelle Pharmaceuticals' rising young stars. He watched her board the plane, when an invisible force suddenly attacked him. Then, an enigmatic stranger appeared out of nowhere in a "living costume" that fought off Trench's assailants. When the battle was over, the stranger handed him a piece of newspaper, then slumped over, dead. The newspaper was dated 10 years in the future with a story about Ashley's making stunning discoveries in adrenaline enhancements. When Trench pulled back the stranger's mask, he saw his own face.

Trench donned the costume and discovered its powers for himself, when terrorists hijacked Ashley's plane. He battled them, and they fired wildly, causing the plane to explode. Since then, he has lived in seclusion and guilt over Ashley's death. Now, he's back -- and Ashley appears to be alive!

1 .... 2.00
1/Variant 3.00
2-12 .... 2.00

Nightwing
DC, 1995

1 .... 4.00
2-4 .... 3.00

Nightwing
DC, 1996

1/2	4.00
1/2/Platinum	7.00
1	11.00
2	6.00
3-5	4.00
6-15	3.00
16-49	2.00
50	4.00
51-98	2.00
99	3.00
100	4.00
101	6.00
102	5.00
103-104	6.00
105	5.00
☞Year 1 Pt. 5	
106	6.00
107-108	2.00
109-128	3.00
1000000	2.00
Ann 1	5.00
GS 1	6.00

Nightwing: Alfred's Return
DC, 1995

1	4.00

Nightwing and Huntress
DC, 1998

1-4	2.00

Nightwing: Our Worlds at War
DC, 2001

This issue is part of the planet-spanning summer crossover, Our Worlds at War, in which the DC Universe super-heroes must face the would-be world conqueror known as Imperiex.

In this "All-Out War" issue, Barbara Gordon, the woman known as Oracle, must travel back in time to stop a computer virus which surfaced at the same time Imperiex made his appearance.

The virus, which apparently comes from the future, is determined to kill Oracle. Luckily, she'll be accompanied on her time travels by Nightwing, as they face prohibition-era gangsters, primeval caveman, and rampaging dinosaurs. Can Nightwing and Oracle stay one step ahead of the virus?

1	3.00

Nightwing Secret Files
DC, 1999

1	5.00

Nightwing: The Target
DC, 2001

Former Batman protègè Dick Grayson has graduated from Robin to Nightwing. Now he spends his days as one of the few honest cops in the corrupt city of Bl͵dhaven.

When Officer Grayson interrupts four cops beating two suspects to death, he is slugged from behind. Waking up in the hospital, he is told that one of the suspects was killed and the police had to knock him out to stop his rampage. The dirty cops are covering for themselves of course, and it is their word against his. Batman warns him that Nightwing's involvement in this case could cast curious eyes at him and his former mentor, so someone else needs to investigate. This one-shot prestige format title finds the former sidekick adopting yet another guise, The Target, a name that is significant on more than one level. Chuck Dixon and Scott McDaniel tell a satisfying, fast-moving crime story within the confines of the super-hero genre.

-- George Haberberger

1	6.00

Nightwing: Ties that Bind
DC

1	13.00

Nightwolf
Devil's Due, 2006

0	1.00
2-3	3.00

Nightwolf
Entropy

Nightwolf began as a feature in Entropy Tales and proved popular enough to receive his own black-and-white title with the talented Peter Krause (The Power of Shazam!) at the creative helm. Our hero is something of a Batman retread with some supernatural underpinnings. Now a successful artist, Paul Hund-Nightwolf's true identity-grew up in the crime-ridden Lowertown section of a big city and saw his friends and his family become victims of the criminals who preyed on the innocent. Paul's family left Lowertown, taking refuge in suburbia, but Paul returned to the city after college, began a lucrative career, acquired an ancient mask, and was transformed into Nightwolf-flashy costume, super-strength, heightened senses, the whole super-hero enchilada! Good stuff, if somewhat derivative.

1-2	2.00

Night Zero
Fleetway-Quality

1-4	2.00

Nikki Blade Summer Fun
ABC

1/A-1/B	3.00

Nimrod
Fantagraphics, 1998

1-2	3.00

Nina's All-Time Greatest Collectors' Item Classic Comics
Dark Horse, 1992
1 ....3.00

Nina's New & Improved All-Time Greatest Collectors' Item Classic Comics
Dark Horse, 1994
1 ....3.00

9-11: Emergency Relief
Alternative, 2002
1 ....15.00

Nine Lives of Felix the Cat
Harvey, 1991
1-5 ....2.00

Nine Lives of Leather Cat
Forbidden Fruit, 1993
1-6 ....4.00

Nine Rings of Wu-Tang
Image, 1999
0 ....2.00
1/A 4.00
1/B 5.00
2-5 ....3.00

1984 Magazine
Warren, 1978
1 ....6.00
2-10 ....4.00

1994 Magazine
Warren, 1980
11-29 ....3.00

1963
Image, 1993
1 ....2.00
1/BR 3.00
1/Gold 5.00
1/Silver 3.00
2-6 ....2.00

Ninety-Nine Girls
Fantagraphics, 1991
1 ....2.00

Nine Volt
Image, 1997
1-4 ....3.00

Ninja
Eternity, 1986

When Cathryn Monroe (Kate, to her friends) was young, she learned the way of the warrior from her grandfather, instead of playing with dolls like other girls. When the time came for her to decide on her future, she joined the military, even though it was against her mother's wishes. Kate excelled in her training and was invited to join an elite killing force. Strangely, it was there that she met the love of her life, Andy. Throughout this series, Monroe faced a struggle between her life of adventure as a Ninja warrior, and her desire for a normal life.

C.J Henderson and Peter Palmer created Ninja for Eternity Comics. The series began its run in October of 1986, featuring art by Kevin Farrell and Roy Richardson.

1-Special 1 .... 2.00

Ninja-Bots Super Special
Pied Piper
1 .... 2.00

Ninja Boy
DC, 2001
1 .... 4.00
2-6 .... 3.00
Ashcan 1 .... 1.00

Ninja Elite
Adventure, 1987
1-8 .... 2.00

Ninja Funnies
Eternity, 1987
1-5 .... 2.00

Ninja High School
Antarctic, 1987

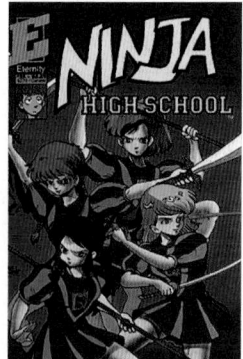

The young ninja, Itchy Koo, is sent to the U.S. in order to convince high school student Jeremy Peeples to marry her. Unfortunately, extraterrestrial Princess Asrial of the Royal Conglomerate (she reminds everyone of her title and stature frequently, so don't you dare forget it!) has come to Earth for just the same reason. The two girls are left to fight it out at Quagmire High School. Throw in two wacky professors, the "Kenterminator," and a mysterious woman in leather, and you've got a hilarious spoof of Japanese comics, complete with Japanese-style animation and plot.

Artist Ben Dunn never could understand the Japanese comic books he collected, but he remembered one series that featured characters who seemed to be eternally in high school. He called it Ninja High School - and even though he later found out the series' real name, he still couldn't remember it. This is his tribute, so to speak, to one of Japan's best exports.

0 .... 3.00
0/Ltd. 4.00
1 .... 7.00
1/2nd 3.00
2 .... 5.00
2/2nd 2.00
3 .... 4.00
3/2nd 2.00
4 .... 4.00
4/2nd 2.00
5-6 .... 4.00
6/2nd 2.00
7-10 .... 4.00
11-22 .... 3.00
23-31 .... 2.00
32-49 .... 3.00
50 .... 4.00

51-99	3.00
100	5.00
101-115	4.00
116-160	3.00
YB 1	6.00
YB 2-4	5.00
YB 5-9/B	4.00
YB 10/A-Summer 1	3.00
3D 1	5.00

Ninja High School in Color
Eternity, 1992

1-3	3.00
4-13	2.00

Ninja High School Perfect Memory
Antarctic, 1993

1	5.00
1/2nd-2	6.00
2/Platinum	5.00

Ninja High School Spotlight
Antarctic, 1996

This isn't Japanese manga, but an incredible simulation! Indiana-based artist Robert DeJesus has mastered the wide-eyed, cute teeny-girl style of manga so thoroughly that his work could have easily been ripped from the pages of any telephone book-sized Japanese comic.

Antarctic Press has created a spotlight series featuring Ninja High School artists such as Robert DeJesus, Fred Perry and Ted Nomura. Now, its Rod Espinosa's moment in the sun as one of everyone's favorite artists is back with a collection of his earlier Ninja High School stories in one comic. The short stories and pinups from various publications in the past include new and never-before-seen artwork that is only available in this special edition. Find out some of the reasons for the continued popularity of the original American manga comic book.

1	4.00
2	3.00
3	4.00
4	3.00

Ninja High School Swimsuit Special
Antarctic, 1992

1-1996	4.00

Ninja High School Talks About Comic Book Printing
Antarctic

1	1.00

Ninja High School Talks About Sexually Transmitted Diseases
Antarctic

1	2.00

Ninja High School: The Prom Formula
Antarctic, 2004

1	6.00

Ninja High School: The Prom Formula
Eternity, 1989

1-2	3.00

Ninja High School: The Special Edition
Eternity

1-4	3.00

Ninja High School Version 2
Antarctic, 1999

1-2	3.00

Ninjak
Valiant, 1994

Colin King, aka Ninjak, is an enforcer in a brutal war between arms merchants. King works for the Weaponeer Organization, arch-enemies with rival arms supplier Webnet. He's a cold, methodical killer, accustomed to living a luxurious lifestyle when not "on duty."

His life changes when he breaks up an arms deal on the docks in Monaco. Meant as a sting against Webnet, he discovers that there is more to this operation than just a few Stinger missiles: Webnet was developing a process called Black Water, which used nanite technology to achieve cold fusion in hydrogen/oxygen molecules.

Soon thereafter, the world seems to go crazy, with Webnet launching a massive retaliation against Weaponeer. Hundreds of people are assassinated, and King flees in a car - which has been rigged to flood its passenger compartment and drown the occupants in Black Water...

0	3.00
0/A	4.00
1	2.00
1/Gold	20.00
2-3	1.00
4	2.00
5-11	1.00
12-13	2.00
14	1.00
15-24	2.00
25	3.00
26	5.00
YB 1	3.00

Ninjak
Acclaim, 1996

1-12	3.00
Ashcan 1	1.00

Ninja Scroll
DC, 2006

1-4	3.00

Ninjutsu, Art of the Ninja
Solson

1	2.00

Nintendo Comics System
Valiant, 1990

1-2	5.00

Nintendo Comics System
Valiant, 1991

1-9	2.00

N.I.O.
Acclaim, 1998

1	3.00

Nira X: Anime
Entity, 1997

0	3.00

Nira X: Annual
Express, 1996

1/A	3.00
1/B	10.00

Nira X: Cyberangel
Express, 1994

1-4	3.00
Ashcan 1	1.00

Nira X: Cyberangel
Express, 1994

1	3.00
1/Ltd.	4.00
2-4	3.00

Nira X: Cyberangel
Express

1	3.00

Nira X: Cyberangel - Cynder: Endangered Species
Express

1	3.00
1/Ltd.	13.00

Nira X: Exodus
Avatar, 1997

Nira X, the incredible Cyberangel first introduced in Zen: Intergalactic Ninja, must discover who among the Cyberangels wants her dead. But Darkkon and Paradoxx are in the tale so blood and gore cannot be far behind for all sides.

This is a black-and-white tale for adults. The publisher Avatar, as with many of it's titles, has multiple covers for each of these issues.

1	3.00

Nira X: Heatwave
Express, 1995

1	4.00
2-3	3.00

Nira X: Soul Skurge
Express, 1996

1	3.00

Noah's Ark
Barbour

1	2.00

Noble Armour Halberder (John and Jason Waltrip's...)
Academy, 1997

1	3.00

Noble Causes: Extended Family One Shot
Image, 2003

1	7.00

Noble Causes
Image, 2002

1/A-1/B	5.00
2/A-4/B	3.00
5	4.00

Noble Causes: Distant Relatives
Image, 2003

1-4	3.00

Noble Causes: Family Secrets
Image, 2002

1-4/B	3.00

Noble Causes: First Impressions
Image, 2001

1	3.00

Noble Causes
Image, 2004

1/A-24	4.00

Nobody
Oni, 1998

1-4	3.00

No Business Like Show Business
3-D Zone

1	3.00

Nocturnal Emissions
Vortex

1	3.00

Nocturnals
Malibu, 1995

1	4.00
2-6	3.00

Nocturnals: Troll Bridge
Oni, 2000

1	5.00

Nocturnals, The: Witching Hour
Dark Horse, 1998

1	5.00

Nocturne
Aircel, 1991

1-3	3.00

Nocturne
Marvel, 1995

1-4	2.00

Nodwick
Henchman, 2000

Presenting humorous modern-day human foibles in a medieval setting, Nodwick is a full-length comic book based upon the characters created for both Dragon Magazine and Dungeon Magazine by cartoonist Aaron Williams. The embodiment of the blue-collar work ethic, the title character, Nodwick, is a henchman who toils with few complaints, and for little reward. Written with tongue firmly planted in cheek, Nodwick often blurs the lines between traditional fantasy genres and current day situations by using modern euphemisms for the sake of parody. Though often spoofing the characters and settings developed for Dungeons and Dragons, Williams' goofy reverence for the game and the lifestyle of its players has endeared him to fans of the popular role-playing game.

1-30	3.00

No Escape
Marvel, 1994

1-3	2.00

Nog the Protector of the Pyramides
Onli

1	2.00

No Guts or Glory
Fantaco, 1991

1	3.00

No Honor
Image, 2000

0-4	3.00

No Hope
Slave Labor, 1993

1-9	3.00

Noid in 3-D
Blackthorne

1-2	3.00

No Illusions
Comics Defence Fund
1 ....1.00

Noir
Alpha, 1994
1 ....4.00

Noir
Creative Force, 1995
1 ....5.00

No Justice, No Piece!
Head, 1997
1-2 ....3.00

Nolan Ryan
Celebrity
1 ....3.00

Nolan Ryan's 7 No-Hitters
Revolutionary, 1993
1 ....3.00

Nomad
Marvel, 1990
1-4 ....2.00

Nomad
Marvel, 1992

Jack Monroe is Nomad. As a boy, he was injected with a derivative of the Super Soldier Serum that created Captain America. For a while, he wore the mask of Bucky, Captain America's sidekick, but he became increasingly unstable and was eventually placed in cryogenic sleep. He reappeared in Captain America #282 as Nomad, a costumed vigilante. However, his vigilante tendencies caused the government to take a harsh view of him, and he was forced to drop out of sight.

In Nomad, Monroe becomes truly worthy of that name. A reluctant "father" to a baby he calls Bucky, he wanders across America, displaying an uncanny ability to find trouble wherever he goes.

1 .... 3.00
2-25 .... 2.00

Noman
Tower, 1966
1 .... 40.00
2 .... 28.00

No Man's Land
Tundra
1 .... 15.00

Non
Red Ink
1-3 .... 3.00

No Need for Tenchi!
Part 1
Viz
1-7 .... 3.00

No Need for Tenchi!
Part 2
Viz
1-7 .... 3.00

No Need for Tenchi!
Part 3
Viz, 1996
1-6 .... 3.00

No Need for Tenchi!
Part 4
Viz, 1997
1-6 .... 3.00

No Need for Tenchi!
Part 5
Viz, 1998
1-5 .... 3.00

No Need for Tenchi!
Part 6
Viz, 1998
1-5 .... 3.00

No Need for Tenchi!
Part 7
Viz, 1999
1-6 .... 3.00

No Need for Tenchi!
Part 8
Viz, 1999
1-5 .... 3.00

No Need For Tenchi!
Part 9
Viz, 1998
1-6 .... 3.00

No Need for Tenchi!
Part 10
Viz, 2001
1-7 .... 3.00

No Need For Tenchi!
Part 11
Viz, 2001
1-4 .... 4.00

No Need For Tenchi!
Part 12
Viz, 2001
1-6 .... 3.00

No Ninja Man
Custom Pic
1-1/2nd 2.00

No No UFO
Antarctic, 1996
1-4 .... 3.00

Noodle Fighter Miki
ADV Manga, 2005
1 .... 10.00

No Pasaran!
NBM
1 .... 14.00
2 .... 12.00

No Profit for the Wise
CFD, 1996
1 .... 3.00

Norb
Mu, 1992
1 .... 9.00

Normalman
Aardvark-Vanaheim, 1984

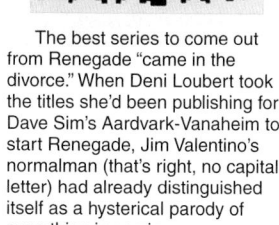

The best series to come out from Renegade "came in the divorce." When Deni Loubert took the titles she'd been publishing for Dave Sim's Aardvark-Vanaheim to start Renegade, Jim Valentino's normalman (that's right, no capital letter) had already distinguished itself as a hysterical parody of everything in comics.

The title character is the son of an accountant who mistakenly thought his planet was going to explode and launched his child into space. Now, normalman is the only normal person on Levram, a planet of super-powered characters.

Once Valentino gets going, nothing is sacred, as issues parody everything from E.C. comics to characters in kids' comics. (Mickey Money, anyone?) One issue even finds Fred Hembeck shooting ads for Hostess starring Cutey Bunny!

Later joining the "comics establishment" as one of Marvel's better creators and a founding member of Image, Valentino here sends it up mercilessly.

-- John Jackson Miller

1	3.00
2-12	2.00
3D 1	3.00

Normalman 3-D
Renegade, 1986

1	2.00

Normalman-Megaton Man Special
Image, 1994

1	3.00

Northern's Hemisphere
Northern's Hemisphere

5-7	2.00

Northern's Hemisphere Undisguised
Northern's Hemisphere

1	3.00

Northguard: The Mandes Conclusion
Caliber, 1989

PACT (Progressive Allied Canadian Technologies) created the UniBand and didn't know what it could do other than kill the person it was designed for. Phillip Wise had similar brain patterns and so was chosen to use the device, but Phillip had a history of reading comic books and this seemed the perfect opportunity to create Canada's first real super-hero.

Edward Holman, The Steel Chameleon, is trying to figure out who kidnapped the young man helping him solve a murder mystery dealing with PACT. That young man, Phillip Wise, has been captured by a group of fanatics, who are not amused with heathen Satanic super-heroes out to spread communism.

Picking up where the Northguard story left off in New Triumph, Mark Shainblum and Gabriel Morrissette have continued their quest and creation of a realistic super-hero.

1-3	2.00

Northstar
Marvel, 1994

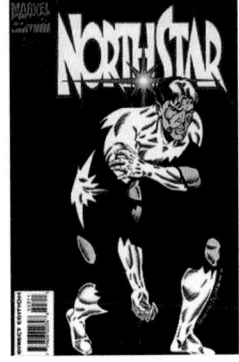

Jean Paul Beubier is Northstar, high-flying speedster, former member of Alpha Flight, and Marvel's first openly gay super-hero. He is now the star of the first mini-series to follow the demise of Alpha Flight, both as a group and as a comic title.

In this series, Jean Paul finds himself assaulted from all sides. The media hounds his every move looking for "something newsworthy," Weapon P.R.I.M.E., a team of super-powered thugs, has been sent to reel him in as an "unacceptably public figure," and someone is out to threaten the people who were major figures in his past. As it turns out, the heart of his difficulties is none other than Arcade, the maniacal gameplayer who has long been an enemy of the X-Men.

1-4	2.00

Northstar Presents
Northstar, 1994

1-2	3.00

Northwest Cartoon Cookery
Starhead, 1995

This comic book/cookbook is definitely an oddity. Still (as is usually the case with Starhead Comix titles), it's a worthwhile one. Seattle-area comix artists are legendary for their "just-getting-by" image, and many readers imagine them with near-bare cupboards containing nothing but a few boxes of macaroni and cheese and an infinite supply of coffee. This comic, however, gives well-known, alternative comix artists a chance to trot out their best family recipes-all illustrated in their own distinctive styles.

J.R. Williams contributes his own favorite: Black Bean Quesadillas, combined with a short strip about his search for the perfect salsa. Ellen Forney gives us her recipe for Whole Wheat Soda Bread, and (as a surprisingly useful bonus), the illustrated instructions for folding a fancy fleur-de-lis napkin. Others maintain the high standard these artists set, with the possible exception of Joe Sacco's "What the Poor Eat," which proves him to be the one non-gourmet of the bunch.

1	3.00

Northwest Mounties
St. John, 1948

1	285.00
2	220.00
3-4	230.00

Northwest Passage
NBM, 2005

1	6.00

Nosferatu
Dark Horse, 1991

1	4.00

Nosferatu
Tome, 1991

1-2	3.00

Nosferatu, Plague of Terror
Millennium
1-4 .... 3.00

Nosferatu: The Death Mass
Antarctic, 1997
1-4 .... 3.00

Nostalgic Mad
E.C.
1 .... 5.00
2 .... 4.00

Nostradamus Chronicles, The: 1559-1821
Tome
1 .... 3.00

Not Approved Crime
Avalon
1 .... 3.00

Not Brand Echh
Marvel, 1967

Not Brand Echh was part of Marvel's expansion in 1967, a boom time for the comic-book industry. Feeling confident in itself, Marvel decided the time was right to have some fun.

The title was a takeoff on the old advertising icon of inferior "Brand X" products. Not Brand Echh promised to bring readers the finest in humor and entertainment, done up in the madcap Marvel style. Nothing was sacred here: Marvel heroes and villains were routinely lampooned, along with Pogo, Peanuts, and of course, the "Brand Echh" competition at DC.

Although it would be canceled a little over a year and a half later, Not Brand Echh left at least one enduring legacy: the stove pot-wearing super-hero Forbush Man. This incredibly incompetent super-hero became a fixture on letters columns and in Marvel bullpen gags for many years to come.

1 .... 45.00
2 .... 18.00
3-5 .... 15.00
6-8 .... 10.00
☛Giant issues start
9-13 .... 25.00

Notenki Memoirs
ADV Manga, 2005
1 .... 10.00

No Time for Sergeants
Dell, 1965
1-2 .... 40.00
3 .... 30.00

(Not Only) The Best of Wonder Wart-Hog
Print Mint, 1973
1 .... 15.00
2-3 .... 12.00

Not Quite Dead
Rip Off, 1993
1-4 .... 3.00

Nova
Marvel, 1976
1 .... 8.00
2 .... 4.00
3-10 .... 3.00
10/35¢ 15.00
11 .... 3.00
11/35¢ 15.00
12 .... 3.00
12/35¢ 15.00
13 .... 3.00
13/35¢ 15.00
14 .... 3.00
14/35¢ 15.00
15-25 .... 3.00

Nova
Marvel, 1994
1 .... 2.00
1/Variant 3.00
2-18 .... 2.00

Nova
Marvel, 1999
1 .... 3.00
2-7 .... 2.00

Nova Hunter
Ryal

Nova Hunter is the colorfully-

illustrated story of Tyros, a large, red, no-guff, renegade law officer on a seedy planet, and his partner Khor, who are sucked into a vast interplanetary conspiracy involving evil smugglers, pure energy beings, and two sisters fighting for control of a galactic empire. Dialogue and narration are kept spare to accommodate the lush, almost painted artwork and big action visuals.

Robert Shaeffer, Max Nicols, and Pat David combined their talents on this series, the debut offering from Ryal Comics.

1 .... 3.00

Novavolo
Jungle Boy, 2000
1-Ann 2001 .... 4.00

Now Comics Preview
Now
1 .... 1.00

Nowheresville
Caliber, 1995
1 .... 4.00

Nowheresville: Death By Starlight
Caliber
1-4 .... 3.00

Nowheresville: The History of Cool
Caliber
1 .... 3.00

Now, on a More Serious Note...
Dawn, 1994
1 .... 2.00

Now We Are Sick
Dreamhaven
1 .... 12.00

Now What?!
Now
1 .... 3.00
2-11 .... 2.00

Nth Man, the Ultimate Ninja
Marvel, 1989
1-16 .... 1.00

Nuance
Magnetic Ink
1-3 .... 3.00

Nuclear War!
NEC, 2000
1-2 .... 4.00

Nukla
Dell, 1965

1	12.00
2	8.00
3	6.00
4	10.00

Null Patrol
Escape Velocity

1-2	2.00

Numidian Force
Kamite, 1991

4	2.00

Nurse Betsy Crane
Charlton, 1961

Considering how much play the medical soap opera theme gets elsewhere in popular culture, it is interesting that comic books have not mined this vein with much conviction. Nurse Betsy Crane, a product of Charlton comics, is one of the few examples. Betsy Crane is (surprise!) a kind-hearted nurse with a knack for picking really cute, really troubled patients. The medical setting allows for an element of Gothic atmosphere and mystery in addition to the usual romance comics histrionics. Also, since Nurse Crane is the titular heroine of the strip, her presence provides continuity, if not genuine character development, that other romance books lack by virtue of the usual anthology format. Dick Giordano, who subsequently went on to become an artist and editor at DC, applied his eye-pleasing style to the covers and stories of this book.

-- Rob Salkowitz

12	15.00
13-20	12.00
21-27	10.00

Nursery Rhymes
Ziff-Davis, 1951

10	75.00

Nurses
Gold Key, 1963

1	50.00
2	40.00
3	30.00

Nurture the Devil
Fantagraphics, 1994

1	0.00
2-3	3.00

Nut Runners
Rip Off, 1991

1-2	3.00

Nuts!
Premiere, 1954

1	175.00
2-5	120.00

Nuts & Bots
Excel Graphics, 1998

1	4.00

Nutty Comics
Harvey, 1946

1	0.00
4	50.00
5-8	40.00

Nutty Comics
Fawcett, 1946

1	80.00

Nutty Life
Fox, 1946

2	60.00

NYC Mech
Image, 2004

1-6	3.00

NYC Mech: Beta Love
Image, 2005

1-2	4.00
3-5	3.00

Nyght School
Brainstorm, 1997

2	3.00

Nyoka the Jungle Girl
Fawcett, 1945

Prior to becoming the star of this third major jungle title (behind Jungle Comics and Sheena, Queen of the Jungle), Nyoka was the centerpiece of a number of movie serials. She was the daughter of one Dr. Meredith (later anthropologist Henry Gordon) who moved to Africa to avoid being confused with his evil twin brother "Slick." Like Tarzan before her, she learned the ways of the jungle from the natives and soon became a white-skinned adventuress in her own right. Her comics appearances portrayed her in shorts and a low-cut blouse accented by a knife and revolver. Although meant as a girl's adventure, Nyoka (and her somewhat skimpy outfits) no doubt also appealed to a sizeable male readership. Nevertheless, it was her quick wits, self-reliance, and occasional use of a solid right hook that made her more than just another leotard-clad damsel in distress.

2	500.00
3	275.00
4-5	200.00
6-10	160.00
11-20	124.00
21-22	92.00
23	9.00
24-25	29.00
26-30	92.00
31-40	72.00
41-50	56.00
51-60	46.00
61-77	40.00

Nyoka the Jungle Girl
Charlton, 1955

14-22	32.00

NYX
Marvel, 2003

1	9.00
1/Variant	8.00
2	7.00
2/Variant	5.00
3	45.00
☛Wolvie's clone	
4	9.00
5	4.00
6-7	3.00

Little Lulu writer John Stanley's last comics series featured the misadventures of a shoeshine boy who traded his shoeshine kit for the presidency of The Tikkletoy Toy Company.

Beautiful women in skimpy clothes, powerful youths struggling to control their awesome abilities: There are many familiar elements in this series.

1-6 .... 3.00

Oblivion
Comico, 1995

1-3 .... 3.00

Oblivion City
Slave Labor, 1991

1-8 .... 3.00
9 .... 4.00

Obnoxio the Clown
Marvel, 1983

1 .... 2.00

Occult Crimes Taskforce
Image, 2006

1-2 .... 3.00

Occult Files of Dr. Spektor
Gold Key, 1973

1 .... 32.00
2-5 .... 14.00
6-10 .... 8.00
11-13 .... 5.00
14 .... 9.00
☛Solar app.
15-17 .... 5.00
18 .... 7.00
☛Solar app.
19-20 .... 5.00
21-22 .... 3.00
23 .... 7.00
☛Solar app.
24 .... 3.00
25 .... 10.00
☛Whitman only

Occult Laff-Parade
Print Mint, 1973

This book details classic stories of those who feel out of place in society getting sucked into the downside of the supernatural and cult-ism with a little adult humor thrown in.

Oak
Fat Cat

1-3 .... 3.00

Oaky Doaks
Eastern Color, 1942

1 .... 210.00

Obergeist: Ragnarok Highway
Image, 2001

This incredible tale from Dan Jolley (JSA: The Liberty File) and Tony Harris (Starman) follows Nazi scientist J␣rgen Steinholtz on his journey to redemption. Steinholtz has committed any number of atrocities in the name of Hilter and the Third Reich, but then he comes face to face with Adam Weiss: seemingly just another Jewish subject to be probed, prodded, and exploited. Steinholtz is forced to see just how horrible his--and the Reich's--crimes are. This six-issue limited series tells a powerful story, one that tugs at the conscience and deals with one of history's darkest eras.

1-6 .... 3.00

Obergeist: The Empty Locket
Dark Horse, 2002

1 .... 3.00

Obie
Store, 1953

1 .... 20.00

Objective Five
Image, 2000

They're young adults -- almost kids, really -- but they're far from helpless. Darryl Gonzalez is lightning fast, a power that anxiety or stress only enhances. Alexis Marks can manipulate electrical fields, absorb electricity, and discharge it in lethal fashion. Another possesses telepathic ability, even though she can neither comprehend nor control it. Still another is hospitalized for his own protection -- or that of others? But in the eyes of the military group secretly training them, they are "Objective Five," and they might just be the next great super-team. That is, if they learn how to harness their powers without killing themselves.

614

Bruce is attracted to Diana, who seems the only bright spot in his life. Diana is handing out pamphlets detailing "The Plan". Soon he is meeting the local cult leader, Padre Leon, and finally the creator himself, Lord Blackstone. But Bruce has learned his lessons well and fears nothing and turns on the spiritual bullies, taking Diana with him. Soon, they're out on the streets, hawking their own "Plan".

"Fingernail of Fear" teaches a lesson to those who would cheat soul-hungry demons from Hell. "Bayooh Blooze" shows the dangers of messing with a tried and true recipe. Other stories and adds keep true to form.

Ocean
DC, 2004

Ocean Comics
Ocean

Ocelot
Fantagraphics

Octavia
-Ism, 2004

Octavia Trilogy
-Ism, 2005

October Yen
Antarctic, 1996

Known for its exploration in American manga, Antarctic Press strikes again with the three-issue limited series October Yen. While telling an epic science fiction tale, the black and white series (written and illustrated by first timer Brandon Graham) wreaks of juvenile artwork, coming across more like a fanboy's dream rather than a seasoned book from a veteran publisher.

October Yen takes place in Earth's distant future. The large mega-company known as the Howe Corporation governs the planet, while two different alien species (Anladores-cat-like humanoids-and Hket-living machines) have made this world their home. An alien terrorist organization known as P.A.T. fights against the Howe Corp., but not quite how one would think. They actually have Earth's-and the universe's-best interests in mind. To that end, the Hket known as Bob fights to stop the Auks (aliens in cahoots with the Howe Corp.) from destroying numerous pocket worlds before the ramifications ripple dangerously through the rest of the universe.

Octobriana
Revolution

Octobriana: Filling in the Blanks
Artful Salamander, 1998

Odd Adventure-Zine
Zamboni, 1997

Oddballs
NBM, 2002

Oddballz
NBM, 2002

Oddjob
Slave Labor, 1999

Oddly Normal
Viper, 2005

Odd Tales
-Ism, 2004

Oeming Sketchbook
Michael Avon Oeming

Of Bitter Souls
Speakeasy Comics, 2005

Offcastes
Marvel, 1993

Offerings
Cry for Dawn, 1993

Official, Authorized Zen Intergalactic Ninja Sourcebook
Express

Official Buz Sawyer
Pioneer, 1988

Official Crisis on Infinite Earths Index
Eclipse, 1986

The Crisis on Infinite Earths was the single most far-reaching storyline in DC history. In twelve dense issues, it managed to kill several popular characters (including Barry Allen, the Flash; and Supergirl) as well as demolish the thousands of "alternate Earths" that had sprung up over the years. What remained was a DC universe unlike any before.

To make sense of it all, ICG published the Official Crisis on Infinite Earths Index. This absolutely indispensable index lays the entire storyline out in great detail. It goes issue by issue, says what characters were involved, what happened to them, and what it all meant. Even those who have read the Crisis on Infinite Earths in its entirety stand to learn a lot by studying this incredibly detailed work.

Official Handbook of the Conan Universe
Marvel, 1986
1 ....2.00
2 ....1.00

Official Handbook of the Invincible Universe
Image, 2007
1 ....5.00

Official Handbook of the Marvel Universe
Marvel, 1983
1-15...2.00

Official Handbook of the Marvel Universe
Marvel, 1985
1-20...2.00

Official Handbook of the Marvel Universe
Marvel, 1989
1-8...2.00

Official Handbook of the Marvel Universe Master Edition
Marvel, 1990
1-5...5.00
6-12...4.00
13-36.......................................5.00

Official Handbook of the Marvel Universe: Alternate Universes 2005
Marvel, 2005
1 ....4.00

Official Handbook of the Marvel Universe: Avengers 2005
Marvel, 2005
1 ....4.00

Official Handbook of the Marvel Universe: Book of the Dead 2004
Marvel, 2004
1 ....4.00

Official Handbook of the Marvel Universe Daredevil Elektra 2004
Marvel, 2004
1 ....4.00

Official Handbook of the Marvel Universe: Fantastic Four 2005
Marvel, 2005
1 ....4.00

Official Handbook of the Marvel Universe: Golden Age Marvel 2004
Marvel, 2004
1 ....4.00

Official Handbook of the Marvel Universe: Horror 2005
Marvel, 2005
1 .... 4.00

Official Handbook of the Marvel Universe: Hulk
Marvel, 2004
1 .... 4.00

Official Handbook of the Marvel Universe: Marvel Knights 2005
Marvel, 2005
1 .... 4.00

Official Handbook of the Marvel Universe: Spider-Man 2004
Marvel, 2004
1 .... 4.00

Official Handbook of the Marvel Universe: Spider-Man 2005
Marvel, 2005
1 .... 4.00

Official Handbook of the Marvel Universe: The Avengers
Marvel, 2004
1 .... 4.00

Official Handbook of the Marvel Universe: Wolverine 2004
Marvel, 2004
1 .... 4.00

Official Handbook of the Marvel Universe: Women of Marvel 2005
Marvel, 2005
1 .... 4.00

Official Handbook of the Marvel Universe: X-Men 2004
Marvel, 2004
1 .... 4.00

Official Handbook of the Marvel Universe: X-Men - Age of Apocalypse 2005
Marvel, 2005
1 .... 4.00

Official Handbook of the Marvel Universe: X-Men 2005
Marvel, 2006
1 .... 4.00

Official Handbook: Ultimate Marvel Universe 2005
Marvel, 2005
1 .... 4.00

Official Handbook: Ultimate Marvel Universe - Ultimates & X-Men 2005
Marvel, 2006
1 .... 4.00

Official Hawkman Index
Eclipse, 1986
1-2 .... 2.00

Official How to Draw G.I. Joe
Blackthorne, 1987
1-3 .... 2.00

Official How to Draw Robotech
Blackthorne, 1987
1-14 .... 2.00

Official How to Draw Transformers
Blackthorne, 1987
1-4 .... 2.00

Official Johnny Hazard
Pioneer, 1988
1 .... 2.00

Official Jungle Jim
Pioneer, 1988
1-9 .... 2.00
10-16 .... 3.00
Ann 1 .... 4.00

Official Justice League of America Index
ICG

This eight-issue series provides a handy resource for the serious fan who wants to know everything about DC's long-running super-hero team series. The Index follows the Justice League of America from its debut in The Brave and The Bold #28 in 1960 through 261 issues of Justice League of America, ending in April of 1987. The index features cover reproductions of every issue, plot synopses, credits, character appearances, and notes and comments.

As a bonus, the Index also lists JLA appearances in other titles, limited series, annuals, and solo appearances by members of the JLA who don't have much of an existence outside of that title, such as the Red Tornado. The Index even does a good job sorting out the plot complications of DC's Crisis On Infinite Earths, which rewrote the continuity of the DC Universe in a way that dramatically impacted a long-running title like JLA.

1-8...2.00

Official Mandrake
Pioneer, 1988
1-9...2.00
10-15.......................................3.00

Official Marvel Index to Marvel Team-Up
Marvel, 1986
1-6...1.00

Official Marvel Index to the Amazing Spider-Man
Marvel, 1985

A nine-part series, this title is a comprehensive index to the Amazing Spider-Man. Covering each issue in turn, this series lists the guest stars, supporting characters, and villains that appear, as well as the cover art, artistic credits, and a detailed synopsis of the events that occur.

1-9...1.00

Official Marvel Index to the Avengers
Marvel, 1987
1-7...3.00

Official Marvel Index to The Avengers
Marvel, 1994
1-6...2.00

Official Marvel Index to the Fantastic Four
Marvel, 1985
1-12.......................................1.00

Official Marvel Index to the X-Men
Marvel, 1987
1-7...3.00

Official Marvel Index to the X-Men
Marvel, 1994
1-5...2.00

Official Modesty Blaise
Pioneer, 1988
1-8...2.00
Ann 1.....................................5.00

Official Prince Valiant
Pioneer, 1988
1-9...2.00
10-18.....................................3.00
Ann 1-King Size 1 ....4.00

Official Prince Valiant Monthly
Pioneer, 1989
1-2...4.00
3-4...5.00
5-8...7.00

Official Rip Kirby
Pioneer, 1988
1-6...2.00

Official Secret Agent
Pioneer, 1988
1-7...2.00

Official Teen Titans Index
Independent, 1985
1-5...2.00

Offworld
Graphic Image
1 ....4.00

Of Mind and Soul
Rage
1 ....2.00

Of Myths and Men
Blackthorne, 1987

This black-and-white title from Renegade Press and writer/artist Timothy J. Tobolski explores the lighter side of magic and super-heroics. "The Pentagram Five" is a team composed of representatives of the four ancient elements-earth, air, fire, and water-and another element that will fall within the purview of a mysterious fifth member. "Super-People" parodies the popular super-heroes of the day. Fun stuff from a bright, young artist!

1-2 ....2.00

Ogenki Clinic
Akita, 1997
1-2 ....4.00
3-6 ....5.00

Ogenki Clinic (Vol. 2)
Akita, 1998
1-6 ....4.00

Ogenki Clinic (Vol. 3)
Sexy Fruit, 1998
1-7 ....4.00

Ogenki Clinic (Vol. 4)
Sexy Fruit, 1999
1-6 ....3.00

Ogenki Clinic (Vol. 5)
Sexy Fruit, 1999
1-7 ....3.00

Ogenki Clinic (Vol. 6)
Sexy Fruit, 2000
1-7 ....3.00

Ogenki Clinic (Vol. 7)
Ironcat, 2000
1-7 ....3.00

Ogenki Clinic (Vol. 8)
Ironcat, 2001
1-8 ....3.00

Ogenki Clinic (Vol. 9)
Ironcat, 2002
1-8..3.00

Ogre
Black Diamond, 1994
1-4..3.00

O.G. Whiz
Gold Key, 1971

The former owner of the Tikkletoy Company was growing dotty as he aged. One day, he wandered into a reception room to read the huge stack of ancient magazines and traded control of the company to a boy in exchange for a shoeshine box.

The boy, O.G. Whiz, suddenly came to realize every child's dream: owning his own toy company, complete with all the toys he could ever desire, a squadron of yes-men who tell him his every idea is brilliant, and a dutiful secretary who makes sure not to allow any visitors when he is in the middle of his afternoon conference with "Mr. Snooze" -- doing sleep research. The only fly in the ointment is the embittered son of the original president, who holds a deep resentment for the two-foot-tall tyke who has suddenly become his boss.

The first issue is apparently the only one written and drawn by its creator, John Stanley, shortly before he left Gold Key to work for Dell.

1...25.00
2...15.00
3-6...10.00
7-11..3.00

Oh.
B Publications, 1995
1-22...3.00

Oh Brother!
Stanhall, 1953
1 .... 40.00
2-5 .... 25.00

Ohm's Law
Imperial
1-3 .... 2.00

Oh My Goddess!
Dark Horse, 1994
1 .... 5.00
2-6 .... 3.00
88-95 .... 4.00
96-105 .... 3.00
106 .... 4.00
107-109 .... 3.00
110-112 .... 4.00

Oh My Goddess! Part II
Dark Horse, 1995
1-8 .... 3.00

Oh My Goddess! Part III
Dark Horse, 1995
1-11 .... 3.00

Oh My Goddess! Part IV
Dark Horse, 1996
1-8 .... 3.00

Oh My Goddess! Part V
Dark Horse, 1997
1-2 .... 3.00
3-4 .... 4.00
5 .... 3.00
6-7 .... 4.00
8 .... 3.00
9-12 .... 4.00

Oh My Goddess! Part VI
Dark Horse, 1998
1 .... 4.00
2-6 .... 3.00

Oh My Goddess! Part VII
Dark Horse, 1999
1-8 .... 3.00

Oh My Goddess! Part VIII
Dark Horse, 2000
1-6 .... 4.00

Oh My Goddess! Part IX
Dark Horse, 2000
1-7 .... 4.00

Oh My Goddess! Part X
Dark Horse, 2001
1-5 .... 4.00

Oh My Goddess! Part XI
Dark Horse, 2001
1-2 .... 4.00
3-6 .... 3.00

Oh My Goddess!: Adventures of the Mini-Goddesses
Dark Horse, 2000
1 .... 10.00

Oh My Goth
Sirius, 1998

The Goth movement, in which young people dress in black, listen to depressing music, and attempt to be pessimistic about life, takes gentle ribbing from one of its own in this title. Voltaire, who began this book to promote his music, commits what might be the ultimate sin in the Goth lifestyle: He doesn't take it seriously. For instance, a Goth musician describes himself thus: "I am Vlad the Impaler. I am 200 years old. I lurk in my dark lair where I seek the blood of hapless victims." But when aliens can't understand him and subject his speech to their Universal Translator, it comes out: "I am Bernie Weinstein. I am 17 1/2 years old. I live in my mother's basement where I drink cheap red wine, when I can get it."

Unfortunately, while Voltaire's use of an Old English typeface for lettering may be appropriate, it is hard to read in large doses.

-- George Haberberger

1-4 .... 3.00

Oh My Goth: Humans Suck!
Sirius, 2000
1-2 .... 3.00

Oink: Blood and Circus
Kitchen Sink, 1998
1-4 .... 5.00

Oink: Heaven's Butcher
Kitchen Sink, 1995
1-3 .... 5.00

Ojo
Oni, 2004
1-5 .... 3.00

OJ's Big Bust Out
Boneyard, 1995
1 ....4.00

Okay Comics
United Feature, 1940
1 ....250.00

Oklahoma Kid
Ajax, 1957
1 ....75.00
2-4..40.00

Oktane
Dark Horse, 1995

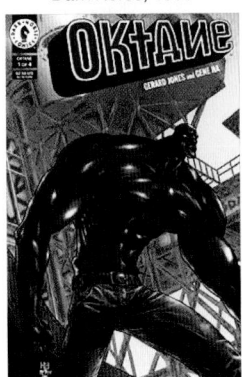

Oktane is a big charcoal-black bodyguard in post-industrial near-future Detroit, providing the muscle for some of the road-warrior type gangsters who dominate the society. Writer Gerald Jones weaves an extremely dense, information-heavy plot that takes Oktane to the ruins of Las Vegas and elsewhere in the course of the four-part mini-series. Gene Ha uses exaggerated anatomy and caricature-like figures against extremely detailed and moody backgrounds to add visual complexity to Jones' panoramic narrative. Oktane provides a good mix of story, big art, and action-enough to sustain excitement through the four-issue story arc.

1-4...3.00

Oldblood
Parody
1-1/2nd...................................3.00

Olympians
Marvel, 1991
1-2..4.00

Olympus Heights
Idea & Design Works, 2004
1-3..4.00

OMAC
DC, 1974

Technology has a long and nasty history of progressing far faster than man's ability to use it wisely. In Jack Kirby's vision of the future, technologies such as genetics and robotics give powerful tools to those who want to do the devil's work. To keep things in line, the World Peace Organization has been founded - a non-partisan group of troubleshooters whose faces are cosmetically blanked to hide their racial origins. A secret agent organization of sorts, they infiltrate groups that are using technology to evil ends. Their point man is a powerhouse called Omac: One Man Army Corps. Omac is linked via a sigil on his chest to an orbiting satellite called "Brother Eye." He receives his incredible powers through that link, as well as information he needs to complete his missions.

This original series lasted only eight issues, but Omac lasted far longer, including appearances in Kamandi and Warlord, and a four-issue remake by John Byrne.

1 .... 40.00
2 .... 15.00
3 .... 12.00
4 .... 10.00
5-8... 7.00

OMAC
DC, 2006
1-6... 3.00

OMAC: One Man Army Corps
DC, 1991
1-4... 4.00

OMAC Project
DC, 2005
1 .... 22.00
1/2nd 7.00
1/3rd....................................... 3.00
2 .... 6.00
2/2nd 3.00
3 .... 4.00
4-6... 3.00

OMAC Project: Infinite Crisis Special
DC, 2006
1 .... 5.00

Omaha: Cat Dancer
Steeldragon, 1984
1 .... 12.00
1/Ashcan 3.00
1/2nd 4.00
2 .... 8.00

Omaha The Cat Dancer
Kitchen Sink, 1986
0 .... 4.00
1 .... 10.00
1/2nd 4.00
1/3rd....................................... 3.00
2 .... 5.00
3-5... 4.00
6-20... 3.00

Omaha The Cat Dancer
Fantagraphics, 1994
1-4... 3.00

O'Malley and the Alley Cats
Gold Key, 1971
1 .... 8.00
2-3... 6.00
4-9... 4.00

Omar Lennyx
Magnecom
1 .... 3.00

Omega Elite
Blackthorne
1 .... 4.00

Omega Flight
Marvel, 2007
1 .... 7.00
2 .... 5.00
3 .... 4.00

Omega Force
South Star, 1992
1 .... 2.00

Omega Force
Entity, 1995
1 .... 3.00

Omega Force II
Entity, 1996
1-3... 3.00

Omega Knights
Underground, 1992

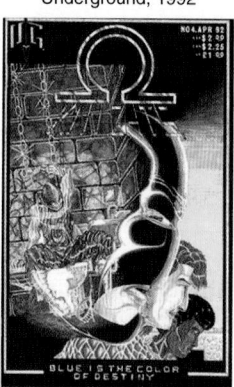

Sundance and his companions in the Omega Knights go about saving Canada (and the world) from various and sundry disasters and evildoers. At least, they did until the series was canceled.

Michael Connery's involved and steadily paced story line had been off to a good start, especially with Dave Marcus' art. The magazine eventually went to color, but was not able to continue despite a very graphic and intriguing story.

1-6 .... 2.00

Omega Man
Omega 7
0 .... 3.00
1 .... 4.00
Ashcan 1 .... 1.00

Omega Men
DC, 1983
1 .... 4.00
2 .... 3.00
3-10 .... 2.00
11-19 .... 1.00
20 .... 2.00
21-38 .... 1.00
Ann 1-2 .... 2.00

Omega Men
DC, 2006
1-3 .... 3.00

Omega the Unknown
Marvel, 1976
1 .... 9.00
2 .... 6.00
2/30¢ 20.00
3 .... 3.00
3/30¢ 20.00
4-8 .... 2.00
9 .... 3.00
9/35¢ 15.00
10 .... 2.00
10/35¢ 15.00

Omen
Chaos!, 1998
1-5 .... 3.00

Omen
Northstar, 1989
1-2 .... 2.00

Omen, The:
Save the Chosen Preview
Chaos!, 1997
1 .... 3.00

Omen, The: Vexed
Chaos!, 1998
1 .... 3.00

Omicron:
Astonishing Adventures
on Other Worlds
Pyramid, 1987

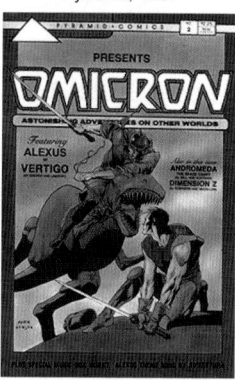

A short lived black-and-white anthology series featuring three regular illustrated features. In Andromeda: Space Cadet by Tim Bell and Mike Hoffman, Andromeda faces challenges as Zeva Squad is sent to rescue one of its own. Alexus of Vertigo by John Brewer and Marc Lamport tells the tale of Alexus, an astronaut marooned on a medieval planet while making the best of a bad situation. Paula Robinson and Rick McCollum's Dimension Z is a place of absolute insanity where one human makes his way home.

1-2 .... 2.00

Omnibus:
Modern Perversity
Blackbird, 1992
1 .... 3.00

Omni Comix
Omni, 1995
1-2 .... 4.00
3 .... 5.00

Omni Men
Blackthorne, 1989
1 .... 4.00

On a Pale Horse
Innovation, 1991
1-5 .... 5.00

Once Upon a Time
in the Future
Platinum
1 .... 10.00

One
Tokyopop, 2004
1-8 .... 10.00

One
Pacific, 1977
1 .... 3.00

One
Marvel, 1985
1-6 .... 2.00

One-Arm Swordsman
Dr. Leung's
1-7 .... 2.00

One-Fisted Tales
Slave Labor, 1990
1-4/3rd 3.00
5 .... 4.00
5/2nd-11 .... 3.00

One Hundred and
One Dalmatians
Disney, 1991
1 .... 3.00

100 Bullets
DC, 1999
1 .... 10.00
2 .... 7.00
3-5 .... 5.00
6-10 .... 4.00
11-49 .... 3.00
50 .... 4.00
51-100 .... 3.00

100 Degrees
in the Shade
Fantagraphics, 1992
1-4 .... 3.00

100 Girls
Arcana, 2004
1-1/Variant 5.00
2-6 .... 3.00

100 Greatest
Marvels of All Time
Marvel, 2001
1-5 .... 8.00
6-10 .... 4.00

101 Other Uses
for a Condom
Apple, 1991
1 .... 5.00

101 Ways to End the Clone Saga
Marvel, 1997
1 ....3.00

100 Pages of Comics
Dell, 1937
1 ....1,200.00

100%
DC, 2002
1-5..6.00

100% True?
DC, 1996
1-2..4.00

One Mile Up
Eclipse, 1991
1-2..3.00

One Millennium
Hunter, 1997
1-5..3.00

One Million Years Ago
St. John, 1953

Joe Kubert and Norman Maurer's One Million Years Ago was a groundbreaking comic, although it was little recognized as such. Kubert and Maurer put themselves into the comic book to introduce readers to the various stories, all set in the world as it might have been at the dawn of mankind.

This comic featured three different stories, the first of which introduced Tor, Kubert's legendary caveman. Tor was more than an adventure hero. His exploits were used to illustrate the dawning of conscience and morality in a world dominated quite literally by the law of the jungle. Kubert even went so far as to break the fourth wall at certain points in the story to point out the nature of the conflicts taking place. The other main features in this title were the improbable caveman comedy "The Wizard of Ugghh" and fantasy/adventure "Danny Dreams." With

issue #2, the comic book would be retitled "3-D Comics," ushering in a short-lived fad.

1 .... 100.00

One Piece
Viz, 2004
1-8... 8.00

One-Pound Gospel
Viz
1-2... 4.00
3-4... 3.00

One-Pound Gospel Round 2
Viz, 1997
1-6... 3.00

One-Shot Parody
Milky Way, 1986
1 .... 2.00

One-Shot Western
Caliber
1 .... 3.00

1001 Nights of Sheherazade
NBM, 2002
1 .... 13.00

1111
Crusade, 1996
1 .... 3.00

1,001 Nights of Bacchus
Dark Horse, 1993
1 .... 5.00

...One to Go
Äardwolf
1 .... 3.00

Oni
Dark Horse, 2001
1-3... 3.00

Oni Double Feature
Oni, 1998

Gen Xer's are featured prominently in this anthology flip

book from Oni Press. "The Secret Broadcast" focuses on a trio of would-be anarchists that run a pirate radio station to free the airwaves from trashy radio programs. Of course, the FCC takes a dim view of unlicensed broadcasts, no matter what the motivation.

Independent film maker and comic fan, Kevin Smith, known for the movies Clerks, Mallrats, and Chasing Amy, brings two characters from Clerks, to the comic pages. Jay and his alter ego, Silent Bob are the main characters in "Walt Flanagan's Dog," a viciously funny story illustrated by Matt Wagner (Mage). Crude, vulgar, and oblivious to everything including their complete lack of potential, Jay and Silent Bob are definitely not role models as they pass time loitering, antagonizing service workers, and selling dope. It's not much of a life, but the resulting story is hilarious.

Later stories in the series included Paul Dini's Jingle Belle, Shannon Wheeler's Too Much Coffee Man, Judd Winick's Frumpy the Clown, and Stan Sakai's Usagi Yojimbo.

-- George Haberberger

1 .... 6.00
1/2nd 3.00
2-6 .... 4.00
7-12 .... 3.00

Onigami
Antarctic, 1998
1-3 .... 3.00

Oni Press Color Special
Oni, 2001
2001-2002 .... 6.00

Oni Press Summer Vacation Supercolor Fun Special
Oni, 2000
1 .... 6.00

Only the End of the World Again
Oni, 2000
1 .... 7.00

On Our Butts
Aeon, 1995
1 .... 3.00

On Raven's Wings
Boneyard, 1994
1-2 .... 3.00

Onslaught: Epilogue
Marvel, 1997
1 .... 3.00

Onslaught: Marvel
Marvel, 1996

1 ....6.00
1/Gold 12.00

Onslaught Reborn
Marvel, 2006

1 ....6.00
2 ....4.00

Onslaught: X-Men
Marvel, 1996

It begins with a message sent forty-five minutes from now. Jean Grey reported that their mansion had been all but leveled, both the blue and gold teams of X-Men were down, and that Professor X had gone insane. The message ended when Jean was herself toppled by a psionic blast. The Onslaught had begun.

Onslaught was the grand Marvel event of 1996, cutting through many of Marvel's titles, changing the face of the X-titles in particular. The saga began in this volume, in which we encounter a villain so powerful that no force on earth seems able to stop him. Worse yet, the villain who was about to destroy the X-Men was once a person whom they had once trusted above all others.

1 ....5.00
1/Gold 10.00
1/Variant 8.00

On The Air
National Broadcasting Company, 1947

1 ....175.00

On the Bus
Slave Labor, 1994

1 ....3.00

On the Road to Perdition
DC, 2003

1-3 ....8.00

On The Spot
Fawcett, 1948

1 .... 250.00

Onyx Overlord
Marvel, 1992

1-4 .... 3.00

Oombah, Jungle Moon Man
Strawberry Jam, 1992

1 .... 3.00

Open Season
Renegade, 1987

Years before "slice-of-life" series would become popular among alternative cartoonists (who all-too-often would provide slices of lives no one would want to know much about), Jim Bricker provided an excellent example in Open Season.

Hapless Joe moves in with Robin, a straight-talking reporter, and Cliff, a drunkard much resembling Bloom County's Steve Dallas. That makes it sitcom city, as the three find that sharing space isn't the bargain they bargained for.

But there are also thoughtful and memorable pieces, such as Joe's gut-wrenching recollection of a high-school dance. There was even a limited stage production of Open Season, and the comics programs from it turn up now and again.
-- John Jackson Miller

1-7 .... 2.00

Open Sore Funnies
Home-Made Euthanasia

1 .... 1.00

Open Space
Marvel, 1989

Open Space is a collection of stories told by some of science-fiction's best writers, loosely tied together by an overarching plot. The plot concerns the release of the Smoots drive, a device which ingeniously circumvents the ultimate speed limit: the speed of light. With the cheap, easy-to-manufacture Smoots drive, the stars become open to everyone. The only problem is that Astranet (the company that created it) doesn't want it released until they can find a way to properly capitalize on it. As far as Astranet is concerned, let humanity rot until then.

But that wasn't good enough for inventor Drake Etchison. He arranged to steal a prototype of the drive and give it to wild card Jack Brody. Jack succeeded in demonstrating the drive to an incredulous world. Meanwhile, Drake was tracked down and murdered - but not before he succeeded in transmitting the plans to a hacker bulletin board. Now, at last, humanity has access to the open space...

The series only lasted four issues, but, if the fifth issue had been published it would have had two events of note: Alex Ross' first professional work and a story by CBG editor Maggie Thompson.

1-4 .... 5.00

Operation: Kansas City
Motion, 1993

1 .... 3.00

Operation: Knightstrike
Image, 1995

1-3 .... 3.00

Operation Peril
ACG, 1950

1	185.00
2	90.00
3-5	80.00
6-10	75.00
11-12	50.00
13-16	40.00

Operation: Stormbreaker
Acclaim, 1997

1	4.00

Operative: Scorpio
Blackthorne, 1989

1	4.00

Opposite Forces
Funnypages, 2002

1-4	3.00

Opposite Forces
Alias, 2005

1	1.00
2-3	3.00

Optic Nerve
Drawn & Quarterly, 1997

1	5.00
2-7	3.00

Optimism of Youth
Fantagraphics, 1991

1	13.00

Ora
Son of a Treebob, 1999

1	3.00

Oracle
Oracle, 1986

1	3.00

Oracle - A Trespassers Mystery
Amazing Montage

1	5.00

Oracle Presents
Oracle, 1986

1-2	3.00

Oral Roberts' True Stories
Telepix, 1956

101	110.00
102	65.00
103-107	50.00
108-113	45.00
114-119	40.00

Orbit
Eclipse

1-3	5.00

Orb Magazine
Orb, 1974

A true product of the '70s, Orb Magazine represents a piece of comic-book history that -- as witnessed by recent trends -- has managed to come full circle: the anthology. The 68-page black-and-white title (which includes a 10-page color insert) can best be compared to Twilight Zone, with its focus on traditional horror, science-fiction, and fantasy stories.

The ongoing serial that receives the magazine's 10-page color treatment is Northern Light -- the story of a modern super-hero facing modern problems. Aside from that, the remaining eight stories (which vary from two to 10 pages) run the gamut of premises, but they do manage to share one thing in common: the macabre. As a bonus, a series of rudimentary Orb posters -- full-page, black and white drawings -- act as interstitial "programming," breaking up each of the publication's episodes.

1-3	1.00

Order
Marvel, 2002

1-6	2.00

Or Else
Drawn and Quarterly, 2005

1	6.00
2-3	4.00

Oriental Heroes
Jademan, 1988

1-55	2.00

Orient Gateway
NBM

1	14.00

Original Adventures of Cholly and Flytrap
Image, 2006

1-2	6.00

Original Astro Boy
Now, 1987

1-20	2.00

Original Black Cat
Recollections, 1988

1-8	2.00
9	3.00
10	1.00

Original Boy: Day of Atonement
Omega 7

This black-and-white title from Alonzo Washington features Omega Man, a black super-hero from the future who travels back in time to stop a plot that would endanger the proceedings at 1995's famous "Million Man March". This was a gathering of black men in Washington D.C. that sent the message of the African-American male's political and social influence. Washington has created an admirable hero in the form of Omega Man-something of a spinoff of the Superman archetype, but his story is intriguing and has multicultural appeal.

1	2.00

Original Crew
Personality, 1991

1-10	3.00

Original Dick Tracy
Gladstone, 1990

1-5	2.00

Original Doctor Solar, Man of the Atom
Valiant, 1995

1	5.00

Original E-Man
First, 1985

1-7	2.00

Original Ghost Rider
Marvel, 1992
1-20...2.00

Original Ghost Rider Rides Again
Marvel, 1991
1-7...2.00

Original Magnus Robot Fighter
Valiant, 1992
1...4.00

Original Man
Omega 7
1...4.00

Original Man: The Most Powerful Man In the Universe
Omega 7
1...2.00

Original Mysterymen Presents (Bob Burden's...)
Dark Horse, 1999
1-4...3.00

Original Sad Sack
Recollections
1...2.00

Original Shield
Archie, 1984
1-4...1.00

Original Sin
Thwack! Pow!
1-3...1.00

Original Sins
Avalon
1...3.00

Original Street Fighter
Alpha
1...3.00

Original Tom Corbett
Eternity, 1990
1-5...3.00

Original Turok, Son of Stone
Valiant, 1995
1...4.00
2...7.00

Original Tzu, The: Spirits of Death
Murim, 1997
1...3.00

Origin of Galactus
Marvel, 1996
1...3.00

Origin of the Defiant Universe
Defiant, 1994
1 .... 2.00

Orion
Dark Horse, 1993

On Lurieh, the mystical psycho-science replaces physical science as the force that drives this advanced society. Seska is a skilled magical transdimensional navigator who maneuvers ships through interdimensional space. Returning to Lurieh in her travels, the reigning religious group attempts to entangle her in their schemes. Their goal is to eliminate all the negative karma in the universe, but the spell has a serious flaw.

She warns her father, a powerful magician from another religion. He casts a spell which binds itself to Seska. He also summons Susano, the god of destruction, to try to prevent the terrible forces unleashed by the release of the karma-eating creature. Can he save the universe?

Masamune Shirow is a master of detail in his beautiful art, and witty in his character's aside comments. He is also the creator of Appleseed and Dominion.

1 .... 4.00
2-5.. 3.00
6 .... 4.00

Orion
DC, 2000
1-25.. 3.00

Orlak Redux
Caliber, 1991
1 .... 4.00

Ororo: Before the Storm
Marvel, 2005
1-4.. 3.00

Orphen
ADV Manga, 2005
1-3 .... 10.00

Osborn Journals
Marvel, 1997
1 .... 3.00

Oscar Comics
Marvel, 1947

Continuing the numbering of Funny Tunes, the first three issues of Oscar Comics carry #24, #25, and #26, respectively, on their covers, although it is blacked out on the third issue with a #3 added below. A second printing, with no blacked-out number, was also produced.

The typical teen-age comedy featured a dark-haired crewcut teen-age boy who was smitten with Kitty, a statuesque blonde who was prominently featured on the covers of each issue.

For the final two issues of the run, the series was retitled Awful Oscar and changed direction to focus on the mischievous antics of a younger red-headed child.

-- **Brent**

1 .... 60.00
2 .... 75.00
3-9 .... 35.00
10 .... 40.00

Othello
Tome
1 .... 4.00

Other Big Thing (Colin Upton's...)
Fantagraphics, 1991
1 .... 3.00
2-3 .... 2.00
4 .... 3.00

Others
Image, 1995

0	1.00
1-4	3.00

Others (Cormac)
Cormac

1	2.00

Other Side
DC, 2006

1-4	3.00

Otherworld
DC, 2005

1-7	3.00

Otis Goes Hollywood
Dark Horse, 1997

1-2	3.00

Otto Space!
Manifest Destiny

1-2	2.00

Ouran High School Host Club
Viz, 2005

1-3	9.00

Our Army at War
DC, 1952

One of the longest-running war comics of all time, Our Army At War enjoyed a continuous, 25-year run from 1952 to 1977. During that time, it brought countless tales of courage, cowardice, and irony - set primarily in World War II.

The highlight of this series was the first appearance of hard-bitten Sgt. Rock in issue #81. Rock, who starred in the remaining run of the series, was DC's premier war hero. He was a hero of unflagging bravery who was tough enough to handle any situation, but who knew the costs of war only too well.

Our Army At War was also notable for its introduction of Enemy Ace in issue #151.

Remarkably, the hero in this case was a German pilot in World War I. Nevertheless, he was a man of extreme honor and courage, and was useful in showing that the real enemy is war itself.

1	1,500.00
2	750.00
3-4	600.00
5-7	500.00
8-11	400.00
12	325.00
13	400.00
14	325.00
15-19	300.00
20	275.00
21-31	200.00
32-40	175.00
41-50	125.00
51-70	100.00
71-80	75.00
81	2,500.00

☛1st Sgt. Rock

82	650.00
83	1,800.00

☛1st Kubert Rock

84	300.00
85	350.00
86-87	300.00
88	325.00
89-90	300.00
91	700.00

☛1st all-Rock issue

92-100	175.00
101-112	125.00
113-118	150.00
119	125.00
120-121	80.00
122-125	75.00
126	100.00
127	75.00
128	275.00

☛Sgt. Rock Origin

129-133	75.00
134-137	60.00
138-150	50.00
151	350.00

☛1st Enemy Ace

152	50.00
153	140.00

☛2nd Enemy Ace

154	40.00
155	75.00

☛3rd Enemy Ace

156-157	40.00
158	60.00

☛1st Iron Major

159-163	40.00
164	80.00

☛Giant-sized

165-167	40.00
168	90.00

☛1st Unknown Soldier

169-176	30.00
177	50.00
178-181	30.00
182-183	40.00
184-185	30.00
186	40.00
187-189	30.00
190	40.00
191-198	25.00
199-202	20.00
203	35.00

☛Giant

204-215	20.00
216	55.00

☛Giant-sized

217-228	15.00
229	35.00

☛Giant-sized

230-234	15.00
235-240	25.00
241	15.00
242	20.00

☛100-page issue

243-253	15.00
254	18.00
255	15.00
256	18.00
257	15.00
258-271	10.00
272	15.00
273-301	10.00

Our Cancer Year
Four Walls Eight Windows, 1994

1	18.00

Our Fighting Forces
DC, 1954

This exciting war comic from the Fifties, Sixties, and Seventies launched many memorable heroes, including Captain Hunter and his Hellcats, and the Unknown Soldier.

However, the real star of this series was The Losers, a squad of hard-fighting soldiers who never gave up - no matter how hopeless the situation. The team consisted of Gunner, Sarge, Johnny Cloud, and their leader, the indomitable Captain Storm.

As a series, Our Fighting Forces gave time to all aspects of the military, from the army infantryman to the ace pilot. The feature stories of Our Fighting Forces hailed the merits of camaraderie, courage, and loyalty, as did the true exploits of U.S. fighting forces and bonus stories printed in each issue.

1	725.00
2	340.00
3	310.00
4-5	250.00
6-9	190.00
10	205.00
11-15	135.00
16-20	115.00
21-30	90.00
31-40	75.00
41	90.00
42-44	70.00
45	235.00
☛1st Gunner & Sarge	
46	95.00
47	80.00
48-50	60.00
51-60	35.00
61-64	28.00
65-70	18.00
71-80	15.00
81-90	10.00
91-99	7.00
100-120	6.00
121-150	5.00
151-181	4.00

Our Flag Comics
Ace, 1941

1	1,700.00
2	925.00
3-5	750.00

Our Gang with Tom & Jerry
Dell, 1942

1	600.00
2	335.00
3-5	190.00
6	195.00
7	130.00
8	175.00
9-10	158.00
11	146.00
12-20	130.00
21-30	115.00
31-36	90.00
37-40	48.00
41-50	32.00
51-59	26.00

Our Love
Marvel, 1949

1	75.00
2	50.00

Our Love Story
Marvel, 1969

In the late 1960s, Marvel branched out from its niche as the leading super-hero comic publisher to start new titles in mystery, Westerns, humor, and romance. Our Love Story was a product of this period and an effort to use the then-formidable cultural power of the "mighty Marvel style" to breathe life into the most conventional and turgid comics genre - love and romance, which by the late 1960s was completely played out and encrusted in cliches.

Our Love Story was nothing if not stylish, with up-to-the-minute romance stories told in the breezy Marvel fashion and illustrated by bullpen luminaries like John Romita, Gene Colan, and Vince Colletta. The high-water mark of the series is the impossibly scarce issue #5, featuring the classic story "My Heart Broke...in Hollywood," Jim Steranko's tour de force kiss-off to Marvel and comic-book work in general.

1	55.00
2-4	25.00
5	75.00
☛Steranko art	
6-8	25.00
9	35.00
10-11	25.00
12	35.00
13	20.00
14-20	12.00
21-37	8.00
38	15.00

Our Secret
Superior, 1949

4	100.00
5-8	55.00

Outbreed 999
Blackout, 1994

1-5	3.00

Outcast
Acclaim, 1995

1	5.00

Outcasts
DC, 1987

1-12	2.00

Outer Edge
Innovation

1	3.00

Outer Limits
Dell, 1964

1	125.00
2-5	65.00
6-10	50.00
11-18	35.00

Outer Orbit
Dark Horse, 2007

1	3.00

Outer Space
Charlton, 1958

17	60.00
☛Was This Magazine Is Haunted	
18-20	75.00
21-25	55.00

Outer Space
Charlton, 1968

1	20.00

Outer Space Babes
Silhouette

1	3.00

Out For Blood
Dark Horse, 1999

1-4	3.00

Outlander
Malibu, 1987

1-7	2.00

Outlanders
Dark Horse, 1988

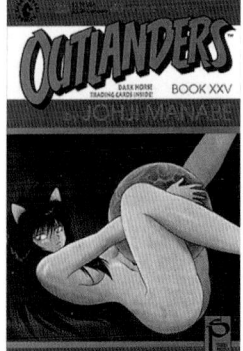

The great Santovasku Empire has returned to the sacred planet of its origin on a pilgrimage, led by the Princess Kahm, heir to the empire. To its horror, the planet has been populated by non-Santovasku vermin. Preparations for the extermination of this repulsive species begin immediately.

Across the galaxy, aliens have invaded Earth! Tetsuya is going to get the scoop on the front lines, no matter what the government says. Best of all, the aliens are led by this fabulous babe! A few extra pictures for himself certainly can't hurt...until she looks his way. Now if he survives long enough to ask her out, he may just be the key to peace between their races.

Johji Manabe is a Japanese manga artist and writer known for his romantic humor set in dramatic settings. He has also written Caravan Kidd and Capricorn.

0-1	3.00
2-21	2.00
22-33	3.00

Outlanders Epilogue
Dark Horse, 1994
1	3.00

Outlaw 7
Dark Horse, 2001
1-3	3.00

Outlaw Fighters
Atlas, 1954
1	85.00
2-5	60.00

Outlaw Kid (1st Series)
Marvel, 1954
1	165.00
2	80.00
3-10	65.00
11-17	54.00
18	58.00
19	54.00

Outlaw Kid (2nd Series)
Marvel, 1970
1	25.00
2-7	10.00
8	15.00
9	8.00
10	20.00
11-20	8.00
21-30	5.00

Outlaw Nation
DC, 2000
1-19	3.00

Outlaw Nation
Boneyard, 1994
1-1/Platinum	5.00

Outlaw Overdrive
Blue Comet

Outlaw Overdrive is a black-and-white comic featuring a collection of characters such as cybernetic assassin Deathrow, and two death-dealing scantily clad females known as the Iron Cupcakes, Windraven, and Shandazar.

Outlaw Overdrive attempts to walk a line between glorifying the ultra-violent blood-bath trend and parodying it with coy resolutions to brutal stories. The art, however, largely relies on gruesome depictions of violent action such as decapitation with a lot of wisecracks added to lighten the mood. The title is clearly aimed at readers who enjoy self-assured, take-no-prisoners attitude, and aren't too meticulous about characters' ethics.

-- George Haberberger

1	3.00

Outlaws
D.S., 1948
1	200.00
2	175.00
3	110.00
4-5	85.00
6	65.00
7-8	90.00
9	200.00

Outlaws
Star, 1952
10	120.00
11-14	90.00

Outlaws
DC, 1991
1-8	2.00

Outlaws of the West
Charlton, 1957
11	20.00
12-20	12.00
21-30	8.00
31-50	5.00
51-60	4.00

61-70	3.00
71-88	2.00

Out of the Night
ACG, 1952
1	400.00
2	285.00
3	150.00
4	230.00
5-10	150.00
11-17	115.00

Out of the Shadows
Standard, 1952
5	350.00
6	225.00
7	160.00
8	285.00
9	160.00
10	145.00
11	160.00
12	215.00
13	190.00
14	160.00

Out of the Vortex
(Comics' Greatest World...)
Dark Horse, 1994
5-12	2.00

Out of this World
Charlton, 1956
1	85.00
2	45.00
3-6	60.00
7	65.00
8-10	60.00
11-12	55.00
13-15	20.00
16	55.00

Out of This World
Eternity
1	4.00

Outposts
Blackthorne, 1997
1	2.00

Outsiders
DC, 1984
1-3	2.00
4-28	1.00
Ann 1	3.00
Special 1	2.00

Outsiders
DC, 1993
0	3.00
1/A	4.00
1/B	3.00
2-12	2.00
13	3.00
14-24	2.00

Outsiders
DC, 2003
1-20	3.00
21-23	4.00
24-43	3.00

Outsiders Double Feature
DC, 2003

1 ....5.00

Out There
DC, 2001

El Dorado City seems like the perfect California town. Somehow, the city maintains its safety and prosperity, while all the nearby towns are sliding into an abyss of crime, drugs, and urban blight. Casey the homecoming queen, her jock boyfriend Zach, Jess the freaky Goth-girl, and Mark the geek are about to discover something horrible about their perfect town -- and it involves goblins, body possession, and the dread Lord Draedalus. What happens when the adults of your town make a deal with the devil, and the only way to stop them is to ally yourself with the kids you hate?

Is saving the world worth risking your school cool?

1 ....3.00
1/Variant...................................4.00
2-18...3.00
Ashcan 1 ....1.00

Overkill: Witchblade/Aliens/ Darkness/Predator
Image, 2000

1-2...6.00

Overload Magazine
Eclipse, 1987

1 ....2.00

Overmen
Excel, 1998

1 ....3.00

Over the Edge
Marvel, 1995

1-10...1.00

Overture
Innovation, 1990

1-2... 2.00

Owl
Gold Key, 1967

1 .... 50.00
2 .... 40.00

Owlhoots
Kitchen Sink

1-2... 3.00

Ox Cow O' War
Spoof

1 .... 3.00

Oz
Caliber, 1995

0 .... 4.00
1 .... 6.00
2-10...................................... 4.00
11-20...................................... 3.00

Oz Collection (Bill Bryan's...)
Arrow

1 .... 3.00

Oz: Daemonstorm
Caliber, 1997

1 .... 4.00

Ozf5 Gale Force
Alias, 2005

1 .... 5.00

Oz: Romance in Rags
Caliber, 1996

1-3... 3.00

Oz Special: Freedom Fighters
Caliber

1 .... 3.00

Oz Special: Lion
Caliber

1 .... 3.00

Oz Special: Scarecrow
Caliber

1 .... 3.00

Oz Special: Tin Man
Caliber

1 .... 3.00

Oz Squad
Brave New Words, 1991

1-4 .... 3.00

Oz Squad
Patchwork, 1994

1-10....................................... 3.00

Oz: Straw & Sorcery
Caliber, 1997

1-3... 3.00

Oz: The Manga
Antarctic, 2005

1-6 .... 3.00

Oz-Wonderland Wars
DC, 1986

1-3 .... 3.00

Ozark Ike
Standard, 1948

11-15 .... 55.00
16-20 .... 44.00
21-25 .... 38.00

Ozzie & Babs
Fawcett, 1947

1 .... 54.00
2 .... 28.00
3-5 .... 24.00
6-13 .... 18.00

Ozzy Osbourne
Rock-It Comics, 1993

This title is one of a series of rock star fantasy-profiles from Rock-It Comics. The spotlight here is on British heavy metal veteran Ozzy Osbourne. Other Rock-It titles featured rockers Lita Ford, World Domination Enterprises, and Metallica.

The Ozzy story begins with him playing a gig at the old English Castle Donington. In the midst of the concert, a storm strikes, and lightning strikes Ozzy. He awakes in Limbo where a host of demons tempt him to give in to despair and drugs, while showing him snippets of his life. In truth, Ozzy did travel a rough road in life, growing up in a lower-class Birmingham neighborhood where he tangled with the police and worked a series of thankless jobs. Later, he hooked up with other musicians to form a progression of bands, culminating in Black Sabbath. That band gave him his reputation as a "devil rocker," but it was not until his solo career that the (mis)label really stuck.

1 .... 6.00

*Although he's not pictured on the cover, "America's Typical Teen"
aka Archie Andrews, makes his first appearance with this issue.*

Pacific Presents
Pacific, 1982
1 .... 4.00
2 .... 3.00
3-4 .... 2.00

Pac (Preter-Human Assault Corps)
Artifacts, 1993
1 .... 2.00

Pact
Image, 1994
1-3 .... 2.00

Pact
Image, 2005
1-4 .... 3.00

Pageant of Comics
St. John, 1947
1-2 .... 50.00

Pagers Comics Anthology
No Talent, 1997
1-6 .... 3.00

Painkiller Jane
Event, 1997

A supercop story with a human touch, Painkiller Jane tells the story of police officer Jane Vasko, killed by mob violence and brought back through "some weird voodoo" as the nearly indestructible scourge of the underworld, Painkiller Jane. Ironically, Jane's invincibility leaves her emotionally hollow and in intense psychic suffering -- almost suicidal sometimes. Her inner conflicts and turmoil add an overlay of drama and humanity to her grim quest for vengeance and justice.

The multilayered story of Painkiller Jane was launched by creators Joe Quesada and Jimmy Palmiotti and deftly developed by Mark Waid and Brian Augustyn. Art by Rick Leonardi and Palmiotti and a beautiful full-color treatment make Painkiller Jane one of the standout independent titles of the mid-1990s.

0 .... 4.00
0/Ltd. 40.00
1 .... 3.00
1/A 4.00
1/Red foil 25.00
2 .... 3.00
2/A 4.00
3 .... 3.00
3/A 4.00
4 .... 3.00
4/A 4.00
5 .... 3.00
5/A 4.00

Painkiller Jane/ Darkchylde
Event, 1998
0 .... 4.00
1 .... 3.00
1/A 30.00
1/B 4.00
1/C 40.00
Ashcan 1 .... 5.00

Painkiller Jane/Hellboy
Event, 1998
1 .... 3.00
1/Ltd. 30.00
1/A 3.00

Painkiller Jane vs. The Darkness: Stripper
Event, 1997
1-1/C 3.00
1/Ltd. 20.00

Paintball Universe 2000
Splattoons
1 .... 3.00

Pajama Chronicles
Blackthorne, 1987
1 .... 2.00

Pakkins' Land
Caliber, 1996
0 .... 2.00
1-6 .... 3.00

Pakkins' Land
Alias, 2005
1-5 .... 3.00

Pakkins' Land: Forgotten Dreams
Caliber, 1998
1-4 .... 3.00

Pakkins' Land: Quest for Kings
Caliber, 1997
1-6 .... 3.00

Palatine
Gryphon Rampant, 1994
1-5 .... 3.00

Palestine
Fantagraphics, 1994
1-9 .... 3.00

Pal-Yat-Chee
Adhesive, 1993
1 .... 3.00

Pamela Anderson Uncovered
Pop
1 .... 3.00

Pancho Villa
L. Miller & Son
1 .... 10.00
2-29 .... 6.00
30-63 .... 4.00

Panda Khan Special
Abacus, 1990
1 .... 3.00

Pandemonium
Chaos!, 1998
1 .... 3.00

Pandora Pill
Acid Rain
1 .... 3.00

Panic
E.C., 1954
1 .... 210.00
2 .... 125.00
3-11 .... 80.00
12 .... 160.00

Panic
Gemstone, 1997
1-12 .... 3.00
Ann 1-2 .... 11.00

Panorama
St.Eve Productions, 1991
1-2 .... 3.00

Pantera
Malibu, 1994
1 .... 4.00

Pantha: Haunted Passion
Harris, 1997
1 ....3.00

Pantheon
Archer Books & Games, 1995
1-2..3.00

Pantheon
Lone Star, 1998
1-6..3.00

Pantheon: Ancient History
Lone Star, 1999
1 ....4.00

Panzer 1946
Antarctic, 2004
1-5..6.00

Paper Cinema: The Box
Grey Blossom Sequentials, 1998
3 ....4.00

Paper Cinema: Waves In Space
Grey Blossom Sequentials, 1998
2 ....4.00

Paper Dolls from the California Girls
Eclipse
1 ....6.00

Paper Museum
Jungle Boy, 2002
1 ....3.00

Paper Tales
CLG Comics, 1993
1-2..3.00

Para-Cops
Excel, 1998
1 ....3.00

Paradax
Vortex, 1987
1-2..2.00

Paradigm
Image, 2002
1-4..4.00
5-8..3.00
9-12..4.00

Paradigm
Gauntlet
1 ....3.00

Paradise Kiss
Tokyopop, 2002
1 ....10.00

Paradise Too
Abstract, 2000
nn-14......................................3.00

Paradise X
Marvel, 2002

After the events of Universe X, Captain America has become one of seven guardians of paradise. This is the paradise created by Mar-Vell to reward humanity but as in the biblical paradise, there are prohibitions to observe. In Universe X, Mar-Vell, the child of Him and Her, defeated Death and was portrayed as mankind's messiah. Now in the realm of the living, since Death has been overcome, people with severe injuries are denied release and linger in agony. These do not appear to be the actions of a benevolent savior.

This series is the final arc in the alternate future of the Marvel universe that started with Earth X and continued in Universe X. This trilogy was always been a high-concept story, but this arc has taken it to the realm of philosophy.
-- George Haberberger
0 ....5.00
1-12..3.00

Paradise X: Devils
Marvel, 2002
1 ....5.00

Paradise X: Heralds
Marvel, 2001
1-3..4.00

Paradise X: A
Marvel, 2003
1 ....3.00

Paradise X: X
Marvel, 2003
1 ....3.00

Paradise X: Ragnarok
Marvel, 2003
1-2..3.00

Paradise X: Xen
Marvel, 2002
1 ....5.00

Paradox Project: Genesis
Paradox Project, 1998
1 ....3.00

Paragon: Dark Apocalypse
AC
1-4..3.00

Parallax: Emerald Night
DC, 1996
1 ....15.00

Paramount Animated Comics
Harvey, 1953
3 ....125.00
4-6..55.00
7 ....100.00
8-10..55.00
11-22......................................45.00

Paranoia
Adventure, 1991
1-6..3.00

Paranoia
Co. & Sons
1 ....4.00

Paraphernalia
Graphitti
1 ....2.00

Parasyte
Mixx, 1999
1-2..12.00

Para Troop
Comics Conspiracy, 1998
0 ....4.00
1-Ashcan 1 ....3.00

Pardners
Cottonwood Graphics, 1990
1-2..8.00

Paris
Slave Labor, 2005
1-2..3.00

Paris the Man of Plaster
Harrier, 1987
1-6..2.00

Parliament of Justice
Image, 2003
1 ....6.00

Paro-Dee
Parody
1 ....3.00

Parody Press Annual Swimsuit Special '93
Parody, 1993
1 ....3.00

Parole Breakers
Avon, 1951

1 ....260.00
2 ....175.00
3 ....160.00

Particle Dreams
Fantagraphics, 1986

1-6..2.00

Partners in Pandemonium
Caliber

1-3...3.00

Partridge Family
Charlton, 1971

1 ....30.00
2 ....16.00
3-4 ....14.00
5 ....20.00
☛Giant-sized
6-14 ....12.00
15-21 ....10.00

Parts of a Hole
Caliber

1 ....3.00

Parts Unknown
Eclipse, 1995

1-4...3.00

Parts Unknown Convention Sketchbook
-Ism, 2005

1 ....10.00

Parts Unknown: Dark Intentions
Knight, 1995

0-4...3.00

Parts Unknown: Hostile Takeover
Image, 2000

1 ....3.00
1/Ashcan 5.00
2 ....3.00
2/Ashcan 5.00
3 ....3.00
3/Ashcan 5.00
4 ....3.00
4/Ashcan 5.00

Parts Unknown II: The Next Invasion
Eclipse, 1993

1 ....3.00

Passover
Maximum, 1996

1 ....3.00

Pat Boone
DC, 1959

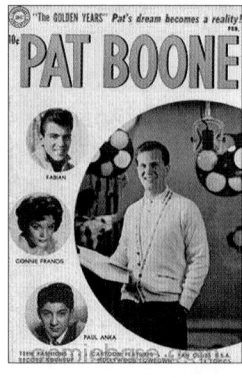

Pat Boone (1934-) was a regular singer on Arthur Godfrey's TV show in 1949 and had become a teen idol even before he began starring in movies of the day. His comic-book series was an oddity, looking more like a teen fan magazine than a comic book. With photo covers and no Comics Code seal, the series clearly aimed for that fan audience. Covers display, in addition to color photos of Boone, black-and-white photos of other popular singers of the day (Jimmie Rodgers, "Kookie" Byrnes, Fabian, Connie Francis, etc.), and regular features include Fan Clubs U.S.A., Record Roundup, TV Topics, and cartoons. And, of course, there are features on Boone himself, such as a preview of his latest picture (Journey to the Center of the Earth).

-- Maggie

1 .... 200.00
2-5 .... 150.00

Patches
Rural Home, 1945

1 .... 300.00
2 .... 125.00
3-7 .... 100.00
8-11 .... 75.00

Pater Contrarius
Robot

1 .... 2.00

Path
CrossGen, 2002

1-23 .... 3.00

Path Prequel
CrossGen, 2002

1 .... 3.00

Pathways to Fantasy
Pacific, 1984

1 .... 2.00

Patient Zero
Image, 2004

1-4 .... 3.00

Patrick Rabbit
Fragments West, 1988

1-7 .... 2.00

Patrick Stewart
Celebrity

1 .... 3.00

Patrick Stewart vs. William Shatner
Celebrity, 1992

1 .... 6.00

Patriots
WildStorm, 2000

1-10 .... 3.00

Pat Savage: The Woman of Bronze
Millennium, 1992

1 .... 3.00

Patsy and Hedy
Marvel, 1952

Patsy Walker and her rival Hedy Wolfe are the stars of this "Good Girl Art" series. Running throughout the 1950s and '60s, it features the two in a more-or-less endless catfight, disagreeing on virtually everything. Nevertheless, the two are friends deep down. Sort of.

One of the more unusual features of this series is the non-stop outfit and hairdo changes that all its characters seem to go through. This comes from the title's practice (taken from Bill Woggon's pioneering work on Katy Keene) of letting readers submit their own ideas for dresses and hair styles, giving the readers credit when they were used (e.g., "Patsy's a Park Avenue pinup in her perky suit by: Inez Colon, N.Y.C., N.Y.").

When her carefree young adult days were over, Patsy Walker will

632

one day become the super-hero known as Hellcat, one of The Defenders.

1	135.00
2	70.00
3-10	48.00
11-20	32.00
21-30	25.00
31-50	23.00
51-60	15.00
61-90	12.00
91-110	10.00
Ann 1	55.00

Patsy & Her Pals
Atlas, 1953

1	125.00
2-4	75.00
5-9	60.00
10-15	55.00
16-19	50.00
20-25	45.00
26-29	40.00

Patsy Walker
Marvel, 1945

1	400.00
2	175.00
3-10	125.00
11-12	70.00
13-14	80.00
15-16	70.00
17	80.00
18	70.00
19-22	80.00
23-24	55.00
25	80.00
26-29	55.00
30	70.00
31-41	30.00
42-50	25.00
51-60	22.00
61-80	16.00
81-100	13.00
101-124	10.00
Special 1	45.00

Pat the Brat
Archie, 1955

1	35.00
2	24.00
3-4	20.00
15-33	14.00

Patty Cake
Permanent Press, 1995

1-9	3.00

Patty Cake
Caliber, 1996

1-Holiday 1	3.00

Patty Cake & Friends
Slave Labor, 1997

1-15	3.00
Special 1	4.00

Patty Cake & Friends
Slave Labor, 2000

1-15	5.00

Patty Powers
Atlas, 1955

4	50.00
5-7	30.00

Paul Terry's Comics
St. John, 1951

85	40.00
86-90	35.00
91-96	25.00
97-105	20.00
106-120	15.00
121-125	10.00

Paul the Samurai
New England, 1992

1	4.00
2	3.00
3	6.00
4	4.00
5-10	3.00

Paul the Samurai
NEC, 1990

1	4.00
2-3	3.00

Pawnee Bill
Story, 1951

1	65.00
2-3	45.00

Payne
Dream Catcher, 1995

1	3.00

Pay-off
D.S., 1948

1	150.00
2	90.00
3-5	75.00

P. City Parade
Horse, 1996

1	5.00

Peacemaker
Charlton, 1967

1	10.00
2-3	6.00
4	8.00
5	6.00

Peacemaker
Modern, 1978

1-2	3.00

Peacemaker
DC, 1988

1-4	2.00

Peacemaker Kurogane
ADV Manga, 2004

1-3	10.00

Peacemakers
Kinetic

1	3.00

Peace Party
Blue Corn

1	3.00

Peace Posse
Mellon Bank

1	3.00

Peanut Butter and Jeremy
Alternative, 2000

1-3	3.00
4/FCBD	2.00

Peanuts
Dell, 1954

1	125.00
4	75.00
5-13	55.00

Peanuts
Gold Key, 1963

1	125.00
2-4	75.00

Peasant and the Devil
Fantagraphics

1	3.00

Pebbles and Bamm-Bamm
Charlton, 1972

1	18.00
2	12.00
3-5	9.00
6-10	7.00
11-20	5.00
21-30	4.00
31-36	3.00

Pebbles & Bamm-Bamm
Harvey, 1993

1-Summer 1	2.00

Pebbles Flintstone
Gold Key, 1963

1	75.00

Pedestrian Vulgarity
Fantagraphics

1	3.00

Pedro
Fox, 1950

1	150.00
2	100.00

Peek-A-Boo 3-D
3-D Zone

1	4.00

Peepshow
Drawn & Quarterly, 1992

1-9	3.00

Pellestar
Eternity, 1987

1-2	2.00

Pendragon
Aircel, 1991
1-2..3.00

Pendulum
Adventure, 1992
1-4..3.00

Pendulum's Illustrated Stories
Pendulum
1-6..5.00

Peng One Shot
Oni, 2005
1..6.00

Penguin & Pencilguin
Fragments West, 1987
1-6..2.00

Penguin Bros.
Labyrinth, 1998
1-2..3.00

Penny
Avon, 1947
1..55.00
2-5..30.00
6..35.00

Penny & Aggie
Alias, 2005
1-4..3.00

Penny Century
Fantagraphics, 1997
1-7..3.00

Pentacle: The Sign of the Five
Eternity, 1991
1-4..2.00

Penthouse Comix
Penthouse International, 1994
1..6.00
1/2nd-33..5.00

Penthouse Max
Penthouse International, 1996
1-3..5.00

Penthouse Men's Adventure Comix
Penthouse, 1995
1-7..5.00

People are Phony
Siegel and Simon, 1976
1..4.00

People's Comics
Golden Gate, 1972
1..4.00

Pep
Archie, 1940

Most readers know Pep as the home of Archie, Jughead, Veronica, Betty, and the rest of the Archies. Indeed, these delightful teens inhabited the majority of Pep's issues, following their introduction in #22.

What is less well-known to the world at large is that Pep started out as a super-hero title, featuring the first appearances of The Shield, The Comet, and many others. The early days of this series even included an appearance by the decidedly un-Archie-like Madam Satan.

Even after Archie's introduction (as a filler in an issue cover-featuring super-heroes fighting a Nazi symbol), The Shield, The Hangman (who replaced The Comet), and Nazis took the cover for another couple of years.

1 .... 6,850.00
2 .... 1,850.00
3 .... 1,375.00
4-5 .... 1,050.00
6 .... 825.00
7-11 .... 800.00
12 .... 925.00
13-15 .... 675.00
16 .... 1,000.00
17 .... 2,700.00
☞1st Hangman
18-21 .... 560.00
22 .... 12,000.00
23 .... 1,150.00
24-25 .... 935.00
26 .... 1,475.00
27-30 .... 750.00
31-35 .... 585.00
36 .... 1,050.00
37-40 .... 410.00
41-47 .... 230.00
48 .... 280.00
49-50 .... 230.00
51-55 .... 185.00
56-60 .... 180.00
61-65 .... 140.00

66-70 .... 100.00
71-80 .... 82.00
81-99 .... 62.00
100 .... 90.00
101-110 .... 40.00
111-120 .... 28.00
121-130 .... 23.00
131-140 .... 19.00
141-160 .... 15.00
161-177 .... 7.00
178-200 .... 6.00
201-220 .... 5.00
221-250 .... 4.00
251-300 .... 2.00
301-411 .... 1.00

Perazim
Antarctic, 1996
1-3 .... 3.00

Percevan: The Three Stars of Ingaar
Fantasy Flight
1 .... 9.00

Peregrine
Alliance, 1994
1-2 .... 3.00

Perfect Love
Ziff-Davis, 1951
1 .... 115.00
2 .... 80.00
3-10 .... 65.00

Perfect Crime
Cross, 1949
1 .... 210.00
2 .... 120.00
3-9 .... 100.00
10-14 .... 85.00
15 .... 90.00
16-25 .... 65.00
26 .... 110.00
27-30 .... 65.00
31-33 .... 60.00

Perg
Lightning, 1993

Ramen Alexander Perg was a policeman in 1800s Chicago. Something turned him against the city he had sworn to protect, leaving him so black and evil that the citizens of Chicago stoned him to death. Apparently, the citizens were so afraid of the policeman that they chained his dead body, put a cross on his chest, and burned him. And it wasn't even a Mob hit! Despite all these precautions, Perg rose the next day as a demonic being, using the cross they'd buried him with as a dagger. But despite appearances, the now-risen Perg fights for the side of Good.

And the dagger? When he plunges it into an evildoer's head, it actually cleanses them of evil. Much of the trouble Perg faces in this series comes from the understandable confusion that Perg's appearance and tactics engender. Despite the fact that those he "cleanses" eventually reawaken free of evil tendencies, drug habits, and the like, Perg is hunted by both the police and other heroes of the Lightning universe.

1-1/Gold	4.00
1/Platinum	3.00
1/Variant	4.00
2-8	3.00

Perhapanauts
Dark Horse, 2005
1-4	3.00

Perhapanauts: Second Chances
Dark Horse, 2006
1-3	3.00

Periphery
Arch-Type
1	3.00

Perramus: Escape from the Past
Fantagraphics, 1991
1-4	4.00

Perry
Lightning, 1997
1	3.00

Perry Mason
Dell, 1964
1-2	40.00

Personality Classics
Personality, 1992
1-4	3.00

Personality Comics Presents
Personality, 1991
1-18	3.00

Personal Love
Famous Funnies, 1950
1	100.00
2	55.00
3-7	45.00
8-9	50.00
10	45.00
11	55.00
12	45.00
13-15	40.00
16-17	45.00
18-30	40.00
31	55.00
32-33	40.00

Pest
Pest Comics
1-7	2.00

Pet
Fantagraphics, 1997
1	3.00

Pete Mangan
L. Miller & Son
51	8.00
52-55	6.00

Peter and the Wolf
NBM
1	16.00

Peter Cannon-Thunderbolt
DC, 1992
1-3	2.00
4-12	1.00

Peter Cottontail
Key, 1954
1	50.00
2	35.00

Peter Kock
Fantagraphics, 1994
1	4.00
2-6	3.00

Peter Pan
Gold Key, 1969
1	20.00
2	12.00

Peter Pan
Tundra
1-2	15.00

Peter Pan
Disney
1	6.00

Peter Pan and the Warlords of Oz
Hand of Doom, 1998
1	3.00

Peter Pan & the Warlords of Oz: Dead Head Water
Hand of Doom, 1999
1	3.00

Peter Pan: Return to Never-Never Land
Adventure, 1991
1-2	3.00

Peter Panda
DC, 1953
1	245.00
2	120.00
3-8	100.00
9	110.00
10	100.00
11-31	60.00

Peter Pan Treasure Chest
Dell, 1953
1	1,500.00

Peter Parker: Spider-Man
Marvel, 1998

In the wake of the much-heralded relaunches of such titles as Avengers and Fantastic Four, Marvel rebooted its main "Spider-verse" titles with The Amazing Spider-Man (Vol. 2) and Peter Parker, Spider-Man.

With the first issue, writer Howard Mackie (Ghost Rider) and artist John Romita, Jr. (Iron Man) do much to return Spidey to his former glory. Peter Parker's life is once again made difficult by the juggling of a multitude of responsibilities as the dutiful nephew of his ever-ailing Aunt May; as the devoted husband of his jet-setting, supermodel wife, Mary Jane Watson-Parker; as the determined photographer for The Daily Bugle; as the distracted employee of a scientific research facility; and as the dedicated super-hero...your friendly, neighborhood Spider-Man. "Duty and responsibility" has long been the theme of the Spider-Man. While our hero got a bit lost for awhile among the clones and the alien symbiotes, this title restored him to his proper place in the Marvel universe.

1	5.00
1/Sunburst	6.00
1/Dynamic	14.00
2/A-2/B	2.00
3-21	4.00
25/Variant	6.00
22-29	4.00
30-49	3.00
50	4.00
51-57	3.00
Ann 1998-1999	4.00

Peter Porkchops
DC, 1949

DC was the preeminent publisher of super-hero comics from the 1940s, but, when superheroes went out of favor toward the end of the decade, staffers had to cast around in the territory of funny animal comics, among other genres, to maintain their readership. Some of their efforts, like Fox and the Crow, were quite successful. Then there were series like Peter Porkchops, an uncomfortable hodgepodge of Porky Pig and Donald Duck that pitted the cagey pig Peter Porkchops against hapless rival Wolfie Wolf. It's hard to imagine that kids would opt for Peter Porkchops, when their same dime could buy them Uncle Scrooge or Bugs Bunny, but enough people bought it to keep it going for a decade. Sandwiched between the predictable antics of Peter and Wolfie in some issues were a few pages of Dizzy Dog by Sheldon Mayer, DC's genuinely funny creator at the time.

-- Rob Salkowitz

1	165.00
2	85.00
3-5	60.00
6-10	50.00
11-20	45.00
21-30	40.00

31-40	32.00
41-50	25.00
51-60	20.00
61-62	18.00

Peter Porker, the Spectacular Spider-Ham
Marvel, 1985

1-17	1.00

Peter Rabbit
Avon, 1947

1	150.00
2	90.00
3-6	70.00
7-10	20.00
11-20	14.00
21-34	10.00

Peter Rabbit 3-D
Eternity

1	3.00

Peter the Little Pest
Marvel, 1969

1	75.00
2-4	50.00

Pete the P.O.'d Postal Worker
Sharkbait, 1997

1	4.00
2-10	3.00

Petticoat Junction
Dell, 1964

1	40.00
2-3	30.00
4	25.00
5	30.00

Petworks vs. WildK.A.T.S.
Parody

1	3.00

Phaedra
Express, 1994

1	3.00

Phage: ShadowDeath (Neil Gaiman's...)
Big, 1996

1-6	2.00

Phantacea: Phase One
Mcpherson, 1987

1	5.00

Phantasmagoria
Tome

1	3.00

Phantasy Against Hunger
Tiger, 1987

1	2.00

Phantom
Gold Key, 1962

1	90.00
2	55.00
3-10	36.00
11-17	28.00
18	32.00
19-28	24.00
30-40	15.00
41-59	12.00
60-70	9.00
71-74	7.00

Phantom
DC, 1988

1-4	2.00

Phantom
DC, 1989

1-13	2.00

Phantom
Wolf, 1992

0/Ltd.	4.00
1	3.00
2-8	2.00

Phantom
Moonstone, 2003

1-8	4.00

Phantom Force
Image, 1993

0-Ashcan 1	3.00

Phantom Force
Genesis West

0	3.00

Phantom Guard
Image, 1997

1-6	3.00

Phantom Jack
Image, 2004

1-4	3.00
4/Error	4.00
5	3.00

Phantom Lady
Fox, 1947

13	2,400.00
14-16	1,500.00
17	3,300.00
18-19	1,050.00
20-22	825.00
23	925.00

Phantom Lady
Ajax, 1954

5	1,000.00
2-4	800.00

Phantom Lady
Verotik, 1994

1	10.00

Phantom of Fear City
Claypool, 1993

1-12	3.00

Phantom of the Opera
Eternity
1 ....2.00

Phantom of the Opera
Innovation, 1991
1 ....7.00

Phantom Quest Corp.
Pioneer, 1997
1 ....3.00

Phantom Stranger (1st Series)
DC, 1952
1 ....1,500.00
2 ....1,000.00
3-6..750.00

Phantom Stranger (2nd Series)
DC, 1969
1 ....125.00
2-3...60.00
4 ....70.00
5-7...50.00
8-13..40.00
14-17..35.00
18-21..25.00
22-41..15.00

Phantom Stranger
DC, 1987
1-4...3.00

Phantom: The Ghost Killer
Moonstone, 2002
nn 6.00

Phantom: The Hunt
Moonstone, 2003
nn 7.00

Phantom: The Singh Web
Moonstone, 2002
nn 7.00

Phantom: The Ghost Who Walks (Lee Falk's...)
Marvel, 1995
1-3...3.00

Phantom: The Treasure of Bangalla
Moonstone, 2002
nn 7.00

Phantom 2040
Marvel, 1995

Begun in 1995 as the companion to a children's animated series (based, in turn, on the long-running King Features newspaper strip), Phantom 2040 continues the legend of The Ghost Who Walks. The lead character is Kit Walker, son of the 23rd person to wear the mask of The Phantom since the tradition began, 500 years earlier. He assumed the role he was destined to play, when a man named Guran gave him a ring which belonged to his long-lost father and then led him to a secret jungle hideout in the midst of the high-tech metropolis where Kit lives.

There Kit learns of his ancestry -- how, long ago, a man donned the mask of The Phantom in order to wage war on pirates. Over the years, the role was passed from father to son, but the lineage was disrupted, when Kit's father disappeared in 2024. Now, however, Kit has assumed the role of the 24th Phantom and is called on to fight more modern sorts of pirates -- those who victimize others using computers and high-tech weaponry.

1-4... 2.00

Phantom Witch Doctor
Avon, 1952
1 .... 300.00

Phantom Zone
DC, 1982
1 .... 2.00
2-4... 1.00

Phase One
Victory, 1986
1-5... 2.00

Phathom
Blatant, 1999
1 .... 3.00

Phatwars
Bon
1 .... 2.00

Phaze
Eclipse, 1988
1-2... 2.00

PhD: Phantasy Degree
Tokyopop, 2005
1-4....................................... 10.00

Phenomerama
Caliber
1 .... 3.00

Phigments
Amazing
1-2... 2.00

Philbert Desanex' Dreams
Rip Off, 1993
1 .... 3.00

Philistine
One Shot, 1993
1-6... 3.00

Phil Rizzuto, Baseball Hero
Fawcett, 1951
1 .... 500.00

Phineus: Magician for Hire
Piffle, 1994
1 .... 3.00

Phobos
Flashpoint, 1994
1 .... 3.00

Phoebe & the Pigeon People
Kitchen Sink
1 .... 3.00

Phoebe: Angel in Black
Angel
1 .... 3.00

Phoebe Chronicles
NBM
1-2....................................... 10.00

Phoenix
Atlas-Seaboard, 1975
1 .... 7.00
2 .... 5.00
3-4... 3.00

Phoenix Restaurant
Fandom House
1 ....4.00

Phoenix Resurrection,
The: Aftermath
Malibu, 1996
1 ....4.00

Phoenix Resurrection,
The: Genesis
Malibu, 1995
1-2...4.00

Phoenix Resurrection,
The: Red Shift
Malibu, 1995
0-0/Ltd. 3.00

Phoenix Resurrection,
The: Revelations
Malibu, 1995
1 ....4.00

Phoenix Square
Slave Labor, 1997
1-2...3.00

Phoenix:
The Untold Story
Marvel, 1984
1 ....8.00

Phonogram
Image, 2006
1-3...4.00

Phony Pages
(Terry Beatty's...)
Renegade, 1986
1-2...2.00

Picnic Party
Dell, 1955
6-7.......................................150.00
8...225.00

Pictorial Confessions
St. John, 1949
1 ....200.00
2 ....125.00
3 ....100.00

Pictorial Love Stories
Charlton, 1949
22-26..................................110.00

Pictorial Romances
St. John, 1950
4 ....160.00
5 ....120.00
6-9...90.00
10...120.00
11...100.00
12-13......................................90.00
14...80.00
15-16......................................90.00
17-20....................................165.00
21-24......................................80.00

Picture News
News in Color and Action, 1946
1 .... 120.00
2 .... 100.00
3.. 80.00
4.. 95.00
5-10....................................... 60.00

Picture Parade
Gilberton, 1953
1 .... 110.00
2-4... 60.00

Picture Progress
Gilberton, 1954
5-9... 38.00

Picture Progress
Gilberton, 1954
1-9... 38.00

Picture Stories From
American History
E.C., 1946
1 .... 140.00
2-4...................................... 110.00

Picture Stories from
Science
E.C., 1947
1 .... 75.00
2 .... 50.00

Picture Stories from the
Bible (New Testament)
E.C., 1944
1 .... 50.00
2-3... 38.00

Picture Stories from the
Bible (Old Testament)
E.C., 1943
1 .... 100.00
2-4... 75.00

Picture Stories from
World History
E.C., 1947
1 .... 210.00
2 .... 160.00

Picture Taker
Slave Labor, 1998
1 .... 3.00

Pie
Wow Cool
1 .... 3.00

Piece of Steak
Tome
1 .... 3.00

Pieces
5th Panel, 1997

Pieces is a fascinating exploration into young angst and what it means to be human by writer/illustrator Todd Richards. Utilizing strikingly different artistic styles, Richards mines our own sense of fear and moral responsibility and reveals the full potential of betrayal in human relationships. In issue #1 for example, "Too Much" tells the story of Todd, who is married to Betty but in an affair with Mary and unable to reconcile his feelings for either. His turmoil, emotional fragmentation and feelings of alienation and mechanistic inevitability are beautifully captured in artwork that is as bizarre as it is enthralling. Richards renders his characters as Cubist figures composed of geometric shapes, mechanical parts, and constantly altering organs, creating a Picasso-like world of the abstract in which his characters live and breathe. Disturbing to read but intriguing nonetheless, Pieces is a mesmerizing anthology.

1-3 .... 3.00

Pied Piper
Graphic Album
Pied Piper
1-3... 7.00

Pied Piper of Hamelin
Tome
1 .... 3.00

Pigeonman
Above & Beyond, 1997
1 .... 3.00

Pigeon-Man,
the Bird-Brain
Ferry Tail, 1993
1 .... 3.00

Pighead
Williamson
1 ....3.00

Pigtale
Image, 2005
1-4 ....3.00

Pilgrim's Progress
Marvel, 1992
1 ....10.00

Pineapple Army
Viz, 1988
1-10 ....2.00

Pinhead
Marvel, 1993
1-6 ....3.00

Pinhead & Foodini
Fawcett, 1951
1 ....180.00
2-3 ....90.00
4 ....75.00

Pinhead vs. Marshal Law: Law in Hell
Marvel, 1993
1-2 ....3.00

Pink Dust
Kitchen Sink, 1998
1 ....4.00

Pink Floyd
Personality
1-2 ....3.00

Pink Floyd Experience
Revolutionary, 1991
1-5 ....3.00

Pink Panther
Gold Key, 1971
1 ....40.00
2 ....17.00
3-5 ....15.00
6-10 ....8.00
11-20 ....6.00
21-40 ....4.00
41-74 ....3.00
75-76 ....15.00
77 ....17.00
78-83 ....8.00
84-87 ....15.00

Pink Panther
Harvey, 1993
1-SS 1 ....2.00

Pinky and the Brain
DC, 1996
1 ....3.00
2-27 ....2.00
Holiday 1 ....3.00

Pinocchia
NBM
1 ....12.00

Pinocchio and the Emperor of the Night
Marvel, 1988
1 ....1.00

Pinocchio Special
Gladstone, 1990
1 ....2.00

Pint-Sized X-Babies
Marvel, 1998
1 ....3.00

Pioneer Picture Stories
Street & Smith, 1941
1 ....165.00
2 ....85.00
3-9 ....75.00

Pipsqueak Papers (Wallace Wood's...)
Fantagraphics
1 ....3.00

Piracy
E.C., 1954
1 ....160.00
2 ....115.00
3-7 ....85.00

Piracy
Gemstone, 1998
1-7 ....3.00

Piranha Is Loose!
Special Studio
1-2 ....3.00

Pirate Club
Slave Labor, 2004
1-8 ....3.00

Pirate Corps
Eternity, 1987
1-4 ....3.00

Pirate Corp$!
Slave Labor, 1989
1-5/2nd 3.00
Special 1 ....2.00
Special 1/2nd 3.00

Pirate Queen
Comax
1 ....3.00

Pirates Comics
Hillman, 1950
1 ....135.00
2 ....100.00
3-4 ....90.00

Pirates of Coney Island
Image, 2006
1-2 ....3.00
3-3/Variant 4.00

Pirates of Dark Water
Marvel, 1991
1-9 ....1.00

P.I.'s, The: Michael Mauser and Ms. Tree
First, 1985
1-3 ....2.00

Pistolero
Eternity
1 ....4.00

Pita Ten Official Fan Club Book
Tokyopop, 2005
1 ....10.00

Pi: The Book of Ants
Artisan Entertainment
1 ....3.00

Pitt
Image, 1993
1/2 ....2.00
1 ....3.00
1/Gold 4.00
2-13 ....2.00
14-20 ....3.00

Pitt
Marvel
1 ....3.00

Pitt Crew
Full Bleed, 1998
1 ....3.00

Pitt: In the Blood
Full Bleed, 1996
1 ....3.00

Pixie and Dixie and Mr. Jinks
Gold Key, 1963
1 ....60.00

Pixies
Magazine Enterprises, 1946
1 ....50.00
2-5 ....30.00

Pixy Junket
Viz

Legend has it that, long ago, a human called Acidhead (it must sound better in Japanese!) was wandering through the forest when he met the queen of the pixies. So enraptured was he by the sight that he disregarded the queen's warning that anyone who kissed her would fall eternally under her spell. He kissed her and became her servant, living blissfully with her in the land of pixies in a state of eternal youth.

300 years passed, until the day when a UFO appears in the skies above the city. Police (in tanks!) are called and monitor from a distance, while humanoid aliens begin excavating the ground where they land. Eventually, they uncover some sort of buried vessel and began airlifting it into their ship. The untimely intervention of a new helicopter severs the hauling line, sending it crashing to the ground. The vessel opens, and inside is a beautiful woman with wings -- a pixy!

1-6 .... 3.00

P.J. Warlock
Eclipse, 1986
1-3 .... 2.00

Places That Are Gone
Aeon, 1994
1-2 .... 3.00

Plague
Tome
1 .... 3.00

Plan 9 from Outer Space
Eternity, 1990
1-1/2nd 5.00

Plan 9 from Outer Space: Thirty Years Later
Eternity, 1991
1-3 .... 3.00

Planet 29
Caliber
1-2 .... 3.00

Planetary
DC, 1999
1 .... 8.00
☞Warren Ellis series
2-26 .... 3.00

Planetary/Batman: Night on Earth
DC, 2003
1 .... 6.00

Planetary: Crossing Worlds
DC, 2004
1 .... 15.00

Planetary/JLA: Terra Occulta
WildStorm, 2002
1 .... 6.00

Planetary/The Authority: Ruling the World
DC, 2000
nn 6.00

Planet Blood
Tokyopop, 2005
1-3 .... 10.00

Planet Comics
Fiction House, 1940
1 .... 12,500.00
2 .... 5,000.00
3 .... 3,250.00
4-7 .... 2,500.00
8-12 .... 2,000.00
13-14 .... 1,500.00
15 .... 2,700.00
☞Scarce
16-18 .... 1,350.00
19-24 .... 1,225.00
25-30 .... 1,000.00
31-40 .... 850.00
41-50 .... 600.00
51-60 .... 500.00
61-70 .... 400.00
71-73 .... 300.00

Planet Comics
Blackthorne, 1988
1-3 .... 2.00

Planet Comics
A-List, 1997
1-3 .... 3.00

Planet Comics
Avalon
1 .... 6.00

Planet Hulk: Gladiator Guidebook
Marvel, 2006
1 .... 4.00

Planet Ladder
Tokyopop, 2002
1-2 .... 10.00

Planet of Geeks
Starhead
1 .... 3.00

Planet of Terror (Basil Wolverton's...)
Dark Horse, 1987
1 .... 2.00

Planet of the Apes
Marvel, 1974
1 .... 20.00
1/2nd 5.00
2 .... 10.00
3 .... 9.00
4-5 .... 8.00
6 .... 6.00

7-29 .... 5.00
Ann 1 .... 4.00

Planet of the Apes
Adventure, 1990
1-1/Ltd. 4.00
1/2nd-24 .... 3.00
Ann 1 .... 4.00

Planet of the Apes
Dark Horse, 2001
1-3/Variant 3.00

Planet of the Apes
Dark Horse, 2001
1-6/Variant 3.00

Planet of the Apes: Blood of the Apes
Adventure, 1991
1-4 .... 3.00

Planet of the Apes: Forbidden Zone
Adventure, 1992
1-4 .... 3.00

Planet of the Apes: Sins of the Father
Adventure, 1992
1 .... 3.00

Planet of the Apes: Urchak's Folly
Adventure, 1991
1-4 .... 3.00

Planet of Vampires
Atlas-Seaboard, 1975
1 .... 12.00
2-3 .... 8.00

Planet Patrol
Edge
1 .... 3.00

Planet Terry
Marvel, 1985
1-12 .... 1.00

Planet-X
Eternity
1 .... 3.00

Planet X Reprint Comic
Planet X, 1987
1 .... 2.00

Plaque X
Aholattafun, 2004
1 .... 3.00

Plasm
Defiant, 1993
0 .... 1.00

Plasma Baby
Caliber
1-3 .... 3.00

Plasmer
Marvel, 1993
1...............................3.00
2-4..............................2.00

Plastic Forks
Marvel, 1990
1-5...............................5.00

Plastic Little
CPM, 1997
1-5...............................3.00

Plastic Man
Comic Magazines, 1943
1.........................3,200.00
2.........................1,300.00
3...........................800.00
4...........................700.00
5...........................565.00
6-10........................450.00
11-20.......................375.00
21-30.......................310.00
31-40.......................240.00
41-50.......................200.00
51-64.......................165.00

Plastic Man
DC, 1966
1...........................150.00
2............................50.00
3............................30.00
4-5..........................20.00
6-10.........................15.00
11-20.........................8.00

Plastic Man
DC, 2004
1-20...........................3.00

Plastic Man
DC, 1988
1-4............................1.00

Plastic Man Lost Annual
DC, 2004
1..............................7.00

Plastic Man Special
DC, 1999
1..............................4.00

Plastron Cafè
Mirage, 1992
1-4............................2.00

Platinum
Komodo
1..............................4.00

Platinum.44
Comax
1..............................3.00

Platinum Grit
Dead Numbat, 1994
1-6............................4.00

Playbear
Fantagraphics, 1995
1-3............................3.00

Playful Little Audrey
Harvey, 1957
1........................... 90.00
2........................... 50.00
3-5......................... 35.00
6-10........................ 24.00
11-21....................... 15.00
22-40....................... 12.00
41-50....................... 10.00
51-60........................ 8.00
61-80........................ 5.00
81-99........................ 3.00
100-103..................... 4.00
104-121..................... 3.00

Playground
Caliber
1............................ 3.00

Playgrounds
Fantagraphics
1............................ 2.00

Pleasure & Passion (Alazar's...)
Brainstorm, 1997
1............................ 3.00

Pleasure Bound
Fantagraphics, 1996
1............................ 3.00

Plop!
DC, 1973
1........................... 18.00
2-3.......................... 8.00
4-5.......................... 7.00
6-10......................... 6.00
11-23........................ 5.00
24........................... 8.00

PMS Book
Ivory Tower
1-1/7th...................... 4.00

Pocahontas (Disney's...)
Marvel, 1995
1............................ 5.00

Pocket Comics
Harvey, 1941
1........................ 1,100.00
2.......................... 775.00
3-4........................ 525.00

Poe
Cheese, 1996
1-11......................... 3.00

Poe
Sirius, 1997
1-Special 1.................. 3.00

Poets Prosper: Rhyme & Revelry
Tome
1............................ 4.00

Pogo Parade
Dell, 1953
1.......................... 275.00

Pogo Possum
Dell, 1949
1.......................... 500.00
2.......................... 400.00
3-5........................ 300.00
6-8........................ 250.00
9-13....................... 200.00
14-16...................... 150.00

Point Blank
WildStorm, 2002
1-5......................... 3.00

Point-Blank
Eclipse
1-2......................... 3.00

Point Pleasant
Ape Entertainment, 2004
1........................... 4.00

Poison Elves: Hyena
Sirius Entertainment, 2004
1-4......................... 3.00

Poison Elves
Mulehide, 1993
8.......................... 15.00
9-10....................... 12.00
11-15...................... 10.00
15/2nd...................... 3.00
16-17....................... 8.00
17/2nd...................... 3.00
18-20....................... 5.00
Deluxe 1................... 35.00

Poison Elves
Sirius, 1995
1........................... 6.00
1/2nd....................... 3.00
2-3......................... 4.00
4-70........................ 3.00
Special 1................... 4.00

Poison Elves: Ventures
Sirius, 2005
1........................... 4.00

Poizon
London Night, 1995
0........................... 3.00
0/Nude...................... 4.00
1/2-1....................... 3.00
1/A........................ 15.00
1/Nude...................... 5.00
2-3......................... 3.00

Pokèmon: The Electric Tale of Pikachu
Viz, 1998
1........................... 4.00
1/2nd-4..................... 3.00

Pokèmon Part 2
Viz, 1999
1-4......................... 3.00

Pokèmon Part 3
Viz, 1999
1-4......................... 4.00

Pokèmon Adventures
Viz, 1999

1-5..6.00

Pokèmon Adventures
Part 2
Viz, 2000

1-6..3.00

Pokèmon Adventures
Part 3
Viz, 2000

1-7..3.00

Pokèmon Adventures
Part 4
Viz, 2001

1-2..3.00
3-4..5.00

Pokèmon Adventures
Part 5
Viz, 2001

1-5..5.00

Pokèmon Adventures
Part 6
Viz, 2001

1-4..5.00

Pokèmon Adventures
Part 7
Viz, 2002

1-5..5.00

Pokèthulhu
Adventure Game
Dork Storm

1..6.00

Police Academy
Marvel, 1989

1-6..1.00

Police Action
Marvel, 1954

1..140.00
2..85.00
3-7..55.00

Police Action
Atlas-Seaboard, 1975

1..11.00
2-3..5.00

Police Against Crime
Premiere, 1954

1..150.00
2..75.00
3-9..50.00

Police Badge #479
Atlas, 1955

5..75.00

Police Comics
Comic Magazines, 1941

Premiering in the fall of 1941, Police Comics featured few police, but lots of crimefighting super-heroes. First and most famous was Plastic Man, who debuted in Police Comics #1. This stretchable super-hero was not only great for visual gag appeal, but would later become the prototype for DC's Elongated Man and Elastic Lad, as well as Marvel's Mister Fantastic (leader of the Fantastic Four). Also appearing in the first issue was future Nazi-fighter Firebrand, the explosive Human Bomb, and the mysterious Phantom Lady (all later members of The Freedom Fighters).

Issue #8 marked the first appearance of the original Manhunter (a police officer turned crimefighter by night, and no relation to the DC character by the same name). He was followed three issues later by The Spirit, who was making the transition from newspaper strips to comic books. Later issues would add teen humor character Candy and others. Beginning with issue #103, they were all dropped and Police Comics became a regular crime comic.

1	6,000.00
2	2,250.00
3	1,700.00
4-5	1,450.00
6-7	1,350.00
8	1,500.00
9-10	1,100.00
11	1,750.00
12-13	985.00
14-20	725.00
21-22	575.00
23-30	500.00
31-40	375.00
41-43	315.00
44-50	260.00
51-60	195.00
61-70	175.00
71-80	160.00
81-93	145.00
94-102	225.00
103	140.00
104-127	110.00

Police Line-Up
Avon, 1951

1..225.00
2..150.00
3-4..115.00

Police Trap
Mainline, 1954

1..165.00
2-4..100.00
5-6..130.00

Polis
Brave New Words

1-2..3.00

Political Action Comics
Comicfix, 2004

1..5.00

Polly and Her Pals
Eternity, 1990

1-5..3.00

Polly and the Pirates
Oni, 2005

1-2..3.00

Polly Pigtails
Parents' Magazine Institute, 1946

1..75.00
2..35.00
3-5..30.00
6-20..25.00
21-30..20.00
31-43..15.00

Ponytail
Dell, 1962

-209..12.00
2-12..8.00

Ponytail
Charlton, 1969

13..6.00
14-20..4.00

Poot
Fantagraphics, 1997

1-3..3.00
4..4.00

Popbot
Idea & Design Works, 2002

1-4..8.00
5-7..10.00

Popcorn!
Discovery

1..4.00

Popcorn Pimps
Fantagraphics, 1996

1..9.00

Popeye
Dell, 1948

E.C. Segar's Popeye the Sailor is one of the classic comics characters of the century and an enduring favorite for more than 70 years. The crusty sailor with the outsized forearms and taste for spinach first appeared in Segar's Thimble Theatre newspaper strip, along with his familiar cast of characters including his sweetheart Olive Oyl, nemesis Bluto, sidekick Wimpy, and many others. Popeye has appeared in comic books since 1937 and his adventures have been carried in titles published by David McKay, Dell, King, Charlton, Gold Key, Whitman, and Ocean. The template for Popeye's success - a goofy blend of humor and adventure, fuelled by unforgettable characters and bizarre dialogue - is almost failure-proof, and comics publishers have used it to delight young fans to the present day.

1	250.00
2	150.00
3-5	125.00
6-10	100.00
11-20	75.00
21-30	60.00
31-50	50.00
51-69	40.00
70-80	30.00
81-92	25.00
93-100	20.00
101-120	15.00
121-138	10.00
139-149	7.00
150-155	5.00
156-157	10.00
158	35.00
159	30.00
162-167	10.00
168-171	18.00
Special 1	2.00

Popeye
(Educational Series)
King, 1972

E 1-E 15	4.00

Popeye
Harvey, 1993

1-Summer 1	2.00

Popeye Special
Ocean, 1987

E. C. Segar's rambunctious, courageous, and gregarious sailor returned to comics in this series from Ocean Comics. A veteran of newspaper comics, animated cartoons in theaters and on television, and of course Robin William's live-action movie, this character is an icon of American humor.

Starting with his origin, (he was born), this title attempted to codify Popeye's life as a series of heroic, (if lighthearted), adventures, rather than simply using the character as a foil for a humorous story. When his mother went to Zaire to introduce the sport of Roller Derby to the natives, Popeye joined the navy. There he met fellow sailors, Wimpy and Brutus and later Brutus' identical twin, Bluto.

The art in this series is unique from other incarnations of the character. Although Popeye still displays the distinctively cartoony features of balloon-like forearms and the double-jaw, the characters are a step removed from the "big-foot" gag style. Ben Dunn, of Warrior Nun Areala fame, Gary Kato who inked Ms. Tree and Superboy's Tom Grummett are some of the artists who contributed to Popeye's decidedly heroic posture.

-- George Haberberger

1-2	2.00

Pop Life
Fantagraphics, 1998

1-2	4.00

Popples
Marvel, 1986

1-4	1.00

Poppo of the
Popcorn Theatre
Fuller, 1955

1	25.00
2	15.00
3-5	12.00
6-13	10.00

Popular Comics
Dell, 1936

1	3,650.00
2	1,285.00
3	1,025.00
4	815.00
5	750.00
6-7	600.00
8-10	565.00
11-15	455.00
16-20	400.00
21-30	345.00
31-40	300.00
41-45	240.00
46	310.00
☛1st Marvel Man	
47-50	240.00
51-60	205.00
61-71	160.00
72-75	140.00
76-78	200.00
79-80	140.00
81-90	130.00
91-100	110.00
101-110	85.00
111	50.00
112-130	80.00
131-145	65.00

Popular Romance
Better, 1949

5	60.00
6-10	40.00
11-21	35.00
22-27	45.00
28-29	35.00

Popular Teenagers
Star, 1950

5	185.00
6-8	170.00
9	110.00
10	105.00
11	85.00
12-13	95.00
14	120.00
15	100.00
16	85.00
17	95.00
18-19	85.00
20-21	95.00
22-23	85.00

Pork Knight: This Little Piggy
Silver Snail, 1986
1 ....2.00

Porky Pig
Dell, 1952
25-30 ....12.00
31-50 ....9.00
51-70 ....7.00
71-81 ....6.00

Porky Pig
Gold Key, 1965
1 ....30.00
2 ....14.00
3-5 ....12.00
6-10 ....8.00
11-20 ....5.00
21-30 ....4.00
31-50 ....3.00
51-109 ....2.00

Pornotopia
Radio, 1999
1 ....3.00

Port
Silverwolf, 1987
1-2 ....2.00

Portable Lowlife
Aeon, 1993
1 ....5.00

Portals of Elondar
Storybook, 1996
1 ....3.00

Portent
Image, 2006
1-4 ....3.00

Portfolios
Delta, 1994
1-3 ....3.00

Portfolios Preview
Delta
Ashcan 1 ....1.00

Portia Prinz of the Glamazons
Eclipse, 1986
1-6 ....2.00

Portrait of a Young Man as a Cartoonist
Hammer & Anvil, 1996
1-8 ....3.00

Possessed
DC, 2003
1-6 ....3.00

Possibleman
Blackthorne, 1987
1-2 ....2.00

Post Apocalypse
Slave Labor, 1994
1 ....3.00

(Post-Atomic) Cyborg Gerbils
Trigon, 1986
1-2 ....3.00

Post Brothers
Rip Off, 1991
19-38 ....3.00

Potential
Slave Labor, 1998
1-2 ....4.00
3 ....5.00
4 ....4.00

Pound
Radio, 2000
1 ....3.00

Pounded
Oni, 2002
1-3 ....3.00

Powder Burn
Antarctic, 1999
1-1/A 3.00
1/CS 6.00

Power
Aircel, 1991
1-4 ....2.00

Power & Glory
Malibu, 1994
1/A-4 ....3.00
WS 1 ....3.00

Power Brigade
Moving Target
1 ....2.00

Power Comics
Holyoke, 1944
1 ....1,500.00
2-4 ....1,250.00

Power Comics
Power, 1977
1-5 ....2.00

Power Comics
Eclipse, 1988
1-4 ....2.00

Power Company
DC, 2002
1-18 ....3.00

Power Company, The: Bork
DC, 2002
1 ....3.00

Power Company, The: Josiah Power
DC, 2002
1 ....3.00

Power Company, The: Manhunter
DC, 2002

On the trail of a stolen shipment of plutonium, Nightwing follows Kirk DePaul, a mercenary and trafficker in stolen goods. DePaul's reputation paints him as an amoral opportunist selling his services to the highest bidder. He also has excellent hand-to-hand fighting skills -- as Nightwing discovers, when DePaul evades his surveillance and confronts him. Aside from his name, DePaul's style is eerily similar to that of Paul Kirk, known as The Manhunter, who died defeating The Council in Detective Comics #443. However, The Council cloned Kirk many times to assemble a cadre of superior warriors. DePaul is one of those clones and, given his genetic source, he may be more than a simple mercenary.

Manhunter was one of seven one-shot books that served to introduce each member of Kurt Busiek's new series, The Power Company. The Power Company is a super-hero group that is incorporated like a law firm, taking some jobs on a for-profit basis and others as pro bono work.

-- George Haberberger

1 ....3.00

Power Company, The: Sapphire
DC, 2002
1 ....3.00

Power Company, The: Skyrocket
DC, 2002
1 ....3.00

Power Company, The: Striker Z
DC, 2002
1 ....3.00

Power Company, The: Witchfire
DC, 2002
1 ....3.00

Power Defense
Miller
1 ....3.00

Power Factor
Wonder, 1986
1-2 ....2.00

Power Factor
Innovation, 1990
1-3 ....2.00
Special 1 ....3.00

Power Girl
DC, 1988
1-4 ....1.00

Powerhouse Pepper Comics
Timely, 1943
1 ....1,025.00
2 ....525.00
3-4 ....485.00
5 ....570.00

Powerless
Marvel, 2004
1-6 ....3.00

Power Line
Marvel, 1988

The Shadow Dwellers were a race that lived alongside ours, but which evolved far more quickly. They were more than human, with powers and lifespans far beyond ours. But we outnumbered them, and they took to living a secret existence in the shadows. They blended into our society -- but never forgot who they really were.

Power Line is the story of three of these Shadow Dwellers: Victor, whose family had been feuding for centuries with the Ravenscores -- and who had seen his family slaughtered just as they tried for peace; Lenore, who used her powers to flee an arranged marriage with one of the Ravenscores; and Ripper, a former wrestler who lost a hand helping Lenore escape. These three fled to New York together, but there is no escape from their true heritage.

The Shadow Line Saga includes the stories of Power Line, Doctor Zero, and St. George.

1-8 .... 2.00

Power Lords
DC, 1983
1-3 .... 1.00

Power Man & Iron Fist
Marvel, 1974
17 .... 8.00
18-20 .... 5.00
21-30 .... 4.00
30/30¢ 20.00
31 .... 4.00
31/30¢ 20.00
32 .... 3.00
32/30¢ 20.00
33 .... 3.00
33/30¢ 20.00
34 .... 3.00
34/30¢ 20.00
35-44 .... 3.00
44/35¢ 15.00
45 .... 3.00
45/35¢ 15.00
46 .... 3.00
46/35¢ 15.00
47-47/Whitman 3.00
47/35¢ 15.00
48 .... 10.00
49-50 .... 6.00
51-52 .... 3.00
53-55 .... 4.00
56 .... 3.00
57 .... 12.00
58-65 .... 3.00
66 .... 20.00
☞2nd Sabretooth
67-77 .... 2.00
78 .... 5.00
79-83 .... 2.00
84 .... 6.00
☞Sabretooth app.
85-125 .... 2.00
Ann 1 .... 4.00

Power of Prime
Malibu, 1995
1-4 .... 3.00

Power of Shazam
DC, 1994
1 .... 3.00
2-42 .... 2.00
43-47 .... 3.00
1000000 .... 4.00
Ann 1 .... 3.00

Power of Strong Man
AC
1 .... 3.00

Power of the Atom
DC, 1988
1-18 .... 1.00

Power Pachyderms
Marvel, 1989
1 .... 1.00

Power Pack
Marvel, 1984
1-2 .... 2.00
3-9 .... 1.00
10 .... 2.00
11-18 .... 1.00
19 .... 2.00
20-26 .... 1.00
27 .... 4.00
28-43 .... 1.00
44-62 .... 2.00
Holiday 1 .... 3.00

Power Pack
Marvel, 2000
1-4 .... 3.00

Power Pack
Marvel, 2005
1-4 .... 3.00

Power Plays
Millennium, 1995
1 .... 3.00

Power Plays
AC, 1985
1-2 .... 2.00

Power Plays
Extrava-Gandt
1-3 .... 2.00

Powerpuff Girls
DC, 2000
1 .... 5.00
2-3 .... 3.00
4-70 .... 2.00

Powerpuff Girls Double Whammy
DC, 2000
1 .... 5.00

Power Rangers Turbo: Into the Fire
Acclaim

This unusually sized book, (similar to children's storybooks) has a heavy card-stock cover featuring yet another iteration of the Power Rangers; this time Power Rangers Turbo. Rather than controlling fighting machines patterned after dinosaurs, these heroes use turbozord power to channel souped-up sports utility vehicles, reflecting this fad's everlasting demand to stay topical.

This title from Acclaim's Young Readers sub-imprint also contained the adventures of the Masked Rider and the funny animal strip, Samurai Pizza Cats.

1 ....5.00

Power Rangers Zeo
Image, 1996
1-2..3.00

Powers
Image, 2000
1..7.00
2..6.00
3..5.00
4-10...4.00
11-37.......................................3.00
Ann 1.....................................4.00

Powers Coloring/ Activity Book
Image, 2001
1...2.00

Powers
Marvel, 2004
1-11...3.00
12/Bendis...............................4.00
12/Oeming-21 ....3.00

Powers That Be
Broadway, 1995
1...2.00
2..3.00
2/Ashcan 1.00
3..3.00
3/Ashcan 1.00
4-9..3.00

Prairie Moon and Other Stories
Dark Horse
1 .... 2.00

Preacher
DC, 1995
1 .... 13.00
2... 6.00
3-5.. 5.00
6-10.. 4.00
11-49...................................... 3.00
50-66...................................... 4.00

Preacher Special: Cassidy: Blood & Whiskey
DC, 1998
1 .... 6.00

Preacher Special: One Man's War
DC, 1998
1 .... 5.00

Preacher Special: Saint of Killers
DC, 1996
1-4... 3.00

Preacher Special: Tall in the Saddle
DC, 2000
1 .... 5.00

Preacher Special: The Good Old Boys
DC, 1997
1 .... 5.00

Preacher Special: The Story of You-Know-Who
DC, 1996
1 .... 5.00

Precious Metal
Arts Industria, 1990
1 .... 3.00

Predator
Dark Horse, 1989
1... 5.00
1/2nd 3.00
2... 4.00
3-4.. 3.00

Predator 2
Dark Horse, 1991
1-2... 3.00

Predator: Bad Blood
Dark Horse, 1993
1-4... 3.00

Predator: Big Game
Dark Horse, 1991
1-4... 3.00

Predator: Captive
Dark Horse, 1998
1 .... 3.00

Predator: Cold War
Dark Horse, 1991
1-4 .... 3.00

Predator: Dark River
Dark Horse, 1996
1-4 .... 3.00

Predator: Hell & Hot Water
Dark Horse, 1997
1-3 .... 3.00

Predator: Hell Come a Walkin'
Dark Horse, 1998
1-2 .... 3.00

Predator: Homeworld
Dark Horse, 1999
1-4 .... 3.00

Predator: Invaders from the Fourth Dimension
Dark Horse, 1994
1 .... 4.00

Predator: Jungle Tales
Dark Horse, 1995
1 .... 3.00

Predator: Kindred
Dark Horse, 1996
1-4 .... 3.00

Predator: Nemesis
Dark Horse, 1997
1-2 .... 3.00

Predator: Primal
Dark Horse, 1997
1-2 .... 3.00

Predator: Race War
Dark Horse, 1993
0-4 .... 3.00

Predator: Strange Roux
Dark Horse, 1996
1 .... 3.00

Predator: The Bloody Sands of Time
Dark Horse, 1992
1-2 .... 3.00

Predator versus Judge Dredd
Dark Horse, 1997
1-3 .... 3.00

Predator vs. Magnus Robot Fighter
Dark Horse, 1992
1 .... 3.00
1/Platinum 10.00
2 .... 3.00

Predator: Xenogenesis
Dark Horse, 1999
1-4 .... 3.00

Prelude to Blue Dog
Ground Zero, 1996
1 ....4.00

Premiere
Diversity
1 ....3.00
1/Gold 4.00
1/Ltd.-2 ....3.00

Preservation of Obscurity
Lump of Squid
1-2 ....3.00

President Dad
Tokyopop, 2004
1-4 ....10.00

Pressed Tongue (Dave Cooper's...)
Fantagraphics, 1994
1-3 ....3.00

Presto Kid
AC
1 ....3.00

Pretear
ADV Manga, 2004
1-4 ....10.00

Pre-Teen Dirty-Gene Kung-Fu Kangaroos
Blackthorne, 1986
1-3 ....2.00

Prey
Monster
1-3 ....2.00

Prey for Us Sinners
Fantaco
1 ....5.00

Prez
DC, 1973

This campy commentary on early Seventies events and culture, written by Joe Simon, imagines a U.S. with a teen-age president elected, as a result of lowering the voting age to 18, in 1971. Evil anti-environmental businessman, Mr. Smiley, sees in the youth vote a chance to sponsor and influence a malleable young candidate. He quickly finds Prez who wins a place in the U.S. Senate together with several other young youth-elected senators. In short time, the senators lower the required age of the president from 35 to 18. Prez, running on the new Flower Party ticket, sweeps the youth vote and becomes the first teen-age president.

By this time, Prez, through the help of American Indian chief, Eagle Free, has seen through Mr. Smiley's machinations. He sets up a young, multi-cultural cabinet and sets about making historic achievements during his time in office. Mr. Smiley is no longer smiling though, and Prez faces more challenges than simple inexperience...

1 .... 12.00
2 .... 6.00
3-4 .... 5.00

Pride & Joy
DC, 1997
1-4 .... 3.00

Pride of the Yankees
Magazine Enterprises, 1949
1 .... 450.00

Priest
Maximum, 1996
1-3 .... 3.00

Primal
Dark Horse, 1992
1-2 .... 3.00

Primal Force
DC, 1994
0-14 .... 2.00

Primal Rage
Sirius, 1996
1-4 .... 3.00

Prime
Malibu, 1993
1/2-1 .... 3.00
1/Hologram............................ 5.00
1/Ltd. 3.00
2-11 .... 2.00
12 .... 4.00
13-26 .... 2.00
Ann 1 .... 4.00
Ashcan 1 .... 1.00

Prime
Malibu, 1995
0-15 .... 2.00

Prime 8 Creation
Two Morrows, 2001
1 .... 4.00

Prime/Captain America
Malibu, 1996
1 .... 4.00

Prime Cuts
Fantagraphics, 1987
1-10 .... 4.00

Prime Cuts (Mike Deodato's...)
Caliber
1 .... 3.00

Primer
Comico, 1982

During the early 1980s, when comics companies were sprouting with a renewed vitality, one of those companies produced a series to give amateurs a chance to break into the business. That company was Comico, the outfit that first published Elementals and Mage. The aptly named Primer was a series much like DC's New Talent Showcase and featured an eclectic mix of super-hero, science-fiction, fantasy, and humor stories.

Primer's most notable achievements include its introduction of Matt Wagner's Grendel in #2 and the first appearance of warrior-nun Evangeline in #6. Sam Kieth, later of Wolverine and The Maxx, got his professional start in comics in a feature in Primer #5.
-- George Haberberger

1 .... 5.00
2 .... 55.00
☛1st Grendel
3-4 .... 4.00
5 .... 50.00
☛1st Sam Kieth art
6 .... 5.00

Primer
Comico, 1996
1 .... 3.00

Prime Slime Tales
Mirage, 1986
1-4 ....2.00

Prime vs. the Incredible Hulk
Malibu, 1995
0 ....5.00

Primitives
Sparetime, 1995
1-3 ....3.00

Primortals (Vol. 1) (Leonard Nimoy's...)
Tekno, 1995
1-16 ....2.00

Primortals (Vol. 2) (Leonard Nimoy's...)
Big, 1996
0-8 ....2.00

Primortals Origins (Leonard Nimoy's...)
Tekno, 1995
1-2 ....2.00

Primus
Charlton, 1972
1 ....7.00
2-4 ....4.00
5-7 ....3.00

Prince: Alter Ego
Piranha Music, 1991
1 ....2.00

Prince and the New Power Generation: Three Chains of Gold
DC
1 ....4.00

Prince and the Pauper
Dell, 1962
1 ....15.00

Prince and the Pauper (Disney's...)
Disney
1 ....6.00

Prince Namor, the Sub-Mariner
Marvel, 1984
1-4 ....2.00

Prince Nightmare
Aaaargh!
1 ....3.00

Princess and the Frog
NBM
1 ....16.00

Princess Karanam and the Djinn of the Green Jug
Mu
1 .... 3.00

Princess Natasha
DC, 2006
1-3 .... 2.00

Princess Prince
CPM Manga, 2000
1-10 .... 3.00

Princess Sally
Archie, 1995
1-3 .... 2.00

Princess Tutu
ADV Manga, 2005
1-2 .... 10.00

Prince Valiant
Marvel, 1994
1-4 .... 4.00

Prince Valiant Monthly
Pioneer
1-4 .... 5.00

Prince Vandal
Triumphant, 1993
1-6 .... 3.00

Priority: White Heat
AC, 1987
1-2 .... 2.00

Prison Break
Realistic Comics, 1951
1 .... 250.00
2 .... 175.00
3 .... 145.00
4-5 .... 125.00

Prisoner
DC, 1988
1-4 .... 4.00

Prisoner of Chillon
Tome
1 .... 3.00

Prisonopolis
Mediawarp, 1997
1-4 .... 3.00

Prison Riot
Avon, 1952
1 .... 200.00

Private Beach: Fun and Perils in the Trudyverse
Antarctic, 1995
1-3 .... 3.00

Private Commissions (Gray Morrow's...)
Forbidden Fruit, 1992
1-2 .... 3.00

Privateers
Vanguard, 1987
1-2 .... 2.00

Private Eye
Atlas, 1951
1 .... 150.00
2-3 .... 90.00
4-8 .... 70.00

Private Eyes
Eternity, 1988
1-3 .... 2.00
4 .... 3.00
5-6 .... 4.00

Prize Comics
Feature, 1940

Prize Comics was the flagship title of Prize Publications during the Golden Age. It featured the usual anthology of super-heroes, adventure strips, jungle action stories, aviation and spy tales, and humor. The main hero features of the book were The Black Owl, later succeeded by his sons, Yank and Doodle, and The Green Lama, who made his first appearance in Prize Comics #7. One of the best loved and remembered characters from the pages of Prize was Frankenstein, a goofy-humor version of Dr. Frankenstein's famous monster, but capable of a wide and powerful storytelling range. The artwork and stories improved steadily, and Prize often featured art that was a step above the crude work of many of the lesser Golden Age publishers. In 1948, Prize became Prize Western Comics and turned to adaptations of movie Westerns, including Streets of Laredo, Roughshod, and Gunsmoke Justice.

1 .... 1,700.00
2 .... 825.00
3-5 .... 625.00
6 .... 545.00
7 .... 1,200.00
8-9 .... 600.00
10-12 .... 510.00

13	550.00
14-20	445.00
21-24	345.00
25-30	280.00
31-35	215.00
36-40	160.00
41-45	130.00
46-50	105.00
51-60	78.00
61-68	62.00

Prize Comics Western
Feature, 1948

69	100.00
70-90	90.00
91-112	80.00
113	125.00
114-119	80.00

Prize Mystery
Key, 1955

1	75.00
2-3	50.00

Pro
Image, 2002

1 ....6.00

Pro Action Magazine
Marvel, 1994

1-3 ....3.00

Probe
Imperial

1-3 ....2.00

Prof. Coffin
Charlton, 1985

19-21 ....2.00

Professional, The: Golgo 13
Viz

1-3 ....5.00

Professor Om
Innovation, 1990

1 ....3.00

Professor Xavier and the X-Men
Marvel, 1995

1-3	2.00
4-18	1.00

Profolio
Alchemy, 1989

1	2.00
2-3	3.00

Profolio
Alchemy

1 ....6.00

Progeny
Caliber

1 ....5.00

Program Error: Battlebot
Phantasy

1 ....2.00

Project
DC, 1997

1-2 .... 6.00

Project A-Ko
Malibu, 1994

This humorous super-hero title was adapted from a series of anime films by Tim Eldred, with illustrations by The Tick's Ben Dunn.

A-Ko Megumi is a redheaded schoolgirl with super-human powers. These come in handy when she oversleeps and needs to zoom into class at Graviton High School for the start of the new year's classes. Her best friend is C-Ko Kotobuki, a little blonde girl with an uncanny knack for pouting, crying, and charming the socks off anyone she encounters. C-Ko is completely devoted to A-Ko and, unfortunately, insists on making A-Ko lunch every day -- although her cooking skills leave much to be desired. B-Ko is the blue-headed rich girl who secretly vies for C-Ko's affections. To impress the C-Ko, she arranges to "save" her from an increasingly silly variety of thugs, robots, and death machines, ultimately taking on the powers of a super-hero herself.

1-4 .... 3.00

Project A-Ko 2
CPM, 1995

1-3 .... 3.00

Project A-Ko versus
CPM, 1995

1-5 .... 3.00

Project Arms
Viz, 2002

1-5 .... 3.00

Project: Dark Matter
Dimm Comics, 1996

1-4 .... 3.00

Project: Generation
Truth, 2000

1-2 .... 1.00

Project: Hero
Vanguard, 1987

1-2 .... 2.00

Project Sex
Fantagraphics, 1991

1 .... 3.00

Project: Superior
Adhouse Books, 2005

1 .... 20.00

Project X
Kitchen Sink

1 .... 3.00

Promethea
DC, 1999

1	6.00
☞Alan Moore series	
1/Variant	7.00
2	4.00
3-22	3.00
23	4.00
24-31	3.00
32	4.00
32/Ltd	125.00

Prometheus' Gift
Cat-Head

1 .... 2.00

Prometheus (Villains)
DC, 1998

1 .... 2.00

Promise
Viz

1 .... 6.00

Propellerman
Dark Horse, 1993

1-8 .... 3.00

Prophecy of the Soul Sorcerer
Arcane, 1998

1-3	3.00
Ashcan 1	2.00

Prophecy of the Soul Sorcerer Preview Issue
Arcane

1 .... 2.00

Prophecy of the Soul Sorcerer
Arcane, 2000

1-3 .... 3.00

Prophet
Image, 1993

0-10 .... 3.00

Prophet
Image, 1995

1	4.00
1/Chromium	5.00

Psi-Judge Anderson
Fleetway-Quality

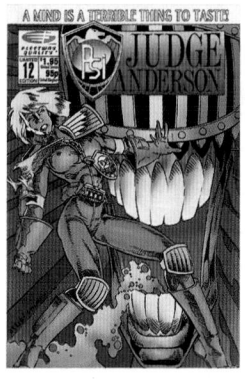

The Judges are the police force of the future. With crime running rampant in the mega-cities, these hard-nosed cops don't have time to fool around when it comes to enforcing the law.

But, whereas other Judges use a draconian approach, Judge Anderson of the Psi Division is (slightly) more subtle. Hers is the power to read minds, which she uses to help convict lowlifes-sometimes because they're just thinking about committing a crime. Unfortunately, this power also has a downside, making her more sensitive to psychic forces. So, when a group of dark Judges from a dead world decides that life itself is a crime, they are able to use her as part of a plan to enter our world.

Reprinted from Britain's 2000 A.D., Psi-Judge Anderson is an action-packed adventure in the tradition of Judge Dredd.

Psi-Lords
Valiant, 1994

Their race's proper name is Starwatchers, but they are more commonly known as the "Psi-Lords," short for "Psionic Overlords." They are a breed that is kept alive and given great powers by molecular machines ("molmechs") in their blood. Indeed, they do not die of old age, a fact that sets them apart from the "temps" (humans) around them, in profound ways.

Starwatchers are capable of using their molecular machines to perform miracles, such as building a space station out of an asteroid belt in six hours. They have also offered their services as peacekeepers to the universe, but it's been more than 14 years since their offers of assistance have been accepted. Somehow, the world doesn't seem to trust its new guardian angels. But when the moon Titan discovers an infestation of Spider Aliens, they turn to the Starwatchers for help. Soon the world will discover whether the Starwatchers are truly friends.

1	4.00
1/VVSS	70.00
1/Gold	20.00
2-4	1.00
5-8	2.00
9	3.00
10	5.00

PS238
Dork Storm, 2002
0-9	3.00

Psyba-Rats
DC, 1995
1-3	3.00

Psychic Academy
Tokyopop, 2004
1-10	10.00

Psycho
DC, 1991
1-3	5.00

Psycho
(Alfred Hitchcock's...)
Innovation
1-3	3.00

Psychoanalysis
E.C., 1955

There were six E.C. titles in its "New Direction," cover-bannered as "an entirely novel and unique reading experience." The cover of each had a frame with the title on top and an identifying icon down the left side. The "New Direction" was one designed to accommodate the Comics Magazine of America's new Comics Code, though the first issue of each did not carry the Code stamp, and all but one lasted for five issues. The six titles were: Aces High, Extra!, Impact, MD, Valor --

and Psychoanalysis, the title that lasted only four issues.

Above Psychoanalysis' title was the line "People Searching for Peace of Mind through ..." and the stories -- all drawn by Jack Kamen -- followed the psychoanalysis, by the same analyst, of Freddy Carter, Ellen Lyman, and Mark Stone. All were cured by series' end. (Whew!)

-- *Maggie*

1	100.00
2-4	85.00

Psychoanalysis
Gemstone, 1999
1-4	3.00
Ann 1	11.00

Psychoblast
First, 1987
1-9	2.00

Psycho Killers
Comic Zone, 1992
1	4.00
1/2nd	3.00
2	4.00
2/2nd	3.00
3	4.00
3/2nd-10	3.00
11	4.00
12-15	3.00

Psycho Killers
PMS Special
Zone, 1993
1	3.00

Psycho (Magazine)
Skywald, 1971
1	20.00
2	12.00
3	10.00
4-10	8.00
11-20	6.00
21-24	5.00
Anl 1972-Anl 1974	5.00

Psychoman
Revolutionary, 1992
1	3.00

Psychonaut
Fantagraphics, 1996
1-3	4.00

Psychonauts
Marvel, 1993
1-4	5.00

Psycho-Path
Venusian, 1990
1-2	2.00

Psycho-Path
The Ultimate Vigilante
Greater Mercury, 1990
1	2.00

Psychotic Adventures
Illustrated
Last Gasp, 1972
1-3	3.00

Psy-Comm
Tokyopop, 2005
1	10.00

Psyence Fiction
Abaculus, 1998

The Psyence Agency, based in Chicago, combines supernatural practices with scientific technology to combat a variety of unexplained phenomenon. The group's field agents are an odd mix of individuals, with a wide array of powers and abilities. In many ways, they are each as much a mystery as their assignments. The beautiful Bianca combines CIA training with a hereditary and powerful cosmic force. Mark Blood is a hard-nosed bounty hunter, as well as a vampire. The volatile man called Rice is a talented marksman, and quite possibly a highly advanced cyborg. The new kid on the block, Gabriel, uses his seemingly normal facade to hide his true demonic nature.

All of these very different, and very dangerous, individuals need to learn to work together quickly, before they are overwhelmed by the mystical forces of evil they seek to defeat.

1/2	1.00
1	3.00

Psylocke & Archangel:
Crimson Dawn
Marvel, 1997
1-4	3.00

PT 109
K.K., 1964
1	12.00

Pteranoman
Kitchen Sink, 1990
1 ....2.00

Public Enemies
D.S., 1948
1 ....115.00
2 ....100.00
3-5..65.00
6-7..55.00

Public Enemies
Eternity
1-2..4.00

Pubo
Dark Horse, 2002
1-3..4.00

Pudgy Pig
Charlton, 1958
1-2..20.00

Puffed
Image, 2003
1-3..3.00

Puke & Explode
Northstar, 1990
1-2..3.00

Pulp (Vol. 1)
Viz, 1997
1 ....6.00

Pulp (Vol. 2)
Viz, 1998
1-12..6.00

Pulp (Vol. 3)
Viz, 1999
1-12..6.00

Pulp (Vol. 4)
Viz, 2000
1-6..6.00

Pulp (Vol. 5)
Viz, 2001
1-12..6.00

Pulp (Vol. 6)
Viz
1-8..6.00

Pulp Action
Avalon
1-8..3.00

Pulp Dreams
Fantagraphics, 1991
1 ....3.00

Pulp Fantastic
DC, 2000
1-3..3.00

Pulp Fiction
A List, 1997

As the medium of comic books enters its seventh decade, the copyrights on some of the earliest material produced by defunct publishers of the 1930s are slipping into public domain, along with the lurid stories that first saw press in the pulp magazines of the same era. A-List Comics has gathered a treasure trove of such material in its lineup of black-and-white reprint books, including Pulp Fiction. On one hand, readers get to enjoy episodes of "Hawk (of the Seas)" from the early issues of Jumbo Comics; some of the first work by comics pioneer Will Eisner (a.k.a. "Willis Rensie"); an extremely rare, early horror tale by Jack Kirby; single-page gag strips by Batman creator, Bob Kane; and vintage stories from the pulps. However, this enjoyment is tempered by the realization that the creators, some of whom are still alive or survived by their estates, will receive no benefit from these reprints.

-- Rob Salkowitz

1-6 .... 3.00

Pulp Western
Avalon
1 .... 3.00

Pulse
Blackjack, 1997
1 .... 2.00

Pulse
Marvel, 2004
1 .... 5.00
2-4 .... 3.00
5 .... 2.00
6-9 .... 3.00
10 .... 6.00
☞House of M
10/Variant............................. 4.00

☞2nd print
11-14 .... 3.00

Pulse: House of M Special Edition
Marvel, 2005
1 .... 1.00

Puma Blues
Aardvark One, 1986
1-23 .... 2.00

Pummeler
Parody, 1992
1 .... 3.00

Pummeler $2099
Parody
1 .... 3.00

Pumpkinhead: The Rites of Exorcism
Dark Horse, 1992
1-4 .... 3.00

Punch & Judy (Vol. 1)
Hillman, 1944
1 .... 125.00
2 .... 70.00
3-12 .... 60.00

Punch & Judy (Vol. 2)
Hillman, 1949
1 .... 40.00
2 .... 125.00
3-9 .... 40.00
10-12 .... 125.00

Punch & Judy (Vol. 3)
Hillman, 1951
1 .... 125.00
2 .... 115.00
3-9 .... 40.00

Punch Comics
Harry A. Chesler, 1941
1 .... 800.00
2 .... 525.00
9 .... 500.00
10 .... 380.00
11 .... 340.00
12 .... 400.00
13 .... 380.00
14-15 .... 330.00
16-17 .... 310.00
18 .... 400.00
19 .... 330.00
20 .... 600.00
21 .... 330.00
22-23 .... 150.00

Punisher
Marvel, 1986
1 .... 13.00
2-3 .... 7.00
4-5 .... 6.00

Punisher
Marvel, 1987

1	7.00
2-3	4.00
4-9	3.00
10	4.00
11-62	2.00
63-74	1.00
75	3.00
76-80	2.00
81-85	1.00
86	3.00
87-90	1.00
91-99	2.00
100	3.00
100/Variant-101	4.00
102-104	2.00
Ann 1	4.00
Ann 2-3	3.00
Ann 4-5	2.00
Ann 6-7	3.00

Punisher
Marvel, 1995

1	3.00
2-18	2.00

Punisher
Marvel, 1998

1	3.00
1/Variant	6.00
2-4	3.00

Punisher
Marvel, 2000

1	4.00
1/Variant	9.00
2	4.00
2/Variant	6.00
3	4.00
4-12	3.00

Punisher
Marvel, 2001

1-37	3.00

Punisher
Marvel, 2004

1	5.00
2	4.00
3-60	3.00

Punisher, The:
A Man Named Frank
Marvel, 1994

1	7.00

Punisher
Anniversary Magazine
Marvel

1	5.00

Punisher Armory
Marvel, 1990

1-10	2.00

Punisher
Back to School Special
Marvel, 1992

1	4.00
2-3	3.00

Punisher/
Batman: Deadly Knights
Marvel, 1994

1	5.00

Punisher/Black Widow:
Spinning
Doomsday's Web
Marvel

1	10.00

Punisher: Bloodlines
Marvel, 1991

1	6.00

Punisher, The:
Blood on the Moors
Marvel

1	17.00

Punisher:
Bloody Valentine
Marvel, 2006

1	4.00

Punisher:
Die Hard in the Big Easy
Marvel, 1992

1	5.00

Punisher, The:
Empty Quarter
Marvel, 1994

1	7.00

Punisher: G-Force
Marvel, 1992

1	5.00

Punisher Holiday Special
Marvel, 1993

1-3	3.00

Punisher Invades the
'Nam: Final Invasion
Marvel, 1994

1	7.00

Punisher Kills the
Marvel Universe
Marvel, 1995

1	20.00
1/2nd	6.00

Punisher, The:
Kingdom Gone
Marvel, 1990

1	17.00

Punisher Magazine
Marvel, 1989

1-16	3.00

Punisher Meets Archie
Marvel, 1994

1	4.00
1/Variant	5.00

Punisher Movie Special
Marvel, 1990

1	6.00

Punisher, The:
No Escape
Marvel, 1990

1	5.00

Punisher, The: Official
Movie Adaptation
Marvel, 2004

1-3	3.00

Punisher, The:
Origin of Micro Chip
Marvel, 1993

1-2	2.00

Punisher/Painkiller Jane
Marvel, 2001

1	4.00

Punisher: P.O.V.
Marvel, 1991

1-4	5.00

Punisher: Red X-Mas
Marvel, 2004

1	4.00

Punisher: Silent Night
Marvel, 2006

1	4.00

Punisher
Summer Special
Marvel, 1991

1-4	3.00

Punisher: The Cell
Marvel, 2005

1	5.00

Punisher, The: The End
Marvel, 2004

1	5.00

Punisher:
The Ghosts of Innocents
Marvel, 1993

1-2	6.00

Punisher: The Movie
Marvel, 2004

1-3	3.00

Punisher: The Prize
Marvel, 1990
1 ....5.00

Punisher: The Tyger
Marvel, 2006
1 ....5.00

Punisher 2099
Marvel, 1993
1 ....2.00
2-15...1.00
16-25...2.00
25/Variant.....................................3.00
26-34...2.00

Punisher Vs Bullseye
Marvel, 2006
1-5..3.00

Punisher vs. Daredevil
Marvel, 2000
1 ....4.00

Punisher War Journal
Marvel, 1988
1 ....5.00
2-7..3.00
8-49..2.00
50..3.00
51-60...2.00
61..3.00
62-64/Variant.................................2.00
65..3.00
66-74...2.00
75..4.00
76..3.00
77-80...2.00

Punisher War Journal
Marvel, 2006
1-5..3.00
6..6.00
7..3.00

Punisher War Zone
Marvel, 1992
1 ....3.00
2-22..2.00
23..3.00
24-41...2.00
Ann 1-2 ....3.00

Punisher/ Wolverine African Saga
Marvel, 1988
1 ....6.00

Punisher X-Mas Special
Marvel, 2007
1 ....4.00

Punisher, The: Year One
Marvel, 1994
1-4..3.00

Punx
Acclaim, 1995
1-3 .... 3.00

Punx (Manga) Special
Acclaim, 1996
1 .... 3.00

Puppet Comics
George W. Dougherty, 1946
1-2... 75.00

Puppet Master
Eternity
1-4 .... 3.00

Puppet Master: Children of the Puppet Master
Eternity, 1991
1-2... 3.00

Puppetoons (George Pal's ...)
Fawcett, 1945
1 .... 300.00
2 .... 150.00
3-19 .... 100.00

Puppy Action!
Northstar
1 .... 3.00

Puppy in My Pocket
Burghley
1-35.. 3.00

Pure Images
Pure Imagination, 1990
1-4.. 3.00

Purgatori
Chaos!, 1998
1/2-Ashcan 1 .... 3.00

Purgatori
Devil's Due, 2000
1-6.. 3.00

Purgatori: Empire
Chaos, 2000
1-3.. 3.00

Purgatori: Goddess Rising
Chaos!, 1999
1-4.. 3.00

Purgatori: The Dracula Gambit
Chaos!, 1997
1-1/Variant............................. 3.00

Purgatori: The Dracula Gambit Sketchbook
Chaos!, 1997
1 .... 3.00

Purgatori: The Vampires Myth
Chaos!, 1996
-1 .... 2.00
1 .... 4.00
1/Ltd. 5.00
1/Variant 8.00
2-6 .... 3.00

Purgatori Vs. Vampirella
Chaos, 2000
nn 3.00

Purgatory USA
Slave Labor, 1989
1 .... 2.00

Purge
Ania, 1993
0-1 .... 2.00

Purge
Amara
0 .... 2.00

Purple Claw
Toby, 1953
1 .... 175.00
2-3 .... 125.00

Purple Claw Mysteries
AC
1 .... 3.00

Purple Hood
John Spencer & Co.
1-2 .... 5.00

Purr
Blue Eyed Dog
1 .... 8.00

Pussycat
Marvel, 1968
1 .... 150.00

PvP
Dork Storm, 2001
1 .... 3.00

PvP
Image, 2003
1 .... 5.00
2-19 .... 3.00

PvP
Image, 2005
0 .... 1.00

20-293.00

Pyrite
Samson
1 .... 1.00

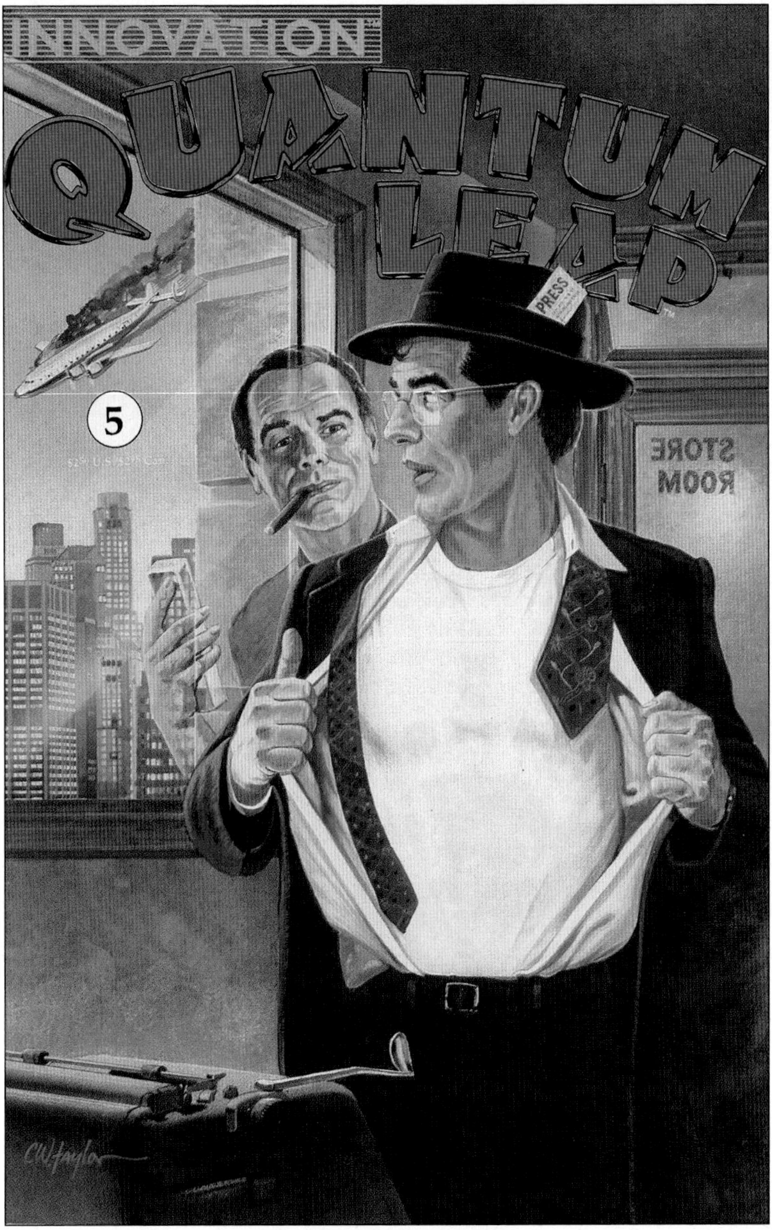

Based on the NBC science-fiction series, Dr. Sam Beckett's
time-travel adventures included a leap into a newspaper reporter.

method of time travel, with Beckett theorizing that time travel might be possible within the span of one's own lifetime. The project was under the threat of losing its funding unless it showed quick results. In desperation, Beckett risked all and stepped into the untested time travel apparatus.

As it turned out, Beckett was right - but not in the way he expected. He now "leaps" randomly in time, winding up in the bodies of different people at various times throughout the last half-century. Beckett must help these people overcome some life difficulty before an unknown force causes him to leap into a different time, place, and identity. His only help in his travels is Al, the project observer who appears as a computer-generated hologram. Somehow, Al must aid Beckett in finding his way back to his own time.

Q-Loc
Chiasmus, 1994

1 .... 3.00

Quack!
Star*Reach, 1976

An anthology from Star*Reach, Quack represents an early attempt to break independent comics creators into the comics-shop scene. Issues #3-5 notably feature The Beavers, a humor strip by Dave Sim, who would later go on to create the long-running Cerebus the Aardvark for Aardvark-Vanaheim.

Other creators contributing to the series include Mad cartoonist (and later Groo creator) Sergio Aragones, Michael T. Gilbert, Steve Leialoha, Scott Shaw! (still spelled with an exclamation point), and Dave Stevens, who would go on to create The Rocketeer.

1-6 .... 3.00

Quadrant
Quadrant, 1983

1-8 .... 2.00

Quadro Gang
Nonsense Unlimited

1 .... 1.00

Quagmire
Kitchen Sink, 1970

1 .... 3.00

Quagmire U.S.A.
Antarctic, 1994

1-3 .... 3.00

Quagmire U.S.A.
Antarctic, 2004

1-5 .... 3.00

Quality Special
Fleetway-Quality

1-2 .... 2.00

Quantum & Woody
Acclaim, 1997

0-17 .... 3.00
Ashcan 1 .... 1.00

Quantum Creep
Parody, 1992

1 .... 3.00

Quantum Leap
Innovation, 1991

Quantum Leap was a popular television show of the early '90s. It starred Dr. Sam Beckett, head of Project Quantum Leap. The goal of the project was to produce a

1 .... 5.00
2-5 .... 4.00
6-13 .... 3.00
Ann 1 .... 4.00
Special 1 .... 5.00

Quantum: Rock of Ages
Dreamchilde Press, 2003

1-4 .... 3.00

Quasar
Marvel, 1989

1 .... 2.00
2-46 .... 1.00
47 .... 2.00
☛1st Thunderstrike
48-49 .... 1.00
50 .... 3.00
51-60 .... 1.00
Special 1-3 .... 2.00

Queen & Country
Oni, 2001

1 .... 9.00
1/FCBD 1.00
2 .... 7.00
3 .... 6.00
4-15 .... 5.00
16-20 .... 4.00
21-24 .... 3.00
25 .... 6.00
26-28 .... 3.00

Queen & Country: Declassified
Oni, 2002

1-3 .... 3.00

Queen & Country: Declassified
Oni, 2005

1 .... 3.00

Queen & Country: Declassified
Oni, 2005
1-3 ....3.00

Queen of the Damned (Anne Rice's...)
Innovation, 1991
1-12 ....3.00

Queen of the West, Dale Evans
Dell, 1954

Perhaps best-known as the wife of King of the Cowboys, Roy Rogers, Dale Evans has had two comics series in her career, one from DC and this slightly longer one from Dell.

Begun in 1953 with appearances in Dell Four Color, Evans' adventures were set in a more modern West, where she could ride her horse Buttermilk while the comic relief followed along in a Jeep.

The stories were a bit less violent than those of Rogers or contemporary Gene Autry, with Evans outsmarting the owlhoots rather than punching their lights out or shooting the guns out of their hands.

-- Brent

3 ....60.00
4-5 ....55.00
6-10 ....48.00
11-22 ....44.00

Queen's Greatest Hits
Revolutionary, 1993
1 ....3.00

Quest for Camelot
DC, 1998
1 ....5.00

Quest for Dreams Lost
Literacy Volunteers, 1987
1 ....2.00

Question
DC, 1987
1-36 .... 2.00
Ann 1 .... 3.00
Ann 2 .... 4.00

Question
DC, 2005
1-6 .... 3.00

Question Quarterly
DC, 1990
1-5 .... 3.00

Question Returns
DC, 1997
1 .... 4.00

Quest of the Tiger Woman
Millennium
1 .... 3.00

Quest Presents
Quest, 1983
1-3 .... 2.00

Questprobe
Marvel, 1984

Scott Adams was a pioneer of the computer game in the early 1980s, taking gamers from desert islands to haunted houses with his ingenious series of adventure games. With personal computers becoming commonplace in the homes of many a comic book reader, Marvel tried its luck with this new form of entertainment, creating the Questprobe series in cooperation with Adams.

The Questprobe computer adventure games featured such prominent Marvel characters as Spider-Man and the Incredible Hulk. As a marketing tool, Marvel also published Questprobe comic books that were related to, but did not provide the answers for, the adventure games.

Unfortunately, both the comics and the games were poorly distributed, and probably very few people who got one ever saw the other.

1-3 .... 2.00

Quick Draw McGraw
Dell, 1960
2 .... 15.00
3-7 .... 10.00
8-12 .... 8.00
13-14 .... 6.00
15 .... 10.00

Quick Draw McGraw
Charlton, 1970
1 .... 10.00
2 .... 7.00
3-5 .... 5.00
6-8 .... 4.00

Quicken Forbidden
Cryptic, 1996
1-13 .... 3.00

Quicksilver
Marvel, 1997
1 .... 3.00
2-13 .... 2.00

Quick-Trigger Western
Atlas, 1956
12-19 .... 100.00

Quincy Looks Into His Future
General Electric
1 .... 2.00

Quit City (Warren Ellis')
Avatar, 2004
1 .... 4.00
1/Foil 15.00

Quit Your Job
Alternative
1 .... 7.00

Quivers
Caliber, 1991
1-2 .... 3.00

Q-Unit
Harris, 1993
1 .... 3.00

Qwan
Tokyopop, 2005
1-3 .... 10.00

One among many crime comics of the late 1940s and early 1950s,
this Hillman series had some of the more imaginative covers.

Rabbit
Sharkbait, 1999
1 .... 3.00

Rabid
Fantaco
1 .... 6.00

Rabid Animal Komix
Krankin' Komix, 1995
1-2 .... 3.00

Rabid Monkey, The
D.B.I. Comics, 1997
1 .... 2.00

Rabid Rachel
Miller
1 .... 2.00

Race Against Time
Dark Angel, 1997
1-2 .... 3.00

Race for the Moon
Harvey, 1958
1 .... 100.00
2-3 .... 150.00

Race of Scorpions
Dark Horse, 1990
1-2 .... 5.00

Race of Scorpions
Dark Horse, 1991
1 .... 2.00
2-4 .... 3.00

Racer X
Now, 1988
1-11 .... 2.00

Racer X
Now, 1989
1-10 .... 2.00

Racer X
WildStorm, 2000
1-3 .... 3.00

Racer X Premiere
Now, 1988
1 .... 4.00

Rack & Pain
Dark Horse, 1994
1-4 .... 3.00

Rack & Pain: Killers
Chaos, 1996
1-4 .... 3.00

Racket Squad in Action
Charlton, 1952
1 .... 150.00
2-4 .... 80.00
5 .... 120.00
6 .... 80.00
7-10 .... 75.00
11 .... 165.00
12 .... 300.00
13 .... 55.00
14 .... 75.00
15-28 .... 55.00
29 .... 60.00

Radical Dreamer
Blackball, 1994
0 .... 3.00
1 .... 2.00
2-4 .... 3.00

Radical Dreamer
Mark's Giant Economy Size, 1995
1-5 .... 3.00

Radioactive Man
Bongo, 1993
1-88 .... 5.00
216-1000 .... 3.00

Radioactive Man
Bongo, 2000
1-9 .... 3.00

Radioactive Man
80 Page Colossal
Bongo, 1995
1 .... 5.00

Radio Boy
Eclipse, 1987
1 .... 2.00

Radiskull & Devil Doll:
Radiskull Love-Hate
One Shot
Image, 2003
1 .... 3.00

Radix
Image, 2001

This adventure begins with a highly trained military unit led by the beautiful and dangerous Colonel Valerie Maxwell. Highly trained as they are, even they weren't ready to face the Radix. It manifests as a ball of green energy but is much more.

Three years later, that encounter still haunts Maxwell and her team members and it may have grave repercussions for their present and their future. Somehow, that encounter echoes into a conflict involving an escaped killer and a dangerous mental patient. That patient is a beautiful blonde in a high-security cell; her eyes glow a vibrant, Radix-like green.

This intense adventure set in a high-tech future is sharply written and beautifully drawn.

1-2 ....3.00

Radrex
Bullet, 1990

1 ....2.00

Ragamuffins
Eclipse, 1985

1 ....2.00

Rage
Anarchy Bridgeworks

1 ....3.00

Raggedy Ann and Andy
Dell, 1946

Though apparently not hotly collected these days, except by collectors of Raggedy Ann material in general, this series was one of the very best ever aimed at pre-teens. With contributors brought together by Editor Oskar Lebeck and with the focus on the Raggedys (whose outspoken driving force was love), the anthology title featured such additional delights as Billy and Bonnie Bee, Dan Noonan's Egbert Elephant and His Friends, and Walt Kelly's Animal Mother Goose.

Created by Johnny Gruelle (1880-1938) in 1918, Raggedy Ann was enormously popular, and Dell's series brought much of the cast of Gruelle's children's works to comic-book format. Lebeck later added such features as children's book adaptations before a creator shift changed the cover feature to John Stanley's creation, Peterkin Pottle. In those stories, fat little Peterkin daydreams elaborate fantasies in which he is the hero. At that point, Stanley also created Raggedy stories that bore little resemblance to the warm fantasies of his predecessors.

-- Maggie

1 .... 180.00
2-4 .... 125.00
5-9 .... 100.00
10-15 .... 75.00
16-19 .... 60.00
20-39 .... 50.00

Raggedy Ann and Andy
Dell, 1964

1 .... 35.00
2-4 .... 20.00

Raggedy Ann and Andy
Gold Key, 1971

1 .... 5.00
2-6 .... 4.00

Raggedyman
Cult, 1993

1-1/Variant............................. 3.00
2-3 .... 2.00
4-6 .... 3.00

Raging Angels
Classic Hippie

1 .... 3.00

Ragman
DC, 1976

1 .... 5.00
2-5 .... 3.00

Ragman
DC, 1991

1-8 .... 2.00

Ragman: Cry of the Dead
DC, 1993

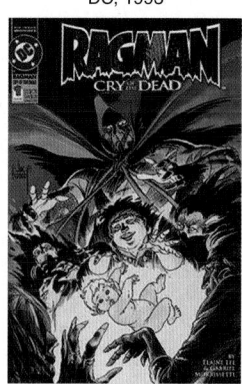

Ragman is Rory Regan, a man who wears a suit composed of a patchwork of rags. Each of these rags is a human soul, stolen from an evildoer and compelled to serve the cause of good at his bidding.

Cry of Dead takes Rory to New Orleans, city of jazz, Mardi Gras, and voodoo. There, he encounters a dread spirit known as Marinette that flies from body to body, driving each one touched to commit ghastly murders. As Ragman, he tries to stop its evil, only to find

himself fighting an opponent capable of devouring the souls in his rags as a snack. In this story of pain, vengeance, and the supernatural, Ragman must find a way to stop Marinette before she tears apart the lives of those closest to him.

1-6 .... 2.00

Ragmop
Planet Lucy, 1995

1-7 .... 3.00

Ragmop
Image, 1997

1-3 .... 3.00

Ragnarok Guy
Sun

1 .... 3.00

Rags Rabbit
Harvey, 1951

11 .... 25.00
12-18 .... 20.00

Rahrwl
Northstar

1 .... 3.00
1/2nd 2.00

Rai
Valiant, 1992

0 .... 4.00
1 .... 8.00
1/Companion 1.00
2 .... 6.00
3 .... 16.00
4 .... 15.00
5 .... 6.00
6-8 .... 3.00
☛adds ...Future Force
25-28 .... 1.00
29-31 .... 2.00
32 .... 3.00
33 .... 5.00

Rai and the Future Force
Valiant, 1993

9 .... 1.00
☛was Rai
9/Gold.................................... 18.00
9/VVSS.................................. 10.00
10-20 .... 1.00
21 .... 2.00
21/VVSS............................... 60.00
22-24 .... 1.00
☛becomes Rai again

Rai Companion
Valiant, 1993

1 .... 1.00

Raiders of the Lost Ark
Marvel, 1981

1-3 .... 2.00

Raider 3000
Gauntlet
1-2..3.00

Raijin Comics
Gutsoon, 2002
1-36..5.00
37-41......................................6.00

Raika
Sun
1-20..3.00

Rain
Tundra

Noted artist Rolf Stark and co-writer Marlene Stevens based this project on Stark's memories of Germany during and after World War II. Stark's jagged and harrowing black-and-white art is the perfect vehicle for the ambitious and kaleidoscopic story that unfolds. Events from protagonist Karl's life as a barely subsisting taxi driver in the present time mingle with disturbing fragments of events and images from his previous life, including his childhood in war-torn Germany and his subsequent experiences wandering the globe.

Both the language and the art are shockingly and deliberately ugly. At the same time, the ugliness is necessary to communicate Stark's harsh vision of reality without sensationalism or sentimentality. Rain occupies territory staked out by Art Spiegelman's Maus and very few others in its use of the comic-book form as literature.

-- Rob Salkowitz

1-6..2.00

Rainbow Brite and the Star Stealer
DC, 1985
1 .... 1.00

Raisin Pie
Fantagraphics, 2002
1-4.. 4.00

Rak
Rak Graphics
1 .... 5.00

Rakehell
Draculina
1 .... 3.00

Ralfy Roach
Bugged Out, 1993
1 .... 3.00

Ralph Kiner, Home Run King
Fawcett, 1950
1 .... 250.00

Ralph Snart Adventures
Now, 1986
1 .... 3.00
2-3.. 2.00

Ralph Snart Adventures
Now, 1986
1-9.. 2.00

Ralph Snart Adventures
Now, 1988

The crazed, loutish, yet strangely lovable Ralph Snart returned in 1988 for a third series. This was to be the longest-running of the Ralph Snart titles. Among the highlights were a wacky 3-D special (complete with glasses) and adventures of "Li'l Ralphie": Snart as a child.

In the Ralph Snart: The Early Years adventures, readers get perspective on how Ralph got to be the bizarre character of later years. He was the kind of kid who would smash all the jack-o'-lanterns in the neighborhood, then go to sleep in his monster costume in order to frighten the wits out of his parents. But for a kid with Ralph's imagination and capacity for getting into trouble, such pranks are a warm-up. He can't even go to the beach with his family without discovering subterranean sand-beings who want to capture him. Is it any wonder that his parents are one step short of checking themselves into the loony bin?

1 .... 2.00
1/3D....................................... 3.00
1/CS 4.00
2-23.. 2.00
24 .... 3.00
25-26 .... 2.00

Ralph Snart Adventures
Now, 1992
1-3.. 3.00

Ralph Snart Adventures
Now, 1993
1-5.. 3.00

Ralph Snart: The Lost Issues
Now, 1993
1-3.. 3.00

Ramar of the Jungle
Charlton, 1954
1 .... 125.00
2-5 .... 75.00

Ramba
Fantagraphics, 1992
1-8.. 3.00

Ramblin' Dawg
Edge, 1994
1 .... 3.00

Rambo
Blackthorne, 1988
1 .... 2.00

Rambo III
Blackthorne
1 .... 2.00
3D 1.. 3.00

Ramm
Megaton, 1987
1-2.. 2.00

Rampage
Slap Happy, 1997
1 .... 10.00

Rampaging Hulk
Marvel, 1998

In an effort to capitalize on the popularity of The Incredible Hulk, which had achieved much greatness during Peter David's 12-year tenure as writer, Marvel launched this second Hulk title in 1998, with writer Glenn Greenberg and artist Rick Leonardi at the helm. Essentially an "Untold Tales" series, The Rampaging Hulk was set in the early years of the Green Goliath's career, when he was still in his savage, "Hulk smash" state of mind. An interesting idea with all the major supporting players of the day - General "Thunderbolt" Ross, Betty Ross Talbot, and Major Glenn Talbot - in place, but Marvel's financial woes, as well as the generally depressed condition of the comic-book marketplace, forced the cancellation of this promising new series with its seventh issue.

1-6 .... 2.00

Rampaging Hulk (Magazine)
Marvel, 1977

1 .... 35.00
2 .... 14.00
3-5 .... 5.00
6-9 .... 4.00

Ramthar (Mike Deodato's...)
Caliber, 1996

1 .... 3.00

Rana 7
NGNG

1-4 .... 3.00

Rana 7: Warriors of Vengeance
NGNG, 1995

1-2 .... 3.00

Random Encounter
Viper, 2005

1-4 .... 3.00

Randy O'Donnell is the M@n
Image, 2001

1-3 .... 3.00

Range Busters
Charlton, 1955

8 .... 50.00
9-10 .... 30.00

Rangeland Love
Atlas, 1949

1 .... 100.00
2 .... 85.00

Range Romances
Quality, 1949

1-2 .... 165.00
3 .... 130.00
4-5 .... 110.00

Rangers Comics
Fiction House, 1941

1 .... 2,750.00
2 .... 850.00
3 .... 650.00
4-5 .... 500.00
6-12 .... 425.00
13-19 .... 350.00
20-24 .... 300.00
25-29 .... 250.00
30-39 .... 175.00
40-59 .... 120.00
60-69 .... 90.00

Rango
Dell, 1967

1 .... 25.00

Rank & Stinky
Parody

1-Special 1 .... 3.00

Ranma 1/2
Viz, 1991

1 .... 25.00
2 .... 10.00
3 .... 8.00
4-5 .... 6.00
6-7 .... 5.00

Ranma 1/2 Part 2
Viz, 1992

1 .... 7.00
2 .... 5.00
3-11 .... 4.00

Ranma 1/2 Part 3
Viz, 1992

1-13 .... 3.00

Ranma 1/2 Part 4
Viz, 1994

1-11 .... 3.00

Ranma 1/2 Part 5
Viz, 1994

1-12 .... 3.00

Ranma 1/2 Part 6
Viz, 1996

1-14 .... 3.00

Ranma 1/2 Part 7
Viz, 1998

1-14 .... 3.00

Ranma 1/2 Part 8
Viz, 1999

1-13 .... 3.00

Ranma 1/2 Part 9
Viz, 2000

1-11 .... 3.00

Ranma 1/2 Part 10
Viz, 2001

1-11 .... 3.00

Ranma 1/2 Part 11
Viz, 2002

1-11 .... 3.00

Ranma 1/2 Part 12
Viz, 2003

1 .... 3.00

Rann-Thanagar War
DC, 2005

1 .... 8.00
1/Variant 5.00
☞2nd printing
2 .... 4.00
3-6 .... 3.00

Rann/Thanagar War: Infinite Crisis Special
DC, 2006

1 .... 5.00

Rant
Boneyard, 1994

1-Ashcan 1 .... 3.00

Raphael Teenage Mutant Ninja Turtle
Mirage, 1987

1 .... 3.00
1/2nd 2.00

Rare Breed
Chrysalis, 1995

1-2 .... 3.00

Rascals in Paradise
Dark Horse, 1994

1-3 .... 4.00

Rat Bastard
Crucial, 1997

Roscoe is an Experimental Life Form, or "ELF" for short. In other words, he's an overgrown rat with a human brain. Roscoe jets around the Manhattan Empire on a flying jet cycle, not looking for trouble, but ready to handle it when it arises.

The Manhattan Empire is a city packed with skyscrapers a thousand stories high, where the religious worship Elvis, gene junkies will rip the spine out of your body, and cults like The Knights of Genetic Purity will murder you, if you're an ELF like Roscoe.

And it's just the sort of place a Rat Bastard would love.

1-1/Ashcan	3.00
2-6	2.00

Rated X
Aircel, 1991

1-Special 1	3.00

Rat Fink Comics
World of Fandom

1-3	3.00

Rat Fink Comix (Ed "Big Daddy" Roth's...)
Starhead

1	2.00

Ratfoo
Spit Wad, 1997

1	3.00

Rat Patrol
Dell, 1967

1-5	40.00
6	25.00

Rat Preview (Justin Hampton's...)
Aeon, 1997

1	1.00

Rats!
Slave Labor, 1992

1	3.00

Ravage 2099
Marvel, 1992

1	2.00
2-18	1.00
19-25	2.00
25/Variant	3.00
26-33	2.00

Rave Master
Tokyopop, 2003

1-18	10.00

Raven, The
Malan Classical Enterprises

1	5.00

Raven
Renaissance, 1993

1-4	3.00

Raven Chronicles
Caliber, 1995

1-14	3.00
15	4.00

Ravens and Rainbows
Pacific, 1983

1	2.00

Ravenwind
Pariah, 1996

1	3.00

Raver
Malibu, 1993

1	3.00
2-3	2.00

Raw City
Dramenon

1	3.00

Rawhide
Dell, 1962

1	200.00

Rawhide
Gold Key, 1963

1	175.00
2	150.00

Rawhide Kid
Marvel, 1955

1	800.00
2	350.00
3-5	185.00
6-10	140.00
11-16	110.00
17	400.00
☞Origin, Kirby art	
18-21	95.00
22	90.00
23	200.00
☞Origin retold, Kirby	

24-30	90.00
31-44	75.00
45	90.00
46	60.00
47-60	35.00
61-70	25.00
71-86	18.00
87-92	15.00
93-99	12.00
100	18.00
101-113	12.00
114-120	10.00
121-133	7.00
133/30¢	20.00
134	7.00
134/30¢	20.00
135-139	7.00
140-140/35¢	15.00
141-151	6.00
Special 1	12.00

Rawhide Kid
Marvel, 1985

1-4	2.00

Rawhide Kid
Marvel, 2003

1	5.00
2	4.00
3-5	3.00

Raw Media Illustrated
ABC, 1998

1-1/Nude	3.00

Raw Media Mags
Rebel, 1994

1-4	5.00

Raw Periphery
Slave Labor

1	3.00

Ray
ADV Manga, 2004

1-3	10.00

Ray
DC, 1992

1	3.00
2-6	2.00

Ray
DC, 1994

0-1	2.00
1/Variant	3.00
2-24	2.00
25	4.00
26-28	2.00
Ann 1	4.00

Ray Bradbury Comics
Topps, 1993

1-Special 1	4.00

Ray Bradbury Comics: Martian Chronicles
Topps, 1994

1	3.00

Ray Bradbury Comics: Trilogy of Terror
Topps, 1994

1 ....3.00

Ray Bradbury Special: Tales of Horror
Topps, 1994

1 ....3.00

Ray-Mond
Deep-Sea

1-2...3.00

Rayne
Sheet Happies, 1995

1-4...3.00

Razor
London Night, 1991

0	3.00
0/A	4.00
0/2nd-1/2	3.00
1	4.00
1/2nd-2	3.00
2/Platinum	4.00
2/Variant	5.00
3	3.00
3/CS	4.00
4	3.00
4/Platinum	4.00
5	3.00
5/Platinum	4.00
6-12	3.00
Ann 1	15.00
Ann 1/Gold	20.00
Ann 2	4.00

Razor
London Night, 1996

1-7...3.00

Razor & Shi Special
London Night, 1994

1 ....3.00
1/Platinum 4.00

Razor Archives
London Night, 1997

1 ....4.00
2-4...5.00

Razor: Burn
London Night, 1995

1-4...3.00

Razor/Cry No More
London Night, 1995

1 ....4.00

Razor/Dark Angel: The Final Nail
London Night, 1994

1 ....3.00

Razorguts
Monster, 1992

1-4...2.00

Razorline: The First Cut
Marvel, 1993

In 1993, Marvel introduced its Razorline series of comics. Created by noted horror writer Clive Barker, this new "Barkerverse" combines humor and horror, super-heroes and the supernatural. This preview edition introduces readers to the first four Razorline titles:

Hokum & Hex is the tale of the failed grandson of a vaudeville magician who becomes this world's guardian against extra-dimensional evil.

HyperKind is a group of unlikely super-heroes who fall in the shadow of their predecessors.

Saint Sinner is a boy driven by a demon to commit murder -- but whose soul is now inhabited also by an angel he killed.

EctoKid is a son of a live woman and a dead man, whose left eye sees our world, and whose left sees the ghost realm.

1 .... 1.00

Razor/Morbid Angel
London Night, 1996

1-3.. 3.00

Razor Nights (Mike Deodato's...)
Caliber, 1996

1 .... 3.00

Razor's Edge
Innovation, 1999

1 .... 3.00

Razor's Edge: Warblade
DC, 2005

1-5.. 3.00

Razor: The Suffering
London Night

1-3.. 3.00

Razor: Torture
London Night, 1995

0 .... 4.00
1-6 .... 3.00

Razor: Uncut
London Night, 1995

13-51 .... 3.00

Razor/Warrior Nun Areala: Faith
London Night, 1996

1 .... 4.00

Razorwire
5th Panel, 1996

This black-and-white anthology title from 5th Panel Comics purports to be "twisted...convoluted...cutting edge." Certainly there's satire, especially in the work of Todd Richards, who takes on the clichTs of super-hero comics, the life of a comic book artist, and the stereotypical musician. Nora Callahan and Kevin Leen's "Tales from the Chaos Inn" is a bit more straight-forward in its storyline, an interesting bit of techno-thriller adventure starring a gun-toting hero who is stunned to meet his genetically engineered brother. David Witt's material explores a realm of nightmares and their impact on a weary traveler. A mixed bag, to be sure, but not without merit.

1-2 .... 2.00

Reaction: The Ultimate Man
Studio Archein

1 .... 3.00

Reacto-Man
B-Movie

1-3.. 2.00

Reactor Girl
Tragedy Strikes, 1991
1-5...3.00

Reagan's Raiders
Solson, 1986
1-3...2.00

Real Adventure Comics
Gilmore, 1955
1...40.00

Real Adventures of Jonny Quest
Dark Horse, 1996
1-12...3.00

Real Americans Admit: "The Worst Thing I've Ever Done!"
NBM
1...9.00

Real Bout High School
Tokyopop, 2002
1-2...10.00

Real Clue Crime Stories
Hillman, 1943
1...275.00
2-4..200.00
5-9..55.00
10-21...45.00
22-33...40.00
34-45...34.00
46-57...28.00
58-73...20.00

Real Deal Magazine
Real Deal
5...2.00

Real Experiences
Atlas, 1950
25..35.00

Real Fact Comics
DC, 1946
1...370.00
2...220.00
3...200.00
4...220.00
5...850.00
☛Making of Batman
6...700.00
☛1st Harlan Ellison
7...105.00
8...380.00
9...160.00
10...150.00
11-12...85.00
13...300.00
14..80.00
15...105.00
16...270.00
17-18...80.00
19..90.00
20...100.00
21..80.00

Real Funnies
Nedor, 1943
1...180.00
2-3...90.00

Real Ghostbusters Summer Special
Now, 1993
1..3.00

Real Ghostbusters 3-D Summer Special
Now, 1993
1..3.00

Real Ghostbusters
Now, 1988
1-28..2.00
3D 1..3.00

Real Ghostbusters
Now, 1991
1..2.00
1/3D..3.00
2-4...2.00
Ann 1992......................................1.00
Ann 1993......................................3.00

Real Girl
Fantagraphics, 1990
1-4...3.00
5-7...4.00

Real Heroes
Parents' Magazine Institute, 1941
1...125.00
2...75.00
3-5...60.00
6...90.00
7-10..45.00
11-16...40.00

Realistic Romances
Realistic Comics, 1951
1...125.00
2-4...50.00
5-17..45.00

Real Life
Fantagraphics, 1990
1..3.00

Real Life Comics
Standard, 1941
1...350.00
2...135.00
3...230.00
4-5...95.00
6-10..85.00
11-20...65.00
21-23...50.00
24..85.00
25-26...50.00
27..72.00
28-30...50.00
31-40...38.00
41-49...32.00

Real Smut
50...145.00
51..28.00
52...165.00
53-59...28.00

Real Life Secrets
Ace, 1949
1...75.00

Real Love
Ace, 1949
25-32...35.00
33-46...30.00
47-76...25.00

Really Fantastic Alien Sex Frenzy (Cynthia Petal's...)
Fantagraphics
1..4.00

Realm Handbook
Caliber
1..3.00

Realm of the Claw
Image, 2003
0..6.00
1/A-2/B.......................................3.00

Realm of the Dead
Caliber
1-3...3.00

Realm
Arrow, 1986
1..5.00
2-3...2.00
4..4.00
5-15..2.00
16-21...3.00

Realm
Caliber
1-13..3.00

Real Schmuck
Starhead
1..3.00

Real Screen Comics
DC, 1945
1...750.00
2...325.00
3...250.00
4-5..175.00
6-10...125.00
11-21...80.00
22-30...55.00
31-39...38.00
40-50...26.00
51-60...18.00
61-70...16.00
71-90...14.00
91-100..10.00
101-128..8.00

Real Smut
Fantagraphics, 1993
1-6...3.00

R

Real Sports Comics
Hillman, 1948
1 ....250.00

Real Stuff
Fantagraphics, 1990

A critically acclaimed alternative comic, Real Stuff is the brainchild of writer Dennis P. Eichhorn, who uses it as a forum to relate episodes from his own life (or perhaps an interesting fictional alternative to his real life). Pencilling is handled by a number of well-regarded artists, ranging from Jaime Hernandez (Love and Rockets) to Pat Moriarty (Big Mouth).

Judging from the stories in Real Life, Eichhorn has often taken the road less traveled. "Death of a Junkie" talks about meeting an old friend at the Seattle Space Needle, following him to his apartment, and discovering a junkie in the back room, dead from an overdose. "Our Thing" follows his misadventures as a high-school student in Idaho, where he and a friend copped booze by following cars from the state-run liquor stores. It's hard to tell if these stories are fiction, elaborations, or the "real stuff." Either way, they're fascinating.

1-20...3.00

Real War Stories
Eclipse, 1987
1-1/2nd.....................................2.00
2 ....5.00

Real Weird War
Avalon
1 ....3.00

Real Weird West
Avalon
1 ....3.00

Real Western Hero
Fawcett, 1948
70 .... 150.00
71 .... 75.00
72-73 .... 60.00
74-75 .... 50.00

Real West Romances
Crestwood, 1949
1 .... 75.00
2-4 .... 60.00
5-6 .... 40.00

Realworlds: Batman
DC
1 .... 6.00

Realworlds: Justice League of America
DC, 2000
1 .... 6.00

Realworlds: Superman
DC
1 .... 6.00

Realworlds: Wonder Woman
DC, 2000
1 .... 6.00

Re-Animator
Aircel
1-3.. 3.00

Re-Animator: Dawn of the Re-Animator
Adventure, 1992

Re-Animator, one of the most popular horror movies of the 1980s, is a gore-fest about a scientist who brings the dead back to life. Dawn of the Re-Animator is a prequel to the movie, detailing the adventures of young Herbert West as he struggles not only to prove that his serum works, and to avoid arrest for murder, and at the same time, to not lose his University funding!

West's troubles begin when he uses the serum on his colleague Dr. Gruber, apparently dead from a heart attack. Unfortunately, there are some rather grisly and eye-popping (literally!) side-effects, none of which seem to include Gruber's reanimation. This, of course, brings him into conflict with the police, the University's Board of Inquiry, and Gruber's estranged daughter.

Meanwhile, the powerful Erich Metler, a man obsessed with immortality, wants the secret of West's formula, and has already unleashed his zombie thugs to retrieve it.

1-4 .... 3.00

Re-Animator in Full Color
Adventure, 1991
1-3... 3.00

Rear Entry
Fantagraphics, 2004
1-10 .... 4.00

R.E.B.E.L.S.
DC, 1994
0-17 .... 2.00

Rebel Sword
Dark Horse, 1994
1-5 .... 3.00

Rebirth
Tokyopop, 2003
1-16 .... 10.00

Recollections Sampler
Recollections
1 .... 1.00

Record of Lodoss War: Chronicles of the Heroic Knight
CPM Manga, 2000
1-11 .... 3.00

Record of Lodoss War: The Grey Witch
CPM, 1998
1-22 .... 3.00

Record of Lodoss War: The Lady of Pharis
CPM
1-8 .... 3.00

Rectum Errrectum
Boneyard
1 .... 4.00

Red
DC, 2003
1-3 .... 3.00

Red Arrow
P.L., 1951

1 ....65.00
2-3 ....50.00

Redblade
Dark Horse, 1993

1-3 ....3.00

Red Circle
Rural Home, 1945

1 ....400.00
2 ....225.00
3-4 ....125.00

Red Circle Sorcery
Red Circle, 1974

6 ....10.00
☛Was Chilling Adventures in Sorcery
7-11 ....5.00

Reddevil
AC

Forty years ago, Reddevil was a super-hero fighting crime and protecting the American way of life during World War II.

Coming out of stasis, Reddevil, as well as other crime-fighters of his era, find themselves in the strange and unfamiliar world of the 1990's. From Catman and the Kitten, to Captain Flash and the Hood, the heroes have outlived all of their friends and relatives, and must now rely on each other.

But if the heroes have survived forty years, might not others have returned as well? Perhaps even an evil criminal genius known as the Claw?

In addition to new material by Dick Ayers, issue number one of this title reprints a story by Jack Cole, featuring the classic Golden Age villain, the Claw.

1 ....3.00

Red Diaries
Caliber, 1997

1-4 .... 4.00

Red Dragon
Comico, 1996

1 .... 3.00

Red Dragon Comics (Vol. 1)
Street & Smith, 1943

5 .... 900.00
6 .... 1,500.00
7 .... 1,000.00
8-9 .... 500.00

Red Dragon Comics (Vol. 2)
Street & Smith, 1947

1 .... 650.00
2 .... 450.00
3 .... 350.00
4-7 .... 250.00

Redeemer
Images & Realities

1 .... 3.00

Redeemers
Antarctic, 1997

1 .... 3.00

Red Flannel Squirrel
Sirius, 1997

1 .... 3.00

Redfox
Harrier, 1986

A female barbarian in a sword-and-sorcery world whose name contains the word "Red." Where have we seen this before? Yes, Red Sonja does leap to mind.

However, Redfox is considerably different from the sturm und drang of Sonja. The style is not deadly serious but, rather, light comedy with the occasional awful pun thrown in for bad measure.

This is somewhat reminiscent of the very early issues of Cerebus the Aardvark in its attempt to do a swords-and-sorcery situation comedy with dramatic moments.

1 .... 4.00
1/2nd 2.00
2-3 .... 3.00
4-20 .... 2.00

Red Heat
Blackthorne, 1988

1 .... 2.00
1/3D 3.00

Red Iceberg
Impact, 1960

1 .... 300.00

Red Mask
Magazine Enterprises, 1954

42 .... 125.00
43 .... 105.00
44-52 .... 95.00
53 .... 75.00

Redmask of the Rio Grande
AC

1-3 .... 3.00

Red Menace
DC, 2007

1-2/Variant 3.00

Red Moon
Millennium, 1995

1-2 .... 3.00

Red Planet Pioneer
Inesco

1 .... 3.00

Red Rabbit
Dearfield, 1947

1 .... 75.00
2 .... 45.00
3-10 .... 35.00
11-17 .... 30.00
18 .... 42.00
19-22 .... 30.00

Red Raven Comics
Timely, 1940

1 .... 10,000.00

Red Razors: A Dreddworld Adventure
Fleetway-Quality

1-3 .... 3.00

Red Revolution
Caliber

1 .... 3.00

Red Rocket 7
Dark Horse, 1997

1-5 .... 3.00
6-7 .... 4.00

Red Ryder Comics
Dell, 1940

Dell's Red Ryder Comics, featuring Fred Harman's intrepid frontier lawman and his sidekick Little Beaver, was one of the most successful and long-running comic strip adaptations. The early issues reprinted Red Ryder Sunday strips along with other classic adventure-hero serials such as Captain Easy and Alley Oop. Eventually, talented writer/artist Harman began producing original material for the 52-page issues ó generally three to four stories per month.

Red Ryder is a tough-as-nails cowboy matching wits and bullets with the typical array of frontier bad-guys, including cattle rustlers, crooked politicians, Mexican banditos, and stagecoach robbers. His no-nonsense approach was lightened up by the comic relief of Little Beaver, a feisty Indian kid.

-- Rob Salkowitz

1	2,200.00
3	1,000.00
4-5	550.00
6	400.00
7-10	350.00
11-20	280.00
21-30	185.00
31-40	125.00
41-50	95.00
51-53	68.00
54-73	60.00
74-77	54.00
78-83	50.00
84-89	45.00
90-95	40.00
96-101	35.00
102-107	30.00
108-110	26.00
111-120	24.00
121-130	22.00
131-140	18.00
141-151	16.00

Red Seal Comics
Harry A. Chesler, 1945

14	475.00
15-16	315.00
17-19	285.00
20-22	250.00

Red Shetland
Graphxpress, 1992

1-4	2.00
5-8	3.00
9-11	4.00

Redskin
Youthful, 1950

1	100.00
2-6	50.00
7-12	45.00

Red Sonja
Marvel, 1976

1	8.00
2-4	3.00
4/35¢-5/35¢	20.00
6	3.00
7-15	2.00

Red Sonja
Marvel, 1983

1-2	1.00

Red Sonja
Marvel, 1983

1-13	2.00

Red Sonja
Dynamite Comics, 2005

0/Black-0/White	3.00
0/Ross	30.00
0/Sketch	150.00
0/Foil	10.00
0/Authentix	20.00
0/DF	25.00
1	20.00
1/Rivera	25.00
1/Adams	35.00
1/Linsner	125.00
1/Ross	40.00
1/Rubi	20.00
1/DF	35.00
5	3.00

Red Sonja:
A Death in Scarlet
Cross Plains, 1999

1	3.00

Red Sonja/Claw:
Devil's Hands
DC, 2006

1-4	3.00

Red Sonja in 3-D
Blackthorne

1	3.00

Red Sonja:
Scavenger Hunt
Marvel, 1995

1	3.00

Red Sonja: The Movie
Marvel, 1985

1-2	1.00

Red Star
Image, 2000

1	4.00
2-9	3.00

Red Star
CrossGen, 2003

1-5	3.00

Red Tornado
DC, 1985

1-4	1.00

Red Warrior
Atlas, 1951

1	100.00
2	50.00
3-6	40.00

Red Wolf
Marvel, 1972

1	35.00
2	18.00
3-5	15.00
6-9	10.00

Reese's Pieces
Eclipse, 1986

1-2	2.00

Reform School Girl
Realistic Comics, 1951

1	1,000.00

Re:Gex
Awesome, 1998

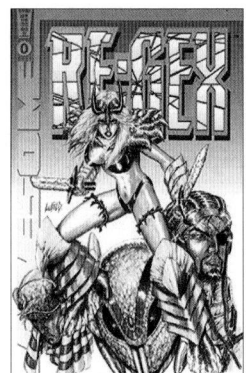

There is a secret war raging in the back streets of our cities and high in our skies. A group of super-powered freedom fighters known as the Re:Gex are battling against the sinister Company in a struggle not only for their own lives but for the future of the world as well. Lead by Scarab, once a warrior for the Company, the group is building its strength, laying plans for attack. Into this conflict comes the beautiful Genie, a woman who is extremely powerful, but a mystery even to herself. Will she save the Re:Gex-or be the worst mistake they've ever made?

0-1/A 3.00

Reggie and Me
Archie, 1966
19	10.00
20	8.00
21-25	6.00
26-30	5.00
31-50	3.00
51-100	2.00
101-126	1.00

Reggie's Revenge
Archie, 1994
1-3 ....2.00

Reggie's Wise Guy Jokes
Archie, 1968
1	8.00
2	5.00
3	4.00
4-5	3.00
6-10	2.00
11-60	1.00

Registry of Death
Kitchen Sink, 1996
1 ....16.00

Regulators
Image, 1995

The tagline for this series is "They Ain't Role Models," and Image ain't kidding. The Regulators are the bad guys, spun off from Jim Valentino's ShadowHawk into their own series. The Regulators consist of Blackjak, Vort-X, Arson, Hardedge, and the most recent addition, Scandal.

For instance, consider the series' first issue which features Blackjak, a womanizing, lying, business-defrauding, super-powered criminal. And to top it all off, he's not bright. The Regulators' recent heists have been foiled by their former employer, Vendetta. Blackjak can't figure out how she thwarted them until he meets a woman named Scandal in a bar, who prompts him to detect the obvious explanation. She then ruthlessly kills a gang of muggers, who, in this continuity, might have been luckier and been in line for their own series, if they'd only been more arrogant.

-- George Haberberger

1-4 .... 3.00

Rehd
Antarctic, 2003
0 .... 3.00

Reid Fleming
Boswell
1	10.00
1/2nd	4.00

Reid Fleming, World's Toughest Milkman
Eclipse, 1986
1	6.00
1/2nd	3.00
1/3rd-1/5th	2.00
1/6th-2	3.00
2/2nd-6	2.00
7-9	3.00

Reign of the Dragonlord
Eternity, 1986
1-2 .... 2.00

Reign of the Zodiac
DC, 2003
1-8 .... 3.00

Reiki Warriors
Revolutionary, 1993
1 .... 3.00

Reinventing Comics
Paradox, 2000
1 .... 23.00

Relative Heroes
DC, 2000

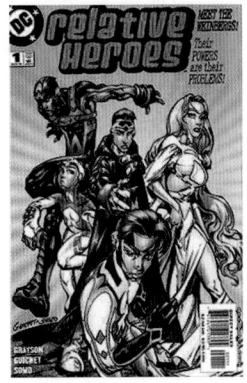

When Deborah and Oren Weinberg unexpectedly die in a car crash, their kids, along with the baby-sitter Damara, pack up the Winnebago and head for Metropolis. Why? To get Superman's advice on becoming super-heroes, of course. After all, kids plus powers, minus parents, pretty much equals super-team road trip, right? Well, that's what older brother Joel thinks, and, as the only one without any powers, he's desperate to hold the family together after their recent tragedy.

Naturally, being orphaned is only the beginning of the kids' problems. They find out the hard way that "cousin" Cameron, a recent addition to the family, is on the run from the Department of Extra-normal Operations. And they've barely made their escape from the D.E.O.'s super-powered strikeforce before being attacked by Damara's "fiance," the angry and bitter God Eryx!

Whoever said that being a kid was easy, huh?

1-6 .... 3.00

Relentless Pursuit
Slave Labor, 1989
1-2	2.00
3	3.00
4	4.00

Reload
DC, 2003
1-3 .... 3.00

Reload/Mek
DC, 2004
1 .... 15.00

Remains
Idea & Design Works, 2004
1-5 .... 4.00

Remarkable Worlds of Phineas B. Fuddle
Paradox, 2000
1-4 ....6.00

Remember Pearl Harbor
Street & Smith, 1942
1 ....350.00

Remote
Tokyopop, 2004
1-7 ....10.00

Ren & Stimpy Show
Marvel, 1992
1/A-1/B 3.00
1/2nd-25 ....2.00
25/Variant 3.00
26-44 ....2.00
Special 1-Holiday 1 ....3.00

Ren & Stimpy Show: Radio Daze
Marvel, 1995
1 ....2.00

Ren & Stimpy Show Special: Around the World in a Daze
Marvel, 1996
1 ....3.00

Ren & Stimpy Show Special: Eenteractive
Marvel, 1995
1 ....3.00

Ren & Stimpy Show Special: Four Swerks
Marvel, 1995
1 ....3.00

Ren & Stimpy Show Special: Powdered Toast Man
Marvel, 1994
1 ....3.00

Ren & Stimpy Show Special: Powdered Toastman's Cereal
Marvel, 1995
1 ....3.00

Ren & Stimpy Show Special: Sports
Marvel, 1995
1 ....3.00

Renegade
Rip Off, 1991
1 ....3.00

Renegade!
Magnecom, 1993
1 ....3.00

Renegade Rabbit
Printed Matter
1-5 .... 2.00

Renegade Romance
Renegade, 1987
1-2 .... 4.00

Renegades
Age of Heroes
1-2 .... 1.00

Renegades of Justice
Blue Masque, 1995
1-2 .... 3.00

Renfield
Caliber, 1994
1 .... 3.00
1/Ltd. 6.00
2-3 .... 3.00
Ashcan 1 .... 1.00

Rennin Comics (Jim Chadwick's...)
Restless Muse, 1997
1 .... 3.00

Reno Browne
Marvel, 1950
50-52 .... 150.00

Replacement God
Handicraft, 1998
6 .... 7.00

Replacement God
Slave Labor, 1995
1 .... 6.00
1/2nd 3.00
2 .... 4.00
3-8 .... 3.00

Replacement God and Other Stories
Image, 1997
1-5 .... 3.00

Reporter
Reporter
1 .... 3.00

Reptilicus
Charlton, 1961
1 .... 100.00
2 .... 50.00

Reptisaurus
Charlton, 1962
3-Special 1 .... 25.00

Requiem for Dracula
Marvel, 1992
1 .... 2.00

Rescueman
Best
1 .... 3.00

Rescuers Down Under (Disney's...)
Disney
1 .... 3.00

Resident Evil
Image, 1998
1 .... 6.00
2-5 .... 5.00

Resident Evil: Code Veronica
DC, 2002
1-3 .... 15.00

Resident Evil: Fire and Ice
WildStorm, 2000
1-4 .... 3.00

Resistance
WildStorm, 2002
1-8 .... 3.00

Restaurant at the End of the Universe
DC, 1994
1-3 .... 7.00

Resurrection Man
DC, 1997
1-27 .... 3.00
1000000 .... 4.00

Retaliator
Eclipse, 1992
1-5 .... 3.00

Retief
Adventure, 1989
1-6 .... 2.00
Book 1 .... 15.00

Retief (Keith Laumer's...)
Mad Dog, 1987
1-6 .... 2.00

Retief and the Warlords
Adventure, 1991
1-4 .... 3.00

Retief: Diplomatic Immunity
Adventure, 1991
1-2 .... 3.00

Retief: Grime and Punishment
Adventure, 1991
1 .... 3.00

Retief of the C.D.T.
Mad Dog
1 .... 2.00

Retief:
The Garbage Invasion
Adventure, 1991
1 ....3.00

Retief: The Giant Killer
Adventure, 1991
1 ....3.00

Retro 50's Comix
Edge
1-2..3.00
3..4.00

Retro Comics
AC

In a time when the market is glutted with new comics titles and characters, Bill Black's Retro series reminds readers that a character doesn't have to be new to be good reading. Incorporating both new and previously published stories about Cat-Man and other classic Golden Age characters, Black creates a new continuity of heroes set in the year 1954. Other titles feature such heroes as Fighting Yank, Captain Flash, and Yankee Girl.

The 6.75 inch by 8.5 inch book, sized differently from most comics, gives the title a pulp-fiction feel, while the black-and-white art gives the campy horror stories a touch of grim realism.

0-3..6.00

Retro-Dead
Blazer, 1995
1 ....3.00

Retrograde
Eternity
1-3..2.00

Retro Rocket
Image, 2006
1-3..3.00

Return of
Disney's Aladdin
Disney
1-2 .... 2.00

Return of Girl Squad X
Fantaco
1 .... 5.00

Return of Gorgo
Charlton, 1963
2-3 .... 75.00

Return of
Happy the Clown
Caliber, 1995
1 .... 4.00
2 .... 3.00

Return of Herbie
Avalon
1 .... 3.00

Return of Konga
Charlton, 1962
1 .... 50.00

Return of Lum
Urusei*Yatsura
Viz, 1994
1-8 .... 3.00

Return of Lum
Urusei*Yatsura, Part 2
Viz, 1995
1-13 .... 3.00

Return of Lum
Urusei*Yatsura, Part 3
Viz, 1996
1-11 .... 3.00

Return of Lum
Urusei*Yatsura, Part 4
Viz, 1997
1-11 .... 3.00

Return of Megaton Man
Kitchen Sink, 1988
1-3 .... 3.00

Return of Shadowhawk
Image, 2004
1 .... 3.00

Return of Tarzan (Edgar
Rice Burroughs'...)
Dark Horse, 1997
1-3 .... 3.00

Return of the Outlaw
Toby, 1953
1 .... 50.00
2-9 .... 25.00
10-11 .... 20.00

Return of the Skyman
Ace, 1987
1 .... 2.00

Return of Valkyrie
Eclipse
1 .... 10.00

Return to Jurassic Park
Topps, 1995
1-9 .... 3.00

Return to the Eve
Monolith
1 .... 3.00

Reveal
Dark Horse, 2002
1 .... 7.00

Revealing Romances
Ace, 1949
1 .... 50.00
2 .... 30.00
3-6 .... 25.00

Revelations
Dark Horse, 1995
1/Ashcan 1.00

Revelations
Dark Horse, 2005
1-6 .... 3.00

Revelations
Golden Realm Unlimited
1 .... 3.00

Revelations
(Clive Barker's)
Eclipse
1 .... 8.00

Revelation:
The Comic Book
Draw Near
1-6 .... 4.00

Revelry in Hell
Fantagraphics, 1990
1 .... 3.00

Revenge of the
Oil Slick Ducks
Canew Ideas
1 .... 1.00

Revenge of the Prowler
Eclipse, 1988
1 .... 2.00
2 .... 3.00
3-4 .... 2.00

Revengers Featuring
Armor and The
Silverstreak
Continuity, 1985
1-3 .... 2.00

Revengers Featuring Megalith
Continuity, 1985
1-6 ....2.00

Revengers: Hybrids Special
Continuity, 1992
1 ....5.00

Reverend Ablack: Adventures of the Antichrist
Creativeforce Designs, 1996
1-2 ....3.00

Revisionary
Moonstone, 2005
1 ....3.00

Revolver
Fleetway-Quality
1-7 ....3.00

Revolver (Robin Snyder's...)
Renegade, 1985
1-Ann 1 ....2.00

Revolving Doors
Blackthorne, 1986
1-3 ....2.00

Revved
Image, 2006
1 ....10.00

Rex Allen
Dell, 1951
2 ....60.00
3-9 ....35.00
10-15 ....30.00
16-19 ....25.00
20-31 ....20.00

Rex Dexter of Mars
Fox, 1940
1 ....1,500.00

Rex Hart
Marvel, 1949
6-8 ....100.00

Rex Hellwig
Black Cat
1 ....3.00

Rex Libris
Slave Labor, 2005
1-2 ....3.00

Rex Morgan, M.D.
Argo, 1950
1 ....75.00
2-3 ....50.00

Rex Mundi
Image, 2003
1-17 ....3.00

RG Veda
Tokyopop, 2005
1-3 .... 10.00

Rhaj
Mu
1-4 .... 2.00

Rhanes of Terror
Buffalo Nickel, 1999
1-4 .... 3.00

Rhudiprrt, Prince of Fur
Mu, 1990
1-4 .... 2.00
5-8 .... 3.00

Rib
Dilemma, 1996
1 .... 2.00

Rib
Caliber, 1997
1 .... 3.00

Ribit!
Comico, 1989
1-4 .... 2.00

Richard Dragon
DC, 2004
1-12 .... 3.00

Richard Dragon, Kung-Fu Fighter
DC, 1975
1 .... 10.00
2-3 .... 4.00
4-5 .... 3.00
6-18 .... 2.00

Richard Speck
Boneyard, 1993
1 .... 3.00

Richie Rich
Harvey, 1960

With his big red bow tie, top coat, and blond hair parted down the middle (turn-of-the-century style), Richie Rich became one of the world's most recognizable comic-book characters.

Richie is a "poor little rich boy," with enough cash to give Scrooge McDuck a run for his money, yet with all the same problems and turmoils as any eight-year-old kid. (Yeah, right! But anyway...)

Richie began as a supporting character in Little Dot, but Harvey could tell it had hit on a successful formula and spun Richie off into his own book. Eventually, he would star in more than 30 titles, digests, specials, and annuals as the flagship character of Harvey's comic book line.

If there's a failing in Harvey worse than its obsession with certain characters and plotlines, it's in the anonymity its creators worked under. Most other publishers had been crediting creators for years while the Richie Rich titles continued to simply magically appear, at least judging from the lack of attribution.

1 .... 3,250.00
2 .... 950.00
3 .... 500.00
4-5 .... 375.00
6-9 .... 250.00
10 .... 175.00
11-15 .... 125.00
16-20 .... 90.00
21-30 .... 65.00
31-40 .... 45.00
41-49 .... 35.00
50-60 .... 25.00
61-70 .... 20.00
71-88 .... 15.00
89-102 .... 10.00
103-126 .... 7.00
127-159 .... 5.00
160-200 .... 3.00
201-254 .... 2.00

Richie Rich
Harvey, 1991
1 .... 5.00
2 .... 3.00
3-10 .... 2.00
11-28 .... 1.00

Richie Rich Adventure Digest Magazine
Harvey, 1992
1-6 .... 2.00

Richie Rich and Billy Bellhops
Harvey, 1977
1 .... 5.00

Richie Rich and Cadbury
Harvey, 1977
1 .... 15.00
2-10 .... 10.00

11-12......................................5.00
13-19......................................4.00
20-29......................................3.00

Richie Rich & Casper
Harvey, 1974

1..12.00
2..6.00
3-5..4.00
6-10..3.00
11-45..2.00

Richie Rich and Casper in 3-D
Blackthorne, 1987

1/A-1/B....................................3.00

Richie Rich & Dollar, the Dog
Harvey, 1977

1..5.00
2..3.00
3-24..2.00

Richie Rich and Dot
Harvey, 1974

1..20.00

Richie Rich and Gloria
Harvey, 1977

1..10.00
2-10..8.00
11-19..5.00
20-25..4.00

Richie Rich and His Girlfriends
Harvey, 1979

1..10.00
2-10..8.00
11-16..5.00

Richie Rich and His Mean Cousin Reggie
Harvey, 1979

1..10.00
2-3..5.00

Richie Rich & Jackie Jokers
Harvey, 1973

1..18.00
2..10.00
3-5..6.00
6-10..4.00
11-30..3.00
31-48..2.00

Richie Rich and Professor Keenbean
Harvey, 1990

1-2..1.00

Richie Rich and the New Kids on the Block
Harvey, 1991

1..2.00

Richie Rich and Timmy Time
Harvey, 1977

1 .... 8.00

Richie Rich Bank Books
Harvey, 1972

1 .... 24.00
2 .... 10.00
3-5 .... 6.00
6-10 .... 4.00
11-20 .... 3.00
21-59 .... 2.00

Richie Rich Best of the Years
Harvey, 1977

1 .... 10.00
2-6 .... 6.00

Richie Rich Big Book (Vol. 2)
Harvey, 1992

1-2.. 2.00

Richie Rich Big Bucks
Harvey, 1991

1 .... 2.00
2-8 .... 1.00

Richie Rich Billions
Harvey, 1974

1 .... 12.00
2 .... 7.00
3 .... 6.00
4-5 .... 5.00
6-10 .... 4.00
11-30 .... 3.00
31-48 .... 2.00

Richie Rich Cash
Harvey, 1974

This series title gets right to the heart of matter, because what is Richie Rich about, if not cash? He's got a lot, his family has a lot, and much madcap adventure involving it ensues over the course of each issue. Stories focus on Richie's interactions with his friends and relatives, such as his prankster cousin Reggie, his young girlfriend Gloria, and his cheerful butler Cadbury. His happy and pleasant parents are on hand, too, usually to do something charitable with all their riches to get the family out of some jam or other. Issues also feature occasional two-page text stories featuring such Harvey characters as Little Dot Polka.

Published by Harvey Publications and one of several regular Richie Rich titles, this series asks the reader to "Cash in on Thrills and Laughs."

1 .... 10.00
2 .... 6.00
3-10 .... 4.00
11-30 .... 3.00
31-47 .... 2.00

Richie Rich Cash Money
Harvey, 1992

1-2 .... 2.00

Richie Rich, Casper and Wendy
Harvey, 1976

1 .... 8.00
1/A-2-1/L-2 .... 5.00

Richie Rich Diamonds
Harvey, 1972

1 .... 15.00
2 .... 9.00
3-5 .... 7.00
6-10 .... 5.00
11-30 .... 4.00
31-40 .... 3.00
41-59 .... 2.00

Richie Rich Digest Magazine
Harvey, 1986

1 .... 4.00
2-10 .... 3.00
11-42 .... 2.00

Richie Rich Digest Stories
Harvey, 1977

1 .... 10.00
2-10 .... 5.00
11-17 .... 3.00

Richie Rich Digest Winners
Harvey, 1977

1 .... 10.00
2-5 .... 5.00

Richie Rich Dollars & Cents
Harvey, 1963

1 .... 250.00
2 .... 125.00

3-5	85.00
6-10	40.00
11-20	25.00
21-30	15.00
31-40	10.00
41-50	7.00
51-60	5.00
61-70	3.00
71-90	2.00
91-109	1.00

Richie Rich Fortunes
Harvey, 1971

1	25.00
2	10.00
3-5	7.00
6-10	5.00
11-20	4.00
21-40	3.00
41-63	2.00

Richie Rich Gems
Harvey, 1974

Everyone knows Richie Rich, that poor little rich boy whose adventures usually involve a whole bunch of money. Here, in some cases, these stories focus on gems, although it should by no means be taken as an unbreakable rule. Typical stories deal with the shiny things, focusing, for example, on his wealthy mom needing to transport a truckload of them into storage -- but they're too heavy! Other stories focus on other members of the Rich family, like Cousin Penny Van Dough, or the girl who spends all her time trying to get Richie to notice her, Mayda Munny. Humor along the lines of the characters' names abounds.

This series does sparkle with fun and excitement.

1	10.00
2	6.00
3-5	4.00
6-10	3.00
11-43	2.00

Richie Rich Giant Size
Harvey, 1992

1-4	2.00

Richie Rich Gold & Silver
Harvey, 1975

1	10.00
2	6.00
3-5	4.00
6-10	3.00
11-42	2.00

Richie Rich Gold Nuggets Digest Magazine
Harvey, 1990

1	3.00
2-4	2.00

Richie Rich Holiday Digest
Harvey, 1980

1	3.00
2-5	2.00

Richie Rich Inventions
Harvey, 1977

1	10.00
2-10	6.00
11-19	4.00
20-26	3.00

Richie Rich Jackpots
Harvey, 1972

1	30.00
2	12.00
3-5	8.00
6-8	6.00
9-19	4.00
20	6.00
21-40	3.00
41-58	2.00

Richie Rich Million Dollar Digest
Harvey, 1980

1-10	10.00

Richie Rich Million Dollar Digest
Harvey, 1986

1	5.00
2-10	3.00
11-34	2.00

Richie Rich Millions
Harvey, 1961

1	200.00
2-3	100.00
4-10	75.00
11-20	50.00
21-30	40.00
31-37	30.00
38-44	25.00
45-48	20.00
49-56	10.00

57-61	7.00
62-80	5.00
81-90	3.00
91-110	2.00
111-113	1.00

Richie Rich Money World
Harvey, 1972

1	85.00
2	35.00
3	25.00
4-5	20.00
6-10	15.00
11-18	10.00
19-28	7.00
29-38	5.00
39-59	3.00

Richie Rich Money World Digest
Harvey, 1991

1-8	2.00

Richie Rich (Movie Adaptation)
Marvel, 1995

1	3.00

Richie Rich Profits
Harvey, 1974

1	25.00
2-3	15.00
4-10	10.00
11-19	8.00
20-29	6.00
30-39	5.00
40-47	4.00

Richie Rich Relics
Harvey, 1988

1-4	3.00

Richie Rich Riches
Harvey, 1972

1	28.00
2	13.00
3-5	8.00
6-10	5.00
11-20	4.00
21-30	3.00
31-59	2.00

Richie Rich Success Stories
Harvey, 1964

1	200.00
2	100.00
3-4	75.00
5-10	50.00
11-20	25.00
21-25	20.00
26-30	15.00
31-40	10.00
41-70	7.00
71-89	5.00
90-100	3.00
101-105	2.00

Richie Rich Vacation Digest
Harvey, 1991
1992-1993 .... 2.00

Richie Rich Vacations Digest
Harvey, 1980
1 .... 10.00
2-8 .... 5.00

Richie Rich Vaults of Mystery
Harvey, 1974

One of the most loved comic-book characters of all time, Richie Rich, the poor little rich boy, has starred in dozens of titles over the decades. Capitalizing on Rich's popularity, the character was even turned into a cartoon series as well as a live-action movie starring Macaulay Culkin. Originally a backup feature star in other Harvey Comics, Richie Rich grew in popularity and even spawned several titles himself.

Richie Rich: Vault$ of Mystery was an all-ages title featuring the adventures of the title character, along with his friends Gloria, Reggie, and a host of others. Though the issue would be rounded out with several short, often one-page, humorous vignettes, the main story would often focus on a mystery requiring Rich's ingenuity and vast wealth in order to solve it. Fans of Richie Rich as well as other youth-oriented mysteries such as Scooby-Doo will delight in the outlandish adventures in Richie Rich: Vault$ of Mystery.

1 .... 25.00
2 .... 15.00
3-5 .... 8.00
6-10 .... 5.00
11-20 .... 4.00

21-47 .... 3.00

Richie Rich Zillionz
Harvey, 1976
1 .... 12.00
2-4 .... 6.00
5 .... 4.00
6-10 .... 3.00
11-33 .... 2.00

Ricky
Standard, 1953
5 .... 20.00

Ride
Image, 2004
1-2 .... 3.00

Ride, The: 2 for the Road One Shot
Image, 2005
1 .... 3.00

Ride: Foreign Parts
Image, 2005
0 .... 3.00

Rider
Ajax, 1957
1 .... 75.00
2-5 .... 40.00

Rifleman
Dell, 1960
2-3 .... 85.00
4-10 .... 70.00
11-20 .... 55.00

Rima, the Jungle Girl
DC, 1974
1 .... 13.00
2-7 .... 7.00

Rime of the Ancient Mariner
Tome
1 .... 4.00

Rimshot
Rip Off, 1990
1-2 .... 2.00
3 .... 3.00

Ring of Bright Water
Dell, 1969
1 .... 7.00

Ring of Roses
Dark Horse, 2005
1-4 .... 3.00

Ring of the Nibelung
DC, 1989
1-4 .... 5.00

Ring of the Nibelung
Dark Horse, 2000
1-4 .... 3.00

Ring of the Nibelung (Vol. 2)
Dark Horse, 2000
1-3 .... 3.00

Ring of the Nibelung (Vol. 3)
Dark Horse, 2000
1-3 .... 3.00

Ring of the Nibelung (Vol. 4)
Dark Horse, 2001
1-4 .... 3.00

Ringo Kid
Marvel, 1970
1 .... 20.00
2 .... 8.00
3-10 .... 5.00
11 .... 4.00
12 .... 10.00
13-27 .... 4.00
27/30¢ 20.00
28 .... 4.00
28/30¢ 20.00
29-30 .... 4.00

Ringo Kid Western
Marvel, 1954
1 .... 175.00
2 .... 90.00
3 .... 60.00
4-5 .... 48.00
6-10 .... 42.00
11-21 .... 36.00

Rin Tin Tin
Dell, 1954
4-10 .... 50.00
11-20 .... 40.00
21-38 .... 35.00

Rin Tin Tin & Rusty
Gold Key, 1963
1 .... 50.00

Rio at Bay
Dark Horse, 1992
1-2 .... 3.00

Rio Conchos
Gold Key, 1965
1 .... 22.00

Rio Graphic Novel
Comico, 1987
1 .... 9.00

Rio Kid
Eternity
1-3 .... 3.00

Rion 2990
Rion
1-4 .... 2.00

Riot
Atlas, 1954

1	165.00
2	120.00
3	105.00
4	140.00
5	145.00
6	105.00

Riot, Act 1
Viz, 1995

1-6	3.00

Riot, Act 2
Viz, 1996

1-7	3.00

Riot Gear
Triumphant, 1993

1-Ashcan 1	3.00

Riot Gear: Violent Past
Triumphant, 1994

1-2	3.00

Ripclaw (Vol. 1)
Image, 1995

1/2	2.00
1/2/Gold-4	3.00

Ripclaw (Vol. 2)
Image, 1995

1-Special 1	3.00

R.I.P. Comics Module
TSR

1-8	3.00

R.I.P.D.
Dark Horse, 1999

1-4	3.00

Ripfire
Malibu, 1995

0	3.00

Rip Hunter... Time Master
DC, 1961

1	350.00
2	140.00
3	115.00
4-5	95.00
6-7	85.00
8-15	70.00
16-20	58.00
21-25	48.00
26-29	40.00

Rip in Time
Fantagor

1-5	2.00

Ripley's Believe It or Not!
Gold Key, 1967

4	26.00
5-10	16.00
11-15	12.00
16-20	10.00
21-30	8.00
31-38	5.00
39	6.00
40-50	5.00
51-70	4.00
71-94	3.00

Ripley's Believe It or Not!
Dark Horse, 2002

1-4	3.00

Ripley's Believe It or Not!: Beauty & Grooming
Schanes

1	3.00

Ripley's Believe It or Not!: Child Prodigies
Schanes

1	3.00

Ripley's Believe It or Not!: Cruelty
Schanes Products, 1993

1-2	3.00

Ripley's Believe It or Not!: Fairy Tales & Literature
Schanes

1	3.00

Ripley's Believe It or Not!: Feats of Wonder
Schanes

1	3.00

Ripley's Believe It or Not Magazine
Harvey, 1953

1	60.00
2	45.00
3-4	40.00

Ripley's Believe It or Not!: Sports Feats
Schanes Products, 1993

1	3.00

Ripley's Believe It or Not!: Strange Deaths
Schanes Products, 1993

1	3.00

Ripley's Believe It or Not True War Stories
Gold Key, 1966

1	24.00

Rip Off Comix
Rip Off, 1977

In a classic salute to everything that is '70s, Rip Off Comix collects several stories - humorous, entertaining and just plain out there - from some of the best-known creators of underground comics. Dave Sheridan, Bill Griffith, and Gilbert Shelton are just a few of the artists lending their characters and unique style of storytelling to this black-and-white compilation.

What make the stories in this title of particular interest to unsuspecting readers are not the striking similarities they share with other mainstream titles, but rather the dated jokes and subject matter that creep into each story's narrative. Abundant references to Nixon, the oil crisis, and such cultural phenomena as New Wave, Pepsi Cola, and the cult classic Alien make for an open window to a time gone but not forgotten.

1	25.00
2	16.00
3	12.00
4	8.00
5-6	6.00
6/2nd	3.00
7	6.00
8-10	5.00
11-23	4.00
24-26	3.00
27-31	4.00

Ripper
Aircel

1-6	3.00

Ripper Legacy
Caliber

1-3	3.00

Riptide
Image, 1995

1-2	3.00

Rise of Apocalypse
Marvel, 1996
1-4 ....2.00

Rising Stars
Image, 1999
0 ....5.00
0/Gold 12.00
1/2 ....3.00
1/Holofoil 8.00
1/Chromium 10.00
1/Kids 7.00
1/Fighting 6.00
1/Funeral 5.00
1/Wizard..................................4.00
2 ....3.00
3-24 ....3.00
Ashcan 1/Conven...................6.00
Ashcan 1 ....3.00

Rising Stars: Bright
Image, 2003
1-3...3.00

Rising Stars: Untouchable
Image, 2006
1 ....3.00

Rising Stars: Visitations
Image, 2002
1 ....9.00

Rising Stars: Voices of the Dead
Image, 2005
1-6...3.00

Rite
Knight, 1997
1 ....3.00

Riverdale High
Archie, 1990
1 ....2.00
2-5 ....1.00

Rivets
Argo, 1956
1 ....30.00
2-3 ....20.00

Rivets & Ruby
Radio, 1998
1-4...3.00

Rivit
Blackthorne, 1987
1 ....2.00

Roach Killer
NBM
1 ....12.00

Roachmill
Blackthorne, 1986
1-6...2.00

Roachmill
Dark Horse, 1988
1-10 .... 2.00

Roadkill
Lighthouse
1-2 .... 2.00

Roadkill: A Chronicle of the Deadworld
Caliber
1 .... 3.00

Road to Hell
Idea & Design Works, 2006
1-3... 4.00

Road Trip
Oni, 2000
1 .... 3.00

Roadways
Cult, 1994
1-4 .... 3.00

Roarin' Rick's Rare Bit Fiends
King Hell, 1994
1-21 .... 3.00

Robbin' $3000
Parody
1 .... 3.00

Rob Hanes
WCG, 1991
1 .... 3.00

Rob Hanes Adventures
WCG, 2000
1-10 .... 3.00

Robin
DC, 1991
1 .... 3.00
1/2nd-1/3rd........................... 2.00
2 .... 3.00
2/2nd-5 .... 2.00
Ann 1-Ann 2 .... 3.00

Robin
DC, 1993
0 .... 2.00
1-1/Variant............................ 4.00
2-14 .... 2.00
14/Variant.............................. 3.00
15-49 .... 2.00
50 .... 3.00
51-74 .... 2.00
75 .... 3.00
76-99 .... 2.00
100 .... 4.00
101-125 .... 2.00
126 .... 5.00
☛Robin quits
127 .... 4.00
☛New Robin
128 .... 3.00
129-138 .... 2.00
139-169 .... 3.00

1000000 .... 4.00
Ann 3..................................... 3.00
Ann 4..................................... 4.00
Ann 5..................................... 3.00
Ann 6..................................... 4.00
Ann 7..................................... 5.00
GS 1 .... 6.00

Robin Plus
DC, 1996
1-2 .... 3.00

Robin 3000
DC, 1992
1-2 .... 5.00

Robin: Year One
DC, 2000
1-4 .... 5.00

Robin/Argent Double-Shot
DC, 1998
1 .... 2.00

Robin II
DC, 1991
1 .... 1.00
1/A-1/C 2.00
1/CS 10.00
1/D... 2.00
2 .... 1.00
2/A-2/C 2.00
2/CS 9.00
3 .... 1.00
3/A-3/B 2.00
3/CS 6.00
4 .... 1.00
4/A 2.00
4/CS 4.00
Deluxe 1 .... 30.00

Robin III: Cry of the Huntress
DC, 1992
1 .... 1.00
1/Variant................................ 3.00
2 .... 1.00
2/Variant................................ 3.00
3 .... 1.00
3/Variant................................ 3.00
4 .... 1.00
4/Variant................................ 3.00
5 .... 1.00
5/Variant................................ 3.00
6 .... 1.00
6/Variant................................ 3.00

Robin Hood
Magazine Enterprises, 1955
52 .... 100.00
53-8 .... 90.00

Robin Hood
Charlton, 1956
28 .... 40.00
29-30 .... 35.00
31-37 .... 30.00
38 .... 45.00

Robin Hood
Dell, 1963

1 ....20.00

Robin Hood
Eternity, 1989

1-4..2.00

Robin Hood
Eclipse, 1991

1-3..3.00

Robin Hood Tales
Quality, 1956

1 ....190.00
2-6....................................185.00

Robin Hood Tales
DC, 1957

7..220.00
8-14....................................185.00

Robin Red
and the Lutins
Ace, 1986

Robin Red is a woodcutter who becomes a hero in Pat Boyette's whimsical fantasy. After Prince Bonny is kidnapped by the garlic-chomping Gringes and taken to the hellish Netherworld, Red is asked to rescue him. Having no weapons himself, he is given a sword by the slumbering wizard Merlin, who was transformed into a tree. Obviously written for children, Robin Red and the Lutins eschews the violent content typical of the genre for mild action and innocuous humor.

1-2..2.00

Robinsonia
NBM

1 ....12.00

Robocop (Magazine)
Marvel, 1987

1 ....3.00

Robocop
Marvel, 1990

1 .... 3.00
2-23 .... 2.00

Robocop
(Movie Adaptation)
Marvel, 1990

1 .... 5.00

Robocop 2
Marvel, 1990

1-3..2.00

Robocop 2
(Magazine)
Marvel, 1990

1 .... 3.00

Robocop 3
Dark Horse, 1993

1-3.. 3.00

Robocop (Frank Miller's)
Avatar, 2003

1 .... 5.00
1/Platinum 7.00
1/Wraparound 5.00
2 .... 4.00
2/Platinum 5.00
3 .... 4.00
3/Platinum 6.00
3/Ryp-4.................................. 4.00
4/Miller................................... 6.00
4/Platinum 5.00
5 .... 4.00
5/Platinum 5.00
5/Wraparound-6 .... 4.00
6/Miller................................... 6.00
6/Platinum 5.00
7 .... 4.00
7/Miller................................... 6.00
7/Platinum 5.00
7/Wraparound-8 .... 4.00
8/Miller................................... 6.00
8/Platinum 5.00
8/Wraparound 4.00

Robocop:
Killing Machine
Avatar, 2004

1 .... 6.00
1/Platinum 15.00
1/Wraparound 6.00

Robocop: Mortal Coils
Dark Horse, 1993

1-4 .... 3.00

Robocop: Prime Suspect
Dark Horse, 1992

1-4 .... 3.00

Robocop: Roulette
Dark Horse, 1993

1-4 .... 3.00

Robocop versus
the Terminator
Dark Horse, 1992

1 .... 3.00
1/Platinum 4.00
2-4 .... 3.00

Robocop: Wild Child
Avatar, 2005

1 .... 3.00
1/Photo.................................. 4.00
1/Platinum 12.00
1/Rivalry 5.00
1/Wraparound 6.00

Robocop: Wild Child -
Detroit's Finest
Avatar, 2005

1 .... 6.00
1/Detroit................................. 7.00
1/Photo.................................. 6.00
1/Platinum 15.00
1/Rivalry 7.00
1/Wraparound 6.00

Robo Dojo
DC, 2002

1-6 .... 3.00

Robo-Hunter
Eagle

1 .... 2.00
2-5 .... 1.00

Robotech
Antarctic, 1997

1-Ann 1.................................. 3.00

Robotech (Wildstorm)
DC, 2003

0-6 .... 3.00

Robotech:
Amazon World-Escape
from Praxis
Academy, 1994

Many worlds within the Robotech Universe besides Earth have felt the ravages of the alien Invid. On Praxis, the Invid have conquered the entire female Amazon population, and are using the planet itself for mysterious experiments.

One small group of captives has managed to escape, but they have found themselves trapped in a large cavern beneath the surface, filled with strange prehistoric plants and animals. While the women navigate the unknown dangers of this strange underworld, the planet seems to be destroying itself with a series of increasingly violent quakes. The tremors are the result of the Invid's experiments, and the female refugees soon discover that the aliens have already abandoned the planet, taking their captives with them. This small group of warriors struggles to get off the planet themselves before it self-destructs, vowing revenge for the deaths of their many sisters and the loss of their homeworld.

1 ....3.00

Robotech: Class Reunion
Antarctic, 1998
1 ....4.00

Robotech: Clone
Academy, 1995
0-5..3.00
Special 1 ....4.00

Robotech: Covert-Ops
Antarctic, 1998
1-2...3.00

Robotech: Cyber World: Secrets of Haydon IV
Academy, 1994
1 ....3.00

Robotech Defenders
DC, 1985
1-2...2.00

Robotech: Escape
Antarctic, 1998
1 ....3.00

Robotech: Final Fire
Antarctic, 1998
1 ....3.00

Robotech: Firewalkers
Eternity, 1993
1 ....3.00

Robotech Genesis
Eternity, 1992
1 ....3.00
1/Ltd. 6.00
2-6..3.00

Robotech in 3-D
Comico, 1985
1 .... 3.00

RoboTech: Invasion
DC, 2004
1-5.. 3.00

Robotech: Invid War
Eternity, 1992
1-9.. 3.00
10-13...................................... 1.00
14-18...................................... 3.00

Robotech: Invid War Aftermath
Eternity, 1993
1-2... 3.00

RoboTech: Love & War
DC, 2003
1-6.. 3.00

RoboTech: Macross Saga
DC, 2003
1-4....................................... 15.00

Robotech Masters
Comico, 1985
1-23....................................... 2.00

Robotech: Mechangel
Academy

Lyss is a Zentraedi assassin, trained by the legendary Breetai Tul and Exadore. She fought on the Zentraedi side during the entire Robotech war, only to change sides at the end. She offered to be shrunk to human size, and proudly served the human side in numerous battles that followed, including the Malcontent Uprisings. During that time, she ran afoul of Eldin Frost, a Colonel in the Brasilia Military Police who began experiments grafting Zentraedi tissues and organs into humans. When Lyss confronted him, she was captured and experimented on for days before escaping.

She never said what they did to her.

Once free, she began methodically targeting the scientists who experimented on her, eventually finding an ally who created a battle suit known as Mechangel. With it, she continued her hunt for Frost and his men.

1-3.. 3.00

Robotech: Megastorm
Antarctic, 1998
1 .... 8.00

Robotech: Prelude to the Shadow Chronicles
DC, 2005
1-5.. 4.00

Robotech: Return to Macross
Eternity, 1993
1-32....................................... 3.00

Robotech: Sentinels - Rubicon
Antarctic, 1998
1-7.. 3.00

Robotech Special
Comico, 1988
1 .... 3.00

Robotech the Graphic Novel
Comico, 1986
1 .... 6.00

Robotech: The Macross Saga
Comico, 1984
1 .... 8.00
2 .... 4.00
3-5 .... 3.00
6-36 .... 2.00

Robotech: The New Generation
Comico, 1985
1-25 .... 2.00

Robotech II: Invid World, Assault on Optera
Academy, 1994
1 .... 3.00

Robotech II: The Sentinels
Eternity, 1988
1 .... 4.00
1/2nd 2.00
2-3 .... 3.00
3/2nd-16 .... 2.00

Robotech II: The Sentinels Book II
Eternity, 1990
1-11 ....2.00
12-20 ....3.00

Robotech II: The Sentinels Book III
Eternity
1-6 ....3.00

Robotech II: The Sentinels Book IV
Academy, 1996
1-6 ....3.00

Robotech II: The Sentinels Cyberpirates
Eternity, 1991
1-4 ....2.00

Robotech II: The Sentinels Special
Eternity, 1989
1-2 ....2.00

Robotech II: The Sentinels Swimsuit Spectacular
Eternity
1 ....3.00

Robotech II: The Sentinels: The Illustrated Handbook
Eternity
1-3 ....3.00

Robotech II: The Sentinels T he Malcontent Uprisings
Malibu, 1989
7-12 ....2.00

Robotech II: The Sentinels: The Untold Story
Eternity
1 ....3.00

Robotech II: The Sentinels Wedding Special
Eternity, 1989
1-2 ....2.00

Robotech: Vermilion
Antarctic, 1997
1-4 ....3.00

Robotech Warriors
Academy, 1995

The Zentraedi are a race of giant warriors created by the technologically advanced Robotech Masters, and used as both explorers and soldiers in the Masters' huge empire. When a Master scientist named Zor sent his prototype space ship into hyperspace, the Zentraedi were called upon to retrieve the ship. The Super-Dimensional Fortress, or SDF-1, contains records of all the knowledge gleaned by Zor during his explorations. Wary of the uses to which his superiors would put the information contained within his ship's data banks, but unwilling to destroy his creation, Zor chose to send the ship on an endless dimension-hopping journey. This is the story of the group of Zentraedi sent after the SDF-1, and the dangers they face as they find themselves exploring the unknown reaches of the universe.

1 .... 3.00

Robotech: Wings of Gibraltar
Antarctic, 1998
1-2 .... 3.00

Robotix
Marvel, 1986
1 .... 1.00

Robotmen of the Lost Planet
Avon, 1952
1 .... 1,000.00

Robo Warriors
CFW
1-8 .... 2.00

Robyn of Sherwood
Caliber, 1998
1 .... 3.00

Rockers
Rip Off, 1988
1-8 .... 2.00

Rocket Comics
Hillman, 1940
1 .... 1,535.00
2-3 .... 775.00

Rocketeer 3-D Comic, The
Disney, 1991
1 .... 5.00

Rocketeer Adventure Magazine
Comico, 1988
1 .... 5.00
2 .... 4.00
3 .... 3.00

Rocketeer Special Edition
Eclipse, 1984
1 .... 2.00

Rocketeer: The Official Movie Adaptation
Disney, 1991
1 .... 3.00
1/Direct 6.00

Rocket Kelly
Fox, 1944
0 .... 185.00
1 .... 140.00
2-5 .... 120.00

Rocketman
AC
1-Ashcan 2 .... 6.00

Rocketman
Ajax, 1952
1 .... 6.00

Rocketman: King of the Rocket Men
Innovation
1-4 .... 3.00

Rocketo
Speakeasy Comics, 2005
1-5 .... 3.00

Rocketo: Journey to the Hidden Sea
Image, 2006
6-7 .... 3.00
10-12 .... 4.00

Rocket Raccoon
Marvel, 1985

1 ....2.00
2-4 ....1.00

Rocket Ranger
Adventure, 1991

In an alternate world where the Nazis succeeded in conquering nearly every country except for the United States, only one brave man can turn the tide for freedom: Rocket Ranger!

Based on the videogame of the same name, this short-lived series detailed the jet-packed adventures of the title character, Tom Cory, (also known as Rocket Ranger) as he fought to end the ever-expanding grasp of the Third Reich. From the battlefields of Eastern Europe to the Nazi "lunarium mines" on the surface of the moon, Rocket Ranger epitomized the feel of the 1940s movie serials from which the videogame was originally inspired. Enthusiasts of the original videogame as well as fans of the similarly themed comic book and subsequent motion picture, The Rocketeer, will love this comic's often B-movie tone.

1-6 ....3.00

Rocket Ship X
Fox, 1951

1 ....525.00

Rocket to the Moon
Avon, 1951

1 ....815.00

Rock Fantasy
Rock Fantasy, 1990

1-15 ....3.00
16 ....5.00
17 ....3.00

Rockheads
Solson

1 .... 2.00

Rockin' Bones
New England, 1992

1-Holiday 1 .... 3.00

Rockinfreakapotamus Presents the Red Hot Chili Peppers Illustrated Lyrics
Telltale, 1997

1 .... 4.00

Rockin Rollin Miner Ants
Fate, 1991

1 .... 2.00

Rockmeez
Jzink Comics, 1992

1-4 .... 3.00

Rock 'n' Roll Comics
Revolutionary, 1989

1 .... 6.00
1/2nd 4.00
1/3rd-1/7th 2.00
2 .... 3.00
2/2nd-2/4th 2.00
1-2 .... 4.00
2/5th-1-4 .... 2.00
3 .... 10.00
1-5-1-6 .... 2.00
4 .... 50.00
1-7 .... 2.00
4/2nd 3.00
5-8 .... 2.00
9 .... 5.00
9/2nd-16 .... 2.00
17 .... 3.00
18 .... 2.00
19-29 .... 3.00
5-2 .... 2.00
30-39 .... 3.00
6-2 .... 2.00
40 .... 3.00
6-3 .... 2.00
41 .... 3.00
6-4 .... 2.00
42-49 .... 3.00
7-2 .... 2.00
50 .... 3.00
7-3 .... 2.00
51-65 .... 3.00

Rock 'N' Roll Comics Magazine
Revolutionary, 1990

1-5 .... 3.00

Rock 'N' Roll
Image, 2006

1 .... 4.00

Rockola
Mirage

1 .... 2.00

Rocko's Modern Life
Marvel, 1994

1-7 .... 2.00

Rocky and His Fiendish Friends
Gold Key, 1962

1 .... 100.00
2-3 .... 75.00
4-5 .... 60.00

Rocky Horror Picture Show: The Comic Book
Caliber, 1990

1 .... 7.00
1/2nd 3.00
2-3 .... 4.00

Rocky Lane Western
Fawcett, 1949

1 .... 450.00
2 .... 175.00
3-9 .... 125.00
10-19 .... 75.00
20-35 .... 55.00
36-45 .... 40.00
46-55 .... 35.00

Rocky Lane Western
Charlton, 1954

56 .... 75.00
57-60 .... 45.00
61-70 .... 35.00
71-87 .... 30.00

Rocky Lane Western (AC)
AC

1 .... 3.00
2 .... 6.00
Ann 1 .... 3.00

Rocky Mountain King
L. Miller & Son

1 .... 10.00
2-5 .... 8.00
6-20 .... 6.00
21-50 .... 5.00
51-65 .... 4.00

Rocky: The One and Only
Fantagraphics, 2006

1 .... 13.00

Rod Cameron Western
Fawcett, 1950

1 .... 325.00
2 .... 150.00
3 .... 125.00
4-10 .... 105.00
11-19 .... 85.00
20 .... 90.00

Roel
Sirius, 1997

1 .... 3.00

Rogan Gosh
DC

1 .... 7.00

Roger Dodger
Standard, 1952
5 ....25.00

Roger Fnord
Rip Off, 1992
1 ....3.00

Roger Rabbit
Disney, 1990
1-18 ....2.00
Special 1 ....4.00

Roger Rabbit in 3-D
Disney
1 ....3.00

Roger Rabbit's Toontown
Disney, 1991
1-5 ....2.00

Roger Wilco
Adventure, 1992
1-2 ....3.00

Rog-2000
Pacific
1 ....2.00

Rogue
Marvel, 1995
1 ....4.00
2-4 ....3.00
Book 1 ....13.00

Rogue
Marvel, 2001
1-4 ....3.00

Rogue
Marvel, 2004
1-12 ....3.00

Rogue
Monster, 1991
1 ....2.00

Rogue Battlebook
Marvel
1 ....4.00

Rogue Satellite Comics
Slave Labor, 1996
1-Special 1 ....3.00

Rogues Gallery
DC
1 ....4.00

Rogues, The (Villains)
DC, 1998
1 ....2.00

Rogue Trooper (1st Series)
Fleetway-Quality
1-49 ....2.00

Rogue Trooper (2nd Series)
Fleetway-Quality
1-9 .... 3.00

Roja Fusion
Antarctic, 1995
1 .... 3.00

Rokkin
DC, 2006
1-6 .... 3.00

Roland: Days Of Wrath
Terra Major, 1999
1 .... 3.00

Rollercoaster
Fantagraphics, 1996
1 .... 4.00

Rollercoasters Special Edition
Blue Comet
1 .... 2.00

Rolling Stones
Personality
1-3 .... 3.00

Rolling Stones: Voodoo Lounge
Marvel, 1995
1 .... 7.00

Roly Poly Comics
Green, 1945
1 .... 225.00
10 .... 150.00
11-14 .... 100.00

Rom
Marvel, 1979

Marvel had a number of titles based on toys in the late 1970s and early 1980s, but the story of Rom has to be the strangest. Based on a robot-like figure from Parker Brothers, Rom had a suitably computer-sounding name (the abbreviation for Read-Only Memory just then coming into general knowledge). The toy died a quick death on the shelves ó but the comics title went on for years, with many readers completely oblivious to its origin!

As for Rom's origin, he's from Galador, a planet which, when threatened by the Dire Wraiths, created cyborg warriors known as Spaceknights. Rom is one, and he travels to earth to banish the shape-shifting Wraiths to Limbo.

Inexplicably, several Marvel creators took Rom and his story seriously enough to incorporate it into their own titles. Chris Claremont, who had shown a weakness for hard-luck cases by bringing Team America into the New Mutants, brought the Dire Wraiths into Uncanny X-Men. And a series simply called Spaceknights would follow nearly two decades after the launch and failure of the Rom toy!

-- John Jackson Miller

1 .... 8.00
2-10 .... 2.00
11-16 .... 1.00
17-18 .... 2.00
19-23 .... 1.00
24-25 .... 2.00
26-53 .... 1.00
54 .... 3.00
55 .... 1.00
56 .... 3.00
57-74 .... 1.00
75 .... 2.00
Ann 1-4 .... 1.00

Romance & Confession Stories
St. John, 1949
1 .... 300.00

Romancer
Moonstone, 1996
1 .... 3.00

Romances of Nurse Helen Grant
Atlas, 1957
1 .... 35.00

Romances of the West
Marvel, 1949
1 .... 150.00
2 .... 100.00

Romance Tales
Marvel, 1949
7 .... 75.00
8-9 .... 55.00

Romance Trail
DC, 1949

1	370.00
2	175.00
3	190.00
4	135.00
5-6	120.00

Roman Holidays
Gold Key, 1973

1	20.00
2-3	10.00

Romantic Adventures
ACG, 1949

ACG's long-running "Romantic Adventures" was by most respects a cookie-cutter affair, full of lovestruck damsels trying to catch the eye of the Man They Love. Even then, Ogden Whitney (creator of Herbie) occasionally appeared to throw his off-kilter personality into the mix. The result were stories like "We Had to be Practical!" wherein two lower-class lovers decide to set their own feelings aside to pursue wealthier matches for themselves.

Other stories, such as "School for Romance," have an almost sadistic streak, with its tale of a teacher who was persecuted daily by the stuffy principal. She later discovered that the principal was a young man in disguise, who covered up his own insecurities by affecting a harsh attitude and style of dress. Naturally, he "had loved her since he first laid eyes on her."

1	70.00
2	35.00
3-5	24.00
6-10	20.00
11-30	16.00
31-45	14.00
46-48	45.00
49-50	14.00
51-67	12.00

Romantic Confessions (Vol. 1)
Hillman, 1949

1	100.00
2	50.00
3-12	40.00

Romantic Confessions (Vol. 2)
Hillman, 1951

1-2	32.00
3	45.00
4-12	32.00

Romantic Hearts
Story, 1951

1	75.00
2	40.00
3-10	35.00

Romantic Hearts
Story, 1953

1	50.00
2	30.00
3-12	25.00

Romantic Love
Avon, 1949

1	130.00
2-5	80.00
6	110.00
7-8	72.00
9-12	80.00
13-23	72.00

Romantic Marriage
Ziff-Davis, 1950

1	125.00
2	70.00
3-9	55.00
10	100.00
11-24	55.00

Romantic Picture Novelettes
Magazine Enterprises, 1946

1	125.00

Romantic Secrets
Fawcett, 1949

1	85.00
2-4	55.00
5-8	40.00
9	55.00
10	40.00
11-23	36.00
24	42.00
25-39	32.00

Romantic Secrets
Charlton, 1955

5	45.00
6-10	22.00
11-20	12.00
21-30	8.00
31-52	6.00

Romantic Story
Charlton, 1949

1	65.00
2	40.00
3	30.00
4-9	20.00
10-22	14.00
23-40	12.00
41-60	10.00
61-80	8.00
81-130	5.00

Romantic Tails
Head, 1998

1	3.00

Romantic Western
Fawcett, 1949

1	90.00
2-3	68.00

Romp One Shot
Image, 2004

1	7.00

Ronald McDonald
Charlton, 1970

1	52.00
2-4	35.00

Ronin
DC, 1983

1	4.00

☞Frank Miller series

2-5	3.00
6	5.00

Rook
Harris, 1995

1-2	3.00

Rook Magazine
Warren, 1979

1	4.00
2-10	3.00
11-14	2.00

Room 222
Dell, 1970

1	30.00
2-4	20.00

Rooter
Custom, 1996

1-6	3.00

Rooter
Custom, 1998

1-2	3.00

Roots of the Oppressor
Northstar

1	3.00

Roots of the Swamp Thing
DC, 1986

1-5	2.00

Roscoe! The Dawg, Ace Detective
Renegade, 1987
1-4..2.00

Rose & Thorn
DC, 2004
1-6..3.00

Rose
Hero, 1992
1...4.00
2...3.00
3-4...4.00
5...3.00

Rose
Cartoon Books, 2000
1-3..6.00

Rose & Gunn
Bishop, 1995
3-5..3.00

Rose & Gunn Creator's Choice
Bishop, 1995
1...3.00

Roswell: Little Green Man
Bongo, 1996
1...4.00
2-6...3.00

Rotogin Junkbotz
Image, 2003
0-3..3.00

Rough Raiders
Blue Comet
1-3...2.00
Ann 1..3.00

Roulette
Caliber
1...3.00

Roundup
D.S., 1948
1...105.00
2-5..75.00

Route 666
CrossGen, 2002
1-22..3.00

Rovers
Malibu, 1987
1-7..2.00

Royal Roy
Marvel, 1985
1-6..1.00

Roy Campanella, Baseball Hero
Fawcett, 1950
1..500.00

Roy Rogers Comics
Dell, 1948

The legendary star of cowboy musicals left his mark on the four-color world of comics with these modern-day Wild West tales. As the daring deputy of Pronghorn (among other occupations), Roy's life was one exciting adventure after another, dealing with everything from stampeding buffaloes to stopping range wars. Of course, getting out of his many scraps would be a lot more difficult without his two "sidekicks." Roy's faithful horse, Trigger, and his courageous dog, Bullet, are always at his side, no matter the danger. So saddle up and get ready for some fun, courtesy of Roy Rogers, King of the Cowboys.

1.......................................600.00
2.......................................275.00
3-5....................................200.00
6-10...................................140.00
11-20.................................105.00
21-30...................................90.00
31-40...................................75.00
41-50...................................55.00
51-60...................................45.00
61-80...................................35.00
81-100.................................30.00
101-145...............................25.00

Roy Rogers' Trigger
Dell, 1951
2...90.00
3-5.......................................48.00
6-17.....................................35.00

Roy Rogers Western
AC
1..5.00

Roy Rogers Western Classics
AC
1-2.......................................3.00
3-4.......................................4.00
5..3.00

RTA: Personality Crisis
Image, 2005
0..4.00

Rubber Blanket
Rubber Blanket
1...6.00
2-3...8.00

Rubber Duck
Print Mint, 1971
1-2...3.00

Rubes Revue
Fragments West
1...2.00

Ruby Shaft's Tales of the Unexpurgated
Fantagraphics
1...3.00

Ruck Bud Webster and His Screeching Commandos
Pyramid
1...2.00

Rude Awakening
Dennis Mcmillan, 1996
1...13.00

Rudolph the Red-Nosed Reindeer
DC
1...10.00

Rudolph the Red-Nosed Reindeer Annual
DC, 1950
1950.....................................115.00
1951......................................90.00
1952-1953.............................75.00
1954-1956.............................60.00
1957-1961.............................48.00
1962......................................75.00

Ruff and Reddy
Dell, 1960
4-8.......................................40.00
9-12.....................................30.00

Rugged Action
Atlas, 1954
1...75.00
2-4.......................................55.00

Rugrats
Marvel UK
1...3.00
2-29...2.00

Rugrats
Comic Adventures
Nickelodeon Magazines, 1997
1 ....4.00
2-10 ....3.00

Rugrats
Comic Adventures
Nickelodeon Magazines, 1998
1 ....3.00

Ruins
Marvel, 1995
1-2 ....5.00

Rulah Jungle Goddess
Fox, 1948
17 ....1,000.00
18 ....750.00
19-22 ....600.00
23-27 ....450.00

Ruler of the Land
ADV Manga, 2004
1-5 ....10.00

Rumble Girls:
Silky Warrior Tansie
Image, 2000
1-6 ....4.00

Rumic World
Viz, 1993
1 ....3.00
2 ....4.00

Rummage $2099
Parody
1 ....3.00

Runaway
Dell, 1964
1 ....16.00

Runaway: A Known
Associates Mystery
Known Associates
1 ....3.00

Runaways
Marvel, 2003
1 ....4.00
2-18 ....3.00

Runaways
Marvel, 2005
1 ....6.00
1/Variant 5.00
2-22 ....3.00

Run, Buddy, Run
Gold Key, 1967
1 ....15.00

Rune
Malibu, 1994
0 .... 3.00
1-2 .... 2.00
3 .... 4.00
4-9 .... 2.00
GS 1 .... 3.00

Rune
Malibu, 1995
0-7 .... 2.00

Rune:
Hearts of Darkness
Malibu, 1996
1-3 .... 2.00

Rune/Silver Surfer
Marvel, 1995
1 .... 3.00
1/Direct 6.00

Runes of Ragnan
Image, 2005
1-3 .... 4.00
4 .... 3.00

Rune vs. Venom
Malibu, 1995
1 .... 4.00

Rune/Wrath
Malibu
1 .... 1.00

Runners: Bad Goods
Serve Man Press, 2003
1-5 .... 3.00

Rurouni Kenshin
Viz, 2003
1-19 .... 8.00

Ruse
CrossGen, 2001

Set in the CrossGen universe, Ruse's early issues did not display the CrossGen Sigil but introduced a fantasy element to the seeming Victorian world of detection, although obviously on a different world than Earth. Detective Simon Archard is a brilliant sleuth in the mold of Sherlock Holmes whose seeming assistant, Emma Bishop, has special powers and is playing some sort of fantasy game. Written by Mark Waid and drawn by Butch Guice, the series immediately plunged the detecting pair into life-threatening controversy.
-- *Maggie*

1-26 .... 3.00

Ruse: Archard's Agents:
Deadly Dare
CrossGen, 2004
1 .... 3.00

Ruse: Archard's Agents:
Pugilistic Pete
CrossGen, 2003
1 .... 3.00

Rush City
DC, 2006
1-3 .... 3.00

Rush Limbaugh
Must Die
Boneyard, 1993
1 .... 5.00

Rust
Now, 1987
1-13 .... 2.00

Rust
Now, 1989
1-7 .... 2.00

Rust
Adventure, 1992
1 .... 3.00
1/Ltd. 5.00
2-4 .... 3.00

Rust
Caliber
1-2 .... 3.00

Rusty
Marvel, 1947
12 .... 55.00
13 .... 40.00
14 .... 60.00
15-17 .... 48.00
18-19 .... 30.00
20 .... 55.00
21-22 .... 60.00

Rusty, Boy Detective
Lev Gleason, 1955
1 .... 50.00
2-5 .... 30.00

Ruule:
Ganglords of Chinatown
Beckett, 2003
1-5 .... 3.00

The first issue of Todd McFarlane's launch of this new ongoing series had multiple variant covers.

Saari
P.L., 1951

1 .... 300.00

Saban Powerhouse
Acclaim, 1997

1-2 .... 5.00

Saban Presents Power Rangers Turbo vs. Beetleborgs Metallix
Acclaim, 1997

1 .... 5.00

Saber Tiger
Viz, 1991

1 .... 13.00

Sabina
Fantagraphics, 1994

1-7 .... 3.00

Sable
First, 1988

1-27 .... 2.00

Sable & Fortune
Marvel, 2006

1-4 .... 3.00

Sable (Mike Grell's...)
First, 1990

1-10 .... 2.00

Sabra Blade
Draculina, 1994

1-1/Variant............................... 3.00

Sabre
Eclipse, 1982

1 .... 3.00
2-14 .... 2.00

Sabre: 20th Anniversary Edition
Image

1 .... 13.00

Sabretooth
Marvel, 1993

Longtime Wolverine foe Sabretooth stars in this, his first solo title. As an arch-assassin, Sabretooth uses his teeth and claws to do his deadly work. Having gained a name for himself with his effectiveness and savage enjoyment of his work, he now earns a comfortable living.

All that is disturbed one night, when his live-in companion arranges for his abduction. Taken into the none-too-gentle care of a figure known as The Tribune, Sabretooth unwillingly undergoes a series of operations. These operations have the effect of increasing his strength, so that he can carry out a special assassination. At the same time, explosive is implanted next to his heart to ensure his compliance. Having little other choice, Sabretooth agrees to the mission. But as soon as it's over, he'll be coming back -- for revenge!

1-4 .... 3.00
Special 1 .... 5.00

Sabretooth
Marvel, 1998

1 .... 6.00

Sabretooth
Marvel, 2004

1-4 .... 3.00

Sabretooth Classic
Marvel, 1994

1-15 .... 2.00

Sabretooth: Mary Shelley Overdrive
Marvel, 2002

1-4 .... 3.00

Sabrina
Archie, 1997

1 .... 3.00
2-32 .... 2.00

Sabrina
Archie, 2000

1-105 .... 2.00

Sabrina Online
Vision

2 .... 4.00

Sabrina the Teenage Witch
Archie, 1971

1 .... 45.00
2 .... 20.00
3-5 .... 12.00
6-10 .... 10.00
11-17 .... 8.00
18-20 .... 6.00
21-30 .... 5.00
31-50 .... 4.00
51-60 .... 3.00
61-77 .... 2.00
Holiday 1 .... 3.00
Holiday 2-3 .... 2.00

Sabrina the Teenage Witch
Archie, 1996

1 .... 2.00

Sachs & Violens
Marvel, 1993

1-1/Platinum 3.00
2-4 .... 2.00

Sacred Ruins: The Mystic Wars
Labyrinth, 2000

1 .... 3.00

Sacrificed Trees
Mansion, 1995

1 .... 3.00

Saddle Justice
E.C., 1948

3 .... 300.00
4 .... 275.00
5-8 .... 250.00

Saddle Romances
E.C., 1949

9-11 .... 275.00

Sade/Razor
London Night

1/2nd 3.00

Sad Sack
Harvey, 1949

1 .... 500.00
2 .... 250.00
3 .... 125.00
4-10 .... 100.00
11-19 .... 70.00
20 .... 50.00
21-30 .... 35.00
31-40 .... 25.00
41-50 .... 15.00
51-70 .... 10.00
71-90 .... 8.00
91-100 .... 5.00
101-150 .... 3.00

151-287	2.00
288-289	3.00
290-291	2.00
292	10.00
293	2.00
3D 1	125.00

Sad Sack & The Sarge
Harvey, 1957

1	80.00
2	45.00
3-5	30.00
6-10	20.00
11-20	16.00
21-30	12.00
31-40	9.00
41-49	7.00
50-60	6.00
61-80	5.00
81-90	3.00
91-96	4.00
97-100	3.00
101-155	2.00

Sad Sack Army Life Parade
Harvey, 1963

A "sad sack" is military slang for a pathetically inept soldier that constantly screws up despite the best intentions. That description crystallizes the essence of the Sad Sack strip, created by George Baker in 1942 at the beginning of U.S. involvement in World War II.

This title features all the mainstays of military comedy. There is the inept private, doomed to grunt work; the long suffering sergeant, whose Army career is in constant jeopardy due to the unfortunate presence of Sad Sack in his platoon; and the self-important general, who possesses the attitude and physical demeanor of Douglas MacArthur, complete with a long cigarette holder and sunglasses.

-- George Haberberger

1	35.00
2	20.00
3	15.00
4-5	12.00

6-10	10.00
11-20	8.00
21-30	6.00
31-40	5.00
41-50	4.00
51-61	3.00

Sad Sack at Home for the Holidays
Lorne-Harvey, 1992

1	2.00

Sad Sack Comics
Harvey

1	15.00
2	12.00
3	10.00
4	10.00
5	10.00
6	8.00
7-9	8.00
10	8.00
11-19	6.00
20-29	4.00
30-39	4.00
40	4.00

Sad Sack Fun Around the World
Harvey, 1974

1	10.00

Sad Sack in 3-D
Blackthorne, 1988

1	2.00

Sad Sack Laugh Special
Harvey, 1958

1	90.00
2	45.00
3-10	25.00
11-20	20.00
21-30	15.00
31-40	12.00
41-60	10.00
61-80	8.00
81-93	6.00

Sad Sack Navy, Gobs 'n' Gals
Harvey, 1972

1	12.00
2	8.00
3-5	6.00
6-8	4.00

Sad Sack's Funny Friends
Harvey, 1955

1	50.00
2	34.00
3	22.00
4-5	20.00
6-10	16.00
11-20	12.00
21-30	10.00
31-40	8.00
41-50	5.00
51-75	3.00

Sad Sack U.S.A.
Harvey, 1972

1	12.00
2-8	6.00

Sad Sack with Sarge & Sadie
Harvey, 1972

1	10.00
2	6.00
3-8	4.00

Sad Sad Sack World
Harvey, 1964

1	45.00
2-10	20.00
11-30	15.00
31-40	12.00
41-46	10.00

Safe Comics
Graphic Graphics, 1998

1-2	3.00

Safest Place in the World
Dark Horse, 1993

1	3.00

Safety-Belt Man
Sirius, 1994

Bill Bardo is a crash-test dummy with a spark of life and a habit of saving people from disaster. Befriended by Dr. Tami Benito, Safety-Belt Man finds himself trying to, not only understand his place in the universe, but also battle to save his friends all too frequently.

Meanwhile, in Divincity, on the other side of time and space, Manidra, Sophia, and Chrad-ha attempt to prove to the powers that be that Bardo is something more than an animated robot. His dharma-duty must be fulfilled through his own self-sacrifice and unflagging service to humanity.

Created by Robb Horan, this is a well-thought-out series rotating different high-caliber artists to keep things jumping.

1-6	3.00

Safety-Belt Man: All Hell
Sirius, 1996
1-6...3.00

Saffire
Image, 2000
1-3...3.00

Saga
Odyssey
1...2.00

**Saga of Crystar,
The Crystal Warrior**
Marvel, 1983
1...2.00
2-11...1.00

Saga of Elf Face
Exter Entrance, 1986
1-3...1.00

Saga of Ra's Al Ghul
DC, 1988
1-4...3.00

Saga of Seven Suns
DC, 2004
1...25.00

**Saga of Squadron
Supreme**
Marvel, 2006
1...4.00

Saga of the Man Elf
Trident, 1989
1-5...2.00

**Saga of the
Original Human Torch**
Marvel, 1990
1-4...2.00

Saga of the Realm
Caliber, 1992
1-3...3.00

Saga of the Sub-Mariner
Marvel, 1988
1-12...2.00

**Saga of the
Swamp Thing**
DC, 1982
1...3.00
2-19...2.00
20...15.00
☞Alan Moore starts
21...12.00
22-25...6.00
26-32...4.00
33...3.00
34...5.00
35-36...3.00
37...55.00
☞1st Hellblazer
38...15.00
39-40...9.00
41-45...4.00
Ann 1...3.00

Ann 2...4.00
Ann 3...3.00

Saigon Chronicles
Avalon
1...3.00

Saikano
Viz, 2004
1-6...10.00

Sailor Moon Comic
Mixxzine, 1998
1...15.00
1/A..12.00
2-4..8.00
5-7..6.00
8..5.00
9..4.00
10-33..3.00

Sailor Moon SuperS
Mixx
1...10.00

Sailor's Story, A
Marvel
1..6.00

**Sailor's Story, A: Winds,
Dreams, and Dragons**
Marvel
1..7.00

Sailor Sweeney
Atlas, 1956
12-14.....................................80.00

Saint
Avon, 1947
1...475.00
2...245.00
3-4...200.00
5..20.00
6..250.00
7..160.00
8-10..145.00
11..100.00
12..120.00

Saint Angel
Image, 2000

On the alien world known as
Kei Nor, floating continents drift

over a world composed entirely of water. For generations, the many species of these great island nations fashioned their own cultures, their own customs, and their own bloody conflicts. On this world, peace rests on a narrow precipice created with questionable alliances and underscored by a deep-rooted fear of an enemy buried within the bowels of the planet. Yet, from the most primitive tribe to the richest kingdom, there exists a widespread legend.

The youth dismiss the legend merely as an old wives' tale, but the elders know the truth: the myth of a warrior, a guardian and protector known only as Saint Angel.

0...3.00
1-4...4.00

St. George
Marvel, 1988
1-8...2.00

Saint Germaine
Caliber, 1997
1-8...3.00

**Saint Germaine:
Restoration**
Caliber, 1997
1...4.00

Saints
Saturn, 1995
0-1...3.00

Saint Sinner
Marvel, 1993
1...3.00
2-8...2.00

St. Swithin's Day
Trident, 1990
1-1/2nd....................................3.00

St. Swithin's Day
Oni, 1998
1...3.00

Saiyuki
Tokyopop, 2004
1...10.00

Saiyuki Reload
Tokyopop, 2005
1-2...10.00

Sakura Taisen
Tokyopop, 2005
1-2...10.00

Salamander Dream
Adhouse Books, 2005
1...15.00

Salamandroid
Harris
Ashcan 1...................................1.00

Salimba
Blackthorne, 1986
1 ....4.00
3D 1-3D 2 ....3.00

Sally Forth
Fantagraphics, 1993
1-8 ....3.00

Sam & Max, Freelance Police
Marvel
1 ....2.00

Sam & Max Freelance Police Special
Comico, 1989
1 ....3.00

Sam and Max, Freelance Police Special
Fishwrap, 1987
1 ....2.00

Sam & Max Freelance Police Special Color Collection
Marvel
1 ....5.00

Sam and Twitch
Image, 1999
1-26 ....3.00

Sam Bronx and the Robots
Eclipse, 1989
1 ....7.00

Sambu Gassho (A Chorus in Three Parts)
Bodo Genki, 1994
1 ....1.00

Sam Hill, Private Eye
Close-Up, 1950
1 ....175.00
2 ....115.00
3-7 ....80.00

Sammy: Tourist Trap
Image, 2003
1-4 ....3.00

Sammy Very Sammy Day One Shot
Image, 2004
1 ....6.00

Sam Noir: Samurai Detective
Image, 2006
1-3 ....3.00

Sam Slade, Robo-Hunter
Fleetway-Quality
1-33 ....2.00

Samson
Fox, 1940
1 ....1,400.00

2 ....550.00
3 ....425.00
4 ....375.00
5-6 ....285.00

Samson
Ajax, 1955
12 ....175.00
13-14 ....155.00

Samson
Samson, 1995
1/2 ....3.00

Samson: The Kid Who Never Got a Haircut
Tyndale
1 ....2.00

Sam Stories: Legs
Image, 1999
1 ....3.00

Samurai
Aircel, 1986
1 ....3.00
1/2nd-12 ....2.00
13-16 ....3.00
17-23 ....2.00

Samurai
Aircel, 1987
1-3 ....2.00

Samurai
Aircel, 1988
1-7 ....2.00

Samurai
Warp, 1997
1 ....3.00

Samurai Champloo
Tokyopop, 2005
1 ....10.00

Samurai 7
Gauntlet
1-3 ....3.00

Samurai Cat
Marvel, 1991
1-3 ....2.00

Samurai Compilation Book
Aircel
1-2 ....5.00

Samurai Deeper Kyo
Tokyopop, 2003
1-16 ....10.00

Samurai: Demon Sword
Night Wynd
1-4 ....3.00

Samurai Executioner
Dark Horse, 2004
1-9 ....10.00

Samurai Funnies
Solson
1-2 ....2.00

Samurai Guard
Colburn, 1999
1-2 ....3.00
Ashcan 1 ....1.00

Samurai: Heaven and Earth
Dark Horse, 2004
1-4 ....3.00

Samurai: Heaven and Earth
Dark Horse, 2006
1 ....3.00

Samurai Jack Special
DC, 2002
1-1/2nd 4.00

Samurai Jam
Slave Labor, 1994
1-4 ....3.00

Samurai: Mystic Cult
Nightwynd, 1992
1-4 ....3.00

Samurai Penguin
Slave Labor, 1986

According to this black-and-white title from Dan Vado, Mark Buck, and Slave Labor Graphics, the life of a penguin is pretty dull—take a swim, eat some fish, get eaten by sharks. That is, until the Samurai Penguin steps in. A disciple of Yoshi, lord and master of the Antarctic penguins, Samurai Penguin is the sharks' natural enemy, and he is willing to sacrifice his life for the good of his fellow flightless waterfowls.

1-8 ....2.00

Samurai Penguin: Food Chain Follies
Slave Labor, 1991
1 ....6.00

Samurai Squirrel
Spotlight, 1986
1-2 ....2.00

Samurai: Vampire's Hunt
Nightwynd, 1992
1-4..3.00

Samuree
Continuity, 1987
1-9..2.00

Samuree
Continuity, 1993
1-4..3.00

Samuree
Acclaim, 1995
1-2..3.00

Sanctuary Part 1
Viz, 1993
1..6.00
2-9..5.00

Sanctuary Part 2
Viz, 1994

Sanctuary follows the rise to power of two former schoolmates, Hojo and Asami. Together, they have vowed to transform the destiny of Japan -- any way they can.

Hojo joins the rough-and-tumble world of organized crime. His wits and charm soon give him a leadership position in the underground Sagara Alliance, while his sex appeal helps him tame the female police chief who would uncover his machinations.

Meanwhile, Asami, with underhanded assistance from Hojo, has won a seat on the Japanese Diet. Asami plans to expose government corruption -- in a political party other than his own, of course.

But Hojo's and Asami's enemies are increasing as quickly as their clout. The result is a fascinating story of loyalty, corruption, friendship, and betrayal.

1-9..5.00

Sanctuary Part 3
Viz, 1994
1-8... 3.00

Sanctuary Part 4
Viz, 1995
1-5... 3.00
6-7... 4.00

Sanctuary Part 5
Viz, 1996
1-13..................................... 4.00

Sanctum
Blackshoe
1/Ltd. 4.00

San Diego Comic-Con Comics
Dark Horse, 1992
1-4... 3.00

Sandmadam
Spoof
1 .... 3.00

Sandman
DC, 1974
1 .... 15.00
2 .... 7.00
3-6 .... 4.00

Sandman
DC, 1989
1 .... 25.00
2-3....................................... 12.00
4-7....................................... 4.00
8 .... 15.00
☛1st Death
8/Ltd. 35.00
9-14..................................... 4.00
15-21................................... 3.00
22 .... 4.00
23-49................................... 3.00
50 .... 5.00
50/Gold............................... 20.00
51-74................................... 3.00
75 .... 4.00
Special 1 .... 5.00

Sandman, The: A Gallery of Dreams
DC, 1994
1 .... 5.00

Sandman: Endless Nights
DC, 2003
1 .... 3.00
1/2nd 18.00

Sandman Midnight Theatre
DC, 1995
1 .... 7.00

Sandman Mystery Theatre
DC, 1993
1 .... 4.00
2-49..................................... 3.00
50 .... 4.00

51-70..................................... 3.00
Ann 1.................................... 4.00

Sandman Mystery Theatre: Sleep of Reason
DC, 2007
1 .... 3.00

Sandman #1 Special Edition
DC, 2006
1 .... 1.00

Sandman Presents,: Bast
DC, 2003
1-3... 3.00

Sandman Presents: Love Street
DC, 1999
1-3... 3.00

Sandman Presents: Lucifer
DC, 1999
1-3... 3.00

Sandman Presents: Petrefax
DC, 2000
1-4... 3.00

Sandman Presents: Taller Tales
DC, 2003
1 .... 20.00

Sandman Presents: Deadboy Detectives
DC, 2001
1-4... 3.00

Sandman Presents: Everything You Always Wanted to Know About Dreams... But Were Afraid To Ask
DC, 2001
1 .... 4.00

Sandman Presents: The Furies
DC, 2004
1 .... 18.00

Sandman Presents: Thessaly - Witch for Hire
DC, 2004
1-4... 3.00

Sandman Presents: The Corinthian
DC, 2001
1-3... 3.00

Sandman Presents: The Thessaliad
DC, 2002
1-4... 3.00

Sandman: The Dream Hunters
DC, 2008
1-4/A 4.00

Sands
Black Eye, 1997
1-3............................3.00

Sandscape
Dreamwave, 2003
1-4............................3.00

Sands of the South Pacific
Toby, 1953
1............................150.00

San Francisco Comic Book
San Francisco Comic Book Co., 1970
1................................6.00
2-7..............................4.00

Santa Claus Adventures (Walt Kelly's...)
Innovation
1................................7.00

Santa Claus Funnies
Dell, 1943
1..............................300.00
2..............................225.00

Santa Claws
Eternity
1................................3.00

Santa Claws
Thorby
1................................3.00

Santana
Malibu, 1994
1................................5.00

Santa's Christmas Comics
Standard, 1952
1..............................100.00

Santa the Barbarian
Maximum, 1996
1................................3.00

Sapphire
Aircel, 1990
1-9............................3.00

Sapphire
NBM, 2001
1-2..........................11.00

Sap Tunes
Fantagraphics
1-2............................3.00

Sarah-Jane Hamilton Presents Superstars of Erotica
Re-Visionary
1................................3.00

Sarge Snorkel
Charlton, 1973
1................................8.00
2................................5.00
3-5..............................4.00
6-17............................3.00

Sarge Steel
Charlton, 1964
1..............................15.00
2..............................10.00
3-5..............................8.00
6-9..............................6.00

Satanika
Verotik, 1995
0................................4.00
1................................5.00
2-3..............................4.00
4-10............................3.00
11................................4.00

Satanika Illustrations
Verotik, 1996
1................................4.00

Satanika Tales
Verotik, 2005
1-2..............................4.00

Satan Place
Thunderhill
1................................4.00

Satan's Planet (A Day in Life On...)
Home-Made Euthanasia
1................................1.00
2................................2.00

Satan's Six
Topps, 1993
1-4..............................3.00

Satan's Six: Hellspawn
Topps, 1994
1-3..............................3.00

Saturday Morning: The Comic
Marvel, 1996
1................................2.00

Saturday Nite
Anson Jew, 1999
1-2..............................3.00

Saucy Little Tart
Fantagraphics, 1995
1................................3.00

Saurians: Unnatural Selection
CrossGen, 2002
1-2..............................3.00

Savage Combat Tales
Atlas-Seaboard, 1975
1..............................16.00
2-3............................10.00

Savage Dragon
Image, 1992
1................................3.00

Savage Dragon
Image, 1993
0................................2.00
1/2..............................3.00
1/2/Platinum 4.00
1-3..............................3.00
4-12............................2.00
13-13/A........................3.00
14................................2.00
15-24............................3.00
25-25/A........................4.00
26-49............................3.00
50................................6.00
51/A-74........................3.00
75................................6.00
76-99............................3.00
100..............................9.00
101-106........................3.00
107..............................4.00
108-123........................3.00
125..............................5.00
126-150........................3.00

Savage Dragon Archives
Image, 1998
1-4..............................3.00

Savage Dragonbert: Full Frontal Nerdity
Image, 2002
1................................6.00

Savage Dragon Companion
Image, 2002
1................................3.00

Savage Dragon/ Destroyer Duck
Image, 1996
1................................4.00

Savage Dragon: God War
Image, 2004
1-3..............................3.00

Savage Dragon/Hellboy
Image, 2002
1................................6.00

Savage Dragon/ Marshal Law
Image, 1997
1-2..............................3.00

Savage Dragon: Red Horizon
Image, 1997
1-3..............................3.00

Savage Dragon: Sex & Violence
Image, 1997
1-2..............................3.00

Savage Dragon/ Teenage Mutant Ninja Turtles Crossover
Mirage, 1993
1 ....3.00

Savage Dragon Vs. The Savage Megaton Man
Image, 1993
1 ....2.00
1/Gold 3.00

Savage Fists of Kung Fu
Marvel
1 ....8.00

Savage Funnies
Vision, 1996
1-2...2.00

Savage Henry
Vortex, 1987
1-13...2.00
14-30.......................................3.00

Savage Henry (Iconografix)
Caliber
1-3...3.00

Savage Henry: Headstrong
Caliber, 1995
1-3...3.00

Savage Hulk
Marvel, 1996
1 ....7.00

Savage Ninja
Cadillac, 1985
1 ....1.00

Savage Return of Dracula
Marvel, 1992
1 ....2.00

Savages
Peregrine, 2001
1 ....3.00

Savages
Comax
1 ....3.00

Savage She-Hulk
Marvel, 1980
1 ....8.00
2 ....5.00
3-5...3.00
6-25...2.00

Savage Sword of Conan
Marvel, 1974

If you're a fan of Conan the Barbarian, there are a few things you should know before you take up Savage Sword of Conan. In Savage Sword, the Conan you know will be a little meaner, the action will be more graphic, and the women will be wearing fewer clothes. If you can deal with this more adult-oriented Conan, then you should love Marvel's rendering of Robert E. Howard's classic character.

In black-and-white, magazine format, Savage Sword of Conan brought several of Howard's most famous Conan adventures to comics form, as well as creating many new Conan epics. From the pits of hell to the cliff nests of monstrous birds, Conan is a savage hero who fears neither man nor monster. Savage Sword of Conan brought readers this legendary character in all his original fury.

1 .... 60.00
2 .... 28.00
3 .... 16.00
4-10 .... 12.00
11-20 .... 8.00
21-29 .... 6.00
30-50 .... 5.00
51-173 .... 3.00
174-235 .... 2.00
Ann 1 .... 17.00
Special 1 .... 6.00

Savage Sword of Mike
Fandom House
1 .... 2.00

Savage Tales
Marvel, 1971
1 .... 150.00
2 .... 32.00
3-4 .... 20.00
5 .... 12.00
6-11 .... 10.00
12 .... 8.00
Ann 1 .... 25.00

Savage Tales
Marvel, 1985
1 .... 4.00
2-5 .... 3.00
6-9 .... 2.00

Savant Garde
Image, 1997
1-7 .... 3.00
Fan ed. 1/A-3/A 1.00

Saved By the Bell
Harvey, 1992
1-5 .... 1.00

Saviour
Trident, 1989
1 .... 4.00
2 .... 2.00
3-5 .... 3.00

Saw: Rebirth
Idea & Design Works
1 .... 4.00

SB Ninja High School
Antarctic, 1992
1/A.. 3.00
1/B.. 5.00
2/A.. 3.00
2/B.. 5.00
3/A.. 3.00
3/B.. 5.00
4-7 .... 3.00

Scab
Fantaco, 1999
1-2 .... 4.00

Scab
Orphan Underground, 1994
1-2 .... 3.00

Scales of the Dragon
Sundragon, 1997
1 .... 2.00

Scalped
DC, 2007
1-30 .... 3.00

Scamp
Dell, 1958
5 .... 25.00
6-10 .... 10.00
11-16 .... 8.00

Scamp
Gold Key, 1968
1 .... 8.00
2-5 .... 4.00
6-20 .... 3.00
21-45 .... 2.00

Scan
Iconografix
1-2 .... 3.00

Scandals
Thorby
1 .... 3.00

Scandal Sheet
Arriba
1 ....3.00

Scarab
DC, 1993

Louis Sendak is an old man who was once a super-hero. Fifty years ago, he was The Scarab, using the powers given him by an otherworldly mask to fight evil. All that is gone now, along with the love of his life, Eleanor.

When Sendak was a boy, his father brought home The Door: an ordinary-looking portal that his father commanded him never to open. His father would occasionally step inside what lay behind it and reappear months later with alien gifts and the smell of faraway lands. One day, Eleanor made the mistake of going through the door and became lost in an endless labyrinth of doors, each stranger than the next. She was powerless to escape, and, even as Scarab, Sendak was unable to open the door and follow her.

All that changes, when an otherworldly assassin known as The Sicari pays Sendak a visit, opening the door, and setting out to murder both Sendak and Eleanor.

0-8...2.00

Scaramouch
Innovation, 1991
1-2..2.00

Scarecrow of Romney Marsh
Gold Key, 1964
1 ....30.00
2-3...20.00

Scarecrow (Villains)
DC, 1998
1 ....2.00

Scare Tactics
DC, 1996
1-12 .... 2.00

Scarface: Scarred for Life
Idea & Design Works, 2006
1 .... 4.00
1/Special 20.00

Scarlet Crush
Awesome, 1998
1-2.. 3.00

Scarlet in Gaslight
Eternity, 1988
1-4.. 2.00

Scarlet Kiss: The Vampyre
All American
1 .... 3.00

Scarlet Scorpion/ Darkshade
AC, 1995
1-2.. 4.00

Scarlet Spider
Marvel, 1995
1-2.. 2.00

Scarlet Spider Unlimited
Marvel, 1995
1 .... 4.00

Scarlett
DC, 1993

Think of it as Buffy the Vampire Slayer with a harder edge (released the year after Joss Whedon's film). For thousands of years, a secret order of the unliving has quietly ruled both the day and the night in many cities across the nation. Now, however, they find themselves threatened by an ancient prophecy that they fear is about to come to fruition. The rogues of their number will go too far, and their actions will help bring about the coming of The Scarlet

Redeemer: a human savior who could destroy their ancient reign.

That savior is Bly Pharis, a popular teen-ager and cheerleader worried more about which party to go to than saving the world. All that changes, when vampires murder her adoptive parents and a strange man named Karis leads her to discover her destiny. Aided by a hardboiled police officer named Montero, Bly goes from being a carefree teen to an avenging vampire-slayer.

1 .... 3.00
2-14 .... 2.00

Scarlet Thunder
Slave Labor, 1995
1-2 .... 2.00
3-4 .... 3.00

Scarlett Pilgrim
Last Gasp
1 .... 1.00

Scarlet Traces: The Great Game
Dark Horse, 2006
1-4 .... 3.00

Scarlet Witch
Marvel, 1994
1-4 .... 2.00

Scarlet Zombie
Comax
1 .... 3.00

Scars (Warren Ellis')
Avatar, 2003
1-6/A....................................... 4.00

Scary Book
Caliber, 1999
1-2 .... 3.00

Scary Godmother
Sirius, 1997

Halloween is a thrilling night for kids, but for Hannah Marie this Halloween is especially exciting. It

is the first time she will be going trick-or-treating with the big kids instead of her parents. However, her cousin Jimmy, charged with her care, resents "babysitting" and the hindrance her presence will be to his candy accumulation. He and his friends decide to take Hannah to a large empty house and tell her that she must leave candy as tribute to the hungry monsters. But Jimmy's scheme to scare Hannah into wanting to go home does not take into account Hannah's own special protector, her Scary Godmother.

This is a story that evokes the special naivete of children (even those given to succumbing to selfishness) and the triumph of innocence. Written and illustrated by Jill Thompson (Black Orchid, Sandman), Scary Godmother is a charming fantasy suitable for everyone and especially appropriate for parents to read to their preschoolers.

-- George Haberberger

1-6...3.00

Scary Godmother: Bloody Valentine
Sirius, 1998
1..4.00

Scary Godmother Holiday Spooktacular
Sirius, 1998
1..3.00

Scary Godmother Revenge of Jimmy
Sirius
1...20.00

Scary Godmother: Wild About Harry
Sirius, 2000
1-3..3.00

Scary Tales
Charlton, 1975
1..5.00
2-10...3.00
11-46.......................................2.00

Scatterbrain
Dark Horse, 1998
1-4..3.00

Scattered
Scattered

The first 23 issues of this title were photocopied fanzines, but, with #24, Scattered made the leap, perhaps prematurely, to the ranks of self-published black-and-white comics. The enthusiasm exhibited by the creators, Jason Dube and Jesse Hamm, is evident, but fundamental spelling errors as well as substandard lettering are annoying hindrances which are difficult to overlook.

The lead feature by Jason Dube is a spiritually oriented story involving angels, demons, and a struggle for Heaven and Hell, with art and characters that seem to have been inspired, at least tangentially, by Neil Gaiman's Sandman. The writing, unfortunately, is less subtle and sophisticated.

Jesse Hamm's contribution, "Stories to Bore and Confuse You," takes itself less seriously and is more successful.

-- George Haberberger

24-30......................................3.00

Scavengers
Fleetway-Quality, 1988
1-5..1.00
6-14..2.00

Scavengers
Triumphant, 1993
0..1.00
0/A-11.....................................3.00

SCC Convention Special
Super Crew
1..2.00

Scenario A
Antarctic, 1998
1-2..3.00

Scene of the Crime
DC, 1999
1-4..3.00

Schizo
Antarctic, 1994
1-3..4.00

School Day Romances
Star, 1949
1..165.00
2-3.....................................120.00
4..185.00

Science Affair, A
Antarctic, 1994
1-2..3.00

Science Comics
Fox, 1940
1.....................................4,000.00
2.....................................1,800.00
3.....................................1,500.00
4.....................................1,350.00
5-8......................................900.00

Science Comics
Humor, 1946
1..125.00
2-3.......................................75.00
4-5.......................................45.00

Science Fair
Antarctic, 2005
1-3..3.00

Science Fair Story of Electronics -- The Discovery That Changed the World!
Radio Shack, 1981
1981-1984.............................1.00

Science Fiction Classics
Dragon Lady
1..6.00

Sci-Fi
Rough Copy
1..3.00

Scimidar
Eternity, 1988
1-3..3.00
4/A-4/B..................................2.00

Scimidar Book II
Eternity, 1989
1-4..3.00

Scimidar Book III
Eternity, 1990
1-4..3.00

Scimidar Book IV: "Wild Thing"
Eternity
1-4..3.00

Scimidar Book V: "Living Color"
Eternity, 1991
1-4..3.00

Scimidar
CFD
1-3.............................3.00

Scimidar Pin-Up Book
Eternity, 1990
1..............................4.00

Scion
CrossGen, 2000

In the interwoven worlds of the CrossGen universe, Avalon looks something like Earth's medieval society, but the people residing there have access to electronic and genetic discoveries that make it clear that Avalon's characters populate quite another world.

The rival powers are the kingdoms of East and West, which have opposed each other for centuries. People of the kingdoms of the Heron Dynasty (West) and Raven Dynasty (East)use Lesser Races as slaves, while members of the Underground want to eliminate such discrimination. Prince Ethan (youngest son of the Heron Dynasty) now bears the Sigil, which grants special powers. Unfortunately, the emergence of the Sigil itself plunged East and West into pitched combat, and Ethan finds himself pulled by powerful forces, including his own desire to fight for freedom of the Lesser Races.

-- Maggie

1-43...........................3.00

Sci-Spy
DC, 2002
1-6.............................3.00

Sci-Tech
DC, 1999
1-4.............................3.00

Scooby-Doo
Marvel, 1977
1-1/35¢ 20.00
2-4 .... 7.00
5-9 .... 4.00

Scooby-Doo
Harvey, 1992
1-Special 2 .... 2.00

Scooby-Doo
Archie, 1995
1-21 .... 2.00

Scooby-Doo
DC, 1997
1 .... 3.00
2-140 .... 2.00
Summer 1 .... 4.00
Special 1 .... 3.00
Special 2 .... 4.00

Scooby-Doo Big Book
Harvey, 1992
1-2 .... 2.00

Scooby-Doo Dollar Comic
DC, 2003
1 .... 1.00

Scooby-Doo Super Scarefest
DC, 2002
1 .... 4.00

Scooby Doo, Where Are You?
Gold Key, 1970
1 .... 100.00
2-8 .... 50.00
9-19 .... 25.00
20-30 .... 15.00

Scooby Doo, Where Are You?
Charlton, 1975
1 .... 15.00
2 .... 10.00
3-5 .... 7.00
6-10 .... 6.00
11 .... 5.00

Scoop Comics
Harry A. Chesler, 1941
1 .... 800.00
2 .... 850.00
3 .... 400.00
8 .... 260.00

Scooterman
Wellzee, 1996
1-3 .... 3.00

Scorched Earth
Tundra, 1991
1-3 .... 3.00

Scorchy
Forbidden Fruit
1 .... 4.00

Score
DC, 1989
1-4 .... 5.00

Scorn: Deadly Rebellion
SCC Entertainment, 1996
0 .... 3.00

Scorn: Heatwave
SCC Entertainment, 1997
1 .... 4.00

Scorpia
Miller
1-2 .... 3.00

Scorpion
Annruel
1 .... 3.00

Scorpion
Atlas-Seaboard, 1975
1-2 .... 16.00
3 .... 10.00

Scorpion Corps
Dagger, 1993
1-10 .... 3.00

Scorpion King
Dark Horse, 2002
1-2 .... 3.00

Scorpion Moon
Express, 1994
1 .... 3.00

Scorpio Rising
Marvel, 1994
1 .... 6.00

Scorpio Rose
Eclipse, 1983
1-2 .... 2.00

Scotland Yard
Charlton, 1955
1 .... 85.00
2-4 .... 60.00

Scout
Eclipse, 1985

SF mercenary Grimjack co-creator (with John Ostrander)

Timothy Truman went on to create, write, and draw Scout, in another science-fiction setting: America following a nuclear holocaust. The title character is an Apache warrior fighting corruption and monsters, and Truman worked to provide a comic book that showed drespect for the culture and religion of Native Americans of the Southwest.

Truman won a Haxtur Award for his work on this series and has done other comics work with a focus on Native Americans, including such historical figures as Simon Girty and Tecumseh and such fictional characters as Jonah Hex and The Lone Ranger -- and that's not to mention such other creations as Truman's Grateful Dead Comix.

-- Maggie

1-15	2.00
16	4.00
17-18	2.00
19	4.00
20-24	2.00

Scout Handbook
Eclipse, 1987
1 .... 2.00

Scout: War Shaman
Eclipse, 1988
1-16 .... 2.00

Scrap City Pack Rats
Out of the Blue, 1986
1-5 .... 2.00

Scratch
Outside, 1986
1-6 .... 2.00

Scratch
DC, 2004
1-5 .... 3.00

Scream Comics
Humor, 1944
1	100.00
2	55.00
3-10	45.00
11-18	42.00
19	52.00

Screamers
Fantagraphics, 1995
1-3 .... 3.00

Screen Monsters
Zone
1 .... 3.00

Screenplay
Slave Labor, 1989
1 .... 2.00

Screwball Squirrel
Dark Horse, 1995

Tex Avery is best known for directing wild theatrical cartoons for Warner Brothers and Walter Lantz. However, he created many characters over the years, and, in 1995, Dark Horse gave Avery and his characters the respect that they deserve with a series of new comics titles featuring Avery's creations.

Screwball Squirrel was a three-issue mini-series that featured the wacky rodent as he harassed his old pal, Meathead the Dog. For instance, when Meathead gets a job as a security officer at a new shopping mall, he soon loses it because of Screwball's outrageous actions. Screwball, a master of mischief, does everything from high-diving into the mall's water fountain to appointing Meathead a knight in the Kingdom of Cholesterol.

In the second half of each issue, readers will find a story featuring another of Avery's creations, such as the City Wolf and Red Riding Hood.

1-3 .... 3.00

Screw Comics
Fantagraphics, 1994
1 .... 4.00

Scribbly
DC, 1948
1	900.00
2	550.00
3-5	430.00
6-10	325.00
11-15	265.00

Scrubs in Scrubland: The Reflex
Scrubland
1 .... 3.00

Scud: Tales from the Vending Machine
Fireman, 1998
1-4 .... 3.00

Scud: The Disposable Assassin
Fireman, 1994
1	10.00
1/2nd-1/3rd	3.00
2-5	4.00
6-20	3.00

Scum of the Earth
Aircel, 1991
1-2 .... 3.00

Scythe
Caliber, 1996
1 .... 3.00

Sea Devils
DC, 1961
1	500.00
2	300.00
3	200.00
4-5	125.00
6-13	75.00
14-20	50.00
21-35	35.00

Seadragon
Elite, 1986
1-6 .... 2.00

Seaguy
DC, 2004
1-3 .... 3.00

Sea Hound
Avon, 1945
1-2 .... 60.00

Sea Hunt
Dell, 1960
4-6	30.00
7-9	25.00
10-13	20.00

Seals
Studio Aries, 2000
Ashcan 1 .... 1.00

Sea of Red
Image, 2005
1-12	3.00
13	4.00

seaQuest
Nemesis, 1994
1	3.00
2-3	2.00

Searchers
Caliber, 1996
1-4 .... 3.00

Searchers, The: Apostle of Mercy
Caliber, 1997
1	3.00
2	4.00

Search for Love
ACG, 1950

1 ....90.00
2 ....60.00

Season of the Witch
Image, 2005

0 ....3.00
1-4 ....4.00

Sebastian 0
DC, 1993

1-3 ....2.00

Sebastian
Disney, 1991

1-2 ....2.00

Second City
Harrier, 1986

1-4 ....2.00

Second Life of Doctor Mirage
Valiant, 1993

1 ....1.00
1/Gold 15.00
2-6 ....1.00
7 ....2.00
8-13 ....1.00
14-17 ....2.00
18 ....4.00

Second Rate Heroes
Foundation

1-2 ....3.00

Secret Agent
Charlton, 1966

9 ....8.00
10 ....6.00

Secret Agent
Gold Key, 1966

1 ....40.00
2 ....25.00

Secret Agents
Personality

1-3 ....3.00

Secret City Saga (Jack Kirby's...)
Topps, 1993

0-4 ....3.00

Secret Defenders
Marvel, 1993

1 ....3.00
2-11 ....2.00
12 ....3.00
13-24 ....2.00
25 ....3.00

Secret Diary of Eerie Adventures
Avon, 1953

1 ....1,425.00

Secret Doors
Dimension

1 ....2.00

Secret Fantasies
Bullseye

1 ....2.00
2 ....3.00

Secret Files
Angel, 1996

0 ....3.00
0/Nude 4.00
1 ....3.00

Secret Files and Origins Guide to the DC Universe 2000
DC, 2000

1 ....7.00

Secret Files & Origins Guide to the DC Universe 2001-2002
DC, 2002

1 ....5.00

Secret Files: Invasion Day
Angel, 1996

1-2/Nude 5.00

Secret Files President Luthor
DC, 2001

1 ....5.00

Secret Files: The Strange Case
Angel

1 ....3.00

Secret Hearts
DC, 1949

1 ....375.00
2 ....190.00
3 ....150.00
4-5 ....155.00
6 ....150.00
7 ....260.00
8-10 ....120.00
11-20 ....90.00
21-26 ....78.00
27-40 ....60.00
41-50 ....42.00
51-60 ....35.00
61-75 ....30.00
76-99 ....25.00
100 ....30.00
101-109 ....25.00
110 ....30.00
111-119 ....18.00
120 ....25.00
121-126 ....18.00
127 ....25.00
128-133 ....14.00
134 ....25.00
135-142 ....14.00
143-148 ....12.00
149 ....14.00
150-152 ....12.00
153 ....14.00

Secret Invasion
Marvel, 2008

1-2 ....4.00

Secret Killers
Bronze Man, 1997

1-4 ....3.00

Secret Love
Ajax, 1955

1 ....50.00
2-3 ....30.00

Secret Love
Four Star, 1957

1 ....45.00
2-4 ....30.00

Secret Loves
Comic Magazines, 1949

1 ....125.00
2 ....110.00
3 ....75.00
4 ....55.00
5 ....75.00
6 ....55.00

Secret Messages
NBM, 2001

1-5 ....3.00

Secret Missions
St. John, 1950

1 ....125.00

Secret Mysteries
Ribage, 1954

16 ....145.00
17-19 ....100.00

Secret Origins
DC, 1961

Ann 1 ....400.00

Secret Origins
DC, 1973

1 ....18.00
2 ....8.00
3-4 ....7.00
5-7 ....6.00

Secret Origins
DC, 1986

In 1986 DC kicked off a series which chronicled the origins of many of its greatest characters. This second series of Secret

Origins told of how everyone from Superman to the Newsboy Legion came into existence. It did this by printing the "secret" origin stories which, in the case of heroes like Wonder Woman, could be quite different than the more widely known origin stories. Published shortly after the events of Crisis on Infinite Earths, the origins were, for the most part, updated and refreshed to reflect the new continuity.

1	5.00
2-50	2.00
Ann 1	3.00
Ann 2-3	2.00
GS 1	5.00
Special 1	2.00

Secret Origins of Krankin' Komix
Krankin' Komix, 1996
1	1.00

Secret Origins of Super-Villains
DC, 1999
GS 1	5.00

Secret Origins Replica Edition
DC, 2000
1	5.00

Secret Plot
Fantagraphics, 1997
1-2	3.00

Secret Romance
Charlton, 1968
1	12.00
2	8.00
3-10	7.00
11-30	5.00
31-39	4.00
40-48	3.00

Secret Romances
Superior, 1951
1	45.00
2	25.00
3-5	18.00
6-20	15.00
21-27	12.00

Secret Six
DC, 1968
1	45.00
2	15.00
3-5	12.00
6	15.00
7	20.00

Secret Six
DC, 2006
1	3.00
2-30	3.00

Secret Society of Super-Villains
DC, 1976

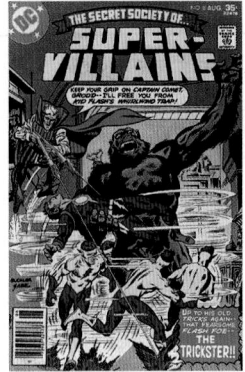

Super-heroes have their own associations, leagues, and teams, so why shouldn't the bad guys have them as well? A wealthy financier, who turns out to be Darkseid himself, sets up some of DC's most unique villains in a high rise in San Francisco. Among the villains teamed up together are Gorilla Grodd, a highly mentally advanced simian with telepathic powers; Mantis, who can drain the energy of her opponents; Hi-Jack, who uses special "playing cards" as a weapon; and Captain Cold, the chilling master of ice. Often infiltrated by super-heroes, this secret society ends up fighting among itself about as often as it fights the heroes it was meant to defeat.

1	10.00
2-8	5.00
9-15	3.00

Secrets of Drawing Comics (Rich Buckler's...)
Showcase, 1994
1-4	3.00

Secrets of Haunted House
DC, 1975
1	35.00
2-4	12.00
5	18.00
6-15	10.00
16-20	6.00
21-30	3.00
31	5.00
32-46	3.00

Secrets of Love and Marriage
Charlton, 1956
1	25.00

2	15.00
3-7	10.00
8	20.00
9-25	10.00

Secrets of Sinister House
DC, 1972
5	40.00

☛Was Sinister House of Secret Love

6-9	20.00
10	25.00
11-15	15.00
16-17	12.00
18	15.00

Secrets of the House of M
Marvel, 2005
1	4.00

Secrets of the Legion of Super-Heroes
DC, 1981
1-3	2.00

Secrets of the Valiant Universe
Valiant, 1994
1	5.00
2-3	3.00

Secrets of Young Brides
Charlton, 1957
5	25.00
6-23	20.00
24-34	15.00
35-44	10.00

Secrets of Young Brides
Charlton, 1975
1	10.00
2-9	7.00

Secret Story Romances
Atlas, 1953
1	100.00
2	75.00
3-21	60.00

Secretum Secretorum
Twilight Twins
0	4.00

Secret Voice
Adhouse Books, 2005
1	5.00

Secret War
Marvel, 2004
1	4.00
1/2nd	5.00
1/3rd	4.00
2	6.00
2/2nd	4.00
3	5.00
4-5	4.00

Secret Wars II
Marvel, 1985

In 1984, Marvel began a 12-issue limited series titled Marvel Super Heroes Secret Wars, in which Earth's heroes were kidnapped by The Beyonder.

Now, intrigued by the victorious heroes in that, the all-powerful Beyonder comes to Earth to gain knowledge and experience. Despite his vast powers, The Beyonder is frightfully naive regarding human nature. Because of this, he reacts badly to the crisis that his presence causes. Because of that, he's inadvertently responsible for great destruction. Out of a series of overreactions and misunderstandings, the second Secret Wars erupts, as Earth's heroes try to force the Beyonder to leave.

1-4	2.00
5	3.00
6-9	2.00

Secret Weapons
Valiant, 1993

1-11	1.00
11/VVSS	30.00
12-15	1.00
16-19	2.00
20	4.00
21	5.00

Sectaurs
Marvel, 1985

1-8	1.00

Section 12
Mythic

1	3.00

Section Zero
Image, 2000

1-3	3.00

Seduction
Eternity

1	3.00

Seduction of the Innocent
Eclipse, 1985

1	3.00
2-6	2.00
3D 1-3D 2	3.00

Seeker
Caliber, 1994

1-2	3.00

Seekers into the Mystery
DC, 1996

1-15	3.00

Seeker 3000
Marvel, 1998

1-4	3.00

Seeker 3000 Premiere
Marvel, 1998

1	2.00

Seeker: Vengeance
Sky, 1993

1-2	3.00

Select Detective
D.S., 1948

1	150.00
2	100.00
3	85.00

Self-Loathing Comics
Fantagraphics, 1996

1-2	3.00

Semper Fi
Marvel, 1988

1-9	1.00

Sensational Police Cases
Avon, 1954

1	250.00
2-4	100.00

Sensational She-Hulk
Marvel, 1989

1	3.00
2-49	2.00
50	3.00
51-60	2.00

Sensational She-Hulk in Ceremony
Marvel, 1989

1-2	4.00

Sensational Spider-Man
Marvel, 1996

-1	2.00
0	5.00
1	2.00
1/CS	4.00
2-11	2.00
11/CS	7.00
12-24	2.00
25-25/A	3.00
26-33	2.00
Ann 1996	3.00

Sensational Spider-Man
Marvel, 2006

23-34	3.00
35	6.00
36	4.00

Sensation Comics
DC, 1942

Sensation Comics was one of the cornerstone DC Golden Age titles and the stomping grounds of one of the company's marquee characters, Wonder Woman. Wonder Woman fights Nazis, super-villains, and criminals in adventures written by creator William Moulton Marston (under the pseudonym Charles Moulton) and drawn in a singular style by Harry G. Peter. Memorable backup characters included prize-fighter-turned-crimefighter Wildcat and playboy masked man Mister Terrific. Issue #34 introduced Sargon the Sorcerer, one of DC's longer-lived occult characters.

As the Golden Age wound down in the early 1950s, Wonder Woman departed for the pages of her own title, and adventure-mystery character Johnny Peril moved over from Comic Cavalcade and Danger Trail. The hard-to-find last several issues were entirely mystery-horror, with the title of the series changing to Sensation Mystery from #110 to the final issue, #116.

1	27,500.00
2	5,200.00
3	2,750.00
4	1,850.00
5	1,550.00
6	1,400.00
7-10	1,140.00
11-20	1,075.00
21-30	840.00
31-34	610.00
35-40	560.00
41-50	495.00
51-60	455.00

61-67 ....395.00
68 ....500.00
☞1st Huntress
69-70 ....395.00
71-80 ....380.00
81 ....425.00
82-90 ....385.00
91-93 ....190.00
94 ....350.00
95-99 ....190.00
100-109 ....450.00

Sensation Comics
DC, 1999
1 ....2.00

Sensation Mystery
DC, 1952
110-116 ....350.00

Sensei
First, 1989
1-4 ....3.00

Sensual Phrase
Viz, 2004
1-10 ....10.00

Sentai
Antarctic, 1994
1-7 ....3.00

Sentinel (Harrier)
Harrier, 1986
1-4 ....2.00

Sentinel
Marvel, 2003
1-12 ....3.00

Sentinel
Marvel, 2003
1-5 ....3.00

Sentinels of Justice
AC

The new Ms. Victory! Commando D! Jet Girl! Together with more than a dozen other heroes (and you thought the Avengers had a huge membership), they are the Sentinels of Justice, protecting the country, the planet—and an all-state girls' swim team? Wherever they are needed, the Sentinels are there. Given their extensive roster, it is not surprising that each issue typically focuses on just a couple members of the team, battling evil and saving damsels in distress wherever they may be.

As one of AC's "compact comics," Sentinels of Justice issues are published at a slightly smaller size than normal, approximately 8 by 5 inches, and yet all the characters are still amply endowed.

1 .... 4.00
2 .... 6.00
3 .... 4.00

Sentinels of Justice Compact
AC
1-3 .... 4.00

Sentinels Presents... Crystal World, The: Prisoners of Spheris
Academy, 1996
1 .... 3.00

Sentinel Squad O*N*E
Marvel, 2006
1-5 .... 3.00

Sentry
Marvel, 2000
1 .... 15.00
1/Variant 20.00
1/Conv 25.00
2 .... 8.00
3-4 .... 4.00
5 .... 4.00

Sentry
Marvel, 2005
1 .... 3.00
2 .... 3.00
3 .... 3.00
4 .... 3.00
5-8 .... 3.00

Sentry/Fantastic Four
Marvel, 2001
1 .... 3.00

Sentry/Hulk
Marvel, 2001
1 .... 3.00

Sentry: Rough Cut
Marvel, 2006
1 .... 4.00

Sentry Special
Innovation, 1991
1 .... 3.00

Sentry/Spider-Man
Marvel, 2001
1 .... 3.00

Sentry/The Void
Marvel, 2001
1 .... 5.00

Sentry/X-Men
Marvel, 2001
1 .... 3.00

Sepulcher
Illustration, 2000
1-2 .... 3.00

Sequential
I Don't Get It, 1999
1-3 .... 3.00

Seraphim
Innovation, 1990
1-3 .... 3.00

Serenity
Dark Horse, 2005
1/Cassaday-1/Jones 12.00
2/Bradstreet-2/DHP 7.00
3/Middleton-3/Yu 5.00

Serenity: Better Days
Dark Horse, 2008
1-2 .... 3.00

Sergeant Barney Barker
Atlas, 1956
1 .... 105.00
2-3 .... 85.00

Sgt. Bilko
DC, 1957
1 .... 350.00
2 .... 150.00
3-5 .... 100.00
6-13 .... 75.00
14-18 .... 60.00

Sgt. Bilko's Pvt. Doberman
DC, 1958
1 .... 150.00
2 .... 110.00
3 .... 90.00
4-5 .... 70.00
6-11 .... 50.00

Sgt. Frog
Tokyopop, 2004
1-10 .... 10.00

Sgt. Fury
Marvel, 1963
1 .... 1,500.00
2 .... 400.00
3-5 .... 225.00
6-10 .... 150.00
11-12 .... 100.00
13 .... 500.00
☞Cap. America app.
13/2nd 2.00
14-15 .... 80.00
16-19 .... 75.00

20-23	50.00
24	30.00
25-27	50.00
28-31	40.00
32-38	25.00
39-40	20.00
41-63	15.00
64-99	12.00
100	25.00
101	12.00
102	10.00
103-110	8.00
111-121	6.00
122-131	5.00
132-133	4.00
133/30¢	20.00
134	4.00
134/30¢	20.00
135-140	4.00
141-142/35¢	15.00
143-151	4.00
152-167	3.00
Ann 1	125.00
Ann 2	55.00
Ann 3	30.00
Ann 4	22.00
Ann 5	10.00
Ann 6-7	9.00

Sgt. Fury: Peacemaker
Marvel, 2006

1-6	4.00

Sgt. Preston of the Yukon
Dell, 1952

5	45.00
6-12	40.00
13	50.00
14-17	40.00
18	45.00
19-29	30.00

Sgt. Rock
DC, 1977

302	25.00
☞Was Our Army at War	
303-307	15.00
308-312	10.00
313-320	8.00
321-329	6.00
329/Whitman	15.00
330	6.00
331-341	5.00
342-350	4.00
351-390	3.00
391-422	2.00
Ann 1-2	4.00
Ann 3-4	3.00

Sgt. Rock
DC, 1991

14-22	2.00
Special 1-Special 2	3.00

Sgt. Rock: Between Hell and a Hard Place
DC, 2003

1	25.00

Sgt. Rock Special
DC, 1988

1-13	3.00

Sgt. Rock's Prize Battle Tales Replica Edition
DC, 2000

1	6.00

Sgt. Rock: The Prophecy
DC, 2006

1-6	3.00

Sergio Aragonès Destroys DC
DC, 1996

1	4.00

Sergio Aragonès Massacres Marvel
Marvel, 1996

1	4.00

Sergio Aragonès Stomps Star Wars
Dark Horse, 2000

1	3.00

Serial Repercussions
Chalk Outlines Studios, 1999

1-3	3.00

Serina
Antarctic, 1996

1-3	3.00

Serius Bounty Hunter
Blackthorne, 1987

1-3	2.00

Serpentina
Lightning, 1998

1/A-1/B	3.00

Serpentyne
Nightwynd, 1992

1-3	3.00

Serra Angel on the World of Magic: The Gathering
Acclaim, 1996

1	6.00

Seth Throb Underground Artist
Slave Labor, 1994

1-7	3.00

Settei
Antarctic, 1993

1-2	8.00

Settei Super Special Featuring: Project A-Ko
Antarctic, 1994

1	3.00

Seven Block
Marvel, 1990

1	5.00

7 Days to Fame
-Ism, 2005

1	4.00

Seven Guys of Justice
False Idol, 2000

1-10	2.00

777: Wrath/ Faust Fearbook
Rebel

1	14.00

Seven Miles a Second
DC, 1996

1	8.00

Seven Seas Comics
Universal Phoenix, 1946

1	575.00
2	490.00
3-6	450.00

Seven Soldiers
DC, 2005

0	5.00
0/Faces	3.00
1	4.00

Seven Soldiers: Frankenstein
DC, 2006

1-4	3.00

Seven Soldiers: Guardian
DC, 2005

1-4	3.00

Seven Soldiers: Klarion the Witch Boy
DC, 2005

1	4.00
2-4	3.00

Seven Soldiers: Mister Miracle
DC, 2005

1-4	3.00

Seven Soldiers: Shining Knight
DC, 2005

1-4	3.00

Seven Soldiers: The Bulleteer
DC, 2006

1-4	3.00

Seven Soldiers: Zatanna
DC, 2005

1-4	3.00

7th Millennium
Allied

1-4	3.00

Seventh Shrine
Image, 2005

1	6.00

7th System
Sirius, 1998
1-6 ....3.00

77 Sunset Strip
Dell, 1962
1 ....150.00

77 Sunset Strip
Gold Key, 1962
1-2 ....100.00

Sewage Dragoon
Parody
1-1/2nd 3.00

Sex & Death
Acid Rain, 1995
1 ....4.00

Sex and Death
Acid Rain
1 ....3.00

Sexcapades
Fantagraphics, 1996
1-3 ....3.00

Sex Drive
M.A.I.N.
1 ....3.00

Sexecutioner
Fantagraphics, 1991
1-3 ....3.00

Sexhibition
Fantagraphics, 1996
1-4 ....3.00

Sex in the Sinema
Comic Zone, 1991
1-4 ....3.00

Sex, Lies and Mutual Funds of the Yuppies From Hell
Marvel
1 ....3.00

Sex Machine
Fantagraphics, 1997
1-3 ....3.00

Sexploitation Cinema: A Cartoon History
Revisionary, 1998
1 ....4.00

Sex Trek: The Next Infiltration
Friendly
1 .... 3.00

Sex Wad
Fantagraphics
1-2 .... 3.00

Sex Warrior
Dark Horse
1-2 .... 3.00

Sex Warrior Isane XXX
Fantagraphics, 2004
1-8 .... 4.00

Sexx Wars
Immortal
1 .... 3.00

Sexy Stories from the World Religions
Last Gasp, 1990
1 .... 3.00

Sexy Superspy
Forbidden Fruit, 1991
1-7 .... 3.00

Sexy Women
Celebrity
1-2 .... 3.00

Seymour
Teddy Bear Press, 1994
1 .... 2.00

SFA Spotlight
Shanda Fantasy Arts, 1999
1-4 .... 3.00
5 .... 5.00

Shade
DC, 1997
1-4 .... 3.00

Shade, The Changing Man
DC, 1977
1 .... 10.00
2-8 .... 4.00

Shade, The Changing Man
DC, 1990
1 .... 3.00

2-49 .... 2.00
50 .... 3.00
51-70 .... 2.00

Shades and Angels
Candle Light
1 .... 3.00

Shades of Blue
AMP, 1999
1-2 .... 3.00

Shades of Gray
Lady Luck, 1994
1-11 .... 3.00

Shades of Gray Comics and Stories
Tapestry, 1996
1-4 .... 3.00

Shade Special
AC, 1984
1 .... 2.00

Shado: Song of the Dragon
DC, 1992
1-4 .... 5.00

Shadow
Archie, 1964
1 .... 30.00
2-8 .... 18.00

Shadow
DC, 1973
1 .... 12.00
2-3 .... 8.00
4 .... 6.00
5 .... 4.00
6 .... 5.00
7-12 .... 4.00

Shadow
DC, 1986
1 .... 3.00
2-4 .... 2.00

Shadow
DC, 1987
1 .... 3.00
2-19 .... 2.00
Ann 1-2 .... 3.00

Shadow (Movie Adaptation)
Dark Horse, 1994

1-2................................3.00

Shadow Agents
Armageddon, 1991

1................................3.00

Shadowwalker
Aircel

1................................2.00

Shadowwalker Chronicles
Ground Zero

1-2................................2.00

Shadow and Doc Savage
Dark Horse, 1995

1-2................................3.00

Shadow and the Mysterious 3
Dark Horse, 1994

1................................3.00

Shadowblade
Hot

1................................2.00

Shadow, The: Blood and Judgment
DC

1................................13.00

Shadow Cabinet
DC, 1994

0................................3.00
1-12................................2.00
13-17................................3.00

Shadow Comics (Vol. 1)
Street & Smith, 1940

The Shadow, created by writer Walter Gibson (aka Maxwell Grant) for Street & Smith's pulp The Shadow Magazine in 1933 (based on a character introduced on radio), is one of the most memorable fictional characters of the 20th century.

As a pioneering costumed crime fighter, the mysterious Shadow and his agents did battle against underworld menaces throughout the 1930s and '40s in the pulps, radio, movies, and comic books. Though the Shadow was a towering influence on Golden Age super-heroes including Batman, his own comic-book adventures paled in comparison to those of his super-peers, not to mention Gibson's biweekly novels or the radio show which at one point starred a young Orson Welles.

At some points, shoddy art and dumbed-down pulp stories failed to capture the most important element of the Shadow's mystique: the overbearing atmosphere of dread and mystery. At other points, the covers reflected the pulp magazine covers and interior stories even featured adaptations of the radio show drawn by Bob Powell using a cyan plate for the "invisible" shadow. It took 30 years before Michael Kaluta and Dennis O'Neil finally tried again for the best aspects of the character in DC's The Shadow series.

-- Rob Salkowitz

1................................2,800.00
2................................1,200.00
3................................800.00
4................................675.00
5-6................................625.00
7................................525.00
8-11................................400.00
12................................325.00

Shadow Comics (Vol. 2)
Street & Smith, 1941

1-2................................325.00
3................................550.00
4-5................................425.00
6-10................................375.00
11-12................................350.00

Shadow Comics (Vol. 3)
Street & Smith, 1943

1-10................................325.00
11-12................................300.00

Shadow Comics (Vol. 4)
Street & Smith, 1944

1-12................................300.00

Shadow Comics (Vol. 5)
Street & Smith, 1945

1................................275.00
2................................325.00
3-7................................300.00
8-12................................275.00

Shadow Comics (Vol. 6)
Street & Smith, 1946

1-12................................250.00

Shadow Comics (Vol. 7)
Street & Smith, 1947

1-12................................250.00

Shadow Comics (Vol. 8)
Street & Smith, 1948

1................................250.00
2-12................................225.00

Shadow Comics (Vol. 9)
Street & Smith, 1949

1-5................................200.00

Shadow Comix Showcase
Shadow Comix, 1996

1................................3.00

Shadow Cross
Darkside, 1995

1................................3.00

Shadowdragon
DC, 1995

Ann 1................................4.00

Shadow Empires: Faith Conquers
Dark Horse, 1994

1-4................................3.00

ShadowGear
Antarctic, 1999

1-3................................3.00

ShadowHawk (Vol. 1)
Image, 1992

1................................3.00
1/A................................2.00
2-3................................3.00
4................................2.00

ShadowHawk (Vol. 2)
Image, 1993

1................................4.00
1/Gold................................3.00
2................................2.00
2/Gold-3................................3.00

ShadowHawk (Vol. 3)
Image, 1993

0-1................................3.00
2................................2.00
3-4................................3.00
12-13................................2.00
14-18................................3.00
Special 1................................4.00

Shadowhawk (Vol. 4)
Image, 2005

1-7................................3.00
8-15................................4.00

Shadowhawk Gallery
Image, 1994

1................................2.00

Shadowhawk One-Shot
Image, 2006

1................................2.00

Shadowhawk Saga
Image

1................................1.00

Shadowhawks of Legend
Image, 1995

1................................5.00

Shadowhawk-Vampirella
Image, 1995
2 ....5.00

Shadow, The: Hell's Heat Wave
Dark Horse, 1995
1-3 ....3.00

Shadow, The: Hitler's Astrologer
Marvel
1 ....13.00

Shadow House
Shadow House, 1997
1-5 ....3.00

Shadowhunt Special
Image, 1996
1/A-1/B 3.00

Shadow, The: In the Coils of Leviathan
Dark Horse, 1993
1-4 ....3.00

Shadow Lady (Masakazu Katsura's...)
Dark Horse, 1998
1-24 ....3.00
Special 1 ....4.00

Shadowland
Fantagraphics, 1989
1-2 ....2.00

Shadowline Special
Image
1 ....1.00

Shadowlord/Triune
Jet City, 1986
1 ....2.00

Shadowman
Valiant, 1992
0/Non-chromium 5.00
0/VVSS 45.00
0 ....3.00
0/Gold 20.00
1 ....8.00
2-3...5.00
4-6...3.00
7 ....2.00
8 ....4.00
9 ....2.00
10-15.......................................1.00
16 ....2.00
17-18.......................................1.00
19 ....5.00
20-24.......................................1.00
25 ....2.00
26-31.......................................1.00
32-39.......................................2.00
40-41.......................................3.00
42 ....4.00
43 ....7.00
YB 1 ....4.00

Shadowman
Acclaim, 1996

Jack Boniface, the former Shadowman, has been replaced in this new series that continues the macabre, voodoo-inspired tales but this time with the customary, sarcastic, black humor of writer Garth Ennis (Preacher, Hitman).

The new Shadowman, a walker between our world and the Deadside, is a quiet, mysterious man named Zero. He was chosen to be the new Shadowman by Nettie, a voodoo priestess killed by Tommy Lee Bones, a maniacal escapee from the Deadside and the beneficiary of some of Ennis' most sardonic and droll dialogue. Death is not the obstacle to Nettie that it is to others, and whatever her reasons for choosing Zero are, they may be eclipsed by Zero's own motives for agreeing to his morbid existence.

-- George Haberberger

1 .... 3.00
1/Variant-5.............................. 3.00
5/Ashcan 1.00
6-20.. 3.00
Ashcan 1 .... 1.00

Shadowman
Acclaim, 1999
1-3... 4.00
4-6... 3.00

Shadow Master
Psygnosis
0 .... 1.00

Shadowmasters
Marvel, 1989
1-4... 4.00

Shadowmen
Trident
1-2... 2.00

Shadow of the Batman
DC, 1985

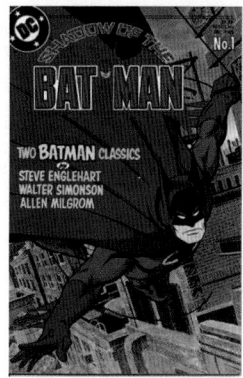

After seeing his parents murdered, Bruce Wayne became an avenging creature of the night. Now, the criminals of Gotham must beware the shadow of the bat.

This series reprints classic Batman stories, featuring work by such talents as Steve Englehart, Walter Simonson, and Allen Milgrom.

As an example of the series, the first issue presents two stories, "By Death's Eerie Light" and "The Master Plan of Dr. Phosphorus," which contain the origin of Dr. Phosphorus and tell of the dangerous first meeting between Batman and the glowing villain. Will Phosphorus succeed in poisoning Gotham's drinking water?

The first issue also includes a backup story titled "Hell Park" in which two men come face-to-face with the demons inside themselves.

1 .... 3.00
2-5 .... 2.00

Shadow of the Torturer (Gene Wolfe's...)
Innovation, 1991
1-6 .... 3.00

Shadowpact
DC, 2006
1-8 .... 3.00

Shadowplay
Idea & Design Works, 2005
1-4 .... 4.00

Shadow Play
Whitman, 1982
1 .... 3.00

Shadow Raven
Poc-It, 1995
1 .... 3.00

Shadow Reavers
Black Bull, 2001
1-2 ....3.00

Shadow Reigns
Aix C.C., 1997
0 ....3.00

Shadow Riders
Marvel, 1992
1 ....3.00
2-4 ....2.00

Shadows
Image, 2003
1-4 ....3.00

Shadows & Light
Marvel, 1998
1-3 ....3.00

Shadows and Light
NBM
1-4 ....11.00

Shadow's Edge
Lion
1 ....4.00

Shadows Fall
DC, 1994
1-6 ....3.00

Shadows from Beyond
Charlton, 1966
50 ....20.00

Shadows from the Grave
Renegade, 1988
1-2 ....2.00

Shadow Slasher
Pocket Change, 1994
0-7 ....3.00

Shadow Slayer
Eternity
0 ....2.00

Shadowstar
Shadowstar, 1985
1-3 ....2.00

Shadow State
Broadway, 1995
1-7 ....3.00
Ashcan 1 ....1.00

Shadow Strikes!
DC, 1989
1 ....3.00
2-31 ....2.00
Ann 1 ....4.00

Shadowtown
Iconografix
1 ....3.00

Shadowtown: Black Fist Rising
Madheart
1 ....3.00

Shadow War of Hawkman
DC, 1985
1 .... 2.00
2-4 .... 1.00

Shadow Warrior
Gateway
1 .... 2.00

Shaiana
Express, 1995
1 .... 3.00
1/Chromium 10.00
1/Holochrome 15.00
2-3 .... 3.00

Shaloman
Mark 1
1-9 .... 2.00

Shaman
Continuity, 1994
0 .... 2.00

Shaman's Tears
Image, 1993
0-1 .... 3.00
1/Platinum 4.00
2 .... 3.00
3 .... 2.00
3/Ashcan 3.00
4-12 .... 2.00

Shanda the Panda
Mu, 1992
1 .... 3.00

Shanda the Panda
Antarctic, 1993
1-15 .... 3.00
16-20 .... 2.00
21-24 .... 3.00
25 .... 5.00
26-33 .... 3.00
34-43 .... 5.00
Ann 1-2 .... 4.00
Ann 3-4 .... 5.00

Shang Chi: Master of Kung Fu
Marvel, 2002
1-6 .... 3.00

Shanghai: Big Machine
Brick House Digital, 2000
1 .... 3.00

Shanghaied: The Saga of the Black Kite
Eternity, 1987
1-3 .... 2.00

Shangri La
Image, 2004
1 .... 8.00

Shanna the She-Devil
Marvel, 1972
1 .... 27.00
2 .... 6.00
3-5 .... 4.00

Shanna the She-Devil
Marvel, 2005
1 .... 6.00
2-7 .... 4.00

Shaolin
Black Tiger
1-5 .... 3.00

Shaolin Cowboy
Burlyman, 2004
1 .... 4.00
1/Variant 5.00
2 .... 4.00
2/Mignola 8.00
3 .... 4.00

Shaolin Sisters
Tokyopop, 2003
1-2 .... 10.00

Shaolin Sisters: Reborn
Tokyopop, 2005
1-3 .... 10.00

Shaquille O'Neal vs. Michael Jordan
Personality
1-2 .... 3.00

Shards
Ascension, 1994
1 .... 3.00

Sharky
Image, 1998
1/A-4/A 3.00

Sharp Comics
Blackerby, 1945
1 .... 235.00
2 .... 210.00

Shatter
First, 1985
1 .... 3.00
1/2nd 2.00

Shatter
First, 1985

Shatter (Sadr al-din Morales) is a "temp cop" in a future world in which technology has not made life more valuable but, rather, has put everything up for sale. In a time of advanced robotics and genetics, underground artists get injections of biological materials in order to foster their talents, and prime samples of RNA are the more precious than gold.

Shatter was introduced in a 1985 special and simultaneously began a six-issue run as a backup for Mike Grell's Jon Sable, Freelance series. Months later, it began this ongoing series. Perhaps more than for the story, Shatter is notable as the first comic-book generated entirely on a computer. It also served as an introduction for the remarkable talents of artist Mike Saenz.

1 ....3.00
2-14 ....2.00

Shattered Earth
Eternity, 1988
1-9 ....2.00

Shattered Image
Image, 1996
1-4 ....3.00

Shatterpoint
Eternity, 1990
1-4 ....2.00

Shaun of the Dead
Idea & Design Works, 2005
1 ....4.00
2-4 ....4.00

Shazam!
DC, 1973
1 ....20.00
2-7 ....10.00
8 ....20.00
☛100-page issue
9-17 ....10.00
18-35 ....7.00

Shazam! and the Shazam Family
DC, 2002
Ann 1 ....6.00

Shazam! Power of Hope
DC, 2000
1-1/2nd 10.00

Shazam: The New Beginning
DC, 1987
1-4 ....2.00

Sheba
Sick Mind, 1996
1-4 ....3.00

Sheba
Sirius, 1997
1-8 ....3.00

Sheba Pantheon
Sirius, 1998
1 ....3.00

She Buccaneer
Monster, 1992
1-2 ....2.00

She-Cat
AC, 1989

She-Cat is a spinoff from the popular Femforce series from AC Comics. In this mini-series, She-Cat has broken off from her old team because she has been experiencing bizarre emotional and physical changes over the last six months. She is also tired of the strong-armed leadership of General Gordon, the leader of Femforce.

The problem lies in the fact that the government doesn't want to let her go. They dispatch a crazed assassin named Barney to bring her back or kill her. She-Cat must rely on the help of a fellow super-hero, Captain Freedom, to help her elude capture and find the secret behind her strange transformation.

1-4 ....3.00

Sheedeva
Fantagraphics, 1994
1-2 ....3.00

Sheena
Marvel, 1984
1-2 ....2.00

Sheena 3-D Special
Blackthorne, 1985
1 ....2.00

Sheena, Queen of the Jungle (Fiction House)
Fiction House, 1942
1 ....1,600.00
2 ....850.00
3 ....575.00
4-5 ....465.00
6 ....415.00

7-10 ....365.00
11-14 ....315.00
15-18 ....210.00

Sheena-Queen of the Jungle
London Night, 1998
1/A-1/C 5.00
1/D...3.00
1/Ltd. 15.00

Sheena, Queen of the Jungle 3-D
Blackthorne, 1985
1 ....3.00

She-Hulk
Marvel, 2004
1 ....12.00
2 ....7.00
3 ....4.00
4-12 ....3.00

She-Hulk
Marvel, 2005
1-2 ....3.00
3 ....4.00
4-7 ....3.00
8 ....22.00
9-28 ....3.00

She Hulk 2
Marvel, 2005
1-2 ....3.00
3 ....4.00
4-14 ....3.00

Sheila Trent: Vampire Hunter
Draculina
1-2 ....3.00

Shell Shock
Mirage, 1989
1 ....13.00

Sheriff of Tombstone
Charlton, 1958
1 ....50.00
2 ....30.00
3-10 ....20.00
11-17 ....18.00

Sherlock Holmes
DC, 1975
1 ....8.00

Sherlock Holmes
Eternity, 1988
1-20 ....2.00
21-23 ....3.00

Sherlock Holmes
Avalon, 1997
1 ....3.00

Sherlock Holmes: Adventures of the Opera Ghost
Caliber
1-2 ....3.00

Sherlock Holmes Casebook
Eternity
1-2 ....2.00

**Sherlock Holmes:
Dr. Jekyll & Mr. Holmes**
Caliber, 1998
1 ....3.00

**Sherlock Holmes
in the Case of the
Missing Martian**
Eternity, 1990
1-4 ....2.00

**Sherlock Holmes
in the Curious Case of
the Vanishing Villain**
Atomeka
1 ....5.00

**Sherlock Holmes
Mysteries**
Moonstone
1 ....3.00

**Sherlock Holmes
of the '30s**
Eternity
1-7 ....3.00

Sherlock Holmes Reader
Tome, 1998
1-4 ....4.00

**Sherlock Holmes:
Return of the Devil**
Adventure, 1992
1-2 ....3.00

Sherlock Jr.
Eternity, 1990
1-3 ....3.00

Sherman's Room
-Ism, 2005
1 ....3.00

**Sherman's
March Through
Atlanta to the Sea**
Heritage Collection
1 ....4.00

Sherlock Holmes
Charlton, 1955
1 ....225.00
2 ....175.00

Sherry the Showgirl
Atlas, 1956
1 ....100.00
2 ....70.00
3-7 ....55.00

She's Josie
Archie, 1963
1 ....85.00
2 ....55.00
3 ....30.00

4-5 ....25.00
6-10 ....20.00
11-16 ....16.00

Sheva's War
DC, 1998
1-5 ....3.00

Shi
Crusade, 1996
0-1/2 ....3.00

**Shi:
Art of War Tour Book**
Crusade, 1998
1 ....5.00

**Shi:
Black, White, and Red**
Crusade, 1998
1-2 ....3.00

**Shi/Cyblade: The
Battle for Independents**
Crusade, 1995
1 ....4.00
1/Variant 5.00

**Shi/Daredevil:
Honor Thy Mother**
Crusade, 1997
1 ....3.00
1/Ltd. 6.00

Shidima
Image, 2001
0/A-4 ....3.00

Shi: East Wind Rain
Crusade, 1997
1-2 ....4.00
Ashcan 1 ....1.00

SHIELD
Marvel, 1973
1 ....15.00
2-5 ....5.00

Shield
Archie, 1983
2 ....1.00

Shield, The: Spotlight
Idea & Design Works, 2004
1-5 ....4.00

Shield -- Steel Sterling
Archie, 1983
3 ....1.00

Shield Wizard Comics
M.L.J., 1940
1 ....2,900.00
2 ....1,350.00
3-4 ....850.00
5 ....740.00
6-8 ....700.00
9-13 ....525.00

Shi: Heaven & Earth
Crusade, 1997
1-Ashcan 1 ....3.00

Shi: Ju Nen
Dark Horse, 2004
1-3 ....3.00

Shi: Kaidan
Crusade, 1996
1-1/A 3.00

**Shiloh:
The Devil's Own Day**
Heritage Collection
1 ....4.00

Shi: Masquerade
Crusade, 1998
1 ....4.00

Shimmer
Avatar, 1998
1 ....4.00

Shi: Nightstalkers
Crusade, 1997
1 ....4.00

**Shion:
Blade of the Minstrel**
Viz, 1990
1 ....10.00

Ship Ahoy
Spotlight, 1944
1 ....135.00

Shi: Pandora's Box
Avatar, 2003
1 ....4.00

Ship of Fools
Image, 1997
0-3 ....3.00

Ship of Fools
Caliber
1-6 ....3.00

Ship of Fools (NBM)
NBM, 1999
1 ....11.00

Shipwrecked!
Disney
1 ....6.00

Shi: Rekishi
Crusade, 1997
1-2 ....3.00

Shi: Sempo
Avatar, 2003
1-2 ....4.00

Shi: Senryaku
Crusade, 1995
1 ....3.00
1/Variant 4.00
2-3 ....3.00

Shi: The Blood of Saints
Crusade, 1996
1 ....3.00
Fan ed. 1/A 2.00

Shi: The Series
Crusade, 1997
1-1/A 4.00
2-16..3.00

Shi:
The Way of the Warrior
Crusade, 1994
1/2 ....3.00
1/2/Platinum 4.00
1..6.00
1/A..5.00
1/B-1/C.....................................8.00
2..5.00
2/A..3.00
2/B..6.00
2/Ashcan...................................5.00
3-4..4.00
4/2nd-5.....................................3.00
5/Variant...................................5.00
6-6/A...3.00
6/Ashcan...................................4.00
7..3.00
7/Variant...................................4.00
8..3.00
8/A..5.00
9-12..3.00
Fan ed. 1/A-Fan ed. 3/A 1.00

Shi/Vampirella
Crusade, 1997
1..3.00

Shi vs. Tomoe
Crusade, 1996
1..4.00
1/Ltd. 5.00

Shi: Year of the Dragon
Crusade, 2000
1..3.00

Shmoo Comics
(Al Capp's...)
Toby, 1949
1..250.00
2-5...175.00

Shock & Spank the
Monkeyboys Special
Arrow
1..3.00

Shock Detective Cases
Star, 1952
20-21.....................................150.00

Shock Illustrated
E.C., 1955
1-2...200.00
3..800.00

Shocking Mystery Cases
Star, 1952
50...325.00
51...150.00
52-60......................................135.00

Shockrockets
Image, 2000
1-6..3.00

Shock SuspenStories
E.C., 1952

From the start, a cover box read, "Jolting tales of tension in the EC tradition" (a caption that also ran on many issues of Crime SuspenStories). Stories of violence and suspense were illustrated by such E.C. standards as Johnny Craig, Reed Crandall, Jack Davis, George Evans, (Editor) Al Feldstein, Graham Ingels, Jack Kamen, Bernie Krigstein, Joe Orlando, Al Williamson, and Wally Wood. Story sources included Edgar Allan Poe and Ray Bradbury, and the Johnny Craig severed-head cover for #22 was questioned as to its taste in Publisher William Gaines' testimony before Congress. "Carrion Death!" in #9 was Reed Crandall's first story for E.C.

The series came to an end with the Comics Magazine Association of America's implementation of the Comics Code, which forbade much of its type of story in newsstand comics.

-- Maggie

1 .... 850.00
2 .... 500.00
3 .... 350.00
4 .... 325.00
5 .... 290.00
6-7 .... 350.00
8 .... 260.00
9-11 .... 210.00
12 .... 225.00
13 .... 350.00
☛Frazetta art
14-15................................... 200.00
16-18................................... 170.00

Shock SuspenStories
(RCP)
Gemstone, 1992
1-16...................................... 2.00
17-18.................................... 3.00
Ann 1.................................... 9.00
Ann 2.................................... 10.00
Ann 3.................................... 9.00
Ann 4.................................... 10.00

Shock the Monkey
Millennium
1 .... 3.00
2 .... 4.00

Shock Therapy
Harrier, 1986
1-5 .... 2.00

Shogun Warriors
Marvel, 1979
1-1/Whitman........................... 5.00
2-20 .... 2.00

Shojo Zen
Zen, 1997
1 .... 3.00

Shonen Jump
Viz, 2002
0-36 .... 5.00

Shoney Bear and
His Friends
Golden Press, 1986
1 .... 2.00

Shoney's Fun and
Adventure Magazine
Paragon, 1983
1-8 .... 1.00

Shooty Beagle
Fantagraphics, 1991
1-3 .... 2.00

Short on Plot!
Mu
1 .... 3.00

Short Order
Head, 1974
1 .... 20.00
2 .... 15.00

Shorts (Pat Kelley's...)
Antarctic, 1997
1-2 .... 3.00

Shortstop Squad
Ultimate Sports Force, 1999
1 .... 4.00

Shotgun Mary
Antarctic, 1995
1 .... 4.00
1/CS 10.00
1/Variant-Ashcan 1 .... 3.00

Shotgun Mary
Antarctic, 1998
1 .... 3.00
1/Variant 4.00
2-3 .... 3.00

Shotgun Mary:
Blood Lore
Antarctic, 1997
1-4 .... 3.00

Shotgun Mary: Deviltown
Antarctic, 1996

1 ....3.00
1/Ltd. 5.00

Shotgun Mary Shooting Gallery
Antarctic, 1996

1 ....3.00

Shotgun Mary: Son of the Beast
Antarctic, 1997

1 ....3.00

Shottloose
Absolute

Shottloose, a black-and-white independent comic, began its run in 1992. The series is an ongoing science fiction tale about two races-green-skinned natives and the alien humans-living together on one planet. The planet is ruled by an evil, twisted president. Anti-government rebels choose one of the humans, a young male, to assassinate the planet's leader. After being convinced that it is the right thing to do, the youthful man makes his attempt. The rest of this admittedly obscure series deals with the relations between the two races as they cope with the loss of a leader.

Shottloose was created by writer Bill Hanley and artist Shane Campos.

1-2..1.00

Shoujo
Antarctic, 2003

1-3..6.00

Showcase
DC, 1956

As the name implies, Showcase is an anthology series designed to spotlight various DC creations. Although many such titles make enjoyable reading, they usually have little importance in the larger worlds of the comics universe. Showcase is an exception to that rule. In #4, it introduces readers to Barry Allen, the Silver Age Flash. Four issues later, it gives us the fantastic first appearance of The Challengers of the Unknown.

Later issues keep up the pace, bringing the first appearances of Anthro, Adam Strange, the Silver Age Green Lantern (Hal Jordan), the Silver Age Atom (Ray Palmer), Hawk and Dove, The Creeper, Rip Hunter, the Sea Devils, and many others.

Having run for 14 years between 1956 and 1970, the series came to an end with #93. It was later revived in 1977, running until issue #104.

1 .... 3,500.00
2-3................................. 1,000.00
4 .... 27,500.00
☛1st Silver Age Flash
5 .... 1,000.00
6 .... 4,000.00
7 .... 2,000.00
8 .... 11,500.00
☛2nd Silver Age Flash
9 .... 7,500.00
10 .... 3,000.00
11-12............................. 1,750.00
13-14 .... 4,500.00
15 .... 2,000.00
16 .... 1,000.00
17 .... 2,750.00
☛1st Adam Strange
18 .... 1,200.00
19 .... 1,500.00
20 .... 1,000.00
21 .... 500.00
22 .... 5,600.00

☛1st Silver Age Green Lantern
23-24 .... 1,750.00
25-26 .... 350.00
27 .... 900.00
28-29 .... 400.00
30 .... 800.00
31-32 .... 400.00
33 .... 375.00
34 .... 1,250.00
35 .... 700.00
36 .... 525.00
37 .... 700.00
38 .... 400.00
39 .... 350.00
40 .... 300.00
41-42 .... 150.00
43 .... 450.00
44 .... 100.00
45 .... 325.00
46-47 .... 100.00
48-52 .... 80.00
53-54 .... 100.00
55 .... 275.00
☛Dr. Fate origin
56 .... 125.00
57 .... 225.00
58 .... 150.00
59 .... 125.00
60 .... 225.00
☛Spectre origin
61 .... 100.00
62 .... 80.00
63 .... 50.00
64 .... 100.00
☛Spectre apperance
65 .... 50.00
66-72 .... 30.00
73 .... 85.00
☛1st Creeper
74 .... 45.00
☛1st Anthro
75 .... 75.00
☛1st Hawk & Dove
76-77 .... 50.00
78 .... 35.00
79-81 .... 45.00
82-84 .... 40.00
85-87 .... 20.00
88-93 .... 15.00
94 .... 20.00
☛New Doom Patrol
95-96 .... 8.00
97-103 .... 6.00
104 .... 5.00
Book 1 .... 20.00

Showcase '93
DC, 1993

1-6 .... 2.00
7-8 .... 3.00
9-12 .... 2.00

Showcase '94
DC, 1994

1-12 .... 2.00

Showcase '95
DC, 1995

1-12 .... 3.00

Showcase '96
DC, 1996
1-12 ....3.00

Showgirls
Atlas, 1957
1 ....100.00
2 ....60.00

Shred
CFW, 1989
1-8 ....2.00

Shrek
Dark Horse, 2003
1-3 ....3.00

Shriek
Fantaco
1-2 ....5.00
Special 1-3 ....4.00

Shriek Show:
Mark of Shadow
-Ism, 2005
1-2 ....3.00

Shrike
Victory, 1987
1-2 ....2.00

Shroud
Marvel, 1994
1-4 ....2.00

Shugga
Fantagraphics
1-2 ....3.00

Shuriken
Victory, 1985
1-8 ....2.00

Shuriken
Eternity, 1991
1-6 ....3.00

Shuriken
Blackthorne
1 ....8.00

Shuriken: Cold Steel
Eternity, 1989
1-6 ....2.00

Shuriken Team-Up
Eternity, 1989
1 ....2.00

Shut Up and Die!
Image, 1998
1-5 ....3.00

Sick Smiles
Aiiie!, 1994

Scott Allie, Lee Purvis, and Marc Mannheimer among others bring us various tales of stories slightly askew in this black-and-white series from Aiie! Comics. Within the Sick Smiles covers are tales that make you think. Mini-dramas which challenge the reader with a story that seems to be normal but then takes a definite left hand twist reminiscent of the best of the Twilight Zone, but for more mature readers.

1-8 .... 3.00

Sidekick
Image, 2006
1-4 .... 4.00

Sidekicks
Fanboy, 2000
1 .... 3.00

Sidekicks:
The Substitute
Oni, 2002
1 .... 3.00

Side Show
Mature Magic, 1987
1 .... 2.00

Sideshow Comics
Pan Graphics
1-5 .... 2.00

Siege
Image, 1997
1-4 .... 3.00

Siegel and Shuster:
Dateline 1930s
Eclipse, 1984
1-2 .... 2.00

Siege of the Alamo
Tome, 1991
1 .... 3.00

Sight Unseen
Fantagraphics, 1997
1 .... 3.00

Sigil
CrossGen, 2000

In the interwoven worlds of the CrossGen universe, this science-fiction title focuses on Samandahl Rey, an old spaceship pilot caring only for himself and his best friend. As a recipient of the powerful Sigil of CrossGen, he finds himself with power -- and obligations, as the Planetary Union needs him to combat the Saurian race.

In an early attack, his best friend is killed and her consciousness migrates to his ship's computer system. Later, Rey takes a quick trip around the CrossGen universe, setting the stage for future series.

-- Maggie

1 .... 4.00
2-42 .... 3.00

Sigma
Image, 1996
1-3 .... 3.00

Signal to Noise
Dark Horse, 1993
1-1/2nd 15.00

Silbuster
Antarctic, 1994
1-19 .... 3.00

Silencers
Caliber, 1991
1-4 .... 3.00

Silencers
Moonstone, 2003
1-2 .... 4.00

Silencers
Image, 2005
1 .... 3.00

Silent Hill: Paint It Black
Idea & Design Works, 2005
0 .... 7.00

Silent City
Kitchen Sink, 1995
1 .... 25.00

Silent Dragon
DC, 2005
1-6..3.00

Silent Hill: Dead/Alive
Idea & Design Works, 2005
1-4..4.00

Silent Hill: Dying Inside
Idea & Design Works, 2004
1-3..4.00
4-5..4.00

Silent Invasion
Renegade, 1986
1-2..2.00
3-12..3.00

Silent Invasion: Abductions
Caliber, 1998
1..3.00

Silent Mobius Part 1
Viz, 1991
1-6..5.00

Silent Mobius Part 2
Viz, 1992
1-5..5.00

Silent Mobius Part 3
Viz, 1992
1-5..3.00

Silent Mobius Part 4
Viz, 1992
1-5..3.00

Silent Mobius Part 5: Into the Labyrinth
Viz, 1999
1-6..3.00

Silent Mobius Part 6: Karma
Viz, 1999
1-7..3.00

Silent Mobius Part 7: Catastrophe
Viz, 2000
1-6..3.00

Silent Mobius Part 8: Love & Chaos
Viz, 2000
1-7..3.00

Silent Mobius Part 9: Advent
Viz, 2001
1-6..3.00

Silent Mobius Part 10: Turnabout
Viz, 2002
1-6..3.00

Silent Mobius Part 11: Blood
Viz, 2002
1-5.. 3.00

Silent Mobius Part 12: Hell
Viz, 2002
1-2.. 3.00

Silent Rapture
Avatar, 1997
1-2.. 3.00

Silent Screamers: Nosferatu
Image, 2000
1.. 5.00

Silent Winter/ Pineappleman
Limelight
1.. 3.00

Silke
Dark Horse, 2001
1-4.. 3.00

Silken Ghost
CrossGen, 2003
1-5.. 3.00

Silly Symphonies
Dell, 1952
1.. 200.00
2.. 175.00
3-4...................................... 125.00
5-9...................................... 110.00

Silly-Cat
Joe Chiappetta, 1997
1.. 1.00

Silly Daddy
Joe Chiappetta, 1995
1-18...................................... 3.00

Silly Tunes
Timely, 1945
1.. 150.00
2.. 85.00
3-7.. 60.00

Silver
Comicolor, 1996
1.. 2.00

Silver Age
DC, 2000
1.. 3.00
GS 1...................................... 6.00

Silver Age: Challengers of the Unknown
DC, 2000
1.. 3.00

Silver Age: Dial H for Hero
DC, 2000
1.. 3.00

Silver Age: Doom Patrol
DC, 2000
1.. 3.00

Silver Age: Flash
DC, 2000
1.. 3.00

Silver Age: Green Lantern
DC, 2000
1.. 3.00

Silver Age: Justice League of America
DC, 2000
1.. 3.00

Silver Age Secret Files
DC, 2000
1.. 5.00

Silver Age: Showcase
DC, 2000
1.. 3.00

Silver Age: Teen Titans
DC, 2000
1.. 3.00

Silver Age: The Brave and the Bold
DC, 2000
1.. 3.00

Silverback
Comico, 1989
1-3.. 3.00

Silverblade
DC, 1987
1-12...................................... 1.00

Silver Cross
Antarctic, 1997
1-3.. 3.00

Silverfawn
Caliber
1.. 2.00

Silverhawks
Marvel, 1987
1-7.. 1.00

Silverheels
Pacific, 1983
1-3.. 2.00

Silver Kid Western
Key, 1954
1.. 60.00
2.. 40.00
3-5.. 30.00

Silver Sable
Marvel, 1992
1-4.. 2.00
5-23...................................... 1.00
24-35.................................... 2.00

Silver Scream
Recollections, 1991
1-3.................................2.00

Silver Star
Pacific, 1983
1-6.................................1.00

Silver Star
(Jack Kirby's...)
Topps, 1993
1.................................3.00

Silverstorm
Aircel, 1990
1-4.................................2.00

Silverstorm
Silverline, 1998
1-4.................................3.00

Silver Streak Comics
Lev Gleason, 1939
1.................................11,000.00
2.................................4,000.00
3.................................3,500.00
4.................................1,750.00
5.................................2,000.00
6.................................13,500.00
7.................................8,300.00
8.................................3,200.00
9.................................1,900.00
10.................................1,500.00
11.................................1,000.00
12-14.................................850.00
15-19.................................700.00
20-23.................................600.00

Silver Surfer
Marvel, 1968

Norrin Radd is an inhabitant of the perfect, boring world of Zenn-La. His only comfort is his love for Shalla Bal. Then tragedy strikes in the form of an alien spaceship bearing Galactus. Zenn-La's best defenses are no match for this devourer of worlds.

1.................................400.00
2.................................160.00
3.................................135.00
4.................................265.00

☞Surfer vs. Thor
5-6.................................75.00
7.................................90.00
8.................................95.00
9-10.................................60.00
11.................................65.00
12.................................50.00
13.................................70.00
14.................................125.00
☞Spider-Man app.
15-18.................................55.00

Silver Surfer
Marvel, 1988
1-2.................................3.00

Silver Surfer
Marvel, 1987
-1-1/2.................................3.00
1/2/Platinum.................................6.00
1.................................7.00
2.................................6.00
3-10.................................4.00
11-14.................................3.00
15.................................4.00
16-24.................................3.00
25.................................4.00
26-31.................................3.00
32-33.................................2.00
34.................................5.00
35.................................4.00
36-38.................................3.00
39-45.................................2.00
46-47.................................3.00
48-49.................................2.00
50.................................5.00
50/2nd-74.................................2.00
75.................................4.00
76-85.................................2.00
85/CS.................................3.00
86-90.................................2.00
91.................................1.00
92-99.................................2.00
100.................................3.00
100/Variant.................................4.00
101-124.................................2.00
125.................................3.00
126-146.................................2.00
Ann 1.................................4.00
Ann 2-7.................................3.00
Ann 1997.................................4.00
Ann 1998.................................3.00

Silver Surfer
Marvel, 2003
1-6.................................2.00
7-14.................................3.00

Silver Surfer
Marvel, 1982
1.................................12.00

Silver Surfer:
Dangerous Artifacts
Marvel, 1996
1.................................4.00

Silver Surfer:
Inner Demons
Marvel, 1998
1.................................4.00

Silver Surfer:
Judgement Day
Marvel, 1988
1.................................15.00

Silver Surfer:
Loftier Than Mortals
Marvel, 1999
1-2.................................3.00

Silver Surfer:
Rebirth of Thanos
Marvel, 2006
1.................................13.00

Silver Surfer/Superman
Marvel, 1996
1.................................6.00

Silver Surfer:
The Enslavers
Marvel, 1990
1.................................17.00

Silver Surfer vs. Dracula
Marvel, 1994
1.................................2.00

Silver Surfer/Warlock:
Resurrection
Marvel, 1993
1-4.................................3.00

Silver Surfer/
Weapon Zero
Marvel, 1997
1.................................3.00

Silver Sweetie
Spoof
1.................................3.00

Silverwing Special
Now, 1987
1.................................1.00

Silverwolf Comic Book
Trivia Comic Book
Silverwolf, 1987
1-3.................................2.00

Simon and Kirby Classics
Pure Imagination, 1986
1.................................2.00

Simon Cat in Taxi
Slab-O-Concrete
1.................................2.00

Simon Spector
(Warren Ellis'...)
Avatar, 2005
1.................................4.00

Simpsons Comics
Bongo, 1992

TV's favorite dysfunctional cartoon family first appeared in Welsh's 1992 one-shot, Simpsons Comics and Stories. In late 1993, they returned, under the new Bongo Entertainment Group. This title is the flagship of a line that includes Itchy & Scratchy Comics, Radioactive Man, Bartman, Treehouse of Horror, and Bart Simpson Comics.

The Simpsons themselves became something of a national craze in the late Eighties and early Nineties. In particular, the family's exuberant young troublemaker, Bart, was featured on countless T-shirts, lunch boxes, and other merchandise accompanied by personal quotes such as, "Don't have a cow, Man!" Created by cartoonist Matt Groening ("rhymes with 'complaining'"), the Simpsons are a sort of comic antidote to the Brady Bunch. They often drive each other to wits' end, but are ultimately just a lovable family of misfits.

The comics series continues the antics of the TV show.

1	5.00
2	4.00
3-10	3.00
11-31	2.00
32	3.00
33-39	2.00
40-150	3.00

Simpsons Comics and Stories
Welsh, 1993

1	4.00

Simpsons Comics (Magazine)
Bongo, 1997

1	4.00
2-25	3.00

Simpsons Comics Presents Bart Simpson
Bongo, 2000

1-26	3.00

Simpsons/Futurama Crossover Crisis Part 2
Bongo, 2005

1	3.00

Simpsons Super Spectacular
Bongo, 2005

1	5.00

Simulators
Neatly Chiseled Features

1	3.00

Sin
Tragedy Strikes, 1992

1-3	3.00

Sinbad
Adventure, 1989

Sinbad, the sailor from the Arabian Nights adventures, is one of the oldest heroes in literature. Heis a daring rogue who lives by his wits and his sword, taking what treasure he can while breaking the hearts of damsels along the way.

Writer R.A. Jones and artists M. C. Wyman, Bruce McCorkindale, and Bobby Blair did justice to the scope and grandeur of the Sinbad legend. In 1989, they introduced this atmospheric and well-illustrated series for Malibuís Adventure Comics line. Rendered in black-and-white, with lush wash tones applied by Blair, their Sinbad adaptation followed the format of the Arabian Nights original right down to the framing story of the princess Shaharazad (sic).

1-4	2.00

Sinbad Book II
Adventure, 1991

1-4	3.00

Sin City
Cozmic

1	2.00

Sin City: A Dame to Kill For
Dark Horse, 1993

"Steam still rises from her skin. Everything she's done and I still can't take my eyes off her."

Ava Lord is the kind of woman who inspires obsession. She knows it and she uses it. She destroys men-some for money, some for sport. And the fact that she's married to mobster Damien Lord doesn't slow her down one bit.

Dwight McCarthy is the latest to fall under her spell. He's a man who thought he was tougher than anyone else, but he fell just the same. In Frank Miller's tale of love, passion, and murder he'll end up paying the inevitable price.

1	4.00
1/2nd-6	3.00

Sin City Angels
Fantagraphics, 2004

1	4.00

Sin City: Family Values
Dark Horse, 1997

1	15.00
1/A	18.00
1/Ltd.	75.00

Sin City: Hell and Back
Dark Horse, 1999

1-9	3.00

Sin City: Just Another Saturday Night
Dark Horse, 1997

1/2-1	3.00

Sin City: Lost, Lonely, & Lethal
Dark Horse, 1996

1	3.00

Sin City: Sex & Violence
Dark Horse, 1997
1 ....3.00

Sin City: Silent Night
Dark Horse, 1995
1 ....3.00

Sin City:
That Yellow Bastard
Dark Horse, 1996
1-5 ....3.00
6 ....4.00

Sin City: The Babe Wore
Red and Other Stories
Dark Horse, 1994
1 ....3.00

Sin City: The Big Fat Kill
Dark Horse, 1994
1-5 ....3.00

Sindy
Forbidden Fruit
1-5 ....3.00

Sinergy
Caliber, 1994
1 ....3.00
1/Ltd. 6.00
2 ....3.00
2/Ltd. 6.00
3 ....3.00
3/Ltd. 6.00
4 ....3.00
4/Ltd. 6.00
5 ....3.00
5/Ltd. 6.00

Single Series
United Feature, 1939
1 ....750.00
2 ....375.00
3 ....300.00
4 ....600.00
5 ....200.00
6 ....300.00
7-11 ....200.00
12-17 ....190.00
18 ....500.00
19 ....300.00
20 ....600.00
21 ....265.00
22 ....200.00
23 ....265.00
24 ....375.00
25 ....300.00
26-28 ....185.00

Singularity 7
Idea & Design Works, 2004
1-4 ....4.00

Sinister House of
Secret Love
DC, 1971
1 ....125.00
2-4 ....75.00

Sinister Romance
Harrier, 1988
1-4 ....2.00

Sinja: Deadly Sins
Lightning, 1996
1 ....3.00
1/A 6.00
1/B 10.00

Sinja: Resurrection
Lightning, 1996
1 ....3.00

Sinnamon
Catfish, 1995
1 ....3.00

Sinnamon
Catfish, 1996
1-4 ....3.00
4/Variant 5.00
5 ....3.00
5/Variant 4.00
6-8 ....3.00

Sinner
Fantagraphics, 1987
1-5 ....3.00

Sinners
DC
1 ....10.00

Sinnin!
Fantagraphics, 1991
1-2 ....2.00

Sin of the Mummy
Fantagraphics
1 ....3.00

Sins of Youth:
Aquaboy/Lagoon Man
DC, 2000
1 ....3.00

Sins of Youth:
Batboy and Robin
DC, 2000
1 ....3.00

Sins of Youth: JLA, Jr.
DC, 2000
1 ....3.00

Sins of Youth:
Kid Flash/Impulse
DC, 2000
1 ....3.00

Sins of Youth
Secret Files
DC, 2000
1 ....5.00

Sins of Youth:
Starwoman and the JSA
(Junior Society)
DC, 2000
1 ....3.00

Sins of Youth:
Superman,
Jr./Superboy, Sr.
DC, 2000
1 ....3.00

Sins of Youth:
The Secret/Deadboy
DC, 2000
1 ....3.00

Sins of Youth:
Wonder Girls
DC, 2000
1 ....3.00

Sinthia
Lightning, 1997
1/A-1/B 3.00
1/Platinum 4.00
2/A-2/B 3.00

Sir Charles Barkley
and the Referee Murders
Hamilton, 1993
1 ....10.00

Siren
Malibu, 1995
0-Special 1 ....2.00

Sirens
Caliber, 1994
1-2 ....4.00

Siren: Shapes
Image, 1998
1-3 ....3.00

Sirens of the Lost World
Comax
1 ....3.00

Sirius Gallery
Sirius, 1997
1-3 ....3.00

Sister Armageddon
Draculina
1-4 ....3.00

Sisterhood of Steel
Marvel, 1984
1-8 ....2.00

Sister Red
ComicsOne, 2004
1-2 ....10.00

Sisters of Darkness
Illustration, 1997
1/A-3 ....3.00

Sisters of Mercy
Maximum, 1995
1-5 ....3.00

Sisters of Mercy
London Night, 1997
0 ....2.00

Sisters of Mercy:
When Razors Cry
Crimson Tears
No Mercy, 1996
1 ....3.00

Sister Vampire
Angel
1 ....3.00

Six
Image, 2004

0 ....6.00

6
Virtual, 1996

1-3 ....3.00

6, The: Lethal Origins
Virtual, 1996

1 ....4.00

Six Degrees
Heretic

1 ....4.00
2-5 ....3.00

Six From Sirius
Marvel, 1984

1-4 ....2.00

Six From Sirius 2
Marvel, 1986

1-4 ....2.00

Six-Gun Heroes
Fawcett, 1950

1 ....325.00
2 ....175.00
3-5 ....120.00
6-15 ....90.00
16-22 ....75.00
23 ....85.00

Six-Gun Heroes
Charlton, 1954

24 ....125.00
25-30 ....65.00
31-40 ....55.00
41-50 ....48.00
51-60 ....32.00
61-70 ....22.00
71-83 ....16.00

Six-Gun Samurai
Alias, 2005

1 ....1.00
2 ....3.00

Six-Gun Western
Atlas, 1957

1 ....120.00
2-3 ....85.00
4 ....60.00

Six Million Dollar Man
Charlton, 1976

1 ....12.00
2 ....6.00
3-5 ....5.00
6-9 ....4.00

Six Million Dollar Man (Magazine)
Charlton, 1976

1 ....10.00
2 ....8.00
3-7 ....5.00

666: The Mark of the Beast
Fleetway-Quality, 1986

1 ....3.00
2-18 ....2.00

Six String Samurai
Awesome, 1998

In this alternate universe, in 1957 the Russians took the United States by nuclear force. Only one piece of the American frontier remained free, a patch of land known as Lost Vegas. Through this desert wasteland wanders the "six string samurai," a latter-day Buddy Holly who handles a guitar or a sword with equal skill. He's a man on a collision course with destiny: It seems that King Elvis, who ruled over the land of Vegas for forty years, has finally taken his last curtain call and the throne now stands empty. But it's a rough road to the big city and the body count is likely to be high, as demonstrated in this postapocalyptic future with a beat we can dance to.

This one-shot was inspired by the independent 1998 film with the same name.

1 ....3.00

68
Image, 2007

1 ....4.00

Sixty Nine
Fantagraphics, 1993

1-4 ....3.00

67 Seconds
Marvel, 1992

1 ....16.00

Sixx
Zygotic

1-4 ....3.00

Sizzle Theatre
Slave Labor, 1991

1 ....3.00

Sizzlin' Sisters
Fantagraphics, 1997

1-2 ....3.00

Skateman
Pacific, 1983

1 ....2.00

Skeleton Girl
Slave Labor, 1995

1-3 ....3.00

Skeleton Hand
ACG, 1952

1 ....260.00
2 ....175.00
3-6 ....145.00

Skeleton Hand
Avalon

1 ....3.00

Skeleton Key
Amaze Ink, 1995

1-30 ....2.00

Skeleton Warriors
Marvel, 1995

1-4 ....2.00

Sketchbook Series
Tundra

1-9 ....4.00
10 ....5.00

Skidmarks
Tundra

0-3 ....3.00

Skid Roze
London Night, 1998

1 ....3.00

Skim Lizard
Puppy Toss

1 ....3.00

Skin
Tundra

1 ....9.00

Skin Graft
Iconografix

1 ....4.00

Skin Graft: The Adventures of a Tattooed Man
DC, 1993

1-4 ....3.00

Skinheads in Love
Fantagraphics, 1992

1 ....2.00

Skinners
Image

1/A-1/C 3.00

Skin13
Express, 1995
1/2/A-1/C 3.00

Skizz
Fleetway-Quality
1-3...2.00

Skreemer
DC, 1989
1 ....2.00
2-6..2.00

Skrog
Comico
1 ....2.00

Skrog
(Yip, Yip, Yay) Special
Crystal
1 ....3.00

Skrull Kill Krew
Marvel, 1995
1-5...3.00

Skulker
Thorby
1 ....3.00

Skull & Bones
DC, 1992
1-3...5.00

Skull Comics
Last Gasp, 1970
1 ....18.00
2 ....10.00
3-6..6.00

Skull the Slayer
Marvel, 1975
1 ....12.00
2 ....5.00
3 ....2.00
4-5..4.00
5/30¢ 20.00
6 ....3.00
6/30¢ 20.00
7-8..3.00

Skunk
Express, 1996
1-6..3.00
GN 1 ....5.00

Skunk
Mu, 1993
1 ....3.00

Sky Ape
(Les Adventures)
Slave Labor, 1997
1-3..3.00
Book 1 ....13.00

Sky Comics
Presents Monthly
Sky Comics, 1992
1 ....3.00

Skye Blue
Mu, 1992
1-3 .... 3.00

Skye Runner
DC, 2006
1-5 .... 3.00

Sky Gal
AC

In the 1940s, Fiction House Books published a title named Jumbo Comics. That series contained eight-page backup stories about a would-be girl pilot named Ginger Maguire, also known as Sky Gal.

In 1993, AC Comics brought the misadventures of Sky Gal back to comic fans. This series contained one new story per issue along with four reprinted stories by the quintessential Sky Gal artist, Matt Baker. Baker drew the madcap adventures of the red-headed girl with a less-developed brain than body. For the era, Sky Gal was quite a risquT character, with many panels flaunting her apparent lack of underwear. Humorous and sexy, she was a perfect example of what became known as "good girl art."

1-3 .... 4.00

Skyman
Columbia, 1941
1-2 .... 800.00
3 .... 400.00

Sky Masters
Pure Imagination, 1991
1 .... 8.00

Skynn & Bones
Brainstorm
1 .... 3.00

Skynn & Bones:
Deadly Angels
Brainstorm, 1996
1 .... 3.00

Sky Pilot
Ziff-Davis, 1951
10-11 .... 85.00

Skyscrapers
of the Midwest
Adhouse Books, 2004
1-2 .... 5.00

Skywolf
Eclipse, 1988
1-3 .... 2.00

Slacker Comics
Slave Labor, 1994
1-18 .... 3.00

Slaine the Berserker
Fleetway-Quality, 1987
1-20 .... 2.00

Slaine the Horned God
Fleetway-Quality, 1990
1 .... 4.00
2-6 .... 3.00

Slaine the King
Fleetway-Quality, 1989
21-28 .... 2.00

Slam Bang Comics
Fawcett, 1940
1 .... 1,375.00
2 .... 575.00
3 .... 850.00
4-7 .... 450.00

Slam Dunk Kings
Personality, 1992
1-4 .... 3.00

Slapstick
Marvel, 1992
1-4 .... 1.00

Slash
Northstar, 1993
1 .... 3.00
1/Special 5.00
2-5 .... 3.00

Slash Maraud
DC, 1987
1-6 .... 2.00

Slaughterman
Comico
1-2 .... 4.00

Slave Girl
Eternity, 1989
1 .... 2.00

Slave Girl Comics
Avon, 1949
1 .... 750.00
2 .... 600.00

Slave Labor Stories
Slave Labor, 1992
1-4 .... 3.00

S

Slave Pit Funnies
Slave Pit, 1995
1 ....5.00

Slayers
CPM Manga, 1998
1-5...3.00

Slayers
Tokyopop, 2002
1-6...3.00

Sleazy Scandals of the Silver Screen
Kitchen Sink, 1993
1 ....3.00

Sledge Hammer
Marvel, 1988
1-2..1.00

Sleeper
DC, 2003
1-12...3.00

Sleeper: Season 2
DC, 2004
1-11...3.00

Sleeping Dragons
Slave Labor, 2000
1-4...3.00

Sleepwalker
Marvel, 1991
1 ....2.00
2-18...1.00
19...2.00
20-24.......................................1.00
25...3.00
26-33.......................................1.00
Holiday 1 ....2.00

Sleepwalking
Hall of Heroes, 1996
1 ....3.00
1/Variant.................................10.00
2-3...3.00

Sleepy Hollow
DC, 2000
1 ....8.00

Sleeze Brothers
Marvel, 1989
1-6...2.00

Sleeze Brothers
Marvel, 1991
1 ....4.00

Slice
Express, 1996
1 ....3.00

Slick Chick
Leader, 1946
1 ....90.00
2-3...60.00

Sliders
Acclaim, 1996
1-7...3.00

Special 1-3 .... 4.00

Slightly Bent Comics
Slightly Bent, 1998
1-2... 3.00

Slimer!
Now, 1989
1-19....................................... 2.00

Slingers
Marvel, 1998
0 .... 1.00
1/A-1/D 3.00
2-12....................................... 2.00

Sloth Park
Blatant, 1998
1 .... 3.00

Slow Burn
Fantagraphics
1 .... 3.00

Slow Death
Last Gasp, 1970
1 .... 20.00
1/Silver 25.00
2 .... 12.00
3-5... 10.00
6-11... 6.00

Slowpoke Comix
Alternative, 1998
1 .... 3.00

Sludge
Malibu, 1993
1-1/Ltd.................................. 3.00
2-11....................................... 2.00
12 .... 4.00
13 .... 2.00

Sludge: Red X-Mas
Malibu, 1994
1 .... 3.00

Slugger
Lev Gleason, 1956
1 .... 30.00

Slug 'n' Ginger
Fantagraphics
1 .... 2.00

Slutburger Stories
Rip Off, 1990
1-2... 3.00

Small Favors
Fantagraphics, 2000
1-4... 4.00

Small Gods
Image, 2004
1 .... 4.00
2-12....................................... 3.00

Small Gods Special
Image, 2005
0 .... 3.00

Small Killing, A
VG, 1993
1 .... 15.00
1/2nd 12.00

Small Press Expo
Insight, 1995
1995-1997 .... 3.00

Small Press Swimsuit Spectacular
Allied, 1995
1 .... 3.00

Smallville
DC, 2003
1-11 .... 4.00

Smash Comics
Quality, 1939
1 .... 1,900.00
2 .... 775.00
3 .... 535.00
4-5....................................... 475.00
6-10..................................... 375.00
11-12................................... 350.00
13 .... 375.00
14 .... 1,700.00
15 .... 825.00
16 .... 800.00
17 .... 900.00
18 .... 1,150.00
19-20................................... 640.00
21-30................................... 585.00
31-40................................... 425.00
41-50................................... 295.00
51-60................................... 200.00
61-70................................... 146.00
71-85................................... 110.00

Smash Comics
DC, 1999
1 .... 2.00

Smax
DC, 2003
1-5... 3.00

Smile
Mixx, 1998
1-12....................................... 4.00
13-29..................................... 5.00

Smile
Kitchen Sink
1 .... 3.00

Smiley
Chaos, 1998
1 .... 3.00

Smiley Anti-Holiday Special
Chaos!, 1999
1 .... 3.00

Smiley Burnett Western
Fawcett, 1950
1 .... 275.00
2-4....................................... 200.00

Smiley's Spring Break
Chaos!, 1999
1 ....3.00

Smiley Wrestling Special
Chaos!, 1999
1 ....3.00

Smilin' Ed
Fantaco, 1982
1-4 ....1.00

Smilin' Jack
Dell, 1948
1 ....65.00
2 ....35.00
3-8 ....30.00

Smith Brown Jones
Kiwi, 1997
1 ....4.00
2-5 ....3.00

Smith Brown Jones: Alien Accountant
Slave Labor, 1998
1-4 ....3.00

Smith Brown Jones: Halloween Special
Slave Labor, 1998
1 ....3.00

Smitty
Dell, 1948
1 ....55.00
2 ....35.00
3-5 ....25.00
6-7 ....20.00

Smoke
Idea & Design Works, 2005
1 ....10.00
2-3 ....7.00

Smoke and Mirrors
Speakeasy Comics, 2005
1 ....3.00

Smokey Bear
Gold Key, 1970
1 ....8.00
2 ....5.00
3 ....4.00
4-13 ....3.00

Smoot
Skip Williamson
1 .... 3.00

Smurfs
Marvel, 1982
1 .... 4.00

Smut the Alternative Comic
Wiltshire
1 .... 3.00

Snack Bar
Big Town
1 .... 3.00

Snagglepuss
Gold Key, 1962
1 .... 45.00
2-4 .... 30.00

Snake
Special Studio, 1989
1 .... 4.00

Snake Eyes
Fantagraphics
1-3 .... 8.00

Snake Plissken Chronicles (John Carpenter's...)
CrossGen, 2003
1/A-2 .... 3.00

Snakes on a Plane
DC, 2006
1-2 .... 3.00

Snak Posse
HCOM, 1994
1-2 .... 2.00

Snap
Harry A. Chesler, 1944
9 .... 125.00

Snap Dragons
Dork Storm, 2002
1-3 .... 3.00

Snap the Punk Turtle
Super Crew
1/2 .... 2.00

Snarf
Kitchen Sink, 1972
1 .... 10.00
2-4 .... 8.00
5-10 .... 6.00
11-14 .... 4.00
15 .... 5.00

Snarl
Caliber
1-3 .... 3.00

Sniffy the Pup
Standard, 1949
5 .... 60.00
6-10 .... 35.00
11-18 .... 25.00

Snoid Comics
Kitchen Sink, 1979
1 .... 2.00

Snooper and Blabber Detectives
Gold Key, 1962
1 .... 100.00
2-3 .... 75.00

S'Not for Kids
Vortex
1 .... 7.00

Snowbuni
Mu, 1991
1 .... 3.00

Snow Drop
Tokyopop, 2004
1-11 .... 10.00

Snowman
Express, 1996
1 .... 5.00
1/A 6.00
1/2nd 3.00
2 .... 4.00
2/A 5.00
2/2nd-3/A 3.00

Snowman: 1944
Entity, 1996
1 .... 3.00

Snow White
Marvel, 1995
1 .... 2.00

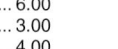

Snow White and the Seven Dwarfs
Gladstone

1 ....4.00

Snuff
Boneyard, 1997

1 ....3.00

Soap Opera Love
Charlton, 1983

1 ....25.00
2-3 ....15.00

Soap Opera Romances
Charlton, 1982

1 ....12.00
2-5 ....8.00

SOB: Special Operations Branch
Promethean, 1994

1 ....2.00

Socketeer
Kardia

1 ....2.00

Sock Monkey
Dark Horse, 1998

1-2 ....3.00

Sock Monkey (Tony Millionaire's...)
Dark Horse, 1999

1-2 ....3.00

Sock Monkey (Tony Millionaire's...)
Dark Horse, 2000

1-2 ....3.00

Sock Monkey (Tony Millionaire's)
Dark Horse, 2003

1-2 ....3.00

Sock Monkey: The Inches Incident
Dark Horse, 2006

1-2 ....3.00

Socrates in Love
Viz, 2005

1 ....9.00

So Dark the Rose
CFD, 1995

1 ....3.00

Sofa Jet City Crisis
Visual Assault

1 ....7.00

S.O.F.T. Corps
Spoof

1 ....3.00

Sojourn
Dreamer, 1998

1-5 ....2.00
6-10 ....3.00

Sojourn
CrossGen, 2001

Part of CrossGen's fantasy universe, Sojourn follows the adventures of Arwyn, a gifted archer on a quest for vengeance.

The Five Lands were ruled by the villain Mordath over 300 years ago, until a brave and mythic warrior defeated him with a single arrow. Now, the Five lands have been overrun again by the evil troll hordes of the resurrected Mordath. Chaos and fire scar the many kingdoms of the Five Lands, and, while Arwyn was saving a young girl's life, Arwyn's own daughter and husband are slaughtered by the marauding monsters.

Putting aside all feelings except hate, Arwyn sets out to kill Mordath with her trusty wolf companion, Kreeg. Sojourn is a tale of classic high fantasy by Ron Marz with a ton of action and impressive art by Greg Land and Drew Geraci.

1 .... 5.00
2-24 .... 3.00
25 .... 1.00
26-34/2nd 3.00
Special 1 .... 4.00

Sojourn Prequel
CrossGen, 2001

1 .... 5.00

Solar Lord
Image, 1999

1-7 .... 3.00

Solarman
Marvel, 1989

1-2 .... 1.00

Solar, Man of the Atom
Valiant, 1991

1 .... 7.00
2-7 .... 5.00
8-9 .... 6.00
10 .... 16.00
☛1st Eternal Warrior

10/2nd 3.00
11 .... 5.00
12 .... 4.00
13 .... 2.00
14 .... 4.00
15-16 .... 2.00
17-32 .... 1.00
33 .... 2.00
34-41 .... 1.00
42-50 .... 2.00
51-56 .... 3.00
57-58 .... 4.00
59 .... 5.00
60 .... 10.00

Solar, Man of the Atom
Acclaim, 1997

1 .... 4.00

Solar, Man of the Atom: Hell on Earth
Acclaim, 1998

Following Man of the Atom and Revelations, this series continues the story of Frank and Helena Selenski, twins who now share the inconceivable power of Solar. It's the power of God, the power to solve all the ills of the world. They soon discover, however, that maybe God has a good reason for not interfering in the world. Everything they do has unforeseen and often cataclysmic results: like when they save the life of one cat, but inadvertently cause the destruction of the city of Seoul.

While the siblings struggle with these ramifications, events quickly get more out of their control. A malevolent entity seems to be chasing them, leaving even more havoc in its wake, while the other super beings in the world take steps to stop what they see as a threat to their entire reality. But can even the combined forces of the Eternal Warriors, Turok, Magnus, and others prevent the coming holocaust?

1-4 .... 3.00

Solar, Man of the Atom: Revelations
Acclaim, 1997
1 ....4.00

Solar Stella
Sirius, 2000
1 ....3.00

Soldier & Marine Comics
Charlton, 1954
11-12 ....30.00
13-15 ....25.00
9 ....45.00

Soldier Comics
Fawcett, 1952
1 ....55.00
2-3 ....30.00
4-5 ....25.00
6-11 ....16.00

Soldiers of Fortune
ACG, 1951
1 ....175.00
2 ....100.00
3-5 ....85.00
6-10 ....75.00
11-13 ....60.00

Soldiers of Freedom
AC, 1987

Clones of the hero known as Captain Freedom are located all over the world, providing each nation with its own protectorate. But now the clones are being systematically killed, slowly destabilizing the world. Behind the deaths is a secret terrorist organization known as Fez carrying out its evil missions around the globe while at the same time providing support to other terrorist organizations. The real Captain Freedom may be able to stop them. There's only one problem: he's one of Fez's prime targets. Also included in this comic is the separate story "Precious Metal" which follows the adventures of a woman known as

Caprice who is caught in the middle of a violent war over Uranium in Northern Chad. She will risk her life to protect the women and children peasants struggling to survive. But will she succeed?

1-2 .... 2.00

Soldier X
Marvel, 2002
1 .... 3.00
2-6 .... 2.00
7-12 .... 3.00

Sold Out
Fantaco, 1986
1-2 .... 2.00

Solitaire
Malibu, 1993
1 .... 2.00
1/CS 3.00
2-12 .... 2.00

Solo
Marvel, 1994
1-4 .... 2.00

Solo
Dark Horse, 1996
1-2 .... 3.00

Solo
DC, 2005
1-12 .... 5.00

Solo Avengers
Marvel, 1987

Solo Avengers is a "split book" in the tradition of Tales of Suspense and Strange Tales. Generally, split books will feature two independent stories, one featuring a standing hero, and the other rotating among lesser-known characters.

In Solo Avengers, Hawkeye assumes the primary role, with other members of the West Coast Avengers taking turns in the second story. The format works well here, giving readers a chance

to really get to know characters who otherwise have to share story time with their many teammates.

1-20 .... 1.00

Solo Ex-Mutants
Eternity, 1987
1-6 .... 2.00

Solomon Kane
Marvel, 1985
1 .... 2.00
2-6 .... 1.00

Solomon Kane in 3-D
Blackthorne
1 .... 3.00

Solson Christmas Special
Solson, 1986
1 .... 3.00

Solson's Comic Talent Starsearch
Solson
1-2 .... 2.00

Solus
CrossGen, 2003
1-8 .... 3.00

Solution
Malibu, 1993
0 .... 3.00
1 .... 2.00
1/Ltd.-2 .... 3.00
3-15 .... 2.00
16 .... 4.00
17 .... 3.00

Someplace Strange
Marvel
1 .... 7.00

Somerset Holmes
Pacific, 1983
1 .... 3.00
2-6 .... 2.00

Some Tales from Gimbley
Harrier, 1987
1 .... 2.00

Something
Strictly Underground
1 .... 3.00

Something at the Window is Scratching
Slave Labor
1 .... 10.00

Something Different
Wooga Central, 1992
1-3 .... 2.00

Something Wicked
Image, 2003
1-3 .... 3.00

Some Trouble of a SeRRious Nature
Crusade, 2001
1 ....4.00

Somnambulo: Sleep of the Just
9th Circle, 1996
1 ....3.00

Son of Vulcan
DC, 1965
1-6 ....3.00

Songbook (Alan Moore's...)
Caliber
1 ....6.00

Song of Mykal, The: Atlantis Fantasyworld 25th Anniversary Comic
Atlantis Fantasyworld, 2001
1 ....3.00

Song of the Cid
Tome
1-2 ....3.00

Song of the Sirens
Millennium
1-2 ....3.00

Songs of Bastards
Conquest
1 ....3.00

Sonic & Knuckles: Mecha Madness Special
Archie, 1995
1 ....2.00

Sonic & Knuckles Special
Archie, 1995
1 ....2.00

Sonic Blast Special
Archie, 1996
1 ....2.00

Sonic Disruptors
DC, 1987

The U.S. had been taken over by a military coup. For years, the military had sat by while gays, communists, and other minorities achieved prominence in the national agenda. Then came the final straw: a female president. The military could stand no more and decided it was time to act.

Today, armed militia patrol the streets and more and more citizens are counted among the "vanished." The only remaining thorn in the governmentís side is The Sonic Disruptors, a group of disc jockeys and revolutionaries who broadcast from an orbital space station. Led by Myron Speece, aka Sheik Rattle Enroll, they beam banned music and revolutionary politics to the world below. Whatís more, the government canít shoot them down as the ship also carries tons of nuclear waste.

Sonic Disruptors was originally scheduled to be a 12-issue maxi-series, but was abruptly cancelled with #7 due to low sales.

1-7 .... 1.00

Sonic Live Special
Archie
1 .... 2.00

Sonic Quest - The Death Egg Saga
Archie, 1997
2 .... 2.00

Sonic's Friendly Nemesis Knuckles
Archie, 1996
1 .... 3.00
2-3 .... 2.00

Sonic the Hedgehog
Archie, 1993
1 .... 20.00
2-3 .... 10.00

Sonic the Hedgehog
Archie, 1993
0 .... 9.00
1 .... 12.00
2-3 .... 9.00
4-5 .... 7.00
6-10 .... 6.00
11-20 .... 4.00
21-50 .... 3.00
51-185 .... 2.00
Special 1 .... 3.00
Special 2-15 .... 2.00

Sonic the Hedgehog in Your Face Special
Archie
1 .... 2.00

Sonic the Hedgehog Triple Trouble Special
Archie, 1995
1 .... 2.00

Sonic vs. Knuckles Battle Royal Special
Archie, 1997
1 .... 2.00

Sonic X
Archie, 2005
1-15 .... 2.00

Son of Ambush Bug
DC, 1986
1-6 .... 2.00

Son of M
Marvel, 2006
1-6 .... 3.00

Son of Mutant World
Fantagor, 1990
1-2 .... 3.00
3-5 .... 2.00

Son of Rampage
Slap Happy, 1998
2 .... 14.00

Son of Satan
Marvel, 1975
1 .... 20.00
2 .... 15.00
3 .... 10.00
3/30¢ 15.00
4 .... 10.00
4/30¢ 15.00
5 .... 10.00
5/30¢ 15.00
6-8 .... 10.00

Son of Sinbad
St. John, 1950
1 .... 250.00

Son of Yuppies From Hell
Marvel
1 .... 4.00

Sons of Katie Elder
Dell, 1965
1 .... 125.00

Sophistikats Katch-Up Kollection
Silk Purrs, 1995
1 .... 6.00

Sorcerer's Children
Sillwill, 1998
1-4 .... 3.00

Sorority Secrets
Toby, 1954
1 .... 50.00

S.O.S.
Fantagraphics
1 .... 3.00

Soul
Flashpoint, 1994
1-1/Gold 3.00

Soulfire
(Michael Turner's ...)
Aspen, 2004

0	5.00
0/Conv	7.00
1	7.00
1/Virgin	8.00
2	6.00
2/Rupps	10.00
3	5.00
4	3.00
4/Variant	4.00
4/Campbell	3.00
4/Lee	4.00
4/Conv	10.00

Soulfire: Beginnings
Aspen, 2003

1	4.00
1/Conv	10.00

Soulfire:
Dying of the Light
Aspen, 2005

0	3.00
0/Conv	15.00
1-2	3.00

Soulfire Preview
Aspen, 2003

1	4.00
1/Conv	8.00

Soul of a Samurai
Image, 2003

1-4	6.00

Soulquest
Innovation, 1989

1	4.00

Soul Saga
Top Cow, 2000

1-5	3.00

Soulsearchers and
Company
Claypool, 1993

Peter David is known for his long run on Marvel's Hulk, for his scripts for the recent form of DC's Supergirl, for his Star Trek prose novels, for co-creating the TV series Space Cases, for his ongoing column in Comics Buyer's Guide -- What he's not as widely known for is his long-time scripting of Claypool's Soulsearchers and Company, devoted to a strange group of paranormal researchers. While they're working on getting rid of "otherworldly weirdness" from Mystic Grove, they're pretty weird themselves. The group comprises Arnold (a talking prairie dog), Baraka (a fire-demon from an Arabic Hell), Bridget (a former Olympic athlete), Janocz (a changeling), Kelly (an apprentice witch), and Peterson (an accountant with a magic bag). Their success as a group has had its ups and downs, but it's usually safe to say that even good days have unsettling aspects.

Thanks to the involvement of David and Editor Richard Howell, the series is loaded with slapstick, parody, and puns. That's fair warning.

-- Maggie

1	4.00
2-82	3.00

Soul to Seoul
Tokyopop, 2005

1-3	10.00

Soul Trek
Spoof, 1992

1-2	3.00

Soulwind
Image, 1997

1-8	3.00

Soupy Sales Comic Book
Archie, 1965

1	80.00

Southern Blood
Jm Comics, 1992

1-2	3.00

Southern Cumfort
Fantagraphics

1	3.00

Southern-Fried
Homicide
Cremo

1	8.00

Southern Knights
Guild, 1983

2-34	2.00
35-36	4.00
Holiday 1-Special 1	2.00

Southern Knights
Primer
Comics Interview

1	2.00

Southern Squadron
Aircel, 1990

1-4	2.00

Southern Squadron
Eternity, 1991

1-4	3.00

Southern Squadron:
The Freedom of
Information Act
Eternity, 1992

1-3	3.00

Sovereign Seven
DC, 1995

1	3.00
1/Variant	4.00
2-36	2.00
Ann 1	4.00
Ann 2	3.00

Sovereign Seven Plus
DC, 1997

1	3.00

Soviet Super Soldiers
Marvel, 1992

1	2.00

Space Action
Ace, 1952

1	525.00
2-3	350.00

Space Squadron
Atlas, 1951

1	400.00
2	340.00
3-5	275.00

Space: 1999
Charlton, 1975

1	10.00
2-4	7.00
5-7	5.00

Space: 34-24-34
MN Design

1	5.00

Space:
Above and Beyond
Topps, 1996

1-3	3.00

Space: Above and
Beyond: The Gauntlet
Topps, 1996

1-2	3.00

Space Ace
Magazine Enterprises, 1952

5	400.00

Space Adventures
Charlton, 1952

Supersophisticated androids that can pass for human? Robots that turn on their creators to take control of their world? Strange alien armies secretly infiltrating the earth? Men rocketing through the galaxy as easily as taking an average Sunday drive in the country? Come on, that stuff is just a bunch of science fiction, right?

You bet it is! Published every two months, Charlton Comics presented a new collection of short stories about mankind's long-dreamed-of exploration of the rest of the solar system...and beyond!

This series is notable for its many stories by Steve Ditko (creator of The Amazing Spider-Man), and for the first appearance of Captain Atom.

1	240.00
2	125.00
3-5	105.00
6-9	90.00
10-12	225.00
13-19	90.00
20	110.00
21	80.00
23	100.00
24-32	70.00
33	325.00
☛1st Captain Atom	
34	150.00
35-40	125.00
41	25.00
42	75.00
43-50	25.00
51-60	18.00
61-72	12.00

Space Ark
AC, 1987

This funny animal series from Bill Black's AC Comics features a cast of animated short-inspired characters in Star Trek-like adventures. Led by a fearless fox named Captain Stone, the crew of the U.S.S. Space Ark journey about the universe "help(ing) make the galaxy a safer and happier place-for the time being." Space Ark is obviously an homage to the cartoons of the 1930s-1950s-the first issue is even dedicated to animation legend Bob Clampett (Sylvester and Tweety)-but, without the benefit of moving pictures, the stories fall a bit flat and the jokes, while occasionally cute, lack a certain "zing"...maybe because there's no Mel Blanc or June Foray to give them life.

1-5	2.00

Space Bananas
Karl Art

0	2.00

Space Beaver
Ten-Buck, 1986

1-11	2.00

Space Busters
Ziff-Davis, 1952

1	525.00
2	450.00

Space Circus
Dark Horse, 2000

1-4	3.00

Space Comics
Avon, 1954

4-5	40.00

Space Cowboy Annual 2001
Vanguard, 2001

1/Frazetta-1/Williamson	5.00

Spaced
Unbridled Ambition, 1985

1-13	2.00

Spaced
Comics and Comix

1	4.00

Space Detective
Avon, 1951

1	775.00
2	575.00
3-4	300.00

Spaced Out
Forbidden Fruit, 1992

1	3.00

Spaced Out
Print Mint

1	3.00

Space Family Robinson
Gold Key, 1962

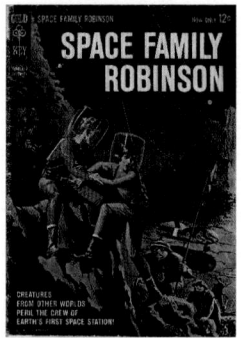

Space Family Robinson was the inspiration for the hit 1960s TV show "Lost In Space." In this original comics version, the family consisted of Craig and June Robinson and their children Tim and Tam. (The TV series' Robot joined the devious Doctor Smith and the stalwart Major West for the TV version.)

In the comics version, the Robinson family was cast adrift in space due to an accident, while the TV Robinsons were the victims of sabotage on the part of Smith. Their goal was to eventually find their way back to Earth, but a series of mishaps and alien encounters always seems to send them spinning off into space just as they were beginning to get back on course.

This series began in 1962, some years before the television show. When the show became a hit, the comic changed its name to "Space Family Robinson Lost in Space" (later even adding "On Space Station One").

1	225.00
2	100.00
3-5	75.00
6-10	50.00
11-15	35.00
16-20	25.00
21-44	20.00
45-54	10.00
55-59	6.00

Space Funnies
Archival, 1990

1	6.00

Spacegal Comics
Thorby

1-2	3.00

Space Ghost
Gold Key, 1967

1	150.00

Space Ghost
Comico, 1987

1	4.00

Space Ghost
DC, 2005

1	22.00
2	10.00
3-6	3.00

Space Giants
Boneyard

1	3.00

Spacegirl Comics
Bill Jones Graphics, 1995

1-2	3.00

Spacehawk
Dark Horse, 1989

1-4	2.00
5	3.00

Space Hustlers
Slave Labor, 1997

1	3.00

Space Jam
DC, 1996

1	6.00

Spaceknights
Marvel, 2000

1-5	3.00

Spaceman
Atlas, 1953

1	400.00
2	260.00
3-6	225.00

Spaceman
Dell, 1962

2	40.00
3	32.00
4-6	24.00
7-8	22.00
9-10	5.00

Spaceman
Oni, 2002

nn	3.00

Space Mouse
Avon, 1953

1	65.00
2	40.00
3-5	30.00

Space: 1999 (Magazine)
Charlton, 1975

1	30.00
2-8	20.00

Space Patrol
Ziff-Davis, 1952

1	550.00
2	390.00

Space Patrol
Adventure

1-3	3.00

Space Slutz
Comic Zone

1	4.00

Space Thrillers
Avon, 1954

1	850.00

Space Time Shuffle a Trilogy
Alpha Productions

1-2	2.00

Space Trip to the Moon
Avalon, 1999

1	3.00

Space Usagi
Mirage, 1992

1-3	3.00

Space Usagi
Mirage, 1993

1-3	3.00

Space Usagi
Dark Horse, 1996

1-3	3.00

Space War
Charlton, 1959

Space War was an anthology title, with each issue containing several different short stories.

These were of the time-honored "surprise-ironic ending" type, set against the backdrop of space. Since each story had just eight pages, the tales often read more like concepts than fiction, such as: "An 'Anywhere Machine' can take its riders to anyplace in space or time: The passengers desire to go to Heaven, but are tricked into going to Hell instead."

In its original form, Space War ran for 27 issues in the late 1950s before changing its name to Fightin' 5. The original series resurfaced in 1978 during Charlton's "reprint years," consisting entirely of old (though generally interesting) stories. This second run succeeded in squeezing out only a few more issues before the series concluded for good.

-- Rob Salkowitz

1	95.00
2-3	55.00
4-6	100.00
7	30.00
8	100.00
9	30.00
10	100.00
11-15	30.00
16-27	16.00
28-32	4.00

Space War Classics
Avalon

1	3.00

Space Western
Charlton, 1952

40	180.00
41	130.00
42	140.00
43-45	130.00

Space Wolf
Antarctic, 1992

1-2	3.00

Space Worlds
Atlas, 1952

6	300.00

Spam
Alpha Productions

1-2	2.00

Spandex Tights
Lost Cause, 1994

1	3.00
2-5	2.00
6	3.00

Spandex Tights
Lost Cause, 1997

1-3	3.00

Spanish Fly
Fantagraphics, 1996

1-5	3.00

Spank
Fantagraphics
2-4 ....2.00

Spank the Monkey
Arrow, 1999
1 ....3.00

Spanner's Galaxy
DC, 1984
1-6 ....1.00

Sparkle Comics
United Feature, 1948
1 ....85.00
2 ....50.00
3-10 ....38.00
11-25 ....26.00
26-33 ....20.00

Sparkler Comics
United Feature, 1940
1 ....315.00
2 ....240.00

Sparkler Comics
United Feature Syndicate, 1941
1 ....1,500.00
2 ....650.00
3-4 ....425.00
5-10 ....375.00
11-20 ....300.00
21-29 ....235.00
30-40 ....165.00
41-50 ....150.00
51-60 ....100.00
61-70 ....75.00
71-90 ....55.00
91-100 ....42.00
101-120 ....30.00

Sparkling Stars
Holyoke, 1944
1 ....100.00
2 ....65.00
3 ....50.00
4-10 ....42.00
11-33 ....35.00

Sparkplug
Heroic, 1993
1-3 ....3.00

Sparky & Tim
Aaron Warner, 1999
1 ....6.00

Sparky Watts
Publication Enterprises, 1942
1 ....300.00
2 ....165.00
3 ....110.00
4 ....85.00
5-6 ....55.00
7 ....42.00
8-10 ....34.00

Sparrow
Millennium, 1995
1-4 ....3.00

Spartan: Warrior Spirit
Image, 1995
1-4 ....3.00

Spartan X: Hell-Bent-Hero-For-Hire (Jackie Chan's...)
Image, 1998
1-4 .... 3.00

Spartan X: The Armour of Heaven (Jackie Chan's...)
Topps, 1997
1 .... 3.00

Spasm
Parody
1 .... 10.00

Spasm
Rough Copy
1-5 .... 3.00

Spawn
Image, 1992

After a stint at DC on such titles as Infinity, Inc. and All-Star Squadron, the multi-talented Todd McFarlane moved to Marvel, bringing his dynamic writing and artistry to a number of titles, most notably the Amazing Spider-Man. Having proved himself, Marvel awarded him his own title, Spider-Man, whose premiere issue was the best-selling comic book of 1991. Eventually, McFarlane set his sights even higher, leaving Marvel to help found Image.

Spawn was McFarlane's first title at Image. Its title character is a former mercenary, dead for five years, who is brought back to life as a cloaked Hellspawn, or "'Spawn." In life, he was Al Simmons, but more than that he remembers only in flashes: a wife, the shadowy organization he worked for, and murders...including his own.

1 .... 5.00
1/A 3.00
2 .... 4.00
3-6 .... 3.00

7-9 .... 4.00
10-50 .... 3.00
51-97 .... 2.00
98-99 .... 3.00
100/A 6.00
100/B-100/F 5.00
101-149 .... 3.00
150 .... 5.00
151-171 .... 3.00
Ann 1 .... 5.00
Fan ed. 1/A-3/B 1.00

Spawn-Batman
Image, 1994
1 .... 4.00

Spawn Bible
Image, 1996
1 .... 2.00

Spawn Blood and Salvation
Image, 1999
1 .... 5.00

Spawn Blood Feud
Image, 1995
1-4 .... 2.00

Spawn: Godslayer
Image, 2006
1 .... 7.00

Spawn Movie Adaptation
Image, 1997
1 .... 5.00

Spawn #1 in 3-D
Image, 2006
1 .... 6.00

Spawn: Simony One-Shot
Image, 2004
1 .... 8.00

Spawn: The Dark Ages
Image, 1999
1-28 .... 3.00

Spawn the Impaler
Image, 1996
1-3 .... 3.00

Spawn the Undead
Image, 1999
1-9 .... 2.00

Spawn/WildC.A.T.S
Image, 1996
1-4 .... 3.00

Spaztic Colon
-Ism, 2005
1-3 .... 4.00

Special Agent
Parents' Magazine Institute, 1947
1 .... 75.00
2 .... 45.00
3-8 .... 35.00

Special Comics
M.L.J., 1941
1 ....2,500.00

Special Edition
DC, 1944
1 ....475.00
2 ....300.00
3-5...350.00
6 ....300.00

Special Edition Comics
Fawcett, 1940
1 ....9,000.00

Special Hugging and Other Childhood Tales
Slave Labor, 1989
1 ....2.00

Special Marvel Edition
Marvel, 1971

Beginning in 1971, Special Marvel Edition spent most of its three-year run as home to a nondescript sereis, first of Thor reprints, then of Sgt. Fury reprints.

Its last two issues were a different story. With #15, Special Marvel Edition introduced Shang-Chi, the Master of Kung Fu. Shang-Chi was a hit, drawing on the kung fu craze of the day. Beginning with #17, Special Marvel Edition was renamed after its new hero, becoming Master of Kung Fu.

By the way, while Shang-Chi is the better-known character today, his introduction actually involved a well-known existing fictional villain, Sax Rohmerís Dr. Fu Manchu. Rohmer (1883-1959) introduced the character in 1912, and Fu Manchuís schemes for world domination were fought (in a number of books over the years) by Sir Denis Nayland Smith and his friends. Smith and Manchu appeared in Shang-Chi stories until Marvel eased them out of continuity.

1 .... 20.00
2-4 .... 15.00
5-14 .... 7.00
15 .... 45.00
☞1st Shang-Chi
16 .... 18.00

Special War Series
Charlton, 1965
1 .... 10.00
2-3 .... 8.00
4 .... 16.00

Species
Dark Horse, 1995
1-4.. 3.00

Species: Human Race
Dark Horse, 1996
1-4.. 3.00

Spectacles
Alternative, 1997
1-4.. 3.00

Spectacular Features Magazine
Fox, 1950
11-12 .... 165.00
3 .... 125.00

Spectacular Scarlet Spider
Marvel, 1995
1-2.. 2.00

Spectacular Spider-Man (Magazine)
Marvel, 1968
1 .... 90.00
2 .... 75.00

Spectacular Spider-Man
Marvel, 1976
-1 .... 2.00
1 .... 25.00
2 .... 15.00
3-3/Whitman 8.00
4-7/Whitman 5.00
7/35¢ 15.00
8-8/Whitman 5.00
8/35¢ 15.00
9-9/Whitman 5.00
9/35¢ 15.00
10-10/Whitman...................... 4.00
10/35¢ 15.00
11-11/Whitman...................... 4.00
11/35¢ 15.00
12-20 .... 4.00
21-26/Whitman 3.00
☞1st Miller Daredevil
27-28 .... 15.00
☞2nd Miller Daredevil
29-55 .... 3.00
56 .... 5.00
57-63 .... 3.00
64 .... 5.00
☞1st Cloak & Dagger
65-82 .... 3.00
83 .... 7.00
☞Punisher app.

84 .... 3.00
85 .... 5.00
86-99 .... 3.00
100 .... 5.00
101 .... 3.00
102-115 .... 2.00
116 .... 3.00
117-129 .... 2.00
130 .... 3.00
131 .... 5.00
132 .... 4.00
133 .... 3.00
134-142 .... 2.00
143 .... 4.00
144-146 .... 2.00
147 .... 8.00
☞New Hobgoblin
148 .... 2.00
149 .... 3.00
150-157 .... 2.00
158 .... 5.00
159 .... 4.00
160-188 .... 2.00
189 .... 4.00
189/2nd 3.00
190-195 .... 2.00
195/CS 3.00
196-199 .... 2.00
200 .... 4.00
201-213 .... 2.00
213/CS 3.00
214-217 .... 2.00
217/Variant 3.00
218-219 .... 2.00
220-221 .... 3.00
222 .... 2.00
223-223/Variant...................... 3.00
224 .... 2.00
225 .... 5.00
225/Variant 4.00
226-228 .... 2.00
229 .... 3.00
229/Variant-230 .... 4.00
231-249 .... 2.00
250 .... 3.00
251-255 .... 2.00
255/Variant 5.00
256-263 .... 2.00
Ann 1 .... 5.00
Ann 2 .... 4.00
Ann 3-7..................................... 3.00
Ann 8 .... 4.00
Ann 9-1997............................... 3.00
Special 1 .... 4.00

Spectacular Spider-Man
Marvel, 2003
1 .... 4.00
1/CanExpo 6.00
2-3.. 3.00
4 .... 4.00
5-7.. 3.00
8-13.. 2.00
14 .... 3.00
15 .... 7.00
☞Avengers Disassembled
16 .... 5.00
☞Avengers Disassmbled
17-19 .... 2.00
20 .... 3.00

☛Organic webshooters
21-27...2.00

Spectacular Spider-Man Adventures
Marvel UK, 1999
1...4.00
2-46...3.00

Spectacular Spider-Man Super Special
Marvel, 1995
1...4.00

Spectacular Stories Magazine
Fox, 1950
3...250.00
4...175.00

Spectre
DC, 1967
1...150.00
2...60.00
3-5...50.00
6-10.......................................40.00

Spectre
DC, 1987
1-5...3.00
6-31...2.00
Ann 1.......................................3.00

Spectre
DC, 1992
0...3.00
1...6.00
2...5.00
3...4.00
4-7...3.00
8...4.00
9-20...3.00
21-36.......................................2.00
37-62.......................................3.00
Ann 1.......................................4.00

Spectre
DC, 2001
1-27...3.00

Spectrescope
Spectre, 1994
1...1.00

Spectrum
New Horizons, 1987
1...2.00

Spectrum Comics Previews
Spectrum, 1983
1...3.00

Speedball
Marvel, 1988
1-10...1.00

Speed Buggy
Charlton, 1975
1...12.00
2-9...8.00

Speed Comics
Harvey, 1939
1....................................... 3,000.00
2....................................... 1,100.00
3.. 525.00
4-5.. 450.00
6-10...................................... 400.00
11-13..................................... 365.00
14-16..................................... 500.00
17.. 550.00
18-20..................................... 365.00
21-30..................................... 300.00
31-37..................................... 250.00
38.. 450.00
39-44..................................... 250.00

Speed Demon
Marvel, 1996
1.. 2.00

Speed Force
DC, 1997
1.. 4.00

Speed Racer
Now, 1987
1.. 3.00
1/2nd-38.................................. 2.00
Special 1 .... 3.00
Special 1/2nd 2.00

Speed Racer
DC, 1999
1-3.. 3.00

Speed Racer
Now
1-3.. 3.00

Speed Racer 3-D Special
Now, 1993
1.. 3.00

Speed Racer Classics
Now, 1988
1-2.. 4.00

Speed Racer Featuring Ninja High School
Now, 1993
1-2.. 3.00

Speed Racer: Return of the GRX
Now, 1994
1-2.. 2.00

Speed Racer: The Original Manga
DC
1.. 10.00

Speed Smith, the Hot Rod King
Ziff-Davis, 1952
1.. 100.00

Speed Tribes
Nemicron, 1998
1.. 3.00

Spellbinders
Fleetway-Quality, 1986
1-12....................................... 2.00

Spellbinders
Marvel, 2005
1-6.. 3.00

Spellbound
Atlas, 1952

In a faraway universe, magic holds sway. Two rival spellbinders command the mystical forces of good and evil, giving them the power to do almost anything they can imagine. All that changed, however, when one of the spellbinder's familiars dared to revolt against him. They stole his rings of order and chaos, and sought out the help of an unknown third spellbinder.

Worlds away, Erica Fortune is a promising English teacher at New York State University. Although she is known to possess paranormal abilities, she has no idea of her true import. That changes when the spellbinder's familiars crash through a dimensional portal into her living room. It's then that she discovers that she is the third great spellbinder, charged with a mystical quest to use her powers for good.

1.. 400.00
2.. 210.00
3-6.. 180.00
7-10...................................... 155.00
11-20..................................... 125.00
21-23..................................... 105.00
24-28...................................... 95.00
29.. 105.00
30-33...................................... 95.00

Spellbound
Marvel, 1988
1-6.. 2.00

Spellcaster
Medusa
1-3.. 3.00

Spelljammer
DC, 1990

1-18..2.00

Spex-7
Shadow Shock, 1994

1...2.00

Sphinx
Print Mint, 1972

1-3...3.00

Spicecapades
Fantagraphics, 1999

1...5.00

Spicy Adult Stories
Aircel, 1991

1-4...3.00

Spicy Tales
Eternity, 1988

1-17..2.00
18-20.......................................3.00
Special 1-2...............................2.00

Spider
Eclipse, 1991

1-3...5.00

Spiderbaby Comix (S.R. Bissette's...)
Spiderbaby, 1996

1...4.00

Spider-Boy
Marvel, 1996

1...3.00

Spider-Boy Team-Uvp
Marvel, 1997

1...2.00

Spider-Femme
Spoof

1...3.00

Spider Garden
NBM

1...13.00

Spider-Girl
Marvel, 1998

In 1998, Marvel tried out another interrelated collection of comics, MC-2. This imprint took the Marvel universe into the future by about 15 years and tried for a lighthearted and fun tone. Spider-Girl, aka May "Mayday" Parker, the daughter of Peter and Mary Jane Parker, was introduced in What If ... ? (Vol. 2) #105. Out of a sense of responsibility to stop the wrongs she sees, May adopts her father's mantle without his knowledge. As Spider-Girl, she fights such villains as Mr. Nobody and Crazy Eight and is assisted by Phil Urich and Dark Devil.

Threatened with cancellation, this series was rescued by fan outcry in 2002.

0 .... 2.00
1/2 .... 3.00
1-1/A.. 4.00
2-5 .... 3.00
6-16 .... 2.00
17 .... 3.00
18-24 .... 2.00
25 .... 3.00
26-58 .... 2.00
59-74 .... 3.00
75 .... 8.00
76-99 .... 3.00
100-Ann 1999...................... 4.00

Spider-Girl Battlebook
Marvel, 1998

1 .... 4.00

Spider-Man
Marvel, 1990

Believe it or not, the first comic-book series called simply Spider-Man didn't appear until 1990. It made a serious splash. Todd McFarlane, who had become a comics superstar for his very spidery-looking renditions of the title character of Amazing Spider-Man, was given the chance to start a Spidey title that would be all his own: "adjectiveless," as it would commonly be called.

Retailers would call it a license to print money, as sales on the first issue went far beyond the wildest expectations. The issue came with special "bagged" editions -- the logic being that if you opened the bag, you destroyed the resale value of the comic book. That particular bit of lunacy didn't survive the end of the 1990s speculator glut, but it had a good deal to do with getting it going in the first place. (It should be noted, in fact, that there is no such thing as a CGC-graded copy of the "bagged edition." CGC has to unbag comics to grade them, making them just like all the others that people -- horrors! -- opened and read.)

McFarlane eventually left the series to form Image, and the title became more closely related to the other Spider-series. It was cancelled in 1998 and restarted as Peter Parker, Spider-Man.

-- John Jackson Miller

-1 .... 2.00
1/2 .... 4.00
1/2/Platinum 6.00
1-1/CS 5.00
1/Platinum 42.00
1/Silver 5.00
1/2nd 50.00
1/Direct/2n 5.00
2-8 .... 3.00
9 .... 6.00
10 .... 4.00
11-12 .... 3.00
13 .... 5.00
14 .... 3.00
15-25 .... 2.00
26 .... 4.00
27-46 .... 2.00
46/CS 3.00
47-49 .... 2.00
50 .... 3.00
50/Variant 4.00
51-51/Variant........................... 3.00
52-56 .... 2.00
57-57/Variant........................... 3.00
58-74 .... 2.00
75 .... 4.00
76-98/B 2.00
Ann 1997-1998...................... 3.00
GS 1 .... 4.00
Holiday 1995 .... 3.00

Spider-Man Adventures
Marvel, 1994

1 .... 2.00
1/Variant 3.00
2-15 .... 2.00

Spider-Man and Arana Special
Marvel, 2006

1 .... 4.00

Spider-Man and Batman
Marvel, 1995

1 .... 6.00

Spider-Man and Daredevil Special Edition
Marvel, 1984
1 ....2.00

Spider-Man and Doctor Octopus: Negative Exposure
Marvel, 2003
1-5..3.00

Spider-Man and His Amazing Friends
Marvel, 1981
1 ....10.00

Spider-Man and Mysterio
Marvel, 2001
1-3..3.00

Spider-Man and Power Pack
Marvel, 2007
1-3..3.00

Spider-Man and the Dallas Cowboys
Marvel, 1983
1 ....10.00

Spider-Man and the Incredible Hulk
Marvel, 1981
1 ....10.00

Spider-Man & the New Mutants
Marvel
1 ....3.00

Spider-Man & Wolverine
Marvel, 2003
1-4..3.00

Spider-Man and X-Factor: Shadowgames
Marvel, 1994
1-3..2.00

Spider-Man/Badrock
Maximum, 1997
1/A-1/B 3.00

Spider-Man Battlebook
Marvel, 1998
1 ....4.00

Spider-Man/Black Cat: The Evil That Men Do
Marvel, 2002
1 ....5.00
2-6..3.00

Spider-Man: Blue
Marvel, 2002
1 ....6.00
2 ....5.00
3-6..4.00

Spider-Man: Breakout
Marvel, 2005
1-5 .... 3.00

Spider-Man: Carnage
Marvel
1 .... 9.00

Spider-Man: Chapter One
Marvel, 1998
0-1 .... 3.00
1/A 4.00
1/B-1/C 14.00
2/A-2/B 3.00
2/C 4.00
3-12... 3.00
Deluxe 1-Deluxe 1/Ltd.......... 30.00

Spider-Man: Christmas in Dallas
Marvel, 1983
1 .... 10.00

Spider-Man Classics
Marvel, 1993
1-12 .... 2.00
13-15 .... 1.00
15/CS 3.00
16 .... 1.00

Spider-Man Collectors' Preview
Marvel, 1994
1 .... 2.00

Spider-Man Comics Magazine
Marvel, 1987
1-13...................................... 2.00

Spider-Man/Daredevil
Marvel, 2002
1 .... 3.00

Spider-Man: Dead Man's Hand
Marvel, 1997
1 .... 3.00

Spider-Man: Death and Destiny
Marvel, 2000
1-3 .... 3.00

Spider-Man/Doctor Octopus: Out of Reach
Marvel, 2004
1 .... 4.00
2-5... 3.00

Spider-Man/Doctor Octopus: Year One
Marvel, 2004
1-5 .... 3.00

Spider-Man/Dr. Strange: The Way to Dusty Death
Marvel, 1992
1 .... 7.00

Spider-Man Family
Marvel, 2005
1 .... 5.00

Spider-Man Family: Amazing Friends
Marvel, 2006
1 .... 5.00

Spider-Man Family Featuring Spider-Clan
Marvel, 2007
1 .... 5.00

Spider-Man: Fear Itself
Marvel, 1992
1 .... 13.00

Spider-Man, Fire-Star and Iceman
Marvel, 1983
1 .... 10.00

Spider-Man: Friends & Enemies
Marvel, 1995
1-4 .... 2.00

Spider-Man: Funeral for an Octopus
Marvel, 1995
1-4 .... 2.00

Spider-Man/Gen13
Marvel, 1996
1 .... 5.00

Spider-Man: Get Kraven
Marvel, 2002
1-6... 2.00

Spider-Man: Hobgoblin Lives
Marvel, 1997
1-3 .... 3.00

Spider-Man: House of M
Marvel, 2005
1 .... 6.00
1/Conv................................... 15.00
2 .... 5.00
2/Variant................................. 4.00
☞2nd print
3-5.. 3.00

Spider-Man/Human Torch
Marvel, 2005
1-5 .... 3.00

Spider-Man: India
Marvel, 2004
1-4 .... 3.00

Spider-Man: Legacy of Evil
Marvel, 1996
1 .... 4.00

Spider-Man Legends
Marvel, 2003
2 .... 20.00

3 .... 25.00
4 .... 14.00

Spider-Man: Lifeline
Marvel, 2001
1-3 .... 3.00

**Spider-Man
Loves Mary Jane**
Marvel, 2006
1-13 .... 3.00

Spider-Man: Made Men
Marvel, 1999
1 .... 6.00

Spider-Man Magazine
Marvel, 1994
1-10 .... 2.00

Spider-Man Magazine
Marvel, 1995
1 .... 3.00

**Spider-Man: Maximum
Clonage Alpha**
Marvel, 1995
1 .... 10.00

**Spider-Man: Maximum
Clonage Omega**
Marvel, 1995
1 .... 10.00

Spider-Man Megazine
Marvel, 1994
1-6 .... 3.00

**Spider-Man 2
Movie Adaptation**
Marvel, 2004
1 .... 4.00

Spider-Man Mysteries
Marvel, 1998
1 .... 1.00

**Spider-Man:
Power of Terror**
Marvel, 1995
1-4 .... 2.00

Spider-Man, Power Pack
Marvel, 1984
1 .... 1.00

**Spider-Man/Punisher:
Family Plot**
Marvel, 1996
1-2 .... 3.00

**Spider-Man,
Punisher, Sabretooth:
Designer Genes**
Marvel, 1993
1 .... 9.00

**Spider-Man:
Quality of Life**
Marvel, 2002
1-4 .... 3.00

**Spider-Man:
Redemption**
Marvel, 1996
1-4 .... 2.00

Spider-Man: Reign
Marvel, 2006
1 .... 20.00
2 .... 18.00

**Spider-Man: Revenge
of the Green Goblin**
Marvel, 2000
1-3 .... 3.00

Spider-Man Saga
Marvel, 1991
1-4 .... 3.00

**Spider-Man:
Son of the Goblin**
Marvel, 2004
1 .... 16.00

**Spider-Man
Special Edition**
Marvel, 1992
1 .... 7.00

**Spider-Man,
Storm and Power Man**
Marvel, 1982
1 .... 2.00

**Spider-Man
Super Special**
Marvel, 1995
1 .... 4.00

**Spider-Man:
Sweet Charity**
Marvel, 2002
1 .... 5.00

Spider-Man Team-Up
Marvel, 1995
1-7 .... 3.00

**Spider-Man
Team-Up Special**
Marvel, 2005
0 .... 3.00

**Spider-Man:
The Arachnis Project**
Marvel, 1994
1-6 .... 2.00

**Spider-Man:
The Clone Journal**
Marvel, 1995
1 .... 3.00

**Spider-Man: The
Death of Captain Stacy**
Marvel, 2000
1 .... 4.00

**Spider-Man:
The Final Adventure**
Marvel, 1995
1-4 .... 3.00

**Spider-Man:
The Jackal Files**
Marvel, 1995
1 .... 2.00

**Spider-Man:
The Lost Years**
Marvel, 1995
0 .... 4.00
1-3 .... 3.00

Spider-Man: The Manga
Marvel, 1997
1 .... 4.00
2-31 .... 3.00

**Spider-Man:
The Mutant Agenda**
Marvel, 1994
0 .... 1.00
1-3 .... 2.00

Spider-Man: The Official Movie Adaptation
Marvel, 2002
1...6.00

Spider-Man: The Other Sketchbook
Marvel, 2005
1...3.00

Spider-Man: The Parker Years
Marvel, 1995
1...3.00

Spider-Man 2099
Marvel, 1992
1...3.00
2-18..1.00
19-25...2.00
25/Variant....................................3.00
26-46...2.00
Ann 1..3.00
Special 1 ....4.00

Spider-Man 2099 Meets Spider-Man
Marvel, 1995
1...6.00

Spider-Man Universe
Marvel, 2000
1-5...5.00
6-7...4.00

Spider-Man Unlimited
Marvel, 1993
1-12..4.00
13-22...3.00

Spider-Man Unlimited
Marvel, 1999
1...3.00

Spider-Man Unlimited
Marvel, 2004
1-15..3.00

Spider-Man Unmasked
Marvel, 1996
1...6.00

Spider-Man: Venom Agenda
Marvel, 1998
1...3.00

Spider-Man vs. Dracula
Marvel, 1994
1...2.00

Spider-Man vs. Punisher
Marvel, 2000
1...3.00

Spider-Man vs. the Hulk
Marvel, 1979
1...7.00

Spider-Man vs. Wolverine
Marvel, 1987
1...6.00
1/2nd...5.00

Spider-Man: Web of Doom
Marvel, 1994
1-3.. 2.00

Spider, The: Reign of the Vampire King
Eclipse, 1992
1-3.. 5.00

Spider Sneak Preview
Argosy, 2001
1 .... 5.00

Spider's Web
Blazing
1 .... 2.00

Spider-Woman
Marvel, 1978

Jessica Drew's father was a visionary scientist who dreamed of someday combining the adaptive abilities of the spider with human genes. His theory was put to the test when he placed his daughter, who was dying of radiation poisoning, n his Genetic Accelerator.

Years later, Jessica found she had incredible strength, could stick to walls, and was able to generate "venom bolts" from her own biosystem. These powers caused others to fear her, and she escaped their wrath only when she was recruited into Hydra. She soon learned the true nature of Hydra, however, and turned against them -- becoming a super-hero.

Spider-Woman's creation was perceived by many as an attempt by Marvel to protect its trademark options, and her frequently dark series never really caught on. A plot device in the series' final issue made it so everyone in the Marvel universe would forget she had ever existed -- which, sadly, wasn't that hard.

1 .... 6.00

2-3 .... 3.00
4-36 .... 2.00
☛1st Siryn
37-38 .... 4.00
☛X-Men app.
39-49 .... 1.00
50 .... 4.00

Spider-Woman
Marvel, 1993
1-4 .... 2.00

Spider-Woman
Marvel, 1999
1-2 .... 3.00
3-18 .... 2.00

Spider-Woman: Origin
Marvel, 2006
1-5 .... 3.00

Spidery-Mon: Maximum Carcass
Parody
1/A-1/C 3.00

Spidey and the Mini-Marvels
Marvel, 2003
1 .... 4.00

Spidey Super Stories
Marvel, 1974
1 .... 20.00
☛Spider-Man origin
2 .... 6.00
3-57 .... 5.00

Spike and Tyke (M.G.M.'s...)
Dell, 1955
4 .... 14.00
5 .... 12.00
6-10 .... 10.00
11-24 .... 8.00

Spike: Asylum
Idea & Design Works, 2006
1-4 .... 4.00

Spike: Lost and Found
Idea & Design Works, 2006
1 .... 7.00

Spike: Old Times
Idea & Design Works, 2005
0 .... 7.00

Spike: Old Wounds
Idea & Design Works, 2006
1 .... 7.00

Spike vs. Dracula
Idea & Design Works, 2006
1-5 .... 4.00

Spin and Marty
Dell, 1958
5 .... 60.00
6-9 .... 45.00

Spineless-Man $2099
Parody
1 .... 3.00

Spine-Tingling Tales (Dr. Spektor Presents...)
Gold Key, 1975
1 ....20.00
2-4 ....8.00

Spinworld
Slave Labor, 1997
1-4 ....3.00

Spiral Path
Eclipse, 1986
1-2 ....2.00

Spiral Zone
DC, 1988
1-4 ....1.00

Spirit
Newspaper, 1940
1 ....700.00
2 ....325.00
3 ....175.00
4-5 ....125.00
6-10 ....100.00
11-20 ....75.00
21-52 ....55.00
53-83 ....45.00
84-135 ....35.00
136-187 ....28.00
188-240 ....20.00
241-290 ....16.00
291-396 ....35.00
397-585 ....30.00
586-634 ....15.00
635-641 ....125.00
642 ....75.00
643-644 ....125.00
645 ....75.00

Spirit
Quality, 1944
1 ....600.00
2 ....350.00
3 ....250.00
4-5 ....185.00
6-10 ....150.00
11 ....125.00
12-17 ....200.00
18-21 ....250.00
22 ....350.00

Spirit
Fiction House, 1952
1 ....250.00
2 ....225.00
3-4 ....175.00
5 ....200.00

Spirit
Super
11-12 ....15.00

Spirit
Harvey, 1966
1 ....50.00
2 ....42.00

Spirit
Kitchen Sink, 1973
1-2 ....14.00

Spirit
Ken Pierce
1-4 .... 18.00

Spirit (Magazine)
Warren, 1974
1 .... 22.00
2 .... 10.00
3 .... 7.00
4-12 .... 6.00
13-15 .... 5.00
16 .... 7.00
17-41 .... 4.00
Special 1 .... 35.00
☛Mail-in only

Spirit
Kitchen Sink, 1983
1 .... 5.00
2-9 .... 4.00
10-11 .... 3.00
12-87 .... 2.00

Spirit
DC, 2007
1-30 .... 3.00

Spirit Casebook
Kitchen Sink
1 .... 13.00

Spirit Collector's Edition Reprints
Will Eisner, 1972
1-40 .... 2.00
Deluxe 1-4 .... 20.00

Spirit Jam
Kitchen Sink, 1998
1 .... 6.00

Spirit of the Tao
Image, 1998
1-13 .... 3.00
Ashcan 1 .... 5.00

Spirit of the Wind
Chocolate Mouse
1 .... 2.00

Spirit of Wonder
Dark Horse, 1996
1-5 .... 3.00

Spirits
Mind Walker, 1995
3 .... 3.00

Spirits of Venom
Marvel, 1993
1 .... 10.00

Spirit: The New Adventures
Kitchen Sink, 1998
1-8 .... 4.00

Spirit: The Origin Years
Kitchen Sink, 1992
1-10 .... 3.00

Spirit World
DC, 1971
1 .... 35.00

Spirou & Fantasio: Z Is for Zorglub
Fantasy Flight
1 .... 9.00

Spitfire and the Troubleshooters
Marvel, 1986
1-9 .... 1.00

Spitfire Comics
Harvey, 1941
1-2 .... 150.00

Spittin' Image
Eclipse
1 .... 3.00

Spit Wad Comics
Spit Wad, 1983
1 .... 3.00

Splat!
Mad Dog, 1987
1-3 .... 2.00

Splatter
Arpad
1 .... 3.00

Splatter
Northstar, 1991
1 .... 5.00
2-8 .... 3.00
Ann 1 .... 5.00

Splitting Image
Image, 1993

Image Comics has had its share of detractors, ranging from such innocuous parodies as WildB.R.A.T.s to the downright nasty Kill Image.

Parody Press has had so much fun making fun of these comic upstarts that it has devoted a substantial amount of its output to spoofing various Image titles. (That is, of course, not to mention that interest in the hot new Image company could spike sales in parodies of its material.)

Perhaps sensing a growth business, Image created Splitting Image to lampoon itself. Although the gang takes good-natured shots at its own characters and public personae, its heart doesn't really seem to be in it. Perhaps, given the slew of Image parodies available, they could have simply left it to the rest of the comic-book industry.

1-2..2.00

Spoof
Marvel, 1970
1..15.00
2..7.00
3..8.00
4-5..7.00

Spoof Comics
Spoof, 1992
0-12..3.00

Spook (1st Series)
Star, 1946
1..200.00

Spook (2nd Series)
Star, 1953
22..225.00
23..150.00
24..160.00
25-30..150.00

Spook City
Mythic, 1997
1..3.00

Spookgirl
Slave Labor, 2000
1..3.00

Spooky
Harvey, 1955
1..200.00
2..110.00
3..65.00
4-5..50.00
6-10..35.00
11-20..24.00
21-29..20.00
30-39..18.00
40-50..15.00
51-70..12.00
71-90..8.00
91-110..6.00
111-130..5.00
131-161..4.00

Spooky
Harvey, 1991
1-4..1.00

Spooky Digest
Harvey, 1992
1-2..2.00

Spooky Haunted House
Harvey, 1972
1..15.00
2-11..10.00

Spooky Mysteries
Your Guide, 1947
1.. 58.00

Spooky Spooktown
Harvey, 1961
1.. 85.00
2.. 45.00
3-5.. 30.00
6-10.. 22.00
11-20.. 15.00
21-29.. 8.00
30-40.. 5.00
41-66.. 3.00

Spooky the Dog Catcher
Paw Prints, 1994
1-3.. 3.00

Sport Comics
Street & Smith, 1940
1.. 350.00
2.. 175.00
3-4.. 150.00

Sports Action
Atlas, 1950
2.. 250.00
3.. 130.00
4-11.. 115.00
12-13.. 125.00
14.. 115.00

Sports Classics
Personality
1.. 3.00
1/Ltd. 6.00
2-5.. 3.00

Sports Comics
Personality
1-4.. 3.00

Sports Hall of Shame in 3-D
Blackthorne
1.. 3.00

Sports Legends
Revolutionary, 1992
1-9.. 3.00

Sports Legends Special - Breaking the Color Barrier
Revolutionary, 1993
1.. 3.00

Sports Personalities
Personality, 1991
1-13.. 3.00

Sport Stars
Parents' Magazine Institute, 1946
1.. 225.00
2.. 145.00
3-4.. 125.00

Sport Stars
Atlas, 1949
1.. 250.00

Sports Superstars
Revolutionary, 1992
1-Ann 1.. 3.00

Spotlight
Marvel, 1978
1.. 8.00
2-4.. 6.00

Spotlight Comics
Harry A. Chesler, 1944
1.. 400.00
2.. 330.00
3.. 340.00

Spotlight on the Genius That Is Joe Sacco
Fantagraphics
1.. 5.00

Spotty the Pup
Avon, 1953
1-3.. 25.00

Spring Break Comics
AC, 1987
1.. 2.00

Spring-Heel Jack
Rebel
1-2.. 2.00

Springtime Tales (Walt Kelly's...)
Eclipse, 1988
1.. 3.00

Spud
Spud, 1996
1.. 4.00

Spunky
Standard, 1949
1.. 75.00
2.. 50.00
3-7.. 30.00

Spunky Knight
Fantagraphics, 1996
1-3.. 3.00

Spunky Knight Extreme
Fantagraphics, 2004
1-4.. 4.00

Spunky Knight XXX
Fantagraphics, 2005
1-4.. 4.00

Spunky the Smiling Spook
Ajax, 1957
1.. 50.00
2-4.. 30.00

Spunky Todd: The Psychic Boy
Caliber
1.. 3.00

Spy and Counterspy
ACG, 1949
1..150.00
2..100.00

SpyBoy
Dark Horse, 1999
1-17...3.00
Special 1 ....5.00

Spyboy 13: Manga Affair
Dark Horse, 2003
1-3...3.00

Spyboy: Final Exam
Dark Horse, 2004
1-4...3.00

Spyboy/Young Justice
Dark Horse, 2002
1-3...3.00

Spy Cases
Atlas, 1950
26...160.00
27-28..105.00
4-7...90.00
8...100.00
9-10...90.00
11-19..75.00

Spy Fighters
Atlas, 1951
1...130.00
2..75.00
3-13...60.00
14-15..65.00

Spy Hunters
ACG, 1949
3...125.00
4-10...75.00
11-15..55.00
16...85.00
17-24..55.00

Spyke
Marvel, 1993
1...3.00
2-4...2.00

Spyman
Harvey, 1966
1..30.00
2-3..24.00

Spy Smasher
Fawcett, 1941
1...2,500.00
2...750.00
3-7...450.00
8-9...350.00
10..375.00
11..350.00

Spy Thrillers
Atlas, 1954
1...125.00
2..85.00
3-4..70.00

Squadron Supreme
Marvel, 1985

Squadron Supreme is a 12-issue mini-series which paints a dark vision of super-heroes determining the fate of the world. Although it uses Marvel characters, it should be thought of as an "alternate reality" story.

It begins when Kyle Richmond (Nighthawk) quits the Defenders, deciding he can help the world more by becoming a congressman. He succeeds and eventually becomes president of the United States. Then, a being called the Overmind strikes, controlling Richmond's mind, the minds of his top advisors, and those of the Squadron Supreme (the government's top super-heroes). Under the Overmind's influence, America wages war against the entire world, eventually conquering it. By the time the Squadron Supreme throws off the Overmind's control, the world is in shambles. They decide to embark on a bold new plan: to use their powers to turn the world into a utopia. The catch: They will become its absolute rulers.

1...2.00
2-12...1.00

Squadron Supreme
Marvel, 2006
1-6...3.00

Squadron Supreme: New World Order
Marvel, 1998
1...6.00

Squalor
First, 1989
1-4...3.00

Squee!
Slave Labor, 1997
1...7.00
1/2nd...3.00
2...5.00
3-4...4.00

Squeeks
Lev Gleason, 1953
1..45.00
2..25.00
3-5..15.00

Sri Krishna
Chakra
1...4.00

Stacia Stories
Kitchen Sink, 1995
1...3.00

Stagger Lee
Image, 2006
1..18.00

Stain
Fathom, 1988
1...3.00

Stainless Steel Armadillo
Antarctic, 1995
1-5...3.00

Stainless Steel Rat
Eagle, 1985
1-6...3.00

Stalker
DC, 1975
1...7.00
2-4...4.00

Stalkers
Marvel, 1990
1-12...2.00

Stalking Ralph
Aeon, 1995
1...5.00

Stamps Comics
Youthful, 1951
1...225.00
2...125.00
3-6...100.00
7...125.00

Stand Up Comix (Bob Rumba's...)
Grey
1...3.00

Stan Lee Meets Dr. Doom
Marvel, 2007
1...4.00

Stan Lee Meets Dr. Strange
Marvel, 2006
1...4.00

Stan Lee Meets Silver Surfer
Marvel, 2007
1 .... 4.00

Stan Lee Meets Spider-Man
Marvel, 2006
1 .... 4.00

Stan Lee Meets Thing
Marvel, 2007
1 .... 4.00

Stanley & His Monster
DC, 1968
109 .... 20.00
110-112 .... 15.00

Stanley and His Monster
DC, 1993
1 .... 3.00
2-4 .... 2.00

Stanley the Snake with the Overactive Imagination
Emerald
1-2 .... 2.00

Star
Image, 1995
1-4 .... 3.00

Starbikers
Renegade
1 .... 2.00

Starblast
Marvel, 1994
1-4 .... 2.00

Star Blazers
Comico, 1987
1-4 .... 2.00

Star Blazers
Comico, 1989
1-2 .... 2.00
3-5 .... 3.00

Star Blazers: The Magazine of Space Battleship Yamato
Argo, 1995
0-1 .... 3.00

Star Blecch: Deep Space Diner
Parody
1/A-1/B 3.00

Star Blecch: Generation Gap
Parody, 1995
1 .... 4.00

Star Brand
Marvel, 1986
1-Ann 1 .... 1.00

Starchild
Taliesen, 1993
0-1 .... 4.00
1/2nd 3.00
2 .... 4.00
2/2nd-14 .... 3.00

Starchild: Crossroads
Coppervale, 1995
1-3 .... 3.00

Starchild: Mythopolis
Image, 1997
0-6 .... 3.00

Starchy
Excel
1 .... 2.00

Star Comics Magazine
Marvel, 1986
1 .... 3.00
2-13 .... 2.00

S.T.A.R. Corps
DC, 1993
1-6 .... 2.00

Star Crossed
DC, 1997
1-3 .... 3.00

Stardust (Neil Gaiman and Charles Vess'...)
DC, 1998
1 .... 7.00
2-4 .... 6.00

Stardusters
Nightwynd, 1991
1-4 .... 3.00

Stardust Kid
Image, 2005
1-3 .... 4.00

Starfire
DC, 1976
1 .... 7.00
2-8 .... 3.00

Star Forces
The Other Faculty
1 .... 3.00

Starforce Six Special
AC, 1984
1 .... 2.00

Stargate
Express, 1996
1 .... 3.00
1/Variant 4.00
2 .... 3.00
2/Variant 4.00
3 .... 3.00
3/Variant 4.00
4 .... 3.00
4/Variant 4.00

Stargate Doomsday World
Entity, 1996
1-3 .... 3.00

Stargate SG1: Aris Boch
Avatar, 2004
1 .... 4.00
1/Platinum 10.00

Stargate SG1 Con Special 2003
Avatar, 2003
1 .... 4.00

Stargate SG1 Con Special 2004
Avatar, 2004
1 .... 3.00
1/A 4.00

Stargate SG-1: Daniel's Song
Avatar, 2005
1 .... 3.00
1/Photo 4.00
1/Wraparound 3.00
1/Glow 20.00
1/Gold Foil 6.00
1/PlatFoil 10.00
1/Adversary 6.00

Stargate SG1: Fall of Rome
Avatar
0/Preview 6.00
1-1/Foil 4.00
1/Platinum 10.00
2 .... 4.00
2/Painted 6.00
2/Photo 4.00
2/Platinum 10.00
3 .... 4.00
3/Painted 6.00
3/Platinum 10.00
3/Photo 4.00

Stargate SG1: P.O.W.
Avatar, 2004
1-3 .... 4.00

Stargate: The New Adventures Collection
Entity, 1997
1 .... 6.00

Stargate Underworld
Entity, 1997
1 .... 3.00

Stargods
Antarctic, 1998
1 .... 3.00
1/CS 6.00
2 .... 3.00
2/CS 6.00

Stargods: Visions
Antarctic, 1998
1 .... 3.00

Star Hawks
Avalon, 1986
1-2 .... 3.00
3-8 .... 3.00

Starhead Presents
Starhead, 1987
1-3...1.00

Star Hunters
DC, 1977
1-7...1.00

Star Jacks
Antarctic, 1994
1...3.00

Star Jam Comics
Revolutionary, 1992
1-10...3.00

Starjammers
Marvel, 1995
1-4...3.00

Starjammers
Marvel, 2004
1-6...3.00

Stark: Future
Aircel, 1986
1-17...2.00

Starkid
Dark Horse, 1998
1...3.00

Stark Raven
Endless Horizons, 2000
1...3.00

Starkweather
Arcana, 2004
1...4.00
1/Ltd. 5.00
2-5...4.00

Starlet O'Hara in Hollywood
Standard, 1948
1...145.00
2...85.00
3-4...70.00

Starlight
Eternity, 1987
1...2.00

Starlight Agency
Antarctic, 1991
1-3...3.00

Starlion: A Pawn's Game
Storm, 1993
1...2.00

Starlord
Marvel, 1996
1-3...3.00

Starlord Megazine
Marvel, 1996
1...3.00

Star-Lord, The Special Edition
Marvel, 1982
1...2.00

Starlove
Forbidden Fruit
1 .... 3.00
2 .... 4.00

Starman (1st Series)
DC, 1988
1-10...................................... 2.00
11-25.................................... 1.00
26.. 2.00
27-45.................................... 1.00

Starman (2nd Series)
DC, 1994
0-1... 5.00
2-3... 4.00
4-40....................................... 3.00
41-46..................................... 2.00
47-49..................................... 3.00
50... 4.00
51-80..................................... 3.00
1000000 .... 4.00
Ann 1..................................... 5.00
Ann 2..................................... 4.00
GS 1 .... 5.00

Starman: Secret Files
DC, 1998
1 .... 5.00

Starman: The Mist
DC, 1998
1 .... 2.00

Star Masters
Marvel, 1995
1-3.. 2.00

Starmasters
AC, 1989
1 .... 2.00

Star Ranger
Centaur, 1937
1 .... 1,150.00
2 .... 525.00
3-6....................................... 450.00
7-10..................................... 360.00
11-12................................... 325.00

Star Ranger Funnies
Centaur, 1939
15 .... 625.00
1 .... 450.00
2-5 .... 375.00

Star Rangers
Adventure, 1987
1-3... 2.00

Star*Reach
Star*Reach, 1974
1-18...................................... 2.00

Star*Reach Classics
Eclipse, 1984
1-6.. 2.00

Starriors
Marvel, 1984
1-4 .... 1.00

Star Rovers
Comax
1 .... 3.00

Stars and S.T.R.I.P.E.
DC, 1999
0-14 .... 3.00

Stars and Stripes Comics
Centaur, 1941
2 .... 2,100.00
3 .... 1,100.00
4 .... 1,000.00
5-6 .... 675.00

Star Seed
Broadway, 1996
7-9 .... 3.00

Starship Troopers
Dark Horse, 1997

This three-issue mini-series from Dark Horse is a prequel to the events recounted in the movie adaptation of the Robert A. Heinlein SF novel Starship Troopers. An intrepid band of scientists and military personnel aboard the spaceship Cortez explore Klendathu, the homeworld of the arachnid race that subsequently invades Earth due to the events related here.

This first-contact story chills and shocks, as it foreshadows the ruthless fighting and graphic battle scenes that are destined to be played out when the arachnids learn of Earth's existence.

-- George Haberberger

1-2 .... 3.00

Starship Troopers: Brute Creations
Dark Horse, 1997
1 .... 3.00

Starship Troopers: Dominant Species
Dark Horse, 1998
1-4 .... 3.00

Starship Troopers: Insect Touch
Dark Horse, 1997
1-3..3.00

Star Slammers
Malibu, 1994
1-4..3.00

Star Slammers Special
Dark Horse, 1996
1..3.00

Starslayer
Pacific, 1982
1..2.00
2..4.00
3..2.00
4..1.00
5..2.00
6-9...1.00
10..2.00
11-34..1.00

Starslayer: The Director's Cut
Acclaim, 1995
1-8..3.00

Star Spangled Comics
DC, 1941

Beginning, appropriately enough, with the adventures of The Star-Spangled Kid and Stripesy, this DC anthology series eventually became home to Joe Simon and Jack Kirby's Guardian and The Newsboy Legion, as well as Robotman, The Tarantula, and a series of solo Robin stories.

In 1949, while still featuring Robin stories, the series' focus shifted to the Revolutionary War adventures of Tomahawk and concluded its run with the adventures of Ghost Breaker, a supernatural investigator.

The series became Star Spangled War Stories following #130.

-- Brent

1....................................4,500.00

2......................................1,800.00
3......................................1,000.00
4-5.......................................875.00
6..800.00
7......................................8,000.00
☞1st Newsboy Legion
8-10...................................1,600.00
11-16.................................1,175.00
17.....................................1,500.00
18-19.................................1,000.00
20-30....................................850.00
31-40....................................525.00
41-50....................................425.00
51-60....................................400.00
61-64....................................375.00
65.....................................1,050.00
☞Robin stories start
66-68....................................690.00
69.......................................800.00
☞1st Tomahawk
70.......................................690.00
71-80....................................575.00
81-83....................................450.00
84.......................................625.00
85-86....................................450.00
87.......................................625.00
88-94....................................500.00
95-99....................................265.00
100......................................300.00
101-110..................................225.00
111-112..................................200.00
113......................................375.00
114......................................325.00
115-131..................................200.00

Star Spangled Comics
DC, 1999
1..2.00

Star Spangled War Stories
DC, 1952

From 1952 until 1977, Star Spangled War Stories was one of DC's line of war comics. In the course of those 20 years, it brought readers tales of Enemy Ace, Viking Prince, and many other notables. Although these features were popular with readers, it was not until issue #151, with the introduction of The Unknown

Soldier that Star Spangled War Stories found its star.

Star Spangled War Stories grew out of an earlier title, Star Spangled Comics. After issue #130 of that title, it switched names to Star Spangled War Stories, although it continued its numbering sequence through issue #133. At that point, it retroactively decided that issue #131 was really a first issue and began numbering its next issues #4, 5, etc. All this was cleared up somewhat when Star Spangled War Stories changed names again (to Unknown Soldier) following issue #205.

132 (1)..................................750.00
133 (2)..................................550.00
3..475.00
4-6......................................285.00
7-10.....................................220.00
11-20....................................185.00
21-30....................................130.00
31-40.....................................90.00
41-50.....................................70.00
51-70.....................................60.00
71-83.....................................55.00
84......................................125.00
☞1st Mlle. Marie
85-87.....................................80.00
88-89.....................................65.00
90......................................325.00
☞1st Dinosaur Island
91..45.00
92......................................110.00
93..45.00
94-99...................................110.00
100.....................................145.00
☞1st Sgt. Gorilla
101-133...................................60.00
134.......................................65.00
135-138...................................60.00
139.......................................50.00
140-143...................................24.00
144.......................................27.00
145.......................................35.00
146-150...................................20.00
151.....................................125.00
☞1st Unknown Soldier
152-153...................................20.00
154.......................................55.00
☞Unknown Soldier origin
155.......................................16.00
156-161...................................14.00
162-180....................................6.00
181-204....................................5.00

Starstone
Aircel
1-3.......................................2.00

Starstream
Gold Key, 1976
1-4.......................................3.00

Starstruck
Marvel, 1985
1...3.00
2-6.......................................2.00

Starstruck
Dark Horse, 1990
1-4 ....3.00

Star Studded
Superior, 1945
1 ....200.00

Startling Comics
Avalon
1 ....3.00

Startling Comics
Better, 1940
1	1,800.00
2	1,000.00
3	800.00
4	575.00
5-9	450.00
10	3,200.00
11	900.00
12	750.00
13-29	450.00
30-40	400.00
41-43	350.00
44-45	500.00
46-53	400.00

Startling Crime Illustrated
Caliber, 1991
1 ....3.00

Startling Stories: Banner
Marvel, 2001

What if the Hulk wasnít really a tragic hero at all, but an uncontrollable mass murderer who leaves death and destruction in his wake? And what if Doc Samson, the benevolent super-powered physicist, wasnít a friend of the Hulk, but a government agent bent on destroying the Hulkóand covering up any evidence of his very existence, by any means necessary?

Thatís the basic premise of writer Brian Azzarelloís (100 Bullets, Hellblazer) four-issue limited series, wherein we see the Hulk in a completely newóand yet scarily familiarólight. Azzarello, with artist Richard Corben, makes a real horror story out of this, bringing the Hulk closer to his literary originsóthe tale of Jekyll and Hydeóthan anyone ever has before. Quite aside from seeing the gory ramifications of a Hulk rampage, we also see the genuine terror of Bruce Banner, who must bear witness to the suffering and devastation the Hulk has wroughtóand know that he is responsible for it. Little wonder then, that by the end of the first issue, we find Banner standing alone on a hilltop, putting a gun in his mouth and preparing to pull the trigger. If you were the reason a killer Hulk existed, what would you do?

-- Stephen C. George

1-4 .... 3.00

Startling Stories: The Thing
Marvel, 2003
1 .... 4.00

Startling Stories: The Thing -- Night Falls on Yancy Street
Marvel, 2003
1-4 .... 4.00

Startling Terror Tales
Star, 1952
10	480.00
11	750.00
12	155.00
13	170.00
14	155.00

Startling Terror Tales
Star, 1953
4-9	160.00
10	210.00
11	160.00

Star Trek
Gold Key, 1967
1	350.00
2	125.00
3	100.00
4	90.00
5-6	75.00
7	60.00
8-9	50.00
10	40.00
11-19	30.00
20-20/Whitman	45.00
21-22	30.00
23-23/Whitman	45.00
24-25/Whitman	35.00
26	25.00
26/Whitman	35.00
27-27/Whitman	30.00
28	20.00
29-29/Whitman	30.00
30-31	20.00

31/Whitman-36/Whitman	30.00
37-38	20.00
38/Whitman-40/Whitman	30.00
41-41/Whitman	25.00
42-43	15.00
44-48/Whitman	25.00
49-50	15.00
51-51/Whitman	25.00
52	15.00
52/Whitman-55/Whitman	25.00
56	15.00
56/Whitman-59/Whitman	25.00
60-60/Whitman	20.00
61	12.00

Star Trek
Marvel, 1980
1	5.00
2	3.00
3-18	2.00

Star Trek
DC, 1984
1	4.00
2-10	3.00
11-56	2.00
Ann 1-3	3.00

Star Trek
DC, 1989

Following hot on the heels of DCís first Star Trek series, this second DC series didnít tie itself as tightly to movie continuity as the first series did, a move that didnít force story changes in mid-stream.

Initially written by Peter David, the series was set in a nebulous time following the events of Star Trek IV and V. David delved more deeply into the continuity of the original TV episodes, including putting Captain Kirk on trial for all the times he had "bent" the Prime Directive or Starfleet regulations during those original missions.

Another memorable storyline, co-written with Bill Mumy (Lost in Spaceís Will Robinson), was a sort of crossover between Star Trek and that competing CBS show. These comics adventures were a real treat for fans of the original TV show, with special guests popping out at every turn.

-- Brent

1	5.00
2	4.00
3-10	3.00
11-23	2.00
24	3.00
25-49	2.00
50	4.00
51-70	2.00
71-74	3.00
75	4.00
76-80	3.00
Ann 1	4.00
Ann 2	3.00
Ann 3-3	4.00

Star Trek: Deep Space Nine
Malibu, 1993

0-1/B	3.00
1/C	4.00
2-24	3.00
25	4.00
26-30	3.00
31-Ann 1	4.00
Ashcan 1	5.00
Special 1	4.00

Star Trek: Deep Space Nine
Marvel, 1996

1-15	2.00

Star Trek: Deep Space Nine, the Celebrity Series: Blood and Honor
Malibu, 1995

1	3.00

Star Trek: Deep Space Nine Hearts and Minds
Malibu, 1994

1-4	3.00

Star Trek: Deep Space Nine: Lightstorm
Malibu, 1994

1	4.00

Star Trek: Deep Space Nine: N-Vector
DC, 2000

1-4	3.00

Star Trek: Deep Space Nine: Rules of Diplomacy
Malibu, 1995

1	3.00

Star Trek: Deep Space Nine/Star Trek: The Next Generation
Malibu, 1994

1-2	3.00
Ashcan 1	1.00

Star Trek: Deep Space Nine: Terok Nor
Malibu, 1995

0	3.00

Star Trek: Deep Space Nine, The Maquis
Malibu, 1995

1-3	3.00

Star Trek: Deep Space Nine, Ultimate Annual
Malibu, 1995

1	6.00

Star Trek: Deep Space Nine, Worf Special
Malibu, 1995

0	4.00

Star Trek: Divided We Fall
DC, 2001

1-4	3.00

Star Trek: Early Voyages
Marvel, 1997

1	3.00
2-17	2.00

Star Trek: Enter the Wolves
WildStorm, 2001

1	6.00

Star Trek: First Contact
Marvel, 1996

1	6.00

Star Trek Generations
DC, 1994

1	4.00
1/Prestige	6.00

Star Trekker
Antarctic, 1991

1	3.00

Star Trek: Mirror Mirror
Marvel, 1997

1	4.00

Star Trek Movie Special
DC, 1984

3-5	2.00

Star Trek: New Frontier: Double Time
DC, 2000

1	6.00

Star Trek: Operation Assimilation
Marvel, 1997

1	3.00

Star Trek VI: The Undiscovered Country
DC, 1992

1	3.00
1/Direct	6.00

Star Trek Special
WildStorm, 2001

1	7.00

Star Trek: Starfleet Academy
Marvel, 1996

1-19	2.00

Star Trek: Telepathy War
Marvel, 1997

1	3.00

Star Trek: The Modala Imperative
DC, 1991

1	3.00
2-4	2.00
Book 1	20.00

Star Trek: The Next Generation
DC, 1988

1	3.00
2-6	2.00

Star Trek: The Next Generation
DC, 1989

1	5.00
2	4.00
3-20	3.00
21-49	2.00
50	4.00
51-71	2.00
72-74	3.00
75	4.00
76-80	3.00
Ann 1-6	4.00
Special 1-3	5.00

Star Trek: The Next Generation/ Deep Space Nine
DC, 1994

1-2	3.00
Ashcan 1	1.00

Star Trek: The Next Generation: Ill Wind
DC, 1995

1-4	3.00

Star Trek: he Next Generation: Perchance to Dream
DC, 2000

1-4	3.00

Star Trek: The Next Generation: Riker
Marvel, 1998

1	4.00

Star Trek: The Next Generation: Shadowheart
DC, 1994

1-4	2.00

Star Trek: The Next Generation: The Killing Shadows
DC, 2000
1-4 ....3.00

Star Trek: The Next Generation: The Modala Imperative
DC, 1991
1-4 ....2.00

Star Trek: The Next Generation: The Series Finale
DC, 1994
1 ....4.00

Star Trek Unlimited
Marvel, 1996
1-10 ....3.00

Star Trek: Untold Voyages
Marvel, 1998
1-4 ....3.00
5 ....4.00

Star Trek: Voyager
Marvel, 1996
1-15 ....2.00

Star Trek: Voyager: Avalon Rising
DC, 2000
1 ....6.00

Star Trek: Voyager: Encounters with the Unknown
DC
1 ....20.00

Star Trek: Voyager: False Colors
DC, 2000
1 ....6.00

Star Trek: Voyager: Splashdown
Marvel, 1998
1-4 ....3.00

Star Trek: Voyager: The Planet Killer
DC, 2001
1-3 ....3.00

Star Trek/X-Men
Marvel, 1996
1 ....5.00

Star Trek/X-Men: Second Contact
Marvel, 1998
1-1/Variant..............................5.00

Star Wars
Marvel, 1977

The long connection between Star Wars and comics began in the mid-1970s, when Marvel Editor Roy Thomas made the acquaintance of director George Lucas, a fan of Carl Barks' Uncle Scrooge comics. Lucas later conveyed his interest in Thomas producing an ad

1 .... 20.00
1/35¢ 800.00
1/2nd-1/Whitman 3rd 4.00
2 .... 10.00
2/35¢ 5.00
2/2nd 4.00
2/Whitman-2/Whitman 3rd ... 10.00
3 .... 8.00
3/35¢ 5.00
3/2nd 4.00
3/Whitman-3/Whitman 3rd 8.00
4 .... 7.00
4/35¢ 5.00
4/2nd 4.00
4/Whitman-5/2nd 7.00
5/Whitman-5/Whitman 2nd..... 4.00
6-6/2nd 7.00
6/Whitman-6/Whitman 2nd..... 4.00
7 .... 7.00
7/Whitman 3.00
8 .... 7.00
8/Whitman 3.00
9 .... 7.00
9/Whitman 3.00
10-19 .... 7.00
20-21 .... 6.00
22-23/Whitman 5.00
24-48 .... 4.00
49 .... 5.00
50-106 .... 4.00
107 .... 25.00
☛Low distribution
Ann 1 .... 8.00
Ann 2-3 .... 5.00

Star Wars (Magazine)
Dark Horse, 1992
1 .... 5.00
2 .... 4.00
3-10 .... 3.00

Star Wars
Dark Horse, 1998
0 .... 10.00
1 .... 4.00
2-49 .... 3.00
50 .... 6.00
☛Title becomes Star Wars Republic
51-83 .... 3.00

Star Wars: A New Hope Manga
Dark Horse, 1998
1-4 .... 10.00

Star Wars: A New Hope: The Special Edition
Dark Horse, 1997
1-4 .... 3.00

Star Wars: Boba Fett
Dark Horse, 1995
1/2 .... 3.00
1/2/Gold................................. 5.00
1-3 .... 4.00

Star Wars: Boba Fett: Agent of Doom
Dark Horse, 2000
1 .... 3.00

Star Wars: Boba Fett: Enemy of the Empire
Dark Horse, 1999
1-4 .... 3.00

Star Wars: Boba Fett One-Shot
Dark Horse, 2006
1 .... 3.00

Star Wars: Boba Fett: Twin Engines of Destruction
Dark Horse, 1997
1 .... 3.00

Star Wars: Chewbacca
Dark Horse, 2000
1-4 .... 3.00

Star Wars: Crimson Empire
Dark Horse, 1997
1 .... 6.00
2-6 .... 5.00

Star Wars: Crimson Empire II: Council of Blood
Dark Horse, 1998
1 .... 4.00
2-6 .... 3.00

Star Wars: Dark Empire
Dark Horse, 1993
1 .... 6.00
1/2nd 3.00

1/Gold 5.00
1/Platinum 6.00
2..4.00
2/2nd 3.00
2/Gold 4.00
2/Platinum 5.00
3..4.00
3/2nd 3.00
3/Gold 4.00
3/Platinum 5.00
4-4/Gold 4.00
4/Platinum 5.00
5..3.00
5/Gold 4.00
5/Platinum 5.00
6..3.00
6/Gold 4.00
6/Platinum 5.00
Ashcan 1 ....1.00

Star Wars: Dark Empire II
Dark Horse, 1994

1..3.00
1/Gold 4.00
2..3.00
2/Gold 4.00
3..3.00
3/Gold 4.00
4..3.00
4/Gold 4.00
5..3.00
5/Gold 4.00
6..3.00
6/Gold 4.00

Star Wars: Dark Force Rising
Dark Horse, 1997

1-6 ....3.00

Star Wars: Dark Times
Dark Horse, 2006

1..3.00

Star Wars: Darth Maul
Dark Horse, 2000

The fourth Star Wars film, Phantom Menace, introduced a villain powerful in both the mystical Force and martial fighting skills.

Since the events of that movie occurred much earlier than the original Star Wars trilogy, the visually frightening Darth Maul was Darth Vader's predecessor as apprentice to Lord Sidious, eventual Emperor and Master of the Dark Side of the Force.

Six months prior to the events of Phantom Menace, Sidious is already plotting his galactic conquests, and pits Maul against two powerful organizations, the Trade Federation and the Black Sun criminal empire. Neither group seems able to stop Maul, as he systematically destroys their installations. But he is only one man, despite his training and powers, and they have legions of warriors to throw at him. But he will face his most powerful adversaries in single combat, including the mysterious Mighella, bodyguard to the Master Black Sun himself.

1-4/Variant.............................. 3.00

Star Wars: Droids
Dark Horse, 1994

1-6 .... 3.00
Special 1 .... 3.00

Star Wars: Droids (Vol. 2)
Dark Horse, 1995

1-8 .... 3.00

Star Wars: Empire
Dark Horse, 2002

1-40 .... 3.00

Star Wars: Empire's End
Dark Horse, 1995

1-2 .... 3.00

Star Wars: Episode I Anakin Skywalker
Dark Horse, 1999

1-1/Variant.............................. 3.00

Star Wars: Episode III: Revenge of the Sith
Dark Horse, 2005

1-4 .... 3.00

Star Wars: Episode I Obi-Wan Kenobi
Dark Horse, 1999

1-1/Variant.............................. 3.00

Star Wars: Episode I Queen Amidala
Dark Horse, 1999

1-1/Variant.............................. 3.00

Star Wars: Episode I Qui-Gon Jinn
Dark Horse, 1999

1-1/Variant.............................. 3.00

Star Wars: Episode I The Phantom Menace
Dark Horse, 1999

1-4/Variant.............................. 3.00

Star Wars: Episode II: Attack of the Clones
Dark Horse

1-4/Variant.............................. 4.00

Star Wars: General Grievous
Dark Horse, 2005

1-4 .... 3.00

Star Wars Handbook
Dark Horse, 1998

1-2 .... 3.00

Star Wars: Heir to the Empire
Dark Horse, 1995

1-6 .... 3.00

Star Wars in 3-D
Blackthorne, 1987

1 .... 3.00

Star Wars: Infinities: A New Hope
Dark Horse, 2001

1-4 .... 3.00

Star Wars: Infinities: Return of the Jedi
Dark Horse, 2003

1-4 .... 3.00

Star Wars: Infinities: The Empire Strikes Back
Dark Horse, 2002

1-4 .... 3.00

Star Wars: Jabba the Hutt
Dark Horse, 1995

The folks at Dark Horse continue to expand their chronicles of the Star Wars universe, giving their readers more insight into the characters from the ever-popular movie trilogy. Finally, it's Jabba the Hutt, the massively corpulent and obscenely gross smuggler who caused so many problems for Han Solo, who gets the spotlight.

Jabba struts (err...oozes...) his stuff, as he proves he's the absolute best at what he does. It's planning, not just money and mercenaries, that keeps him at the top of the Empire's criminal world, and Jabba never, ever, leaves anything to chance. Knowing the weaknesses of his enemies (not to mention his friends), and always taking advantage of that knowledge, is what makes Jabba one of the most feared and successful criminals in the galaxy.

1-4 .... 3.00

Star Wars: Jango Fett: Open Seasons
Dark Horse, 2002
1-4 .... 3.00

Star Wars: Jedi - Aayla Secura
Dark Horse, 2003
1 .... 5.00

Star Wars: Jedi Academy: Leviathan
Dark Horse, 1998
1-4 .... 3.00

Star Wars: Jedi Council: Acts of War
Dark Horse, 2000
1-4 .... 3.00

Star Wars: Jedi - Dooku Clone Wars
Dark Horse, 2003
1 .... 5.00

Star Wars: Jedi - Mace Windu
Dark Horse, 2003
1 .... 5.00

Star Wars: Jedi Quest
Dark Horse, 2001
1-4 .... 3.00

Star Wars: Jedi - Shaak Ti
Dark Horse, 2003
1 .... 5.00

Star Wars: Jedi vs. Sith
Dark Horse, 2001
1-6 .... 3.00

Star Wars: Jedi - Yoda
Dark Horse, 2004
1 .... 5.00

Star Wars: Knights of the Old Republic
Dark Horse, 2006
1 .... 12.00
2-4 .... 6.00
5-6 .... 5.00
7-8 .... 4.00
9-40 .... 3.00

Star Wars: Knights of the Old Republic 25¢ Flip Book
Dark Horse, 2006
1 .... 2.00

Star Wars: Legacy
Dark Horse, 2006
0 .... 1.00
1 .... 12.00
2-7 .... 3.00

Star Wars: Mara Jade
Dark Horse, 1998
1-6 .... 3.00

Star Wars: Obsession
Dark Horse, 2004
1 .... 8.00
2 .... 4.00
3-5 .... 3.00

Star Wars: Purge
Dark Horse, 2005
1 .... 25.00

Star Wars: Qui-Gon & Obi-Wan: Last Stand on Ord Mantell
Dark Horse, 2000
1/A-3/B 3.00

Star Wars: Qui-Gon & Obi-Wan: The Aurorient Express
Dark Horse, 2002
1-2 .... 3.00

Star Wars: Rebellion
Dark Horse, 2006
1 .... 8.00
3-5 .... 3.00

Star Wars: Return of the Jedi
Marvel, 1983
1-4 .... 4.00

Star Wars: River of Chaos
Dark Horse, 1995
1-4 .... 3.00

Star Wars: Shadows of Empire: Evolution
Dark Horse, 1998
1-5 .... 3.00

Star Wars: Shadows of the Empire
Dark Horse, 1995
1-6 .... 3.00

Star Wars: Shadow Stalker
Dark Horse, 1997
1 .... 3.00

Star Wars: Splinter of the Mind's Eye
Dark Horse, 1995
1-4 .... 3.00

Star Wars: Starfighter: Crossbones
Dark Horse, 2002
1-3 .... 3.00

Star Wars: Tag & Bink are Dead
Dark Horse, 2001
1-2 .... 3.00

Star Wars: Tag & Bink Episode I - Revenge of the Clone Menace
Dark Horse, 2006
1 .... 3.00

Star Wars Tales
Dark Horse, 1999
1-4 .... 5.00
5-21 .... 6.00
22/Art 7.00
22/Photo 6.00
23/Art 7.00
23/Photo 6.00
24/Art 7.00
24/Photo 6.00

Star Wars: Tales: A Jedi's Weapon
Dark Horse, 2002
1 .... 2.00

Star Wars Tales- A Jedi's Weapon
Dark Horse
1 .... 1.00

Star Wars: Tales from Mos Eisley
Dark Horse, 1996
1 .... 3.00

Star Wars: Tales of the Jedi
Dark Horse, 1993
1 .... 4.00
1/Special 6.00
2 .... 4.00
2/Special 5.00
3 .... 3.00
3/Special 5.00
4 .... 3.00
4/Special 5.00
5 .... 3.00
5/Special 5.00

**Star Wars:
Tales of the Jedi:
Dark Lords of the Sith**
Dark Horse, 1994
1-6...3.00

**Star Wars:
Tales of the Jedi:
Fall of the Sith Empire**
Dark Horse, 1997
1-5...3.00

**Star Wars: Tales of the
Jedi: Redemption**
Dark Horse, 1998
1-5...3.00

**Star Wars:
Tales of the Jedi: The
Freedon Nadd Uprising**
Dark Horse, 1994
1-2...3.00

**Star Wars:
Tales of the Jedi: The
Golden Age of the Sith**
Dark Horse, 1996
0...1.00
1-5...3.00

**Star Wars: Tales of the
Jedi: The Sith War**
Dark Horse, 1995
1-6...3.00

**Star Wars: The Bounty
Hunters: Aurra Sing**
Dark Horse, 1999
1...3.00

**Star Wars: The Bounty
Hunters: Kenix Kil**
Dark Horse, 1999
1...3.00

**Star Wars:
The Bounty Hunters:
Scoundrel's Wages**
Dark Horse, 1999
1...3.00

**Star Wars: The Empire
Strikes Back: Manga**
Dark Horse, 1999
1-4.......................................10.00

**Star Wars:
The Jabba Tape**
Dark Horse, 1998
1...3.00

**Star Wars:
The Last Command**
Dark Horse, 1997
1...4.00
2-6...3.00

**Star Wars:
The Protocol Offensive**
Dark Horse, 1997
1 .... 5.00

**Star Wars: The
Return of Tag & Bink
Special Edition**
Dark Horse, 2006
1 .... 3.00

**Star Wars: Underworld:
The Yavin Vassilika**
Dark Horse, 2000
1/A-5/B 3.00

Star Wars: Union
Dark Horse, 1999
1 .... 14.00
2... 10.00
3... 7.00
4... 5.00

Star Wars: Vader's Quest
Dark Horse, 1999
1-4... 3.00

**Star Wars:
Valentines Story**
Dark Horse, 2003
1 .... 4.00

**Star Wars:
X-Wing Rogue Leader**
Dark Horse, 2005
1-3... 3.00

**Star Wars:
X-Wing Rogue Squadron**
Dark Horse, 1995
1/2 .... 3.00
1/2/Platinum 5.00
1-4... 4.00
5-24.. 3.00
25 .... 4.00
26-35...................................... 3.00
Special 1 .... 1.00

Star Weevils
Rip Off
1 .... 1.00

Star Western
Avalon
1-5... 6.00

S.T.A.T.
Majestic, 1993
1-1/Variant.............................. 2.00

Static
DC, 1993
1 .... 2.00
1/CS-1/Silver 3.00
2-13.. 2.00
14 .... 3.00
15-24...................................... 2.00
25 .... 4.00
26-30...................................... 3.00
31 .... 1.00
32-47...................................... 3.00

**Static Shock!:
Rebirth of the Cool**
DC, 2001

Virgil Hawkins is trying to enjoy his summer vacation, despite the fact that his old super-buddies are trying to get him back into action. Virgil is taking time off recovering from the loss of one of his teammates that he feels he could have prevented. But things are changing quickly. Someone is hunting those people who were empowered at The Big Bang and is not letting them go. Now, Static has to power-up and get going before all his old friends are gone.

With the promising premiere of the WB network's Static Shock animated series, Milestone pulled Static out of the mothballs and back into action.

1-4 .... 3.00

Stay Puffed
Image, 2004
1 .... 4.00

Steady Beat
Tokyopop, 2005
1 .... 10.00

Stealth Force
Malibu, 1987
1-8 .... 2.00

Stealth Squad
Petra, 1995
0-4 .... 3.00

Steampunk
DC, 2000

Cole Blaquesmith fell asleep for 100 years. Upon waking, he finds himself in a nightmare techno-Victorian world controlled by Mortimer Absinthe. Somehow, this madman has managed to twist the world into a reflection of his own deranged psyche. He has even gone so far as to replace our hero's heart with a steam-powered engine! Trapped in a world where he does not belong, Blaquesmith fights to make things right again, all the while driven by a hatred for the scheming Lord Absinthe.

Writer Joe Kelly and artist Chris Bachalo are the "creatives" behind this dense tale of fantasy and science fiction. Publishing under the Cliffhanger imprint (a division of Wildstorm Productions), the comic book packs each panel with an imagery that borders on confusing. With this project, the creative duo hope to reach a different kind of audience -- one willing to wade through intense storytelling and confusing plot twists to reach an ultimate payoff. But be warned: This title is not for the casual reader.

1-4	3.00
5	4.00
6-11	3.00
12	4.00

Steampunk: Catechism
DC, 2000

1	3.00

Stech
Silverwolf, 1986

1	2.00

Steed and Mrs. Peel
Eclipse, 1990

1-3	5.00

Steel
DC, 1994

0-46	2.00
47-52	3.00
Ann 1-2	4.00

Steel Angel
Gauntlet

1	3.00

Steel Claw
Fleetway-Quality, 1986

1-5	2.00

Steeldragon Stories
Steeldragon

1	2.00

Steele Destinies
Nightscapes, 1995

1-3	3.00

Steelgrip Starkey
Marvel, 1986

1-6	2.00

Steel Pulse
True Fiction, 1986

1-3	2.00
4	4.00

Steel Sterling
Archie, 1984

4-7	1.00

Steel, the Indestructible Man
DC, 1978

1	5.00
2-5	2.00

Steel: The Official Comic Adaptation of the Warner Bros. Motion Picture
DC, 1997

1	5.00

Steeltown Rockers
Marvel, 1990

1-6	1.00

Stellar Comics
Stellar

1	3.00

Stellar Losers
Antarctic, 1993

1-3	3.00

Stephen Darklord
Rak, 1987

1-3	2.00

Steps to a Drug Free Life
David G. Brown, 1998

1	1.00

Stern Wheeler
Spotlight

1	2.00

Steve Canyon Comics
Harvey, 1948

1	110.00
2	75.00
3-6	55.00

Steve Canyon Magazine (Milton Caniff's...)
Kitchen Sink, 1983

1-4	3.00
5-7	4.00
8-12	5.00
13	6.00
14	5.00
3D 1	2.00

Steven
Kitchen Sink, 1996

1-4	3.00
5-8	4.00

Steven Presents Dumpy
Fantagraphics, 1999

1	3.00

Steven's Comics
DK Press

1	1.00
3	3.00
2	2.00
4	4.00

Steve Roper
Famous Funnies, 1948

1	65.00
2	45.00
3-5	35.00

Steve Zodiak and the Fireball XL-5
Gold Key, 1964

1	65.00

Stevie
Magazine Publications, 1952

1	45.00
2-6	25.00

Stewart the Rat
About, 2003

1	4.00

Stickboy
Fantagraphics, 1990

1-5	3.00

Stickboy
Revolutionary, 1990

1-4	3.00

Stickboy
Starhead, 1993

1-6	3.00

Stig's Inferno
Vortex, 1989

1-2	2.00
3-4	4.00
5-7	2.00

Stimulator
Fantagraphics, 1991

1	3.00

Sting
Artline
1 ....3.00

Sting of the Green Hornet
Now, 1992
1-4/CS..................................3.00

Stinktooth
Stinktooth, 1991
1 ....1.00

Stinz
Fantagraphics, 1989
1 ....4.00
2-5...3.00

Stinz
Brave New Words, 1990
1-3...3.00

Stinz
Mu, 1994
1-4...3.00
5..5.00
6..6.00
7..5.00

Stoker's Dracula
Marvel, 2004
1-4...4.00

Stone
Image, 1998
1-2...3.00
2/A..6.00
2/B..4.00
3-4...3.00

Stone
Image, 1999
1..3.00
1/Variant...............................7.00
2-3...3.00

Stone Cold Steve Austin
Chaos, 1999
1-4...3.00

Stone Protectors
Harvey, 1994
1-3...2.00

Stonewall in the Shenandoah
Heritage Collection
1 ....4.00

Stoney Burke
Dell, 1963
1..25.00
2..20.00

Stories by Famous Authors Illustrated
Seaboard, 1950
1-13.....................................200.00

Stories from Bosnia
Drawn and Quarterly
1 ....4.00

Stories of Romance
Atlas, 1956
5 .... 55.00
6-13..................................... 35.00

Stories of the Fantastic
NBM
1-2... 10.00
3 .... 13.00

Storm
Marvel, 1996
1-4... 3.00

Storm Battlebook
Marvel, 1998
1 .... 4.00

Stormbreaker: The Saga of Beta Ray Bill
Marvel, 2005
1-6... 3.00

Storm
Marvel, 2006
1-6... 3.00

Stormquest
Caliber, 1955
1-6... 2.00

Stormwatch
Image, 1993
0-1/Gold 3.00
2-8... 2.00
9 .... 3.00
10 .... 2.00
10/A-10/B 3.00
11-16..................................... 2.00
17-36..................................... 3.00
37 .... 4.00
38-49..................................... 3.00
50 .... 5.00
Special 1 .... 4.00
Special 2 .... 3.00

Stormwatch
Image, 1997

After 50 issues of its initial run, StormWatch started over in a second series in 1997. Under the direction of writer Warren Ellis, the team of super-powered U.N. peacekeepers has taken on a sharp edge, and the action sequences make them seem every inch the professional soldiers they claim to be. When they take down a group of terrorists at the opening of "Strange Weather," the three-part storyline that kicked off the series, it's like watching six James Bonds swing into action: They're fast, efficient, and sport none of the angst and infighting that characterize so many other super-groups.

The burden of politics is largely carried by Weatherman One, their eye-in-the-sky leader. Not that politics is a small part of their problem. As a result of StormWatch acting against U.S.-based terrorists without official sanction in the opening battle of this series, they have been banned from U.S. territory.

1-12 .... 3.00

Stormwatcher
Eclipse, 1989
1-4 .... 2.00

Stormwatch: PHD
DC, 2007
1-2/Variant............................. 3.00

Stormwatch Sourcebook
Image, 1994
1 .... 3.00

StormWatch: Team Achilles
WildStorm, 2002
1-23....................................... 3.00

Story of Electronics: The Discovery that Changed the World!
Radio Shack, 1980
1 .... 3.00

Story of Martha Wayne
Argo
1 .... 25.00

Straight Arrow
Magazine Enterprises, 1950
1 .... 260.00
2 .... 150.00
3 .... 175.00
4-5 .... 75.00
6-10 .... 70.00
11-20 .... 62.00
21 .... 55.00
22 .... 110.00
23-30 .... 50.00
31-40 .... 42.00
41-50 .... 30.00
51-55 .... 24.00

Straitjacket Studios Presents
Straitjacket
0 ....3.00

Strand
Trident, 1990
1-2 ....3.00

Stranded On Planet X
Radio, 1999
1 ....3.00

Strange
Marvel, 2004
1-6 ....4.00

Strange Adventures
DC, 1950

For most of its 244-issue run, Strange Adventures was host to a rather unremarkable collection of science-fiction and monster stories. Several of the characters that got their start here, however, were remade into some of DC's most inventive and original heroes.

First came the Atomic Knights in issue #117. These long-running characters were a sort of post-apocalyptic Knights of the Round Table. Later, their origin was revised, a la Miracleman, to state that the adventures had all been computer-inspired delusions of the lead character. Issue #180 saw the introduction of Animal Man, a rather plain hero who took on the powers of animals around him. Writer Grant Morrison gave him a surreal bent, and used him to represent man's struggle with nature. Finally came the eerie Deadman in issue #205, a great character from the start. Deadman was the spirit of a murdered aerialist who inhabits the bodies the living in order to fight evil.

1	2,500.00
2	1,150.00
3	850.00
4	800.00
5-6	650.00
7	625.00
8	550.00
9	1,250.00

☛1st Captain Comet

10	400.00
11	500.00
12	400.00
13	500.00
14	650.00
15	500.00
16	450.00
17	275.00
18-20	450.00
21-23	350.00
24	375.00
25	350.00
26-29	300.00
30	425.00
31-38	275.00
39	400.00
40-41	250.00
42	275.00
43	250.00
44	325.00
45-46	250.00
47	200.00
48	250.00
49	200.00
50	225.00
51	200.00
52-53	225.00
54	150.00
55	200.00
56-60	150.00
61-70	125.00
71-74	100.00
75	75.00
76-78	100.00
79	150.00
80-83	100.00
84	125.00
85-90	100.00
91	90.00
92-93	80.00
94	75.00
95	90.00
96	65.00
97	90.00
98	75.00
99	90.00
100	125.00
101	65.00
102-103	90.00
104-106	65.00
107	75.00
108-109	65.00
110	75.00
111	65.00
112	60.00
113	90.00
114	125.00

☛1st Star Hawkins

115-116	60.00
117	550.00

☛1st Atomic Knights

118	75.00
119	90.00
120	200.00

☛2nd Atomic Knights

121-123	75.00
124	90.00
125-126	75.00
127	50.00
128	75.00
129	90.00
130-131	50.00
132	75.00
133-135	65.00
136-137	50.00
138	55.00
139-140	50.00
141	55.00
142-145	50.00
146	40.00
147-148	50.00
149	40.00
150-160	50.00
161-167	35.00
168	30.00
169	35.00
170	50.00
171-172	30.00
173	40.00
174	30.00
175	40.00
176-177	30.00
178	25.00
179	30.00
180	150.00

☛1st Animal Man

181	25.00
182-183	30.00
184	60.00

☛Animal Man app.

185-186	25.00
187	20.00
188	25.00
189	30.00
190	100.00

☛Animal Man app.

191	20.00
192-193	25.00
194	20.00
195	35.00

☛Animal Man app.

196-197	25.00
198	20.00
199	30.00
200	25.00
201	40.00
202-204	20.00
205	125.00

☛Deadman begins

206	60.00

☛Adams Deadman

207	50.00
208-212	60.00
213	40.00
214	60.00
215	45.00
216	40.00
217-219	20.00
220	25.00
221-223	20.00
224-230	15.00
231-244	10.00

Strange Adventures
DC, 1999

1-4 ....3.00

Strange Attractors
Retrografix, 1993

1 ....4.00
1/2nd 3.00
2 ....4.00
2/2nd 3.00
3 ....4.00
3/2nd-15 ....3.00

Strange Attractors: Moon Fever
Caliber, 1997

1-3 ....3.00

Strange Avenging Tales (Steve Ditko's...)
Fantagraphics, 1997

1 ....3.00

Strange Bedfellows
Hippy, 2002

1-2 ....6.00

Strange Brew
Aardvark-Vanaheim

1 ....3.00

Strange Combat Tales
Marvel, 1984

1-4 ....3.00

Strange Confessions
Ziff-Davis, 1952

1 ....285.00
2-4 ....200.00

Strange Day
Alternative, 2005

1 ....4.00

Strange Days
Eclipse, 1984

1-3 ....2.00

Strange Detective Tales: Dead Love
Oddgod Press, 2005

1 ....4.00

Strange Embrace
Atomeka, 1993

1-3 ....4.00

Strange Fantasy
Farrell, 1952

1 ....300.00
2 ....250.00
3 ....200.00
4-6 ....125.00
7 ....150.00
8 ....125.00
9 ....150.00
10 ....125.00
11-14 ....100.00

Strange Girl
Image, 2005

1-12 ....3.00

Strangehaven
Abiogenesis, 1995

1 ....5.00
1/2nd 3.00
2 ....4.00
2/2nd 3.00
3 ....4.00
3/2nd-18 ....3.00

Strange Heroes
Lone Star, 2000

1-2 ....3.00

Strange Journey
America's Best, 1957

1 ....105.00
2-4 ....75.00

Strange Killings: Body Orchard (Warren Ellis')
Avatar, 2002

1-6 ....4.00

Strange Killings: Necromancer (Warren Eilis')
Avatar, 2004

1-2 ....4.00

Strange Killings: Strong Medicine (Warren Ellis')
Avatar, 2003

1-3 ....4.00

Strange Looking Exile
Robert Kirby

1-3 ....2.00

Strangelove
Express

1-2 ....3.00

Strange Mysteries
Superior, 1951

1 ....375.00
2 ....200.00
3-5 ....175.00
6-9 ....145.00
10 ....130.00
11-18 ....115.00
19 ....125.00
20-21 ....90.00

Strange Planets
Super, 1958

1 ....60.00
9 ....35.00
10-12 ....20.00
13-16 ....15.00

Stranger in a Strange Land
Rip Off, 1989

1-2 ....2.00
3 ....3.00

Strangers
Malibu, 1993

1 ....2.00
1/Hologram 5.00
1/Ltd. 4.00

2-4 ....2.00
5 ....3.00
6-12 ....2.00
13 ....4.00
14-24 ....2.00
Ann 1 ....4.00

Strangers
Image, 2003

1-6 ....3.00

Strangers in Paradise
Antarctic, 1993

0 ....75.00
1 ....65.00
1/2nd 5.00
1/3rd 3.00
2 ....24.00
3 ....18.00

Strangers in Paradise
Abstract, 1994

1 ....30.00
1/Gold 4.00
1/2nd 3.00
2 ....15.00
2/Gold 3.00
3 ....12.00
3/Gold 3.00
4 ....10.00
4/Gold 3.00
5 ....10.00
5/Gold 3.00
6 ....8.00
6/Gold 3.00
7 ....8.00
7/Gold 3.00
8 ....8.00
8/Gold 3.00
9 ....8.00
9/Gold 3.00
10 ....8.00
10/Gold 3.00
11 ....5.00
11/Gold 3.00
12 ....5.00
12/Gold 3.00
13 ....4.00
13/Gold-14 ....3.00

Strangers in Paradise
Homage, 1996

1 ....4.00
2-78 ....3.00
Special 1 ....4.00

Strangers in Paradise Sourcebook
Abstract, 2003

1 ....3.00

Stranger's Tale, A
Vineyard

1 ....2.00

Stranger than Fiction
Impact, 1998

1-4 ....2.00

Strange Sports Stories
DC, 1973

1	18.00
2	9.00
3-6	7.00

Strange Sports Stories
Adventure, 1992

1-3	3.00

Strange Stories
Avalon

1	3.00

Strange Stories from Another World
Fawcett, 1952

2	300.00
3-5	220.00

Strange Stories of Suspense
Atlas, 1955

5	220.00
6	130.00
7	135.00
8	140.00
9	130.00
10	135.00
11-13	110.00
14-16	120.00

Strange Suspense Stories
Charlton, 1952

The perennial also-ran publisher Charlton experienced a flash of brilliance in 1967, when artist and art director Dick Giordano was promoted to editor and brought a wave of talented young writers and artists into the fold. Strange Suspense Stories is a revival of one of Charlton's most successful titles of the 1950s: a blend of horror, science fiction, and mystery in the mold of E.C.'s Shock SuspenStories. The 1960s revival issues feature some of the earliest professional work of Dennis O'Neill (at that time using the alias Sergius O'Shaughnessy), who went on to become the longtime editor of Batman, and Jim Aparo, who did memorable work at DC in the 1970s and 1980s. Strange Suspense Stories during Giordano's editorship provided solid storytelling and art, with tales that anticipated DC's efforts in House of Mystery several years later.

1	450.00
2	325.00
3-5	275.00
16	150.00
17	110.00
18	160.00
19	200.00
20	160.00
21	110.00
22	135.00
27	60.00
28-30	50.00
31-33	100.00
34	200.00
35	100.00
36	145.00
37	100.00
38	45.00
39-41	80.00
42-44	20.00
45	80.00
46	20.00
47-48	80.00
49	20.00
50-51	75.00
52-54	50.00
55-60	20.00
61-74	14.00
75	90.00
76-77	20.00

Strange Suspense Stories
Charlton, 1967

1	20.00
2-9	12.00

Strange Tales
Marvel, 1951

Strange Tales began as a straightforward horror comic book, gradually switching to include super-hero appearances by the likes of The Human Torch. In issue #110, it made a breakthrough, introducing readers to Stephen Strange, better known as "Doctor Strange, Master of the Mystic Arts."

Strange Tales featured a pair of stories each month. Initially, Dr. Strange battled cosmic foes in one story and The Torch, often teamed with The Thing, starred in the other. The Torch stories were replaced, in #135, when Strange Tales introduced Nick Fury, Agent of S.H.I.E.L.D.

With issue #169, Doctor Strange took over the entire issue and its numbering.

In the mid-1970s, the series returned picking up its numbering with #169 and featuring single stories each month featuring first Brother Voodoo, then Warlock. These new characters failed to catch on, though, and the series concluded with issue #188.

1	2,750.00
2	800.00
3-5	700.00
6-10	550.00
11-20	350.00
21-30	275.00
31-44	225.00
45-58	200.00
59	225.00
60	200.00
61	225.00
62-63	175.00
64	200.00
65-66	175.00
67-78	200.00
79	250.00
80	200.00
81-83	175.00
84	200.00
85-88	175.00
89	400.00

☞Kirby Fin Fang Foom

90-92	175.00
93-96	150.00
97	350.00

☞Aunt May & Uncle Ben

98-100	150.00
101	900.00

☞Human Torch starts

102	425.00

☞Human Torch app.

103-105	300.00
106	225.00
107	250.00
108-109	225.00
110	1,250.00

☞1st Dr. Strange

111	350.00
112-113	150.00
114	350.00
115	450.00

☞Dr. Strange origin

116	125.00

117-118	100.00
119-123	125.00
124-125	75.00
126	90.00
127-129	75.00
130	90.00
131-134	75.00
135	125.00

☞1st S.H.I.E.L.D.

136	75.00
137-147	50.00
148	75.00

☞Ancient One origin

149-150	50.00
151	75.00
152-158	50.00
159	60.00
160-168	50.00
169	15.00

☞Series restarted

170	10.00
171-177	7.00
178	15.00

☞Warlock origin

179-181	10.00
182-185	3.00
185/30¢	20.00
186	3.00
186/30¢	20.00
187-188	3.00
Ann 1	325.00
Ann 2	350.00

Strange Tales
Marvel, 1987

Strange Tales returned in 1987, with each issue featuring a pair of stories starring Cloak & Dagger and Doctor Strange, respectively. With action-packed adventures including appearances by the Punisher and the Defenders, this second volume of Strange Tales enjoyed an eventful, if relatively brief run.

1	2.00
2-12	1.00
13-14	2.00
15-16	1.00
17	2.00
18-19	1.00

Strange Tales
Marvel, 1994

1	7.00

Strange Tales
Marvel, 1998

1-4	5.00

Strange Tales: Dark Corners
Marvel, 1998

1	4.00

Strange Tales of the Unusual
Atlas, 1955

1	300.00
2-3	165.00
4	125.00
5	150.00
6	125.00
7	135.00
8	125.00
9	135.00
10-11	125.00

Strange Terrors
St. John, 1952

1	500.00
2	250.00
3	350.00
4	500.00
5	350.00
6	500.00
7	525.00

Strange Weather Lately
Metaphrog, 1997

1-6	4.00
7-9	3.00
10	4.00

Strange Wink (John Bolton's...)
Dark Horse, 1998

1-3	3.00

Strange World of Your Dreams
Prize, 1952

1	400.00
2-3	300.00
4	240.00

Strange Worlds (Avon)
Avon, 1950

1	1,000.00
2-9	800.00
18-19	175.00
20	55.00
21-22	40.00

Strange Worlds
Atlas, 1958

1	525.00
2	300.00
3	235.00
4	210.00
5	180.00

Strange Worlds
Eternity

1	4.00

Strange Worlds
North Coast

1	4.00

Strangling Desdemona
Ningen Manga

1	3.00

Strapped (Derreck Wayne Jackson's...)
Gothic Images, 1994

1-4	2.00

Strata
Renegade, 1986

1-5	2.00

Stratonaut
Nightwynd, 1991

1-4	3.00

Stratosfear
Caliber

1	3.00

Strawberry Shortcake
Marvel, 1985

1-6	1.00

Straw Men
All American, 1989

1-8	2.00

Stray
DC, 2001

1	6.00

Stray Bullets
El Capitan, 1995

1	4.00
1/2nd-21	3.00
22-35	4.00

Stray Cats
Twilight Twins, 1999

1	3.00

Stray Toasters
Marvel

1-4	5.00

Streak of Chalk
NBM

1	16.00

Street Fighter (Devil's Due)
Devil's Due, 2004

7	3.00
7/Foil	8.00
8	3.00
8/Foil	13.00
9	3.00
9/Foil	8.00
10	3.00
10/Foil	4.00
11	3.00
11/Variant	4.00

11/Foil	13.00
12	3.00
12/Variant	4.00
13	3.00
13/Variant	4.00
14	3.00
14/Variant	4.00

Streetfighter
Ocean, 1986
1-4	2.00

Street Fighter
Malibu, 1993
1	3.00
1/Gold	5.00
2	3.00
2/Gold	4.00
3	3.00
3/Gold	4.00

Street Fighter
Image, 2003
1	3.00
1/A/2nd	5.00
1.1	2.00
1/A-3	3.00
3/C	5.00
3/A-4	3.00
4/C	5.00
4/A-5	3.00
5/A	5.00
6	3.00
6/Dynamic	5.00

Street Fighter: The Battle for Shadaloo
DC
1	4.00

Street Fighter II (Tokuma Shoten)
Tokuma Shoten, 1994
1	3.00

Street Fighter II
Viz, 1994
1-8	3.00

Street Fighter II: The Animated Movie
Viz
1-5	3.00

Street Heroes 2005
Eternity, 1989
1-3	2.00

Street Music
Fantagraphics
1-6	3.00

Street Poet Ray
Blackthorne, 1989
1-2	2.00

Street Poet Ray
Marvel, 1990
1-4	3.00

Streets
DC, 1993
1-3	5.00

Street Sharks
Archie, 1996
1-3	2.00

Street Sharks
Archie, 1996
1-3	2.00

Street Wolf
Blackthorne, 1986
1-3	2.00

Strictly Independent!
One Shot, 1996
1-2	2.00

Strictly Private
Eastern Color, 1942
1-2	135.00

Strike!
Eclipse, 1987
1-6	2.00

Strikeback!
Malibu, 1994
1-3	3.00

Strikeback!
Image, 1996
1-6	3.00

Strike Force America
Comico, 1992
1	3.00

Strike Force America
Comico
1	3.00

Strike Force Legacy
Comico, 1993
1	4.00

Strikeforce: Morituri
Marvel, 1986
1-4	2.00
5-12	1.00
13	2.00
14-23	1.00
24-31	2.00

Strikeforce: Morituri: Electric Undertow
Marvel, 1989
1-5	4.00

Striker
Viz, 1998
1-4	3.00

Striker: Secret of the Berserker
Viz
1-4	3.00

Strike! Versus Sgt. Strike Special
Eclipse, 1988
1	2.00

Strippers and Sex Queens of the Exotic World
Fantagraphics, 1994
1-4	4.00

Strips
Rip Off, 1989
1-10	3.00
Special 1-2	4.00

Strong Guy Reborn
Marvel, 1997
1	3.00

Stronghold
Devil's Due, 2005
1	5.00

Strontium Bitch
Fleetway-Quality
1-2	3.00

Strontium Dog
Eagle, 1985
1-4	2.00

Strontium Dog
Fleetway-Quality, 1987
1	2.00
2-12	1.00
13-Special 1	2.00

Str̦del War
Rough Copy
1	3.00

Stryfe's Strike File
Marvel, 1993
1-1/2nd	2.00

Stryke
London Night
0	3.00
0/A	4.00
1	3.00

Strykeforce
Image, 2004
1-5	3.00

St. Tail Comic
Mixx, 2000
1-9	3.00

Students of the Unusual
3 Finger Prints, 2005
1-4	3.00
5-6	4.00

Studio Comics Presents
Studio, 1995
1	3.00

Stuff of Dreams
Fantagraphics
1-3	4.00

Stumbo Tinytown
Harvey, 1963
1	85.00
2	50.00
3	35.00

4-5	25.00
6-13	18.00

Stunt Dawgs
Harvey, 1993

1	1.00

Stuntman Comics
Harvey, 1946

1	685.00
2-3	425.00

Stupid
Image, 1993

1	2.00

Stupid Comics
Oni, 2000

1	3.00

Stupid Comics
Image, 2003

1-3	3.00

Stupid Heroes
Mirage, 1994

1-3	3.00

Stupidman
Parody

1	3.00

Stupidman: Burial for a Buddy
Parody

1/A-1/B	3.00

Stupidman: Rain on the Stupidmen
Parody

1/A-1/B	3.00

Stupid, Stupid Rat Tails
Cartoon Books, 1999

This three-issue mini-series, a great addition to Jeff Smith's Bone saga, focuses on the wild and woolly adventures of Big Johnson Bone, Frontier Hero, sort of a cross between Tomahawk and Yosemite Sam. As our story opens, this particular Bone is making his way across the untamed countryside with a monkey he won in a card game. In short order, he meets those eponymous rat-tails, the perennial vexation of Bones everywhere. Although he escapes unscathed, he soon comes upon a group of cute woodland creatures who have been plagued by the monsters. Can Big Johnson Bone save himself, his monkey, and these cute-as-a-bug critters from the rat-tail menace--and their vile queen? As usual, Smith's Bone creations are at once touching, hilarious, and exciting to follow. Your Bone collection won't be complete without this one!

-- *Stephen C. George*

1-3	3.00

Stygmata
Express, 1994

0-3	3.00

Subhuman
Dark Horse, 1998

1-4	3.00

Submarine Attack
Charlton, 1958

11	24.00
12-20	16.00
21-30	12.00
31-40	9.00
41-54	7.00

Sub-Marine
Timely, 1941

1	25,000.00
2	7,000.00
3	5,000.00
4	4,500.00
5	3,500.00
6-11	2,500.00
12-15	1,500.00
16-20	1,200.00
21-31	1,000.00
32	1,250.00
33-35	900.00
36-41	700.00
42	1,000.00

Sub-Mariner
Marvel, 1968

1	125.00
2	45.00
3-4	35.00
5	30.00
6-7	25.00
8	75.00
☛vs. The Thing	
8/2nd	2.00
9	30.00
10	25.00
11-13	20.00
14	50.00
☛Toro dies	
15-30	20.00
31-33	15.00
34	70.00
☛Hulk, Surfer app.	

35	35.00
☛Hulk, Surfer app.	
36-40	15.00
41-Special 1	10.00
Special 2	15.00

Submissive Suzanne
Fantagraphics, 1998

1-6	3.00

Subspecies
Eternity, 1991

1-4	3.00

Substance Affect
Crazyfish

1	3.00

Substance Quarterly
Substance, 1994

1-3	3.00

Subtle Violents
Cry for Dawn, 1991

1	15.00
1/A	160.00

Suburban High Life
Slave Labor, 1987

1-3	2.00

Suburban High Life
Slave Labor, 1988

1	6.00

Suburban Nightmares
Renegade, 1988

1-4	2.00

Suburban She-Devils
Marvel, 1991

1	2.00

Suburban Voodoo
Fantagraphics, 1992

1	3.00

Succubus
Fantagraphics

1	3.00

Sucker the Comic
Troma

1	3.00

Suckle
Fantagraphics, 1996

1	15.00

Sugar & Spike
DC, 1956

1	1,700.00
1/2nd	3.00
2	700.00
3-5	500.00
6-10	350.00
11-20	250.00
21-30	150.00
31-40	125.00
41-50	75.00
51-60	55.00
61-80	50.00
81-98	35.00

Sugar Bowl Comics
Famous Funnies, 1948

1	75.00
2	42.00
3	55.00
4-5	42.00

Sugar Buzz
Slave Labor, 1998

1-4	3.00

Sugar Ray Finhead
Wolf, 1994

1-11	3.00

Sugarvirus
Atomeka

1	4.00

Suicide Squad
DC, 1987

1-22	1.00
23	15.00
☛1st Oracle	
24-49	1.00
50	2.00
51-66	1.00
Ann 1	2.00

Suicide Squad
DC, 2001

1-30	3.00

Suikoden III:
The Successor of Fate
Tokyopop, 2004

1-8	10.00

Suit
Virtual, 1996

1	3.00
1/A-2/A	4.00

Sullengray
Ape Entertainment, 2005

1	4.00

Sultry Teenage
Super Foxes
Solson

1-2	2.00

Summer Fun
Dell, 1959

2	175.00

Summer Love
Charlton, 1965

46	95.00
47	70.00
48	15.00

Sunburn
Alternative, 2000

1	3.00

Sun Devils
DC, 1984

1-12	2.00

Sundiata:
A Legend of Africa
NBM

1	16.00

Sundown
Arcana, 2005

1	3.00

Sunfire & Big Hero Six
Marvel, 1998

1-3	3.00

Sun Fun Komiks
Sun, 1939

1	175.00

Sun Girl
Marvel, 1948

1	1,000.00
2-3	675.00

Sunglasses After Dark
Verotik, 1995

1-5	3.00
6	4.00

Sunny,
America's Sweetheart
Fox, 1947

11	475.00
12-14	375.00

Sunrise
Harrier, 1986

1-2	2.00

Sun-Runners
Pacific, 1984

1-Special 1	2.00

Sunset Carson
Charlton, 1951

1	530.00
2	380.00
3-4	280.00

Super Bad
James Dynomite
Idea & Design Works, 2006

1-4	4.00

Superboy
DC, 1949

Encouraged by the long-lasting popularity of Superman, DC decided to launch several follow-up titles. Titles such as Superman's Girl Friend Lois Lane, and Superman's Pal Jimmy Olsen concentrated on supporting cast, and Superboy went back into his own past, telling of Clark Kent's adventures as a teenager.

The stories here were lighthearted and often gimmicky. A Bizarro-Superboy, Super-Baby, Super-Dog, and even a Super-Monkey were concocted for this series. Superboy's main problems, however, were balancing the need to save the world, protecting his secret identity, and fending off the romantic advances of Lana Lang and others.

With issue #231, the title became known as Superboy and the Legion of Super-Heroes. With issue #259, Superboy faded from view, and the title's name changed officially to The Legion of Super-Heroes.

1	7,000.00
2	2,000.00
3	1,500.00
4-5	1,000.00
6-10	800.00
11-15	600.00
16-20	450.00
21-30	350.00
31-38	275.00
39-50	225.00
51-60	175.00
61-67	125.00
68	500.00
☛1st Bizarro	
69-77	100.00
78	175.00
☛Mxyzptlk origin	
79	100.00
80	150.00
☛Meets Supergirl	
81-85	90.00
86	200.00
☛Legion app.	
87-88	90.00
89	275.00
☛1st Mon-El	
90-93	90.00
94-97	75.00
98	100.00
99	75.00
100	175.00
☛Phtm. Zone villains	
101-120	60.00
121-128	50.00
129	75.00
130-137	40.00
138	55.00
☛Giant-sized	
139-140	40.00
141-146	35.00
147	50.00
☛Saturn Girl origin	
148-155	25.00
156	65.00
☛Giant-size	
157-164	25.00

165	50.00

☛Giant-size

166-168	25.00
169-173	20.00
174	30.00
175-178	20.00

☛Giant-sized

179-181	15.00
182	20.00
183-196	12.00
197	20.00

☛Legion stories start

198-199	12.00
200	15.00
201	12.00
202	30.00
203-204	12.00
205	40.00
206-207	12.00
208	15.00
209	10.00
210	15.00
211-212	10.00
213-221	7.00
222-230	5.00
Ann 1	175.00
SP 1	4.00

Superboy
DC, 1990

1-18	2.00
Special 1	3.00

Superboy
DC, 1994

0	2.00
1	3.00
2-24	2.00
25	3.00
26-99	2.00
100	3.00
1000000	4.00
Ann 1	3.00
Ann 2	4.00
Ann 3	3.00
Ann 4	4.00

Superboy and the Legion of Super-Heroes
DC, 1977

231-241	5.00
241/Whitman	8.00
242	5.00
242/Whitman	8.00
243	5.00

243/Whitman	8.00
244	5.00
244/Whitman	8.00
245	5.00
245/Whitman	8.00
246	5.00
246/Whitman	8.00
247	5.00
247/Whitman	8.00
248	5.00
248/Whitman	8.00
249-250	5.00
251	4.00
251/Whitman	7.00
252	4.00
252/Whitman	7.00
253	4.00
253/Whitman	7.00
254	4.00
254/Whitman	7.00
255	4.00
255/Whitman	7.00
256	4.00
256/Whitman	7.00
257	4.00
257/Whitman	7.00
258	4.00
258/Whitman	7.00

Superboy & the Ravers
DC, 1996

1-19	2.00

Superboy Plus
DC, 1997

1-2	3.00

Superboy/ Risk Double-Shot
DC, 1998

1	2.00

Superboy/Robin: World's Finest Three
DC, 1996

1-2	5.00

Superboy's Legion
DC, 2001

1-2	6.00

Super Brat
Toby, 1954

1	40.00
2-4	25.00

Supercar
Gold Key, 1962

1	250.00
2-4	200.00

Super Cat
Star, 1953

56-58	120.00

Super Cat
Ajax, 1957

1	55.00
2-4	35.00

Super Circus
Cross, 1951

1	85.00
2	55.00
3-5	45.00

Super Comics
Dell, 1938

1	1,600.00
2	600.00
3	510.00
4-5	400.00
6-10	315.00
11-25	260.00
26-29	182.00
30	265.00
31-40	138.00
41-50	124.00
51-70	78.00
71-90	58.00
91-100	48.00
101-110	34.00
111-121	25.00

Supercops
Now, 1990

1	3.00
2-4	2.00

Super Cops
Red Circle, 1974

1	2.00

Super DC Giant
DC, 1970

13	75.00
14-16	30.00
17	125.00
18-19	50.00
20	40.00
21	175.00
22	25.00

☛Westerns

23	40.00
24	30.00

☛Supergirl comics

25-26	25.00
27	15.00

Super Deluxe Hero Happy Hour: The Lost Episode
Idea & Design Works, 2006

1	10.00

Super Duck Comics
Archie, 1944

1	350.00
2	145.00
3	105.00
4-5	85.00
6-10	68.00
11-20	56.00
21-30	45.00
31-50	32.00
51-70	24.00
71-94	20.00

Superfan
Mark 1

1	2.00

Superfist Ayumi
Fantagraphics, 1996

1-2	3.00

Super Friends
DC, 1976

1	20.00
2	9.00
3-5	7.00
6-10	6.00
11-13	4.00
13/Whitman	8.00
14	6.00
14/Whitman	12.00
15	4.00
15/Whitman	12.00
16	6.00
16/Whitman	12.00
17-20	4.00
20/Whitman	12.00
21	6.00
21/Whitman	12.00
22	6.00
22/Whitman	12.00
23	6.00
23/Whitman	12.00
24-25	4.00
25/Whitman	8.00
26-31	4.00
32	5.00
32/Whitman	10.00
33-47	4.00
Special 1	5.00

Super Funnies
Superior, 1953

1	300.00
2	100.00
3-4	50.00

Supergirl
DC, 1972

1	15.00
2	10.00
3-10	8.00

Supergirl
DC, 1983

14-23	3.00
DOT 1-2	4.00

Supergirl
DC, 1996

1	10.00

☛Matrix, Linda merge

1/2nd	3.00
2-3	4.00
4-7	3.00
8-49	2.00
50	4.00
51-72	2.00
73-75	3.00
76-80	3.00
1000000	4.00
Ann 1	3.00
Ann 2	4.00

Supergirl (4th series)
DC, 2005

0	5.00
1	7.00
1/Turner	10.00
1/Sketch	4.00

☛2nd print

2-4	3.00
5	4.00
6-38	3.00

Supergirl and the Legion of Super-Heroes
DC, 2006

17-25	3.00

Supergirl/ Lex Luthor Special
DC, 1993

1	3.00

Supergirl
DC, 1994

The "Supergirl" of this series is not the original, but is instead a synthetic being, created in homage to Superman. Her earliest memory is of a red-headed man, looking much like today's Lex Luthor. She was then sent to Earth to help Superman fight a trio of alien terrorists. Horribly beaten in that battle, she reverted to what may have been her natural form: a claylike blank, whom Superman eventually nursed back to health. She then repaid the debt, helping Superman fight Brainiac in the "Panic in the Sky" storyline that ran throughout the Superman titles. Unfortunately, she soon fell in with this Earth's Lex Luthor, who keeps her as something of a super-powered love slave.

In this series, Supergirl is still discovering her powers, all the while denying that her sweetheart, Lex, is the monster people say he is. In time, however, she will discover that her "darling Lex" has some very dark plans for her.

1-4	3.00

Supergirl Movie Special
DC

1	1.00

Supergirl Plus
DC, 1997

1	3.00

Supergirl/ Prysm Double Shot
DC, 1998

1	2.00

Supergirl: Wings
DC, 2001

1	6.00

Super Goof
Gold Key, 1965

1	24.00
2-3	12.00
4-10	10.00
11-20	7.00
21-30	5.00
31-57	3.00
58-59	4.00
60	15.00
61	70.00
62	15.00
63	3.00
64-66	5.00
67-69	8.00
70-74	15.00

Super Green Beret
Milson, 1967

1	30.00
2	24.00

Superheroes
Dell, 1967

1	20.00
2-4	12.00

Super Heroes Battle Super Gorillas
DC, 1976

1 ....10.00

Super Heroes Stamp Album
USPS, 2000

1-6 ....3.00
7-10 ....4.00

Super Heroes Versus Super Villains
Archie, 1966

1 ....50.00

Super Hero Happy Hour
GeekPunk, 2002

1-4 ....3.00

SupeRichie
Harvey, 1975

1 ....5.00
2-5 ....3.00
6-18 ....2.00

Super Information Hijinks: Reality Check
Tavicat, 1995

Collin Meeks is just an average kid in 2012 Los Angeles. His concerns hang between his "bottom of the gene pool" family and the True Virtual Reality unit that just came for him in the mail. But Collin's attempt to share his interest in science with his family by creating their perfect virtual realities for them only confirms his previous fears about them.

Then comes the fateful night when his cat, Catreece, curls up for a nap in the VR helmet. Collin comes back to his room to discover she has created her own ideal virtual reality. When he joins her, he must decide which is more unsettling-that she now has a curvaceous feminine body, or that she is the one who has been

watching his videos of classic musicals during the day!

1-5 .... 3.00

Super Information Hijinks: Reality Check!
Sirius, 1996

1-10 .... 3.00

Superior Seven
Imagine This, 1992

1-5 .... 2.00

Superior Stories
Nesbit, 1955

1 .... 120.00
2-4 .... 50.00

Super Magic
Street & Smith, 1941

1 .... 1,200.00

Super Magician (Vol. 1)
Street & Smith, 1941

2 .... 325.00
3 .... 250.00
4-5 .... 225.00
6-7 .... 200.00
8 .... 225.00
9-10 .... 200.00
11-12 .... 175.00

Super Magician (Vol. 2)
Street & Smith, 1943

1 .... 225.00
2-12 .... 110.00

Super Magician (Vol. 3)
Street & Smith, 1944

1-12 .... 100.00

Super Magician (Vol. 4)
Street & Smith, 1945

1-12 .... 90.00

Super Magician (Vol. 5)
Street & Smith, 1946

1-8 .... 75.00

Superman
DC, 1939

When Jor-El, the top scientist of the planet Krypton, realized that his

world was doomed, he sent his baby son, Kal-El, off into space in a rocket ship. The ship traveled far from the red sun of the exploding planet Krypton, eventually landing on Earth. There, the baby was found by a kindly old couple, the Kents, who dubbed him Clark and raised him as their own son. Our worldís yellow sun gave Clark incredible powers, eventually turning him into the legendary hero Superman.

Siegel and Shusterís creation was already the headliner in Action Comics when this solo Superman series began. Running for over forty-five years, this title introduced readers to Mr. Mxyzptlk, Kryptonite, and some of the most delightfully gimmicky Superman stories of all time. The series concluded in 1986 when John Byrne began a reinvention of Superman in The Man of Steel Mini-Series. It later picked up again as Adventures of Superman.

1 .... 160,000.00
2 .... 16,000.00
3 .... 9,200.00
4 .... 6,500.00
5 .... 6,000.00
6-7 .... 3,500.00
8-10 .... 2,850.00
11-13 .... 2,200.00
14 .... 4,500.00
☛U.S. flag cover
15 .... 2,050.00
16-20 .... 1,650.00
21 .... 1,500.00
22-23 .... 1,100.00
24 .... 1,400.00
25 .... 1,050.00
26 .... 1,250.00
27-29 .... 950.00
30 .... 1,350.00
☛1st Mr. Mxyzptlk
31-40 .... 825.00
41-50 .... 650.00
51-52 .... 525.00
53 .... 1,800.00
☛Superman origin
54-60 .... 500.00
61 .... 1,000.00
☛1st Kryptonite
62-70 .... 475.00
71-75 .... 450.00
76 .... 1,100.00
☛Batman team-up
77-80 .... 400.00
81-90 .... 375.00
91-95 .... 360.00
96-99 .... 325.00
100 .... 1,500.00
101-110 .... 280.00
111-120 .... 240.00
121-130 .... 195.00
131-139 .... 155.00
140 .... 175.00
☛1st Bizarro Jr.

141-145	115.00
146	160.00
☛Superman origin	
147	135.00
148	115.00
149	125.00
☛Legion app.	
150-161	68.00
162-180	58.00
181-186	55.00
187	60.00
188-192	55.00
193	60.00
194-198	55.00
199	180.00
☛1st race with Flash	
200	60.00
201	24.00
202	30.00
203-211	24.00
212	50.00
☛Superbabies	
213-216	24.00
217	30.00
218-221	20.00
222	30.00
223-226	20.00
227	30.00
228-231	20.00
232	30.00
233	40.00
☛Kryptonite destroyed	
234-238	18.00
239	30.00
☛Giant-sized	
240-244	18.00
245	22.00
246-251	18.00
252	60.00
☛100-page issue	
253	18.00
254	22.00
255-264	9.00
265-271	8.00
272	20.00
☛100-page issue	
273-277	7.00
278	17.00
☛100-page issue	
279-283	5.00
284	7.00
285-286	5.00
287-292	4.00
293-299	3.00
300	11.00
301-321	3.00
321/Whitman	5.00
322	3.00
322/Whitman	5.00
323	3.00
323/Whitman	5.00
324	3.00
324/Whitman	5.00
325	3.00
325/Whitman	5.00
326	3.00
326/Whitman	5.00
327	3.00
327/Whitman	5.00
328	3.00

328/Whitman	5.00
329	3.00
329/Whitman	5.00
330	3.00
330/Whitman	5.00
331	3.00
331/Whitman	5.00
332	3.00
332/Whitman	5.00
333	3.00
333/Whitman	5.00
334	3.00
334/Whitman	5.00
335	3.00
335/Whitman	5.00
336	3.00
336/Whitman	5.00
337	3.00
337/Whitman	5.00
338	3.00
338/Whitman	5.00
339	3.00
339/Whitman	5.00
340	3.00
340/Whitman	5.00
341	3.00
341/Whitman	5.00
342	3.00
342/Whitman	5.00
343	3.00
343/Whitman	5.00
344	3.00
344/Whitman	5.00
345	3.00
345/Whitman	5.00
346	3.00
346/Whitman	5.00
347	3.00
347/Whitman	5.00
348	3.00
348/Whitman	5.00
349	3.00
349/Whitman	5.00
350	3.00
350/Whitman	5.00
351-399	2.00
400	5.00
401-422	2.00
423	5.00
Ann 1	600.00
Ann 1/2nd	5.00
Ann 2	325.00
Ann 3	210.00
Ann 4	180.00
Ann 5	105.00
Ann 6	90.00
Ann 7	62.00
Ann 8	46.00
Ann 9-10	5.00
Ann 11	4.00
Ann 12	3.00
Special 1-3	4.00

Superman
DC, 1987

One of the temptations for a character like Superman is to make him seem more and more powerful, with each new feat outdoing the last. Over the years since his first appearance in Action Comics #1, this has certainly been the case, going even so far at one point as to show Superman moving Earth back into its orbit. However, such a daunting character has a hard time finding an adequate challenge, and in time can get a little boring. DC comics realized this and decided to reinvent the Superman character, altering his origin somewhat and scaling back his powers to a more comprehensible level.

With this second volume, we see a far more interesting Superman than ever before. He has to try a little harder, and alterego Clark Kent is a more interesting character. Killed in an event that made national news, this new, modern Superman even settled down with Lois Lane, a feat sheíd been trying to accomplish for more than 50 years.

0	3.00
1-2	4.00
3-5	3.00
6-8	2.00
9	4.00
10-49	2.00
50	4.00
50/2nd-52/2nd	2.00
53	3.00
53/2nd-72	2.00
73	3.00
73/2nd	2.00
74	4.00
74/2nd	2.00
75	5.00
☛Death of Superman	
75/CS	12.00
75/Platinum	40.00

Superman 3-D
DC, 1998

Most 3-D comics employ the three-dimensional effect throughout the entire story. But this title uses the 3-D illusion intermittently to indicate the strange machinations of Mainframe, a group of computer-themed cyborgs. The leader, Override, intends to digitize this dimension using technology stolen from Jude, one of the Hairies.

When Jack Kirby returned to DC Comics in the early 1970s he imbued the Jimmy Olsen title with a new vitality replete with fantastic characters that were inspired by the popular culture of the time. One of his concepts was the Hairies, a group of high-tech outcasts that employed the counter-culture slang and stereotypical appearance of hippies. The leader of the Hairies was a brilliant scientist known as Jude who piloted a massive vehicle called the Mountain of Judgement. Twenty-five years later, Jude's rebellious daughter (and friend of Jimmy Olsen), Misa, consider the Hairies to be the Establishment.

Misa, along with Jimmy Olsen and Superman come to Jude's aid opposing Mainframe and resurrecting the long-buried rancor between father and daughter.

-- George Haberberger

Superman Adventures
DC, 1996

Superman/Aliens 2: God War
DC, 2002

Superman: A Nation Divided
DC

The year is 1863, perhaps the darkest time in American history, as North battles South in a war that could tear apart a nation. That's when General Ulysses S. Grant sees things begin to turn in his favor thanks to the incredible abilities of a young enlistee from Kansas by the name of Atticus Kent. For how can an army lose when led by a man who shrugs off gunfire, stops a locomotive in its tracks, and flies?

This DC Elseworlds adventure drops Superman into the middle of the Civil War, and shows what might have happened if he had been around--and not just during the war, but afterwards. For instanc, what might have happened if President Lincoln had had the Last Son of Krypton at his side?

Superman & Batman: Generations
DC, 1999

Superman & Batman: Generations II
DC, 2001

Superman & Batman: Generations III
DC, 2003

Superman & Batman Magazine
Welsh, 1993
1 ....3.00
2 ....2.00
3 ....3.00
4-8 ....2.00

Superman and Batman: World's Funnest
DC, 2000
1 ....7.00

Superman & Bugs Bunny
DC, 2000
1-4 ....3.00

Superman & Savage Dragon: Chicago
DC, 2002
1 ....6.00

Superman & Savage Dragon: Metropolis
DC, 1999
nn 5.00

Superman Archives
DC, 1989
1-3 ....40.00
4-6 ....50.00

Superman: At Earth's End
DC, 1995
1 ....5.00

Superman/Batman Secret Files
DC, 2003
1 ....5.00

Superman/Batman
DC, 2003
1 ....8.00
1/Retailer ed........................125.00
1/2nd-1/3rd...........................4.00
2 ....6.00
3 ....5.00
3/2nd 3.00
4 ....4.00
5 ....3.00
6 ....4.00
7 ....3.00
8 ....10.00

☛1st new Supergirl
8/2nd 7.00
☛Sketch cover
8/3rd 6.00
☛Wonder Woman cover
8/4th 3.00
9 .... 5.00
9/2nd 4.00
9/3rd 3.00
10 .... 5.00
10/2nd 4.00
11 .... 5.00
12 .... 4.00
13 .... 5.00
13/Supergirl........................... 7.00
14 .... 5.00
15 .... 4.00
16 .... 5.00
17 .... 4.00
18 .... 3.00
19 .... 4.00
20 .... 3.00
21 .... 4.00
22-24 .... 3.00
26 .... 4.00
27-31 .... 3.00
Ann 1 .... 4.00

Superman: Birthright
DC, 2003
1-12 .... 3.00

Superman: Bizarro's World
DC
1 .... 10.00

Superman: Blood of My Ancestors
DC, 2003
1 .... 7.00

Superman Confidential
DC, 2007
1-10 .... 3.00

Superman: Day of Doom
DC, 2003
1 .... 10.00

Superman: Distant Fires
DC, 1998
1 .... 6.00

Superman/Doomsday: Hunter/Prey
DC, 1994
1-3 .... 6.00

Superman: Emperor Joker
DC, 2000
1 .... 4.00

Superman: Endgame
DC, 2001
1 .... 15.00

Superman Family
DC, 1974
164 .... 35.00
☛100-page issue
165-169 .... 13.00
☛100-page issue
170-177 .... 11.00
178-180 .... 5.00
181-200 .... 4.00
201-222 .... 3.00

Superman/ Fantastic Four
DC, 1999
1 .... 10.00

Superman for All Seasons
DC, 1998
1-4 .... 5.00

Superman for Earth
DC, 1991
1 .... 5.00

Superman Forever
DC, 1998
1 .... 6.00
1/Variant 7.00

Super Manga Blast!
Dark Horse, 2000
1-18 .... 5.00
19-59 .... 6.00

Superman Gallery
DC, 1993
1 .... 3.00

Superman/Gen13
WildStorm, 2000
1-3 .... 3.00

Superman (Giveaways)
DC, 1980

1-5..1.00

Superman, Inc.
DC, 2000

1...................................7.00

Superman IV Movie Special
DC, 1987

1...2.00

Superman: Kal
DC

1...6.00

Superman: Kansas Sighting
DC, 2004

1-2...................................7.00

Superman: King of the World
DC, 1999

1...4.00
1/Gold 5.00

Superman: Krisis of the Krimson Kryptonite
DC, 1996

1...13.00

Superman: Last Son of Earth
DC, 2000

1-2...6.00

Superman: Last Stand on Krypton
DC, 2003

1...7.00

Superman: Lex 2000
DC, 2001

1...4.00

Superman: Lois Lane
DC, 1998

1...2.00

Superman/Madman Hullabaloo
Dark Horse, 1997

1-3..3.00

Superman Meets the Motorsports Champions
DC, 1999

1...1.00

Superman Meets the Quik Bunny
DC

1...1.00

Superman: Metropolis
DC, 2003

1-12...3.00

Superman Metropolis Secret Files
DC, 2000

1.............................. 5.00

Superman Monster
DC

1.............................. 6.00

Superman Movie Special
DC, 1983

1.............................. 2.00

Superman: No Limits!
DC, 2001

1.............................. 15.00

Superman: Our Worlds at War Secret Files
DC, 2001

1.............................. 6.00

Superman: Peace on Earth
DC, 1999

1-1/2nd.............................. 10.00

Superman Plus
DC, 1997

1.............................. 3.00

Superman: President Lex
DC, 2003

1.............................. 18.00

Superman: Red Son
DC, 2003

1.............................. 7.00
2-3.............................. 6.00

Superman Red/ Superman Blue
DC, 1998

1.............................. 4.00
Deluxe 1 .... 5.00

Superman Returns: Krypton to Earth
DC, 2006

1-4.............................. 4.00

Superman Returns: The Movie Adaptation
DC, 2006

1.............................. 7.00

Superman: Return to Krypton
DC, 2004

1.............................. 18.00

Superman: Save the Planet
DC, 1998

1.............................. 3.00
1/Variant.............................. 4.00

Superman: Secret Files
DC, 1998

1-2.............................. 5.00

Superman: Secret Files 2004
DC, 2004

1.............................. 5.00

Superman Secret Files and Origins 2004
DC, 2005

0.............................. 6.00
☛Infinite Crisis tie

Superman Secret Files 2005
DC, 2006

1.............................. 5.00

Superman: Secret Identity
DC, 2004

1-4 .... 6.00

Superman's Girl Friend Lois Lane
DC, 1958

1	2,600.00
2	625.00
3	415.00
4-5	300.00
6-10	220.00
11-18	125.00
19	215.00
20	125.00
21-29	86.00
30-50	48.00
51-67	34.00
68	44.00
69	34.00
70	175.00

☛1st SA Catwoman

71	105.00

☛Catwoman app.

72-73	15.00
74	34.00
75-76	15.00
77	24.00
78	15.00
79-85	10.00
86	16.00
87-94	10.00
95	25.00

☛Giant-sized

96-103	8.00
104	16.00
105-106	14.00
107-110	6.00
111	10.00
112	6.00
113	14.00
114-120	6.00
121	5.00
122-123	8.00
124-137	5.00
Ann 1	75.00
Ann 2	50.00

Superman/Shazam: First Thunder
DC, 2005

1-4 .... 4.00

Superman: Silver Banshee
DC, 1998
1-2...2.00

Superman's Metropolis
DC, 1997
1..6.00

Superman's Nemesis: Lex Luthor
DC, 1999
1-4...3.00

Superman's Pal Jimmy Olsen
DC, 1954
1..4,000.00
2..1,250.00
3...675.00
4-5...475.00
6-10.......................................335.00
11-20......................................235.00
21-30......................................150.00
31-40......................................100.00
41-50..75.00
51-56..50.00
57-70..30.00
71...25.00
72-73..30.00
74-75..25.00
76...30.00
77-88..25.00
89-90..20.00
91-94..16.00
95...25.00
96-99..16.00
100..25.00
101-103.....................................12.00
104..35.00
☛Weird Adventures
105-112.....................................12.00
113..25.00
☛Anti-Superman ish
114-119.....................................12.00
120-126.....................................10.00
127..16.00
128-130.....................................10.00
131-132.......................................8.00
133..10.00
134..25.00
135-140.....................................12.00
141-150.....................................10.00
151...8.00
152-163.......................................7.00

Superman Spectacular
DC
1..3.00

Superman: Speeding Bullets
DC, 1993

As the doomed planet Krypton erupted into a fiery conflagration, a single craft escaped with that world's sole survivor. The orphaned infant arrived on Earth to be found and cared for by a loving couple...and Alfred, their faithful butler! Yes, in this Elseworlds story, it was Thomas and Martha Wayne who became Superman's adoptive parents, until, evoking the origin of Batman, they were killed by a mugger.

This amalgam of Superman's character with Batman's life serves to highlight the fundamental differences in temperament between these two stalwarts of the DC Universe. With solid, pleasing art by Eduardo Barreto, the writer, J. M. DeMatteis, examines the how different Superman would have been had he endured the trauma of Batman's experiences.

-- George Haberberger

1 .... 5.00

Superman: Strength
DC, 2005
1-3.. 6.00

Superman/Tarzan: Sons of the Jungle
Dark Horse, 2001
1-3.. 3.00

Superman: The Dark Side
DC, 1998

This Elseworlds series is an elaborate "What If..." scenario. Namely, what if Superman, while being sent as a baby through space toward Earth, were diverted by malevolent forces to a different world instead. That world was Apokolips, where the baby Kal-El was taken in by the evil Darkseid. Once grown, the baby became-not the familiar defender of truth, justice, and the American Way-but an almost all-powerful knight only too-willing to serve his dark master's wishes.

1-3.. 5.00

Superman: The Doomsday Wars
DC, 1999
1 .... 5.00
1/Ltd. 25.00
2-3 .... 5.00

Superman: The Earth Stealers
DC, 1988
1 .... 3.00

Superman: The Last God of Krypton
DC, 1999
1 .... 5.00

Superman: The Legacy of Superman
DC, 1993
1 .... 3.00

Superman: The Man of Steel
DC, 1991

He was born as Kal-El, on the planet Krypton where his father, Jor-El, was that world's greatest scientist. When Jor-El, realized that their world was doomed, he placed his son in a lone spaceship and sent it to Earth. There, the boy was found by a kind elderly couple, the Kents, who named him Clark, and raised him as if he were their own son. As the boy grew, he developed extraordinary powers: super-strength, X-ray vision, the ability to fly, and more. When he sheds his identity of Clark Kent, he becomes Superman: The Man of Steel.

The most recent Superman series, this title continues to bring readers the adventures of the world's best-known super-hero, intertwining its stories with the stories contained in Superman (2nd Series), Action Comics, and Adventures of Superman. To keep things straight, each issue features a triangle-number on the cover showing the sequence of the stories.

0	3.00
1	6.00
2-3	3.00
4-16	2.00
17	3.00
18	4.00
18/2nd-18/3rd	2.00
19-21	3.00
22	2.00
22/Variant	3.00
23-30	2.00
30/Variant	3.00
31-49	2.00
50	3.00
51-99	2.00
100	3.00
100/Variant	4.00
101-134	2.00
1000000-Ann 5	3.00
Ann 6	4.00

Superman: The Man of Steel Gallery
DC, 1995

1	4.00

Superman: The Man of Tomorrow
DC, 1995

1-14	2.00
15	3.00
1000000	2.00

Superman: The Odyssey
DC, 1999

1	5.00

Superman: The Secret Years
DC, 1985

At one point, DC ran both Superman and Superboy comics at the same time. Although it was interesting to read Superboy to see what Clark Kent was like in high school, the stories lacked a certain element of suspense. After all, readers knew what eventually happened to almost every character in the stories, having seen their futures in the Superman series.

Superman: The Secret Years cleverly manages to bring us new insights on Clark Kent, while still keeping us guessing. It does this by concentrating on Clark's time at college-a previously unexplored time of Clark's life-and simultaneously introducing an entirely new cast of supporting characters. The result is so interesting that it's a shame that this was only a four-issue mini-series.

1-4	2.00

Superman: The Trial of Superman
DC

1	15.00

Superman: The Wedding Album
DC, 1996

1	6.00
1/Direct	5.00
1/Gold	10.00

Superman/Thundercats
DC, 2004

1	6.00

Superman/Toyman
DC, 1996

1	2.00

Superman: Under a Yellow Sun
DC, 1994

1	6.00

Superman vs. Aliens
DC, 1995

1-3	5.00

Superman Vs. Predator
DC, 2000

1-3	5.00

Superman vs. the Amazing Spider-Man
DC

1	20.00

Superman vs. the Revenge Squad
DC

1	13.00

Superman vs. The Terminator: Death to the Future
Dark Horse, 1999

1-4	3.00

Superman Villains Secret Files
DC, 1998

1	5.00

Superman vs. Darkseid: Apokolips Now
DC, 2003

1	3.00

Superman: War of the Worlds
DC, 1998

1	6.00
1/Ltd.	19.00

Superman: Where is Thy Sting?
DC, 2001

1	7.00

Superman/ Wonder Woman: Whom Gods Destroy
DC, 1996
1-4 ....5.00

Superman Y2K
DC, 2000
nn 5.00

Super Mario Bros.
Valiant, 1990
1-6 ....2.00
Special 1 ....3.00

Super Mario Bros.
Valiant, 1991
1-5 ....2.00

Supermarket
Idea & Design Works, 2006
1-4 ....4.00

Supermen of America
DC, 1999
1 ....4.00
1/CS 5.00
2-4 ....3.00

Supermodels in the Rainforest
Sirius, 1998
1-3 ....3.00

Supermouse, The Big Cheese
Pines, 1948
1 ....200.00
2 ....125.00
3 ....85.00
4-6 ....65.00
7-10 ....35.00
11-20 ....25.00
21-40 ....18.00
41-45 ....15.00
GS 1 ....75.00
GS 2 ....50.00

Super-Mystery Comics (1st Series)
Ace, 1940
1 ....1,700.00
2 ....950.00
3 ....675.00
4 ....450.00
5 ....500.00
6 ....450.00

Super-Mystery Comics (2nd Series)
Ace, 1941
1 ....2,000.00
2-6 ....350.00

Super-Mystery Comics (3rd Series)
Ace, 1942
1-6 ....300.00

Super-Mystery Comics (4th Series)
Ace, 1944
1 ....300.00
2-6 ....250.00

Super-Mystery Comics (5th Series)
Ace, 1945
1-6 ....250.00

Super-Mystery Comics (6th Series)
Ace, 1946
1 ....225.00
2-4 ....200.00
5 ....250.00
6 ....200.00

Super-Mystery Comics (7th Series)
Ace, 1947
1-6 ....200.00

Super-Mystery Comics (8th Series)
Ace, 1948
1-6 ....200.00

Supernatural Freak Machine
Idea & Design Works, 2005
1-2 ....4.00

Supernatural Law
Exhibit A, 1999
24-38 ....3.00

Supernaturals
Marvel, 1998
1/A-1/D 4.00
1/E 5.00
1/Ltd. 30.00
2/A-4/E 4.00
Ashcan 1 ....3.00

Supernaturals Tour Book
Marvel, 1998
1 ....3.00

Supernatural Thrillers
Marvel, 1972
1 ....27.00
2-4 ....10.00
5 ....27.00
☛1st Living Mummy
6-15 ....10.00

Superpatriot
Image, 1993
1-4 ....2.00

SuperPatriot: America's Fighting Force
Image, 2002
1-4 ....3.00

Superpatriot: Liberty & Justice
Image, 1995
1 ....3.00
2-4 ....3.00

Superpatriot: War on Terror
Image, 2004
1 ....4.00
2 ....3.00

Super Powers
DC, 1984
1 ....2.00
2-5 ....1.00

Super Powers
DC, 1985
1-6 ....1.00

Super Powers
DC, 1986
1-4 ....1.00

Super Pup
Avon, 1940
4-5 ....25.00

Super Rabbit
Timely, 1943
1 ....500.00
1/2nd 35.00
2 ....275.00
2/2nd 25.00
3-5 ....175.00
6 ....150.00
7-10 ....100.00
10/2nd 22.00
11-14 ....90.00

Super Sexxx
Fantagraphics
1 ....3.00

Super Shark Humanoids
Fish Tales, 1992
1 ....3.00

Supersnipe Comics
Street & Smith, 1942

Koppy McFad is the kid with the most comic books in America. With these treasures to feed his 10-year old imagination, plus red pajamas and a mask, Koppy pictures himself as the masked avenger Supersnipe -- solver of crimes, doer of great deeds, allowed to stay up late and have as much ice cream as he wants. Supersnipe had such immediate appeal that the character promptly took over the former Army and Navy Comics in the middle of World War II, and entertained kids throughout the 1940s.

Supersnipeís adventures ran to epic length, often 32 pages of a 48-page issue (the remainder given over to assorted humorous backups). With quick pacing, imaginative plots, and well-crafted art to rival the best kid strips of the era (including Disneyís), Supersnipe gained a cult following of fans and anchored the otherwise-average Street and Smith comics line.

-- Rob Salkowitz

6	600.00
7	390.00
8	415.00
9	440.00
10	365.00
11-12	335.00

Supersnipe Comics (Vol. 2)
Street & Smith, 1944

1	250.00
2-3	220.00
4-12	210.00

Supersnipe Comics (Vol. 3)
Street & Smith, 1946

1	190.00
2-12	165.00

Supersnipe Comics (Vol. 4)
Street & Smith, 1947

1-12	130.00

Supersnipe Comics (Vol. 5)
Street & Smith, 1949

1	105.00

Super Soldier
DC, 1996

1	2.00

Super Soldier: Man of War
DC, 1997

1	2.00

Super Soldiers
Marvel, 1993

1	3.00
2-8	2.00

Supersonic Soul Puddin Comics & Stories
Four Cats Funny Books, 1995

1	4.00

Super Sonic vs. Hyper Knuckles
Archie

1	2.00

Super Spy
Centaur, 1940

1	1,000.00
2	600.00

Superstar: As Seen on TV
Image, 1999

1	6.00

Superswine
Caliber

1-2	3.00

Super Taboo
Fantagraphics, 1995

1-2	3.00

Super-Team Family
DC, 1975

1	12.00
2-4	6.00
5-10	4.00
11-15	3.00

Super-Villain Classics
Marvel, 1983

1	3.00

Super-Villain Team-Up
Marvel, 1975

Marvel had a great idea with Super-Villain Team-Up: take the worlds' nastiest, most evil characters-villains that have conceived the most ingenious and malevolent plans for destruction-and have them join forces to plot even nastier deeds.

So in Super-Villain Team-Up, we see Dr. Doom, the Hate-Monger, the Red Skull, the Shroud, Arnim Zola, and others joining forces to wreak even greater havoc than could be accomplished by each alone.

1	7.00
2	5.00
3-5	4.00
5/30¢	20.00
6	3.00
6/30¢	20.00
7	3.00
7/30¢	20.00
8-12/Whitman	3.00
12/35¢	15.00
13	5.00
13/35¢	15.00
14-14/Whitman	3.00
14/35¢	15.00
15-17	3.00

Super Western Comics
Youthful, 1950

1	70.00

Superworld Comics
Hugo Gernsback, 1940

1	4,000.00
2	2,350.00
3	1,825.00

Suppressed!
Tome

1	3.00

Supreme
Image, 1992

0-1/Gold	3.00
2-12	2.00
13-40	3.00
41	4.00
41/Ltd.	15.00
41/AmEnt	9.00
41/2nd-56	3.00
Ann 1	4.00

Supreme: Glory Days
Image, 1994

1-2	3.00

Supreme Power
Marvel, 2003

1	4.00
1/Special	5.00
2-4	3.00
5	4.00
6-18	3.00

Supreme Power: Hyperion
Marvel, 2005

1-5	3.00

Supreme Power: Nighthawk
Marvel, 2005

1-6	3.00

Supreme: The Return
Awesome, 1999

1-6	3.00

Supremie
Parody
1 ....3.00

Sure-Fire Comics
Ace, 1940
1 ....1,025.00
2 ....485.00
3 ....375.00
4 ....500.00

Surfcrazed Comics
Pacifica
1 ....3.00
3 ....4.00
4 ....3.00

Surf 'n' Wheels
Charlton, 1969
1-6 ....12.00

Surf Sumo
Star Tiger, 1997
1-1/2nd....................................3.00

Surge
Eclipse, 1984
1-4...2.00

Surreal School Stories
Gratuitous Bunny, 1995
1-5...2.00

Surrogates
Top Shelf Productions, 2005
1 ....3.00

Surrogate Saviour
Hot Brazen Comics, 1995
1-3...3.00

Survive!
Apple
1 ....3.00

Survivors
Fantagraphics
1-2...3.00

Survivors
Prelude, 1986
1-2...2.00

Survivors
Burnside, 1987
1 ....2.00

Sushi
Shunga, 1990
1-8 .... 3.00

Suspense
Atlas, 1949
1 .... 370.00
2 .... 190.00
3 .... 210.00
4 .... 155.00
5-6 .... 165.00
7-10 .... 155.00
11-13 .... 120.00
14 .... 190.00
15-17 .... 120.00
18 .... 130.00
19-20 .... 120.00
21 .... 115.00
22 .... 130.00
23-24 .... 115.00
25 .... 160.00
26-29 .... 115.00

Suspense Comics
Continental, 1943
1 .... 2,500.00
2 .... 1,850.00
3 .... 6,000.00
4-6 .... 1,400.00
7-10 .... 1,050.00
11 .... 1,925.00
12 .... 1,050.00

Suspense Detective
Fawcett, 1952
1 .... 260.00
2 .... 155.00
3-5 .... 125.00

Suspira: The Great Working
Chaos, 1997
1-4 .... 3.00

Sussex Vampire
Caliber
1 .... 3.00

Sustah-Girl: Queen of the Black Age
Onli
1 .... 2.00

Suzie Comics
M.L.J., 1945
49 .... 125.00
50-55 .... 80.00
56 .... 75.00
57-100 .... 55.00

Swamp Fever
Big Muddy
1 .... 3.00

Swamp Thing
DC, 1972
1 .... 60.00
2 .... 30.00
3-4 .... 20.00
5-6 .... 15.00
7 .... 12.00
8-10 .... 10.00
11-24 .... 5.00

Swamp Thing
DC, 1986
46 .... 4.00
47-49 .... 3.00
50 .... 4.00
51 .... 3.00
52 .... 4.00
53 .... 5.00
☞Batman appearance
54-81 .... 3.00
82-83 .... 2.00
84 .... 5.00
☞Sandman appearance
85-89 .... 2.00
90 .... 3.00
91-99 .... 2.00
100 .... 3.00
101-124 .... 2.00
125 .... 3.00
126-140 .... 2.00
140/Platinum 6.00
141-149 .... 2.00
150 .... 3.00
151-158 .... 2.00
159-171 .... 3.00
Ann 4-5.................................... 4.00
Ann 6 .... 3.00
Ann 7 .... 4.00

Swamp Thing
DC, 2000
1 .... 4.00
2-20 .... 3.00

Swamp Thing
DC, 2004

1	4.00
2-29	3.00

Swamp Thing: Roots
DC

1	8.00

Swan
Little Idylls, 1995

1-4	3.00

Swarm
Mushroom

1	3.00

Sweatshop
DC, 2003

1-6	3.00

Sweeney
Standard, 1949

4-5	45.00

Sweet
Adept

Yes, this is another 1990s female vampire, but Leland Myrick manages to put an interesting spin on the overdone premise. Instead of yet another story about an ultracool street vampire preying on humanity, Sweet takes the victim's point of view...a willing, eager victim at that. Artwork is spare but not lacking, and the characters, though nameless, are developed and intriguing.

The story revolves around a male college student who is visited one night by the seductive female vampire and becomes obsessed with her. He prevents her from taking other victims, but it is out of jealousy rather than altruism. He pursues her, trying to thwart her from attacking anyone else but himself.

1	4.00

Sweetchilde
New Moon

1	3.00

Sweet Childe: Lost Confessions
Anarchy Bridgeworks

1	3.00

Sweetheart Diary
Fawcett, 1949

1	90.00
2	50.00
3-4	75.00
5-10	45.00
11-14	32.00

Sweetheart Diary
Charlton, 1955

32	35.00
33-41	25.00
42-60	15.00
61-65	12.00

Sweethearts
Fawcett, 1948

68	85.00
69-70	50.00
71-80	40.00
81-99	34.00
100	40.00
101-115	30.00
116-122	25.00

Sweethearts
Charlton, 1954

23-30	12.00
31-39	10.00
40	16.00
41	9.00
42	35.00
43-45	9.00
46	15.00
47-50	9.00
51-60	7.00
61-70	6.00
71-100	4.00
101-137	3.00

Sweetie Pie
Ajax, 1955

1	45.00
2	25.00

Sweet Love
Harvey, 1949

1	55.00
2	35.00
3-4	25.00
5	40.00

Sweet Lucy
Brainstorm, 1993

1-2	3.00

Sweet Lucy: Blonde Steele
Brainstorm

1	3.00

Sweet Lucy Commemorative Edition
Brainstorm, 1994

1	4.00

Sweetmeats
Atomeka

1	4.00

Sweet Sixteen
Parents' Magazine Institute, 1946

1	100.00
2	75.00
3-13	50.00

Sweet XVI
Marvel, 1991

1-6	1.00
Special 1	2.00

Swerve
Slave Labor, 1995

1-2	2.00

Swift Arrow
Ajax, 1954

1	85.00
2	50.00
3-5	35.00

Swift Arrow
Ajax, 1957

1	45.00
2-3	35.00

Swift Arrow's Gunfighters
Ajax, 1957

4	35.00

Swiftsure
Harrier, 1985

1-18	2.00

Swiftsure & Conqueror
Harrier, 1985

1-8	2.00
9	3.00
10-18	2.00

Swimsuits & Mermaids
Image Guild

1-1/2nd	4.00

Swing with Scooter
DC, 1966

1	30.00
2	18.00
3	15.00
4-5	12.00
6-10	10.00
11-20	8.00
21-30	6.00
31-36	5.00

Switchblade
Silverline, 1997

1	3.00

Sword in the Stone
Gold Key, 1964
1 .... 30.00

Sword of Damocles
Image, 1996
1-2 .... 3.00

Sword of Dracula
Image, 2003
1-6 .... 3.00

Sword of Sorcery
DC, 1973

This was a title that had everything going for it. It had great artwork by the likes of Howard Chaykin and Neal Adams (the latter working under the moniker "The Crusty Bunkers"). Then-publisher Denny O'Neil did a fine job on the writing, with crisp, action-filled scripts.

Best of all, the subject matter was great, featuring comic adaptations of Fritz Leiber's adventure tales starring Fafhrd and the Grey Mouser. These were easily two of the best characters in the genre, with the figure of Fafhrd (a surprisingly charming barbarian) playing well against the clever thief Grey Mouser. Their adventures were equally balanced between swordfighting and quick thinking, a mix that years later would inspire the game sensation, Advanced Dungeons & Dragons.

This should have been the perfect adventure series, but it inexplicably lasted only five issues.

1 .... 10.00
2-3 .... 8.00
4-5 .... 6.00

Sword of the Atom
DC, 1983
1-Special 3 .... 2.00

Sword of the Samurai
Avalon, 1996
1 .... 3.00

Sword of Valor
A+

You'll find Viking hordes, Arthurian knights, wizard-cursed swords, Shogun warriors, and even a little bit of time travel in this anthology series, in which barbarians and other sword-wielding heroes run amok. Each issue is 48 pages of sword-and-sorcery adventure.

This title featured some popular artists, such as Jim Aparo, John Buscema, and Walt Simonson, as well as others less known but no less talented. Many of the stories are self-contained shorts, but a few, such as Kuno, son of Steel, continue from issue to issue.

1-4 .... 3.00

Swordsmen and Saurians
Eclipse
1 .... 20.00

Swords of Cerebus
Aardvark-Vanaheim
1-2/2nd 5.00
3-4/2nd 6.00
5-6 .... 5.00

Swords of Cerebus Supplement
Aardvark-Vanaheim
1 .... 1.00

Swords of Shar-Pei
Caliber
1-2 .... 3.00

Swords of Texas
Eclipse, 1987
1-4 .... 2.00

Swords of the Swashbucklers
Marvel, 1985
1-12 .... 2.00

Swords of Valor
A-Plus
1-4 .... 3.00

Sylvia Faust
Image, 2004
1-2 .... 3.00

Symbols of Justice
High Impact, 1995
1 .... 3.00

Syn
Dark Horse, 2003
1-5 .... 3.00

Synn, the Girl from LSD
AC, 1990
1 .... 4.00

Synthetic Assassin
Night Realm
1 .... 2.00

Syphons
Now, 1986
1-7 .... 2.00

Syphons
Now, 1993
0 .... 1.00
1-3 .... 3.00

Syphons: The Sygate Stratagem
Now, 1994
1-3 .... 3.00

System
DC, 1996
1-3 .... 3.00

System Seven
Arrow, 1987
1-3 .... 2.00

Kevin Eastman and Peter Laird's amphibian-based crimefighters
were originally created as a parody of Frank Miller's work on Daredevil.

Archie. That's Tales Calculated to Drive You Bats, a true "humor in a jugular vein" offering from Archie Comics in the early 1960s. Campy, funny, and fun, Tales Calculated to Drive You Bats offers goofy takes on familiar movie monsters such as Dracula, the Wolf-Man and the Mummy. One-to-four-page stories keep the gags moving at a frantic clip, and, if Archie humor tickles your funny bone, then Tales Calculated to Drive You Bats will certainly appeal. Strangely enough, Tales Calculated to Drive You Bats didn't make much of an impression on the newsstands and vanished unable to capitalize on the "funny ha-ha-funny-strange" formula that propelled early 1960s TV series like The Munsters and The Addams Family to nationwide popularity.

-- Rob Salkowitz

Taboo
Spiderbaby, 1995
1-3 .... 10.00
4-9 .... 15.00

Taboux
Antarctic, 1996
1-2 .... 4.00

Tabula Rasa
Image, 2006
1 .... 5.00

Tactics
ADV Manga, 2004
1-2 .... 10.00

Taffy Comics
Rural Home, 1945
1 .... 150.00
2 .... 110.00
3 .... 90.00
4-5 .... 75.00
6-10 .... 50.00
11-12 .... 40.00

Tailgunner Jo
DC, 1988
1-6 .... 1.00

Tails
Archie, 1995
1-3 .... 2.00

Tainted
DC, 1995
1 .... 5.00

Tainted Blood
Weirdling, 1996
1 .... 3.00

Taken Under Compendium
Caliber
1 .... 3.00

Takion
DC, 1996
1-7 .... 2.00

Tale of Halima
Fantagraphics
1-2 .... 3.00

Tale of Mya Rom
Aircel
1 .... 2.00

Tale of One Bad Rat
Dark Horse, 1994
1 .... 4.00
2-4 .... 3.00

Tale of the Body Thief (Anne Rice's...)
Sicilian Dragon, 1999
1-12 .... 3.00

Tales Calculated to Drive You Bats
Archie, 1961

Imagine the gallows wit of Charles Addams filtered through the comic style and sensibility of

1 .... 75.00
2 .... 50.00
3-7 .... 30.00
Ann 1 .... 50.00

Tales Calculated to Drive You Mad
E.C., 1997
1-8 .... 4.00

Tales Designed to Thrizzle
Fantagraphics, 2005
1 .... 5.00

Tales from Ground Zero
Excel
1 .... 5.00

Tales From Necropolis
Brainstorm
1 .... 3.00

Tales From ... Riverdale Digest Magazine
Archie, 2005
7-17 .... 2.00

Tales from Shock City
Fantagraphics, 2001
nn 4.00

Tales From Sleaze Castle
Gratuitous Bunny
1-3 .... 3.00

Tales From the Age of Apocalypse
Marvel, 1996
1 .... 6.00

Tales from the Age of Apocalypse: Sinister Bloodlines
Marvel, 1997
1 .... 6.00

Tales from the Aniverse
Massive, 1992

1-3...2.00

Tales from the Aniverse
Arrow

1-6...2.00

Tales from the Bog
Aberration, 1995

1-Ashcan 1 ....3.00

Tales from the Bog
(Director's Cut)
Aberration, 1998

1..3.00

Tales from the
Bully Pulpit One Shot
Image, 2004

1..7.00

Tales from the
Clonezone
Dark Horse

1..2.00

Tales From the Crypt
E.C., 1950

20..775.00
21..900.00
22..700.00
23-25...................................520.00
26-30...................................400.00
31..460.00
32..300.00
33..675.00
☛Crypt Keeper origin
34-46...................................295.00

Tales from the Crypt
Gladstone, 1990

1-6...3.00

Tales from the Crypt
Cochran, 1991

1..4.00

Tales from the Crypt
Cochran, 1991

1-7...2.00

Tales from the Crypt
Gemstone, 1992

1-15...2.00
16-30...3.00
Ann 1...9.00
Ann 2.......................................10.00
Ann 3.......................................11.00
Ann 4.......................................13.00
Ann 5.......................................14.00

Tales from the Edge!
Vanguard, 1993

1..4.00
2..5.00
3-7...3.00
8..4.00
9..5.00
10..4.00
11..5.00

12 .... 4.00
13 .... 3.00
14 .... 5.00
15 .... 6.00
Summer 1................................ 4.00

Tales from the Fridge
Kitchen Sink, 1973

1 .... 3.00

Tales from the
Great Book
Famous Funnies, 1955

1 .... 30.00
2-4 .... 24.00

Tales from the Heart
Entropy, 1988

1 .... 4.00
2-11 .... 3.00

Tales from the
Heart of Africa:
The Temporary Natives
Marvel, 1990

1 .... 4.00

Tales from the Kids
David G. Brown, 1996

1 .... 2.00

Tales From the
Leather Nun
Last Gasp

1 .... 14.00

Tales From the
Mahabharata
Amar Chitra Katha

16 .... 4.00

Tales from the
Outer Boroughs
Fantagraphics

1-3 .... 2.00
4-5 .... 3.00

Tales from the Plague
Eclipse

1 .... 4.00

Tales from the
Ravaged Lands
Magi, 1996

0 .... 2.00
1-6 .... 3.00

Tales from the
Stone Troll Cafè
Planet X, 1986

1 .... 2.00

Tales from the Tomb
Dell, 1962

1 .... 125.00

Tales from the Tomb
(Magazine, Vol. 1)
Eerie, 1969

6 .... 40.00
7-8 .... 34.00

Tales from the Tomb
(Magazine, Vol. 2)
Eerie, 1970

1-6 .... 30.00

Tales from the Tomb
(Magazine, Vol. 3)
Eerie, 1971

1-6 .... 25.00

Tales from the Tomb
(Magazine, Vol. 4)
Eerie, 1972

1-5 .... 25.00

Tales from the Tomb
(Magazine, Vol. 5)
Eerie, 1973

1-6 .... 20.00

Tales from the Tomb
(Magazine, Vol. 6)
Eerie, 1974

1-6 .... 20.00

Tales from the Tomb
(Magazine, Vol. 7)
Eerie, 1975

1-3 .... 15.00

Tales from the Tube
Print Mint

1 .... 3.00

Tales of a
Checkered Man
D.W. Brubaker

1 .... 2.00

Tales of Asgard
Marvel, 1968

1 .... 30.00

Tales of Asgard
Marvel, 1984

1 .... 2.00

Tales of Beatrix Farmer
Mu, 1996

1 .... 3.00

Tales of Blue & Grey
Avalon

1 .... 3.00

Tales of Evil
Atlas-Seaboard, 1975

1 .... 9.00
2-3 .... 7.00

Tales of Ghost Castle
DC, 1975

1 .... 10.00
2-3 .... 9.00

Tales of G.I. Joe
Marvel, 1988

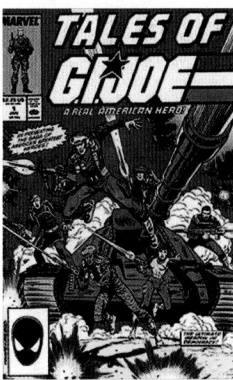

OK, who by now doesn't know that The G.I. Joes are a group of heroes who fight to save the world from the menace of COBRA? Each Joe is a master in a given specialty, from explosives to heavy weaponry. Operating from bases around the world, they are ever-vigilant, looking to stop the evil plans of COBRA Commander and his hired henchmen.

Originally, a line of Hasbro dolls (err -- maybe we should make that "action figures"), the Joes proved amazingly popular in both their television cartoon show and in the Marvel comic book series G.I. Joe, a Real American Hero. Tales of G.I. Joe reprints the first 15 issues of that series.

1-15..1.00

Tales of Horror
Toby, 1952

1...250.00
2...175.00
3-13......................................150.00

Tales of Jerry
Hacienda

1-10..3.00

Tales of Lethargy
Alpha

1-3...3.00

Tales of Ordinary Madness
Dark Horse, 2004

1-4...3.00

Tales of Screaming Horror
Fantaco, 1992

1...4.00

Tales of Sex and Death
Print Mint, 1971

1-2...3.00

Tales of Shaundra
Rip Off

1.. 13.00

Tales of Suspense
Marvel, 1959

Like many early Marvel titles, Tales of Suspense began as a collection of horror/science-fiction stories and eventually evolved into a super-hero title. Tales of Suspense made the big change in issue #39, when Stan Lee introduced Tony Stark, the billionaire inventor who would become Iron Man. An immediate hit, Iron Man soon joined the Avengers, becoming a key character in the Marvel Universe.

Beginning with issue #59, Tales of Suspense went to a double-feature format, co-starring Captain America in his first solo stories of the Silver Age. The issues that followed would be remembered as Marvel classics.

Following issue #99, Marvel decided to "graduate" these two characters to their own titles. Iron Man started over with issue #1 (after the bridging Iron Man and Sub-Mariner #1), and Captain America inherited Tales of Suspense's numbering sequence, starting with issue #100.

1 .... 1,400.00
2 .... 540.00
3 .... 475.00
4 .... 450.00
5-10 .... 325.00
11-20 .... 240.00
21-32 .... 150.00
33-38 .... 135.00
39 .... 3,500.00
☞1st Iron Man
40 .... 1,100.00
41 .... 650.00
42-45 .... 325.00
☞1st Crimson Dynamo
46-47 .... 210.00

48 .... 265.00
☞1st red/gold armor
49 .... 210.00
50 .... 155.00
51 .... 105.00
52 .... 140.00
53 .... 120.00
☞Watcher origin
54-56 .... 62.00
57 .... 170.00
☞Cap America appearance
58-59 .... 210.00
☞Cap stories start
60 .... 120.00
61-62 .... 82.00
63 .... 180.00
☞Bucky origin
64 .... 72.00
65-66 .... 125.00
☞Red Skull origin
67-70 .... 52.00
71-80 .... 42.00
81-99 .... 32.00

Tales of Suspense
Marvel, 1995

1 .... 7.00

Tales of Suspense: Captain America/ Iron Man
Marvel, 2005

1 .... 6.00

Tales of Tellos
Image, 2004

1-3 .... 4.00

Tales of Terror
Eclipse, 1985

1-13 .... 2.00

Tales of Terror Annual
E.C., 1951

1 .... 2,500.00
2 .... 2,000.00
3 .... 1,500.00

Tales of the Armorkins
Co. & Sons

1 .... 3.00

Tales of the Beanworld
Eclipse, 1985

1 .... 4.00
2-10 .... 3.00
11-19 .... 2.00
20-21 .... 3.00

Tales of the Closet
Hetric-Martin, 1987

1-8 .... 3.00

Tales of the Crimson Lion
Gary Lankford, 1987

1 .... 2.00

Tales of the Cyborg Gerbils
Harrier, 1987
1 .... 2.00

Tales of the Darkness
Image, 1998
1/2 .... 3.00
1/2/A 4.00
1-4 .... 3.00

Tales of the Fehnnik
Antarctic, 1995
1 .... 3.00

Tales of the Fehnnik
Radio, 1998
1 .... 3.00

Tales of the Great Unspoken
Top Shelf
1 .... 4.00

Tales of the Green Beret
Dell, 1967
1 .... 25.00
2-5 .... 18.00

Tales of the Green Berets
Avalon
1-7 .... 3.00

Tales of the Green Hornet
Now, 1990
1-2 .... 2.00

Tales of the Green Hornet
Now, 1992
1-4 .... 2.00

Tales of the Green Hornet
Now, 1992
1-3 .... 3.00

Tales of the Green Lantern Corps
DC, 1981
1 .... 2.00
2-3 .... 1.00
Ann 1 .... 2.00

Tales of the Jackalope
Blackthorne, 1986
1-7 .... 2.00

Tales of the Kung Fu Warriors
CFW, 1989
1-14 .... 2.00

Tales of the Legion
DC, 1984
314-324 .... 1.00
325 .... 2.00
326-354 .... 1.00
Ann 4-5 .... 2.00

Tales of the Mans
Skit
Ashcan 1 .... 1.00

Tales of the Marvels: Blockbuster
Marvel, 1995
1 .... 6.00

Tales of the Marvels: Inner Demons
Marvel, 1995
1 .... 6.00

Tales of the Marvels: Wonder Years
Marvel, 1995
1-2 .... 5.00

Tales of the Marvel Universe
Marvel, 1997
1 .... 3.00

Tales of the Mysterious Traveler
Charlton, 1956
1 .... 220.00
2 .... 170.00
3 .... 135.00
4-5 .... 115.00
6-10 .... 92.00
11-13 .... 80.00
14-15 .... 3.00

Tales of the Mysterious Traveler
Eclipse
1 .... 3.00

Tales of the New Teen Titans
DC, 1982
1 .... 2.00
2-4 .... 1.00

Tales of the Ninja Warriors
CFW, 1988
1-16 .... 2.00

Tales of the Sun Runners
Sirius, 1986
1-3 .... 2.00

Tales of the Teenage Mutant Ninja Turtles
Mirage, 1987
1 .... 3.00
2-7 .... 2.00

Tales of the Teenage Mutant Ninja Turtles
Mirage, 2004
1-5 .... 3.00

Tales of the Teen Titans
DC, 1984
41-42 .... 2.00

43 .... 3.00
44 .... 6.00
45-59 .... 2.00
60-91 .... 1.00
Ann 4 .... 2.00

Tales of the Unexpected
DC, 1956

From silly science-fiction tales to poignant fantasy stories, Tales of the Unexpected sought to serve up something for everyone. In the best DC fantasy tradition, this series showcased stories and art that inspired a generation of fiction writers.

The series became simply The Unexpected with #105, featuring artwork by horror master Bernie Wrightson, among others.

As the market for non-super-hero titles continued to dry up in the late 1970s, The Unexpected became home to House of Secrets and The Witching Hour features.

-- Rob Salkowitz

1 .... 750.00
2 .... 385.00
3 .... 275.00
4-5 .... 225.00
6-10 .... 165.00
11-20 .... 125.00
21-30 .... 100.00
31-39 .... 85.00
40 .... 650.00
☛Space Ranger starts
41-42 .... 275.00
43 .... 450.00
☛Space Ranger cover
44-45 .... 200.00
46-50 .... 150.00
51-55 .... 125.00
56-60 .... 100.00
61-70 .... 85.00
71-74 .... 60.00
75-82 .... 50.00
83-90 .... 30.00
91-100 .... 22.00
101-104 .... 20.00
☛Becomes Unexpected

Tales of the Unexpected
DC, 2006
1-3 ....4.00

Tales of the Vampires
Dark Horse, 2003
1-5 ....3.00

Tales of the Witchblade
Image, 1996
1/2 ....4.00
1/2/A 8.00
1/2/Gold 5.00
1-1/Gold 3.00
1/Platinum 5.00
2-9 ....3.00
Deluxe 1 ....15.00

Tales of the Zombie
Marvel, 1973
1 ....25.00
2 ....18.00
3-5 ....15.00
6-10 ....10.00
Ann 1 ....15.00

Tales of Toad
Print Mint, 1970
1 ....20.00
2-3 ....15.00

Tales of Torment
Mirage, 2004
1 ....3.00

Tale Spin
Disney, 1991
1-7 ....2.00

Tale Spin Limited Series
Disney, 1991
1-4 ....2.00

Talespin
Disney
1 ....4.00

Tales Sleepy Hollow:
The Lost Chronicles of
"I Hunt Monsters"
Antarctic, 2005
1 ....3.00

Tales to Astonish
Marvel, 1959
1 ....2,000.00
2 ....635.00
3-5 ....440.00
6-10 ....355.00
11-20 ....265.00
21-26 ....200.00
27 ....3,600.00
☞1st Hank Pym
28-34 ....175.00
35 ....1,900.00
☞1st Ant-Man
36 ....625.00
37-40 ....350.00
41-43 ....230.00

44 ....500.00
☞1st Wasp
45-48 ....150.00
49 ....250.00
☞1st Giant Man
50-56 ....95.00
57 ....125.00
☞Spider-Man appearance
58 ....95.00
59 ....150.00
☞Giant-Man vs. Hulk
60 ....175.00
☞Hulk stories start
61 ....75.00
62 ....90.00
☞1st Leader
63-65 ....75.00
66-69 ....70.00
70 ....100.00
☞Namor stories start
71-81 ....55.00
82 ....78.00
☞Iron Man appearance
83-90 ....55.00
91 ....52.00
☞Silver Surfer appearance
92-93 ....75.00
☞Silver Surfer appearance
94-99 ....50.00
100 ....75.00
101 ....85.00

Tales to Astonish
Marvel, 1979
1-14 ....2.00

Tales to Astonish
Marvel, 1994
1 ....7.00

Tales to Offend
Dark Horse, 1997
1 ....3.00

Tales Too Terrible to Tell
NEC, 1990

According to the editor, nobody on staff at New England Comics expected to make a dime off a 76-page comic book sporting a $2.95 cover price. But money apparently wasn't the issue. This was a labor of love: a tribute to the pre-Code horror comics of the 1950s. E.C.'s contemporaries -- smaller companies that went out of business years ago and whose material has now become public domain -- originally published the stories reprinted within these pages.

Also featured are a cover gallery and "terrology": a short history of pre-Code horror comics, compliments of the editor and staff at NEC.

1 ....3.00
1/2nd-7 ....4.00

Taleweaver
WildStorm, 2001
1 ....4.00
2-6 ....3.00

Talismen: SCSI Voodoo
Blink
1-3 ....3.00

Talk Dirty
Fantagraphics, 1992
1-3 ....3.00

Talking Orangutans
in Borneo
GT-Labs, 1999
1 ....4.00

Tall Tails
Golden Realm, 1993
1-2 ....2.00
3-7 ....3.00

Tally-Ho Comics
Bailey, 1944
1 ....350.00

Talonz
Stop Dragon, 1987
1 ....2.00

Talos of the
Wilderness Sea
DC, 1985
1 ....2.00

Tammas
Pandemonium, 1986
1 ....2.00

Tangent Comics/
Doom Patrol
DC, 1997
1 ....3.00

Tangent Comics/
Green Lantern
DC, 1997
1 ....3.00

Tangent Comics/JLA
DC, 1998
1 ....2.00

Tangent Comics/ Metal Men
DC, 1997
1 ....3.00

Tangent Comics/ Nightwing
DC, 1997
1 ....3.00

Tangent Comics/ Nightwing: Night Force
DC, 1998
1 ....2.00

Tangent Comics/ Powergirl
DC, 1998
1 ....2.00

Tangent Comics/Sea Devils
DC, 1997
1 ....3.00

Tangent Comics/Secret Six
DC, 1997
1 ....3.00

Tangent Comics/Tales of the Green Lantern
DC, 1998
1 ....2.00

Tangent Comics/ The Atom
DC, 1997
1 ....3.00

Tangent Comics/ The Batman
DC, 1998
1 ....2.00

Tangent Comics/ The Flash
DC, 1997
1 ....3.00

Tangent Comics/ The Joker
DC, 1997
1 ....3.00

Tangent Comics/ The Joker's Wild
DC, 1998
1 ....2.00

Tangent Comics/ The Superman
DC, 1998
1 ....2.00

Tangent Comics/ The Trials of the Flash
DC, 1998
1 ....2.00

Tangent Comics/ Wonder Woman
DC, 1998
1 .... 2.00

Tangents
NBM
1 .... 17.00

Tangled Web
Marvel, 2001
1-22 .... 3.00

Tank Girl
Dark Horse, 1991
1 .... 4.00
2-4 .... 3.00

Tank Girl 2
Dark Horse, 1993

Tank Girl is not the sweet, little, freckle-faced cherub from next door. She's sort of the ultimate tomboy, with a shaven head, "bollocks to that!" attitude, and a multi-ton piece of advanced armament, courtesy of the Australian military.

Hewlett and Martin's heroine is back in this second Tank Girl compilation, along with friends Jet Girl, Sub Girl, and assorted stuffed animals. In a series of weird adventures, they escape from a mental institute (where the authorities try to revert them to childhood and inject them with lemonade), deal with the resignation of their artist creators, and more.

Tank Girl originally appeared in the pages of Britain's Deadline magazine.

1-4 .... 3.00

Tank Girl: Apocalypse
DC, 1995
1-4 .... 2.00

Tank Girl Movie Adaptation
DC
1 .... 6.00

Tank Girl: The Odyssey
DC, 1995
1-4 .... 3.00

Tank Vixens
Antarctic, 1994
1-4 .... 3.00

Tantalizing Stories
Tundra, 1992
1-5 .... 2.00
6 .... 3.00

TaoLand
Sumitek, 1994
1 .... 2.00
2-5 .... 6.00

TaoLand Adventures
Antarctic, 1999
1-2 .... 4.00

Tap
Promethean, 1994
1-3 .... 3.00

Tapestry
Superior Junk, 1994
1-5 .... 2.00

Tapestry Anthology
Caliber, 1997
1 .... 3.00

Tapping the Vein
Eclipse
1 .... 8.00
2-3 .... 7.00
4-5 .... 8.00

Target: Airboy
Eclipse, 1988
1 .... 2.00

Target Comics
Novelty, 1940
1 .... 3,500.00
2 .... 1,650.00
3-4 .... 1,100.00
5 .... 3,100.00
6 .... 1,450.00
7 .... 3,300.00
8-9 .... 1,100.00
10 .... 1,375.00
11 .... 1,200.00
12 .... 1,100.00
13 .... 615.00
14 .... 585.00
15-24 .... 500.00
25-34 .... 450.00
35-36 .... 95.00
37-48 .... 68.00
49-56 .... 56.00
57-66 .... 50.00
67-90 .... 45.00
91-102 .... 38.00
103-105 .... 32.00

Target: The Corruptors
Dell, 1962
2-3 ....25.00

Target Western Romances
Star, 1949
106 ....200.00
107 ....175.00

Targitt
Atlas-Seaboard, 1975
1 ....9.00
2 ....8.00
3 ....7.00

Tarot Cafe
Tokyopop, 2005
1-4 ....10.00

Tarot: Witch of the Black Rose
Broadsword, 2000
1 ....5.00
2-29 ....3.00
29/Variant 4.00
30 ....3.00
30/Variant 20.00
31 ....3.00
31/Deluxe 20.00
31/Photo 15.00
32 ....3.00
32/Variant 5.00
33-55 ....3.00
33/Deluxe 20.00

Tarzan
Dell, 1948

This Tarzan series spanned several decades, beginning with Dell's Tarzan #1, published in 1948, then moving to Dell's Gold Key label 13 years later, and finally to DC.

Dell's run of Tarzan was probably the truest to Edgar Rice Burroughs' original vision of the character. A white baby, raised by apes, Tarzan eventually became the jungle's lord and protector. In this series, he had not yet met future love interest Jane, although he did have a kid sidekick, simply called "Boy." For the most part, his

adventures centered around fending off poachers, aiding his friends among the tribes, and stopping various plots launched by both white hunters and black tribesmen.

Many issues of this series included a backup storyline, "Brothers of the Spear," a buddy-comic starring white Dan-El (Daniel) and Natongo, an African. These two friends embarked on adventures exploring the mysterious jungle.

1 .... 900.00
2 .... 525.00
3-5 .... 385.00
6-9 .... 290.00
10 .... 260.00
11 .... 235.00
12-15 .... 220.00
16-20 .... 160.00
21-30 .... 135.00
31-54 .... 80.00
55-70 .... 50.00
71-79 .... 42.00
80-99 .... 30.00
100 .... 40.00
101-110 .... 28.00
111-120 .... 25.00
121-131 .... 20.00

Tarzan
Gold Key, 1962
132-154 .... 14.00
155 .... 18.00
156-162 .... 10.00
163-164 .... 8.00
165 .... 10.00
166-167 .... 8.00
168 .... 10.00
169-170 .... 8.00
171 .... 10.00
172-200 .... 7.00
201-206 .... 6.00

Tarzan
DC, 1972
207 .... 17.00
208 .... 10.00
209-210 .... 6.00
211-229 .... 4.00
230-235 .... 8.00
236-258 .... 3.00

Tarzan
Marvel, 1977
1 .... 3.00
1/35¢ 15.00
2-2/Whitman 2.00
2/35¢ 15.00
3 .... 2.00
3/35¢ 15.00
4 .... 2.00
4/35¢ 15.00
5 .... 2.00
5/35¢ 15.00
6-29 .... 2.00
Ann 1 .... 3.00
Ann 2-3 .... 2.00

Tarzan
Dark Horse, 1996
1-20 .... 3.00

Tarzan (Disney's...)
Dark Horse, 1999
1-2 .... 3.00

Tarzan and the Jewels of Opar (Edgar Rice Burroughs'...)
Dark Horse, 1999
1 .... 11.00

Tarzan: A Tale of Mugambi (Edgar Rice Burroughs'...)
Dark Horse, 1995
1 .... 3.00

Tarzan/Carson of Venus
Dark Horse, 1998
1-4 .... 3.00

Tarzan Digest
DC, 1972
1 .... 3.00

Tarzan Family
DC, 1975
60-61 .... 5.00
62-66 .... 4.00

Tarzan/John Carter: Warlords of Mars
Dark Horse, 1996
1-4 .... 3.00

Tarzan, Lord of the Jungle
Gold Key, 1965
1 .... 40.00

Tarzan: Love, Lies and the Lost City
Malibu, 1992
1-3 .... 4.00

Tarzan of the Apes
Marvel, 1984
1-2 .... 3.00

Tarzan of the Apes (Edgar Rice Burroughs'...)
Dark Horse, 1999
1 .... 13.00

Tarzan's Jungle Annual
Dell, 1952
1 .... 100.00
2 .... 75.00
3-7 .... 55.00

Tarzan: The Beckoning
Malibu, 1992
1-7 .... 3.00

Tarzan: The Lost Adventure (Edgar Rice Burroughs'...)
Dark Horse, 1995
1-4 ....3.00

Tarzan: The Rivers of Blood (Edgar Rice Burroughs'...)
Dark Horse, 1999
1-4 ....3.00

Tarzan: The Savage Heart
Dark Horse, 1999
1-4 ....3.00

Tarzan The Warrior
Malibu, 1992
1-5 ....3.00

Tarzan vs. Predator at the Earth's Core
Dark Horse, 1996
1-4 ....3.00

Tarzan Weekly
Byblos
1 ....5.00

T.A.S.E.R.
Comicreations, 1992
1-2 ....2.00

Task Force One
Image, 2006
1-4 ....4.00

Taskmaster
Marvel, 2002

This limited series from Udon Studios and Marvel Comics fleshes out the character of the Taskmaster, the Avengers foe who can mimic the skills and abilities of, well, anybody. Essentially, he's a criminal-for-hire, and he's been double crossed by Sunset Bain, the woman who hired him to break into Stark Labs. He wants answers, and he will have them, along with the million dollars he was promised for pulling the job, one way or another. It's good, old-fashioned anti-hero fun in the Mighty Marvel Manner!

1-4 .... 3.00

Tasmanian Devil and His Tasty Friends
Gold Key, 1962
1 .... 75.00

Tastee-Freez Comics
Harvey, 1957
1-6 .... 25.00

Tasty Bits
Avalon, 1999
1 .... 3.00

Tattered Banners
DC, 1998
1-4 .... 3.00

Tattoo
Caliber
1-2 .... 3.00

Tattoo Man
Fantagraphics
1 .... 3.00

Taxx
Express
1/2 .... 2.00
1 .... 3.00

T-Bird Chronicles
Me Comix
1-2 .... 2.00

Team 7
Image, 1994
1-4 .... 3.00
Ashcan 1 .... 1.00

Team 7: Dead Reckoning
Image, 1996
1-4 .... 3.00

Team 7: Objective: Hell
Image, 1995
1-3 .... 3.00

Team America
Marvel, 1982
1-12 .... 1.00

Team Anarchy
Dagger, 1993
1-7 .... 3.00

Team Nippon
Aircel, 1989
1-7 .... 2.00

Team One: Stormwatch
Image, 1995
1-2 .... 3.00

Team One: WildC.A.T.S
Image, 1995
1-2 .... 3.00

Team Superman
DC, 1999
1 .... 3.00

Team Superman Secret Files
DC, 1998
1 .... 5.00

Team Titans
DC, 1992
1/A 4.00
1/B-1/E 3.00
2-24 .... 2.00
Ann 1 .... 4.00
Ann 2 .... 3.00

Team X
Marvel, 1999
2000 .... 4.00

Team X/Team 7
Marvel, 1997
1 .... 5.00

Team Yankee
First, 1989
1-6 .... 2.00

Team Youngblood
Image, 1993
1-9 .... 2.00
10 .... 3.00
11 .... 2.00
12-22 .... 3.00

Team Zero
DC, 2006
1-6 .... 3.00

Tears
Boneyard, 1992
1-2 .... 3.00

Teaser and the Blacksmith
Fantagraphics
1 .... 4.00

Tech High
Virtually Real Enterprises, 1996
1-3 .... 3.00

Tech Jacket
Image, 2003
1-6 .... 3.00

Techno Maniacs
Independent
1 .... 2.00

Technopolis
Caliber
1-4 .... 3.00

Technopriests
DC, 2004
1 .... 15.00

Teddy Roosevelt and His Rough Riders
Avon, 1950
1 ....125.00

Teen-Age Brides
Home, 1953
1...40.00
2...25.00
3-7..20.00

Teen-Age Confidential Confessions
Charlton, 1960
1...20.00
2...12.00
3-5..10.00
6-9..8.00
10-22.......................................6.00

Teen-Aged Dope Slaves and Reform School Girls
Eclipse
1...10.00

Teen-Age Diary Secrets
St. John, 1949
4...150.00
5-9.......................................125.00

Teenage Hotrodders
Charlton, 1963
1...35.00
2-10.......................................20.00
11-24......................................15.00

Teen-Age Love
Charlton, 1958
4...30.00
5...16.00
6-10.......................................14.00
11-20..9.00
21-30..7.00
31-50..5.00
51-70..4.00
71-96..2.00

Teenage Mutant Ninja Turtles
Mirage, 1984

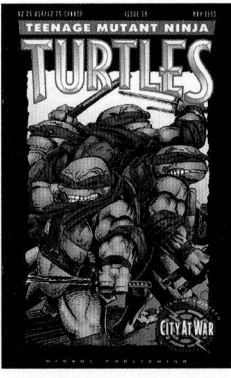

Kevin Eastman and Peter Laird set out to do what amounted to a

parody of the work of Frank Miller, whose work was brilliant, distinctive, and popular. So they combined two Miller concepts — his work on Marvel's Daredevil and his work on DC's Ronin. They then extrapolated from what had happened during the event that had created Daredevil in the first place: the drum of radioactive material striking Matt Murdock and blinding him in the street. What happened to that radioactive material? asked Eastman and Laird. Why, it drained into the sewer and affected the turtles that had been flushed there. And what did they get? "Teenage Mutant Ninja Turtles"! They could never have expected that their joke would develop a cult of devoted fans and attract the attention of a merchandiser, eventually turning them into an international phenomenon.

The Turtles: Donatello, Raphael, Michelangelo, and Leonardo, along with their rat sensei Splinter, became one of the hottest tickets in town. Stars of stage, screen, and countless comics (including this, the original), they combine humor and action in a way that appeals to young children and hip intellectuals.

1 .... 300.00
1/Counterfeit........................... 2.00
1/2nd 15.00
1/3rd 8.00
1/4th 4.00
1/5th 3.00
2 .... 28.00
2/Counterfeit........................... 2.00
2/2nd 6.00
2/3rd 3.00
2/4th 4.00
3-3/Misprint 15.00
3/2nd 3.00
4 .... 12.00
4/2nd 2.00
5 .... 4.00
5/2nd 2.00
6 .... 3.00
6/2nd 2.00
7 .... 5.00
7/2nd 2.00
8 .... 4.00
9-10.. 3.00
11 .... 4.00
12-15..................................... 3.00
16-62..................................... 2.00

Teenage Mutant Ninja Turtles
Mirage, 1993
1-13....................................... 3.00
Special 1 .... 4.00

Teenage Mutant Ninja Turtles
Image, 1996
1 .... 4.00
2-23....................................... 3.00

Teenage Mutant Ninja Turtles Adventures
Archie, 1988
1-3... 3.00

Teenage Mutant Ninja Turtles Adventures
Archie, 1989
1-3... 3.00
4-72....................................... 2.00
Special 5 .... 3.00
Special 6 .... 2.00

Teenage Mutant Ninja Turtles Adventures
Archie, 1996
1-3... 2.00

Teenage Mutant Ninja Turtles Animated
Dreamwave, 2003
1-7... 3.00

Teenage Mutant Ninja Turtles Authorized Martial Arts Training Manual
Solson, 1986
1-4... 3.00

Teenage Mutant Ninja Turtles Classics Digest
Archie, 1993
1-8... 2.00

Teenage Mutant Ninja Turtles/Flaming Carrot Crossover
Mirage, 1993
1-4... 3.00

Teenage Mutant Ninja Turtles III The Movie: The Turtles are Back... In Time
Archie
1 .... 3.00
1/Prestige 5.00

Teenage Mutant Ninja Turtles II: The Secret of the Ooze
Mirage
1 .... 6.00

Teenage Mutant Ninja Turtles Meet the Conservation Corps
Archie
1 .... 3.00

Teenage Mutant Ninja Turtles Michaelangelo Christmas Special
Mirage, 1990

1 ....2.00

Teenage Mutant Ninja Turtles Movie II
Archie, 1991

1 ....3.00

Teenage Mutant Ninja Turtles Mutant Universe Sourcebook
Archie, 1993

1-3 ....2.00

Teenage Mutant Ninja Turtles Present: April O'Neil
Archie, 1993

1-3 ....1.00

Teenage Mutant Ninja Turtles Presents: Donatello and Leatherhead
Archie, 1993

1-3 ....1.00

Teenage Mutant Ninja Turtles Presents Merdude and Michaelangelo
Archie, 1993

1-3 ....1.00

Teenage Mutant inja Turtles-Savage Dragon Crossover
Mirage, 1995

1 ....3.00

Teenage Mutant Ninja Turtles: The Movie
Archie, 1990

1 ....3.00
1/Direct 5.00
1/Prestige 6.00

Teenage Mutant Ninja Turtles: The Movie (Mirage)
Mirage, 1990

1 ....6.00

Teenagents (Jack Kirby's...)
Topps, 1993

1-4 ....3.00

Teen-Age Romance
Atlas, 1960

77-81 ....15.00

Teen-Age Romance
Marvel, 1961

82-86 ....20.00

Teen-Age Romances
St. John, 1949

1 .... 250.00
2-3 .... 160.00
4-8 .... 150.00
9 .... 160.00
10-12 .... 145.00
13-22 .... 160.00
23-30 .... 125.00
31-45 .... 105.00

Teen-Age Temptations
St. John, 1952

1 .... 250.00
2-9 .... 125.00

Teen Comics
Marvel, 1947

22-23 .... 55.00
24 .... 60.00
25 .... 55.00
26 .... 60.00
27 .... 55.00
28 .... 60.00
29 .... 55.00
30 .... 60.00
31-35 .... 55.00

Teen Comics
Personality, 1992

1-6 .... 3.00

Teen Confessions
Charlton, 1959

1 .... 75.00
2 .... 40.00
3-10 .... 30.00
11-30 .... 25.00
31 .... 125.00
32-50 .... 20.00
51-58 .... 15.00
59 .... 20.00
60-97 .... 12.00

Teenie Weenies
Ziff-Davis, 1951

10-11 .... 125.00

Teens at Play
Fantagraphics, 2004

1 .... 5.00

Teen Tales: The Library Comic
David G. Brown, 1997

1 .... 1.00

Teen Titans
DC, 1966

1 .... 260.00
2 .... 100.00
3-5 .... 40.00
6-10 .... 32.00
11-17 .... 28.00
18-22 .... 33.00
23-25 .... 18.00
26-30 .... 12.00
31 .... 20.00
☛Giant-sized
32-38 .... 18.00
39-43 .... 12.00
44-47 .... 7.00
48 .... 12.00
☛1st Harlequin
49 .... 7.00
50 .... 20.00
☛Batgirl returns
51-53 .... 6.00

Teen Titans
DC, 1996

1 .... 4.00
2-10 .... 3.00
11 .... 2.00
12 .... 3.00
13-24 .... 2.00
Ann 1 .... 4.00
Ann 1999 .... 5.00

Teen Titans
DC, 2003

1/2 .... 16.00
1 .... 12.00
1/2nd 5.00
1/3rd 4.00
1/4th 8.00
2-15 .... 3.00
16 .... 5.00
17 .... 4.00
18-19 .... 3.00
20 .... 4.00
☛Identity Crisis tie
21-41 .... 3.00
Ann 1 .... 12.00

Teen Titans Go!
DC, 2003

1-12 .... 2.00
13-14 .... 3.00
15-38 .... 2.00

Teen Titans/ Legion Special
DC, 2004

1 .... 4.00

Teen Titans/ Outsiders Secret Files
DC, 2003

1 .... 6.00

Teen Titans/Outsiders Secret Files 2005
DC, 2005

1 .... 5.00

Teen Titans Spotlight
DC, 1986

1-21 .... 1.00

Tekken Forever
Image, 2001

1/A-1/B 3.00

Tek Knights
Artline

1 .... 3.00

Tekno*Comix Handbook
Tekno, 1996

1 .... 4.00

Teknophage (Neil Gaiman's...)
Tekno, 1995
1	2.00
1/Variant	3.00
2-10	2.00

Teknophage versus Zeerus
Big, 1996
1	3.00

TEKQ
Gauntlet
1-4	3.00

Tekworld
Marvel, 1992
1	3.00
2-24	2.00

Telepathic Wanderers
Tokyopop, 2005
1	10.00

Television Comics
Standard, 1950
5	45.00
6-8	35.00

Television Puppet Show
Avon, 1950
1	100.00
2	75.00

Tell It to the Marines
Toby, 1952
1	135.00
2	90.00
3-5	68.00
6-7	58.00
8-11	50.00
12-15	40.00

Tellos
Image, 1999
1-4/A	3.00
4/B	4.00
5-10	3.00
Ashcan 1	2.00

Tellos: Maiden Voyage
Image, 2001
1	6.00

Tellos: Sons & Moons
Image, 2002
1	6.00

Tellos: The Last Heist
Image, 2001
1	6.00

Telltale Heart
Mojo
1	5.00

Tell Tale Heart and Other Stories
Fantagraphics
1	3.00

Telluria
Zub
1-3	3.00

Tempest
DC, 1996

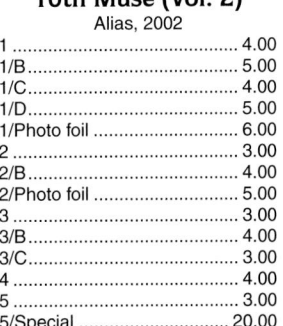

This mini-series explains how Garth -- formerly Aqualad, the protege of Aquaman and a member of the Teen Titans -- received his elemental powers and mystic abilities.

Garth, who has been a member of the DC universe since the Silver Age, steps out of the shadow of his mentor, as Atlan, Aquaman's long-absent father, reveals his ancestry. During a battle with rogue warriors in Garth's birth-city, Atlan is spirited away in a mysterious vortex along with the silent soldiers, leaving many unanswered questions. Left behind is what appears to be Tula, Garth's lost love, who was killed during the Crisis on Infinite Earths.

-- George Haberberger

1-4	2.00

Template
Head, 1995
0-Special 1	3.00
Spec 1/Ashcan	1.00
Special 1/Varia	3.00

Temple Snare
Mu
1	2.00

Temptress: The Blood of Eve
Caliber
1	3.00

Tempus Fugitive
DC, 1990
1-4	5.00

Tenchi Muyo!
Pioneer, 1997
1-6	3.00

Tender Love Stories
Skywald, 1971
1	15.00
2-4	10.00

Tender Romance
Key, 1953
1	100.00
2	60.00

Tense Suspense
Fago, 1958
1	55.00
2	40.00

Tenth
Image, 1997
0	3.00
∫	5.00
1	3.00
1/A	4.00
2-4	3.00

Tenth
Image, 1997
0	3.00
0/A	8.00
1	3.00
2-3/A	3.00
3/B	8.00
4-14/A	3.00

Tenth
Image, 1999
1-1/A	3.00
1/B	10.00
2-4	3.00

Tenth
Image, 1999
1	3.00
1/A	6.00
1/B-4	3.00

Tenth Configuration
Image, 1998
1	3.00

10th Muse
Image, 2000
1-9/B	3.00

10th Muse (Vol. 2)
Alias, 2002

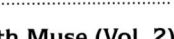

1	4.00
1/B	5.00
1/C	4.00
1/D	5.00
1/Photo foil	6.00
2	3.00
2/B	4.00
2/Photo foil	5.00
3	3.00
3/B	4.00
3/C	3.00
4	4.00
5	3.00
5/Special	20.00
6-8	3.00

Tenth, The: Resurrected
Dark Horse, 2001
1/A-4 ....3.00

Ten Years of
Love & Rockets
Fantagraphics, 1992
1..2.00

Terminal City
DC, 1996
1..3.00
2-9...3.00

Terminal City:
Aerial Graffiti
DC, 1997
1-5..3.00

Terminal Point
Dark Horse, 1993
1-3..3.00

Terminator
Now, 1988
1-17...2.00

Terminator
Dark Horse, 1990
1-4..3.00

Terminator
Dark Horse, 1991
1..3.00

Terminator
Dark Horse, 1998
1-4..3.00

Terminator (Magazine)
Trident
1-4..3.00

Terminator 2:
Judgment Day
Marvel, 1991
1-3..2.00

Terminator 2: Judgment
Day (Magazine)
Marvel, 1991
1..3.00

Terminator 3
Beckett, 2003
1-6..6.00

Terminator, The:
All My Futures Past
Now, 1990
1-2..3.00

Terminator: Endgame
Dark Horse, 1992
1-3..3.00

Terminator:
Hunters and Killers
Dark Horse, 1992
1-3..3.00

Terminator, The:
One Shot
Dark Horse, 1991
1 .... 6.00

Terminator:
Secondary Objectives
Dark Horse, 1991
1-4 .... 3.00

Terminator, The:
The Burning Earth
Now, 1990
1 .... 8.00
2-3... 5.00
4-5 .... 6.00

Terminator, The:
The Dark Years
Dark Horse, 1999
1-4 .... 3.00

Terminator, The:
The Enemy Within
Dark Horse, 1991
1-4 .... 3.00

Terraformers
Wonder Color, 1987
1-2 .... 2.00

Terranauts
Fantasy General, 1986
1 .... 2.00

Terra Obscura
DC, 2003
1-5 .... 3.00
6 .... 4.00

Terra Obscura (Vol. 2)
DC, 2004
1-6 .... 3.00

Terrarists
Marvel, 1993
1-4 .... 3.00

Terrific Comics
Continental, 1944
1 .... 3,500.00
2-3 .... 2,000.00
4 .... 3,600.00
5 .... 4,500.00
6 .... 1,800.00

Terrific Comics
Ajax, 1954
14 .... 200.00
16 .... 150.00

Terrifying Tales
Star, 1953
11 .... 350.00
12 .... 310.00
13 .... 350.00
14-15 .... 275.00

Territory
Dark Horse, 1999
1-4 .... 3.00

Terror
Leadslinger, 1991
1 .... 3.00

Terroress
Helpless Anger, 1990
1 .... 3.00

Terror Illustrated
E.C., 1955
1 .... 100.00
2 .... 75.00

Terror, Inc.
Marvel, 1992
1-13 .... 2.00

Terror on the
Planet of the Apes
Adventure, 1991

The "Planet of the Apes" movies told the compelling tale of a future where apes had gained intelligence, and had risen up to wrest control of the world from the humans who used to keep them as pets. The movies that embodied this vision were so successful that a total of five "Planet of the Apes" movies were eventually made.

Now, Terror on the Planet of the Apes takes the adventure one step further. Following years of fighting, small enclaves of men and apes have begun to learn to live together in peace. But old hatreds and fears are not easily put aside. The Lawgiver, who had long been a stabilizing influence in the village suddenly leaves on an unexplained mission into the Forbidden Zone. The militant ape leader, Brutus, decides the time is right for a revival of the old evils of racism and hatred-and in a horrific parallel to our own history, he organizes a band of hooded riders to bring terror and death to the humans.

1-4 .... 3.00

Terrors of the Jungle
Star, 1952

17	525.00
18	385.00
19-21	345.00
4-10	300.00

Terror Tales
Eternity, 1991

1	3.00

Terry and the Pirates
Avalon

1-2	3.00

Terry and the Pirates Comics
Harvey, 1947

3	285.00
4	160.00
5	100.00
6-10	65.00
11-20	55.00
21-25	45.00
26-28	28.00

Terry-Bears Comics
St. John, 1952

1	55.00
2-3	35.00

Terry-Toons Comics
Timely, 1942

1	1,025.00
2	380.00
3-5	255.00
6-10	200.00
11-20	125.00
21-37	85.00
38	700.00
39	250.00
40-50	110.00
51-59	70.00

Terry-Toons Comics
St. John, 1947

60	70.00
61-71	60.00
72-83	55.00
84-86	48.00

Terry-Toons Comics
Pines, 1952

1	110.00
2	55.00
3-9	50.00

Tessie the Typist
Marvel, 1944

1	325.00
2	190.00
3	60.00
4-8	125.00
9-13	138.00
14-23	40.00

Testament
DC, 2006

1-13	3.00

Test Dirt
Fantagraphics

1	3.00

Test Drive
M.A.I.N.

1	3.00

Texan
St. John, 1948

1	100.00
2	75.00
3	65.00
4-10	50.00
11	75.00
12	85.00
13-15	50.00

Texas Chainsaw Massacre
DC, 2007

1-2	3.00

Texas Kid
Leading, 1951

1	95.00
2	60.00
3-5	50.00
6-10	40.00

Texas Rangers in Action
Charlton, 1956

5	30.00
6-7	22.00
8	32.00
9-10	22.00
11	36.00
12	16.00
13	28.00
14-20	16.00
21-30	12.00
31-40	9.00
41-50	7.00
51-60	5.00
61-70	4.00
71-79	2.00

Tex Benson
3-D Zone

1-2	3.00

Tex Benson
Metro

1-4	2.00

Tex Dawson, Gunslinger
Marvel, 1973

1	12.00

Tex Farrell
D.S., 1948

1	75.00

Tex Granger
Parents' Magazine Institute, 1948

18	55.00
19	45.00
20-24	35.00

Tex Morgan
Marvel, 1948

1	150.00
2	105.00
3-6	60.00
7-9	105.00

Tex Ritter Western
Charlton, 1950

1	375.00
2	230.00
3	100.00
4-5	72.00
6-10	55.00
11-20	40.00
21	22.00
22	40.00
23-30	22.00
31-46	20.00

Tex Taylor
Marvel, 1948

1	175.00
2	90.00
3	80.00
4-6	95.00
7-9	110.00

Teykwa
Gemstone, 1988

1	2.00

Thacker's Revenge
Explorer

1	3.00

Thane of Bagarth
Avalon

1	3.00

Thanos
Marvel, 2003

1	4.00
2-12	3.00

Thanos Quest
Marvel, 1990

1-2/2nd	5.00
Special 1	4.00

That Chemical Reflex
CFD

1-3	3.00

That Wilkin Boy
Archie, 1969

Ever eager to meet the demands of readers across America clamoring for more Archie products, Archie Comics launched

Meet Bingo, That Wilkin Boy at the tail end of the 1960s. Similar in style but more contemporary in sensibility than the '50s-oriented Archie gang, Bingo Wilkin was a typical teen of the 1970s suburbs. The stories revolved almost exclusively around his clownish efforts to pry his eager young girlfriend Samantha from the grip of her psychotic, overprotective father. Of most interest to today's retro-'70s fans are the wardrobe, vocabulary, cars, and numerous pop-culture references, which rival the Partridge Family for sheer, unmitigated shtik value. When the dawn of the Reagan era cast its light over all that was '70s, That Wilkin Boy vanished from the stands.

-- *Rob Salkowitz*

1	15.00
2	9.00
3-5	6.00
6-10	5.00
11	4.00
12-20	6.00
21-26	5.00
27-30	4.00
31-52	3.00

THB
Horse, 1994

1	12.00
1/2nd	6.00
2	10.00
3-4	8.00
5-6	6.00
69	5.00

T.H.E. Cat
Gold Key, 1967

1	12.00
2-4	10.00

TheComicStore.com Presents
TheComicStore.com

1	1.00

There's a Madman in My Mirror
Bench, 1999

1	4.00

Thespian
Dark Moon, 1995

1	3.00

They Call Me...The Skul
Virtual, 1996

1	3.00
1/A	4.00
2	3.00

They Came from the '50s
Eternity

1	10.00

They Were 11
Viz

1-4	3.00

They Were Chosen to be the Survivors
Spectrum, 1983

1-4	2.00

Thief
Penguin Palace, 1995

1	3.00

Thief of Sherwood
A-Plus

1	2.00

Thieves
Silverwolf, 1986

1	2.00

Thieves & Kings
I Box, 1994

1	4.00
1/2nd-3	3.00
3/2nd	2.00
4-20	3.00
21-24	2.00
25-36	3.00

Thing
Marvel, 2006

1-8	3.00

Thing
Charlton, 1952

1	735.00
2-4	585.00
5-9	540.00
10-14	390.00
15-17	295.00

Thing
Marvel, 1983

1	6.00
2-10	2.00
11-13	1.00
14	2.00
15-36	1.00

Thing: Freakshow
Marvel, 2002

1-4	3.00

Thing from Another World
Dark Horse, 1993

1-4	3.00

Thing From Another World: Climate of Fear
Dark Horse, 1994

1-4	3.00

Thing From Another World, The: Eternal Vows
Dark Horse, 1993

1-4	3.00

Thing/She-Hulk: The Long Night
Marvel, 2002

1	3.00

3rd Degree
NBM

1	3.00

Third Eye (Dark One's...)
Sirius, 1998

1-2	5.00

Third World War
Fleetway-Quality

1-6	3.00

Thirteen
Dell, 1961

Thirteen (subtitled "...Going on Eighteen") targeted a young, female audience. The main character is Val, a 13-year-old girl who lives with her family, including an older sister whom she strives to emulate. Val's best friend is a heavy-set girl named Judy, who's down-to-earth and sometimes comes up with the right advice to solve Val's many troubles.

Each issue contains several short stories about the wacky situations in which the girls find themselves. If Val isn't trying to wear makeup too soon or trying to date the grocery delivery boy, she is thinking up ways to make her friend, Stu, stop following her. In some, Judy has a story of her own.

The series was created by longtime Little Lulu artist-writer John Stanley, and it's not an intellectual leap to consider Val an older Lulu.

1	35.00
2	24.00
3-4	20.00
5-10	18.00
11-25	14.00
26-29	8.00

13:
Assassin Comics Module
TSR

1-8..2.00

13 Days of Christmas,
The: A Tale of the
Lost Lunar Bestiary
Sirius

1......................................3.00

Thirteen O'Clock
Dark Horse

1......................................3.00

Thirteen Something!
Global

1......................................2.00

13th Son:
Worse Thing Waiting
Dark Horse, 2005

1-4......................................3.00

30 Days of Night
Idea & Design Works, 2002

1......................................55.00
1/2nd...................................7.00
2......................................25.00
3......................................10.00
Ann 2004...............................5.00

30 Days of Night:
Bloodsucker Tales
Idea & Design Works, 2004

1......................................4.00
2-7....................................4.00
8......................................3.00

30 Days of Night:
Dead Space
Idea & Design Works, 2006

1......................................4.00
2-3....................................4.00

30 Days of Night:
Return to Barrow
Idea & Design Works, 2004

1......................................12.00
1/2nd..................................4.00
2......................................8.00
3......................................5.00
4-6....................................4.00

Dark Days: A 30 Days
of Night Sequel
Idea & Design Works, 2003

1......................................8.00
2......................................5.00
3-6....................................4.00

30 Days of Night:
Spreading the Disease
Idea & Design Works, 2006

1......................................4.00

39 Screams
Thunder Baas, 1986

1-6.. 2.00

32 Pages
Sirius, 2001

1... 3.00

This Is Heat
Aeon

1... 3.00

This Is Not an Exit
Draculina

1-2.. 3.00

This Is Sick!
Silver Skull

1-2.. 3.00

This Is Suspense
Charlton, 1955

23 .... 145.00
24 .... 75.00
25-26 .... 45.00

This is War
Standard, 1952

5 .... 100.00
6 .... 75.00
7-9 .... 50.00

This Magazine
Is Haunted
Fawcett, 1951

1 .... 350.00
2 .... 265.00
3 .... 200.00
4-5 .... 175.00
6-8 .... 150.00
9 .... 125.00
10 .... 200.00
11-12 .... 125.00
13 .... 200.00
14 .... 125.00
15 .... 100.00
16 .... 225.00
17 .... 250.00
18 .... 225.00
19 .... 215.00
20 .... 100.00
21 .... 200.00

This Magazine is
Haunted (2nd Series)
Charlton, 1957

12-14 .... 300.00
15-16 .... 200.00

Thor
Marvel, 1966

In Journey into Mystery #83, Dr. Don Blake discovered the cane that transformed him into Thor, the Asgardian god of thunder -- and readers would come to know that Odin had banished his prideful son into Blake's oblivious form. Armed with his mystical uru hammer Mjolnir, Thor battled foes on Earth and in Asgard, and made Journey into Mystery his own title in 1966.

Jack Kirby's work remains the most memorable part of the series early years, with Walter Simonson's reinterpretation reinvigorating the title in the 1980s. It's a title that often needed reinvigorating, with a dull alter ego for Thor and such overworn polot devices as Thor losing his hammer and turning back into Blake. In the mid-1990s, while Thor was off in "Heroes Reborn," the series returned to being Journey Into Mystery, Vol. 1 -- there had been a Volume 2 in between!

-- JJM

126 .... 125.00
127-140 .... 45.00
141-160 .... 32.00
161-164 .... 25.00
165 .... 40.00
☞Warlock app.
166 .... 36.00
167 .... 24.00
☞Galactus origin
168-169 .... 36.00
☞Galactus origin
170-177 .... 20.00
178-179 .... 18.00
180 .... 24.00
☞Thor vs. Mephisto
181 .... 23.00
182-192 .... 12.00
193 .... 55.00
☞Silver Surfer appearance
194-199 .... 12.00

200 ....16.00
201-205 ....9.00
206-224 ....7.00
225 ....14.00
☛1st Firelord
226 ....7.00
227-246 ....5.00
246/30¢ 20.00
247 ....5.00
247/30¢ 20.00
248 ....5.00
248/30¢ 20.00
249-260/Whitman 5.00
260/35¢ 15.00
261-261/Whitman 5.00
261/35¢ 15.00
262-262/Whitman 5.00
262/35¢ 15.00
263-263/Whitman 5.00
263/35¢ 15.00
264-264/Whitman 5.00
264/35¢ 15.00
265-299 ....3.00
300 ....8.00
301-336 ....2.00
337 ....7.00
☛1st Beta Ray Bill
338 ....3.00
339 ....5.00
340 ....4.00
341 ....3.00
342 ....4.00
343-348 ....2.00
349 ....3.00
350-373 ....2.00
374 ....3.00
375-400 ....2.00
401-410 ....1.00
411 ....3.00
412 ....2.00
413-431 ....1.00
432-433 ....2.00
434-449 ....1.00
450 ....3.00
451-473 ....1.00
474-475 ....2.00
475/Variant 3.00
476-481 ....2.00
482 ....3.00
483-499 ....2.00
500 ....3.00
501-502 ....2.00
Ann 2 ....65.00
Ann 2/2nd 3.00
Ann 3 ....12.00
Ann 4 ....10.00
Ann 5-6 ....8.00
Ann 7 ....7.00
Ann 8 ....6.00
Ann 9-12 ....4.00
Ann 13-19 ....3.00

Thor
Marvel, 1998

1 ....5.00
1/A 20.00
1/B 5.00
1/C 6.00
1/D 8.00
1/E 5.00

2-2/A 3.00
3-11 ....2.00
12 ....3.00
12/DF 15.00
13-25 ....2.00
25/Gold 5.00
26-31 ....2.00
32 ....4.00
33-34 ....2.00
35 ....3.00
36-61 ....2.00
62-79 ....3.00
80 ....28.00
☛Avengers Disassembled
81 ....5.00
82-84 ....4.00
85 ....3.00
Ann 1999-2001 ....4.00

Thor
Marvel, 2007

1 ....3.00
1/Suydam-1/Zombie 7.00
1/2nd 4.00
1/3rd-2 ....3.00
2/Dell Otto 5.00
2/2nd-14 ....3.00

Thor Battlebook
Marvel, 1998

1 ....4.00

Thor: Blood Oath
Marvel, 2005

1-6 ....3.00

Thor Corps
Marvel, 1993

1-4 ....2.00

Thorion of the New Asgods
Marvel, 1997

1 ....2.00

Thorr-Sverd
Vincent

1-3 ....1.00

Thor: Son of Asgard
Marvel, 2004

1-12 ....3.00

Thor: The Legend
Marvel, 1996

1 ....4.00

Thor: Vikings
Marvel, 2003

1-5 ....4.00

Those Annoying Post Bros.
Vortex, 1994

1 ....3.00
2-18 ....2.00
39-48 ....3.00
Ann 1 ....5.00

Those Crazy Peckers
U.S.Comics, 1987

1 ....2.00

Those Magnificent Men In Their Flying Machines
Gold Key, 1965

1 ....25.00

Those Unstoppable Rogues
Original Syndicate, 1995

1 ....4.00

Those Who Hunt Elves
ADV Manga, 2003

1 ....10.00

Thrax
Event, 1996

1-2 ....3.00

Threat!
Fantagraphics, 1986

1-10 ....2.00

Three
Invincible

1-4 ....2.00

3-D Action
Atlas, 1954

1 ....250.00

3-D Adventure Comics
Stats Etc., 1986

1 ....2.00

3-D Alien Terror
Eclipse, 1986

1 ....3.00

3-D Dolly
Harvey, 1953

1 ....175.00

3-D-ell
Dell, 1953

1 ....265.00
2-3 ....190.00

3-D Exotic Beauties
3-D Zone, 1990

1 ....4.00

3-D Heroes
Blackthorne

1 ....3.00

3-D Hollywood
3-D Zone

1 ....3.00

Three Dimensional Adventures
DC

1 ....900.00
1/2nd 3.00

Three Dimensional E.C. Classics
E.C., 1954

1 ....550.00

Three Dimension Comics
St. John, 1953

1 ....100.00

2-3 .... 80.00

3-D Sheena, Jungle Queen
Real Adventures, 1953
1 .... 325.00
4-5 .... 250.00

3-D Space Zombies
3-D Zone
1 .... 4.00

3-D Substance
3-D Zone
1 .... 3.00
2 .... 4.00

3-D Tales of the West
Atlas, 1954
1 .... 250.00

3-D Three Stooges
Eclipse
1-3 .... 3.00

3-D True Crime
3-D Zone, 1992
1 .... 4.00

3-D Zone
3-D Zone, 1986
1-20 .... 3.00

.357!
Mu, 1990
1 .... 3.00

3 Geeks
3 Finger Prints, 1997
1-7 .... 3.00
8 .... 4.00
9-11 .... 3.00

300
Dark Horse, 1998
1-2 .... 4.00
3-4 .... 3.00
5 .... 4.00

3 Little Kittens: Purr-Fect Weapons (Jim Balent's...)
Broadsword, 2002
1-3/A 3.00

Three Mouseketeers
DC, 1956
1 .... 140.00
2 .... 58.00
3-10 .... 50.00
11-26 .... 40.00

Three Mouseketeers (2nd series)
DC, 1970
1 .... 35.00
2-4 .... 18.00
5-7 .... 22.00

Three Musketeers
Eternity, 1988
1-3 .... 2.00

Three Musketeers
Marvel, 1993
1-2 .... 2.00

3 Ninjas Kick Back
Now, 1994
1-3 .... 2.00

303
Avatar, 2004
0 .... 1.00
1 .... 5.00
☛Garth Ennis series
1/Wraparound 10.00
2 .... 4.00
2/Platinum 10.00
2/Wraparound-3 .... 4.00
3/Wraparound 5.00
4 .... 4.00
4/Wraparound 5.00
5 .... 4.00
5/Incentive 7.00
5/Wraparound 4.00

Three Stooges
Jubilee, 1949
1 .... 700.00
2 .... 500.00

Three Stooges
St. John, 1953
1 .... 400.00
2 .... 300.00
3 .... 275.00
4-7 .... 200.00

Three Stooges
Gold Key, 1961
6 .... 65.00
7 .... 48.00
8-10 .... 40.00
11-20 .... 28.00
21-30 .... 22.00
31-40 .... 18.00
41-55 .... 15.00

Three Stooges in 3-D
Eternity
1 .... 4.00

Three Stooges in Full Color
Eternity
1 .... 6.00

Three Stooges Meet Hercules
Dell, 1962
1 .... 75.00

3x3 Eyes
Innovation, 1991
1 .... 3.00
2-5 .... 2.00

3x3 Eyes: Curse of the Gesu
Dark Horse, 1995
1-5 .... 3.00

3x3 Eyes: Descent of the Mystic City
Dark Horse, 2004
1 .... 19.00

Threshold
Sleeping Giant, 1996
1-2 .... 3.00

Threshold
Sleeping Giant, 1997
1-3 .... 3.00

Threshold (3rd Series)
Avatar, 1998
1-50 .... 5.00

Threshold of Reality
Maintech, 1986
1-3 .... 1.00

Threshold: The Stamp Collector
Sleeping Giant, 1997
1-2 .... 3.00

Thriller
DC, 1983
1-12 .... 2.00

Thrilling Adventure Stories
Atlas-Seaboard, 1975
1 .... 18.00
2 .... 25.00

Thrilling Adventure Strips
Dragon Lady, 1986
5-10 .... 3.00

Thrilling Comics
Better, 1940
1 .... 2,000.00
2 .... 800.00
3 .... 650.00
4-10 .... 500.00
11-18 .... 425.00
19 .... 500.00
☛1st American Crusader
20 .... 425.00
21-30 .... 350.00
31-40 .... 310.00
41 .... 700.00
☛Hitler cover
42-52 .... 270.00
53-70 .... 225.00
71-80 .... 90.00

Thrilling Comics
DC, 1999
1 .... 2.00

Thrilling Crime Cases
Star Publications, 1950
41 .... 140.00
42-45 .... 65.00
46-48 .... 55.00
49 .... 200.00

Thrilling Romances
Standard, 1949
5 ....60.00
6-8......................................40.00
9-10....................................45.00
11-26..................................40.00

Thrilling Science Fiction
Paragon
1 ....10.00

Thrilling Science Tales
AC
1-2.......................................4.00

Thrilling True Story of the Baseball Giants
Fawcett, 1952
1 ....425.00

Thrilling True Story of the Baseball Yankees
Fawcett, 1952
1 ....400.00

Thrilling Wonder Tales
AC, 1991
1 ....3.00

Thrill Kill
Caliber
1 ....3.00

Thrillkiller
DC, 1997
1 ....3.00
2-3..3.00

Thrillkiller '62
DC, 1998
1 ....5.00

Thrillogy
Pacific, 1984
1 ....2.00

Thrill-O-Rama
Harvey, 1965
1 ....25.00
2 ....16.00
3 ....14.00

Thrills of Tomorrow
Harvey, 1954
17 ....80.00
18 ....65.00
19-20..................................195.00

Through Gates of Splendor
Spire, 1974
1 ....8.00

Thumb Screw
Caliber
1-3..4.00

Thump'n Guts
Kitchen Sink, 1993
1 ....3.00

Thun'da Comics
Magazine Enterprises, 1952
1 ....850.00

---

2 ....165.00
3 ....135.00
4-6.......................................95.00

Thun'Da, King of the Congo
AC
1 ....3.00

Thun'da Tales (Frank Frazetta's...)
Fantagraphics, 1986
1 ....2.00

T.H.U.N.D.E.R.
Solson
1 ....2.00

THUNDER Agents
Tower, 1965
1 ....140.00
2 ....75.00
3-5...55.00
6-8...42.00
9-10.......................................35.00
11-15......................................38.00
16-19......................................22.00
20 ....15.00

T.H.U.N.D.E.R. Agents
J.C., 1983
1-2..2.00

Thunder Agents (Wally Wood's)
Deluxe, 1984
1-5..2.00

Thunderbolt
Charlton, 1966
1 ....16.00
51 ....10.00
52-60.......................................9.00

Thunderbolt and Jaxon
DC, 2006
1-5..3.00

Thunderbolts
Marvel, 1997

The disappearance of The Avengers and The Fantastic Four due to Onslaught left the citizens of New York concerned about who would protect them from the villains that seem to infect the city. Into the breach came The Thunderbolts, six new heroes professing to take up the mantle for their fallen comrades. They were: Atlas, Mach-1, Meteorite, Songbird, and Techno, and their leader, Citizen V. The Thunderbolts first appeared in The Incredible Hulk #449, where they bravely engaged the gamma ray-spawned monster.

Debuting to the acclaim of the media and the populace by rousting a band of scavengers called The Rat Pack, and then soundly defeating The Wrecking Crew, the city government sought to give them an official sanction and whatever assistance they need. There is no doubt that The Thunderbolts seem to be exactly what New York needs. But things are not always what they seem...

-1 ....2.00
0 ....1.00
1 ....4.00
2-5...3.00
6-11...2.00
12 ....6.00
13-24.......................................2.00
25 ....3.00
26-49.......................................2.00
50 ....3.00
51-76.......................................2.00
77-78.......................................3.00
79-81.......................................2.00
100 ....4.00
101-102...................................3.00
103 ....8.00
104-109...................................3.00
110-140...................................5.00
Ann 1997-Ashcan 1 ....3.00

Thunderbolts: Life Sentences
Marvel, 2001
1 ....4.00

Thunderbunny
Archie, 1984
1 ....2.00

Thunderbunny
Warp, 1985
1-12...2.00

Thundercats
Marvel, 1985
1 ....4.00
2-24...2.00

Thundercats/ Battle of the Planets
DC, 2003
1 ....5.00

Thundercats: Dogs of War
DC, 2003
1 ....3.00

Thundercats:
Enemy's Pride
DC, 2004
1-5 ....3.00

Thundercats:
Hammerhand's Revenge
DC, 2003
1-5 ....3.00

Thundercats Origins:
Heroes & Villains
DC, 2004
1 ....4.00

Thundercats Origins:
Villains & Heroes
DC, 2004
1 ....4.00

Thundercats:
Reclaiming Thundera
DC, 2003
1 ....13.00

Thundercats: The Return
DC, 2003
1-5 ....3.00

ThunderCats
(DC/WildStorm)
DC, 2002
0-5 ....3.00

Thunder Girls
Pin & Ink, 1997
1-3 ....3.00

Thundergod
Crusade, 1996
1-3 ....3.00

Thundermace
Rak, 1986
1-7 ....2.00

Thundersaurs: The
Bodacious Adventures
of Biff Thundersaur
Innovation
1 ....2.00

Thunderskull!
(Sidney Mellon's...)
Slave Labor, 1989
1 ....2.00

Thunderstrike
Marvel, 1993
1 ....3.00
2-8 ....1.00
9-13 ....2.00
13/A 3.00
14 ....2.00
14/A 3.00
15 ....2.00
15/A 3.00
16 ....2.00
16/A 3.00
17-24 ....2.00

Tick
NEC, 1988
1 .... 15.00
1/2nd-1/3rd................... 3.00
1/4th 2.00
1/5th 3.00
2 .... 8.00
2/Variant..................... 15.00
2/2nd 3.00
2/3rd-2/4th................... 2.00
2/5th 3.00
3 .... 6.00
3/2nd-3/4th................... 3.00
4 .... 8.00
4/2nd 2.00
4/3rd-4/5th................... 3.00
5 .... 8.00
5/2nd 3.00
6 .... 5.00
6/2nd-6/3rd................... 3.00
7 .... 5.00
7/2nd-7/3rd................... 3.00
8-8/Variant................... 8.00
8/2nd-12 .... 3.00
12/Ltd. 20.00
13 .... 4.00
Special 1 .... 50.00
Special 2 .... 25.00

Tick & Arthur
NEC, 1999
1 .... 4.00

Tick & Artie
NEC, 2002
1/A-1/B 4.00

Tick Big Blue Destiny
NEC, 1997
1 .... 3.00
1/A 5.00
1/Ashcan 3.00
1/B 19.00
2-2/Variant................... 3.00
3-5 .... 4.00

Tick Big Red-n-Green
Christmas Spectacle
NEC, 2001
1 .... 4.00

Tick Big Summer Annual
NEC, 1999
1 .... 4.00

Tick, The:
Circus Maximus
NEC, 2000
1-4 .... 4.00

Tick: Days of Drama
New England, 2005
1 .... 5.00

Tick, The:
Heroes of the City
NEC, 1999
1 .... 4.00

Tick Incredible
Internet Comic
NEC, 2001
1 .... 4.00

Tick, The:
Karma Tornado
NEC, 1993
1 .... 4.00
1/2nd 3.00
2 .... 4.00
2/2nd 3.00
3 .... 5.00
3/2nd 3.00
4 .... 5.00
4/2nd 5.00
5 .... 5.00
5/2nd 3.00
6 .... 4.00
6/2nd 3.00
7 .... 4.00
7/2nd 3.00
8 .... 4.00
8/2nd-9/2nd................... 3.00

Tick: Luny Bin Trilogy
NEC, 1998
0 .... 2.00
1-3 .... 4.00

Tick's Back
NEC, 1997
0 .... 3.00
0/A 5.00
0/B 8.00
0/C 10.00

Tick's Big Back
to School Special
NEC, 1998
1 .... 4.00

Tick's Big Cruise Ship
Vacation Special
NEC, 2000
1 .... 4.00

Tick's Big
Father's Day Special
NEC, 2000
1 .... 4.00

Tick's Big
Halloween Special
NEC, 1999
1 .... 4.00

Tick's Big
Mother's Day Special
NEC, 2000
1 .... 4.00

Tick's Big
Romantic Adventure
NEC, 1998
1 .... 3.00

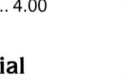

Tick's Big Summer Fun Special
NEC, 1998

1 ....4.00

Tick's Big Tax Time Terror
NEC, 2000

1 ....4.00

Tick's Big Year 2000 Special
NEC, 2000

1 ....4.00

Tick's Big Yule Log Special
NEC, 1997

1 ....4.00
2000/Ltd. 5.00
2001 ....4.00

Tick's Giant Circus of the Mighty
NEC, 1992

1-2...3.00

Tick's Golden Age Comic
NEC, 2002

1/A-2/B 5.00

Tick's Massive Summer Double Spectacle
NEC, 2000

1-2/B 4.00

Tick-Tock Follies
Slave Labor, 1996

1 ....3.00

Tick Tock Tales
Magazine Enterprises, 1946

1 ....75.00
2 ....40.00
3-10.......................................35.00
11-33.....................................30.00

Tic Toc Tom
Detonator Canada, 1995

1-3...3.00

Tiger
King, 1970

1 ....10.00
1/2nd 6.00
2 ....5.00
3-6...4.00

Tiger 2021
Anubis, 1994

Ashcan 1 ....4.00

Tiger Girl
Gold Key, 1968

1 ....35.00

Tigerman
Atlas-Seaboard, 1975

1 ....9.00
2-3...8.00

Tigers of Terra
Mind-Visions, 1990

1-8 ....3.00
9-12 ....4.00

Tigers of Terra
Antarctic, 1993

0-23 ....3.00
24 ....4.00
25 ....3.00

Tigers of Terra
Antarctic, 2000

1 ....3.00

Tigers of Terra: Technical Manual
Antarctic, 1995

1-2...3.00

Tiger Woman
Millennium, 1994

1-2...3.00

Tiger Woman, The: The Last Place on Earth
Caliber

1 ....3.00

Tiger-X
Eternity, 1988

1-3...2.00
Special 1-Special 1/2nd 2.00

Tiger-X Book II
Eternity, 1989

1-4...2.00

Tigra
Marvel, 2002

This four-issue mini-series spotlights the feisty were-woman Tigra, from the regular Avengers comic. The story follows Greer Nelson, a woman with the uncanny ability to transform into a tiger-like werewolf, albeit a sexy, sultry one as drawn by Mike Deodarto, Jr. Christina Z (long-time writer of Witchblade) combines elements of super-hero adventure, crime drama and psychological profile together in order to weave an interesting tale centered around Tigra's past. The mini-series succeeds in revealing heretofore, unknown facts about this current member of the Avengers. The mini-series is also highlighted with cameo appearances from some of her most famous teammates, including the Wasp and Captain America.

1-4 ....3.00

Tigress
Hero, 1992

1-5...3.00
6 ....4.00

Tigress
Basement, 1998

1 ....3.00

Tijuana Bible
Starhead, 1997

1-9...3.00

Tilazeus Meets the Messiah
Aiiie

1 ....3.00

Timber Wolf
DC, 1992

1-5...2.00

Time Bandits
Marvel, 1982

1 ....2.00

Time Breakers
DC, 1997

1-5...2.00

Time City
Rocket, 1992

1 ....3.00

Timecop
Dark Horse, 1994

1-2...3.00

Timedrifter (Gerard Jones'...)
Innovation, 1990

1-3...2.00

Time for Love
Charlton, 1967

1 ....7.00
2-5...5.00
6-10...4.00
11-30.......................................3.00
31-47.......................................2.00

Time Gates
Double Edge

1-3...2.00

Timejump War
Apple, 1989
1-3..2.00

Time Killers
Fleetway-Quality
1-7..3.00

Timeless Tales
(Bob Powell's...)
Eclipse, 1989
1..2.00

Timely Presents:
All-Winners
Marvel, 1999
1..4.00

Timely Presents:
Human Torch
Marvel, 1999
1..4.00

Time Machine
Eternity, 1990
1-3..3.00

Time Masters
DC, 1990

This mini-series was a post-Crisis on Infinite Earths updating of the Silver Age character Rip Hunter, Time Master. Co-written by Bob Wayne and science-fiction novelist Lewis Shiner, it featured Rip and his team battling The Illuminati, a centuries-old, ultimate secret society behind any number of conspiracy theories, to prevent an upcoming nuclear war. It included cameos by other DC universe heroes, including Superman, and the leader of the Illuminati was a long-time DC villain.

While intended to define time travel and its limitations in the post-Crisis universe, many of those aspects were quickly ignored, such as the one-time-trip-per-person method of time travel. The post-

Crisis Rip Hunter had previously appeared in Booster Gold, and there was suspicion that The Linear Man (from Superman and Zero Hour) named Hunter was in fact an older Rip Hunter.

1-8..2.00

Time Out of Mind
Graphic Serials
1-3..2.00

Timeslip Collection
Marvel, 1998
1..3.00

Timeslip Special
Marvel, 1998
1..6.00

Timespell
Club 408 Graphics, 1997
0-4..3.00
Ashcan 1..1.00

Timespell:
The Director's Cut
Club 408 Graphics, 1998
1..3.00

Timespirits
Marvel, 1984
1-8..2.00

Time Traveler Ai
CPM Manga, 1999
1-6..3.00

Time Traveler Herbie
Avalon
1..3.00

Time Tunnel
Gold Key, 1967
1..40.00
2..35.00

Time Twisted Tales
Rip Off
1..2.00

Time Twisters
Fleetway-Quality
1-21..2.00

Timewalker
Acclaim, 1995
0..5.00
1..2.00
1/VVSS..75.00
2-3..1.00
4-15..2.00
YB 1..3.00

Time Wankers
Fantagraphics, 1991
1-5..2.00

Time Warp
DC, 1979
1..4.00
2-5..2.00

Time Warrior
Blazing, 1993
1..3.00

Time Warriors:
The Beginning
Fantasy General
1..2.00

Tim Holt
Magazine Enterprises, 1948
1..350.00
2..175.00
3..130.00
4-5..95.00
6..155.00
7-10..90.00
11..220.00
12-19..72.00
20..95.00
21-30..58.00
31-41..48.00

Tim Holt
Western Annual
AC
1..3.00

Tim McCoy
Charlton, 1947
16..275.00
17-21..225.00

Timmy the Timid Ghost
(1st Series)
Charlton, 1956
3..36.00
4-10..20.00
11-20..18.00
21-45..10.00

Timmy the Timid Ghost
(2nd Series)
Charlton, 1967
1..10.00
2-10..6.00
11-26..4.00

Tim Tyler
Standard, 1948
11..40.00
12-18..30.00

Tincan Man
Image, 1999
1-Ashcan 1..3.00

Tiny Deaths
YUGP, 1997
1-2..2.00

Tiny Tessie
Marvel, 1949
24 ....50.00

Tiny Toon Adventures
DC, 1994
1-7...2.00

Tiny Tot Comics
E.C., 1946
1 ....225.00
2 ....155.00
3-5 ....125.00
6-10 ....100.00

Tipper Gore's Comics and Stories
Revolutionary, 1989
1-5...2.00

Tippy Teen
Tower, 1965
1 ....25.00
2 ....14.00
3 ....8.00
4-5 ....6.00
6-27 ....5.00

Tip Top Comics
St. John, 1936
1 ....7,200.00
2 ....2,400.00
3 ....1,600.00
4-5 ....1,000.00
6-10 ....760.00
11-20 ....560.00
21-30 ....350.00
31-40 ....250.00
41-50 ....200.00
51-60 ....140.00
61-80 ....110.00
81-100 ....85.00
101-110 ....72.00
111-120 ....60.00
121-130 ....52.00
131-150 ....45.00
151-180 ....40.00
181-200 ....35.00
201-225 ....28.00

Tip-Topper Comics
United Features, 1949
1 ....45.00
2 ....30.00
3-5 ....25.00
6-10 ....15.00
11-28 ....14.00

Titan A.E.
Dark Horse, 2000
1-3...3.00

Titans
DC, 1999
1 ....3.00
2-24 ....3.00
25 ....4.00
26-50 ....3.00
Ann 1..4.00

Titans/Legion of Super-Heroes: Universe Ablaze
DC, 2000
1-4 .... 5.00

Titan Special
Dark Horse, 1994
1 .... 4.00

Titans: Scissors, Paper, Stone
DC, 1997
1 .... 5.00

Titans Secret Files
DC, 1999
1-2 .... 5.00

Titans Sell-Out! Special
DC, 1992
1 .... 4.00

Titans/Young Justice: Graduation Day
DC, 2003
1-3 .... 3.00

Tiyu
Express, 1996
1 .... 10.00

T-Man
Quality, 1951
1 .... 210.00
2 .... 110.00
3 .... 100.00
4-5 .... 105.00
6 .... 110.00
7-8 .... 100.00
9-10 .... 85.00
11 .... 65.00
12-13 .... 55.00
14 .... 65.00
15-19 .... 55.00
20 .... 70.00
21-26 .... 55.00
27-38 .... 50.00

T-Minus-1
Renegade, 1988
1 .... 2.00

TMNT Mutant Universe Sourcebook
Archie
1-2 .... 2.00

TMNT: Teenage Mutant Ninja Turtles
Mirage, 2001
1-9 .... 3.00
10 .... 4.00
11-18 .... 3.00

To Be Announced
Strawberry Jam, 1986
1-7 .... 2.00

Today's Brides
Ajax, 1955
1 .... 45.00

2-4 .... 30.00

Today's Romance
Standard, 1952
5 .... 30.00
6 .... 24.00
7-8 .... 15.00

Todd Mcfarlane Presents: Kiss Psycho Circus
Image, 1998
1 .... 7.00
2-5 .... 5.00

Todd Mcfarlane Presents: Ozzy Osbourne
Image, 1999
1 .... 5.00

Todd McFarlane Presents: The Crow Magazine
Image, 2000
1 .... 5.00

To Die For
Blackthorne
1 .... 2.00
1/3D.. 3.00

Toe Tags Featuring George Romero
DC, 2004
1-6 .... 3.00

Toka
Dell, 1964
1 .... 25.00
2 .... 15.00
3-10 .... 10.00

Tokyo Babylon
Tokyopop, 2004
1 .... 10.00

Tokyo Boys & Girls
Viz, 2005
1-2 .... 9.00

Tokyo Mew Mew
Tokyopop, 2003
1 .... 10.00

TokyoPop (Vol. 3)
Mixx, 1999
1-7 .... 5.00

TokyoPop (Vol. 4)
Mixx, 2000
1-3 .... 5.00

Tokyo Storm Warning
DC, 2003
1-3 .... 3.00

Tokyo Tribes
Tokyopop, 2004
1-4 .... 10.00

Tomahawk
DC, 1950

Tomahawk made his first appearance in Star Spangled Comics #69. Adventures of Tomahawk and his sidekick, Dan Hunter, at the time of America's Revolutionary War were an immediate hit, and Tomahawk received his own series in 1950. In its 22-year run, Tomahawk and the Rangers starred in countless adventures, some of them (in Comics Code days) featuring dinosaurs, fantasy aliens, and the like.

The buckskin-clad Tom Hawk had been raised by Indians and used what he'd learned to fight the British. However, time finally caught up with him, and he settled down to a quiet life. His son, Hawk, took over the starring role in the series, and the cover bore the name Son of Tomahawk for the last 10 issues of its 140-issue run.

```
1 .........................................850.00
2 .........................................400.00
3-5 ......................................290.00
6-10 ....................................195.00
11-20 .................................125.00
21-27 .................................100.00
28 ........................................110.00
29 ........................................130.00
```
☛Frazetta art
```
30 ..........................................90.00
31-40 ...................................70.00
41-50 ...................................56.00
51-56 ...................................45.00
57 ..........................................85.00
```
☛Frazetta art
```
58-60 ...................................40.00
61-80 ...................................32.00
81-90 ...................................25.00
91-100 .................................15.00
101-110 ...............................10.00
111-120 .................................8.00
121-132 .................................6.00
133-140 .................................5.00
```

Tom & Jerry 50th Anniversary Special
Harvey, 1991
```
1 ................................................ 3.00
```

Tom & Jerry Adventures
Harvey, 1992
```
1 ................................................ 1.00
```

Tom & Jerry and Friends
Harvey, 1991
```
1-4 ............................................. 1.00
```

Tom & Jerry Big Book
Harvey, 1992
```
1-2 ............................................. 2.00
```

Tom & Jerry Comics
Dell, 1949
```
60 ............................................. 50.00
61-65 ....................................... 40.00
66-70 ....................................... 36.00
71-80 ....................................... 28.00
81-90 ....................................... 24.00
91-100 ..................................... 18.00
101-110 ................................... 14.00
111-120 ................................... 12.00
121-130 ..................................... 9.00
131-150 ..................................... 7.00
151-170 ..................................... 6.00
171-190 ..................................... 5.00
191-200 ..................................... 4.00
201-230 ..................................... 3.00
231-300 ..................................... 2.00
301-327 ..................................... 1.00
328-329 ..................................... 5.00
330 ......................................... 20.00
331-341 ..................................... 7.00
342-341 ................................... 15.00
```

Tom & Jerry
Harvey, 1991
```
1 ................................................ 2.00
2-8 ............................................. 1.00
9-Ann 1 ..................................... 2.00
```

Tom & Jerry Digest
Harvey, 1992
```
1 ................................................ 2.00
```

Tom & Jerry Giant Size
Harvey, 1992
```
1-2 ............................................. 2.00
```

Tom & Jerry Picnic Time
Dell, 1958
```
1 .............................................. 75.00
```

Tom & Jerry's Back to School
Dell, 1956
```
1 .............................................. 90.00
```

Tom & Jerry's Toy Fair
Dell, 1958
```
1 .............................................. 65.00
```

Tom & Jerry Summer Fun
Dell, 1954
```
1 ............................................ 100.00
```

```
2-4 ........................................ 50.00
```

Tom & Jerry Summer Fun
Gold Key, 1967
```
1 .............................................. 35.00
```

Tom & Jerry's Winter Fun
Dell, 1954
```
3 .............................................. 50.00
4-7 ........................................... 40.00
```

Tom & Jerry Winter Carnival
Dell, 1952
```
1 ............................................ 150.00
2 ............................................ 125.00
```

Tomato
Starhead, 1994
```
1-2 ............................................. 3.00
```

Tomb of Darkness
Marvel, 1974
```
9 .............................................. 20.00
```
☛Cont'd from Beware
```
10-20 ....................................... 10.00
20/30¢ ..................................... 20.00
21 ............................................ 10.00
21/30¢ ..................................... 20.00
22-23 ....................................... 10.00
```

Tomb of Dracula
Marvel, 1972

Vlad Dracula, who had been bloodthirsty in life, became more so in death. Born as a prince of Wallachia, he grew into a fierce warrior given to impaling his enemies on stakes. This cruel practice earned him the name "Vlad the Impaler." Eventually Dracula's army was defeated and he was mortally wounded. He was taken to a gypsy woman to be healed, but little did anyone know that, in reality, the woman was a vampire. Three days after his lifeless body was buried, Dracula rose again as a vampire.

Tomb of Dracula was a remarkable horror series which enjoyed a long and well-deserved run. Written by Marv Wolfman and featuring the distinctive art of Gene Colan, it was a great example of a horror comic book done right. The plots were dark but not obsessive, and the characters were well-developed. Ultimately, it was hard to know whether to cheer for Dracula's assailants or to hope he would triumph again to bring horror to next month's issue.

1	100.00
2-3	35.00
4	30.00
5-6	18.00
7	15.00
8-9	12.00
10	100.00
☛1st Blade	
11	10.00
12	12.00
13	35.00
☛Blade origin	
14	12.00
15-16	10.00
17	12.00
18	10.00
19	12.00
20-21	10.00
22-25	8.00
25/2nd	2.00
26-29	8.00
30	10.00
31-32	8.00
33-41	7.00
42-43	6.00
43/30¢	18.00
44	6.00
44/30¢	18.00
45	6.00
45/30¢	18.00
46	6.00
46/30¢	18.00
47	6.00
47/30¢	18.00
48-49	6.00
50	10.00
51-56	6.00
57-57/35¢	12.00
58	6.00
58/35¢	12.00
59	6.00
59/35¢	12.00
60	6.00
60/35¢	12.00
61-69	5.00
70	8.00

Tomb of Dracula
Marvel, 2004
1-4	3.00

Tomb of Dracula (Magazine)
Marvel, 1979
1	15.00
2-6	6.00

Tomb of Dracula
Marvel, 1991
1-4	5.00

Tomb of Ligeia
Dell, 1965
1	12.00

Tomb of Terror
Harvey, 1952
1	500.00
2-3	300.00
4-12	250.00
13-14	340.00
15	550.00
16	300.00

Tomb Raider: Arabian Nights
Image, 2004
1	6.00

Tomb Raider Cover Gallery
Image, 2006
1	3.00

Tomb Raider/ Darkness Special
Image, 2001
1	4.00
1/A	6.00

Tomb Raider: Epiphany
Image, 2003
1	5.00

Tomb Raider Gallery
Image, 2000
1	3.00

Tomb Raider: Greatest Treasure of All One Shot
Image
1	7.00

Tomb Raider: Journeys
Image, 2002
1-12	3.00

Tomb Raider Magazine
Image, 2001
1	5.00

Tomb Raider: Takeover One Shot
Image, 2003
1	3.00

Tomb Raider: The Series
Image, 1999
0	3.00
0/Dynamic	5.00
1/2-1/D	3.00
1/Holofoil	7.00
1/Another Unive	5.00
1/Tower Gold	6.00
1/Tower	5.00
2	3.00
2/Tower	5.00
2/Tower foil	7.00
3	3.00
3/Monster Mart	7.00
3/Gold Mart	125.00
4	3.00
4/Dynamic	4.00
4/Dynamic with	8.00
5	3.00
5/Dynamic	6.00
6-7	3.00
7/Museum	125.00
8-9	3.00
9/White	4.00
9/Dynamic	6.00
9/Dynamic blue	7.00
9/Sketch	10.00
10	3.00
10/Gold foil	12.00
10/Red foil	10.00
11	3.00
11/Graham	7.00
12	3.00
12/Graham	8.00
13-15	3.00
15/Dynamic	10.00
16-46	3.00
47	4.00
47/Variant	3.00
48	4.00
48/Variant-50	3.00
Ashcan 1	5.00

Tomb Raider/Witchblade
Image, 1997
1-1/A	6.00
1/B	20.00
1/2nd	3.00

Tomb Tales
Cryptic, 1997
1-2	3.00

Tom Corbett
Eternity, 1990
1-4	2.00

Tom Corbett Book Two
Eternity, 1990
1-4	2.00

Tom Corbett, Space Cadet
Dell, 1953
4-11	55.00

Tom Corbett, Space Cadet
Prize, 1955

1 ....200.00
2-3 ....140.00

Tom Judge: End of Days
Image, 2003

1 ....4.00

Tom Landry
Spire, 1973

1 ....3.00

Tommi Gunn
London Night, 1996

1 ....3.00

Tommi Gunn: Killer's Lust
London Night, 1997

1-1/Nude 3.00

Tom Mix
Ralston-Purina, 1940

1 ....2,500.00
2 ....1,250.00
3-9 ....800.00
10-11 ....500.00

Tom Mix Western
Fawcett, 1948

1 ....1,400.00
2 ....550.00
3-5 ....375.00
6-10 ....285.00
11-25 ....225.00
26-40 ....115.00
41-61 ....75.00

Tom Mix Western
AC

1-2 ....3.00

Tommy and the Monsters
New Comics

1 ....2.00

Tommy Looks At Farming
B.F. Goodrich, 1955

1 ....20.00

Tommy of the Big Top
Best, 1948

10 ....30.00
11-12 ....24.00

Tomoe
Crusade, 1996

0 ....3.00
0/Ltd. 4.00
0/Variant-1 ....3.00
1/Ltd. 4.00
1/2nd-3 ....3.00

Tomoe: Unforgettable Fire
Crusade, 1997

1 ....3.00
1/Ltd. 4.00

Tomoe/Witchblade: Fire Sermon
Crusade, 1996

1 ....4.00
1/A 5.00

Tomorrow Knights
Marvel, 1990

1-6 ....2.00

Tomorrow Man
Antarctic, 1993

1 ....3.00

Tomorrow Man & Knight Hunter: Last Rites
Antarctic, 1994

1-6 ....3.00

Tomorrow Stories
DC, 1999

1 ....4.00
1/Variant 6.00
2-12 ....3.00

Tomorrow Stories Special
DC, 2006

1-2 ....7.00

Tom Strong
DC, 1999

1 ....4.00
1/Variant 5.00
2-36 ....3.00

Tom Strong's Terrific Tales
DC, 2002

1 ....4.00
2-12 ....3.00

Tom Terrific
Pines, 1957

1 ....135.00
2-6 ....95.00

Tongue*Lash
Dark Horse, 1996

1-2 ....3.00

Tongue*Lash II
Dark Horse, 1999

1-2 ....3.00

Tony Bravado, Trouble-Shooter
Renegade, 1989

1-2 ....2.00
3-4 ....3.00

Tool & Die
Flashpoint, 1994

1 ....3.00

Too Much Coffee Man
Adhesive, 1993

A cult favorite, Too Much Coffee Man appeals to everyone who can get through the day only with the aid of heavy doses of hot, steaming, caffeine-in-a-cup. Too Much Coffee Man (TMCM to his fans) is a sort of heroic Everyman with a coffee habit and a huge cup of coffee for a hat. He can't leap tall buildings, run faster than a speeding bullet, or, for that matter, do any of the standard super-things. Still, he is ready to fly to Mars on a minute's notice, if the need arises: a positive mental attitude attributable to the power of caffeine.

Now if only he could shake that edgy, paranoid feeling.

Shannon Wheeler published the early adventures of TMCM in a series of mini-comics. Although scarcely four inches tall with only eight story pages, they packed a surprising amount of fun into their shrunken size. The series won the 1995 Eisner for Best New Series.

1 ....12.00
2 ....8.00
3 ....6.00
4-5 ....5.00
6-8 ....3.00
MC 1 ....10.00
MC 1/2nd 3.00
MC 2 ....8.00
MC 2/2nd 3.00
MC 3 ....8.00
MC 3/2nd 3.00
MC 4 ....6.00
MC 4/2nd-Special 2 ....3.00

Too Much Hopeless Savages
Oni, 2003

1-4 ....3.00

Toon Warz: The Fandom Menace
Sirius, 1999

1/A-1/D 3.00

Tooth and Claw
Image, 1999

1-3 .... 3.00
Ashcan 1 .... 2.00

Top 10
DC, 1999

1 .... 5.00
1/Variant 6.00
2-12 .... 3.00

Top Cat
Dell, 1961

1 .... 60.00
2 .... 35.00
3-5 .... 25.00
6-10 .... 20.00
11-20 .... 15.00
21-31 .... 12.00

Top Cat
Charlton, 1970

1 .... 20.00
2 .... 12.00
3-5 .... 8.00
6-10 .... 5.00
11-20 .... 4.00

Top Comics: Flintstones
Gold Key, 1967

1-2 .... 10.00
3-4 .... 15.00

Top Comics: Flipper
Gold Key, 1967

1 .... 10.00

Top Comics: Lassie
Gold Key, 1967

1 .... 10.00

Top Comics: Mickey Mouse
Gold Key, 1967

1-2 .... 10.00
3-4 .... 15.00

Top Comics: Tweety & Sylvester
Gold Key, 1967

1-2 .... 10.00

Top Comics: Yogi Bear
Gold Key, 1967

1 .... 16.00

Top Cow 2003 Compilation Special
Image, 2003

1 .... 3.00

Top Cow 2005 Preview Book
Top Cow, 2005

0 .... 1.00

Top Cow: Book of Revelation 2003
Image, 2003

1 .... 4.00

Top Cow Classics in Black and White: Aphrodite IX
Image, 2000

1 .... 3.00

Top Cow Classics in Black and White: Ascenscion
Image, 2000

1-1/A 3.00

Top Cow Classics in Black and White: Fathom
Image, 2000

1 .... 3.00

Top Cow Classics in Black and White: Magdalena
Image, 2002

1 .... 3.00

Top Cow Classics in Black and White: Midnight Nation
Image, 2001

1 .... 3.00

Top Cow Classics in Black and White: Rising Stars
Image, 2000

1 .... 3.00

Top Cow Classics in Black and White: The Darkness
Image, 2000

1 .... 3.00

Top Cow Classics in Black and White: Tomb Raider
Image, 2000

1 .... 3.00

Top Cow Classics in Black and White: Witchblade
Image, 2000

1 .... 3.00
1/A 5.00
25 .... 3.00

Top Cow Con Sketchbook 2004
Image, 2004

1 .... 3.00

Top Cow Productions Inc./Ballistic Studios Swimsuit Special
Image, 1995

1 .... 3.00

Top Cow Secrets
Image, 1996

WS 1 .... 3.00

Top Cow Special
Image

1 .... 3.00

Top Dog
Marvel, 1985

Top Dog is an adorable canine who was found by a boy named Joey. The two have since become the best of friends, but they also share a secret: Top Dog can talk! This is the sort of thing that could cause great controversy, so they have to pretend that Top Dog is just a regular dog, when they're around other people.

Joey and Top Dog share tons of fun and many adventures, in part because Top Dog is an expert at getting into trouble. On the other hand, he also has a way of winning people over and saving the day. Even Joey's bratty sister Liz will occasionally crack a smile when Top Dog comes to the rescue.

1-14 .... 1.00

Top Eliminator
Charlton, 1967

25-29 .... 10.00

Top Flight Comics
St. John, 1952

1 .... 60.00

Topix (Vol. 1)
Catechetical Guild, 1942

1 .... 225.00
2 .... 120.00
3 .... 90.00
4-8 .... 70.00

Topix (Vol. 2)
Catechetical Guild, 1943
1-10......................................55.00

Topix (Vol. 3)
Catechetical Guild, 1944
1-10......................................45.00

Topix (Vol. 4)
Catechetical Guild, 1945
1-10......................................36.00

Topix (Vol. 5)
Catechetical Guild, 1946
1-4..32.00
5..75.00
6-15......................................32.00

Topix (Vol. 6)
Catechetical Guild, 1948
4-14......................................30.00

Topix (Vol. 7)
Catechetical Guild, 1948
1-20......................................26.00

Topix (Vol. 8)
Catechetical Guild, 1949
1-30......................................26.00

Topix (Vol. 9)
Catechetical Guild, 1950
1-30......................................22.00

Topix (Vol. 10)
Catechetical Guild, 1951
1-15......................................20.00

Top Love Stories
Star, 1951
3..185.00
4-9......................................150.00
10-19..................................135.00

Top-Notch Comics
M.L.J., 1939
1......................................3,500.00
2......................................1,500.00
3......................................1,000.00
4..825.00
5..900.00
6-8......................................650.00
9......................................3,000.00
☛1st Black Hood
10....................................1,000.00
☛2nd Black Hood
11-15..................................625.00
16-20..................................550.00
21-30..................................425.00
31-45..................................250.00

Topps Comics Presents
Topps, 1993
0..2.00
1..1.00

Tops
Lev Gleason, 1949
1......................................1,100.00
2..900.00

Top Secret
Hillman, 1952
1 .... 150.00

Top Secrets
Street & Smith, 1947
1 .... 200.00
2-10 .... 125.00

Top Shelf
Primal Groove, 1995
1 .... 5.00

Top Shelf
Top Shelf, 1996
1-7 .... 7.00

Tops in Adventure
Ziff-Davis, 1952
1 .... 300.00

Top 10: Beyond the Farthest Precinct
DC, 2005
1-5 .... 3.00

Tor
DC, 1975
1 .... 8.00
2-6 .... 4.00

Tor
Marvel, 1993
1-4 .... 6.00

Tor 3-D
Eclipse, 1986
1-2 .... 3.00

Torch of Liberty Special
Dark Horse, 1995
1 .... 3.00

Torchy
Innovation, 1992
1-9 .... 3.00
Summer 1 .... 3.00

Torchy
Quality, 1949
1 .... 1,000.00
2-3 .... 405.00
4 .... 510.00
5-6 .... 640.00

Torg
Adventure, 1992
1-4 .... 3.00

Tori Do
Penguin Palace, 1994
1-1/2nd 2.00

To Riverdale and Back Again
Archie, 1990
1 .... 3.00

Tor Johnson: Hollywood Star
Monster
1 .... 3.00

Tor Love Betty
Fantagraphics, 1991
1 .... 3.00

Torment
Aircel
1-3 .... 3.00

Torpedo
Hard Boiled, 1993
1-4 .... 3.00

Torrid Affairs
Eternity, 1988
1-2/B..................................... 2.00
3-5 .... 3.00

Torso
Image, 1999

Mention the name "Eliot Ness," and most people of a certain age immediately think of The Untouchables. That's certainly understandable; after all, the saga of the war The Untouchables had with the mob is perhaps the best-known true-crime drama of the 20th century. However, Ness' career didn't end with the arrest of Al Capone; in fact, his most challenging and horrifying case came later in Cleveland circa 1935.

Headless torsos and other dismembered body parts began washing up in a concentrated area of Lake Erie. Most of the victims were transients or derelicts living in shantytowns. This story is a stylish recounting of one of the most fascinating, and forgotten, chapters in American crime history. Eliot Ness is about to experience something beyond his wildest dreams or his worst nightmares. A disconcerting chill moves down the spine when one realizes that the story is based on actual events. This series is intended for mature readers.

1-2 .... 4.00
3-6 .... 5.00

Tortoise and The Hare
Last Gasp
1 ....3.00

To See the Stars
NBM
1 ....14.00

Total Eclipse
Eclipse, 1988
1-5...4.00

Total Eclipse: The Seraphim Objective
Eclipse, 1988
1 ....2.00

Total Justice
DC, 1996
1-3...2.00

Totally Alien
Trigon
1-5...3.00

Totally Horses!
Painted Pony, 1997
1-5...2.00

Total Recall
DC, 1990
1 ....3.00

Total War
Gold Key, 1965
1 ....40.00
2 ....35.00

Totems
DC, 2000
1 ....6.00

Totems
Cartoon Frolics
1-3...3.00

Totem: Sign of the Wardog
Alpha Productions, 1991
1-2...2.00

Totem: Sign of the Wardog
Alpha Productions, 1992
1-2...3.00
Ann 1......................................4.00

Touch
DC, 2004
1-6...3.00

Touch of Silk, a Taste of Leather, A
Boneyard, 1994
1 ....3.00

Touch of Silver, A
Image, 1997
1-6... 3.00

Tough
Viz, 2005
1-4.. 10.00

Tough Guys and Wild Women
Eternity, 1989
1-2... 2.00

Tough Kid Squad
Timely, 1942
1 .... 7,500.00

Tower of Shadows
Marvel, 1969
1 .... 55.00
2-5..................................... 25.00
6-8..................................... 15.00
9 .... 8.00
Special 1 .... 22.00

Townscapes
DC, 2004
1 .... 18.00

Toxic!
Apocalypse
1-19...................................... 3.00

Toxic Avenger
Marvel, 1991

The Toxic Avenger is a hero for our polluted times. A lightning bolt and a barrel of toxic waste transformed nerdy Melvin Junko into a muscle-bound mass of walking sludge, a defender of the weak and defenseless. Now, with his trusty mop in hand, the Toxic Avenger is cleaning up his city, and there's a lot that needs to be cleaned up: environmentally, politically, and justice-wise. His mop wipes up much of it, though it surely doesn't hurt that Melvin's new body absorbs flying toxins -- like bullets -- without any effect.

Six years after Troma's release of the Lloyd Kaufman film whose promotional line read, "Melvin was a 90 lb. weakling until nuclear waste turned him into ... The Toxic Avenger," this Marvel series began.

1-11 .... 2.00

Toxic Crusaders
Marvel, 1992
1-8 .... 1.00

Toxic Gumbo
DC, 1998
1 .... 6.00

Toxic Paradise
Slave Labor
1 .... 5.00

Toxin
Marvel, 2005
1-6 .... 3.00

Toxine
Nose, 1991
1 .... 3.00

Toyboy
Continuity, 1986
1-7 .... 2.00

Toyland Comics
Fiction House, 1947
1 .... 200.00
2-3 .... 125.00

Toy Story (Disney's...)
Marvel, 1995
1 .... 5.00

Toytown Comics
Toytown, 1945
1 .... 150.00
2 .... 100.00
3-7 .... 75.00

Traci Lords: The Outlaw Years
Boneyard
1 .... 3.00

Tracker
Blackthorne, 1988
1-2 .... 2.00

Tragg and the Sky Gods
Whitman, 1975
1 .... 5.00
2-9 .... 3.00

Trail Blazers
Street & Smith, 1941
1 .... 170.00
2 .... 130.00
3-4 .... 120.00

Trailer Trash
Tundra, 1996
1 .... 2.00
4-8 .... 3.00

Trakk: Monster Hunter
Image, 2003
1-2..3.00

Tramps Like Us
Tokyopop, 2004
1-7..10.00

Tranceptor
NBM
1 ....12.00

Trancers
Eternity, 1991
1-2..3.00

Tranquility
Dreamsmith, 1998
1-3..3.00

Tranquilizer
Luxurious
1-2..3.00

Transformers
Marvel, 1984
1......................................10.00
2-3...5.00
4-20.......................................3.00
21-69......................................2.00
70-76......................................5.00
77-79....................................10.00
80 ....18.00

Transformers
Idea & Design Works, 2005
0-5..1.00

Transformers Animated Movie Adaptation
Idea & Design Works, 2006
1-3..4.00

Transformers: Armada
Dreamwave, 2002
1-7..3.00
7/A..4.00
8-18..3.00

Transformers Armada: More Than Meets the Eye
Dark Horse, 2004
1-3..5.00

Transformers: Beast Wars
Idea & Design Works, 2006
1-4..3.00

Transformers Comics Magazine
Marvel, 1987
1-10..2.00

Transformers: Energon
Dark Horse, 2004
19-30......................................3.00

Transformers: Escalation
Idea & Design Works, 2006
1-2.. 4.00

Transformers: Evolutions
Idea & Design Works, 2006
1-4... 3.00

Transformers/Gen13
Marvel
Ashcan 1 .... 1.00

Transformers: Generation 1
Dreamwave, 2002
1/Autobot-1/Decepticon.......... 4.00
1/Chromium........................... 6.00
1/2nd-1/3rd........................... 3.00
2/Autobot-2/Decepticon.......... 4.00
2/2nd-6/Decepticon 3.00

Transformers: Generation 1
Dreamwave, 2003
1 .... 3.00
1/Counterfeit......................... 6.00
2-6 .... 3.00

Transformers: Generation 1
Dreamwave, 2003
0 .... 3.00
1 .... 4.00
1/SilvSnail 5.00
2-10...................................... 3.00

Transformers: Generation 1 Preview
Dreamwave, 2002
1/A-1/B 4.00

Transformers: Generation 2
Marvel, 1993

For a comic book based on a line of toys, The Transformers retained its popularity for a remarkable length of time. The comic's initial run lasted for more than seven years -- 80 issues in all. In that time, the heroes -- a team of mechanical beings called the Autobots -- waged a desperate war against the evil transformers known as Decepticons, led by the dreaded Megatron.

As this new series begins, the Autobots come to realize that their old war against the Decepticons was only an insignificant part of their true struggle. Thousands of years ago, when the Autobots left their home planet of Cybertron to lie dormant on Earth, the Cybertronian Empire began expanding throughout the galaxy. The Decepticons they left behind were those that they had considered unworthy for true rule. These were the villains that the Autobots had done such fierce battle with in the first series; now they had to take on the Empire itself!

1 .... 2.00
1/Variant................................ 3.00
2-12 .... 2.00

Transformers: Generations
Idea & Design Works, 2006
1-9... 2.00
10 .... 3.00

Transformers/G.I.Joe
Dreamwave, 2003
1 .... 3.00
2-6 .... 3.00

Transformers, The: Headmasters
Marvel, 1987
1-4 .... 1.00

Transformers in 3-D
Blackthorne, 1987
1-3 .... 3.00

Transformers: Infiltration
Idea & Design Works, 2006
1-6 .... 3.00

Transformers: Infiltration Cover Gallery
Idea & Design Works, 2006
1 .... 6.00

Transformers: Micromasters
Dreamwave, 2004
1-3 .... 3.00

Transformers: More than Meets the Eye Official Guide
Dreamwave, 2003
1-8 .... 5.00

Transformers Movie
Marvel, 1986

1-3 .... 1.00

Transformers Spotlight: Hot Rod
Idea & Design Works, 2006

1 .... 4.00

Transformers Spotlight: Nightbeat
Idea & Design Works, 2006

1 .... 4.00

Transformers Spotlight: Shockwave
Idea & Design Works, 2006

1 .... 4.00

Transformers Spotlight: Six Shot
Idea & Design Works, 2006

1 .... 4.00

Transformers: Stormbringer
Idea & Design Works, 2006

1-4 .... 3.00

Transformers 2004 Summer Special
Dreamwave, 2004

1 .... 5.00

Transformers: The War Within
Dreamwave, 2002

1/Variant 7.00
2-5 .... 3.00
5/A 5.00
6 .... 3.00
Ashcan 1 .... 3.00

Transformers: The War Within
Dreamwave, 2003

1-6 .... 3.00

Transformers: The War Within
Dreamwave, 2004

1-3 .... 3.00

Transformers Universe
Marvel, 1986

1 .... 20.00
1/DirCut-2 .... 10.00
2/FanClub 25.00
2/Conv 20.00
3 .... 5.00
4 .... 2.00

Transit
Vortex, 1987

1-5 .... 2.00

Transmetropolitan
DC, 1997

1 .... 8.00
2 .... 6.00

3-5 .... 4.00
6-60 .... 3.00

Transmetropolitan: Filth of the City
DC, 2001

1 .... 6.00

Transmetropolitan: I Hate it Here
DC, 2000

1 .... 6.00

Transmutation of Ike Garuda
Marvel, 1992

1-2 .... 4.00

Trans Nubians
Adeola

1 .... 3.00

Trash
Fleetway-Quality

1-2 .... 3.00

Trauma Corps
Anubis, 1994

1 .... 3.00

Travelers
South Jersey Rebellion Productions

1-3 .... 2.00

Traveller's Tale, A
Antarctic, 1992

1-3 .... 3.00

Travels of Jaimie McPheeters
Gold Key, 1963

1 .... 12.00

Treasure Chest of Fun and Fact (Vol. 1)
George A. Pflaum, 1946

In 1946, publisher George A. Pflaum began offering Treasure Chest of Fun and Fact to Catholic parochial schools. In addition to religious-themed stories (the parts

of the Mass, the lives of the saints, stories from the Bible), the series also had adventure serials to sustain its (mostly) biweekly publication.

The best-known and longest-running featured the adventures of Chuck White, a parochial student who, through the course of the series, went to college, became a reporter, and much later, became a doting uncle whose nephew could take on the title role.

Sports was also a popular topic for stories in the pages of Treasure Chest, with profiles on sports legends and pieces on improving students' athletic abilities.

Among the title's artists were such names as Reed Crandall, Graham Ingels, and Lloyd Ostendorf. The Crandall-illustrated series "This Godless Communism," which appeared in Vol. 17's even-numbered issues, is of particular interest to many collectors.

-- *Brent Frankenhoff*

1 .... 275.00
2 .... 150.00
3 .... 85.00
4-6 .... 70.00

Treasure Chest of Fun and Fact (Vol. 2)
George A. Pflaum, 1946

1 .... 55.00
2-20 .... 50.00

Treasure Chest of Fun and Fact (Vol. 3)
George A. Pflaum, 1947

1 .... 40.00
2-20 .... 35.00

Treasure Chest of Fun and Fact (Vol. 4)
George A. Pflaum, 1948

1-20 .... 32.00

Treasure Chest of Fun and Fact (Vol. 5)
George A. Pflaum, 1949

1 .... 32.00
2-20 .... 30.00

Treasure Chest of Fun and Fact (Vol. 6)
George A. Pflaum, 1950

1-20 .... 30.00

Treasure Chest of Fun and Fact (Vol. 7)
George A. Pflaum, 1951

1 .... 30.00
2-20 .... 26.00

Treasure Chest of Fun and Fact (Vol. 8)
George A. Pflaum, 1952
1-20 ....26.00

Treasure Chest of Fun and Fact (Vol. 9)
George A. Pflaum, 1953
1-20 ....26.00

Treasure Chest of Fun and Fact (Vol. 10)
George A. Pflaum, 1954
1-20 ....24.00

Treasure Chest of Fun and Fact (Vol. 11)
George A. Pflaum, 1955
1-20 ....24.00

Treasure Chest of Fun and Fact (Vol. 12)
George A. Pflaum, 1956
1-20 ....24.00

Treasure Chest of Fun and Fact (Vol. 13)
George A. Pflaum, 1957
1-20 ....24.00

Treasure Chest of Fun and Fact (Vol. 14)
George A. Pflaum, 1958
1-20 ....24.00

Treasure Chest of Fun and Fact (Vol. 15)
George A. Pflaum, 1959
1-20 ....24.00

Treasure Chest of Fun and Fact (Vol. 16)
George A. Pflaum, 1960
1-20 ....20.00

Treasure Chest of Fun and Fact (Vol. 17)
George A. Pflaum, 1961
1 ....20.00
2 ....100.00
3 ....20.00
4 ....65.00
5 ....20.00
6 ....65.00
7 ....20.00
8 ....65.00
9 ....20.00
10 ....65.00
11 ....20.00
12 ....65.00
13 ....20.00
14 ....65.00
15 ....20.00
16 ....65.00
17 ....20.00
18 ....65.00
19 ....20.00
20 ....65.00

Treasure Chest of Fun and Fact (Vol. 18)
George A. Pflaum, 1962
1-20 .... 20.00

Treasure Chest of Fun and Fact (Vol. 19)
George A. Pflaum, 1963
1-20 .... 20.00

Treasure Chest of Fun and Fact (Vol. 20)
George A. Pflaum, 1964
1-20 .... 18.00

Treasure Chest of Fun and Fact (Vol. 21)
George A. Pflaum, 1965
1-20 .... 18.00

Treasure Chest of Fun and Fact (Vol. 22)
George A. Pflaum, 1966
1-20 .... 18.00

Treasure Chest of Fun and Fact (Vol. 23)
George A. Pflaum, 1967
1-20 .... 18.00

Treasure Chest of Fun and Fact (Vol. 24)
George A. Pflaum, 1968
1-18 .... 18.00

Treasure Chest of Fun and Fact (Vol. 25)
George A. Pflaum, 1969
1-16 .... 15.00

Treasure Chest of Fun and Fact (Vol. 26)
George A. Pflaum, 1970
1-8 .... 15.00

Treasure Chest of Fun and Fact (Vol. 27)
George A. Pflaum, 1969
1-8 .... 15.00

Treasure Chests
Fantagraphics, 1999
1-5 .... 3.00

Treasure Chest Summer (Vol. 1)
George A. Pflaum, 1966
1-6 .... 5.00

Treasure Comics
Prize, 1945
1 .... 175.00
2-6 .... 100.00
7-8 .... 200.00
9 .... 100.00
10 .... 175.00
11 .... 100.00

Treasury of Dogs, A
Dell, 1956
1 .... 25.00

Treasury of Horses, A
Dell, 1955
1 .... 25.00

Treasury of Victorian Murder, A
NBM
1 .... 9.00

Treehouse of Horror (Bart Simpson's...)
Bongo, 1995
1 .... 4.00
2-4 .... 3.00
5 .... 4.00
6-7 .... 5.00
8 .... 4.00
9-10 .... 5.00

Trekker
Dark Horse, 1987
1-9 .... 2.00
Special 1 .... 3.00

Trekker
Image, 1999
Special 1 .... 3.00

Trek Teens
Parody, 1993
1-1/A 3.00

Trenchcoat Brigade
DC, 1999
1-4 .... 3.00

Trencher
Image, 1993
1-4 .... 2.00

Trencher X-Mas Bites Holiday Blow-Out
Blackball, 1993
1 .... 3.00

Trespassers
Amazing Montage
1-5 .... 3.00

Triad Universe
Triad, 1994
1-2 .... 2.00

Trial Run
Miller
1-7 .... 2.00
14-15 .... 3.00

Trials of Shazam!
DC, 2006
1-4 .... 3.00

Triarch
Caliber
1-2 .... 3.00

Tribe
Image, 1993

1-1/Variant	3.00
2-3	2.00

Tribe
Good, 1996

0	3.00

Trickster King Monkey
Eastern, 1988

1	2.00

Trident
Trident, 1989

1-8	4.00

Trident Sampler
Trident

1-2	1.00

Trigger
DC, 2005

1-8	3.00

Triggerman
Caliber, 1996

1-2	3.00

Trigger Twins
DC, 1973

1	18.00

Trilogy Tour
Cartoon, 1997

1	2.00

Trilogy Tour II
Cartoon, 1998

1	5.00

Trinity Angels
Acclaim, 1997

1-12	3.00
Ashcan 1	1.00

Triple Dare
Alternative, 1998

1	3.00

Triple Threat
Holyoke, 1946

1	150.00

TripleïX
Dark Horse, 1994

1-6	4.00
7	5.00

Triple-X Cinema: A Cartoon History
Re-Visionary, 1997

1-3	4.00

Triumph
DC, 1995

1-4	2.00

Triumphant Unleashed
Triumphant, 1993

0	3.00
0/A	1.00
0/Variant	4.00
1	3.00

Triumvirate
Catacomb

1	3.00

Troll
Image, 1993

1	3.00

Troll II
Image, 1994

1	4.00

Troll: Halloween Special
Image, 1994

1	3.00

Troll: Once a Hero
Image, 1994

1	3.00

Trollords: Death and Kisses
Apple, 1989

1-5	2.00
6	3.00

Trollords
Tru, 1986

1-15	2.00
Special 1	2.00

Trollords
Comico, 1988

1-3	2.00
4	3.00

Troll Patrol
Harvey, 1993

1	2.00

Trombone
Knockabout

1	3.00

Tropo
Blackbird

1-5	3.00

Trouble
Marvel, 2003

1-5	3.00

Trouble Express
Radio, 1998

1-2	3.00

Trouble Magnet
DC, 2000

1-4	3.00

Troublemakers
Acclaim, 1996

Pharmaceutical giant G&G accepted volunteers from among their most gifted young employees, and turned their offspring into a new phase of human evolution. The program, called ZEUS: Control, consists of four teenagers-Christine and Zachary Helvin, Parker Matthews and Jane Ngo.

Unlike the angst-ridden super-powered outcasts from titles in the same vein, like Gen13 and Excalibur, the ZEUS youth have believable, boy-and-girl-next-door personalities, with the kind of interaction and camaraderie you'd expect from normal teenagers. Troublemakers is a winning series from writer Fabian Nicieza.

1-19	3.00
Ashcan 1	1.00

Troubleman
Image, 1996

1-3	2.00

Troubleshooters Inc.
Nightwolf, 1995

1-2	3.00

Trouble With Girls
Malibu, 1987

1	3.00
2-14	2.00
Ann 1	3.00
Holiday 1	3.00

Trouble With Girls
Comico, 1989

1	3.00
2-23	2.00

Trouble With Girls, The: The Night of the Lizard
Marvel, 1993

1	3.00
2-4	2.00

Trouble with Tigers
Antarctic, 1992
1-2..3.00

Trout Fission
Tall Tale, 1998
1-2..2.00

Troy
Tome
1..3.00

TRS-80 Computer Whiz Kids
Archie
1..2.00

Truckin'
Print Mint, 1972
1-2..3.00

True Adventures of Adam and Bryon
American Mule, 1998
1-3..3.00

True Aviation Picture Stories
Parents' Magazine Institute, 1942
1..100.00
2..80.00
3-5..60.00
6-14..50.00

True Comics
Parents' Magazine Institute, 1941

This title boldly promises, "Truth is stranger and thousand times more thrilling than fiction!" Fact stranger than fiction? Yes. A thousand times more thrilling? Not exactly since its narration using a documentary-style point of view that wrings emotions out of the story. Published during World War II, it feels like news correspondence from the front. Initially, one would expect jingoism or propaganda rallying the home front to stay the course during that fateful time in our nation's history. Be assured that none of those themes are present since the Axis Powers were politically expedient targets. The principles of democracy should be told with spirit and passion that otherwise would be a labor in vain.

1 .... 210.00
2 .... 105.00
3 .... 150.00
4-5 .... 100.00
6 .... 105.00
7-10 .... 58.00
11-20 .... 56.00
21-30 .... 45.00
31-50 .... 35.00
51-54 .... 30.00
55 .... 50.00
56-60 .... 30.00
61-70 .... 25.00
71 .... 45.00
72-73 .... 35.00
74-77 .... 25.00
78 .... 35.00
79 .... 25.00
80-84 .... 80.00

True Complete Mystery
Superior, 1949
5 .... 145.00
6 .... 110.00

True Confidences
Fawcett, 1949
1 .... 80.00
2-4 .... 60.00

True Confusions
Fantagraphics
1 .... 3.00

True Crime Comics (1st series)
Magazine Village, 1947
2 .... 900.00
3 .... 825.00
4 .... 750.00
5-6 .... 550.00

True Crime Comics
Magazine Village, 1949
1 .... 850.00

True Crime Comics
Eclipse
1-2 .... 3.00

True Faith
DC
1 .... 13.00

True Gein
Boneyard, 1993
1 .... 3.00

True Glitz
Rip Off
1 .... 3.00

True Life Secrets
Charlton, 1951
1 .... 50.00
2 .... 25.00
3-5 .... 18.00

6-10 .... 15.00
11-20 .... 12.00
21-29 .... 9.00

True Life Tales
Marvel, 1949
8 .... 50.00
2 .... 40.00

True Love
Eclipse, 1986
1-2 .... 2.00

True Love Pictorial
St. John, 1952
1 .... 75.00
2 .... 100.00
3-5 .... 175.00
6-9 .... 100.00
10-11 .... 75.00

True Love Problems & Advice Illustrated
Harvey, 1949
1 .... 75.00
2 .... 50.00
3-10 .... 35.00
11-31 .... 25.00
32-44 .... 20.00

True Movie and Television
Toby, 1950
1 .... 300.00
2 .... 400.00
3-4 .... 150.00

True North
Comic Legends Defense Fund, 1988
1 .... 4.00

True North II
Comic Legends Defense Fund, 1990
1 .... 5.00

True Secrets
Atlas, 1950
3 .... 80.00
4-9 .... 60.00
10-21 .... 50.00
22-40 .... 40.00

True Sin
Boneyard
1 .... 3.00

True Sport Picture Stories (Vol. 1)
Street & Smith, 1942
5 .... 185.00
6-12 .... 120.00

True Sport Picture Stories (Vol. 2)
Street & Smith, 1943
1-12 .... 100.00

True Sport Picture Stories (Vol. 3)
Street & Smith, 1945
1-12 ....85.00

True Sport Picture Stories (Vol. 4)
Street & Smith, 1947
1-12 ....75.00

True Sport Picture Stories (Vol. 5)
Street & Smith, 1949
1-2 ....75.00

True Spy Stories
Caliber
1 ....3.00

True Story, Swear to God
Image, 2006
1-2 ....3.00

True Swamp
Peristaltic, 1994
1-5 ....3.00

True Sweetheart Secrets
Fawcett, 1950
1 ....40.00
2-11 ....25.00

True 3-D
Harvey, 1953
1-2 ....30.00

True Travel Tales
-Ism, 2004
1-4 ....3.00

True War Experiences
Harvey, 1952
1 ....75.00
2-4 ....40.00

Trufan Adventures Theatre
Paragraphics, 1986
1-2 ....2.00

Truly Tasteless and Tacky
Caliber
1 ....3.00

Trump
Playboy, 1957

When Harvey Kurtzman left the editorship of Mad, he started a glossy, upscale version for Hugh Hefner's Playboy empire. Though it lasted only two issues, it demonstrated what Kurtzman could achieve, given a financial base. Featuring four-color comics satire by the likes of Wally Wood, Will Elder, and Jack Davis, the magazine was a toothsome delight that didn't have the time to find an audience sufficient to support it.

After all, the magazine -- as hefty as an issue of Playboy and packed from cover to cover with the finest comics comedy of the day -- cost half a dollar! Who could afford it?

Frankly, even at collector prices today, this is a delicious view of what Kurtzman and his crew found worthy of satire in the 1950s, and issues are filled with such bonuses as photos of some of the creators themselves.

1 ....175.00
2 ....125.00

Truth
Dark Horse, 1999
0 .... 1.00
1 .... 18.00

Truth, Justin, and the American Way
Image, 2006
1-4 .... 3.00

Truth: Red, White & Black
Marvel, 2003
1 .... 5.00
2-7 .... 4.00

Truth Serum
Slave Labor, 2002
1-3 .... 3.00

Trypto the Acid Dog
Renegade
1 .... 2.00

TSC Jams
TSC
0-1 .... 4.00

TSR Worlds
DC, 1990
Ann 1 .... 2.00

Tsukuyomi - Moon Phase
Tokyopop, 2005
1 .... 10.00

Tsunami Girl
Image, 1999
1-3 .... 3.00

Tsunami, the Irresistible Force
Epoch
1 .... 2.00

T2: Cybernetic Dawn
Malibu, 1995
0-4 .... 3.00

T2: Nuclear Twilight
Malibu, 1995
0-4 .... 3.00

Tubby
Dell, 1953
5 .... 45.00
6-10 .... 30.00
11-20 .... 26.00
21-40 .... 24.00
41-49 .... 20.00

Tubby and His Clubhouse Pals
Dell, 1956
1 .... 75.00

Tubby and the Little Men From Mars
Gold Key, 1964
1 .... 75.00

Tuesday
Kim-Rehr, 2003
1-3 .... 3.00

Tuff Ghosts, Starring Spooky
Harvey, 1962
1 .... 35.00
2-5 .... 18.00
6-10 .... 12.00
11-30 .... 10.00
31-40 .... 8.00
41-43 .... 6.00

Tuff Sh*t
Print Mint
1 .... 3.00

Tuffy
Standard, 1949
5 .... 24.00
6-9 .... 18.00

Tug & Buster
Art & Soul, 1995
1-7 .... 3.00

Tug & Buster
Image, 1998
1 .... 3.00

Tumbling Boxes
Fantagraphics, 1994
1 .... 3.00

Tundra Sketchbook Series
Tundra
1-9 .... 4.00
10 .... 5.00
11-12 .... 4.00

Turbo Jones: Pathfinder
Fleetway-Quality
1 ....10.00

Turistas: Other Side of Paradise -- Book One
Idea & Design Works, 2006
1 ....4.00

Turok
Acclaim, 1998
1-4 ....3.00

Turok Adon's Curse
Acclaim
1 ....5.00

Turok: Child of Blood
Acclaim, 1998
1 ....4.00

Turok, Dinosaur Hunter
Acclaim, 1993

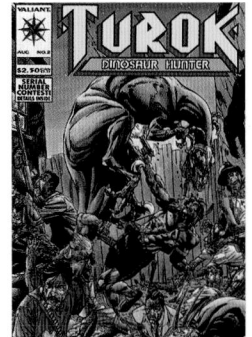

Fitting neatly into the Unity storyline and resurrecting a Gold Key character, Turok, Dinosaur Hunter was a worthy addition to the Valiant lineup. A Native American hunter, Turok wandered through caverns that took him into a world where Stone Age men coexisted with dinosaurs. Turok easily befriended the natives, but renegade robots from the far future also found a way into this world and they quickly proceeded to threaten the land. Magnus Robot Fighter appeared to help him defeat the robots, but not before they technologically enhanced several dinosaurs, which destroyed Turok's adopted tribe.

Turok swore vengeance on the leader of these sentient dinosaurs, the villainous Mon-Ark. But, before Turok could kill him, the Unity war ended, and both were transported through time to South America in 1987. Mon-Ark had learned to kill for the sake of killing, and only Turok had the skills and determination to bring him down.

0	5.00
1	2.00
1/Gold	14.00
1/VVSS	20.00
2-10	1.00
11	2.00
12-19	1.00
20	2.00
21	1.00
22-38	2.00
39	3.00
40-42	4.00
43-44	3.00
45	6.00
46	9.00
47	18.00
YB 1	4.00

Turok: Evolution
Acclaim, 2002
1 .... 3.00

Turok: Redpath
Acclaim, 1997
1 .... 4.00

Turok: Seeds of Evil
Acclaim
1-1/Direct................................ 5.00

Turok/Shadowman
Acclaim, 1999
1 .... 4.00

Turok: Shadow of Oblivion
Acclaim, 2000
1 .... 5.00

Turok, Son of Stone
Dell, 1956

Out on a hunting trip, Turok and Andar discover a mystical land where dinosaurs still roamed the earth. Soon the duo were trapped there, and had to use their skills to their utmost if they were to survive. Always, the two hoped to someday find the way back home to their families.

First appearing in 1954's Four Color Comics #596, Turok had one more appearance in Four Color Comics before starting this, his first

series. Many years later, a revived and updated Turok would become part of the Valiant Universe, with the title "Turok, Dinosaur Hunter."

3	155.00
4-5	125.00
6-7	110.00
7/15¢	135.00
8-10	110.00
11-20	75.00
21-30	48.00
31-40	38.00
41-50	28.00
51-60	22.00
61-70	15.00
71-90	10.00
91-110	8.00
111-130	6.00
GS 1	100.00

Turok: Spring Break in the Lost Land
Acclaim, 1997
1 .... 4.00

Turok: Tales of the Lost Land
Acclaim, 1998
1 .... 4.00

Turok: The Empty Souls
Acclaim, 1996
1-1/Variant.............................. 4.00
Ashcan 1 .... 1.00

Turok the Hunted
Acclaim, 1996
1-2 .... 5.00

Turok, Timewalker: Seventh Sabbath
Acclaim, 1997
1-2 .... 3.00

Turtle Soup
Mirage, 1987
1 .... 5.00

Turtle Soup
Mirage, 1991
1-4 .... 3.00

Turtle Soup
Astonish, 2003
1 .... 4.00

Tusk World Tour Book 2001
Tusk, 2001
nn 5.00

Tutenstein
Marvel, 2004
1 .... 1.00

Tuxedo Gin
Viz, 2003
1-14 .... 10.00

TV Casper and Company
Harvey, 1963

1	75.00
2-5	30.00
6-10	20.00
11-20	15.00
21-31	10.00
32-46	8.00

TV Funnies
(Walter Lantz...)
Dell, 1958

261-271	4.00

TV Stars
Marvel, 1978

1	15.00
2-4	7.00

TV Western
AC, 2001

1	6.00

Tweety and Sylvester
Dell, 1951

4-11	20.00
12-37	15.00

Tweety and Sylvester
Gold Key, 1964

1	35.00
2-5	20.00
6-10	8.00
11-20	5.00
21-40	4.00
41-100	3.00
101-102	2.00
103-104	5.00
105-106	12.00
107	17.00
108-116	8.00
117-121	10.00

24 Hour Comics
About, 2004

1	12.00

24: Midnight Sun
Idea & Design Works, 2005

0	7.00

24: Nightfall
Idea & Design Works, 2006

1	4.00
2	4.00

24 One-shot
Idea & Design Works, 2004

1	7.00

20 Nude Dancers
20 Year Two
Tundra

1	4.00

21
Image, 1996

1-3	3.00

21 Down
DC, 2002

1-12	3.00

21st Centurions
AC, 2005

1	4.00

22 Brides
Event, 1996

1	3.00
1/Ltd.	4.00
2-4	3.00
4/A	4.00
CS 1	35.00

Twice-Told Tales of Unsupervised Existence
Rip Off, 1989

1	2.00

Twilight
DC, 1991

1-3	5.00

Twilight
Avatar, 1997

1-2	3.00

Twilight Avenger
Elite, 1986

1-2	2.00

Twilight Avenger
Eternity, 1988

1-8	2.00

Twilight Experiment
DC, 2005

1-6	3.00

Twilight Girl
Cross Plains, 2000

1-3	3.00

Twilight Man
First, 1989

1-4	3.00

Twilight People
Caliber

1-2	3.00

Twilight X
Pork Chop

1-3	2.00

Twilight X
Antarctic, 1993

1-5	3.00

Twilight-X: Interlude
Antarctic, 1992

1-6	3.00

Twilight-X: Interlude
Antarctic, 1993

1-5	3.00

Twilight X Quarterly
Antarctic, 1994

1-3	3.00

Twilight X: Storm
Antarctic, 2003

1-6	4.00

Twilight: X War
Antarctic, 2005

1	3.00

Twilight Zone
Dell, 1962

-207	250.00
-210	200.00

Twilight Zone
Gold Key, 1962

1	90.00
2	55.00
3	42.00
4-10	35.00
11-20	30.00
21-27	16.00
28-30	10.00
31-40	8.00
41-51	6.00
52-70	5.00
71-92	4.00

Twilight Zone
Now, 1991

1-1/Direct	3.00
2-8	2.00
9	3.00
9/Prestige	5.00
10-16	2.00
SF 1	4.00

Twilight Zone
Now, 1993

1-Ann 1993	3.00

Twilight Zone 3-D Special
Now, 1993

1	3.00

Twilight Zone Premiere
Now, 1991

1-1/Direct	3.00
1/Prestige	5.00
1/2nd-1/Direct/2n	3.00

Twin Earths
R. Susor

1-2	6.00

Twist
Dell, 1962

1	5.00

Twist
Kitchen Sink, 1988

1-3	2.00

Twisted
Alchemy

1	4.00

Twisted 3-D Tales
Blackthorne, 1986
1 ....3.00

Twisted Sisters
Kitchen Sink, 1994
1-4..4.00

Twisted Tales
Pacific, 1954
1 ....4.00
2-3D 1 ....3.00

Twisted Tales of Bruce Jones
Eclipse, 1985
1-4..2.00

Twisted Tantrums of the Purple Snit
Blackthorne
1-2..2.00

Twister
Harris
1 ....3.00

Twitch (Justin Hampton's...)
Aeon
1 ....3.00

Two-Bits
Image, 2005
1 ....1.00

Two Faces of Tomorrow
Dark Horse, 1997
1-13..3.00

Two-Fisted Science
General Tektronics Labs, 2001
1 ....3.00

Two-Fisted Tales
E.C., 1950

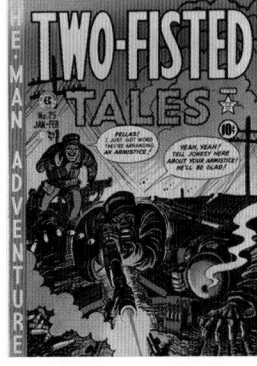

The title picked up the numbering of The Haunt of Fear and, with the Frontline Combat title, was E.C.'s outstanding venture into publishing adventure comics. Many of the stories had a focus on stories of army combat

(including such armed forces as the Roman army and such battles as Agincourt). Cover logos over the span of issues included "He-Man Adventure," "War and Fighting Men," and simply "Adventure." Two special issues were devoted to the Civil War.

Detailed attention was paid to historic accuracy of story backgrounds, and stories were outstanding. Classic E.C. artists for the title included Johnny Craig, Jack Davis, Reed Crandall, Will Elder, George Evans, Al Feldstein, Bernie Krigstein, Harvey Kurtzman, John Severin, Alex Toth, and Wally Wood.

— *Maggie*

18	700.00
19	500.00
20	325.00
21-22	260.00
23-25	210.00
26-30	160.00
31-35	130.00
36-41	115.00
Ann 1	550.00
Ann 2	400.00

Two-Fisted Tales (RCP)
Gemstone, 1992

1-15	2.00
16-24	3.00
Ann 1	9.00
Ann 2	10.00
Ann 3	11.00
Ann 4	13.00
Ann 5	14.00

Two Fools
Last Gasp
1 .... 1.00

Two-Gun Kid
Marvel, 1948

In 1948, Marvel Comics saw its super-hero comics in decline. The Next Big Things were romance, crime, and Western comics. Marvel jumped onto the Western bandwagon with Two-Gun Kid, later followed by such titles as Kid Colt Outlaw and the Rawhide Kid.

The Two-Gun Kid was a famed gunslinger who spent much of his time in his secret identity of Matt Hawk, a lawyer. When danger threatened, however, he would don a mask and cowhide vest, strap on his shooting irons, and ride off to stop the bad guys. Like all good Western heroes, however, he avoided killing. Instead, he preferred shooting the guns right out of the villains' hands, then turning them over to the local sheriff.

Issues of this long-running series were written by Larry Lieber (Stan Lee's brother) and included art by Dick Ayers and Bill Everett (creator of the Sub-Mariner).

1	660.00
2	300.00
3-4	220.00
5	200.00
6-10	165.00
11-12	125.00
13-20	90.00
21-30	80.00
31-44	60.00
45-46	55.00
47	45.00
48	50.00
49-50	40.00
51	50.00
52	40.00
53-54	20.00
55	40.00
56	20.00
57	40.00
58-59	20.00
60	30.00
☛Two-Gun Kid origin	
61-80	12.00
81-92	8.00
93-129	4.00
129/30¢	20.00
130	4.00
130/30¢	20.00
131	4.00
131/30¢	20.00
132-136	4.00

Two-Gun Kid: Sunset Riders
Marvel, 1995
1-2 .... 7.00

2-Gun Western
Atlas, 1956
4 .... 100.00

Two Gun Western
Marvel, 1950

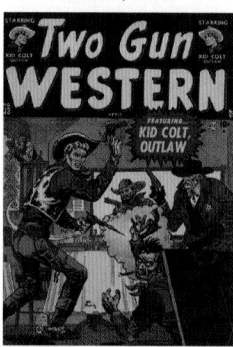

Two Gun Western from the early 1950s is the first of two series by that name from Atlas (pre-Marvel), neither of which featured the popular Atlas character, Two-Gun Kid. (He had his own title). Confused?

The star of Two Gun Western was Kid Colt, Outlaw, later to anchor his own series. Two Gun Western introduced other continuing Western characters: The Apache Kid (featuring early art by future Marvel bullpen stalwart John Buscema) and The Black Rider. Issues of the early '50s series are distinguished by covers and interior art by the great Joe Maneely, whose gritty but ornate style redeemed the cowboys-and-Indians, cattle-rustler, and evil land-baron plots that were tired even then.

5 .... 90.00
6-14 .... 70.00

2-Headed Giant
A Is A, 1995
1 .... 3.00

2 Hot Girls on a Hot Summer Night
Fantagraphics, 1991
1-4 .... 3.00

2 Live Crew Comics
Fantagraphics
1 .... 3.00

Two Over Ten
Second 2 Some Studios, 2001
1-5 .... 3.00

Two Step
DC, 2003
1-3 .... 3.00

2000 A.D. Monthly
Eagle, 1985
1-6 .... 2.00

2000 A.D. Monthly
Eagle, 1986
1-3 .... 2.00

2000 A.D. Presents
Fleetway-Quality, 1986
4-25 .... 2.00

2000 A.D. Showcase
Fleetway-Quality
25-54 .... 2.00

2000 A.D. Showcase
Fleetway-Quality
1-11 .... 3.00

2002 Tokyopop Manga Sampler
Mixx, 2002
1 .... 1.00

Two Thousand Maniacs
Aircel
1-3 .... 3.00

2099 A.D.
Marvel, 1995
1 .... 4.00

2099 A.D. Apocalypse
Marvel, 1995
1 .... 5.00

2099 A.D. Genesis
Marvel, 1996
1 .... 5.00

2099: Manifest Destiny
Marvel, 1998
1 .... 6.00

2099 Special: The World of Doom
Marvel, 1995
1 .... 2.00

2099 Unlimited
Marvel, 1993
1-10 .... 4.00
Ashcan 1 .... 1.00

2099: World of Tomorrow
Marvel, 1996
1-8 .... 3.00

2001 Nights
Viz, 1990
1-10 .... 4.00

2001, A Space Odyssey
Marvel, 1976
1-7 .... 5.00
7/35¢ 20.00
8 .... 12.00
8/35¢ 20.00
9 .... 5.00
9/35¢ 20.00
10 .... 5.00
10/35¢ 20.00
GS 1 .... 12.00

2010
Marvel, 1984
1-2 .... 2.00

2112 (John Byrne's...)
Dark Horse, 1991
1-1/3rd 10.00

2024
NBM
1 .... 17.00

2020 Visions
DC, 1997
1-12 .... 3.00

2 to Chest
Dark Horse, 2004
1 .... 3.00

Two x Justice
Graphic Serials
1 .... 2.00

Tykes
Alternative, 1997
1-Ashcan 1 .... 3.00

Tyler Kirkham Sketchbook
Image, 2006
1 .... 3.00

Typhoid
Marvel, 1995
1-4 .... 4.00

Tyrannosaurus Tex
Monster, 1991
1-3 .... 3.00

Tyrant (S.R. Bissette's...)
Spider Baby, 1994
1-3 .... 3.00
3/Gold 4.00
4-6 .... 3.00

Tzu the Reaper
Murim, 1997
1-3 .... 3.00

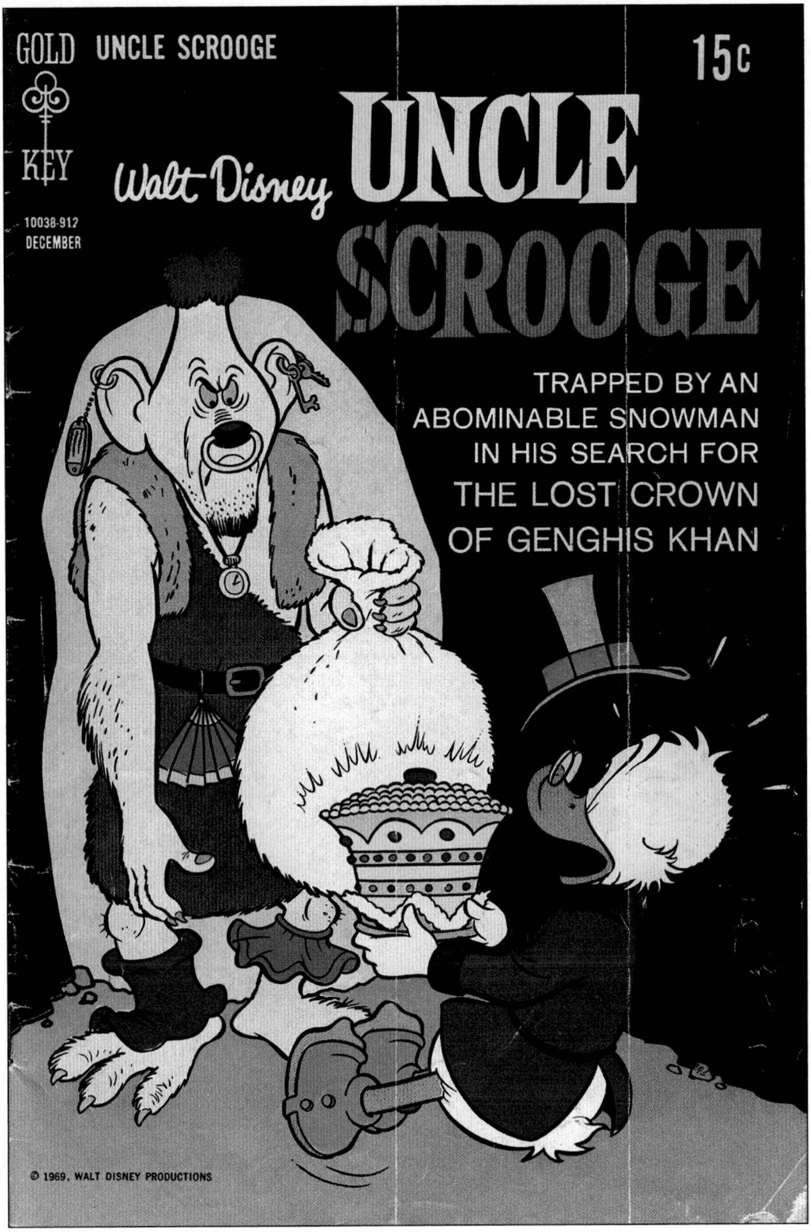

Writer and artist Carl Barks sent Donald Duck's miserly uncle on fantastic adventures around the world.

Uberdub
Caliber, 1991

1-3 .... 3.00

UFO & Outer Space
Whitman, 1978

14 .... 8.00
15-20 .... 6.00
21-25 .... 5.00

UFO Encounters
Golden Press

1 .... 2.00

UFO Flying Saucers
Gold Key, 1968

According to this series, the term "flying saucer" was first used in 1947. By the early '70s (when this series was published), flying saucers were all the rage. At times, it seemed as if, every time small-town locals would go for a walk, they'd have a "close encounter" with space aliens.

UFO Flying Saucers recounted scores of these alien and UFO ("Unidentified Flying Object") sightings. Often, the stories would take great care to point out the corroboration of the story or the impeccable reputation of the person reporting the sighting. The series even went so far as to suggest Biblical tales might have had their origin in alien encounters. In an attempt to give some balance, however, it also ran a debunking column titled "The Hoaxmaster Knows and Tells All," which recounted various UFO scams over the years.

With #14, this series became UFO & Outer Space.

1 .... 25.00
2-4 .... 15.00
5-13 .... 10.00

Ultiman Giant Annual
Image, 2001

1 .... 5.00

Ultimate Adventures
Marvel, 2002

1-4 .... 2.00
5-6 .... 3.00

Ultimate Daredevil & Elektra
Marvel, 2003

1 .... 3.00
2-4 .... 2.00

Ultimate Elektra
Marvel, 2004

1-5 .... 2.00

Ultimate Extinction
Marvel, 2006

1-5 .... 3.00

Ultimate Fantastic Four
Marvel, 2004

1 .... 5.00
2 .... 4.00
3 .... 3.00
4 .... 2.00
5 .... 3.00
6 .... 2.00
7 .... 3.00
8 .... 4.00
9-13 .... 2.00
13/Sketch.............................. 6.00
14-18 .... 2.00
19 .... 5.00
20 .... 4.00
21 .... 6.00
21/Variant 8.00
22 .... 16.00
23 .... 7.00
24-55 .... 3.00
Ann 1-2.................................... 4.00

Ultimate Fantastic Four/ X-Men Special
Marvel, 2006

1 .... 3.00

Ultimate Iron Man
Marvel, 2005

1/Kubert.................................. 5.00
1/Hitch 4.00
1/Sketch.................................. 6.00
2-5 .... 3.00

Ultimate Marvel Flip Magazine
Marvel, 2005

1-11 .... 4.00
12-20 .... 5.00

Ultimate Marvel Magazine
Marvel, 2001

1 .... 6.00
2-11 .... 4.00

Ultimate Marvel Team-Up
Marvel, 2001

1-16 .... 3.00

Ultimate Nightmare
Marvel, 2004

1 .... 3.00
2-5 .... 2.00

Ultimate Power
Marvel, 2006

1-3 .... 3.00

Ultimates
Marvel, 2002

1 .... 7.00
2 .... 9.00
3 .... 6.00
4 .... 10.00
5 .... 8.00

6	7.00
7	6.00
8	5.00
9	6.00
10	4.00
11	3.00
12	2.00
13	4.00

Ultimates 2
Marvel, 2005

1-1/2nd	3.00
1/Sketch	35.00
2-11	3.00
12-Ann 2	4.00

Ultimate Secret
Marvel, 2005

1-4	3.00

Ultimate Six
Marvel, 2003

1	4.00
2	3.00
3	2.00
4	3.00
5	2.00
6	3.00
7	2.00

Ultimate Spider-Man
Marvel, 2000

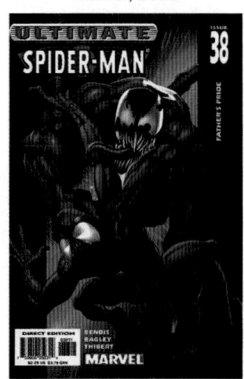

In an effort to make its heroes more accessible to a new audience, Marvel Comics launched its "Ultimate" line with Ultimate Spider-Man in October 2000. The concept is simple: The Ultimate titles - which soon included Ultimate X-Men and a Marvel Team-Up-style series titled Ultimate Marvel: Spider-Man and... - start from scratch. They reintroduce the classic Marvel super-heroes with new origins, new or tweaked looks, and refurbished supporting casts and allow readers to get in on the ground floor of a universe that is separate from Marvel's long-running mainstream continuity.

Ultimate Spider-Man begins with "puny Peter Parker" at once suffering humiliation at the hands of high-school bully Flash Thompson and his popular entourage and basking in the warmth of the love of his surrogate parents: his uncle and aunt, Ben and May Parker. While touring Osborn Industries on a class field trip, Peter is bitten by one of the medical research facility's test specimens - a spider - and injected with an experimental drug called Oz that gives him super-powers that mirror the natural abilities of a spider. The spider-powers are both a blessing and a curse to Peter. They allow him to stand up for himself at school and to make money for his financially strapped household. But his newfound popularity at Midtown High and his growing fame as a masked professional wrestler called "The Amazing Spider-Man" cause him to lose sight of his priorities and lead to the tragedy that will be the most significant event in the young hero-to-be's life.

Writer Brian Michael Bendis (Powers) and artist Mark Bagley (Thunderbolts) take Spider-Man back to his roots.

1/2	8.00
1/2/A	18.00
1	65.00
1/White	375.00
1/Kay-Bee	4.00
1/FCBD	3.00
1/Checkers	7.00
1/Payless	6.00
1/Target	175.00
2	30.00
2/Swinging	25.00
3	16.00
4	8.00
5	55.00
6	9.00
6/Niagara	35.00
7	9.00
8	8.00
8/Payless	6.00
9-10	6.00
11	5.00
12	4.00
13	5.00
14	4.00
15	5.00
16-21	3.00
22	4.00
23-26	3.00
27	4.00
28	3.00
29	4.00
30	3.00
31	4.00
32	3.00
33	4.00

34-46	3.00
47	4.00
48-49	3.00
50	4.00
51	2.00
52	5.00
53	3.00
54-55	2.00
56	4.00
57-59	2.00
60	8.00
61	5.00
62	8.00
63	5.00
☛Gwen Stacy returns	
64	4.00
65	5.00
66	2.00
67	3.00
68-71	2.00
72	4.00
73-77	2.00
78-99	3.00
100	4.00
101-103	3.00
Ann 1	4.00
Ann 2	3.00
SP 1	4.00

Ultimate Tales Flip Magazine
Marvel, 2005

1-11	4.00
12-20	5.00

Ultimate Vision
Marvel, 2007

0-2	3.00

Ultimate War
Marvel, 2003

1-4	3.00

Ultimate Wolverine Vs. Hulk
Marvel, 2006

1-2	3.00

Ultimate X-Men
Marvel, 2000

1/2	5.00
1	14.00
1/Sketch	20.00
1/Checkers	30.00
1/NYPost	8.00
1/Universal	60.00
2	7.00
3	6.00
4-5	5.00
6-10	4.00
11-12	3.00
13	4.00
14	3.00
15	4.00
16-17	3.00
18	5.00
19	4.00
20-26	3.00
27-32	2.00
33	5.00

34	4.00
35	3.00
36	4.00
37	3.00
38	2.00
39	3.00
40	2.00
41	5.00
42	4.00
43-49	2.00
50	5.00
50/Conv	15.00
51-59	2.00
60-61	3.00
61/Coipel	5.00
62-74	3.00
75	4.00
76-77	3.00
Ann 1-2	4.00

Ultimate X-Men/ Fantastic Four Special
Marvel, 2006

1	3.00

Ultra
Image, 2004

1	4.00
2-8	3.00

UltraForce
Malibu, 1994

0	3.00
0/Variant	1.00
1	3.00
1/Hologram	5.00
2-5	2.00
6-10	3.00
Ashcan 1	1.00

UltraForce
Malibu, 1995

0-15	2.00

UltraForce/Avengers
Malibu, 1995

1	4.00

UltraForce/ Avengers Prelude
Malibu, 1995

1	3.00

UltraForce/Spider-Man
Malibu, 1996

1-1/Variant	4.00

Ultragirl
Marvel, 1996

1-3	2.00

Ultrahawk
D.M.S.

1	2.00

Ultra Klutz
Onward, 1986

1-31	2.00

Ultra Klutz '81
Onward, 1981

1	2.00

Ultra Klutz Dreams
Bad Habit

1	3.00

Ultraman (Ultracomics)
Harvey, 1993

1	2.00
1/CS	3.00
1/Direct	4.00
2	2.00
2/CS-2/Direct	3.00
3	2.00
3/CS-3/Direct	3.00

Ultraman
Nemesis, 1994

-1-1	3.00
1/A-5	2.00

Ultraman Classic: Battle of the Ultra-Brothers
Viz

1-5	5.00

Ultraman Tiga
Dark Horse, 2003

1-5	4.00
6-7	3.00
8-10	4.00

Ultra Monthly
Malibu, 1993

1-6	1.00

Ultraverse/ Avengers Prelude
Malibu, 1995

1	3.00

Ultraverse Double Feature: Prime and Solitaire
Malibu, 1995

1	4.00

Ultraverse: Future Shock
Malibu, 1997

1	3.00

Ultraverse Origins
Malibu, 1994

1	1.00

Ultraverse Premiere
Malibu, 1993

0	1.00

Ultraverse Unlimited
Malibu, 1996

1-2	3.00

Ultraverse Year One
Malibu, 1994

1	5.00

Ultraverse Year Two
Malibu, 1995

1	5.00

Ultraverse Year Zero: The Death of The Squad
Malibu, 1995

1-4	3.00

Umbra
Image, 2006

1-3	6.00

Umbrella Academy: Apocalypse Suite
Dark Horse, 2007

1	8.00
1/2nd	4.00
2-6	3.00

Unbound
Image, 1998

1	3.00

Uncanny Origins
Marvel, 1996

1-14	1.00

Uncanny Tales
Marvel, 1952

1	700.00
2	400.00
3-5	325.00
6-10	285.00
11-20	210.00
21-25	165.00
26	225.00
27-28	165.00
29-40	80.00
41-56	65.00

Uncanny Tales
Marvel, 1973

1	20.00
2-12	12.00

Uncanny X-Men
Marvel, 1970

In the age of the atom, more and more children were being born with strange abilities that set them apart from the rest of humanity. These people were known as mutants, and Professor Charles Xavier decided that he must make it his mission to shelter these mutants from society's fears and teach them to use their abilities for the good of mankind. Thus, he gathered together the heroes that would become known as the X-Men.

The original X-Men (Cyclops, The Beast, The Angel, and Marvel Girl) were eventually replaced by a new team in Giant Size X-Men #1. That team, which added members Thunderbird, Nightcrawler, Colossus, Banshee, Storm, and Wolverine, would become a comic-book sensation.

Readers should note that, with #142, this series, originally known simply as X-Men (1st Series), changed its name officially to "The Uncanny X-Men."

-1	2.00
142	25.00
☞Future Past	
143	8.00
144	6.00
145	7.00
146-148	6.00
149-157	5.00
158	6.00
☞Rogue app.	
159-161	5.00
162	6.00
163-166	5.00
167	4.00
☞Rogue joins team	
168-175	5.00
176-177	4.00
178	5.00
179	4.00
180	3.00
181	4.00
182-183	5.00
184-186	4.00
187-188	3.00
189-190	4.00
191	5.00
192	4.00
193	5.00
194-199	3.00
200	6.00
201	5.00
☞Portacio art	
202-209	4.00
210-211	5.00
☞Wolverine vs. Sabretooth	
212-213	8.00
☞Wolverine vs. Sabretooth	
214-215	3.00
216	4.00
217-218	3.00
219-220	4.00
221	7.00
☞1st Mr. Sinister	
222	5.00
☞Wolverine vs. Sabretooth	
223	4.00
224-231	3.00
232	4.00
233-243	3.00
244	5.00
☞1st Jubilee	

245-247	3.00
248	5.00
☞1st Jim Lee X-Men	
248/2nd	2.00
249-258	3.00
259	4.00
260-265	3.00
266	14.00
☞1st Gambit	
267-268	6.00
269	3.00
270	4.00
270/2nd	2.00
271-275	3.00
275/2nd	2.00
276-280	3.00
281-281/2nd	2.00
282	3.00
282/2nd	1.00
283	5.00
284	4.00
285	3.00
286	2.00
287	3.00
288-291	2.00
292	3.00
293	2.00
294/CS	3.00
295/CS	2.00
296/CS	3.00
297-299	2.00
300	3.00
301-302	2.00
303	3.00
304-306	2.00
307	5.00
308-328	2.00
329	4.00
330-352	2.00
353	3.00
354-362	2.00
363	4.00
364	3.00
365-374	2.00
375	3.00
376-378	2.00
379	3.00
380-381	2.00
381/Dynamic	7.00
382	2.00
383	3.00
384-386	2.00
387	3.00
388-399	2.00
400	4.00
401-403	2.00
404	4.00
405-415	2.00
416	3.00
417-421	2.00
422	4.00
423-429	2.00
430-438	3.00
439	2.00
440-441	3.00
442	2.00
443	3.00
444	4.00
445-449	2.00
450	7.00

☞1st X-23	
451	6.00
☞X-23 app.	
452	3.00
453-454	2.00
455	4.00
456-459	2.00
460-461	3.00
461/Kubert	15.00
☞House of M	
462-493	3.00
Ann 1	50.00
Ann 2	45.00
Ann 3	14.00
Ann 4	6.00
Ann 5	5.00
Ann 6	7.00
Ann 7	5.00
Ann 8	4.00
Ann 9	10.00
Ann 10	8.00
Ann 11-12	4.00
Ann 13	3.00
Ann 14	6.00
Ann 15	4.00
Ann 16	2.00
Ann 17-18	3.00
Ann 1995	4.00
Ann 1996-1998	3.00
Ann 2000-2001	4.00

Uncanny X-Men in Days of Future Past
Marvel

1	4.00

Uncensored Mouse
Eternity, 1989

1-2	3.00

Uncle Charlie's Fables
Lev Gleason, 1952

1	50.00
2	30.00
3-5	24.00

Uncle Joe's Commie Book Featuring Cutey Bunny
Rip Off, 1995

1	3.00

Uncle Joe's Funnies
Centaur, 1938

1	250.00

Uncle Milty
Victoria, 1950

1	325.00
2	200.00
3-4	165.00

Uncle Sam
DC, 1997

1-2	5.00

Uncle Sam and the Freedom Fighters
DC, 2006

1-6	3.00

Uncle Sam Quarterly
Quality, 1941

1	1,500.00
2	750.00
3	600.00
4	550.00
5-8	500.00

Uncle Scrooge
Dell, 1953

Uncle Scrooge McDuck is one of the most popular comics characters of all time and was created by the genius artist-writer Carl Barks as a plot device for a Donald Duck story. While the first Scrooge story, "Christmas on Bear Mountain," was cover-featured, that comic book itself was simply another in the tryout Dell Four Color Series. (It was #178, released at the end of 1947). The grumpy rich uncle quickly grew into a fully rounded character, as Barks introduced such plot elements as The Beagle Boys and Scrooge's gigantic money bin.

Scrooge went from being the character who got Donald and Donald's nephews into adventures to being the focal point of a variety of imaginative adventures.

- Maggie

4	310.00
5	220.00
6-7	185.00
8	140.00
9-10	125.00
11-15	100.00
16-20	80.00
21-30	65.00
31-40	55.00
41-50	45.00
51-70	40.00
71	38.00
72-100	32.00
101-120	20.00
121-140	18.00
141-160	12.00
161-171	10.00
172-176	15.00
177-178	25.00
179	225.00
180	35.00
181-185	15.00
186-197	10.00
198	15.00
199-200	10.00
201-219	6.00
220-240	5.00
241-260	4.00
261-299	3.00
300-308	2.00
309-318	7.00

Uncle Scrooge
Gemstone, 2003

319-349	7.00

Uncle Scrooge Adventures
Gladstone, 1987

1	5.00
2	3.00
3-4	2.00
5	6.00
6-8	2.00
9	5.00
10-13	2.00
14	5.00
15-19	2.00
20-21	5.00
22	2.00
23	3.00
24-25	2.00
26	3.00
27	2.00
28	3.00
29	2.00
30	3.00
31-32	2.00
33	3.00
34-54	2.00

Uncle Scrooge and Donald Duck
Gold Key, 1965

1	50.00

Uncle Scrooge & Donald Duck
Gladstone, 1998

1-2	2.00

Uncle Scrooge and Money
Gold Key, 1967

1	6.00

Uncle Scrooge Classics
Whitman, 1979

1	3.00

Uncle Scrooge Comics Digest
Gladstone, 1986

1	3.00
2-5	2.00

Uncle Scrooge Goes to Disneyland
Gladstone, 1985

1	275.00
1/A-1/A/2nd	5.00
1/2nd	6.00

Uncle Scrooge the Golden Fleecing
Whitman

1	8.00

Uncle Sham
Print Mint

1	4.00

Uncle Slam & Fire Dog
Action Planet, 1997

1-2	3.00

Uncut Comics
Uncut Comics, 1997

1	1.00
1/A-2	2.00

Undercover Genie
DC, 2003

1	15.00

Undercover Girl
Magazine Enterprises, 1952

5	230.00
6-7	220.00

Underdog
Charlton, 1970

1	60.00
2	38.00
3-5	30.00
6-10	25.00

Underdog
Gold Key, 1975

1	35.00
2	20.00
3	12.00
4-5	8.00
6-10	6.00
11-20	5.00
21-23	4.00

Underdog
Spotlight, 1987

1-2	3.00

Underdog
Harvey, 1993

1-Summer 1	2.00

Underdog 3-D
Blackthorne

1	3.00

Underground
Aircel

1	2.00

Underground (Andrew Vachss'...)
Dark Horse, 1993

1-4	4.00

Underground Classics
Rip Off, 1985

1	6.00
2	10.00
2/2nd	2.00
2/3rd	3.00
3	8.00
3/2nd	2.00
4	3.00
5	8.00
6	5.00
7	6.00
8	5.00
9-11	4.00
12	5.00
12/2nd	3.00
13-15	4.00

Underlords
Eidolon Entertainment, 2005

1-4	3.00

Undersea Agent
Tower, 1966

1	32.00
2	22.00
3-6	18.00

Underside
Caliber

1	3.00

Undertaker
Chaos, 1999

Much of the World Wrestling Federation's backdrop borrows from the epic good vs. evil plot of standard super-hero comics. So was is only natural that they make a foray into this classic, four-color medium. The endeavor for the WWF features the grim and gruesome Undertaker.

Readers quickly learn that The Undertaker is the sole guardian of Stygian, Hell's prison. He seeks to gain all three Books of the Dead, of which he currently holds the third volume, to keep control of his chaotic dungeon. His quest takes him to the squared-circle of the wrestling arena, where he battles those demons in human guise that have escaped his realm. Opposing him in this Herculean task are the arcane Embalmer and the mysterious Paul Bearer. "Remember," Death Scribe writes, "in Hell, you can trust no one."

0	3.00
1/2-1	4.00
1/A	6.00
1/B	8.00
1/Variant	4.00
2-Holiday 1	3.00

Under Terra
Predawn

2-6	2.00

Undertow
NBM

1	9.00

Underwater
Drawn and Quarterly, 1994

1	3.00

Underworld
Marvel, 2006

1-5	3.00

Underworld
D.S., 1948

1	400.00
2-6	250.00
7-9	175.00

Underworld
DC, 1987

1-4	3.00

Underworld
Death

1	2.00

Underworld Crime
Fawcett, 1952

1	200.00
2-7	100.00

Underworld: Evolution
Idea & Design Works, 2006

1	7.00

Underworld Unleashed
DC, 1995

1	4.00
2-3	3.00

Underworld Unleashed: Abyss: Hell's Sentinel
DC, 1995

1	3.00

Underworld Unleashed: Apokolips: Dark Uprising
DC, 1995

1	2.00

Underworld Unleashed: Batman: Devil's Asylum
DC, 1995

1	3.00

Underworld Unleashed: Patterns of Fear
DC, 1995

1	3.00

Undie Dog
Halley's

1	2.00

Unearthly Spectaculars
Harvey, 1965

1	20.00
2-3	16.00

Uneeda Comix
Print Mint

1	20.00

Unexpected
DC, 1968

105	50.00

☛Was Tales of ...

106-113	35.00
114-116	30.00
117-127	25.00
128	45.00

☛Wrightson art

129-139	20.00
140-156	15.00
157-162	30.00

☛100 pages

163-188	10.00
189-190	7.00
191	10.00
192-206	7.00
207-222	5.00

U.N. Force
Gauntlet, 1995

1-5	3.00

Unforgiven
Mythic

1	3.00

Unfunnies (Mark Millar's)
Avatar, 2004

1	5.00
2	4.00

Unfunny X-Cons
Parody, 1992

1-1/2nd	3.00

Unholy (Brian Pulido's ...)
Avatar, 2005

1	4.00
1/Foil	5.00
1/Platinum	10.00
1/Haunted	6.00
1/Premium	8.00
1/Wraparound	5.00
2	4.00

Unicorn Isle
Apple, 1986
1-5...2.00

Unicorn King
Kz Comics, 1986
1..2.00

Union
Image, 1993
0-1...3.00
2-4...2.00

Union
Image, 1995
1-9...3.00

Union: Final Vengeance
Image, 1997
1..3.00

Union Jack
Marvel, 1998
1-3...3.00

Union Jack (2nd series)
Marvel, 2006
1-4...3.00

Union Jacks
Anacom
1..2.00

United Comics
United Feature Syndicate, 1940
1..125.00
8-20..25.00
21..18.00
22..25.00
23..18.00
24..25.00
25-26.....................................18.00

United States Marines
Magazine Enterprises, 1943
1..100.00
2..150.00
3..125.00
4..100.00
5-8..40.00

Unity
Valiant, 1992
0..5.00
0/Red 75.00
1..4.00
1/Gold 10.00
1/Platinum 12.00
YB 1 ....4.00

Unity: The Lost Chapter
Valiant, 1995
1..5.00

Unity 2000
Acclaim, 1999
1..3.00
1/A...5.00
2-3...3.00

Universal Monsters: Dracula
Dark Horse, 1993
1 .... 5.00

Universal Monsters: Frankenstein
Dark Horse, 1993
1 .... 4.00

Universal Monsters: The Creature from the Black Lagoon
Dark Horse, 1993
1 .... 5.00

Universal Monsters: The Mummy
Dark Horse, 1993
1 .... 5.00

Universal Pictures Presents Dracula
Dell, 1963
1 .... 160.00

Universal Soldier
Now, 1992
1 .... 2.00
1/Direct-1/Variant 3.00
2 .... 2.00
2/Direct................................... 3.00
3 .... 2.00
3/Direct................................... 3.00

Universe
Image, 2001
1-7 .... 3.00
8 .... 5.00

Universe X
Marvel, 2000

In the wake of the events of Earth X, Captain America has reclaimed Earth for humanity. But he's got a long row to hoe, as he watches over Mar-Vell (the baby who is the key to the world's salvation) and as Reed Richards works to find a cure for the virus that has mutated the human population of Earth into a race of supermen. You see, Virus X made mankind invulnerable to disease or death, and Mar-Vell and Richards' efforts will spark the return of humanity and mortality to a populace that doesn't necessarily want to...um...devolve. Still, Captain America knows that Mar-Vell - the perfect child of Him and Her - is mankind's last, best hope. As the living symbol of all that is good and pure, he will protect the child from scorn and attack.

This sequel limited series finds the Marvel universe of the future struggling to regain some semblance of order. Since it's the work of Jim Krueger (Footsoldiers), Alex Ross (Kingdom Come), and Dougie Braithwaite (Green Arrow), it's one heckuva story.

0-X... 4.00

Universe X: Beasts
Marvel, 2001
1 .... 4.00

Universe X: Cap
Marvel, 2001
1 .... 5.00

Universe X: Iron Men
Marvel, 2001
1 .... 4.00

Universe X: Omnibus
Marvel, 2001
1 .... 4.00

Universe X: Spidey
Marvel, 2001
1 .... 10.00
1/A... 6.00
1/B... 10.00
1/C... 90.00

Unknown Soldier
DC, 1977
205-210 .... 5.00
211-229 .... 4.00
230-247 .... 3.00
248-249 .... 5.00
250-267 .... 3.00
268 .... 5.00

Unknown Soldier
DC, 1988
1-12 .... 3.00

Unknown Soldier
DC, 1997
1-4 .... 3.00

Unknown World
Fawcett, 1952
1 .... 250.00

Unknown Worlds
ACG, 1960

The series "Unknown Worlds" was published by the American Comic Group and made its debut in 1960. The series lasted for 57 issues and featured a wide variety of odd stories in the science-fiction, monster, and fantasy genres. It was an offshoot of other of ACG's popular titles: Forbidden Worlds and Adventures into the Unknown.

Since it began in 1960, the series had stories that were handicapped by the constraints of the Comics Code (then very much in force, prohibiting many of the most popular horror and crime themes). It made up for the lack of artistic freedom, in some ways, by the exceptional imagination (and sometimes plain weirdness) of Editor Richard Hughes and his artists, including Ogden Whitney (Herbie), Steve Ditko, Johnny Craig, and Al Williamson, all of whom made contributions to later issues.

1	90.00
2	60.00
3	45.00
4-5	40.00
6-8	35.00
9	50.00
10	35.00
11-20	28.00
21-30	20.00
31-40	16.00
41-57	12.00

Unknown Worlds of Frank Brunner
Eclipse, 1985

1-2	2.00

Unknown Worlds of Science Fiction
Marvel, 1975

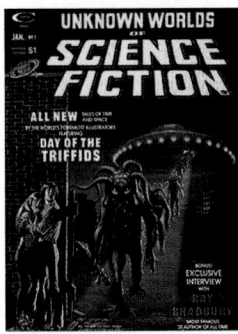

The 1975 follow-up to Marvel Comics' ill-fated Worlds Unknown, Unknown Worlds of Science Fiction picked up where its predecessor left off. Packaged in the happier $1 black-and-white-magazine format, the bimonthly publication contained a number of self-contained stories (approximately 10 per issue) revolving around one central theme: science fiction. Those stories were crafted by some of the genre's greatest writers. Work by names like Harlan Ellison, Roger Zelazny, and "Chip" Delany populated the pages.

While Magazine Management Co. published the periodical, the "Stan Lee presents:" found on the series' title page was a telling sign as to the true backer behind the project. Losing out to the spandex-clad, super-hero-saturated market, some of the greatest names to come out of the House of Ideas -- e.g., John Romita, Chris Claremont, and Tony Isabella -- provided their talents to the publication.

1	12.00
2-6	7.00
Special 1	10.00

Unleashed!
Triumphant

1	3.00

Unlimited Access
Marvel, 1997

1	3.00
2-3	2.00
4	3.00

Unseen
Standard, 1952

5	225.00
6-7	180.00
8-11	150.00
12-14	160.00

Unsupervised Existence
Fantagraphics

1-7/2nd	2.00

Untamed
Marvel, 1993

1	3.00
2-3	2.00

Untamed Love
Comic Magazines, 1950

1-2	125.00
3-4	100.00
5	125.00

Untamed Love (Frank Frazetta's...)
Fantagraphics, 1987

1	2.00

Untold Legend of Captain Marvel
Marvel, 1997

1-3	3.00

Untold Legend of the Batman
DC, 1980

1	3.00
1/2nd	1.00
1/3rd-3	2.00

Untold Origin of Femforce
AC, 1989

1	5.00

Untold Origin of Ms. Victory
AC, 1989

1	3.00

Untold Tales of Chastity
Chaos, 2000

1	3.00

Untold Tales of Lady Death
Chaos, 2000

1	3.00

Untold Tales of Purgatori
Chaos, 2000

1	3.00
-1	1.00
1	2.00
2-25	1.00
Ann 1996-1997	2.00

Untold Tales of the New Universe: Justice
Marvel, 2006

1	3.00

Untold Tales of the New Universe: D.P. 7
Marvel, 2006

1	3.00

Untold Tales of the New Universe: Nightmask
Marvel, 2006
1 ....3.00

Untold Tales of the New Universe: Psi-Force
Marvel, 2006
1 ....3.00

Untold Tales of the New Universe: Star Brand
Marvel, 2006
1 ....3.00

Untouchables
Dell, 1962
3-4...50.00

Untouchables
Caliber, 1997
1-4...3.00

Untouchables
Eastern
1-2...1.00

Unusual Tales
Charlton, 1955
1 ....125.00
2 ....75.00
3-5..45.00
6-11...80.00
12...56.00
13...30.00
14-15.......................................56.00
16...30.00
17-21.......................................22.00
22...35.00
23...14.00
24-27.......................................30.00
28-29.......................................14.00
30-40.......................................10.00
41-49...6.00

Up from Bondage
Fantagraphics, 1991
1 ....3.00

Up From the Deep
Rip Off, 1971
1 ....3.00

Urban Hipster
Alternative, 1998
1 ....3.00

Urban Legends
Dark Horse, 1993
1 ....3.00

Urotsukidoji: Legend of the Overfiend
CPM, 1998
1-3...3.00

Urth 4
Continuity, 1989
1-4 .... 2.00

Urza-Mishra War on the World of Magic: The Gathering
Acclaim, 1996
1-2 .... 6.00

U.S. 1
Marvel, 1983
1-12 .... 1.00

USA Comics
Timely, 1941
1 .... 12,000.00
2 .... 4,400.00
3 .... 3,100.00
4-5 .... 2,500.00
6 .... 3,550.00
7 .... 3,400.00
8-10 .... 2,250.00
11-12 .... 1,500.00
13-17 .... 1,250.00

U.S.Agent
Marvel, 1993

A killer known as the Scourge of the Underworld has been systematically targeting felons for execution. But when the Scourge discovers that its latest target has truly gone straight, it can't bring itself to pull the trigger.

But, as U.S.Agent discovers, the "Scourge of the Underworld" is actually any one of the many members of a secret society. When this latest "Scourge" -- a beautiful woman -- can't bring herself to kill an innocent man, she becomes a target herself. She places herself under the protection of U.S.Agent, who must find a way to save her.

The overly earnest U.S.Agent received his powers from the Power Broker's "Strength Augmentation Treatment." Originally donning the mask of the "Super Patriot," he stepped in briefly as a new Captain America. When that stint ended in tragedy, he eventually took on the duties of a member of the West Coast Avengers.

1-4 .... 2.00

USAgent
Marvel, 2001
1-3 .... 3.00

Usagi Yojimbo
Fantagraphics, 1986
1 .... 8.00
1/2nd 3.00
2-3 .... 5.00
4-5 .... 4.00
6-10 .... 3.00
10/2nd 2.00
11-38 .... 3.00
Special 1 .... 4.00
Summer 1 .... 5.00

Usagi Yojimbo
Mirage, 1993
1 .... 5.00
2-5 .... 4.00
6-16 .... 3.00

Usagi Yojimbo
Dark Horse, 1996
1 .... 4.00
2-120 .... 3.00
Special 4 .... 4.00

U.S. Air Force
Charlton, 1958
1 .... 45.00
2 .... 25.00
3-5 .... 15.00
6-10 .... 12.00
11-20 .... 10.00
21-37 .... 8.00

User
DC, 2001
1-3 .... 6.00

U.S. Fighting Air Force
Superior, 1952
1 .... 55.00
2-3 .... 38.00
4-5 .... 30.00
6-10 .... 25.00
11-28 .... 20.00

U.S. Fighting Men
Super, 1963
10-11 .... 15.00
12-18 .... 12.00

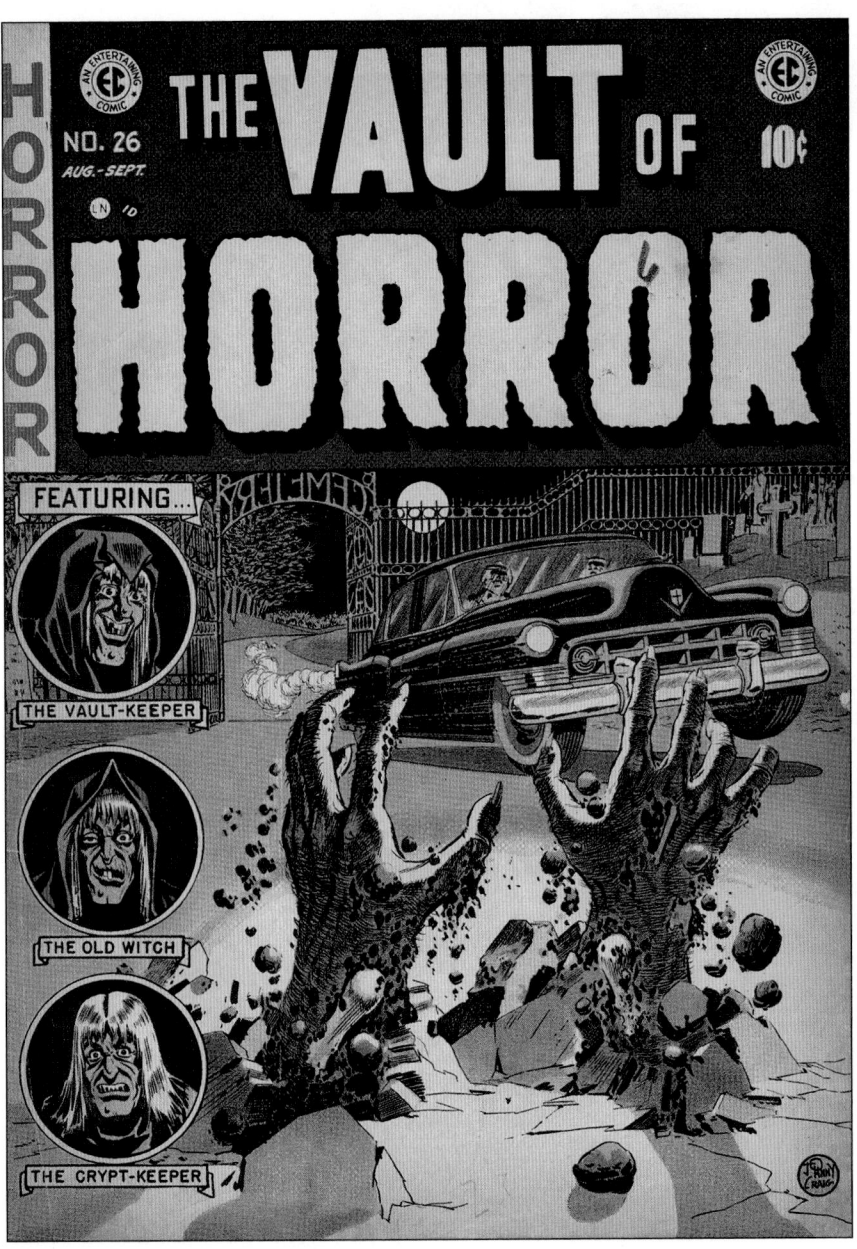

One of E.C.'s trio of horror titles, this series began as War Against Crime.

V
DC, 1985

V is for "Visitors": They appeared suddenly over the skies of Earth in gleaming spaceships. When they touched down, all mankind rejoiced that the Visitors looked just like ourselves and said they'd come as our friends. In return for natural resources that we held in abundance, they would give us the secrets of revolutionary technology.

Soon, the Visitors were part of our society and our governments. It wasn't long before mankind began to wonder if our new friends weren't really our new masters. Then, a few brave humans sneaked aboard a Visitor ship and discovered their shocking secret: The Visitors' humanoid appearance was a masquerade

that disguised their true, lizard-like forms. Moreover, our "friends" had unfriendly plans in store for us.

Now, mankind has begun to fight to take back its planet. No more V for Visitors; now it's V for Victory!

1	2.00
2-18	1.00

Vacation in Disneyland
Dell, 1958

1	125.00

Vagabond
Image, 2000

1/A-1/B	3.00

Vagabond (Viz)
Viz, 2001

1-15	5.00

Vaistron
Slave Labor, 2005

1-2	3.00

Valentine
Redeye, 1997

1	3.00

Valentino
Renegade, 1985

1-3	2.00

Valerian
Fantasy Flight, 1996

1	3.00

Valeria, the She-Bat (Continuity)
Continuity, 1993

1-4	3.00
5	2.00

Valeria the She-Bat (Windjammer)
Acclaim, 1995

1-2	3.00

Valhalla
Antarctic, 1999

1	3.00

Valiant Efforts
Valiant Comics, 1991

1	2.00

Valiant Reader
Valiant, 1993

1	1.00

Valiant Varmints
Shanda Fantasy Arts

1	5.00

Valiant Vision Starter Kit
Valiant, 1994

1	3.00

Valkyr
Ironcat, 1999

1-5	3.00

Valkyrie
Eclipse, 1987

1-3	2.00

Valkyrie
Eclipse, 1988

1-3	2.00

Valkyrie
Marvel, 1997

1	3.00

Valley of the Dinosaurs
Harvey, 1975

1	10.00
2-5	6.00
6-11	4.00

Valor
E.C., 1955

1	190.00
2	140.00
3-4	115.00
5	105.00

Valor
DC, 1992

1-12	1.00
13-23	2.00

Valor
Gemstone, 1998

1-5	3.00

Valor Thunderstar and His Fireflies
Now, 1986

1-3	2.00

Vamperotica
Brainstorm, 1994

1	8.00

1/Gold-1/Platinum 10.00
1/2nd......................................4.00
1/3rd......................................3.00
2 ....5.00
3-16..3.00
16/Nude 5.00
17...3.00
17/A..5.00
18..3.00
18/Nude 5.00
19-19/A 3.00
19/Nude 5.00
20..3.00
20/Nude 5.00
21-22......................................3.00
22/Nude 5.00
23-24......................................3.00
24/Nude 5.00
25-45......................................3.00
45/Variant...............................4.00
46-49......................................3.00
Ann 1.......................................4.00
Ann 1/Gold..............................8.00
SS 1 ....4.00

Vamperotica Magazine
Brainstorm
1...5.00
1/Nude 6.00
1/Variant................................10.00
2 ....5.00
2/Nude-2/Variant....................6.00
3...5.00
3/Nude-10/Variant..................6.00
11-12/Nude 3.00

Vamperotica Presents Countess Vladimira
Brainstorm, 2001
1...3.00

Vampfire
Brainstorm, 1996
1...3.00

Vampfire: Erotic Echo
Brainstorm, 1997
1-2/Nude 3.00

Vampfire: Necromantique
Brainstorm, 1997
1-2...3.00

Vampi
Harris, 2000
1...3.00
1/A-1/C....................................5.00
1/D...6.00
1/E...8.00
1/F...15.00
2-5...3.00
6-24...4.00
25...3.00
25/Ltd....................................10.00
Ashcan 1 ....4.00
Ashcan 1/A............................10.00

Vampire Companion
Innovation
1-3...3.00

Vampire Game
Tokyopop, 2003
1-13...................................... 10.00

Vampire Girls: Bubble Gum & Blood
Angel
1-2... 3.00

Vampire Girls: California 1969
Angel Entertainment, 1996
0.. 3.00
0/A-0/Nude........................... 5.00
1.. 3.00

Vampire Girls, Poets of Blood: San Francisco
Angel
1-2/Nude 5.00

Vampire Lestat (Anne Rice's...)
Innovation, 1990
1... 5.00
1/2nd-12................................ 3.00

Vampirella (Magazine)
Warren, 1969

From 1969 until 1983, Warren Publications brought us Vampirella, the sultry female vampire. What had started out as a gag piece first turned into a serious horror comics magazine, then eventually grew into a cult phenomenon.

"Vampi," as she is known to her fans, was the perfect mix of heroine and night creature. She hails from the planet Drakulon, where the rivers flow with blood. Although not one of the classically undead herself, she, nevertheless, needs to drink blood (or a special serum which replaces it) in order to survive.

In addition to its thrilling namesake, this adult-oriented black-and-white magazine featured other great tales of horror and science-fiction in each issue. Starlin, Brunner, Wrightson, and others contributed their talents to this unusual and memorable horror comics magazine.

1 .... 325.00
1/2nd 15.00
2 .... 125.00
3 .... 200.00
4-5 .... 75.00
6-9 .... 70.00
10 .... 30.00
11-15 .... 43.00
16-25 .... 30.00
26 .... 20.00
27 .... 30.00
28-36 .... 25.00
37-45 .... 20.00
46 .... 25.00
47-50 .... 20.00
51-70 .... 17.00
71-99 .... 16.00
100 .... 30.00
101-111 .... 16.00
112 .... 45.00
113 .... 195.00
Ann 1 .... 175.00
Special 1 .... 30.00

Vampirella
Harris, 1992
0-0/Silver 5.00
0/Gold-1 .... 15.00
1/2nd 5.00
2 .... 12.00
3 .... 10.00
4-5 .... 8.00

Vampirella & the Blood Red Queen of Hearts
Harris, 1996
1 .... 10.00

Vampirella: Ascending Evil
Harris
1 .... 3.00
2-4 .... 3.00

Vampirella: Blood Lust
Harris, 1997
1-2 .... 5.00

Vampirella Classic
Harris, 1995
1-5 .... 3.00

Vampirella Commemorative Edition
Harris, 1996
1 .... 3.00

Vampirella: Crossover Gallery
Harris, 1997
1 .... 3.00

Vampirella: Death & Destruction
Harris, 1996
1-1/A.................................... 3.00
1/Ltd. 5.00

2-Ashcan 1 ....3.00

Vampirella/Dracula & Pantha Showcase
Harris, 1997

1-1/A 2.00

Vampirella/Dracula: The Centennial
Harris, 1997

1-2............................6.00

Vampirella: Hell on Earth Battlebook
Harris, 1999

1 ....4.00

Vampirella: Julie Strain Special
Harris, 2000

1 ....4.00
1/A............................15.00
1/B............................25.00

Vampirella/Lady Death
Harris, 1999

1 ....4.00
1/A............................5.00
1/Ltd. 10.00

Vampirella Lives
Harris, 1996

1-1/B 4.00
1/C 10.00
2-2/A 3.00
2/B............................4.00
3 ....3.00
3/A............................4.00

Vampirella Monthly
Harris, 1997

0-1............................4.00
1/A-1/C............................5.00
1/D 60.00
1/E............................10.00
1/F............................20.00
2 ....3.00
2/A............................10.00
3 ....3.00
3/A............................10.00
4 ....3.00
4/A............................4.00
4/B-7 ....3.00
7/A............................10.00
7/B............................4.00
7/C 5.00
7/D 12.00
7/E............................10.00
8-10............................3.00
10/A............................6.00
10/B............................5.00
11-12/A 3.00
12/B............................15.00
12/Variant............................6.00
13-16/A 3.00
16/B............................4.00
16/C 5.00
16/D 3.00
16/E-17 ....4.00
17/A............................3.00

17/B-17/C 4.00
17/D............................ 3.00
17/E............................ 4.00
18............................ 3.00
18/A-18/B 5.00
19............................ 3.00
19/A............................ 5.00
20............................ 3.00
20/A............................ 5.00
21............................ 3.00
21/A............................ 5.00
21/B-22............................ 4.00
22/A............................ 3.00
22/B............................ 4.00
23............................ 3.00
23/A............................ 7.00
23/B............................ 5.00
23/C............................ 20.00
23/D............................ 10.00
24-24/A............................ 3.00
24/B............................ 10.00
25-26/A............................ 3.00
Ashcan 1-Ashcan 3............................ 5.00
Ashcan 3/A............................ 15.00
Ashcan 4-Ashcan 6............................ 3.00
Book 1 .... 8.00

Vampirella: Morning in America
Harris, 1991

1-4............................ 4.00

Vampirella of Drakulon
Harris, 1994

0-3............................ 3.00

Vampirella/ Painkiller Jane
Harris, 1998

1 .... 4.00
1/A............................ 5.00
1/B-1/Gold............................ 25.00
Ashcan 1 .... 3.00

Vampirella Pin-Up Special
Harris, 1995

1-1/A............................ 3.00

Vampirella: Sad Wings of Destiny
Harris, 1996

1 .... 4.00
1/Gold............................ 5.00

Vampirella/ ShadowHawk: Creatures of the Night
Harris, 1995

1-2............................ 5.00

Vampirella/Shi
Harris, 1997

1 .... 3.00

Vampirella: Silver Anniversary Collection
Harris, 1997

1/A-4/B 3.00

Vampirella's Summer Nights
Harris, 1992

1 .... 4.00

Vampirella Strikes
Harris, 1995

1-1/C 3.00
1/Ltd. 10.00
2-Ann 1/B 3.00

Vampirella 30th Anniversary Celebration
Harris, 1999

1 .... 3.00

Vampirella 25th Anniversary Special
Harris, 1996

1-1/A 6.00

Vampirella vs Hemorrhage
Harris, 1997

1-1/A 4.00
1/Ashcan 1.00
2-3 .... 4.00

Vampirella vs Pantha
Harris, 1997

1/A-Ashcan 1............................ 4.00

Vampirella/Wetworks
Harris, 1997

1 .... 3.00

Vampire Miyu
Antarctic, 1995

1 .... 4.00
2-6............................ 3.00
Ashcan 1 .... 1.00

Vampires Lust
CFD, 1996

1 .... 3.00
1/Nude............................ 4.00

Vampire's Prank
Acid Rain

1 .... 3.00

Vampire Tales
Marvel, 1973

1 .... 35.00
2-7............................ 18.00
8-10............................ 20.00
11 .... 25.00
☞Scarce
Ann 1 .... 30.00
☞Scarce

Vampire the Masquerade: Toreador
Moonstone, 2003

1 .... 6.00

Vampire Verses
CFD, 1995

1-1/3rd............................ 3.00
1/Ltd. 5.00
2-2/3rd............................ 3.00

2/Ltd. 5.00
3-3/2nd..................................3.00
3/Ltd. 5.00
4-4/2nd..................................3.00
4/Ltd. 5.00

Vampire Vixens
Acid Rain

1 ....3.00

Vampire World
Acid Rain

The vampire queen, Lady Pietra of Castle Claudio, has established a pact with the nearby village. In exchange for the vampire's protection from other magical creatures, such as ogres, cyclops, and demons, the villagers will willingly provide sacrificial blood victims four times a year. Even though the pact has been mutually beneficial for centuries, there is no love lost between the two factions. Pietra, in fact, has become quite bored with her role in maintaining the status quo.

So when the demonic Shiguku threatens to destroy the mountain on which Castle Claudio sits, Pietra does not hesitate to use the villagers as expendable pawns in her plan to defeat the mountain wraith. After all, she may be bored, but not even Pietra is foolish enough to risk herself against something as powerful as Shiguku.

Amid all the mythical creatures and evil plotting, is also a tragic story of love, hope, and ultimate betrayal.

1 ....3.00

Vampire Yui
Ironcat, 2000

1 ....3.00

Vampiric Jihad
Apple

1 ....5.00

Vampornella
Adam Post

1 .... 3.00

Vampress Luxura
Brainstorm, 1996

1 .... 3.00
1/Gold.................................... 8.00

Vamps
DC, 1994

1-6 .... 3.00

Vamps: Hollywood & Vein
DC, 1996

1-6 .... 3.00

Vamps: Pumpkin Time
DC, 1998

1-3 .... 3.00

Vampurada
Tavicat, 1995

1 .... 2.00

Vampyres
Eternity, 1989

1-4 .... 2.00

Vampyre's Kiss
Aircel, 1990

1-4 .... 3.00

Vampyre's Kiss, Book II
Aircel, 1990

1-4 .... 3.00

Vampyre's Kiss, Book III
Aircel, 1991

1-4 .... 3.00

Vandala
Chaos!, 2000

1 .... 3.00

Vanguard
Image, 1993

1-6 .... 2.00

Vanguard
Image, 1996

1-4 .... 3.00

Vanguard: Ethereal Warriors
Image, 2000

1 .... 6.00

Vanguard Illustrated
Pacific, 1983

1-6 .... 2.00
7 .... 4.00

Van Helsing One-Shot
Dark Horse, 2004

1 .... 3.00

Vanity
Pacific, 1984

1-2 .... 2.00

Vanity Angel
Antarctic, 1994

1-6 .... 4.00

Varcel's Vixens
Caliber, 1990

1-3 .... 3.00

Variations on the Theme
Scarlet Rose

1-4 .... 3.00

Varick: Chronicles of the Dark Prince
Q, 1999

1 .... 2.00

Variety Comics
Rural Home, 1944

1 .... 125.00
2 .... 65.00
3 .... 50.00

Variogenesis
Dagger, 1994

0 .... 4.00

Varla Vortex
Boneyard

1 .... 3.00

Varmints
Blue Comet

1 .... 2.00
Special 1 .... 3.00

Vast Knowledge of General Subjects, A
Fantagraphics, 1994

1 .... 5.00

Vault of Doomnation
B-Movie, 1986

1 .... 2.00

Vault of Evil
Marvel, 1973

1 .... 60.00
2-4 .... 25.00
5-10 .... 15.00
11-23 .... 12.00

Vault of Horror
E.C., 1950

The E.C. line of comics became well-known — in some views, notorious — for its line of horror titles. This was a continuation of the numbering for the crime series War against Crime, and it featured The Vault-Keeper as host. Cover copy for the first three issues read "Introducing a New Trend in Magazines … Illustrated SuspenStories we dare you to read!"

Artists for whom the E.C. line was known did work in the series: Johnny Craig, Harvey Kurtzman, Al Feldstein, Graham Ingels, Jack Davis, Jack Kamen, Reed Crandall, George Evans, Bernie Krigstein, Al Williamson, Joe Orlando, and Wally Wood. Some of the stories were adaptations of stories by the likes of H.P. Lovecraft, Edgar Allan Poe, and Ray Bradbury. The series came to an end with the Comics Magazine Association of America's implementation of the Comics Code, which forbade "all scenes of horror" in newsstand comics.

— Maggie

12	4,000.00
13	800.00
14	725.00
15	600.00
16	500.00
17-19	360.00
20-25	275.00
26-30	225.00
31-40	185.00

Vault of Horror
Gladstone, 1990

1-7	3.00

Vault of Horror
Cochran, 1991

1-5	2.00

Vault of Horror (RCP)
Gemstone, 1992

1-15	2.00
16-29	3.00
Ann 1	9.00
Ann 2	10.00
Ann 3	11.00
Ann 4	13.00
Ann 5	14.00

Vault of Screaming Horror
Fantaco

1	4.00

Vault of Whores
Fantagraphics

1	3.00

V-Comics
Fox, 1942

1	850.00
2	600.00

VC's
Fleetway-Quality

1-5	2.00

Vector
Now, 1986

1-4	2.00

Vegas Knights
Pioneer

1	2.00

Vegetable Lover
Fantagraphics, 1992

1	3.00

Vegman
Checker, 1998

1-2	3.00

Velocity
Image, 1995

1-3	3.00

Velocity
Eclipse

5	3.00

Velvet
Adventure, 1993

1-4	3.00

Velvet Artichoke Theatre
Velvet Artichoke, 1998

1	2.00

Velvet Touch
Antarctic, 1993

1-6	4.00

Vendetta: Holy Vindicator
Red Bullet

1-4	3.00

Vengeance of the Aztecs
Caliber

1-5	3.00

Vengeance of Vampirella
Harris, 1994

As writer Tom Sniegoski said, "The days of Vampirella standing around looking winsome are over." 1994's Vengeance of Vampirella shows how far the beautiful bloodsucker had come since her

days as a gag piece in the original Vampirella (Magazine). This series finds her at her most savage: a hunter of evil beasts, who is herself a night dweller.

This instinct was awakened in her following her meeting with Dracula in Harris' previous Vampirella series. That series met an early end, as Harris fell further and further behind its announced ship dates. In Vengeance of Vampirella, both Harris and Vampi get to make a fresh start of it -- and the results are startling.

0	3.00
1/2-1	4.00
1/A	3.00
1/Gold	10.00
1/2nd-6	3.00
6/A	4.00
7-25/A	3.00
25/B-25/Gold	5.00
25/Platinum	6.00
25/Ashcan	5.00

Vengeance Squad
Charlton, 1975

1	9.00
2-6	5.00

Vengeful Skye
Davdez, 1998

1	3.00

Venger Robo
Viz

1-7	3.00

Venom
Marvel, 2003

1	10.00
2	3.00
3-7	2.00
8	3.00
9	4.00
10-18	3.00

Venom: Along Came a Spider
Marvel, 1996

During the Marvel Super Heroes Secret Wars, Spider-Man

was given a new black costume, which seemed to give him enhanced powers. It was eventually revealed that the costume was a living entity. When Spider-Man rejected the symbiotic relationship the entity wanted, the spurned costume melded with Peter Parker's jealous rival Eddie Brock to become the villain known as Venom.

Later, in an attempt to reunite with Eddie Brock, the symbiote winds up attached to Brock's ex-wife Ann Weying, transforming her into She-Venom. Now, Brock must team with Spider-Man in order to save his ex-wife from the symbiote.

The series also features a backup story about Hybrid, an aptly named character that is yet another piece of the symbiote melded with a paraplegic shooting victim.

-- George Haberberger

1-4 ....3.00

Venom: Carnage Unleashed
Marvel, 1995
1-4 ....3.00

Venom: Deathtrap: The Vault
Marvel
1 ....7.00

Venom: Finale
Marvel, 1997
1-3 ....2.00

Venom: Funeral Pyre
Marvel, 1993
1-3 ....3.00

Venom: Lethal Protector
Marvel, 1993
1 ....3.00
1/Black 75.00
1/Gold 5.00
2-6 ....3.00

Venom: License to Kill
Marvel, 1997
1-3 ....2.00

Venom: Nights of Vengeance
Marvel, 1994
1-4 ....3.00

Venom: On Trial
Marvel, 1997
1-3 ....2.00

Venom: Seed of Darkness
Marvel, 1997
-1 ....2.00

Venom: Separation Anxiety
Marvel, 1994
1-4 .... 3.00

Venom: Sign of the Boss
Marvel, 1997
1-2 .... 2.00

Venom: Sinner Takes All
Marvel, 1995
1-5 .... 3.00

Venom Super Special
Marvel, 1995
1 .... 4.00

Venom: The Enemy Within
Marvel, 1994
1-3 .... 3.00

Venom: The Hunger
Marvel, 1996
1-4 .... 2.00

Venom: The Hunted
Marvel, 1996
1-3 .... 3.00

Venom: The Mace
Marvel, 1994
1-3 .... 3.00

Venom: The Madness
Marvel, 1993
1-3 .... 3.00

Venom: Tooth and Claw
Marvel, 1996
1-3 .... 2.00

Venom vs. Carnage
Marvel, 2004
1 .... 6.00
2-4 .... 3.00

Venture
AC, 1986
1-3 .... 2.00

Venture
Image, 2003
1-4 .... 3.00

Venture San Diego Comic-Con Special Edition
Venture, 1994
1 .... 3.00

Venumb
Parody, 1993
1-1/Deluxe 3.00

Venus
Marvel, 1948

Venus, one of the original "Good Girl" comics of the late 1940s and early '50s, is an interesting example of the changes that comics went through, as the Golden Age came to an end. Venus was originally conceived as a super-heroine: the actual incarnation of Venus, the goddess of love, with powers to charm and beguile her (generally male) antagonists. The series then shifted focus toward "Romantic Tales of Fantasy," continuing the Venus character but putting her in more down-to-earth romantic situations. Finally, the format changed to science fiction and horror. Venus reappeared in later issues as a backup feature in her own comic book.

Venus featured occasional painted covers, above-average art by Bill Everett (creator of Namor, the Sub-Mariner), and stories by the Atlas house writer, one Stan Lee. She was briefly revived in the 1970s in Marvel Premiere.

-- Rob Salkowitz

1 .... 1,425.00
2 .... 800.00
3 .... 675.00
4-5 .... 650.00
6-9 .... 640.00
10 .... 780.00
11 .... 800.00
12 .... 550.00
13-19 .... 820.00

Venus Domina
Verotik, 1997
1-3 .... 5.00

Venus Interface (Heavy Metal's...)
HM Communications
1 .... 6.00

Venus Wars
Dark Horse, 1991
1 ....3.00
2-14 ....2.00

Venus Wars II
Dark Horse, 1992
1-15 ....3.00

Verbatim
Fantagraphics, 1993
1-2 ....3.00

Verdict
Eternity, 1988
1-4 ....2.00

Vermillion
DC, 1996
1-12 ....2.00

Veronica
Archie, 1989

Those famous teenagers Archie Andrews, Jughead Forsythe, and Betty Cooper first showed up in Pep #22. A few months later, Pep #26 introduced Veronica Lodge, the dark-haired rich girl who would become Betty's rival for Archie's affection.

Veronica got her own series in 1989 as part of a relaunch of the Archie Comics line. She stars here in a series of adventures and misadventures suitable for readers of all ages. And while she and Betty may fight for dates with Archie, they'll always be friends in the end-especially when it's time to head to the mall to catch a 50%-off clothing sale.

For a fun experiment in pop psychology, compare the sales per issue between Veronica -- and the simultanously published Betty!

1-20 ....2.00
21-35 ....1.00
36-193 ....2.00

Veronica's Digest Magazine
Archie, 1992
1-6 .... 2.00

Verotika
Verotik, 1994
1 .... 4.00
2-14 .... 3.00
15 .... 4.00

Verotik Illustrated
Verotik, 1997
1-3 .... 7.00

Verotik Rogues Gallery of Villains
Verotik, 1997
1 .... 4.00

Verotik World
Verotik, 2002
1 .... 4.00
1/Variant 5.00
2-3 .... 4.00
3/Variant 10.00

Version
Dark Horse, 1993
1.1-2.7 .... 3.00

Vertical
DC, 2004
1 .... 5.00

Vertigo Gallery, The: Dreams and Nightmares
DC
1 .... 4.00

Vertigo Jam
DC, 1993
1 .... 4.00

Vertigo Pop! Bangkok
DC, 2003
1-4 .... 3.00

Vertigo Pop! London
DC, 2002
1-4 .... 3.00

Vertigo Pop! Tokyo
DC, 2002
1-3 .... 3.00

Vertigo Preview
DC
1 .... 2.00

Vertigo Rave
DC, 1994
1 .... 2.00

Vertigo Secret Files & Origins: Swamp Thing
DC, 2000
1 .... 5.00

Vertigo Secret Files: Hellblazer
DC, 2000
1 .... 5.00

Vertigo Veritè: The Unseen Hand
DC, 1996
1-4 .... 3.00

Vertigo Visions: Doctor Occult
DC, 1994
1 .... 4.00

Vertigo Visions: Dr. Thirteen
DC, 1998
1 .... 6.00

Vertigo Visions: Prez
DC, 1995
1 .... 4.00

Vertigo Visions: The Geek
DC, 1993
1 .... 4.00

Vertigo Visions: The Phantom Stranger
DC, 1993
1 .... 4.00

Vertigo Visions: Tomahawk
DC, 1998
1 .... 5.00

Vertigo Voices: The Eaters
DC
1 .... 5.00

Vertigo: Winter's Edge
DC, 1998
1 .... 8.00
2-3 .... 7.00

Vertigo X Preview
DC, 2003
1 .... 1.00

Very Best of Dennis the Menace
Marvel, 1982
1 .... 3.00
2-3 .... 2.00

Very Mu Christmas, A
Mu, 1992
1 .... 3.00

Very Vicky
Iconografix, 1993
1-8 .... 3.00

Vespers
Mars Media Group, 1995
1 .... 3.00

Vext
DC, 1999
1-6..3.00

V for Vendetta
DC, 1988
☞Alan Moore series
1-10..3.00

Vibe
Young Gun, 1994
1...2.00

Vic & Blood
Mad Dog, 1987
1-2..2.00

V.I.C.E.
Image, 2005
1-5..3.00

Vicious
Brainstorm
1...3.00

Vic Jordan
Argo, 1945
1...60.00

Vicki
Atlas-Seaboard, 1975
1...28.00
2...18.00
3-4..12.00

Vicki Valentine
Renegade, 1985
1-4..2.00

Victim
Silverwolf, 1987
1...2.00

Victims
Eternity, 1983
1-6..2.00

Victorian
Penny-Farthing, 1998
1/2..1.00
1-25..3.00

Victoria's Secret Service
Alias, 2005
0...1.00

Vic Torry
Avalon
1...3.00

Vic Torry and His Flying Saucer
Fawcett, 1950
1...410.00

Victor Vector & Yondo
Fractal, 1994
1-3..2.00

Victory (Topps)
Topps, 1994
1...3.00

Victory
Image, 2003
1-4 .... 3.00

Victory Comics
Hillman, 1941
1 .... 1,875.00
2 .... 1,200.00
3 .... 850.00
4 .... 400.00

Victory
Image, 2004
1/A-4/C 3.00

Vic Verity
Verity, 1945
1 .... 100.00
2-4 .... 75.00
5-7 .... 50.00

Video Classics
Eternity
1-2 .... 4.00

Video Girl AI
Viz, 2003
1-5 .... 16.00
6-8 .... 13.00
9-13 .... 10.00

Video Hiroshima
Aeon, 1995
1 .... 3.00

Video Jack
Marvel, 1987

Video Jack is a six-issue limited series from Epic Comics. The central character is a teenage boy named Jack Swift. Jack is addicted to television. He lives in a town that once resembled Mayberry, from the old Andy Griffith television show. Lately, the town has caught up with the times. Prostitution, pornography, rape, drugs, and general lawlessness are the order of the day. In response, an old man who practices black magic has taken it upon himself to rid his town of those who have no morals. Jack's friend is the man's nephew,

and invites Jack to check out the man's video set-up. Then, in a bizarre mishap of the old man's magic and the video technology, Jack finds himself cast into an alternate dimension. Or is it his home, somehow changed?

Video Jack is the brainchild of Carry Gates and Keith Giffen (Trencher, Maxx).

1-6 .... 1.00

Vietnam Journal
Apple, 1987
1-16 .... 2.00

Vietnam Journal: Bloodbath at Khe Sanh
Apple, 1993
1-4 .... 3.00

Vietnam Journal: Tet '68
Apple, 1992
1-6 .... 3.00

Vietnam Journal: Valley of Death
Apple, 1994
1 .... 3.00

Vigilante
DC, 1983
1-3 .... 2.00
4-23 .... 1.00
24 .... 2.00
25-50 .... 1.00
Ann 1-2................................... 2.00

Vigilante
DC, 2005
1-6 .... 3.00

Vigilante 8: Second Offense
Chaos, 1999
1 .... 3.00

Vigilante: City Lights, Prairie Justice
DC, 1995
1-4 .... 3.00

Vigil: Bloodline
Duality, 1998
1-8 .... 3.00

Vigil: Desert Foxes
Millennium, 1995
1-2 .... 4.00

Vigil: Eruption
Millennium, 1996
1-2 .... 3.00

Vigil: Fall from Grace
Innovation, 1992
1-2 .... 3.00

Vigil: Kukulkan
Innovation
1 .... 3.00

Vigil: Rebirth
Millennium, 1994
1-2 .... 3.00

Vigil: Scattershots
Duality, 1997
1-2 .... 4.00

Vigil: The Golden Parts
Innovation
1 .... 3.00

Vigil: Vamporum Animaturi
Millennium, 1994
1 .... 4.00

Vignette Comics
Harrier
1 .... 2.00

Viking Glory: The Viking Prince
DC
1 .... 15.00

Vile
Raging Rhino
1 .... 3.00

Villains & Vigilantes
Eclipse, 1986
1-4 .... 2.00

Villains United
DC, 2005
1 .... 12.00
1/2nd 8.00
1/3rd 3.00
2 .... 5.00
3-5 .... 3.00
6 .... 4.00

Villains United: Infinite Crisis Special
DC, 2006
1 .... 5.00

Villa of the Mysteries
Fantagraphics, 1998
1-3 .... 4.00

Vimanarama!
DC, 2005
1-3 .... 3.00

Vincent J. Mielcarek Jr. Memorial Comic
Cooper Union, 1993
1 .... 3.00

Vintage Comic Classics
Recollections, 1990
1 .... 2.00

Vintage Magnus Robot Fighter
Valiant, 1992
1-4 .... 5.00

Violator
Image, 1994
1-3 .... 3.00

Violator vs. Badrock
Image, 1995
1-4 .... 3.00

Violent Cases
Titan, 1992
1 .... 15.00
1/2nd 10.00
1/3rd 13.00

Violent Messiahs
Hurricane, 1997
1-3 .... 3.00

Violent Messiahs
Image, 2000
1/2/A-8 .... 3.00

Violent Messiahs: Genesis
Image, 2001
1 .... 6.00

Violent Messiahs: Lamenting Pain
Image, 2002
1-4 .... 3.00

Violent Tales
Death, 1997
1 .... 3.00

VIP
TV, 2000
1 .... 3.00

Viper
DC, 1994
1-4 .... 2.00

Viper Force
Acid Ram, 1995
1 .... 3.00

Virtex
Oktomica, 1998
1-3 .... 3.00
Ashcan 1 .... 1.00

Virtua Fighter
Marvel, 1995
1 .... 3.00

Virtual Bang
Ironcat, 1998
1-2 .... 3.00

Virus
Dark Horse, 1993

PFARRER·COBB·PALMIOTTI

The commercial tug Electra is caught in a storm that necessitates dumping her $10 million cargo. The amoral and sometimes incompetent captain is pleased. Then, while trying to get back on course, his crew finds a Chinese research vessel adrift and fully equipped with valuable electronics. But, when the Electra's crew attempts to salvage the vessel, they come upon a ghastly scene: The entire crew of the Chinese ship is dead, either having been brutally murdered or having taken their own lives in desperation. Worse, the equipment on board seems to have a mind of its own. Strange accidents soon kill or wound two of the ship's new visitors, sinking the Electra in the process.

Trapped on a derelict ghost ship, the Electra's crew begins to discover the ship's dark secret -- a secret so horrible that the Red Chinese are ready to bomb their own ship to keep it hidden -- a secret known as Virus.

1-4 .... 3.00

Visage Special Edition
Illusion, 1996
1 .... 2.00

Vision

Marvel, 1994
1-4 .... 2.00

Vision & Scarlet Witch
Marvel, 1982
1-4 .... 2.00

Vision & Scarlet Witch
Marvel, 1985
1 .... 2.00
2-12 .... 1.00

Visionaries
Marvel, 1988
1-6..1.00

Visions
Caliber
1..5.00

Visions: David Mack
Caliber
1..6.00

Visions of Curves
Fantagraphics, 1994
1-3..5.00

Visions: R.G. Taylor
Caliber
1..3.00

Visitations
Image
1..7.00

Visitor
Valiant, 1995
1-10...2.00
11-12..3.00
13..5.00

Visitor vs. The Valiant Universe
Valiant, 1995
1..3.00
1/$2.50......................................10.00
2..3.00
2/$2.50......................................10.00

Visual Assault Omnibus
Visual Assault
1-3..3.00

Vixen 9
Samson
1..3.00

Vixen Warrior Diaries
Raging Rhino
1..3.00

Vixen Wars
Raging Rhino
1-10...3.00

Vogue
Image, 1995
1-4..3.00

Void Indigo
Marvel, 1984
1-2..2.00

Volcanic Nights
Palliard
1..3.00

Volcanic Revolver
Oni, 1999
1-3.. 3.00

Voltron
Solson
1-3.. 1.00

Voltron: Defender of the Universe
Image, 2003
0-5.. 3.00

Voltron: Defender of the Universe
Devil's Due, 2004
1-11.. 3.00

Volunteer Comics Summer Line-Up '96
Volunteer, 1996
1.. 3.00

Volunteer Comics Winter Line-Up '96
Volunteer, 1996
1.. 3.00

Volunteers Quest for Dreams Lost
Literacy
1.. 2.00

Von Fange Brothers: Green Hair and Red "S's"
Mikey-Sized Comics, 1996
1.. 2.00

Von Fange Brothers: The Uncommons
Mikey-Sized Comics, 1996
1.. 2.00

VonPyre
Eyeful
1.. 3.00

Voodoo
Farrell, 1952
1.. 350.00
2.. 275.00
3-5...................................... 225.00
6-10.................................... 205.00
11-20.................................. 170.00
Ann 1.................................. 500.00

Voodoo
Image, 1997
1-4.. 3.00

Voodoo Ink
Deja-Vu, 1989
0-5.. 2.00

Voodoom
Oni, 2000
1 .... 5.00

VoodooZealot: Skin Trade
Image, 1995
1 .... 5.00

Vortex
Vortex, 1982
1-15 .... 2.00

Vortex
Comico, 1991
1-4.. 3.00

Vortex
Hall of Heroes, 1993
1-6.. 3.00

Vortex
Entity, 1996
1 .... 3.00

Vortex the Wonder Mule
Cutting Edge
1-2.. 3.00

Vox
Apple, 1989
1-7.. 2.00

Voyage to the Bottom of the Sea
Gold Key, 1964
1 .... 60.00
2 .... 45.00
3-5 .... 35.00
6-10 .... 25.00
11-14 .... 18.00
15-16 .... 12.00

Voyage to the Deep
Dell, 1962
1 .... 28.00
2-4 .... 14.00

Voyeur
Aircel, 1991
1-4 .... 3.00

Vroom Socko
Slave Labor, 1993
1 .... 3.00

Vulgar Vince
Throb
1 .... 2.00

Vultures of Whapeton
Conquest
1 .... 3.00

George Pérez' 1986 revamp of DC's Amazon warrior brought the character closer to her Grecian mythology roots.

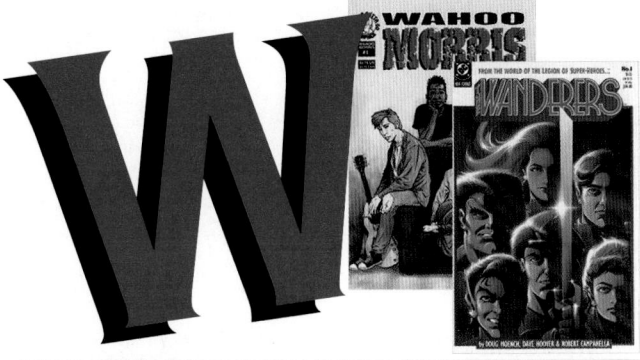

everyone (including the reader), Wacky is a good witch and even, sometimes, a funny one.

Young readers will especially enjoy the simple plots and easy-to-follow storylines. In addition to the Wacky Witch herself, the comic book also occasionally features backup stories by supporting characters like those porcine comrades-in-arms, The Three Tusketeers, Nott ën Ham, Greta Ghost, Dreadful Dragon, Batty Bat, and one or two other creatures with alliterative names.

-- Stephen C. George

1	12.00
2	7.00
3-5	5.00
6-10	4.00
11-21	3.00

Wagon Train
Dell, 1960

4-6	38.00
7-9	34.00
10-13	25.00

Wagon Train
Gold Key, 1964

1	38.00
2-4	25.00

Wahh
Frank & Hank

1-2	3.00

Wahoo Morris
Too Hip Gotta Go Graphics, 2005

1	3.00

Wahoo Morris
Too Hip Gotta Go Graphics, 1988

1-3	3.00

Waiting for the End of the World
Rodent

1-3	1.00

Waiting Place
Slave Labor, 1997

1-6	3.00

Wake
NBM

1	10.00
2	9.00
3	10.00

Waldo World
Fantagraphics

1-2	3.00

Walking Dead
Image, 2003

1	45.00
2	32.00
3	15.00
4	12.00
4/A	6.00

W
Good, 1996

1	3.00

Wabbit Wampage
Amazing, 1987

1	2.00

Wacky Adventures of Cracky
Gold Key, 1972

Gold Key's own animal characters bring delight to children in this series of adventures. Cracky the Parrot is joined by Kaws the Crow, as they entertain readers in a talking-animal world reminiscent of Disney's own talking critters of comics and films. Cracky is the wise and thoughtful bird whose brainy ideas and jobs are afflicted by the bumblings of Kaw in short stories that will remind older readers of Martin and Lewis.

Cracky appeared in various other Gold Key titles but, thanks to being an original, rather than a licensed, character, never possessed the staying power of the vast number of movie and TV characters, such as Warner Brothers' Daffy Duck and Foghorn Leghorn and Disney's Donald Duck.

1	5.00
2-5	3.00
6-12	2.00

Wacky Duck
Timely, 1946

3-6	125.00

Wacky Duck
Timely, 1948

1-2	100.00

Wacky Races
Gold Key, 1969

1	40.00
2	26.00
3-7	20.00

Wacky Squirrel
Dark Horse, 1987

1-Summer 1	2.00

Wacky Witch
Gold Key, 1971

Oh yes, "wacky" is the operative term in this charming Gold Key comic. The green-skinned witchy heroine, the personal sorceress to King Dingaling, spends most of her adventures running screwball errands for His Majesty, or else getting herself and others out of jams that her own magic has gotten them into. Lucky for

5 ....4.00
6-33...3.00

Walking Dead
Aircel, 1989

1 ....5.00
2-4...3.00
Special 1 ....4.00

Walk Through October
Caliber, 1995

1 ....3.00

Wall of Flesh
AC

This title is a campy and oddly humorous tribute to the really bad horror comics of the 1950s. Unlike the various EC titles, which often managed to bring something original and unpredictable to the genre, Wall of Flesh is essentially just a gross horror device with the merest of plot required to show it and an ending you can see a mile off. Normally this would be the kiss of death for a horror comic, but in Wall of Flesh's case, these are the very qualities that make it so much fun.

AC Comics, which is better known for its female super-hero team Femforce, delves into the vaults of pre-code horror to bring you the infamous Wall of Flesh, as well as other delightfully bad horror stories by Joe Kubert, Wally Wood, and Dick Ayers. Not even the forgettable stories that NEC spotlights in its Extinct! series manage to sink so low-or have quite so much fun at it-as Wall of Flesh.

1 ....4.00

Wally
Gold Key, 1962

1 ....30.00
2-4...22.00

Wally the Wizard
Marvel, 1985

1-12 .... 1.00

Walt Disney Comics Digest
Gold Key, 1968

1 .... 60.00
2-5... 40.00
6-13... 25.00
14-20....................................... 20.00
21-43....................................... 15.00
44 .... 40.00
45-50....................................... 15.00
51-57....................................... 10.00

Walt Disney Giant
Gladstone, 1995

1-7 .... 2.00

Walt Disney Presents
Dell, 1958

2 .... 50.00
3 .... 45.00
4-6 .... 35.00

Walt Disney's Autumn Adventures
Disney, 1991

1-2.. 3.00

Walt Disney's Christmas Parade
Dell, 1949

1 .... 600.00
2 .... 450.00
3 .... 155.00
4 .... 140.00
5 .... 125.00
6 .... 110.00
7 .... 100.00
8-9 .... 200.00

Walt Disney's Christmas Parade
Gold Key, 1962

1 .... 75.00
2-8 .... 50.00
9 .... 20.00

Walt Disney's Christmas Parade
Gladstone, 1988

1-2.. 3.00

Walt Disney's Christmas Parade
Gemstone, 2003

1-3.. 9.00

Walt Disney's Comics and Stories
Dell, 1940

This title was published off and on for more than 50 years, cycling through numerous publishers, from Dell and Gold Key, to Gladstone, to Disney, and back to Gladstone. What didn't change is the timeless quality of these great stories.

Walt Disney's Comics and Stories featured countless Disney characters, including Winnie the Pooh, Chip 'n' Dale, Mickey Mouse, Dumbo, and Goofy. Of course, many regard the highlight of the entire series as being the legendary "Barks Ducks." These were the stories featuring Donald Duck and his assorted duck friends, drawn by the immortal Carl Barks. Even decades later, they have lost none of their power to delight and inspire readers.

After issue #600, Gladstone took the title off newsstands and switched to an upscale, prestige format for the title. That move, and publishers' difficulties in making a profit with the license, ended the series. In 2003 Gemstone brought it back again continuing the numbering.

1 .... 20,000.00
2 .... 7,500.00
3 .... 3,400.00
4 .... 2,050.00
5 .... 1,250.00
6-7 .... 1,100.00
8-9 .... 900.00
10 .... 850.00
11-15 .... 750.00
16-17 .... 650.00
18 .... 625.00
19-30 .... 580.00
31 .... 3,700.00
☛Barks Donald starts
32 .... 2,000.00
33 .... 1,200.00
34 .... 950.00
35-36 .... 840.00
37 .... 435.00

38	650.00
39-40	580.00
41-46	500.00
47-50	475.00
51-60	375.00
61-70	305.00
71-80	240.00
81-87	215.00
88	270.00
89-90	210.00
91-97	190.00
98	365.00

☛Unc. Scrooge starts

99	190.00
100	200.00
101-112	155.00
113-116	90.00
117	130.00
118-123	85.00
124	130.00
125	190.00
126-129	130.00
130-133	125.00
134	200.00
135-139	105.00
140	225.00

☛1st Barks Gyro

141-150	94.00
151-170	88.00
171-200	80.00
201-240	75.00
241-260	60.00
261-283	50.00
284-285	25.00
286	28.00
287	25.00
288-289	28.00
290	25.00
291-293	28.00
294-296	25.00
297-308	28.00
309-311	25.00
312	28.00
313-334	14.00
335	25.00
336-341	14.00
342-351	25.00
351/Poster	30.00
351/No poster	20.00
352	25.00
352/Poster-352/No poster	30.00
353	25.00
353/Poster	30.00
353/No poster	20.00
354	25.00
354/Poster-354/No poster	30.00
355	25.00
355/Poster-355/No poster	30.00
356	25.00
356/Poster	30.00
356/No poster	20.00
357	25.00
357/Poster-357/No poster	30.00
358	25.00
358/Poster-358/No poster	30.00
359	25.00
359/Poster	30.00
359/No poster	20.00
360	25.00
360/Poster	30.00

360/No poster	20.00
361-400	25.00
401-429	14.00
430	10.00
431-432	12.00
433	10.00
434-436	12.00
437-438	10.00
439-440	12.00
441-443	10.00
444-445	6.00
446-465	10.00
466	6.00
467-478	10.00
479	30.00
480	125.00
481-484	30.00
485-510	10.00
511	15.00
512-513	12.00
514-516	8.00
517-518	5.00
519	14.00
520-549	10.00
550	6.00
551-554	4.00
555-556	3.00
557-573	4.00
574-577	5.00
578-579	3.00
580	5.00
581-584	3.00
585	5.00
586-597	3.00
598-599	4.00
600-611	6.00
612-648	7.00

Walt Disney's Comics & Stories
Gemstone, 2003

634-661	7.00

Walt Disney's Comics and Stories Penny Pincher
Gladstone, 1997

1-4	1.00

Walt Disney's Comics Digest
Gladstone, 1986

1	6.00
2-7	4.00

Walt Disney's Holiday Parade
Disney, 1991

1-2	3.00

Walt Disney Showcase
Gold Key, 1970

The 1970s were a high point for Walt Disney movie-making, and Walt Disney Showcase threw the spotlight on many of the various productions as they came out. Included were features on Swiss Family Robinson, Bedknobs and Broomsticks, Unidentified Flying Oddball, The Black Hole, and many others.

Naturally, there was always room for Disney's cartoon features, and Mickey Mouse, Goofy, and the rest of the gang were frequent guests in this series. Characters who couldn't support a title all to themselves, such as Pluto and Tinkerbell, would get their own issues here.

1	16.00
2	10.00
3-4	9.00
5-6	12.00
7-8	9.00
9	10.00
10	12.00
11-13	8.00
14	12.00
15	8.00
16-18	12.00
19	10.00
20	9.00
21-23	8.00
24-29	7.00
30	15.00

☛Magica de Spell

31-32	9.00
33-39	7.00
40-41	8.00
42	7.00
43	9.00
44-48	10.00
49-54	7.00

Walt Disney's Spring Fever
Disney, 1991

1	3.00

Walt Disney's Summer Fun
Disney

1 ....3.00

Walt Disney's Three Musketeers
Gemstone, 2004

1 ....4.00

Walt Disney's Vacation Parade
Dell, 1950

1 ....550.00
2 ....160.00
3-5 ....90.00

Walt Disney's World of Adventure
Gold Key, 1963

1 ....8.00
2-3 ....5.00

Walter
Dark Horse, 1996

1-4 ....3.00

Walter Kitty in... the Hollow Earth
Vision, 1996

1-2 ....2.00

Walt The Wildcat
MotioN Comics, 1995

1 ....3.00

Wambi, Jungle Boy
Fiction House, 1942

1 ....500.00
2-3 ....300.00
4-5 ....175.00
6-10 ....150.00
11-14 ....125.00
15-18 ....100.00

Wanda Luwand & the Pirate Girls
Fantagraphics

1 ....3.00

Wanderers
DC, 1988

1-13 ....2.00

Wandering Star
Pen and Ink, 1993

1 ....8.00
1/2nd 4.00
1/3rd 3.00
2 ....5.00
2/2nd 2.00
3 ....4.00
3/2nd 2.00
4 ....4.00
4/2nd 2.00
5 ....4.00
5/2nd 2.00
6-21 ....3.00

Wandering Stars
Fantagraphics

1 ....2.00

Wanted
Celebrity, 1989

1-5 ....2.00

Wanted
Image, 2003

1 ....12.00
1/A 9.00
1/B 8.00
1/C 3.00
1/D 6.00
1/E 5.00
2 ....3.00
2/B 4.00
2/C 5.00
3 ....3.00
3/A 4.00
4-6 ....3.00

Wanted Comics
Toytown, 1947

9 ....120.00
10-11 ....72.00
12 ....105.00
13 ....72.00
14-15 ....65.00
16-17 ....60.00
18 ....140.00
19-22 ....60.00
23-30 ....48.00
31-34 ....40.00
35 ....65.00
36-38 ....40.00
39 ....105.00
40-49 ....40.00
50-52 ....65.00
53 ....40.00

Wanted: Dossier One-Shot
Image, 2004

1 ....3.00

Wanted, the World's Most Dangerous Villains
DC, 1972

1 ....10.00
2-3 ....8.00
4-9 ....6.00

War
Charlton, 1975

Begun in July of 1975, this forty-nine-issue Charlton series turned out a respectable set of war stories, ranging from Alexander the Great to Viet Nam. At its best, it rose above the roar of the guns to address the real human tragedy of war, as in "A Reason For Dying," the story of a black slave who escapes to fight for the Union in the Civil War-only to be killed by the white man he helped raise while a slave. As that man kneels over the body of his old friend, he hears that they've won the battle-and realizes how hollow "victory" can be.

1 ....8.00
2-10 ....5.00
11-22 ....3.00
23-49 ....2.00

War
Marvel, 1989

1-4 ....4.00

War Action
Atlas, 1952

1 ....100.00
2 ....60.00
3-10 ....50.00
11-14 ....60.00

War Adventures
Atlas, 1952

1 ....100.00
2-13 ....75.00

War Against Crime
E.C., 1948

1 ....430.00
2-3 ....250.00
4-5 ....225.00
6-9 ....210.00
10 ....1,500.00
11 ....775.00

War Against Crime
Gemstone, 2000

1-5 ....3.00
Ann 1 ....14.00

War and Attack
Charlton, 1964

1 ....30.00
54-63 ....10.00

War Angel: Book of Death (Brian Pulido's)
Avatar

1 ....3.00
1/Platinum 15.00
1/Wraparound 3.00

Warblade: Endangered Species
Image, 1995

Reno Bryce is Warblade, a member of Jim Lee's WildC.A.T.S, and has the power to transform his body into any form, including turning his hands into deadly blades. These blades are sharp enough to cut through almost anything. He shares this ability with a few others, most notably a Native American named Ripclaw, who is a member of the mutant team Cyberforce.

In Endangered Species, Warblade takes a hiatus from his team in order to follow leads concerning the Daemonites, the WildC.A.T.S' mortal enemies. Meanwhile, Ripclaw investigates strange disappearances concerning the youthful members of his tribe. Both mysteries share the same solutions, so the two heroes combine forces to attack the aliens and humans responsible for developing an impenetrable armor that would almost guarantee a Daemonite victory on Earth if it were completed.

1-4 ....3.00

Warcat
Coconut, 1997

Ashcan 1-Special 1 ....3.00

Warchild
Maximum, 1994

1/A-4 .... 3.00

War Combat
Marvel, 1952

1 .... 60.00
2 .... 35.00
3-5 .... 22.00

War Comics
Dell, 1940

1 .... 350.00
2 .... 175.00
3-4 .... 125.00

War Comics
Atlas, 1950

1 .... 125.00
2 .... 75.00
3-10 .... 50.00
11 .... 60.00
12-20 .... 50.00
21-32 .... 45.00
33-49 .... 40.00

War Criminals
Comic Zone

1 .... 3.00

Warcry
Image

1 .... 3.00

War Dancer
Defiant, 1994

1-6 .... 3.00

Warfront
Harvey, 1951

As the saying goes, "War is Hell," and the short stories presented in this title are aimed at proving the statement true.

These stories remind readers that wars are fought by real people, not just nameless, faceless statistics in the news. Whether it is an average guy from the Midwest or a much-decorated hero, every soldier is a hero. Warfare is fought by people's friends and family. It is fought in the dirt and the mud, with real guns, real blood, and very real death. Wars are fought against other soldiers who are also someone's friends and someone's family.

1 .... 75.00
2 .... 45.00
3-5 .... 35.00
6-10 .... 32.00
11-20 .... 28.00
21-35 .... 24.00
36-39 .... 18.00

War Fury
Comic Media, 1952

1 .... 100.00
2-4 .... 75.00

Wargod
Speakeasy Comics, 2005

0 .... 5.00

Warhammer Monthly
Games Workshop, 1998

0 .... 1.00
1-51 .... 3.00
52-85 .... 4.00

Warhawks Comics Module
TSR, 1990

1-9 .... 3.00

Warheads
Marvel, 1992

1-14 .... 2.00

Warheads: Black Dawn
Marvel, 1993

1-2 .... 3.00

War Heroes
Dell, 1942

1 .... 120.00
2 .... 100.00
3-6 .... 80.00
7-11 .... 60.00

War Heroes
Ace, 1952

1 .... 50.00
2 .... 35.00
3-7 .... 30.00

War Heroes
Charlton, 1963

1-2 .... 25.00
3-5 .... 12.00
6-20 .... 8.00
21-27 .... 5.00

War Heroes Classics
Recollections, 1991

1 .... 2.00

War Is Hell
Marvel, 1973

1 .... 25.00
2 .... 18.00
3-5 .... 14.00
6-8 .... 10.00
9-15 .... 8.00

Warlands
Image, 1999

A touch of manga and a dollop of elf are mixed with high fantasy in this world-spanning tale pitting an exiled princess against her sister queen, while evil forces gather that could tear their world apart.

Somehow, four warriors must find a way to avoid civil war and unite the battling factions. At the same time, they must protect an ancient power from a powerful, evil man.

The stakes are high and the odds long, but they'll put their hearts into it through the bitter end.

The series was created by Pat Lee and Adrian Tsang.

1-12	3.00
Deluxe 1	15.00

Warlands: Dark Tide Rising
Dreamwave, 2002

1-6	3.00

Warlands Epilogue: Three Stories
Image, 2001

1	6.00

Warlands: The Age of Ice
Dreamwave, 2001

0	2.00
1-3	3.00

Warlash
CFD, 1995

1	3.00

Warlock
Marvel, 1972

1	32.00
2-3	15.00
4-5	8.00
6-8	7.00
9-11	10.00
12	8.00

12/30¢	15.00
13	8.00
13/30¢	15.00
14	8.00
14/30¢	15.00
15	8.00

Warlock
Marvel, 1982

1	4.00
2-6	3.00
Special 1	2.00

Warlock
Marvel, 1992

1-6	3.00

Warlock
Marvel, 1998

1-4	3.00

Warlock
Marvel, 1999

1-4	2.00

Warlock
Marvel, 2004

1-4	3.00

Warlock and the Infinity Watch
Marvel, 1992

Following the events of The Infinity Gauntlet, Adam Warlock was left in possession of The Infinity Gems, making him the most powerful being in the universe. But Warlock realizes that no single being, even such a remarkable one as he, should ever be in control of so much power. He divides the gems, giving one each to a number of unlikely protectors and one to a party he keeps a secret. The final gem, The Soul Gem, is always with him. Together with Warlock, these protectors are the Infinity Watch. By distributing the gems in this fashion, Warlock hopes that they will be safe from ever falling into a single person's hands again.

But that is not to be. Someone has begun to overtake members of the Watch, gathering their powers to himself. Warlock must stop him or risk the destruction of the galaxy. But, when Warlock finally encounters this foe, he discovers a familiar face.

1	3.00
2-24	2.00
25	3.00
26-42	2.00

Warlock Chronicles
Marvel, 1993

1	3.00
2-8	2.00

Warlock 5
Aircel, 1986

1-22	2.00

Warlock 5
Sirius, 1998

1-4	3.00

Warlock 5 Book II
Aircel, 1989

1-7	2.00

Warlocks
Aircel, 1988

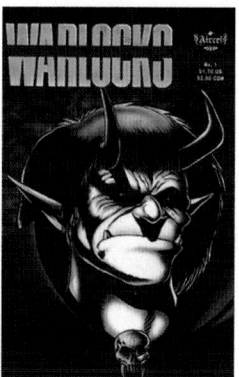

Warlocks is a black-and-white terror series written and drawn by Barry Blair (Samurai, Leather & Lace).

Leading off the series was Blair's "Anarchy Unbound," a supernatural tale set in the Amazon Jungle. Two young people, one teen-age girl and a younger boy, are in search of their long-lost father. They accidentally run into a young savage and are coaxed to follow him. To their surprise, they find an old man who tells a tale of horror and demonic possession; he's possessed by an evil demon who travels around the jungle.

The good news is that the children are told of how the demon can be defeated. The bad news is that the demon has now taken possession of their father.

1-Special 1 ....2.00

Warlord
DC, 1976

1 ....10.00
2 ....4.00
3-6 ....3.00
7-22 ....2.00
22/Whitman 8.00
23-29 ....2.00
30-47 ....1.00
48 ....2.00
49-130 ....1.00
131 ....2.00
132 ....1.00
133 ....2.00
Ann 1 ....3.00
Ann 2-Ann 6 ....1.00

Warlord
DC, 1992

1-6 ....2.00

Warlord
DC, 2006

1-10 ....3.00

War Machine
Marvel, 1994

1 ....2.00
1/Variant 3.00
2-8 ....2.00
8/CS 3.00
9-14 ....2.00
15 ....3.00
16-25 ....2.00
Ashcan 1 ....1.00

War Machine
Marvel, 2001

1-12 ....2.00

War Man
Marvel, 1993

1-2 ....3.00

War of the Gods
DC, 1991

1-4/Direct 2.00

War of the Worlds
Caliber, 1996

1-5 ....3.00

War of the Worlds
Eternity, 1990

1-6 ....2.00

War of the Worlds, The: The Memphis Front
Arrow, 1998

1-5 ....3.00

Warp
First, 1983

1-7 ....2.00
8-Special 3 ....1.00

Warp-3
Equinox, 1990

1 .... 2.00

War Party
Lightning, 1994

1 .... 3.00

Warp Graphics Annual
Warp

1 .... 3.00

Warpwalking
Caliber

1-4 .... 3.00

War Report
Farrell, 1952

1 .... 50.00
2-5 .... 25.00

Warrior Bugs
Artcoda, 2002

1 .... 3.00

Warrior
Ultimate Creations, 1996

1-4 .... 3.00

Warrior Comics
Blackerby, 1945

1 .... 100.00

Warrior Nun Areala
Antarctic, 1994

1-1/Ltd. 5.00
1/2nd 3.00
2-3 .... 4.00
3/CS 8.00
3/Ltd. 5.00

Warrior Nun Areala
Antarctic, 1997

1 .... 3.00
1/Variant 6.00
2-6 .... 3.00

Warrior Nun Areala
Antarctic, 1999

1-2 .... 3.00

Warrior Nun Areala and Avengelyne
Antarctic, 1996

1/A 3.00
1/B 6.00

Warrior Nun Areala and Glory
Antarctic, 1997

1 .... 3.00
1/CS 6.00

Warrior Nun Areala/ Razor: Revenge
Antarctic, 1999

1 .... 3.00
1/Deluxe 6.00

Warrior Nun Areala: Resurrection
Antarctic, 1998

1-6 .... 3.00
Ashcan 1 .... 1.00

Warrior Nun Areala: Rheintöchter
Antarctic, 1997

1-2 .... 3.00

Warrior Nun Areala: Rituals
Antarctic, 1995

1 .... 3.00
1/Variant 4.00
2-6 .... 3.00

Warrior Nun: Black & White
Antarctic, 1997

1-21 .... 3.00

Warrior Nun Brigantia
Antarctic, 2000

1-3 .... 3.00

Warrior Nun Dei
Antarctic

1 .... 6.00

Warrior Nun Dei: Aftertime
Antarctic, 1997

Sister Dei is a young Warrior Nun assigned to the distant planet Sullen Dun. It is this planet that has been determined to be the source of the demon invasion on Earth, despite the presence of the Hinterland, a well-fortified base established to prevent that occurrence.

Father Caedius, the administrator of the Hinterland, has taken a brusque and antagonistic attitude toward Sister Dei, and she has her own suspicions about him.

Ben Dunn's Warrior Nun mythos, an unusual mix of horror

and mysticism with a smattering of Catholicism, has proved popular enough to expand to interpretations by other writers and artists. This three-issue mini-series features full-color computer-painted art by Patrick Thornton.
-- George Haberberger

1-3..3.00

Warrior Nun: Frenzy
Antarctic, 1998
1-2..3.00

Warrior Nun: Scorpio Rose
Antarctic, 1996
1-4..3.00

Warrior Nun vs Razor
Antarctic, 1996
1 ....4.00

Warrior of Waverly Street
Dark Horse, 1996
1-2..3.00

Warriors
Adventure, 1987

This black-and-white anthology series offers stories featuring characters from Adventurers. The stories are short, but involving, and present various takes on the worlds of wizards, knights, and sword-swinging mercenaries. In one tale, a pair of prisoners must escape from their captors before they become part of a blood sacrifice. In another, a young spellcaster hopes a sorceress will take him as her pupil; she tests him an unexpected question, which the young man can't answer honestly. Different creative teams on each story lend variety in dialogue, story structure, and art styles.

1-5..2.00

Warriors of Plasm
Defiant, 1993
1-13.................................... 3.00

Warriors of Plasm Graphic Novel
Defiant, 1993
1 .... 7.00

Warrior's Way
Bench, 1998
1-3.................................... 3.00

War Sirens and Liberty Belles
Recollections
1 .... 5.00

War Sluts
Pretty Graphic
1-2.................................... 4.00

War Stories
DC, 2004
1 .... 20.00

War Story: Archangel
DC, 2003
1 .... 5.00

War Story: D-Day Dodgers
DC, 2001
1 .... 5.00

War Story: Johann's Tiger
DC, 2001
1 .... 5.00

War Story: Nightingale
DC, 2002
1 .... 5.00

War Story: Screaming Eagles
DC, 2002
1 .... 5.00

Warstrike
Malibu, 1994
1-7.................................... 2.00
GS 1 .... 3.00

Wartime Romances
St. John, 1951
1 .... 200.00
2-8.................................... 100.00
9-13.................................... 80.00
14-18.................................... 60.00

War Victory Adventures
Harvey, 1942
1 .... 250.00
2 .... 175.00
3 .... 150.00

Warworld!
Dark Horse, 1989
1 .... 2.00

Warzone
Express, 1994
1-3.. 3.00

Warzone 3719
Pocket Change
1 .... 2.00

Washmen
New York
1 .... 2.00

Washouts
Renaissance, 2002
1 .... 3.00

Wash Tubbs Quarterly
Dragon Lady
1 .... 5.00
2-5.. 6.00

Waste L.A.: Descent
John Gaushell, 1996
1-3.. 3.00

Wasteland
DC, 1987
1 .... 2.00
2-18...................................... 2.00

Watchcats
Harrier
1 .... 2.00

Watchmen
DC, 1986

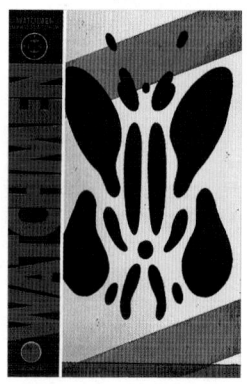

Someone - or something - is stalking costumed crime-fighters. "The Crimebusters" have long been out of action, having been outlawed by the Anti-Vigilante Act. We meet them now in the twilight of their lives, when a closer look also shows that these once-honored heroes were not so heroic, after all. In fact, in many cases, they're borderline psychotics, if not outright insane. And now someone is picking them off, one by one ...

This classic 12-issue maxi-series by writer Alan Moore explores both the darkest and the best in human nature. It has a maturity and insight rarely seen in the world of comics. Watchmen will change forever the way you think of super-heroes.

1 ....8.00
☛Moore, Gibbons series
2-3..5.00
4-12..4.00

Waterloo Sunset
Image, 2004
1-4..7.00

Waterworld: Children of Leviathan
Acclaim, 1997
1-4..3.00

Wavemakers
Blind Bat, 1990
1 ....3.00

Wave Warriors
Astroboys
1 ....2.00

Waxwork
Blackthorne
1 ....2.00
3D 1 ....3.00

Way of the Rat
CrossGen, 2002
1-24..3.00

Way Out Strips
Fantagraphics, 1994
1-3..3.00

Way Out Strips
Tragedy Strikes, 1992
1-3..3.00

Wayward Warrior
Alpha Productions, 1990
1-3..2.00

WCW World Championship Wrestling
Marvel, 1992

If you love watching World Championship Wrestling on

television or in person, this comic-book adaptation of the "sport" will make you feel right at home. The running commentary narration is smoothly done. Artists capture the look and the feel of the fighters. The plotting is as coherent as any WCW show.

The only difference between this and televised bouts is the focus on the young people in the audience. Instead of a faceless throng booing, cheering, and never seen except when a wrestler is thrown into the audience, young fans are sometimes the focus, as they reach out to their heroes in the ring and meet a real person with real problems. True, this series does not explain WCW or attempt to tone down the violence, but, if you already enjoy seeing 200-400-pound men getting their heads bashed with two-by-fours, this title is good reading.

1-12...................................... 1.00

We 3
DC, 2004
1-3.. 3.00

Weapons File
Antarctic, 2005
1-3.. 5.00

Weapon X
Marvel, 1995
1-4.. 2.00

Weapon X
Marvel, 2002
1-8.. 2.00
9-28.. 3.00

Weapon X: Days of Future Now
Marvel, 2005
1-5.. 3.00

Weapon X: The Draft: Kane
Marvel, 2002
1 .... 2.00

Weapon XXX: Origin of the Implants
Friendly, 1992
1-3.. 3.00

Weapon Zero
Image, 1995
1-5.. 3.00

Weapon Zero
Image, 1996
1-14...................................... 3.00
15 .... 4.00

Weapon Zero/ Silver Surfer
Top Cow, 1997
1-1/A...................................... 3.00

Weasel Guy: Road Trip
Image, 1999
1-1/A...................................... 3.00
2 .... 4.00

Weasel Patrol
Eclipse
1 .... 2.00

Weather Woman
CPM Manga, 2000
1-1/A...................................... 3.00

Weaveworld
Marvel, 1991

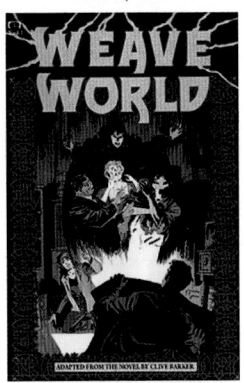

Weaveworld adapts Clive Barker's fantastic (often gruesome) novel by the same name. It all begins with working-class Cal Mooney discovers a special carpet that contains another world within its threads. It's called the Fugue -- the Weaveworld -- created by magical beings known as Seerkind. Fleeing from an entity known as The Scourge, these beings have created the Weaveworld, then hidden themselves within it.

Almost a century later, the guardian of the Fugue -- an elderly grandmother -- lies dying. As her final act, she entrusts The Fugue to her granddaughter, Suzanna Parish. It's then that the dark sorceress Immacolata decides to exact her revenge upon her fellow Seerkind. Using human and demonic accomplices, she strives for possession of Weaveworld -- and only Cal and Suzanna stand in her way.

1-3 .... 5.00

Web
DC, 1991
1-14 .... 1.00
Ann 1 .... 3.00

Webber's World
Allstar
1 .... 5.00

Web-Man
Argosy
1 .... 3.00

Web of Evil
Quality, 1952
1 .... 550.00
2-7 .... 325.00
8-11 .... 250.00
12-21 .... 150.00

Web of Mystery
Ace, 1951
1 .... 325.00
2 .... 185.00
3-10 .... 155.00
11-26 .... 132.00
27 .... 116.00
28-29 .... 86.00

Web of Scarlet Spider
Marvel, 1995
1-4 .... 2.00

Web of Spider-Man
Marvel, 1985
1 .... 8.00
2 .... 6.00
3 .... 5.00
4-10 .... 4.00
11-28 .... 3.00
29 .... 5.00
30 .... 4.00
31-32 .... 5.00
33-35 .... 3.00
36 .... 4.00
37 .... 3.00
38 .... 5.00
39-47 .... 3.00
48 .... 8.00
☛1st Demogoblin
49 .... 2.00
50 .... 3.00
51-57 .... 2.00
58 .... 3.00
59 .... 8.00
60-61 .... 3.00
62-89 .... 2.00
90 .... 5.00
90/2nd 3.00
91-99 .... 2.00
100 .... 4.00
101-105 .... 2.00
106/CS 5.00
106 .... 1.00
107-113 .... 2.00
113/CS 4.00
114-116 .... 2.00
117 .... 3.00
117/Variant 5.00
118 .... 3.00
118/2nd-119 .... 2.00

119/CS 6.00
120 .... 4.00
121-124 .... 2.00
125 .... 3.00
125/Variant 4.00
126-129 .... 2.00
129/CS 5.00
Ann 1 .... 7.00
Ann 2 .... 6.00
Ann 3-10 .... 3.00
SS 1 .... 4.00

Webspinners: Tales of Spider-Man
Marvel, 1999
1-1/B 3.00
1/Sunburst 5.00
2/A-18 .... 3.00

Wedding Bells
Quality, 1954
1-12 .... 50.00

Wedding of Dracula
Marvel, 1993
1 .... 2.00

Wedding of Popeye and Olive
Ocean, 1998
1 .... 3.00

Weezul
Lightning, 1996
1/A-1/B 3.00

Weird
DC, 1988
1-4 .... 2.00

Weird (Magazine)
DC, 1997
1 .... 3.00

Weird
Avalon
1-4 .... 3.00

Weird Adventures
P.L., 1951
1 .... 325.00
2 .... 250.00
3 .... 225.00

Weird Adventures (Ziff)
Ziff-Davis, 1951
10 .... 225.00

Weird Business
Mojo
Ashcan 1 .... 1.00

Weird Chills
Key, 1954
1 .... 600.00
2 .... 450.00
3 .... 300.00

Weird Comics
Fox, 1940
1 .... 4,500.00
2 .... 2,000.00
3-5 .... 1,000.00
6-8 .... 925.00
9-10 .... 800.00
11-19 .... 600.00
20 .... 650.00

Weirdfall
Antarctic, 1995
1-3 .... 3.00

Weird Fantasy
E.C., 1950
1 .... 1,150.00
2 .... 500.00
3-4 .... 425.00
5 .... 335.00
6-10 .... 240.00
11-13 .... 180.00
14 .... 300.00
15 .... 200.00
16-19 .... 170.00
20 .... 200.00
21 .... 285.00
22 .... 140.00

Weird Fantasy
Gemstone, 1992
1 .... 3.00
2-10 .... 2.00
11-22 .... 3.00
Ann 1 .... 9.00
Ann 2 .... 10.00
Ann 3 .... 9.00
Ann 4 .... 10.00
Ann 5 .... 11.00

Weird Horrors
St. John, 1952
1 .... 300.00
2-3 .... 200.00
4-5 .... 160.00
6-7 .... 300.00
8-9 .... 225.00

Weird Melvin
Marc Hansen Stuff!, 1995
1-5 .... 3.00

Weird Mysteries
Gilmore, 1952
1 .... 600.00
2 .... 750.00
3 .... 550.00
4 .... 600.00
5 .... 625.00
6 .... 550.00
7 .... 450.00
8 .... 350.00
9 .... 300.00
10 .... 250.00
11 .... 225.00
12 .... 300.00

Weird Mystery Tales
DC, 1972

1	30.00
2	20.00
3	15.00
4-10	12.00
11-20	10.00
21	15.00
22-24	10.00

Weirdo
Last Gasp, 1981

1	15.00
2	10.00
3	8.00
4-10	6.00
11-20	5.00
21-26	4.00

Weirdom Comix
Weirdom, 1968

1	3.00
2-15	2.00

Weird Romance
Eclipse, 1988

1	2.00

Weird Science
E.C., 1950

1	1,450.00
2	625.00
3-4	575.00
5-10	360.00
11-14	230.00
15-18	260.00
19-22	335.00

Weird Science
Gladstone, 1990

1-4	2.00

Weird Science
Gemstone, 1992

1	3.00
2-14	2.00
15-22	3.00
Ann 1	9.00
Ann 2	10.00
Ann 3	11.00
Ann 4	10.00
Ann 5	11.00

Weird Science-Fantasy Annual
E.C., 1952

1	2,000.00
2	1,200.00

Weird Science-Fantasy
E.C., 1954

23-24	235.00
25	270.00
26	220.00
27	235.00
28	260.00
29	450.00

Weird Science-Fantasy (RCP)
Gemstone, 1992

1-11	2.00
Ann 1	9.00
Ann 2	13.00

Weird Secret Origins 80-Page Giant
DC, 2004

1	6.00

Weird Sex
Fantagraphics, 1999

1	3.00

Weird Space
Avalon

1-4	3.00

Weird Suspense
Atlas-Seaboard, 1975

1	12.00
2	8.00
3	7.00

Weird SuspenStories
Superior, 1951

1-3	300.00

Weirdsville
Blindwolf, 1997

Poor Tommy! It's never easy for a kid to move to a new town, but things are especially hard, when his family moves him to the strange place called Weirdling. This tiny town definitely lives up to its name.

On his first outing to the local market, Tommy meets two brothers afraid to cross the road (because the crossing light is possessed by a homicidal demon). He also meets the pitiful dairy prophet preaching about an apocalyptic bovine conspiracy. Then, there's the talking snake looking for his baby rattle (don't worry; he thinks biting or spitting venom is gross!) and the poor guy all slimed up in goo at the bottom of the well. Not surprisingly, flying saucers and federal agents make their appearance, as well.

1-9	3.00

Weird Tales Illustrated
Millennium

1	3.00
1/Deluxe	5.00
2	3.00

Weird Tales of the Future
Aragon, 1952

1	600.00
2	750.00
3-4	600.00
5	750.00
6	350.00
7	600.00
8	425.00

Weird Tales of the Macabre
Atlas-Seaboard, 1975

1	20.00
2	30.00

☞Scarce

Weird Terror
Comic Media, 1952

1	500.00
2-4	300.00
5	230.00
6	260.00
7	230.00
8	260.00
9-10	200.00
11	260.00
12	190.00
13	200.00

Weird Thrillers
Ziff-Davis, 1951

1	600.00
2	450.00
3	850.00
4	400.00
5	300.00

Weird Trips Magazine
Kitchen Sink

1	4.00

Weird War Tales
DC, 1971

1	125.00
2	75.00
3	45.00
4-5	30.00
6-10	20.00
11-20	12.00
21-31	8.00
32-50	6.00
51-92	5.00
93	6.00
94-101	5.00
102-124	4.00

Weird War Tales
DC, 1997

1-4...3.00
Special 1 ....5.00

Weird West
Fantaco, 1992

1-3...3.00

Weird Western Tales
DC, 1972

The series started staidly enough, with old timer Pow Wow Smith and the title All-Star Western. Stories soon featured Gray Morrow's El Diablo, a mysterious gun-fighter with supernatural powers. Though Billy the Kid roamed the pages, when the grotesque and lethal Jonah Hex was introduced in #10, it quickly became clear that more unusual changes were in the works.

Stories involved adventure and mystery set in the old West. Scalphunter showed up in #39, a light-skinned Indian who faced persecution by both white settlers and his own people. The romps of Bat Lash sometimes lightened the mood, but the title was designed to attract fans of, yes, weird Westerns.

12...45.00
13...30.00
14-15.......................................20.00
16-28.......................................12.00
29...16.00
30-42...8.00
43-50...6.00
51-70...5.00

Weird Western Tales
DC, 2001

1-4...3.00

Weird Wonder Tales
Marvel, 1973

1...14.00
2-3...7.00
4-7...5.00
8-15...4.00
15/30¢ 20.00

16 .... 4.00
16/30¢ 20.00
17 .... 4.00
17/30¢ 20.00
18-22.................................... 4.00

Weird Worlds
DC, 1972

1 .... 12.00
2-5 .... 7.00
6 .... 8.00
7 .... 6.00
8-10 .... 5.00

Welcome Back, Kotter
DC, 1976

1 .... 10.00
2-10 .... 3.00

Welcome Back to the House of Mystery
DC, 1998

1 .... 6.00

Welcome to the Little Shop of Horrors
Roger Corman's Cosmic Comics, 1995

1-3 .... 3.00

Welcome to the Zone
Kitchen Sink

1 .... 10.00

Wendel
Kitchen Sink

1 .... 3.00

Wendy and the New Kids on the Block
Harvey, 1991

1-3 .... 2.00

Wendy Digest Magazine
Harvey, 1990

1-5 .... 2.00

Wendy, the Good Little Witch
Harvey, 1960

1 .... 60.00
2 .... 40.00
3-5 .... 28.00
6-10 .... 22.00
11-15 .... 14.00
16-20 .... 12.00
21-25 .... 8.00
26-30 .... 6.00
31-40 .... 5.00
41-50 .... 4.00
51-60 .... 3.00
61-93 .... 2.00
94-97 .... 1.00

Wendy the Good Little Witch
Harvey, 1991

1-15 .... 2.00

Wendy in 3-D
Blackthorne

1 .... 3.00

Wendy Whitebread, Undercover Slut
Fantagraphics, 1990

1-1/4th 3.00
1/5th 4.00
2 .... 3.00

Wendy Witch World
Harvey, 1961

1 .... 90.00
2-5 .... 50.00
6-10 .... 35.00
11-20 .... 26.00
21-30 .... 22.00
31-35 .... 18.00
36-44 .... 15.00
45-49 .... 12.00
50-53 .... 8.00

Werewolf
Dell, 1966

1 .... 8.00
2-3 .... 5.00

Werewolf
Blackthorne, 1988

1-4 .... 2.00

Werewolf at Large
Eternity, 1989

1-3 .... 2.00

Werewolf By Night
Marvel, 1972

When the moon is full and the wolfsbane blooms, luckless Jack Russell transforms from a quiet young man into the vicious Werewolf by Night. Much like The Incredible Hulk, Jack has little control or memories of his behavior when he goes hairy, and his knack for transforming into a man-beast with a penchant for causing mayhem and fear wreaks havoc with his personal relationships.

Werewolf by Night made his first appearance in Marvel Spotlight #2 and soon graduated to his own series, which came out around the same time as other Marvel monster titles of the '70s Tomb of Dracula and Frankenstein. He crossed over into other series such as Marvel Team-Up and appeared in a few giant-sized specials. The title also introduced Moon Knight, who would go on to become a popular star feature in his own right.

— *Rob Salkowitz*

1	80.00
2	30.00
3	15.00
4	18.00
5-10	15.00
11-14	12.00
15	15.00
16-17	12.00
18-20	10.00
21-31	8.00
32	60.00

☞1st Moon Knight

33	30.00
34	8.00
35-36	5.00
37	10.00
38	5.00
38/30¢	15.00
39	5.00
39/30¢	15.00
40-41	5.00
42	12.00
43	18.00

Werewolf By Night
Marvel, 1998
1-6	3.00

Werewolf in 3-D
Blackthorne, 1988
1	3.00

Werewolf the Apocalypse: Black Furies
Moonstone, 2003
1	6.00

Werewolf the Apocalypse: Bone Gnawers
Moonstone, 2003
1	6.00

West Coast Avengers
Marvel, 1984
1	3.00
2-4	2.00

West Coast Avengers
Marvel, 1985
1-3	2.00
4	3.00
5-46	1.00
Ann 1-3	2.00

Western Tales of Terror
Hoarse and Buggy, 2004
1-5	4.00

Western Action
Atlas-Seaboard, 1975
1	9.00

Western Adventure Comics
Ace, 1948
1	135.00
2	70.00
3	75.00
4	60.00

Western Comics
DC, 1948
1	625.00
2	300.00
3	225.00
4-5	200.00
6-7	165.00
8	200.00
9-10	165.00
11-20	110.00
21-30	85.00
31-40	60.00
41-50	45.00
51-60	38.00
61-85	35.00

Western Crime Busters
Trojan, 1950
1	175.00
2	100.00
3-5	85.00
6-7	175.00
8	85.00

Western Crime Cases
Star, 1951
9	125.00

Westerner
Toytown, 1948
14	75.00
15-25	50.00
26	75.00
27-30	50.00
31-41	40.00

Western Fighters (Vol. 1)
Hillman, 1948
1	165.00
2-3	48.00
4	55.00
5-6	32.00
7	55.00
8-9	32.00
10	55.00
11	125.00
12	30.00

Western Fighters (Vol. 2)
Hillman, 1949
1	45.00
2-12	24.00

Western Fighters (Vol. 3)
Hillman, 1950
1-11	20.00
12	35.00

Western Fighters (Vol. 4)
Hillman, 1951
1-7	30.00
3D 1	160.00

Western Gunfighters (1st series)
Atlas, 1956
20-21	75.00
22	100.00
23-24	75.00
25-27	55.00

Western Gunfighters (2nd Series)
Marvel, 1970
1	28.00
2-3	15.00
4	18.00
5-7	15.00
8-16	7.00
17-33	5.00

Western Hearts
Standard, 1949
1	120.00
2-10	80.00

Western Hero
Fawcett, 1949
76	150.00
77-82	100.00
83-95	75.00
96-112	60.00

Western Kid (2nd Series)
Marvel, 1971
1	17.00
2-5	8.00

Western Killers
Fox, 1948
60	140.00
61-64	110.00

Western Life Romances
Marvel, 1949
1	125.00
2	85.00

Western Love
Prize, 1949
1	200.00
2	150.00
3-4	100.00
5	150.00

Western Outlaws
Atlas, 1954
1	150.00
2	90.00
3-10	60.00
11	70.00
12-13	60.00
14	70.00
15-21	60.00

Western Outlaws and Sheriffs
Marvel, 1949

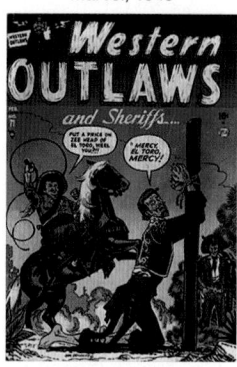

Western Outlaws and Sheriffs, formerly Best Western Comics, was an especially graphic and brutal pre-Comics Code Western series from Atlas (later Marvel), at that time one of the bottom-feeders in the comics-publishing food chain.

Western Outlaws and Sheriffs specialized in stories featuring whippings, hangings, scalpings, and -- on one notable occasion -- cannibalism. This was the Western genre's equivalent of the crime comics on the stands at the same time, glorifying the violence and lawlessness of the criminals and offering an equal measure of rough justice in the end.

-- Rob Salkowitz

60	125.00
61-67	100.00
68-72	75.00
73	80.00

Western Picture Stories
Comics Magazine, 1937

1	1,100.00
2-4	550.00

Western Roundup
Dell, 1952

1	165.00
2	120.00
3-5	75.00
6-10	65.00
11-17	55.00
18	65.00
19-23	55.00
24	60.00
25	80.00

Western Team-Up
Marvel, 1973

1	8.00

Western Thrillers
Fox, 1948

1	275.00
2	110.00
3-6	100.00

Western Thrillers
Atlas, 1954

1	100.00
2-4	65.00

Western True Crime
Fox, 1949

4-6	85.00

Western Winners
Marvel, 1949

5	175.00
6-7	150.00

West of the Dakotas
Comic Book Stories, 2002

1	5.00

Westside
Antarctic, 2000

1	3.00

West Street Stories
West Street, 1995

0-1	3.00

Wetworks
Image, 1994

1	3.00
1/3D	5.00
1/Ltd.-3	2.00
4-24	3.00
25-25/A	4.00
26-32	3.00
32/A	4.00
33-43	3.00
3D 1	5.00

Wetworks Sourcebook
Image, 1994

1	3.00

Wetworks/Vampirella
Image, 1997

1-1/A	3.00

Whack
St. John, 1953

1	175.00
2-3	85.00

Whacked!
River Group, 1994

1	3.00

Wha... Huh?
Marvel, 2005

0	4.00

Wham
Centaur, 1940

1	1,000.00
2	675.00

Wham-O Giant Comics
Wham-O, 1967

1	100.00

What If...? (Vol. 1)
Marvel, 1977

One of the most imaginative titles to come from Marvel, What If... was a more engaging, serious take on DC's "imaginary stories." As series host, The Watcher reminded readers each issue of one or more events from Marvel's history -- and then told the story of an alternate reality in which things happened differently.

Some were silly -- such as the Marvel Bullpen becoming the Fantastic Four or Sgt. Fury fighting World War II in space -- but others were poignant. "What If The Avengers Had Become the Pawns of Korvac" in #32 stands as one of the bleakest, most horrifying tales ever to come from Marvel. (A follow-up later appeared in Classic X-Men.) The story of the survival of Spider-Man's clone in #30 is better than the entire "Clone Saga" that appeared in later Spidey comics. And Tony Isabella's "What If Gwen Stacy Had Lived" in #24 has torn at the heartstrings of many Spidey fans over the years.

Too many stories would follow the "let's kill all the super-heroes" mold, but many from this first series, which is far superior to the second volume, are among Marvel's best. Look for #34's all-humor issue, which remains one of the funniest comics ever published by Marvel.

-- John Jackson Miller

1	15.00
2	10.00
3-5	8.00
6-10	5.00
11-12	4.00
13	5.00
14-15	4.00
16	3.00
17	4.00

While Fifty Million Died
Tome
1 ....3.00

Whip Wilson
Bell Features, 1950
9 ....350.00
10-11 ....200.00

Whirlwind Comics
Nita, 1940
1 ....1,250.00
2-3 ....850.00

Whispers and Shadows
Oasis, 1984
1-8 ....2.00

Whisper
Capital, 1983
1 ....3.00
2 ....2.00

Whisper
First, 1985
1-37 ....2.00
Special 1 ....3.00

White Devil
Eternity, 1988
1-8 ....3.00

White Fang
Disney, 1990
1 ....3.00
1/Direct 6.00

White Like She
Dark Horse, 1994
1-4 ....3.00

White Orchid
Atlantis
1 ....3.00

Whiteout
Oni, 1998
1-4 ....3.00

Whiteout: Melt
Oni, 1999
1-4 ....3.00

White Princess
of the Jungle
Avon, 1951
1-2 ....400.00
3-4 ....300.00
5 ....350.00

White Raven
Visionary, 1995
1 ....3.00

White Rider and
Super Horse
Star, 1950
4 ....100.00
5-6 ....80.00

White Tiger
Marvel, 2007
1-2 ....3.00

White Trash
Tundra
1-4 ....4.00

Whiz Comics
Fawcett, 1940

Whiz Comics was Fawcett Publications' first comic-book title. It was an anthology series, featuring one story each about such characters as Ibis the Invincible, Lance O'Casey, Golden Arrow, Spy Smasher, Dan Dare, Scoop Smith, and Dr. Voodoo. There was never an issue numbered #1, although an ashcan exists; the first to hit the newsstand was #2, and it cover-featured the character for whom it's best known: Captain Marvel. The story of how Billy Batson became The Big Red Cheese by shouting, "Shazam!" was first told in this issue, and in #25 the series featured the origin story of another Marvel Family member: Captain Marvel Jr. (Freddy Freeman, no relation to Billy). ("Shazam," by the way, was an acronym for the names of those from whom Captain Marvel drew his powers: Solomon, Hercules, Atlas, Zeus, Achilles, and Mercury.)

The Marvel Family's career went on hiatus in a consent decree in the 1950s and, by the time the field was eager to read new adventures, the name of Captain Marvel had been usurped by Marvel Comics. As a result, the version from the Silver Age to today appears in titles like Shazam!, rather than in a Captain Marvel-titled series.

-- Maggie

1 ....70,000.00
☛1st Captain Marvel
2 ....5,200.00
3 ....3,400.00
4 ....2,800.00
5 ....2,250.00
6 ....1,650.00
7 ....1,725.00
8-9 ....1,650.00

10 ....1,250.00
11-12 ....1,100.00
13-14 ....1,075.00
15 ....1,250.00
16-18 ....1,100.00
19-20 ....750.00
21 ....800.00
22-24 ....600.00
25 ....6,200.00
☛1st Capt. Marvel Jr.
26 ....550.00
27-30 ....525.00
31-32 ....460.00
33 ....525.00
34 ....365.00
35 ....410.00
36-40 ....365.00
41-43 ....260.00
44 ....300.00
45-50 ....260.00
51-60 ....210.00
61-70 ....175.00
71-82 ....150.00
83-100 ....130.00
101-120 ....110.00
121-152 ....100.00
153-155 ....200.00

Whiz Kids
Image, 2003
1 ....5.00

Whoa, Nellie!
Fantagraphics, 1996
1-3 ....3.00

Whodunnit?
Eclipse, 1986
1-3 ....2.00

Who Is Next?
Standard, 1953
5 ....100.00

Who is the Crooked Man
Crusade, 1996
1 ....4.00

Who Really Killed JFK
Revolutionary, 1993
1 ....3.00

Who's Who in Star Trek
DC, 1987
1-2 ....2.00

Who's Who
in the DC Universe
DC, 1990
1-16 ....5.00

Who's Who
in the DC Universe
Update 1993
DC, 1992
1-2 ....6.00

Who's Who in the
Impact Universe
DC, 1991
1-3 ....5.00

Who's Who in the Legion of Super-Heroes
DC, 1988

1-7..2.00

Who's Who: The Definitive Directory of the DC Universe
DC, 1985

1-26...2.00

Who's Who Update '87
DC, 1987

1-5...2.00

Who's Who Update '88
DC, 1988

1-4...2.00

Whotnot
Fantagraphics

1-3...3.00

Why I Hate Saturn
DC

1..15.00

Wicked
Image, 1999

1-7...3.00
Ashcan 1 ....5.00

Wicked
Millennium, 1994

1-3...3.00

Wicked, The: Medusa's Tale
Image, 2000

1..4.00

Widow
Avatar, 2000

0..4.00

Widow: Flesh and Blood
Ground Zero, 1992

1-3...3.00

Widow: Metal Gypsies
London Night, 1995

1..4.00

Wiindows
Cult, 1993

1..4.00
2-17...3.00

Wilbur
Archie, 1944

1..260.00
2..115.00
3-4...85.00
5..375.00
6-10...85.00
11-21...52.00
22-30...36.00
31-50...24.00
51-60...15.00
61-70...10.00
71-88...8.00
89-90...4.00

Wild
Atlas, 1954

1 .... 150.00
2 .... 85.00
3-5 .... 75.00

Wild
Eastern

1 .... 2.00

Wild!
Mu, 2003

1-14 .... 4.00

Wild Animals
Pacific, 1982

1 .... 2.00

Wild Bill Elliott
Dell, 1950

2-3 .... 75.00
4-10 .... 55.00
13-17 .... 40.00

Wild Bill Hickok
Avon, 1949

1 .... 165.00
2 .... 75.00
3-5 .... 60.00
6-9 .... 50.00
10-12 .... 60.00
13-14 .... 50.00
15-20 .... 40.00
21-28 .... 35.00

Wild Bill Hickok
Super, 1952

10-12 .... 60.00

Wild Bill Pecos
AC, 1989

1 .... 4.00

Wild Boy of the Congo
Ziff-Davis, 1951

10 (#1).. 120.00
11 (#2).. 100.00
12 (#3).. 80.00
4 .... 60.00
5-6 .... 50.00
7 .... 60.00
8-10 .... 50.00
11 .... 65.00
12-15 .... 50.00

WildB.R.A.T.s
Fantagraphics, 1992

1 .... 3.00

Wildcards
Marvel, 1990

1-4 .... 5.00

WildC.A.T.s
Image, 1992

0 .... 3.00
1 .... 4.00
1/3D.. 5.00
1/Gold.. 10.00
1/Variant 5.00
2 .... 4.00
3-10 .... 3.00

11 .... 15.00
11/Holofoil 22.00
12 .... 8.00
13 .... 6.00
14-24 .... 3.00
25 .... 5.00
26-49 .... 3.00
50 .... 4.00
50/Variant 5.00
Ann 1 .... 3.00
Special 1 .... 4.00

WildCats
DC, 1999

1-1/F... 3.00
1/Sketch 10.00
2-28 .... 3.00
Ann 2000............................... 4.00

WildCats
DC, 2006

1-1/2nd variant 3.00

WildC.A.T.S Adventures
Image, 1994

1-3.. 2.00
4-10.. 3.00

WildC.A.T.S Adventures Sourcebook
Image, 1995

1 .... 3.00

WildC.A.T.S/Aliens
Image, 1998

1-1/A 5.00

WildCats/Cyberforce: Killer Instinct
DC, 2004

1 .... 15.00

WildC.A.T.S (Jim Lee's...)
Image, 1995

1 .... 2.00

WildCats: Ladytron
DC, 2000

1 .... 6.00

WildCats: Mosaic
DC, 2000

1 .... 4.00

WildCats: Nemesis
DC, 2005

1-9 .... 3.00

WildC.A.T.S Sourcebook
Image, 1993

1-2.. 3.00

WildC.A.T.S Trilogy
Image, 1993

1 .... 3.00
2-3 .... 2.00

WildCats Version 3.0
DC, 2002

1-24 .... 3.00

WildC.A.T.s/X-Men: The Golden Age
Image, 1997

1-1/A	5.00
1/Scroll	8.00
1/C	5.00
1/w. glasses	7.00
1/F	5.00
1/Scroll w. gla	9.00

WildC.A.T.s/X-Men: The Modern Age
Image, 1997

1	5.00
1/A	6.00
1/Nightcrawler	8.00
1/w. glasses	7.00
1/D	5.00
1/E	8.00

WildC.A.T.s/X-Men: The Silver Age
Image, 1997

1-1/B	5.00
1/3D-1/D	7.00
1/E	5.00

Wildcore
Image, 1997

Wildcore is the special strike team of the government's Department PSI. Comprising both human paranormals and members of the alien race, Kherubim, Wildcore battles the D'rahn, another alien race, and former allies against the Daemonites, who first appeared in WildC.A.T.s.

The members include: Taboo, a woman with a symbiote constructed from vampire DNA grafted to her; Zealot, a full-blooded Kherubim warrior and formerly a member of WildC.A.T.S; and Ferrian, another Kherubim, who can divine psychic impressions from objects through touch. Marc Slayton, a Kherubim half-breed who has lived for 3000 years, is the leader of Wildcore and is code-named Backlash. Before

he obtained his own title he was a core member of StormWatch.

Although the individual powers of the team members are diverse and distinct, their emotional interactions are not so different from those of normal men and women.

-- George Haberberger

1-1/A	3.00
1/B	5.00
2-Ashcan 1	3.00

Wild Dog
DC, 1987

1-4	2.00
Special 1	3.00

Wilderness
4Winds

Deluxe 1	25.00

Wildflower
Sirius, 1998

1-5	3.00

Wild Frontier
Charlton, 1955

1	60.00
2-6	40.00
7	50.00

Wild Frontier (Shanda)
Shanda, 1956

1	60.00
2	3.00

Wild Girl
DC, 2005

1-6	3.00

Wildguard: Casting Call
Image, 2003

1-6	3.00

Wildguard: Fire Power
Image, 2004

1/A-1/B	4.00

WildGuard: Fool's Gold
Image, 2005

1-2	4.00

Wild Kingdom
Mu, 1991

1-7	3.00
8-14	4.00

Wild Knights
Eternity, 1988

1-10	2.00

Wild Life
Antarctic, 1993

1-12	3.00

Wild Life
Fantagraphics, 1994

1-2	3.00

Wildlifers
Radio, 1999

1	5.00

Wildman
Miller

1-11	2.00

Wildman (Grass Green's...)
Megaton

1-2	2.00

Wild Party
Kitchen Sink

1	22.00

Wild Person in the Woods
G.T. Labs, 1999

A black-and-white comic-book novelization compresses the more than 20 years of Birute Galdikas' field work into fewer than 20 pages. This follows her extensive adventures in the lush jungles of Borneo, tracking and observing orangutans in the wild. Jim Ottaviani once again has captured the feel of a scientist doing her work and expresses her motions and feelings during a sweeping period of time.

With the benefit of Anne Timmons' illustrations, this book is an excellent story, bordering on biographical fact and containing extensive end notes and references at the end of the tale to help prospective researchers become aware of what's going on in the world today.

1	3.00

Wild Side
United, 1998

1-6	4.00

Wildsiderz
DC, 2005

0	2.00
0/Variant	3.00
1/A cover	4.00
1/B cover	5.00
1/Lenticular	6.00
2	4.00

Wildstar
Image, 1995

1-4 .... 3.00

Wild Stars
Collector's, 1984

1 .... 1.00

Wild Stars
Collector's, 1988

1 .... 2.00

Wild Stars
Little Rocket, 2001

1-7 .... 3.00

Wildstar: Sky Zero
Image, 1993

1	3.00
1/Gold	4.00
2	2.00
3-4	3.00

WildStorm!
Image, 1995

1-4 .... 3.00

WildStorm Annual
DC, 2000

2000 .... 4.00

WildStorm Chamber of Horrors
Image, 1995

1 .... 4.00

WildStorm Fine Art Spotlight: Jim Lee
DC, 2007

1 .... 4.00

WildStorm Halloween '97
Image, 1997

1 .... 3.00

WildStorm Rarities
Image, 1994

1 .... 5.00

WildStorm Rising
Image, 1995

1	3.00
2	2.00

WildStorm Sampler
Image

1 .... 1.00

WildStorms Player's Guide
Image, 1996

1 .... 2.00

WildStorm Spotlight
Image, 1997

1-4 .... 3.00

Wildstorm Summer Special
DC, 2001

1 .... 6.00

WildStorm Swimsuit Special
Image, 1994

1-1997 .... 3.00

WildStorm Thunderbook
DC, 2000

1 .... 7.00

Wildstorm Ultimate Sports Official Program
Image, 1997

1 .... 3.00

WildStorm Universe 97
Image, 1996

1-3 .... 3.00

WildStorm Universe Sourcebook
Image, 1995

1-2 .... 3.00

Wildstorm Winter Special
DC, 2005

1 .... 5.00

Wild Thing
Marvel, 1993

1	3.00
2-7	2.00

Wild Thing
Marvel, 1999

1-5 .... 2.00

Wild Things
Metro, 1986

1-3 .... 2.00

Wild Thingz
ABC

0/A	3.00
0/B	6.00
0/Platinum	3.00

Wild Think
Wild Think, 1987

1 .... 2.00

Wild Times: Deathblow
DC, 1999

In a multi-title WildStorm Productions event, Wild Times takes five of the publisher's most popular titles and drops them into pivotal points in American history (the Wild West, World War II, Prohibition, the Cold War and the 1960s), retelling their origins to fit accordingly. Think of it as a "What if this character or group had lived in this particular era" type of story.

Receiving the treatment this time around is the popular character of Deathblow. It's 1899 and Michael Cray, a.k.a. Deathblow, is the last of a dying breed of old-time gunslingers. Selling his services and six guns to Sister Maria, a nun fighting to protect the world from a virtual Hell on Earth at the hands of Jason Brittles, the story plays out more like a past life experience for each of the characters rather than an alternate reality. A surprise appearance by DC Comics' Jonah Hex only sweetens the tale.

1 .... 3.00

Wild Times: DV8
DC, 1999

1 .... 3.00

Wild Times: Gen13
DC, 1999

1 .... 3.00

Wild Times: Grifter
DC, 1999

1 .... 3.00

Wild Times: Wetworks
DC, 1999

1 .... 3.00

Wild West
Marvel, 1948

1	200.00
2	125.00

Wild West
Charlton, 1966
58 ....10.00

Wild West C.O.W.-Boys of Moo Mesa
Archie, 1993
1-3 ....1.00

Wild Western
Atlas, 1948
3 ....160.00
4 ....110.00
5 ....125.00
6-8 ....75.00
9 ....100.00
10 ....110.00
11-19 ....75.00
20-30 ....55.00
31-40 ....45.00
41-47 ....40.00
48 ....50.00
49-51 ....40.00
52 ....50.00
53 ....40.00
54-55 ....50.00
56-57 ....40.00

Wild, Wild West
Gold Key, 1966
1 ....70.00
2 ....45.00
3-7 ....35.00

Wild, Wild West
Millennium, 1990
1-4 ....3.00

Wild Women
Paragon
1 ....5.00

Wild Zoo
Radio, 2000
1-7 ....3.00
8 ....4.00

Will Eisner Presents
Eclipse, 1990
1-3 ....3.00

Will Eisner Reader
DC, 2000
1 ....10.00

Will Eisner's 3-D Classics: Spirit
Kitchen Sink, 1985
1 ....2.00

Will Eisner's John Law: Angels and Ashes, Devils and Dust
Idea & Design Works, 2006
1 ....4.00

Will Eisner's Quarterly
Kitchen Sink, 1983
1 ....3.00
2 ....4.00
3-8 ....2.00

William Shatner
Celebrity
1 ....6.00

Willie Comics
Marvel, 1946
5 ....75.00
6-12 ....50.00

Willow
Marvel, 1988
1-3 ....2.00

Willow (Angel)
Angel, 1996
0 ....3.00
0/Nude 10.00

Will Rogers
Fox, 1950
5 ....175.00
2 ....200.00

Will to Power
Dark Horse, 1994

This series matches Comics' Greatest World's biggest Boy Scout against its most dangerous vigilante. It all takes place in Arcadia, a city built on corruption. The vigilante called X has staked out a territory of his own here. Prowling the docks and rooftops, he's caused considerable trouble for the mob bosses. Unable to stop him themselves, they've decided to call in some help from out of town.

Titan is a well-intentioned super-man currently working for the government. Through the influence of corrupt politicians, he is assigned to clean up Arcadia -- starting with the "X-Killer." Titan is indestructible and unstoppable, but X is a man obsessed. When these two meet, the results are (literally) explosive! Following that confrontation, Titan would go on to meet the other denizens of Comics' Greatest World.

1 ....2.00
2-12 ....1.00

Wimmen's Comix
Renegade, 1972
1 ....10.00
2-4 ....8.00
5-8 ....5.00
9-10 ....4.00
11-18 ....3.00

Windburnt Plains of Wonder
Lohman Hills, 1996
1 ....12.00

Wind in the Willows
NBM, 1999
1-2 ....16.00

Windraven
Heroic
1 ....3.00

Windraven Adventures
Blue Comet, 1993
1 ....3.00

Winds of Winter
Antarctic, 2001
1 ....5.00

Windsor
Win-Mil
1-2 ....2.00

Windy and Willy
DC, 1969
1 ....25.00
2-4 ....15.00

Wingbird Akuma-She
Verotik, 1998
1 ....4.00

Wingbird Returns
Verotik, 1997
1 ....10.00

Wingding Orgy
Fantagraphics, 1997
1-2 ....4.00

Winged Tiger
Cartoonists Across America, 1999
3 ....3.00

Winging It
Solo
1 ....2.00

Wings
Mu, 1992
1 ....3.00

Wings Comics
Fiction House, 1940
1 ....1,500.00
2 ....800.00
3-5 ....460.00
6-10 ....365.00
11-15 ....320.00
16-20 ....275.00
21-30 ....215.00
31-40 ....175.00
41-50 ....135.00

51-60	110.00
61-80	100.00
81-100	90.00
101-124	75.00

Wings Comics (A-List)
A-List, 1997

1-4	3.00

Winnie the Pooh
Gold Key, 1977

1	20.00
2	10.00
3-17	7.00
18-19	10.00
20	125.00
21-28	10.00
29-33	20.00

Winnie Winkle
Dell, 1948

1	50,00
2	30.00
3-7	25.00

Winning in the Desert
Apple

1-2	3.00

Winter Men
DC, 2005

1-5	3.00

Winter Soldier: Winter Kills
Marvel, 2007

1	4.00

Winterstar
Echo, 1996

1	3.00

Winterworld
Eclipse, 1987

1-3	2.00

Wireheads
Fleetway-Quality

1-2	3.00

Wisdom
Marvel, 2007

1	4.00

Wisdom of the Gnomes
Celebrity, 1989

1-2	3.00

Wise Son: The White Wolf
DC, 1996

1-4	3.00

Wish
Tokyopop, 2002

1	10.00

Wish Upon a Star
Warp, 1994

1	1.00

Wisp
Oktomica, 1999

1	3.00

Witch
Eternity

1	2.00

Witchblade
Image, 1995

Witchblade, created by Marc Silvestri and published by Image Comics, began in December 1995. Police Detective Sara Pezzini's life was changed forever, when she discovered the Witchblade, a bio-mechanical weapon. At first, Sara was afraid of the Witchblade but soon became accustomed, if not addicted, to the powerful killing tool. Finding herself haunted by nightmares concerning friends who were murdered, she decides to use the Witchblade to avenge those senseless crimes. But she must keep the knowledge of the Witchblade secret from her friends as well as those who know of its existence and would kill to acquire it.

Although Image co-founder and artist Marc Silvestri created Witchblade, he did not write or draw the issues. Nevertheless, Witchblade managed to combine hints of sex and violence into a collector's phenomenon, with a fury of bidding driving up the prices of early issues.

1/2	15.00
1	25.00
1/B	15.00
2	18.00
2/A	15.00
2/2nd	4.00
3	10.00
4-5	8.00
6-7	6.00
8-10	5.00
11-14	4.00
14/Gold	6.00
15	4.00
16-18/A	3.00
19-24	3.00
24/Variant	5.00
25	3.00
25/A	4.00
25/B	8.00
25/C	15.00
26-29	3.00
29/Variant	5.00
30-32	3.00
32/Variant	15.00
33-41	3.00
41/A	10.00
42-49	3.00
50	5.00
50/Silvestri-50/Turner	5.00
51-74	3.00
75-75/Variant	5.00
76-80	3.00
80/Holiday	5.00
80/Cho-80/Land	3.00
80/Conv	5.00
81-91	3.00
92	5.00
93-99	3.00
100/Turner-100/Anime	5.00
101-102	3.00
500	5.00
Deluxe 1-3	25.00

Witchblade/Dark Minds: Return of Paradox
Image, 2004

1	10.00

Witchblade/Aliens/ The Darkness/Predator
Dark Horse, 2000

1-3	3.00

Witchblade: Animated One Shot
Image, 2003

1	3.00

Witchblade: Blood Oath
Image, 2004

1	5.00

Witchblade/Darkchylde
Image, 2000

1	3.00

Witchblade/Darkness Special
Image, 1999

1/2/Platinum	35.00
1	4.00

Witchblade: Destiny's Child
Image, 2000

1-3	3.00

Witchblade/Elektra
Marvel, 1997

1	3.00

Witchblade Gallery
Image, 2000

1	3.00

Witchblade Infinity
Image, 1999
1 .... 4.00

Witchblade/Lady Death
Image, 2001
1 .... 5.00

Witchblade: Movie Edition
Image, 2000
1-1/C 3.00

Witchblade: Nottingham
Image, 2003
1 .... 5.00

Witchblade: Obakemono
Image, 2002
1 .... 10.00

Witchblade 10th Anniversary Cover Gallery
Image, 2005
1 .... 3.00

Witchblade/Tomb Raider
Image, 1998
1/2 .... 5.00

Witchblade & Tomb Raider
Image, 2005
1 .... 3.00

Witchblade/Tomb Raider
Image, 1998
1/A 4.00
1/B 5.00
1/C 7.00

Witchblade/Wolverine
Image, 2004
1 .... 3.00

Witchcraft
Avon, 1952
1 .... 420.00
2 .... 315.00
3 .... 235.00
4 .... 265.00
5 .... 300.00
6 .... 235.00

Witchcraft
DC, 1994
1-3 .... 3.00

Witchcraft: La Terreur
DC, 1998
1-3 .... 3.00

Witches
Marvel, 2004
1-4 .... 3.00

Witches' Cauldron: The Battle of the Cherkassy Pocket
Heritage Collection
1 .... 4.00

Witches Tales
Harvey, 1951
1 .... 310.00
2 .... 260.00
3-10 .... 210.00
11-16 .... 190.00
17-19 .... 225.00
20-24 .... 190.00
25-28 .... 165.00

Witches' Western Tales
Harvey, 1955
29-30 .... 125.00

Witchfinder
Image, 1999
1-2 .... 3.00

Witch Hunter
Malibu, 1996
1 .... 3.00

Witching
DC, 2004
1-10 .... 3.00

Witching Hour
DC, 1969
1 .... 150.00
2 .... 70.00
3 .... 50.00
4-6 .... 25.00
7 .... 18.00
8-13 .... 15.00
14-51 .... 10.00
52-66 .... 8.00
67-85 .... 5.00

Witching Hour
DC, 2000
1-3 .... 6.00

Witching Hour (Anne Rice's...)
Millennium, 1992
1-13 .... 3.00

Within Our Reach
Star*Reach
1 .... 8.00

With the Marines on the Battlefronts of the World
Toby, 1953
1 .... 70.00
2 .... 40.00

Witness
Marvel, 1948
1 .... 1,250.00

Witty Comics
Chicago Nite Life News, 1945

As the golden age of comics began to wind down in the mid-1940s, lots of publishers tried their hand at grabbing a share of the shrinking market. Witty Comics is an also-ran so obscure that it barely registers on the radar, but not because it was necessarily any worse than any other offering on the stands at the time. Witty Comics featured a typical Golden Age line-up led by a costumed hero (the undistinguished Pioneer), backed up by an assortment of adventurers (Dick Royce, jungle aviator). Also included are detectives (Steve Hagen, private eye), teen humor (Sir Gallagher, goofy teen inventor), non-fiction featurettes ("Live and Learn"), and gag strips (the oddly-named "Poopsicles" and "Weeny and Pop"). However, by 1945, the formula that had made outfits like DC, Quality, and Fawcett successful was passe, with readers looking for newer thrills (like the insurgent crime, "Good Girl Art," and romance comics then appearing on the stands), and Witty did not last into 1946.

-- Rob Salkowitz

1 .... 90.00
2 .... 55.00
3-7 .... 50.00

Wizard in Training
Upper Deck, 2002
0 .... 3.00

Wizard of 4th Street
Dark Horse, 1987
1-6 .... 2.00

Wizard of 4th Street
David P. House
1-3 .... 2.00

Wizard of Time
DPH, 1986
1-2..2.00

Wizards of the Last Resort
Blackthorne, 1987
1-4..2.00

Wizard Works
Fantasy General, 1986

Wizard Works was one of a number of titles launched simultaneously in 1985 by Fantasy General Comics. It was a boom time for black-and-white comics, and Fantasy General planned to make its mark with titles like Heavy Armor, Alpha Track, Charlie the Caveman, and Future Course. However, each appeared and disappeared with little notice.

For its part, Wizard Works was planned as a four-issue anthology with several fantasy-based features running in serial format. Few rose above rehashing old movie plot lines ("Sorcerer of the Black Void" virtually lifting Poltergeist) or telling middling fantasy-elf tales. Whereas titles like Elfquest manage to create a world full of engaging characters, Wizard Works seems more an earnest, well-meaning work of fan fiction.

1-4..2.00

WJHC
Wilson Place, 1998
1 ....2.00

Wogglebug
Arrow, 1988
1 ....3.00

Wolf & Red
Dark Horse, 1995
1-3..3.00

Wolff & Byrd, Counselors of the Macabre
Exhibit A, 1988
1 .... 4.00
2-23 .... 3.00

Wolff & Byrd, Counselors of the Macabre's Greatest Writs
Exhibit A
1 .... 3.00

Wolff & Byrd, Counselors of the Macabre's Secretary Mavis
Exhibit A, 1998
1-2 .... 3.00
3-4 .... 4.00

Wolff & Byrd: Supernatural Law
Exhibit A
1 .... 8.00

Wolf Gal (Al Capp's...)
Toby, 1951
1-2 .... 195.00

Wolfman
Dell, 1964
1 .... 24.00
1/2nd 20.00

Wolfpack
Marvel, 1988

Legend has it that a lost tribe of Israel promised its god that there would always be ten righteous men in the world. To balance this, nature provided for the Nine: evil men whose purpose was to corrupt and destroy the Ten. The Nine proved almost impossible to resist, and, in desperation, one of the Ten formed a renegade band, a wolfpack, whose members hid in the hills.

Millennia later, the pack's spiritual descendants were a group of youngsters in the Bronx, gathered together by Mr. Mack to fight drug pushers and other thugs.

First appearing in Marvel Graphic Novel #31, the team carries on the fight in this 12-issue limited series. Only this time, Mr. Mack is gone, and the Wolfpack must learn to survive on its own.

1-12 .... 1.00

Wolf Run: A Known Associates Mystery
Known Associates
1 .... 3.00

Wolph
Blackthorne, 1987
1 .... 2.00

Wolverbroad vs. Hobo
Spoof, 1992
1 .... 3.00

Wolverine
Marvel, 1982

His past is shrouded in mystery. The man named Logan was a secret agent once but eventually resigned. After that, he became the unwilling subject of a brutal experiment -- an experiment that bonded adamantium to his skeleton and gave him retractable claws that can cut through steel. Now, he is best known as Wolverine, a member of The Uncanny X-Men and one of the most dangerous men on the planet.

He fell in love with the beautiful Marika Yashida, daughter of one of the richest and most powerful families in Japan. Although they had planned to marry, she spurned him at the last moment. Now, Wolverine receives word that she has been summoned back to

Japan and forced to fulfill a debt of honor by marrying the head of another clan. When Wolverine decides to see for himself, he learns her terrible secret and becomes embroiled in the dark underground of the Japanese mob.

1	25.00
2	18.00
3	17.00
4	16.00

Wolverine
Marvel, 1988

-1	2.00
1/2	3.00
1/2/Ltd.	8.00
1	10.00
2	6.00
3-5	5.00
6	4.00
7-9	5.00
10	8.00
11-14	4.00
15	5.00
16-19	4.00
20	5.00
21-23	4.00
24-40	3.00
41	4.00
41/2nd-42/2nd	2.00
43	3.00
44	2.00
45-49	3.00
50	4.00
51-56	2.00
57	3.00
58-74	2.00
75	4.00
76-79	2.00
80	8.00
81-84	2.00
85	3.00
85/Variant	4.00
86-87	2.00
87/Deluxe	4.00
88	2.00
88/Deluxe	4.00
89	2.00
89/Deluxe	4.00
90	2.00
90/Deluxe	4.00
91-98	2.00
99	4.00
100	5.00
100/Variant	8.00
101-124	2.00
125	4.00
125/A-125/B	10.00
126-130	2.00
131	5.00
131/A	3.00
132-133	2.00
133/Variant	4.00
134-144	2.00
145	4.00
145/Gold foil	25.00
145/Silver foil	30.00
145/Nabisco	400.00

146	5.00
147-149	2.00
150	3.00
151-165	2.00
166	3.00
166/A	40.00
167-189	2.00
Ann 1995	4.00
Ann 1996-1997	3.00
Ann 1999-2000	4.00
Ann 2001	3.00
Special 1	4.00

Wolverine
Marvel, 2003

1	7.00
2	5.00
3	4.00
4-9	3.00
10	2.00
11-15	3.00
16	2.00
17	3.00
18-20	2.00
20/Variant	90.00
☛Retailer incentive	
20/Texas	20.00
☛Texas con premium	
21-26	2.00
26/Silvestri	15.00
27	2.00
27/Quesada	25.00
28	2.00
29-36	3.00
36/Quesada	12.00
37-40	3.00
41	4.00
42-48	3.00
49-50	4.00

Wolverine and the Punisher: Damaging Evidence
Marvel, 1993

It's been a year since Conchita's death in the Punisher's last war with the Kingpin. As an anniversary present, the Punisher has been hitting the Kingpin's operations with unprecedented ferocity. Most recently, he took

down one of the Kingpin's South American operations, and slew his chief assassin.

Now, the Kingpin decides it's time to cut his losses. He recruits Pierce and his Reavers to take out the Punisher once and for all. But, as fate would have it, the Reavers are currently engaged in a battle to take down the X-Men's Wolverine. After defeating one of those high-tech mercenaries, Wolverine learns of the contract out on the Punisher and decides to come to his aid. Thus it's all the more surprising to him when he discovers that "the Punisher" is not the man he seemed to be when last they met in Hearts of Darkness.

1-3	2.00

Wolverine Battlebook
Battlebooks, 1998

1	4.00
1/A	5.00

Wolverine Battles the Incredible Hulk
Marvel, 1989

1	5.00

Wolverine: Black Rio
Marvel, 1998

1	6.00

Wolverine: Blood Hungry!
Marvel, 1993

1-1/2nd	7.00

Wolverine: Bloodlust
Marvel, 1990

1	5.00

Wolverine: Bloody Choices
Marvel, 1993

1	8.00

Wolverine/Captain America
Marvel, 2004

1	4.00
2-4	3.00

Wolverine: Days of Future Past
Marvel, 1997

1-3	3.00

Wolverine: Doombringer
Marvel, 1997

1	6.00
1/Variant	15.00

Wolverine/Doop
Marvel, 2003

1-2	3.00

Wolverine: Evilution
Marvel, 1994

1	6.00

Wolverine/Gambit: Victims
Marvel, 1995
1-4 ....3.00

Wolverine: Global Jeopardy
Marvel, 1993
1 ....3.00

Wolverine/Hulk
Marvel, 2002
1-4 ....4.00

Wolverine: Inner Fury
Marvel, 1992
1 ....6.00

Wolverine: Killing
Marvel, 1993
1 ....6.00

Wolverine: Knight of Terra
Marvel, 1995
1 ....7.00

Wolverine: Netsuke
Marvel, 2002
1-4 ....4.00

Wolverine and Nick Fury: Scorpio Rising
Marvel, 1994
1 ....5.00

Wolverine/Nick Fury: The Scorpio Connection
Marvel
1 ....13.00

Wolverine: Origins
Marvel, 2006
1-35 ....3.00

Wolverine Poster Magazine
Marvel
1 ....5.00

Wolverine/Punisher
Marvel, 2004
1-5 ....3.00

Wolverine/Punisher Revelation
Marvel, 1999
1-4 ....3.00

Wolverine: Rahne of Terra
Marvel, 1991
1 ....6.00

Wolverine Saga
Marvel, 1989
1-4 ....4.00

Wolverine: Save the Tiger!
Marvel, 1992
1 .... 3.00

Wolverine: Snikt!
Marvel, 2003
1-5 .... 3.00

Wolverine: Soultaker
Marvel, 2005
1-5 .... 3.00

Wolverine: The End
Marvel, 2004
1 .... 7.00
1/Texas................................. 15.00
2 .... 6.00
3 .... 5.00
4 .... 4.00
5-6 .... 3.00

Wolverine: The Jungle Adventure
Marvel, 1990
1 .... 5.00

Wolverine: The Origin
Marvel, 2001

![ORIGIN cover - PART III OF VI - THE BEAST WITHIN - JENKINS - KUBERT - ISANOVE]

For years we have watched as Wolverine struggled to untangle the mysteries of his past. He is the most enigmatic hero in Marvel Comics history, and his true story has never been told...until now.

This mini-series tells the tale of a sickly boy, a girl named Rose, and a poor child nicknamed "Dog." How are these three friends torn apart by love and tragedy? And in the end, how does one of the children grow up to become the hero known as Wolverine?

Written by Eisner Award-winner Paul Jenkins, Origin reveals the secrets at last.

1 .... 25.00
2 .... 12.00
3 .... 8.00
4 .... 5.00

5 .... 4.00
6 .... 5.00

Wolverine Unleashed
Marvel, 2002
1 .... 5.00
2-10 .... 4.00
11-19 .... 3.00

Wolverine vs. Night Man
Marvel
0 .... 15.00

Wolverine vs. Spider-Man
Marvel, 1995
1 .... 3.00

Wolverine/Witchblade
Image, 1997
1 .... 5.00
1/A 3.00

Wolverine: Xisle
Marvel, 2003
1-5 .... 3.00

Wombles
Redan
1-2 .... 3.00

Women in Fur
Shanda Fantasy Arts
2 .... 5.00

Women in Love
Fox, 1949
1 .... 170.00
2 .... 140.00

Women in Rock Special
Revolutionary, 1993
1 .... 3.00

Women of Marvel Poster Book
Marvel, 2006
1 .... 5.00

Women on Top
Fantagraphics, 1991
1 .... 2.00

Women Outlaws
Fox, 1948
1 .... 450.00
2-3 .... 350.00
4-8 .... 275.00

Wonder Boy
Ajax, 1955
17 .... 275.00
18 .... 225.00

Wonder Comics (Fox)
Fox, 1939
1 .... 15,000.00
2 .... 5,000.00

Wonder Comics
Nedor, 1944

1	1,100.00
2	590.00
3-5	540.00
6-10	425.00
11-14	500.00
15-20	440.00

Wonderland
Arrow, 1985

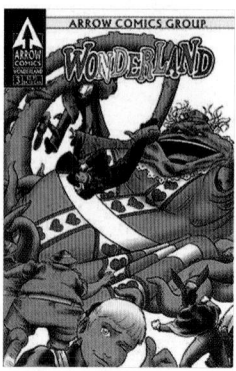

Ever wonder what it would be like if the characters from Lewis Carroll's Alice in Wonderland and the characters from L. Frank Baum's Oz books teamed up? Well, you don't have to. Arrow Comics released Dark Oz and this title, in which Dorothy Gale, Alice, the Hatter, the Cheshire Cat and various other characters from both sets of children's stories team up to fight the Red Queen (who, as you might suspect, is bent on taking off everyone's heads). Alas, this black-and-white independent is a bit too impressed with itself, the dialogue isn't really in keeping with that of either set of books, and the two sets of characters don't exactly gel. This same concept was attempted--and much more successfully so--when DC Comics sent its funny-animal heroes, Captain Carrot and his Amazing Zoo Crew, off to fight in the limited series known as the Oz-Wonderland War.

-- Stephen C. George

1-3	3.00

Wonderland
Wonderland Educational, 1962

1	4.00
2-37	3.00

Wonderlanders
Oktomica, 1999

1	3.00

Wonder Man
Marvel, 1986

1	2.00

Wonder Man
Marvel, 1991

1	2.00
2-24	1.00
25	3.00
26-29	1.00
Ann 1	2.00
Ann 2	3.00

Wonder Man
Marvel, 2007

1	3.00

Wonders and Oddities (Rick Geary's...)
Dark Horse, 1988

1	2.00

Wonder Wart-Hog, Hog of Steel
Rip Off

Wonder Wart-Hog, Hog of Steel is a black-and-white alternative comic series created by Gilbert Shelton, better known for his stories about The Fabulous Furry Freak Brothers. Clearly a take-off on such characters as Superman and Batman, he possesses a secret identity (in his case, Philbert Desanex) -- who looks more meek and mild (and smaller) than The Hog of Steel.

The stories abound in comics references, and this series contains multiple adventures per issue. However, although the character was created decades ago and first came to the attention of the general public in Harvey Kurtzman's Help! magazine, and later in publications like Drag Cartoons, his solo comics titles have been few.

-- Maggie

1-3	3.00

Wonder Woman
DC, 1942

In 1942, an Amazonian princess nursed a downed American pilot, Steve Trevor, back to health. Blessed with great strength and agility, she accompanied him back to the U.S. as Wonder Woman, woman warrior against the forces of war and evil.

In addition to her great strength and speed, Wonder Woman has awesome accessories: an invisible plane, Feminium bracelets (which she uses to deflect bullets and shrapnel), and a magical golden lasso. DC's earliest major female super-hero reigned for more than 40 years in this, her first series. Ironically, it took her alter-ego, Diana Prince, almost as long to advance from a low-ranking army nurse to a major.

1	17,000.00
2	3,100.00
3	1,900.00
4	1,200.00
5	1,050.00
6-10	900.00
11-20	650.00
21-23	450.00
24	600.00
25	450.00
26-30	425.00
31-40	415.00
41-44	400.00
45	500.00
46-50	400.00
51-60	310.00
61-70	240.00
71-79	190.00
80-90	155.00
91-100	120.00
101-104	90.00
105	600.00
☛1st Wonder Girl	
106-110	80.00
111-130	70.00
131-149	56.00
150-159	50.00
160-161	30.00
162	40.00

854

163-170	30.00
171-180	25.00
181-190	33.00
191-200	40.00
201-210	14.00
211	25.00

☞100-page issue

212-213	11.00
214	30.00

☞100-page issue

215-218	11.00
219-236	7.00
237-250	6.00
250/Whitman	12.00
251	6.00
251/Whitman	12.00
252	6.00
252/Whitman	12.00
253-255	6.00
255/Whitman	12.00
256	6.00
256/Whitman	12.00
257	6.00
257/Whitman	12.00
258	6.00
258/Whitman	12.00
259	6.00
259/Whitman	12.00
260	6.00
260/Whitman	12.00
261	5.00
261/Whitman	15.00
262	5.00
262/Whitman	10.00
263	5.00
263/Whitman	15.00
264	5.00
264/Whitman	10.00
265-268	5.00
269-279	4.00
280	3.00
281-283	5.00
284-299	3.00
300	6.00
301-329	3.00

Wonder Woman
DC, 1987

0	6.00
1	4.00
2-10/A	3.00
11-84	2.00
85	10.00

☞1st Deodato art

86	4.00
87-93	3.00
94-99	2.00
100	3.00
100/Variant	4.00
101-119	2.00
120	3.00
121-199	2.00
200	4.00
201-213	2.00
214	25.00

☞Inf. Crisis tie

215	10.00
216	7.00
217	6.00
218	5.00

219	15.00

☞Max Lord dies

219/2nd	3.00

☞2nd print

220	12.00
220/2nd-1000000	3.00
Ann 1-2	2.00
Ann 3	3.00
Ann 4	4.00
Ann 5	3.00
Ann 6	4.00
Ann 7-8	3.00
Special 1	2.00

Wonder Woman
DC, 2006

1	6.00
1/Variant-25	3.00

Wonder Woman: Amazonia
DC, 1998

1	8.00

Wonder Woman: Blue Amazon
DC, 2003

1	7.00

Wonder Woman: Donna Troy
DC, 1998

1	2.00

Wonder Woman Gallery
DC, 1996

1	4.00

Wonder Woman: Our Worlds At War
DC, 2001

In the "Worlds At War" crossover event, aliens from a number of different worlds are fighting with earth as the major battleground. Earth's mightiest super-heroes join the battle, but many pay a cost that is too dear for anyone to bear. In this one-shot, Wonder Woman comes to terms with the death of someone extremely close to her. But the story is not about the amazing Amazon, so much as it is a history primer of all Amazons, as well as the explanation of various incongruities that have sprouted up in Princess Diana's 60-year history. Writer Phil Jimenez produces one of the best Wonder Woman stories since Diana's re-boot in the mid-1980s. In the space of a single comic, he manages to cogently explain the entire Wonder Woman saga, making room for a World War II era Wonder Woman, reconciling the Amazon's relationship with Donna Troy (of Teen Titans fame), and establishing a much more cohesive mythology for the character. It's a great jumping-in point for any WW fan eager to catch up on the latest doings of DC's greatest heroine.

-- Stephen C. George

1	3.00

Wonder Woman Plus
DC, 1997

1	3.00

Wonder Woman Secret Files
DC, 1998

1-3	5.00

Wonder Woman: Spirit of Truth
DC, 2000

1-1/2nd	10.00

Wonder Woman: The Once and Future Story
DC, 1998

1	5.00

Wonderworld Comics
Fox, 1939

3	5,000.00
4	3,000.00
5-6	1,600.00
7-8	2,000.00
9-10	1,600.00
11	1,200.00
12-15	1,000.00
16-20	750.00
21-28	500.00
29-33	350.00

Wonderworld Express
That Other Comix Co., 1984

1	2.00

Wonderworlds
Innovation, 1992

1	4.00

Wood Boy (Raymond E. Feist's ...)
Image, 2005

1	3.00

Woodstock: The Comic
Marvel

1 ....6.00

Woodsy Owl
Gold Key, 1973

Aging Generation X-ers may have fond childhood memories of Saturday morning cartoons that served some higher purpose beyond selling action figures of the leading characters. For example, there were the environment-friendly adventures of Woodsy Owl ("Give a hoot! Don't pollute!"), the upstanding animated symbol of all that was precious about our unspoiled wilderness. Alas, nostalgia isn't what it used to be. Turns out that behind Woodsy's pristine forest home was a nasty old paper mill churning out issues of Woodsy Owl comics in a range of bright and doubtless carcinogenic colors. Gold Key, purveyors of fine, wholesome comics for young readers and shameless adapters of every single animated series ever ("Secret Squirrel," anyone?) brought the Woodsy one's adventures to the newsstand through the mid-70s.

-- Rob Salkowitz

1 ....8.00
2 ....5.00
3-5 ....4.00
6-10 ....3.00

Woody Woodpecker
(Walter Lantz...)
Dell, 1952

16-20 ....14.00
21-50 ....12.00
51-72 ....9.00
73-75 ....25.00
76-100 ....15.00
101-120 ....10.00
121-130 ....6.00
131-170 ....3.00
171-187 ....2.00

188-189 .... 10.00
190-191 .... 25.00
193-201 .... 15.00

Woody Woodpecker
Harvey, 1991

1 .... 2.00
2-8 .... 1.00
9-12 .... 2.00

Woody Woodpecker 50th Anniversary Special
Harvey, 1991

1 .... 3.00

Woody Woodpecker Adventures
Harvey, 1992

1-3 .... 1.00

Woody Woodpecker and Friends
Harvey, 1991

1-4 .... 1.00

Woody Woodpecker Digest
Harvey, 1992

1 .... 2.00

Woody Woodpecker Giant Size
Harvey, 1992

1 .... 2.00

Woody Woodpecker's Back to School
Dell, 1952

1 .... 100.00
2-6 .... 75.00

Woody Woodpecker's Christmas Parade
Gold Key, 1968

1 .... 20.00

Woody Woodpecker's County Fair
Dell, 1956

5 .... 75.00
2 .... 60.00

Woody Woodpecker Summer Fun
Gold Key, 1966

1 .... 50.00

Woody Woodpecker Summer Special
Harvey, 1990

1 .... 2.00

Woofers and Hooters
Fantagraphics

1 .... 3.00

Woolworth's Happy Time Christmas Book
Whitman, 1952

1 .... 30.00

Words & Pictures
Maverick, 1994

1-2 .... 4.00

Wordsmith
Renegade, 1985

1-12 .... 2.00

Wordsmith
Caliber, 1996

1-6 .... 3.00

Word Warriors
Literacy Volunteers

1 .... 2.00

Worgard: Viking Berserkir
Stronghold, 1997

1 .... 3.00

Workshop
Blue Comet

1 .... 3.00

World Around Us
Gilberton, 1958

1 .... 35.00
2-12 .... 25.00
13 .... 40.00
14 .... 35.00
15-25 .... 25.00
26 .... 35.00
27-33 .... 25.00
34 .... 35.00
35 .... 40.00
36 .... 25.00

World Bank
Public Services International

1 .... 3.00

World Below
Dark Horse, 1999

1-4 .... 3.00

World Below, The: Deeper and Stranger
Dark Horse, 1999

1-4 .... 3.00

World Class Comics
Image, 2002

1 .... 5.00

World Exists for Me
Tokyopop, 2005

1 .... 10.00

World Famous Heroes
Centaur, 1941

1 .... 750.00
2 .... 350.00
3-4 .... 275.00

World Hardball League
Titus, 1994

1-2 .... 3.00

World is His Parish, The: The Story of Pope Pius XII
George A. Pflaum, 1954

1 .... 100.00

World of Archie
Archie, 1992

It's nice to know that in a world where Superman dies (then gets better), Green Lantern becomes a mass murderer, and Spider-Man is said to be a clone of himself, some things stay resolutely the same. Thus it is in the World of Archie. This series, started in 1995, brings readers more humorous adventures featuring Archie and all his pals.

Although generations have grown up and old reading his adventures, Archie remains a perpetual teenager at Riverdale High. The blonde Betty is still a wholesome heartthrob, and rich girl Veronica Lake is still her jealous rival for Archie's affections. Jughead still craves lunch above all other human pursuits, Reggie is still a fink, and the whole gang is still good for a laugh after all these years.

1-22 .... 2.00

World of Fantasy
Atlas, 1956

1	350.00
2	300.00
3	250.00
4	200.00
5-6	160.00
7-12	150.00
13-15	125.00
16-19	100.00

World of Ginger Fox
Comico

1 .... 7.00

World of Hartz
Tokyopop, 2004

1 .... 10.00

World of Krypton
DC, 1979

1-3 .... 2.00

World of Krypton
DC, 1987

1-4 .... 2.00

World of Metropolis
DC, 1988

1-4 .... 2.00

World of Mystery
Atlas, 1956

1	300.00
2	100.00
3-4	125.00
5-7	100.00

World of Smallville
DC, 1988

As a boy, Clark Kent grew up in Smallville, and, even today, it is the one place which Superman loves the most. His parents, Ma and Pa Kent, still live there in the house he grew up in, and the streets are filled with people who remember him from when he was a boy.

Still, even this little town has its secrets. One of them, Clark is shocked to learn, is that his mother was once married to someone other than his father. Therein lies a story -- exactly the sort of tale that small town life is full of.

World of Smallville was one of three interlocking mini-series which shed light on the forces that shaped Superman. The others were World of Krypton, which described his birth world, and World of Metropolis, which was set in the grown Clark Kent's home city.

1-4 .... 2.00

World of Suspense
Atlas, 1956

1	225.00
2-3	125.00
4-6	100.00
7	125.00
8	100.00

World of Warcraft
DC, 2008

1-16 .... 3.00

World of Wheels
Charlton, 1967

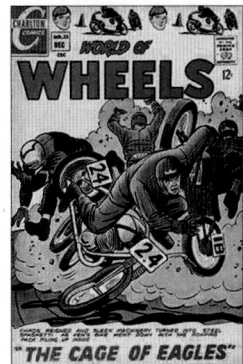

During a brief dark period in comics history (late 50s-late 60s), there arose a tedious genre of "racing comics" featuring the endlessly repetitive adventures of hot rodders, drag racers, professional auto and motorcycle speedsters, and their assorted rivals, hangers-on and romantic interests. Perhaps no publisher was better suited to bring this genre to life than Charlton Comics, a firm not often known for its originality and attention to quality. World of Wheels was a continuation of their Dragstrip Hotrodders book, now featuring the adventures of teenage stunt-cycle sensation Ken King. World of Wheels delivered what the fans wanted, though-lots and lots of technical detail about cars, engines and racing.

-- Rob Salkowitz

17-20	12.00
21-32	8.00

World of Wood
Eclipse, 1986

1-5 .... 2.00

World of X-Ray
Pyramid

1 .... 2.00

World of Young Master
New Comics, 1989

1 .... 2.00

World's Best Comics
DC, 1941

1 .... 18,000.00

World's Best Comics: Silver Age DC Archive Sampler
DC, 2004

1 .... 1.00

Worlds Beyond
Fawcett, 1951
1 ....250.00

Worlds Collide
DC, 1994
1 ....3.00
1/CS-1/Platinum.....................4.00

World's Finest
DC, 1990
1-3...5.00

World's Finest Comics
DC, 1941
2 ....4,000.00
3 ....2,900.00
4-5 ....1,975.00
6-7 ....1,450.00
8 ....1,275.00
9 ....1,300.00
10 ....1,050.00
11-16 ....895.00
17 ....875.00
18-20 ....805.00
21-30 ....610.00
31-40 ....530.00
41-60 ....430.00
61-64 ....320.00
65 ....540.00
66-70 ....370.00
71 ....900.00
☛1st Superman/Batman team
72-73 ....550.00
74-80 ....375.00
81-90 ....235.00
91-93 ....175.00
94 ....525.00
☛Superman/Batman team origin
95-99 ....175.00
100 ....260.00
101-110 ....105.00
111-121 ....85.00
122-142 ....75.00
143-150 ....52.00
151-152 ....50.00
153-155 ....45.00
156 ....55.00
☛Bizarro, Joker app.
157-161 ....45.00
162-177 ....38.00
178-180 ....30.00
181-190 ....25.00
191-197 ....20.00
☛Superman/Flash race
198-199 ....80.00
☛Superman/Flash race
200-212 ....16.00
213-228 ....14.00
229-270 ....6.00
271-300 ....4.00
301-323 ....3.00

World's Finest:
Our Worlds at War
DC, 2001
1 ....3.00

World's Funnest Comics
Moordam, 1998
1 ....3.00

World's Greatest Songs
Atlas, 1954
1 ....250.00

Worlds of Fear
Fawcett, 1952
2 ....325.00
3 ....250.00
4-9 ....200.00
10 ....475.00

Worlds of H.P. Lovecraft: Beyond The Wall of Sleep
Tome
1 ....3.00

Worlds of H.P. Lovecraft, The: Dagon
Caliber
1 ....3.00

Worlds of H.P. Lovecraft: The Alchemist
Tome
1 ....3.00

Worlds of H.P. Lovecraft, The: The Music of Erich Zann
Caliber
1 ....3.00

Worlds of H.P. Lovecraft, The: The Picture in the House
Caliber
1 ....3.00

Worldstorm
DC, 2006
1 ....3.00

Worlds Unknown
Marvel, 1973
1 ....17.00
2 ....10.00
3 ....7.00
4-8 ....5.00

World's Worst Comics Awards
Kitchen Sink, 1990
1-2 ....3.00

World War II: 1946
Antarctic, 1999
1-12 ....3.00

World War II: 1946/Families of Altered Wars
Antarctic, 1998
1-2/2nd 4.00

World War III
Ace, 1953
1 ....400.00
2 ....350.00

World without End
DC, 1990

Years before Defiant produced Warriors of Plasm, John Higgins and Jamie Delano envisioned another world where all was biology and living flesh. Here, the world is simply known as the Host, a pulsating vastness into which all other life is deeply connected. Architecture, technology -- indeed, the nature of power itself -- are all composed of organic matter.

Just as in Earth's Dark Ages, this world is controlled by a system of guilds, with each holding sway over some profession or facet of life. And, just as happened on Earth, they all seek to enforce their own world view or else risk losing power.

Here, the power is all male, with eugenics and ritual used to ensure the "purity" of maleness. But out on the wild fringes, far from the eyes of the city, rumors are strong of a rogue being that could destroy their world.

1-6 ....3.00

Wormwood Gentleman Corpse
Idea & Design Works, 2006
1-4 ....4.00

Wormwood Gentleman Corpse: The Taster
Idea & Design Works, 2006

1 ....4.00

Woron's Worlds
Illustration, 1993

1/A-3/B 3.00

Worst from Mad
E.C., 1958

nn 400.00
2..300.00
3..200.00
4..175.00
5-6...250.00
7-8...175.00
9..250.00
10-12.....................................175.00

Wow Comics
Fawcett, 1940

1 ....13,800.00
2..2,125.00
3..1,200.00
4..925.00
5..560.00
6..775.00
7-8...610.00
9..1,150.00
10..610.00
11-15......................................325.00
16-17......................................260.00
18..300.00
19-20......................................260.00
21-30......................................175.00
31-37......................................115.00
38..240.00
39-40......................................115.00
41-50..80.00
51-58..66.00
59-60..52.00
61-69..42.00

W.O.W. The World of Ward
Allied American Artists

1 ....4.00

Wraithborn
DC, 2005

1-5...3.00
6..4.00

Wraith
Outlander Comics Group, 1991

1-2...2.00

Wrath
Malibu, 1994

1 ....2.00
1/Ltd. 3.00
2-9...2.00
GS 1 ....3.00

Wrath of the Spectre
DC, 1988

1-4...3.00

Wretch
Caliber, 1997

1-4 .... 3.00

Wretch
Slave Labor, 1997

1-6 .... 3.00

Writers' Bloc Anthology
Writers' Bloc

1 .... 3.00

Wulf the Barbarian
Atlas-Seaboard, 1975

Young Prince Wulf rode with his parents that fateful day. Out on his first hunt, he and his family were ambushed by a huge force of trolls. When the king fell, Wulf's mother gave the prince to a trusted retainer and sword master, who somehow managed to break free and get the boy to safety. Looking back over his shoulder, the boy caught a final glimpse as his mother was murdered by a troll he has grown to call "the Grinner." Wulf swore a blood oath that day that he would have his revenge.

Arriving in the town of Azerbajia, the sword master relentlessly schooled the boy in the art of combat. Eventually the boy grew to become a skilled warrior. He was finally discovered by trolls sent by the dark wizard, Mordek Mal Moriak. That gave Wulf a chance to fulfill part of that oath by killing the Grinner. But Wulf would not rest until the sorcerer behind it lay dead under Wulf's sword.

1 .... 12.00
2 .... 9.00
3-4 .... 8.00

Wu Wei
Angus

1-6 .... 3.00

WW 2
NEC, 2000

1-2 .... 4.00

WW2 Rommel
New England, 2005

1 .... 4.00

WWF: World Wrestling Foundation
Valiant

1-4 .... 3.00

WWW.
NBM

1 .... 11.00

Wyatt Earp
Marvel, 1955

1 .... 120.00
2 .... 70.00
3-10 .... 50.00
11-20 .... 42.00
21-29 .... 30.00
30-34 .... 5.00

Wyatt Earp
Dell, 1958

4-13 .... 30.00

Wyatt Earp: Dodge City
Moonstone, 2005

1-2 .... 3.00

Wyatt Earp, Frontier Marshal
Charlton, 1956

12 .... 35.00
13-18 .... 18.00
19 .... 40.00
☛Giant-sized
20-30 .... 14.00
31-40 .... 10.00
41-50 .... 8.00
51-72 .... 6.00

Wynonna Earp
Image, 1996

1-5 .... 3.00

Wyoming Territory
Ark, 1989

1 .... 2.00

Wyrd the Reluctant Warrior
Slave Labor, 1999

1-6 .... 3.00

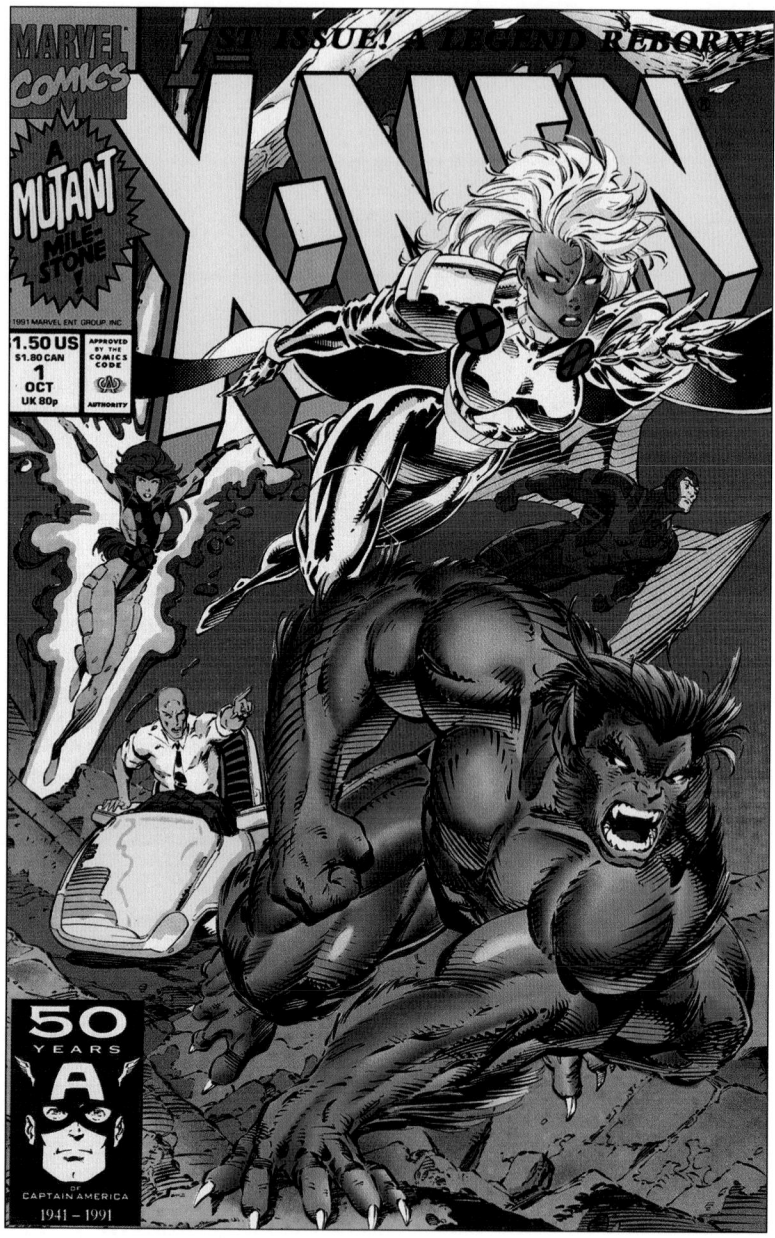

While Spider-Man #1 (1990) had multiple variations of its Todd McFarlane cover,
X-Men #1 (1991) had four different covers that, put together, formed one larger image.

crossover, Excalibur ended, replaced by the alternate-reality "X-Calibre." In this reality, Magneto is one of the good guys, and has recruited a swashbuckling version of Nightcrawler to help him seek out other mutants that might aid their cause. In particular, they seek the fabled land of Avalon, where the mutant Destiny holds the precognitive ability that may be the key to restoring reality and ending the Age of Apocalypse. Along the way, however, he'll face powerful enemies, including this reality's version of Angel, now a haughty nightclub owner of a crossroads bar called (appropriately enough) Heaven.

1-4 .... 2.00

Xena
Brainstorm, 1995
1 .... 3.00

Xena: Warrior Princess (Vol. 1)
Topps, 1997
0-1 .... 3.00
1/A 4.00
1/Variant 4.00
2 .... 3.00
2/Variant 4.00

Xena: Warrior Princess
Dark Horse, 1999
1-14/Variant 3.00

Xena: Warrior Princess: And the Original Olympics
Topps, 1998
1-3 .... 3.00

Xena: Warrior Princess: Bloodlines
Topps, 1998
1-2 .... 3.00

Xena: Warrior Princess/ Joxer: Warrior Prince
Topps, 1997
1-3/Variant 3.00

Xena: Warrior Princess: The Dragon's Teeth
Topps, 1997
1-3/Variant 3.00

Xena: Warrior Princess: The Orpheus Trilogy
Topps, 1998
1-3/Variant 3.00

Xena: Warrior Princess: The Warrior Way Of Death
Dark Horse, 1999
1-2/Variant 3.00

X
Dark Horse, 1994
1-3 .... 3.00
4-7 .... 2.00
8-25 .... 3.00
Hero ed. 1 .... 1.00

X-Men: Colossus: Bloodline
Marvel, 2005
1-5 .... 3.00

X-Men: Kitty Pryde: Shadow & Flame
Marvel, 2005
1-5 .... 3.00

X-Men: The 198
Marvel, 2006
1-5 .... 3.00

Xanadu
Thoughts & Images, 1988
1-5 .... 2.00

Xanadu
3-D Zone, 1986
1-4 .... 2.00

Xanadu: Across Diamond Seas
Mu, 1994
1-5 .... 3.00

Xanadu Color Special
Eclipse, 1988
1 .... 2.00

Xander in Lost Universe (Gene Roddenberry's...)
Tekno, 1995
0-8 .... 2.00

Xanth Graphic Novel
Father Tree, 1990
1 .... 10.00

X-Babies: Murderama
Marvel, 1998
1 .... 3.00

X-Babies: Reborn
Marvel, 2000
1 .... 4.00

X-Calibre
Marvel, 1995

For four issues during Marvel's 1995 "Age of Apocalypse"

Xena: Warrior Princess vs. Callisto
Topps, 1998

1	3.00
1/A	5.00
1/Variant-3/Variant	3.00

Xena, Warrior Princess: Wrath of Hera
Topps, 1998

1-2/Variant	3.00

Xena: Warrior Princess, Year One
Topps, 1998

1	5.00
1/Gold	10.00

X-Men: Days of Future Past
Marvel, 2004

1	20.00

Xene
Eyeball Soup Designs, 1996

1-4	5.00

Xenobrood
DC, 1994

0-6	2.00

Xeno-Men
Blackthorne, 1987

1	2.00

Xenon
Eclipse, 1987

Asuka Kano was a high-school student who fell into the clutches of the Black Sea Organization. As their unwilling test subject, he was transformed into Xenon, a cyborg designed as a new kind of weapon. Although this trauma, and that of a plane crash he was involved in, wiped out much of his memory, he's slowly beginning to remember who he is. Of course,

that doesn't solve the problem of what he's become.

But, as if his new metal body weren't enough to contend with, there's Ryuji Goda, leader of the Cheerleaders gang, who hated Asuka even before he became a cyborg. Worse, the Black Sea Organization unleashed Number 204, a previous assassin cyborg, on a mission to remedy the "little mistake" they made when Xenon got away.

It was one of the earliest manga titles to make it to U.S. shores.

1-23	2.00

Xeno's Arrow
Cup o' Tea, 1999

1-4	3.00

Xenotech
Mirage, 1994

1-3	3.00

Xenozoic Tales
Kitchen Sink, 1987

1	8.00
1/2nd	3.00
2-5	6.00
6-10	5.00
11-14	4.00

Xenya
Sanctuary, 1994

1-3	3.00

Xero
DC, 1997

1-12	2.00

X-Factor
Marvel, 1986

X-Factor started with a couple of really bad ideas -- three if you considered there to already be too many X-titles. John Byrne preferred the original X-Men cast and wanted to bring back Jean Grey, who died in the classic "Dark Phoenix" storyline in X-Men #137. So he retroactively cloned her

before that story took place -- rendering the classic story meaningless -- in an issue of The Avengers and shipped her over to star in the first issue of X-Factor with her former partners.

Bad idea #2 came in the group's cover: Since there was so much mutant paranoia, these heroes posed as mutant-exterminators who, in reality, collected suspected mutants and took them into protection. Some contemporary readers found the concept offensive. Sure, good guys can save people while pretending to be bad guys (see "Schindler's List") -- but early X-Factor storylines seemed not to be well-thought through. Later stories would recognize the trouble with the cover story, and steps were taken to put it to rest.

A much-altered X-Factor series finally gave up the ghost in 1998.

-- John Jackson Miller

-1	2.00
1	3.00
2-4	2.00
5	3.00
6	5.00
7	3.00
8-22	2.00
23	5.00
24	8.00
25-49	2.00
50-53	3.00
54-59	2.00
60	3.00
60/2nd	2.00
61-69	3.00
70-91	2.00
92	4.00
93-100	2.00
100/Variant	3.00
101-106	2.00
106/Variant	3.00
107-124	2.00
125	3.00
126-129	2.00
130	3.00
131-149	2.00
Ann 1-6	3.00
Ann 7	2.00
Ann 8-9	3.00

X-Factor
Marvel, 2002

1-4	3.00

X-Factor: Prisoner of Love
Marvel, 1990

1	5.00

X-Factor
Marvel, 2006

1	7.00
2-7	3.00

8...8.00
9-24...3.00
25-26.......................................6.00
27-50.......................................3.00

X-Farce
Eclipse, 1992
1...3.00

X-Farce vs. X-Cons: X-tinction
Parody, 1993
1-1.5......................................3.00

X-51
Marvel, 1999
0...1.00
1-12..2.00

X-Files
Topps, 1995
-2--1.......................................10.00
0/A-0/C..................................4.00
1/2...10.00
1...8.00
1/2nd......................................3.00
2...5.00
3...4.00
3/2nd......................................3.00
4...4.00
4/2nd-33.................................3.00
33/Variant...............................5.00
34-41/Variant..........................3.00
Ann 1-Ashcan 1 ....4.00
Special 1-5..............................5.00

X-Files (Magazine)
Manga, 1996
1...4.00
2-23..3.00

X-Files Comics Digest
Topps, 1995
1-3...4.00

X-Files Ground Zero
Topps, 1997
1-4...3.00

X-Files, The: Season One
Topps, 1997
1-9...5.00

X-Files, The: Afterflight
Topps, 1997
1...6.00

X-Flies Bug Hunt
Twist and Shout, 1996
1-4...3.00

X-Flies Conspiracy
Twist and Shout, 1996
1...3.00

X-Flies Special
Twist and Shout, 1995
1...3.00

X-Force
Marvel, 1991

Following the introduction of Cable into the New Mutants, that team took on a decidedly more aggressive role in fighting evil. With Cable as their new leader, the mutants that chose to remain were joined by mysterious new recruits Domino, Shatterstar, and Warpath. Following the conclusion of The New Mutants in #100, this new team became known as X-Force.

Cable led his new team as he would a military strike force. Each operation was carefully planned and run "by the numbers." Even then, danger has a habit of striking without warning, and the new team has suffered its share of defeats. But the battle continues and, as it does, readers uncover more of the secrets of the enigmatic group called X-Force.

-1-1/2nd................................ 2.00
2... 3.00
3-24.. 2.00
25 .... 3.00
26-30...................................... 2.00
31-33...................................... 1.00
34-38...................................... 2.00
38/Variant............................... 3.00
39-49/Deluxe.......................... 2.00
50 .... 3.00
50/A... 4.00
50/Variant-98.......................... 2.00
99 .... 3.00
100-129.................................. 2.00
Ann 1-3................................... 3.00
Ann 1995................................ 4.00
Ann 1996-1997....................... 3.00
Ann 1998-1999....................... 4.00

X-Force (Vol. 2)
Marvel, 2004
1 .... 4.00
2-6.. 3.00

X-Force: Shatterstar
Marvel, 2005
1-4.. 3.00

X-Force/Youngblood
Marvel, 1996
1 .... 5.00

XIII
Alias, 2005
1 .... 1.00
2-5.. 3.00

Ximos: Violent Past
Triumphant, 1994
1-2 .... 3.00

Xiola
Xero, 1994
0-3 .... 2.00
Ashcan 1 .... 1.00

XL
Blackthorne
1 .... 4.00

X-Lax
Thwack! Pow!
1 .... 1.00

X-Man
Marvel, 1995

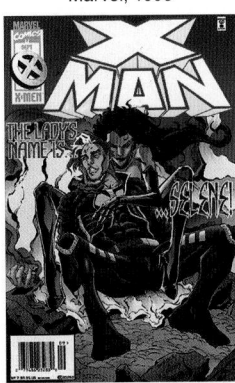

In early 1995, Marvel launched a series of alternate X-Men titles as part of an "Age of Apocalypse" storyline. The story began in a reality in which Professor X had been killed and, thus, had never been able to train a group of young mutants to become The X-Men. In the years that followed, a villainous mutant named Apocalypse gathered his fellow mutants to become the rulers of North America and launched murderous "culls" of the humans that remained.

X-Man is the story of a mutant named Nathan - better known in this reality as Cable - who leads a band of mutants in a challenge to Apocalypse's rule. His crew, which includes several who would otherwise have become notable X-Men villains, fought to stop

Apocalypse from mass-murdering both humans and mutants.

Remarkably, when the fight is won, Nate actually crosses over into the timestream which today's X-Men occupy.

-1	2.00
1	3.00
1/2nd	2.00
2-4	3.00
5-14	2.00
15	3.00
16-24	2.00
25	3.00
26-74	2.00
75	3.00
Ann 1996-1998	4.00

X-Man: All Saints' Day
Marvel, 1997

1	6.00

Xmas Comics
Fawcett, 1941

1	2,600.00
2	1,100.00

Xmas Comics
Fawcett, 1949

4	550.00
5-7	375.00

X-Men
Marvel, 1963

Stan Lee co-created the X-Men, one of Marvel's first super-groups, as a youthful counterpart to the full-grown heroes in The Avengers. With membership consisting of Scott Summers (Cyclops), Jean Grey (Marvel Girl), Warren Worthington III (Angel), and Hank McCoy (The Beast), The X-Men are students, enrolled in Professor Xavier's School for Gifted Youngsters. The secret is that these youngsters are mutants. Their genetic structure is different from that of normal people, and they have been blessed with strange super-powers as a result.

They are called The X-Men because of that "something X-tra" that each possesses.

Although reasonably popular in its early days, the original run of The X-Men had almost faded from existence when it was suddenly revitalized by the introduction of the "New X-Men" in Giant-Size X-Men #1. It then went on to become one of Marvel's most successful titles.

1	7,000.00
☞1st X-Men	
2	1,900.00
3	1,030.00
4	900.00
5	550.00
6	500.00
7	475.00
8-10	360.00
11	300.00
12	500.00
☞1st Juggernaut	
13	275.00
14	250.00
15-16	190.00
17-20	100.00
21-27	90.00
28	155.00
☞1st Banshee	
28/2nd	2.00
29-34	90.00
35	150.00
☞Spider-Man appearance	
36-37	65.00
38	80.00
39-40	90.00
41-48	65.00
49-51	75.00
52	65.00
53-57	72.00
58	100.00
☞1st Havok	
59-62	70.00
62/2nd	2.00
63	70.00
63/2nd	2.00
64-65	70.00
66	80.00
☞Last new issue	
67-80	35.00
81-85	40.00
86-93	35.00
94	500.00
☞2nd New X-Men	
95	85.00
☞Thunderbird dies	
96	55.00
97-98	48.00
98/30¢	125.00
99	48.00
99/30¢	125.00
100	60.00
☞Phoenix origin starts	
100/30¢	135.00
101	55.00
☞Phoenix origin	
102-105	28.00

105/35¢	60.00
106	28.00
106/35¢	60.00
107	28.00
107/35¢	60.00
108	35.00
☞1st Byrne X-Men	
109	30.00
☞1st Weapon alpha	
110-115	20.00
116-119	16.00
☞1st Alpha Flight	
120-121	28.00
122-128	12.00
129	20.00
☞1st Kitty, Empire Frost	
130-135	12.00
136	11.00
137	14.00
☞Phoenix dies	
138	8.00
139-141	11.00
☞Future Past	

X-Men
Marvel, 1991

-1	3.00
-1/A	4.00
1/Beast	5.00
1/Colossus	3.00
1/Cyclops	4.00
1/Magneto	3.00
1/Collector's	5.00
2	4.00
3-20	3.00
21-24	2.00
25	5.00
25/Gold	25.00
25/Ltd.	30.00
26-29	2.00
30	3.00
31-49	2.00
50	3.00
50/Variant	4.00
51-54	2.00
54/Silver	25.00
55-62	2.00
62/A	3.00
63-79	2.00
80	3.00
80/Holofoil	10.00
80/DF	7.00
81-98	2.00
99-100/G	3.00
101-104	2.00
105	3.00
106-113	2.00
114	5.00
115-144	2.00
145-147	3.00
148	2.00
149	3.00
150	4.00
151	3.00
152	2.00
153-156	3.00
157-158	2.00
159	3.00
160-164	2.00
165	3.00

166-169	2.00
170-220	3.00
Ann 1-3	3.00
Ann 1995	4.00
Ann 1996-Ann 1998	3.00
Ann 1999-Ann 2001	4.00
Ashcan 1	1.00

X-Men Adventures
Marvel, 1992

1	3.00
2-15	2.00

X-Men Adventures
Marvel, 1994

1	2.00
2-8	1.00
9-13	2.00

X-Men Adventures
Marvel, 1995

1-13	2.00

X-Men: Age of Apocalypse
Marvel, 2005

0	4.00

X-Men: Age of Apocalypse
Marvel, 2005

1	4.00
2-6	3.00

X-Men Alpha
Marvel, 1995

In 1995, Marvel preempted its X-titles to take readers into an alternate universe created when Legion (Professor Xavier's son) went back in time and killed Professor X before he could found the X-Men. The result was a dark world in which Apocalypse and his mutant cohorts declared war on humans and began a genocidal rule of North America. This was the Age of Apocalypse.

The story kicked off with this special "X-Men Alpha" edition, and would later conclude with X-Men Omega. In X-Men Alpha we meet the new X-Men, led by Magneto, who would otherwise be their mortal enemy. Magneto and Rogue have wed and have a son, Charles. Meanwhile, Wolverine and Jean Grey are a couple on the run, Angel runs a secret bar in the clouds that he calls Heaven, the Summers brothers, Cyclops and Havok, work for Apocalypse, and only a mysterious stranger exists to tell this brave new world what might have been.

1	3.00
1/Gold	20.00

X-Men/Alpha Flight
Marvel, 1985

1-2	3.00

X-Men/Alpha Flight
Marvel, 1998

1-2	3.00

X-Men/Alpha Flight: The Gift
Marvel, 1998

1	4.00

X-Men and Power Pack
Marvel, 2005

1-4	3.00

X-Men & The Micronauts
Marvel, 1984

1	3.00
2-3	2.00
4	1.00

X-Men Animation Special: The Pryde of the X-Men
Marvel, 1990

1	11.00

X-Men Anniversary Magazine
Marvel, 1993

1	4.00

X-Men: Apocalypse vs. Dracula
Marvel, 2006

1-4	3.00

X-Men Archives
Marvel, 1995

1-4	3.00

X-Men Archives Featuring Captain Britain
Marvel, 1995

1-7	3.00

X-Men Archives Sketchbook
Marvel, 2000

1	3.00

X-Men at the State Fair
Marvel

1	2.00

X-Men: Books of the Askani
Marvel, 1995

1	3.00

X-Men: Children of the Atom
Marvel, 1999

This limited series retells the origins of the original X-Men -- Cyclops, the Beast, the Angel, Iceman, and Marvel Girl -- and the story of their recruitment by Professor Charles Xavier for his School for Gifted Youngsters. The story focuses on the outcast status of mutants in the Marvel universe -- how they are curiosities and experiments-in-waiting, how they are hated and feared -- before Professor X enters their lives, helps them master their mutant abilities, and sells them on his dream of a world in which mutants and humans live in perfect harmony.

Meanwhile, master of magnetism Magneto is recruiting young mutants, too. He wants to establish a brotherhood that will crush humanity and make non-mutants pay for their intolerance of mutants. How will young, would-be X-Men respond to Magneto's offer? There are surprises in this retelling of X-history.

1-6	3.00

X-Men Chromium Classics: Days of Future Past
Marvel

1	14.00

X-Men Chromium Classics: Death of the Phoenix
Marvel

1 ....14.00
1/A...30.00

X-Men Chromium Classics: Origin of the X-Men
Marvel

1 ....14.00

X-Men Chronicles
Fantaco, 1981

1 ....2.00

X-Men Chronicles
Marvel, 1995

1-2..4.00

X-Men: Clandestine
Marvel, 1996

1-2..3.00

X-Men Classic
Marvel, 1990

46-110.....................................2.00

X-Men Classics
Marvel, 1983

1-3..4.00

X-Men Collector's Edition
Marvel

2 ....1.00

X-Men: Deadly Genesis
Marvel, 2006

1 ....6.00
1/Quesada 14.00
1/Hairsine................................7.00
2-6..4.00

X-Men: Declassified
Marvel, 2000

1 ....4.00

X-Men: Earthfall
Marvel, 1996

1 ....3.00

X-Men: Evolution
Marvel, 2002

An adaptation of the hit Warner Brothers animated series, which itself is based on the original Marvel comics, "X-Men: Evolution" is a nearly straightforward interpretation of the world's most popular mutants. Mutants are nothing more than humans with extraordinary powers--born with an "X" gene, they stand out from normal homo sapiens. They are homo superior. Keeping the classic ideological conflict between Professor Xavier and Magneto at its core, the comic adaptation of the cartoon delivers for both longtime fans and new readers. The major difference here is that the classic X-Men characters such as Wolverine, Storm, Cyclops and Nightcrawler have been reverted to their high school and college years, allowing the series to focus on the everyday struggles facing both mutants and teenagers. Less continuity-laden than the comics it is originally based on, "Evolution" focuses on more accessible stories with a trendy edge and lots of action.

1-9.. 2.00

X-Men: Fairy Tales
Marvel, 2006

1-4.. 3.00

X-Men/Fantastic Four
Marvel, 2005

1-5.. 4.00

X-Men: First Class
Marvel, 2006

1-4.. 3.00

X-Men Firsts
Marvel, 1996

1 .... 5.00

X-Men Forever
Marvel, 2001

1-6.. 4.00

X-Men: God Loves, Man Kills -- Special Edition
Marvel, 2003

1 .... 5.00

X-Men: Hellfire Club
Marvel, 2000

This limited series tells, in fairly broad strokes, the history of one of the X-Men's most powerful adversaries and, when necessity has demanded it, uneasy allies. From its Colonial era origins to the formation of Sebastian Shaw's Inner Circle of power-hungry mutants, writer Ben Raab (Excalibur) and artist Charlie Adlard (Mars Attacks) give some much-needed backstory to this dangerously ambitious group of villains.

-- *Stephen C. George*

1-4 .... 3.00

X-Men in the Savage Land
Marvel

1 .... 7.00

X-Men: Liberators
Marvel, 1998

1 .... 3.00
1/Ltd. 20.00
2-4 .... 3.00

X-Men: Lost Tales
Marvel, 1997

1-2 .... 3.00

X-Men: Messiah Complex
Marvel, 2007

1 .... 4.00

X-Men: Millennial Visions
Marvel, 2000
1-1/A 4.00

X-Men Movie Adaptation
Marvel, 2000
1 ....6.00

X-Men Movie Premiere Prequel Edition
Marvel, 2000
1 ....2.00

X-Men Movie Prequel: Magneto
Marvel, 2000
1 ....6.00

X-Men Movie Prequel: Rogue
Marvel, 2000
1-1/Variant...............................6.00

X-Men Movie Prequel: Wolverine
Marvel, 2000
1-1/Variant...............................6.00

X-Men Mutant Search R.U. 1?
Marvel, 1998
1 ....2.00

X-Men Omega
Marvel, 1995
1 ....6.00
1/Gold 25.00

X-Men: Phoenix
Marvel, 1999
1 ....4.00
2-3..3.00

X-Men: Phoenix -- Endsong
Marvel, 2005
1 ....8.00
☛Green costume
1/Variant-2..............................6.00
2/Variant..................................5.00
☛Green costume
3 ....4.00
4-5..5.00

X-Men: Phoenix -- Legacy of Fire
Marvel, 2003
1-3..3.00

X-Men: Phoenix -- Warsong
Marvel, 2006
1-4..3.00

X-Men Poster Magazine
Marvel, 1994
1-4..5.00

X-Men Prime
Marvel, 1995
1 .... 5.00

X-Men Rarities
Marvel, 1995
1 .... 6.00

X-Men: Road to Onslaught
Marvel, 1996
1 .... 3.00

X-Men: Ronin
Marvel, 2003
1 .... 4.00
2-5.. 3.00

X-Men Special Edition
Marvel, 1983
1 .... 5.00

X-Men Spotlight On... Starjammers
Marvel, 1990

Springing from the pages of the Uncanny X-Men, they are the Starjammers, a band of pirates and adventurers fighting a war in a far-off galaxy. Led by an Earth man named Corsair, this group of aliens bring their swashbuckling fury to the very heart of the Shi-ar fleet. Their goal: to overthrow the false ruler of the Shi-ar, and place Lilandra, a compatriot and the rightful ruler of the Shi-ar back on the throne.

1-2.. 5.00

X-Men: Survival Guide to the Mansion
Marvel, 1993
1 .... 7.00

X-Men: The Early Years
Marvel, 1994
1 .... 3.00
2-16.. 2.00
17 .... 3.00

X-Men: The End - Dreamers and Demons
Marvel, 2004
1 .... 4.00
2-6 .... 3.00

X-Men: The End - Heroes & Martyrs
Marvel, 2005
1-6 .... 3.00

X-Men: The End - Men and X-Men
Marvel, 2006
1-6 .... 3.00

X-Men: The Hidden Years
Marvel, 1999

From #67-93 of the original X-Men series, Marvel reprinted issues #12-45, due to low sales. As a result, fans have discussed for years what happened to the mutant heroes during the lengthy hiatus. The answers are here, as artist John Byrne is joined by original series artist Tom Palmer to fill in the gaps with tales from The X-Men's hidden years.

The adventure begins, as The X-Men manage to awaken Professor Xavier from a deep coma only to discover the professor is not his usual self. Meanwhile, Iceman decides to walk away from the team, and Cyclops, The Beast, Marvel Girl, and Angel must return to The Savage Land to thwart the evil plans of Magneto, who was believed dead.

Each issue captures the magic of the X-Men's early adventures while giving fans a chance to watch two master storytellers at work.

1 .... 4.00
2-22 .... 3.00

X-Men: The Magneto War
Marvel, 1999

This series kicks off an X-Men crossover story in which super-mutant Magneto decides to rid the world of human beings once and for all-a mission that, of course, flies in the face of Professor Xavier's dream of the peaceful coexistence of homo sapien and homo superior. Here, with the help of a group of Magneto's former Acolytes, we learn the X-Men's darkest dreams involving Magneto, Xavier fears for the lives of his Children of the Atom, Wolverine relives the loss of his adamantium, and Rogue watches helplessly as Gambit and Magneto fight for her love. Mutants, mutants everywhere as yet another X-Men "event" takes off.

1 ....3.00

X-Men: The Manga
Marvel, 1998

1-15..3.00
16-26..4.00

X-Men: The Movie Special
Marvel, 2000

1 ....1.00

X-Men: The 198 Files
Marvel, 2006

1 ....4.00

X-Men: The Search for Cyclops
Marvel, 2000

3/A-4 ....3.00

X-Men: The Ultra Collection
Marvel, 1994

1-5..3.00

X-Men: The Wedding Album
Marvel, 1994

1 .... 3.00

X-Men: True Friends
Marvel, 1999

1-3.. 3.00

X-Men 2 Movie
Marvel, 2003

1 .... 4.00

X-Men 2 Movie Prequel: Nightcrawler
Marvel, 2003

1 .... 4.00

X-Men 2 Movie Prequel: Wolverine
Marvel, 2003

1 .... 4.00

X-Men 2099
Marvel, 1993

1 .... 2.00
1/Gold...................................... 3.00
1/2nd-5................................... 2.00
6-7.. 1.00
8-24.. 2.00
25 .... 3.00
25/Variant............................... 4.00
26-35...................................... 2.00
Special 1 .... 4.00

X-Men 2099: Oasis
Marvel, 1996

1 .... 6.00

X-Men Ultra III Preview
Marvel, 1995

1 .... 3.00

X-Men Universe
Marvel, 1999

Keepin' up with all those X-Men titles gettin' ya down? Well, how

about gettin' a bunch of 'em in one convenient package?

That's the premise behind X-Men Universe: Each issue collects an installment from three different series that feature Marvel's merry band of mutants ... or one of its many derivations. Through this hefty anthology title, fans can catch up on the core titles (Uncanny X-Men and X-Men Vol. 2), the spin-offs (Generation X and X-Force), and the limited series (The Astonishing X-Men, which starred popular X-heroes Cyclops, Phoenix, Wolverine, Archangel, X-Man, and Cable).

1-11 .... 5.00
12-17...................................... 4.00

X-Men Universe: Past, Present and Future
Marvel, 1999

1 .... 3.00

X-Men Unlimited
Marvel, 1993

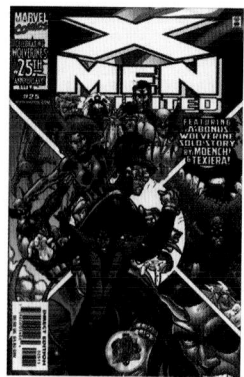

At the time Marvel released X-Men Unlimited, it was already publishing many "X" titles: X-Factor, X-Force, X-Men, Excalibur, The Uncanny X-Men, and X-Men Adventures. Why, then, another title? To judge by X-Men Unlimited, perhaps the answer was "to do it right!" It does so at a premium price, but X-Men Unlimited uses the best of everything: the best paper, the best art, and, yes, the best stories. In a series of giant-sized issues, X-Men gives fans The X-Men full of life, richly characterized, and exhibiting the sort of team synergy that has made them more than the sum of their parts.

1-31 .... 3.00
32-43 .... 4.00
44-50 .... 3.00

X-Men Unlimited
Marvel, 2004
1-14 ....3.00

X-Men vs. Dracula
Marvel, 1993
1 ....2.00

X-Men Vs. Exiles
Malibu, 1995
0 ....3.00
0/Gold 5.00

X-Men vs. the Avengers
Marvel, 1987
1 ....4.00
2-4 ....3.00

X-Men vs. the Brood
Marvel, 1996
1-2 ....3.00

X-Men/WildC.A.T.S: The Dark Age
Marvel, 1998
1/A-1/B 5.00

X-Men: Wrath of Apocalypse
Marvel, 1996
1 ....5.00

X-Men: Year of the Mutants Collector's Preview
Marvel, 1995
1 ....2.00

X-Nation 2099
Marvel, 1996
1 ....4.00
2-6 ....2.00

X/1999
Viz, 1996
1-6 ....3.00

X-O Manowar
Valiant, 1992

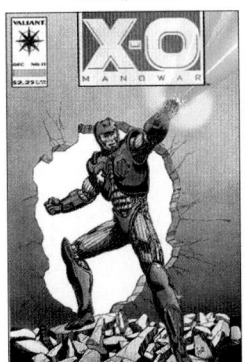

X-O Manowar is the name of the most powerful of a line of alien armors. Although the X-O Commando and other armors are formidable, indeed, the wearer of the X-O Manowar becomes one of the most powerful beings in the universe. But there's more: The X-O Manowar armor is more than mere technology - it's actually alive and sentient.

In the Valiant universe, connections between characters over vast periods of time are almost common. As such, it should not be surprising that the futuristic X-O Manowar armor is worn by a barbarian named Aric, who heads a corporation in 1990s America. His adventures cover similar ground, from star-spanning battles with Magnus and Solar to hunting dinosaurs with fellow warrior Turok.

0 .... 2.00
0/Gold................................... 35.00
1/2 .... 8.00
1/2/Gold............................... 55.00
1 .... 7.00
2-4 .... 6.00
5 .... 5.00
6 .... 4.00
7-8 .... 3.00
9 .... 2.00
10-15 .... 1.00
15/Pink 8.00
16-27 .... 1.00
28 .... 2.00
29-35 .... 1.00
36 .... 2.00
37-41 .... 1.00
42-54 .... 2.00
55-62 .... 3.00
63-65 .... 4.00
66 .... 5.00
67 .... 7.00
68 .... 12.00
YB 1 .... 4.00

X-O Manowar (Vol. 2)
Acclaim, 1996
1-21 .... 3.00
Ashcan 1 .... 1.00

X-O Database
Valiant, 1993
1 .... 4.00
1/VVSS................................. 30.00

X-O Manowar/Iron Man: In Heavy Metal
Acclaim, 1996
1 .... 3.00

Xombi
DC, 1994

Xombi is David Kim, "your average man who can't die." David's body can rebuild itself, whether the damage is a minor cut or the stripping away of all his flesh. Within minutes, he's back to normal -- whatever that is.

This title began with Xombi #0, which formed part of Milestone's Shadow War crossover series. The series began in its own right a few months later with Xombi #1. That issue told of how David, a promising young research scientist in the field of nanotechnology (microscopic machines), had the bad luck to be working late when his building was overrun by strange, mystical beings. They slaughtered everyone in the building in an effort to steal disks and devices from David's lab. After being critically wounded by the attackers, David begs his assistant to inject him with nanomachines programmed to rebuild his body. Surprisingly, this not only saves his life, but now prevents him from dying at all!

0 .... 3.00
1 .... 2.00
1/Platinum 3.00
2-13 .... 2.00
14-16 .... 3.00
17 .... 1.00
18-20 .... 3.00
21 .... 4.00

X: One Shot to the Head
Dark Horse, 1994
1 .... 3.00

X-Patrol
Marvel, 1996
1 .... 2.00

X-Presidents
Random House, 2000
1 .... 13.00

X-Ray Comics
Slave Labor, 1998
1-3..3.00

XSE
Marvel, 1996
1 ....2.00
1/A...3.00
2-4..2.00

Xstacy:
The First Look Edition
Fresco
1 ....3.00

Xstacy: The Libretto
Fresco
1 ....3.00

X-Statix
Marvel, 2002
1 ....3.00
2-7..2.00
8-26..3.00

X-Statix Presents
Dead Girl
Marvel, 2006
1-5..3.00

X-Terminators
Marvel, 1988
1-4..2.00

X, The Man With
X-Ray Eyes
Gold Key, 1963
1 ....50.00

X-Treme X-Men
Marvel, 2001
1-35..3.00
36-39..4.00
40-46..3.00
Ann 2001...................................5.00

X-Treme X-Men:
Savage Land
Marvel, 2001

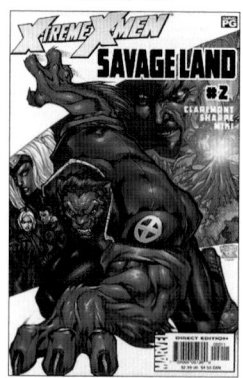

X-Treme X-Men certainly
doesn't break any new ground,

but for longtime X-fans, it must be
a blessing to see the team back in
the hands of old X-writer Chris
Claremont. Those turned off by
the constantly (ahem) mutating X-
storylines might want to pass on it
however.

The 4-part "Savage Land" mini-
series delves into the jungle that is
Rogue's mental state, the Beast's
new feral edge, a group of
Dinosaur people, the return of a
Savage land Mutate (Brainchild)
and another battle for ownership of
the Savage Land. A pretty
standard day in the X-career really.

1-4 .... 3.00

X-Treme X-Men X-pose
Marvel, 2003
1-2 .... 3.00

X-TV
Comic Zone, 1998
1-2 .... 3.00

X-23
Marvel, 2005
1 .... 7.00
1/Variant................... 3.00
2 .... 4.00
2/Variant................... 6.00
3 .... 5.00
4 .... 4.00
5 .... 3.00

X-23:
Target X
Marvel, 2007
1-2 .... 3.00

X-Universe
Marvel, 1995

X-Universe was one of several
mini-series and one-shots pumped
onto the stands in 1995 to service
Marvel's sprawling multi-title
crossover du jour, The Age of
Apocalypse (and perhaps also to
feed the perceived market appetite

for first issues). X-Universe served
as a road crew, filling in potholes in
the fifty-lane-wide plot and
providing background explanations
for goings-on in the other titles.

X-Universe claims to reveal the
fate of the Marvel universe during
the Age of Apocalypse, an
alternate-history plotline that came
about with the premature death of
X-Men mentor Professor Xavier
and the subsequent enslavement
of the world by Apocalypse. X-
Universe features Sue Storm, Ben
Grimm, Don Blake, Tony Stark,
and Gwen Stacy in non-super-
powered roles, but the storyline is,
by design, only comprehensible to
those who have invested in every
issue of the crossover saga.

-- Rob Salkowitz

1-2 .... 4.00

X-Venture
Victory, 1947
1-2 .... 2.00

XXXenophile
Palliard, 1989
1 .... 8.00
1/2nd-1/3rd............... 3.00
2 .... 5.00
2/2nd 3.00
3 .... 4.00
3/2nd 3.00
4 .... 4.00
4/2nd-10 .... 3.00
11 .... 4.00

XXXenophile Presents
Palliard, 1992
1-4 .... 3.00

XXX Women
Fantagraphics
1-4 .... 3.00

XYZ Comics
Kitchen Sink, 1972
1 .... 25.00
1/2nd 12.00
1/3rd 8.00
1/4th-1/5th 6.00
1/6th 5.00
1/7th 3.00

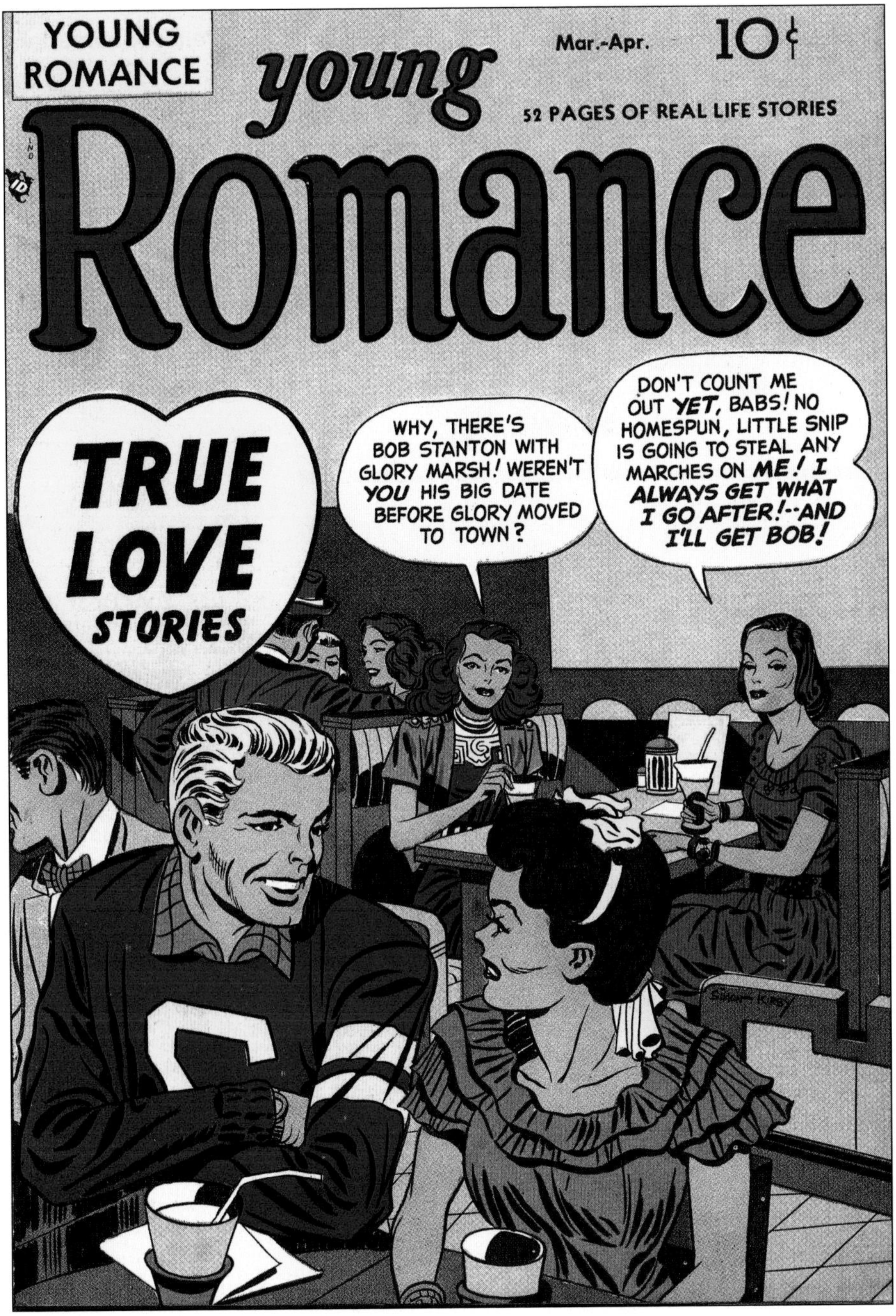

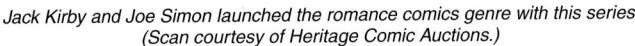
Jack Kirby and Joe Simon launched the romance comics genre with this series.
(Scan courtesy of Heritage Comic Auctions.)

Yellow Jar
NBM
1 .... 13.00

Yellow Submarine
Gold Key, 1969
1 .... 110.00

Yenny
Alias, 2005
1 .... 5.00
1/Variant 3.00

Yikes! (Weissman)
Weissman, 1995
1-5 .... 3.00

Yin Fei the Chinese Ninja
Dr. Leung's, 1988
1-8 .... 2.00

Yogi Bear (Dell/Gold Key)
Dell, 1961
4-9 .... 40.00
10-11 .... 55.00
12 .... 30.00
13 .... 55.00
14-20 .... 30.00
21-31 .... 20.00
32-42 .... 15.00

Yogi Bear
Charlton, 1970
1 .... 22.00
2-3 .... 15.00
4-6 .... 12.00
7 .... 15.00
8-10 .... 12.00
11-20 .... 8.00
21-35 .... 6.00

Yogi Bear
Marvel, 1977
1 .... 6.00
2-5 .... 4.00
6-9 .... 3.00

Yogi Bear
Harvey, 1992
1 .... 2.00
2-6 .... 1.00

Yogi Bear
Archie, 1997
1 .... 2.00

Yogi Bear Big Book
Harvey, 1992
1-2 .... 2.00

Yogi Bear GS
Harvey, 1992
1-2 .... 2.00

Yogi Berra Baseball Hero
Fawcett, 1951
1 .... 550.00

Yosemite Sam
Gold Key, 1970
1 .... 35.00

Y2K: The Comic
NEC, 1999
1 .... 4.00

Yahoo
Fantagraphics, 1988
1 .... 3.00
2-3 .... 2.00
4-6 .... 3.00

Yakuza
Eternity, 1987
1-4 .... 2.00

Yamara
Steve Jackson Games
1 .... 10.00

Yang
Charlton, 1973
1 .... 9.00
2-13 .... 5.00
15-17 .... 3.00

Yankee Comics
Harry A. Chesler, 1941
1 .... 1,025.00
2 .... 570.00
3 .... 415.00
4 .... 310.00
4/A 55.00
5 .... 40.00

Yarn Man
Kitchen Sink, 1989
1 .... 2.00

Yattering and Jack
Eclipse
1 .... 10.00

Yawn
Parody, 1992
1-1/2nd 3.00

Yeah!
DC, 1999
1-8 .... 3.00

Year of the Monkey (Aaron Warner's...)
Image, 1997
1-2 .... 3.00

Year One: Batman/Ra's al Ghul
DC, 2005
1-2 .... 6.00

Year One: Batman-Scarecrow
DC, 2005
1-2 .... 6.00

Yellow Claw
Atlas, 1956
1 .... 850.00
2 .... 675.00
3 .... 625.00
4 .... 550.00

Yellow Dog Comix
Print Mint, 1968
1 .... 50.00
2 .... 30.00
3-9/10 .... 25.00
11/12 .... 20.00
13/14 .... 30.00
15-25 .... 15.00

Yellowjacket Comics
Frank, 1944
1 .... 450.00
2 .... 350.00
3-5 .... 225.00
6 .... 300.00
7 .... 750.00
8-10 .... 250.00

  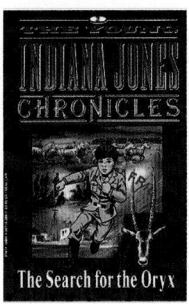 

2-5	20.00
6-10	15.00
11-20	10.00
21-50	4.00
51-65	3.00
66-67	8.00
68	20.00
69-70	17.00
71-78	10.00
79-81	17.00

Yotsuba!
ADV Manga, 2005

1-3	10.00

You Are Here
DC

1	20.00

You Can Draw Manga
Antarctic, 2004

1-12	5.00

Young Hearts
Marvel, 1949

1-2	60.00

Young Allies Comics
Timely, 1941

1	11,500.00
2	3,000.00
3	2,100.00
4	3,000.00
5	1,300.00
6-8	875.00
9	900.00
10	875.00
11-14	720.00
15-20	615.00

Young All-Stars
DC, 1987

1-3	3.00
4-31	2.00
Ann 1	3.00

Young Avengers
Marvel, 2005

1	10.00
1/DirCut	6.00
1/Conv	15.00
2	7.00
3	4.00
4-12	3.00

Young Avengers Special
Marvel, 2006

1	3.00

Youngblood
Image, 1992

0	2.00
0/Gold	4.00
1	3.00
1/2nd	2.00
2-4	3.00
5	2.00
6	4.00
7-10	3.00
SS 1	4.00
YB 1	3.00

Youngblood
Image, 1995

1-15	3.00

Youngblood
Awesome, 1998

1/A-1/L	3.00
1/M	4.00
1/N-2	3.00

Youngblood Battlezone
Image, 1993

1	2.00
2	3.00

Youngblood: Bloodsport
Arcade, 2003

1	4.00
1/Park-1/Variant	3.00

Youngblood: Strikefile
Image, 1993

1-11	3.00

Youngblood/X-Force
Image, 1996

1/A-1/C	5.00

Young Brides
Prize, 1952

1	175.00
2	100.00
3-6	90.00
7-18	85.00
19-21	25.00

22-25	20.00
26	75.00
27-28	20.00
29-30	30.00

Youngbroads: Stripfile
Parody, 1994

1	3.00

Youngbrother
Multicultural, 1994

1	2.00

Young Bug
Zoo Arsonist, 1996

1-3	3.00

Young Cynics Club
Dark Horse, 1993

1	3.00

Young Death
Fleetway-Quality, 1992

1-3	3.00

Young Dracula
Caliber, 1993

1-3	4.00

Young Dracula: Prayer of the Vampire
Boneyard, 1997

1-4	3.00

Young Eagle
Fawcett, 1950

1	105.00
2	55.00
3-6	50.00
7-10	45.00

Young Eagle
Charlton, 1956

3-5	40.00

Young Girl on Girl: Passion and Fashion
Angel

1	3.00
1/Nude	4.00

Young Gun
AC

1	3.00

Young Guns 2004 Sketch Book
Marvel, 2005
1 ....4.00

Young Guns Reloaded Sketchbook
Marvel, 2007
1 ....4.00

Young Hero
AC, 1989
1-2 ....3.00

Young Heroes in Love
DC, 1997
1 ....2.00
1/Ltd. 6.00
2-16 ....2.00
17-1000000 ....3.00

Young Indiana Jones Chronicles
Dark Horse, 1992
1-12 ....3.00

Young Indiana Jones Chronicles
Hollywood, 1992
1-3 ....3.00

Young Justice
DC, 1998
1 ....4.00
2-49 ....3.00
50 ....4.00
51-55 ....3.00
1000000 ....4.00
GS 1 ....5.00

Young Justice in No Man's Land
DC, 1999
1 ....4.00

Young Justice: Our Worlds At War
DC, 2001
1 ....3.00

Young Justice Secret Files
DC, 1999
1 ....5.00

Young Justice: Sins of Youth
DC, 2000
1-2 ....3.00

Young Justice: The Secret
DC, 1998
1 ....2.00

Young King Cole Vol. 1
Novelty, 1945
1 ....200.00
2-4 ....100.00

Young King Cole Vol. 2
Novelty, 1946
1 ....200.00
2-7 ....100.00

Young King Cole Vol. 3
Novelty, 1947
1 ....150.00
2-12 ....80.00

Young Lawyers
Dell, 1971
1-2 ....10.00

Young Love
Crestwood, 1949
1 ....200.00
2 ....100.00
3 ....80.00
4-5 ....65.00
6-10 ....52.00
11-20 ....45.00
21-30 ....36.00
31-40 ....26.00
41-50 ....20.00
51-60 ....18.00
61-70 ....14.00
71-73 ....12.00

Young Love
DC, 1963
39 ....30.00
40-50 ....24.00
51-70 ....20.00
71-90 ....14.00
91-100 ....10.00
101-106 ....7.00
107 ....25.00
108-114 ....20.00
115-126 ....12.00

Young Lovers
Charlton, 1957
16-17 ....80.00
18 ....400.00

Young Lovers
Avalon
1 ....3.00

Young Lust
Print Mint, 1970
1 ....5.00
2-8 ....3.00

Young Master
New Comics, 1987
1-9 ....2.00

Young Men
Marvel, 1950
4 ....120.00
5-10 ....70.00
11-23 ....52.00
24 ....1,600.00
☛Cap, Namor origin
25 ....775.00
25/2nd 2.00
26-28 ....750.00

Young Rebels
Dell, 1971
1 ....15.00

Young Romance
Prize, 1947
1 ....325.00
2 ....200.00
3-5 ....150.00
6-10 ....125.00
11-20 ....95.00
21-30 ....75.00
31-40 ....60.00

41-48	55.00
49-51	24.00
52-60	55.00
61-71	45.00
72-77	16.00
78-90	40.00
91-92	35.00
93-94	15.00
95-97	35.00
98	15.00
99	35.00
100	15.00
101	12.00
102-104	30.00
105-124	14.00

Young Romance
DC, 1963

125	42.00
126-140	18.00
141-150	15.00
151-159	12.00
160-170	10.00
171-197	9.00
198-201	20.00
202-208	8.00

Youngspud
Spoof, 1992

1	3.00

Young Witches
Fantagraphics, 1991

1-4	3.00

Young Witches III, The: Empire of Sin
Fantagraphics, 1993

1-3	3.00

Young Witches VI, The: Wrath of Agatha
Fantagraphics

1-2	4.00

Young Witches IV, The: The Eternal Dream
Fantagraphics, 1993

1-3	3.00

Young Witches, The: London Babylon
Fantagraphics, 1992

1-6	4.00

Young Zen: City of Death
Express

1	3.00

Young Zen Intergalactic Ninja
Express

1	4.00
2	3.00

Your Big Book of Big Bang Comics
Image, 1998

1	11.00

You're Under Arrest!
Dark Horse, 1995

1-8	3.00

Your Hytone Comix
Apex Novelties, 1971

1	8.00

Your United States
Lloyd Jacquet Studios, 1946

1	25.00

Youthful Hearts
Youthful, 1952

1	180.00
2-3	150.00

Youthful Romances (Pix Parade)
Pix Parade, 1949

1	150.00
2-6	100.00
7-14	80.00

Youthful Romances (Ribage)
Ribage, 1953

15-18	70.00
5-8	60.00

Y's Guys
October, 1999

1	3.00

Y: The Last Man
DC, 2002

Everything on Earth with a Y chromosome dies. Suddenly. People, pets, wild animals: Half the population keels over with no explanation. Except for American Yorick Brown, an amateur escape artist. With his monkey, Ampersand, he sets out to find his girlfriend who's trapped in Australia -- and to try to figure out how to save the human race. "I don't know if I'm the only man on earth ... but I swear I'm not going to be the last." It's science fiction and social commentary, as Brian K. Vaughan and Pia Guerra begin the story of Brown's life in a world of women whose lives have been fundamentally changed.

The series was an immediate favorite of many readers, and the story quickly moved beyond such social problems as restructuring government and into the more personal matters of what Brown needs to do to survive and keep hope alive.

-- Maggie Thompson

1	30.00
2	15.00
3	5.00
4-5	4.00
6-52	3.00

Yuggoth Cultures (Alan Moore's)
Avatar, 2003

1-3	4.00

Yummy Fur
Vortex, 1986

1	6.00
2	5.00
3-5	4.00
6-32	3.00

Yuppies from Hell
Marvel

1	3.00

Yuppies, Rednecks and Lesbian Bitches From Mars
Fantagraphics, 1997

1-7	3.00

YuYu Hakusho
Viz, 2003

1-8	8.00

Scott McCloud's adventures of a teenage boy from an alternate Earth was part of the independent comics boom of the 1980s.

Zatanna
DC, 1993

"Zatanna is a half-human, half-Atlantean sorceress and onetime lover of John Constantine (Hellblazer). Despite her special abilities, she tries to eke out a relatively normal existence in San Francisco as a booking agent. Over the last few days, however, she has noted a huge increase in the number of darkling spirits in San Francisco and decides to investigate. In doing so, she encounters an ancient enemy and a mystical plan that threatens to spill the darkling realm into our world.

An entertaining mini-series, "Come Together" gives the writers a chance to develop Zatanna. Aside from freeing her from the device of having to speak her spells backward, they add dimension to her personality, turning her into a much stronger character.

1-4 .... 2.00

Zatanna: Everyday Magic
DC, 2003

1 .... 6.00

Zatanna Special
DC, 1987

1 .... 2.00

Zatch Bell!
Viz, 2005

1-3 .... 10.00

Zaza the Mystic (Avalon)
Avalon

1 .... 3.00

Zealot
Image, 1995

1-3 .... 3.00

Zegra, Jungle Empress
Fox, 1948

2 .... 525.00
3-5 .... 450.00

Z
Keystone Graphics, 1994

1-3 .... 3.00

Zago
Fox, 1948

1 .... 525.00
2-3 .... 410.00
4 .... 305.00

Zaibatsu Tears
Limelight, 2000

1-3 .... 3.00

Zane Grey's Stories of the West
Dell, 1955

27 .... 50.00
28-35 .... 45.00
36-39 .... 40.00

Zap Comix
Last Gasp, 1967

0 .... 300.00
0/2nd 110.00
0/3rd 45.00
0/4th 20.00
0/5th 12.00
0/6th 6.00
0/7th 4.00
0/8th-0/10th 3.00
1 .... 3,000.00
1/2nd 110.00
1/3rd 70.00

1/4th 28.00
1/5th 8.00
1/6th 6.00
1/7th 4.00
1/8th 3.00
2 .... 55.00
2/2nd 34.00
2/3rd 8.00
2/4th-2/5th 4.00
3 .... 35.00
3/2nd 18.00
3/3rd 7.00
3/4th-3/5th 4.00
4 .... 28.00
4/2nd 8.00
4/3rd-4/5th 4.00
5 .... 28.00
5/2nd 8.00
5/3rd 4.00
5/4th 3.00
6 .... 16.00
6/2nd 5.00
6/3rd-6/4th 4.00
7 .... 10.00
7/2nd 4.00
7/3rd-7/4th 3.00
8 .... 10.00
8/2nd-8/3rd 4.00
9 .... 10.00
9/2nd-9/3rd 4.00
10 .... 5.00
11 .... 4.00
12-13 .... 5.00
14 .... 4.00

Zell Sworddancer
3-D Zone
1 ....2.00

Zell, Sworddancer
Thoughts & Images, 1986
1 ....2.00

Zendra
Penny-Farthing, 2000
1-4..3.00

Zen Illustrated Novella
Entity
1-2..3.00

Zen, Intergalactic Ninja
Zen, 1987
1 ....3.00
1/2nd-6..................................2.00

Zen, Intergalactic Ninja
Zen, 1990
1-4..2.00

Zen, Intergalactic Ninja
Zen, 1992
1-5..2.00
Holiday 1 ....3.00

Zen Intergalactic Ninja
Archie, 1992
1-3..1.00

Zen Intergalactic Ninja
Archie, 1992
1-7..1.00

Zen Intergalactic Ninja
Express, 1993
0-0/A 3.00
0/B..4.00
0/Ltd.-1....................................3.00
1/Variant..................................4.00
2-4..3.00
Ashcan 1..................................1.00
Spring 1....................................3.00

Zen Intergalactic Ninja All-New Color Special
Express, 1994
0 ....4.00

Zen Intergalactic Ninja Color
Express, 1994
1-3..4.00
4-7..3.00

Zen Intergalactic Ninja Color (2nd Series)
Express, 1995
1-2..3.00

Zen, Intergalactic Ninja Earth Day Annual
Zen, 1993
1 ....3.00

Zen Intergalactic Ninja Milestone
Express, 1994
1 ....3.00

Zen Intergalactic Ninja Starquest
Express, 1994
1-7 ....3.00

Zen Intergalactic Ninja Summer Special: Video Warrior
Express, 1994
1 ....3.00

Zen Intergalactic Ninja: Tour of the Universe Special, the Airbrush Art of Dan Cote
Express, 1995
1 ....4.00

Zenith: Phase I
Fleetway-Quality
1-3...2.00

Zenith: Phase II
Fleetway-Quality
1-2...2.00

Zen: The New Adventures
Zen, 1997
1 ....3.00

Zero
Zero Comics, 1975
1-3...3.00

Zero Girl
Homage, 2001
1-5...3.00

Zero Girl: Full Circle
DC, 2003
1-5...3.00

Zero Hour
Dog Soup, 1995
1 ....3.00

Zero Hour: Crisis in Time
DC, 1994
4-2 ....2.00
1 ....3.00
0 ....2.00
Ashcan 1 ....1.00

Zero Patrol
Continuity, 1984
1-2...2.00

Zero Patrol
Continuity, 1987
1-5...2.00

Zero Street
Amaze Ink, 2000
1 ....3.00

Zero Tolerance
First, 1990
1-4 ....2.00

Zero Zero
Fantagraphics, 1995

Over the years, Marvel and DC have had several "tryout" titles for new artists. Normally, these are anthologies featuring established characters. The more daring ones might even go so far as to let the auditioning team use its own characters and stories. Still, none of these titles comes close to the degree of freedom accorded the artists in Zero Zero.

Begun in 1995, Zero Zero is a spotlight for experimental cartoonists, published by Fantagraphics-one of the most daring comic publishers. The stories contained here are not meant for readers who like super-hero cliches or straightforward storylines. Depending on the artist, illustrations range from stark and angst-ridden to minimalist and surreal. The storylines similarly bounce from one-page black humor to stream-of-consciousness narrative. It's definitely not for everyone, but readers can find exciting surprises inside.

1-7 ....4.00
8 ....6.00
9-26 ....4.00

Zetraman
Antarctic, 1991
1-3 ....2.00

Zetraman: Revival
Antarctic, 1993
1-3 ....3.00

Ziggy Pig & Silly Seal
Timely, 1944
1 ....150.00
2-3 ....80.00
4-6 ....75.00

Zig Zag
Adhouse Books, 2005
1 ....6.00

Zillion
Eternity, 1993
1-4...3.00

Zip Comics
M.L.J., 1940
1 ....3,500.00
2 ....1,600.00
3 ....1,250.00
4-5.......................................900.00
6-8.......................................750.00
9 ....800.00
10...750.00
11-17...................................600.00
18...625.00
19...600.00
20...900.00
21-26...................................540.00
27...800.00
28-30...................................540.00
31-40...................................375.00
41-47...................................280.00

Zip Comics
Cozmic
1 ....4.00

Zip Jet
St. John, 1953
1 ....650.00
2 ....450.00

Zippy Quarterly
Fantagraphics, 1993
1-2...5.00
3-13...4.00

Zodiac P.I.
Tokyopop, 2003
1 ....10.00

Zoids:
Chaotic Century
Viz, 2002
1-6...7.00

Zolastraya and the Bard
Twilight Twins, 1987
1-5...2.00

Zombie
Marvel, 2006
1-4 .... 4.00

Zombie 3-D
3-D Zone
1 .... 4.00

Zombie Boy
Antarctic, 1996
1-3... 3.00

Zombie Boy
Timbuktu
1 .... 2.00

Zombie Boy
Rises Again
Timbuktu, 1994
1 .... 3.00

Zombie King
Image, 2005
0 .... 3.00

Zombie Love
ZuZupetal
1-3... 3.00

Zombies!
Idea & Design Works, 2006
1-5... 4.00

Zombies:
Eclipse of the Undead
Idea & Design Works, 2006
1-2... 4.00

Zombies vs. Robots
Idea & Design Works, 2006
1 .... 4.00

Zombie War
Tundra, 1992
1 .... 4.00

Zombie War
Fantaco, 1992
1-2... 4.00

Zombie War:
Earth Must
Be Destroyed
Fantaco, 1993
1-4... 3.00

ZombieWorld:
Champion of the Worms
Dark Horse, 1997
1-3... 3.00

ZombieWorld:
Dead End
Dark Horse, 1998
1-2... 3.00

ZombieWorld:
Eat Your Heart Out
Dark Horse, 1998
1 .... 3.00

ZombieWorld:
Home for the Holidays
Dark Horse, 1997
1 .... 3.00

ZombieWorld:
Tree of Death
Dark Horse, 1999
1-4... 3.00

ZombieWorld:
Winter's Dregs
Dark Horse, 1998
1-4... 3.00

Zomboy
Inferno, 1996
1 .... 3.00

Zomoid Illustories
3-D Zone
1 .... 3.00

Zone
Dark Horse
1 .... 2.00

Zone Continuum
Caliber, 1994
1 .... 3.00
1/A-1/B 2.00
2 .... 3.00

Zone Continuum
Caliber
1-2... 3.00

Zone Zero
Planet Boy
1 .... 3.00

Zoo Funnies
Children Comics, 1945

1	120.00
2-3	70.00
4-6	60.00
7-9	52.00
10-12	40.00
13-15	38.00

Zoo Funnies
Charlton, 1953

1	42.00
2	30.00
3	24.00
4-7	20.00
8-13	32.00

Zoo Funnies
Charlton, 1984

1	2.00

Zoom's Academy for the Super Gifted
Astonish, 2000

1-3	4.00

Zooniverse
Eclipse, 1986

1-6	2.00

Zoot!
Fantagraphics, 1992

1-6	3.00

Zoot Comics
Fox, 1946

1	175.00
2-5	150.00
6-9	125.00
10-11	100.00
12-14	90.00
13/A-14/A	425.00
15-16	85.00

Zorann: Star-Warrior!
Blue Comet, 1994

0	3.00
1	2.00

Zori J's 3-D Bubble Bath
3-D Zone

1	4.00

Zori J's Super-Swell Bubble Bath Adventure-Oh Boy!
3-D Zone

1	3.00

Zorro
Dell, 1959

8-9	70.00
10-12	68.00
13-15	65.00

Zorro
Gold Key, 1966

1	70.00
2-4	38.00
5-7	34.00
8-9	28.00

Zorro
Marvel, 1990

1	3.00
2-12	2.00

Zorro
Topps, 1993

0	3.00
1	4.00
2	8.00
3-11	3.00

Zorro
NBM, 2005

1-6	3.00

Zorro: Matanzas!
Image

Ashcan 1	1.00

Zot!
Eclipse, 1984

Zachary T. Paleozogt ("Zot") was a boy who grew up on a more advanced alternate version of Earth. His parents inexplicably abandoned him before he was 10, after which he was cared for by his eccentric uncle Max. Max was a great teacher, and Zot quickly excelled in both school and sports. Most importantly, he became the world arcade marksman champion. He used these skills to become a hero on his home world. He eventually crossed over into our world to stop a robotic rampage. Here, he encountered young Jenny Weaver, a kind teen-ager who would eventually become his girlfriend. The two embarked on a series of high-flying adventures, beginning with the search for the gold key which opens the legendary "Doorway at the Edge of the Universe."

Zot! is delightfully innocent fun by Scott McCloud, best known for his book "Understanding Comics." Later issues also included a backup spoof featuring Matt Feazell's Cynicalman.

1	5.00
2-11	3.00
12-35	2.00
36	3.00

Zu
Mu, 1995

1-19	3.00

Zugal
Bryan Evans

1	3.00

Zulunation
Tome, 1995

1-3	3.00

Zwanna, Son of Zulu
Dark Zulu Lies

1	2.00

ZZZ
Alan Bunce, 2000

Canadian Alan Bunce neatly handles the dual linguistics of his native country with this whimsical title, which relies solely on pictures to relate its hero's whimsical dreams. In the first issue, the hero, who looks somewhat like one of the Smurfs, falls down a magical, mystery hole into a treasure trove, where he releases a playful genie. Soon, the two are running around, tripping and tumbling in slapstick fashion, made even funner by the genie's magic trickery. It's almost a shame our hero has to wake up at the end.

Zzz is a delightful fantasy title appropriate for kids of all ages-and nationalities.

1	2.00

Are Your Favorites Among the 1000

FIND OUT...

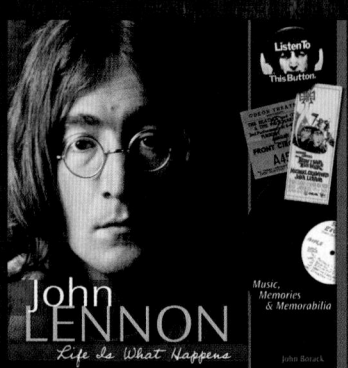
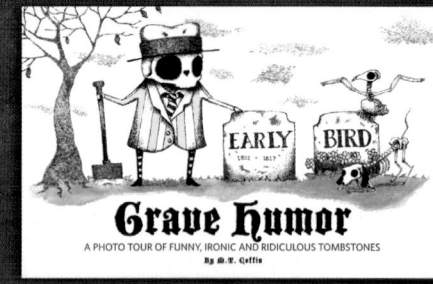
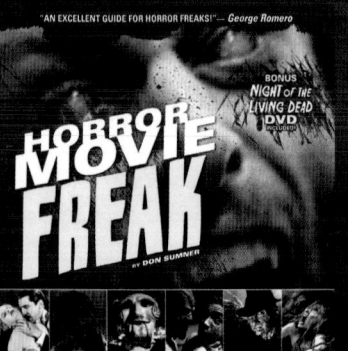
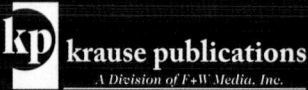

COMIC DEALERS:

Supplies that are:
- always in stock
- delivered on time
- consistent quality
- great prices
- Bags & Boards come in printed packing bags

NEW BAGS, BACKINGS & BOXES

1.2 mil Polypropylene **COMIC BAGS** with flap

New Comic Bags 6-7/8 × 10-3/8″		Regular Comic Bags 7-1/8 × 10-3/8″	
2,500	$75.00+	2,500	$75.00+
5,000	145.00+	5,000	145.50+
10,000	280.00+	10,000	280.00+
Code: SPPNC		SPPMAR	

24 pt Double White **COMIC BACKINGS**

New Comic Backings 6-11/16 × 10-3/8″		Regular Comic Backings 6-15/16 × 10-3/8″	
1,000	$43.50+	1,000	$45.00+
5,000	215.00+	5,000	222.50+
10,000	425.00+	10,000	440.00+
Code: KSBS24N		KSBS24R	

Lower Prices

50	$187.50+
100	325.00+

Code: XLC300

New Design Long **COMIC BOX**
275 lb. test, double-wall corrugated

7-5/8 × 11 × 25-3/4″

NOTE: + symbol indicates a price that does not include freight costs.

Order, see freight chart, or request a quote at BagsUnlimited.com/dealer

BAGS Unlimited inc

THE COLLECTION PROTECTION SUPPLY COMPANY   1-800-767-2247